A Guide to Human Rights Law in Scotland

A Guide to Human Rights Law in Scotland

The Honourable Lord Reed
Senator of the College of Justice in Scotland

Jim Murdoch
Professor of Public Law, University of Glasgow

Print on Demand Edition

Tottel
publishing

Published by
Tottel Publishing Ltd
Maxwelton House
41-43 Boltro Road
Haywards Heath
West Sussex
RH16 1BJ

Tottel Publishing Ltd
9-10 St Andrew Square
Edinburgh
EH2 2AF

ISBN 13: 978-1-84592-556-7
ISBN 10: 1-84592-556-4
© Reed Elsevier (UK) Ltd 2001
Formerly published by LexisNexis Butterworths

This edition transferred to print-on-demand 2006 by Tottel Publishing Ltd.

British Library Cataloguing-in-Publication Data.
A catalogue record for this book is available from the British Library.

Typeset by Phoenix Photosetting, Chatham, Kent
Printed and bound in Great Britain by
CPI Antony Rowe Limited, Eastbourne, East Sussex

Preface

Even prior to the Human Rights Act 1998 and the Scotland Act 1998, the European Convention on Human Rights had begun to have a significant influence on the development of Scots law: an influence which could be seen in such diverse areas of the law as criminal procedure, family law, contempt of court and the liability in negligence of public authorities. Its influence has been intensified by the two Acts of 1998 which gave effect to the substantive provisions of the Convention in Scots law as 'Convention rights' and made it unlawful for all public bodies below the level of the Westminster Parliament, including the courts, to act incompatibly with those rights.

This is an important development for a variety of reasons; and, especially so in Scotland, given the fact that Convention rights have been made binding upon the Scottish Parliament and Executive. One aspect of the Convention's importance is that it imposes an obligation on Contracting States to safeguard basic rights, and as a corollary an obligation to justify any interference with such rights. The incorporation of Convention rights into domestic law is therefore particularly significant in a Contracting State such as the United Kingdom whose constitution does not contain any catalogue of basic rights: for the first time, fundamental rights have been given a special status in our law. It is also important to understand that the Convention is what its name suggests: a *European* Convention. It is an international instrument, creating obligations for the United Kingdom under international law and forming part of a world-wide framework of human rights instruments. The purpose of giving it domestic effect under the Human Rights Act 1998 was to 'bring rights home': in other words, to spare applicants the necessity of going to the European Court of Human Rights, by requiring domestic courts (and other public authorities) to ensure that Convention requirements were met within the domestic legal order. The purpose of giving the Convention effect under the Scotland Act 1998 was to prevent the Scottish Parliament and Executive from placing the United Kingdom in breach of its international obligations. So the Convention has a Janus-like aspect: it has to be interpreted and applied by our domestic courts as part of our domestic law; but its meaning and effect in any particular case may be ultimately determined by an international court whose members are drawn from all 43 Contracting States, and which can be regarded to some extent as performing, so far as fundamental rights are concerned, the role of a European constitutional court.

The effect given to the Convention has implications for the relationship between the courts and other institutions of government, and for the relationship between law and public opinion. That has become apparent even in the short period since the Scotland Act and the Human Rights Act came into force. The full implications will become clear only after a much longer period. What is perhaps striking about the Scottish experience to date is that political institutions, the courts and public opinion have all, by and large, responded positively: an effort has been made to master unfamiliar material and to address the issues in a measured and careful manner, without insularity or complacency.

It is too early to judge what effect the incorporation[1] of the Convention will have upon Scots law and society. Experience to date suggests that both the hopes and the fears expressed by some commentators prior to incorporation are likely to prove to have been exaggerated. However, the incorporation of the Convention has already resulted in a number of changes to our law of some significance, particularly concerning the machinery of the administration of justice. Many of these changes have been the result of legislation rather than of court decisions. So far as the courts are concerned, most of the issues which have arisen have challenged the procedure and institutions by which decisions are taken; and most of the decisions of the courts have been based on principles which are fundamental to our own criminal or constitutional law. More controversial issues may lie ahead, when the implications of the Convention for areas of substantive law, such as family law and the law of privacy, may have to be addressed[2]. The Convention is, however, unlikely often to steer our legal system in unfamiliar or unwelcome directions: it expresses the values of a tolerant and inclusive society as those values are judged in the Europe of the twenty-first century; and it would seem to be reasonable to expect those values to be in line, on the whole, with those which are generally accepted in contemporary Scotland.

The need to learn about Convention jurisprudence has encouraged the publication of a plethora of books on the subject. The aims of the present work are modest. It is intended as an introduction to Convention materials for Scots lawyers and law students. It does not attempt the depth of critical analysis to be found in the leading monographs on Convention law. It attempts rather to present, in a relatively short volume, an explanation of the domestic legislation giving effect to the Convention (Chapter 1), the institutions and procedures established by the Convention (Chapter 2), the general principles of Convention law (Chapter 3), the application of the Convention by the European Court of Human Rights and by British courts in each of its main subject-areas (Chapters 5 to 8), and the text of the relevant domestic and Convention provisions (the Appendices). The book is intended for the lawyer or student who requires a concise guide to the Convention as interpreted by the European Court of Human Rights and as applied in Scotland.

The book does not in general attempt to connect the Convention material to pre-existing Scots law, for which reference can be made to the standard textbooks. Most of the book is also devoted to the Convention materials rather than to the terms of the domestic legislation giving effect to it. This reflects the fact that there has to date been relatively little judicial discussion of the Scotland Act or the Human Rights Act, at least when compared with the volume of Convention jurisprudence. It is, however,

---

1 A convenient shorthand expression, but one which is not strictly accurate.
2 A process which has already begun, particularly in England and Wales: see below, Ch. 6.

important to emphasise at the outset that it is the two Acts which form part of our domestic law, rather than the Convention itself; and in practice the most important and difficult questions will often concern the application of the domestic provisions rather than the interpretation of the Convention. A practitioner who has investigated the law on a particular Convention right has performed only one part of his task: he must equally consider how the Convention right has been given effect in Scots law via the provisions of the Scotland Act or the Human Rights Act.

We received invaluable assistance from Patricia Orr, Gavin Simpson (now legal officer with the Office of High Representative, Bosnia and Herzcegovina) and Sarah Summers (now legal researcher at the University of Zurich) in researching the Convention materials, and are most grateful to them for their help. At a later stage, the assistance in the preparation of the table of cases of Roddy Hart and Jamie McRorie, two other recent Glasgow law graduates, proved indispensable. The encouragement and patience of the staff of Butterworths Scotland is acknowledged. We are also most grateful to the staff of the Human Rights Library of the Council of Europe in Strasbourg. The usual disclaimers apply.

We have attempted generally to state the law as at 31 August 2001.

Robert Reed and Jim Murdoch
September 2001

Contents

Table of statutes

All references in this table are to paragraph numbers.

Table of statutory instruments

All references in this table are to paragraph numbers.

Table of European legislation and international/UN conventions

All references in this table are to paragraph numbers.

xvii

Table of cases

All references in this table are to paragraph numbers.

United Kingdom Cases

Other Domestic Jurisdictions and International Tribunals

Judgments of the European Court of Human Rights

All references in this table are to paragraph numbers. For a discussion of citation of judgments, see paras 2.44–2.45.

Commission and Court Decisions on Admissibility and Commission Reports on the Merits – Alphabetical list

All references in this table are to paragraph numbers. For a discussion of citation of decisions and reports, see paras 2.44 and 2.46.

Commission and Court Decisions on Admissibility and Commission Reports on the Merits – Numerical list

All references in this table are to paragraph numbers. For a discussion of citation of decisions and reports, see paras 2.44 and 2.46.

List of abbreviations

A	Series A Publications of the European Court of Human Rights [see para 2.45]
AC	Appeal Cases Law Reports
AJIL	American Journal of International Law
All ER	All England Law Reports
asp	Act of the Scottish Parliament
B	Series B Publications of the European Court of Human Rights [see para 2.44]
BCLC	Butterworths Company Law Cases
BCLR	Butterworths Constitutional Law Reports
BYBIL	British Yearbook of International Law
CA	Court of Appeal
CD	Collection of Decisions of the European Commission of Human Rights [see para 2.44]
CLJ	Cambridge Law Journal
Colum Hum Rts L Rev	Columbia Human Rights law Review
Comms L	Communications Law
CP(S)A	Criminal Procedure (Scotland) Act 1995
CPT	European Committee for the Prevention of Torture and Inhuman and Degrading Treatment or Punishment
Cr App R	Criminal Appeal Reports
Crim LR	Criminal Law Review
Ct of S	Court of Session
DR	Decisions and Reports of the European Commission of Human Rights [see para 2.44]
ECR	European Court Reports
E Europ HRRev	East European Human Rights Review
Ed Law	Education and the Law
EHRLR	European Human Rights Law Review
EJIL	European Journal of International Law
ELRev	European Law Review
EMLR	Entertainment and Media Law Reports
ET	Employment Tribunal
ETS	European Treaty Series
EuGRZ	Europäische Grundrechte Zeitschrift
EPL	European Public Law
Fam	Family Division Law Reports
Fam Law	Family Law
FCR	Family Court Reporter
FLR	Family Law Reports
HCJ	High Court of Justiciary
HLR	Housing Law Reports
HRA	Human Rights Act 1998
HRLJ	Human Rights Law Journal
HRLR	Human Rights Law Reports
HRQ	Human Rights Quarterly
HR & UKP	Human Rights and UK Practice
ICC	International Criminal Court
ICLQ	International and Comparative Law Quarterly

ICR	Industrial Case Reports
IH	Inner House, Court of Session
Imm A R	Immigration Appeal Reports
Int Jo Children's Rights	International Journal of Children's Rights
Interights Bull	Interights Bulletin
IR	Irish Reports
IRLR	Industrial Relations Law Reports
JC	Justiciary Cases
JCPC	Judicial Committee of the Privy Council
JLSS	Journal of the Law Society of Scotland
J Env L	Journal of Environmental Law
J L & Ed	Journal of Law and Education
JPL	Journal of Planning and Environment Law
JR	Juridical Review
KB	King's Bench Law Reports
LQR	Law Quarterly Review
Med L Rev	Medical Law Review
Med Sci Law	Medicine, Science and the Law
MLR	Modern Law Review
NLJ	New Law Journal
Nott L J	Nottingham Law Journal
NQHR	Netherlands Quarterly of Human Rights
OH	Outer House, Court of Session
OJEC	Official Journal of the European Communities
OSCE	Organisation for Security and Co-operation in Europe
PL	Public Law
QB	Queen's Bench Law Reports
QBD	Queen's Bench Division
SA	Scotland Act 1998
SC	Session Cases
SCC	Supreme Court Cases [Canada]
SCCR	Scottish Criminal Case Reports
SI	Statutory Instrument
SLPQ	Scottish Law and Practice Quarterly
SLT	Scots Law Times
SSI	Scottish Statutory Instrument
Stat Law Rev	Statute Law Review
STC	Simons Tax Cases
Tech and Con Ct	Technology and Construction Court
Web JCLI	Web Journal of Current Legal Issues
WLR	Weekly Law Reports
YB	Yearbook of the European Convention on Human Rights

CHAPTER 1

The ECHR and Scots law

INTRODUCTION

1.01 As one of the constituent parts of the United Kingdom, Scotland has been affected by the European Convention on Human Rights ('the Convention') along with the remainder of the United Kingdom, particularly since the acceptance of the right of individual petition in 1966[1]. Scotland is of course a separate jurisdiction from England and Wales and Northern Ireland, with its own distinctive legal history and traditions, its own body of common law and statute law, its own system of courts and its own legal profession. In consequence, the impact of the Convention in Scotland has not been identical to that elsewhere in the United Kingdom. The cases which have gone to the Strasbourg institutions from Scotland have often arisen within a particularly Scottish context; and the treatment of the Convention by the Scottish courts has also had a distinctive history.

1 This was delayed so as to prevent any challenge to the War Damage Act 1965, which deprived the pursuers of the fruits of their victory in *Burmah Oil Co (Burmah Trading) Ltd v Lord Advocate* 1964 SC (HL) 117.

1.02 The distinctiveness of the impact of the European Convention on Human Rights in Scotland is unlikely to diminish in the new constitutional context established by the Scotland Act 1998 and the Human Rights Act 1998. The Scotland Act 1998, in particular, by providing Scotland with a Parliament empowered to legislate in most areas of domestic affairs, seems likely to bring about a greater divergence between the law in Scotland and that elsewhere in the United Kingdom. As the Scottish Parliament and Executive cannot (in general) competently act in contravention of the Convention, however, the Scotland Act 1998 is apt to create a body of case law on the Convention which will complement that created both in Scotland and elsewhere under the Human Rights Act 1998.

1.03 This chapter will consider the Convention and Scots law under the following headings:

- Scottish cases in Strasbourg;
- the Convention in the Scottish courts prior to the 1998 Acts;
- the Scotland Act 1998 and the Convention;
- the Human Rights Act 1998.

SCOTTISH CASES IN STRASBOURG

1.04 Cases in Strasbourg which emanate from Scotland do not always have a distinctively Scottish dimension. Where the law and practice in Scotland are effectively identical to those elsewhere in the United Kingdom, the national background of a case is of no particular importance. This is reflected in the fact that the law in Scotland has often been altered in response to Strasbourg decisions in cases from other parts of the United Kingdom, just as the law in England and Wales and Northern Ireland is liable to require alteration in consequence of a Strasbourg decision in a Scottish case. Nevertheless, a survey of Scottish cases is likely to be of value to Scottish practitioners, particularly as the issues raised by Scottish applicants have in practice tended to arise from a distinctively Scottish context.

1.05 Several of the Scottish cases decided by the European Court of Human Rights have concerned aspects of criminal procedure: notably the composition of a jury[1]; the examination of witnesses before the Appeal Court[2]; legal aid for criminal appeals[3]; legal representation in criminal appeals[4]; and the 'sifting' procedure whereby the court decides whether to grant leave to appeal[5]. These issues have been considered under reference to Article 6(1)[6], (3)(c)[7] and (d)[8] of the European Convention on Human Rights. 'Just satisfaction' has been considered in several of these cases[9].

1 *Pullar v United Kingdom* 1996-III, 783.
2 *Pullar v United Kingdom* 1996-III, 783.
3 *Granger v United Kingdom* (1990) A 174.
4 *Boner v United Kingdom* (1994) A 300-B; *Maxwell v United Kingdom* A 300-C (1994).
5 40285/98, *Martin v United Kingdom* (7 September 1999).
6 *Pullar v United Kingdom* 1996-III, 783; *Martin v United Kingdom* (7 September 1999).
7 *Granger v United Kingdom* (1990) A 174: *Maxwell v United Kingdom* (1994) A 300-C; 40285/98, *Martin v United Kingdom* (7 September 1999).
8 *Pullar v United Kingdom* 1996-III, 783.
9 *Granger v United Kingdom* (1990) A 174; *Boner v United Kingdom* (1994) A 300-B; *Maxwell v United Kingdom* (1994) A 300-C.

1.06 Several cases have concerned aspects of prisoners' rights, such as correspondence[1], visits[2], leave[3] and prison conditions[4]. These issues have been examined under reference to Articles 3[5], 8[6], 10[7], 13[8] and 25[9] of the European Convention on Human Rights. 'Just satisfaction' has been considered in all these cases.

1 *Boyle and Rice v United Kingdom* (1988) A 131; *McCallum v United Kingdom* (1990) A 183; *Campbell v United Kingdom* (1992) A 233-A.
2 *Boyle and Rice v United Kingdom* (1988) A 131.
3 *Boyle and Rice v United Kingdom* (1988) A 131.
4 *McCallum v United Kingdom* (1990) A 183.
5 *McCallum v United Kingdom* (1990) A 183.
6 *Boyle and Rice v United Kingdom* (1988) A 131; *McCallum v United Kingdom* (1990) A 183; *Campbell v United Kingdom* (1992) A 233-A.
7 *McCallum v United Kingdom* (1990 A 183).
8 *Boyle and Rice v United Kingdom* (1988) A 131; *McCallum v United Kingdom* (1990) A 183.
9 *Campbell v United Kingdom* (1992) A 233-A.

1.07 The law relating to children was examined in one case which concerned procedure at a children's hearing and parental rights in relation to an illegitimate child[1]. These issues were examined in relation to Articles 6(1), 8 and 14 of the European Convention on Human Rights. 'Just satisfaction' was also considered. In another case corporal punishment in schools was examined in relation to Article 3 of the Convention and Article 2 of Protocol 1[2]. A subsequent judgment[3] dealt with 'just satisfaction'. Another case considered procedures in the Court of Session for the enforcement of a contact order made by an English court in the light of Articles 6 and 8 of the Convention[4].

1 *McMichael v United Kingdom* (1995) A 307-B.
2 *Campbell and Cosans v United Kingdom* (1982) A 48.
3 *Campbell and Cosans v United Kingdom* (1983) A 60.
4 *Glaser v United Kingdom* (19 September 2000).

1.08 The protection of property has been considered in one case concerning the nationalisation of an industry, the adequacy of compensation and the assessment of compensation by a statutory tribunal[1]. These issues were examined in relation to Articles 6(1) and 13 of the European Convention on Human Rights and Article 1 of Protocol 1 (taken alone and in conjunction with Article 14 of the Convention).

1 *Lithgow v United Kingdom* (1986) A 102.

1.09 Two cases arising from the participation of servicemen in nuclear tests raised a wide variety of issues concerning the duties of the Government to protect both the servicemen themselves and their future children; access to records; the recovery of documents; and (before the Commission) the interception of communications and the effectiveness of domestic remedies[1]. These issues were examined under Articles 2, 3, 6(1), 8, 10, 11, 13, 14 and 26 of the European Convention on Human Rights.

1 *McGinley and Egan v United Kingdom* 1998-III, 1334; 23413/94, *LCB v United Kingdom* 1998-III, 1390. The Commission's decision on admissibility in *McGinley and Egan* is 21825/93 (28 November 1995). Its decision on admissibility in *LCB* is reported at (1995) DR 83, 31. An application for revision of the *McGinley and Egan* judgment was refused by the E Ct HR in *McGinley and Egan v United Kingdom (No 2)* (11 January 2000).

1.10 A larger number of Scottish cases were considered by the European Commission on Human Rights prior to the establishment of the new court in November 1998. Although many are not reported in any published series of reports, they are available on the internet[1]. Broad categories have been used in the following survey to indicate the principal subject matter of the cases, but it should be appreciated that these are not watertight compartments.

1 At www.echr.coe.int .

1.11 The largest group of cases concerned aspects of criminal procedure. A large number of these concerned the availability of legal aid for trials[1] or appeals[2], and the related problem of appellants being unrepresented. These issues have been examined under Articles 6(1) and (3)(c) of the European Convention on Human Rights. Some of these cases have ended in friendly settlements[3]. In relation to pre-trial procedure, cases have concerned: the questioning of a suspect by the police without a solicitor being present[4]; detention without access to a solicitor[5]; detention under prevention of terrorism legislation[6]; the adequacy of time and facilities for the preparation of the defence[7]; absence of access to police statements and Crown precognitions[8]; the late instruction of counsel[9]; the refusal of an adjournment of the trial[10]; the obtaining ex parte of a warrant to take hair samples[11]; the forcible execution of such a warrant[12]; and conviction on a charge of obstructing the execution of a warrant to obtain bodily samples and teeth impressions[13]. These issues have been examined under the Convention, Articles 3[14], 5[15], 6(1)[16], (3)(b)[17], (c)[18] and (d)[19] and 7[20]. In relation to trial procedure, cases have concerned: the composition of the jury[21]; the impartiality of the jury[22]; newspaper reporting of the trial[23]; the adequacy of legal representation at the trial[24]; alleged errors of fact in the judge's charge[25]; and deletions from the indictment[26]. These issues have been considered under the Convention, Article 6. Conviction on a basis of concert rather than as an actor has been examined under Article 6[27]. Conviction on an individual basis under an indictment libelling mobbing and rioting has been examined under Article 7[28]. In relation to appeal procedure, cases have concerned: the handcuffing of an appellant during the hearing of his appeal[29]; access to the transcript of the trial[30]; access to a translation of the trial judge's charge and report to the Appeal Court[31]; the withdrawal of counsel[32]; the increase of sentence by the Appeal Court[33]; its refusal to allow the abandonment of an appeal[34]; its impartiality[35]; its refusal of an adjournment[36]; its alleged refusal to allow an appeal to be presented[37]; its receipt of a witness statement[38]; its substitution of a conviction in amended terms[39]; the absence of a right of appeal to the House of Lords[40]; and the absence of a right to compensation[41]. These issues have been examined under the Convention, Article 6 (and, in respect of a right to compensation, Articles 5(5) and 13[42]). The length of proceedings has been examined under Article 6(1) in a case in which there was a delay in bringing a case to trial[43]. 'Just satisfaction' was also considered. An increase in statutory sentencing powers has been examined under Article 7[44]. The ability of a Secretary of State's reference to cure defects in an earlier appeal hearing has also been considered[45]. The question of whether a person has a right to have criminal proceedings instituted against other persons has been considered in relation to Articles 5, 6[46] and 13[47].

1   11711/85, *McDermitt v United Kingdom* (1987) DR 52, 244; 12322/86, *Bell v United Kingdom* (13 October 1987); 12370/86, *S v United Kingdom* (9 December 1987); 12917/87, *Drummond v United Kingdom* (9 December 1987).

2   16212/90, *R v United Kingdom* (17 April 1991); 14778/99, *Higgins v United Kingdom* (1992) DR 73, 95; 18711/91, *B v United Kingdom* (4 May 1993); 25523/94, *Murdoch v United Kingdom* (12 April 1996); 23934/94, *Middleton v United Kingdom* (12 April 1996); 22112/93, *Wotherspoon v United Kingdom* (12 April 1996); 24487/94, *Given v United Kingdom* (12 April 1996); 25648/94, *Robson v United Kingdom* (15 May 1996); 28891/95, *McAteer v United Kingdom* (2 July 1997); 31021/96, *Taylor v United Kingdom* (22 October 1997), 28944/95, *Faulkner v United Kingdom* (4 March 1998).

3   11711/85, *McDermitt v United Kingdom* (1987) DR 52, 244; 14778/99, *Higgins v United Kingdom* (1992) DR 73, 95.

4   25648/94, *Robson v United Kingdom* (15 May 1996).

5   13081/87, *Windsor v United Kingdom* (14 December 1988); 25648/94, *Robson v United Kingdom* (15 May 1996).

6   11641/85, *C v United Kingdom* (12 July 1986); 15096/89, *McGlinchey v United Kingdom* (2 July 1990).

7 13081/87, *Windsor v United Kingdom* (14 December 1988); 23934/94, *Middleton v United Kingdom* (12 April 1996).
8 22112/93, *Wotherspoon v United Kingdom* (12 April 1996).
9 12834/87, *Boyle v United Kingdom* (3 March 1988).
10 26282/95, *Burns v United Kingdom* (4 September 1996).
11 34723/97, *Mellors v United Kingdom* (21 May 1998).
12 34723/97, *Mellors v United Kingdom* (21 May 1998).
13 34723/97, *Mellors v United Kingdom* (21 May 1998).
14 34723/97, *Mellors v United Kingdom* (21 May 1998).
15 11641/85, *BC v United Kingdom* (12 July 1986); 15096/89, *McGlinchey v United Kingdom* (2 July 1990).
16 13081/87, *Windsor v United Kingdom* (14 December 1988); 25648/94, *Robson v United Kingdom* (15 May 1996).
17 11396/85, *JWR v United Kingdom* (11 December 1986); 13081/87, *Windsor v United Kingdom* (14 December 1988); 23934/94, *Middleton v United Kingdom* (12 April 1996); 22112/93, *Wotherspoon v United Kingdom* (12 April 1996).
18 13081/87, *Windsor v United Kingdom* (14 December 1988); 34723/97, *Mellors v United Kingdom* (21 May 1998).
19 22112/93, *Wotherspoon v United Kingdom* (12 April 1996).
20 34723/97, *Mellors v United Kingdom* (21 May 1998).
21 24399/94, *Mennie v United Kingdom* (16 October 1994).
22 23934/94, *Middleton v United Kingdom* (12 April 1996).
23 23934/94, *Middleton v United Kingdom* (12 April 1996).
24 25523/94, *Murdoch v United Kingdom* (12 April 1996); 23934/94, *Middleton v United Kingdom* (12 April 1996); 25648/94, *Robson v United Kingdom* (15 May 1996).
25 32874/96, *Moore v United Kingdom* (11 September 1997).
26 24399/94, *Mennie v United Kingdom* (16 October 1994).
27 12323/86, *Campbell v United Kingdom* (1988) DR 57, 148.
28 21266/93, *K v United Kingdom* (30 June 1993).
29 12323/86, *Campbell v United Kingdom* (1988) DR 57, 148.
30 18077/91, *Montes and Lopez v United Kingdom* (2 December 1992).
31 18077/91, *Montes and Lopez v United Kingdom* (2 December 1992).
32 12834/87, *Boyle v United Kingdom* (3 March 1988).
33 12002/86, *Grant v United Kingdom* (1988) DR 55, 218.
34 12002/86, *Grant v United Kingdom* (1988) DR 55, 218.
35 12002/86, *Grant v United Kingdom* (1988) DR 55, 218.
36 25523/94, *Murdoch v United Kingdom* (12 April 1996).
37 24487/94, *Given v United Kingdom* (12 April 1996); 26282/95, *Burns v United Kingdom* (4 September 1996); 28944/95, *Faulkner v United Kingdom* (4 March 1998).
38 24399/94, *Mennie v United Kingdom* (16 October 1994), applying *Pullar v United Kingdom* 1996-III, 783.
39 24399/94, *Mennie v United Kingdom* (16 October 1994).
40 24399/94, *Mennie v United Kingdom* (16 October 1994).
41 24399/94, *Mennie v United Kingdom* (16 October 1994).
42 24399/94, *Mennie v United Kingdom* (16 October 1994).
43 21437/93, *Dougan v United Kingdom* 1997 SCCR 56.
44 14099/88, *Gillies v United Kingdom* (14 April 1989).
45 16732/90, *WK v United Kingdom* (11 January 1993).
46 13081/87, *Windsor v United Kingdom* (14 December 1988).
47 18077/91, *Montes and Lopez v United Kingdom* (2 December 1992).

1.12 Aspects of civil procedure have been considered in a number of cases. These include cases concerned with: a vexatious litigant order (and the European Convention on Human Rights, Article 6(1))[1]; summary warrant procedure in connection with taxes[2] and rates[3] (and its compatibility with Article 6(1)); child maintenance review procedures[4]; directors' disqualification proceedings (in particular, the disclosure of information, the giving of reasons and the effectiveness of judicial review, under Article 6(1))[5]; an unfair dismissal hearing before an industrial tribunal following acquittal in criminal proceedings (compatibility with Article

6(1) and (2))[6]; the Warsaw Convention (as applied in *Abnett v British Airways plc*[7]) (examined under Articles 1, 2, 3, 5, 6(1), 8, 13 and 14 of the European Convention on Human Rights, and Article 1 of Protocol 1)[8]; the treatment of a party litigant[9]; the adequacy of rights of appeal from the Lands Tribunal for Scotland[10]; procedure at a public inquiry (compatibility with Article 6(1) and (2))[11]; and the effect of developments in the common law on prior transactions (compatibility with Article 1 of Protocol 1)[12].

1 11559/85, *H v United Kingdom* (1985) DR 45, 281.
2 25373/94, *Smith v United Kingdom* (29 November 1995).
3 25602/94, *ANM & Co v United Kingdom* (29 November 1995).
4 24875/94, *Logan v United Kingdom* (1996) DR 86, 74.
5 28530/95, *X v United Kingdom* (19 January 1998).
6 11882/85, *C v United Kingdom* (1987) DR 54, 162.
7 1997 SC (HL) 26.
8 37650/97, *Manners v United Kingdom* (21 May 1998); 38698/97, *Sykes v United Kingdom* (21 May 1998).
9 13475/87, *Kay v United Kingdom* (2 May 1989).
10 13135/87, *S and Others v United Kingdom* (1988) DR 56, 268.
11 22301/93, *McKenzie v United Kingdom* (1 December 1993).
12 37857/97, *Bank of Scotland v United Kingdom* (21 October 1998), considering *Smith v Bank of Scotland* 1997 SC (HL) 10.

1.13   Several cases have concerned prisoners' rights. Particular issues have included: interference with correspondence with a solicitor[1]; or with the court[2]; restrictions on lawyers' visits[3]; restrictions on television interviews[4]; solitary confinement[5]; imprisonment in a remote location[6]; the transfer of prisoners to Scotland[7]; denial of access to a telephone[8]; lockdown conditions[9]; parole, in particular the system of periodical reviews and the withdrawal of a release recommendation following an incident which resulted in the prisoner's being charged and acquitted[10]; and the position of child offenders in relation to remission[11]. These issues have been considered under the European Convention on Human Rights, Articles 3[12], 5[13], 6[14], 8[15], 10[16], 13[17] and 25[18].

1 10621/83, *McComb v United Kingdom* (1986) DR 50, 81 (friendly settlement); 20075/92, *Leech v United Kingdom* (31 August 1994) (considering *Leech v Secretary of State for Scotland* 1993 SLT 365).
2 11392/85, *Hodgson v United Kingdom* (4 March 1987).
3 12323/86, *Campbell v United Kingdom* (1988) DR 57, 148.
4 12656/87, *K v United Kingdom* (13 May 1988).
5 12323/86, *Campbell v United Kingdom* (1988) DR 57, 148.
6 14462/88, *Ballantyne v United Kingdom* (12 April 1991).
7 15817/89, *Wakefield v United Kingdom* (1990) DR 66, 251.
8 18077/91, *Montes and Lopez v United Kingdom* (2 December 1992).
9 18942/91, *Windsor v United Kingdom* (6 April 1993); 25525/94, *Advic v United Kingdom* (6 September 1995).
10 20755/92, *Howden v United Kingdom* (10 October 1994), applying *Wynne v United Kingdom* A 294 (1994) and considering *Howden v Parole Board for Scotland* 1992 GWD 20-1186.
11 11077/84, *Nelson v United Kingdom* (1986) DR 49, 170.
12 18942/91, *Windsor v United Kingdom* (6 April 1993); 25525/94, *Advic v United Kingdom* (6 September 1995).
13 20755/92, *Howden v United Kingdom* (10 October 1994); 11077/84, *Nelson v United Kingdom* (1986) DR 49, 170.
14 12323/86, *Campbell v United Kingdom* (1988) DR 57, 148; 10621/83, *McComb v United Kingdom* (1986) DR 50, 81 (friendly settlement); 20946/92, *Veenstra v United Kingdom* (31 August 1994); 20755/92, *Howden v United Kingdom* (10 October 1994).

15 10621/83, *McComb v United Kingdom* (1986) DR 50, 81 (friendly settlement); 11392/85, *Hodgson v United Kingdom* (4 March 1987); 15817/89, *Wakefield v United Kingdom* (1 October 1990); 14462/88, *Ballantyne v United Kingdom* (12 April 1991); 20946/92, *Veenstra v United Kingdom* (8 August 1994); 20075/92, *Leech v United Kingdom* (31 August 1994).
16 12656/87, *K v United Kingdom* (13 May 1988).
17 18942/91, *Windsor v United Kingdom* (6 April 1993); 20075/92, *Leech v United Kingdom* (31 August 1994).
18 12323/86, *Campbell v United Kingdom* (1988) DR 57, 148.

1.14 Immigration law has been considered in one case under the European Convention on Human Rights, Article 8, concerned with re-admission as a returning resident[1]. No special issue of Scots law arose.

1 25525/94, *Advic v United Kingdom* (6 September 1995).

1.15 The law governing mentally disordered offenders was considered in a case under the European Convention on Human Rights, Article 5(1)(e) and (4) concerned with the absence of a judicial remedy allowing the periodic review of detention[1].

1 10213/82 *Gordon v United Kingdom* (1985) DR 47, 36 (following *X v United Kingdom*, Judgment of 5 November (1981) A 46).

1.16 Other cases have concerned a variety of issues, including: the interception of communications[1]; a closed shop agreement[2]; the effects of a child maintenance order on access to the children and on religious observance[3]; the suspension of invalidity benefits during imprisonment[4]; corporal punishment in schools and 'philosophical convictions'[5]; the failure of the state to provide financial assistance for private education[6]; a prohibition, by an order made under the *nobile officium*[7], of the broadcasting of a television programme until the completion of a criminal trial[8]; compensation for the compulsory purchase of land[9]; differences between valuations for rating in Scotland and in England[10]; the security vetting of prospective employees[11]; the keeping of dossiers on individuals by the Security Services and others[12]; an employer's right to reprimand an employee who wrote to a newspaper without permission[13]; dismissal for a theft of which the employee had not been convicted[14]; the loss of tied accommodation[15]; privilege under the law of defamation[16]; and the Crown's refusal to disclose a post-mortem report to a relative of the deceased[17]. Other cases have illustrated issues which may arise in relation to company law[18] and in relation to the taking of children into care[19].

1 21482/93, *Christie v United Kingdom* (1994) DR 78, 119: European Convention on Human Rights, Article 8.
2 9520/81, *Reid v United Kingdom* (1983) DR 34, 107: ECHR, Art 11.
3 24875/94, *Logan v United Kingdom* (1996) DR 86, 74: Arts 8 and 9.
4 27537/95, *Carlin v United Kingdom* (3 December 1997): Protocol 1, Art 1.
5 8566/79, *X, Y and Z v United Kingdom* (1982) DR 31, 50: Protocol 1, Art 2.
6 9461/81, *X and Y v United Kingdom* (1982) DR 31, 210: Protocol 1, Art 2.
7 Ie the High Court of Justiciary's inherent equitable jurisdiction.
8 34324/96, *BBC Scotland, McDonald, Rodgers and Donald v United Kingdom* (23 October 1997).
9 13135/87, *S v United Kingdom* (1988) DR 56, 268.
10 13473/87, *P v United Kingdom* (11 July 1988): Protocol 1, Art 1 and Art 14 of the Convention.
11 12015/86, *Hilton v United Kingdom* (1988) DR 57, 108: ECHR, Art 8. This decision contains a discussion of the status of the BBC under the Convention.

12 12015/86, *Hilton v United Kingdom* (1988) DR 57, 108.
13 16936/90, *Todd v United Kingdom* (7 November 1990): ECHR, Art 10.
14 28530/95, *X v United Kingdom* (19 January 1998): ECHR, Art 6(2).
15 28530/95, *X v United Kingdom* (19 January 1998): ECHR, Art 8.
16 22301/93, *McKenzie v United Kingdom* (1 December 1993): ECHR, Art 6.
17 11516/85, *B v United Kingdom* (13 May 1986): ECHR, Arts 8 and 10.
18 11413/85, *A v United Kingdom* (13 May 1986): Protocol 1, Art 1.
19 19579/92, *B Family v United Kingdom* (4 April 1993): Arts 3, 5, 6, 8 and 13 of the
    Convention, and Protocol 1, Art 2.

THE CONVENTION IN THE SCOTTISH COURTS PRIOR TO THE 1998 ACTS

1.17   Although Scotland has contributed significantly to the jurisprudence of the European Court of Human Rights and the European Commission on Human Rights, the Scottish courts were relatively slow to make use of the Convention. In *Surjit Kaur v Lord Advocate*[1] Lord Ross expressed the view that a Scottish court was not entitled to have regard to the Convention, either as an aid to construction or otherwise, unless and until its provisions were given statutory effect. Although obiter dictum[2] this view was approved by the Inner House (again, obiter) in *Moore v Secretary of State for Scotland*[3]. This restrictive approach[4] discouraged reference to the Convention in Scottish cases for many years, although such references appeared in the speeches in the House of Lords in *Lord Advocate v Scotsman Publications Ltd*[5]. This was in contrast to the approach adopted in England and Wales, not least by Scottish judges sitting in the House of Lords[6].

1 1980 SC 319.
2 There was conceded to be no ambiguity in the legislation in issue in *Surjit Kaur v Lord
   Advocate* 1980 SC 319, and thus no room for the use of the Convention as an aid to interpretation: see 1980 SC at 329.
3 1985 SLT 38.
4 The presumption that Parliament does not intend to legislate in a manner inconsistent
   with the treaty obligations entered into by the Crown appears to have been accepted in
   Scots law prior to *Surjit Kaur* and *Moore*: see eg *Mortensen v Peters* (1906) 8 F (J) 93.
5 1989 SC (HL) 122.
6 Eg *Waddington v Miah* [1974] 1 WLR 683 at 694 per Lord Reid; *A-G v British Broadcasting
   Corp* [1981] AC 303 at 352 per Lord Fraser of Tullybelton.

1.18   The European Convention on Human Rights began, however, to have a direct impact upon the Scottish courts, particularly through a number of decisions of the European Court of Human Rights concerned with Scottish criminal proceedings. The first of these decisions, *Granger v United Kingdom*[1], resulted in the issue of a Practice Note by the Lord Justice-General, providing for a procedure whereby the High Court of Justiciary (as a court of appeal) could recommend the review of a decision of the legal aid authorities to refuse legal aid for representation at an appeal hearing. Subsequently, the cases of *Boner v United Kingdom*[2] and *Maxwell v United Kingdom*[3] resulted in a significant alteration of the criminal appeal system in Scotland, so as to end the automatic right of appeal against conviction or sentence and to introduce a requirement that leave to appeal be obtained. The High Court's awareness of the implications of the Convention was reflected in *Anderson v HM Advocate*, where Lord Hope of Craighead referred to Article 6 as describing 'principles which . . . have, for a long time, been established as part of the law of this country[4].

1 *Granger v United Kingdom* (1990) A 174.
2 *Boner v United Kingdom* (1994) A 300-B.
3 *Maxwell v United Kingdom* (1994) A 300-C.
4 1996 JC 29 at 34.

1.19 Following his appointment as Lord President and Lord Justice-General, Lord Hope made clear extra-judicially his concerns over the difference in approach to the European Convention on Human Rights which was at least believed to exist between the Scottish and English courts, and the consequent reluctance of Scottish counsel to make use of the Convention in argument[1]. Subsequently, in *T, Petitioner*[2], he took the opportunity to review the status of the Convention in Scots law. In relation to *Surjit Kaur*[3], he stated:

'Lord Ross's opinion, although widely quoted in the textbooks as still representing the law of Scotland on this matter, has been looking increasingly outdated in the light of subsequent developments, and in my opinion, with respect, it is time that it was expressly departed from[4].'

Lord Hope then reviewed the series of English cases in the House of Lords, culminating in *R v Secretary of State for the Home Department, ex p Brind*[5], which had established that in construing any provision in domestic legislation which is ambiguous in the sense that is capable of a meaning which either conforms to or conflicts with the Convention, the courts will presume that Parliament intended to legislate in uniformity with the Convention, not in conflict with it. Lord Hope concluded:

'I consider that the drawing of a distinction between the law of Scotland and that of the rest of the United Kingdom on this matter can no longer be justified. In my opinion the courts in Scotland should apply the same presumption as that described by Lord Bridge [in *ex p Brind*], namely that, when legislation is found to be ambiguous in the sense that it is capable of a meaning which either conforms to or conflicts with the Convention, Parliament is to be presumed to have legislated in conformity with the Convention, not in conflict with it[6].'

1 1991 JR 122 at 126–127; 'From Maastricht to the Saltmarket', Society of Solicitors in the Supreme Courts of Scotland, Biennial Lecture 1992, at 16–17. See also Lord Hope of Craighead 'Devolution and Human Rights' [1998] EHRLR 367.
2 1997 SLT 724.
3 *Surjit Kaur v Lord Advocate* 1980 SC 319.
4 1997 SLT at 733.
5 [1991] 1 AC 696.
6 1997 SLT 724 at 734.

1.20 Since *T, Petitioner* the European Convention on Human Rights has been cited with increasing frequency in the Scottish courts, particularly in the High Court of Justiciary. A notable example is *McLeod v HM Advocate*[1], concerned with the disclosure of documents to the defence in criminal proceedings, where the court carried out a close examination of the Strasbourg case law under Article 6(1) and was concerned to decide the case in a way which was consistent with Article 6(1). Other criminal cases involving the Convention have concerned: the compatibility with Articles 5(2) and 6(3)(a) of procedures for dealing with persons who did not speak English[2]; delay in the hearing of an appeal[3]; the adequacy of legal aid[4]; the withdrawal of legal aid[5]; contempt of court[6]; and the procedural rules governing the raising of a devolution issue[7]. The second-last mentioned case contains an instructive observation by the Lord Justice-General, Lord Rodger of Earlsferry[8], that, although a boundary has always existed between freedom of expression and the requirements of the due course of justice, Article 10 may have had the consequence of displacing that boundary from the familiar place where once it ran: the boundary may have been redrawn at a point which would not have been chosen by people looking at the matter primarily from the standpoint of the administration of justice. This is a useful reminder that, although the Convention gives expression to values which already infuse the law of Scotland, and may be regarded as commonplaces of all western legal systems, it does not always express or balance those values in the same way as Scots law has traditionally done.

1 1998 SCCR 77.
2 *Ucak v HM Advocate* 1998 SCCR 517.
3 *Ucak v HM Advocate* 1998 SCCR 517.
4 *Gayne v Vannet* 2000 SCCR 5.
5 *Shaw, Petitioner; Milne, Petitioner* 1998 SCCR 672.
6 *Cox and Griffiths, Petitioners* 1998 SCCR 561; *Al Megrahi v Times Newspapers Ltd* 1999 SCCR 824.
7 *HM Advocate v Dickson* 1999 SCCR 859.
8 *Cox and Griffiths, Petitioners* 1998 SCCR 561 at 568.

1.21   The European Convention on Human Rights has also featured in a number of civil cases. In *Booker Aquaculture Ltd v Secretary of State for Scotland* [1], Article 1 of Protocol 1 to the Convention was considered in the context of the implementation of European Community legislation. Article 8 of the Convention has also been referred to in the context of sexual harassment[2], and in numerous cases concerned with immigration[3]. The dismissal of an action on the ground of irrelevancy has also been considered in the light of Article 6[4].

1 2000 SC 9.
2 *Ward v Scotrail Railways Ltd* 1999 SC 255.
3 E g *Abdadou v Secretary of State for the Home Department* 1998 SC 504; *Akhtar v Secretary of State for the Home Department* 2001 SLT 1239.
4 *Crooks v Haddow* (1 March 2000, unreported) Ct of S.

1.22   As is apparent from the foregoing discussion, the European Convention on Human Rights has already influenced the law and practice in Scotland in many fields. Even before the commencement of the Scotland Act 1998 or the Human Rights Act 1998, the Convention had begun to be used more creatively by the courts in Scotland, with the consequence that its influence on the law of Scotland was certain to increase.

THE SCOTLAND ACT 1998 AND THE CONVENTION

1.23   The Government elected in May 1997 had a manifesto commitment to a programme of constitutional reform, including devolution to Scotland and the incorporation of the European Convention on Human Rights into UK law. The White Paper on devolution[1], published in July 1997, left open the precise implications for devolution of incorporating the Convention, although making it clear that the Scottish Executive and Parliament would implement the UK's international obligations[2]. There were two broad approaches by means of which this could be achieved in respect of the Convention: by enabling the UK Government to override acts of the Scottish Executive or Parliament which would contravene the Convention, or by making it legally impossible for the Scottish Executive or Parliament to contravene the Convention. The White Paper on the Human Rights Bill[3], published in October 1997, made it clear that the latter approach was to be adopted:

> 'The Government has decided that the Scottish Parliament will have no power to legislate in a way which is incompatible with the Convention; and similarly that the Scottish Executive will have no power to make subordinate legislation or to take executive action which is incompatible with the Convention. It will accordingly be possible to challenge such legislation and actions on the ground that the Scottish Parliament or Executive has incorrectly applied its powers. If the challenge is successful then the legislation or action would be held to be unlawful.'[4]

These proposals were reflected in the provisions of the Scotland Bill, which were enacted (with substantial modifications) in the Scotland Act 1998[5]. It should be made clear at the outset that SA 1998 is complex and raises many difficult questions, and that the following account attempts only to give an outline of the principal features relevant to the Convention[6]. There are numerous qualifications and exceptions on matters of detail, for which reference should be made to SA 1998 itself.

1   *Scotland's Parliament* (Cm 3658) (1997).
2   *Scotland's Parliament* (Cm 3658) (1997), paras 4.19–4.20.
3   *Rights Brought Home* (Cm 3782) (1997).
4   *Rights Brought Home* (Cm 3782) (1997), para 2.21.
5   Scotland Act 1998 (c 46).
6   It should be borne in mind that the Convention is not the only human rights instrument which is relevant to the Scottish Parliament and Executive: see e g SA 1998, Sch 5, Pt I, para 7 (2).

Acts of the Scottish Parliament

1.24   The Scotland Act 1998, s 29(1) provides that an Act of the Scottish Parliament is not law so far as any provision of the Act is outside the legislative competence of the Parliament. Section 29(2) provides that a provision is outside that competence as far as any of the following paragraphs applies:

(a)   it would form part of the law of a country or territory other than Scotland, or confer or remove functions exercisable otherwise than in or as regards Scotland;

(b)   it relates to reserved matters;

(c)   it is in breach of the restrictions in Sch 4;

(d)   it is incompatible with any of the Convention rights or with Community law;

(e)   it would remove the Lord Advocate from his position as head of the system of criminal prosecution and investigation of deaths in Scotland.

1.25   Paragraphs (a) and (e) are not concerned with the European Convention on Human Rights. In relation to paragraph (b), the observation and implementation of obligations under the Convention are not reserved matters[1]. In relation to paragraph (c), Scotland Act 1998, Sch 4 provides that an Act of the Scottish Parliament cannot modify, or confer power by subordinate legislation to modify, any of a number of provisions including the Human Rights Act 1998[2]. SA 1998, Sch 4 also protects s 29 itself from modification by the Scottish Parliament[3]. In relation to paragraph (d), the expression 'the Convention rights' is defined[4] as having the same meaning as in HRA 1998 (where it is further defined)[5].

1 Scotland Act 1998, Sch 5, para 7(2).
2 SA 1998, Sch 4, para 1(1) and (2)(f).
3 SA 1998, Sch 4, para 4.
4 SA 1998, s 126(1).
5 Human Rights Act 1998, s 1.

1.26   The Scotland Act 1998 contains provisions to ensure that Bills are scrutinised before their introduction in the Scottish Parliament, and to allow for their further scrutiny prior to their submission for Royal Assent. Under SA 1998, s 31 a member of the Scottish Executive in charge of a Bill must, on or before introduction of the Bill in the Parliament, state that in his view the provisions of the Bill would be within the legislative competence of the Parliament[1]. In addition, the Presiding Officer[2] must, on or before the introduction of the Bill, decide whether or not in his view the provisions of the Bill would be within the legislative competence of the Parliament and state his decision[3]. In this way, the compatibility of any Bill with the Convention must be scrutinised both within the Scottish Executive and by an independent officer of the Scottish Parliament at an early stage. These statutory requirements are reflected in the Standing Orders of the Scottish Parliament[4]. Rule 9.3.1 requires a Bill, on its introduction, to be accompanied by a written statement signed by the Presiding Officer indicating whether or not in his or her view the provisions of the Bill would be within the legislative competence of the Parliament and, if in his or her view any of the provisions would not be within such competence, indicating which those provisions are and the reasons for that view. Rule 9.3.3 requires a Bill introduced by a member of the Scottish Executive also to be accompanied by a written statement signed by the member of the Scottish Executive in charge of the Bill which states that in his or her view the provisions of the Bill would be within the legislative competence of the Parliament. The statement must also include

Explanatory notes summarising the effect of the Bill and a Policy Memorandum which sets out:

(i)   the policy objectives of the Bill;
(ii)   whether alternative ways of meeting those objectives were considered and, if so, why the approach taken in the Bill was adopted;
(iii)   the consultation, if any, which was undertaken on those objectives and the ways of meeting them or on the detail of the Bill and a summary of the outcome of that consultation; and
(iv)   an assessment of the effects, if any, of the Bill on human rights and other matters. The Policy Memorandum may well be significant in assessing the compatibility of legislation with the Convention, particularly in applying the test of proportionality[5].

1 Scotland Act 1998, s 31(1).
2 SA 1998, s 19.
3 SA 1998, s 31(2).
4 Available on www.scottish.parliament.uk/parl_bus/stol.htm .
5 See paras 3.70ff.

1.27   Once a Bill has been passed, it is for the Presiding Officer to submit it for Royal Assent[1]. There is, however, a period of four weeks beginning with the passing of a Bill during which the Advocate General[2], the Lord Advocate or the Attorney General can refer to the Judicial Committee of the Privy Council for decision to the question of whether a Bill or any provision of a Bill would be within the legislative competence of the Parliament[3]. For this purpose the Judicial Committee will consist of the Lords of Appeal in Ordinary together with any other member of the Committee who has held high judicial office[4]. A Law Officer cannot, however, make a reference if he has notified the Presiding Officer that he does not intend to make a reference in relation to the Bill[5]. The Presiding Officer cannot submit a Bill for Royal Assent at any time when any of the Law Officers is entitled to make a reference, or when any such reference has been made but has not been decided or otherwise disposed of by the Judicial Committee[6]. If the Judicial Committee decides that the Bill or any provision of it would not be within the legislative competence of the Parliament, then the Presiding Officer cannot submit the Bill for Royal Assent in its unamended form[7]. The Bill can, however, be reconsidered by the Parliament following an adverse decision by the Judicial Committee; and any Bill amended on reconsideration can then be approved or rejected by the Parliament[8]. Where a Bill is approved following its reconsideration, there is then a further four-week period during which it can again be referred by a law officer to the Judicial Committee[9]. In principle, the process of referral, decision, amendment on reconsideration, approval and re-referral can be repeated indefinitely[10]. In the event that a reference to the Judicial Committee results in a reference to the European Court of Justice for a preliminary ruling, special provisions apply[11].

1 Scotland Act 1998, s 32(1).
2 SA 1998, s 87.
3 SA 1998, s 33(1) and (2)(a).
4 SA 1998, s 103(2).
5 SA 1998, s 33(3).
6 SA 1998, s 32(2)

7 SA 1998, s 32(3).
8 SA 1998, s 36(4).
9 SA 1998, s 33(2).
10 SA 1998, s 36(6).
11 SA 1998, s 34, read with SA 1998, ss 32(3)(b) and 36(4)(b).

1.28   The Scotland Act 1998 does not state expressly whether the above arrangements provide the only means whereby the compatibility of a Bill with the European Convention on Human Rights can be tested, or whether legal proceedings could be brought by third parties (eg against the member of the Scottish Executive responsible for making a statement under s 31(1); or against the Presiding Officer in respect of his decision under s 31(2); or against the Law Officers in respect of their exercise of their discretion under s 33(1); or against the Parliament itself in respect of its decision whether to pass a Bill or to approve a Bill amended on reconsideration). It is clear that legal proceedings can in principle be taken against a Law Officer or a member of the Scottish Executive; and SA 1998 provides for proceedings against the Parliament or the Presiding Officer, although only a restricted range of remedies is available[1]. A person seeking to challenge a Bill might, however, have difficulty in establishing title and interest to sue[2]. There is also a question whether issues concerning the legislative competence of the Parliament can, consistently with the scheme of SA 1998, be raised (other than by a Law Officer) except as a 'devolution issue' under SA 1998, s 98. Any person wishing to challenge a Bill on the basis of the Convention would in addition have to be a 'victim' for the purposes of Article 34 of the Convention[3]. That test would also apply to a challenge, based on the Convention, of a failure to introduce a Bill[4].

1 Scotland Act 1998, s 40. See *Whaley v Watson* 2000 SC 340.
2 See 592 HL Official Report (5th series) cols 1364–1377, and *Whaley v Watson* 2000 SC 340.
3 SA 1998, s 100(1). See para 1.84 below on the meaning of 'victim'.
4 Crown Proceedings Act 1947, s 21, would also be relevant to the remedies available: see SA 1998, Sch 8, para 7. CPA 1947 generally restricts the remedies available against the Scottish Ministers: SA 1998, Sch 8, para 7. This appears to have been overlooked in *Napier v The Scottish Ministers* (26 June 2001, unreported), Ct of S. See *Scott v The Scottish Ministers* (26 October 2001, unreported), Ct of S.

1.29   Issues which have arisen in practice as to the compatibility of Acts of the Scottish Parliament with the European Convention on Human Rights are described below under the heading 'Devolution issues'. Legislation has been introduced in a number of areas where existing law was thought to be incompatible with the Convention[1].

1 Eg the Bail, Judicial Appointments etc (Scotland) Act 2000; the Regulation of Investigatory Powers (Scotland) Act 2000; and the Convention Rights (Compliance) (Scotland) Act 2001.

Acts of the Scottish Administration

1.30   In order to understand how the European Convention on Human Rights applies under the Scotland Act 1998 to the Scottish Administration, it is necessary to begin with a rather complicated taxonomy. The Scottish Administration comprises the Scottish Executive (whose members are referred to collectively as the Scottish Ministers[1]), junior Scottish Ministers[2] and the staff of the Scottish Administration[3] (ie civil servants).

The members of the Scottish Executive are the First Minister, ministers appointed by the First Minister under SA 1998, s 47, the Lord Advocate and the Solicitor General for Scotland[4]. Statutory functions (ie functions conferred by any enactment, including an Act of the Scottish Parliament or an Act of the Westminster Parliament[5]) may be conferred on the Scottish Ministers as a whole, or on the First Minister alone, or on the Lord Advocate alone[6]. Statutory functions conferred on the Lord Advocate alone after he ceases to be a Minister of the Crown, together with any functions exercisable by him immediately before he ceases to be a Minister of the Crown, comprise his 'retained functions'[7].

1 Scotland Act 1998, s 44(2).
2 SA 1998, s 49.
3 SA 1998, s 51.
4 SA 1998, s 44(1).
5 SA 1998, ss 52(7) and 126(1).
6 SA 1998, s 52(1), (2), (5)(a) and (6)(b).
7 SA 1998, s 52(6).

1.31   The Scotland Act 1998, s 53 provides for the general transfer of existing ministerial functions to the Scottish Ministers. It applies to three specified categories of function which appear to cover all the functions exercisable by a Minister of the Crown[1] – subject to the important exception of the retained functions of the Lord Advocate – and provides that those functions 'shall, so far as they are exercisable within devolved competence', be exercisable by the Scottish Ministers. The expression 'within devolved competence' is explained in SA 1998, s 54. This provides first that the making of any provision by subordinate legislation is outside devolved competence if the provision would be outside the legislative competence of the Parliament if it were included in an Act of the Scottish Parliament.

In relation to any function other than a function of making, confirming or approving subordinate legislation, SA 1998, s 54 provides that it is outside devolved competence to exercise the function (or exercise it in any way) so far as a provision of an Act of the Scottish Parliament conferring the function (or, as the case may be, conferring it so as to be exercisable in that way) would be outside the legislative competence of the Parliament. These complex provisions are intended to have the effect (informally referred to as 'washing') that the functions transferred to the Scottish Ministers – other than the retained functions of the Lord Advocate – do not include any function which would be outside the legislative competence of the Scottish Parliament, and do not include any power to exercise a function in a way which would be outside the legislative competence of the Parliament.

Accordingly, in broad terms, if the exercise of an existing function of a Minister of the Crown is incompatible with any Convention right, then the function is not transferred to the Scottish Ministers. For example, since the Sheriff Courts (Scotland) Act 1971 conferred on the Secretary of State a power to appoint temporary sheriffs which was incompatible with the European Convention on Human Rights, that power was not transferred to the Scottish Ministers but remained with the Secretary of State[2]. Equally, if the exercise in a particular way of an existing function of a Minister of the Crown is incompatible with any Convention right, then the power to exercise it in that way is not transferred to the Scottish Ministers. The major exception to the last two propositions comprises any function exercisable by the Lord Advocate immediately before he ceased to be a Minister of the Crown: these functions are retained by him. One effect of these provisions is that the power to exercise Crown powers incompatibly with the Convention – for example, where that was required by an Act of the Westminster Parliament – was not devolved by the Scotland Act 1998, but did not disappear either: it was retained by the Crown, ie by the United Kingdom Government. Prosecution functions were, however, treated differently, because they were not to be retained by the United Kingdom Government – they continue to be exercised by the Lord Advocate; but because he is now a member of the Scottish Executive and, as such, covered by the provision (in SA 1998, s 57(2)) that a member of the Scottish Executive has no power to do any act incompatible with Convention rights, an exception was created (in s 57(3)) to enable him, and him alone, to act in breach of the Convention when that was necessary to implement Westminster legislation.

1 Subject to specified exceptions, eg functions exercisable in relation to cross-border public
   authorities: Scotland Act 1998, s 88(1).
2 *Starrs v Ruxton* 1999 SCCR 1052, 1079–1080, 1100–1101.

1.32   Compatibility with the European Convention on Human Rights is further addressed in the Scotland Act 1998, s 57(2). It provides that a member of the Scottish Executive has no power to make any subordinate legislation, or to do any other act, so far as the legislation or act is incompatible with any of the Convention rights. Compliance with the Convention is thus made by SA 1998 in to a question of vires. Nevertheless, the right to object under SA 1998 to a violation of the Convention can be waived[1].

1 *Clancy v Caird* 2000 SC 441; contrast *Millar v Dickson* 2001 SLT 988.

1.33   The term 'act' in s 57(2) of the Scotland Act 1998 has generally been given a wide construction. It has been said that the implementation of any executive or administrative decision must involve an 'act'[1]. In the context of criminal proceedings, it has been held to include the Lord Advocate's moving the court to grant a remedy[2]; and, generally, all actions taken or avoided by the Lord Advocate in the course of the prosecution of offences[3]. It has been held (in both civil and criminal proceedings) to include failure to act[4]. It has been treated (by concession) as including the initiation[5] and continuation[6] of a prosecution; the calling of an indictment[7]; the leading of evidence[8]; and an application for a confiscation order[9]; but it has been held not to include informal involvement in administrative arrangements for the transmission of trial proceedings by closed circuit television, the transmission having been authorised by the court and the arrangements being under the supervision of the court[10]. This approach is consistent with the intention[11] that the Scottish Executive should have no power to take executive action which is incompatible with the European Convention on Human Rights[12]. Perhaps more controversially, the questions whether the Scottish Ministers have failed to act so as to reform an aspect of the legal system which is said to be incompatible with the Convention have also been treated as constituting a devolution issue[13].

1 HM Advocate v Burns 2000 SCCR 884.
2 HM Advocate v Scottish Media Newspapers Ltd 1999 SCCR 599, 603. The making of an application for a confiscation order is an 'act': *HM Advocate v Burns* 2000 SCCR 884.
3 HM Advocate v Robb 1999 SCCR 971, 976.
4 HM Advocate v Robb at 975; *Clancy v Caird* 2000 SC 441.
5 HM Advocate v Robb 1999 SCCR 971.
6 Starrs v Ruxton 1999 SCCR 1052; *McNab v HM Advocate* 1999 SCCR 930; *McLean v HM Advocate* 2000 SCCR 112; *Paton v Ritchie* 2000 SCCR 151; *Buchanan v McLean* 2001 SCCR 475; *Millar v Dickson* 2001 SCCR 741.
7 HM Advocate v Little 1999 SCCR 625.
8 HM Advocate v Robb 1999 SCCR 971 at 976; *Paton v Ritchie* 2000 SCCR 151 at 154; *McKenna v HM Advocate* 2000 SCCR 159. A devolution issue can competently challenge the giving of notice of an intention to lead evidence, although it will normally (but not invariably) be premature to raise the issue prior to trial: see the cases cited (which might be contrasted with *HM Advocate v Campbell* 1999 SCCR 980 at 983). This is discussed further at para 1.51 below.
9 HM Advocate v McIntosh 2001 SCCR 191.
10 British Broadcasting Corporation, Petitioners 2000 SCCR 5333. See also *Hoekstra v HM Advocate (No 3)* 2000 SCCR 676.
11 See para 1.23 above.
12 Subject to the limited exception provided by Scotland Act 1998, s 57(3); as to which, see *Starrs v Ruxton* 1999 SCCR 1052 and *Millar v Dickson* 2001 SLT 988.
13 S v Miller 2001 SLT 531; see also *Clancy v Caird* 2000 SC 441.

1.34   Although the term 'act' has been given a wide construction, there remains the critical question whether the act is incompatible with any of the rights under the European Convention on Human Rights. In particular, it may be necessary to consider whether the act itself infringes any Convention right or gives rise to a real risk of such an infringement, or whether any infringement of Convention rights will not be the direct result of the act in question[1].

This issue gave rise to particular difficulty during the period prior to 2 October 2000, when the Scotland Act 1998 was fully in force but the Human Rights Act 1998 was not. In that situation, an 'act' such as the initiation or continuation of a prosecution, or the tendering of evidence by the prosecution, might ultimately result in a breach of the accused's Convention rights, if the law applied by the court (in deciding whether to allow the proceedings to continue, or to admit the evidence in question) did not meet Convention standards. In such a situation, the immediate cause of the breach of Convention rights would be a decision of the court, but the act of the prosecution would be a *sine qua non* of such a decision.

The approach taken by the High Court of Justiciary in most[2] (but not all[3]) such cases was to treat the act of the prosecution as incompatible with the Convention and therefore ultra vires, if it would inevitably result in an infringement (by the court) of the accused's Convention rights. This approach was questioned by some members of the Privy Council in *Montgomery v HM Advocate*[4]. It was suggested[5] that, although the Convention imposed an obligation upon the State as a whole, in the context of the Scotland Act 1998 it was necessary to identify the particular organ of government responsible for the infringement of the Convention right: if the infringement was the direct result of an act of the court, rather than an act of the prosecutor, there would be no devolution issue. In particular, the prosecutor could not infringe the right to a fair trial under the Convention, Article 6(1), since his acts are 'capable of creating the conditions for an unfair determination of the charge but they cannot in themselves cause such an extent and therefore infringe the provisions of article 6(1)'[6].

Another suggestion[7] was that the Scotland Act 1998 should be interpreted as prohibiting the Lord Advocate (or any other member of the Scottish Executive) from acting in a manner which is incompatible with the obligations owed by the state under the Convention, whether the act is one which gives rise to a present and immediate incompatibility or is one which will inevitably lead to an incompatibility in the future. The point was discussed again in *Stott v Brown*[8], concerned with the leading in evidence of an answer obtained from the accused under compulsory powers. The Judicial Committee decided that a devolution issue would arise under the Scotland Act 1998 if a question were raised as to the compatibility of the prosecutor's actings under the Convention. The Judicial Committee expressly left open the question whether, even if the admission of the evidence in question would be incompatible with the accused's Convention rights, the prosecutor could nevertheless lawfully (as far as SA 1998 was concerned) lead such evidence. The point was again left open in *HM Advocate v McIntosh*[9]. The way in which this issue – whether the Convention, as given effect in domestic law, imposes an obligation only upon the court or also upon the prosecutor – has arisen in these cases reflects the constitutional position following devolution; and the fact that the prosecution service exercises devolved functions whereas the courts do not. The issue may, however, be of more general importance. Although the Human Rights Act 1998 makes it unlawful for a court to act in a way which is incompatible with the Convention (unless it requires to do so in order to implement primary legislation[10]), it remains to be seen how that provision will be interpreted; and it is conceivable that there may be situations in which the court will have to apply law which is incompatible with the Convention, and in which the question will arise whether the authority which has invited the court to apply that law has ipso facto acted in a way which is incompatible with a Convention right[12].

1 See e g *HM Advocate v Robb* 1999 SCCR 971, 976–977; *HM Advocate v McKenna* 2000 SCCR 159; *HM Advocate v Burns* 2000 SCCR 884.
2 E g *Montgomery v HM Advocate* 2000 SCCR 1044; *Brown v Stott* 2000 SCCR 314; *McIntosh, Petitioner* 2000 SCCR 1017.
3 *HM Advocate v Burns* 2000 SCCR 884. See now *Mills and Cochrane v HMA* (1 August 2001, unreported), HCJ.
4 2000 SCCR 1044.
5 Per Lord Hoffmann.
6 Per Lord Hoffmann.
7 Per Lord Hope of Craighead.
8 2001 SCCR 62.
9 2001 SCCR 191.
10 Human Rights Act 1998, s 6.
11 This issue has implications in particular for Parliamentary sovereignty, which HRA 1998, s 6(2) seeks to preserve. It may also have implications for the retrospectivity of the Human Rights Act 1998. In *R v Lambert* [2001] 3 WLR 206 the House of Lords proceeded on the basis that a person convicted prior to 2 October 2000, on the basis of an interpretation of a statute which was correct at the time but non-compliant with HRA 1998, could not then appeal against his conviction in reliance on ss 7(1)(b) and 22(4), since the act complained of was that of the trial judge (in directing the jury) rather than that of the prosecutor. The Committee's opinion that s 6 was not intended to result in the quashing of convictions which were good as the law stood at the time may have implications for arguments focussing upon the act of the prosecutor in inviting the court to apply law which is non-compliant with Convention rights.

1.35   The general rule laid down in the Scotland Act 1998, s 57(2) is subject to an important exception: it does not apply to an act of the Lord Advocate in prosecuting any offence[1], nor in his capacity as head of the systems of criminal prosecution and investigation of deaths in Scotland which, because of the Human Rights Act 1998, s 6(2), is not unlawful under s 6(1). In other words, if, as the result of primary legislation, the Lord Advocate could not have acted differently, or if he was acting so as to give effect to or enforce provisions of primary legislation (or provisions made under primary legislation) which cannot be read or given effect in a way which is compatible with the rights under the European Convention on Human Rights, then it is not unlawful for him so to act[2]. The reason for the creation of this exception, and for its being confined to the Lord Advocate, has been explained above[3]. It is to be noted that SA 1998, s 57(2) has opened the possibility of review of the Lord Advocate's exercise of his discretionary powers as public prosecutor, which the courts have in the past refused to review[4].

1   This is not restricted to the initiation of a criminal prosecution: *HM Advocate v Robb* 1999 SCCR 971 at 975.
2   On the interpretation of Human Rights Act 1998, s 6, see *HM Advocate v Robb* 1999 SCCR 971, 975; *Starrs v Ruxton* 1999 SCCR 1052 at 1080, and 1104–1105; *Millar v Dickson* 2001 SCCR 741.
3   Paragraph 1.31 above.
4   Judicial review, which is a residual remedy, will not, however, be appropriate where a decision to prosecute is in breach of Convention right and that decision can be challenged in the trial process or on appeal: *Montgomery v HM Advocate* 2000 SCCR 144 at 1091–1092 per Lord Hope of Craighead.

1.36   As mentioned above, the Scotland Act 1998, s 57(2) refers to acts of 'a member of the Scottish Executive'. Since junior Scottish Ministers are appointed 'to assist the Scottish Ministers in the exercise of their functions'[1], their acts and omissions are presumably to be treated as those of the Scottish Ministers. Similarly, it is to be expected that the *Carltona*[2] principle will apply to the Scottish Ministers, so that acts done by civil servants in the name of a Scottish Minister and on his behalf will be treated as his acts. The acts of members of the Procurator Fiscal Service have in practice been treated as the acts of the Lord Advocate[3].

1   Scotland Act 1998, s 49.
2   *Carltona v Works Comrs* [1943] 2 All ER 560.
3   *Starrs v Ruxton* 1999 SCCR 1052; *Buchanan v McLean* 2001 SCCR 475; *Millar v Dickson* 2001 SCCR 741.

1.37   Issues which have arisen as to the compatibility of acts of the Scottish Administration with the European Convention on Human Rights are discussed below under the heading 'Devolution issues'.

Devolution issues

1.38   The Scotland Act 1998, Sch 6 contains elaborate provisions for dealing with 'devolution issues'. These are defined[1] as meaning:

(a)   a question whether an Act of the Scottish Parliament or any provision of such an Act is within the legislative competence of the Parliament;

(b)   a question whether any function (which a person has purported, or is proposing, to exercise) is a function of the Scottish Ministers, the First Minister or the Lord Advocate;

(c)   a question whether the purported or proposed exercise of a function by a member of the Scottish Executive is, or would be, within devolved competence;

(d)   a question whether a purported or proposed exercise of a function by a member of the Scottish Executive is, or would be, incompatible with any of the Convention rights or with Community law;

(e)   a question whether a failure to act by a member of the Scottish Executive is incompatible with any of the Convention rights or with Community law;

(f)   any other question about whether a function is exercisable within devolved competence or in or as regards Scotland and any other question arising by virtue of the Act about reserved matters.

Putative devolution issues which are frivolous or vexatious can be filtered out[2].

1 Scotland Act 1998, Sch 6, para 1.
2 SA 1998, Sch 6, para 2.

1.39 Devolution issues may arise in any proceedings before courts or tribunals anywhere in the United Kingdom[1]. They may, for example, arise in proceedings for judicial review instituted for the purpose of challenging legislation of the Scottish Parliament or acts of Scottish Ministers, or collaterally (eg by way of defence in criminal proceedings). They can thus arise in proceedings at any level in the judicial hierarchy. Although most devolution issues are likely to arise in proceedings in Scotland, it is conceivable that they may also arise in proceedings in England and Wales or in Northern Ireland. The Scotland Act 1998, Sch 6 accordingly contains separate provisions in respect of each jurisdiction. They are, however, broadly similar. The present discussion will focus on the Scottish provisions.

1 See the discussion in 594 HL Official Report (5th series) cols 77–79 at 94.

1.40 The provisions cover both proceedings for the determination of a devolution issue[1] and other proceedings in which a devolution issue arises[2]. In each case, provision is made for the involvement in the proceedings of the Advocate General and the Lord Advocate.

1 Scotland Act 1998, Sch 6, para 4.
2 SA 1998, Sch 6, para 5.

1.41 When a devolution issue arises in civil proceedings before a court other than the House of Lords or any court consisting of three or more judges of the Court of Session, that court has a discretion (subject to any rules made under the Scotland Act 1998) to refer the devolution issue to the Inner House[1]. Alternatively, the court can decide the issue itself, and it can thereafter come before the higher courts by way of appeal. Similarly, tribunals must make a reference if there is no appeal from their decision, but otherwise have a discretion[2]. The position in criminal proceedings is similar: a court other than any court consisting of two or more judges of the High Court of Justiciary has a discretion (subject to any rules made) either to refer the devolution issue to the High Court of Justiciary, or to decide the issue itself[3]. The reference procedure is designed to allow a court, when faced with an issue of difficulty or of some general importance, to refer the issue to a higher court[4]. It is a stage in the proceedings before the original court, rather than a free-standing procedure. If the proceedings come to an end (eg because an indictment falls) the reference comes to an end along with the proceedings[5].

1 Scotland Act 1998, Sch 6, para 7. This is subject to rules made under SA 1998, Sch 6, para 37.
2 SA 1998, Sch 6, para 8.
3 SA 1998, Sch 6, para 9.
4 *HM Advocate v Touatti* 2001 SCCR 392.
5 *HM Advocate v Touatti* 2001 SCCR 392.

1.42   The court to which the issue is referred must then determine it: it cannot refer the issue to a yet higher court[1]. The court to which the reference is made answers the question posed in the reference. It is, however, for the original court to make the operative decision, using the guidance given by the court to which the reference was made. It is also for the original court, and not the parties, to decide whether to make the reference[2]. When the Inner House decides a devolution issue on a reference by a lower court, an appeal lies to the Judicial Committee of the Privy Council[3]. Similarly, when the High Court of Justiciary decides a devolution issue on a reference by a lower court, an appeal again lies to the Judicial Committee, but in this instance it is necessary to obtain the leave of the High Court or, failing such leave, the special leave of the Judicial Committee[4]. The reason why leave is required in this instance, but not from a decision of the Inner House, may be that an appeal ordinarily lies from any final decision of the Inner House to the House of Lords without leave, whereas there has hitherto been no right of appeal beyond the High Court of Justiciary.

1 This is implicit in Scotland Act 1998, Sch 6, paras 10 and 11.
2 *HM Advocate v Touatti* 2001 SCCR 392.
3 SA 1998, Sch 6, para 12.
4 SA 1998, Sch 6, para 13.

1.43   If, on the other hand, a devolution issue arises in proceedings before a court consisting of three or more judges of the Court of Session, or two or more judges of the High Court of Justiciary (typically, but not necessarily, on appeal from a lower court or tribunal), then they can either refer the issue to the Judicial Committee[1] or decide the issue themselves. If they decide the issue themselves, an appeal will normally lie in civil proceedings to the House of Lords; but where in civil proceedings there is no right of appeal to the House of Lords, and in all criminal proceedings, an appeal will lie to the Judicial Committee with leave of the court concerned or, failing such leave, with special leave of the Judicial Committee[2]. Reasons should be given for the refusal of leave[3]. If the devolution issue was argued before a lower court but not before the High Court of Justiciary it cannot be ressurected by means of an appeal to the Judicial Committee[4].

1 Scotland Act 1998, Sch 6, paras 10 and 11.
2 SA 1998, Sch 6, para 13.
3 *Follen v HM Advocate* 2001 SCCR 255.
4 *Follen v HM Advocate* 2001 SCCR 255.

1.44   Where a devolution issue arises in the House of Lords, it must be referred to the Judicial Committee unless the House considers it more appropriate, having regard to all the circumstances, that it should determine the issue[1].

1 Scotland Act 1998, Sch 6, para 32.

1.45   The Lord Advocate, the Advocate General, the Attorney General or the Attorney General for Northern Ireland may require any court or tribunal to refer to the Judicial Committee any devolution issue which has arisen in proceedings before it to which he is a party[1]. A Law Officer may also refer to the Judicial Committee any devolution issue which is not the subject of proceedings[2].

1 Scotland Act 1998, Sch 6, para 33.
2 SA 1998, Sch 6, para 34.

1.46   The Scotland Act 1998 provides for subordinate legislation for prescribing such matters as the stage in proceedings at which a devolution issue is to be raised or referred, the sisting of proceedings for the purpose of a reference, and the manner and time within which any intimation is to be given[1]. Rules have been issued, and are discussed below.

1 Scotland Act 1998, Sch 6, para 37.

1.47   One noteworthy aspect of the procedure is that the Judicial Committee will in general (but not always) be the final court of appeal in respect of devolution issues, including questions as to the compatibility of Acts of the Scottish Parliament or acts of Scottish Ministers with the European Convention on Human Rights. Decisions of the Judicial Committee are thus likely to become an important source of domestic law on the Convention; and the Act provides that they are to be 'binding in all legal proceedings (other than proceedings before the Committee)'[1]. It remains to be seen whether this will be interpreted as meaning that its decisions are to be binding on the House of Lords.

1 Scotland Act 1998, s 103(1).

1.48   Subordinate legislation has been made regulating the procedure to be followed where a devolution issue is sought to be raised. The present discussion will focus on the rules applicable to criminal proceedings in Scotland[1], and to civil proceedings before the Court of Session[2]. There are also rules in respect of civil proceedings in the sheriff court[3] and in respect of proceedings before the Judicial Committee[4].

1 Act of Adjournal (Devolution Issue Rules) 1999, SI 1999/1346, as amended by Act of Adjournal (Criminal Procedure Rules Amendment) (Miscellaneous) 2000, SSI 2000/65. This inserted a new Ch 40 in the Act of Adjournal (Criminal Procedure Rules) 1996, SI 1996/513.

2 Act of Sederunt (Devolution Issue Rules) 1999, SI 1999/1345, as amended by Act of Sederunt (Rules of the Court of Session Amendment) (Miscellaneous) 2000, SSI 2000/66. This inserted a new Ch 25A in the Act of Sederunt (Rules of the Court of Session) 1994, SI 1994/1443.
3 Act of Sederunt (Proceedings for Determination of Devolution Issues Rules) 1999, SI 1999/1347.
4 The Judicial Committee (Devolution Issues) Rules Order 1999, SI 1999/665.

1.49 So far as criminal proceedings are concerned, the rules are contained in Chapter 40 of the Act of Adjournal (Criminal Procedure Rules) 1996 (as amended). In relation to proceedings on indictment, the Act of Adjournal requires a party to those proceedings who proposes to raise a devolution issue to give notice within seven days of service of the indictment. The notice must give sufficient specification of the alleged devolution issue to enable the court to determine whether any devolution issue actually arises[1]. The notice has to be given to the court, the other parties to the proceedings and the Advocate General[2]. The devolution issue is then to be considered at a hearing held in accordance with the procedure followed under existing law[3].

A challenge to a provision in an Act of the Scottish Parliament as being incompatible with any of the Convention rights might, for example, take the form of a plea to the competency or relevancy of an indictment based on the provision. A complaint that the Lord Advocate was acting in a manner which was incompatible with Convention rights might take the form of a plea of oppression. In either case, the issue could (and normally should) be dealt with, in solemn proceedings in the High Court, at a preliminary diet[4]. For such a diet to be held, notice normally has to be given within 15 days of service of the indictment: the shorter period allowed in respect of a devolution issue may reflect the need to notify the Advocate General (who is likely to have no prior knowledge of the proceedings) in adequate time for the hearing[5]. These relatively short time limits generally reflect the tight timetable of solemn procedure, which requires the indictment to be served 29 days prior to the trial[6], and envisages the holding of any preliminary diet during the intervening period.

A broadly similar procedure applies where a party wishes to raise a devolution issue in summary proceedings[7] or in other types of criminal proceedings[8]. A devolution issue cannot be raised in criminal proceedings except in accordance with these time limits, unless the court on cause shown otherwise determines[9]. Following the service of the notice, the court may determine that no devolution issue in fact arises[10]. If a devolution issue does arise, then the court can determine it, or it can make a reference to the High Court of Justiciary (unless the court itself consists of two or more judges of the High Court of Justiciary[11], in which case a reference can be made to the Judicial Committee of the Privy Council[12]). The one exception is that where a court determines that a devolution issue may be raised during a trial, it cannot make a reference, but must determine the issue itself. This avoids what might otherwise be insuperable practical problems[13]. The scheme of the Act of Adjournal is directed towards ensuring that devolution issues are raised prior to trial, whenever possible. This partly reflects the practical problems which are liable to arise, as just mentioned, if devolution issues are to be raised during a trial. It may also reflect the fact that an erroneous determination of a devolution issue during a trial leading to an acquittal in proceedings on indictment could not be appealed so as to affect the acquittal[14]. The Act of Adjournal has been challenged as being ultra vires, on the basis inter alia that the time limits are incompatible with the Convention. The challenge was unsuccessful[15].

1 Act of Adjournal (Criminal Procedure Rules) 1996, SI 1996/513, r 40.6.
2 SI 1996/513, r 40.2(1).
3 This is implied rather than expressed: see *HM Advocate v Montgomery* 1999 SCCR 959.
4 Under the Criminal Procedure (Scotland) Act 1995, s 72. See *HM Advocate v Montgomery* 1999 SCCR 959. In solemn proceedings in the sheriff court, the issue could be dealt with at a first diet: CP(S)A 1995, s 71(2).
5 The Advocate General has seven days from receipt of the notice to decide whether to become party to the proceedings: SI 1996/513, r 40.2(3).
6 CP(S)A 1995, s 66(6).
7 SI 1996/513, r 40.3.
8 SI 1996/513, r 40.4. This would cover petitions to the *nobile officium*. It may also cover appeals.
9 SI 1996/513, r 40.5. As to what constitutes 'cause shown', see *HM Advocate v Montgomery* 1999 SCCR 959. As that case indicates (at 965D), 'ordinary' time limits or rules may apply as well as the particular requirements imposed by SI 1996/513, Ch 40.
10 SI 1996/513, rr 40.2(2), 40.3(2) and 40.4(3).
11 SI 1996/513, r 40.7(1).
12 SI 1996/513, r 40.9(1).
13 If, for example, a devolution issue were raised during a trial before a jury, and a reference were made, the jury would have to be sent away while the case was dealt with before the High Court of Justiciary (and, possibly, the Judicial Committee). The adjournment of the trial would be liable to last weeks, if not months, making it impractical to resume the trial (even assuming that the jury could be reassembled).
14 The Lord Advocate cannot appeal against an acquittal in proceedings on indictment: CP(S)A 1995, s 106(1). He can, however, refer a point of law which has arisen in relation to a charge to the High Court for its opinion; but the opinion does not affect the acquittal: CP(S)A 1995, s 123. He also has a limited right of appeal against procedural decisions during the course of proceedings on indictment: CP(S)A 1995, s 131. The Advocate General has a right to refer any devolution issue to the High Court for its opinion, following an acquittal or a conviction: but the opinion does not affect the acquittal or conviction: CP(S)A 1995, s 288A (inserted by SA 1998, Sch 8, para 32). A decision taken prior to trial can be appealed: CP(S)A 1995, s 74.
15 *HM Advocate v Dickson* 1999 SCCR 859; affd *Dickson v HM Advocate* 2001 SCCR 397.

1.50   The new rules applicable to civil proceedings in the Court of Session[1] adopt a broadly similar scheme. The devolution issue must be specified in detail in pleadings. The issue must be raised before any evidence is led, unless the court on cause shown otherwise determines[2]. Intimation of the devolution issue must be given to the Lord Advocate and to the Advocate General[3], who then have 14 days to decide whether to take part in proceedings[4], and a further 7 days to lodge written submissions[5]. The issue is then dealt with at a hearing before proof or trial. This procedure is in some respects analogous to the procedure followed in the Court of Session under existing practice where a party wishes to raise a preliminary point (eg as to jurisdiction or title to sue) or a question of relevancy.

1 Act of Sederunt (Devolution Issue Rules) 1999, SI 1999/1345, as amended. As to the sheriff court, see the Act of Sederunt (Proceedings for Determination of Devolution Issues Rules) 1999, SI 1999/1347.
2 SI 1999/1347, r 25A.3(1).
3 SI 1999/1347, r 25A.5(1).

4 SI 1999/1347, r 25A.5(4).
5 SI 1999/1347, r 25A.6(1).

1.51 In both criminal and civil procedure, then, the rules aim to ensure, as far as possible, that devolution issues are raised and determined prior to trial. In practice, however, this may not be possible or appropriate: there may be situations where the devolution issue cannot reasonably be identified in advance of trial; and even if the devolution issue can be identified prior to trial, it may not always be possible (or necessary) to determine it until the significance of the point raised can be assessed in the context of the trial. This is liable in particular to be a difficulty in relation to issues relating to evidence. In general, the court's role in ruling on the admissibility of evidence and directing the jury (if any) on the use to be made of evidence should operate, at the trial, as a means of preventing evidence being considered and relied upon in such a way as to deprive an accused person of a fair trial[1]. For that reason, questions under Article 6 relating to the admissibility of evidence should generally be raised at the trial[2]. There are, however, circumstances in which a devolution issue relating to evidence can be raised and determined prior to trial[3].

1 *HM Advocate v Robb* 1999 SCCR 971 at 977; *HM Advocate v Campbell* 1999 SCCR 980; *Paton v Ritchie* 1999 SCCR 151; *McKenna v HM Advocate* 2000 SCCR 159.
2 *HM Advocate v Robb* 1999 SCCR 971, 977; *HM Advocate v Campbell* 1999 SCCR 980; *Paton v Ritchie* 1999 SCCR 151; *McKenna v HM Advocate* 2000 SCCR 159. Cf *R v A* [2001] 1 WLR 789 per Lord Hope of Craighead at para 11: 'As a general rule a question as to whether the admission or exclusion of evidence at a criminal trial is incompatible with the right to a fair trial under Article 6 of the Convention is best considered after the trial has been completed. But ... [i]t is undesirable that vulnerable witnesses such as the complainant in a rape trial who has already given evidence should be exposed to the risk of having to give evidence again at a new trial. This is what would happen if the verdict at the first trial were to be set aside on the ground that the respondent did not receive a fair trial'.
3 See e g *Stott v Brown* 2001 SCCR 62.

1.52 There appears to have been, at the date of writing, only one case in which legislation passed by the Scottish Parliament has been challenged as being incompatible with the European Convention on Human Rights[1]. The challenge, which concerned the Mental Health (Public Safety and Appeals) (Scotland) Act 1999[2], was unsuccessful.

1 *A v The Scottish Ministers* (15 October 2001, unreported), JCPC.
2 1999 asp 1.

1.53 There have been a number of other civil cases before the Court of Session in which a devolution issue has been raised. In one case, the independence of a temporary judge was challenged, unsuccessfully[1]. In another case, it was held at first instance that a decision taken under planning legislation failed to comply with the European Convention on Human Rights, Article 6, since neither the reporter nor the Scottish Ministers constituted an independent and impartial tribunal, and the scope of any appeal to the courts was too limited to meet the requirements of Article 6. The decision was reversed on appeal[2]. A third case concerned the compatibility with Article 5 of arrangements for the recall into custody of a prisoner released on licence.[3] In another case, before an employment tribunal, the exclusion of employment tribunals from the legal aid scheme was held not to raise a devolution issue[4]. Other cases have concerned aspects of the children's hearing system[5], prison disciplinary hearings[6], and prison conditions[7].

1 *Clancy v Caird* 2000 SC 441.
2 *County Properties Ltd v The Scottish Ministers* 2001 SLT 1125. See also *Lafarge Redland Aggregates Ltd v The Scottish Ministers* 2001 SC 298.
3 *Varey v The Scottish Ministers* 2001 SC 162.
4 *Gerrie v Ministry of Defence* (22 October 1999, unreported), ET.
5 *S v Miller* 2001 SLT 531.
6 *Matthewson v The Scottish Ministers* (28 June 2001, unreported), Ct of S.
7 *Napier v The Scottish Ministers* (26 June 2001, unreported), Ct of S.

1.54 The criminal courts, on the other hand, have had to deal with a great many cases in which devolution issues have been raised, some of which have been of considerable importance. The principal issues raised relating to the European Convention on Human Rights can be summarised as follows:

1   Whether a criminal trial can take place before a temporary sheriff, the point being whether the temporary sheriff possesses sufficient independence to comply with Article 6(1)[1]; or whether it can take place in the district court, in view of the part played by the clerk of court in the running of the court[2].
2   Whether a summary criminal trial can take place compatibly with Article 6(1) when the legal aid available to the defence is based on fixed fees which are said to be inadequate[3].
3   Whether there has been excessive delay in proceedings, contrary to Article 6(1)[4].
4   Whether the Crown can use as evidence against an accused a statement which he was required to provide to the police under s 172 of the Road Traffic Act 1988[5].
5   Whether the Crown can, consistently with Article 6(1), lead evidence of a police interview with the accused[6], or of an identification parade[7], the accused not having had access to a solicitor during the interview or identification parade.
6   Whether pre-trial publicity has prevented the holding of a trial which would be compatible with Article 6[8].
7   Whether hearsay evidence can be admitted[9].
8   Whether evidence given anonymously can be admitted[10].
9   Whether the statutory presumptions applicable where a confiscation order is sought in respect of the proceeds of drug trafficking are incompatible with Articles 6(2) or 8 of the Convention or with Article 1 of Protocol 1[11].
10 Whether the Crown can cite as a witness an expert instructed on behalf of the defence[12].

There have also been cases concerning the granting of a search warrant[13]; the impartiality of a judge[14] or a jury[15]; the refusal of bail[16]; contempt of court[17]; the specification of criminal charges[18]; the libelling of a breach of bail[19]; a visit by a jury to the locus of an offence[20]; the disclosure of a prior conviction during the course of a trial[21]; the handcuffing of a witness[22]; the consequences of a procedural irregularity during the course of appeal proceedings[23]; and the broadcasting of trial proceedings[24].

1 *Starrs v Ruxton* 1999 SCCR 1052. As to waiver of the right to an independent and impartial tribunal, see *Millar v Dickson* 2001 SCCR 741.
2 *Clark v Kelly* 2000 SCCR 821.
3 *Buchanan v McLean* 2001 SCCR 475.
4 *HM Advocate v Little* 1999 SCCR 625; *McNab v HM Advocate* 1999 SCCR 930; *McLean v HM Advocate* 2000 SCCR 112; *Docherty v HM Advocate* 2000 SCCR 717; *Robb v HM Advocate* 2000 SCCR 354; *HM Advocate v McGlinchey* 2000 SCCR 593; *Crummock (Scotland) Ltd v HM Advocate* 2000 SCCR 453; *HM Advocate v Hynd* 2000 SCCR 644; *Reilly v HM Advocate* 2000 SCCR 879; *Smith v HM Advocate* 2000 SCCR 926; *Gibson v HM Advocate* 2001 SCCR 51; *Hendry v HM Advocate* 2001 SCCR 59; *Mitchell v HM Advocate* 2001 SCCR 110; *Martin v HM Advocate* (19 December 2000, unreported) HCJ; *Thompson v HM Advocate* (19 December 2000, unreported), HCJ; *HM Advocate v P* 2001 SCCR 210; *Dyer v Watson* 2001 SCCR 430; *Kane v HM Advocate* 2001 SCCR 621; *HM Advocate v Wright* 2001 SCCR 509; *O'Brien v HM Advocate* 2001 SCCR 542; *HM Advocate v Valentine* 2001 SCCR 727. The correctness of the approach adopted in these cases has been questioned: *HM Advocate v Rourke* (10 October 2001, unreported), HCJ. See also *Mills and Cochrane v HM Advocate* (1 August 2001, unreported), HCJ.
5 *Brown v Stott* 2001 SCCR 62.
6 *HM Advocate v Robb* 1999 SCCR 971; *Paton v Ritchie* 2000 SCCR 151; *Dickson v HM Advocate* 2001 SCCR 397.
7 *HM Advocate v Campbell* 1999 SCCR 980.
8 *Montgomery v HM Advocate* 2000 SCCR 1044; *HM Advocate v Fraser* 2000 SCCR 412; *Aspinall v HM Advocate* (27 March 2000, unreported), HCJ.
9 *McKenna v HM Advocate* 2000 SCCR 159; *HM Advocate v Nulty* 2000 SCCR 431; *HM Advocate v Bain* 2001 SCCR 461.
10 *HM Advocate v Smith* 2000 SCCR 910.
11 *HM Advocate v McIntosh* 2001 SCCR 191; *HM Advocate v McSalley* 2000 JC 48; *HM Advocate v Burns* 2000 SCCR 884.
12 *Wales v HM Advocate* 2001 SCCR 633.
13 *Birse v HM Advocate* 2000 SCCR 505.
14 *Hoekstra v HM Advocate (No 2)* 2000 SCCR 367.
15 *Crummock (Scotland) Ltd v HM Advocate* 2000 SCCR 453.
16 *Burn, Petitioner* 2000 SCCR 384; also *Selfridge v Brown* 2000 JC 9.
17 *HM Advocate v Scottish Media Newspapers Ltd* 1999 SCCR 599.
18 *McLean v HM Advocate* 2000 SCCR 112.
19 *Boyd v HM Advocate* 2000 SCCR 962.
20 *Hoekstra v HM Advocate (No 1)* 2000 SCCR 263.
21 *Andrew v HM Advocate* 2000 SLT 402.
22 *Trotter v HM Advocate* 2000 SCR 968.
23 *Hoekstra v HM Advocate (No 1)* 2000 SCCR 263.
24 *British Broadcasting Corporation, Petitioners* 2000 SCCR 533.

Other aspects

1.55 There are a number of miscellaneous matters arising under the Scotland Act 1998 which require to be borne in mind.

1.56 The Scotland Act 1998 contains a number of provisions which should ensure broad congruence with the Human Rights Act 1998. First, in relation to standing, SA 1998 does not enable a person to bring any proceedings on the ground that an act is incompatible with rights under the European Convention on Human Rights, or to rely on the Convention rights in proceedings, unless he would be a victim for the purposes of Article 34 of the Convention (within the meaning of HRA 1998) if proceedings in respect of the act were brought in the European Court of Human Rights[1]. This imports the same test as HRA 1998, s 7(7)[2]. Secondly, in relation to damages, the Scotland Act 1998 does not enable a court or tribunal to award any damages in respect of an act which is incompatible with the Convention rights which it could not award if HRA 1998, s 8(3) and (4) applied[3]. There are, however, several points where a contrast can be drawn. These are described below[4].

1 Scotland Act 1998, s 100(1).
2 See para 1.83 below.
3 SA 1998, s 100(3).
4 See paras 1.63, 1.65, 1.76 and 1.101 below. See also Jamieson 'Relationship between the Scotland Act and the Human Rights Act' 2001 SLT (News) 43 (the author of which was one of the principal architects of the SA 1998).

1.57 In the event that a court or tribunal decides that an Act of the Scottish Parliament is outwith its competence, or that subordinate legislation is ultra vires, the court or tribunal has a wide power to make an order removing or limiting any retrospective effect of the decision, or suspending the effect of the decision for any period and, on any conditions, to allow the defect to be corrected[1].

The Scotland Act 1998 also provides for subordinate legislation to make 'such provision as the person making the legislation considers necessary or expedient' in consequence of an Act of the Scottish Parliament which is not, or may not be, within its competence, or any purported exercise by a member of the Scottish Executive of his functions which is not, or may not be, an exercise or a proper exercise of those functions[2]. Such subordinate legislation can have retrospective effects[3]. It should be noted that these powers, so far as concerned with the Scottish Executive, are not confined to devolution issues but can apply where, on ordinary grounds of administrative law, a Scottish Minister has acted ultra vires[4]. The exercise of these powers may be liable to give rise to a variety of issues under the European Convention on Human Rights.

1 Scotland Act 1998, s 102. This provision was discussed in 593 HL Official Report (5th series) cols 595–606. It was said during the passage of the Bill that the discretion is intended to be exercised only exceptionally in criminal proceedings.
2 SA 1998, s 107.
3 SA 1998, s 114(3).
4 This is the intended effect: 594 HL Official Report (5th series) col 599.

1.58 An important transitional provision, to cover the period between the coming into force of the Scotland Act 1998 and the date when the Human Rights Act 1998 was fully in force, was SA 1998, s 129(2)? It provided that during that transitional period, ss 29 (2)(d), 57(2) and (3), 100 and 126(1) and Sch 6 to SA 1998 were to have effect as they would have effect after the time when HRA 1998 was fully in force.

THE HUMAN RIGHTS ACT 1998

1.59   The White Paper *Rights Brought Home* announced the Government's intention to 'give people in the United Kingdom opportunities to enforce their rights under the European Convention in British Courts rather than having to incur the cost and delay of taking a case to the European Human Rights Court in Strasbourg'[1].

1   Cm 3782 (1997) p 1.

1.60   The Human Rights Act 1998 seeks to fulfil that intention through, in particular, the introduction of the following obligations:

1   So far as it is possible to do so, primary legislation and subordinate legislation must be read and given effect in a way which is compatible with the Convention rights[1].

2   If the court is satisfied that a provision of primary legislation is incompatible with a Convention right, it may make a declaration of that 'incompatibility'[2]. In that event, a Minister of the Crown may by order make such amendments to the legislation as he considers necessary to remove the incompatibility[3].

3   It is unlawful for a public authority (including a court or tribunal) to act in a way which is incompatible with a Convention right[4].

4   A Minister of the Crown in charge of a Bill in either House of Parliament must, before the Second Reading of the Bill, make a statement about the compatibility of the Bill with Convention rights[5].

It should be made clear at the outset that HRA 1998 is complex and raises difficult questions, and that the following account attempts only to give an outline of the principal features. There are numerous qualifications and exceptions on matters of detail, for which reference should be made to HRA 1998 itself, and the extensive secondary literature on it.

1   Human Rights Act 1998, s 3.
2   HRA 1998, s 4.
3   HRA 1998, s 10.
4   HRA 1998, s 6.
5   HRA 1998, s 19.

1.61   The Human Rights Act 1998, s 1 defines the Convention rights to which effect is given. These are the rights and fundamental freedoms set out in Articles 2 to 12 and 14 of the Convention; Articles 1 to 3 of Protocol 1, and Articles 1 and 3 of Protocol 6, as read with Articles 16 to 18 of the Convention[1]. The 'Convention rights' therefore do not include Articles 1 and 13 of the Convention. That has been said to be because HRA 1998 itself gives effect to Articles 1 and 13[2]. The articles setting out Convention rights are to have effect for the purposes of HRA 1998 subject to any designated derogation or reservation, as provided by HRA 1998, ss 14 and 15[3].

1   Human Rights Act 1998, s 1(1).
2   583 HL Official Report (5th series) col 475; 582 HL Official Report (5th series) col 1308; 312 HC Official Report (6th series) cols 978–981. As to European Convention on Human Rights, Art 1, see *Douglas v Hello! Ltd* [2001] 2 WLR 992, para 91, per Brooke LJ. As to Art 13, see *Montgomery v HM Advocate* 2000 SCCR 1044, 1093 per Lord Hope of Craighead, and

Stott v Brown 2001 SCCR 62 per Lord Hope of Craighead. It should be borne in mind that HRA 1998 itself has to be interpreted in accordance with the Convention in so far at least as it may be ambiguous, given the purpose of the 1998 Act and its background in the White Paper (see para 1.59 above), and bearing in mind the principle in *T, Petitioner* (see para 1.19 above).

3 HRA 1998, s 1(2). See paras 1.94–1.95 below.

1.62   The Human Rights Act 1998, s 2 provides that a court or tribunal determining a question which has arisen in connection with a Convention right must take into account any judgment, decision or declaration or advisory opinion of the European Court of Human Rights, any opinion of the Commission given in a report adopted under Article 31 of the European Convention on Human Rights (ie any opinion on the merits of an application), any opinion of the Commission in connection with Articles 26 or 27(2) of the Convention (ie any decision on admissibility) or any decision of the Committee of Ministers taken under Article 46 of the Convention, so far as relevant to the proceedings. In practice, the most important of these sources are judgments of the European Court of Human Rights. The Commission ceased to exist under the revised structure established by Protocol 11 to the Convention (with effect from 1 November 1998). Its admissibility decisions and Article 31 reports are a useful source, but have less authority than judgments of the Court. Decisions of the Committee of Ministers (which are taken under Article 46 in connection with its supervision of the implementation of a judgment) are unlikely to be of practical significance. The Strasbourg judgments etc are not binding on national courts or tribunals, but it is intended that they should normally apply the Convention jurisprudence[1]. Any authoritative report is sufficient evidence of a judgment etc[2]. It has been said that in the absence of some special circumstances the court should follow any clear and constant jurisprudence of the European Court of Human Rights[3].

1 583 HL Official Report (5th Series) cols 514–515 (18 November 1997); 584 HL Official Report (5th Series) cols 1270–1271 (19 January 1998); 313 HC Official Report (6th Series) cols 388, 402 and 413 (3 June 1998).

2 Act of Adjournal Criminal Procedure Rules 1996, SI 1996/513, r 41.2, inserted by the Act of Adjournal (Criminal Procedure Rules Amendment No 2) (Human Rights Act 1998) 2000, SSI 2000/315; RCS 1994, r 81.2, inserted by the Act of Sederunt (Rules of the Court of Session Amendment No 6) (Human Rights Act 1998) 2000, SSI 2000/316; Act of Sederunt (Evidence of Judgments etc) (Human Rights Act 1998) 2000, SSI 2000/314.

3 *R (Alconbury Developments Ltd) v Secretary of State for the Environment, Transport and the Regions* [2001] 2 WLR 1389 at para 26 per Lord Slynn of Hadley.

1.63   The Human Rights Act 1998, s 3 requires primary legislation and subordinate legislation[1] to be read and given effect in a way that is compatible with the Convention rights, so far as it is possible to do so[2]. This provision is of great significance, particularly because it applies to legislation whenever enacted[3], and may therefore require established interpretations to be re-examined. As Lord Steyn has said: 'Traditionally the search has been for the true meaning of a statute. Now the search will be for a possible meaning that would prevent the need for a declaration of incompatibility'[4]. The obligation imposed by s 3 does not affect the validity, containing operation or enforcement of any incompatible primary legislation, or of any incompatible subordinate legislation if (disregarding the possibility of revocation) primary legislation prevents removal of the incompatibility[5]. HRA 1998 therefore does not impliedly repeal previous legislation enacted by the UK Parliament which is incompatible with the Convention, or prevent the enactment of subsequent legislation by the UK Parliament which is incompatible with the Convention. It has to be borne in mind that Acts of the Scottish Parliament, and certain instruments made by Scottish Ministers, are 'subordinate legislation' as defined in the Act[6]. This principle of interpretation is different from that which applies in determining whether Acts of the Scottish Parliament are within the legislative competence of the Parliament, or whether subordinate legislation is within the powers conferred on Scottish Ministers by the Scotland Act 1998: where any provision in such legislation could be read in such a way as to be outside competence, it is to be read as narrowly as is required for it to be within competence, if such a reading is possible[7]. Depending on the circumstances, one or other of these principles of interpretation may be relevant, or both.

1 The question whether this might cover rules made under a private Act of Parliament was considered, but not decided, in *Royal Society for the Prevention of Cruelty to Animals v Attorney General* [2001] 3 All ER 530.
2 Human Rights Act 1998, s 3(1). See *A v The Scottish Ministers* (15 October 2001, unreported), JCPC, per Lord Hope or Craighead.
3 HRA 1998, s 3(2)(a). Thus the Scotland Act 1998 must be construed in accordance with the HRA 1998, s 3.
4 [1998] EHRLR 153. This may give rise to difficult questions, for example where a statutory provision employs concepts which have a wider currency beyond the provision in question.
5 HRA 1998, s 3(2)(b) and (c).
6 HRA 1998, s 21(1).
7 SA 1998, s 101. It should also be borne in mind that the Interpretation Act 1978 applies only in part to Acts of the Scottish Parliament: see SA 1998, Sch 8, para 16.

1.64 The Human Rights Act 1998, s 3 has been considered in a number of cases. In *R (Wardle) v Crown Court at Leeds*[1], Lord Hope of Craighead said:

> 'Section 3(1) of the 1998 Act provides that, so far as it is possible to do so, primary legislation and subordinate legislation must be read and given effect in a way which is compatible with Convention rights. This means that, if according to its ordinary construction [a provision] is incompatible with any of the Convention rights, a possible meaning for [the provision] must be found that will prevent the need for a declaration of incompatibility. But one must first be satisfied that the ordinary construction of the [provision] gives rise to an incompatibility.'[2]

Lord Clyde also observed:

> 'I should also record one area for dispute which may have to be resolved in the future, namely whether s 3 requires reading in or only reading down. The point is one on which different views have been expressed, for example by Richard A Edwards on the one hand ('Reading down legislation under the Human Rights Act' (2000) 20 LS 353) and Richard Clayton and Hugh Tomlinson *The Law of Human Rights* (2000) Vol 1, p 163, para 4.20 on the other.'[3]

In *R v A (No 2)*[4] some members of the House of Lords appear to have proceeded on the basis that 'reading in' was possible. It has been held that it is not possible to construe a provision containing a proviso or exception in such a way that the exception invariably applies[5]. The relationship between s 3 and ss 4 and 5 is discussed below[6].

1 [2001] 2 WLR 865.
2 [2001] 2 WLR 865, para 79.
3 [2001] 2 WLR 865, para 115.
4 [2001] 2 WLR 1546. See in particular para 45 per Lord Steyn: 'It is therefore possible under s 3 to read [the statutory provision in question] as subject to the implied provision that evidence or questioning which is required to ensure a fair trial under Article 6 of the Convention should not be treated as inadmissible'. Contrast para 108 per Lord Hope of Craighead. See also *R v Lambert* [2001] 3 WLR 206, especially per Lord Hope of Craighead at paras 78–94.
5 *Gunn v Newman* 2001 SC 525; 2001 SLT 776, IH. It may also be that a provision conferring a discretion cannot be construed in such a way that there is no discretion: cf the pre-Human Rights Act 1998 case of *R (Montana) v Secretary of State for the Home Dept* [2001] 1 WLR 552.
6 Paragraphs 1.69–1.70 below.

1.65   The Human Rights Act 1998, s 4 enables[1] certain courts to make a declaration that a provision of primary legislation is incompatible with a Convention right; and such a declaration can also be made in respect of a provision of subordinate legislation where primary legislation prevents removal of the incompatibility. In Scottish proceedings, the courts which have the power to make a declaration of incompatibility are the House of Lords, the Judicial Committee of the Privy Council, the High Court of Justiciary sitting otherwise than as a trial court, and the Court of Session[2]. A declaration of incompatibility does not affect the validity, containing operation or enforcement of the provision in respect of which it is given, and is not binding on the parties to the proceedings in which it is made[3]. The award of expenses in cases in which a declaration of incompatibility is sought may raise difficult questions[4]. Although an Act of the Scottish Parliament falls within the definition of 'subordinate legislation', the Parliament has no power to enact legislation which is incompatible with the Convention rights[5]: a declaration of incompatibility is accordingly not the appropriate remedy. The same would appear to apply to subordinate legislation made by a Scottish Minister, notwithstanding that it may fall within the definition of 'subordinate legislation' in HRA 1998, since a Scottish Minister has no power to make subordinate legislation which is incompatible with the Convention rights[6].

1 As to the discretion conferred, see para 1.66 below.
2 Human Rights Act 1998, s 4(5).
3 HRA 1998, s 4(6).
4 Cf *Motsepe v IRC* (1997) 6 BCLR 692, 705 (Constitutional Court of South Africa), per Ackermann J: 'One should be cautious in awarding costs against litigants who seek to enforce their constitutional rights against the state, particularly where constitutionality of a statutory provision is attacked, lest such orders have an unduly inhibiting or "chilling effect" on other potential litigants in this category. This cautious approach cannot, however, be allowed to develop into an inflexible rule so that litigants are induced into believing that they are free to challenge the constitutionality of provisions in this court, no matter how spurious the grounds for doing so may be or how remote the possibility that this court will grant them access. This can neither be in the interests of the administration of justice nor fair to those who are forced to oppose such attacks'. An additional problem which arises under HRA 1998 is that the point may arise in a litigation between private parties.

5 Scotland Act 1998, s 29.
6 SA 1998, s 57(2).

1.66   Rather than imposing a duty, the Human Rights Act 1998, s 4(2) confers a power on the court to make a declaration of incompatibility if it is satisfied that a provision is incompatible with a Convention right. The granting of such a declaration may not be sought by the parties to the proceedings in question, for whom it might well have no practical effect. In *S v Miller*[1] the court was invited simply to indicate a view that the provision in question was incompatible with the Convention, without making a formal declaration. The court, however, observed that such an approach would in effect circumvent the provisions of s 5(1), requiring notice to be given to the Crown, for whom an indication of the court's view that the United Kingdom was in breach of its obligations under the Convention would be a matter of significance. It would also have the effect of depriving the responsible authorities of the powers which Parliament intended they should have (under HRA 1998, s 10 and Sch 2) to deal with incompatible legislation. It was said to be unsurprising that, during the passage of the Human Rights Bill through Parliament, the Lord Chancellor had indicated[2] that he expected that, where a court had found a provision to be incompatible, it would declare that incompatibility.

1 2001 SLT 531.
2 583 HL Official Report (5th series) col 546 (18 November 1997).

1.67   Declarations of incompatibility have been granted in respect of the Mental Health Act 1983, s 73[1]; and the Consumer Credit Act 1974, s 127(3)[2].

1 *R (H) v Mental Health Review Tribunal, North and East London Region* [2001] 3 WLR 512.
2 *Wilson v First County Trust Ltd (No 2)* [2001] 3 WLR 42.

1.68   The Human Rights Act 1998, s 5 entitles the Crown to notice where a court is considering whether to make a declaration of incompatibility. In such a case, a Minister of the Crown, or member of the Scottish Executive, or Northern Ireland Minister or Department, is entitled to be joined as a party to the proceedings. The court can fix a diet for a hearing on the question of incompatibility as a separate hearing from any other hearing in the proceedings, and can sist the proceedings if it considers it necessary to do so while the question of incompatibility is being determined[1].

1 For the procedure in the High Court of Justiciary, see the Criminal Procedure Rules 1996, SI 1996/513, Ch 41 inserted by the Act of Adjournal (Criminal Procedure Rules Amendment No 2) (Human Rights Act 1998) 2000, SSI 2000/315. For the procedure in the Court of Session, see RCS 1994, Ch 82, inserted by the Act of Sederunt (Rules of the Court of Session Amendment No 6) (Human Rights Act 1998) 2000, SSI 2000/316.

1.69   It has been held that the court can (indeed, must) direct *ex proprio motu* that notice be given under the Human Rights Act 1998, s 5 if there is an apparent incompatibility which has not been raised by the parties to the case. In such a case (under English procedure), it was said that an *amicus curiae* should be appointed to put before the court the argument for making the declaration of incompatibility if it is opposed by the Crown[1]. The court also proceeded on the basis that notice should be given to the Crown before the court decided how the statutory provision in question should be interpreted in the light of s 3 of HRA 1998, the question whether a declaration should be made under s 4 being dependent on the court's decision as to the interpretation of the provision. The same approach was adopted in a Scottish case where it was considered that the issue of inter-pretation under s 3 and the issue of incompatibility might be so bound up with one another as to mean that, in substance, when determining the interpretation question the court was already engaged in part of the process of 'considering whether to make a declaration of incompatibility', with the result that the Crown was entitled to notice in terms of s 5(1)[2].

1 *Wilson v First County Trust Ltd* [2001] QB 407.
2 *Gunn v Newman* 2001 SLT 776.

1.70   The purpose of the Human Rights Act 1998, s 5 is to ensure that the appropriate minister has an opportunity to address the court on the objects and purposes of the legislation in question and any other matters which may be relevant[1]. Given that that is the real purpose of s 5, it would be unsatisfactory, and possibly productive of injustice, if the court were to determine the interpretation of the provision in question having heard only the parties to the action, subsequently to find that it changed its mind, after notice had been given to the Crown and in the light of addi-tional arguments presented by the Crown in a hearing about a declaration of incompatibility[2]. There is also a danger that delay and inefficiency will result if the Crown is not involved at an appropriately early stage of proceedings where the court may have to consider whether to make a declaration of incompatibility[3]. It has also been said, in an English case, that so as to give the Crown as much notice as possible, whenever a party is seeking a declaration of incompatibility or acknowledges that a declara-tion of incompatibility may be made, it should give the Crown as much informal notice as practical of the proceedings and the issues involved; and at the same time should send a copy of such informal notice to the court, so that the court is alerted to the fact that it will have to consider whether a formal notice should be given, and to the other parties[4].

1 *R v A* [2001] 1 WLR 789.
2 *Gunn v Newman* 2001 SLT 776.
3 *Gunn v Newman* 2001 SLT 776.
4 *Poplar Housing and Regeneration Community Association Ltd v Donoghue* [2001] 3 WLR 183.

1.71   The Human Rights Act 1998, s 6(1) makes it unlawful in general for a public authority to act in a way which is incompatible with a Convention right[1]. That provision does not apply to an act if:

(a)   as the result of one or more provisions of primary legislation, the authority could not have acted differently[2]; or

(b)   in the case of one or more provisions of, or made under, primary legislation which cannot be read or given effect in a way which is compatible with the Convention rights, the authority was acting so as to give effect to or enforce those provisions[3].

These exceptions are designed to preserve the principle of Parliamentary sovereignty, and should be read together with ss 3 and 4. An 'act' is defined by s 6(6) to include a failure to act, but does not include a failure to:

(a) introduce in, or lay before, Parliament a proposal for legislation; or

(b) make any primary legislation or remedial order.

These exceptions again preserve Parliamentary sovereignty.

1 This is perhaps less straightforward than it might appear at first sight. Human Rights Act 1998, s 6(1) focuses upon an act. The Convention may require the entirety of proceedings to be considered. Where a right of appeal exists, there may be room for argument as to whether the requirements of the European Convention on Human Rights, Article 6 must be met at first instance, or whether it is sufficient if they are met at the stage of an appeal.

2 This exception appears to cover the situation where the public authority is required by primary legislation to act as it has done, even though that act is incompatible with a Convention right. See *Starrs v Ruxton* 1999 SCCR 1052.

3 This exception appears to cover the situation where the public authority is not required by primary legislation to act as it has done, but where it was acting so as to implement the legislation and all possible ways of implementing the legislation would involve a breach of Convention rights. See *Millar v Dickson* 2001 SCCR 741. In relation to secondary legislation, it appears that 'which' may be governed by 'primary legislation' rather than by 'provisions': cf HRA 1998, s 4(3) and (4).

1.72 The Human Rights Act 1998, s 6(3)–(5) makes provision for identifying a 'public authority' for the purposes of the section. 'Public authority' includes:

(a) a court or tribunal[1], and

(b) any person certain of whose functions are functions of a public nature,

but does not include either House of Parliament or a person exercising functions in connection with proceedings in Parliament[2]. It has been said that s 6 is designed to invite the civil courts of the United Kingdom, as far as possible, to treat as a 'public authority' those bodies which the Strasbourg institutions would treat as bodies whose acts engage the responsibility of the state[3].

1 'Tribunal' is defined as meaning any tribunal in which legal proceedings may be brought: Human Rights Act 1998, s 21(1). It has been said that s 6(3)(a) is not intended to include the courts of the Church of Scotland: 585 HL Official Report (5th series) col 794 (5 February 1998); 312 HC Official Report (6th series) cols 1064–1067 (20 May 1998). It is well established that religious courts or tribunals are not public bodies for the purposes of judicial review under English law; but it is equally well established that their decisions are susceptible to judicial review under Scots law, subject to important qualifications in respect of the courts of the Church of Scotland: see Clyde and Edwards *Judicial Review* (2000) paras 9.06–9.07. Ways in which churches may act as 'public authorities' were discussed at HC Official Report (6th series) col 1015 (20 May 1998).

2 'Parliament' does not include the House of Lords in its judicial capacity: HRA 1998, s 6(4).

3 585 HL Official Report (5th series) col 794 (5 February 1998); similarly 314 HC Official report (6th series) cols 406, 432–433 (17 June 1998). For other observations see 582 HL Official Report (5th series) cols 1231–1232, 1309–1310; 583 HL Official Report (5th series) cols 796–797 (3 November 1997); 306 HC Official Report (6th series) col 778 (16 February 1998); 312 HC Official Report (6th series) col 1018 (20 May 1998). See also *Rights Brought Home* (Cm 3782) (1997) para 2.2.

1.73 There has as yet been little judicial discussion of the scope of the expression 'public authority'. In an English case concerned with a housing association, it was said that the fact that a body performed an activity which otherwise a public body would be under a duty to perform could not mean that such performance was necessarily a public function. While activities of housing associations need not involve the performance of public functions, in the case in question the role of the association, in providing accommodation for the defendant and then seeking possession, was so closely assimilated to that of the local authority that it was performing public and not private functions. It was therefore a functional public authority at least to that extent[1]. That decision was distinguished in a later case concerned with a charitable foundation operating nursing and residential care homes, which had decided to close one of its homes and relocate the residents to another home. It was held that state funding and regulation, and the fact that local authorities were permitted to contract out the provision of services to such a body, did not mean that it exercised public functions[2]. It has been held that an adjudicator acting under the system of adjudication established by the Housing Grants, Construction and Regeneration Act 1996 is not a public authority[3]. A parochial church council has been held to be a public authority[4]. The RSPCA has been held not to be a public authority[5]. A private company operating as a statutory sewerage undertaker has been treated as a public authority[6].

1 *Poplar Housing and Regeneration Community Association Ltd v Donoghue* [2001] 3 WLR 183.
2 *Heather v Leonard Cheshire Foundation* (15 June 2001, unreported), QBD.
3 *Austin Hall Building Ltd v Buckland Securities Ltd* (11 April 2001, unreported), Tech and Con Ct.
4 *Aston Cantlow and Wilmcote with Billesley Parochial Church Council v Wallbank* [2001] 3 All ER 393.
5 *Royal Society for the Prevention of Cruelty to Animals v Attorney General* [2001] 3 All ER 530.
6 *Marcic v Thames Water Utilities Ltd* [2001] 3 All ER 698.

1.74   The effect of defining 'public authority' so as to include the courts has been much discussed[1]. It appears that the courts will have the duty of acting compatibly with the European Convention on Human Rights not only in cases involving other public authorities but also in developing the common law in deciding cases between private parties, but that they will proceed by adapting and developing the common law, rather than by inventing new rights or remedies in the absence of existing domestic principles. Thus in *Venables v News Group Newspapers Ltd*, a case brought by a private individual against newspaper publishers, it was said:

> 'It is clear that, although operating in the public domain and fulfilling a public service, the defendant newspapers cannot sensibly be said to come within the definition of public authority in section 6(1) of the Human Rights Act 1998. Consequently, Convention rights are not directly enforceable against the defendants: see section 7(1) and section 8 of the 1998 Act. That is not, however, the end of the matter, since the court is a public authority (see section 6(3)) and must itself act in a way compatible with the Convention (see section 6 (1)) and have regard to European jurisprudence: see section 2.
>
> ... the decisions of the European Court of Human Rights in *Glaser's*[2] case and *X and Y v The Netherlands*[3], seem to dispose of any argument that a court is a not to have regard to the Convention in private law cases ...
>
> ... I am satisfied that I have to apply article 10 directly to the present case.
>
> That obligation on the court does not seem to me to encompass the creation of a free standing cause of action based directly upon the articles of the Convention ... The duty of the court, in my view, is to act compatibly with Convention rights in adjudicating upon existing common law causes of action, and that includes a positive as well as a negative obligation[4].'

On this approach, it would appear that one private party cannot bring (or defend) proceedings against another private party on the basis of a Convention right, but in proceedings based on the common law[5] he can argue that the court should develop the law in the light of the Convention. For example, in an action of defamation, the pursuer might argue that the defence of qualified privilege should be restricted in the light of Articles 6 and 8; and the defender might argue that the defence should be expanded in the light of Article 10[6]. In an action of removing from privately owned land, on the other hand, it would not (on this approach) appear to be possible for the defenders to resist eviction from land on which they were trespassing, solely on the basis that their Convention right to respect for their home and family life should prevail against the pursuer's right of property. It appears from the terms of the Human Rights Act 1998, s 6 (and s 3) that the court is required to consider issues arising under the Convention whether or not they are raised by parties[7].

1 Buxton 'The Human Rights Act and Private Law' (2000) 116 LQR 48; Wade 'Horizons of Horizontality' (2000) 116 LQR 217; Lester and Pannick 'The Impact of the Human Rights Act on Private Law: The Knight's Move' (2000) 116 LQR 380; and Beatson and Grosz 'Horizontality: A Footnote' (2000) 116 LQR 385.
2 *Glaser v United Kingdom* (19 September 2000, unreported), E Ct HR.
3 (1985) A 91.
4 [2001] 2 WLR 1038, paras 24–27 per Dame Elizabeth Butler-Sloss P. See also *Douglas v Hello! Ltd* [2001] 2 WLR 992. This approach reflects the Government's intention: 583 HL Official Report (5th series) cols 783–784 (24 November 1997).
5 In any action involving a statute, s 3 of the Human Rights Act 1998 would apply, whether the parties were private or public.
6 On this approach, HRA 1998, s 6 reinforces the influence which the Convention already has in developing the common law in litigation between private parties: see e g *Reynolds v Times Newspapers Ltd* [2001] 2 AC 27.
7 As was acknowledged in *Wilson v First County Trust Ltd (No 1)* [2001] QB 407 per Sir Andrew Morritt V-C and per Chadwick LJ.

1.75   In relation to a particular act, a person is not a public authority by virtue only of being a person certain of whose functions are functions of a public nature if the nature of the act is private[1].

1 Human Rights Act 1998, s 6(5). The intention is to distinguish between 'obvious' public authorities such as central and local government and the police, all of whose acts are unlawful if incompatible with the European Convention on Human Rights, and entities which are public authorities only by virtue of HRA 1998, s 6(3)(b), whose acts are unlawful by reason of being incompatible with the Convention only if not of a private nature. See 583 HL Official Report (5th series) col 1231 (16 November 1997) cols 798, 796, 810–812 (24 November 1997); 314 HL Official Report (6th series) cols 409–410 and 433 (17 June 1998). One therefore has to be able to certify (1) public authorities which are not so only by virtue of HRA 1998, s (6)(3)(b); (2) functions of a public nature; and (3) acts of a private nature. Each of these categories presents obvious problems, particularly perhaps from a Scottish perspective, where the 'public/private' distinction drawn in English administrative law has not been adopted. Some guidance can be taken from examples described in Parliament during the passage of the Bill. For example, it was said that Railtrack exercised public functions in its role as a safety regulator, but acted privately in its role as a property developer; and that a GP was a public authority in relation to his NHS functions, but not in relation to his private patients: 583 HL Official Report (5th series) cols 811–812. The analytical basis for these distinctions was not clearly explained. The concepts of public authorities, public functions and private acts are not significant in Convention jurisprudence; the main issue is whether the facts disclose a violation of the Convention for which the state is responsible (which may be a direct consequence of its own acts, or because it has failed to provide a

remedy or to address a problem caused by the acts or omissions of private parties). English case law on 'public bodies' in the context of judicial review would appear to be relevant to HRA 1998, s 6, as also may be the case law of other systems with analogous constitutional instruments, such as those of Canada, New Zealand and the United States. For decided cases to date under HRA 1998, s 6 see para 1.73 above.

1.76   The Scottish Parliament and the Scottish Ministers will be 'public authorities' within the meaning of the Human Rights Act 1998, s 6. The application of s 6 to these bodies is, however, more complicated than in respect of most other bodies, and depends on the interplay of the Scotland Act 1998 and HRA 1998. The Parliament has no power to enact legislation which is incompatible with a Convention right[1]. Scottish Ministers have no power to make any subordinate legislation which is incompatible with a Convention right[2]. Subject to one exception, Scottish Ministers have no power to do any other act which is incompatible with a Convention right[3]. That exception is an act of the Lord Advocate in prosecuting an offence or in his capacity as head of the system of criminal prosecution and investigation of deaths in Scotland which, because of HRA 1998, s 6(2), is not unlawful under s 6(1). In other words, the only circumstances in which a Scottish Minister has the power to act in a way which is incompatible with a Convention right is where the Lord Advocate acts (in prosecuting, or in his investigation of deaths function) in a way in which he is constrained to act by primary legislation, or is giving effect to or enforcing primary legislation (or provisions made under such legislation) which is incompatible with Convention rights. It remains to be seen whether the courts will regard section 6 as applicable to Acts of the Scottish Parliament and acts done by Scottish Ministers (and is providing an alternative route to a challenge under SA 1998), or not[4].

1 Scotland Act 1998, s 29.
2 SA 1998, s 57(2).
3 SA 1998, s 57(2).
4 See now *Mills and Cochrane v HM Advocate* (1 August 2001, unreported), HCJ; *HM Advocate v Rourke* (10 October 2001, unreported), HCJ. SA 1998, s 57(2) and (3) would appear impliedly to restrict the applicability of HRA 1998, s 6(2), so far as concerns matters falling within the scope of the SA 1998, s 57(2). Challenges to Acts of the Scottish Parliament or acts of the Scottish Executive based on the Convention will raise 'devolution issues' within the meaning of SA 1998, Sch 6.

1.77   The consequences of a breach of Human Rights Act 1998 s 6, are dealt with in ss 7–9. HRA 1998, s 7 provides that a person who claims that a public authority[1] has acted (or proposes to act) in a way which is made unlawful by s 6(1) may:

(a)   bring proceedings against the authority under the Act in the appropriate court or tribunal[2], or
(b)   rely on the Convention right or rights concerned in any legal proceedings, but only if he is (or would be) a victim of the unlawful act[3].

The appropriate court or tribunal (in so far as not determined by any enactment[4]) is any civil court or tribunal which has jurisdiction to grant the remedy sought[5]. In relation to s 7(1)(b), it has been said by the House of Lords, in an English case concerned with criminal proceedings, that if a defendant's right to a fair trial under the European Convention on Human Rights, Article 6 has been infringed, a conviction will be held to be unsafe[6]. This is not, however, an absolute rule: if there is no doubt about guilt, it is not every case where an unfairness can be identified that will necessarily and inevitably lead to a quashing of the conviction[7]. The admission of evidence obtained in contravention of Article 8 does not automatically render the conviction unsafe[8].

1   See para 1.71ff above.
2   Defined by Human Rights Act 1998, s 7(2) as meaning 'such court or tribunal as may be determined in accordance with rules (as to which, see s 7 (9)–(13)). The rules are contained in the Human Rights Act 1998 (Jurisdiction) (Scotland) Rules 2000, SI 2000/301. Care may need to be taken in deciding whether an ordinary action or an application for judicial review is appropriate: cf the discussion (in the different context of English law) in *R (Pretty) v DPP* (18 October 2001, unreported), QBD; *R (Wilkinson) v Responsible Medical Officer, Broadmoor Hospital* (22 October 2001, unreported), CA; and *R (Rushbridger) v Attorney General* (22 June 2001, unreported).
3   See para 1.83 below.
4   The Regulation of Investigatory Powers Act 2000, s 65(2)(a) makes provision in this regard.
5   The Human Rights Act 1998 (Jurisdiction) (Scotland) Rules 2000, SSI 2000/301, r 3.
6   *R v Forbes* [2001] 1 AC 473, para 30. A breach of Article 6 during appellate proceedings would not of course place in question the original conviction: cf *Granger, Petitioner* 2001 SCCR 337.
7   *R v Lambert* [2001] 3 WLR 206 at 259 per Lord Clyde.
8   *R v Loveridge* (11 April 2001, unreported), CA.

1.78   In relation to proceedings brought under the Human Rights Act 1998 itself (ie under s 7(1)(a)), s 7(2) defines 'proceedings against an authority' as including a counterclaim or similar proceeding. If the proceedings are made by way of a petition for judicial review in Scotland, the applicant is to be taken to have title and interest to sue in relation to the unlawful act only if he is, or would be, a victim of that act[1]. Proceedings under s 7(1)(a) must be brought before the end of:

(a)   the period of one year beginning with the date on which the act complained of took place; or

(b)   such longer period as the court or tribunal considers equitable having regard to all the circumstances,

but that is subject to any rule imposing a stricter time limit in relation to the procedure in question[2].

1   See para 1.84 below; interventions can, however, be made by other persons, where a matter of public interest is raised, in accordance with RCS 1994, r 58.8A, inserted by the Act of Sederunt (Rules of the Court of Session Amendment No 5) (Public Interest Intervention in Judicial Review) 2000, SSI 2000/317.
2   Human Rights Act 1998, s 7(5). The rationale for such a short limitation period when a fundamental right is relied on is not entirely clear, particularly when no such time limit applies if the point can be raised under the Scotland Act 1998; and it tends to require a distinction to be maintained between Convention rights and the remainder of the law.

1.79   Apart from bringing proceedings under Human Rights Act 1998, s 7(1)(a) (eg an action for breach of statutory duty, or an application for judicial review), s 7(1)(b) makes it possible to rely on the Convention rights in any legal proceedings (for example, as part of a defence to a criminal prosecution or a civil action brought by a public authority[1]).

'Legal proceedings' are defined[2] to include proceedings brought by or at the instigation of a public authority, and an appeal against the decision of a court or tribunal. It has been said that this is not intended to be an exhaustive definition[3]. By virtue of s 22(4), s 7(1)(b) applies to proceedings brought by or at the instigation of a public authority whenever the act in question took place, but otherwise does not apply to an act taking place before s 7 came into force[4]. To that extent, s 6 can have retroactive effect.

1 See 306 HC Official Report (6th series) col 780 (16 February 1998).
2 Human Rights Act 1998, s 7(6).
3 314 HC Official Report (6th series) col 1057 (24 June 1998).
4 HRA 1998, s 22(4). For commencement, see s 22. The HRA 1998 was brought fully into force on 2 October 2000. On the interpretation of s 22(4), read with s 7(1)(b) (in particular, on the issue whether an appeal forms part of the same proceedings as the trial), see *R v DPP, ex p Kebilene* [2000] AC 326. As to whether a re-trial forms part of the same proceedings as an appeal (for the purposes of the Contempt of Court Act 1981) see *Galbraith v HM Advocate* 2000 SCCR 939–940.

1.80   The effect of the Human Rights Act 1998, s 22(4) was first considered fully in *Wilson v First County Trust Ltd (No 2)*[1]:

> 'The effect of s 22(4) is not in doubt. It provides (by the second limb of the section) that, in general, s 7(1) does not apply to an act taking place before 2 October 2000. So, for example, a person who claims that a public authority has acted in a way which is incompatible with a Convention right (contrary to s 6(1) of the Act) cannot bring proceedings against the authority under the Act (pursuant to s 7(1)(a)) if the unlawful act took place before 2 October 2000[2]. Nor, it seems, can a person who claims that a court or tribunal has acted in a way which is incompatible with a Convention right (contrary to s 6(1) of the Act) rely on that as a ground of appeal against the decision of that court or tribunal in a case where the decision complained of was made before 2 October 2000[3]: see s 7(1)(b) and s 7(6)(b) of the Act. If the act which is said to be unlawful under s 6(1) has taken place before 2 October 2000, it is only where the person who claims to be the victim of that act is party to proceedings brought by or at the instigation of a public authority that he can rely on that section.
>
> Once the effect of s 22(4) of the 1998 Act is analysed, it is not difficult to see the purpose for which that section was enacted. Parliament took the view no doubt as a matter of policy that public authorities should not be exposed to proceedings in respect of acts (alleged to be incompatible with Convention rights) which had taken place before ss 6 and 7 had come into force. Nor should the decisions of courts and tribunals made before those sections had come into force be impugned on the ground that the court or tribunal was said to have acted in a way which was incompatible with Convention rights. But, where the public authority was itself the claimant in, or the instigator of, proceedings, there was no reason why another party to those proceedings should not rely on allegation that the authority had acted in a way which s 6 made unlawful, whenever the alleged unlawful act had taken place[4].'

Section 22(4) was similarly interpreted by a majority of the House of Lords in the subsequent case of *R v Lambert*[5].

1 [2001] 3 WLR 42.
2 See eg *R (Ben-Abdelaziz) v Haringey London Borough Council* [2001] 1 WLR 1485; *Stewart v*

Perth and Kinross Council (15 June 2001, unreported), Ct of S. *Pearce v Governing Body of Mayfield School* [2001] IRLR 669.

3 Approved by the House of Lords in *R v Lambert* [2001] 3 WLR 206.

4 See e g *AstonCantlow and Wilmcote with Billesley Parochial Church Council v Wallbank* [2001] 3 All ER 393.

5 [2001] 3 WLR 206. In the light of this decision a number of earlier English criminal cases must be regarded as having been incorrectly decided on the issue of retrospectivity. A number of other cases would also appear to have been incorrectly decided on this issue e g *Advocate General for Scotland v MacDonald* 2001 SLT 819; *J A Pye (Oxford) Ltd v Graham* [2001] 2 WLR 1293; *King v Walden* [2001] STC 822

1.81 An application for judicial review of a decision taken by a public authority prior to 2 October 2000 cannot in general therefore be brought on the basis that the decision was incompatible with a Convention right[1]. On the other hand, a breach of the Convention which began prior to 2 October 2000 may continue after that date[2]. The court's obligation to act compatibly with Convention rights in deciding a dispute between private parties (including, in particular, its obligation under Human Rights Act 1998, s 3, and its power to make a declaration of incompatibility under s 4) applies whether the events giving rise to the dispute occurred prior to or after 2 October 2000[3].

1 *R (Ben-Abdelaziz) v Haringey London Borough Council* [2001] 1 WLR 1485; *Stewart v Perth and Kinross District Council* (15 June 2001, unreported) Ct of S.

2 E g *R (Wright) v Secretary of State for The Home Department* (20 June 2001, unreported), QBD (failure to carry out adequate investigation into death of prisoner in custody in 1996).

3 *Wilson v First County Trust Ltd (No 2)* [2001] 3 WLR 42.

1.82 The appropriate stage in proceedings at which a Convention issue should be raised has not been much discussed, but will depend on the circumstances[1]. It has been said that as a general rule a question as to whether the admission or exclusion of evidence at a criminal trial is incompatible with the right to a fair trial under Article 6 is best considered after the trial has been completed. It is, however, undesirable that vulnerable witnesses, such as the complainant in a rape trial, should be exposed to the risk of having to give evidence a second time at a re-trial, as would happen if the verdict of the first trial were to be quashed on the ground that the accused did not receive a fair trial. In such a case, it is desirable that the issue should be determined before the trial. Similarly, if the issue is one of general public importance which is likely to affect other trials, it should be determined as soon as possible[2].

1 Cf para 1.51 above.

2 *R v A* [2001] 1 WLR 789, para 11 per Lord Hope of Craighead. See also *R (Kathro) v Rhondda Cynon Taff County Borough Council* (16 July 2001, unreported), QBD (Article 6 challenge to planning decision).

1.83 For the purposes of the Human Rights Act 1998, s 7, a person is a victim of an unlawful act only if he would be a victim for the purposes of Article 34 of the Convention if proceedings were brought in the European Court of Human Rights in respect of that act[1]. The relevant principles established by the Strasbourg institutions are discussed in chapter 2[2].

1 Human Rights Act 1998, s 7(7). The thinking behind s 7(7) was explained at 314 HC Official Report (6th Series) cols 1083–1086 (24 June 1998).

2 Paragraphs 2.29–2.30 below.

1.84   Nothing in the Human Rights Act 1998 creates a criminal offence[1].

1 Human Rights Act 1998, s 7(8).

1.85   The Human Rights Act 1998, s 8 enables the court (defined as including a tribunal[1]) to grant appropriate remedies in relation to any act (or proposed act) of a public authority which the court finds is (or would be) unlawful under s 6(1)[2]. Where the court finds that any act (or proposed act) of a public authority is (or would be) unlawful, it may grant such relief or remedy, or make such order, within its powers as it considers just and appropriate[3]. The HRA 1998 therefore does not create any new remedy (other than the declaration of incompatibility). Damages[4] may be awarded only by a court which has power to award damages, or to order the payment of compensation in civil proceedings[5]. No award of damages is to be made unless, taking account of all the circumstances of the case, including any other relief or remedy granted, or order made, in relation to the act in question (by that or any other court) and the consequences of any decision in respect of that act, the court is satisfied that the award is necessary to afford just satisfaction to the person in whose favour it is made[6]. In determining whether to award damages, or the amount of an award, the court must take into account the principles applied by the European Court of Human Rights in relation to the award of compensation under Article 41 of the European Convention on Human Rights[7]. Where a public authority is found liable in damages under HRA 1998, s 8, the law of contribution (under the Law Reform (Miscellaneous Provisions) (Scotland) Act 1940) applies in relation to joint and several liability[8]. It is unclear at present whether HRA 1998, s 8 creates a new type of breach of statutory duty for which damages can be recovered, or introduces into our law the concept known to other jurisdictions of damages for the infringement of a constitutional right[9]. The remedy has novel features, in so far as it is discretionary, residual and to be awarded taking account of the principles applied by the Strasbourg court, some of which are unfamiliar to our law of damages[10]. Another interesting question is whether the court, when it is faced with infringements of Convention rights which cannot instantly be brought to an end, but require some sort of programme of work to be undertaken, will be prepared to grant remedies which require such a programme to be commenced and subjected to some sort of judicial oversight[11].

1 Human Rights Act 1998, s 8(6).
2 HRA 1998, s 8(6).
3 HRA 1998, s 8(1). The Lord Chancellor could not be held liable for wasted expenses (estimated at £1m) incurred when a hearing had to be aborted due to a lack of impartiality, because the Court of Appeal had ordered a re-hearing and no breach of a Convention right had therefore occurred: *In re Medicaments and Related Classes of Goods (No 4)* (26 July 2001, unreported), CA.
4 Ie for an act of a public authority which is unlawful under HRA 1998, s 6(1); HRA 1998, s 8(6)
5 HRA 1998, s 8(2). So, for example, the High Court of Justiciary will be unable to award damages. The wording of s 8(2) might arguably be construed as permitting the sheriff court, in criminal proceedings, to award damages (since the sheriff court is a court which has the power to award damages in civil proceedings), but that does not appear to be what is intended: 583 HL Official Report (5th series) col 855 (24 November 1997). HRA 1998, s 8(1) in any event keeps the court 'within its powers', which presumably refers to the powers of the court in the context of the proceedings before it.

6   HRA 1998, s 8(3). In interpreting and applying s 8 it will have to borne in mind that many acts which are contrary to HRA 1998, s 6(1) are in any event civil wrongs sounding in damages under the law of delict.
7   HRA 1998, s 8(4). The aim has been said to be that people should receive damages equivalent to what they would have gained had they taken their case to Strasbourg: 582 HL Official Report (5th series) col 1232 (3 November 1997). In reality, it is difficult to identify specific 'principles'. The European Court of Human Rights carries out a broad equitable assessment of the facts of the individual case and decides whether compensation is appropriate in those circumstances. One might extrapolate from the case law that compensation is not awarded unless the loss or damage is proved to have been caused by the violation in question; that compensation is not awarded where the finding of a violation constitutes sufficient just satisfaction; that compensation can be awarded for pecuniary and non pecuniary loss, including mental distress; and that interest on compensation can be awarded (but rarely is). See para 2.31 below. See also *Damages under the Human Rights Act 1998* (Scot Law Com No 180; Law Com No 266; Cm 4853).
8   HRA 1998, s 8(5).
9   For an example, see *Kearney v Minister for Justice* [1986] IR 116.
10 Eg whether the applicant is viewed as deserving or not, or whether the breach of the Convention was procedural or substantive, technical or flagrant. For an example, see *Marcic v Thames Water Utilities Ltd* [2001] 3 All ER 698; *Marcic v Thames Water Utilities Ltd (No 2)* [2001] 4 All ER 326.
11 Other jurisdictions, such as the United States of America, Canada, South Africa and Ireland, have developed what have been called 'structural orders' or 'structural injunctions'. See eg *DB v Minister for Justice* [1999] IR 29. For an English example, see *Marcic v Thames Water Utilities Ltd* [2001] 3 All ER 698

1.86   The Human Rights Act 1998, s 9 concerns judicial acts. A 'judicial act' is defined[1] to mean a judicial act of court[2], including an act done on the instructions, or on behalf, of a judge[3]. Proceedings under HRA 1998, s 7(1)(a) in respect of a judicial act may be brought only:

(a)   by exercising a right of appeal;
(b)   on a petition for judicial review; or
(c)   in such other forum as may be prescribed by rules[4].

That does not affect any rule of law which prevents a court from being the subject of judicial review[5]. The general intention of these provisions appears to be that decisions of courts and tribunals should be challenged only by way of appeal or (where competent) judicial review, unless another forum is prescribed by rules. The relevant rule[6] prescribes the Court of Session, for the purposes of s 9(1)(c), in cases where proceedings in respect of the judicial act in question could not, at any time since the date of that act, have competently been brought under s 9(1)(a) or (b). Damages cannot be awarded in proceedings under the Human Rights Act 1998 in respect of a judicial act done in good faith, otherwise than to compensate a person to the extent required by Article 5(5) of the Convention[7]. Any such award of damages is to be made against the Crown, but no award may be made unless the appropriate person, if not a party to the proceedings, is joined[8], ie sisted.

1   Human Rights Act 1998, s 9(5).
2   Court includes a tribunal: HRA 1998, s 9(5).
3   'Judge' includes a member of a tribunal, a justice of the peace and a clerk or other officer entitled to exercise the jurisdiction of a court: HRA 1998, s 9(5).
4   HRA 1998, s 9(1).
5   HRA 1998, s 9(2). For example, the High Court of Justiciary is not subject to the supervisory jurisdiction of the Court of Session.
6   Human Rights Act 1998 (Jurisdiction) (Scotland) Rules 2000, SI 2000/301, r 4.

7 HRA 1998, s 9(3). As to ECHR, Article 5(5), see para 4.101 below.
8 HRA 1998, s 9(4). The 'appropriate person' means the minister responsible for the court concerned, or a person or government department nominated by him: HRA 1998, s 9(5).

1.87 The Human Rights Act 1998, s 10 enables the Government[1] to take urgent action to amend legislation declared to be incompatible with the Convention. It also applies where there has been an adverse finding of the European Court of Human Rights in proceedings against the United Kingdom.

1 It seems that powers under the Human Rights Act 1998, s 10 can also be exercised by a Scottish Minister in relation to matters falling within devolved competence: see the complex provisions of the Scotland Act 1998, s 53 and Sch 4, paras 1, 12 and 13. Similar powers are conferred in any event on the Scottish Ministers by the Convention Rights (Compliance) (Scotland) Act 2001.

1.88 The section applies in two situations:

(a) where a provision of legislation has been declared under the Human Rights Act 1998, s 4 to be incompatible with a Convention right and, if an appeal lies, all persons who may appeal have stated in writing that they do not intend to do so; or the time for bringing an appeal has expired and no appeal has been brought within that time; or an appeal brought within that time has been determined or abandoned; or

(b) it appears to a Minister of the Crown[1] or Her Majesty in Council that, having regard to a finding of the European Court of Human Rights made after the coming into force of HRA 1998, s 10 in proceedings against the United Kingdom, a provision of legislation is incompatible with an obligation of the United Kingdom arising from the Convention[2].

In these circumstances, if a Minister of the Crown considers that there are compelling reasons for proceeding under HRA 1998, s 10, he may by order[3] make such amendments to the legislation as he considers necessary to remove the incompatibility[4]. This power would extend to legislation enacted by the Scottish Parliament. In the case of subordinate legislation, if the Minister considers it necessary to amend the primary legislation under which the subordinate legislation was made, in order to enable the incompatibility to be removed, and if he considers that there are compelling reasons for proceeding under s 10, then he may by order make such amendments to the primary legislation as he considers necessary[5]. Section 10 also applies where the provision in question is in subordinate legislation and has been quashed, or declared invalid, by reason of incompatibility with a Convention right and the Minister proposes to make a remedial order under para 2 (b) of Sch 2[6]. Schedule 2 makes further provision about remedial orders, and indicates that such an order may have retrospective effects and may make 'different provision for different cases'[7].

1 Defined by the Human Rights Act 1998, s 21(1) as having the same meaning as in the Ministers of the Crown Act 1975. A member of the Scottish Executive is not a Minister of the Crown; but see para 1.87, n 1 above.
2 HRA 1998, s 10(1).
3 Ie by statutory instrument: HRA 1998, s 20(1).

4 HRA 1998, s 10(2). If the legislation is an Order in Council, the power conferred by s 10(2) or (3) is exercisable by Her Majesty in Council: s 10(5). The discretionary nature of the power conferred by s 10(2) was discussed at 583 HL Official Report (5th series) col 1139 (27 November 1997) and 314 HC Official Report (6th series) cols 1127–1133 (24 June 1998). See also cols 1137–1138 as to the standard set by 'compelling' and 'necessary',
5 HRA 1998, s 10(3).
6 HRA 1998, s 10(4).
7 HRA 1998, Sch 2, para 1. The exercise of such a power could give rise to issues under the Convention (eg under Article 6(1)), but it may be that HRA 1998, s 6 would not apply (see s 6(3) and (6)). Judicial review of the exercise of the s 10 power may nevertheless be available. The exercise of s 10 powers falls within the ambit of the Joint Select Committee on Human Rights.

1.89   The Human Rights Act 1998, s 11 safeguards existing human rights by providing that a person's reliance on a Convention right does not restrict any other right or freedom conferred on him by or under any law having effect in any part of the United Kingdom, or his right to make any claim or bring any proceedings which he could make or bring apart from ss 7–9.

1.90   The Human Rights Act 1998, ss 12 and 13 respond to concerns expressed by, respectively, the media and the churches during the progress of the Bill, as to the impact which its provisions might have upon their activities[1]. The Government did not intend either section to require the courts to violate the principles contained in the Convention and its jurisprudence[2].

1 Most commentators have doubted whether these concerns were well founded.
2 In relation to Human Rights Act 1998, s 12, see 315 HC Official Report (6th series) col 543 (2 July 1998). In relation to s 13, see 312 HC Official Report (6th series) cols 1019–1022 (20 May 1998). The approach adopted in *Douglas v Hello! Ltd* [2001] 2 WLR 992 and *Ashdown v Telegraph Group Ltd* (18 July 2001, unreported), CA avoids any conflict between s 12 and the European Convention on Human Rights.

1.91   The Human Rights Act 1998, s 12 applies if a court[1] is considering whether to grant any relief[2] which, if granted, might affect the exercise of the Convention right[3] to freedom of expression[4]. In such a situation, if the person against whom the application for relief is made ('the respondent') is neither present nor represented, no such relief is to be granted unless the court is satisfied that the applicant has taken all practicable steps to notify the respondent, or that there are compelling reasons why the respondent should not be notified[5]. No such relief is to be granted so as to restrain publication before trial unless the court is satisfied that the applicant is likely to establish that publication should not be allowed[6]. The court must have particular regard to the importance of the Convention right to freedom of expression[7]. Where the proceedings relate to material which the respondent claims, or which appears to the court, to be journalistic, literary or artistic material (or to conduct connected with such material[8]), the court must also have particular regard to:

(a)   the extent to which the material has, or is about to, become available to the public; or it is, or would be, in the public interest for the material to be published[9];
(b)   any relevant privacy code[10].

Section 12 has been considered in recent English cases[11].

1 Including a tribunal: Human Rights Act 1998, s 12(5).
2 'Relief' includes any remedy or order, other than in criminal proceedings: HRA 1998, s 12(5). Criminal courts are, however, required (in the same way as other courts) not to act incompatibly with Convention rights, including Article 10: HRA 1998, s 6(1). Section 12 is not intended to derogate from the Convention: see 315 HC Official Report (6th series) col 540 (2 July 1998). It appears to have been envisaged that s 12 might enhance press freedom in situations in which the Convention did not apply: 315 HC Official Report (6th series) col 536 (but cf col 561).
3 European Convention on Human Rights, Article 10.
4 HRA 1998, s 12(1).
5 HRA 1998, s 12(2). This reflects current practice.
6 HRA 1998, s 12(3). This reflects Convention jurisprudence: see para 7.24 below.
7 HRA 1998, s 12(4).
8 This expression was discussed at 315 HC Official Report (6th series) col 540 (2 July 1998); cf *Goodwin v United Kingdom* 1996-II, 483.
9 This reflects Convention jurisprudence: see para 7.16 below.
10 The intention was to emphasise the importance of self-regulation of the newspaper and broadcasting media: 315 HC Official Report (6th series) cols 538–541 (2 July 1998). Privacy is addresses in cl 3 of Code of Practice ratified by the Press Complaints Commission in November 1997.
11 *Ashdown v Telegraph Group Ltd* (18 July 2001, unreported), CA; *Douglas v Hello! Ltd* [2001] 2 WLR 992; *Imutran Ltd v Uncaged Campaigns Ltd* [2001] 2 All ER 385; *A-G v Times Newspapers Ltd* [2001] 1 WLR 885. See paras 7.25–7.26 below.

1.92   The Human Rights Act 1998, s 13 provides that if a court's[1] determination of any question arising under HRA 1998 might affect the exercise by a religious organisation (itself or its members collectively) of the Convention right to freedom of thought, conscience and religion[2], it must have particular regard to the importance of that right. It is important to emphasise that this provision is not intended to derogate from the Convention[3]: its purpose is merely to 'signal to the courts that they must pay due regard to the rights guaranteed by Article 9[4]'.

1 Including a tribunal: Human Rights Act 1998, s 13(2).
2 Ie Article 9: see 312 HC Official Report (6th series) col 1063 (20 May 1998).
3 See para 1.91 n 2 above.
4 312 HC Official Report (6th series) col 1022 (20 May 1998). See para 7.10.

1.93   The Human Rights Act 1998, ss 14–17 deal with designated derogations or reservations from the European Convention on Human Rights[1]. Article 15 of the Convention enables a contracting state to derogate from certain of its obligations under the Convention in specified circumstances. Article 57 of the Convention enables a contracting state, when signing the Convention or when depositing its instrument of ratification, to make a reservation in respect of any provision to the extent that any law then in force in its territory is not in conformity with the provision. Derogations and reservations can also be made in respect of protocols to the Convention[2].

1 Cf Human Rights Act 1998, s 1(2): para 1.61 above.
2 Where permitted by the terms of the protocols. See eg Art 5 of Protocol 1; Art 7 of Protocol 7; contrast Arts 3 and 4 of Protocol 6.

1.94   The Human Rights Act 1998, s 14 as amended[1] defines the expression 'designated derogation' to mean any derogation by the United Kingdom from an article of the Convention, or of any protocol to the

Convention, which is designated for the purposes of the 1998 Act in an order[2] made by the Secretary of State[3]. Further provisions are designed to ensure that derogations for the purposes of HRA 1998 continue to reflect the United Kingdom's international obligations from time to time under the Convention and its protocols[4].

1 The UK's derogation from Article 5(3) of the Convention, relating to the detention of persons suspected of terrorism, was terminated following the entry into force of the Terrorism Act 2000, and the Human Rights Act 1998, s 14 and Sch 3 were amended accordingly with effect from 1 April 2001: Human Rights (Amendment) Order 2001, SI 2001/1216.
2 Ie a statutory instrument: HRA 1998, s 20(1) and (3).
3 HRA 1998, s 14(1). The order ceases to have effect unless approved by Parliament.
4 HRA 1998, s 14 (3)–(6).

1.95 The Human Rights Act 1998, s 15 defines the expression 'designated reservation' to mean the United Kingdom's reservation to Article 2 of Protocol 1 to the European Convention on Human Rights[1], and any other reservation by the United Kingdom to an article of the Convention, or of any protocol to the Convention, which is designated for the purposes of the Act in an order[2] made by the Secretary of State[3]. Further provisions are designed to ensure that designated reservations for the purposes of HRA 1998 continue to reflect the United Kingdom's international obligations from time to time under the Convention and its protocols[4].

1 This relates to the education of children in accordance with the wishes of their parents. The reservation is set out in the Human Rights Act 1998, Sch 3, Pt II.
2 Ie a statutory instrument: HRA 1998, s 20(1) and (3).
3 HRA 1998, s 15(1).
4 HRA 1998, s 15 (3)–(5).

1.96 The Human Rights Act 1998, s 16 as amended[1] provides for a designated derogation to cease to have effect for the purposes of the Act after a period of five years[2], unless extended by an order made by the Secretary of State[3]. This reflects the emergency nature of derogations under Article 15 of the European Convention on Human Rights.

1 By the Human Rights (Amendment) Order 2001, SI 2001/1216.
2 Human Rights Act 1998, s 16(1).
3 HRA 1998, s 16(2). See also s 20(1) and (4).

1.97 The Human Rights Act 1998, s 17 makes similar provisions in respect of designated reservations.

1.98 The Human Rights Act 1998, s 18 makes provision in respect of the appointment of serving United Kingdom judges to the European Court of Human Rights.

1.99 The Human Rights Act 1998, s 19 requires a Minister of the Crown[1] in charge of a Bill in either House of Parliament to make a statement[2], before the second reading of the Bill, either to the effect that in his view the provisions of the Bill are compatible with the Convention rights ('a statement of compatibility') or to the effect that although he is unable to make a statement of compatibility the Government nevertheless wishes the House to proceed with the Bill[3]. A statement of compatibility has been made in respect of every Bill introduced since HRA 1998 received Royal Assent, with the exception of the Local Government Bill introduced in the Commons on 13 March 2000[4]. An analogous practice has been adopted in respect of statutory instruments[5].

1 As defined by Human Rights Act 1998, s 21(1).
2 The statement must be in writing and be published in such manner as the Minister making it considers appropriate: HRA 1998, s 19 (2).
3 HRA 1998, s 19(1). Although this provision does not apply to the Scottish Parliament, analogous provision is made by Scotland Act 1998, s 31(1). A statement made to the Westminster Parliament probably does not give rise to a justiciable issue, by virtue of Parliamentary privilege under the Bill of Rights 1688. That privilege does not, however, apply to the Scottish Parliament: *Whaley v Watson* 2000 SC 340. As to the possible effects of a compatibility statement in legal proceedings, see Lord Hoffmann (1999) 62 MLR 159 at 162.
4 This exception arose from a Lords amendment to reaffirm the provisions of s 2A of the Local Government Act 1986 (concerning sex education in schools), which appeared to be incompatible with Convention rights (e g possibly those of homosexuals and their families, under Art 8, or those of teachers under Art 10).
5 See House of Lords Select Committee on Delegated Powers and Deregulation, 1st Report, Session 1999–2000, Annex 6; also 608 HL Official Report (5th series) written answers col 76 (10 January 2000).

1.100 The remaining provisions of the Human Rights Act 1998 are supplemental and can be discussed briefly. Section 20 concerns the order-making powers contained in the Act. Section 21 defines certain terms used in the Act, and also abolishes the death penalty for military offences. Section 22 is the commencement section[1].

1 On the Human Rights Act 1998, s 22(4), see para 1.80 above.

1.101 There are a number of important differences between cases brought under the Scotland Act 1998 on the basis of the European Convention on Human Rights and cases brought under HRA 1998. The House of Lords is the court of last resort for issues raised under HRA 1998 (except in Scottish criminal cases), whereas the Judicial Committee of the Privy Council is normally the court of last resort for devolution issues. Devolution issues can be dealt with by a preliminary reference, whereas issues raised under HRA 1998 cannot. A one-year limitation period applies to proceedings brought against a public authority under HRA 1998[1], whereas no such period applies to proceedings under SA 1998. The powers given to the court under HRA 1998 where a public authority acts unlawfully are arguably different from those available under SA 1998[2]. The legislative power given under SA 1998 to remedy ultra vires acts is wider than that under HRA 1998[3].

1 Human Rights Act 1998, s 7(5).
2 Compare HRA 1998, s 8 with the Scotland Act 1998, s 102.
3 Compare HRA 1998, s 10 with SA 1998, s 107.

1.102 Early Scottish cases under the Human Rights Act 1998 have included cases concerned with civil jury trials[1], disciplinary proceedings[2], employment in the armed services[3], criminal procedure[4], the children's hearing system[5], and land obligations[6].

1 *Gunn v Newman* 2001 SC 525 (OH), 2001 SLT 776 (IH); *McLeod v British Railways Board* 2001 SC 534; *Sandison v Graham Begg Ltd* (30 March 2001, unreported), Ct of S. See para 5.81 below.

2 *Tehrani v United Kingdom Central Council for Nursing, Midwifery and Health Visiting* 2001 SC 581.
3 *Advocate General for Scotland v MacDonald* 2001 SLT 819.
4 *Al Megrahi v HM Advocate* 2001 SCCR 701; *McMaster v HM Advocate* 2001 SCCR 517; *Degnan v HM Advocate* 2001 SCCR 810.
5 *S v Miller* 2001 SLT 531; *S v Miller (No 2)* (7 August 2001, unreported), Ct of S.
6 *Strathclyde Joint Police Board v The Elderslie Estates Ltd* (17 August 2001, unreported), Lands Tr.

1.103 Cases under the Human Rights Act 1998 before other United Kingdom courts have concerned, amongst other matters: criminal law and procedure[1], sentencing[2], the law of evidence[3], confidentiality[4], copyright[5], courts martial[6], prisoners' rights[7], the law relating to children[8], medical treatment[9], immigration[10], housing law[11], the law relating to burial[12], landlord and tenant[13], planning law[14], construction law[15], taxation[16], consumer credit law[17], the law of limitation[18], damages[19], defamation[20], charities[21], employment tribunals[22], disciplinary tribunals[23], the law of marriage[24], nuisance[25] and harassment[26].

1 *R v Lambert* [2001] 3 WLR 206 (burden of proving statutory defence); *R (Wardle) v Crown Court at Leeds* [2001] 2 WLR 865 (custody time limits); *R v Charles* (31 January 2001, unreported), CA (time limit for seeking leave to appeal); *R v Williams* (14 March 2001, unreported), CA (whether misdirection constituting breach of Article 6(2) automatically rendered conviction unsafe); *R (DPP) v Havering Magistrates Court* [2001] 1 WLR 805 (withdrawal of bail for breach of condition); *R v Davis* [2001] 1 Cr App R 8 (disclosure of information to defence); *R v Smith (Joe)* [2001] 1 WLR 1031 (disclosure of information to defence); *R (DPP) v Acton Youth Court* [2001] 1 WLR 1828 (whether judge who has made preliminary ruling in favour of Crown can conduct trial); *R v H (Assault of child: Reasonable chastisement)* [2001] 2 FLR 431; *Attorney General's Reference (No 2 of 2001)* [2001] 1 WLR 1869 (delay); *R v Qureshi* (23 July 2001, unreported), CA (whether court can inquire into jury's deliberations); *R v Hayward* [2001] QB 862 (trial in absentia); *R (Rushbridger) v Attorney General* (22 June 2001, unreported), QBD (whether entitled to know in advance whether publication of articles would result in prosecution); *R v M* (5 October 2001, unreported), CA (determining fitness to plead); *R v Shayler* (28 September 2001, unreported), CA (official secrets and Article 10); *R (Pretty) v DPP* (18 October 2001, unreported), QBD (assisted suicide); *R v Loosely* (25 October 2001, unreported), HL (entrapment).
2 *R v Offen* [2001] 1 WLR 253 (automatic life sentences for repeat offenders); *R (Anderson) v Secretary of State for the Home Department* (22 February 2001, unreported), QBD (fixing of tariff element of mandatory life sentence); *R v Lichniak* [2001] 3 WLR 933 (mandatory life sentence); *A and W* [2001] 2 Cr App R 18 (homosexual offences).
3 *R v Forbes* [2001] 1 AC 473 (admissibility of street identification evidence); *Attorney-General's Reference (No 3 of 1999)* [2001] 2 AC 91 (admissibility of evidence based on DNA sample which should have been destroyed); *R v A (No 2)* [2001] 2 WLR 1546 (evidence of rape complainer's previous sexual history); *R v Loveridge* (11 April 2001, unreported), CA (video taken of defendants in police cell area); *Re Al-Fawwaz* [2001] 4 All ER 149 (anonymous evidence); *R v Craven* [2001] 2 Cr App R 181 (fresh evidence adduced by Crown); *Attorney-General's Reference (No 7 of 2000)* [2001] 1 WLR 1879 (self-incrimination).
4 *Ashworth Hospital Authority v MGN Ltd* [2001] 1 WLR 515 (disclosure of journalist's source); *Douglas v Hello! Ltd* [2001] 2 WLR 992 (publication of photographs taken surreptitiously at wedding); *Venables v News Group Newspapers Ltd* [2001] 2 WLR 1038 (publication of information relating to identity, whereabouts and appearance of persons convicted of murder); *Imutran Ltd v Uncaged Campaigns Ltd* [2001] 2 All ER 385 (publication of leaked documents); *Attorney-General v Times Newspapers Ltd* [2001] 1 WLR 885 (publication of book by former member of SIS); *Re X (Disclosure of information)* [2001] 2 FLR 440 (disclosure of evidence in care proceedings); *Clibbery v Allan* [2001] 2 FLR 819 (disclosure of evidence given at hearing in chambers); *R (Pamplin) v Law Society* (30 March 2001, unreported), QBD (disclosure by police to Law Society of interview with solicitor's clerk); *A Health Authority v X* (discovery: medical conduct) [2001] 2 FLR 673.

  5 *Ashdown v Telegraph Group Ltd* (18 July 2001, unreported), CA (unauthorised publication of politician's diary); *Imutran Ltd v Uncaged Campaigns Ltd* [2001] 2 All ER 385 (publication of leaked documents by animal rights group).
  6 *R v Spear* [2001] QB 804; *R v Williams* (30 July 2001, unreported), Courts-Martial Appeal Ct.
  7 *R (Carroll) v Secretary of State for the Home Department* (16 February 2001, unreported), QBD (strip searches); *R (Greenfield) v Secretary of State for the Home Department* [2001] 1 WLR 1731 (prison discipline); *R (Pearson) v Secretary of State for the Home Department* (4 April 2001, unreported), CA (disqualification of prisoners from voting); *R (Mellor) v Secretary of State for the Home Dept* [2001] 3 WLR 533 (artificial insemination facilities); *R (P)* v *Secretary of State for the Home Department* [2001] 1 WLR 2002 (separation of female prisoners from their children); *R (Daly) v Secretary of State for the Home Department* [2001] 2 WLR 1622 (prisoners' correspondence); *R (Wright) v Secretary of State for the Home Dept* (20 June 2001, unreported), QBD (right of relatives to have investigation into death of prisoner); *R (Amin) v Secretary of State for the Home Department* (5 October 2001, unreported), QBD (right of relatives to have investigation into death of prisoner).
  8 *In re K (A Child) (Secure Accommodation Order: Right to Liberty)* [2001] Fam 377; *Payne v Payne* [2001] 2 WLR 1826 (removal from jurisdiction); *In re C (Secure Accommodation Order: Representation)* [2001] 2 FLR 169; *Re W and B (Care Plan)* [2001] 2 FLR 582.
  9 *In re A (Children) (Conjoined Twins: Surgical Separation)* [2001] Fam 147; *R (K) v Camden and Islington Health Authority* [2001] 3 WLR 553 (detention of patient with mental disorder); *NHS Trust A v M* [2001] Fam 348 (withdrawal of treatment); *R (H) v Mental Health Review Tribunal, North and East London Region* [2001] 3 WLR 512 (discharge of restricted patient: onus of proof); *R (Heather) v Leonard Cheshire Foundation* (15 June 2001, unreported), QBD (closure of nursing home: whether a 'public authority'); *R(C) v Mental Health Review Tribunal London South and South West Region* (3 July 2001, unreported), CA (speedy determination of lawfulness of detention); *R (Van Brandenburg) v East London and the City Mental Health NHS Trust* [2001] 3 WLR 588.
 10 *R (X) v Secretary of State for the Home Department* [2001] 1 WLR 740 (removal of illegal entrant suffering from mental illness); *K v Secretary of State for the Home Department* [2001] Imm AR 11 (removal of AIDS sufferer); *Kacaj v Secretary of State for the Home Department* (19 July 2001, unreported), IAT (Article 3 and standard of proof; non-state actors; relevance of breaches of other Convention rights outwith UK); *R (Farrakhan) v Secretary of State for the Home Department* (1 October 2001, unreported), QBD (Article 10 and entry to UK); *R (Saadi) v Secretary of State for the Home Department* (19 October 2001, unreported), CA (detention of asylum seekers); *R (Samaroo) v Secretary of State for the Home Department* (17 July 2001, unreported), CA (deportation).
 11 *Poplar Housing and Regeneration Community Association Ltd v Donoghue* [2001] 3 WLR 183 (order for possession); *R (Johns and McLellan) v Bracknell Forest DC* [2001] 33 HLR 45 (introductory, ie non-secure tenancies); *St Brice v Southwark London Borough Council* (17 July 2001, unreported), CA (order for possession); *Lambeth LBC v Howard* [2001] 33 HLR 58.
 12 *In re Crawley Green Road Cemetery, Luton* [2001] Fam 308; *In re Durrington Cemetery* [2001] Fam 33.
 13 *Malekshad v Howard de Walden Estates Ltd* [2001] 3 WLR 824 (leasehold enfranchisement).
 14 *R (Alconbury Developments Ltd) v Secretary of State for the Environment, Planning and the Regions* [2001] 2 WLR 1389 (called-in applications); *R (Kathro) v Rhondda Cynon Taff County Borough Council* (6 July 2001, unreported), QBD (local authority determining its own application); *R (Vetterlein) v Hampshire County Council* (14 June 2001, unreported), QBD (planning permission and quality of life); *Porter v South Buckinghamshire District Council* (12 October 2001, unreported), CA (enforcement of development control and right to respect for home).
 15 *Austin Hall Building Ltd v Buckland Securities Ltd* (11 April 2001, unreported) Tech and Con Ct (adjudication proceedings).
 16 *R (Professional Contractors Group Ltd) v Inland Revenue Commissioners* [2001] STC 618 (lifting the corporate veil); *Goldsmith v Customs and Excise Commissioners* [2001] 1 WLR 1673 (condemnation of forfeited goods); *Aston Cantlow and Wilmcote with Billesley Parochial Church Council v Wallbank* [2001] 3 All ER 393 (liability to repair church); *King v Walden* [2001] STC 822 (penalty assessments: delay); *Customs and Excise Commissioners v Hall* [2001] STC 1188 (penalty assessments); *Bennett v Customs and Excise Commissioners (No 2)* [2001] STC 137 (whether fresh assessment can be made following successful appeal against original assessment); *R v Dimsey* [2001] 3 WLR 843 (tax avoidance

legislation); *R (Banque Internationale à Luxembourg) v Inland Revenue Commissioners* [2000] STC 708 (investigation of tax avoidance).

17 *Wilson v First County Trust Ltd* [2001] QB 407; *Wilson v First County Trust Ltd (No 2)* [2001] 3 WLR 42.

18 *JA Pye (Oxford) Ltd v Graham* [2001] 2 WLR 1293; *Family Housing Association v Donnellan* (12 July 2001, unreported), Ch D.

19 *Greenfield v Irwin* [2001] 1 WLR 1279 (whether damages recoverable for financial loss due to birth of healthy child); *Briody v St Helen's and Knowsley Area Health* Authority (29 June 2001, unreported), CA (whether damages recoverable to pay for surrogacy).

20 *Loutchansky v Times Newspapers Ltd* [2001] 3 WLR 404 (whether defendants pleading qualified privilege entitled to rely on facts not known to them at time of publication); *Branson v Bower* (24 May 2001, unreported), CA (distinction between fact and comment); *Berezovsky v Forbes* (31 July 2001, unreported), CA ('repetition' rule and 'conduct' rule).

21 *Royal Society for the Prevention of Cruelty to Animals v Attorney General* [2001] 3 All ER 530 (whether exclusion from membership of pro-hunting campaigners compatible with Arts 10 and 11).

22 *Scanfuture UK Ltd v Secretary of State for Trade and Industry* [2001] IRLR 416.

23 *Preiss v General Dental Council* [2001] 1 WLR 1926.

24 *Bellinger v Bellinger* (17 July 2001, unreported), CA (whether male-to-female transexual could marry male).

25 *Marcic v Thames Water Utilities Ltd* [2001] 3 All ER 698.

26 *Thomas v News group Newspapers Ltd* (18 July 2001, unreported), CA (harassment by newspaper articles).

CONCLUSION

1.104   As a result of the Scotland Act 1998, Convention rights have been given what may be regarded as a constitutional status in Scotland: they are legally superior to Acts of the Scottish Parliament, and provide standards by which those Acts must be judged. The Parliament has no power to make law which is incompatible with the Convention rights. The Convention also provides standards by which the acts of Scottish Ministers will be judged: in general, they have no power to act in a way which is incompatible with Convention rights. In this way, Convention rights will be pivotal to Scottish constitutional law.

1.105   More generally, as elsewhere in the United Kingdom, the European Convention on Human Rights will profoundly influence public law in Scotland in so far as it becomes binding on public authorities as a result of the Human Rights Act 1998. Since the courts themselves are public authorities for the purposes of the Act[1], the Convention will guide the courts in the development of the common law generally as well as the interpretation of statutes. Over time, this will inevitably have a significant effect upon the whole of our law.

1 Human Rights Act 1998, s 6(3)(a).

CHAPTER 2

European Protection of Human Rights

THE COUNCIL OF EUROPE AND THE PROTECTION OF HUMAN RIGHTS

A developing international concern for human rights

2.01 Before 1945, legal protection for the individual against state interference with what now would be termed 'human rights' was largely a matter for domestic law. By the early part of the nineteenth century, international law had begun to develop an interest in the prohibition of slavery, in the treatment of aliens and in humanitarian intervention, and later that century issues such as the care of injured combatants and prisoners of war were being addressed by multilateral treaties. While the establishment of the League of Nations after the 1914–18 war gave additional impetus to the international protection of minorities and employees' rights[1], the individual continued to be unable to rely directly upon international law for relief. The excesses of totalitarianism before and during the 1939–45 war, however, prompted a fresh and more dynamic concern for human rights through the establishment of innovative charters of guarantees and new institutions for their enforcement. Of key importance in the development of this new international legal order was the United Nations whose Charter of June 1945 specifically sought to 'reaffirm faith in fundamental human rights' by 'promoting and encouraging respect for human rights and for fundamental freedoms for all without distinction as to race, sex, language or religion'[2]. To this end, the United Nations adopted the Universal Declaration of Human Rights in December 1948. In international law, this marked a fundamental shift in approach by appearing to limit nation-state sovereignty through the recognition that a state's treatment of its citizens within its territorial boundaries was now of legitimate concern[3].

This instrument gave expression to a new global emphasis on the protection of individual liberty and the provision of basic economic and social needs. However, it tended to blur an important distinction. Civil and political rights were grounded in Western liberal democratic tradition, and stressed protection for personal integrity (through respect for the right to life, protection against torture or inhuman treatment, and guarantees against arbitrary deprivation of liberty), procedural propriety in the determination of civil rights and criminal liability, protection for democratic processes (including participation in political activities, association with others, and expression), and the promotion of religious tolerance and plurality of belief. The first constitutional catalogues of civil and political rights appeared in the American states (in 1776 and in 1780, Virginia and Massachusetts respectively incorporated Bills of Rights), and were followed by the French Declaration of the Rights of Man and the Citizen of 1789, and Amendments I–X of the Constitution of the United States of America of 1791. These rights are usually deemed 'first generation' rights in the sense that they constituted the first attempts to develop a reasonably coherent philosophy of human rights. On the other hand, claims for economic and social rights – 'second generation' rights since historically they appeared later than claims to civil and political rights – formed the basis of socialist or communist conceptions of human rights and were concerned more with the satisfaction of essential human needs such as the rights to housing, to minimum standards of income or social welfare provision, to work, to education, and to health care. From a European perspective, economic and social rights emerged from the Industrial Revolution. In 1792, for example, Thomas Paine in *The Rights of Man* proposed social welfare insurance and provision of employment for the poor. By 1848, working-class movements (such as the Chartists in Britain) were advocating not only universal (male) suffrage but also the rights to fair remuneration and fair working conditions. These calls were replicated in other countries undergoing industrialisation and urbanisation: Ferdinand Lassalle, the founder of the German Labourers' Association, argued that civil and political rights were empty concepts from the perspective of the labourer who would only achieve political freedom through education; economic security, in turn, would come through nationalisation of industry which would allow the state to effect social equality and genuine shared prosperity. Ultimately, writers such as Karl Marx would adopt a more radical stance towards economic and social rights.

1 Covenant of the League of Nations, Arts 22 and 23. Minorities' rights in non-self-governing territories were subject to monitoring by a mandates commission which considered reports from those countries appointed as mandatories for the colony or territory; employees' rights were the concern of the International Labour Organisation (ILO) which continues to operate as an intergovernmental agency. For a brief overview of the historical development of international human rights, see Humphrey 'The International Law of Human Rights in the Middle Twentieth Century' in Marten (ed) *The Present State of International Law and Other Essays* (International Law Association, 1973), reproduced in Lillich & Newman *International Human Rights: Problems of Law and Policy* (1979) pp 1–12; Robertson and Merrills *Human Rights in the World* (4th edn, 1996) pp 14–21; and for more detailed treatment, Steiner and Alston *International Human Rights in Context* (2nd edn, 2000), pp 56–135.
2 Preamble; and Art 1(3). Articles 55 and 56 further commit states to take joint and separate action with a view to promoting economic and social development and universal observance of human rights 'without distinction as to race, sex, language or religion'.
3 See further, Brownlie *Principles of Public International Law* (5th edn, 1998) pp 557–605; for discussion of the Declaration, see Alfredsson and Eide *The Universal Declaration on Human Rights: A Common Standard of Achievement* (1999).

2.02 These conceptually differing approaches towards human rights eventually resulted in the adoption of two separate international human rights instruments in 1966 which entered into force ten years later. The International Covenant on Civil and Political Rights focuses upon the protection of the individual against state encroachment of physical integrity and political liberties[1], while the International Covenant on Economic, Social and Cultural Rights seeks to emphasise state responsibilities in providing basic human needs such as housing, public health, education and employment. International legal and political initiatives could not bridge, however, the ever-widening gulf between liberal democracy and communism after 1945, and the dichotomy between two competing concepts of human rights became more marked as each side sought to advance its own distinct philosophy of rights, leading in turn to a further weakening of any notion of the universal applicability of human rights and its gradual replacement by an acceptance that human rights were in reality largely culturally specific. This standpoint was indeed strengthened by new arguments advanced by Third World countries from the 1970s onwards that human rights could also be considered as group or community rights. These states sought to advance claims to such matters as self-determination, development and peace as part of their own struggles for political, social and economic advancement, thus producing a 'third generation' of rights[2]. This lack of intellectual clarity and philosophical agreement at an international level[3] was to some extent masked by the welter of international treaties under the auspices of the United Nations which appeared in the years before the fall of communism in Europe[4], yet the continuation of these ideological fault-lines and lack of effective enforcement machinery prevented the establishment of a genuinely universal human rights legal order.

1 There are two additional Optional Protocols: the first (which also entered into force in 1976) provides for a system of individual complaint, and the second (which entered into force in 1991) for abolition of the death penalty. See further Alston (ed) *The United Nations and Human Rights* (1992); Nowak *UN Covenant on Civil and Political Rights: CCPR Commentary* (1993); Harris and Joseph (eds) *The International Covenant on Civil and Political Rights and United Kingdom Law* (1995); and Craven *The International Covenant on Economic, Social and Cultural Rights* (1995).
2 For discussion of group rights, see eg Crawford *The Rights of Peoples* (1988); Thornberry *International Law and the Rights of Minorities* (1992); Dinstein and Tabory (eds) *The Protection of Minorities and Human Rights* (1992); Brölmann, Lefeber and Zieck *Peoples and Minorities in International Law* (1993); Oestreich 'Liberal Theory and Minority Group Rights' [1999] 21 HRQ 108–132; and Donnelly 'Human Rights, Democracy and Development' [1999] 21 HRQ 608–632.
3 See further Cranston *What are Human Rights?* (2nd edn, 1973); Donnelly *Universal Human Rights in Theory and Practice* (1989); Shestack 'The Jurisprudence of Human Rights' in Meron (ed) *Human Rights in International Law: Legal and Policy Issues* (1984) pp 69–105; Wilson (ed) *Human Rights, Culture and Context: Anthropological Perspectives* (1997); and Shestack 'Philosophical Foundations of Human Rights' [1998] 20 HRQ 201. For discussion of (post-communist) conceptions of 'second generation' rights, see Eide, Krause and Rosas (eds) *Economic, Social and Cultural Rights* (1995). Other approaches to human rights exist. For a survey of feminist perspectives, see Alfredsson and Tomaševski (eds) *A Thematic Guide to Documents on the Human Rights of Women* (1995); and Fraser 'Becoming Human: The Origins and Development of Women's Human Rights' [1999] 21 HRQ 853.
4 Including conventions on the prevention and punishment of genocide (1948); the treatment of prisoners of war (1949); status of refugees (1951); political rights for women (1952); slavery (1956); forced labour (1957); consent to marriage (1962); racial discrimination (1965); apartheid (1973); discrimination against women (1979); torture (1984); and children's rights (1989). For a survey, see Marie 'International Instruments Relating to Human Rights' (1999) 20 HRLJ 115; and, for materials and background, see Lawson *Encyclopaedia of Human Rights* (2nd edn, 1996); and Steiner and Alston *International Human Rights in Context* (2nd edn, 2000).

2.03 Against this picture, the Helsinki Final Act of 1975 may be seen as a crucial milestone in the development of a common approach to human rights between east and west. This Act arose out of the Conference on

Security and Co-operation in Europe and was accepted by all European states from both sides of the Iron Curtain (with the exception of Albania), and Canada and the USA. It established what is now known as the Organisation for Security and Co-operation in Europe (the OSCE)[1]. More particularly, the triumph of democracy by the close of the twentieth century allowed a fresh reassessment of the importance of economic and social rights in a climate of increasing material prosperity and free of the historical baggage of political confrontation. There is now a greater recognition of the importance of the aims behind such rights, but also acceptance that economic and social rights require to be enforced in an appropriate manner and cannot readily be protected through judicial means as if they were civil and political rights. At the same time as these advances in international human rights were taking place, regional arrangements were also being established[2]. New developments in human rights law also continued. The *Pinochet* judgment[3] was one key landmark; and the steps taken to establish an International Criminal Court another[4]. The legacy of a century marked by armed conflict and systematic violation of human rights to its successor is a fresh determination to enforce respect for human dignity at national, regional and international levels.

1 The OSCE was originally known as the Conference on Security and Co-operation in Europe (CSCE) until the 1994 Budapest Conference. It became a permanent institution by virtue of the Treaty of Paris, 1990. The OSCE was originally concerned with three separate issues – *détente* and disarmament, economic co-operation, and human rights; its current focus is upon consolidation of democracy, the rule of law, and conflict prevention. It seeks to achieve its mandate through intergovermental conferences rather than through any more formal machinery. Human rights monitoring takes place through the so-called 'Human Dimension Mechanism', and there is a High Commissioner for National Minorities. See further Mastny *Helsinki, Human Rights, and European Security* (1986). For an overview of the human rights aspects of the OSCE system, see Buergenthal 'CSCE Human Dimension: The Birth of a System' in European University Institute *Collected Courses of the Academy of European Law* vol I-2 (1992) pp 171–209; Bothe, Ronziti and Rosas (eds) *The OSCE in the Maintenance of Peace and Security* (1997); and Gottehrer *Ombudsman and Human Rights Protection Institutions in OSCE Participating States* (1998).
2 For discussion of other regional systems of human rights protection, see, e g, Harris and Livingstone (eds) *The Inter-American System of Human Rights* (1998); Davidson *The Inter-American Human Rights System* (1997); MacCarthy-Arnolds and others *Africa, Human Rights, and the Global System* (1994); Ankumah *The African Commission on Human and People's Right* (1996).
3 See *R v Bow Street Metropolitan Stipendiary Magistrate ex p Pinochet Ugarte (No 3)* [2000] 1 AC 147; for the background to these proceedings, see Wilson 'Prosecuting Pinochet: International Crimes in Spanish Domestic Law' (1999) 21 HRQ 927; and Woodhouse (ed) *The Pinochet Case: A Legal and Constitutional Analysis* (2000).
4 For discussion of developments in international law, see Sunga *International Responsibility in International Law for Serious Human Rights Violations* (1992); de Guzman 'The Road from Rome: The Developing Law of Crimes against Humanity' (2000) 22 HRQ 335. For relevant documents on the ICC, see Bassiouni *The Statute of the International Criminal Court* (1998).

The work of the Council of Europe

2.04   The Council of Europe is an intergovernmental organisation founded upon the principles of pluralist democracy, respect for human rights, and the rule of law. Established in 1949 in the aftermath of the 1939–45 war and in a period when the Cold War between west and east was rapidly escalating, it was one of several European initiatives which sought to bring western liberal democracies closer together to strengthen shared values and to prevent the spread of totalitarianism and further violations of human rights. With the increase in membership after the fall of communist regimes, the Council of Europe now has 43 member states[1]. Its founding charter refers to the furtherance of European co-operation not only in the political sphere but also in regard to economic and social progress[2]. The activities of the Council of Europe include the promotion of Europe's cultural identity and diversity and the consolidation of democratic stability through legislative and constitutional reform[3]. Its work thus covers a broad range of activities leading to a number of European initiatives[4] in the areas of legal co-operation[5], media[6], local democracy[7], environmental and regional planning[8], economic, social and health issues[9], and education, culture and heritage[10].

1 The original ten members of the Council of Europe were Belgium, Denmark, France, Ireland, Italy, Luxembourg, Netherlands, Norway, Sweden and the United Kingdom. Greece and Turkey also joined in 1949, followed by Iceland and Germany (1950), Austria (1956), Cyprus (1961), Switzerland (1963), Malta (1965), Portugal (1976), Spain (1977), Liechtenstein (1978), San Marino (1988) and Finland (1989). The last west European state to become a member was Andorra in 1994. The organisation rapidly expanded after 1989 with the membership of Hungary (1990), Poland (1991), Bulgaria (1992), Estonia, Lithuania, Slovenia, the Czech Republic, Slovakia and Romania (1993), Latvia, Albania, Moldova, Ukraine and the Former Yugoslav Republic of Macedonia (1995), Russia and Croatia (1996), Georgia (1999), and Armenia and Azerbaijan (2001). Applications for membership from Bosnia and Hercegovina, the Federal Republic of Yugoslavia, and Monaco are currently being considered. Belarus's observer status at the Parliamentary Assembly was suspended in 1997. For monitoring of undertakings entered into by states upon their accession, see 'Compliance with Commitments Entered into by Member States', docs Monitor/Inf (97) 1, Monitor/Inf(98) 1 and 2 and Monitor/Inf (99) 1.

2 Statute of the Council of Europe, Art 1. For the background and early development of the Council of Europe, see Robertson *The Council of Europe* (1961) pp 1–24, 160–184; Beddard *Human Rights and Europe* (3rd edn, 1993) pp 19–40. For a more recent perspective, see Huber *A Decade Which Made History – The Council of Europe 1989–1999* (1999).

3 See generally: Council of Europe *The Council of Europe: Activities and Achievements* (2001).

4 There are now some 180 European conventions which are published in the series of *European Conventions and Agreements* (7 vols, 1971–1999), and available at http://conventions.coe.int/. The European Court of Human Rights may refer to relevant treaties in its judgments: see paras 2.33 and 3.22, below.

5 Through, in particular, harmonisation of domestic legislation in line with the principles of human rights, democracy and the rule of law by improving the delivery of justice. Of particular note is the European Commission for Democracy through Law (the 'Venice Commission') established in 1990 which considers constitutional and administrative measures of assistance in the consolidation of democratic stability. The Commission publishes a *Bulletin on Constitutional Case-Law* summarising constitutional developments and judgments in European states, and is available at www.venice. coe.int/site/interface/english.htm . In addition, several treaties regulate medical law issues, including the European Convention on Human Rights and Biomedicine (ETS 164 (1997)) and co-operation in penal matters (cf *Co-operation in Penal Matters – Conventions* (vol 1) (1997)).

6 In particular, by seeking to strengthen freedom of expression and the free flow of information: see eg the European Convention on Transfrontier Television (ETS 132 (1989)) and the amending Protocol (ETS 171 (1998)), and the European Convention Relating to Questions on Copyright Law and Neighbouring Rights in the Framework of Transfrontier Broadcasting by Satellite (ETS 153 (1994)). See further http://www. humanrights.coe.int/media .

7 That is, with a view to promoting local democracy and regional diversity: see in particular European Charter of Local Self-Government (ETS 122 (1985)) and European Outline Convention on Transfrontier Co-operation between Territorial Communities or

Authorities (ETS 106 (1983)) and its additional Protocols (ETS 159 (1995)) and (ETS 169 (1998)). See further, www.local.coe.int .

8 Through promoting international co-operation with a view to protecting the natural environment and promoting the development of spatial planning: see in particular the Convention on Protection of European Wildlife and Natural Habitats (ETS 104 (1982)) and the Convention on Civil Liability for Damage Resulting from Activities Dangerous to the Natural Environment (ETS 150 (1993)).

9 By aiming to promote social rights and equality of treatment through, for example, guaranteeing adequate social welfare protection, the promotion of employment and training, combatting discrimination, and harmonising health policies: see in particular the European Social Charter (1961) discussed further at para 2.39 below.

10 The Convention on the Recognition of Qualifications concerning Higher Education in the European Region (ETS 165 (1997)) seeks to facilitate movement in higher education. The European Cultural Convention (ETS 18 (1954)) provides a framework for international co-operation in the fields of culture, heritage, education and youth. See also the European Convention on the Protection of Archaeological Heritage (ETS 143 (1992)).

The Council of Europe and the protection of human rights

2.05   The Council of Europe has been able to achieve at a regional level innovative systems of effective protection of human rights. Its success in promoting respect for civil and political rights, first through the establishment and progressive development of an enforcement machinery under the European Convention on Human Rights[1] and then through the entry into force of the European Convention for the Prevention of Torture or Inhuman and Degrading Treatment or Punishment, is without parallel. The Council of Europe has also been mindful of the need to promote social cohesion through the promotion of social standards under the European Social Charter, and to encourage equality of treatment of members of national minorities through its more recent Framework Convention for the Protection of National Minorities and the work of the European Commission against Racism and Intolerance. Its success is in part attributable to a number of disparate factors which emerged in Europe over a 50-year period: the constitutional willingness of emerging democracies (after both 1945 and 1989) to incorporate international human rights treaties into domestic law as a safeguard against any repetition of human rights excesses of the past; a political desire to follow basic tenets of liberal democracy as outward symbols of shared values (after 1945, in opposition to the continuing totalitarianism in East Europe, and for states which joined after 1989, as members of a new and democratic Europe); recognition that assumption of responsibilities required by membership of the Council of Europe was a prerequisite for consideration for further membership of the European Union[2]; and – perhaps most significantly – growing trust in the European enforcement machinery itself which encouraged the ever-increasing assumption of unilateral obligations by states.

1 For discussion of the ECHR's impact upon international legal developments elsewhere, see, Buergenthal 'The European and Inter-American Human Rights Courts: Beneficial Interaction' in Mahoney, Matscher, Petzold and Wildhaber (eds) *Protecting Human Rights: The European Perspective* (2000) pp 123–133; Cassese 'The Impact of the European Convention on Human Rights on the International Criminal Tribunal for the Former Yugoslavia' in Mahoney, Matscher, Petzold and Wildhaber (eds) *Protecting Human Rights: The European Perspective* (2000) pp 213–236; and Lester 'The Export of the Convention to the Commonwealth', in Mahoney, Matscher, Petzold and Wildhaber *Protecting Human Rights: The European Perspective* (2000) pp 753–762.

2 Cf TEU, Art 49 which confirms that accession is dependent upon respect for democracy, human rights and the rule of law.

The Council of Europe and the European Union

2.06 The Council of Europe and the European Union were conceived in the same political climate, share similar political ideals and aspirations, and have institutional structures which at first appearance have common features: decision-making bodies comprising ministers of member states, consultative and deliberative parliamentary assemblies, and judicial organs exercising European jurisdiction. But the Council of Europe and the European Union diverge in membership, organisation and emphasis. The European Union – the 'Europe of the 15' – currently affects the lives of 375 million Europeans while the Council of Europe's 43 member states contain a population of some 800 million. The Council of Europe is an organisation of nation states whose structures reflect retention of national sovereignty, since its Committee of Ministers can only make recommendations or approve conventions for further determination by member states, and the Parliamentary Assembly is deliberative only and has no legislative authority[1]. Above all, the European Union's principal focus is upon economic and political integration, while the Council of Europe's most significant success lies in the promotion of human rights.

Yet, greater convergence is now evident. The Council of Europe's aims of closer legal and political co-operation and the strengthening of pluralist democracy have been given greater urgency since 1989 with the rapid and substantial increase in membership of central and eastern European states. More significantly, the EU is embracing enhanced expectations in the protection of human rights[2]. While the original EEC Treaty made no direct provision for human rights, in a number of cases from 1969 onwards the European Court of Justice began to recognise that fundamental rights formed an integral part of the new Community legal order[3]. The explicit aims of the European Union now include those of strengthening 'the protection of the rights and interests of the nationals of its Member States' and of maintaining and developing the Union 'as an area of freedom, security and justice'[4]. In consequence, it is now recognised that since the European Union was 'founded on the principles of liberty, democracy, respect for human rights and fundamental freedoms, and the rule of law, principles which are common to the Member States', the EU is bound to respect as general principles of Community law the guarantees of the European Convention on Human Rights and common constitutional traditions[5]. This early recognition of human rights principles was given explicit approval by the Amsterdam Treaty which specifically now empowers the European Court of Justice to ensure that European institutions respected fundamental rights and freedoms. Further moves to strengthen the protection of human rights have taken place as a result of the meeting of the European Council in 1999 in Cologne. This has led to the drafting of a new European Union Charter of Fundamental Rights which seeks to provide in a single text the range of rights enjoyed by EU citizens (and others resident in the EU) under six chapters: dignity; freedoms; equality; solidarity; citizens' rights; and justice. The rights are of both a civil and political as well as an economic and social nature, and are based upon sources which include the European Convention on Human Rights and the European Social Charter, as well as the Community Charter of Fundamental Social Rights of Workers and other international conventions ratified by the EU or member states[6]. From the perspective of the Council of Europe, however, there is a real risk that such a charter could lead to uncertainty through conflicting interpretations by the courts in Luxembourg and in Strasbourg[7]. The Charter's future is uncertain. The European Council meeting in Nice in December 2000 deferred taking a decision on whether the Charter should be legally binding until resolution of the debate on the wider issue of the EU's future.

1 The decision-making authority of the Council of Europe is the Committee of Ministers composed of the Foreign Ministers of member states (with each minister presiding over the Committee for a period of six months); its consultative body is the Parliamentary Assembly which is made up of parliamentarians drawn from domestic legislatures and which may propose recommendations for consideration in turn by the Committee of Ministers. Treaties, declarations and conclusions, resolutions, recommendations and decisions of the Committee of Ministers, and opinions, recommendations, resolutions and orders of the Parliamentary Assembly are published in the *Official Gazette* of the Council of Europe. Day-to-day activities of the Council of Europe are carried out by an international civil service or secretariat comprising some 1,700 officials and employees under the authority of the Council's Secretary General who is elected for a fixed period by the Parliamentary Assembly. The Council of Europe also has a Congress of Local and Regional Authorities of Europe, a consultative body which seeks to represent these authorities. Relevant websites are: www.stars.coe.int (Parliamentary Assembly); www.cm.coe.int (Committee of Ministers); and www.coe.int/cplre (Congress of Local and Regional Authorities).
2 See further, eg Clapham *Human Rights in the Private Sphere* (1993); Betten and MacDevitt *The Protection of Fundamental Social Rights in the European Union* (1996); and Peers 'Human Rights and the Third Pillar' in Alston (ed) *The EU and Human Rights* (1999) pp 167–186. For a survey of ECJ human rights jurisprudence, see Guild and Lesieur *The European Court of Justice on the European Court of Human Rights* (1998).
3 Case 29/69, *Stauder v City of Ulm* [1969] ECR 419.
4 TEU, Art 2.
5 TEU, Art 6(1). EU member states were not considered responsible by the Strasbourg organs for actions taken in respect of EU obligations: see, eg 13258/87, *M & Co v Germany* (1990) DR 64, 138 (writ of execution issued by domestic authorities to give effect to judgment of European Court of Justice). A similar principle applies in respect of other international obligations entered into by member states: eg 21090/92, *Heinz v The Contracting States also Parties to the European Patent Convention* (1994) DR 76, 125. However, in *Matthews v United Kingdom* 1999-I, 251, the European Court of Human Rights examined the question of whether states which were bound by the European Convention on Human Rights had positive responsibilities in determining the manner in which they discharged their rights or duties under EU law within the context of electoral law: see further para 7.61 below.
6 See Doc C364/01, OJ 18 December 2000, available at www.europarl.eu.int/charter/pdf/text_en.pdf . See further, de Búrca 'The Drafting of the European Union Charter of Fundamental Rights (2001) 26 EL Rev 126–138.
7 Cf Council of Europe Parliamentary Assembly Recommendation No 1439 (2000) proposing again that the EU should incorporate the ECHR into EU law to prevent inconsistency in interpretation of fundamental rights. For discussion of existing divergences in approach, see Lawson 'Confusion and Conflict? Diverging Interpretation of the ECHR in Strasbourg and Luxembourg' in Lawson and de Blois (eds) *The Dynamics of the Protection of Human Rights in Europe* vol III (1994) pp 219–252; and for consideration (from a Strasbourg perspective) of how the EU and Council of Europe human rights systems could be brought together, see Clapham 'On Complementarity: Human Rights in the European Legal Orders' (2000) 4 HRLJ 313; and Krüger and Polakiewicz 'Köharenter Menschenrechtsschutz in Europa'(2001) 28 EuGRZ 92. For consideration of the impact of Strasbourg jurisprudence on the EU, see Peukert 'The Importance of the European Convention on Human Rights for the European Union' in Mahoney, Matscher, Petzold and Wildhaber (eds) *Protecting Human Rights: The European Perspective* (2000) pp 1107–1122.

THE EUROPEAN CONVENTION ON HUMAN RIGHTS

2.07   The European Convention on Human Rights[1] was opened for ratification in November 1950 and entered into force in September 1953[2]. Its preamble affirms the Council of Europe's aim of achieving greater unity between states inter alia through 'the maintenance and further realisation of human rights and fundamental freedoms'. Such rights are considered to be 'the foundation of justice and peace in the world [which] are best maintained on the one hand by an effective political democracy and on the other by a common understanding and observance of the human rights upon which they depend'. To these ends, the Convention involves 'the first steps for the collective enforcement of certain of the rights stated in the Universal Declaration'[3]. The focus of the Convention is thus upon civil and political rights rather than economic and social rights, and upon those civil and political rights which are recognised and shared by developed western legal systems. In consequence, Convention guarantees reflect values which are commonplace in European legal systems: equality before the law, fair hearings, impartiality of judges, no retroactive lawmaking, protection against discrimination and against wrongful deprival of liberty, recognition of the concept of marriage, freedom of conscience and expression, respect for privacy and belief, and protection of property rights. Such ideas had been articulated and developed by the judiciary in many domestic legal systems long before the Convention's ratification, but were to be given heightened status and enhanced protection through international protection.

1   The formal name of the treaty is 'The Convention for the Protection of Human Rights and Fundamental Freedoms'. For current ratifications etc see http://conventions.coe.int . The Convention is currently in force in 41 states (Armenia and Azerbaijan have signed the Convention and its optional protocols, but not yet ratified them). The Convention is also applied in Bosnia and Hercegovina by virtue of Annexe VI of the Dayton Accord, and in Kosovo by virtue of regulations made under the authority of UN Security Council Resolution 1244 (1999): see O'Flaherty and Gisvold *Post War Protection of Human Rights in Bosnia and Hercegovina* (1998); Lawyers' Committee for Human Rights 'A Fragile Peace: Laying the foundations for Justice in Kosovo' (1999) E Europ H R Rev 1. For an overview of Bosnian Human Rights Chamber case law, see Neussl 'Bosnia and Hercegovina Still Far from the Rule of Law' (1999) 20 HRLJ 290. Chamber judgments are available at www.gwdg.de/~ujvr/hrch/hrch.htm .
2   For further background, see Beddard *Human Rights and Europe* (3rd edn, 1993) pp 19–32; for discussion of the UK's involvement in the drafting and ratification, see Janis, Kay and Bradley *European Human Rights Law: Text and Materials* (2nd edn, 2000) pp 16–22.
3   For discussion of the preamble, see van Boren 'The Preamble of the Convention on Human Rights and Fundamental Freedoms' in Coomans and others (eds) *Human Rights from Exclusion to Inclusion; Principles and Practice* (2000) pp 401–412. The Court may refer to the preamble for guidance in interpreting substantive guarantees: see, eg *Brumarescu v Romania* (28 October 1999), para 61 (principle of the rule of law implies legal certainty).

Optional nature of additional substantive guarantees under Protocols 1, 4, 6 and 7

2.08   The drafters of the Convention were concerned to ensure that the treaty reflected those substantive rights which commanded general support, and thus there was lengthy initial consideration at the drafting stage as to whether the treaty should include certain rights which had more of an economic or social than a civil and political flavour, such as the rights to marry and to found a family (which ultimately were included in the Convention as Article 12) and to the peaceful enjoyment of property and to education (two provisions which were eventually rejected)[1]. The approach taken thus involved a deliberate decision to reject rights which did not command support from each of the original member states. Further addition to the catalogue of protected human rights was not, however, precluded, and was to be secured by means of additional optional protocols[2]. The rights to property and to education (along with the right to free elections) were thus eventually secured by Protocol 1[3], opened for signature in 1952. Additional substantive guarantees were provided in 1963 through Protocol 4 which protects freedom of movement and prohibits imprisonment for debt, expulsion of nationals and the collective expulsion of aliens; in 1983 with Protocol 6 which abolishes the death penalty; and in 1984 with Protocol 7 which provides for additional procedural safeguards relating to the expulsion of aliens, rights of appeal in criminal matters, compensation for wrongful conviction, protection against being tried or punished twice, and the principle of equality between spouses. Protocols 4 and 7 have not been ratified by the United Kingdom, and consequently these rights are not incorporated into domestic law by virtue of the Scotland Act 1998 or Human Rights Act 1998[4]. Protocol 12, which proposes to strengthen protection against discrimination, was opened for signature in November 2000[5].

1 For the background to the drafting of the Convention, see Robertson *Human Rights in Europe* (3rd edn, 1993) pp 1–24 and Marston 'The United Kingdom's Part in the Preparation of the European Convention on Human Rights'(1993) 42 ICLQ 796. See too Council of Europe *Collected Edition of the Travaux Préparatoires of the European Convention on Human Rights* (7 vols, 1975–1985).

2 Protocols 1, 4, 6 and 7 are concerned with substantive guarantees, while Protocols 2, 3, 5, 8, 9 and 11 made amendments to the Convention's enforcement machinery. Protocol 10 did not enter into force, and has been superseded by the procedural reforms occasioned by Protocol 11. Proposals for developments are normally considered by a Steering Committee for Human Rights, a Committee of Experts for the Improvement of Procedures for the Protection of Human Rights (currently examining means of improving further the Court's working methods) and a Committee of Experts for the Development of Human Rights (which has finished work on the drafting of an additional Protocol 12).

3 Opened for signature in March 1952. As at 31 August 2001, Protocol 1 has been ratified by all member states with the exception of Andorra, Armenia, Azerbaijan and Switzerland.

4 In addition, as at 31 August 2001, Protocol 4 has not been ratified by Andorra, Armenia, Azerbaijan, Greece, Liechtenstein, Malta, Spain, Switzerland and Turkey; and Protocol 7 has not been ratified by Andorra, Armenia, Azerbaijan, Belgium, Germany, Irelands, Liechtenstein, Malta, the Netherlands, Poland, Portugal, Spain, and Turkey.

5 The Protocol provides for a general prohibition of discrimination by providing (in Art 1, para (1)) that 'the enjoyment of any right set forth by law shall be secured without discrimination on any ground such as sex, race, colour, language, religion, political or other opinion, national or social origin, association with a national minority, property, birth or other status'; and (in para (2)) that 'no one shall be discriminated against by any public authority on any ground such as those mentioned in paragraph 1'. The Protocol requires ratification by ten states before it can enter into force. For discussion of Art 14's prohibition of discrimination in the enjoyment of Convention rights, see paras 3.40–3.65 below.

Enforcement mechanisms under the European Convention on Human Rights

2.09   The Convention 'creates, over and above a network of mutual, bilateral undertakings, objective obligations [which] benefit from a "collective enforcement" '[1]. However, it is up to each state to decide the extent of the obligations it wishes to accept, and thus the level of human rights protection available to individuals can vary between European states[2]. Three distinct mechanisms to ensure states respect their obligations are found. First, a reporting procedure requires states to furnish the Secretary General of the Council of Europe with details of the implementation of Convention guarantees in domestic law under Article 52 (formerly Article 57); second, a state may bring an allegation of a violation by another state to the notice of the Strasbourg institutions in terms of Article 33 (formerly Article 24); and third, individuals and other non-governmental bodies may raise complaints of violations directly under Article 34 (formerly Article 25). While these first two methods of enforcement were replicated elsewhere in international law at the time of the Convention's entry into force, this latter right of individual application was at the time a bold innovation which remedied the traditional lack of standing of individuals in international law.

1   *Ireland v United Kingdom* (1978) A 25, at para 239.
2   This will not only be dependent upon state ratification of optional protocols, but also any declarations or reservations made at the time of ratification and any subsequent use of the right to derogate under Art 15; and in addition, the recognition of a 'margin of appreciation' by the Court will influence the practical level of domestic human rights protection: see below, paras 3.06 and 3.85–3.96. For further discussion, see van Dijk 'The Law of Human Rights in Europe: Instruments and Procedures for a Uniform Implementation' in *Collected Courses of the Academy of European Law* vol VI-2 (1997) pp 1–120.

Reporting procedures

2.10   Reporting procedures involve the scrutiny of periodic or ad hoc reports by independent agencies (or 'treaty bodies'). This device is an established way of monitoring the progressive implementation of rights (such as economic, social and cultural rights) which are more open in content, of overcoming problems with reliance upon inter-state complaint which may be weakened by political practicalities, and of providing a more complete assessment of compliance with international obligations than that which can be achieved by piecemeal examination of particular issues highlighted by individual complaint. To these ends, reporting procedures exist under a number of international treaties[1]. In particular, substantial use has been made of these by the Human Rights Committee under the International Covenant on Civil and Political Rights[2]. The European Convention on Human Rights, Article 52[3] makes provision for the Secretary General of the Council of Europe to request ratifying states to 'furnish an explanation of the manner in which its internal law ensures the effective implementation of any of the provisions of this Convention'. While the treaty provision is short and to the point, 'the conclusion must ... be that the Secretary General has an independent, autonomous and discretionary power of investigation conferred upon him', although in making any use of this power he would be expected to proceed 'in an objective and impartial manner'[4]. However, this is an underutilised and (in comparison with equivalent provisions in other treaties) a much weaker device[5] with no provision for formal scrutiny of information supplied, presumably since the drafters considered that reliance upon domestic implementation of Convention guarantees and the right of individual application would cure the *lacuna* traditionally found in human rights enforcement machinery[6].

1　These include procedures under the International Covenant on Civil and Political Rights, Art 40; the International Covenant on Economic, Social and Political Rights, Art 16; the Convention on the Rights of the Child, Art 44; and the European Social Charter, Art 21. For further discussion, see Dimitrijevic 'The Monitoring of Human Rights and the Prevention of Human Rights Violations through Reporting Procedures' in Bloed, Leicht, Nowak and Rosas (eds) *Monitoring Human Rights in Europe* (1993) pp 6–7.

2　See further, McGoldrick *The Human Rights Committee* (1991); Alston (ed) *The United Nations and Human Rights* (2000).

3　Art 57 (original treaty).

4　Mahoney 'Does Article 57 of the European Convention on Human Rights Serve any Useful Purpose?' in Matscher and Petzold (eds) *Protecting Human Rights: The European Dimension* (2nd edn, 1990) pp 373–393 at 380 and 385.

5　Article 52 has been used sparingly, ie in 1964 (in relation to all provisions of the Convention and Protocol 1); in 1970 (in respect of Art 5(5)); in 1975 (to review state obligations under Arts 8–11); in 1983 (with regard to guarantees for children and minors in care); and in 1988 (in respect of Art 6(1)). On each occasion replies were summarised and circulated to the Parliamentary Assembly, but in addition the 1975 replies were subjected to a comparative study by the Secretariat and circulated to the Commission and Court: Mahoney pp 373–393 at 374–375. In December 1999 the Russian Federation was also requested to furnish a report on the manner in which the Convention was being implemented in Chechnya.

6　Cf Dimitrijevic 'The Monitoring of Human Rights and the Prevention of Human Rights Violations through Reporting Procedures' in Bloed, Leicht, Nowak and Rosas (eds) *Monitoring Human Rights in Europe* (1993) pp 7–10, who suggests that an enhanced system of monitoring compliance through reporting and scrutinising under the European Convention would be desirable, first to ensure compliance with rights which may not necessarily be 'cognisable under contentious proceedings' (such as the rights to education and to free elections at reasonable intervals under Protocol 2) and second to help assimilate central and eastern European states which have recently ratified the Convention. Mahoney 'Does Article 57 of the European Convention on Human Rights Serve any Useful Purpose?' in Matscher and Petzold (eds) Protecting Human Rights: The European Dimension (2nd edn, 1990) at pp 391–392 suggests that 'the lack of precision in the text as to the exercise of the function conferred needs to be cured by rules of application laying down set procedures to be followed by the Secretary General' before Art 52's potential can be realised.

Inter-state cases

2.11　Inter-state complaint is similarly a recognised method of calling states to account for failure to discharge their obligations. Under what is now the Convention, Article 33[1], a contracting state is able to complain of an alleged violation of the treaty by any other state; and, in turn, accepts the jurisdiction of the Strasbourg institutions to consider such a complaint brought against it. In bringing an application against another state alleging breach of any provision of the Convention, the state 'is not to be regarded as exercising a right of action for the purposes of enforcing its own rights but rather as [raising] an alleged violation of the public order of Europe' since the responsibilities assumed upon ratification by states 'are essentially of an objective character, being designed rather to protect the fundamental rights of individual human beings … than to create subjective and reciprocal rights' between ratifying states[2]. Unlike most other multilateral treaties, the aim of a human rights treaty is to seek to confer rights directly upon non-state beneficiaries who need not even be nationals of the states in question, but, paradoxically, while individuals and groups are the beneficiaries of such treaties, states are responsible in international law to other state parties. Enforcement may thus become a matter for other contracting states who may have no particular link with the victims of state violations, but this may be unlikely unless the nature of the violation is compelling and the state interest in upholding the responsibility coincides with other diplomatic interests[3]. Probably on account of the political nature of such a remedy, the use of inter-state complaint under the European Convention on Human Rights has been limited[4] despite less rigorous requirements of admissibility[5]. The unwillingness on the part of governments to make use of Article 33 thus reflects the dominance of political over human rights considerations[6], but also implicitly acknowledges that there may well be compelling political factors which will limit a state's readiness to take the necessary action to comply with a Court judgment[7].

1 Art 24 (original treaty).
2 788/60, *Austria v Italy* (1961) YB 4 112 at 140.
3 Dimitrijevic 'The Monitoring of Human Rights and the Prevention of Human Rights Violations through Reporting Procedures' in Bloed, Leicht, Nowak and Rosas (eds) *Monitoring Human Rights in Europe* (1993) p 1.
4 The 22 interstate applications lodged (considered in 14 separate cases after the joining of related applications) involved complaints against the United Kingdom in relation to Cyprus and to Northern Ireland; a complaint against Italy in respect of the trial of German-speaking nationals; complaints against Greece in response to action taken by its military dictatorship; complaints against Turkey after the occupation of northern Cyprus; and complaints against Turkey in respect of violations by its military dictatorship and of the infliction of torture. Eleven of these cases were ultimately determined by the Committee of Ministers. *Ireland v United Kingdom* (1978) A 25, discussed at para 4.20, below, led to a finding of violation of Art 3 by the Court. *Denmark v Turkey* (5 April 2000) was struck out by the Court after a friendly settlement was achieved (allegations of ill-treatment in violation of Art 3 inflicted against a Danish citizen detained in Turkey and that the interrogation techniques allegedly applied in the individual's case formed part of a widespread practice in the state: the settlement took the form of an *ex gratia* payment, acknowledgment of 'occasional and individual' (*sic*) infliction of torture and ill-treatment, recognition that training of police officers is crucial in preventing violations of Art 3, and establishment of a bilateral dialogue between the two states with a view to improving human rights). *Cyprus v Turkey* (10 May 2001) (discussed at paras 4.25, 4.36, 6.52, 7.08 and 7.14 below) involved challenges to the occupation of northern Cyprus by Turkey since 1974 and led to the Court's finding of multiple violations of Convention guarantees (including Turkey's failure to carry out effective investigations into the fate of Greek Cypriots who had disappeared while in custody; the continuing refusal to allow the return of any Greek Cypriot displaced persons to their homes; degrading discriminatory treatment; limiting access to places of worship and participation in religious life through restrictions on movement; censorship of school books destined for use by Greek Cypriot primary schoolchildren; lack of provision of secondary school facilities; and (in respect of Turkish Cypriots) violations of fair trial guarantees through authorisation of the trial of civilians by military courts).
5 Cf Arts 33 and 35. There is no need to establish any particular state interest in the complaint (for example, that any of its nationals are a victim); and the only admissibility requirements to be satisfied are exhaustion of domestic remedies and the six-month rule.
6 For further discussion see Van Dijk and van Hoof *Theory and Practice of the European Convention on Human Rights* (3rd edn, 1998) pp 40–44; Krüger and Nørgaard 'The Right of Application' in Macdonald, Matscher and Petzold (eds) *The European System for the Protection of Human Rights* (1993) pp 657–675; and Prebensen 'Inter-State Complaints under Treaty Provisions' (1999) 20 HRLJ 446.

7 Supervision of the enforcement of Court judgments is entrusted to the Committee of Ministers: see para 2.32 below. However, it is difficult to see how a political situation such as the Turkish occupation of northern Cyprus will be remedied by the respondent state to meet the Court's decisions in *Loizidou v Turkey* 1996-VI, 2216 and in *Cyprus v Turkey* (10 May 2001): the Convention system is not equipped to deal with serious and systematic violations of human rights, and the more likely outcomes in this situation would be a state denunciation of the Convention in terms of Art 58 (as occurred after the Commission's report in 4448/70, *Denmark, Norway and Sweden v Greece* (1970) YB 13, 108) or a decision to expel the country from the Council of Europe. See further White 'Tackling Political Disputes Through Individual Applications' [1998] EHRLR 61; Jambrek 'Judicial Complaints v Structural Violence: Reactive and Proactive Role of the Strasbourg Court of Law' in Council of Europe *In our Minds: the Effectiveness of Human Rights Protection 50 years after the Universal Declaration* (1998) pp 75–81; and Magliveras *Exclusion from Participation in International Organisations* (1999) pp 79–87.

The right of individual application

2.12 This general unwillingness on the part of states to enforce inter-state obligations may be remedied by giving individuals and groups the right to instigate complaints directly. In international law, recognition of the right of a person or body to challenge national legislation or administrative practice before an international forum was an innovation with far-reaching potential, and not all states found it easy to accept that an individual should enjoy equality of status with state parties in this regard[1]. Recognition of this right initially came somewhat reluctantly[2]. Under the European Convention on Human Rights, states could accept the optional right of individual application either without limit of time or for a specified period in terms of what is now Article 34[3] whereby 'any person, non-governmental organisation or group of individuals claiming to be a victim of a violation' of a Convention guarantee[4] could bring a complaint before the Strasbourg organs. Such a provision marked a fundamental change in the relationship between the individual and the state. The United Kingdom first recognised the right of individual application in 1966 in respect of any act or decision occurring after the date of this recognition[5]. The potential afforded by this innovation in international human rights protection was soon exploited by individual applicants, and its very success led to incremental reforms of judicial procedures and ultimately in 1998 to radical reform by virtue of Protocol 11.

1 Other international and regional human rights instruments have extended the use of recognition of individual complaint, and in particular, under the Optional Protocol to the International Covenant on Civil and Political Rights the ability of the Human Rights Committee to deal with 'communications' from individuals and groups has now been recognised by the majority of contracting states (but not by the United Kingdom): see McGoldrick *The Human Rights Committee* (1991) pp 120 ff. For a comparison of individual complaints machineries under the European Convention and the International Covenant, see Müllerson 'The Efficiency of the Individual Complaint Procedures' in Bloed, Leicht, Nowak and Rosas (eds) *Monitoring Human Rights in Europe* (1993) pp 29–42.
2 In general, northern (west) European states were the first to recognise the right of individual petition: Sweden, Iceland, Denmark, Belgium, Germany, Norway, Luxembourg and the Netherlands all had done so by the end of 1960. France and Spain only recognised this right in 1981, while Greece and Turkey only did so in 1985 and 1987 respectively.
3 Art 25 (original treaty).
4 For discussion of 'victim', see paras 2.29–2.30 below. Cf 34324/96, *BBC Scotland, McDonald, Rodgers and Donald v United Kingdom* (23 October 1997) (question whether a state public

service broadcaster could qualify as a 'victim' left open). The provision also specifies that states 'undertake not to hinder in any way the effective exercise of this right'. Violation of this provision may also be established: cf *Akdivar v Turkey* 1996-IV, 1192, paras 103–106 (police questioning, videoing etc of individuals in respect of applications made to the Commission). However, a state's failure to respect any interim measures requested to protect the situation of an applicant under Rule of Court 39 will not lead to a violation: *Cruz Varas v Sweden* (1991) A 201, paras 99–103 (no violation of Art 34 in respect of failure to adhere to request to delay expulsion of the applicants). See also *European Agreement Relating to Persons Participating in Proceedings of the European Court of Human Rights* (1996) (covering immunity from legal process in respect of documents etc submitted to the Court, and the freedom of movement of applicants; but not yet ratified by the United Kingdom).

5 That is, 14 February 1966: cf *LCB v United Kingdom* 1998-III, 1390, para 35 (Court had no jurisdiction to determine events taking place before this date). The United Kingdom thereafter renewed recognition at five-yearly intervals. See further Lester 'UK Acceptance of the Strasbourg Jurisdiction: What Really went on in Whitehall in 1966' [1998] PL 237. After the Court's judgment in *Tyrer v United Kingdom* (1978) A 26, however, the right of individual petition was not renewed in relation to the Isle of Man until 1993.

Overview of the machinery established to deal with inter-state cases and individual complaints

2.13 The entry into force of Protocol 11 on 1 November 1998 resulted in a significant overhaul of the enforcement machinery provided by the Convention. This was made necessary by a dramatic increase in individual applications to Strasbourg[1], reflecting both a growing awareness of the Convention amongst individuals and legal practitioners and a significantly enlarged membership of the Council of Europe. The new procedures are designed to improve efficiency in the disposal of applications: a full-time Court has replaced a part-time Commission and Court and thus has removed much of the duplication of effort inherent in the original arrangements which continued to some extent to reflect a need to secure state confidence in international supervision. However, some basic understanding of the original enforcement machinery[2] is necessary to appreciate the relative importance of the case law of the Commission and Court and the former role played by the Committee of Ministers.

1 The annual number of applications lodged (and provisional files opened) had reached almost 600 (and over 2,700 respectively) by 1982, some 1,000 (and 4,100) by 1988, and over 2,000 (and 9,300) by 1993. The majority of applications continued to be introduced without legal assistance: in 1998, of the 5,981 applications registered by the Commission, 45% had been introduced through a lawyer (a percentage which has, however, increased significantly from the period 1955–1970 when the average figure was around 10%). In contrast, the number of applications made by persons detained had decreased. Well over a third (and on occasion one half) of applications in most years until 1978 concerned individuals who were detained: the figure for 1998 was 10%. See further (1998) YB 41 18–19.

2 The Commission continued to function under transitional arrangements until the end of October 1999 to deal with cases which had been declared admissible before the entry into force of Protocol 11 in November 1998.

Enforcement procedure before November 1998

2.14 The original treaty provided for shared responsibility between a Commission responsible for scrutiny of admissibility, fact-finding, conciliation and a preliminary opinion on the merits; a Court whose jurisdiction was optional and (where this was recognised) charged with giving a binding judgment and determination of any award of compensation or 'just satisfaction'; and the Committee of Ministers which would give a final decision on cases not brought before the Court and supervise state compliance with obligations where a violation had been established. Both the Commission and the Court were thus judicial institutions[1]; the Committee of Ministers, however, was a political body[2]. This procedure, in turn, reflected the innovative nature of the Convention when it first entered into force, for states were naturally cautious in embarking upon the novel experiment of voluntarily subjecting themselves to any more radical enforcement machinery. The evolution of the Strasbourg machinery into the full-time Court now provided by Protocol 11 has been incremental as state confidence has grown alongside a firm commitment to the ideals expressed in the treaty's Preamble.

1 Members of the Commission and Judges of the Court were elected by the Committee of Ministers from a list drawn up by the Parliamentary Assembly of persons of 'high moral character' who possessed the qualifications required for high judicial office or who were of recognised competence in national or international law: Arts 21(3) and 39 (original treaty, as amended by Protocol 8).

2 For discussion of the Committee of Ministers, see references at para 2.32 below. Cf Opsahl's comments that 'if control mechanisms are to be just, the legal ones should be allowed to do their job; but if they are to be effective, the political ones are better', in Eide and Hagtvet (eds) *Human Rights in Perspective: A Global Perspective* (1992) pp 60–65, discussed by van Boven 'General Course on Human Rights' *Collected Courses of the Academy of European Law vol IV-2* (1995) pp 62–65 who concludes that the legal and the political processes should be seen as complementary, not contradictory.

FUNCTIONS OF THE EUROPEAN COMMISSION ON HUMAN RIGHTS

2.15 The Commission was responsible for consideration of the admissibility of any application lodged and thereafter for examination of the merits of the complaint[1]. The Commission was first established in 1954, and was a part-time institution serviced by its Secretariat, normally holding some eight sessions per annum. Members held office for an initial period of six years, sitting in their individual capacities and not as representatives of states[2]. The vast majority of applications lodged – almost 90 per cent – were rejected by the Commission as inadmissible, either at the outset of the proceedings or after observations of the relevant state had been considered[3]. Where admissibility criteria had been satisfied, the Commission's task was thereafter threefold: first, it would establish the facts (and, to this end, in exceptional cases could undertake an investigation); second, it would place itself at the disposal of the parties with a view to securing a friendly settlement (achieved in some 10 per cent of cases declared admissible, and normally in the form of an offer by a state to pay financial compensation or to amend domestic law or practice); and third, where no friendly settlement was effected, it would issue a report on the facts as established giving its opinion as to whether there had been a violation[4]. Most of this work took place through the consideration of written submissions. Committees (of three members) would examine admissibility; Chambers (of seven members) would normally determine more difficult questions of admissibility and the merits of applications declared admissible[5]. A decision that an application was inadmissible was conclusive and could not be re-opened. The Commission's report on the merits of a complaint, however, was strictly only an opinion and thus not binding. The Committee of Ministers could ultimately decide (by a two-thirds majority) whether there had been a violation of the treaty and, if so, the time by which a state had to take satisfactory measures to comply with the decision[6]. However, within three months from the date of transmission of the report to the Committee of Ministers, the case could be referred to the European Court of Human Rights if the respondent state had recognised the Court's optional jurisdiction[7]. A referral could be made either by the Commission or by the state against which the complaint was lodged or, in an appropriate case, by the state whose national was alleged to be a victim[8]. From 1994 onwards, additionally, an individual applicant could refer the case to the Court with leave of a screening panel where the relevant state party had recognised this optional provision[9].

1 See further Fribergh and Villiger 'The European Commission of Human Rights' in Macdonald, Matscher and Petzold (eds) *The European System for the Protection of Human Rights* (1993) pp 605–620.
2 Arts 21–23 (original treaty as amended by Protocols 5 and 8).
3 By the end of the Commission's work, 39,047 applications had been registered and 33,123 decisions taken. The number of applications declared inadmissible (or struck off the list *de plano*) was 26,226; and a further 2,733 applications were declared inadmissible after communication to the respondent government. Only 4,161 applications were declared admissible (of which a further 12 were rejected in the course of examination of the merits): (1998) YB 41, 20. For discussion of admissibility criteria, see paras 2.24–2.28 below.
4 Arts 28–31 (original treaty as amended by Protocols 3 and 8). See further, Krüger and Nørgaard 'Reflections concerning Friendly Settlement under the ECHR' in Matscher and Petzold (edd) *Protecting Human Rights: The European Dimension* (2nd edn, 1990) pp 329–334; and Kiss 'Conciliation' in Macdonald, Matscher and Petzold (eds) *The European System for the Protection of Human Rights* (1993) pp 703–711.
5 Protocol 8.
6 Art 32 (original treaty). The Committee met *in camera*. Protocol 10 would have reduced the majority required for such a decision to that of a simple majority, but never entered into force. For discussion of the Committee's role under the Convention, see further Jacobs and White *The European Convention on Human Rights* (2nd edn, 1996) pp 393–399; Ravaud 'The Committee of Ministers' in Macdonald, Matscher and Petzold (eds) *The European System for the Protection of Human Rights* (1993) pp 645–656; and Drzemczewski 'Decision on the Merits: By the Committee of Ministers' in Macdonald, Matscher and Petzold (eds), above, pp 733–754.
7 Under Art 46 (original treaty).
8 Art 48 (original treaty).
9 In terms of Protocol 9.

THE EUROPEAN COURT OF HUMAN RIGHTS

2.16 The Court was first established in 1959[1]. The optional nature of its jurisdiction and the relative paucity of applications to the Commission in the early years (reflecting the optional nature of recognition of the right of individual application) resulted in a slow start to its work: the first case was referred to it in 1960[2], and between then and the end of 1975, only another 10 cases followed. In time, all states had come to recognise its jurisdiction or had indicated (in the case of new member states of the Council of Europe) an intention of doing so as a condition of membership[3]. The corresponding exponential growth in workload is remarkable. In the next ten years – 1976 until 1985 – the Court was seised of a further 81 cases; and in the final full year of the 'old' Court alone – 1997 – of 119 cases. Before implementation of the reforms of Protocol 11, no less than 837 judgments had been delivered[4]. The vast majority of referrals were made by the Commission where it considered that an authoritative ruling by the Court was appropriate; less than 40 cases have been on account of state referrals alone[5]. Its additional function of giving advisory opinions on interpretation of the Convention at the request of the Committee of Ministers was never exercised[6].

This steady growth in workload was reflected in organisational and procedural reforms. As the number of member states grew, so did the Court, which was comprised of a number of judges equal to that of member states[7]. The Court was essentially a part-time institution which was serviced by its full-time Registry. It normally sat in Chambers of seven (and subsequently nine) judges which would include the judge appointed in respect of the respondent state; in certain cases, however, a case would be considered by a Grand Chamber of 17 (and subsequently 21) judges or, in exceptional cases, by the plenary court[8]. The first stage in any case was the submission of written memorials or other documentation by the parties (and, in certain cases, by other states or organisations where the President of the Court determined that this would be in the interests of the proper administration of justice)[9]. At any subsequent hearing, the Commission was not formally a party to the proceedings but appeared through its delegates to assist the Court in its deliberations; any applicant who had indicated a wish to take part in proceedings was normally legally represented by a practising or academic lawyer. The state concerned was heard last. The Court was able to reconsider whether a decision that an issue was admissible had been correctly decided by the Commission, to re-open deliberations on the question of the merits of an application, and in certain cases to deliberate upon a question of application of a treaty provision which had not been considered by the Commission[10]. Decisions were given by simple majority and were binding upon states but were essentially declaratory: supervision of implementation of measures required by any decision (and of any Court determination as to the payment of costs and expenses and payment of 'just satisfaction') was a matter for the Committee of Ministers[11].

1 See further Mahoney and Prebensen 'The European Court of Human Rights' in Macdonald, Matscher and Petzold (eds), *The European System for the Protection of Human Rights* (1993) pp 621–643.
2 That is, *Lawless v Ireland* (1960–1961) A 1–3.
3 Cf the formula used by the Parliamentary Assembly in considering commitments undertaken as a condition of membership that it attached 'great importance' to recognition of the right of individual application: see further doc Monitor/Inf (99) 1.
4 As well as 190 decisions rejecting applications under Protocol 9, Art 5(2): European Court of Human Rights *Survey: Forty Years of Activity 1959–1998* (1999) p 25.
5 European Court of Human Rights *Survey: Forty Years of Activity* p 3. Only two of those cases involved a referral by a state whose national was alleged to have been a victim.
6 In terms of Protocol 2. This function continues (Art 47).
7 Art 38 (original treaty). Judges were elected (or re-elected) by the Parliamentary Assembly for a period of nine years from a list of three persons drawn up by member states, and sat in their own individual capacity: Arts 39 and 40 (original treaty, as amended).
8 Art 43 (original treaty); and (former) Rule of Court 'A' 51.
9 In terms of (former) Rule of Court A 37(2).
10 *De Wilde, Ooms and Versyp v Belgium* (1971) A 12, paras 47–52. A decision of the Commission that an issue was inadmissible could not, however, be reopened: see eg *Fusco v Italy* 1997-V, 1727, para 16. See further van Dijk and van Hoof *Theory and Practice of the European Convention on Human Rights* (3rd edn, 1998) pp 203–213. See also *Guzzardi v Italy* (1980) A 39, paras 58–63 (identification of Art 5 issue by the Commission and the Court which had not been specifically raised by the applicant); *Phillips v United Kingdom* (5 July 2001) at para 38 (the Court is 'master of the characterisation to be given in law to the facts of a case').
11 Arts 52–54 (original treaty).

European Convention on Human Rights (ECHR)
Detailed overview

New control mechanism
Full-time Court

Former control mechanism
Two distinct procedural stages before part-time Commission
and then before part-time Court or Committee of Ministers

Inter-state applications: Article 33

Individual applications: Article 34

Individual applications: Article 25

Inter-state applications: Article 24

Court: committee of 3 judges

Inadmissible: unanimous decision: end of case:

Commission: committee of 3 members

Court chamber

Commission (chamber or plenary)

Examination of admissibility: Articles 29 and 35

Inadmissible: end of case

Examination of admissibility: Articles 26 and 27

Case admissible

Case admissible

Establishment of facts and friendly settlement proceedings

Friendly settlement: end of case

Establishment of facts and friendly settlement negotiations

No friendly settlement

No friendly settlement

Court judgement: Articles 29 and 44 (2) (and just satisfaction if necessary: Article 41)

Referral/transmission to Grand Chamber of Court: Article 43

Commission report Articles 31

Request accepted in exceptional cases by panel of 5 judges: Article 43

Court: filter by committee of 3 when case brought by individual applicant

Rejection: Court judgment stands

Seizure of Court by Commission or State concerned within 3 months: Articles 46 and 48

Committee of Ministers seized: Article 32 (1)

Grand Chamber judgment: Articles 43 (3) and 44

Court judgment: Articles 51-53 (and just satisfaction if necessary: Article 50)

Committee of Ministers decision: Article 32

Committee of Ministers supervises execution of judgment: Article 46 (2)

Committee of Ministers supervises execution of judgment: Article 54

Committee of Ministers supervises execution of its decision: Article 32 (3)

⟶ Compulsory jurisdiction
‑ ‑ ‑ ➤ Optional jurisdiction
·········➤ Optional procedure under Protocol No. 9.

Concept and design: P. Drzemczewski
Graphic: Publications unit, Directorate of Human Rights

Enforcement machinery after November 1998: the changes occasioned by Protocol 11

2.17   By the early 1990s, there was substantial recognition that the existing procedures were inefficient, with needless duplication between Commission and Court, and productive of excessive delay[1]. The Commission's increasing willingness to refer cases to the Court for determination was resulting in lengthening delays: it was not uncommon for applications to take some five years between Commission registration and Court judgment. Protocol 11 in essence abolished the Commission, restricted the functions of the Committee of Ministers to supervision of the enforcement of decisions, and made significant reforms to the Court, which became a full-time body[2].

1 See, further, Council of Europe *Report of the Committee of Experts for the Improvement of Procedures for the Protection of Human Rights*, Doc H (89) 2, reproduced in Janis, Kay and Bradley *European Human Rights Law: Text and Materials* (1st edn, 1995) pp 88–105; Council of Europe *Reform of the Control System of the European Convention on Human Rights*, Doc H (92) 14 (see (1993) 14 HRLJ 31); *Explanatory Report to Protocol No 11*, Doc H (94) 5 (reprinted in Janis, Kay and Bradley, above, pp 106–118; Drzemczewski 'A Major Overhaul of the European Human Rights Convention Control Mechanism: Protocol No 11' (1995) *VI Protection of Human Rights in Europe: Book 2* (1997) pp 122–244.

ORGANISATION AND FUNCTIONS OF THE 'NEW' COURT

2.18   The appointment, organisation and functions of the Court are now to be found in Articles 19–51 of the revised European Convention on Human Rights as supplemented by new Rules of Court[1]. The Court has jurisdiction in both inter-state cases and individual applications[2] (that is, applications from any person, non-governmental organisation or group of individuals claiming to be a victim of a breach of the Convention)[3], and retains the function of giving advisory opinions[4]. It continues to consist of a number of judges equal to that of state parties to the Convention, elected as before for renewable periods of six years by the Parliamentary Assembly[5]. Judges are still to be 'of high moral character and must either possess the qualifications required for appointment to high judicial office or be jurisconsults of recognised competence'[6]. A new retirement age of 70 has, however, been introduced[7]. The procedures will continue to be both written and oral, but while Rules of Court provide that hearings will be held in public unless the Court in exceptional circumstances decides otherwise[8], the practice is now (on account of the caseload facing the Court and the relatively routine nature of many applications, particularly those concerning the length of domestic proceedings)[9] to require oral argument only in cases where the Court feels this is helpful for the proper disposal of a case. Many other elements of the pre-1998 machinery have continued and the substantive rules on admissibility remain unaffected. However, the Committee of Ministers has lost its decision-making authority and its role is now limited to supervision of execution of final judgments of the Court[10]. The organisation of the new Court also reflects many features found in procedures prior to the introduction of Protocol 11. Considerable use is made of devolution of authority. The Court may sit in committees (of three judges), Chambers (of seven judges together with substitute judges and which will include the President of the Section), a Grand Chamber (of 17 judges and three substitute judges and which will include the President of the Court), or in plenary[11]. Under Rules of Court, the Court is divided into four sections each headed by a Section President. Membership of Sections is fixed for three years and seeks to achieve gender and geographic balance[12] and representation of the different legal traditions found across the continent. All decisions are taken by majority vote and reasons for admissibility decisions and for judgments must be given; any judge who considers the judgment does not represent in whole or in part the unanimous opinion of the Court is entitled to deliver a separate opinion[13].

1 Rules of Court are available at www.echr.coe.int/Eng/EDocs/RulesOfCourt.html . See further Clements 'Striking the Right Balance: The New Rules of Procedure for the European Court of Human Rights' [1999] EHRLR 266. See further Mowbray 'The Composition and Operation of the New European Court of Human Rights' [1999] PL 219.
2 ECHR, Art 32.
3 ECHR, Art 34. For discussion of 'victim' see para 2.29–2.30 below.
4 ECHR, Art 47–49. Requests for advisory opinions are considered by the Grand Chamber: Art 31. The Council of Europe Convention on Human Rights and Biomedicine additionally will confer power on the Court to give advisory opinions at the request of states when the treaty enters into force.
5 ECHR, Arts 20 and 22. Each state nominates three candidates; the Parliamentary Assembly selects one candidate by a majority of votes. Judges need not be nationals of the state in respect of which they have been elected: currently, the San Marinan judge is Italian, and the Liechtenstein judge is Swiss. Not until 1998 did the United Kingdom Government nominate a Scottish qualified candidate for this office (although one Scot, Professor A E Anton, did serve albeit for a matter of weeks as a member of the Commission in the early 1980s). A Scottish judge first sat on the Court, on an ad hoc basis, in *Hashmann and Harrup v United Kingdom* (25 November 1999). For discussion of the procedure in operation, see Schermers 'Election of Judges to the European Court of Human Rights' (1998) 23 EL Rev 568; and Flauss 'L'Assemblée Parlementaire du Conseil de l'Europe et l'Élection de la Nouvelle Cour Européenne des Droits de l'Homme' in Haller, Krüger and Petzold *Law in Greater Europe: Towards a Common Legal Area* (2000) pp 190–207.
6 EHCR, Art 21(1). Judges sit in their individual capacity, and must not engage in any activity which is incompatible with their independence or impartiality: paras (2) and (3). See the *Sixth Protocol to the General Agreement on Privileges and Immunities of the Council of Europe* (ETS No 162) (1996) for privileges and immunities of judges (not yet ratified by the UK); and the *European Agreement Relating to Persons Participating in Proceedings of the European Court of Human Rights* (ETS No 161) (1996).
7 EHCR, Art 23(6).
8 Rule of Court 33. For example, the hearing in the cases of *T v United Kingdom* and *V v United Kingdom* (16 December 1999), was held in private.
9 See para 5.90 below.
10 EHCR, Art 46(1).
11 EHCR, Art 26 and 27 (the plenary Court meets to elect its President and Vice-Presidents; adopt its Rules of Court; set up Chambers; and elect Chamber Presidents, the Court Registrar and Deputy Registrars). See further Rules of Court 24–30.
12 Rule of Court 25(2).
13 ECHR, Art 45.

2.19 A registered application is assigned to a Section, whose President allocates it to a particular judge (the 'judge rapporteur') who is responsible for preparing the case, communicating with any relevant party as appropriate, and (if the case is declared admissible) taking steps to try to secure a friendly settlement. Before taking a decision on admissibility, the petition may be communicated to the respondent state to allow it to submit observations[1]. The application is thereafter normally considered by a Committee comprising three judges which may (by unanimous vote) decide to declare an individual application inadmissible or strike it from its list[2]. Alternatively, the rapporteur may decide that the application should be dealt with by a Chamber from the outset. An applicant may request that interim measures be taken to protect his situation pending determination of his complaint[3]. Any application not considered inadmissible by unanimous vote of a committee will be transferred to a Chamber for any further examination of admissibility deemed necessary and ultimately for a decision on the merits[4] where a friendly settlement has not been achieved[5]. When an application has been admitted by a Chamber, the parties may be invited to submit further evidence and written observations (including any claim for just satisfaction under Article 41)[6]. The President of the Chamber may invite or grant leave to any other state or person not a party to the proceedings to submit written pleadings (and, exceptionally, to address the Chamber) where this is in the interests of the proper administration of justice[7]. It is still open for a case to be struck out where the Court considers it no longer justified to continue with the application and such a measure is not incompatible with respect for human rights[8].

1 See Rules of Court 49(2) and 53(3).
2 EHCR, Art 28. See further Rules of Court 45, 47, 49 and 52–57, and 62.
3 See further Rule of Court 39. For a recent example, see 71555/01, *Einhorn v France* (19 July 2001) (interim measures in respect of a person facing deportation to the USA – on charges carrying the death penalty – and imposed following upon a suicide attempt; measures lifted after one week upon satisfaction of certain conditions). Cf Zwart *The Admissibility of Human Rights Petitions: The Case Law of the European Commission of Human Rights and the Human Rights Committee* (1994) pp 34–37 (interim measures will be appropriate where the applicant faces irreparable harm of a very serious nature; the harm is imminent and irremediable; and the applicant has a prima facie case). See also Buquicchio-de Boer 'Interim Measures by the European Commission of Human Rights' in de Salvia and Villiger (eds) *The Birth of European Human Rights Law* (1998) pp 229–236.
4 In certain cases, the determination of admissibility may depend upon examination of the merits, and the two issues may be conjoined: e g *Ferrazzini v Italy* (12 July 2001), paras 18–19 (opportunity taken by Grand Chamber to review existing case law on the applicability of Art 6 to tax proceedings).
5 ECHR, Art 29. A Chamber rather than a committee must decide the question of admissibility of any inter-state application: para (2). Where an agreement is reached between the parties (normally in the form of an agreement to pay compensation and to amend domestic law or practice) and the Court is satisfied that the settlement is based on respect for human rights, the case will be struck off the list: ECHR, Art 37(1) and Rule of Court 62(3). Negotiations with a view to friendly settlement are confidential, and may not subsequently be referred to in contentious proceedings: Art 38(2) and Rule of Court 62(2).
6 See further Rule of Court 60. For discussion of 'just satisfaction', see para 2.31 below.
7 Rule of Court 61. An individual whose rights a state sought to protect in taking action which forms the subject of the application may be invited to submit comments: e g *Feldek v Slovakia* (12 July 2001) paras 68–71 (defamation action raised by a minister against the applicant in respect of statements concerning the minister's background). Where the applicant is a national of a Council of Europe state other than the respondent state, this state will be invited to submit observations. For discussion of NGO interventions, see Nowicki 'Non-Governmental Organisations (NGOs) before the European Commission of Human Rights' in de Salvia and Villiger (eds) *The Birth of European Human Rights Law* (1998) 267–273.
8 ECHR, Art 3. Striking out may occur where a state unilaterally offers a settlement considered acceptable to the Court and is not dependent upon acceptance of the offer by the applicant. For a recent example, see *Akman v Turkey* (26 June 2001) paras 23–32 (acceptance that the state had violated Art 2; and *ex gratia* offer of payment to the victim's father).

2.20   The Grand Chamber has three functions. First, it may give advisory opinions to the Committee of Ministers but not on matters concerning substantive guarantees under the Convention[1]. Second, and more importantly, it considers all inter-state cases, and individual applications where a Chamber has decided to relinquish jurisdiction. A Chamber may so decide where it feels that the case pending before it raises a serious question of interpretation or 'where the resolution of a question before it might have a result inconsistent with a judgment previously delivered by the Court', but may not do so if one of the parties to the case objects[2]. The provision is designed to help ensure consistency in jurisprudence, but the 'veto' power seems inconsistent with this aim[3]. Third, the Grand Chamber acts in effect as an appellate court from decisions of a Chamber where a party to a case requests within three months of a Chamber decision that the case be sent to the Grand Chamber. The Convention provides that such a request is to be made only 'in exceptional cases', and is to be considered by a panel of five judges of the Grand Chamber to determine whether the case 'raises a serious question affecting the interpretation or application of the Convention, ... or a serious issue of general importance'[4]. The composition of the Grand Chamber which will re-hear the case is somewhat contentious, for both the President of the Chamber and the 'national' judge (who will have been involved in the Chamber proceedings) will again sit[5]; further, should liberal use be made of this provision, delay in the final disposal of applications will continue, with the reforms becoming largely self-defeating[6]. The practical result is that judgments of Chambers will not become final until the expiry of the three-month period or until the parties have confirmed that they do not intend requesting a referral to the panel: consequently, care must be taken with the use of recent judgments of a Chamber.

1   ECHR, Arts 31, 47–49 (cf Art 47(2): opinions may not deal with issues as to the content or scope of substantive rights and freedoms).
2   ECHR, Art 30. Five cases were relinquished in 2000. There is some early indication that cases which involve a background of some political complexity are being relinquished: 52207/99 *Banković and Others v Belgium and 16 other states* (NATO bombing of Radio-Television Serbia during the Kosovo campaign) and 48787/99, *Ilaşcu and Others v Moldova and Russia* (4 July 2001) (responsibility of respondent states for situation in Transnistra where the applicants are being held in unlawful detention) have both been relinquished in favour of the Grand Chamber.
3   See Schermers 'Election of Judges to the European Court of Human Rights' (1998) 23 EL Rev 568.
4   ECHR, Art 43. The panel of five judges comprises the President of the Court, the Section Presidents (with the exception of the Section President who presided over the Section to which the Chamber that gave the judgment belongs), and another judge selected by rotation from judges who were not members of the original Chamber. Two cases were referred by the panel in 2000. It is open to the Grand Chamber to take into account new material not previously submitted as well as fresh arguments: cf *K and T v Finland* (12 July 2001), para 147.
5   ECHR, Art 27(3).
6   Drzemczewski and Meyer-Ladewig 'Principal Characteristics of the New ECHR Control mechanism, as Established by Protocol No 11' (1994) 15 HRLJ 81 at p 85.

FACT-FINDING BY THE EUROPEAN COURT OF HUMAN RIGHTS

2.21   Under the original machinery, fact-finding was the responsibility of the Commission[1]. Article 38(1)(a) of the revised Convention provides that the Court is to 'pursue the examination' of any case declared admissible 'together with the representatives of the parties, and if need be, undertake an investigation, for the effective conduct of which the States concerned shall furnish all necessary facilities'. In normal circumstances, the Court makes use of any appropriate domestic evidence such as official reports[2], transcripts of inquiries[3], and similar sources. While the Court's task is not to substitute its own assessment of the facts, it is not bound by determinations made by domestic courts, and remains free to make its own assessment depending upon all the evidence before it[4]. Where the facts are in dispute, the Court will carry out an investigation, again making use of existing documentary evidence and also in exceptional cases by holding a hearing into the alleged facts[5], but there is no power to secure the production of evidence or to compel the attendance of witnesses and, on occasion, the assessment of facts can present particular difficulties[6]. The requisite standard of proof in Article 3 cases is one of beyond reasonable doubt[7]. In some circumstances, there is a duty upon a state authority to provide a response. Where an individual in good health has been detained by state authorities but is released suffering from injuries, for example, the state must provide a 'plausible explanation' to avoid an issue arising under Article 3[8]. The requisite standard of proof may be reached through the co-existence of sufficiently strong, clear and concordant inferences or presumptions which the state has not been able to rebut[9], bearing in mind the seriousness and nature of the allegations made and the particular circumstances of each case[10].

1 ECHR, Arts 28(1) and 31 (original treaty). While the Court remained free to arrive at its own assessment, it would only depart from the Commission's findings in exceptional circumstances: e g *Akdivar v Turkey* 1996-VI, 1192, para 78; *Kaya v Turkey* 1998-I, 297, para 75. See further Rogge 'Fact-Finding' in Macdonald, Matscher and Petzold (eds) *The European System for the Protection of Human Rights* (1993) pp 677–701; and Krüger 'Gathering Evidence' in de Salvia and Villiger (eds) *The Birth of European Human Rights Law* (1998) pp 249–259.

2 E g *Yaşa v Turkey* 1998-VI, 2411, paras 95–96.

3 E g *McCann and Ors v United Kingdom* (1995) A 324, paras 107–121.

4 *Ribitsch v Austria* (1995) A 336, para 32. However, it will only depart from the findings of domestic courts in the most compelling of cases: cf *Klaas v Germany* (1993) A 269, para 29.

5 Cf *Aksoy v Turkey* 1996-VI, 2260 (the Commission made two visits to Turkey to gather and assess documentary evidence and oral testimony to establish the circumstances surrounding the alleged torture of the applicant). Fact-finding of this sort will now be undertaken by the Court: see Rule of Court 42.

6 Cf *Denizci and Others v Cyprus* (23 May 2001) at para 315: 'In a case where there are contradictory and conflicting factual accounts of events, the Court is acutely aware of its own shortcomings as a first instance tribunal of fact. [There are] problems of language . . .; there is also an inevitable lack of detailed and direct familiarity with the conditions pertaining in the region. In addition, [there are no] powers of compulsion as regards attendance of witnesses'.

7 *Ireland v United Kingdom* (1978) A 25, at paras 160–161.

8 *Aksoy v Turkey* 1996-VI, 2260, para 61.

9 *Aydin v Turkey* 1997-VI, 1866 at para 70.

10 *Yaşa v Turkey* 1998-VI, 2411 at para 96.

WORKLOAD OF THE NEW COURT

2.22   The new Court's annual workload continues to grow at a rate which reflects heightened awareness of the Convention on the part of applicants[1]. Its caseload increased by some 40 per cent in 1999 alone and by a further 20 per cent in 2000[2], and the number of judgments delivered in the first two years of the restructured European Court of Human Rights (177 in 1999 and no less than 695 in 2000)[3] surpassed the number achieved by its predecessor in 40 years of existence[4]. It is clear that a further sharp increase in its workload is likely: certain states which have recently ratified the Convention still account for relatively few pending applications[5]. There are already indications that these procedural reforms may prove, at the end of the day, to be inadequate. An 'evaluation group' has already been established to examine what additional changes may be required[6]: at the very least, greater devolution of responsibility to the committees and Chambers and greater willingness in the selection of cases to be considered by the Grand Chamber may be considered appropriate.

1 In its first 14 months (ie from November 1998 until the end of 1999) just over 25,000 provisional files were opened by the Court Registry, leading to 9,371 registered applications. The Court considered some 4,250 applications (of which 731 were declared admissible and 3,389 inadmissible, and 130 were struck off). Just under 1,600 applications were communicated to states in this period: Registrar of the European Court of Human Rights *Survey of Activities 1998* (1999) 25; *Survey of Activities 1999* (2000) 49.
2 In the year 2000, 6,769 applications were struck out or declared inadmissible and 1,082 were declared admissible: Press Release, 22 January 2001.
3 Sixty-three of the 177 judgments in 1999, and 26 of the 695 judgments in 2000 were decisions of the Grand Chamber. In 1999, at least one violation was established in 120 of the judgments, and in 2000 in 424 of the judgments: Registrar of the European Court of Human Rights *Survey of Activities 1999* 52; *Survey of Activities 2000* (provisional edn) (2001) 73.
4 Between 1 November 1998 and 5 December 2000, the new Court had delivered 838 judgments – one more than the previous, part-time Court had delivered in the 40 years between its establishment in 1959 and its demise on 31 October 1998.
5 Registered applications for the year 2000 (a total of 10,436) indicate differences which are probably attributable to the levels of knowledge on the part of legal advisers and individuals in new member states. On the one hand, significant applications are now being made in respect of Poland (777), the Russian Federation (1,325), and Ukraine (728); on the other, only a handful were made in respect of Albania (3), Georgia (7) and FYRO Macedonia (18). By December 2000, the new Court had a total of 15,858 registered applications pending. It was receiving an average of 135 phone calls and 760 letters a day. See further Information Note, 22 January 2001.
6 Further to the Ministerial Conference held in Rome in November 2000, additional resources have also been made available to the new Court for 2001: Press Release, 22 January 2001.

2.23 It may still be too early to assess the approaches taken by the new Court to established jurisprudence[1]. Certainly, there are indications of development in protection against torture and inhuman and degrading treatment[2], of clarification of some of the uncertainty in determining the scope of Article 6[3], and of reiteration of the importance of free speech in a democracy[4]. On the other hand, certain decisions seem excessively cautious[5]. The majority of established violations in 1999 and 2000, the first full two year's of the 'new' Court's work, still concerned a handful of states such as France, Italy and Portugal which continue to fail to meet fair hearing guarantees under Article 6, Turkey which faced condemnation for 'disappearances' and ill-treatment in places of detention under Articles 2 and 3 and criticism of measures designed to repress free speech under Article 10, and the United Kingdom[6]. British applications again raised an eclectic mixture of issues: in 1999, 12 of the 120 judgments in which violations were established concerned British law and practice on topics involving the trial and subsequent imprisonment of juveniles for murder in adult courts,[7] the independence and impartiality of courts martial[8], the lack of a public hearing in arbitration proceedings[9], the lack of legal aid in proceedings which resulted in imprisonment for non-payment of the community charge[10], the dismissal of homosexuals from the armed forces[11], the power to bind over to be of good behaviour in English law[12], and the right to free elections[13]. In 2000, 16 judgments involved violations by Britain in a range of cases involving the lack of bail in serious offences[14], review of discretionary life sentences[15], the length of time between reviews of the lawfulness of detention[16], the independence and impartiality of judges[17], the issue of public interest immunity certificates[18], the drawing of adverse inferences from an accused's silence[19], racial prejudice on the part of jurors[20], the use of statements made under threat of penalty during prosecutions[21], the length of criminal proceedings[22], the lack of impartiality of the Gaming Board in determining licences[23], the absence of a legal basis for the use of a police listening device[24], denial of access to a lawyer during detention[25], redirection of mail to a court-appointed trustee[26], convictions for homosexual group sex[27], and further cases involving military discipline[28].

1   For a critical assessment of the new Court, see O'Boyle 'Establishing the New European Court of Human Rights: Progress to Date' (1999) 4 HRLR 3; and Drzemczewski 'The European Human Rights Convention: Protocol No 11 – Entry into Force and First Year of Application' (2000) 21 HRLJ 1. Half of the judges appointed in 1998 have had prior experience as members of the 'old' Court or Commission (with this expertise drawn in equal numbers from each institution). For further discussion, see Bratza and O'Boyle 'Opinion: The Legacy of the Commission to the New Court under the Eleventh Protocol' [1997] EHRLR 211. For a suggestion that the new Court should seek consistency and continuity in jurisprudence, see Berger 'la Nouvelle Cour Européenne des Droits de l'Homme: D'une Jurisprudence à l'Autre?' in Flécheux (ed) *Mélanges en Hommage à Louis Edmond Pettiti* (1998) pp 129–163.
2   E g *Selmouni v France* 1999-V, 149; *Dougoz v Greece* (6 March 2001); and *Peers v Greece* (19 April 2001), discussed at paras 4.20 and 4.35 below.
3   *Pellegrin v France* (8 December 1999), discussed at para 5.16 below.
4   E g *Bladet Tromsø v Norway* 1999-III, 289, discussed at para 7.27 below.
5   E g *Janowski v Poland* (21 January 1999), discussed at para 7.29 below; *Labita v Italy* (6 April 2000), discussed at para 4.24 below; and *Refah Partisi (The Welfare Party), Erbekan, Kazan and Tekdal v Turkey* (31 July 2001) discussed at para 7.54 below.
6   In these two years, and excluding cases involving length of proceedings, the greatest number of judgments on the merits and settlements were in respect of Turkey (51), the United Kingdom (39), France (32), Italy (24), Austria (21), and Greece (15).
7   *T v United Kingdom* and *V v United Kingdom* (16 December 1999), discussed at paras 4.31, 4.88 and 5.65, below.
8   *Cable and Ors v United Kingdom* (18 February 1999), *Hood v United Kingdom* (18 February 2000), *Moore and Gordon v United Kingdom*, and *Smith and Ford v United Kingdom* (29 September 1999), discussed at para 5.41 below.
9   *Scarth v United Kingdom* (22 July 1999), discussed at para 5.89 below.
10 *Perks and Ors v United Kingdom* (12 October 1999), discussed at para 5.127 below.
11 *Lustig-Prean and Beckett v United Kingdom* and *Smith and Grady v United Kingdom* (27 September 1999), discussed at para 6.44 below.
12 *Hashman and Harrup v United Kingdom* (25 November 1999), discussed at para 7.23 below.
13 *Matthews v United Kingdom* 1999-I, 251, discussed at para 7.61 below.
14 *Caballero v United Kingdom* (8 February 2000), discussed at para 4.76 below.
15 *Curley v United Kingdom* (28 March 2000); discussed at para 4.99 below. *Walsh v United Kingdom* (4 April 2000).
16 *Oldham v United Kingdom* (26 September 2000), discussed at para 4.87 below.
17 *McGonnell v United Kingdom* (8 February 2000), discussed at para 5.39 below.
18 *Rowe and Davis v United Kingdom; Fitt v United Kingdom*; and *Jasper v United Kingdom* (16 February 2000), discussed at para 5.59 below.

19 *Condron v United Kingdom* (2 May 2000), discussed at para 5.79 below.
20 *Sander v United Kingdom* (9 May 2000), discussed at para 5.43 below.
21 *IJL, GMR and AKP v United Kingdom* (19 September 2000), discussed at para 5.97 below.
22 *Howarth v United Kingdom* (21 September 2000), discussed at para 5.97 below.
23 *Kingsley v United Kingdom* (7 November 2000), discussed at para 5.83 below.
24 *Khan v United Kingdom* (12 May 2000), discussed at para 6.25 below.
25 *Magee v United Kingdom* (6 June 2000), discussed at para 5.70 below; and *Averill v United Kingdom* (6 June 2000), discussed at para 5.124 below.
26 *Foxley v United Kingdom* (20 June 2000), discussed at para 6.27 below.
27 *A D T v United Kingdom* (31 July 2000), discussed at para 6.41 below.
28 *Stephen Jordan v United Kingdom* (14 March 2000).

Admissibility criteria

2.24   ECHR, Article 35 details the criteria for admissibility of an application lodged by an individual. Detailed discussion of these criteria is outwith the scope of this work, as is consideration of the practicalities of lodging an application[1]. The principal issues considered in determining admissibility include: prior exhaustion of available domestic remedies; lodging an application within six months of the taking of the final decision; and compatibility *ratione temporis, ratione loci, ratione personae,* and *ratione materiae.* In addition, the Court will not deal with any application which is anonymous, or is substantially the same as a matter that has already been examined and which contains no relevant new information, or is 'manifestly ill-founded' or considered an abuse of the right of petition[2].

1 For a fuller discussion of the practicalities of making an application to the Court, see Zwart *The Admissibility of Human Rights Petitions: The Case Law of the European Commission on Human Rights and the Human Rights Committee* (1994); Reid *A Practitioner's Guide to the European Convention on Human Rights* (1998) pp 19–29; van Dijk and van Hoof *Theory and Practice of the European Convention on Human Rights* (3rd edn, 1998) pp 44–65 and 97–192; Clements, Mole and Simmons *European Human Rights: Taking a Case Under the Convention* (2nd edn, 1998) pp 12–40; and Leach *Taking a Case to the European Court of Human Rights* (2001) pp 61–92.
2 ECHR, Art 35(1) requires an applicant to have exhausted domestic remedies and to have made a complaint within six months of the date on which the final decision was taken. These requirements apply to all applications, including inter-state applications. The additional requirements apply in respect of individual complaints. Thus an inter-state case cannot be declared inadmissible for being substantially the same as a previous application or as abusive: 8007/77, *Cyprus v Turkey* (1978) DR 13, 85; and (1983) DR 72, 5.

Exhaustion of domestic remedies

2.25   The requirement that an applicant has sought to exhaust domestic remedies is further recognition of the supervisory nature of the Strasbourg court. The purpose is to afford an opportunity to states to prevent or put right an alleged violation of a Convention guarantee before the matter is considered by an international institution[1]. However, an applicant need only have recourse to 'remedies which are available and capable of remedying the breaches alleged'. In other words, 'the existence of the remedies in question must be sufficiently certain not only in theory but in practice'[2]. The burden is upon the state which claims that this requirement has not been met by an applicant to establish that an effective remedy existed; but once this has been achieved, the onus is then on the applicant to show why the remedy advanced by the state was not an effective one in the circumstances. In examining this matter, the Court takes a realistic account 'not only of the formal remedies in the legal system of the Contracting Party concerned but also of the context in which they operate and the personal circumstances of the applicant'[3]. Further, since the context in which the requirement of exhaustion is being considered is that of human rights protection, the rule is applied 'with some degree of flexibility and without excessive formalism'[4].

1   *Akdivar and Ors v Turkey* 1996-IV, 1192, para 66.
2   *Beïs v Greece* 1997-II, 555, para 32. For discussion of the effect of the Human Rights Act 1998 on exhaustion of domestic remedies, see 63716/00, *Sawoniuk v United Kingdom* (29 May 2001) (failure to take proceedings in domestic courts where the applicant would have been able to rely directly on the provisions of the Convention: application inadmissible on account of failure to exhaust domestic remedies).
3   *Beïs v Greece* 1997-II, 555, at para 32. The respondent government's failure to argue exhaustion of domestic remedies will bar it from relying upon this point subsequently: see e g *Steel and Others v United Kingdom* 1998-VII, 2719, paras 62–65 (withdrawal of a prosecution against the applicants who had been arrested during a peaceful protest and who in turn had not sought to bring an action of civil damages for false imprisonment: in view of the respondent government's failure to raise a preliminary objection on the grounds of failure to exhaust domestic remedies, the Court itself decided to consider the lawfulness of the detention, and concluded that this had been unlawful in domestic law since there had been no indication that the protest had been anything other than peaceful). See further Robertson 'Exhaustion of Local Remedies in International Human Rights Litigation: the Burden of Proof Reconsidered' (1990) 39 ICLQ 191.
4   *Akdivar and Ors v Turkey* 1996-IV, 1192, at para 69; *Aksoy v Turkey* 1996-VI, 2260, paras 53 and 54.

The six months rule

2.26   The primary purpose of the requirement that an application must be made within six months from the taking of a final decision is to help ensure legal certainty. The rule is closely related to the admissibility requirement of exhaustion of domestic remedies: the period begins to run from the point when the final outcome of domestic procedures is made known to the applicant or his legal representative[1]. Where there are no effective domestic remedies the period will begin to run from the date of the state action[2] or, in certain cases, from the date of the applicant's knowledge of a violation[3]. The rule is inapplicable where there is a continuing situation giving rise to a violation, for example in the form of a legislative provision[4] (rather than a situation attributable to a particular decision or event)[5]. An application is lodged on the date of the applicant's first letter (rather than the date of formal registration by the Court), provided that the letter sufficiently indicates the purpose of the application[6].

1   *Worm v Austria* 1997-V, 1534, at para 32. Cf 37555/97, *O'Hara v United Kingdom* (14 March 2000) (domestic proceedings challenging the lawfulness of detention in 1986 which, if successful, would have resulted in the payment of compensation concluded in 1996: six-month period in the circumstances ran from the dismissal of the appeal and not from the date of release from detention).
2   Eg 14807/89, *Agrotexim and Ors v Greece* (1992) DR 72, 148.
3   Cf 12015/86, *Hilton v United Kingdom* (1988) DR 57, 108 (applicant became aware of possible subjection to vetting process only nine years after the event: six-month rule ran from the date of knowledge).
4   Cf *Dudgeon v United Kingdom* (1981) A 45, para 42 (applicant directly affected by legislation penalising homosexual conduct).
5   Eg 12659/87, *Gama da Costa v Portugal* (1990) DR 65, 136.
6   *Papageorgiou v Greece* 1997-VI, 2277, at para 32.

Compatibility with Convention guarantees

2.27 An application which is incompatible with a state's international obligations will be rejected. There are four aspects to compatibility (that is, whether a complaint falls within the scope of the state's international obligations): compatibility *ratione temporis, ratione loci, ratione personae,* and *ratione materiae.* Compatibility *ratione temporis* concerns the question whether the facts giving rise to an allegation of violation occurred after the state's acceptance of the obligation (or recognition of the right of individual petition where this is expressly limited to events occurring after the relevant date)[1]; compatibility *ratione loci* requires the violation to have taken place within the jurisdiction of the respondent state[2] or over territory effectively controlled by the state[3]; compatibility *ratione personae* rules out complaints not directed against a state authority or public body or involving the exercise (or failure to exercise) state responsibility[4] or complaints by individuals who cannot qualify as 'victims'[5]; and compatibility *ratione materiae* excludes a complaint seeking to enforce a right which is not included in the Convention[6] or one which falls outwith the scope of a particular provision[7].

1 As with the UK's recognition: Cf *LCB v United Kingdom* 1998-III, 1390 (no jurisdiction to examine complaints under Arts 2, 8 and 13 concerning monitoring of exposure to radiation since these were based on events before the UK's acceptance of the right of individual petition).
2 Cf Art 56 (a state may extend the territorial application of the Convention to dependent territories by means of a declaration). The United Kingdom made such a declaration in 1953 in respect of some 43 territories including the Isle of Man and the Channel Islands (cf *Gillow v United Kingdom* (1986) A 109, paras 60–62 (failure to extend the territorial application of Protocol 1 to Guernsey: application inadmissible under this provision).
3 Eg *Cyprus v Turkey* (10 May 2001) paras 75–81 (applicant's allegations of violations of rights in Turkish-occupied northern Cyprus related to facts which fell within the 'jurisdiction' of Turkey within the meaning of Art 1: the state exercised effective overall control of the region through its military presence, and its responsibility extended beyond that for the acts of its own soldiers and officials to include the acts of the local administration which survived by virtue of Turkish military and other support).
4 A state may still be responsible for the actions of private bodies where it has failed to secure Convention rights under Art 1 'to everyone within their jurisdiction', and thus 'cannot absolve itself from responsibility by delegating its obligations to private bodies or individuals': *Costello-Roberts v United Kingdom* (1993) A 247-C, paras 26–28 at para 27 (disciplinary measures in a private school engaged state responsibility). Cf *Nielsen v Denmark* (1988) A 144, paras 57–73 (government's objection that the committal to a psychiatric hospital by the applicant's mother did not involve the exercise of state responsibility rejected as the merits of the complaint did not fall clearly outside the Convention's provisions; on the merits, the Court ruled that the hospitalisation had not involved a deprivation of liberty but the exercise of a parent's custodial rights).
5 See below, paras 2.29–2.30.
6 Eg *Johnston v Ireland* (1986) A 112, paras 51–54 (Art 12 does not support a right to divorce).
7 Eg *Botta v Italy* 1998-I, 412, at para 35 (asserted right to gain access to the beach during holidays involved 'interpersonal relations of such broad and indeterminate scope' which fell outwith Art 8).

Additional admissibility requirements

2.28 In addition, the Court will reject an application which is anonymous[1], or is substantially the same as a matter that has already been examined and which contains no relevant new information[2], or is considered an abuse of the right of petition[3]. Further, significant numbers of applications are rejected on admissibility criteria on preliminary examination as 'manifestly ill-founded', that is the facts are unsubstantiated or do not disclose an interference with a Convention right or the interference can be considered as justifiable[4].

1 Eg 10983/84, *Confédération des Syndicats médicaux français–Fédération nationale des Infirmiers v France* (1986) DR 47, 225 (application on behalf of unidentified individuals).
2 Eg 8206/78, *X v United Kingdom* (1981) DR 25, 147.
3 This aspect has a close relationship with Art 17's prohibition on the abuse of rights: cf *Sidiropoulos and Others v Greece* 1998-IV, 1594, paras 28–29 (objection that the applicants were seeking to raise a question concerning the political relations between two countries rejected). See too 11208/84, *McQuiston v United Kingdom* (1986) DR 46, 182 (an application may be an abuse of the right of petition if motivated by the desire for publicity and not supported by any facts).
4 Eg 37664/97, 37665/97 and others, *R C and A W A and Ors v United Kingdom* (1998) DR 94, 119 (prohibition of possession of small-calibre pistols involved a complaint relating to the right to pursue a hobby and not one falling within the scope of Protocol 1, Art 1: manifestly ill-founded).

Meaning of 'victim'

2.29   In terms of Article 34, the Court 'may receive applications from any person, non-governmental organisation or group of individuals claiming to be the victim' of a violation of a substantive Convention guarantee by a state. A person can claim to be a 'victim' of an interference with the exercise of a right guaranteed under the Convention 'in the absence of an individual measure of implementation, [also] if they run the risk of being directly affected by it'[1]. Since the Human Rights Act 1998, s 7(1) provides that a person is to be regarded as a victim of an unlawful act under the statute only if he would be a 'victim' under Convention case law, more detailed discussion of this issue is appropriate. Bearing in mind the need to ensure that Convention guarantees are practical and effective, the necessary standing to qualify as a 'victim' is interpreted broadly.

1 *Norris v Ireland* (1988) A 142, at para 31. See also *Klass and Ors v Germany* (1978) A 28, paras 32–34.

2.30   The relevant principles established by the Strasbourg institutions can be summarised as follows[1]:

(1) The Convention does not permit an *actio popularis*. Individuals, associations or campaigning groups cannot therefore complain against a law *in abstracto* simply because they feel that it contravenes the Convention[2]. The applicant must be directly affected in some way by the matter complained of.

(2) The range of persons directly affected by a legal situation can, however, be extremely wide. For example, all users or potential users of a state's postal or telecommunication services could claim to be directly affected by legislation which provided for secret surveillance[3]. In another case, all women of childbearing age could claim to be victims of an injunction against the provision of information about abortion facilities[4].

(3) 'Victims' is not restricted to persons who can establish that their rights have actually been violated. A person who establishes that there is a reasonable likelihood that his rights have been violated

can be treated as a 'victim'[5]. It can also suffice if persons run the risk of being directly affected by the legal situation of which complaint is made[6]. Thus persons can be 'victims' even if they have not been individually affected by the implementation of the law complained of. Individuals have been held to be 'victims' by virtue of legal situations which, for example, criminalised homosexual behaviour or stigmatised untraditional families, even in the absence of the practical enforcement of the laws in question[7]. On the other hand, where there will be no violation of a convention right unless a particular decision is taken (eg as to deportation), a person cannot claim to be a 'victim' unless and until such a decision is in fact made[8].

(4)   A 'victim' need not be prejudiced by the act or omission in question, provided that he is directly affected by it[9]. The existence of prejudice is, however, relevant to the award of a remedy under Article 41[10].

(5)   A person may be a 'victim' if he is directly affected by the violation of another person's rights (eg the spouse of a person who is to be deported, allegedly in breach of Article 8)[11]. A person may also be an 'indirect victim' if, broadly speaking, he is prejudiced by the violation of another person's rights (notably, if he is the spouse or parent of a person killed in violation of Article 2)[12]. This should be distinguished from the question whether a person is entitled, under Strasbourg procedure, to bring proceedings in a representative capacity (eg if he is the parent of a young child or the guardian of a person of unsound mind)[13]. These categories tend to merge, and clear principles are difficult to state with confidence.

(6)   Legal persons, such as companies, can be 'victims'[14]. Shareholders cannot claim to be 'victims' in respect of a violation of the rights of the company, other than in exceptional circumstances (eg if it is impossible for the company to bring a complaint)[15]. A company can be a 'victim' even if dissolved or in receivership[16].

(7)   Unincorporated associations can be 'victims' if their own rights are violated[17], but not on the basis that an individual member's rights have been violated[18]. In Strasbourg proceedings, associations are permitted to bring complaints on behalf of their members[19]: it is necessary to bear in mind, in relation to such cases, that the association acts as a representative of the victim, and is not itself a 'victim'. The refusal of domestic law to recognise the legal personality of an organisation (in the particular case, a church) can itself constitute a violation of the Convention[20].

(8)   Governmental organisations, such as local authorities, cannot be 'victims'[21]. This follows from the terms of Article 34, which permits applications to be received from 'any person, non-governmental organisation or group of individuals claiming to be a victim of a violation by one of the High Contracting Parties of the rights set forth in the Convention or the protocols thereto'.

(9)   A person may not be treated as a 'victim' if the violation of his Convention rights has been acknowledged and redressed by the domestic authorities[22].

1 For a fuller account, see eg Van Dijk and Van Hoof *Theory and Practice of the European Convention on Human Rights* (3rd edn, 1998) pp 46–60.
2 *Klass v Germany* (1978) A 28, para 33.

3 *Klass v Germany* (1978) A 28, para 33.

4 *Open Door and Dublin Well Woman v Ireland* (1990) A 246, para 44.

5 *Halford v United Kingdom* 1997-III, 1004, paras 47–48 ; *Klass v Germany* (1978) A 28, paras 30–32; 12015/86, *Hilton v United Kingdom* (1988) DR 57, 108.

6 *Campbell and Cosans v United Kingdom* (1982) A 48, para 26; *Soering v United Kingdom* (1989) A 161, paras 81–91; *Marckx v Belgium* (1979) A 31, paras 25–27.

7 *Dudgeon v United Kingdom* (1982) A 45, para 41; *Marckx v Belgium* (1979) A 31, paras 25–27; cf *X, Y and Z v United Kingdom* 1997-II, 619, paras 36–43.

8 *Vijayanathan and Pusparajah v France* (1992) A 241–B, para 46; 9214/80, 9473/81 and 9474/81, *X, Cabales and Balkandali v United Kingdom* (1982) DR 29, 176; contrast *Soering v United Kingdom* (1989) A 161.

9 *Eckle v Germany* (1982) A 51, para 66; *Ludi v Switzerland* (1992) A 238, paras 31–34.

10 *Eckle v Germany* (1983) A 65, paras 20–24; *Ludi v Switzerland* (1992) A 238, para 52.

11 *Abdulaziz, Cabales and Balkandali v United Kingdom* (1982) A 94, 29 DR 176, para 65; *X, Y and Z v United Kingdom* 1997-II, 619.

12 E g *McCann v United Kingdom* (1995) A 324, para 151.

13 E g *Campbell and Cosans v United Kingdom* (1980) A 48 Comm Rep para 112.

14 E g *Observer Ltd and Guardian Newspapers Ltd v United Kingdom* (1991) A 216, para 49.

15 *Agrotexim and Ors v Greece* (1995) A 330-A, paras 59–72.

16 *Pine Valley Developments Ltd v Ireland* (1991) A 222, paras 40–43.

17 E g 11603/85 *Council of Civil Service Unions v United Kingdom* (1987) DR 50, 228.

18 7805/77 *X and Church of Scientology v Sweden* (1979) DR 16, 68; 10581/83 *Norris v Ireland*, (1988) DR 44, 132.

19 15404/89 *Purcell v Ireland* (1991) DR 70, 262; 11308/84 *Vereniging Rechtswinkel Utrecht v Netherlands* (1986) DR 46, 200.

20 *Catholic Church of Canea v Greece* 1997-VIII, 2843, paras 32–42.

21 13252/87 *Rothenthurm Commune v Switzerland* (1989) DR 59, 251.

22 E g *Eckle v Germany* (1982) A 51.

Payment of 'just satisfaction'

2.31   In terms of Article 41[1], the Court 'shall, if necessary, afford just satis-faction' to a person whose Convention rights have been found to have been violated 'if the internal law of the [state concerned] allows only partial reparation to be made'[2]. The Human Rights Act 1998, s 8 provides that before a court may award damages in relation to any act by a public authority which is found to be unlawful, it must be satisfied that the award is necessary to afford just satisfaction to the person in whose favour it is made[3]. The intention is that domestic courts should take into account the principles applied by the Strasbourg court in determining both whether an award should be made and also the level of compensation[4]. Article 41 'just satisfaction' awards can often be significantly lower than awards made by domestic courts since the Court determines its assess-ments in line with its own principles rather than with the scales used by domestic courts[5]. The problem for domestic courts is that Strasbourg case law on this issue is not always consistent[6].

In Strasbourg, an award of just satisfaction must be specifically requested by an applicant[7]. It is granted at the discretion of the Court, normally at the same time as a violation is established unless the Court deems it more appropriate to dispose of all or part of the Article 41 issue at a later stage[8]. 'Just satisfaction' covers pecuniary damage, non-pecuniary damage, and costs and expenses. The Court makes its assess-ment 'on an equitable basis, and having regard to its usual criteria'[9]. In respect of pecuniary damage, there must be a causal connection between the violation established and the loss alleged by an applicant, and the

Court will not speculate as to what the outcome of a matter would have been had there not been a breach of a state's obligations[10]. A wide range of factors may be relevant in assessing pecuniary damage, including, for example, depreciation in the value of property on account of pollution[11], real (rather than speculative) loss of development opportunities[12] or of earnings[13] or rental income[14], the costs of publishing a court judgment in a newspaper[15], criminal fines imposed upon an applicant[16], and depreciation in the real value of a compensation award on account of delay in payment[17]. However, the calculation of actual loss sustained may often be a difficult exercise for the Court, and in such circumstances it is likely to proceed upon the basis of consideration of what is 'equitable' in all the circumstances[18]. Non-pecuniary damage is awarded to compensate anxiety, pain and suffering arising from, for example, violation of respect for private life[19], unlawful detention[20], ill-treatment of detainees[21] or failure to carry out an investigation into their disappearance[22], undue delay in the administration of justice[23], and interference with freedom of religion[24]. The Court again seeks to determine what is 'a just and equitable amount of compensation' in all the circumstances of the case[25], and this is reflected in a tendency to deny claims for compensation in Article 6 cases which have involved only procedural breaches of fair hearing guarantees, and in other cases where applicants are considered not to be worthy, for example if they had been involved in terrorist activities[26]. The Court does not expressly award aggravated damages, but may take into account the seriousness of violations established and reflect this in the amount of compensation awarded for non-pecuniary damage[27]. However, in many instances the Court will simply conclude that the finding of a violation is in itself sufficient compensation[28], in particular, if the aim of the applicant in bringing a case was to secure a change in domestic law[29]. Further, the court may aggregate pecuniary and non-pecuniary damage without specifying how its assessment has been reached[30]. Finally, an award of costs and expenses may be made where an applicant has incurred these in order to prevent or to rectify a violation of Convention guarantees before the Strasbourg court, as long as it can be shown that the costs were 'actually and necessarily incurred and that they are reasonable as to quantum'[31].

1   Art 50 (original treaty).
2   See further Mas 'The Right to Compensation under Article 50' and Sansonetis 'Costs and Expenses', in Macdonald, Matscher and Petzold (eds) *The European System for the Protection of Human Rights* (1993) pp 775–790 and 755–773; and Tomuschat 'Just Satisfaction under Article 50 of the European Convention on Human Rights' in Mahoney, Matscher, Petzold and Wildhaber (eds) *Protecting Human Rights: The European Perspective* (2000) pp 1409–1430.
3   The Human Rights Act 1998, s 8(2) provides that damages may only be awarded by a court which has power to award damages or (in civil proceedings) to order the payment of compensation: see para 1.85 above.
4   Cf 582 HL Official Report (5th series) col 1232 (3 November1997) (Lord Chancellor). See further Feldman 'Remedies for Violation of Convention Rights after the Enactment of the Human Rights Act' [1998] EHRLR 691; Amos 'Damages for Breach of the Human Rights Act 1998' [1999] EHRLR 178.
5   *Osman v United Kingdom* 1998-VIII, 3124, para 164.
6   For recent discussions of the topic, see Reid *A Practitioner's Guide to the European Convention on Human Rights* (1998) pp 397–426; Carnwath 'ECHR Remedies from a Common Law Perspective' (2000) 49 ICLQ 517; *Damages under the Human Rights Act* (Law Com Discussion Paper no 266 and Scot Law Com Paper no 180) (Cm 4853) (2000), available at www.scotlawcom.gov.uk/ .

7 Cf *F E v France* 1998-VIII, 3332, paras 63–65 (award of non-pecuniary damage made, but no ruling on costs and expenses as the applicant had not submitted any such claim).

8 Eg *Guillemin v France* 1997-I, 149, paras 62–63 (issue in respect of pecuniary damage not ready for resolution; but sum awarded in respect of non-pecuniary damage since the applicant had indisputably sustained such); *Cyprus v Turkey* (10 May 2001) (question of damage not ready for resolution after the establishment of widespread and serious violations of rights in northern Cyprus).

9 *Aït-Mouhoub v France* 1998-VIII, 3214, at para 68.

10 Eg *Mauer v Austria* 1997-I, 76, para 40 (allegation that the applicant's plans for expanding his business had suffered: since the applicant had not established the existence or extent of such damage, no pecuniary damage awarded); *Findlay v United Kingdom* 1997-I, 263, paras 84–85 (impossible to speculate what the outcome of court-martial proceedings might have been, and thus no award in respect of pecuniary and non-pecuniary damage); *Radio ABC v Austria* 1997-VI, 2188, para 41 (claim based upon speculative assumption that the applicant company would have received a licence); *Kopp v Switzerland* 1998-II, 524, para 83 (causal connection between telephone interception and alleged loss not established).

11 *Lopèz Ostra v Spain* (1994) A 303-C, paras 62–65.

12 Eg *De Geoffre de la Pradelle v France* (1992) A 253-B, para 39 (exploitation of land hindered by lack of access to a court to challenge planning restrictions); cf *Podbielski v Poland* 1998-VIII, 3387, para 44 (claim based on lost business opportunities which were speculative in nature).

13 Eg *Young, James and Webster v United Kingdom* (1982) A 55, para 11.

14 Cf *Pammel v Germany* 1997-IV, 1096, para 78 (pecuniary loss of interest only which could not be calculated precisely but would be made on an equitable basis).

15 *De Haes and Gijsels v Belgium* 1997-I, 198, paras 61–63.

16 Eg *Jersild v Denmark* (1994) A 298, paras 42–43.

17 *Akkuş v Turkey* 1997-IV, 1300, paras 35–36.

18 Cf *Sporrong and Lönnroth v Sweden* (1984) A 85, paras 27–32.

19 Eg *Z v Finland* 1997-I, 323, para 122 (disclosure that the applicant was HIV positive without the consent of the patient); *Halford v United Kingdom* 1997-III, 1004, para 76 (interception of telephones); but cf *Kopp v Switzerland* 1998-II, 524, para 80 (finding of a violation of Art 8 on account of interception of communications constituted sufficient compensation in itself); *Smith and Grady v United Kingdom* (25 July 2000) paras 12–13 (dismissal of homosexuals from the armed forces).

20 *Johnson v United Kingdom* 1997-VII, 2391, para 77 (mental health detention: applicant's behaviour taken into account in the calculation of the award); but cf *Nikolova v Bulgaria* 1999–II, 203, paras 70–76 (unlawful detention on remand; finding of violation of Art 5(3) and (4) was sufficient compensation since the Court was not prepared to speculate whether the applicant would have been detained had there been no violations).

21 Eg *Aydin v Turkey* 1997-VI, 1866, para 131 (rape of the applicant while in police custody).

22 Eg *Kaya v Turkey* 1998-I, 297, para 122.

23 Eg *Stamoulakatos v Greece (No 2)* 1997-VII, 2640, paras 46–49; *Pailot v France* 1998-II, 787, para 76.

24 Eg *Larissis and Others v Greece* 1998-I, 362, para 74.

25 *Halford v United Kingdom* 1997-III, 1004, at para 76.

26 Reid *A Practitioner's Guide to the European Convention on Human Rights* (1998) p 402, citing, eg *McCann and Ors v United Kingdom* (1995) A 324, para 219.

27 Eg *Selçuk and Asker v Turkey* 1998-II, 891, paras 117–118 (destruction of houses and other property by armed forces).

28 Eg *Mantovanelli v France* 1997-II, 424, para 40.

29 Eg *Dudgeon v United Kingdom* (1983) A 59, para 21.

30 Eg *Tsirlis and Kouloumpas v Greece* 1997-III, 909, para 80 (compensation for unlawful detention).

31 *Niederöst-Huber v Switzerland* 1997-I, 101, at para 40. Legal fees will be scrutinised with care: e g *Z v Finland* 1997-I, 323, paras 123 and 126 (certain costs and expenses awarded, but other legal expenses were not necessarily incurred); cf *Robins v United Kingdom* 1997-V, 1801, paras 42–44 (an applicant sought compensation for the time spent preparing the case at the level equivalent to that of a solicitor or barrister: the Court's award appears to have included a token award in this respect). The applicant's attendance at Strasbourg will be reimbursed under this heading where this serves a useful purpose: *Sunday Times*

(No 1) v United Kingdom (1980) A 38, para 33; but cf *Halford v United Kingdom* 1997-III, 1004, para 79 (attendance of the applicant in Strasbourg covered by an award of pecuniary loss).

The Role of the Committee of Ministers in the Supervision of the Execution of Judgments

2.32 Final judgments are binding on the state which is a party to a case[1]. The obligation to comply with a judgment of the Court may involve payment of any sum of money which has been awarded to an applicant in the form of just satisfaction[2], and may in addition extend to the taking of specific or general measures to comply with a judgment[3]. The Committee of Ministers has retained its responsibility for supervising the execution of judgments by verifying whether states have so complied[4]. To this end, a judgment will remain on the agenda of the Committee of Ministers until it is satisfied that appropriate action has been taken[5]; in certain cases, interim resolutions may be adopted which seek to assess the extent to which progress is being made[6]. Specific measures taken for the benefit of an individual may include, for example, the re-opening of a criminal case by re-examination of the evidence[7], an undertaking not to execute a criminal sentence and to annul the record of a conviction[8], and the granting of indefinite leave to remain in a country to an individual facing expulsion[9]. A judgment may also require the implementation of general measures involving constitutional, legislative or administrative reform[10].

1 Art 46(1); Arts 32 and 54 (original treaty).
2 See para 2.31 above.
3 For a survey of the effects of judgments or cases in domestic law, see European Court of Human Rights, *Survey: Forty Years of Activities 1959–1998* (1999) pp 86–113; and Lambert *Les Effects des Arrêts de la Cour Européenne des Droits de l'Homme* (1999).
4 Art 46(2). The task is discharged by the Committee of Ministers working in co-operation with the Directorate General of Human Rights and the relevant national authorities. See further Zwaak 'The Implementation of Decisions of the Supervisory Organs under the European Convention on Human Rights' and Alkema 'Implementing the Decisions of the Supervisory Bodies of the ECHR – Exploring Present Possibilities' in Barkhuysen, van Emmerik, and van Kempen (eds) *The Execution of Strasbourg and Geneva Human Rights Decisions in the National Legal Order* (1999) pp 75–88 and 89–99; and Council of Europe 'Control of the Execution of Judgments and Decisions under the European Convention on Human Rights' Doc H/Conf (2000) 8. For (a now dated) discussion of UK compliance, see Churchill and Young 'Compliance with Judgments of the European Court of Human Rights and Decisions of the Committee of Ministers: The Experience of the United Kingdom, 1975–1987' (1991) 62 BYBIL 283; for discussion of the impact upon domestic legal systems, see Gearty (ed) *European Civil Liberties and the European Convention on Human Rights* (1997).
5 Eg Resolution DH (88) 003 (in relation to the judgment in *Marckx v Belgium* in 1979 concerning establishment of maternal affiliation and discrimination in inheritance rights on the grounds of illegitimacy: period of eight years and nine months between judgment and final resolution which noted various amendments to domestic law).
6 Eg Interim Resolution DH (2000) 27 (concerning the judgment in *Saunders v United Kingdom*: interim guidance note from the Attorney General on the handling of prosecutions and enactment of amending legislation which is still to be brought into force); Interim Resolution DH (99) 680 (concerning the judgment in *Loizidou v Turkey*: the resolution 'deplor[ed]' Turkey's failure to pay the sums awarded as just satisfaction, 'stress[ed]' the nature of the obligation, and 'strongly urg[ed]' Turkey to review its position; a note by the Directorate General of Human Rights indicated that the failure to pay just satisfaction was a situation which was 'unprecedented').

7 Eg Resolution DH (89) 002 (in relation to the judgment in *Unterpertinger v Austria*).
8 Eg Resolution DH (85) 004 (in relation to the Commission's report in 9193/80, *Marijnissen v Netherlands* (29 June 1980)).
9 Eg Resolution DH (98) 10 (concerning the judgment in *D v United Kingdom*).
10 Eg Resolution DH (99) 555 (concerning the judgment in *Ciraklar v Turkey* in 1998: amendment to the Constitution to alter the composition of national security courts); Resolution DH (92) 40 (concerning the judgment in *Huvig v France*: new legislative provisions concerning the interception of telecommunications); and Resolution DH (99) 20 (concerning 19092/91, *Yağiz v Turkey*, report of 1995: administrative circular introducing new rules for regulation of police detention and procedural safeguards).

OTHER COUNCIL OF EUROPE HUMAN RIGHTS INITIATIVES

2.33   The Council of Europe's work in human rights extends beyond the European Convention on Equality and Human Rights. These additional instruments and initiatives complement the protection of the individual[1], although greater synthesis may be desirable[2]. Some understanding of these treaties and bodies (and of other international human rights provisions)[3] is necessary, for the Court may refer to these in its deliberations[4].

1 There are other human rights initiatives of the Council of Europe in addition to the bodies and treaties considered below. In particular, a Steering Committee for Equality between Women and Men seeks to promote equal treatment and to prevent the trafficking of women and children for the purpose of sexual exploitation: see further 'Positive Action in the Field of Equality between Women and Men', Doc EG-S-PA (2000) 7, and para 4.41, below. In central and east Europe, the Council's Programmes for Democratic Stability seek to raise awareness of human rights amongst judges, lawyers and police officers, and provides expert opinions on the compatibility of legislation with European human rights norms.
2 Cf comments of Tarschys, Secretary General of the Council of Europe, that greater coherence and the development of a 'truly comprehensive "system" of [European] Human Rights protection' were still needed: in Council of Europe *In Our Hands: The Effectiveness of Human Rights Protection 50 Years after the Universal Declaration* (1998) at p 21. See further Imbert 'Complementarity of Mechanisms Within the Council of Europe: Perspectives of the Directorate of Human Rights' (2000) 21 HRLJ 292.
3 The key international instruments of relevance in civil and political rights include the International Convention on the Elimination of All Forms of Racial Discrimination (1965); the International Covenant on Civil and Political Rights (1966); the Convention on the Elimination of All Forms of Discrimination against Women (1979) (and the Optional Protocol of 1999); the Declaration on the Elimination of All Forms of Intolerance and of Discrimination Based on Religion or Belief (1981); the Convention Against Torture and other Cruel, Inhuman or Degrading Treatment or Punishment (1984); the United Nations Convention on the Rights of the Child (1989); and the Declaration on the Rights of Persons Belonging to National or Ethnic, Religious and Linguistic Minorities (1992). For examples of the use of such instruments, see e g *Streletz, Kessler and Krenz v Germany* (22 March 2001), paras 98–106 (the applicants' conduct also constituted offences under international law).
4 Eg *Van der Mussele v Belgium* (1983) A 70, para 32 (reference to ILO Convention in discussion of Art 4); *Sigurdur A Sigurjónsson v Iceland* (1993) A 264, para 35 (references to the Universal Declaration of Human Rights, European Social Charter and ILO Conventions in discussion of Art 11). See further, para 3.22 below. For discussion of the use of European Committee against Torture (CPT) reports, see para 4.39, below. Discussion of other conventions, etc in Strasbourg case law has received little academic attention. It can be justified on occasion to ensure that a state which enters into other international obligations does not thereby infringe existing responsibilities under the European Human Rights Convention: cf 21072/92, *Gestra v Italy* (1995) DR 80, 89; and *Matthews v United Kingdom* 1991-I, 251, discussed below at para 7.61. More positively, however, it can help ensure a 'progressive' interpretation of Convention guarantees 'plus ample que celle qui était

manifestement dans l'intention des auteurs du texte': Conforti 'Quelques Réflexions sur les Rapports de la Convention Européenne des Droits de l'Homme avec d'Autres Conventions' in de Salvia and Villiger (eds) *The Birth of European Human Rights Law* (1998) pp 47–52 at 48. Regular liaison between Council of Europe organs and UN treaty-based bodies takes place: Weitzel and Strasser 'The Relationship between the European Convention on Human Rights and Other International Enforcement Mechanisms', in de Salvia and Villiger (eds) above, pp 347–363 at 348–349.

Furthering protection for physical integrity: the European Committee for the Prevention of Torture and Inhuman or Degrading Treatment or Punishment

2.34   European states have accepted new obligations with a view to furthering the protection of persons deprived of their liberty by allowing access to places of detention to an international body[1]. The European Convention for the Prevention of Torture and Inhuman or Degrading Treatment or Punishment is now an established safeguard for detainees and an influential source of new minimum standards and expectations[2]. This treaty is designed to complement the European Convention on Human Rights; further, the body established by the treaty, the European Committee for the Prevention of Torture and Inhuman or Degrading Treatment or Punishment (the CPT), has started to pose some challenge to the Commission's traditional reluctance to criticise detention conditions, and may indeed now have succeeded in encouraging the new Court to adopt a more critical approach and to revise existing jurisprudence[3]. The Committee achieves its goal not through a system of complaint and confrontation but through the process of dialogue and discussion with state officials following upon visits to places of detention[4]. The key to its success lies in this power of visit. While in general reporting systems rely primarily upon the good faith of state parties, the strategy of allowing an independent body to investigate detention conditions is of particular value where the primary goal is the prevention of human rights violations. The work of the Committee is surrounded by a guarantee of confidentiality, and thus information on discussions during meetings with officials or on Committee findings and recommendations may not be disclosed. However, states now invariably request publication of reports and governmental responses[5]. In its work, the CPT has also developed codes of standards or expectations which it employs during visits to help assess existing practices and to encourage states to meet its criteria of acceptable arrangements and conditions. These emerging standards are for the most part more detailed and more demanding than those found in other international obligations, and are now having some impact through the implementation of recommendations for the introduction of legislative, administrative and organisational reforms at domestic level[6].

1 Other Council of Europe initiatives seeking to promote protection for detainees include recommendations and resolutions of the Committee of Ministers on such matters as the recruitment and training of prison staff (Resolution (66) 26); custody pending trial (Recommendation No (80) 11); and the custody and treatment of dangerous prisoners (Recommendation No (82) 17).
2 ETS No 126 (1987) The inspiration for the Committee is drawn from the work of the International Committee of the Red Cross which pioneered the notion of protecting detained persons through a system of visits to places of detention by an expert and

impartial body. The proposal for a European treaty was made to the Council of Europe by the International Commission of Jurists and by the Swiss Committee against Torture. Prompt ratification followed the Convention's adoption in 1987, and the treaty came into force in 1989. See, further, Evans and Morgan 'The CPT: An Introduction' in Morgan and Evans *Protecting Prisoners: The Standards of the CPT in Context* (1999) pp 3–30. For discussion of the impact of CPT standards on the European Prison Rules, see Murdoch 'CPT Standards within the Context of the Council of Europe' in Evans and Morgan, above, pp 106–110. A yearbook is now published which features membership, reports, etc.

3 See para 4.39 below. For an example of the CPT's influence in the disposal of fair trial issues under Art 6, see para 5.70 below.

4 The CPT has authority to visit places of detention where individuals – of whatever age, or whatever nationality, or on whatever ground – have been deprived of their liberty on account of official or state action. This will thus include deprivation of liberty which takes place in private as well as in public institutions such as police stations, prisons, mental hospitals holding patients subject to compulsory detention, immigration centres, and military detention centres. Visits may take place even in times of war or other public emergency (although in certain circumstances where there is armed conflict visits by the International Committee of the Red Cross may replace those by the CPT). The Committee first visited Scottish prisons and police stations in 1994. For its findings (which included critical observations on Barlinnie Prison, Glasgow), see CPT/Inf (96) 11 (available at www.cpt.coe.int).

5 See further Murdoch 'The European Convention for the Prevention of Torture and Inhuman or Degrading Treatment or Punishment: Activities in 1999' (2000) 25 EL Rev HR 212. In certain circumstances, the Committee may issue a public statement on conditions in any particular country. The earliest reports in respect of the CPT's frequent visits to Turkey have never been published, although some flavour of the CPT's findings are apparent in the two public statements issued by the Committee. Reports (and further information on the CPT) are available at www.cpt.coe.int .

6 See further paras 4.38 and 6.50 below.

Protecting minorities and combating racism

2.35   The re-drawing of the boundaries of nation states after the 1914–18 war first promoted international legal concern for the protection of the rights of minorities in Europe[1]. The establishment of independent states after the collapse of communism in central and eastern Europe from 1989 onwards gave political expression to the democratic aspirations of ethnic groups but also led to xenophobia and racism. European state boundaries contain – as in the past – minorities which are ethnically linked with the population of other nation states or which (as with Romany gipsies or the *Sama* of Lapland) share a distinct racial origin without a 'homeland'. In Europe, protection of cultural pluralism and prevention of discrimination are again of some concern[2].

1 That is, through peace treaties or League of Nations treaties concluded with states which were formerly part of the Austro–Hungarian empire, or through declarations made before admission to the League of Nations: Robertson and Merrills *Human Rights in the World* (4th edn, 1996) pp 20–23; and Evans *Religious Liberty and International Law in Europe* (1997) pp 75–171.

2 See further Council of Europe *The Protection of Minorities* (1994); and Matscher (ed) *Vienna International Encounter on Current Issues Regarding National Minorities* (1997). For discussion of domestic law, see Poulter *Ethnicity, Law and Human Rights: The English Experience* (1998); and, for international law, see Lerner *Group Rights and Discrimination in International Law* (1991); Phillips and Rosas (eds) *Universal Minority Rights* (1995); and Trechsel 'Human Rights and Minority Rights – Two Sides of the Same Coin?' in Mahoney, Matscher, Petzold and Wildhaber (eds) *Protecting Human Rights: The European Perspective* (2000) pp 1437–1453.

The Framework Convention for the Protection of National Minorities

2.36 The Framework Convention for the Protection of National Minorities, which entered into force in February 1998, is the first binding treaty in international law to seek to protect national minorities in states[1]. The Preamble acknowledges the historical background and political impetus behind the treaty: the disintegration of former central and east European states and the realisation that there were limits to the extent that emerging democracies would promote pluralism within their frontiers. Implicit, too, is the concern that a charter of civil and political rights such as the European Convention on Human Rights is not an appropriate instrument for the protection of minority groups[2]. The Preamble specifically refers to the consideration that 'a pluralist and genuinely democratic society should not only respect the ethnic, cultural, linguistic and religious identity of each person belonging to a national minority, but also create appropriate conditions enabling them to express, preserve and develop this identity' and, further, that cultural diversity should be seen as a matter of enrichment rather than division[3]. In these respects, the Framework Convention echoes the underlying assumption found in the European Convention on Human Rights that pluralism and tolerance are the hallmarks of democratic society.

Article 1 of the Framework Convention refers to 'the protection of national minorities and of the rights and freedoms of persons belonging to national minorities'. No collective rights are thus envisaged, although it is recognised that 'the protection of a national minority can be achieved through protection of the rights of individuals belonging to such a minority'[4]. There is no definition, however, of what constitutes a national minority since the framers found it difficult to arrive at a formulation which would have commanded general political support and have avoided problems with legal interpretation[5]. The substantive provisions are found in Articles 4–19, and comprise a range of undertakings including the promotion of effective equality and of the conditions necessary for the preservation and development of religion, language and cultural traditions. The Framework Convention also makes provision for freedoms of assembly, association, expression, thought, conscience and religion, access to the media and to education, linguistic freedoms, and participation in public, cultural and social life. These rights are not directly applicable, and are best considered as a series of programme goals assumed by states[6] rather than as imposing obligations enforceable by judicial means. An Advisory Committee comprising persons with recognised expertise in the field of the protection of national minorities and who serve in their individual capacities for four years is charged with the monitoring on behalf of the Committee of Ministers of the implementation of action taken by states based upon periodic reports submitted by state parties[7].

1 ETS No 157 (1995). The Vienna Declaration of Heads of State and Government of 1993 provided the impetus for the treaty. See further, Council of Europe *Framework Convention for the Protection of National Minorities: Collected Texts* (1999). As at 31 August 2001, the treaty has been ratified by all Council of Europe states with the exception of Andorra, Belgium, France, Georgia, Greece, Iceland, Latvia, Luxembourg, Netherlands, and Portugal, and is in force in Bosnia and Hercegovina. In respect of the United Kingdom, the treaty entered into force in May 1998.

2 Cf Explanatory Report, para 1, which notes that as early as 1961 the Parliamentary Assembly had recommended that guarantees for national minorities be included by way of an additional Protocol to the ECHR. The Court's decision in the *Belgian Linguistics* case (1968) A 6, illustrates the limits of the Human Rights Convention in this respect: see para 6.52, below. In *Cyprus v Turkey* (10 May 2001), however, the Court found multiple violations of the rights of the enclaved Greek Cypriot community living in northern Cyprus: see paras 4.36, 6.52 and 7.08 below.

3 The inspiration for this comes from the United Nations Declaration on the Rights of Persons belonging to National or Ethnic, Religious and Linguistic Minorities of 1992: Commentary, para 24.

4 Commentary, at para 31. Art 3 guarantees to every person belonging to a national minority the right to decide whether to be treated as so belonging: that is, it is open to individuals to decide whether they wish to seek the protection of the Framework Convention: Explanatory Report, para 34.

5 Commentary, para 12. The first United Kingdom Report adopts a distinctly Anglo-centric view: the British Government's report proceeds upon the basis that 'national minorities' are to include 'our ethnic communities (or visible minorities) and the Scots, Irish and Welsh, who are defined as a racial group by virtue of their national origins': doc ACFC/SR (99) 13, at para 2.

6 Explanatory Report, para 11.

7 Arts 24–26. See further Committee of Ministers Resolution (97) 10; and *Rules of Procedure of the Advisory Committee on the Framework Convention for the Protection of National Minorities* (1998).

The European Charter for Regional or Minority Languages

2.37 The European Charter for Regional or Minority Languages, adopted in 1992 and entering into force in 1998[1], encourages states to undertake to base legislative and administrative policies on principles designed to protect regional and minority languages[2], and to adopt measures to promote their use in public life (that is, in education and judicial proceedings, by administrative authorities and the public service, in respect of the media, and in cultural, economic and social life)[3]. States submit periodic reports on policies and measures adopted which are scrutinised by a committee of experts who prepare a report for consideration by the Committee of Ministers[4].

1 ETS NO 148 (1992). See further Dunbar 'Implications of the European Charter for Regional or Minority Languages for British Linguistic Minorities' (2000) 25 EL Rev HR 46; and Dunbar 'Minority Language Rights in International Law' (2001) 50 ICLQ 90. For an international perspective, see de Varennes *Language, Minorities and Human Rights* (1996).

2 Defined by Art 1(a) as those languages that are 'traditionally used within a given territory of a State by nationals of that State who form a group numerically smaller than the rest of the State's population, and different from the official language(s) of that State; [but] it does not include either dialects of the official language(s) of the State or the languages of migrants'.

3 Arts 7–14.

4 Arts 15 and 16. Committee members are appointed in accordance with Art 17, and serve for a renewable period of six years and are to be persons of 'the highest integrity and recognised competence'. State reports are made public, and the reports of the committee of experts may be made public by the Committee of Ministers.

The European Commission against Racism and Intolerance

2.38 The European Commission against Racism and Intolerance (ECRI) seeks to combat racism, xenophobia, anti-semitism and intolerance by combating discrimination and prejudice on grounds of race, colour, language, religion, nationality and national or ethnic origin[1]. The Commission, which is composed of independent members, examines the relevant situation in states and prepares reports with recommendations for action by governments. Initially, draft texts of these reports are communicated to aid what the Commission hopes will be a process of confidential dialogue; the final report is made public two months after it has been transmitted unless the state concerned expressly requests that this should not take place[2]. Thereafter, the Commission will monitor what action is taken by national authorities in respect of any proposals made[3]. The Commission may also make general policy recommendations and disseminate examples of good practice to states[4].

1 The decision to establish the Commission was taken at the Summit of Heads of State and Government in Vienna in 1993, and the Committee began its work in 1994. Members of the Commission are nominated by states on the basis of recognised expertise in the area of tackling intolerance.

2 For reports to the United Kingdom, see Docs CRI (99) 5 and CRI (2001) 6 (the latter report recommended action to address a hostile climate concerning asylum seekers and refugees, to make effective criminal law provisions on incitement to racial hatred and civil rules on anti-discrimination, to tackle institutionalised racism in the police service, and to ensure the education system reflects the needs of a diverse society).

3 The Commission arranges contact visits to states to allow its rapporteurs to meet government officials and non-governmental organisations. See further ECRI's annual reports (e g Annual Report for 2000, CRI (2001) 20, available at www.ecri.coe.int) .

4 Including general policy recommendations on intolerance against Roma and Muslims, the establishment of specialised bodies at national level, and combating the dissemination of racist etc material on the internet; and good practices on combatting racism and intolerance in the media: see further Council of Europe 'Compilation of ECRI's General Policy Recommendations' Doc CRI (2001) 7.

Economic and social rights: the European Social Charter

2.39 Guarantees for social and economic human rights concerning conditions of employment and social cohesion are found in the European Social Charter of 1961 and its three additional Protocols[1]. The Charter guarantees a series of rights concerning in the areas of housing, health, education, employment[2] and social protection[3], the most crucial of which relate to the right to work (Article 1), to organise (Article 5) and to bargain collectively (Article 6), to social security (Article 12) and to social, legal and economic protection (Article 16). States may decide at the time of ratification which obligations they wish to undertake although there is a 'hard core' of rights (as well as a minimum number) to which they must subscribe[4]. The revised European Social Charter of 1996[5] aims to broaden protection against discrimination and to provide additional economic and social rights in the workplace[6], the right to decent housing, and the right to protection against poverty and social exclusion.

Supervision is by means of international scrutiny of reports submitted at periodic intervals by states. These are initially considered by the European Committee of Social Rights (formerly the Committee of Independent Experts) whose reports in turn provide a legal assessment of the extent of state compliance with their obligations under the Charter. This report is then transmitted to a Governmental Committee which may prepare recommendations for the Committee of Ministers to adopt by way of recommendations to states if it appears that there has been non-compliance[7]. Since July 1998, this process may now involve the examination of collective complaints[8].

1 ETS No 35 (1961), ETS No 128 (1988), ETS No 142 (1991) and ETS No 158 (1995). See further Gomien, Harris and Zwaak *Law and Practice of the European Convention on Human Rights and the European Social Charter* (1996) pp 377–437; Council of Europe *European Social Charter: Short Guide* (2000); and Council of Europe *European Social Charter: Collected Texts* (2nd edn, 2000).

2 Including rights to: vocational guidance and vocational training; protection in the work environment; just conditions of work; fair remuneration (including the right of women and men to equal pay for work of equal value); organise and bargain collectively; information and consultation (including participation in the determination and improvement of the working conditions and working environment).

3 Including rights to social security; to social and medical assistance, and to benefit from social welfare services. Other rights confer special protection outwith the work environment for children and young persons, mothers and families, handicapped and elderly persons, and migrant workers and their families.

4 The United Kingdom has accepted all obligations except for Arts 2(1), 4(3), 7(1), (4), (7) and (8), 8(2)–(4) and 12 (2)–(4). It has not as yet ratified the Additional Protocol of 1988 or the Amending Protocol of 1991, the Collective Complaints Protocol of 1995, or the Revised European Social Charter of 1996.

5 ETS No 163 (1996). The revised Social Charter will progressively replace the first Charter as states in time ratify this new instrument which was opened for signature in 1996 and entered into force on 1 July 1999.

6 Including the right to protection in cases of termination of employment, and the right of workers with family responsibilities to equal opportunities and treatment.

7 Since 1992, the Parliamentary Assembly has also based its social policy reports on the conclusions of the Committee of Independent Experts. See further www.humanrights. coe.int/cseweb/GB/index.htm . For discussion of the United Kingdom's record, see Ewing 'Social Rights and Human Rights: Britain and the Social Charter – the Conservative Legacy' [2000] EHRLR 91.

8 See further Council of Europe *European Social Charter: Short Guide* (2000) pp 15–17. Complaints may now be lodged by management, labour and non-governmental organisations (NGOs). For the first decision on admissibility of a collective complaint, see 1/1998 *International Commission of Jurists v Portugal* (1 February 1999). See further Cullen 'The Collective Complaints Mechanism of the European Social Charter' (2000) 25 EL Rev HR 18.

Promoting awareness and respect: the Council of Europe Commissioner for Human Rights

2.40   The Council of Europe Commissioner for Human Rights was first appointed in 1999[1] and is charged with the promotion of human rights by raising awareness of human rights and ensuring their effective respect in Council of Europe member states. This office is designed to complement existing institutions and to play a preventive role (for example, by identifying shortcomings in domestic law and practice). The Commissioner is expected to exercise his functions with complete independence and impartiality while at the same time respecting the competence of the various Council of Europe supervisory bodies. He is thus a non-judicial officer who does not investigate individual complaints but can still act (within the general authority of promoting human rights) on any relevant information made available to him. He submits an annual report on his work to the Committee of Ministers and the Parliamentary Assembly of the Council of Europe, and takes into account views expressed by these institutions concerning the Commissioner's activities. The Commissioner may also issue recommendations, opinions and reports on any matters within his competence[2].

1 The office was approved at the Summit of Heads of State and Government in October 1997, and the resolution setting out the Commissioner's terms of reference was adopted by the Committee of Ministers in May 1999. The Commissioner for Human Rights is elected by the Parliamentary Assembly, by a majority of votes cast, from a list of three candidates drawn up by the Committee of Ministers and hold office for a non-renewable term of office of six years. Candidates must be nationals of a Council of Europe member state and have recognised expertise in the field of human rights. For discussion of the use of such offices in domestic human rights protection, see Reif 'The Promotion of International Human Rights Law by the Office of Ombudsman' in Reif (ed) *The International Ombudsman Anthology* (1999) pp 271–315.

2 Documents concerning the work of the Commissioner are available at www. commissioner.coe.int . For discussion of the office (and its possible future development) see Trechsel 'A European Commissioner for Human Rights for the European Court of Human Rights?' in Haller, Krüger and Petzold *Law in Greater Europe: Towards a Common Legal Area* (2000) pp 178–189.

RESEARCHING HUMAN RIGHTS LAW

Strasbourg case law

2.41　In giving effect to Convention rights, the Human Rights Act 1998, s 2 requires courts and tribunals to take into account Court judgments, decisions, declarations or advisory opinions; Commission reports on the merits of applications; Commission decisions on admissibility; and decisions of the Committee of Ministers on a case which has not been decided by the Court[1]. The most important of these sources of ECHR law will be Court judgments and Commission decisions on admissibility and reports on the merits of applications. However, since there are few provisions which have not now been examined exhaustively by the Court, Commission reports are likely to be of limited assistance[2]. Further, the substantial increase in the new Court's workload is generating considerable opportunity for clarification of admissibility criteria which should now be considered as indicative of current interpretation.

1 Human Rights Act 1998, s 2 and Scotland Act 1998, s 129(2) (which requires courts to apply HRA 1998, s 2). See further para 1.62 above.

2 For example, Court judgments dominate interpretation of Arts 5 and 6 (although Commission decisions on admissibility are still of importance in discussion of the scope of Art 5 in determining what constitutes a 'deprivation of liberty': see paras 4.47–4.49 below). In contrast, Protocol 1, Art 3's guarantees of fair elections still require considerable discussion of Commission jurisprudence. Until comparatively recently, Arts 2 and 3 had generated little in the way of Court discussion, but the relative importance of Commission decisions and reports in these areas has now been weakened considerably on account of a number of cases involving (in particular) Turkey and the United Kingdom.

NAMES OF APPLICANTS

2.42　Court decisions on admissibility and judgments are cited by the name of the applicant and the respondent state, but rules of court provide that 'applicants who do not wish their identity to be disclosed to the public shall so indicate and shall submit a statement of the reasons justifying such a departure from the normal rule of public access to information in proceedings before the Court', and that anonymity may be authorised by the President of the Chamber 'in exceptional and duly justified cases'[1]. In such instances, applicants will be identified by the letters of their surnames (or, in earlier practice, by the use of a formula such as *X v United Kingdom*). A judgment is cited by the surname of the applicant, and with the addition of the applicant's first name where this is necessary to distinguish it from an earlier case[2].

1 Rule of Court 47(3).
2 Thus *Murray v United Kingdom* (1994) A 300-A; and *John Murray v United Kingdom* 1996-I, 30. Cases involving the same applicant are distinguished thus eg *Olsson v Sweden (No 1)* (1988) A 130, and *Olsson v Sweden (No 2)* (1992) A 250.

Primary sources

2.43   Official publications of the Council of Europe are generally available in print. The University of Glasgow Library is the only institution in Scotland with Council of Europe depositary status, and this collection is open for general consultation. However, most significant documents are now available over the Internet[1], and since only a selection of the 'new' Court's judgments and reports on admissibility will now be available in printed reports, use of the Council of Europe's electronic database will be increasingly necessary. Strasbourg case law is also reported in *European Human Rights Reports*, *European Human Rights Law Review* and *Human Rights Law Journal*.

1 All sites referred to in this chapter are as accessed at 31 August 2001.

COMMISSION DECISIONS AND REPORTS, AND CITATIONS

2.44   Until 1999, the Commission gave *decisions* on the admissibility of applications, and issued *reports* on their merits. In this work, Commission decisions and reports are cited by application number and names of the parties: eg 9267/81, *Moureaux and Ors v Belgium* (1983) DR 33, 97. Where a decision or report is unpublished, the date is given[1]: eg 21221/93, *L J v Finland* (28 June 1995). Fuller citations (and relevant references to *European Human Rights Reports*) appear in the list of cases.

A selection of key cases is found in *Collection of Decisions* (from 1959 until 1974) in 46 volumes and in *Decisions and Reports* (from 1975 until 1998): in 94 volumes (volumes 76 onwards appeared in two versions: the 'A' volume contained the text in the official working language for the application (that is, in either English or French) with volume 'B' appearing subsequently with translations). In addition, the *Yearbook of the European Convention on Human Rights* contains certain decisions and reports not readily accessible elsewhere. Further, *Series B* reports include the Commission's report in cases considered by the Court (as well as other relevant documents including written submissions to the Court), but this series terminated with volume 104 in 1995. Commission reports thereafter appear as an appendix to Court judgments in the *Series A* reports (and their continuation in *Reports of Judgments and Decisions*).

Citation of decisions and reports is thus somewhat complex[2]. Where a decision or report appears in more than one publication, only one reference is required, with the preferred citation in the case of decisions that of the *Collection* or *Decisions and Reports*. All applications are allocated a reference number, and *decisions* are normally cited by this number alone, unless it is considered necessary to specify the name of the respondent state. Decisions are cited in the following manner:

No 1706/62, Dec 4.10.66, Collection 21, p 34.
No 7624/76, *X v Austria*, Dec. 6.7.77, D.R. 19, p 100.
No 1850/63, Dec. 29.3.66, Yearbook 9, p 241 [where a decision is published solely in the *Yearbook*].
No 7162/75, Dec. 18.5.76, unpublished.

Reports may appear in a variety of official publications as follows, and are generally cited without the application number (although, in this work, the number is also given):

Köplinger v Austria, Comm. Report 1.10.68, para 24, Yearbook 12, p 484
Jespers v Belgium, Comm. Report 14.12.81, para 55, D.R. 27, p. 87
Golder v United Kingdom, Comm. Report 1.6.73, para 53, Eur Court HR, Series B no 16, p 38 [for a report published solely in the Series B reports]
Benthem v the Netherlands, Comm. Report 8.10.83, para 95, Eur Court HR, Series A no 97, p 24 [for reports published in Series A and appended to the judgments of the Court]
F.E v France, Comm. Report 22.4.1998, para 46, Eur Court HR, Reports 1999, p 3362 [for a report published in *Reports of Judgments and Decisions* and appended to the judgments of the Court].

1 Unreported decisions and reports are available from the Council of Europe's Human Rights Information Centre. Unpublished reports from 1986 onwards (and some pre-1986 unpublished reports) are available on the HUDOC website: see para 2.48 below.
2 See Council of Europe 'Directive Concerning Quotations, References and Abbreviations in the Decisions and Reports of the Commission' (December 1996).

COURT JUDGMENTS, DECISIONS ON ADMISSIBILITY, AND CITATIONS

2.45 Judgments of the Court from 1961 onwards appear in English and French in the *Series A* reports of the European Court of Human Rights and, from 1996 onwards, in the continuation of this series in *Reports of Judgments and Decisions*. In this work, Court judgments are cited for the sake of brevity as, for example *T v Italy* (1992) A 245-C (the reference to the number of the report); or *Texeira de Castro v Portugal* 1998-IV, 1451 (the latter number being the first page of the report). Fuller citations (and relevant references to *European Human Rights Reports*) appear in the list of cases.

Cases (and relevant judicial observations) before 1999 are cited by the Court in its judgments in the following format:

Eur Court HR, *T v Italy* judgment of 12 October 1992, Series A no 245-C, p 41, para 25
Eur Court HR, *Fouquet v France* judgment of 31 January 1996, Reports 1996-I, p 38, para 44.

Where it is clear from the context that reference is being made to a Court decision, 'Eur Court HR' is omitted.

DECISIONS ON ADMISSIBILITY AND JUDGMENTS OF THE 'NEW' COURT

2.46 From November 1998, the *Reports of Judgments and Decisions* will contain a selection of decisions on admissibility and judgments of the new Court. However, only those decisions and judgments considered as being of some significance will appear: it is understood that around one judgment in seven will be selected. At present, there is a delay between the date of decision or judgment and publication of the official report of approximately two years, and where a judgment has not appeared in print, the date of the judgment is given in this work: if the case has been reported in *European Human Rights Reports*, the reference also appears in the list of cases. In these circumstances, use of the Court's website is likely to be necessary to obtain the text of the judgment. Note, however, that many decisions and judgments will not be translated into both official languages, and thus some material will be available only in French. Remember, too, that judgments given by Chambers remain provisional for up three months[1], so that care must be taken in relying upon recent cases (as with several cases cited in this work which attempts to state the law as at 31 August 2001). Official citation of decisions and judgments of the Court from November 1998 is as follows[2]:

CHAMBER JUDGMENT ON MERITS

Campbell v Ireland, no 45678/98, §24, ECHR 1999-II.

GRAND CHAMBER JUDGMENT ON MERITS

Campbell v Ireland [GC], no 45678/98, §24, ECHR 1999-II.

CHAMBER DECISION ON ADMISSIBILITY

Campbell v Ireland (dec.), no 45678/98, ECHR 1999-II.

GRAND CHAMBER DECISION ON ADMISSIBILITY

Campbell v Ireland (dec.) [GC], no 45678/98, ECHR 1999-II.

CHAMBER JUDGMENT ON PRELIMINARY OBJECTIONS

Campbell v Ireland (preliminary objections), no 45678/98, §15, ECHR 1999-II.

CHAMBER JUDGMENT ON JUST SATISFACTION

Campbell v Ireland (just satisfaction), no 45678/98, §15, ECHR 1999-II.

CHAMBER JUDGMENT ON REVISION

Campbell v Ireland (revision), no 45678/98, §15, ECHR 1999-II.

CHAMBER JUDGMENT ON INTERPRETATION

Campbell v Ireland (interpretation), no 45678/98, §15, ECHR 1999-II.

1 Article 43 provides that any party to the case may, within three months from the date of a Chamber judgment, request that the case be referred to the Grand Chamber of the Court. The request is considered by a panel of five judges who will examine whether the case raises a serious question affecting the interpretation or application of the Convention or any other serious issue of general importance which would justify referral to the Grand Chamber. Chamber judgments thus become final upon a rejection of any such request, on the expiry of the three-month period, or earlier if the parties declare that they do not intend to make a request to refer.
2 Court Instruction on Citation of Case-law of 3 April 2000.

2.47   Where it is necessary to consider resolutions of the Committee of Ministers, these are available in printed collections[1] and in the appropriate volume of the *Yearbook of the European Convention on Human Rights*. The Yearbook also contains relevant texts from the Parliamentary Assembly of the Council of Europe.

1 *Collection of Resolutions adopted by the Committee of Ministers in the Application of Arts 32 and 54 of the European Convention for the Protection of Human Rights and Fundamental Freedoms: 1959–1983* (and subsequent volumes).

WEBSITES

2.48   Much Strasbourg jurisprudence is now available electronically. The Council of Europe's human rights home page is at www. humanrights.coe.int . Ready access to information on the Court is available through the Court's website at www.echr.coe.int and in particular to the texts of Court judgments at www.echr.coe.int/Eng/ Judgments.htm and to the HUDOC search facility (which allows access to Commission and Court case law) at www.echr.coe.int/Hudoc.htm . Note, however, that many decisions and judgments are available only in French. Resolutions of the Committee of Ministers from 1996 onwards are available at http://cm.coe.int/indexes/doc.0.html .

DIGESTS

2.49   The *Digest of Strasbourg Case-Law Relating to the European Convention on Human Rights* in looseleaf format (1984–1985; 6 volumes), although updated periodically, is now considerably out of date. An earlier *Digest of Case Law Relating to the European Convention on Human Rights 1955–1967* (1970) is unlikely now to be of any practical assistance. A modern aid to research, Kempees *A Systematic Guide to the Case-Law of the European Court of Human Rights* (1996–2000) is published in 4 volumes (vols 1 and 2: 1960–1994; vol 3: 1995–1996; and vol 4 1997–1998) and contains relevant extracts from Court judgments.

Secondary sources

2.50   *Human Rights Information Bulletins* are published by the Directorate General of Human Rights some four times per year. The Court also (from November 1998 onwards) publishes monthly *Information Notices on the Case-Law of the Court*. These documents may be accessed at www.humanrights.coe.int/Bulletin/eng/presenting.htm and at www.echr.coe.int/Eng/InformationNotes/InformationNotes.htm respectively.

The *Yearbook of the European Convention on Human Rights* contains summaries of Court judgments. Case summaries (together with useful bibliographies) of judgments up until 1993 appear in Berger *Case Law of the European Court of Human Rights* (1989–1995) in 3 volumes (vol 1: 1960–1987; vol 2: 1988–1990; and vol 3: 1991–1993), and with key judgments in later cases in *Jurisprudence de la Cour Européenne des Droits de l'Homme* (7th edn, 2000). The influential NGO based in London, the Aire

Centre, represents applicants from across Europe before the Strasbourg Court, and publishes useful bulletins on the European Convention on Human Rights at www.airecentre.org .

The leading textbooks on the Convention appear in English, French or German; most are written (or co-written) by lawyers working in the Council of Europe, former members of the Commission, or judges of the Court. See in particular:

> De Salvia and Villiger (eds) *The Birth of European Human Rights Law: L'Éclosion du Droit européen des Droits de l'Homme* (1998).
>
> Frohwein and Peukert *Europäische Menschenrechtskonvention: EMRK-Kommentar* (2nd edn, 1996).
>
> Harris, O'Boyle, and Warbrick *Law of the European Convention on Human Rights* (1995).
>
> Macdonald, Matscher, and Petzold (eds) *The European System for the Protection of Human Rights* (1993).
>
> Pettiti, Imbert, and Decaux *La Convention Européenne des Droits de l'Homme* (2nd edn, 1999).
>
> Reid *A Practitioner's Guide to the European Convention on Human Rights* (1998).
>
> Van Dijk and Van Hoof *Theory and Practice of the European Convention on Human Rights* (3rd edn, 1998).
>
> Villiger *Handbuch der Europäischen Menschenrechtskonvention (EMRK), unter der besonderen Berücksichtigung der schweizerischen Rechtslage* (2nd edn, 1999).

Several journals now contain articles on substantive Convention guarantees and summaries of recent decisions and judgments. The leading English-language publications include *European Human Rights Law Review* and *European Law Review*. The *Human Rights Law Journal* and its two foreign-language counterparts, *Revue Universelle des Droits de l'Homme* and *Europäische Grundrechte Zeitschrift*, contain articles and notes of recent judgments. The *European Law Review, International and Comparative Law Quarterly, Netherlands Quarterly of Human Rights* and *Revue trimestrielle des Droits de l'Homme* all carry regular articles and commentary on Strasbourg case law.

Other human rights treaties and instruments; and related jurisprudence

2.51   Access to other human rights instruments[1] and reports may provide assistance in addressing issues of Convention rights in domestic tribunals. The Court itself makes reference to other relevant international treaties in its judgments[2]; and the Scottish courts have themselves proved willing to consider other Commonwealth jurisprudence.

The following websites in particular provide access to a range of international, regional and national materials[3]: www.1.umn.edu/humanrts/ ; www.diana.law.yale.edu/ ; www.hri.ca/ and www.hrdc.net/accesshr/ .

---

1 For a survey, see Marie 'International Instruments Relating to Human Rights' (1999) 20 HRLJ 115–133.

2 See paras 2.33 above and 3.22 below.
3 All sites are as accessed at 31 August 2001.

Jurisprudence of European domestic courts

2.52 Domestic human rights case law from other European countries is of particular relevance in the application of the Convention, but linguistic difficulties may prove a practical barrier to easy access. However, certain publications of the Council of Europe's Venice Commission may be of some assistance: see www.venice.coe.int/site/interface/english.htm . The *Yearbook of the European Convention on Human Rights* also contains summaries to the use of the ECHR in influencing or implementing domestic legislation and executive acts in member states, and of decisions of domestic courts concerning Convention guarantees. The *Human Rights Law Journal* (and particularly its two foreign-language counterparts *Revue Universelle des Droits de l'Homme*, and *Europäische Grundrechte Zeitschrift*) also contain human rights decisions of European domestic courts. An additional source of assistance is *European Current Law* which includes summaries of domestic developments.

Many websites now give access to decisions of constitutional courts (and equivalent bodies) in European jurisdictions[1]. Those currently providing coverage of recent decisions (rather than mere descriptive material) in English, French, German, Italian or Spanish include the following:

> Austrian Constitutional Court: www.vfgh.gv.at [German]
> Belgium Court of Arbitration: www.arbitrage.be [French]
> Bulgarian Constitutional Court: www.bild.net/ccourt/index-en.htm [English]
> Czech Constitutional Court: www.concourt.cz [English]
> Estonian Supreme Court: www.nc.ee [English]
> French Constitutional Council: www.conseil-constitutionnel.fr [English]
> Georgian Supreme Court: www.constcourt.gov.ge [English]
> German Federal Constitutional Court: www.bverfg.de [German]
> Hungarian Constitutional Court: www.mkab.hu [English]
> Italian Constitutional Court: www.cortecostituzionale.it [Italian]
> Lithuanian Constitutional Court: www.lrkt.lt [English]
> Netherlands Supreme Court: www.hogeraad.nl [English]
> Norwegian Supreme Court: www.domstol.no/hoyesterett/ [English]
> Polish Constitutional Tribunal: www.trybunal.gov.pl [English]
> Slovakian Constitutional Court: www.concourt.sk [English]
> Spanish Constitutional Court: www.tribunalconstitucional.es [Spanish]
> Swiss Federal Court: www.bger.ch [French; German; Italian]

Decisions of the Human Rights Chamber of Bosnia and Hercegovina (in applying the European Convention on Human Rights) are found in English at: www.gwdg.de/~ujvr/hrch/hrch.htm .

1 A full list of worldwide links is available via the Council of Europe's Venice Commission's website.

Commonwealth jurisprudence

2.53   The Interights website at www.interights.org/ provides access to the Commonwealth Human Rights Case Law database. Sites providing access to Commonwealth courts' interpretation of human rights treaties and domestic human rights charters include:

Australia: www.austlii.edu.au/ and www.vicnet.net.au/~victorp/vphuman.htm
Canada: www.canada.justice.gc.ca/loireg/charte/const_en.html
New Zealand: www.austlii.edu.au/nz/cases/NZCA/
South Africa: www.concourt.gov.za/

International and other non-Commonwealth jurisprudence

2.54   The leading English language periodicals and reports (each of which also contains material on the ECHR) include *Netherlands Quarterly of Human Rights*, the *Human Rights Quarterly*, and *International Human Rights Reports*. The UN's main portal is at www.un.org/ Materials from the Human Rights Committee is accessed via www1.umn.edu/humanrts/hrcommittee/hrc-page.html . The website of the World Court (formerly the International Court of Justice) in The Hague is available at www.icj.law.gla.ac.uk/; that of the UN High Commissioner for Refugees at www.unhcr.ch ; and that of the International Labour Organisation at www.ilo.org .

Other potentially useful sites include:

United States jurisprudence: www.gsulaw.gsu.edu/metaindex/
Amnesty International: www.amnesty.org/
Human Rights Watch: www.hrw.org/

CHAPTER 3

Applying the European Convention on Human Rights

THE OBLIGATIONS OF THE UNITED KINGDOM

Ratification of the European Convention on Human Rights by the United Kingdom

3.01 The European Convention on Human Rights and its protocols provide a range of substantive rights and freedoms designed to enhance individual protection against arbitrary state authority. However, the extent of the state obligations which apply within a particular legal order is dependent upon the application or otherwise of any declaration, reservation or derogation made by the state in question, as well as the range of optional protocols ratified. In other words, while there may be one system of European human rights protection enforceable by legal means before the European Court of Human Rights, the extent of state responsibility is directly dependent upon the extent of state assumption of such responsibility. In this sense, then, while there is a scheme for the protection of human rights within Europe, the nature of the rights protected varies across the continent[1].

1 Prior to the entry into force of Protocol 11, the nature of the enforcement machinery available to individuals to challenge states also was dependent upon individual state acceptance of the right of individual application and of the Court's optional jurisdiction but, since November 1998, one universal system of enforcement machinery now exists. The state of signatures and ratifications of the ECHR and its protocols is found in the most recent *Human Rights Information Bulletin* of the Council of Europe's Directorate of Human Rights or on the internet at: www.coe.int . See further paras 2.09–2.21 above.

3.02 The European Convention on Human Rights, Article 1 provides that 'the High Contracting parties shall secure to everyone within their jurisdiction the rights and freedoms defined [in arts 2–18]'. 'Everyone within [the] jurisdiction' encompasses any individual or legal person satisfying the test of 'victim' who is affected by the acts of national authorities whether within or outwith the national or legal boundaries of a state[1]. The test is that of effective or de facto control. In *Loizidou v Turkey*, for example, the European Court of Human Rights accepted that the respondent state, which was occupying northern Cyprus and which had on several occasions refused the applicant (who was now living in southern Cyprus) access to her property, had a responsibility in terms of Article 1 for 'securing' the Convention rights and freedoms of the applicant and others affected by the occupation of northern Cyprus[2]. Further, Article 56[3] provides that a state may declare by notification to the Secretary General of the Council of Europe that the Convention applies to any territory for whose international relations it is responsible, and additionally, that it accepts the competence of the Court to receive application from individuals, non-governmental organisations or groups who claim to be victims of any violation of Convention guarantees[4]. These two matters are distinct. The United Kingdom has notified its acceptance of the application of the Convention to certain territories. Separate and additional notification is required under each optional protocol[5]. Any territorial extension of the Convention's application is, however, subject to due regard being taken of 'local requirements'[6]. In *Tyrer v United Kingdom*, an attempt was made to justify the continuation of judicially-authorised corporal punishment and thus escape Article 3 condemnation on grounds of 'local requirements' by claiming that its use was supported by public opinion and was also necessary to deter crime and uphold public order. The Court considered such arguments to be more to do with 'circumstances and conditions' than 'requirements' since it could not be shown that the maintenance of law and order specifically required such a punishment[7].

1 *Drozd and Janousek v France and Spain* (1992) A 240, para 91.
2 1996-VI, 2216, para 56.
3 Formerly Art 63.
4 European Convention on Human Rights, Art 56(4).
5 Cf *Gillow v United Kingdom* (1986) A 109, para 62 (no express declaration had been made under Protocol 1 to extend these provisions to Guernsey, and thus the Court had no jurisdiction to consider arguments based upon the right to property).
6 European Convention on Human Rights, Art 56(3).
7 (1978) A 26, para 38: the Court also ruled that even were a local requirement to have been established (that is, that corporal punishment was necessary to maintain law and order), this would not in any case have allowed a state to make use of such a punishment since states cannot derogate from ECHR, Art 3 which contains an absolute prohibition of torture or inhuman or degrading treatment.

3.03 So far as the United Kingdom itself is concerned, the substantive rights conferred on individuals derive in the first place from the European Convention on Human Rights, Articles 2–18, which was ratified on 8 March 1951 and came into force on 23 September 1953. Further rights derive from Protocol 1, which was ratified on 3 November 1952 and came into force on 18 May 1954, and Protocol 6, which came into force on 1 March 1985 and was ratified by the United Kingdom on 27 January 1999. These rights are those given effect as 'Convention rights' by the Human Rights Act 1998 and the Scotland Act 1998.

3.04 A state cannot avoid its responsibilities under the European Convention on Human Rights by delegating or devolving functions of a public nature. For example, the state remains responsible for a breach of the Convention committed in the course of providing education, even if the education is being provided in a private school[1]. On the other hand, the state is not responsible for acts which cannot be imputed to a public authority: a decision by a parent to hospitalise a child, for example, is not one which directly involves the authority of the state[2].

1 *Costello-Roberts v United Kingdom* (1993) A 247-C.
2 *Nielsen v Denmark* (1988) A 44.

Reservations and derogations

3.05 The European Convention on Human Rights, Article 57[1] permits any state, when signing the Convention or when depositing its instrument of ratification, to make a reservation in respect of any particular provision of the Convention to the extent that any law then in force in its territory is not in conformity with the provision. Reservations of a general character are not permitted; and any reservation must contain a brief statement of the law concerned[2]. This provision applies also to protocols to the Convention. Effect is given to reservations, under the domestic law of the United Kingdom, by virtue of the Human Rights Act 1998, ss 1(2), 15 and 17[3]. The United Kingdom has made a reservation in respect of Protocol 1, Article 2[4].

1 Formerly Art 64.
2 As to these requirements, see *Belilos v Swizerland* (1988) A 132, paras 58–59; *Weber v Switzerland* (1990) A 177; *Chorherr v Austria* (1993) A 266-B, para 19.
3 As to which, see para 1.95 above.
4 The reservation is set out in the Human Rights Act 1998, Sch 3, Pt 2. It is discussed at para 6.54 below. In the light of the *Belilos* judgment, it is questionable whether the UK reservation complies with the European Convention on Human Rights, Art 57(2). See also 28915/95, *S P v United Kingdom* (17 January 1997).

3.06 The European Convention on Human Rights, Article 15 permits any contracting state, 'in time of war or other public emergency threatening the life of the nation'[1] to take measures derogating from its obligations under the Convention 'to the extent strictly required by the exigencies of the situation'[2], provided that such measures are not inconsistent with its other obligations under international law. No derogation can, however, be made from Article 2, except in respect of deaths resulting from lawful acts of war, or from Articles 3, 4 (paragraph 1) and 7. This provision applies also to protocols to the Convention. Effect is given to derogations, under the domestic law of the United Kingdom, by the Human Rights Act 1998, ss 1(2), 14 and 16. The United Kingdom made a derogation from the Convention, Article 5(3)[3] following the decision of the European Court of Human Rights in *Brogan and Ors v United Kingdom*[4] that the detention of the applicants for more than four days under the Prevention of Terrorism (Temporary Provisions) Act 1984 contravened Article 5(3). The validity of the derogation has been upheld by the European Court of Human Rights[5]. It was withdrawn following the entry into force of the Terrorism Act 2000.

1 See *Lawless v Ireland (No 3)* (1961) A 3.
2 See *Ireland v United Kingdom* (1978) A 25; *Brannigan and McBride v United Kingdom* (1993) A 258-B.
3 The derogation was set out in the Human Rights Act 1998, Sch 3, Pt 1 as originally enacted. See further para 4.46 below.
4 (1988) A 145-B.
5 *Brannigan and McBride v United Kingdom* (1993) A 258-B. The subject of derogations is discussed in detail in Harris, O'Boyle and Warbrick *Law of the European Convention on Human Rights* (1995) pp 489–507.

Positive and negative obligations

3.07 Under the European Convention on Human Rights, Article 1 contracting states undertake to '*secure* to everyone within their jurisdiction' the rights and freedoms set out in the Convention (and its protocols) upon ratification. In consequence, the state is under a negative obligation to refrain from interfering with the protected rights; and that negative obligation is reflected, for example, in the language used in several of the articles of the Convention:

'No-one shall be deprived of his life intentionally . . .' (Art 2).
'No-one shall be subjected to torture . . .' (Art 3).
'No-one shall be held in slavery. . .' (Art 4).
'No-one shall be deprived of his liberty except . . .' (Art 5).
'No-one shall be held guilty . . .' (Art 7).
'There shall be no interference by a public authority . . .' (Art 8).
'Freedom to manifest one's religion or beliefs shall be subject only to such limitations as . . .' (Art 9).
'Everyone has the right to freedom of expression . . . without interference by public authorities' (Art 10).
'No restrictions shall be placed on the exercise of these rights . . .' (Art 11).
'No-one shall be deprived of his possessions except . . .' (Protocol 1, Art 1).

The overarching obligation to *secure* rights is, however, not confined to a requirement that states refrain from interfering with protected rights: it can also place the state under an obligation to take positive steps. This too is reflected in the language used in some of the articles of the Convention:

'Everyone's right to life shall be protected by law' (Art 2).
'Everyone charged with a criminal offence has . . . [the right] to be given [legal assistance] free when the interests of justice so require' (Art 6).

Whether a positive obligation exists does not, however, depend on the semantic form in which a guarantee is expressed, but upon whether it is necessary to construe the guarantee as imposing a positive obligation in order to secure effective protection of the right in question[1].

1 As to the 'effectiveness principle' of interpretation, see para 3.24 below.

3.08   Positive obligations can arise in a variety of circumstances and can take a variety of forms. The state – which includes national courts, as well as the legislature, the executive and other public authorities – may be under an obligation to take positive steps to alter domestic law or practice so as to ensure that the legal system meets the standards of the European Convention on Human Rights, for example in relation to the system of criminal proscution[1], the substance of the criminal law[2], criminal procedure[3], or private law[4]. The scope of the Convention to impose positive obligations on the state, including the courts, in respect of questions of private law, is particularly significant as it entails that the Convention, and the Human Rights Act 1998, can be relevant to disputes between private individuals[5]. The duty to secure Convention rights can also impose upon the state (including the courts) a duty to take some positive step of an executive or operational nature: for example, to undertake a criminal investigation[6], or to obtain an expert report before depriving a father of his right to access to his child[7]. The fact that the Convention imposes positive as well as negative obligations is reflected in the terms of the Human Rights Act 1998[8].

1 Eg *Kaya v Turkey* 1998-I 297, para 93; *Yasa v Turkey* 1998-VI 2411, paras 113–115.
2 Eg *Dudgeon v United Kingdom* (1981) A 44, para 49 (prohibition of homosexual conduct in private); *A v United Kingdom* 1998-VI, 2692, paras 23–24 (breach of the European Convention on Human Rights, Art 3 through domestic recognition of a defence of 'reasonable chastisement').
3 Eg *V v United Kingdom* (16 December 1999).
4 Eg *Marckx v Belgium* (1979) A 31, para 44 (differential status of illegitimate children); *Young, James and Webster v United Kingdom* (1981) A 44, para 49 (domestic law permitted employer to dismiss employees in contravention of ECHR, Art 11); *Hoffmann v Austria* (1993) A 255-C, para 29 (decision of court in resolving dispute concerning custody of children amounted to 'interference' with ECHR, Art 8 rights, despite private nature of litigation).
5 In an ECHR, Art 8 case, the court observed: 'These obligations may even involve the adoption of measures designed to secure respect for private life even in the sphere of the relations of individuals between themselves': *X and Y v Netherlands* (1985) A 91, para 23. For a detailed study, see Clapham *Human Rights in the Private Sphere* (1993).
6 Eg *Aydin v Turkey* 1997-VI, 1866, paras 103–109.
7 *Elsholz v Germany* (13 July 2000), paras 62–66.
8 Section 6(6).

3.09   In deciding whether or not a positive obligation exists, 'the Court will have regard to the fair balance that has to be struck between the general interest of the community and the competing private interests of the individual, or individuals, concerned'[1]. Positive obligations have been found to exist in a variety of situations. In *Osman v United Kingdom*[2] the European Court of Human Rights held that the European Convention on Human Rights, Article 2 imposed a positive obligation on the state to 'secure the right to life by putting in place effective criminal law provisions to deter the commission of offences against the person, backed up by law enforcement machinery for the prevention, suppression and sanctioning of breaches of such provisions'[3]. In the particular circumstances of that case, the police were therefore under an obligation to take reasonable steps to prevent a foreseeable murderous attack. However the Court also said that this obligation had to be 'interpreted in a way which does not impose an impossible or disproportionate burden on the authorities'[4] and also in a manner which was consistent with the rights of suspects. In *Aydin v Turkey*[5] the Court held that, where an individual made a complaint of torture or inhuman or degrading treatment, the state was under a positive obligation to carry out 'a thorough and effective investigation capable of leading to the identification and punishment of those responsible, and including effective access for the complainant to the investigatory procedure'[6]. Article 3 has also been held to impose a positive obligation of a similar character[7]. Article 6 imposes a number of positive obligations: for example, to establish independent and impartial courts which deal with proceedings within a reasonable time; and to provide legal aid[8] and interpreters where necessary. The right of access to a court, which is implicit in Article 6[9], also has far-reaching implications for the courts in their development of the law, including private law[10]. The obligation to 'respect' private and family life, under Article 8, is also capable of imposing specific positive obligations, depending on the particular circumstances. For example, it can impose on the state an obligation to give legal recognition to a change of gender by a post-operative transsexual[11]; or to provide access to social work records of a person's childhood[12]; or to amend the law of succession[13]. Positive obligations have also been held to arise from Articles 9[14] and 10[15]. Article 11 can impose on the state a positive obligation to protect peaceful demonstrators from violent counter-demonstrators[16].

1 *McGinley and Egan v United Kingdom* 1998-III, 1334, para 98.
2 1998-VIII, 3124.
3 1998-VIII, 3124, para 115. See also *McCann, Savage and Farrell v United Kingdom* (1996) A 324, para 161; *Z v United Kingdom* (10 May 2001).
4 *Osman v United Kingdom* 1998-VIII, 3124, para 116.
5 1997-VI, 1866.
6 Para 103. See also *X and Y v Netherlands* (1985) A 91, para 23 (positive obligation to prosecute rapist, in order to secure rights of victim).
7 *A v United Kingdom* 1998-VI, 2692.
8 This is an express obligation in respect of criminal proceedings, but also on implied obligation in respect of civil proceedings: *Airey v Ireland* (1979) A 32, para 26.
9 E g *Ashingdane v United Kingdom* (1985) A 93, para 55.
10 A good illustration, in a case concerning a public authority, is *Osman v United Kingdom* 1998-VIII, 3124. An example involving private individuals is *Fayed v United Kingdom* A (1994) 294-B.
11 *B v France* (1992) A 232-C, paras 44–63; contrast *Rees v United Kingdom* (1986) A 106, para 37, *Cossey v United Kingdom* (1990) A 184, paras 36–39, and *Sheffield and Horsham v United Kingdom* 1998-V, 2011, paras 51–61. The difference between the French case and the British cases arises essentially from the greater seriousness of the effect of existing French law, as compared with United Kingdom law, on the privacy of transsexuals.
12 *Gaskin v United Kingdom* (1989) A 160, paras 42–49.
13 *Marckx v Belgium* (1979) A 31, para 31.
14 33490/96 and 34055/96, *Dubowska and Skup v Poland* (1997) DR 89, 156 .
15 *Gaskin v United Kingdom* (1989) A 160.
16 *Plattform Ärtze für das Leben v Austria* (1988) A 139, para 32.

3.10   In some circumstances it may be difficult to distinguish between positive and negative obligations. Whether the state has interfered with a protected right or has failed to protect it can in some cases appear to be a distinction without a difference. In such cases the result should not depend on a semantic classification. The principles applicable are 'broadly similar', however the issue is described[1].

1 *López Ostra v Spain* (1994) A 303-C, para 51; *Rees v United Kingdom* (1987) A 106, para 37.

LIMITS TO THE ENJOYMENT OF CONVENTION RIGHTS

Abuse of rights

3.11   The European Convention on Human Rights, Article 17 provides:

> 'Nothing in this Convention may be interpreted as implying for any State, group or person any right to engage in any activity or perform any act aimed at the destruction of any of the rights and freedoms set forth herein or at their limitation to a greater extent than is provided for in the Convention.'

This provision prevents the Convention from being used as a basis for asserting a right to act in a way which is aimed at destroying the Convention rights of others. For example, the Convention could not be used as a basis for asserting the right to distribute racist pamphlets or to stand as candidates in elections on a racist platform[1]. On the other hand, those who have acted in a way which was aimed at destroying the Convention rights of others are not thereafter generally barred from asserting their own Convention rights, such as their right to a fair trial[2].

1 8348/78, *Glimmerveen and Hagenbeek v Netherlands* (1979) DR 18, 187; *Lehideux and Isorni v France* 1998-VIII, 2864.
2 *Lawless v Ireland* (1961) A 3, para 7; *SW v United Kingdom* (1995) A 355-B (not following the reasoning of Mrs Liddy in the Commission). On the European Convention on Human Rights, Art 17, see Cooper and Williams 'Hate Speech, Holocaust Denial and International Human Rights Law' (1999) EHRLR 593 at 605–607. The Court takes account of the conduct of applicants in deciding whether to await compensation under Art 41: see para 2.31 above.

Waiver of rights

3.12 The waiver of Convention rights is an issue which has not been greatly explored in the Strasbourg jurisprudence, possibly because of the requirement that applicants must exhaust domestic remedies if their complaints are to be admissible[1]. The law on waiver is correspondingly lacking in clarity, and raises difficult questions.

1 European Convention on Human Rights, Art 35.

3.13 Certain Convention rights cannot be waived[1]. It is doubtful, for example, whether the right to liberty guaranteed by Article 5 can be waived[2]. It also seems unlikely that waiver could operate in respect of other basic rights such as those guaranteed by Articles 2, 3 and 4[3]. On the other hand, some at least of the rights guaranteed by Article 6 are capable of being waived[4]. In general, it appears that a Convention right can be waived provided that 'neither the letter nor the spirit of [the] provision prevents a person from waiving [the right] of his own free will', and further provided that the waiver is 'made in an unequivocal manner, and [does] not run counter to an important public interest'[5].

1 *Albert and Le Compte v Belgium* (1983) A 58, para 35.
2 *De Wilde, Ooms and Versyp v Belgium* (1971) A 12, para 65.
3 In relation to the European Convention on Human Rights, Art 4, see *Van der Mussele v Belgium* (1984) A 70.
4 See para 3.14 below.
5 *Schuler-Zraggen v Switzerland* (1993) A 263, para 58; *Hakansson and Sturesson v Sweden* (1991) A 171, para 66.

3.14 Most of the Strasbourg case law on waiver has concerned the European Convention on Human Rights, Article 6. The requirement that a criminal trial be before a tribunal 'established by law' has been said to be 'of essential importance and its exercise cannot depend on the parties alone'[1]. The requirement that the tribunal be 'independent and impartial' gives rise to complex questions. In *Bulut v Austria*[2] the Court found that, as a matter of domestic law, there had been an effective waiver of the right to object to a judge with a prior involvement in the case: the domestic court was therefore 'established by law'[3]. The Court considered, however, that, 'regardless of whether a waiver was made or not' it had still to decide whether, from the standpoint of the Convention, the domestic court was 'impartial'[4]. In that regard, the Court accepted that the judge in question was subjectively impartial; and, applying the objective test, it was not open to the applicant to complain that he had legitimate reasons to doubt the court's impartiality, given his failure to object to its composition[5]. This judgment might be interpreted as meaning that the Convention right to an independent and impartial tribunal cannot be waived, but that failure to object to the tribunal bars the applicant from founding on his own alleged doubts as to its impartiality[6]. In the subsequent case of *McGonnell v United Kingdom*, however, the judgment (of a Chamber of the Court) might be understood as accepting that the right to an independent and impartial tribunal could be waived[7]. The right to a hearing in public can be waived[8], as can also the right to be legally represented[9]. The right to have a criminal charge determined by a tribunal (rather than 'settled' by payment of a fiscal fine) can be waived[10].

1 *Pfeifer and Plankl v Austria* (1992) A 227, para 38.
2 1996-II, 346. In the earlier case of *Oberschlick v Austria* (1991) A 204, the Court did not determine whether the right to an independent and impartial tribunal could be waived, but held that there had not been an effective waiver.
3 *Bulut v Austria* 1996-II, 346, para 29.
4 *Bulut v Austria* 1996-II, 346, para 30.
5 *Bulut v Austria* 1996-II, 346, paras 32–36.
6 This approach would reflect the fundamental importance of an independent judiciary as an aspect of the *ordre public* within the Council of Europe: cf *De Wilde , Ooms and Versyp v Belgium* (1971) A 12, para 65. The *Bulut* judgment has, however, been criticised, not without justification, as 'ambiguous': Van Dijk and Van Hoof *Theory and Practice of the European Convention on Human Rights* (3rd edn, 1998) p 456. See also *Millar v Dickson* 2001 SLT 988 per Lord Clyde at para 81.
7 (8 February 2001), paras 44 and 45.
8 *Albert and Le Compte v Belgium* (1983) A 58, para 35. This principle was applied, in the context of a construction contract adjudication, in *Austin Hall Building Ltd v Buckland Securities Ltd* (11 April 2001, unreported) Tech and Con Ct.
9 *Melin v France* (1993) A 261-A, para 25.
10 *Deweer v Belgium* (1980) A 35, para 49.

3.15　As already mentioned, the waiver of a right guaranteed by the European Convention of Human Rights – in so far as it is permissible – must be established in an unequivocal manner[1]. In the case of procedural rights a waiver, in order to be effective, requires 'minimum guarantees commensurate to its importance'[2]. For example, a purported waiver of a procedural right without the benefit of legal advice is unlikely to be valid[3]. Waiver need not be express: 'tacit' waiver can be inferred from conduct[4].

1 *Pfeifer and Plankl v Austria* (1992) A 227, para 37.
2 *Pfeifer and Plankl v Austria* (1992) A 227, para 37.
3 *Pfeifer and Plankl v Austria* (1992) A 227 para 38.
4 See e g *Colozza v Italy* (1985) A 89, para 28; *Hakansson and Sturesson v Sweden* (1991) A 171, para 67; *McGonnell v United Kingdom* (8 February 2000) paras 44–45.

3.16　In three cases under the Scotland Act 1998 the courts have considered the issue of waiver of the right under the European Convention on Human Rights, Article 6 to an independent and impartial tribunal. In *Clancy v Caird*[1], the Inner House held, on the basis of *Oberschlick v Austria (No 1)*[2] and *Bulut v Austria*[3], that the right to an independent and impartial tribunal could be waived[4], and had been tacitly waived by a failure to object timeously to the judge in question, the possible ground of objection to the judge's independence being something of which the pursuer's legal representatives must be taken to have been aware. In *Millar v Dickson*[5] it was accepted by a majority of the Privy Council that the right to an independent and impartial tribunal could be waived (the power being conceded). The Privy Council however made it clear that waiver depends on the making of an informed choice, and that waiver could not be imputed to a party on the basis that he or his agent was deemed to know the law. In *County Properties Ltd v The Scottish Ministers*[6] it was held that waiver should not be inferred from a failure to object at the earliest possible opportunity (the calling-in of a planning application), the objection having been taken prior to any substantive hearing.

1 2000 SC 441.
2 (1991) A 204.
3 1996-II, 346.
4 As discussed in para 3.14 above, it may be questionable whether that is the correct interpretation to place upon the Strasbourg cases.
5 2000 SLT 988.
6 2000 SLT 965; revd 2001 SLT 1125.

THE INTERPRETATION OF THE CONVENTION

Introduction

3.17   The European Convention on Human Rights is an international convention, and therefore falls to be interpreted in accordance with the principles set out in the Vienna Convention on the Law of Treaties, Articles 31–33. These principles are discussed below. In practice, one of these principles has proved to be especially important: that the Convention should be interpreted 'in the light of its object and purpose'[1]. That principle has been elaborated in the Convention jurisprudence under reference to three particular expressions: that the Convention should guarantee rights that are 'practical and effective'; that certain of its terms should be interpreted as 'autonomous concepts'; and that it should be interpreted and applied as a 'living instrument'. The Convention jurisprudence also manifests a number of other general principles, derived from continental administrative law, notably those of legal certainty, non-discrimination (an express requirement, under Article 14) and proportionality. The first and third of these are particularly (but not exclusively) related to provisions in the Convention which call, respectively, for interferences with protected rights to be 'prescribed by law' (or some equivalent formulation) and 'necessary'. It is thus possible to describe a number of guiding principles of interpretation:

– the Vienna Convention
– the effectiveness principle
– autonomous concepts
– living instrument
– legal certainty
– non-discrimination
– necessity and proportionality.

These principles are distinguished and described below, for the purpose of explaining the approach required in the interpretation of the

Convention. It should, however, be emphasised at the outset that they are not rigidly distinct, let alone forming some sort of systematic or hierarchical schema to be applied. In reality, the interpretation of the Convention is a single exercise, directed towards rendering the Convention effective, and imbued by the general standards of legal certainty, non-discrimination and proportionality.

1 Vienna Convention, Art 31(1).

3.18 At the level of the European Court of Human Rights, a number of other principles apply which are specific to its function as an international court:

- the subsidiarity principle
- the margin of appreciation doctrine
- the fourth instance doctrine.

As will be explained[1], these three principles do not apply to national courts, such as Scottish courts applying the Scotland Act 1998 or the Human Rights Act 1998.

1 At para 3.91 below.

The Vienna Convention

3.19 Although the Vienna Convention postdates the European Convention on Human Rights, and does not have retroactive effect, it expresses the pre-existing principles of international law governing the interpretation of treaties. It is accepted by the European Court of Human Rights that it should be guided by the Vienna Convention Articles 31–33[1].

1 *Golder v United Kingdom* (1975) A 18, para 29.

3.20 Those articles are in the following terms:

Article 31

General rule of interpretation

1. A treaty shall be interpreted in good faith in accordance with the ordinary meaning to be given to the terms of the treaty in their context and in the light of its object and purpose.
2. The context for the purpose of the interpretation of a treaty shall comprise, in addition to the text, including its preamble and annexes:
   (a) any agreement relating to the treaty which was made between all the parties in connection with the conclusion of the treaty;
   (b) any instrument which was made by one or more parties in connection with the conclusion of the treaty and accepted by other parties as an instrument related to the treaty.
3. There shall be taken into account, together with the context:
   (a) any subsequent agreement between the parties regarding the interpretation of the treaty or the application of its provisions;
   (b) any relevant rules of international law applicable in relations between the parties.
4. A special meaning shall be given to a term if it is established that the parties so intended.

Article 32

Supplementary means of interpretation

> Recourse may be had to supplementary means of interpretation, including the preparatory work of the treaty and the circumstances of its conclusion, in order to confirm the meaning resulting from the application of art 31, or to determine the meaning when the interpretation according to art 31:
> (a) leaves the meaning ambiguous or obscure; or
> (b) leads to a result which is manifestly absurd or unreasonable.

Article 33

Interpretation of treaties authenticated in two or more languages

> 1. When a treaty has been authenticated in two or more languages, the text is equally authoritative in each language, unless the treaty provides or the parties agree that, in case of divergence, a particular text shall prevail.
> 2. A version of the treaty in a language other than one of those in which the text was authenticated shall be considered an authentic text only if the treaty so provides or the parties so agree.
> 3. The terms of the treaty are presumed to have the same meaning in each authentic text.
> 4. Except where a particular text prevails in accordance with paragraph 1, where a comparison of the authentic texts discloses a difference of meaning which the application of arts 31 and 32 does not remove, the meaning which best reconciles the texts, having regard to the object and purposes of the treaty, shall be adopted.

3.21   The Vienna Convention, Article 31 contains the fundamental principle that the Convention must be interpreted in accordance with the ordinary meaning of its terms in their context[1] and in accordance with its object and purpose. As regards the 'object and purpose' of the Convention, the European Commission on Human Rights said in *Golder v United Kingdom*:

> 'The over-riding function of this Convention is to protect the rights of the individual and not to lay down as between States mutual obligations, which are to be restrictively interpreted having regard to the sovereignty of these States. On the contrary, the role of the Convention and the function of its interpretation is to make the protection of the individual effective[2].'

That approach is equally implicit in the judgments of the European Court of Human Rights. The Court has also emphasised that the Convention is 'an instrument designed to maintain and promote the ideals and values of a democratic society'[3]. More generally, the Court's approach, and its insistence upon a progressive and realistic application of the Convention, is encapsulated in its description of the Convention as 'a constitutional instrument of European public order'[4].

1 E g *Johnston v Ireland* (1987) A 112 and *Rees v United Kingdom* (1986) A 106, para 49 ('right to marry'); *Campbell and Cosans v United Kingdom* (1982) A 48, para 30 ('inhuman or degrading treatment').
2 (1973) B 16, at p 40.
3 *Kjelsden, Busk, Madsen and Pedersen v Denmark* (1976) A 23, para 53. See further, para 3.69 below.
4 *Loizidou v Turkey* (1995) A 310, para 75.

3.22   In accordance with the Vienna Convention, Article 31(2), Council of Europe measures may be relevant to the interpretation of the European Convention on Human Rights[1]. The Vienna Convention, Article 31(3) requires account to be taken of any relevant rules of international law. In practice, international instruments are often referred to by the European Court of Human Rights and can be an important source of guidance, whether or not they have been signed or ratified by all or most or any of the Council of Europe states[2] or are binding in international law[3]. These have included United Nations instruments[4], International Labour Organisation instruments[5], and other international conventions[6]. The Court has also considered European Union standards[7]. Indeed, in interpreting the European Convention on Human Rights as a 'living instrument'[8] and therefore taking account of prevailing attitudes within the Council of Europe, the Court has had regard to a wide range of instruments, including resolutions of the European Parliament and of the Parliamentary Assembly of the Council of Europe[9], and a report of the World Council of Churches[10]. The Scottish courts have also been prepared to consider a wide range of expressions of prevailing attitudes[11]. These various sources are, however, merely an aid to the interpretation of the language used in the European Convention on Human Rights: they cannot be used to 'read into' the Convention a right which it does not contain[12]. Furthermore, although the existence or absence of a generally shared approach to an issue among contracting states is often highly relevant to the application of the Convention, this does not mean that absolute uniformity is required[13].

1 As in *Marckx v Belgium* (1979) A 31 (reference to Committee of Ministers Resolution (70) 15 on Social Protection of Unmarried Mothers and their Children); *Autronic AG v Switzerland* (1990) A 178 (European Convention on Transfrontier Television); *National Union of Belgian Police v Belgium* (1975) A 19, and *Sigurgur A Sigurjónsson v Iceland* (1993) A 264 (European Social Charter); *S v Switzerland* (1991) A 220 (Standard Minimum Rules for the Treatment of Prisoners).

2 See eg *Marckx v Belgium* (1979) A 31, para 41; *S v Switzerland* (1991) A 220, para 48.

3 Many of the UN instruments are supported only by a General Assembly resolution, and are therefore not binding.

4 As in *Soering v United Kingdom* (1989) A 161 (UN Convention against Torture); *Costello-Roberts v United Kingdom* (1993) A 247 (UN Convention on the Rights of the Child); *V v United Kingdom* (16 December 1999) (UN Convention on the Rights of the Child; Standard Minimum Rules for the Administration of Juvenile Justice); and *Brannigan and McBride v United Kingdom* (1993) A 258-B (International Covenant on Civil and Political Rights); *Funke v France* (1993) A 256-A (International Covenant on Civil and Political Rights); *Saunders v United Kingdom* 1996-VI, 2044 (International Covenant on Civil and Political Rights); *KH-W v Germany* (22 March 2001) (International Covenant on Civil and Political Rights; Universal Declaration on Human Rights; the Nuremberg principles adopted by General Assembly Resolution 95 (I) of 1946); *Sigurgur A Sigurjónsson v Iceland* (1993) A 264 (International Covenant on Economic, Social and Cultural Rights); *Jersild v Denmark* (1994) A 298 (International Convention on the Elimination of All Forms of Racial Discrimination).

5 As in *Van der Mussele v Belgium* (1983) A 70 (ILO Convention on Forced or Compulsory Labour).

6 Eg *Marckx v Belgium* (1979) A 31 (Brussels Convention on the Establishment of Maternal Affiliation of Natural Children); *Autronic AG v Switzerland* (1990) A 178 (International Telecommunication Convention); *Powell and Rayner v United Kingdom* (1990) A 172 (the Rome Convention on Damages caused by Foreign Aircraft to Third Parties on the Surface).

7 As in *Goodwin v United Kingdom* 1996-II, 483.

8 See para 3.27 below.

9 *Cossey v United Kingdom* (1990) A 184.

10 *Kokkinakis v Greece* (1993) A 260-A, para 48.
11 As in *Starrs v Ruxton* 1999 SCCR 1052.
12 See eg 8945/80, *S v Germany* (1983) DR 39, 43, and compare the International Covenant on Civil and Political Rights, Art 14(7).
13 See eg *F v Switzerland* A 128 (1987) para 33; and cf the margin of appreciation doctrine, discussed at para 3.85 ff below.

3.23 The Vienna Convention, Article 31(4) contains the principle that terms can be 'autonomous concepts'. Article 32 permits reference to be made to the *travaux préparatoires*: this is unusual in practice, in part because of the 'living instrument' principle derived from the need to fulfil the Convention's object and purpose, but it is not unknown[1]. In relation to Article 33, it is important to remember that the English and French texts of the Convention are equally authoritative. If the different language versions are capable of different interpretations, the European Court of Human Rights will adopt the meaning best adapted to fulfilling the object and purpose of the Convention[2].

1 Eg *Johnston v Ireland* (1987) A 112; *Lithgow v United Kingdom* (1986) A 102, para 117.
2 *Wemhoff v Germany* (1968) A 7, Law, para 8; *Pakelli v Germany* (1983) A 64, para 31.

The effectiveness principle

3.24 The European Court of Human Rights has said, on many occasions, that the European Convention Human Rights 'is intended to guarantee not rights that are theoretical or illusory but rights that are practical and effective'[1]. This has a number of consequences. In the first place, the Convention is concerned with the reality of a situation rather than its formal appearance: 'the Court is compelled to look behind the appearances and investigate the realities of the procedure in question'[2]. This is one of the reasons why the Court has given an autonomous meaning to many of the terms of the Convention, rather than adopting the formal classification given by national legal systems. For example, the commencement of criminal proceedings, for the purpose of the 'reasonable time' guarantee in Article 6, depends on the application of tests developed by the Strasbourg Court, rather than upon the moment at which proceedings formally commence under domestic law[3]. Secondly, the principle of effectiveness has resulted in the Court's interpreting the Convention as including numerous implied rights, without which the express rights conferred would be less effective. Article 6, for example, has been interpreted as including an implied right of access to a court, without which the procedural guarantees applicable to court proceedings under Article 6 might be rendered pointless[4]; and, for the same reason, as including an implied right to legal aid where necessary in civil proceedings[5]. Similarly, the right to legal representation in criminal proceedings, under Article 6(3)(c), has been interpreted as including an implied right to be represented by a lawyer who is competent[6]. Thirdly, the principle of effectiveness is reflected in the Court's interpretation of the Convention as imposing positive objections on contracting states (including their courts) to alter their law (including their private law) and practice and to take executive action in certain circumstances[7]. Fourthly, the principle of effectiveness is reflected in the Court's willingness, in certain circumstances, to consider an alleged violation of the Convention rights on the basis of the facts existing at the time of its own decision, rather than confining itself to a review on the basis of the facts existing at the time of the decision complained of[8]. More generally, the principle of effectiveness pervades the interpretation and application of the Convention, rather as the concept of 'purposive interpretation' pervades European Community law.

1 See e g *Airey v Ireland* (1979) A 32, para 24.
2 *Deweer v Belgium* (1980) A 35, para 44.
3 See e g *Deweer v Belgium* (1980) A 35, paras 41–42.
4 *Golder v United Kingdom* (1975) A 18, paras 26–36.
5 *Airey v Ireland* (1979) A 32, para 26.
6 *Artico v Italy* (1980) A 37, para 36.
7 See para 3.07 above.
8 E g *Chahal v United Kingdom* 1996-V, 1831 (deportation).

Autonomous concepts

3.25 Many of the terms contained in the European Convention on Human Rights have been interpreted by the European Court of Human Rights as having a specific meaning in the context of the Convention, independent of any meaning which they might have in domestic legal systems. This approach not only secures uniformity of interpretation of the terms in question throughout the contracting states: it also ensures that the effectiveness of the Convention cannot be compromised by contracting states' interpreting or applying its provisions in a restrictive manner. An example is the expression 'criminal charge' in Article 6 of the Convention[1]. The relationship between the interpretation of Convention terms as autonomous concepts and the need to look at the realities of a situation in accordance with the effectiveness principle is illustrated by the decision in *V v United Kingdom*[2] that the Home Secretary's fixing of the tariff to be served by juvenile offenders sentenced to detention during Her Majesty's Pleasure contravened Article 6. The Government argued that the offender was sentenced by the judge, and that the fixing of the tariff was merely an aspect of the administration of the sentence already imposed by the court. The European Court of Human Rights considered that the fixing of the tariff amounted in reality to a sentencing exercise, however it was formally classified under English law, and therefore formed part of the 'determination' of the criminal charge and attracted the safeguards of Article 6.

1 See e g *Öztürk v Germany* (1984) A 73, para 53.
2 (16 December 1999).

3.26 Certain expressions used in the European Convention on Human Rights can be regarded as a hybrid between autonomous concepts and terms interpreted according to domestic law. For example, the expression 'prescribed by law' (or its equivalents) refers to domestic law in order to determine whether the act in question was in accordance with domestic law, but is also interpreted as requiring that the domestic law in question must satisfy certain requirements implicit in the Convention[1]. A particularly complex concept is that of 'civil rights and obligations' (Article 6). 'Civil' has an autonomous meaning, so that the classification of the right or obligation under domestic law is not conclusive[2]. Domestic law, on the other hand, determines the content of the right in question[3]. Domestic law's denial that there is a right (eg because of an immunity or defence pleaded by the defender) will not, however, prevent there being a civil right for the purposes of Article 6, if the domestic law in question is so disproportionately restrictive as to be incompatible with the right of access to a court[4]. This is another illustration, of particular difficulty, of the Court's insistence on looking at the practical realities of the situation and interpreting the Convention so as to make it practical and effective.

1 See para 3.34 below.
2 *König v Germany* (1978) A 27, para 88.
3 Para 89.
4 Eg *Fayed v United Kingdom* (1994) A 294-B.

A living instrument

3.27   The European Court of Human Rights has described the European Convention on Human Rights, in a phrase which it has often repeated, as 'a living instrument which . . . must be interpreted in the light of present-day conditions'[1]. Another way of expressing the same idea is to say that the Convention must be given a 'dynamic' or 'evolving' interpretation. This is essentially because the Convention uses expressions whose meaning and application inevitably change over time, reflecting changes in European society and its prevailing ideas, values and standards. This approach evidently limits the relevance of the *travaux préparatoires* as an aid to interpretation.

1 *Tyrer v United Kingdom* (1978) A 26, para 31.

3.28   An example is the expression 'necessary in a democratic society', which is one of the tests of the compatibility with the European Convention on Human Rights of interferences with the rights guaranteed by Articles 8–11. What is 'necessary in a democratic society' evidently changes as society changes. This has been reflected in an evolution in the Court's approach to certain issues, such as the treatment of homosexuals[1]. In one such case, concerned with the criminalisation of homosexual acts, the Court observed:

> '[T]here is now a better understanding, and in consequence an increased tolerance, of homosexual behaviour to the extent that in the great majority of the member states of the Council of Europe it is no longer considered to be necessary or appropriate to treat homosexual practices of the kind now in question as in themselves a matter to which the sanctions of the criminal law should be applied; the Court cannot overlook the marked changes which have occurred in this regard in the domestic law of the member states.'[2]

Similarly, the Court has made it clear that the treatment of transsexuals should be kept under review, observing:

> 'Since the Convention has always to be interpreted and applied in the light of current circumstances, it is important that the need for appropriate legal measures in this area should be kept under review.'[3]

1 See eg *Dudgeon v United Kingdom* (1981) A 45; 25186/94 *Sutherland v United Kingdom* (1 July 1997).
2 *Dudgeon v United Kingdom* (1981) A 45, para 60.
3 *Cossey v United Kingdom* (1990) A 184, para 42; similarly *Rees v United Kingdom* (1986) A 106, para 47; cf *Sheffield and Horsham v United Kingdom* 1998-V, 2011, para 60.

3.29 Another example is the concept of 'inhuman or degrading treatment', in the European Convention on Human Rights, Article 3. In a case under Article 3 concerned with corporal punishment, the Court observed:

> '[T]he Convention is a living instrument which, as the Commission rightly stressed, must be interpreted in the light of present-day conditions. In the case now before it the Court cannot but be influenced by the developments and commonly accepted standards in the penal policy of the member states of the Council of Europe.'[1]

Another example is the concept of the 'family', in Article 8. In a case concerned with the status of 'illegitimate' children, the Court observed:

> 'It is true that, at the time when the Convention of 4 November 1950 was drafted, it was regarded as permissible and normal in many European countries to draw a distinction in this area between the "illegitimate" and "legitimate" family. However, the Court recalls that this Convention must be interpreted in the light of present-day conditions. In the instant case, the Court cannot but be struck by the fact that the domestic law of the great majority of the member states of the Council of Europe has evolved and is continuing to evolve, in company with the relevant international instruments, towards full juridical recognition of the maxim *mater semper certa est.'[2]

Many other examples could be given[3]. The 'living instrument' principle is one which pervades the interpretation and application of the Convention.

1 *Tyrer v United Kingdom* (1978) A 26, para 31. Other relevant European Convention on Human Rights, Art 3 cases include *Soering v United Kingdom* (1989) A 161 (extradition to face capital punishment) and *V v United Kingdom* (16 December 1999) (the treatment of child offenders).
2 *Marckx v Belgium* (1979) A 31, para 41.
3 Eg *Winterwerp v Netherlands* (1979) A 33 ('persons of unsound mind'); *Borgers v Belgium* (1991) A 214 ('fair trial').

3.30 The principle of evolutive interpretation, however, remains a principle of interpretation: in other words, it respects the text of the treaty, and reflects changes in the meaning of the language used. It does not permit courts applying the European Convention on Human Rights to give free rein to their own moral or political views. As the Court said in a case in which it was invited to imply into Articles 8 or 12 a right to divorce:

> 'It is true that the Convention and its protocols must be interpreted in the light of present-day conditions. However, the Court cannot, by means of an evolutive interpretation, derive from these instruments a right that was not included therein at the outset. This is particularly so here, where the omission was deliberate.'[1]

1 *Johnston v Ireland* (1986) A 112, para 53. See also *Soering v United Kingdom* (1989) A 161.

3.31 As is apparent from the passages quoted in paragraphs 3.28–3.29 above, the principle of evolutive interpretation is closely related to the search for a common European standard, reflecting the European Convention on Human Rights status as 'a constitutional instrument of European public order'[1]. It therefore requires account to be taken of law and practice throughout the contracting states, and of international agreements entered into by those states. The former of these, in particular, is liable to be a problem for a national court, because of the difficulty of obtaining accurate information[2]. The provision of such information is one of the tasks which can usefully be performed by a third party intervener[3].

1 *Loizidou v Turkey* (1995) A 310, para 75.
2 Particularly where, as in Scotland, there is no institute of comparative law. The relationships being formed between domestic legal firms and firms overseas and between Scottish and European law schools, may prove useful in this regard.
3 This task has been usefully performed by organisations such as Liberty and Stonewall in recent Strasbourg cases. Public authorities such as the Equal Opportunities Commission are also in a position to make a useful contribution.

3.32 It follows from the 'living instrument' principle that no strict doctrine of precedent applies to decisions of the European Court of Human Rights or of the Commission. Nevertheless, the Court refers to its previous decisions and generally builds upon them incrementally, in much the same way as a British court. In practice, a heavy onus normally lies on a party seeking to persuade the Court to depart from its previous case law[1].

1 See e g *Cossey v United Kingdom* (1990) A 184, para 35; *Wynn v United Kingdom* (1994) A 294-A, para 36. See further Wildhaber 'Precedent in the European Court of Human Rights' in Mahoney, Matscher, Petzold and Wildhaber (eds) *Protecting Human Rights: The European Perspective* (2000) pp 1529–1545.

Legal certainty

3.33 Legal certainty might be defined, in broad terms, as the ability to act within a settled framework without fear of arbitrary or unforeseeable state interference. As such, it is a fundamental aspect of the constitutional order of the contracting states, reflected for example in the British concept of the rule of law, the French concept of the *état de droit*, and the German concept of the *Rechtsstaat*. It is expressed in numerous more precise principles of national law, such as (in the United Kingdom) the principles of interpretation of criminal statutes, the presumption against retrospectivity and the protection of legitimate expectations[1]. It is a fundamental principle of European Community law. It also forms an important element of Convention law. It finds particular expression in a number of articles of the European Convention on Human Rights which are discussed below. It is not, however, confined to those provisions. Those specific provisions, as the Court has said, require domestic law 'to be compatible with the rule of law, a concept inherent in all the articles of the Convention'[2].

1 Partly under the influence of European Community law, itself influenced by the German principle of *Vertrauenschutz*.
2 *Amuur v France* 1996-III, 826, para 50.

3.34   A number of provisions in the European Convention on Human Rights contain an express requirement that measures interfering with protected rights must be lawful. A number of different expressions are used in the English text[1]: 'in accordance with law'[2], 'prescribed by law'[3], 'provided for by law'[4] and 'in accordance with law'[5]. No significance has been given to those differences in wording[6]. In order to satisfy the Convention texts, the interference must be in accordance with domestic law, and that law must itself meet certain Convention requirements. The texts therefore call for scrutiny of both the extent to which state activity is covered by domestic legal rules, and also the quality of those rules themselves.

1 The French text uses the phrase 'prévues par la loi' throughout.
2 European Convention on Human Rights, Art 8.
3 ECHR, Arts 9–11.
4 ECHR, Protocol 1, Art 1.
5 ECHR, Protocol 4, Art 2.
6 *Sunday Times (No 1) v United Kingdom* (1979) A 30, paras 48–49.

3.35   First, the act in question must have a basis in domestic law. This includes not only legislation, but also common law[1] and European Community law[2]. It does not necessarily include non-statutory guidance or codes of practice[3].

1 Eg *Sunday Times (No 1) v United Kingdom* (1979) A 30, para 47.
2 *Groppera Radio AG v Switzerland* (1990) A 173.
3 27237/95, *Govell v United Kingdom* (14 January 1998); *Khan v United Kingdom* (12 May 2000). Contrast *Silver and Ors v United Kingdom* (1983) A 61, paras 85–88. See also *R (Matthias Rath Bv) v Advertising Standards Authority* [2001] HRLR 22 (ASA codes of practice: prescribed by law).

3.36   Secondly, the law must meet certain requirements, notably of accessibility and foreseeability. These are essentially aspects of a single objective: legal certainty. In relation to accessibility, the European Court of Human Rights said in the *Sunday Times* case:

> 'First, the law must be adequately accessible: the citizen must be able to have an indication that is adequate in the circumstances of the legal rules applicable to a given case.[1]'

In relation to foreseeability, the Court said in the same case:

> 'Secondly, a norm cannot be regarded as a "law" unless it is formulated with sufficient precision to enable the citizen to regulate his conduct: he must be able – if need be with appropriate advice – to foresee, to a degree that is reasonable in the circumstances, the consequences which a given action may entail. Those consequences need not be foreseeable with absolute certainty: experience shows this to be unattainable. Again, whilst certainty is highly desirable, it may bring in its train excessive rigidity and the law must be able to keep pace with changing circumstances. Accordingly, many laws are inevitably couched in terms which, to a greater or lesser extent, are vague and whose interpretation and application are questions of practice.'

The level of precision required will be dependent on 'the content of the instrument in question; the field it is designed to cover and the number and status of those to whom it is addressed'[2]. The law can confer a discretion, but in order to conform to the notion of the rule of law there must be some safeguard against arbitrariness in its application[3]:

> 'A law which confers a discretion is not in itself inconsistent with [the requirement of foreseeability], provided that the scope of the discretion and the manner of its exercise are indicated with sufficient clarity, having regard to the legitimate aim in question, to give the individual adequate protection against arbitrary interference'.[4]

1 *Sunday Times (No 1) v United Kingdom* (1979) A 30, para 49.
2 *Rekvényi v Hungary* (20 May 1999) para 34. Particular issues arise in the context of secret surveillance: see *Malone v United Kingdom* (1984) A 82; *Kruslin v France* (1990) A 176-B; *Kopp v Switzerland* 1988-II, 524, para 34.
3 *Malone v United Kingdom* (1984) A 82, paras 67–68.
4 *Margareta and Roger Andersson v Sweden* (1992) A 26-A, para 75.

3.37   These requirements do not give rise to any particular difficulty in relation to the common law. Indeed, as the European Court of Human Rights has pointed out, 'it would be wrong to exaggerate the difference between common-law countries and Continental countries'[1]. The development of a common law offence, for example, is not inconsistent with legal certainty, provided that any development is reasonably foreseeable and consistent with the essence of the offence[2]. Nor are jury awards of damages in defamation cases inconsistent with legal certainty: although there are no specific legal guidelines, that is 'an inherent feature of the law of damages', which has to make allowances for 'an open-ended variety of factual situations'; and an irrational award could be set aside by the appeal court[3]. The Court has accepted that the English concept of breach of the peace is defined with sufficient precision for the foreseeability criterion to be satisfied[4]. On the other hand, the power of the English courts to bind persons over to be of good behaviour (ie not to act *contra bonos mores*) did not satisfy that criterion, because of its complete lack of precision[5]. These cases also indicate that the surrounding factual circumstances, as well as the legal definition in question, can be taken into account in assessing whether the foreseeability criterion is satisfied[6].

1 *Kruslin v France* (1990) A 176-B, para 29.
2 *SW v United Kingdom* (1995) A 355-B.
3 *Tolstoy Miloslavsky v United Kingdom* (1995) A 316-B, paras 37–44. On the other hand, the award in the case in question was disproportionate to the aim of protecting reputation and therefore failed the requirement of being 'necessary in a democratic society'. This case illustrates how the Convention can impact upon litigation between private parties.
4 *McLeod v United Kingdom* 1998-VII, 2774, para 42; *Steel v United Kingdom* 1998-VII, 2719, paras 55–57.
5 *Hashman and Harrup v United Kingdom* (25 November 1999).
6 See *Hashman and Harrup v United Kingdom* (25 November 1999) paras 35 and 40.

3.38   The requirement of legal certainty is also reflected in the European Convention on Human Rights, Article 5, which requires any deprivation of liberty to be 'lawful' and 'in accordance with a procedure prescribed by law'. The principles already discussed apply also to these requirements:

> '[T]he expressions "lawful" and "in accordance with a procedure prescribed by law" in art 5(1) stipulate not only full compliance with the procedural and substantive rules of national law, but also that any deprivation of liberty be consistent with the purpose of art 5 and not arbitrary. In addition, given

the importance of personal liberty, it is essential that the applicable national law meets the standard of "lawfulness" set by the Convention, which requires that all law, whether written or unwritten, be sufficiently precise to allow the citizen – if need be, with appropriate advice – to foresee, to a degree that is reasonable in the circumstances, the consequences which a given action may entail.'[1]

1 *Steel v United Kingdom* 1998-VII, 2719, para 54.

3.39   In the context of the criminal law, the need for legal certainty is reflected in the European Convention on Human Rights, Article 7:

'Article 7(1) of the Convention is not confined to prohibiting the retrospective application of the criminal law to an accused's disadvantage. It also embodies, more generally, the principle that only law can define a crime and prescribe a penalty (*nullum crimen, nulla poena, sine lege*) and the principle that the criminal law must not be extensively construed to an accused's detriment, for instance by analogy: it follows from this that an offence must be clearly defined in law.'[1]

This requirement embodies the criteria already discussed: accessibility and foreseeability[2]. It is not incompatible with the development of common law or other offences by judicial case law:

'However clearly drafted a legal provision may be, in any system of law, including criminal law, there is an inevitable element of judicial interpretation. There will always be a need for elucidation of doubtful points and for adaptation to changing circumstances. Indeed, in the United Kingdom, as in the other Convention states, the progressive development of the criminal law through judicial law-making is a well entrenched and necessary part of legal tradition. Article 7 of the Convention cannot be read as outlawing the gradual clarification of the rules of criminal liability through judicial interpretation from case to case, providing the resultant development is consistent with the essence of the offence and could reasonably be foreseen.'[3]

In the opinion of the Commission, Article 7 implies that the consistent elements of an offence (eg 'the particular form of culpability required for its completion') may not be essentially changed to the detriment of the accused by judicial decision, but does not prevent the clarification of the existing elements of the offence or their adaptation to new circumstances which can reasonably be brought within the original concept of the offence[4]. Article 7 is considered more fully in chapter 5 below[5].

1 *Kokkinakis v Greece* (1993) A 260-A, para 52.
2 *SW v United Kingdom* (1995) A 355-B, para 32. The exceptional problems arising from the prosecution of former East German officials and border guards, following German reunification, are discussed in *Streletz v Germany* and *K-H W v Germany* (22 March 2001).
3 *SW v United Kingdom* (1995) A 355-B, para 36 (marital rape).
4 8710/79, *X Ltd and Y v United Kingdom* (1982) DR 28, 77, para 9.
5 At paras 5.13ff below.

Non-discrimination

3.40   The principle of non-discrimination is of fundamental importance in the constitutional law of most European states. In Germany, for example, equality is guaranteed by the Basic Law (*Grundgesetz*) of 1949, Article 3; and, in France, equality is one of the *principles généraux du droit*. Non-discrimination is equally fundamental as an unwritten principle of European Community law, belonging to 'that philosophical, political and legal substratum common to the Member States from which though the case law an unwritten Community law emerges'[1]. In Community law, as in national systems such as French law, the principle requires a consideration of differential treatment in the light of the stated reasons for the measure in question: 'it is thus only within the sphere of the ends pursued that the principle must be respected; it will be infringed only if one treats differently two situations which are similar with regard to their ends'[2]. As will appear, the approach adopted under the European Convention on Human Rights is essentially similar, and turns in much the same way upon an assessment of the comparability of situations in the light of the objectives of the measure in question, and upon an assessment of the justification for their differential treatment in the light of those objectives, applying the principle of proportionality[3] (and, at the Strasbourg level, the doctrine of the margin of appreciation)[4]. In accordance with the principle of effectiveness[5], the focus is upon substantive equality rather than formal equality[6].

1 Case 11/70 *Internationale Handelsgesellschaft* [1970] ECR 1125 1146 per Dutheillet de Lamothe AG.
2 Case 13/63 *Italy v Commission* [1963] ECR 165, 190 per Lagrange AG.
3 See para 3.71 below.
4 See para 3.85 below.
5 See para 3.24 above.
6 See para 3.43 below.

3.41   The principle of non-discrimination is expressed in the European Convention on Human Rights in Article 14[1]:

> 'The enjoyment of the rights and freedoms set forth in this Convention shall be secured without discrimination on any ground such as sex, race, colour, language, religion, political or other opinion, national or social origin, association with a national minority, property, birth or other status.'

The list of prohibited grounds for discrimination is qualified by the phrase 'any ground such as', and is not exhaustive but merely illustrative[2]. As is apparent from its terms, Article 14 does not confer any free-standing or substantive right: it expresses a principle to be applied in relation to the substantive rights conferred by other provisions. In other words, Article 14 can only be considered in conjunction with one or more of the substantive guarantees contained in Articles 2–12 of the Convention or in one of the protocols[3]. Article 14 is nevertheless of fundamental importance: 'a measure which in itself is in conformity with the requirements of the article enshrining the right or freedom in question may however infringe this Article when read in conjunction with art 14 for the reason that is of a discriminatory nature'[4].

1 The Commission has also considered discriminatory treatment, taken with the intention of humiliating or debasing an individual, as treatment sufficiently degrading to violate the European Convention on Human Rights, Art 3: 4403/70, *East African Asians v United Kingdom* (1970) CD 36, 92; (1973) DR 78, 5. Other Council of Europe initiatives also seek to

tackle prejudice, eg the Framework Convention for the Protection of National Minorities: see paras 2.35–2.38 above. On 26 June 2000 the Committee of Ministers agreed Protocol 12, which creates a new right not to be discriminated against in the enjoyment of any right set forth by law. The protocol was opened for signature on 4 November 2000. It is available at www.cm.coe.int/ .

2 *Engel v Netherlands* (1976) A 22, para 72.

3 For example, the lack of access for disabled persons to a beach did not fall within the ambit of any substantive Convention right, and therefore did not violate ECHR, Art 14: *Botta v Italy* 1998-I, 412, paras 37–39.

4 *Belgian Linguistics Case* (1968) A6, Law, para 9. For example, discrimination in sentencing could contravene ECHR, Art 5 read in conjunction with Art 14, although each sentence considered in isolation might be unobjectionable: 22761/93, *RM v United Kingdom* (1994) DR 77, 98. The Commission observed (at 105) that the position is 'as though art 14 formed an integral part of each of the provisions laying down the specific rights and freedoms'. Even if a state exceeds its obligations under the Convention, it will contravene Art 14 in conjunction with the substantive provision in issue if it does so in a discriminatory fashion: *Belgian Linguistics Case* (1968) A6, Law, para 9. See eg *Abdulaziz, Cabales and Balkandali v United Kingdom* (1989) A 94, paras 70–89.

3.42   As already mentioned, the application of the European Convention on Human Rights, Article 14 turns in the first place upon an assessment of the comparability of the situations in questions. The persons in question must be in a 'relevantly similar'[1] position. The onus of establishing this rests on the applicant[2].

1 *National and Provincial Building Society v United Kingdom* 1997-VII, 2325, para 88.

2 See eg *Menteş v Turkey* 1997-VIII, 2689, para 95: *Fredin v Sweden* (1991) A 192. A great variety of comparisons have been considered, eg Scottish prisoners compared with prisoners elsewhere in the United Kingdom: 11077/84, *Nelson v United Kingdom* (1986) DR 49, 170; married couples compared with unmarried couples: 11089/84, *Lindsay v United Kingdom* (1986) DR 49, 181: domiciled persons, seeking to rely upon a foreign divorce, compared with non-domiciled persons: *Johnston v Ireland* (1986) A 112, para 60; trainee barristers compared with intrants to other professions: *Van der Mussele v Belgium* (1983) A 70; victims of negligent delicts compared with victims of intentional delicts: *Stubbings v United Kingdom* 1996-IV, 1487; citizens compared with non-citizens: *Gaygusuz v Austria* 1996-IV, 1129, paras 46–50, cf *Moustaquiem v Belgium* (1991) A 193, para 49; homosexuals compared with heterosexuals: 25186/94, *Sutherland v United Kingdom* (1 July 1997); transsexuals compared with persons of a given biological sex: *Sheffield and Horsham v United Kingdom* 1998-V, 2011; and 'illegitimate' compared with 'legitimate' children: *Marckx v Belgium* (1997) A 31.

3.43   If the applicant establishes that the situations in question are comparable, the remaining issue is whether the difference in their treatment has an 'objective and reasonable'[1] justification. The onus of establishing such a justification lies on the state[2]. A difference in treatment is therefore not automatically discriminatory: public authorities 'are frequently confronted with situations and problems which, on account of differences inherent therein, call for different legal solutions: moreover, certain legal inequalities tend only to correct factual inequalities'[3]. A difference in treatment will therefore be discriminatory only if it does not pursue a legitimate aim, or if there is no 'reasonable relationship of proportionality between the means employed and the aim sought to be realised'[4]. As always, this assessment of proportionality requires the court to strike a fair balance between the protection of the interests of the community and respect for the rights and freedoms safeguarded by the Convention. It is also necessary to bear in mind the 'living instrument' principle: distinctions in treatment which were formerly acceptable may come to be considered no longer compatible with the European Convention on Human Rights, Article 14[5]. The European Court of Human Rights will also apply the 'margin of appreciation' doctrine[6].

1 *Belgian Linguistics Case* (1968) A 6.
2 See eg 25186/94, *Sutherland v United Kingdom* (1 July 1997); *Markcx v Belgium* (1979) A 31, paras 32–43.
3 *Belgian Linguistics Case* (1968) A 6. See eg 11089/84, *Lindsay v United Kingdom* (1986) DR 49, 181.
4 *Belgian Linguistics Case* (1968) A 6. See eg 11089/84, *Lindsay v United Kingdom* (1986) DR 49, 181; *Darby v Sweden* (1991) A 187, para 31.
5 Eg as to the status of 'illegitimate' children: *Inze v Austria* (1988) A 126, para 41; or the age of consent for homosexual relations: 25186/94, *Sutherland v United Kingdom* (1 July 1997).
6 *Lithgow v United Kingdom* (1986) A 102, para 177. *Belgium Linguistics Case* (1968) A 6.

3.44 In practice, the European Court of Human Rights will not normally consider any complaint of discrimination under the European Convention on Human Rights, Article 14 when it has already established that there has been a violation of a substantive guarantee raising substantially the same point[1].

1 Eg in *Lustig-Prean and Beckett v United Kingdom* (27 September 1999), concerned with the policy of excluding homosexuals from the armed forces: the Court declined to consider the European Convention on Human Rights, Art 14 issue, noting that this matter 'amounts in effect to the same complaint (as under Art 8), albeit seen from a different angle' (para 108). Similarly a complaint of racial bias on the part of a jury was disposed of under Art 6 alone: *Gregory v United Kingdom* 1997-I 296, paras 43–50. In *X and Y v Netherlands* (1985) A 91, para 32, the Court indicated that the position will be different where 'a clear inequality of treatment in the enjoyment of the right in question is a fundamental aspect of the case'.

3.45 The European Convention on Human Rights, Article 14 potentially has a very wide scope. This can be illustrated by *Thlimmenos v Greece*, which concerned a person who had been refused admission as a chartered accountant because of a criminal conviction arising from his refusal to wear military uniform due to his religious beliefs as a Jehovah's Witness[1]. The majority of cases under the European Convention on Human Rights, Article 14, however, concern more predictable situations, such as discrimination based on sex or sexual orientation. There have also been a significant number of cases concerned with 'illegitimate' children. These and other issues are discussed in the following paragraphs.

1 (6 April 2000).

3.46 The European Court of Human Rights has frequently expressed the view that the advancement of the equality of the sexes is a major goal in the member states of the Council of Europe. As such is has stated that very weighty reasons would have to be put forward before the Convention organs could regard as compatible with the Convention, a difference in treatment based exclusively on the ground of sex[1]. Unsurprisingly therefore, this ethos underpins much of the Court's jurisprudence. In *Burghartz v Switzerland*, for example, the Court held that a Swiss law which permitted a wife to use her surname before their family name, but which prohibited her husband from doing so, lacked an objective and reasonable basis and thus constituted discrimination based on sex which was incompatible with Articles 8 and 14[2]. In *Karlheinz Schmidt* the Court had to consider a German law which obliged men, but not women, to serve in the fire brigade or to make a financial contribution[3]. The Court noted that in view of the continuing existence of a sufficient number of volunteers, no male person was obliged in practice to serve in a fire brigade. It held that the financial contribution had become the only effective duty and in the imposition of such a financial burden, a difference of treatment could hardly be justified. As such there had been a violation of Article 14 taken in conjunction with Article 4, paragraph 3[4]. This case can be contrasted with the decision of the Commission in *Spöttl v Austria*, where the applicant argued that the obligation to perform military service constituted discrimination prohibited by Article 4 in conjunction with Article 14, as women were not subject to such a duty. The Commission, however, held this complaint to be inadmissible. It observed that in so far as the applicant complained about the difference in treatment between men and women with regard to the obligation to perform military service, the difference in treatment was justified by objective reasons, which were within the broad margin of appreciation available to states in respect of their national defence policy[5]. The Commission distinguished this case from the judgment of the Court in *Karlheinz Schmidt* on the basis that, in that case, the obligation to serve in the fire brigade existed only in theory, that the men were only liable to a levy as a compensatory contribution, and the Court's finding in that case was limited to the assertion that a difference in treatment on the ground of sex in the imposition of a financial burden could not be justified.

1 *Schuler-Zgraggen v Switzerland* (1993) A 263, para 67; *Burghartz v Switzerland* (1994) A 280-B, para 27; *Karlheinz Schmidt v Germany* (1994) A 291-B, para 24.
2 (1994) A 280-B.
3 (1994) A 291-B, paras 21–30.
4 Paras 28–29.
5 22956/93, *Spöttl v Austria* (1996) DR 85, 58.

3.47   Ensuring equality between the sexes has also been an important consideration underlying many of the Strasbourg authorities' judgments in relation to allocation of benefits. In *Van Raalte v Netherlands*, the applicant was an unmarried man with no children. He complained that a law which exempted childless women over the age of 45 from paying social security contributions towards child benefit, but which had no such provisions for exempting men, was discriminatory[1]. The European Court of Human Rights held that while states enjoyed a certain margin of appreciation under the European Convention on Human Rights as regards the introduction of exemptions to such contributory obligations, Article 14 requires that such a measure 'applies even-handedly to both men and women unless compelling reasons have been adduced to justify a difference in treatment'[2]. In this case the Court was not persuaded that such reasons existed, and thus it held that there had been a violation of Article 14 when taken together with Protocol 1, Article 1. In *Schuler-Zgraggen*, which concerned the decision of the domestic court to refuse the applicant invalidity benefit, the applicant alleged that the domestic court had violated Article 14 in conjunction with Article 6 when it based its judgment on the assumption that many married women gave up their jobs when their first child was born and resumed it later. The court had then inferred from this that the applicant would have given up work even if she had not had health problems. The applicant considered that if she had been a man, the court would never have made such an assumption, which was in any case contradicted by several scientific studies. The Court noted that this assumption was 'the sole basis for the reasoning', and thus it introduced a difference in treatment based on the grounds of sex only that lacked any reasonable and objective justification[3]. *In MacGregor v United Kingdom*[4], a case which concerned personal tax allowances, the Commission held admissible a complaint that a female tax payer with a young child and totally incapacitated husband was unable to claim additional personal allowance granted to males under the Income and Corporate Taxes Act 1988, s 259. A friendly settlement was reached when the United Kingdom accepted that there were no grounds for the discrimination.

1 1997-I, 173.
2 *Van Raalte v Netherlands* 1997-I, 173, paras 41–45 at 42.
3 (1993) A 263, para 67.
4 30548/96, (1 July 1998).

3.48   There have been a number of cases against the United Kingdom concerning discrimination in the allocation of benefit entitlements to widows and widowers. Social security legislation meant that a widower was not entitled to the same benefits that a bereaved widow would have had (widowed mother's allowance). In the first case, *Cornwell v United Kingdom*, after the Commission had declared the claim admissible from the data upon which complaint had been raised, a friendly settlement was reached on the basis that the applicant widower was paid the same amount as a widow would have received[1]. Following this agreement the case was struck out of the list. Since this decision a number of cases have been taken against the United Kingdom in respect of this social security legislation. The United Kingdom has admitted that these provisions are discriminatory and has been reaching friendly settlements in all of these cases[2].

1 *Cornwell v United Kingdom* (25 April 2000).
2 Eg *Leary v United Kingdom* (25 April 2000), para 11.

3.49   The cases where the European Court of Human Rights has not held differences in the treatment of the sexes to be a violation of the European Convention on Human Rights, Article 14 have generally concerned issues on which there is no common standard among member states, and thus where the states have a wider margin of appreciation. One of the most contentious areas has been regarding distinctions in treatment between unmarried fathers and mothers. The Convention does not necessarily require that an unmarried father enjoy equality of treatment with a mother in the recognition of parental rights[1]. Article 5 of Protocol 7 specifically provides that 'spouses shall enjoy equality of rights and responsibilities', and thus the implication is that where a state has not ratified this protocol certain differences in treatment are not incompatible with the Convention.

1 The weaker standing of an unmarried father is found elsewhere in Europe: eg 9639/82, *B, R & J v Germany* (1984) DR 36, 130 (differences in treatment could be justified by the greater protection afforded to the family based on marriage in light of the European Convention on Human Rights, Art 12).

3.50 That this is an evolving area of Convention jurisprudence is evident from the different approaches taken by the European Commission on Human Rights and the European Court of Human Rights. In relation to the issue of parental leave, for example, the Commission used the strong wording of the judgments of the Court in such cases as *Karlheinz Schmidt* and *Burghartz*, emphasising the need for sexual equality to rule that failure to permit parental leave payments for fathers, when mothers were entitled to payment, was a violation of Article 14[1]. It noted that 'the lack of a common standard cannot absolve the Contracting States which have opted for a specific scheme of parental leave payments from granting these benefits in a non-discriminatory manner[2]. In *Petrovic v Austria*, however, the Court reached a different conclusion. In this case, a father had his claim for parental leave allowance rejected by an employment office since at that time only mothers could qualify. While agreeing with the Commission that payment of social welfare assistance by the state was made with a view to promoting family life and thus Article 8 was applicable, the Court did not accept that the discrimination violated Article 14. Of crucial importance was the lack of any common European standard in social security provision for parental leave to be paid to fathers although most states were according a high priority to equality of the sexes and were moving gradually towards implementation of this in child care matters. Accordingly the state was entitled to a wider margin of appreciation, in its assessment of the need for a difference of treatment, than would otherwise have been the case[3].

1 20458/92, *AP v Austria* (15 October 1996).
2 20458/92, *AP v Austria* (15 October 1996) at para 37.
3 1998-II, 579, paras 22–43. The Commission had determined a violation by a majority of 25 to 5; for the two dissenting judges on the Court, the lack of any standard European norm 'was not conclusive'; while states were not under a duty in terms of the European Convention on Human Rights, Art 8 to pay any such allowance, if they chose to do so it would not be appropriate to do so in a discriminatory manner.

3.51 In *McMichael v United Kingdom*, the European Court of Human Rights upheld the distinction in Scots law[1] between the automatic conferment of parental rights to a married father and the requirement placed upon an unmarried father to take some form of positive step to acquire these (such as through an application to a court). It held that this requirement was a proportionate response to achieve the legitimate aim of distinguishing between fathers who had some justifiable claim and those whose status lacked sufficient merit[2].

1 Formal equality as regards the exercise of parental rights is specifically rejected by Scots law. Under the Children (Scotland) Act 1995, a father will automatically enjoy parental rights (including in terms of s 2 the rights to have the child living with him or otherwise to regulate the child's residence; to control, guide and direct the child's upbringing in a manner appropriate to the child's stage of development; to maintain personal relations and direct contact with the child on a regular basis where the child is not living with him; and to act as the child's legal representative) only if married to the mother (at the time of conception or subsequently); if unmarried, to acquire such rights he must draw up an agreement with the mother and have this registered (s 4) or alternatively apply for parental rights through a court order (s 11). See also *Re W (Minors) (Abduction: father's rights)* [1999] Fam 1.
2 (1995) A 308, para 98.

3.52 Distinctions based upon illegitimacy are seldom considered to a have a legitimate aim. In *Marckx v Belgium*, domestic law still required an unmarried mother to follow certain legal procedure in order to establish a legal bond with her child; further, the rights of inheritance on intestacy of a recognised illegitimate child were less than those of a child recognised as legitimate. The European Court of Human Rights noted that the text of ECHR, Article 8 did not distinguish between family units constituted through marriage and those outside wedlock. Moreover it considered that to imply any such interpretation would have been inconsistent with the general principle that Convention guarantees apply to 'everyone', as well as contrary to the prohibition of Article 14 of any discrimination in the enjoyment of Convention rights on grounds including 'birth'[1]. The Court confirmed this approach in *Camp and Bourimi v Netherlands*[2], which concerned the situation of a child whose unmarried father had died without having recognised the child or leaving a will. The child was born illegitimate, however despite the subsequent granting of letters of legitimation, domestic law prevented the child inheriting from his father. Although the Court held that there had been no violation of Article 8 when considered alone, it noted that matters of intestate succession between near relatives fell within the scope of Article 8 as they represented a feature of family life. As such the Court held that it was appropriate to consider Article 14 in conjunction with Article 8. The Court noted that the protection of the rights of other heirs might constitute a legitimate claim, however the child was treated differently not only from children born in wedlock, but also from children who although born out of wedlock had been recognised by their fathers. As such the child's exclusion from his father's inheritance was disproportionate and consequently there had been a breach of Article 14 when taken together with Article 8.

1 (1979) A 31, (various violations of the European Convention on Human Rights, Art 8 taken alone, of Art 8 taken in conjunction with Art 14, and of Art 14 taken in conjunction with Protocol 1, Art 1).
2 (3 October 2000). See also *Mazurek v France* (1 February 2000).

3.53 Differences in treatment based upon sexual orientation are subject to particular scrutiny and are unlikely to satisfy the requirement of legitimate aim. Often the treatment complained about will have a discriminatory aspect at its core[1]. Consequently, it is important to note that although many of the judgments of the European Court of Human Rights have not concerned ECHR, Article 14 directly, they have had a considerable impact in influencing and indeed forming the approach against discrimination based on sexual orientation.

1 E g *Lustig-Prean and Beckett v United Kingdom* (27 September 1999), where the discriminatory practice of prohibiting homosexuals from serving in the armed services was considered only in relation to the European Convention on Human Rights, Art 8.

3.54 Initially many of the cases which the Strasbourg authorities had to consider concerned sanctions imposed by the criminal law[1]. In *Sutherland v United Kingdom*, for example, the Commission considered that different ages for the minimum age of consent between heterosexual and homosexual activity violated the European Convention on Human Rights, Article 8 when taken along with Article 14. Domestic law prohibited homosexual acts between males over the age of 16 but under the age of 18 years, while the minimum age for heterosexual activity was 16. The Commission could find no objective and reasonable justification for the distinction, even after attaching some weight to recent deliberations by Parliament which had considered the argument that certain young men between the ages of 16 and 18 did not yet have a settled sexual orientation and thus required protection, and further that society was 'entitled to indicate its disapproval of homosexual conduct and its preference that children follow a heterosexual way of life': neither reason was considered sufficient. The Commission noted that current medical findings suggested sexual orientation was already fixed in both sexes by the age of 16 and thus the suggestion of recruitment was inadequate. Moreover, the Commission reiterated the Court's statement in *Dudgeon v United Kingdom* that preference for a heterosexual lifestyle could not constitute an objective or reasonable justification[2].

1 *Dudgeon v United Kingdom* (1981) A 45; *Norris v Ireland* (1988) A 142; *Modinos v Cyprus* (1993) A 259 (all concerned the criminalisation of sex between men).
2 25186/94, (1 July 1997) paras 55–66.

3.55 It has been suggested that in the area of sexual orientation discrimination the impact of the European Court of Human Rights' decisions was lessened by virtue of the fact that its judgments in cases such as *Dudgeon* were 'confined to the single issue of the criminalisation of same-sex relations[1]. More recent cases, however, have signalled an expansion of the Court's jurisprudence into other areas of the law. The decision of the Court in *Smith and Grady v United Kingdom*, concerning employment, while not concerning Article 14, is instrumental in demonstrating the Court's commitment to the prohibition of discrimination in the application of any Convention right on the ground of sexual orientation. In the case, the Court held that the dismissal of gay and lesbian military personnel on the basis of their sexual orientation violated the right to respect for private life protected by Article 8[2]. This approach is in contrast to the reticence of the European Court of Justice, which has not found sexual orientation discrimination to be unlawful under EC sex discrimination law[3].

1 Wintemute *Sexual Orientation and Human Rights; The United States Constitution, the European Convention and the Canadian Charter* (1995).
2 See also *Lustig-Prean and Beckett v United Kingdom* (27 September 1999).
3 Case 249/96, *Grant v South-West Trains* [1998] ECR I-621. See Bamforth 'Sexual Orientation Discrimination after *Grant v South-West Trains*' [2000] MLR 694; and *Advocate General of Scotland v MacDonald* 2001 SLT 819.

3.56 The European Court of Human Rights took another important step in prohibiting such discrimination in *Sulgueiro da Silva Mouta v Portugal* when it held for the first time that discrimination on the ground of homosexuality violated the European Convention on Human Rights, Article 14. It ruled that the refusal to grant custody of the daughter of a marriage to the father, who was by then living in a homosexual relationship, on the particular ground that such an environment could not be a healthy one in which to raise a child, violated Article 8 when taken together with Article 14[1]. This case emphasises that discrimination on the ground of sexual orientation falls within the ambit of Article 14 and that it 'cannot be tolerated under the convention'[2].

1 (21 December 1999).
2 For an examination of the possible implications for Scots law see Norrie 'Stay Standing if you Like Gay People' (2000) SCOLAG 34.

3.57 The treatment of transsexuals has necessitated consideration of the discrimination provisions. In *Sheffield & Horsham v United Kingdom*[1], the applicants, who were both transsexuals, claimed that the failure of the Government to recognise in law that they were of the female sex constituted a violation of the European Convention on Human Rights, Article 8 alone and in conjunction with Article 14. The Court held, however, that the United Kingdom was entitled to rely on the margin of appreciation to defend its refusal to recognise in law a post-operative transsexual's sexual identity. Minimal inquiries as to pre-operative status were held not to be a disproportionate interference with applicants' Article 8 rights. The Court also ruled that there had been no violation of Article 14 taken together with Article 8. Relying again on the margin of appreciation, the Court held that the measures taken by the state had struck a fair balance between safeguarding the interests of transsexuals and the interests of the community and were not disproportionate. Moreover, it noted that these considerations 'which are equally encompassed in the notion of "reasonable and objective justification" for the purpose of Article 14 of the Convention, must also be seen as justifying the difference in treatment which the applicants experienced'[2]. The approach of the Court appears to rest on the assumption that as yet there is no consensus within Europe on the status of transsexuals, and consequently that it is preferable to allow states some latitude in regulating this area[3]. The assertion that there is no consensus in Europe was questioned in the joint dissenting opinion of several of the judges who noted that only the United Kingdom, Ireland, Albania and Andorra expressly prohibited any changes to birth certificates in such circumstances, and indeed that the majority of European countries allowed such amendments[4]. Nevertheless, neither the Commission nor the strong dissenting opinions focused expressly on Article 14, and it therefore seems likely that any moves in the future to improve the status of transsexuals are likely to rely on the substantive provision protecting private life, rather that Article 14.

1 1998-V, 2011.
2 *Sheffield and Horsham v United Kingdom* 1998-V, 2011 at para 76.
3 *Sheffield and Horsham v United Kingdom* 1998-V, 2011 at paras 55–61.
4 Joint partly dissenting opinion of Judges Bernhardt, Thorvilhjalmsson, Spielmann, Palm, Wildhaber, Makarczyk and Voicu.

3.58 The European Court of Human Rights has on several occasions ruled that discriminatory treatment on religious grounds is incompatible with the European Convention on Human Rights. Interestingly, in several of the cases, Article 14 has not been considered in conjunction with Article 9, the provision guaranteeing, inter alia, freedom of religion, but in connection with other substantive provisions. In *Hoffman v Austria*[1], for example, the applicant had been denied custody of her child because of her involvement with the Jehovah's Witnesses. The Court held that it was unacceptable for a domestic court to base a decision on the ground of a difference in religion. Although the point at issue was essentially one of religion, the Court considered it under Articles 8 and 14 as it concerned the determination of child custody, an aspect of family life. As it had already considered the matter under Articles 8 and 14, the Court held that there was no need to consider the point under Article 9.

1   (1993) A 255-C.

3.59   In *Canea Catholic Church v Greece*[1] the European Court of Human Rights had to consider a situation where a church could not take legal proceedings in order to protect its property rights while the Orthodox Church and the Jewish Community were able to do so. The Court found that there could be no objective and reasonable justification for this discriminatory treatment and thus there was a violation of Article 6(1) taken in conjunction with Article 14.

1   1997-VIII, 2843.

3.60   Religious beliefs may also involve consideration of discriminatory treatment in employment and give rise to questions under the European Convention on Human Rights, Article 14. In *Thlimmenos v Greece*, the applicant had been refused admission as a chartered accountant on the ground of a conviction for insubordination. As a Jehovah's Witness professing pacifism, he had refused to wear military uniform at a time of general mobilisation for which he had been imprisoned for more than two years. While the European Court of Human Rights noted that access to a profession is not covered by the Convention, the applicant's complaint concerned the lack of distinction between convictions based upon religious beliefs and other convictions for criminal offences. In effect, the complaint alleged discrimination on the basis of the exercise of freedom of religion. While states could legitimately exclude certain classes of offenders from various professions, any conviction for refusing to wear military uniform on the basis of religious convictions could not suggest dishonesty or moral turpitude and thus did not follow a legitimate aim. Further, the disqualification was in the nature of an additional and disproportionate sanction. Accordingly, there was a violation of Article 14 taken in conjunction with Article 9 on account of the lack of objective and reasonable justification for the disqualification[1].

1   (6 April 2000).

3.61   The right to education, protected by the European Convention on Human Rights, Protocol 1, Article 2, has many facets. It encompasses not only the right of access to educational institutions but also the right to effective education and official recognition of the successful completion of studies[1]. There is considerable scope for the use of anti-discrimination provisions in this area. The Strasbourg authorities, however, have proven reluctant to examine in detail the effectiveness principle, an indication, perhaps, of the width of the margin of appreciation in relation to this provision. In *SP v United Kingdom*, the Commission declared inadmissible a complaint by a child with special needs who claimed that he was denied his right to education[2]. His mother has argued that the teaching staff at the various schools, which her son had attended, had failed to take into account her son's special needs, and that this had contributed to the behavioural problems that her son had experienced. The Commission, however, did not believe that he had been denied his right to education[3]. Thus while the Strasbourg authorities have recognised the need for equal treatment in education, they have so far declined to examine in any detail the conditions which are necessary to ensure that this equality is effective[4].

1 *Belgian Linguistics Case* (1968) A 6.
2 28915/95, *SP v United Kingdom* (17 January 1997).
3 For an examination of how the discrimination provisions affect special needs students, see Black-Branch, 'Equality, Non-Discrimination and the Right to Special Education; From International Law to the Human Rights Act' [2000] EHRLR 297.
4 See also 29046/95, *McIntyre v United Kingdom* (21 October 1998) (the Commission declared inadmissible a complaint by a physically disabled applicant that she had been denied the right to education as a result of the school's refusal to install a lift to allow her to access the same facilities as her able-bodied peers); 25959/94, *Cohen v United Kingdom* (28 February 1996) (refusal of local authority to pay cost of transport of a child with special needs to the school of choice was within the margin of appreciation and the facts did not disclose a violation of the European Convention on Human Rights, Art 14, thus the case was inadmissible).

3.62 One of the most instrumental judgments in outlining the scope of the European Convention on Human Rights, Article 14 in this area is the *Belgian Linguistics Case*. In this case the Court held that Article 14, even when read in conjunction with Protocol 1, Article 2, did not have the effect of guaranteeing to a child or his parents the right to obtain instructions in the language of his choice. The Court noted that the scope of the right was in fact more limited, and was to ensure that the right to education be secured by each contracting state to everyone within its jurisdiction without discrimination on the ground, for instance, of language. The Court also noted that 'to interpret the two provisions as conferring on everyone within the jurisdiction of a state a right to obtain education in the language of his choice would lead to absurd results, for it would be open to anyone to claim any language of instructions in any of the territories of the contracting parties'[1].

1 *Belgian Linguistics Case* (1968) A 6, para 11.

3.63 In *Kjeldsen, Busk Madsen and Pedersen v Denmark*, the European Court of Human Rights had to consider a Danish law which introduced compulsory sex education into primary schools[1]. The applicants, who were all parents with school age children, complained that the law violated Protocol 1, Article 2 when taken alone and in conjunction with Article 14. The applicants noted that Danish law made provision to allow parents to have their children exempted from religious education, and the failure to permit such an exemption with regard to sex education constituted discrimination contrary to Article 14. The Court rejected this argument, holding that there was a difference in kind between religious instruction, which necessarily disseminated tenets, and sex education, which was concerned with 'mere knowledge'[2]. Accordingly the discrimination objected to by the applicants was founded on dissimilar factual circumstances and was consistent with the requirements of Article 14. The issue of religious education in schools has also provoked some controversy. The Commission has acknowledged that Protocol 1, Article 2 permits parents to excuse children from lessons or acts of worship on the grounds of faith or religion[3]. The restrictive interpretation of this provision by the Court, however, means that it is unlikely that the Court would hold that a state has a positive obligation to provide alternative worship for such children. As such, some commentators have suggested that non-discrimination provisions may be more useful[4].

1   (1976) A 23.
2   *Kjeldsen, Busk Madsen and Pedersen v Denmark* (1976) A 23, para 56.
3   4733/71, *Karnell and Hardt v Sweden* (1971) YB 14, 676 at 690.
4   See Cumper 'School Worship: Praying for Guidance' [1998] EHRLR 45.

3.64   The European Court of Human Rights has often proven unwilling to find a violation of the European Convention on Human Rights, Article 14 on account of an allegation of discrimination by a state against minorities. Often this disinclination rests on a combination of difficulties in proving the allegations beyond reasonable doubt, combined with an acknowledgment of the sensitive political issues at stake. This is illustrated by a number of cases taken against the Turkish Government by applicants alleging discrimination against the Kurdish minority in southeast Turkey. *In Tanrikulu v Turkey*[1], for instance, the applicant claimed that her husband was killed because he was a Kurd and that he was thus a victim of discrimination on the ground of national origin. Although the Court found a violation of Article 2, it considered, relying on the Commission's findings, that there was no evidence to support a finding that there had been a violation of Article 14.

1   1999-IV, 457.

3.65   The European Court of Human Rights has also had to consider the treatment of gipsies. *In Buckley v United Kingdom*[1], the applicant was a gipsy living with her three children on land which she owned. Her land was part of six plots, which were occupied by gipsies; one plot had received planning permission for the residential use of three caravans. The remaining sites were occupied without planning permission and the occupants had been subject to enforcement proceedings. The applicant alleged that she was prevented from living with her family in caravans on her own land and was thus prevented from following the traditional lifestyle of a gipsy, contrary to Article 8. The Commission held that the measures taken were disproportionate and that there had been a violation of Article 8. The Court, however, disagreed, holding that the measures were proportionate[2]. The Court considered the applicant's complaint that there had been a violation of Article 14 in conjunction with Article 8, but held that it did not appear that the applicant was at any time penalised or subject to any detrimental treatment for attempting to follow a traditional gipsy lifestyle. In fact it noted that the national policy was aimed at enabling gipsies to care for their own needs[3]. *In Velikova v Bulgaria*, the Court had to consider an application of a gipsy on behalf of the man with whom she had been living prior to his death. Mr Tonshev had died following detention in police custody, and the applicant alleged that he had suffered discrimination because of his ethnic origin[4]. The Court held that there had been a violation of Article 2, as the state had not carried out an effective investigation into his death. In relation to Article 14, the Court noted that the applicant's complaint was 'grounded on a number of serious arguments' and further that the respondent state had failed to 'provide plausible reasons why the investigation omitted certain fundamental and indispensable steps which could have shed light on the events'. In spite of these findings, however, the Court concluded that the material before it did not enable it to 'conclude beyond reasonable doubt' that Mr Tonshev's killing and the lack of a meaningful investigation into it were 'motivated by racial prejudice, as claimed by the applicant'[5].

1 1996-IV, 1271.
2 *Buckley v United Kingdom* 1996-IV, 1271, at para 84.
3 *Buckley v United Kingdom* 1996-IV, 1271, at para 88. See also *Chapman v United Kingdom* (18 January 2001); *Jane Smith v United Kingdom* (18 January 2001).
4 (18 May 2000).
5 *Velikova v Bulgaria* (18 May 2000), para 94.

Necessity and proportionality

3.66   The concept of 'necessity' is involved (expressly or implicitly) in several articles of the European Convention on Human Rights, but it has subtly different connotations in different contexts. A broad distinction can be drawn between those articles which guarantee rights principally of a civil and political nature, that are subject to widely expressed qualifications, and those articles which guarantee rights (primarily those concerning physical integrity and human dignity) which are either subject to no express qualification or subject only to stringent qualifications.

3.67   Rights of the former kind are found in the European Convention on Human Rights, Articles 8–11. Paragraph 1 of each of these articles guarantees, in turn, respect for private and family life, home and correspondence; freedom of thought, conscience and religion; freedom of expression; and freedom of assembly and association. Paragraph 2 of each of these articles, however, goes on to identify particular interests or 'legitimate aims' which may justify interference with the protected rights, always provided that any such interference is 'in accordance with the law' (or 'prescribed by law') and 'necessary in a democratic society'[1]. Questions arising under these articles are determined using a well-established checklist:

1   What is the scope of the particular guarantee?
2   Has there been any interference with the right guaranteed?
3   Does the interference have a legitimate aim?
4   Is the interference 'in accordance with the law'?
5   Is the interference 'necessary in a democratic society'?

1 The same formula is used in the European Convention on Human Rights, Protocol 4, Art 2(3) concerning free movement of persons. This protocol has not been ratified by the United Kingdom.

3.68   In relation to the first and second of these questions, interpretation of the European Convention on Human Rights by the Commission and the Court has clarified the scope of each guarantee and the circumstances in which an interference will be considered to have been established. In relation to the third question, the legitimate aims, so far as Articles 8–11 are concerned, are listed in paragraph 2 of each of the articles in question: the interests of national security, public safety or the economic well-being of the country, the prevention of disorder or crime, the protection of health or morals, and the protection of the rights and freedoms of others. In practice, an interference purporting to have a legitimate aim will be accepted as falling within the scope of one of the listed objectives. In relation to the fourth question, the concept of 'accordance with the law' has been discussed earlier[1].

1 See para 3.34 above. See further Kempees ' "Legitimate Aims" in the Case Law of the European Court of Human Rights' in Mahoney, Matscher, Petzold and Wildhaber (eds) *Protecting Human Rights: The European Perspective* (2000) pp 659–675.

3.69 In most cases, the real difficulty lies in the fifth question, ie in deciding whether an interference is 'necessary in a democratic society'. In considering this phrase, it is important to bear in mind both the word 'necessary' and the words 'in a democratic society'. The Strasbourg Court has said:

> 'The Court has noted that, whilst the adjective "necessary", within the meaning of art 10(2), is not synonymous with "indispensable", neither has it the flexibility of such expressions as "admissible", "ordinary", "useful", "reasonable" or "desirable" and that it implies the existence of a "pressing social need" '.[1]

The Court has also identified certain characteristics of a 'democratic society', for example describing pluralism, tolerance and broadmindedness as hallmarks of a democratic society[2], and describing freedom of expression as one of the essential foundations of a democratic society[3]. Deciding whether an interference is 'necessary in a democratic society' may involve considering whether the law or practice in question is out of line with standards generally prevailing elsewhere in the Council of Europe states (either domestically, or in international conventions which they have accepted), as it is more difficult to justify a measure as being 'necessary in a democratic society' if the great majority of other Council of Europe states adopt a different approach.

1 *Sunday Times (No 1) v United Kingdom* (1979) A 30, para 59; *Handyside v United Kingdom* (1976) A 24, para 48. This formulation has been repeated in the context of the European Convention on Human Rights, Art 8(2): *Dudgeon v United Kingdom* (1981) A 45.
2 *Handyside v United Kingdom* (1976) A 24, para 49; *Dudgeon v United Kingdom* (1981) A 45, para 53.
3 *Handyside v United Kingdom* (1976) A 24, para 49; *Bowman v United Kingdom* 1998-I, 175, paras 42–43.

3.70 The question whether an interference is necessary in a democratic society is thus ineluctably a question of judgment. In the domestic law of the United Kingdom, questions of this nature, arising in the exercise of the courts' supervisory jurisdiction, have been resolved by applying what has come to be known as the *Wednesbury* test of unreasonableness[1]. Under the European Convention on Human Rights, the test applied is a rather more searching one: the requirement of 'proportionality'.

1 From *Associated Provincial Picture Houses Ltd v Wednesbury Corporation* [1948] 1 KB 223.

3.71 This concept has its origins in continental administrative law: it is found in German law, in the principle of *Verhältnissmässigkeit*, and a similar principle can also be seen in French law. It is also a well-established principle of European Community law, where it can be summarised as meaning that 'an official measure must not have any greater effect on private interests than is necessary for the attainment of its objective'[1]. If one were to substitute 'individual rights' for 'private interests', that formulation would encapsulate the essence of what is meant by proportionality in the context of the European Convention on Human Rights, Articles 8–11. As is apparent from this formulation, an assessment of proportionality is dependent on the specification of objectives and on the giving of reasons for decisions: equally, it is a means of ensuring that reasons are given. Proportionality is also related to the principle of non-discrimination, discussed earlier[2]. Discrimination can be defined as differential treatment of comparable situations which is not objectively justified, but this notion of justification involves the concept of proportionality. Proportionality is clearly a question of degree, and so involves a judicial evaluation of the situation in question. Accordingly, the requirements of proportionality will vary according to the circumstances of the case. In particular, proportionality does not require the effects of a general measure to be precisely tailored to each individual case affected where that would impose an unreasonable burden on the authorities involved. In general, although proportionality involves a closer examination of the merits of the case in issue than is traditional in the administrative law of the United Kingdom, that examination remains one of a supervisory rather than appellate character.

1 Case 125/77 *Koninklijke Scholten-Honig v Hoofproduktschap voor Akkerbouwprodukten* [1978] ECR 1991, 2030.
2 At para 3.40 above.

3.72 Authoritative guidance as to the criteria to be used in assessing proportionality under domestic law were given by Lord Clyde in *De Freitas v Permanent Secretary of Ministry of Agriculture, Fisheries, Lands and Housing*[1], and has been adopted by the House of Lords in subsequent cases under the Human Rights Act 1998[2]. The court should ask itself:

> 'Whether: (i) the legislative objective is sufficiently important to justify limiting a fundamental right; (ii) the measures designed to meet the legislative objective are rationally connected to it; and (iii) the means used to impair the right or freedom are no more than is necessary to accomplish the objective.'

1 [1999] 1 AC 69.
2 Eg *R v A (No 2)* [2001] 2 WLR 1546.

3.73 In the context of the European Convention on Human Rights, Articles 8–11, every interference with a protected right must be proportionate to the legitimate aim pursued. In order to determine this question, the Strasbourg court decides, in the light of the arguments and evidence available to it, 'whether the reasons given by the national authorities to justify the actual measures of "interference" they take are relevant and sufficient'[1]. In a case concerned with Article 10, the Court summarised its approach as follows:

'The Court will look at the interference complained of in the light of the case as a whole and determine whether the reasons adduced by the national authorities to justify it are relevant and sufficient and whether the means employed were proportionate to the legitimate aim pursued. In doing so the Court has to satisfy itself that the national authorities did apply standards which were in conformity with the principles embodied in art 10 and, moreover, that they based themselves on an acceptable assessment of the relevant facts[2].'

1 *Handyside v United Kingdom* (1976) A 24, para 50.
2 *Jersild v Denmark* (1995) A 298, para 31; *Vogt v Germany* (1995) A 323, para 52.

3.74   'Sufficiency' requires that there be not only a rational connection between the means employed and the aim sought to be achieved, but also that a fair balance be struck between the demands of the general interest of the community and the requirements of the protection of the individual's fundamental rights. For example, a measure which involves a grave interference with an important right, such as a parent's right to contact with a child, will not be regarded as proportionate if some less drastic measure would have achieved the desired objective[1]. Similarly, the reading of prisoners' correspondence, outwith their presence, was not proportionate when the desired objective (to ensure that no prohibited material was included with letters) could have been achieved by merely opening the correspondence in the prisoner's presence[2]. In addition, for an interference to meet such requirements procedural safeguards may be necessary to ensure due protection of the individual's interests[3].

1 Eg *Olsson v Sweden (No. 1)* (1988) A 130, para 72; cf *Olsson (No 2) v Sweden* (1992) A 250, paras 87–91.
2 *Campbell v United Kingdom* (1993) A 233-A.
3 *McMichael v United Kingdom* (1995) A 308, para 87; *Buckley v United Kingdom* 1996-IV, 1271, para 76.

3.75   The search for a fair balance between the demands of the general interest of the community and the requirements of the protection of the individual's fundamental rights is, of course, not confined to the European Convention on Human Rights, Articles 8–11. As the Court has said, 'The search for this balance is inherent in the whole of the Convention'[1]. In that sense, proportionality can be regarded as a concept which permeates the entirety of the Convention. It is relevant, for example, to the question whether a difference in treatment can be justified under Article 14[2], or whether an interference with property rights violated the right guaranteed by Protocol 1, Article 1[3]. For example, an interference with property rights will not be regarded as compatible with the latter right if it imposes an individual and excessive burden without the possibility of compensation[4]. Proportionality is also the basis upon which the Court determines whether the Convention should be construed as imposing a positive obligation upon a contracting state in a particular situation[5]. It is also the principal basis upon which the Court sets limits to rights which are implicit in the Convention, such as the right under Article 6 to access to a court[6].

1 *Sporring and Lönnroth v Sweden* (1982) A 52, para 69.
2 *Belgian Linguistics Case* (1968) A 6.

3 *Sporring and Lönnroth v Sweden* (1982) A 52, para 69.
4 *Sporring and Lönnroth v Sweden* (1982) A 52, para 73. This approach has antecedents in French administrative law.
5 Eg *Rees v United Kingdom* (1986) A 106, para 37.
6 Eg *Ashingdane v United Kingdom* (1985) A 93, para 57.

3.76 The onus of establishing that an interference is justified, and there-fore the onus of establishing that an interference is proportionate, rests on the state[1]. The standard of justification required depends, in practice, on the particular context. In principle, the stronger the 'pressing social need', the less difficult it will be to justify the interference. For example, national security is in principle a powerful consideration[2]. Certain legitimate aims, such as national security, also require the state to be allowed (at the inter-national level) a wide margin of appreciation, making it more difficult for the Strasbourg court to determine that the interference was unjustified. The concept of the 'margin of appreciation' is discussed below[3]. On the other hand, interferences with certain types of right are more difficult to justify than others. For example, where the case concerns 'a most intimate aspect of private life', such as sexual behaviour, 'there must exist particu-larly serious reasons before interferences on the part of the public author-ities can be legitimate for the purposes of art 8(2)'[4]. Similarly, interferences with correspondence with a legal adviser, or with the confidentiality of such correspondence, require a compelling justification[5]. Interferences with freedom of expression, particularly in respect of the discussion of matters of public interest, similarly require a convincing justification[6]. In addition to the nature of the right interfered with, the degree of interfer-ence is of course another material factor[7].

1 Eg *Smith and Grady v United Kingdom* (27 September 1999), para 99.
2 See eg *Leander v Sweden* (1987) A 116, para 59; but contrast *Smith and Grady v United Kingdom* (27 September 1999) para 89, where the counteracting factor was the serious nature of the interference with an intimate aspect of private life.
3 At para 3.85.
4 *Dudgeon v United Kingdom* (1981) A 45, para 52.
5 Eg *Campbell v United Kingdom* (1992) A 233-A; *Niemietz v Germany* (1992) A 251-B.
6 Eg *Barthold v Germany* (1985) A 90, para 55.
7 Eg *Smith and Grady v United Kingdom* (27 September 1999), para 91.

3.77 The foregoing discussion has been concerned with rights which are subject to widely expressed qualifications, and especially with those con-ferred by the European Convention on Human Rights, Articles 8–11, where interferences must be 'necessary in a democratic society'. Other rights are subject to qualifications which are more stringently expressed, or to no express qualification at all. For example, Article 2 of the Convention guar-antees the right to life, subject to an exception where the deprivation of life results from the use of force which is 'no more than absolutely necessary' for certain specified purposes. In that context, it has been said that the words 'absolutely necessary' indicate that 'a stricter and more compelling test of necessity must be employed from that normally applicable when determining whether State action is "necessary in a democratic society" under paragraph 2 of arts 8–11 of the Convention'[1]. Similarly, although Article 3 (which prohibits torture) contains no reference to necessity, there are circumstances in which treatment (eg of prisoners, or of the mentally ill) can be justified by necessity which would otherwise be inhuman or degrading; and so the Court has said that 'in respect of a person deprived of his liberty, any recourse to physical force which has not been made *strictly necessary* by his own conduct diminishes human dignity and is in principle an infringement of the right set forth in art 3 of the Convention'[2]. Article 5, on the other hand, permits the lawful arrest or detention of a person 'when it is *reasonably considered necessary* to prevent his committing an offence or fleeing after having done so'. Article 6, which guarantees the right to a fair trial, in principle requires a public hearing, but permits the exclusion of the press and the public 'in the interests of morals, public order or national security in a democratic society, where the interests of juveniles or the protection of the private life of the parties so require, or to the extent *strictly necessary* in the opinion of the court in special circumstances where publicity would prejudice the interests of justice'. This qualification has been applied in a realistic manner, the Court emphasising the strictness of the requirements only in circumstances where a strict approach was appropriate to the nature of the proceedings in issue[3]. Similarly, although Article 15 permits derogations in times of emergency 'to the extent strictly required by the exigencies of the situation', the Court has construed that phrase as meaning 'reasonably considered to be strictly required'[4]. In practice, accordingly, the Court has had regard to the nature of the context, as well as to the language of the text, in deciding how strict a test of necessity is appropriate. To the extent that a strict test of necessity is imposed, the test of proportionality is correspondingly stringent. In relation to Article 2(2), for example, any force used 'must be *strictly* proportionate to the achievement of the aims' specified[5].

1 *McCann v United Kingdom* (1996) A 324, para 149.
2 *Ribitsch v Austria* (1995) A 377, para 38.
3 E g *Diennet v France* (1995) A 325-A. Contrast *Campbell and Fell v United Kingdom* (1984) A 80, para 87; and, in relation to juveniles, *V v United Kingdom* (16 December 1999) paras 76–77, 90.
4 *Ireland v United Kingdom* (1978) A 25, paras 213–220.
5 *McCann v United Kingdom* (1996) A 324, para 149.

3.78   Finally, proportionality is employed as a general supervisory principle which can be used as a yardstick in determining whether a measure is compatible with the European Convention on Human Rights. For example, the Court has suggested on a number of occasions that a criminal sentence which was disproportionate might constitute inhuman or degrading treatment, contrary to Article 3[1]. Under Article 4 (which prohibits slavery and forced labour), the Court has held that a requirement that intrants to the legal profession provide free legal services could amount to forced labour only if the burden imposed was disproportionate[2]. Under Article 6, the Court has held that a system of 'fiscal fines' operating in Belgium was incompatible with the right to a fair trial because of a 'flagrant disproportion' between the modest sum demanded and the alternative consequences of lengthy criminal proceedings during which the applicant's business would have been closed down[3].

1 *Soering v United Kingdom* (1989) A 161, para 104 (the death sentence); cf *V v United Kingdom* (16 December 1999) para 97.
2 *Van der Mussele v Belgium* (1984) A 70, para 37.
3 *Deweer v Belgium* (1980) A 35, para 51.

THE APPLICATION OF THE CONVENTION — THE RELATION BETWEEN STRASBOURG AND NATIONAL AUTHORITIES

Introduction

3.79 In applying the European Convention on Human Rights, the European Court of Human Rights adopts an approach which reflects its character as an international court enforcing an international convention. Certain general principles are characteristic of that approach: the principle of subsidiarity; the doctrine of the margin of appreciation; and the fourth instance doctrine. As will become apparent, and as discussed below in relation to the margin of appreciation in particular, none of these principles is appropriate to the role of a national court. It is necessary to understand them, however, in order to understand the reasoning underlying the Strasbourg case law: in particular, the margin of appreciation doctrine underlies what may sometimes appear to be a lack of consistency in the case law, and limits the circumstances in which decisions on particular facts can be treated as authoritative precedents.

The principle of subsidiarity

3.80 The principle of subsidiarity describes three related aspects of the Convention system. First, the European Convention on Human Rights represents a floor rather than a ceiling – in other words, a minimum level of protection of fundamental rights, rather than a maximum – and in that sense is intended to be subsidiary to any higher level of protection adopted by contracting states under domestic or international law. This is reflected in Article 53:

> 'Nothing in this Convention shall be construed as limiting or derogating from any of the human rights and fundamental freedoms which may be ensured under the laws of any High Contracting Party or under any other agreement to which it is a Party.'

This approach is also reflected, under United Kingdom law, in the Human Rights Act 1998, s 11.

3.81 Secondly, the European Convention on Human Rights sets minimum standards, but does not prescribe the means by which those standards are to be achieved. The choice of means remains within the competence of national authorities. Thus, in a case concerned with a complaint of discriminatory treatment contrary to Article 14, the Court said:

> 'In attempting to find out, in a given case, whether or not there has been an arbitrary distinction, the Court cannot disregard those legal and factual

features which characterise the life of the society in the State which, as a Contracting Party, has to answer for the measure in dispute. In so doing, it cannot assume the role of the competent national authorities, for it would thereby lose sight of the subsidiary nature of the international machinery of collective enforcement established by the Convention. The national authorities remain free to choose the measures which they consider appropriate in those matters which are governed by the Convention. Review by the Court concerns only the conformity of these measures with the requirements of the Convention[1].'

1 *Belgian Linguistics Case* (1968) A 6.

3.82 Thirdly, the European Convention on Human Rights looks primarily to national authorities, and national courts, in particular, as the means by which the substantive rights conferred by the Convention should be protected. Thus Article 1 places on contracting states the obligation to 'secure to everyone within their jurisdiction the rights and freedoms defined in Section 1 of this Convention' (ie Articles 2–18). Article 13 guarantees a right to an effective remedy at the national level:

'Everyone whose rights and freedoms as set forth in this Convention are violated shall have an effective remedy before a national authority notwithstanding that the violation has been committed by persons acting in an official capacity.'

Article 35 permits the European Court of Human Rights to deal with an application only after all domestic remedies have been exhausted. These provisions are not incorporated into the Human Rights Act (where Article 35 would of course have no place in any event), but it has been said that that is because the Act itself gives effect to Articles 1 and 13 'by securing to people in the United Kingdom the rights and freedoms of the Convention'[1] and 'by establishing a scheme under which Convention rights can be raised before our domestic courts'[2].

1 583 HL Official Report (5th series) col 475 (the Lord Chancellor, Lord Irvine of Lairg).
2 583 HL Official Report (5th series) col 475 (the Lord Chancellor, Lord Irvine of Lairg). As to Art 13, see also 584 HL Official Report (5th series) cols 1265–1267 (the Lord Chancellor). See also para 1.61, n 2 above.

3.83 Finally, and perhaps most importantly, the principle of subsidiarity is also reflected in the margin of appreciation[1] and fourth instance doctrines[2].

1 See para 3.85 below.
2 See para 3.84 below.

The fourth instance doctrine

3.84 By the 'fourth instance' doctrine is meant the principle that the European Court of Human Rights will not act as an appellate court (the expression 'fourth instance' derives from there being typically two levels of appellate court, beyond the court of first instance, within national legal systems). The Court therefore treats the assessment of national law as primarily a matter for the national courts[1]; and it will not interfere with their findings of fact, unless they have drawn arbitrary conclusions from the evidence before them[2].

1 Eg *Winterwerp v Netherlands* (1979) A 33, para 46.
2 Eg *Edwards v United Kingdom* (1993) A 247-B, para 34.

The margin of appreciation

3.85   The assessment of the compatibility of a measure with the European Convention on Human Rights involves judgment. To determine whether a measure is necessary and proportionate, for example, is not a mechanical exercise: once all the facts are known, there remains an irreducible value judgment which has to be made. In accordance with the principle of subsidiarity, the European Court of Human Rights exercises a degree of restraint in determining whether the judgment made by national authorities (including national courts) is compatible with the state's obligations under the Convention. That restraint is exercised by means of the doctrine of the margin of appreciation. The concept of the margin of appreciation is thus one of the principal means by which the European Court of Human Rights recognises its subsidiary role in protecting human rights, and the right of free societies, within limits, to choose for themselves the human rights policies that suit them best[1]. If the concept were extended too far, however, then it could be argued that the Court had abdicated its responsibilities. Hence it is inevitably a concept which is sometimes difficult to apply in practice and which is apt to give rise to controversy[2].

1 See Ryssdall 'The Coming of Age of the European Convention on Human Rights' [1996] EHRLR 18, 24–26.
2 For a critical perspective on the use made of the concept, see eg Van Dijk and Van Hoof *Theory and Practice of the European Convention on Human Rights* (3rd edn, 1998) pp 82–95; Jones 'The Devaluation of Human Rights Under the European Convention' [1995] PL 430; Lavender 'The Problem of the Margin of Appreciation' [1997] EHRLR 380; Lester 'Universality versus Subsidiarity: A Reply' [1998] EHRLR 73. Some recent case law is carefully analysed, and defended, in Mahoney 'Universality versus Subsidiarity in the Strasbourg Case Law on Free Speech: Explaining Some Recent Judgments' [1998] EHRLR 364. Other leading articles on the margin of appreciation include Mahoney 'Judicial Activism and Judicial Self-Restraint in the European Court of Human Rights: Two Sides of the Same Coin' [1990] 3 HRLJ 57; and MacDonald 'The Margin of Appreciation', in Macdonald, Matscher and Petzold *The European System for the Protection of Human Rights* (1993) p 83.

3.86   The concept was first explained by the European Court of Human Rights in the case of *Handyside v United Kingdom*[1], which concerned the prosecution of a publisher for obscenity. The issue was whether that interference with freedom of expression was 'necessary in a democratic society ... for the protection of morals', as required by Article 10(2). The Court said:

> 'The Court points out that the machinery of protection established by the Convention is subsidiary to the national systems safeguarding human rights. The Convention leaves to each Contracting State, in the first place, the task of securing the rights and freedoms it enshrines. The institutions created by it make their own contribution to this task but they become

involved only through contentious proceedings and once all domestic remedies have been exhausted [art 35].

These observations apply, notably, to art 10(2). In particular, it is not possible
to find in the domestic law of the various Contracting States a uniform
European conception of morals. The view taken by their respective laws of
the requirements of morals varies from time to time and from place to place,
especially in our era which is characterised by a rapid and far-reaching
evolution of opinions on the subject. By reason of their direct and continuous contact with the vital forces of their countries, State authorities are in
principle in a better position than the international judge to give an opinion
on the exact content of these requirements as well as on the "necessity" of a
"restriction" or "penalty" intended to meet them . . . [I]t is for the national
authorities to make the initial assessment of the reality of the pressing social
need implied by the notion of "necessity" in this context.

Consequently, art 10(2) leaves to the Contracting States a margin of appreciation. This margin is given both to the domestic legislator ("prescribed by
law") and to the bodies, judicial amongst others, that are called upon to
interpret and apply the laws in force.

Nevertheless, art 10(2) does not give the Contracting States an unlimited
power of appreciation. The Court, which, with the Commission, is responsible for ensuring the observance of those States' engagements, is empowered to give the final ruling on whether a "restriction" or "penalty" is
reconcilable with freedom of expression as protected by art 10. The domestic
margin of appreciation thus goes hand in hand with a European supervision. Such supervision concerns both the aim of the measure challenged and
its "necessity"; it covers not only the basic legislation but also the decision
applying it, even one given by an independent court . . .

It follows from this that it is in no way the Court's task to take the place of
the competent national courts but rather to review under art 10 the decisions
they delivered in the exercise of their power of appreciation'[2].

1 (1976) A 24.
2 (1976) A 24, paras 48–50.

3.87   The concept of the margin of appreciation thus reflects a recognition
on the part of the European Court of Human Rights that – in certain
circumstances, and within certain limits – national authorities (including
national courts) are better placed than the court itself to determine the
outcome of the process of balancing individual and community interests,
by reason of 'their direct and continuous contact with the vital forces of
their countries'[1]. This reflects both the principle of subsidiarity – the
primary role of national authorities in ensuring the effective securing of
Convention guarantees – and the 'fourth instance' doctrine: that the Court
exercises a supervisory jurisdiction at an international level, rather than
being a final court of appeal of a domestic character. The margin of appreciation is not however a negation of the Court's supervisory function,
since the Court has been at pains to emphasise that the margin (where it
exists) is limited, and that the Court itself takes the final decision when it
reviews the assessment of the national authorities[2].

1 *Handyside v United Kingdom* (1976) A 24, para 48.
2 *Klass v Germany* (1978) A 28, para 49.

3.88 The existence and width of any margin of appreciation depends entirely on the context. The width of the margin of appreciation depends fundamentally upon the extent to which it is appropriate for an international court to respect the view taken by the national authorities. That depends upon a number of factors, notably the language of the Convention provision, the existence or not of consensus among the majority of contracting states, the nature of the right protected, the nature of the obligation placed upon the state, the nature of the activity interfered with, the nature of the aim pursued by the restriction and the surrounding circumstances.

3.89 A wide margin therefore tends to be recognised in situations where national authorities must be allowed a wide measure of discretion, for example in dealing with public emergencies or issues of national security[1]. For the same reason, a wide margin tends to be recognised in contexts in which the European Court of Human Rights accepts that widely differing views can legitimately be held, consistently with the European Convention on Human Rights: for example, in relation to moral issues such as the censorship of books or films[2], or issues of economic policy[3], or issues of social policy on which there is no European consensus. Thus, in a case concerned with the reform of the law of landlord and tenant, the Court said (in relation to Protocol 1, Article 1):

> 'Because of their direct knowledge of their society and its needs, the national authorities are in principle better placed than the international judge to appreciate what is "in the public interest". Under the system of protection established by the Convention, it is thus for the national authorities to make the initial assessment both of the existence of a problem of public concern warranting measures of deprivation of property and of the remedial action to be taken. Here, as in other fields to which the safeguards of the Convention extend, the national authorities accordingly enjoy a certain margin of appreciation.
>
> Furthermore, the notion of "public interest" is necessarily extensive. In particular, as the Commission noted, the decision to enact laws expropriating property will commonly involve consideration of political, economic and social issues on which opinions within a democratic society may reasonably differ widely. The Court, finding it natural that the margin of appreciation available to the legislature in implementing social and economic policies should be a wide one, will respect the legislature's judgment as to what is "in the public interest" unless that judgment be manifestly without reasonable foundation. In other words, although the Court cannot substitute it own assessment for that of the national authorities, it is bound to review the contested measures under art 1 of protocol 1 and, in so doing, to make an inquiry into the facts with reference to which the national authorities acted[4].'

1 *Leander v Sweden* (1987) A 116.
2 Eg *Handyside v United Kingdom* (1976) A 24; *Wingrove v United Kingdom* 1996-V, 1937.
3 Eg *James v United Kingdom* (1986) A 98, para 46.
4 *James v United Kingdom* (1986) A 98, para 46.

3.90 On the other hand, the European Court of Human Rights tends to adopt a less deferential approach in contexts where there is less justification under the European Convention on Human Rights for allowing national authorities a wide discretion, for example in cases concerned with intimate aspects of private life[1] or freedom of political debate[2]. In relation to freedom of expression, for example, the Court has explained how the width of the margin of appreciation depends on the context, and in particular on the nature of the expression restricted and on the nature of the justification for the restriction. In a case concerned with blasphemy, the Court said:

> 'Whereas there is little scope under art 10(2) of the Convention for restrictions on political speech or on debate on questions of public interest, a wider margin of appreciation is generally available to the Contracting States when regulating freedom of expression in relation to matters liable to offend intimate personal convictions within the sphere of morals or, especially, religion. Moreover, as in the field of morals, and perhaps to an even greater degree, there is no uniform European conception of "the requirements of the protection of the rights of others" in relation to attacks on their religious convictions. What is likely to cause substantial offence to persons of a particular religious persuasion will vary significantly from time to time and from place to place, especially in an era characterised by an ever-growing array of faiths and denominations. By reason of their direct and continuous contact with the vital forces of their countries, State authorities are in principle in a better position than the international judge to give an opinion on the exact content of these requirements with regard to the rights of others as well as on the "necessity" of a "restriction" intended to protect from such material those whose deepest feelings and convictions would be seriously offended[3].'

Where, however, the justification for the interference is a less subjective concept, on which a broad consensus exists at a European level, such as the need to maintain the authority of the judiciary, the Court will exercise stricter supervision[4]. In some contexts, such as Articles 2 and 3, the Court has not as yet recognised any margin of appreciation at all, and the scope for the doctrine would appear to be extremely limited in a context of that kind, since it does not normally involve a balancing of the interests of the individual against a wider interest, let alone a situation where such a balance is best struck by national authorities exercising a discretion.

1 *Dudgeon v United Kingdom* (1982) A 45; *Smith and Grady v United Kingdom* (27 September 1999).
2 Eg *Bowman v United Kingdom* 1998-I, 175.
3 *Wingrove v United Kingdom* 1996-V, 1937, para 58.
4 *Sunday Times v United Kingdom (No 1)* (1979) A 30, para 59; *Rasmussen v Denmark* (1984) A 87, paras 40–41.

Proportionality, the margin of appreciation and national courts

3.91 Since the doctrine of the margin of appreciation is a principle guiding the exercise of a supervisory jurisdiction at the international level, it has no application to the function of national courts. It is, on the contrary, a doctrine which reflects the way in which the function of an international court differs from that of a national court. In the first place, the margin of appreciation doctrine is essentially a basis for demarcating between the area in which an international court will interfere and the area in which it will not interfere. More specifically, it is a basis for judging the extent to which proportionality – the balance between individual rights and the community interest – should be assessed at the national level rather than the international level. National courts do not make that judgment: of necessity, they have to assess proportionality at the national level. A different way of expressing the same point is that the European Court of Human Rights exercises a supervisory jurisdiction over the actions of contracting states. A national court forms part of the state whose actions are reviewed: its decisions, just as much as those of central government or other public authorities, are the focus of review at the Strasbourg level, to assess whether they are compatible with the European Convention on Human Rights. This is reflected in the Human Rights Act 1998, s 6, which requires the courts, as public authorities, to act compatibly with Convention rights. The national court therefore does not stand back from 'the state' and allow 'the state' the margin of appreciation which would be applied by the European Court of Human Rights. On the contrary, the margin of appreciation doctrine is based on the expectation that national authorities will have taken a decision, with the benefit of local knowledge, which they consider to be proportionate and compatible with the Convention. In particular, in cases where a decision has been taken by a public authority other than the national court, and that decision has then been scrutinised by the national court, the margin of appreciation doctrine applies to that primary scrutiny when it in turn is subjected to secondary scrutiny at the Strasbourg level, on the basis that the primary scrutiny has been carried out by a national body with better knowledge of national circumstances and requirements. The decisions of national courts would cease to merit such respect at the international level if national courts themselves applied the Strasbourg margin of appreciation to the decisions of other public authorities.

3.92 The margin of appreciation doctrine therefore has no direct application to the reasoning which should be followed by courts applying the Scotland Act 1998 or the Human Rights Act 1998. That is not to say, however, that it is irrelevant. The Strasbourg law on the margin of appreciation cannot be entirely irrelevant to decision making by domestic courts, since those courts must not exceed the degree of latitude which will be allowed at the Strasbourg level. In other words, if a situation is to be avoided in which a domestic court rules that there has been no contravention of a Convention right, but the European Court of Human Rights subsequently rules to the contrary, then the domestic court must operate within the limits of the margin of appreciation allowed by the Strasbourg court.

3.93 Although national courts cannot apply the doctrine of the margin of appreciation when they have to consider the compatibility with the European Convention on Human Rights of the acts of other public authorities, there is at the same time nothing in the Convention, or in the Human Rights Act 1998, which requires national courts simply to substitute their own views for those of other bodies with legislative or executive responsibilities. Neither the Convention nor the Act obliterates the separation of powers. When considering the compatibility with the Convention of legislation or the acts of other public authorities, the courts have to apply the tests laid down in the Convention and the Strasbourg jurisprudence, notably the test of proportionality. That is a more stringent test than *Wednesbury* reasonableness. As the Strasbourg court has said, even where it allows a wide margin of appreciation, that:

> 'does not mean that the [Court's] supervision is limited to ascertaining whether the respondent state has exercised its discretion reasonably, carefully and in good faith: what the Court has to do is to look at the interference complained of in the light of the case as a whole and determine whether it was "proportionate to the legitimate aim proposed" and whether the reasons adduced by the national authorities to justify it are "relevant and sufficient"'[1].

Indeed the *Wednesbury* test has led the European Court of Human Rights to decide (in particular circumstances) that judicial review was not an 'effective remedy' within the meaning of Article 13, the Court observing that the threshold for review

> 'was placed so high that it effectively excluded any consideration by the domestic courts of the question whether the interference with the applicants' rights answered a pressing social need or was proportionate to the national security and public order aims pursued, principles which lie at the heart of the Court's analysis of complaints under art 8 of the Convention'[2].

Nevertheless, applying the Convention tests, national courts can continue to exercise a jurisdiction which is of a supervisory nature and which recognises that other bodies may be better placed than the courts to take a decision, by reasons of expertise or a democratic mandate. As Sir John Laws has observed, 'it is necessary to distinguish the idea of a margin of appreciation, which is apt for an international court reviewing a national decision, from the different idea of a discretion left to elected authorities on democratic grounds'[3]. The margin of appreciation doctrine, which is a doctrine of judicial review at the international level, thus has its analogy at the national level, with the same rationale of reflecting the separation of powers within a constitutional framework, and therefore respecting the competence and responsibilities of other bodies within that framework[4].

1 *Vogt v Germany* (1995) A 323, para 52.
2 *Smith and Grady v United Kingdom* (27 September 1999), para 138 (commenting on *R v Ministry of Defence, ex p Smith* [1996] QB 517).
3 'Wednesbury' in *The Golden Metwand and the Crooked Cord: Essays in Public Law in Honour of Sir William Wade QC* (1998) p 201.
4 For an illustration, see *R (Pretty) v DPP* (18 October 2001, unreported), QBD, paras 55–62.

3.94   The fact that the national courts' jurisdiction to consider the compatibility with the European Convention of Human Rights of legislation or executive action accords a degree of deference to the choices made by the legislature or the executive has been recognised by the courts. In *R v DPP, ex p Kebilene*, Lord Hope of Craighead said:

> '[The doctrine of the margin of appreciation] is an integral part of the supervisory jurisdiction which is exercised over state conduct by the international court. By conceding a margin of appreciation to each national system, the court has recognised that the Convention, as a living system, does not need to be applied uniformly by all States but may vary in its application

according to local needs and conditions. This technique is not available to the national courts when they are considering Convention issues arising within their own countries. But in the hands of the national courts also the Convention should be seen as an expression of fundamental principles rather than as a set of mere rules. The questions which the courts will have to decide in the application of these principles will involve questions of balance between competing interests, and issues of proportionality. In this area difficult choices have to be made by the executive or the legislature between the rights of the individual and the needs of society. In some circumstances it will be appropriate for the courts to recognise that there is an area of judgment within which the judiciary will defer, on democratic grounds, to the considered opinion of the elected body or person whose act or decision is said to be incompatible with the Convention. This point is well made at p 74, para 3.21 of *Human Rights Law and Practice* (1999), of which Lord Lester of Herne Hill and Mr Pannick are the general editors, where the area in which these choices may arise is conveniently and appropriately described as the "discretionary area of judgment". It will be easier for such an area of judgment to be recognised where the Convention itself requires a balance to be struck, much less so where the right is stated in terms which are unqualified. It will be easier for it to be recognised where the issues involve questions of social or economic policy, much less so where the courts are especially well placed to assess the need for protection[1].'

Those observations were cited and applied in *A v The Scottish Ministers*, a case concerned with the compatibility with the Convention of the Mental Health (Public Safety and Appeals)(Scotland) Act 1999. The Lord President, Lord Rodger of Earlsferry, said:

'What we must therefore decide is whether, even though the members were conscious of the need to have regard to the human rights of the patients, the Parliament nonetheless failed to maintain the necessary fair balance by giving too much weight to the perceived danger to members of the public and, thereby, giving too little weight to the requirements of the protection of the patients' right to freedom and in particular their rights under art 5 (1)(e) and (4). In determining that issue, as the authorities show, it is right that the court should give due deference to the assessment which the democratically elected legislature has made of the policy issues involved[2].'

Similar observations have been made in other cases[3].

1 [2000] 2 AC 326.
2 2001 SC 1. See now *A v The Scottish Ministers* (15 October 2001, unreported), JCPC.
3 E g *Stott v Brown* 2001 SCCR 62, 79 per Lord Bingham of Cornhill, 86–87 per Lord Steyn; *McIntosh Petitioner* 2001 SCCR 191, para 36 per Lord Bingham of Cornhill.

3.95 The appropriate degree of deference, if any, will however depend upon the circumstances. In a (pre-Human Rights Act 1998) case in which an illegal entrant challenged the refusal of exceptional leave to remain on the basis that the Secretary of State had wrongly rejected his claim that he would, if returned to his country of origin, be subjected to treatment contrary to the European Covention on Human Rights, Article 3, Simon Brown LJ observed:

'This is not an area in which the court will pay any especial deference to the Secretary of State's conclusion on the facts. In the first place, the human right involved here – the right not to be exposed to a real risk of art 3 ill-treatment – is both absolute and fundamental: it is not a qualified right requiring a balance to be struck with some competing social need. Secondly, the court here is hardly less well placed than the Secretary of State himself to evaluate the risk once the relevant material is placed before it ... In circumstances such as these, what has been called the "discretionary area of judgment" – the area of judgment within which the court should defer to the Secretary of State as the person primarily entrusted with the decision on the applicant's removal (see Lord Hope of Craighead's speech in *R v DPP, ex p Kebilene*) – is a decidedly narrow one[1].'

On the other hand, in a case concerned with housing legislation, the court observed that the economic and other implications of any policy in this area were extremely complex and far-reaching; and the question whether the court's statutory duty to make an order for possession was legitimate and proportionate fell within the area of policy where the court should defer to the decision of Parliament[2].

1 *R v Secretary of State for the Home Department, ex p Turgut* [2001] 1 All ER 719, 729. See also *R v A (No 2)* [2001] 2 WLR 1546, para 36 per Lord Steyn: '[W]hen the question arises whether in the criminal statute in question Parliament adopted a legislative scheme which makes an excessive inroad into the right to a fair trial the court is qualified to make its own judgment and must do so.'

2 *Poplar Housing and Regeneration Community Association Ltd v Donoghue* [2001] 3 WLR 183.

CHAPTER 4

Physical integrity: life, torture and inhuman treatment, servitude and liberty of person

INTRODUCTION

4.01 Protection of the physical integrity of the individual[1] is a central concern of any system of protection of civil rights. The widespread loss of life, use of torture and inhuman treatment, imposition of enforced labour, and arbitrary use of detention occasioned by totalitarianism provided compelling justification for the European Convention on Human Rights first four substantive guarantees: those of the right to respect for life (Art 2), prohibition of torture or inhuman or degrading treatment or punishment (Art 3), prohibition of slavery and forced or compulsory labour (Art 4), and the right to liberty and security of person (Art 5)[2]. Increasingly, these articles are seen as having a close inter-relationship[3]. While explained by the past, they are interpreted in accordance with modern requirements: the European Court of Human Rights gives the highest priority to these guarantees and there is little scope for application of any state margin of appreciation[4]. The Court has also proved capable of creative interpretation, extrapolating from the text positive duties such as carrying out adequate investigations into death or allegations of ill-treatment, and providing opportunities for periodic review of continuing detention. Further developments are by no means improbable since the Convention requires to be interpreted as a 'living instrument'[5]. Advances in the protection of personal integrity have also been achieved through additional optional protocols, as with Protocol 6 which abolishes the death penalty in times of peace, and Protocol 4, Article 1 which removes inability to fulfil a contractual obligation from being a legitimate ground for deprivation of liberty[6]. Additionally, applicants have successfully relied upon Article 8's guarantee of respect for private and family life to broaden protection of physical integrity[7]. These provisions are in addition to any principles of international human rights law applied in domestic legal systems[8].

1 'Physical integrity' can be used, as here, in a general sense to denote concern for the protection of the human body against all forms of state interference (for example, Berger *Jurisprudence de la Cour Européenne des Droits de l'Homme* (7th edn, 2000) deals with Arts 2–5 and Art 2 of Protocol 4 under the title of 'La Liberté Physique'); alternatively, in a narrower sense it may refer solely to infliction of physical or psychological harm: thus Gomien, Harris and Zwack in *Law and Practice of the European Convention on Human Rights* (1996) use the term as a shorthand reference for torture or inhuman or degrading treatment or punishment. See, further, Feldman 'Human Dignity as a Legal Value' [1999]

PL 682 and [2000] PL 61; and Buxton 'The Human Rights Act and Private Law' (2000) 116 LQR 48.

2 The historical legacy of these guarantees is still reflected in the text in some measure, for example in the preservation of state practices such as infliction of the death penalty or imposition of compulsory military service which were commonplace at the time of drafting but which are either now in disuse or of rapidly decreasing importance. Article 15, which protects inter alia the most crucial aspects of Arts 2, 3 and 4 from state derogation in time of emergency, represents a further example of the central importance of physical integrity to the framers of the European Convention on Human Rights.

3 Cf *Kurt* v *Turkey* 1998-III, 1152, at para 123: 'Prompt judicial intervention [under Arts 5(3) and (4)] may lead to the detection and prevention of life-threatening measures or serious ill-treatment which violate the fundamental guarantees contained in Articles 2 and 3 of the Convention. . . . What is at stake is both the protection of the physical liberty of individuals as well as their personal security in a context which, in the absence of safeguards, could result in a subversion of the rule of law and place detainees beyond the reach of the most rudimentary forms of legal protection.'

4 In *McCann and Ors v United Kingdom* (1995) A 324, paras 146 and 147, the European Court of Human Rights offered justification for strict construction of ECHR, Arts 2 and 3 by identifying their paramount importance in the scheme of Convention protection. Cf Callewaert 'Is there a Margin of Appreciation in the Application of Articles 2, 3 and 4 of the Convention?' (1998) 19 HRLJ 6. The detailed text of Art 5 also provides restricted latitude for states in decision-making: Mahoney 'The Doctrine of the Margin of Appreciation under the European Convention on Human Rights: Its Legitimacy in Theory and Application in Practice' (1998) 19 HRLJ 1 at p 5.

5 The question of whether the imposition of capital punishment may itself constitute torture still seems an open one, and may still be avoided in the pending case of 46221/99, *Öcalan v Turkey*, recently declared admissible by the Court (14 December 2000). However, issues such as abortion which fail to command any common European consensus are unlikely to be brought within the sphere of Convention protection: see further paras 4.13 and 4.15 below.

6 The United Kingdom has not yet ratified Protocol 4.

7 In particular, in respect of the administration of corporal punishment and failure to provide protection against environmental pollution: see paras 6.35 and 6.46.

8 Cf *R v Bow Street Metropolitan Stipendiary Magistrate, ex p Pinochet Ugarte (No 3)* [2000] 1 AC 147; and deGuzman 'The Road from Rome: The Developing Law of Crimes against Humanity' (2000) 22 HRQ 335.

RIGHT TO LIFE: ARTICLE 2 AND PROTOCOL 6

Scope of the right to life

4.02   The formulation of Article 2 reflects a deliberate determination to provide a more detailed elaboration than the equivalent phrase in the Universal Declaration of Human Rights that 'everyone has the right to life, to liberty and security of person'[1], but the result is merely to clarify that the right to life under the European Convention on Human Rights is by no means absolute. The primary focus of Article 2 is upon the regulation of the taking of life by state officials in terms of paragraph (2). The article establishes a demanding test whereby any force deployed by the state must not have been in excess of what was 'absolutely necessary'. This calls for a careful and exacting scrutiny of the circumstances in which life has been taken, and thus involves a need to ensure due diligence in the investigation of death. Significantly and additionally, however, Article 2 may impose positive duties upon a state to take appropriate steps to safeguard life. At the very least, domestic law must make provision for the punishment of the intentional taking of life[2]. These duties may in certain circumstances also involve the provision of protection for individuals against imminent threats of violence from others, and more recent jurisprudence indeed suggests there may additionally be a positive state responsibility to minimise the risk of harm from noxious and potentially lethal pollutants[3]. However, it has not yet been accepted that this article can be implemented to require the prohibition or punishment of abortion or euthanasia or assisted suicide[4]. Further, the European Court of Human Rights seems reluctant to interpret the provision in such a way as to place restrictions upon decision-making in economic or social spheres since Article 2 cannot be used to found any claim of an essentially economic or social nature, for example, to require the provision of adequate social welfare benefits[5]. On the other hand, where a state has undertaken to make health care available generally within a state, the denial of health care may possibly give rise to an issue under Article 2 where this can be shown to place an individual's life at risk[6].

No derogation from Article 2 by a state in time of war or other public emergency is permissible except in the case of deaths resulting from lawful acts of war[7]. Within the United Kingdom (and following its decision to ratify Protocol 6 which abolishes use of the death penalty[8]), the utility of Article 2 is thus likely to be confined to questions of intentional or negligent killing of individuals by state officials, investigation of homicides, issues relating to the deportation or extradition of individuals, and issues relating to medical treatment.

1 Universal Declaration of Human Rights, Art 3.
2 Cf Harris, O'Boyle and Warbrick *Law of the European Convention on Human Rights* (1995) p 38: the authors suggest that while passive euthanasia (eg by withdrawing treatment) is unlikely to give rise to an Art 2 issue; 'a different answer would be likely in the case of active euthanasia, whereby death is accelerated by a positive act'. For discussion of the issues surrounding euthanasia, see McLean (ed) *Death, Dying and the Law* (1996); and Otlowski *Voluntary Euthanasia and the Common Law* (1997). See further *NHS Trust A v M* [2001] 2 WLR 942 and *R (Pretty) v DPP* (18 October 2001, unreported), QBD discussed at para 4.14 below and for discussion of abortion, see para 4.13 below.
3 See para 4.12 below.
4 See paras 4.10 and 4.13 below.
5 The guarantee cannot be interpreted as requiring particular economic or social measures: eg 7697/76, *X v Belgium* (1977) DR 9, 194 (release of convicted prisoner). Cf 5207/71 *X v Germany* (1971) YB 14, 698 (question whether eviction of chronically ill applicant from her home could give rise to Art 2 considerations left open); 40772/98, *Pančenko v Latvia* (28 October 1999) (complaint concerning precarious economic and social situation arising from refusal of residence permit declared inadmissible: the European Convention on Human Rights does not guarantee the right to a rent-free residence, the right to work, or the right to medical assistance or financial assistance). Nor can Art 2 be used to challenge political decision-making: 28204/95, *Tauira and Ors v France* (1995) DR 83, 112 (resumption of nuclear testing: the applicants were not 'victims'); 22869/93, *Tugar v Italy* (1995) DR 83, 26 (no state responsibility for sale of mines to Iraq).
6 Cf 32647/96, *Passannante v Italy* (1998) DR 94, 91 (where a state has assumed responsibilities for health care, an excessive delay which is likely to have an impact on a patient's health may give rise to an Art 8 issue; *Cyprus v Turkey* (10 May 2001), para 219 (no violation established under Art 2, and issue of access to medical facilities considered under Art 8; no need in this case to consider the extent of any possible positive duty under Art 2 to make available a certain standard of health care). See also *D v United Kingdom* 1997-III, 777 (threatened deportation of prisoner in the advanced stages of AIDS to a country without appropriate care facilities: deportation would have violated Art 3). For domestic discussion see *Re A (Children) (Conjoined Twins: Surgical Treatment)* [2001] Fam 147; *NHS Trust A v M* [2001] Fam 348. See further para 4.14 below.

7 Art 15(2). International law distinguishes between *ius ad bellum* (war undertaken for the legitimate defence of a state or action taken by the Security Council of the UN) and *ius in bello* (or armed conflict in the most general sense). The meaning of 'war' for the purposes of Art 15 has not been considered to date, but may be addressed in a pending application 52207/99, *Banković and Ors v Belgium and 16 other states* (NATO bombing of Radio-Television Serbia during the Kosovo campaign: communicated). The political background to events may influence determination as to whether there has been a violation of Art 2: see, eg 17579/90, *Kelly v United Kingdom* (1993) DR 74, 139, discussed at para 4.05, below.

8 The White Paper, *Rights Brought Home* (Cm 3782) originally proposed that ratification of this Protocol would proceed on a free vote in Parliament. Consequently, the Human Rights Bill at first did not propose to include abolition of the death penalty in its scope. However, the Government subsequently proposed an amendment to the Bill during its parliamentary stages to include this Protocol, and formally ratified the Protocol on 20 May 1999 (with entry into force on 1 June 1999).

The meaning of 'victim' for the purposes of Article 2

4.03 Applications involving alleged violations of the European Convention on Human Rights may be brought by those who can claim legitimately to qualify as 'victims' in terms of Article 34[1]. In the context of Article 2, applications may normally be brought by a deceased's spouse[2], children[3] or sibling[4], or even nephew[5]. A violation may also be alleged by an individual who has been the subject of a attempted homicide[6].

1 See further, paras 2.29–2.30 above.
2 Eg *Aytekin v* Turkey 1998-VII, 2807.
3 Eg *Osman v United Kingdom* 1998-VIII, 3124.
4 Eg *Ergi v Turkey* 1998-IV, 1751 at para 61 (application of brother of deceased who had complained about murder of sister involved a 'genuine and valid exercise' of right of individual application).
5 Eg *Yaşa v Turkey* 1998-VI, 2411, paras 61–66 (person sufficiently concerned to wish to complain of the murder of a close relation met the 'victim' requirement in the particular circumstances of the case).
6 Eg *Osman v United Kingdom* 1998-VIII, 3124 (discussed at para 4.10 below); *Yaşa v Turkey*, 1998-VI, 2411 (attempted murder of applicant); cf *Venables v News Group Newspapers Ltd* [2001] 2 WLR 1038 (potential victim of lethal violence).

State use of lethal force

4.04 The use of force by state agents such as police officers or military personnel which results in the loss of life[1], whether deliberate or not[2], gives rise to considerations as to the purpose of the use of force and the level of force used. The four sets of circumstances outlined in the European Convention on Human Rights, Article 2, paragraph (2) involve situations in which the state may use force which results in the deprivation of life: to protect against violence, to effect an arrest, to prevent escape of a prisoner, or to quell rioting or insurrection. At first glance, these categories appear potentially wide; but a more careful reading of the text and recent jurisprudence narrow considerably the lawfulness of any such exercise of state authority. The provision 'does not primarily define instances where it is permitted intentionally to kill an individual, but describes the situations where it is permitted to "use force" which may result, as an unintended outcome, in the deprivation of life'[3]. The key issue is likely to be whether any use of force falling within one of the recognised categories and which does result in the loss of life can meet the test of absolute necessity. This calls for the assessment both of training, planning and operational control of any police or security service operation resulting in death, and also of the particular circumstances surrounding the actual use of force[4]. The European Court of Human Rights, will examine these questions by assessing all the evidence placed before it and, if necessary, will carry out its own investigation[5].

1 It is only in exceptional circumstances that physical ill-treatment by state officials which does not in the event result in death will result in a breach of the European Convention on Human Rights, Art 2: *Ilhan v Turkey* (27 June 2000), paras 73–78 (the applicant suffered brain damage following at least one blow to the head by a rifle butt inflicted by gendarmes who were seeking to arrest him; the degree and type of force used and the unequivocal intention or aim behind the use of force were relevant factors in assessing whether infliction of injury short of death was incompatible with the object and purpose of Art 2, but here the European Court of Human Rights was not persuaded that the force was of such a nature or degree as to breach Art 2, noting that disposal of such allegations was more appropriate under Art 3 in almost all such cases).

2 1044/82, *Stewart v United Kingdom* (1984) DR 39, 162, reversing an earlier decision that Art 2 required any killing to have been carried out intentionally.

3 *McCann and Ors v United Kingdom* (1995) A 324 at para 148.

4 *McCann and Ors v United Kingdom* (1995) A 324 at paras 149 and 150. The central issue is whether the facts indicate that force has been no more than 'absolutely necessary', rather than the legal standard of justification for the use of force: paras 154–155. (The dissenting judgments placed weight on the conclusions of the inquiry jury which had enjoyed the benefits of hearing the witnesses involved and which had thereafter considered that the killings had been lawful; the minority also considered that it had not been shown that the planning and control of the operation had been faulty.)

5 *McCann and Ors v United Kingdom* (1995) A 324 at paras 171–173 (this exercise does not involve assessment of criminal liability, and thus there is no onus upon the state to prove beyond reasonable doubt that the operation was in accordance with Art 2).

4.05 Planning and operational direction must seek to minimise the risk of loss of life to avoid the taking of life being considered negligent. In *McCann and Ors v United Kingdom,* the European Court of Human Rights questioned whether the control and organisation of an anti-terrorist operation against an active service unit of the IRA in Gibraltar had taken adequate account of the terrorists' rights under the European Convention on Human Rights, Article 2 and concluded that there were less onerous alternatives available to prevent any terrorist outrage, that there had been a failure to make sufficient allowance for erroneous intelligence assessments, and that the reflex action of soldiers in shooting to kill lacked 'the degree of caution in the use of firearms to be expected from law enforcement personnel in a democratic society'. Consequently, in the eyes of the majority of the Court, the killing of the suspects had not been shown to have been 'absolutely necessary'[1]. Proportionality between means and end sought to be achieved may thus, for example, require selection of an appropriate range of weapons to ensure that the use of force is not disproportionate[2]. The principle applies also to minimising the risk of incidental loss of life to other civilians. In *Ergi v Turkey*, the Court was not satisfied that the state had taken 'all feasible precautions in the choice of means and methods' to avoid the risk of death since the location of security forces during the military action was such as to place others at substantial risk of being caught up in cross-fire[3].

1 *McCann and Ors v United Kingdom* (1995) A 324, paras 195–214 (at para 200: use of lethal force on account of an honestly held belief albeit one which subsequently turns out to be a

mistaken belief is acceptable, since to approach the matter otherwise 'would be to impose an unrealistic burden on the State and its law enforcement personnel in the execution of their duty, perhaps to the detriment of their lives and those of others'). See, too, *Ogur v Turkey* (20 May 1999), paras 73–84 (death of night watchman during military operation). In 17579/90, *Kelly v United Kingdom* (1993) DR 74, 139, the Commission accepted that the shooting of an individual in a stolen car as he tried to drive through a security checkpoint in Belfast could be justified as having been for the purpose of apprehending individuals reasonably believed to be terrorists. The Commission was also influenced by the speed at which the situation arose, which had given the soldiers little or no warning, and by the political background of terrorist killings.

2 *Güleç v Turkey* 1998-IV, 1698, paras 69–73 at para 71 (use of armoured vehicles because of an 'incomprehensible and unacceptable' lack of less powerful weapons (such as truncheons, riot shields, water cannon, rubber bullets or tear gas) against violent demonstration resulting in death was not a use of force which was deemed to have been 'absolutely necessary').

3 1998-IV, 1751, paras 79–81 at para 79.

4.06   In any evaluation of the actual force used, consideration of actions of state officials facing split-second decision-making as to whether to use potentially lethal force is not without difficulty. A state official such as a police officer, too, has the right to respect for life, and to use self-defence to protect himself[1]. The European Court of Human Rights has recognised that it would be inappropriate for it to seek to substitute its own detached assessment for that of the officers involved[2], but its appraisals have not always achieved a convincing consensus. In *McCann and Ors v United Kingdom*[3], a bare majority of the Court was prepared to accept that the decisions of the soldiers to open fire had been justified, and in *Andronicou and Constantinou v Cyprus* (where it had been considered that the planning and control of a police operation against a gunman involved in a domestic dispute with his fiancée had been carried out in such a manner as to minimise as far as possible any risk of death) a majority also accepted that the police officers who had opened fire on the gunman had honestly believed that there was a real and immediate danger to the life of another individual and to themselves, even though the belief was mistaken[4]. In contrast, the situation in *Gül v Turkey* provides an illustration of the use of lethal force which the Court was satisfied could not have been considered as 'absolutely necessary'. As part of a security operation, police officers had sought entry to a flat in order to carry out a search but, as the occupier was unlocking the door, the police officers opened fire and fatally injured the occupier who was behind the door. As far as the planning of the operation was concerned, the Court considered that there was insufficient evidence to establish that the officers had been under instructions to use lethal force. However, it also held that the firing of shots at the door could not have been justified by any reasonable belief on the part of the officers that their lives were at risk from the occupants of the flat, let alone that that this was required to secure entry to the flat. In short, their reaction in opening fire with automatic weapons on an unseen target in a residential block inhabited by innocent civilians could only be considered as a grossly disproportionate response[5].

1 Cf 2758/66, *X v Belgium* (1969) YB 12, 174; 10044/82, *Stewart v United Kingdom* (1984) DR 39, 162; and 11257/84, *Wolfgram v Germany* (1986) DR 49, 213.

2 *Andronicou and Constantinou v Cyprus* 1997-VI, 2059, para 192.

3 (1995) A 324.

4 1997-VI, 2059 at paras 181–186, and 191–194. The principal concern of the dissenting

judges appears to have been the specialised nature of the police response team involved in the operation. For earlier Commission cases, see too 10044/82, *Stewart v United Kingdom* (1984) DR 39, 162 (discharge of a plastic baton round during a riot); and 17579/90, *Kelly v United Kingdom* (1993) DR 74, 139 (shooting of a joyrider who failed to stop at an army checkpoint).
5 (14 December 2000), paras 81–83.

Deaths in police custody and 'disappeared persons'

4.07   Where an individual previously in good health dies while in police custody, there is a duty upon state authorities to provide a plausible explanation[1]. This jurisprudence has been based upon the principle developed under the European Convention on Human Rights, Article 3 that a state must account for injuries sustained by a detainee while in custody[2], an obligation which is 'particularly stringent' in the case of death[3]. The failure of state authorities to provide a plausible explanation for the fate of a detainee will thus give rise to issues which go beyond merely the question of unlawful deprivation of liberty under Article 5[4]. Similarly, cases involving persons who were last seen in the custody of state officers and who subsequently 'disappear' in circumstances where there is sufficient evidence to support a conclusion that a detainee must be presumed to have died while in custody will give rise to issues under Article 2. Here, though, sufficient circumstantial evidence must exist 'based on concrete elements, from which it may be concluded to the requisite standard of proof that a detainee must be presumed to have died while in custody'[5]. In *Cakici v Turkey*, the security forces had claimed to have found the body of the applicant's brother amongst the corpses of a group of suspected terrorists, while the applicant claimed his brother had last been seen some 15 months before when taken into custody. The European Court of Human Rights held that there had been violations of Article 2 both on the basis of a presumption of death after unacknowledged detention by state officials, and also on account of an inadequate investigation into the disappearance and alleged discovery of the body[6]. The same principle may also apply in the absence of a victim's body. In *Timurtas v Turkey* the applicant's son had been taken into custody and then had disappeared, but the state had disputed the fact that he had ever been in custody. The Court accepted that upon the facts established by the Commission there was sufficient evidence for to it to conclude beyond all reasonable doubt that he had died while in the custody of the security forces[7]. In *Tas v Turkey*, the state conceded that an individual had been taken into custody but had been unable to provide any custody or other records showing where he had been subsequently detained, claiming that he had escaped from custody. However, since the report of this alleged escape was unsubstantiated and the signatories of the report had not been traced, the Court held that no plausible explanation for what had happened had been provided. Given the length of time which had elapsed since his disappearance and also the political situation in that part of Turkey, the Court considered that the individual must be presumed dead following his detention by the security forces, and thus liability for his death was attributable to the state[8].

1 *Tanli v Turkey* (10 April 2001), paras 139–154 (death of applicant's son who had been in good health during interrogation: respondent state was deemed responsible for his death

because of its failure to provide such an explanation; and there was a further violation of the European Convention on Human Rights, Art 2 because of the state's failure to carry out an effective investigation).
2 See para 4.27 below.
3 *Tas v Turkey* (14 November 2000), at para 63.
4 *Tas v Turkey* (14 November 2000), para 64. Initially, the Court had treated 'disappeared persons' cases under Art 5 rather than under ECHR, Arts 2 and 3: cf *Kurt v Turkey* 1998-III, 1152, paras 106–109, 126–129 (at para 128: the failure of the state authorities to offer any credible and substantiated explanation for the whereabouts or the fate of the applicant's son who had last been seen in the custody of security forces led to the conclusion that he had been held 'in unacknowledged detention in the complete absence of the safeguards contained in Article 5'). In *Timurtas v Turkey* (13 June 2000), paras 99–106, the Court (in addition to a violation of ECHR, Art 2) found that the disappearance of the applicant's son during an unacknowledged detention disclosed a particularly grave violation of ECHR, Art 5 in particular because of the lack of a prompt and effective inquiry into the circumstances of the disappearance and the lack of accurate and reliable records of detention of persons taken into custody by police officers.
5 *Çakici v Turkey* (8 July 1999), at para 85. See also *Cyprus v Turkey* (10 May 2001), paras 129–136 (detention of Greek Cypriots at a time when military operations involving Turkish or Turkish Cypriot forces were accompanied by widespread arrests and killings).
6 (8 July 1999), paras 85–87.
7 (13 June 2000), paras 81–86 (a further violation of ECHR, Art 2 was established because of the inadequacy of the official investigation: paras 87–90). See too *Ertak v Turkey* (9 May 2000); and *Çiçek v Turkey* (27 February 2001). For discussion of international law, see Nowak 'Monitoring Disappearances: The Difficult Path from Clarifying Past Cases to Effectively Preventing Future Ones' [1996] EHRLR 348.
8 (14 November 2000), paras 62–67. The investigation was considered neither prompt nor adequate nor effective, and thus resulted in a further violation of ECHR, Art 2: paras 68–72. Cf partly dissenting opinion of Judge Gölcüklü, the ad hoc Turkish judge, who was of the opinion that it had not been proved beyond reasonable doubt that the applicant's son had died in police custody; and further that the Court should not have departed from its decision in *Kurt v Turkey* 1998-III, 1152 to approach such cases solely under ECHR, Art 5.

Positive obligations: protection of life through effective domestic investigation – the procedural aspect of Article 2

4.08   Domestic law ordinarily protects the right to life through enforcement of the criminal law[1] and the availability of a civil right to compensation for unlawful killing. Implicit in the European Convention on Human Rights, Article 2 is a positive obligation on the part of state authorities to ensure that such domestic provisions should be effective in their operation[2]. The European Court of Human Rights has recognised that in practical terms the prohibition against unlawful or arbitrary deprivation of life would be largely meaningless without some requirement of a domestic procedural investigation into the facts, at least where agents of the state have been responsible for the taking of life[3]. Article 2 thus includes a positive duty upon states to ensure that an investigation is held involving 'independent and public scrutiny capable of leading to a determination on whether the force used was or was not justified in a particular set of circumstances' in which the applicant may participate[4]. In consequence, even where it has not been established that the force used was unjustified, there may still be a violation of Article 2 if any investigation is deemed ineffective. For example, in *Kaya v Turkey,* the applicant alleged that his brother had been deliberately killed by security forces while the government suggested that he had died in the course of a gun battle during a skirmish between terrorists and security forces. The Commission had found any possibility of establishing the facts considerably compromised by the failure of the applicant and other key witnesses to give oral evidence, and had concluded that it could not be established beyond reasonable doubt that security forces had intentionally killed him. The Court did not consider that there were any exceptional circumstances justifying departure from these findings of fact, and agreed that there was insufficient evidence to establish any violation of Article 2 on this issue. However, both the Commission and the Court considered that the Turkish authorities had failed to carry out any effective investigation into the killing. In particular, the public prosecutor had accepted without question the version of the facts given by security forces and had failed to carry out any independent verification of evidence. In these circumstances, there was a violation of Article 2[5].

Several other cases involving Turkey have identified significant inadequacies in responsibilities to carry out effective domestic investigations[6] under Article 2 (and also in terms of Articles 3, 5 and 13) including failures on the part of public prosecutors to attempt to locate[7] and properly interview[8] witnesses or to obtain and assess real evidence[9], thus leading to conclusions of perfunctory investigation[10] or bias[11] in the carrying out of inquiries. To this end, the Court will consider the adequacy of decisions by domestic courts which have ruled on the criminal liability of state officials who have used lethal force. In *Gül v Turkey*, a criminal court had heard only brief oral evidence from the three police officers charged with the fatal shooting of the householder. The acquittal of the officers had been based upon two expert reports requested by the court, each of which proceeded upon the assumption that the police officers were not at fault rather than upon any apparent technical expertise of the authors of the report. For the Court, the decision to acquit in these circumstances without any further explanation as to why these reports had been considered sufficient had meant that the domestic court had 'effectively deprived itself of its jurisdiction to decide the factual and legal issues of the case'[12].

It is not, though, for the Court to specify in detail what procedures should be adopted, nor to conclude that one unified procedure which combines fact-finding, criminal investigation and prosecution is necessary. However, domestic arrangements must strike an appropriate balance when seeking to take into account other legitimate interests such as national security or the protection of material relevant to other investigations in ensuring that Article 2 safeguards are provided in an accessible and effective manner. This was made clear in a series of four related cases, *Hugh Jordan v United Kingdom, McKerr v United Kingdom, Kelly and Ors v United Kingdom* and *Shanaghan v United Kingdom*, in which the Court considered the deaths of fourteen individuals arising out of four separate incidents in Northern Ireland, three involving the use of lethal force by police officers and soldiers, and the fourth concerning the murder of a terrorist suspect by unknown individuals following the disclosure of intelligence by the armed forces. As far as the state's responsibility for these deaths was concerned, the Court wished to avoid duplicating proceedings which were still pending in the civil courts since these courts were considered to be better placed and equipped to establish factual matters. On the other hand the Court did examine whether Northern Irish procedures into the allegations of unlawful killings had been capable of leading to the identification and punishment of those responsible under the procedural aspect of Article 2. Here, significant shortcomings in transparency and effectiveness had run counter to the state's aim of allaying suspicions and rumours through proper investigation and indeed had helped fuel allegations of a shoot-to-kill policy[13].

1 Cf 16734/90, *Dujarin v France* (1992) DR 32, 190. See also van Dijk and van Hoof *Theory and Practice of the European Convention on Human Rights* (3rd edn, 1998) at pp 297–298: 'The protection provided by the law, however, is a reality only if that law is implemented. Omission on the part of the authorities to trace and prosecute the offender in case of an unlawful deprivation of life is, therefore, in principle subjected to review by the Strasbourg organs.'

2 Cf 23412/94, *The Taylor, Crampton, Gibson and King Families v United Kingdom* (1994) DR 79, 127 (death of applicants' children by a mentally ill nurse: the criminal prosecution of the nurse and the holding of an independent but private inquiry which published its findings satisfied the requirements of the European Convention on Human Rights, Art 2). In *McCann v United Kingdom* (1995) A 324, paras 160–164, the Court did not find it necessary to decide whether a right of access to a court to bring civil proceedings could be inferred from ECHR, Art 2 since this was an issue better determined under Arts 6 and 13, neither of which had been invoked by the applicants. Nor was it necessary to determine what form an investigation into the taking of life should assume since the domestic proceedings in the present case seemed satisfactory. In England, an application for judicial review of the decision to hold in private the inquiry into the killing of patients by Dr Harold Shipman, based in part on ECHR, Art 10, was successful: *R (Wagstaff) v Secretary of State for Health* [2001] 1 WLR 292. An inquiry in public was also considered appropriate in *R (Wright) v Secretary of State for the Home Department* (20 June 2001, unreported), QBD concerned with the death of a prisoner and in the similar case of *R (Amin) v Secretary of State for the Home Department* (5 October 2001, unreported), QBD.

3 This principle derives in part from international legal standards: cf *Hugh Jordan v United Kingdom* (4 May 2001), paras 87–92; *McKerr v United Kingdom* (4 May 2001), paras 92–97; *Kelly and Ors v United Kingdom* (4 May 2001), paras 75–80; and *Shanaghan v United Kingdom* (4 May 2001), paras 69–74 (consideration inter alia of relevant international law and practice including the UN Principles on Extra-Legal Executions of 1989 and the UN Force and Firearms Principles of 1990).

4 *Kaya v Turkey* 1998-I, 297 at paras 86–87. It is not clear whether any such investigation must be instigated as a matter of course by the state, or may be prompted by the taking of civil proceedings by a near relative. An administrative body carrying out an investigation into killings by police or security forces which is hierarchically subordinate to executive authority will not be considered 'independent': *Güleç v Turkey* 1998-IV, 1698, paras 80–82; *Gül v Turkey* (14 December 2000), para 91. See too 39473/98, *Xhavara and Ors v Italy and Albania* (11 January 2001) (responsibility of state authorities for a collision at sea which resulted in the deaths of 58 Albanian illegal immigrants: no evidence that the boat carrying the immigrants had been deliberately sunk by the Italian warship, and no reason to believe that the Italian investigation had been inefficient: inadmissible).

5 *Kaya v Turkey* 1998-I, 297, paras 61–92. See too *Yaşa v Turkey* 1998-VI, 2411, paras 92–108 (not possible to conclude beyond reasonable doubt that individuals had been killed by security services; but criminal inquiries had made no real progress or yielded any tangible results some five years after the event, and thus investigations were inadequate).

6 Including the adequacy of post mortem examinations which are expected to provide 'a complete and accurate record of possible signs of ill-treatment and an objective analysis of clinical findings' in terms of the UN Principles on Extra-legal Executions: *Salman v Turkey* (27 June 2000), at para 73; *Gül v Turkey* (14 December 2000), at para 89. For an example where an investigation was considered adequate, see *Ekinci v Turkey* (18 July 2000), paras 77–87.

7 Eg *Aydin v Turkey* 1997-VI, 1866, para 106.

8 E g *Menteş and Ors v Turkey* 1997-VIII, 2689, para 91 (misgivings as to selection of witnesses etc); *Kurt v Turkey* 1998-III, 1152, para 127 (questions sought to lead witnesses); *Selçuk and Asker v Turkey* 1998-II, 891, para 97 (officer in charge not interviewed).

9 E g *Kaya v Turkey* 1998-I, 297, paras 89–90 (failure to collect evidence at the locus, and to check custody records).

10 E g *Ergi v Turkey* 1998-IV, 1751, paras 82–85 and 98, 155; *Kurt v Turkey* 1998-III, 1152, para 141 (police conclusions accepted at face value).

11 E g *Aydin v Turkey* 1997-VI, 1866, para 106 (deferential attitude towards security services).

12 (14 December 2000), paras 93–94 at para 94.

13 *Hugh Jordan v United Kingdom* (4 May 2001), paras 110–145; *McKerr v United Kingdom* (4 May 2001), paras 116–161; *Kelly and Ors v United Kingdom* (4 May 2001), paras 99–139; and *Shanaghan v United Kingdom* (4 May 2001), paras 93–125. The applicants specifically referred to the Scottish system of inquiry conducted by a judge of criminal jurisdiction as an appropriate model for satisfying the procedural aspect of ECHR, Art 2, but the Court merely noted that this is not the only method available (at paras 143; 159; 137; and 123 respectively). The inadequacies identified in several or all of the cases variously included a lack of independence of the police officers investigating the incident from police officers or security force personnel involved in the incidents; lack of public scrutiny (and information to the victim's family) of reasons by the public prosecutor not to proceed against any police officer or soldier; police officers or soldiers who had used lethal force could not have been required to attend the inquests as witnesses; inquest procedures had not allowed any verdict or findings which could play an effective role in securing a prosecution; inquest proceedings had not commenced promptly and had not been not pursued with reasonable expedition; and the non-disclosure of witness statements prior to the appearance of the victim's families at inquests had prejudiced their ability to participate in proceedings (and, in two of the cases, had contributed to long adjournments in the proceedings). Additional failings in individual cases had included the absence of legal aid for the representation of the victim's family; the effect of a public interest immunity certificate which had prevented the inquest examining crucial matters; and (in the fourth case) the inquest was excluded from considering concerns of security force collusion in the targeting and killing of the victim. The Court also considered the CPT's Report on its visit to the United Kingdom in 1999 which was critical of the effectiveness of police and Police Complaints Authority investigations into allegations of police ill-treatment of individuals: *Report to the United Kingdom*, CPT/Inf (2000) 1, paras 9–58. The UK Government's response is published at CPT/Inf (2000) 7. This report was referred to in *R (Manning) v Director of Public Prosecutions* [2001] QB 330, where the Divisional Court quashed the DPP's decision not to prosecute prison officers who had forcibly searched a prison inmate immediately before his death, and ordered the DPP to reconsider the matter.

4.09   As cases such as *Gül v Turkey* illustrate, the responsibility to carry out an adequate investigation is closely related to the issue as to the existence of an effective remedy in domestic law to enforce the substance of the guarantee in terms of the European Convention on Human Rights, Article 13[1], and initially, as to whether an applicant has exhausted any such remedies in terms of Article 35[2]. A claim for compensation for unlawful killing by state officials may also fall within Article 6's guarantee of access to a court for determination of civil rights and obligations. In *Kaya v Turkey*, the applicant alleged that he would have been unable to seek compensation in the Turkish courts on account of the state's untested but firm contention that his brother had been a terrorist. Since the applicant had never attempted to raise any such action, the European Court of Human Rights determined that it was not possible to determine the substance of this complaint, but that in any case this issue was more appropriately considered as falling within the scope of Article 13[3].

In an English case concerned with the death of a prisoner, the court derived from the Strasbourg decisions the following propositions:

1   Articles 2 and 3 enshrine fundamental human rights. When it is arguable that there has been a breach of either article, the state has an obligation to procure an effective official investigation.
2   The obligation to procure an effective official investigation arises by necessary implication in Articles 2 and 3. Such investigation is required, in order to maximise future compliance with these articles.
3   There is no universal set of rules for the form which an effective official investigation must take. The form which the investigation takes will depend on the facts of the case and the procedures available in the particular state.
4   Where the victim has died and it is arguable that there has been a breach of Art 2, the investigation should have the general features identified by the Court in *Hugh Jordan v United Kingdom*[4].
5   The holding of an inquest may or may not satisfy the implied obligation to investigate arising under Art 2. This depends upon the facts of the case and the course of events at the inquest[5].

1 *Yaşa v Turkey* 1998-VI, 2411, at para 114 (the European Convention on Human Rights, Art 13 imposes obligation to carry out 'a thorough and effective investigation capable of leading to the identification and punishment of those responsible and in which the complainant has effective access to the investigation proceedings'). Cf *Ogur v Turkey* (20 May 1999), paras 88–93 (case file inaccessible to applicant whose son had been shot dead during armed operations purportedly against terrorists at a mining site where the son had worked as a nightwatchman). In *Hugh Jordan v United Kingdom* (4 May 2001), paras 159–165; *McKerr v United Kingdom* (4 May 2001), paras 170–176; *Kelly and Ors v United Kingdom* (4 May 2001), paras 153–159; and *Shanaghan v United Kingdom* (4 May 2001), paras 134–140, the Court found that no separate issue arose under ECHR, Art 13, noting that civil proceedings were still pending (or had been settled or discontinued) and that complaints concerning the investigation into the deaths had already been examined under the procedural aspect of ECHR, Art 2.
2 *Gül v Turkey* (14 December 2000), para 95 (decisions of the criminal court meant that no effective criminal investigation could have been considered to have been conducted, and thus the applicant was denied both an effective remedy in respect of his son's death as well as access to any other available remedies including a claim for compensation); *Aytekin v Turkey* 1998-VII, 2807 at paras 82 and 84 (domestic remedies must be 'accessible', 'capable of providing redress', and offering 'reasonable prospects of success'; but an alleged violation of ECHR, Art 2 'cannot be remedied exclusively through an award of damages to the relatives of the victim'); *Tanrikulu v Turkey* 1999-IV, 457, at para 117 ('the remedy required by Article 13 must be 'effective' in practice as well as in law, in particular in the sense that its exercise must not be unjustifiably hindered by the acts or omissions of the authorities').
3 *Kaya v Turkey* 1998-I, 297, at para 107. Similar considerations apply to allegations of violations of ECHR, Art 3: see *Aksoy v Turkey* 1996-VI, 2260, para 98.
4 (4 May 2001), paras 106–109: (1) the investigation must be independent; (2) the investigation must be effective; (3) the investigation must be reasonably prompt; (4) there must be a sufficient element of public scrutiny; and (5) the next of kin must be involved to the appropriate extent.
5 *R (Wright) v Secretary of State for the Home Department* (20 June 2001, unreported), QBD. On the facts of the case, neither the inquest nor a civil action (in which liability had been admitted) was regarded as satisfying the requirements of Arts 2 and 3, and the Home Secretary was ordered to set up an independent investigation into the circumstances of the death. The Court also indicated that the inquiry should be held in public. A similar decision was reached in *R (Amin) v Secretary of State for the Home Department* (5 October 2001, unreported), QBD.

Positive obligations: protection against threats of severe violence or harm which may result in death

4.10   The scope of positive duties upon a state under the European Convention on Human Rights, Article 2, paragraph (1) to ensure that the right to life is 'protected by law' has recently been further extended to cover situations where there is a real threat of loss of life. This development, of potentially wide scope, remains at an early stage: the risk is of inappropriate judicial involvement in policy-making[1]. Initially, there was reluctance to accept that Article 2 imposed any general duty upon the state to provide indefinite police protection to individuals against threats from others[2], but in *Osman v United Kingdom*, the European Court of Human Rights indicated that Article 2 may indeed place upon a state a positive obligation to take appropriate steps to try to protect life, although any such positive duty 'must be interpreted in such a way which does not impose an impossible or disproportionate burden on the authorities'. In *Osman*, the applicant alleged that the police had taken insufficient measures to provide protection in the face of threats of violence from an unstable teacher who had developed an unhealthy attraction for a pupil. On the particular facts of the case, the Court eventually considered that the police could not be assumed to have known of any real and immediate risk to the life of the deceased, nor could it reasonably have been assumed that any action taken by the police would have neutralised any such risk. Consequently, there was no violation under this heading[3]. However, the Court was prepared to establish a positive obligation on states to contrive an effective response where there is a real or immediate risk of death through the criminal actions of an individual known to the authorities (or where the authorities ought to have known his identity) where such a threat could have been addressed by use of 'measures within the scope of their powers which, judged reasonably, might [have been] expected to avoid that risk'[4]. This principle has been applied in cases involving Turkey where the Court has accepted that the state has failed to take reasonable measures to counter real and immediate threats to the lives of individuals at particular risk[5], and may also extend to protecting the public in general from the risk posed by individuals known to be dangerous[6]. It seems also to apply to the taking of reasonable measures to protect prisoners from self-harm, for example by force-feeding[7] or by placing prisoners on suicide watch[8]. Indeed, a relevant ground for considering whether pre-trial detention is justified in terms of Article 5(3) can include the need to protect an accused person against threats of violence through public disorder[9].

---

1 In particular, where such may interfere with allocation of limited resources. See further, O'Sullivan 'Allocation of Scarce Resources and the Right to Life under the ECHR' [1998] PL 389; and McBride 'Protecting Life: A Positive Obligation to Help' (1999) 24 EL Rev HR 43.

2 6040/73, *X v Ireland* (1973) YB 16, 338 at 392 (withdrawal after three years of police protection against a terrorist organisation which had attempted to kill the applicant; the European Convention on Human Rights, Art 2 'cannot be interpreted as imposing a duty on a State to give protection of this nature, at least not for an indefinite period of time. . . .'). Cf 9348/81, *W v United Kingdom* (1983) DR 32, 190, at para 12 (claim that the state had not provided adequate and effective security for the population of Northern Ireland rejected on account of level of presence of security forces; ECHR, Art 2 could not require 'positive obligation to exclude any possible violence').

3 1998-VIII, 3124, at paras 119–121.

4 1998-VIII, 3124, at para 116. Cf 22998/93, *Danini v Italy* (1996) DR 87, 24 (not foreseeable that the applicant's daughter was in real and imminent danger of being killed by an individual who had made threats against her); *Denizci and Others v Cyprus* (23 May 2001), paras 375–377 (nothing to suggest an individual's life was at real and immediate risk: no violation of Art 2 on this account).

5 See too *Akkoç v Turkey* (10 October 2000), paras 77–94 (failure to protect the applicant's husband who was at particular risk of falling victim to an unlawful attack because of his political activities; state authorities had been aware of this risk since the public prosecutor had been informed of threats to the lives of the applicant and her husband had been made, and ought further to have been aware of the possibility that this risk derived from the activities of persons acting with the acquiescence of elements in the security forces: conclusion that in the circumstances the authorities had failed to take reasonable measures available to them to prevent a real and immediate risk to the life of the applicant's husband and accordingly there had been a violation of ECHR, Art 2); *Kilic v Turkey* (28 March 2000), paras 62–77; *Kaya v Turkey* (28 March 2000), paras 85–101. See also *Venables v News Group Newspapers Ltd* [2001] 2 WLR 1038.

6 26561/95, *Rebai v France* (1997) DR 88, 72 (no indication that prisoner who set fire to a cell resulting in his death and that of two other prisoners posed a danger to others; nor had authorities failed to protect the lives of cellmates who died); cf 37703/97, *Mastromatteo v Italy* (14 September 2000) (murder of the applicant's son by prisoners on home leave after being released by judges without seeking background information or a prescribed psychological report: application declared admissible).

7 Cf 10563/83, *X v Germany*. See further para 4.26 below.

8 *Tanribilir v Turkey* (16 November 2000), paras 68–80 (no negligence on the part of police officers in preventing the suicide of a prisoner which could not have been reasonably foreseeable; and the authorities had carried out an effective investigation); *Keenan v United Kingdom* (3 April 2001), paras 88–101 (not possible to conclude that the applicant's son had been at immediate risk of suicide, and the prison authorities had done all that could have been reasonably expected of them: no violation of ECHR, Art 2; but a violation of ECHR, Art 3 because of defects in health care).

9 Eg *I A v France* 1998-VII, 2951, para 108: see para 4.79 below.

DECISIONS OF DOMESTIC COURTS ON THE PROTECTION OF INDIVIDUALS FROM THREATS OF SEVERE VIOLENCE

4.11   In the English case of *Venables v News Group Newspapers Ltd*, the risk to the safety of two individuals (who had, as children, been convicted of a horrific murder) was held to justify the grant of an injunction preventing the press from revealing their identities or whereabouts, following their release. Reliance was placed by the court upon the *Osman* judgment in extending the existing common law to give effect to the state's positive duties under the European Convention on Human Rights, Articles 2 and 3[1].

1 [2001] 2 WLR 1038. Other relevant decisions of domestic courts are noted at paras 4.08 and 4.09 above and 4.30 below.

Serious risks to health

4.12   Recent applications have also sought to broaden the responsibility of the state for minimising or reducing any serious risks to health. In other words, a real threat to an individual's continuing existence may give rise to an issue under the European Convention on Human Rights, Article 2, even where no actual loss of life has occurred. The emergence of such a duty is an extension of, and closely related to, the requirement under Article 8 to take steps to ensure effective respect for family life, for example by providing protection against serious environmental pollution[1]. These initial cases have concerned exposure to radiation, but the principle could equally apply to harmful omissions from toxic pollution, and conceivably to other avoidable noxious substances. Whether the principle can be extended in time to require action to minimise other less direct but still obvious risks to life (for example, by taking appropriate measures at identified road traffic accident blackspots) remains unclear[2]. The positive duty is to prevent life from being avoidably put at risk by taking such steps within the scope of state authority as can be considered reasonably to be expected in the light of the information available[3]. In domestic law, the tests of proximity and foreseeability of harm could presumably be applied to determine the extent of any duty. Relevant Strasbourg decisions seem to imply a requirement that the state is aware (or ought to be aware) of the identity of the applicant before any positive obligation to protect his life can be deemed to exist. However, the requirement placed upon the applicant to establish a causal link between a real and serious threat to life and the acts or omissions complained of may restrict the practical use of this development[4]. In *LCB v United Kingdom*, the applicant's father had taken part as a conscript serviceman in nuclear weapon testing some eight years before her birth. At four years old, the applicant had been diagnosed as having leukaemia, and medical records indicated that there was a possibility that the condition was linked to her father's exposure to radiation. She complained that there had been a failure on the part of state authorities to warn and advise her parents and to monitor her health. The European Court of Human Rights accepted that such positive action on the part of state officials could have been required, but only where it appeared likely that her father's exposure to radiation had indeed endangered risk to her health. Here, however, it was not possible to establish any causal link between the applicant's illness and the exposure, and consequently there was no violation of Article 2[5].

1 *López Ostra v Spain* A303-C, para 51, and *Guerra and Ors v Italy* 1998-I, 210; paras 56–60; see further para 6.46 below. In the *Guerra* case, paras 61–62, the Court declined to examine the merits in terms of the European Convention on Human Rights, Art 2 but determined that ECHR, Art 8 required effective protection of respect for private and family life; and failure to provide applicants who lived within 1 km of the factory with essential information allowing them to assess the risks of living in this area was a violation. The Court appeared to ignore the fact that employees of the polluting factory had died of cancer through the release of highly toxic substances.
2 Cf 32165/96, *Wöckel v Germany* (1998) DR 93, 82 (ECHR, Art 2 does not require a general prohibition on smoking to protect life).
3 *LCB v United Kingdom* 1998-III, 1390, para 36. Presumably, the exercise of state authority must be consistent with Convention guarantees such as ECHR, Arts 5 and 8. For example, in *Osman v United Kingdom* 1998-VIII, 3124, para 121, discussed above at para 4.10, it was considered that there had been insufficient evidence available to the police to justify arrest.
4 Cf *McGinley and Egan v United Kingdom* 1998-III, 1334, paras 85–90 (ECHR, Art 6 issue could arise in relation to access to documents relevant to determination of pension rights).
5 1998-III, 1390, paras 35–41. The Court had no jurisdiction to examine complaints under ECHR, Arts 2, 8 and 13 concerning the monitoring of her father's exposure to radiation since these were based on events before the UK's acceptance of the right of individual petition. Cf International Covenant on Civil and Political Rights, Art 7: 'No one shall be subjected to torture or to cruel, inhuman or degrading treatment or punishment. In particular, no one shall be subjected without his free consent to medical or scientific experimentation.'

Abortion

4.13 The lack of clarity under the European Convention on Human Rights as to when any right to life begins is shared by other international instruments and reflects a lack of general agreement amongst states on this issue[1]. On this account, abortion of an unborn foetus is unlikely to be considered as a violation of Article 2[2]. The issue has been essentially avoided by Strasbourg[3], either since the issue has not been argued directly by applicants[4], or the applicants have not been recognised as 'victims'[5], or on account of the need to include countervailing interests – in particular, that of the woman carrying the foetus – in any assessment[6]. The conclusion is that abortion is not specifically excluded from Article 2 consideration, but that it would be difficult to identify the circumstances in which any violation could be deemed to have taken place[7].

1   Cf UN Convention on the Rights of the Child, Art 6(1): 'Every child has the inherent right to life.' 'Child' is defined by Art 1 as 'every human being below the age of eighteen years'. Attempts to extend the convention to include foetuses were resisted since international consensus was lacking: see Alston 'The Unborn Child and Abortion under the Draft Convention on the Rights of the Child' (1990) 12 HRQ 156. Cf the American Convention on Human Rights, Art 4: 'Every person has the right to have his life respected. This right shall be protected by law, and in general, from the moment of conception.'

2   The Commission noted in 17004/90, *H v Norway* (1992) DR 73, 155 that because of differences in their domestic laws, member states 'must have a certain discretion' in the regulation of abortion. However, it then went on to indicate that it did not wish to rule out the possibility of a foetus receiving protection under the European Convention on Human Rights, Art 2 in certain but undefined circumstances. Earlier, in 8416/78, *Paton v United Kingdom* (1980) DR 19, 244, the Commission had concluded that the term 'everyone' in the treaty applied only to persons actually born, and thus a foetus could not be said to enjoy ECHR rights.

3   For a fuller discussion, see Domien, Harris and Zwaak *Law and Practice of the European Convention on Human Rights and the European Social Charter* (1996) pp 102–103; van Dijk and van Hoof *Theory and Practice of the European Convention on Human Rights* (3rd edn, 1998) pp 300–302. For discussion of respect of the beliefs of medical staff under ECHR, Art 9, see Hammer 'Abortion Objection in the UK Within the Framework of the ECHR' [1999] EHRLR 564.

4   As in *Open Door and Dublin Well Woman v Ireland* (1992) A 246-A, paras 66–79 (at paras 78–79: question essentially concerned right to receive and impart information on abortion under ECHR, Art 10; but the Court declined to consider whether restrictions could be justified by the state as protecting the 'rights of others').

5   As in 867/60, *X v Norway* (1961) YB 4, 270 and 7045/75, *X v Austria* (1976) DR 7, 87 (applicant unable to qualify as a 'victim' in a general challenge to abortion legislation). In 17004/90, *H v Norway* (1992) DR 73, 155, the applicant had sought to challenge the decision of his partner to abort the child she was carrying (the applicant being the father of the foetus) but the Commission refused to accept that the regulation by domestic law of abortion exceeded the discretion available to states. In 8416/78, *Paton v United Kingdom* (1980) DR 19, 244, the Commission did accept that the father of the foetus was 'so closely affected' by the termination of his wife's pregnancy that he could qualify as a 'victim'. In *Open Door and Dublin Well Woman v Ireland* (1992) A 246-A, para 44, the Court also considered for the purposes of ECHR, Art 8 that women of child-bearing age qualified as 'victims' since they could be affected by the restrictions on the availability of material on abortion. In Scots civil law, no legal personality is recognised until birth, although a child is entitled to raise an action in delict for injuries sustained while *in utero*: *Hamilton v Fife Health Board* 1993 SC 369. However, this principle cannot be extended to give a father who would qualify as a legal guardian of a child upon its birth the right to prevent any damage to the foetus, at least not to prevent the termination of the pregnancy by way of abortion: *Kelly v Kelly* 1997 SC 285 (husband sought to prevent his wife from seeking an abortion but the court considered he lacked title to sue: an unborn foetus had no rights which could be vindicated).

6   As in 6959/75, *Brüggeman and Scheuten v Germany* (1977) DR 10, 100, paras 60–61 (challenge to restrictions on availability of abortion under ECHR, Art 8; domestic law required specific situations of distress to the pregnant women to be shown before abortion was lawful. The Commission could not accept that pregnancy pertained exclusively to the sphere of private life since the foetus has some claim to consideration, and thus that not every regulation of abortion constituted an interference with respect for private life. However, the Commission avoided consideration whether the foetus was an entity permitting interference 'for the protection of others').

7 Cf 24844/94, *Reeve v United Kingdom* (1994) DR 79, 146 (issue of access to court under ECHR, Art 6(1) to pursue a claim for negligence on the part of a health authority, in the absence of which the applicant's parents could have decided upon an abortion).

Decisions of domestic courts concerning medical treatment

4.14   The European Convention on Human Rights, Article 2 has been considered in other medical contexts in recent cases before the English courts. In *Re A (Children) (Conjoined Twins: Surgical Separation)*, the issue was whether the court should grant a declaration that a hospital could lawfully carry out an operation to separate twins who were conjoined at the pelvis and shared a common aorta. In the absence of such an operation, it was clear that both twins would die within three to six months. If the operation were carried out, one twin had a reasonable prospect of a worthwhile life, but the other was certain to die within minutes. The parents were opposed to the operation. The court's decision, granting the declaration, was primarily concerned with domestic civil and criminal law, but also considered the issue in relation to Article 2. It was held that the word 'intentionally' in Article 2(1) should be given its natural and ordinary meaning. So construed, it applied only to cases where the purpose of the prohibited action was to cause death. The purpose of the operation was to save life, even though the extinction of another life was a virtual certainty. English law adequately protected the right to life, notwithstanding that in such exceptional circumstances it regarded an act which had as its foreseen consequence the earlier ending of one twin's life (for the sake of saving the other twin's life) as justified by the doctrine of necessity[1].

In *NHS Trust A v M* the court had to consider the compatibility with Article 2[2] of the withdrawal of feeding from patients in a permanent vegetative state. The court proceeded on the basis that the principles laid down in *Airedale NHS Trust v Bland*[3] had to be reconsidered in the light of the Human Rights Act 1998 (and the same would apply, in a Scottish context, to the principles laid down in *Law Hospital NHS Trust v Lord Advocate*[4]). The court accepted that a patient in a permanent vegetative state continued to be protected by Article 2. It also accepted that the intention of the withdrawal of treatment was to bring about the death of the patient. The court considered that the issue was whether, in such a case, Article 2 imposed upon the state a positive obligation to take steps to prolong the patient's life. In that regard, reference was made to the opinion of the Commission in the *Osman* case:

'Whether risk to life derives from disease, environmental factors or from the intentional activities of those acting outside the law, there will be a range of policy decisions, relating, inter alia, to the use of State resources, which it will be for Contracting States to assess on the basis of their aims and priorities, subject to these being compatible with the values of democratic societies and the fundamental rights guaranteed in the Convention[5].'

The court concluded:

> 'In a case where a responsible clinical decision is made to withhold treatment, on the grounds that it is not in the patient's best interests, and that clinical decision is made in accordance with a respectable body of medical opinion, the state's positive obligation under Article 2 is, in my view, discharged'[6].

1   [2001] Fam 147. The court also considered the matter under the European Convention on Human Rights, Arts 3 and 8. Cf 7154/75, *Association X v United Kingdom* (1978) DR 14, 31 (deaths of children as side-effect of vaccination scheme not 'intentional' deprivation of life).
2   And also ECHR, Arts 3 and 8.
3   [1993] AC 789.
4   1996 SC 301.
5   1998-VIII, 3124, Opinion of the Commission, at para 91.
6   [2001] Fam 348; again, the court considered the matter additionally under ECHR, Arts 3 and 8. This approach, based upon the distinction between acts and omissions, has been criticised as excessively formal: Bainham 'Dehydration and Human Rights' [2001] 60 CLJ 53. Whether there is an obligation on a state to provide life-preserving medical treatment must, however, depend on the scope of the positive obligation imposed by ECHR, Art 2. As to assisted suicide, see *R (Pretty) v DPP* (18 October 2001, unreported), QBD.

Imposition of the death penalty

4.15   The specific reference to capital punishment in the European Convention on Human Rights, Article 2, paragraph (1) is an historical legacy rather than an indication of contemporary practice. Many European states permitted and applied the death penalty in the middle of the twentieth century; 50 years on, the practice has been almost universally abandoned[1]. Protocol 6 abolishes the death penalty[2], but retains the right of any state to make legal provision for capital punishment 'in respect of acts committed in time of war or of imminent threat of war', providing always that any such sentence 'shall be applied only in the instances laid down in the law and in accordance with its provisions'[3]. Most member states of the Council of Europe have now ratified this optional protocol; and those which have not done so would find it politically difficult to impose such a sentence[4], even assuming that other Convention concerns (such as whether an individual has had a fair trial[5] or whether detention conditions on death row are acceptable[6]) have been met. The question of the compatibility of carrying out a sentence of death with the Convention will be addressed in the forthcoming case of *Öcalan v Turkey*[7].

1   Of Council of Europe member states, all have abolished the death penalty entirely or in peacetime, with the exception of Armenia, Russia and Turkey which are considering whether to do so, each having applied a moratorium on executions. The last judicial executions appear to have taken place in Ukraine in 1997 and in the Chechen Republic in Russia in 1999. The only European non-member state still to carry out executions is Belarus (where some 24 executions took place in 1999). See further Council of Europe *The Council of Europe and the Death Penalty* (2001).
2   The European Convention on Human Rights, Protocol 6 opened for signature in April 1983, and entered into force in March 1985. It was ratified by the United Kingdom on 20 May 1999 with effect from 1 June 1999. Ratification followed acceptance in May 1998 by the

Commons of a backbench amendment inserting Protocol 6 in the Human Rights Bill. The Government had wished to retain the right of Parliament to consider whether the death penalty should be used and was concerned that any ratification of Protocol 6 would prevent reintroduction of capital punishment at a later stage without renunciation of the Convention as a whole: see (1998) NLJ 810. The Crime and Disorder Act 1998, s 36 abolished the death penalty for treason, and the Human Rights Act 1998, s 21(5) in respect of military offences. See further, Krüger 'Protocol No 6 to the ECHR' and Ravaud and Trechsel 'The Death Penalty and the Case-Law of the Institutions of the ECHR' in Council of Europe *The Death Penalty – Abolition in Europe* (1999) pp 69–78, 79–90. For discussion of practice elsewhere, see Hood *The Death Penalty* (2nd edn, 1996); and Schabas *The Death Penalty as Cruel Treatment and Torture* (1996); and of international moves towards abolition of the death penalty, see Schabas *The Abolition of the Death Penalty in International Law* (2nd edn, 1997); and Fine 'Moratorium 2000: An International Dialogue toward a Ban on Capital Punishment' (1999) 30 Colum Hum Rts L Rev 421.

3   ECHR, Protocol 6, Arts 1 and 2. No derogation or reservation is possible: Arts 3 and 4. Gomien, Harris and Zwaak *Law and Practice of the European Convention on Human Rights and the European Social Charter* (1996) at p 96 conclude that any legislation permitting the death penalty in time of war would require to have been enacted during peacetime, and could not be altered during war.

4   See Wohlwend 'The Efforts of the Parliamentary Assembly' in Council of Europe *The Death Penalty – Abolition in Europe* (1999) pp 55–68; Committee of Ministers Declaration 'For a European death-penalty-free area' (9 November 2000).

5   In *Damjanovic v Federation of Bosnia and Hercegovina*, case CH/96/30 (1996), the Human Rights Chamber of Bosnia and Hercegovina, in applying the ECHR, held that a death sentence imposed by a Bosnian military court violated Art 2 largely because of Art 6 considerations: judges were able to be dismissed by the executive and there was no evidence that in practice they enjoyed any safeguards of independence (and indeed a military court was more likely to be subjected to external pressures). The case can be found at: www.gwdg.de/~ujvr/hrch/hrch.htm .

6   Cf *Soering v United Kingdom* (1989) A 161, discussed at para 4.16 below. See also 10479/83, *Kirkwood v United Kingdom* (1984) DR 37, 158. Four applications challenging conditions of detention of prisoners sentenced to death before abolition of capital punishment in 2000 have been declared admissible: e g 39483/98, *Nazarenko v Ukraine* (25 May 1999).

7   46221/99. In November 1999, the Court requested, by way of an interim measure under Rule of Court 39, that the respondent state would not execute the applicant who had been sentenced to death for terrorist crimes until the Court had determined the issues raised in the application. The case was declared admissible on 14 December 2000. Recent Commonwealth cases to examine the death penalty include *Pratt and Morgan v A-G of Jamaica* [1994] 2 AC 1 and *Lewis and Ors v A-G of Jamaica* [2001] 2 AC 50. Arguments concerning the death penalty are considered in the South African case of *The State v Makwanyane and Mchunu* (1995) 16 HRLJ 4.

Deportation to face a charge carrying the death penalty

4.16   The case of *Öcalan v Turkey*[1] aside, any issue concerning the death penalty is now likely to be restricted to the question of extradition to a state where there is a real risk of the imposition of capital punishment. This is, however, an issue more properly considered under the European Convention on Human Rights, Article 3. In *Soering v United Kingdom*, the European Court of Human Rights declined to accept that the imposition of a sentence of death would in itself violate the prohibition of inhuman or degrading treatment under this provision[2]. The applicant (a German national) had been detained in the United Kingdom pending determination of a request by the United States of America for his extradition to face two charges of murder allegedly committed when the applicant was 18. There was a substantial likelihood that, if convicted, the sentence would have been one of capital punishment. The Court's ruling that extradition would trigger an Article 3 violation was confined to condemnation of the holding conditions pending execution (or 'death row phenomenon') rather than of the sentence itself. Although 'the Convention is to be read as a whole and Article 3 should therefore be construed in harmony with the provisions of Article 2', the Court concluded not that any infliction of the death penalty must avoid suffering amounting to inhuman or degrading treatment or punishment, but rather that the intention of the drafters of the treaty was to exclude any general prohibition of the death penalty since the text of Article 2(1) specifically permits capital punishment. Certainly, the subsequent abolition of capital punishment in Europe 'could be taken as establishing the agreement of the Contracting States to abrogate the exception' provided by Article 2 and thus encourage the evolutive interpretation of Article 3. However, the very existence of Protocol 6 indicated that states intended to abolish the death penalty not by judicial re-interpretation but by 'the normal method of amendment', that is, by optional ratification of the additional protocol. Thus the Court concluded that Article 3 could not be interpreted as imposing any general prohibition against infliction of the death penalty[3]. This aspect of the judgment appears unduly narrow, and contrasts with the approach adopted in certain state courts in the USA where the cruelty involved in the method of execution can be considered unconstitutional[4]. The irony is that this optional protocol, which was designed to speed up abolition of the death penalty, was treated by the Court as a restraint upon its prohibition through the development of legal interpretation. Political rather than legal determination was to end the use of the death penalty in Europe. This dictum has become increasingly at odds with the policy of the Council of Europe over the last decade that capital punishment is unacceptable. There is thus no clear guidance as to whether there should be a prohibition upon extradition from a Council of Europe state to another country where there is a substantial risk that the death penalty may be carried out using a manner of execution which gives rise to particular concerns as to the level of pain inflicted[5] or where infliction of the penalty would violate other aspects of international law[6].

1   46221/99 (14 December 2000).
2   (1989) A 161, paras 101–104. The applicant had not directly raised this issue: his argument under the European Convention on Human Rights, Art 3 was based upon the detention conditions on death row prior to execution. The Canadian Supreme Court has recently ruled that individuals may not be extradited to the USA without assurances that capital punishment would not be sought if convicted: *United States v Burns* 2001 SCC 7.
3   *Soering v United Kingdom* (1989) A 161, at para 103. However, there must be substantial doubt as to whether the treaty drafters (or ratifying states) ever themselves contemplated the extension of ECHR protection to extradition to non-ratifying states such as the USA in the way achieved by *Soering*. Cf 44190/98, *Nivette v France* (3 July 2001) (assurances received by the respondent state were such as to exclude the danger that the death penalty would be imposed if the applicant were extradited to the USA: inadmissible).
4   E g *Fierro v Gomez* 77 F 3d 301 (1996) (execution by lethal gas deemed unconstitutional by a federal court in the USA but the Supreme Court remanded the case back for consideration after the state in question amended its law to provide that lethal injection be administered unless the condemned requested lethal gas; on remand, the lower court held the case was moot since Fierro had not selected to die by gassing). If a simulated execution is likely to be considered as resulting in an ECHR, Art 3 violation, why should an actual execution involving similar levels of pre-execution stress and anxiety (even before consideration of the physical pain involved in the killing itself) escape Art 3 censure? On the other hand, the UN Convention against Torture and Other Cruel, Inhuman or Degrading Treatment or

Punishment, Art 1(1) specifically excludes 'pain or suffering arising only from, inherent in or incidental to lawful sanctions' from the definition of 'torture'.

5 Cf 10227/82, *H v Spain* (1983) DR 37, 93 (extradition proceedings are not a 'determination' of a criminal charge in terms of ECHR, Art 6; the state could only consider whether formal procedures for extradition were satisfied and not the question of guilt); 10479/83, *Kirkwood v United Kingdom* (1983) DR 37, 158 (terms of ECHR, Art 2 does not support a contention that extradition to a state without prior binding assurance that death penalty will not be applied would result in ECHR, Art 3 violation); 58128/00, *Ismaili v Germany* (15 March 2001) (allegation that there is a substantial risk that the death penalty may be applied must be established; here, the country seeking extradition had indicated that the crime the applicant was accused of did not carry this penalty, an assurance which had been confirmed by the German courts: inadmissible).

6 The imposition of a death sentence on an individual for a crime committed as a minor (under 18) is prohibited by the International Covenant on Civil and Political Rights, Art 6(5) and by the UN Convention on the Rights of the Child, Art 37(a). The USA, Saudi Arabia, Iran, Yemen and Nigeria still execute persons convicted of crimes committed as minors. Denials of consular access to detainees facing a sentence of death in the USA were addressed by the World Court in *Germany v United States of America* (the 'La Grand case') (27 June 2001). See further Hudson 'Does the Death Row Phenomenon Violate a Prisoner's Human Rights under International Law?' (2000) 11 EJIL 833.

TORTURE AND INHUMAN OR DEGRADING TREATMENT OR PUNISHMENT

General principles of interpretation

4.17   The European Convention on Human Rights, Article 3 'enshrines one of the fundamental values of the democratic societies making up the Council of Europe'[1]. The text of Article 3 is succinct; the prohibition against torture or inhuman or degrading treatment or punishment is absolute; and no derogation is permitted in time of war or other emergency[2]. The European Court of Human Rights has adopted a dynamic rather than static interpretation, judging state action according to generally accepted European standards[3]. Further, the Court 'takes the view that the increasingly high standard being required in the area of protection of human rights and fundamental liberties correspondingly and inevitably requires greater firmness in assessing breaches of the fundamental values of democratic societies', so that earlier classifications of acts as 'inhuman' or 'degrading' could well now justify the label 'torture'[4]. However, at the same time the Court has resisted attempts to lower the threshold test to bring more instances of state practice into Article 3 consideration. Nor can Article 3 be used to found any claim essentially of a social or economic nature[5]. Potential issues under Article 3 include the use of force during interrogation, infliction of punishment, conditions of detention, expulsion (extradition and deportation to other states), and particular discriminatory practices. In exceptional circumstances, destruction of home and possessions may also be considered to give rise to a violation of the guarantee[6]. Two questions arise in the application of Article 3: first, whether the physical or mental treatment has achieved a minimum level of severity to give rise to a violation of the provision; and second, where this threshold test has been satisfied, thereafter whether the circumstances amount to torture, to inhuman treatment or punishment, or to degrading treatment or punishment. Both questions involve an assessment often essentially subjective in nature: there can be an unresolved tension between recognition of the Convention as a 'living instrument' to be interpreted in a purposive manner reflecting contemporary expectations, and awareness of the historical legacy which underpinned inclusion of this guarantee at the heart of protection of physical integrity[7]. Further, practical considerations such as state interests in dealing with prisoners considered to pose particular security risks[8] or in tackling terrorism[9] can play a part in assessment. Established jurisprudence is also under increasing challenge from the approaches of the Council of Europe's Committee for the Prevention of Torture in discharging its mandate of enhancing the protection of detainees. In short, interpretation of a right intended to be absolute in nature and of fundamental importance in a democratic society can in practice pose particular difficulties of interpretation.

1 *Soering v United Kingdom* (1989) A 161 at para 88. Cf Universal Declaration of Human Rights, Art 5, and International Covenant on Civil and Political Rights, Art 7. Torture is now recognised as a crime under customary international law.
2 European Convention on Human Rights, Art 15(2).
3 *Tyrer v United Kingdom* (1978) A 26, at para 31 (the Court 'cannot but be influenced by the developments and commonly accepted standards in [European] penal policy'). A recent attempt to extend the scope of ECHR, Art 3 to include the subjection by a victim of a rape to cross-examination by the accused was eventually struck out after a friendly settlement: 41518/98 *JM v United Kingdom* (28 September 2000) (*ex gratia* payment and introduction of amending legislation).
4 *Selmouni v France* 1999-V, 149, para 101.
5 40772/98, *Pančenko v Latvia* (28 October 1999) (complaint concerning precarious economic and social situation arising from refusal of residence permit declared inadmissible: the ECHR does not guarantee the right to a rent-free residence, the right to work, or the right to medical assistance or financial assistance).
6 *Selçuk and Asker v Turkey* 1998-II, 891, paras 72–80; *Bilgin v Turkey* (16 November 2000), paras 100–104.
7 For further discussion of ECHR, Art 3, see Addo and Grief 'Is there a Policy Behind the Decisions and Judgments relating to Article 3?' (1995) 20 EL Rev 178 and 'Some Practical Issues Affecting the Notion of Absolute Right in Article 3 ECHR' (1998) 23 EL Rev HR 17.
8 Cf 8463/78, *Kröcher and Möller v Switzerland* (1981) DR 26, 24 (terrorist suspects ordered by investigating judge to be held incommunicado; legal advisers could only visit with the permission of the judge; the suspects were subjected to constant surveillance; no newspapers or radio allowed etc. The Commission accepted that the cumulative effect of security measures should also be assessed in determining whether there was an ECHR, Art 3 violation, but considered that the measures had been justified on security grounds).
9 Cf *Brannigan and McBride v United Kingdom* (1994) A 258-B (sustained questioning and medical examination of suspects held incommunicado over periods of four to six days; no ECHR, Art 3 issue identified by the applicants, nor any Art 3 point taken by the Commission). See too *Tomasi v France* (1992) A 241-A, at para 115 ('The requirements of the investigation and the undeniable difficulties inherent in the fight against crime, particularly with regard to terrorism, cannot result in limits being placed on the protection to be afforded in respect of the physical integrity of individuals').

Threshold test: determining whether the minimum level of severity has been reached

4.18   A European Convention on Human Rights, Article 3 violation will only arise where the specific treatment complained of meets a minimum level of severity. Even failing actual infliction of any such treatment, the threat of infliction may also trigger Article 3 consideration providing it is 'sufficiently real and immediate'[1]. The issue is considered by reference to all the circumstances of the 'treatment' in question, including its duration and its physical and mental effects, as well as the sex, age and health of the victim[2]. If the suffering involved is considered excessive in the light of prevailing general standards[3] (including contemporary medical standards in the case of involuntary therapeutic treatment[4]), then this threshold test is satisfied. The lack of any evidence of a positive intention to humiliate or to debase an individual is not in itself conclusive as the absence of any such purpose does not rule out a finding of a violation of Article 3[5]. The test has been used to rein in any tendency to trivialise Article 3 by seeking to apply it to matters which arguably lack the requisite degree of seriousness at the historical heart of the article[6] and still exemplified by certain recent cases involving the behaviour of the Turkish state[7]. In *Costello-Roberts v United Kingdom*, for example, a bare majority of the European Court of Human Rights decided that the infliction of corporal punishment in a school was not serious enough to amount to a breach of Article 3, in contrast to the dissenting judgments which placed greater emphasis on consideration of the particular victim (a 'lonely and insecure 7-year-old boy') and of the circumstances surrounding the punishment (which was inflicted after a delay of three days) rather than upon any objective assessment of the treatment itself[8]. There also seems to be an insistence that the treatment is assessed in terms of its immediate or short-term impact only: long-term harm or prolonged exposure to poor material conditions in places of detention has not readily in the past given rise to an Article 3 issue except in the most extreme and extraordinary of cases[9], although the Court's recent judgment in *Peers v Greece* suggests some revision of previous case law may now be taking place[10].

1 *Campbell and Cosans v United Kingdom* (1982) A 48, at para 26.
2 5310/71, *Ireland v United Kingdom* (1976) YB 19, 512, para 162.
3 Cf *Tyrer v United Kingdom* (1978) A 26, paras 31 and 38 (contentions that corporal punishment was supported overwhelmingly by the local population not considered by the Court as a relevant factor). In 3344/67, *Greek case* (1969) YB 12, 186, at para 11, the Commission stressed the importance of local culture in finding that a 'certain roughness of treatment' of persons detained by state officials was tolerated and taken for granted, so 'underlin[ing] the fact that the point up to which prisoners may accept physical violence as being neither cruel nor excessive, varies between different societies and even between different sections of them'. This approach is at odds with the fundamental aim of the European Convention on Human Rights, Art 3, and is clearly now inappropriate.
4 *Herczegfalvy v Austria* (1992) A 244, paras 82–83 at para 82 ('as a general rule, a measure which is a therapeutic necessity [in terms of established principles of medicine] cannot be regarded as inhuman or degrading').
5 *Peers v Greece* (19 April 2001), para 74.
6 E g *Raninen v Finland* 1997-VIII, 2804, paras 55–59 (handcuffing of conscientious objector while being taken to a barracks not sufficiently serious to result in an ECHR, Art 3 violation). There is unlikely to be an Art 3 issue where an appeal court has increased the length of a sentence: cf *Howarth v United Kingdom* (21 September 2000), para 31 (the fact that the applicant (an adult of full age) had completed his non-custodial sentence before being sentenced to imprisonment did not disclose any violation of Art 3). See also *R (X) v Secretary of State for the Home Dept* [2001] 1 WLR 740 (removal of illegal entrant suffering from mental illness); contrast *R (Husain) v Asylum Support Adjudicator* (5 October 2001, unreported), QBD.
7 E g *Selçuk and Asker v Turkey* 1998-II, 891, paras 72–80 and *Bilgin v Turkey* (16 November 2000), paras 100–104 (premeditated destruction of applicants' homes and personal

property: findings of inhuman treatment); *Tekin v Turkey* 1998-IV, 1504, paras 48–54 (ill-treatment while detained blindfolded in cold and dark cell).
8 (1993) A 247-C, paras 31–32 (distinguishing the facts from those in *Tyrer v United Kingdom* (1978) A 26, discussed at para 4.33 below); and joint partly dissenting opinion of Judges Ryssdal, Vilhjálmsson, Matscher and Wildhaber.
9 As in *Soering v United Kingdom* (1989) A 161, discussed at para 4.37 below.
10 (19 April 2001), discussed at para 4.35 below.

APPLICATION OF THE THRESHOLD TEST BY DOMESTIC COURTS

4.19   It has been said in an English case that the European Convention on Human Rights, Article 3 requires the victim to be aware of the inhuman and degrading treatment which he or she is experiencing or at least to be in a state of physical or mental suffering[1].

1 *NHS Trust A v M* [2001] Fam 348, para 49. It may be questionable whether that is correct in all circumstances. See also the domestic cases cited in para 4.18 above.

Classifying violations of Article 3: 'torture'; and 'inhuman' or 'degrading' treatment or punishment

4.20   The distinctions between 'torture', 'inhuman' and 'degrading treatment or punishment' reflect differences in the intensity of suffering as judged by contemporary standards and assessment of state purpose. Use of the term 'torture' attaches a 'special stigma to deliberate inhuman treatment causing very serious and cruel suffering'[1], although often such a determination will be essentially subjective. In the early but influential *Greek* case, the Commission defined 'torture' as inhuman treatment inflicted for a specific purpose, while 'inhuman' was understood as suggesting the unjustified infliction of severe pain, and 'degrading treatment or punishment' consisted of that which grossly humiliates or that which forces an individual to act contrary to his will or conscience[2]. In the first case under the European Convention on Human Rights, Article 3 to be considered by the Court, *Ireland v United Kingdom*, this approach was merely refined. Individuals deprived of their liberty under prevention of terrorism powers in Northern Ireland had been subjected to five interrogation techniques (hooding, wall-standing, exposure to continuous noise, deprivation of sleep and deprivation of food) during questioning by members of the security forces. The Commission had accepted that this ordeal had incurred 'intense physical and mental suffering' and 'acute psychiatric disturbances' such as to amount to torture. However, the Court considered that the circumstances did not display 'suffering of the particular intensity and cruelty' required for a finding of torture (defined as 'deliberate inhuman treatment causing very serious and cruel suffering'), holding instead that the treatment had amounted to inhuman treatment or punishment through the infliction of intense physical and mental suffering. The least severe form of Article 3 violation, degrading treatment or punishment, was defined as treatment 'designed to arouse in the victims feelings of fear, anguish and inferiority capable of humiliating and debasing them and possibly breaking their physical or moral resistance'[3].
Subsequent decisions have applied this interpretation which proceeds

by assessing the degree or intensity of the suffering inflicted. Consistency in jurisprudence is, however, compromised by recognition that heightened expectations may require reassessment of earlier decisions: in particular, what in the past may have amounted to 'inhuman or degrading' treatment may now justify a finding of 'torture'[4]. The early judgment of *Tyrer v United Kingdom* concerned the birching of a 15-year-old youth following a juvenile court decision. The punishment was inflicted three weeks after the court decision by a police officer. The Court emphasised that the degree of humiliation must be judged according to the particular circumstances of the case: here, the fact that the birching was administered on the applicant's bare buttocks was an aggravating factor. Further, any publicity surrounding the treatment or punishment would also be of relevance in deciding whether the treatment was degrading, although the absence of publicity will not in itself prevent an Article 3 violation since 'it may well suffice that the victim is humiliated in his own eyes, even if not in the eyes of others'. In all the circumstances, the institutionalised nature of the violence taken along with the probable long-term psychological harm occasioned justified a finding of 'degrading' treatment[5]. In the first Court finding of torture involving an EU member state, *Selmouni v France*, the applicant had been arrested on suspicion of involvement in drug-trafficking. He had been held in police custody for some three days during which he was beaten with a baseball bat or similar implement, urinated upon and sexually assaulted. Medical examination was consistent with his allegations. The Court considered that this type of particularly serious and cruel physical and mental violence should now be regarded as 'torture'[6]. Similarly, in *Salman v Turkey*, the Court considered the infliction of 'falaka' (as well as a blow to the chest) during interrogation amounted to torture on account of the very serious and cruel suffering involved[7]. More recent cases have also stressed the importance of consideration of state motive or purpose in assessing the level of violation[8], suggesting that in relation to the definition of 'torture', the Court is beginning to develop an alternative or at least a parallel approach which adopts the stricter test of the United Nations Convention against Torture[9]. In *Aksoy v Turkey* which produced the first finding of torture by the Court, the applicant had been stripped naked by police officers and then suspended by his arms which had been tied behind his back. The treatment itself had involved severe pain and subsequent temporary paralysis of both arms; its deliberate infliction had also required 'a certain amount of preparation and exertion' by state officials; its purpose appeared to be to extract information or a confession from the applicant. In these circumstances, the conclusion was that the treatment amounted to torture[10]. In contrast, in *Denizci and Others v Cyprus*, the ill-treatment administered to the applicants in Cypriot police stations was classified as 'inhuman' rather than as 'torture' since it had been impossible to establish the manner in which the beatings were inflicted, and it had not been established that the aim of the officers had been to extract confessions[11].

1 5310/71, *Ireland v United Kingdom* (1976) YB 19, 512, at para 167.
2 3321/67–3323/67 and 3344/67, 1969 YB 12, 186.
3 (1978) A 25, at para 167 (these five techniques had been 'applied in combination, with premeditation and for hours at a stretch'). Judge Fitzmaurice in a separate opinion seems

to have accepted that to classify the techniques as 'torture' would be to trivialise the guarantee. Judge Zekia's opinion suggests that both an objective and a subjective test can be applied: the beating up of an 'elderly sick man' could result in torture while the same violence administered to a 'wrestler or even a young athlete' may not even result in a violation of the European Convention on Human Rights, Art 3 if considered as 'mere rough handling'. Zekia's approach itself brings with it substantial dangers in minimising the practical utility of the guarantee while ostensibly attempting to protect it, and is now out of line with the more robust approach taken to violence inflicted on detainees in *Ribitsch v Austria* (1995) A 336, discussed at para 4.23 below.

4   *Selmouni v France* (28 July 1999), para 101.
5   (1978) A 26, paras 32–34. The case involved the Isle of Man for which the United Kingdom had assumed Convention responsibilities in terms of ECHR, Art 56.
6   1999-V, 149, paras 91–106; see Uildriks 'Police Torture in France' (1999) 17 NQHR 411. See also *Ilhan v Turkey* (26 July 2000), paras 84–88 (applicant was kicked and beaten and struck at least once on the head with a rifle, resulting in severe bruising and head injuries which caused brain damage, and delay of some 36 hours before he was brought to a hospital).
7   (27 June 2000), paras 113–116.
8   Cf *Akkoç v Turkey* (10 October 2000) at para 115 (torture may also involve a purposive element as recognised in the UN Convention against Torture, Art 1).
9   The United Nations Convention against Torture and Other Cruel, Inhuman or Degrading Treatment or Punishment, Art 1(1) imposes a four-part test: (a) the intentional infliction (b) of severe pain or suffering whether physical or mental (c) for any purpose including, for example, to obtain information, inflict punishment or intimidate him or a third person, (d) by a public official or person acting in an official capacity.
10 1996-VI, 2260, at para 64. See, too, *Aydin v Turkey* 1997-VI, 1866, paras 80–86 (17-year-old Kurdish girl stripped, beaten, sprayed with cold water and subsequently raped by soldiers; the Court accepted (at para 85) that the detention had been with a view to interrogation, and thus the suffering inflicted should be seen as having been calculated to serve the same purpose). Cf *Ireland v United Kingdom* (1976) YB 19, 512, at para 168, where the Court acknowledged that the object of the ill-treatment was 'the extraction of confessions, the naming of others and/or information', but seemed thereafter to discount the importance of this motive.
11 (23 May 2001), paras 383–387.

Infliction of ill-treatment during deprivation of liberty

4.21   The use of force against detainees by state officials will give rise to issues under the European Convention on Human Rights, Article 3[1]. Case law has considered the extent of state responsibility for unauthorised behaviour of officials, the nature of the treatment which violates the guarantee, and the extent of state responsibilities for investigating allegations of ill-treatment. A state may not escape liability by asserting that the acts complained of were unauthorised or outwith the authority of an official where they form part of a pattern of conduct amounting to an administrative practice. In the *Greek case*, the Commission had established that members of the security police had inflicted torture or ill-treatment on detainees as a matter of administrative practice. The Commission rejected the government's contention that a state could only be in breach of its obligations if the state itself had inflicted the treatment or had at an executive level shown toleration towards the challenged practices, deciding instead that state responsibility could arise under Article 3 for the action of any public official, even where the official was acting without express authorisation or even contrary to instructions[2].

1 See further McBride 'Imperfect Limits to Unacceptable Treatment' (2000) 25 EL Rev HR 31.
2 3321–3/67 and 3344/67, *Greek case* (1969) YB 12, 194. Cf *Ireland v United Kingdom* [Commission] (1976) YB 19, 512 at 758–762 (the level of official tolerance of unauthorised ill-treatment may also be relevant in considering whether an applicant has exhausted domestic remedies, for if it is established that such tolerance existed at executive level, 'this fact alone would be a strong indication that the complainant has no possibility of obtaining redress through any national organ, including the courts'); and (1978) A 25, para 159.

Use of force

4.22 Recourse to physical force by state officials which has not been rendered strictly necessary by a detainee's own conduct is now considered a violation of the European Convention on Human Rights, Article 3[1]. It may perhaps be easier to justify the need to adopt physical means of restraint at the point of deprivation of liberty (rather than during subsequent detention), and recent European Court of Human Rights decisions suggest that where justification for the use of force is lacking, ill-treatment at this stage may still be considered a less serious violation of the guarantee. In *Egmez v Cyprus*, the state had accepted that the applicant had been intentionally subjected by police officers to violence at the time of his arrest and during its immediate aftermath. The Court determined that the facts disclosed a finding of 'inhuman' treatment rather than torture since the injuries had been inflicted over a short period of heightened tension at the time of arrest, no convincing evidence had been adduced to show that the ill-treatment had resulted in any long-term consequences, and it had not been shown that the officers' aim had been to extract a confession [2]. In *Rehbock v Slovenia*, a doctor had examined the applicant the day following his arrest by police officers and had diagnosed a double fracture of the jaw and facial contusions. In view of the particularly serious nature of the injury, the Court considered that it was for the state authorities to demonstrate convincingly that the use of force had not been excessive. Here, no convincing or credible arguments which would have explained or justified the degree of force used during the arrest had been furnished, and the conclusion was that the force used had been excessive and unjustified and had thus amounted to inhuman treatment[3].

1 *Ribitsch v Austria* (1995) A 336, para 38; *Tekin v Turkey* 1998-IV, 1504, para 53. The treatment must still meet a minimum level of severity: cf *Raninen v Finland* 1997-VIII, 2804, paras 55–59 (unnecessary handcuffing of detainee unlawfully deprived of liberty caused no mental or physical effects and thus there was no violation of the European Convention on Human Rights, Art 3).
2 (21 December 2000), paras 77–79 (there was also some uncertainty concerning the gravity of the injuries caused in part by the 'retouching' of photographs submitted by the applicant). See too 15299–15300/89, *Chrysostomos and Papachrysostomou v Turkey* (1993) DR 86, 4 (use of rough treatment by police officers did not meet the minimum threshold test for ECHR, Art 3 in view of the public disorder at the time the applicants were taken into custody).
3 (28 November 2000), paras 68–78; cf paras 79–81: no violation of ECHR, Art 3 during detention (as opposed to the time of arrest) was established.

4.23 Infliction of violence may indeed be aggravated when it is premeditated or inflicted for a particular purpose such as to extract a confession or information[1] or when it is accompanied by unacceptable detention conditions[2]. There is still, perhaps, some reluctance to accept that non-physical methods of treatment administered during detention may as readily give rise to concerns under the European Convention on Human Rights, Article 3[3], or if these do so, that they occasion as much suffering[4]. The European Court of Human Rights may carry out its own investigation with a view to establishing the facts, and will make its assessment based on all the information available[5]. The isolation in which a detainee is likely to find himself and the likelihood of official denial or excuse may render this assessment a difficult one[6], but the facts may bear no reasonable interpretation other than that force has been applied by police officers or other state officials. Consequently, the Court has developed the principle that where an individual alleges that he has been ill-treated while in custody, the state is under an obligation to provide a complete and sufficient explanation as to how any injuries were caused: any injury to a person in custody gives rise to a strong factual presumption which places the onus on the state to produce evidence establishing facts that cast doubt on the allegations made by a detainee[7]. To this end the Court has also recently endorsed suggestions that a detainee should have the benefit of an independent medical examination upon his release[8]. In *Tomasi v France*, the state was unable to provide any alternative explanation for the injuries sustained by the applicant over a period of 48 hours whilst in police custody on a charge of murder related to terrorist activities. The Court took this into account along with other evidence, such as the applicant's complaints when brought for judicial examination and the evidence contained in independent medical reports, in declaring itself convinced beyond reasonable doubt that the injuries had been inflicted by police officers, and that their number and severity bore testament to ill-treatment[9]. In *Klaas v Germany*, on the other hand, the applicant's claims that injuries sustained while being detained on a drink-driving offence were occasioned by excessive police force were contested by the police as having been self-inflicted by the applicant, and in the circumstances, the Court was unwilling to depart from the findings of the domestic courts that this was a plausible explanation[10]. In *Ribitsch v Austria*, the state had accepted that injuries had been sustained while the applicant was in police custody but a domestic court had determined that it was not possible to establish culpable conduct on the part of any police officer. The Court accepted in principle that its role was not to substitute its own assessment of the facts for those established domestically, but neither was it formally bound by such a domestic determination. Taking into account all the circumstances of the case, the Court considered that the state's explanation was incomplete and unconvincing, and thus that the state had not satisfactorily established that the injuries sustained by the applicant were caused otherwise than by ill-treatment while in custody[11]. This principle also extends to persons detained in a prison 'having regard to the fact that they are deprived of their liberty and remain subject to the control and responsibility of the prison administration'[12].

---

1 *Aksoy v Turkey* 1996-VI, 2260, para 64.
2 *Tekin v Turkey* 1998-IV, 1504, para 53 (prisoner held blindfolded in cold, dark cell and with wounds and bruising).
3 Cf 47240/99 *Ebbinge v Netherlands* and 39195/98, *Jager v Netherlands* (14 March 2000) (two suspects had been subjected to psychologically disorientating police interrogation methods which appeared objectionable in the context of criminal investigations but

which did not support the suggestion that this had resulted in mental pain and suffering sufficient to amount to ill-treatment).

4 *Ireland v United Kingdom* (1978) A 25, discussed at para 4.20 above. Cf *Magee v United Kingdom* (6 June 2000), and see para 5.70 below for discussion of Art 6 concerns as to the fairness of evidence obtained through 'psychologically coercive' detention conditions.

5 *Cruz Varas and Ors v Sweden* (1991) A 201, para 75.

6 Cf *Labita v Italy* (6 April 2000), at para 125: 'the Court recognises that it may prove difficult for prisoners to obtain evidence of ill-treatment by their prison warders'.

7 E g *Berktay v Turkey* (1 March 2001), para 167.

8 *Akkoç v Turkey* (10 October 2000), at para 118: 'the Court further endorses the comments expressed by the Commission concerning the importance of independent and thorough examinations of persons on release from detention. [The CPT] has also emphasised that proper medical examinations are an essential safeguard against ill-treatment of persons in custody. Such examinations must be carried out by a properly qualified doctor, without any police officer being present and the report of the examination must include not only the detail of any injuries found but the explanations given by the patient as to how they occurred and the opinion of the doctor as to whether the injuries are consistent with those explanations'.

9 (1992) A 241-A, para 115.

10 (1993) A-269, paras 30–31.

11 (1995) A 336, paras 27–40.

12 *Satik and Ors v Turkey* (10 October 2000) at para 54; cf para 58 (when prison authorities have recourse to outside assistance in dealing with an internal incident some form of independent monitoring of the action is necessary to ensure that the force used is proportionate).

4.24   Allegations of ill-treatment must be supported by appropriate evidence[1]. This is assessed adopting the standard of proof beyond reasonable doubt and which 'may follow from the coexistence of sufficiently strong, clear and concordant inferences or of similar unrebutted presumptions of fact'[2]. The problem of establishing sufficiency of evidence is illustrated by the judgment of the Grand Chamber of the Court in *Labita v Italy*. The applicant had been detained pending trial for approximately two years and seven months on suspicion of being a member of the Mafia. He had alleged that he had been subjected to ill-treatment that had been systematically inflicted on prisoners, an allegation supported by an independent judicial report but which had not resulted in the prosecution of any official since those responsible had not been identified. The Grand Chamber of the Court decided by a majority of nine votes to eight that there was insufficient evidence to support a conclusion that the applicant had been subjected to physical and mental ill-treatment: the applicant had not produced any conclusive evidence or supplied a detailed account of the abuse to which he had allegedly been subjected, he had never suggested that he had ever been refused permission to see a doctor, and he had inexplicably taken more than a year to complain about his treatment, notwithstanding the fact that he had made several applications through his lawyers to the judicial authorities shortly after the alleged ill-treatment had diminished or ceased[3]. A strong dissenting minority opinion stresses the practical difficulties facing a prisoner who seeks to allege ill-treatment both in producing sufficient evidence to justify his complaints as well as running the potential risk of reprisals. In the present case, the minority considered that it had been understandable that prisoners would not have wished to have asked to be examined by doctors since medical staff had not been seen as independent. More particularly, the standard used by the majority for assessing the sufficiency of evidence was 'inadequate, possibly illogical and even unworkable'. The Court should have applied what the minority deemed a 'serious presumption' that the ill-treatment was indeed inflicted during detention, with the burden of proof of providing a satisfactory and convincing explanation being placed clearly upon the state authorities who alone could have had knowledge of events: in any event, where the domestic authorities have failed to carry out an effective investigation and to make the findings available to the Court, the standard to which the applicant must prove his case should be a lower one. If state authorities could in future 'count on the Court's refraining in cases such as the instant one from examining the allegations of ill-treatment for want of sufficient evidence, they will then have an interest in not investigating such allegations, thus depriving the applicant of proof "beyond reasonable doubt"' and limiting any state responsibility to a violation of the procedural aspect of Article 3[4], a much less serious finding than one which has established the actual infliction of ill-treatment. In any case, application of a standard of proof 'beyond all reasonable doubt' was inappropriate since the Court was not determining guilt or innocence but providing protection for individuals in custody and redress in cases of violation. This dissenting opinion appears persuasive, both in its principled reasoning and in its conclusion on the particular facts[5].

1 *Klaas v Germany* (1993) A 269, para 30.
2 *Ireland v United Kingdom* (1978) A 25, para 161 (conduct of parties when evidence is being obtained may be taken into account in the assessment).
3 (6 April 2000), paras 113–129 (allegations of being slapped, blows, squeezing of the testicles and baton blows and of insults, unnecessary body searches, acts of humiliation such as being required to remain in handcuffs during medical examinations, intimidation and threats). Similarly (paras 130–136), the Court held that there was insufficient evidence to conclude that there had been any violation of ECHR, Art 3 concerning the frequency and conditions of transfers from a prison on account of the applicant's failure to supply detailed information; however, since investigations into his allegations were slow and not sufficiently effective, the Court considered that there had been a violation of the procedural aspect of ECHR, Art 3.
4 Discussed at para 4.27 below.
5 *Labita v Italy* (6 April 2000), joint partly dissenting opinion, paras 1–3 (the minority considered that the matters that led the majority to establish a procedural violation of ECHR, Art 3 were in themselves sufficiently clear and evident to justify finding a violation of the substantive guarantee: the suggestion that only treatment which left scars detectable on medical examination were worthy of consideration was inappropriate since (at para 2) 'there would not necessarily have been any signs left by insults, threats or acts of humiliation, by being kept handcuffed during medical examinations, or being required to run along a slippery corridor leading to the exercise yard while warders hurled insults', treatment which nevertheless could damage an individual's mental integrity; assertions concerning the psychological ill-treatment were corroborated by evidence contained in the judicial report concerning the general situation in the prison; and in any event, the respondent state had acknowledged before the Commission that the applicant had been ill-treated, describing the prison warders' conduct as 'appalling').

'Disappeared persons'

4.25 The European Court of Human Rights has accepted that, in certain circumstances, it may also be possible to conclude that the level of mental anguish endured by a family member of a 'disappeared person' last known to have been in state custody is itself sufficient to amount to a violation of the European Convention on Human Rights, Article 3 'on account of the suffering [having] a dimension and character distinct from the emotional distress which may be regarded as inevitably caused to relatives of a victim of a serious human rights violation'. The particular nature of the breach of the guarantee 'does not so much lie in the fact of the "disappearance" of the family member but rather concerns the authorities' reactions and attitudes to the situation when it is brought to their attention'[1]. Unacknowledged deprivation of liberty is also considered a particularly serious violation of Article 5, and a state has responsibilities to 'take effective measures to safeguard against the risk of disappearance and to conduct a prompt effective investigation into an arguable claim that a person has been taken into custody and has not been seen since'[2].

1 *Çakici v Turkey* (8 July 1999), paras 94–99 at para 98 (no violation established); *Timurtas v Turkey* (13 June 2000), paras 91–98 at para 95 (disappearance of the applicant's son amounted to inhuman and degrading treatment contrary to the European Convention on Human Rights, Art 3 in relation to the applicant in particular because of the lack of promptness and efficiency in carrying out an investigation and the display of a 'callous disregard'; relevant factors in establishing whether a family member of a 'disappeared' person qualifies as a victim of an Art 3 violation included the proximity of family tie ('a certain weight will attach to the parent–child bond'), the particular circumstances of the relationship, whether the family member witnessed any of the events, involvement in seeking information about the disappeared person, and the manner of any response from the authorities); *Tas v Turkey* (14 November 2000), paras 79–80 at para 80 ('indifference and callousness of the authorities to the applicant's concerns (as to the fate of his son) and the acute anguish and uncertainty which he has suffered as a result and continues to suffer' were sufficient to amount to a violation of Art 3); and *Cyprus v Turkey* (10 May 2001), paras 156–158 at para 157 (military operations in northern Cyprus had resulted in significant loss of life, deprivation of liberty and enforced separation of families, matters still 'vivid in the minds of the relatives of persons whose fate has never been accounted for' and who 'endure the agony of not knowing whether family members were killed in the conflict or are still in detention or, if detained, have since died': violation of Art 3).
2 *Kurt v Turkey* 1998-III, 1152, at para 124.

Involuntary treatment of patients

4.26   Involuntary therapeutic treatment in accordance with contemporary medical standards is unlikely to give rise to any issue under the European Convention on Human Rights, Article 3. In *Herczegfalvy v Austria*, the applicant complained of treatment which had included his being handcuffed to a bed, but the European Court on Human Rights declined to treat this as meeting the threshold test of severity[1]. This principle would almost certainly apply to cases involving the forcible feeding of a prisoner or mental health patient, at least in situations where there is evidence to suggest that the individual's mental capacity is diminished[2]. This scenario, however, can be contrasted with one in which there has been a failure to provide acceptable standards of detention or treatment[3].

1 (1992) A 244, at paras 82–83 ('as a general rule, a measure which is a therapeutic necessity [in terms of established principles of medicine] cannot be regarded as inhuman or degrading'). Cf 70417/01, *Avci and Others v Turkey* (detainees chained to their beds in a casualty department in which they had been placed following a hunger strike: communicated). See too 18835/91, *Grare v France* (2 December 1992) (side-effects of medication were unpleasant but not serious enough to violate the European Convention on Human Rights, Art 3). Cf *Keenan v United Kingdom* (3 April 2001), paras 108–115 (inadequate monitoring and lack of informed psychiatric treatment of sufficient seriousness to amount to a breach of ECHR, Art 3). See also *NHS Trust A v M* [2001] Fam 348; and *Nielsen v Denmark* (1988) A 144, discussed in relation to Art 5 at para 4.47 below. For domestic application, see *NHS Trust A v M* [2001] Fam 348. See further Douraki 'La Protection Internationale des Malades

Mentaux contre les Traitements Abusifs' in Flécheux (ed) *Mélanges en Hommage à Louis Edmond Pettiti* (1998) pp 309-322.

2 However, such a situation may conceivably also give rise to positive duties under ECHR, Art 2 to protect health where there is a serious risk of death if this is ignored: cf 10565/83, *X v Germany* (9 May 1984) (force-feeding of prisoner). But see Harris O'Boyle and Warbrick *Law of the European Convention on Human Rights* (1995) at p 40 ('it is submitted that a state should not be liable under Article 2 for an omission that respects the physical will and integrity of an individual who is capable of taking a decision [to go on hunger strike] as to matters of life and death'). See also *NHS Trust A v M* [2001] 2 WLR 942.

3 Cf *Aerts v Belgium* 1998-V, 1939: see para 4.39 below; 6840/74, *A v United Kingdom* (1980) DR 10, 5 (complaint concerning lack of appropriate regime etc in Broadmoor Hospital declared admissible).

Positive obligations: investigating allegations of ill-treatment – the procedural aspect of Article 3

4.27   Under the European Convention on Human Rights, Article 3, there may exist a positive obligation on the state to carry out an effective investigation of an arguable claim that an individual has been seriously ill-treated by the police or by other state forces. The result is that in situations where it has not been possible to establish any actual infliction of ill-treatment, there may still be found a violation of Article 3 if any subsequent state investigation of an arguable claim that ill-treatment has taken place is deemed inadequate: that is, that the investigation has been insufficiently thorough to lead to the identification and punishment of those responsible[1]. Further, the choice of person or body charged with the investigation must be able to guarantee an independent determination of the material facts[2]. As with the requirement under Article 2 to carry out an investigation in cases of use of lethal force, the justification for this principle is also to seek to render the Convention guarantee effective in practice[3]. In *Assenov and Ors v Bulgaria*, a 14-year-old boy had been taken to a police station after being arrested for unlawful gambling. It was not in dispute that he had been hit in the police station by his father with a strip of wood (apparently to show to the police officers that he was prepared to punish the applicant), but it was also alleged that thereafter the applicant had been beaten by police officers using truncheons. The Court accepted that in light of the time which had elapsed and the lack of any proper investigation, it could not be established that the police officers had caused the applicant's injuries. However, the perfunctory nature of inquiries into these serious allegations had not resulted in a sufficiently thorough and effective investigation, and accordingly there had been a violation of this procedural aspect of Article 3[4].

1 *Assenov and Ors v Bulgaria* 1998-VIII, 3264, para 102. See also *Veznedaroglu v Turkey* (11 April 2000), paras 23–35 (impossible to establish whether injuries had been caused by police torture, but inertia of authorities in carrying out an investigation gave rise to a violation of the European Convention on Human Rights, Art 3).

2 *Satik and Ors v Turkey* (10 October 2000), paras 60–62.

3 *Assenov and Ors v Bulgaria* 1998-VIII, 3264, para 102.

4 1998-VIII, 3264, paras 101–106. The issue of exhaustion of domestic remedies was considered at paras 82–86 (although a private prosecution against the police officers was not possible, the applicant had attempted without success to persuade the authorities to carry out a full criminal investigation; and since civil compensation cannot in itself be deemed

fully to rectify a violation of ECHR, Art 3, the applicant was deemed to have exhausted domestic remedies without requiring to raise any civil action). There appears to have been no discussion in this case of positive duties upon the police officers to protect the individual from violence inflicted by his father (cf *A v United Kingdom* 1998-VI, 2692, discussed at para 4.29 below).

4.28 As with this development under the European Convention on Human Rights, Article 2[1], this requirement is closely related to the issues of the availability of an effective domestic remedy for the purposes of Article 13 and of whether any such domestic remedies have been exhausted in terms of Article 35[2]. However, there is now an important but not altogether convincing distinction to be drawn following the Grand Chamber's decision in *Ilhan v Turkey*. The applicant had alleged breaches of Article 3 on account both of his treatment and of the lack of an effective investigation. After finding that the applicant had been subjected to torture at the hands of the security forces, the European Court of Human Rights declined to consider the question of the lack of an investigation under Article 3 but instead considered this as more appropriate for disposal under Article 13 since a finding of actual ill-treatment under Article 3 had been established. The Court first distinguished *Assenov v Bulgaria* on account of the inability in this earlier case to conclude that the applicant's injuries had been caused by the police as alleged. The Court contrasted Article 3 which is phrased in substantive terms with Article 2 which contains the requirement that the right to life be 'protected by law' and which may concern 'situations where the initiative must rest on the State for the practical reason that the victim is deceased and the circumstances of the death may be largely confined within the knowledge of state officials'. It then concluded that Article 13 of the Convention should generally be expected to provide redress to an applicant through the provision of necessary procedural safeguards to protect an individual against ill-treatment. Thus a procedural breach of Article 3 through the failure to carry out an effective investigation would only be appropriate in circumstances where an investigation had not permitted the determination of the material facts to allow disposal of the complaint under the substantive guarantee of Article 3[3]. This decision is perhaps not entirely satisfactory. Subsequent cases seem difficult to reconcile with its approach[4], and there is the apparent anomaly that inadequate investigations in cases such as *Assenov and Ors* may result in findings of violations both of Article 3 and also of Article 13 on the same grounds[5].

1 See para 4.08 above.
2 Cf *Aksoy v Turkey* 1996-VI, 2260, paras 51–57 and 98 at para 98 (the notion of an effective remedy under the European Convention on Human Rights, Art 13 'includes the duty to carry out a thorough and effective investigation capable of leading to the identification and punishment of those responsible for any ill-treatment and permitting effective access for the complainant to the investigatory procedure'; here the Court considered that it was unreasonable to expect the applicant to have used civil, criminal and administrative remedies in light of the physical paralysis of his arms and the psychological feelings of powerlessness consequent upon the infliction of torture by police officers).
3 (26 July 2000), paras 89–93 at paras 91 and 92, followed in *Büyükdağ v Turkey* (21 December 2000), paras 45–69.
4 Cf *Satik and Ors v Turkey* (10 October 2000), paras 60–62 (the Court concluded that, in view of the absence of a plausible explanation on the part of the authorities for the injuries sustained, the applicants had been beaten and injured by state officials resulting in a

violation of ECHR, Art 3; moreover, in view of the investigation's serious shortcomings, there was also a violation of Art 3).

5 1998-VIII, 3264, paras 117–118 (notion of an effective remedy not only entails a thorough and effective investigation under ECHR, Art 3 but also effective access to the investigatory procedure and to compensation under Art 13).

Positive obligations: protection by domestic law against infliction of ill-treatment

4.29   ECHR, Article 3 imposes positive obligations upon a state to ensure the effective protection of physical integrity through the enforcement of domestic law in response to ill-treatment inflicted by private individuals, a duty which also exists in respect of less serious interferences with physical and moral integrity under Article 8[1]. This principle applies in respect of children against the infliction of violence by parents or others in a family setting or exercising powers *in loco parentis*. In *A v United Kingdom*, the applicant, a nine-year-old boy, had been beaten repeatedly by his stepfather with a cane. This had resulted in significant bruising. An English court had accepted the defence of reasonable chastisement, and the stepfather had been acquitted. The Court accepted that the beatings were of sufficient severity as to give rise to an Article 3 issue, and that the state had failed to take adequate measures in the form of effective deterrence to protect the applicant from inhuman or degrading punishment, since the defence of 'reasonable chastisement' did not provide sufficient safeguards against abuse[2]. This case thus concerns the positive responsibilities upon states to ensure that domestic legal systems adequately protect Article 3 interests. The Commission in its report had sought to stress that the finding of a violation should not be seen as imposing any duty upon states to provide protection against any form of physical rebuke including the most mild; the Court's decision can be taken, however, as a signal to states that family and criminal law must protect with greater vigilance the rights of children. In Scots law, the extent of parental rights to inflict corporal punishment on children remains unclear. Statute provides a defence of 'moderate and reasonable chastisement'[3], but this probably requires to be interpreted in light of contemporary views on the suitability and extent of such authority[4]. The positive duty to protect individuals through enforcement of the criminal law also applies to interferences with physical and moral integrity arising under Article 8[5].

A public authority's failure to take reasonable steps to protect a vulnerable individual may similarly give rise to an Article 3 violation. In *Z and Ors v United Kingdom*, the applicants were four siblings in a family which had been monitored by the social services because of concerns about their well-being. Support had been given to the family over a period of four-and-a-half years, but no steps had been taken to place the children in care, despite police and social services reports which had highlighted significant neglect and emotional abuse. Only when their mother had threatened to hit them had the children finally been placed in emergency foster care. Before the Court, the United Kingdom Government indeed accepted that the neglect and abuse suffered by the four children had reached the threshold of inhuman and degrading treatment, and further that it had failed in its positive obligation to provide the applicants with adequate protection.

The Court reiterated that Article 3 imposed a positive duty upon states to provide protection against inhuman or degrading treatment inflicted by others. In the case of vulnerable children, this would extend to the taking of reasonable steps to prevent ill-treatment of which the authorities had or ought to have had knowledge. While the Court acknowledged that social services often faced difficult and sensitive decisions in attempting to respect and thus preserve family life, the circumstances of the case were such as to leave no doubt as to the failure of the authorities to protect the applicants from serious and long-term neglect and abuse[6].

1 See para 6.35 below.
2 1998-VI, 2692, paras 20–24 (the state conceded that there had been a breach of the European Convention on Human Rights, Art 3, but requested the Court to confine itself to the facts of the case without making any general statement about corporal punishment of children: the Court (paras 25–28) decided it was not necessary in this case to consider the separate complaint under Art 8). See McCafferty 'The Duty to Act – Article 3 of the Human Rights Convention *v* the Non-Intervention Principle' [1999] Fam Law 717.
3 Children and Young Persons (Scotland) Act 1937, s 12(1). Cf *Gray v Hawthorn* 1964 JC 69. No child may be placed with a foster parent without written agreement from the foster parent that corporal punishment will not be administered: Fostering of Children (Scotland) Regulations 1996, SI 1996/3263, reg 8.
4 Scottish Law Commission *Report on Family Law* (Scot Law Com no 135) (1992) at para 2.102 (report recommended that the defence should not be available where a stick, belt or similar object was used, or where there was actual or a real risk of causing serious injury, or pain or discomfort lasting more than a short time; Parliament declined to take any action). The Scottish Executive Justice Department published a consultation paper in 1999, *The Physical Punishment of Children in Scotland*, which proposed that Scots law should make clear that physical punishment reaching the minimum level of severity for ECHR, Art 3 could never be justified as 'reasonable chastisement'. This would thus require explicit consideration of the nature and context of the treatment, its duration and frequency, its physical and mental effects and (in some instances) the sex, age, and state of health of the victim.
5 See para 6.35 below.
6 (10 May 2001), paras 73–75.

DECISIONS OF DOMESTIC COURTS ON PROTECTION AGAINST ILL-TREATMENT

4.30 Following *A v United Kingdom*, the English Court of Appeal has held that a jury should now be directed in detailed terms as to factors relevant to whether the chastisement in question was reasonable and moderate and that they should consider:

(i)   the nature and context of the defendant's behaviour;
(ii) its duration;
(iii) the physical and mental consequences in respect of the child;
(iv) the age and personal characteristics of the child; and
(v)   the reasons given by the defendant for administering the punishment[1].

It has also been accepted in domestic law that Article 3 imposes a positive duty upon the state to protect individuals from ill-treatment at the hands of other private individuals[2].

1 *R v H (Assault of Child: Reasonable Chastisement)* [2001] 2 FLR 431. The case concerned the beating of a young child with a leather belt. An acquittal on such facts might well raise an issue under the European Convention on Human Rights, Art 3, even if the jury had received such directions.
2 *Venables v News Group Newspapers Ltd* [2001] 2 WLR 1038; cf *A v United Kingdom* 1998-VI, 2692. Other domestic cases are noted at paras 4.08–4.09 above, 4.35 and 4.37 below.

Juvenile justice and punishment of minors

4.31　The European Convention on Human Rights, Article 3 cannot readily be used to challenge substantive or procedural provisions concerning juvenile justice. In the related cases of *T v United Kingdom* and *V v United Kingdom*, two ten-year-old children who had abducted and murdered an infant claimed that their prosecution in an adult court with all its attendant formality had caused psychiatric harm and a high degree of public humiliation, and further that the attribution of criminal responsibility at such a young age in English law was itself contrary to this provision. The majority of the European Court of Human Rights decided, however, that there had been no Article 3 violation. The intention of the state in holding the trial in an adult court had not been to humiliate or cause any suffering. An inquiry into the death of the victim involving the attendance and participation of the applicants would have had a harmful effect on any child of their age, and their suffering had not gone significantly beyond that which would have been engendered in any process. Further, although English law had one of the lowest ages of criminal responsibility in Europe, there was no common European standard and, accordingly, it could not be said that domestic law differed so disproportionately as to give rise to a violation[1].

1　(16 December 1999), paras 60–78 and 92–100; and (16 December 1999), paras 62–80 and 93–101. These cases represented the Court's first ever consideration of the ECHR's application to child defendants. They also raised important issues under Arts 5 and 6 regarding elements of the UK's trial and sentencing procedures: see further, paras 4.88 and 5.65 below. The age of criminal responsibility in Scotland is eight years: Criminal Procedure (Scotland) Act 1995, s 41. The Scottish Executive's Advisory Group on Youth Crime recommended that consideration be given to raising this to 12 years. A discussion paper has been issued by the Scottish Law Commission: Discussion Paper No 115.

4.32　Issues under the European Convention on Human Rights, Article 3 issues may, however, arise in exceptional cases in relation to the sentence imposed and its implementation, since a sentence disproportionate to the gravity of the offence or which fails to take into account the relative age of a young person sentenced to a lengthy period of imprisonment may breach the guarantee. In *Weeks v United Kingdom*, a 17-year-old youth who had used a starting pistol to rob a shopkeeper of 35p had been sentenced to life imprisonment. The justification for this sentence had been reconsidered at length by the English Court of Appeal and accepted as appropriate to protect the public and, indeed, additionally to help ensure the applicant's early release from prison, and the European Court of Human Rights thus accepted that the sentence did not give rise to an Article 3 issue[1]. The Court has also acknowledged that failure to respect the process of maturation in the case of a juvenile sentenced to a period of imprisonment which could last for the remainder of the individual's natural life can give rise to Article 3 considerations[2]. On the other hand, Article 3 does not prohibit a state from subjecting a young person convicted of a serious offence to an indeterminate sentence allowing for his continued detention where it is deemed necessary for the protection of the public. In *T v United Kingdom* and *V v United Kingdom*, the applicants further claimed that that the length of the tariff to be served by way of retribution and deterrence (set originally at 15 years before being quashed on review) amounted to

inhuman and degrading treatment. However, the Court found the punitive element in their sentences to be acceptable, bearing in mind the
responsibility of the state to protect the public from violent crime[3].

1 (1987) A 114, para 47. See too 44190/98, *Nivette v France* (14 December 2000) (allegation that
   an adult, if extradited to the USA, faced the danger of having to serve a full life sentence:
   communicated).
2 *Hussain v United Kingdom* 1996–I, 252, para 61; *Singh v United Kingdom* 1996–I, 280, para 53.
   See further para 4.88 below. The mandatory life sentence in respect of adult murderers
   does not contravene the European Convention on Human Rights, Art 3: *R v Lichniak* [2001]
   3 WLR 933.
3 (16 December 1999), paras 92–100; (16 December 1999), paras 93–101.

Corporal punishment

4.33 The essence of corporal punishment is 'institutionalised violence',
that is, a deliberate assault carried out by state authority where an individual is 'treated as an object in the power of the authorities'[1]. Use of
corporal punishment of minors is out of line with a strong European
consensus that such punishment is now unacceptable. This factor carried
particular weight in *Tyrer v United Kingdom* where the European Court of
Human Rights ruled that the birching of a 15-year-old boy on his bare
buttocks upon the order of an Isle of Man juvenile court was 'degrading'[2].
On the other hand, cases involving the administration of corporal punishment by schoolteachers always ran the risk of appearing to trivialise the
nature of the European Convention on Human Rights, Article 3[3]. In the
first case to challenge this practice, *Campbell and Cosans v United Kingdom*,
the Court was able to avoid any Article 3 issue since on the particular facts
neither child of the two applicants had been physically punished,
although the Court did accept that a 'sufficiently real and immediate'
threat of infliction of treatment violating the guarantee could be sufficient
to breach Article 3[4]. Other applications complaining about the actual
infliction of corporal punishment in schools eventually turned upon the
level of violence used. The Commission in *Warwick v United Kingdom*
accepted that the heavy bruising caused to a 16-year-old girl who had
been caned three times on the hand in the presence of the male deputy
headmaster violated Article 3[5]. In other similar cases the Commission
declared the complaints admissible, or expressed the opinion that a violation had occurred before the cases were resolved by friendly settlement
pending reform of domestic law[6].

1 *Tyrer v United Kingdom* (1978) A 26, para 33.
2 See Zellick 'Corporal Punishment in the Isle of Man' (1978) 27 ICLQ 665.
3 Cf *Costello-Roberts v United Kingdom* (1993) A 247–C, para 32 (a seven-year-old boy 'slip-
   pered' by a headmaster was unable to show any severe or long-lasting effects, and thus no
   issue under the European Convention on Human Rights, Art 3); see para 4.18 above.
4 (1982) A 48, paras 26 and 30. The case did result in a violation of ECHR, Protocol 1, Art 2:
   see para 6.55 below.
5 9471/81, (1986) DR 60, 5 (the Committee of Ministers subsequently failed to agree that
   there had been a violation).
6 Cf *Y v United Kingdom* (1992) A 247–A (friendly settlement reached by applicant and
   government after expression of opinion of violation by Commission). Corporal
   punishment was abolished in state schools and for publicly funded pupils in independent schools by the Education (Scotland) Act 1980, s 48A(1). See further Ghandi 'Spare
   the Rod: Corporal Punishment in Schools and the ECHR' (1984) 33 ICLQ 488; Phillips
   'The Case for Corporal Punishment in the UK: Beaten into Submission in Europe?'
   (1994) 43 ICLQ 153.

Conditions of detention

4.34 It has largely proved difficult to bring general detention conditions within the scope of the European Convention on Human Rights, Article 3, possibly on account of acceptance (at least in the case of persons convicted of an offence) that there is always 'an inevitable element of suffering or humiliation' in the very nature of legitimate punishment[1]. Thus failure to ameliorate living conditions which were 'undoubtedly unpleasant or even irksome'[2] was unlikely to meet the minimum level of severity required for a violation of Article 3. The lack of critical approach to the material environment in places of detention extended beyond prisons. Even highly unsatisfactory conditions in mental hospitals have escaped Article 3 censure[3]. Similarly, it has been difficult to use this provision to challenge specific holding conditions. State interests (for example, security considerations or the interests of justice) have been considered to justify solitary confinement involving sensory deprivation[4]; and while prolonged solitary confinement may be considered undesirable, this is evaluated in terms of 'the particular conditions of its application, including its stringency, duration and purpose, as well as its effects on the person concerned'[5]. Only extreme or excessive state action[6], or a failure to take humanitarian measures[7] or to provide medical treatment in accordance with reasonable professional requirements[8], or a finding of extreme physical or psychological effects of imprisonment in an individual case caused by special holding conditions[9] have resulted in findings of breach of the provision.

Further, while dicta suggested there was a positive duty upon states to 'maintain a continuous review of the detention arrangements employed with a view to ensuring the health and well-being of all prisoners with due regard to the ordinary and reasonable requirements of imprisonment'[10], the practical impact of this has perhaps been limited. In *Assenov and Ors v Bulgaria*, for example, a 17-year-old youth had been detained for almost 11 months in a police station in conditions which even the public prosecutor accepted as likely to be harmful to physical and mental development if prolonged, but given the absence of any objective evidence of actual harm, the European Court of Human Rights was unable to accept that the conditions of detention were sufficiently severe as to violate Article 3[11]. In *Kudla v Poland*, the applicant complained that he had not been given adequate psychiatric treatment during his four years spent as a remand prisoner and despite a psychiatric report that continuing detention carried a likelihood that he would attempt suicide. While it was accepted that his mental condition had rendered him more vulnerable than other detainees and that detention might have exacerbated his feelings of distress, anguish and fear, the Court did not find it established that the applicant had been subjected to ill-treatment that had attained a sufficient level of severity to come within the scope of the article since he had received frequent psychiatric assistance[12]. The maintenance of good order in prisons, too, was enough to justify physical intrusions such as the provision of urine samples in order to control drug abuse[13].

1 *Tyrer v United Kingdom* (1978) A 26, at para 29.
2 *Guzzardi v Italy* (1980) A 39, para 107 (detention on island involving nightly curfew, poor living conditions, restricted medical facilities and opportunities for religious

observances, etc may have been 'irksome' but did not amount to a violation of the European Convention on Human Rights, Art 3).

3 Eg 6870/75, *Y v United Kingdom* (1977) DR 10, 37; *Aerts v Belgium* 1998-V, 1939, discussed at para 4.39 below; cf 6840/74, *X v United Kingdom* (1977) DR 10, 5.

4 8463/78, *Kröcher & Möller v Switzerland* (1981) DR 26, 24; 7854/77, *Bonzi v Switzerland* (1978) DR 12, 185.

5 10263/83, *R v Denmark* (1985) DR 41, 149 at 153. Cf 17525/90, *Delazarus v United Kingdom* (16 February 1993) (complaint about segregation of a prisoner from other prisoners for 14 weeks and holding conditions: declared inadmissible).

6 Eg *Ireland v United Kingdom* (1978) A 25, paras 167–181 (use of sensory deprivation interrogation techniques against terrorist suspects); *Tekin v Turkey* 1998-IV, 1504, paras 48–54 (the applicant had been held for two days blindfolded in a cold and dark cell and ill-treated so as to leave him with wounds and bruising, circumstances which clearly gave rise to an Art 3 violation).

7 Eg 8317/78, *McFeely v UK* (1980) DR 20, 44 (prison authorities to exercise custodial authority in such a way as to safeguard health etc of all prisoners, even those taking part in unlawful protest involving refusal to wash); cf 9044/80, *Chartier v Italy* (1982) DR 33, 41 (continuing detention of long-term prisoner suffering from hereditary obesity and other disorders not a violation of ECHR, Art 3 in light of the medical treatment provided, but the Commission noted that 'particularly serious' cases may require greater sensitivity to humanitarian considerations); 22564/93, *Grice v United Kingdom* (1994) DR 77, 90 (no indication that detention of a prisoner suffering from AIDS had any impact upon his health); 25096/94, *Remer v Germany* (1995) DR 82, 117 (80-year-old sentenced to imprisonment for 22 months, but no allegation of ill-health on account of detention); 63716/00, *Sawoniuk v United Kingdom* (29 May 2001) (imprisonment of 80-year-old convicted under the War Crimes Act for murder: no prohibition in the Convention against the detention in prison of persons who attain an advanced age, and inadmissible); and 64666/01, *Papon v France* (8 June 2001) (imprisonment of 90-year-old applicant with heart problems: declared inadmissible, the Court noting that no European state had an upper age limit for detention, and while in certain circumstances detention of an elderly person may give rise to an Art 3 issue, here the applicant's general state of health and conditions of detention did not constitute treatment of the requisite level of severity to bring it within the scope of Art 3). Nor can ECHR, Art 5(4) be used to require the release of a detainee because of his state of health: *Kudla v Poland* (26 October 2000), para 93; *Jabłoński v Poland* (21 December 2000), para 82. See further Reynaud *Human Rights in Prisons* (1986) pp 37–113. For CPT expectations in the case of prisoners unsuited for continued detention on the grounds of serious ill-health, see CPT/Inf (93) 12, para 70.

8 *Hurtado v Switzerland* (1994) A 280-A (failure to provide medical treatment until eight days after the applicant's arrest which had involved the use of force and had resulted in a fracture of a rib: the Commission accepted that this failure to safeguard the physical well-being of detainees amounted to degrading treatment, but a friendly settlement was later achieved). Cf 6870/75, *B v United Kingdom* (1981) DR 32, 5 (failure to provide any treatment while a patient in a secure mental hospital justified on account of clinical advice; the Commission concluded albeit with some reservations that the facts did not disclose a violation of ECHR, Art 3); 18824/91, *Lockwood v United Kingdom* (14 October 1992) (four-month delay in seeking second medical opinion, but this had no impact upon the prisoner's health).

9 Eg *Soering v United Kingdom* (1989) A161, discussed at para 4.37 below. Cf 36790/97 *Zhu v United Kingdom* (12 September 2000) (detainee held for 18 months pending deportation in prison where he alleged he was unable to communicate and suffered racial assaults; complaint declared inadmissible as the authorities had made some effort to alleviate the applicant's situation, and the behaviour of other inmates had not been sufficiently serious to give rise to an ECHR, Art 3 issue).

10 10448/83, *Dhoest v Belgium* (1987) DR 55, 5 at 21; *Hurtado v Switzerland* (1994) A 280-A (the applicant had defecated in his trousers at the time of arrest and had been forced to wear soiled clothing for a day: the failure to provide clean clothes was in the opinion of the Commission 'humiliating and debasing for the applicant and therefore degrading': friendly settlement achieved).

11 1998-VIII, 3264, paras 128–135.

12 (26 October 2000), paras 90–100; cf at para 93 (ECHR, Art 3 cannot 'be interpreted as laying down a general obligation to release a detainee on health grounds or to place him in a civil hospital to enable him to obtain a particular kind of medical treatment').

13 20872/92, *AB v Switzerland* (1995) DR 80, 66; 21132/93, *Peters v Netherlands* (1994) DR 77, 75; 34199/96, *Galloway v United Kingdom* (9 September 1998).

4.35   The work of the Council of Europe's Committee for the Prevention of Torture (the CPT) increasingly had the potential to prompt revisal of this jurisprudence as it continued to take a more demanding view of detention conditions[1], and to be more critical of interrogation practices[2]. There is now, indeed, some early indication from the new, full-time European Court of Human Rights that it is prepared to reconsider the former Commission's approach of rejecting complaints of poor detention conditions[3]. In the *Kudla v Poland* judgment, for example, the Court noted there was a general expectation that state authorities will ensure that a detainee is held in conditions which are

> 'compatible with respect for his human dignity, that the manner and method of the execution of the measure do not subject him to distress or hardship of an intensity exceeding the unavoidable level of suffering inherent in deten-tion and that, given the practical demands of imprisonment, his health and well-being are adequately secured by, among other things, providing him with the requisite medical assistance'[4].

In *Price v United Kingdom*, the applicant, a four-limb-deficient thalidomide victim suffering from kidney problems, had been committed to prison for seven days for failure to answer questions during civil proceedings for debt recovery. No steps had been taken by the judge before imposing the penalty to ascertain whether adequate detention facilities were available to cope with the applicant's severe level of disability. The first night she had been held in a police cell which had been too cold for her medical condition, and since she could not use the bed in the cell, she had been forced to sleep in her wheelchair. For the remainder of her sentence, she had been held in a prison hospital where the lack of female medical staff had meant it had been necessary for male prison officers to assist her with toileting. For the Court, the detention of 'a severely disabled person in conditions where she is dangerously cold, risks developing sores because her bed is too hard or unreachable, and is unable to go to the toilet or keep clean without the greatest of difficulty' constituted degrading treatment within the meaning of Article 3[5].

Of considerable significance now are recent determinations that general detention conditions have indeed been sufficiently poor as to amount to violations of the European Convention on Human Rights, Article 3. In *Dougoz v Greece*, the applicant had been held in a detention centre and then a police station pending his expulsion, on each occasion for several months. Echoing the approach of the European Committee for the Prevention of Torture[6], the Court considered that the cumulative effects of the holding conditions had to be assessed. It also relied upon the CPT's own opinion that the cellular accommodation and detention regime at the police station were unsuitable for detention exceeding a few days. In these circumstances, the Court accepted that the serious overcrowding and appalling sanitary conditions amounted to degrading treatment in viola-tion of the applicant's rights under Article 3[7]. In *Peers v Greece*, a British prisoner had been held in a segregation wing where, for at least two months, he had been largely confined to a cell lacking ventilation and windows and which in consequence would at times become unbearably hot. The applicant also had been forced to use the cell's toilet in the presence of another inmate (and similarly be present when his cellmate was using the toilet). These two factors were sufficient for the Court to consider that the applicant's human dignity had been diminished. The conditions had given rise to feelings of anguish and inferiority capable of humiliating and debasing the applicant and possibly breaking his physical or moral resistance, and the failure of the authorities to take steps to improve the applicant's conditions of detention were considered to have amounted to degrading treatment[8]. This latter case may be of some interest in Scotland where 'slopping out' continues as a daily routine for many prisoners. The European Committee for the Prevention of Torture has on several occasions criticised overcrowding, lack of integral sanitation and inadequate regime activities in British prisons[9]. The compatibility with Article 3 of conditions in a Scottish prison has been challenged in proceedings before the Court of Session[10].

1 See paras 4.38 and 4.39 below.
2 See, eg *Magee v United Kingdom* (6 June 2000), paras 38–46, discussed below at para 5.70.
3 Several such applications have been declared admissible since 1999: eg 44558/98 *Valašinas v Lithuania* (14 March 2000). Cf 25498/94, *Merrina v Italy* (8 June 1999) (strict conditions of detention imposed because of the applicant's links with the mafia considered inadmissible under the European Convention on Human Rights, Art 3, but admissible under Art 8).
4 *Kudla v Poland* (26 October 2000), at para 94.
5 (10 July 2001), paras 25–30 at para 30. Cf separate opinion of the British judge, Judge Bratza, joined by Judge Costa: 'the primary responsibility for what occurred lies not with the police or with the prison authorities … but with the judicial authorities who committed the applicant to an immediate term of imprisonment for contempt of court'. See too *Keenan v United Kingdom* (3 April 2001), paras 108–115 (inadequate monitoring and lack of informed psychiatric treatment of sufficient seriousness to amount to a breach of Article 3); 50390/99, *McGlinchey and Ors v United Kingdom* (conditions of detention of detainee suffering from withdrawal symptoms and allegation of refusal of treatment as a disciplinary sanction: communicated).
6 CPT/Inf (94) 20, paras 54–59.
7 (6 March 2001), paras 45–49.
8 (19 April 2001), paras 67–75.
9 See para 4.38 below.
10 *Napier v The Scottish Ministers* (26 June 2001, unreported), Ct of S.

Discriminatory treatment

4.36   The European Convention on Human Rights, Article 14 provides general protection against discrimination in the enjoyment of Convention guarantees[1], but discriminatory treatment may itself amount to treatment sufficiently degrading so as to constitute a violation of Article 3. In the *East African Asians* case, British passport holders who had been forced to leave Uganda and Kenya had been denied entry to the United Kingdom. The Commission determined that denial of entry had been on account of their race or colour, and held that this amounted to institutionalised racism which in turn amounted to degrading treatment[2]. A similar conclusion was reached in *Cyprus v Turkey*, where the Court found that Greek Cypriots living in Turkish-controlled northern Cyprus had been subjected, because of race and religion, to state action which violated 'the very notion of respect for the human dignity of its members'. This enclaved population over a lengthy period had been and continued to be 'isolated, restricted in their movements, controlled and with no prospect of renewing or developing their community', treatment which was sufficiently debasing to qualify as degrading treatment within the meaning of Article 3[3]. In contrast, in the earlier case of *Abdulaziz, Cabales and Balkandali v United Kingdom*, the Court determined that treatment the applicants alleged had been discriminatory on the ground of sex 'did not denote any contempt or lack of respect for the personality of the applicants and that it was not designed to, and did not, humiliate or debase', but had been taken solely to achieve goals of immigration policy. The treatment thus could not be seen as 'degrading'[4]. However, in the recent case of *Smith and Grady v United Kingdom*, the European Court of Human Rights seemed to suggest that discriminatory treatment, even in the absence of any state intention to humiliate, may still result in a violation of Article 3. Here, service personnel had been subjected to intimate questioning concerning their homosexuality before being dismissed from the armed forces. The Court considered this intrusive treatment to be of a 'particularly grave' nature but not such as to reach the minimum level of severity required to bring it within the scope of Article 3 on the particular facts. At the same time, it specifically refused to 'exclude that treatment which is grounded upon a predisposed bias on the part of a heterosexual majority against a homosexual minority ... could, in principle, fall within the scope of Article 3'[5]. The conclusion is that to be considered a violation of Article 3, discriminatory treatment must attain a level which is considered grossly humiliating[6].

1   See paras 3.40–3.65 above.
2   4403/70 et al (1973) DR 78, 5. The Commission's Report was only made public in 1994.
3   (10 May 2001), paras 305–311 at para 309: there was 'an inescapable conclusion that the interferences at issue were directed at the ... Greek-Cypriot community for the very reason that they belonged to this class of persons'.
4   (1985) A 94, at para 91.
5   (27 September 1999), paras 118–123 at para 121.
6   Cf 51564/99, *Conka and Ors v Belgium* (13 March 2001) (allegation by Roma due to be expelled that numbers were marked on their arms using indelible ink; explanation accepted that this was for the purpose of identification and not of humiliation: inadmissible on this issue).

Deportation or extradition to another country where there is a risk of infliction of torture or inhuman or degrading treatment

4.37   A state may not deport or extradite an individual to another country if there is a significant risk that he will face the infliction of torture or inhuman or degrading treatment if removed. This applies in equal measure where claims for refugee status have been refused[1], where extradition is sought to bring an individual to trial on criminal charges, or where deportation after a sentence of imprisonment has been ordered. It provides protection where 'substantial grounds have been shown for believing that the person concerned, if extradited, faces a real risk of being subjected to torture or to inhuman or degrading treatment or punishment in the requesting country'[2] or loss of life at the hands of state officials or even private individuals[3]. In assessing the element of risk, the European Court of

Human Rights will consider all available material placed before it or obtained *ex proprio motu*[4]. In certain cases, the use of interim measures under Rule of Court 39 may be appropriate to protect the situation of the applicant pending determination of the case by the Court[5]. Several recent applications have challenged threatened expulsion to countries with a clear record of human rights violations[6], but even the law and practice of established democracies may still give rise to an Article 3 issue, and the principle is also of application where an individual is removed to an intermediary country which is bound by the European Convention on Human Rights[7].

The leading case is *Soering v United Kingdom*[8], which concerned the possible extradition of the applicant to the United States to face a charge carrying the death penalty. The Court accepted the applicant's submissions that, if extradited, there was a real risk that he would be subjected to inhuman or degrading treatment in the light of his age and mental state and the lengthy time that inmates spent on death row with the consequent 'ever present and mounting anguish of awaiting execution'. Further, the Court specifically considered that the manner of imposition of the death penalty, the personal circumstances of the individual (such as his age or state of mind, as in *Soering*), or the disproportionate nature of the penalty in relation to the offence may all support challenges to extradition to face a capital charge under Article 3[9]. However, the applicant must always be able to substantiate the risk of ill-treatment. In *Cruz Varas v Sweden*, a family of Chilean citizens had unsuccessfully sought political asylum. Thereafter, Sweden had deported the husband back to Chile and then had commenced steps to deport the wife and son. The Court emphasised that 'the existence of the risk must be assessed primarily with reference to those facts which were known or ought to have been known . . . at the time of the expulsion' although the Court could also have regard to information which becomes available after any expulsion in helping to establish or disprove whether the fears of an applicant were well founded. Here, the lack of credibility of the husband was a decisive factor in ruling that there was no violation of Article 3. There was no direct evidence that agents of the Pinochet regime had inflicted ill-treatment on him, nor was there any indication that he had been involved in clandestine political activity[10]. The risk of ill-treatment can also involve the threat of withdrawal of appropriate care and support where 'compelling humanitarian considerations' exist, even although Article 3 cannot be used to establish any entitlement to a minimum level of medical treatment. In *D v United Kingdom*, the Court ruled that the deportation of a prisoner to St Kitts would have constituted a violation of the guarantee. The applicant had been in the advanced stages of AIDS, and deportation would almost certainly have resulted in acute physical and mental suffering as well as hastening his death on account of the lack of appropriate social and medical facilities in St Kitts[11]. The consequence is that, in deciding whether to extradite or deport an individual, states must pay particular attention to such matters as political climate and (if relevant) medical care facilities, even if this results in lengthy detention pending determination of these matters[12].

1 Cf van Dijk and van Hoof *Theory and Practice of the European Convention on Human Rights* (3rd edn, 1998) at p 328: the norms of the European Convention on Human Rights, Art 3 and the Convention Relating to the Status of Refugees 1951 overlap 'in that if a person has a well-founded fear of being persecuted – in the sense of Article 1(A) of the Refugee

Convention – in his country of origin, his forced return to this country would violate Article 3'. See also Mole *Asylum and the European Convention on Human Rights* (2001).

2　*Soering v United Kingdom* (1989) A 161, at para 91.

3　*HLR v France* 1997-III, 745, para 40; 5961/72, *Amekrane v United Kingdom* (1973) YB 16, 356; followed in *Kacaj v Secretary of State for the Home Department* (19 July 2001, unreported), IAT.

4　*Cruz Varas v Sweden* (1991) A 201, para 75.

5　Eg *Soering v United Kingdom* (1989) A 161; 51342/99, *Kalantari v Germany* (28 September 2000).

6　Such as Turkey (cf 33124/96, *Incedursun v Netherlands* (22 June 1999) (friendly settlement achieved)) and Iran (cf 43258/98, *GHH and Ors v Turkey* (31 August 1999) (declared admissible); 37014/97, *Aspichi Dehwarni v Netherlands* (27 April 2000) (friendly settlement achieved); and China 58073/00, *Jin v Hungary* (11 January 2000) (declared admissible). The International Rehabilitation Council for Torture Victims, based in Denmark, estimates that torture continues to be practised regularly in some 100 countries.

7　43844/98, *T I v United Kingdom* (7 March 2000) (the applicant initially but unsuccessfully had claimed asylum in Germany, then had made a similar application in Britain; at the request of the UK, Germany agreed to take responsibility for further consideration of his request following an international convention (the Dublin Convention) concerning the attribution of responsibility between member states for deciding asylum requests. The Court declared the application inadmissible on the facts, but confirmed that the removal of the applicant to Germany did not absolve the UK Government of its obligations under ECHR, Art 3 to ensure that he was not subjected to inhuman or degrading treatment).

8　(1989) A 161.

9　*Soering v United Kingdom* (1989) A 161, paras 91–111 at para 111. See Sherlock 'Extradition, Death Row, and the Convention' (1990) 15 EL Rev 87; and Hudson 'Does the Death Row Phenomenon Violate a Prisoner's Human Rights under International Law?' (2000) 11 EJIL 833. See too *Jabari v Turkey* (11 July 2000), paras 38–42 (deportation to Iran of Iranian national facing a charge of adultery for which the penalty was death by stoning or flogging would have violated ECHR, Art 3; the Court was not persuaded that the Turkish authorities had conducted any meaningful assessment of the applicant's claim, and also gave due weight to the UN High Commissioner for Refugees' conclusion that her fears were credible). There are numerous domestic cases on this topic: see e g *R v Secretary of State for the Home Dept, ex p Turgut* [2001] 1 All ER 719.

10　(1991) A 201, at paras 75–84 (the Court also noted the evolution of democracy in Chile which was resulting in the voluntary return of large numbers of refugees). See too *Vilvarajah v United Kingdom* (1991) A 215, paras 107–115 (return of Tamils to Sri Lanka at time of improved situation in country; likelihood of ill-treatment by state officials was judged to be only a 'possibility' and thus there was no real risk of ill-treatment); *Ahmed v Austria* 1996-VI, 2195, paras 41–47 (violation of ECHR, Art 3 established were the applicant to be returned to Somalia where his father and brother had been executed on account of assistance given to his uncle who was a leading political opponent of the regime; forfeiture of refugee status after conviction for crime could not be a material consideration in the assessment); *HLR v France* 1997-III, 745, paras 33–43 (an applicant arrested on drugs charges while in transit claimed that any forcible return to Columbia would pose a real risk to his life from other drug dealers on whom he had informed; the Court accepted that ECHR, Art 3 could apply even where the threat emanates from private individuals rather than state agents (although a general situation of violence did not involve an Art 3 violation) but the applicant had not shown the authorities were unable to give protection. Note the dissenting opinion of Judge Pekkanen suggesting that to require an 'informer' to provide more concrete evidence of the risk of death from criminals is 'unrealistic'); *Hilal v United Kingdom* (6 March 2001), paras 59–68 (expulsion to Tanzania of the applicant who had been denied asylum in the UK: the applicant had previously been tortured, and his return to a country with endemic human rights problems and life-threatening detention conditions would violate ECHR, Art 3); and 58128/00, *Ismaili v Germany* (15 March 2001) (possibility of ill-treatment solely on the basis of political instability in the country seeking extradition insufficient: inadmissible).

11　1997-III, 777, paras 50–54. See too *BB v France* 1998-VI, 2595 (case ultimately struck off the list; but the Commission had considered that the deportation of the applicant (who was suffering from AIDS) to the Congo would have been a violation of ECHR, Art 3 because of the lack of appropriate health care). Cf 40900/98, *Karara v Finland* (29 May 1998) (illness of the applicant was not at an advanced stage: inadmissible); 41874/98, *Tatete v Switzerland* (6 July 2000) (illegal immigrant suffering from AIDS sent back to the Congo: friendly settlement); and 46553/99, *S C C v Sweden* (15 February 2000) (refusal of residence permit for Zambian national infected by HIV declared inadmissible: treatment was available in Zambia where most of the applicant's relatives still lived). See also *K v Secretary of State for the Home Department* [2001] Imm AR 11 (removal of AIDS sufferer to Uganda: no violation of ECHR, Art 3). For applications not involving HIV/AIDS patients, see 23634/94, *Tanko v Finland* (19 May 1994) DR 77, 133 (expulsion of an individual suffering from glaucoma; no indication that there was any need for an immediate operation, or that medication would not be available if deported to Ghana: inadmissible); and *Bensaid v United Kingdom* (6 February 2001), paras 32–41 (expulsion of a schizophrenic would not lead to a violation as appropriate (albeit not as favourable) health care would be available in the country to which he was to be deported). Contrast *R (X) v Secretary of State for the Home Dept* [2001] 1 WLR 740 (removal of illegal entrant suffering from mental illness to country where increased risk of self-harm and deterioration in mental health: no violation of ECHR, Art 3).

12   Cf *Chahal v United Kingdom* 1996-V, 1831, paras 73–107 (detention of Sikh activist for six years justified in terms of Art 5(1) because of ECHR, Art 3 considerations (see para 4.67 below); the Court used Amnesty International reports etc in finding that return to India would result in a real risk of torture and persecution); and 41874/98, *Tatete v Switzerland* (18 November 1999) illegal immigrant suffering from AIDS sent back to the Congo: declared admissible). The CPT has considered the issue of appropriate procedural safeguards in such circumstances: *Seventh General Report* CPT/Inf (97) 10, paras 32–34.

Fact-finding and standard-setting by the European Committee for the Prevention of Torture and Inhuman or Degrading Treatment or Punishment ('the CPT')

4.38   The European Committee for the Prevention of Torture[1] has been more vigorous in its condemnation of detention conditions and treatment of detainees than the Commission or the European Court of Human Rights. The essential contrast lies in the view taken of detention conditions in both prisons and mental health institutions. The Commission and Court have refused to accept that a state has any positive legal duty to minimise the side-effects of imprisonment: indeed, there is perceived to be an inevitable element of 'humiliation' implicit in the infliction of any punishment. In contrast, the Committee accepts that 'people are sent to prison as a punishment, not for punishment'[2], and thus by extension that the 'act of depriving a person of liberty entails a correlative duty for the state to safeguard physical and mental welfare until such time as liberty is restored'[3]. The CPT has thus condemned both general holding conditions which would escape Commission or Court criticism, such as the holding conditions in certain parts of Barlinnie Prison in Glasgow which it labelled inhuman and degrading[4], and specific conditions or treatment such as solitary confinement which could lead to 'isolation syndrome'[5]. This more critical attitude reflects the proactive concerns of the CPT to make recommendations to help prevent ill-treatment and to counteract the psychological effects of incarceration. It is also a consequence of the availability of medical expertise in the Committee. The CPT has now issued detailed statements of expectations in respect of detention in police stations[6], prisons[7] and mental health institutions[8], and of categories of detainees, including foreign nationals held under aliens legislation[9], juveniles[10] and females[11].

1   See para 2.34 above, CPT reports are available at www.cpt.coe.int . For discussion of the equivalent treaty in international law, see Boulesbaa *The UN Convention on Torture and the Prospects for Enforcement* (1999).
2   *United Kingdom Report* CPT/Inf (91) 15, para 57.
3   *Portuguese Report (No 2)* CPT/Inf (96) 31, para 104.

4 See *United Kingdom Report* CPT/Inf (96) 11, para 343: 'Conditions of detention in C Hall were quite unsatisfactory. The vices of overcrowding, inadequate lavatory facilities and poor regime activities were all to be found there; in addition, many of the cells were in a poor state of repair. As the CPT has already had occasion to make clear in the past, to subject prisoners to such a combination of negative elements amounts, in its view, to inhuman and degrading treatment.' Reference was made to this report in *Napier v The Scottish Ministers* (26 June 2001, unreported), Ct of Sess.

5 Eg *Swiss Report* CPT/Inf (93) 3, paras 48–52 (non-voluntary isolation lasting up to seven years without socio-therapeutic stimulation for prisoners); *German Report* CPT/Inf (93) 13, para 72 (solitary confinement should be of minimum duration); *Bulgarian Report* CPT/Inf (97) 1, paras 109–110 (14-day segregation in dark and unventilated cell of 2 square metres 'inhuman').

6 The CPT has encouraged states to develop more rigorous procedural codes to ensure that domestic guarantees exist providing adequate safeguards against ill-treatment by police officers during detention in general, and interrogation in particular. There should thus be a right to have notification of detention made to a close relative or other third party; notification of detention and access to a legal representative; medical examination by a doctor of the detainee's own choice; notification by police officers of detainees' rights; and the maintenance of comprehensive custody records. Holding conditions in police stations should be of a reasonable size to accommodate the number of persons placed in them; detainees should be provided with a means of rest and a mattress and clean blankets if they are being held overnight; cell design should ensure adequate lighting and ventilation etc. The interrogation of suspects in police custody should be regulated in some detail by domestic law and supplemented by a code of conduct for interrogations covering such issues as the systematic informing of the detainee of the details of the officers conducting the interrogation, rest periods between and breaks during interrogation, the places where interrogation may take place, and clarification of whether a suspect may be required to remain standing during the interrogation. There should also be an efficient and effective system of police complaints which entails an independent mechanism for investigating allegations of misconduct and which may be made use of by persons who have suffered deprivation of liberty by police officers without undue deterrence. See further Murdoch 'CPT Standards and the Council of Europe' in Morgan and Evans (eds) *Protecting Prisoners: The Standards of the European Committee for the Prevention of Torture in Context'* (1999) pp 103–136.

7 For example, prisoners should have access to programmes of activities which enable them to spend at least eight hours or more each day outside their cells, while engaged in purposeful activities of a varied nature such as group association activities, education, sport, and work with vocational value; accommodation must meet 'the requirements of health and hygiene, due regard being paid to climatic conditions' and offer 'a reasonable amount of space, lighting, heating and ventilation'; prisoners should have regular access to proper toilet facilities offering sufficient privacy; prisoners should be entitled to the same level of medical care as persons living in the community at large with 'equivalence of care' between community and prison health services in general medicine, physiotherapy, and nursing care; and pre-trial remand prisoners should be able to wear their own clothing rather than prison issue. See further Evans and Morgan *Preventing Torture: A Study of the European Convention for the Prevention of Torture and Inhuman or Degrading Treatment or Punishment* (1998) pp 307–315.

8 8th General Report CPT/Inf (98) 12, paras 25–58.

9 7th General Report CPT/Inf (97) 10, paras 24–36.

10 9th General Report CPT/Inf (99) 12, paras 20–41.

11 10th General Report CPT/Inf (2000) 13, paras 21–33.

Use of CPT reports in Article 3 cases

4.39 While limited use has been made of CPT country reports by applicants seeking to challenge detention conditions under the European Convention on Human Rights, Article 3, the potential for such use exists both for helping establish the factual circumstances of detention and also in encouraging revision of existing Article 3 case law[1]. In its first report to the United Kingdom, the Committee criticised holding conditions in certain English prisons and considered that the cumulative effect of over-crowding, lack of integral sanitation and inadequate regime activities all amounted to 'inhuman and degrading treatment'[2]. In *Raphaie v United Kingdom*, the applicant made several complaints about his treatment while detained in two English prisons[3]. The Commission eventually declared the application inadmissible as being time-barred, but did appear willing to use the CPT's report to provide additional corroboration of factual assertions[4]. Use of CPT reports to challenge existing jurisprudence and thus seek enhanced Article 3 protection has hitherto proved more difficult[5]. Initially, the Commission and Court seem to have rejected conclusions of the CPT out of hand. In *LJ v Finland*, the Commission had regard to the CPT's criticisms that the material conditions of detention in an isolation unit were 'poor' and that there was insufficient 'mental and physical stimulation', but simply concluded that the facts 'did not disclose any appearance of a violation' of Article 3[6]. In *Amuur v France*, the applicants maintained that transit zone detention facilities did not meet Committee recommendations in support of their complaint of violations of Article 5 guarantees of liberty of the person, but while the relevant CPT report[7] was referred to in the factual and legal background, the Court did not rely upon it in its decision[8]. In *Aerts v Belgium*, the applicant had been detained by a court in a prison psychiatric annexe under mental health provisions, although the judge had instructed that he be placed in a named institution rather than continue to be held in a prison. Subsequent attempts through the courts to have him sent to the particular institution which had been selected on account of its appropriate regime were unsuccessful on account of a shortage of places. After failing to be awarded legal aid to challenge prison detention conditions, he made an application to the Commission, relying upon a CPT report which had been highly critical of the prison during a recent visit. The CPT's report had concluded that 'in every regard, the level of care of patients held in the annexe was below the minimum acceptable level from the ethical and human point of view'[9]. The Commission acknowledged that the CPT's criticisms gave weight to its conclusion that the conditions in which the applicant had been held constituted degrading treatment contrary to Article 3[10]. The Court, however, did not accept that there was evidence that the applicant's mental health had deteriorated, nor that the conditions of detention had resulted in any serious effects on the applicant's mental health. The issue was primarily one of proof, and while the applicant was ultimately unsuccessful in this application, the point remains that the Court relied upon the CPT report as being of particular importance in establishing not only the factual basis of holding conditions but also for the first time the seriousness of their shortcomings in assessing whether there had been a violation of Article 3[11]. The potential for further use of published CPT reports in this manner certainly exists[12], and cases such as *Dougoz v Greece* and *Peers v Greece* suggest that the Court has finally begun to place greater weight upon the conclusions of the CPT in particular cases[13]. Indeed, reliance has been placed on a CPT report in proceedings before the Court of Session[14].

1 It is not inconceivable that an individual could have his case examined both by the CPT and by the Court since CPT involvement does not formally prevent any application under the European Convention on Human Rights. While Art 35 (2)(b) provides that the

Court cannot deal inter alia with any matter which 'has already been submitted to another procedure of international investigation', the European Convention for the Prevention of Torture, Art 17(1) and (2) protect the competence of the Court in considering questions of violation of ECHR, Art 3. The ECPT Explanatory Memorandum, para 92, states that 'it is not envisaged that a person whose case has been examined by the Committee would be met with a plea based on [Art 35(2)(b)] if he subsequently lodges a petition with the [Court] of Human Rights'.

2 *United Kingdom Report* CPT/Inf (91) 15, para 57. The Government's response to the CPT was that improvement was necessary, but that the assessment was wrong: *Response of the United Kingdom Government* CPT/Inf (91) 16, preface, para 5.

3 The applicant had been forced to share a cell designed for single occupancy with one or two others and which had no integral sanitation; prisoners had to satisfy the needs of nature by using a chamber pot in the presence of other prisoners; the emptying of the chamber pots took place at the same time as the washing of eating utensils; he had been confined to the cell for 23 hours a day; cockroaches and rats had been present in one prison where he was permitted only 45 minutes of daily exercise; and he had been held in the psychiatric wing without having been given a reason for this placement.

4 20035/92 (2 December 1993). Cf 17525/90, *Delazarus v United Kingdom* (16 February 1993) where the applicant was unable to rely upon similar CPT condemnation since he had been held in a single cell. See also *Salman v Turkey* (27 June 2000), at para 113 ('the bruising and swelling on the left foot combined with the grazes on the left ankle were consistent with the application of "falaka", which [the CPT] reported was one of the forms of ill-treatment in common use, *inter alia*, in [the particular detention centre]'). See also *Dougoz v Greece* (6 March 2001), paras 46–49 (use of CPT report to corroborate applicant's allegations of degrading treatment because of serious overcrowding and appalling sanitary conditions: violation).

5 Cf 19066/91, *S, M & MT v Austria* (1993) DR 74, 179 (the CPT's views that immigration detainees were being held in acceptable conditions cited by the Commission in holding that no ECHR, Art 3 violation).

6 21221/93 (28 June 1995).

7 *French Report* CPT/Inf (93) 2.

8 1996-III, 827.

9 *Belgian Report* CPT/Inf (94) 15, para 191 (author's translation).

10 25357/94 (20 May 1997), paras 39–55, 66–83. (The majority of the Commission accepted the criticisms of an inadequate treatment regime, overcrowding and promiscuity contained in the CPT report, while the minority seized upon the failure of the CPT report to condemn the prison conditions expressly as 'inhuman or degrading treatment', suggesting that the conditions had not reached the level of severity required for Art 3. The Commission also accepted that there had been a failure to provide an adequate treatment regime and thus there had been a violation of Art 5(1). The Commission minority opinion fails to recognise the exhortation contained in the Explanatory Report to the European Convention for the Prevention of Torture at para 91 that the CPT should avoid formulating 'interpretations of the provisions of the European Convention on Human Rights').

11 1998-V, 1939, paras 61–67. There was, however, a breach of Art 5(1)(e) because of a lack of proper relationship between the grounds and conditions of detention (paras 45–50.)

12 Cf 52750/99, *Lorsé and Ors v Netherlands* (18 January 2000) (detention in a top-security institution whose regime was labelled by the CPT as amounting to 'inhuman treatment' on account of its excessive severity resulting in an insufficiency of privacy and human contact which could lead to the deterioration of prisoners' psychological and physical condition). The Court has also begun to endorse certain CPT standards: e g *Akkoç v Turkey* (10 October 2000), at para 118 ('[The CPT] has also emphasised that proper medical examinations are an essential safeguard against ill treatment of persons in custody').

13 See para 4.35 above.

14 *Napier v The Scottish Ministers* (26 June 2001, unreported). Reference was also made to a CPT report in *R (Manning) v Director for Public Prosecutions* [2001] QB 330.

PROTECTION AGAINST SLAVERY OR SERVITUDE

Scope of Article 4

4.40   The practical utility of the European Convention on Human Rights, Article 4's prohibition of slavery or servitude or imposition of any requirement to perform forced or compulsory labour is likely to be limited. The guarantee is clearly designed to prevent exploitation through the imposition of compulsion to work[1]. It does not prohibit obligations to provide unpaid services as part of professional responsibilities, unless these can be considered to be unjust, oppressive or unreasonably detrimental[2]. In *Van Der Mussele v Belgium*, the applicant had been required to undertake representation of a client as a pupil advocate without remuneration or even reimbursement of expenses incurred. The European Court of Human Rights considered that this requirement fell outwith the scope of 'forced or compulsory labour' since it was a professional obligation required for qualification as an advocate and known to the applicant before he had voluntarily sought to enter this profession[3].

1 The terms 'slavery', 'servitude' or 'forced or compulsory labour' are not defined, but are given their normal meanings in international law: cf *Van der Mussele v Belgium* (1983) A 70 para 32 (drafters of the ECHR followed International Labour Organisation Convention No 29 concerning Forced or Compulsory Labour (1930) and the Court would thus take this into account in interpreting the European Convention on Human Rights, Art 4; here, the definition of 'forced or compulsory labour' in the Convention on Forced Labour as work or services 'extracted from any person under the menace of any penalty and for which the said person has not offered himself voluntarily' would be applied, bearing in mind that the Convention is a 'living instrument' to be interpreted in accordance with present-day requirements). See too 7641/76, *X and Y v Germany* (1978) DR 10, 224 (reference to ILO Conventions Nos 29 and 105). The Slavery Convention of 1926 defines slavery as the 'status or condition of a person over whom many or all of the powers attaching to the right of ownership are exercised'; the Supplementary Convention of 1956 refers also to practices such as serfdom and debt bondage. In *Van Droogenbroeck v Belgium* (1982) A 50, at para 59, the Court observed that if a situation arose where release from detention was 'conditional on the possession of savings from pay for work done in prison . . . one is not far away from an obligation in the strict sense of the term [used in the Article]'. Article 15 provides that a state may not derogate from its obligations under Art 4(1) (which refers to slavery and servitude) in time of emergency. Cf *Cyprus v Turkey* (10 May 2001), paras 137–141 (no evidence that missing persons were still being held in custody and in conditions amounting to slavery or servitude in respect of occupation of northern Cyprus by Turkish forces).
2 20781/92, *Ackerl and Ors v Austria* (1994) DR 78,116 (requirement imposed on judges to carry out work of absent colleagues without additional remuneration arose from freely accepted terms of their appointment: inadmissible); 39109/97, *Doyen v France* (1998) DR 94, 151 (requirement placed upon *avocats* to be on call one day in every 200 to assist detainees in police custody: inadmissible).
3 (1988) A 70, para 40 See too 1468/62, *Iversen v Norway* (1963) YB 6, 278 (dentist required to serve in Lapland for one year as part of professional obligations to ensure provision of dental services in remote communities: application inadmissible).

TRAFFICKING IN HUMAN BEINGS

4.41   Trafficking in human beings for the purpose of sexual exploitation clearly violates physical integrity and human dignity, and several central and east European states in particular are now affected by this phenomenon (as countries of either origin, transit or destination of women and minors) and normally as the direct result of poverty or armed conflict. However, trafficking does not readily fall within the scope of the European Convention on Human Rights, Article 4, and in any case may be better addressed by co-ordinated action at national level[1].

1   See Committee of Ministers Recommendation No R (91) 11 (concerning sexual exploitation, pornography and prostitution of, and trafficking in, children and young adults) and Recommendation No R (2000) 11 (on action against trafficking in human beings for the purpose of sexual exploitation). See also Parliamentary Assembly Recommendation 1325 (1997) on traffic in women and forced prostitution. For a compilation of principal texts, see 'Trafficking in Human Beings', doc EG (2000) 2 (2 vols). As far as EU law is concerned, the Treaty of Amsterdam, Art 29 makes reference to the trafficking of persons and offences against children. Action is proposed in a Council Framework Decision (COM(2000) 854–2001/0025(CNS)).

Recognised exclusions

4.42   There are specific exclusions in the European Convention on Human Rights, Article 4, paragraph (3)[1] from the definition of 'forced or compulsory labour' of 'any work required to be done in the ordinary course of detention' justified under Article 5[2], or of work forming part of civic obligations[3], military service (or civil service in lieu where this is recognised by a state[4]) or services in time of any emergency 'threatening the life or well-being of the community'. However, if the selection of individuals required to carry out such work is determined by discriminatory criteria, then work or labour which is otherwise in the 'normal course of affairs' could be rendered abnormal and thus unlawful[5]. In *Karlheinz Schmidt v Germany*, compulsory service as a fireman was considered to be a normal civic obligation in terms of this exclusion and, by extension, the financial levy payable in place of carrying out this service also fell to be treated as being within the scope of the paragraph. However, the European Court of Human Rights noted that these linked requirements were imposed only upon men, even though women could and did serve as volunteer firefighters; further, since there were sufficient volunteers (of both sexes) to staff the service, the reality was that no male was ever required to serve, so that payment of the financial levy was in practice effectively the only legal responsibility. In such circumstances, the Court considered that the difference of treatment on the ground of sex could not be justified and thus constituted a violation of Article 14 taken in conjunction with Article 4(3)[6]. On the other hand, the Commission has shown less sympathy to applicants seeking to challenge exemptions on the basis of discriminatory treatment in circumstances where service or labour – as opposed to payment – is required by domestic law[7].

1   Cf 22956/93, *Spöttl v Austria* (1996) DR 85, 58 (para (3) is to be read as delimiting the very content of Art 4 by indicating what is excluded from 'forced or compulsory labour' rather than limiting the *exercise* of the right).
2   8500/79, *X v Switzerland* (1979) DR 18, 238. Cf European Prison Rules, Recommendation (87) 3, rr 71–76 (regulating work done by convicted prisoners who may be compelled to work) and r 96 (unconvicted prisoners may be offered work, but may not be compelled to work). Cf *Van Droogenbroeck v Belgium* (1982) A 50, paras 58–59 (applicant had been 'placed at disposal of government' as a recidivist offender following a court decision and required to carry out work; work required had not exceeded that ordinarily required in such instances).
3   Eg 9686/82, *X v Germany* DR 39, 90 (1984) (duty upon firearms licence holder to provide practical help to eradicate rabies).

4 Cf Recommendation No R (87) 8 of the Committee of Ministers concerning military service; 10600/83, *Johansen v Norway* (1985) DR 44, 155 (Art 4(3)(b) does not require states to provide substitute civilian service for conscientious objectors). Only some four European states which retain military service do not recognise the alternative of civilian service. Most of the applications concerning conscientious objectors have arisen under Art 9: see para 7.06 below. See further, Rodotà 'Conscientious Objection to Military Service', and Quinn 'Conscientious Objection in Labour Relations', in Council of Europe *Freedom of Conscience: Proceedings of the Leiden Seminar* (1993) pp 95–122. By 2000, only three Council of Europe states (Albania, FYRO Macedonia, and Turkey) with military service did not recognise alternative civilian service: see Council of Europe 'Report of the Committee on Legal Affairs and Human Rights on the Exercise of the Right of Conscientious Objection to Military Service' doc 8809 (13 July 2000).
5 *Van der Mussele v Belgium* (1983) A 70, at para 53.
6 (1994) A 291-B, paras 22–23, 28–29.
7 E g 2299/64, *Grandrath v Germany* (1967) YB 10, 626 (Jehovah's Witness leader of 'bible study' could be required to undertake military or civilian service although ordained clergy of Protestant and Roman Catholic churches were exempted).

Contracts of service entered into by minors

4.43 An issue in terms of the European Convention on Human Rights, Article 4 has arisen in respect of minors who had signed up for lengthy periods of service with the military forces. In *W, X, Y and Z v United Kingdom*, four serving sailors and soldiers who had entered contracts of service for nine years and who had been refused requests for discharge sought to persuade the Commission that these contractual undertakings entered into when they were aged 15 or 16 and below the age of full contractual capacity constituted 'forced or compulsory labour'. The Commission accepted that the specific exemption for military service contained in paragraph (3) could not be taken to exclude military service questions entirely from consideration under paragraph (2). However, since the applicants had entered the armed forces voluntarily and with the consent of their parents, there was no sense in which the situation they found themselves amounted to 'servitude'[1]. Paragraph (3) thus covers both voluntary and compulsory military service. Yet the decision itself appears unduly narrow and contrary to the spirit of the guarantee. There would probably now be some doubt as to whether the Commission's approach to parental consent should continue to be followed[2].

1 3435-38/67 (1968) YB 11, 562
2 Cf Grosz, Beatson, and Duffy *Human Rights: the 1998 Act and the European Convention* (1999) at p 194: 'Even with parental consent, the practice looks highly questionable in the light of subsequent Court judgments which have emphasised the importance of showing clear consent to any waiving of rights and to developments on the rights of the child, especially the International Convention of 1989.' The decision is also at odds with a current UN proposal to raise the minimum age of recruitment and deployment of armed personnel to 18, reflecting an emerging common international consensus on this issue.

LIBERTY AND SECURITY OF PERSON

Introduction

4.44 Guarantees against arbitrary deprivation of liberty lie at the heart of the protection of human rights. In part, the substantial case law generated by the European Convention on Human Rights, Article 5 reflects the variety of systems of criminal justice and of procedural and substantive provisions throughout Europe, for police powers, criminal procedure, juvenile justice, and mental health provisions are all affected by this guarantee. Strasbourg has upheld a number of challenges to British law and practice concerning detention of terrorist suspects, the imposition of discretionary life sentences, release and recall of prisoners on licence, and involuntary mental health placements. Scots law relating to bail has been amended so as to remove certain respects in which it failed to comply with Article 5[1]. The content of the guarantee is in any case by no means static, and recent Court decisions continue to emphasise the crucial importance accorded to liberty and security of person through cautious advances in established Article 5 jurisprudence[2].

1 The question of release on bail must now be considered in all cases, including murder, as required by the European Convention on Human Rights, Art 5(3): Bail and Judicial Appointments etc (Scotland) Act 2000. 'Prompt' access to a court, which is also required by ECHR, Art 5(3), could still pose a problem: see para 4.73 below. Uncertainty as to whether an arrest has been effected as exemplified by cases such as *Swankie v Milne* 1973 JC 1 may cause difficulties with 'prescribed by law': see para 4.51 below.
2 See Murdoch 'Safeguarding the Liberty of Person: Recent Strasbourg Jurisprudence'(1993) 42 ICLQ 494; and 'A Survey of Recent Case Law under Article 5 ECHR' (1998) 23 EL Rev HR 31.

4.45   The European Convention on Human Rights, Article 5 provides a list of grounds for deprivation of liberty and associated procedural and substantive rights. First, paragraph (1) recognises some fifteen permissible grounds for deprivation of liberty as expressed in six sub-paragraphs. These permitted grounds for deprivation of liberty are exhaustive. They constitute exceptions to a fundamental guarantee of individual freedom and thus are given a narrow interpretation[1]. Second, paragraphs (2) to (4) confer guarantees designed to ensure a prompt and effective determination of the lawfulness of the deprivation. Third, paragraph (5) provides for an enforceable right to compensation in the event of unlawful detention or failure to accord a detainee these procedural rights. These safeguards are complemented in the case of unacknowledged deprivation of liberty by additional positive obligations on the part of the state to 'take effective measures to safeguard against the risk of disappearance and to conduct a prompt effective investigation into an arguable claim that a person has been taken into custody and has not been seen since'[2].

1 *Quinn v France* (1995) A 311, para 42.
2 *Kurt v Turkey* 1998-III, 1152, at para 124; *Taş v Turkey* (14 November 2000), at para 84. See too *Cyprus v Turkey* (10 May 2001), para 131. Cf *Şarli v Turkey* (22 May 2001) para 69, (where it is not established beyond reasonable doubt that state authorities were responsible for a deprivation of liberty in terms of Art 5, the responsibility for carrying out an effective investigation arises under Art 13).

Derogation in time of emergency

4.46   The European Convention on Human Rights, Article 15 allows a state to derogate from its obligations in time of war or other public emergency 'to the extent strictly required by the exigencies of the situation, provided that such measures are not inconsistent with its other obligations under international law'[1]. The United Kingdom has made use of this to prevent further challenge under Article 5 to extended powers of detention under prevention of terrorism legislation. The most recent derogation dating from 1988 appeared in the Human Rights Act 1998, Sch 3[2], but the United Kingdom gave notice in February 2001 that this derogation would be withdrawn following upon the entry into force of the Terrorism Act 2000[3]. Exercise of a state's right of derogation under Article 5 will be scrutinised with particular care[4]. Domestic provisions designed to tackle organised crime or the threat posed by terrorism may pose delicate questions under Article 5. State action designed to safeguard the rule of law must itself be subject to tests of legality: the means employed should not themselves breach the ends sought to be achieved. While the Convention recognises the need 'for a proper balance between the defence of the institutions of democracy in the common interest and the protection of individual rights', any balancing process cannot be taken to the extent of stretching the notions involved 'to the point of impairing the very essence of the right[s] guaranteed'[5].

1 European Convention on Human Rights, Art 15(1). No derogation from Art 2 (except in respect of deaths resulting from lawful acts of war), 3, 4(1) and 7 may be made. Notification of the measures taken, the reasons therefor, and when the measures have ceased to operate is to be given to the Secretary General of the Council of Europe. See further Svensson-McCarthy *The International Law of Human Rights and States of Exception* (1998) pp 285–325; and Macdonald 'Protecting Human Rights in Emergency Situations: Making Article 15 Work' in Mahoney, Matscher, Petzold and Wildhaber (eds) *Protecting Human Rights: The European Perspective* (2000) pp 817–835.

2 See para 3.06 above.

3 For a copy of the Note Verbale, see *Human Rights Information Bulletin No 52*, H/Inf (2001) 3, 3–4. The Terrorism Act 2000 entered fully into force on 19 January 2001, and the derogation was then withdrawn. The Human Rights Act 1998 was amended accordingly with effect from 1 April 2001. See para 1.94 above. The derogation is still in force in the Channel Islands and in the Isle of Man pending the enactment of local legislation.

4 Cf *Ireland v United Kingdom* (1978) A 25, paras 202–224. The initial derogation was withdrawn only in 1984, several years after the abandonment of the policy of internment. A further derogation was lodged after the decision in *Brogan and Ors v United Kingdom* (1988) A 145-B, and subsequently upheld by the Court in *Brannigan and McBride v United Kingdom* (1993) A 258-B. A complaint challenging the continuation of the UK's derogation (before its withdrawal in February 2001) was declared inadmissible: 41571/98, *Marshall v United Kingdom* (10 July 2000). Cf 37555/97, *O'Hara v United Kingdom* (14 March 2000) (arrest and detention took place before the lodging of the derogation in 1988: government concession that the requirements of ECHR, Art 5 (3) had not been complied with). See further, Marks 'Civil Liberties at the Margin: The United Kingdom Derogation and the ECHR' (1995) 15 OJLS 69.

5 *Brogan and Ors v United Kingdom* (1988) A 145-B, at para 59 (in connection with the nature of terrorist crime).

Meaning of 'deprivation of liberty'

4.47 The focus of the European Convention on Human Rights, Article 5 is on the loss of personal freedom[1]. 'Liberty and security of person' is best considered as a unitary concept conferring protection against arbitrary interference with freedom of person of either a substantive or a procedural nature by a public authority[2]. Thus the reference to 'security' cannot be interpreted as implying any duty upon states to provide material assistance[3]. Indeed, within the context of Article 5, the term is largely superfluous, but protection for 'security' in the sense of positive obligations on a state to protect physical safety does exist within the scope of positive state duties under other provisions[4]. In order to give rise to an Article 5 question, the facts must constitute a deprivation of liberty and not merely a restriction on the freedom of movement[5]. This threshold test which determines the application of the guarantee is not without difficulty. The distinction between restriction of movement and loss of liberty has been described as one of 'degree or intensity' rather than 'nature or substance'[6]; and, on occasion, the Commission has also implied that the primary purpose of state action may be the determining factor. The handful of decisions and judgments on this issue do not provide clear guidance as to where the boundary lies[7]. Voluntary submission to detention probably does not affect the assessment[8]. New developments in domestic law – such as the introduction of electronic tagging in lieu of detention on remand – remain untested[9]. It will certainly be critical that an alleged deprivation of liberty is the direct result of state rather than private action and is motivated by state rather than private interests. For example, in *Nielsen v Denmark*, a 12-year-old boy had been admitted to a psychiatric hospital by his mother for treatment for neurosis. The Commission determined that the five-and-a-half-month-long detention of a boy who was not mentally ill and who was capable of appreciating the situation amounted to a 'deprivation of liberty' but, by a bare majority, the European Court of Human Rights disagreed since the crucial point was that hospitalisation took place under an exercise of parental authority, and the state's role was at most merely to provide assistance to the mother[10]. On the other hand, in *Riera Blume and Others v Spain*, the Court held that the involvement of the police in the handing over of members of a religious sect to their families upon their release from custody and following a judge's recommendation that the families should arrange voluntary psychiatric treatment had been sufficient to give rise to state responsibility for a deprivation of liberty. The applicants had been taken by police officers to a hotel where for ten days they had been subjected to 'de-programming', and where police officers had questioned them in the presence of their legal representatives. These officers had thus been aware that the applicants were being held against their will (rather than being subjected to 'de-programming' on a voluntary basis as proposed by the court) and had done nothing to assist their release. The Court applied a test of whether the participation of the police had been 'so decisive that without it the deprivation of liberty would not have occurred', and held that while the 'direct and immediate' responsibility for the detention was borne by the applicants' families and an association dedicated to counteracting the influence of such sects, it was also true that without the 'active co-operation' of the police it could not have taken place. Accordingly the 'ultimate responsibility' for the deprivation of liberty lay with the national authorities[11].

1 26536/95, *Boffa v San Marino* (1998) DR 92, 27.
2 *Bozano v France* (1986) A 111, para 54. See too *Cyprus v Turkey* (10 May 2001), at para 226: 'the applicant state's' complaint relates to the vulnerability of what is an aged and dwindling population to the threat of aggression and criminality and its overall sense of insecurity. However, the Court considers that these are matters which fall outside the scope of Article 5 of the Convention and are more appropriately addressed in the context of its overall assessment of the living conditions of [these individuals] seen from the angle of the requirements of Article 8.'
3 See Murdoch 'A Survey of Recent Case Law under Article 5 ECHR' (1998) 23 EL Rev HR 31 at pp 31–33.

4 'Security' has thus been relocated to the European Convention on Human Rights, Arts 2, 3, 8, 10 and 11: see paras 4.10, 4.12 and 4.29 above and paras 6.35, 7.15 and 7.49 below. However, remnants of the idea still are found by implication in Art 5 in such cases as *Guenat v Switzerland*, discussed at para 4.48 below, and in the justification for deprivation of liberty falling within the category of Art 5 (1)(e).

5 E g 16360/90, *SF v Switzerland* (1994) DR 76, 13 (following refusal to enter Switzerland, applicant was obliged to stay on Italian territory entirely surrounded by Swiss territory: not a 'deprivation of liberty' but mere restriction on movement).

6 *Guzzardi v Italy* (1980) A 39, para 93 (detention on island and subjection to night curfew, restrictions on movement, limited facilities etc).

7 Cf Murdoch 'Safeguarding the Liberty of Person: Recent Strasbourg Jurisprudence' (1993) 42 ICLQ 494 at 495–499; and 'A Survey of Recent Case Law under Article 5 ECHR' (1998) 23 EL Rev HR 31 at pp 31–33.

8 *De Wilde, Ooms and Versyp v Belgium* (1971) A 12, para 65.

9 Relevant domestic legislation regulating electronic tagging is found in the Crime and Punishment (Scotland) Act 1997 and the Crime and Disorder Act 1998. In *Giulia Manzoni v Italy* 1997-IV, 1184, the question as to the status of detention at home imposed as a preventive measure was raised, but no decision on this issue was required since the applicant was not ultimately subjected to such an order; (at para 22) the Court merely remarked that the range of preventive measures available in Italian law 'all restrict individual liberty to a greater or lesser extent'. In *Raimondo v Italy* (1994) A 281-A, para 39, the Court decided that an obligation to remain at home between 9 pm and 7 am each day did not amount to a loss of liberty.

10 (1988) A 144. In the event of a dispute as to the facts, it must also be established beyond reasonable doubt that the state authorities were responsible for a deprivation of liberty: *Şarli v Turkey* (22 May 2001), para 69.

11 (14 October 1999), paras 16–18, and 30–35.

4.48 The question of the guarantee's applicability will arise most often in the exercise of powers of criminal investigation, ancillary to which are rights to detain (in order, for example, to carry out a personal search, to fingerprint, or to place a suspect in an identification parade). Whether such limited interference with liberty or movement for such specific purposes is enough to trigger the guarantees provided by the European Convention on Human Rights, Article 5 may not always have a clear answer[1]. Detention to compel the taking of a blood test may do so even although the detention is of short duration[2]; but, in contrast, instances of restriction of movement incidental to the carrying out of criminal investigations to enable police officers to carry out a search[3] or to question suspects[4] may not result in a finding of detention[5]. Similarly, exercise of police discretionary authority to protect individuals from harm may not result in an Article 5 issue. In *Guenat v Switzerland*, police officers had invited an individual who had been thought to be acting abnormally to accompany them from his home to a police station. After various unsuccessful attempts to contact doctors at the clinic where the applicant had been receiving treatment, a psychiatrist had arranged for his compulsory detention in a mental health hospital. The applicant claimed that he had been arrested arbitrarily and detained for some three hours in the police station without being given any explanation for his arrest, but the majority of the Commission considered that there had been no deprivation of liberty since the police action had been prompted by humanitarian considerations, no physical force had been used and the applicant had remained free to walk about the police station[6]. Certainly, however, such considerations cannot justify the imposition of extensive interference with an individual's rights, as illustrated by the *Riera Blume and Others v Spain* judgment discussed above[7] where the length of the detention and the absence of immediate physical risk seemed to be of significance.

1 Cf Trechsel 'Right to Liberty and Security of the Person' [1980] 1 HRLJ 88, at 96: 'It is the very short arrest which raises specific problems. In point of fact, ... under the legislation of several High Contracting parties there seems to exist certain forms of short-term police arrest which are hardly covered by the exceptions exhaustively listed in Article 5(1). [Such short term arrests cannot] fall outside the scope of Article 5... It is quite another question, however, whether in such cases all the specific guarantees of Article 5 apply, in particular the right to have the lawfulness of detention ascertained by a court [in terms of Article 5(4)].' However, as long as the relevant level of 'reasonable suspicion' exists, detention to question individuals suspected of having committed an offence would now be seen as an integral part of the criminal process and thus justified by the European Convention on Human Rights, Art 5(1)(c): see para 4.57 below.
2 8278/78, *X v Austria* (1979) DR 18, 154 at 156. The decision may have been influenced by the consideration that ECHR, Art 5 (1)(b) itself would have permitted detention of such a kind if there had been non-compliance with the lawful order of a court or if effected in order to secure the fulfilment of an obligation prescribed by law.
3 9179/80 (6 July 1981). Cf *Berktay v Turkey* (1 March 2001), paras 128–133 (detention of the applicant in his home during the carrying out of a police search by five police officers: deprivation of liberty established.
4 8819/79, *X v Germany* (1981) DR 24, 158 at 161 (no deprivation of liberty in the case of a ten-year-old girl who had been taken from school with two friends to a police station for two hours and kept for part of this time in an unlocked cell while police questioned her about thefts, since the object of the police action was to obtain information).
5 Cf *Baumann v France* (22 May 2001) para 63 (seizure of passport by police officers amounted to a restriction on the right of free movement which gave rise to an issue under Art 2 of Protocol 4).
6 24722/94, (1995) DR 81, 130 at 134. His complaint that he had been wrongfully admitted to a psychiatric institution after a medical examination instructed by the police and without being informed of the reasons for such a measure was rejected on the ground of non-exhaustion of domestic remedies.
7 At para 4.47 above.

4.49 Consideration of when a deprivation of liberty can be said to exist is further complicated by the suggestion that lack of procedural safeguards in domestic law may also be a critical factor in deciding whether the European Convention on Human Rights, Article 5 applies. In *Amuur v France*, asylum seekers had been held in an airport's transit zone for 20 days under constant police surveillance. They had been technically free to return to their country of origin which had given assurances that they would not be ill-treated. The Commission concluded that no deprivation of liberty had occurred since the degree of physical constraint was not substantial enough: the European Court of Human Rights, on the other hand, decided that Article 5 did apply. While states had a legitimate interest in preventing unauthorised immigration, any exercise of the power to hold aliens in a transit zone could not be prolonged excessively. A state was under some obligation to provide decision-making procedures for determining refugee status along with speedy judicial review of reasons for prolonging detention. Here, the length of time that the applicants were held and the lack of legal and social assistance had amounted to a deprivation of liberty[1].

1 1996-III, 826, paras 41–49. Cf 19066/91, *SM and MT v Austria* (1993) DR 74, 179 (no deprivation of liberty as applicants were free to leave the airport at any time). The decision in *Amuur* mirrors the approach adopted by the CPT that individuals in such circumstances are de facto being held in a 'place of detention': cf CPT/Inf (91) 10, para 89; and CPT/Inf (99) 10, para 10 (persons held in transit or international zones in Vienna and Frankfurt airports).

Grounds for deprivation of liberty under Article 5(1)

4.50 To be lawful in terms of the European Convention on Human Rights, Article 5, any detention must fall within at least one of the fifteen distinct purposes provided for in the six sub-paragraphs of paragraph (1). It is possible for a particular deprivation of liberty to fall within two or more of the categories[1] or for the nature and classification of the detention subsequently to change[2]. Lord Hope of Craighead observed in *R (Wardle) v Crown Court at Leeds*:

> 'As the European Court said in *W v Switzerland*[3], continued detention can be justified in a given case only if there are specific indications of a genuine requirement of public interest which, notwithstanding the presumption of innocence, outweighs the rule of respect for individual liberty. To this end art 5(1) provides a right to liberty, which is subject to six specified exceptions and to two overriding requirements. The first requirement is that any deprivation of liberty must be in accordance with a procedure prescribed by law. The second requirement is that it must be lawful. To be lawful in this context, the detention must not only be lawful under domestic law. It must satisfy the requirements of the Convention that the domestic law on which the decision is based must be sufficiently accessible to the individual and must be sufficiently precise to enable the individual to foresee the consequences of the restriction[4].'

1 Eg *X v United Kingdom* (1981) A 46, paras 36–39; and *Eriksen v Norway* 1997–III, 839, para 76.
2 Eg 11256/84, *Egue v France* (1988) DR 57, 47 (for a deprivation to be lawful, it must at any given moment fall within one of the six categories).
3 (1993) A254-A.
4 [2001] 2 WLR 865 at para 83.

Ensuring that detention is 'lawful' and 'in accordance with a procedure prescribed by law'

4.51 Each of the six sub-paragraphs providing for permissible grounds of deprivation of liberty is in turn qualified by the requirement that any detention be both 'lawful' and also 'in accordance with a procedure prescribed by law', and thus the European Convention on Human Rights, Article 5 calls for scrutiny of domestic law, although the Court has recognised its task 'is subject to limits inherent in the logic of the European system of protection, since it is in the first place for the national authorities, notably the courts, to interpret and apply domestic law'[1]. 'Lawfulness' requires both compliance with substantive legal rules[2] as well as absence of abuse of authority or bad faith[3] since deprivation of liberty may not be justified if the real purpose behind the purported state action falls outwith the scope of paragraph (1)[4]. Domestic procedures also require to be 'prescribed by law': that is, legal rules must be 'adequately accessible' and 'formulated with sufficient precision' to permit individuals to regulate their behaviour accordingly[5]. However, a determination by an appellate court that a lower court erred in law does not in itself affect the lawfulness of any intervening loss of liberty, for Article 5 cannot be used by persons to challenge detention which is subsequently deemed to have been based on errors of fact or law[6]. Further, domestic law and procedures must also satisfy the purpose of the paragraph in protecting an individual from arbitrary loss of liberty[7]. Deprivation of liberty is thus 'only justified where other, less severe measures, have been considered and found to be insufficient to safeguard the individual or public interest which might require that the person concerned be detained': in other words, the loss of liberty must also be shown to have been necessary in the particular circumstances[8]. The Court has also stressed that the absence of administrative recording of the fact of detention is itself incompatible with the very purpose of Article 5[9].

Recent decisions of the European Court of Human Rights help illustrate these requirements. Domestic law must be sufficiently detailed to allow individuals reasonably to foresee that the consequences of any behaviour could lead to application of the law[10]. This is of particular relevance when considering potentially wide concepts such as 'breach of the peace'. In *Steel and Ors v United Kingdom*, protestors who had been detained for refusing to be bound over to keep the peace claimed that English law did not regulate with sufficient precision either the type of behaviour that could trigger the imposition or lead to the subsequent violation of such an order. The Court, however, accepted that recent clarification (and restriction) by the English courts of the concept of breach of the peace did satisfy this test[11]. Clearly, failure by state officials to adhere to domestic law will lead to a violation of Article 5. Thus in *K-F v Germany*, a delay of some 45 minutes in releasing an individual detained to allow police the opportunity of checking identity, after the maximum period of 12 hours' detention had expired, rendered the detention unlawful. The absolute nature of the permissible length of detention placed police officers under a duty to take all necessary precautions to ensure compliance with the law[12]. This situation, though, can be contrasted with one in which there is some limited and reasonable delay on account of practical considerations before implementation of a court order to release a detained person[13]. Most obviously, detention (or continuation of detention) without legal justification will give rise to a violation of Article 5. For example, in *Baranowski v Poland*, the prosecutor had decided to continue the applicant's detention on remand solely by reference to a practice without legal foundation which considered a request made by a prisoner for release as one which it was not necessary to determine once the indictment had been served. The applicant accordingly had been held in custody after the expiry of the period authorised by a court, and thus there had been a breach of the guarantee[14]. However, flaws in a detention order will not necessarily render the period of detention unlawful, as long as the detention is based upon a judicial authorisation[15]. More difficult questions can arise where a legal system distinguishes between void and voidable judicial decisions. In *Benham v United Kingdom*, English law allowed courts to enforce the payment of the community charge or 'poll tax' by imprisonment where it was established that failure to pay was because of wilful refusal or culpable neglect. The applicant had served 11 days' imprisonment before being released on bail pending his appeal. This appeal ultimately proved successful as it was accepted that the magistrates had been mistaken in finding that culpable neglect had been established. The applicant argued that in these circumstances his deprivation of liberty had been unlawful in domestic law since the magistrates' decision had been taken in excess of their jurisdiction.

The Commission agreed that the detention had not been 'lawful' in domestic law. By a substantial majority, however, the Court ruled that no Article 5 violation had been established. The mere setting aside of a detention order on appeal could not be conclusive; instead, the distinction in domestic law between decisions within the power of a court (but which could be later held to be erroneous) and decisions that fell outwith its jurisdiction (and thus were void from the outset) was considered crucial. Had the magistrates not discharged their task in considering whether the applicant's non-payment was culpably negligent, then their decision might have fallen into the latter category which would have rendered the detention unlawful. Here, though, the appeal court had merely decided that the evidence presented could not sustain the magistrates' decision, rather than having ruled that the magistrates had taken a fundamentally flawed decision[16].

Further, it is not enough in itself that the deprivation of liberty is permitted by domestic law: the particular loss of liberty must be considered as necessary in the circumstances to avoid the appearance of arbitrariness in the application of the law. Thus in *Litwa v Poland*, while it was accepted that the detention of the applicant in a 'sobering up' centre had been in accordance with domestic procedures, the Court nevertheless found a violation of Article 5 because of considerable doubts that the applicant had been posing a danger to himself or to others, and further since no consideration had been given to other available alternatives. Detention was the most extreme of the measures available under domestic law to deal with an intoxicated person, and the police could have taken the applicant either to a public care establishment or even back to his home. In these circumstances, a violation of Article 5 was established[17].

Determining the issue of the lawfulness of certain state action may also involve delicate questions of public policy. In *Sánchez-Ramirez v France*, the applicant (popularly known as 'Carlos the Jackal') had been attacked and handcuffed in Sudan and flown to a military air base in France where he had been served with an arrest warrant. He claimed that his deprivation of liberty had not been lawful, and challenged the involvement of French officials in his forcible removal from Sudan. The Commission, by a majority, dismissed his application as inadmissible since action by Sudanese officials clearly fell to be excluded *ratione personae*. For the Commission, the key point was that the arrest warrant served in France clearly had been 'lawful'. The Convention did not include any provision concerning the taking of extradition proceedings by a state, and thus it followed that even a 'disguised extradition' could not constitute a violation of France's obligations. Collaboration between the French and Sudanese authorities 'particularly in the field of the fight against terrorism, which frequently necessitates co-operation between States' thus did not raise any Article 5 issue[18]. The reasoning is unconvincing, and avoids questions which are likely to arise under other guarantees such as Article 3[19]. The Commission's approach also contrasts sharply with the Court's criticism of such instances of 'disguised extradition', at least where two contracting states are involved[20]. The Court will have an opportunity to clarify the effect of abduction on the lawfulness of deprivation of liberty in the case of *Öcalan v Turkey*[21].

1 *Bozano v France* (1986) A 111, para 58.
2 Including, in certain circumstances, any directly applicable EC legislation: eg 6871/75, *Caprino v United Kingdom* (1978) DR 12, 14. Cf 54942/00, *Kelly v United Kingdom* (life imprisonment imposed after two serious offences in terms of the Crimes (Sentences) Act 1997; trial judge rejected factors which the applicant considered constituted 'exceptional circumstances' within the meaning of the statute: communicated).
3 Cf the European Convention on Human Rights, Art 18 which provides that restrictions on freedoms 'shall not be applied for any purpose other than those for which they have been prescribed'. In *Bozano v France* (1986) A 111, para 60, the Court labelled the actions of the French police as a disguised form of extradition which thereby failed to be 'lawful'.
4 Cf *Lukanov v Bulgaria* 1997-II, 529, paras 40–46 (detention of former Communist prime minister of Bulgaria was in reality a form of political reprisal not justified under ECHR, Art 5(1)). See too *Denizci v Cyprus* (23 May 2001), paras 323 and 392 (detention of applicants by police officers without legal authority prior to their expulsion to northern Cyprus: no lawful basis for the deprivation of liberty had been advanced by the respondent state, and thus there was a violation of Art 5).
5 Cf *Steel and Ors v United Kingdom* 1998-VII, 2719, at para 75; *Hashman & Harrup v United Kingdom* (25 November 1999), para 31.
6 *Benham v United Kingdom* 1996-III, 738, para 42.
7 *K-F v Germany* 1997-VII, 2657, para 63; *Erkalo v Netherlands* 1998-VI, 2464, para 56.
8 *Witold Litwa v Poland* (4 April 2000), at para 78; *Varbanov v Bulgaria* (5 October 2000), at para 46.
9 *Çiçek v Turkey* (27 February 2001), para 165 (unexplained disappearance of the applicant's two sons after their detention).
10 *Ječius v Lithuania* (31 July 2000), paras 57–64 (issue whether detention whilst the applicant had been accorded access to his case file had been authorised by domestic law: effects of this law were vague enough to cause confusion amongst competent authorities and thus the detention was therefore not lawful). Cf *Tsirlis and Kouloumpas v Greece* 1997-III, 909 paras 56–63 (detention of conscientious objectors in violation of settled domestic law). See also See also *Dougoz v Greece* (6 March 2001), paras 55–58 (opinion of a senior public prosecutor that a ministerial decision applied by analogy in the case of the applicant did not constitute a 'law' of sufficient 'quality' within the meaning of the Court's jurisprudence).
11 1998-VII, 2719, paras 51–78. At para 55, the Court noted that English law provides that a breach of the peace is committed 'only when an individual causes harm, or appears likely to cause harm, to persons or property or acts in a manner the natural consequence of which would be to provoke others to violence'. Cf *Hashman and Harrup v United Kingdom* (25 November 1999), paras 29–41, discussed further at para 7.23 below (order by which the applicants were bound over to keep the peace and not to behave *contra bonos mores* was not 'prescribed by law' as required by ECHR, Art 10).
12 1997-VII, 2657, paras 71–73.
13 *Giulia Manzoni v Italy* 1997-IV, 1184, para 25. Cf *Quinn v France* (1995) A 311, paras 39–43 (a court had ordered the applicant to be released 'forthwith', but he remained for a further eleven hours in detention without steps being taken to implement this instruction: the Court regarded this as clearly unlawful); *Labita v Italy* (6 April 2000), paras 166–174 (detention of the applicant continued for 12 hours after his acquittal, a period only partly attributable to the need for the relevant administrative formalities to be carried out: violation of ECHR, Art 5(1)).
14 (28 March 2000), paras 42–58.
15 Cf *Ječius v Lithuania* (31 July 2000), paras 65–69 (regardless of the possible flaws in the wording of the order, its meaning must have been clear to the applicant). Minor clerical errors in detention orders, etc may in certain circumstances be overlooked: *Douiyeb v Netherlands* (4 August 1999), paras 39–55 (erroneous reference to statutory provision on one occasion but other references were correct: no violation).
16 1996-III, 738, paras 35–47 and 59–77 (the imprisonment thus fell within sub-paragraph (b) since the detention was to secure the payment of a legal obligation, and accordingly, no ECHR, Art 5 violation existed; however, a violation of Art 6(1) and (3)(c) taken together was established in view of the failure to provide free legal representation at the court hearing). See, too, *Perks and Ors v United Kingdom* (12 October 1999), paras 64–71 at para 67 (defects 'only a fettered exercise of discretion' and thus not 'unlawful' in the sense of being beyond the court's jurisdiction).
17 (4 April 2000), paras 72–80.

18 28780/95 (1996) DR 86, 155 at 162. See, too, 14009/88, *Reinette v France* (1989) DR 63, 189 (co-operation between authorities of a contracting state and a state which was not a Council of Europe member resulting in deprivation of liberty of the applicant in an aircraft: question of lawfulness of action judged solely by reference to actions of French officials); 28574/95, *Ullah v United Kingdom* (1996) DR 87, 118 (detention of an individual pending the making of a deportation order who had been held for some 18 days before being advised that he was being released since, in the opinion of the Secretary of State, the deportation decision was not in accordance with the law as full consideration had not been given to his previous applications for leave to remain. His subsequent action for damages for false imprisonment failed in the Court of Appeal which found that his detention would have remained lawful since the conditions precedent to its lawfulness were satisfied. For the Commission, it was 'far from clear' (even despite the Secretary of State's letter) that the deportation notice was unlawful; the lawfulness of the actual detention was not dependent upon the validity of the notice; and even although there had been procedural irregularities in the making of the order, they were not of a nature in domestic law to affect the validity of the detention. There was no question in this case as to excess of jurisdiction or bad faith, and thus this part of the application was manifestly ill-founded.) For discussion, see Frowein 'Male Captus Male Dentus – a Human Right' in Lawson and de Blois (eds) *The Dynamics of the Protection of Human Rights in Europe* vol III (1994) pp 175–185.

19 For the approach taken by the English courts in such instances, see *R v Horsferry Road Magistrates' Court, ex p Bennett* [1994] 1 AC 42, HL.

20 Cf *Bozano v France* (1986) A 111, para 60.

21 46221/99 (14 December 2000) (arrest of the applicant in Africa during an operation conducted in disputed circumstances: application declared admissible in respect of ECHR, Art 5 complaints).

DECISIONS OF THE DOMESTIC COURTS ON 'LAWFULNESS'

4.52   The importance of ensuring that deprivation of liberty is in accordance with domestic law is illustrated by the decision of the House of Lords in *R v Governor of Brockhill Prison, ex p Evans*. The applicant's release date was calculated by the Governor on the basis of the existing case law. On her application for judicial review, the Divisional Court held that the earlier case law was erroneous, and that she had been detained in custody for 59 days after she had been entitled to be released. On her application for damages, the House of Lords held that false imprisonment was a tort of strict liability, and that the Governor was accordingly liable in damages notwithstanding that he had complied with the law as the courts had at that time declared it to be. This conclusion was observed to be consistent with the European Convention on Human Rights, Article 5: detention after the date when the applicant was entitled to be released was unlawful under domestic law, and therefore also unlawful within the meaning of Article 5[1].

The requirement that individuals be protected from an arbitrary loss of liberty – ie that the loss of liberty be necessary in the particular circumstances – is illustrated by the English case of *R v Offen*, which concerned the statutory requirement that a life sentence be imposed on any person convicted of two serious offences unless there are exceptional circumstances relating to either of the offences or to the offender. The Court of Appeal considered that that requirement, as it had until then been interpreted by the courts, could operate in a disproportionate manner which would contravene Article 5 (and possibly Article 3 also). Construing the requirement in accordance with the Human Rights Act 1998, s 3, however, the problem disappeared:

'In our judgment, [the statutory provision] will not contravene Convention rights if courts apply the section so that it does not result in offenders being sentenced to life imprisonment when they do not constitute a significant risk to the public[2].'

The English courts have also held that the mandatory life sentence in respect of persons convicted of murder is not arbitrary[3].

1 [2000] 3 WLR 843.
2 [2001] 1 WLR 253 at p 277.
3 *R v Lichniak* [2001] 3 WLR 933.

ECHR, Article 5, paragraph (1)(a): Detention after conviction by a competent court

4.53 This provision justifies detention imposed following upon conviction of a criminal offence[1] by a court[2]. It thus covers loss of liberty after conviction but pending appeal[3], detention imposed as an alternative to the original sentence[4], and detention classified by domestic law as a disciplinary rather than a criminal matter[5]. The sub-paragraph will be satisfied if the deprivation of liberty follows upon a conviction, even if the aim of the court in imposing the detention is other than retributive. In *Bizzotto v Greece*, for example, a drug addict had been sentenced to imprisonment for eight years (later reduced to six years on appeal) with an order that he be placed in an institution offering treatment for drug addiction. However, since no secure facilities offering appropriate medical facilities existed, the applicant had been detained in an ordinary prison. Eighteen months later, he sought release on licence, claiming to have been cured of his dependency. The Commission considered that the failure to provide the treatment regime ordered by the domestic court rendered the deprivation of liberty unlawful, but the European Court of Human Rights considered that the detention fell within the scope of the European Convention on Human Rights, Article 5(1)(a) since the detention was as a consequence of his conviction for drug trafficking, rather than on account of his addiction under sub-paragraph (e), even although the humanitarian and reformative purpose behind the court's order was acknowledged[6].

1 Including disciplinary offences: *Engel v Netherlands* (1976) A 22, para 68. For discussion of Art 3 issues in the imposition of sentences which are grossly disproportionate to the offence, see para 4.32 above.
2 A 'court' need not 'be understood as signifying a court of law of the classic kind, integrated within the judicial machinery of the country', but its members must enjoy a certain amount of stability (although perhaps only for a specified period), independence from the executive, and provide 'guarantees of judicial procedure' in the discharge of their functions. Cf *Drodz and Janousek v France and Spain* (1992) A 240, paras 105–107 (the applicants had been convicted in Andorra but required to serve their sentences in either France or Spain. The Court concluded that the Andorran court was the court which had determined the conviction for para (1)(a) purposes, even although Andorra was not a contracting state to the Convention).
3 Cf *Monnell and Morris v United Kingdom* (1987) A 115, paras 47–48 (time spent in prison awaiting disposal of appeal ordered by court not to count towards sentence; the Court ruled that this did not give rise to a violation of the European Convention on Human Rights, Art 5 such a risk was an inherent part of the domestic appeals system and was designed to further the legitimate interest of discouraging unmeritorious appeals).
4 7994/77, *Kötalla v Netherlands* (1978) DR 14, 238 (life imprisonment imposed as an alternative to infliction of the death penalty). Where a prisoner is required to serve additional days prior to being released on licence, as a consequence of a disciplinary

offence, the jurisdictional basis of his detention is the original sentence of the court, the postponement of his release being an aspect of the administration of that sentence. The court's sentence therefore satisfies the requirements of ECHR, Art 5(1) so far as the additional days are concerned: *R (Greenfield) v Secretary of State for the Home Dept* (22 February 2001, unreported), DC.

5 *Engel v Netherlands* (1976) A 22, para 68.
6 1996-V, 1724, paras 31–35. See, too, *Ashingdane v UK* (1985) A 93, para 44 (treatment under mental health detention under para (1)(e)); and *Bouamar v Belgium* (1988) A 129, para 50 (detention not justified under para (1)(d) since lack of proper facilities for educational supervision of minor in adult prison).

4.54 The European Convention on Human Rights, Article 5, paragraph (1)(a) may also justify subsequent loss of liberty after release, but any recall to prison must result directly from the original sentence and have a sufficient causal link with the original sentencing court's decision[1]. For example, in *Weeks v United Kingdom,* the applicant had been sentenced to life imprisonment for armed robbery, released on licence, and subsequently recalled. The European Court of Human Rights considered that this further loss of liberty could be brought within the sub-paragraph since there existed a requisite link between the re-detention and the original decision of the trial court to impose this sentence because of the applicant's perceived dangerousness. The recall had thus been ordered for a purpose consistent with these original aims of the trial court[2]. However, establishment of any requisite link hitherto has in practice not proved to be a demanding requirement and may, for example, include the preventive detention of a recidivist after conviction[3].

1 *Van Droogenbroeck v Belgium* (1982) A 50, para 40.
2 *Weeks v United Kingdom* (1987) A 114, paras 42–51.
3 9167/80, *X v Austria* (1981) DR 26, 248. See too *Eriksen v Norway* 1997-III, 839, discussed at para 4.58 above. But cf 46295/99, *Stafford v United Kingdom* (29 May 2001) (revocation of licence on two occasions for breach of a requirement to remain within the UK and after conviction for forgery; after the sentence had been served, he remained in prison on the basis of the revocation of the licence despite a Parole Board recommendation that he should be released but in accordance with a Court of Appeal decision that domestic law conferred a broad discretion on the Secretary of State whose decision not to release the applicant was in accordance with the policy whereby the risk of re-offending was taken into account, such risk not having been expressed as being limited to offences of a violent or sexual nature: admissible under Art 5(1) and (4)).

ECHR, Article 5, paragraph (1)(b): non-compliance with the lawful order of a court or to secure the fulfilment of a legal obligation

4.55 The European Convention on Human Rights, Article 5(1)(b) permits deprivation of liberty 'for non-compliance with the lawful order of a court or in order to secure the fulfilment of any obligation prescribed by law'[1]. Deprivation of liberty upon refusal to be bound over to keep the public peace, as provided for in English criminal law, is a 'lawful order' or 'obligation'[2], although arguably (as with imprisonment imposed for failure to pay a fine) the distinction between sub-paragraphs (a) and (b) in such instances is a slim one. Court-authorised detention to obtain a blood test[3] or to allow compilation of a psychiatric opinion[4] or the taking of an affidavit[5] is also covered, as is detention with a view to secure compliance with an order to deliver up property[6] or to pay a fine[7]. It may also justify detention for refusal to give evidence in court, as long as other Convention considerations have been met[8].

Detention in order to secure the fulfilment of a prescribed legal obligation cannot be given too loose an interpretation as this could undermine the aim of the Convention in protecting individual liberty. Any such obligation thus must be of a 'specific and concrete nature', as illustrated by the early case of *Lawless v Ireland*. Anti-terrorist legislation permitted individuals to be detained if they were considered to be engaging in 'activities prejudicial to the security of the state'. The applicant had been held for five months on the ground that this was necessary to secure compliance with the general duty upon citizens not to commit offences against the public peace or state security. The European Court of Human Rights considered that since no specific legal obligation was involved, the detention could not be brought within Article 5 (1)(b)[9]. On the other hand, in *McVeigh, O'Neill and Evans v United Kingdom*, the duty imposed by British anti-terrorist legislation was to 'submit to further examination'. The Commission accepted that this was a specific and concrete obligation to provide information for the purpose of permitting officials to establish status at the point of entry into the United Kingdom and not (as claimed by the applicants) in substance merely an obligation to submit to detention. It did consider, however, that there had to be specific circumstances warranting detention to secure the fulfilment of the obligation before sub-paragraph (b) could be satisfied[10].

1 This sub-paragraph should be read alongside the European Convention on Human Rights, Art 1 Protocol 4 where ratified by a particular state (the United Kingdom has not yet ratified this protocol).
2 *Steel & Ors v United Kingdom* 1998-VII, 2719, para 69. The length of detention of the first applicant (44 hours) was also accepted as proportionate to the aim of preventing the risk of serious physical injury in assessment of ECHR, Art 10: at para 105. See further para 7.33 below.
3 8278/78, *X v Austria* (1979) DR 18, 154.
4 6659/74, *X v Germany* (1975) DR 3, 92.
5 5025/71, *X v Germany* (1971) YB 14, 692.
6 6944/75, (30 September 1976).
7 6289/73, *Airey v Ireland* (1977) DR 8, 42. Presumably imprisonment following upon a sentence to pay a fine where the court at that time imposes a period of imprisonment in default would fall within ECHR, Art 5 (1) (a).
8 Cf *K v Austria* (1993) A 255-B (in the opinion of the Commission, the order to testify was made in violation of ECHR, Arts 6 and 10, and therefore could not justify detention under para (1)(b): case struck out after a friendly settlement).
9 (1961) A 3, Law, para 9.
10 8022/77, 8025/77 and 8027/77, *McVeigh and Ors v United Kingdom* (1981) DR 25, 15, paras 168–175.

ECHR, Article 5, paragraph (1)(c): Arrest or detention for the purpose of bringing a suspect before the competent legal authority; or to prevent the commission of an offence or the fleeing of a criminal suspect

4.56   Three separate state interests justifying detention are covered in the European Convention on Human Rights, Article 5, sub-paragraph (1)(c): first, 'the lawful arrest or detention of a person effected for the purpose of bringing him before the competent legal authority on reasonable suspicion of having committed an offence'; second, 'when it is reasonably considered necessary to prevent his committing an offence'; and third, when detention is considered necessary to prevent flight after the commission of any offence. These three headings are exhaustive, and this sub-paragraph cannot be used to justify detention in order to secure extradition[1], or effected solely in order to extract information about others[2].

1 7317/75, *Lynas v Sweden* (1976) DR 6, 141.
2 *Ireland v United Kingdom* (1978) A 25, para 196.

DETENTION ON REASONABLE SUSPICION OF HAVING COMMITTED AN OFFENCE

4.57 The European Convention on Human Rights, Article 5(1)(c) first recognises the state's right to detain a person on reasonable suspicion of having committed an offence[1]. This sub-paragraph should be read alongside the Article 5(3) entitlements to be brought promptly before a judge or other officer exercising judicial power and to trial within a reasonable time or to release pending trial[2], and other Convention guarantees which protect the situation of a suspect detained in police custody[3]. A state must be able to show more than that a suspicion was honestly held to justify any deprivation of liberty.

> 'Having a "reasonable suspicion" presupposes the existence of facts or information which would satisfy an objective observer that the person concerned may have committed the offence. What may be regarded as "reasonable" will however depend upon all the circumstances'[4].

Further, detention which was at first justified by reasonable suspicion may cease being so if the suspicion ceases to exist[5]. In other words, the fact that a person detained 'on reasonable suspicion' is not ultimately brought before a judge does not bring the detention outwith the scope of the sub-paragraph as long as the relevant level of suspicion existed at the outset of detention.

> 'The object of questioning during detention [under the sub-paragraph] is to further the criminal investigation by way of confirming or dispelling the concrete suspicion grounding the arrest [, and thus] facts which raise a suspicion need not be of the same level as those necessary to justify a conviction or even the bringing of a charge, which comes at the next stage of the process of criminal investigation'[6].

In *Brogan and Ors v United Kingdom*, the applicants argued that they had been held under prevention of terrorism legislation on suspicion of involvement in unspecified acts of terrorism, a contention rejected by the Court which found that detention had been with the aim of furthering police investigations 'by way of confirming or dispelling the concrete suspicions' of commission of particular offences[7]. In *Murray v United Kingdom*, the applicant had been arrested under a provision allowing an officer to detain on the ground of a suspicion 'honestly and reasonably held'. She claimed that this was insufficient to meet the standards of the sub-paragraph, and that the real reason for her arrest had not been to bring her before a 'competent legal authority' but to interrogate her for the general purpose of intelligence gathering, contrary to the applicable domestic law. The Court held that there was sufficient information to provide a 'plausible and objective basis' for suspicion of involvement in offences, and that the purpose of the arrest had been 'genuinely' to bring her before a judge even although she was released without charge[8]. This ruling has been applied subsequently in other instances of serious crimes[9] as well as less serious offences[10]. The focus is now clearly upon ensuring the existence of an adequate level of suspicion at the time when deprivation of liberty takes place, with paragraph (3) coming into play where a decision is taken to proceed with a criminal process[11].

1 That is, the facts invoked must be able to be reasonably considered as constituting a crime at the time when they occurred: cf *Wloch v Poland* (19 October 2000), paras 109–117 (applicant's detention on remand was based on a suspicion that he had been involved in acts qualified as the offence of trading in children, even although there were serious difficulties as regards interpretation of the relevant legal provision, there was nothing to suggest that reliance upon the provision was arbitrary or unreasonable: no violation of the European Convention on Human Rights, Art 5(1)).

2 *Lawless v Ireland* (1961) A 3, Law, para 14.

3 Such as protection against inhuman or degrading treatment, and fair trial considerations which may require the right of access to a legal representative during interrogation: see paras 4.21–4.24 above and paras 5.69 and 5.70 below. For discussion of CPT standards in respect of police custody, see *Second General Report* CPT/Inf (92) 3, paras 36-43, and *Sixth General Report* CPT/Inf (96) 21, paras 14-16.

4 *Fox, Campbell and Hartley v United Kingdom* (1990) A 182, paras 32–36, at para 32.

5 *Stögmüller v Austria* (1969) A 9, Law, para 4; cf *De Jong, Baljet and Van Den Brink v Netherlands* (1984) A 77, at para 44 ('whether the mere persistence of suspicion suffices to warrant the prolongation of a lawfully ordered detention on remand is covered, not by [this sub-paragraph] as such, but by Article 5 (3), which forms a whole with Article 5(1)(c),... to require provisional release once detention ceases to be reasonable....'). Cf *Labita v Italy* (6 April 2000), paras 155–159 (the applicant had been arrested on suspicion of being a member of the Mafia solely on the grounds of uncorroborated allegations by a former Mafioso who had decided to co-operate; while a suspect may be detained at the beginning of proceedings on the basis of statements made by *pentiti*, these statements necessarily become less relevant with the passage of time unless supported by corroboration).

6 *Murray v United Kingdom* (1994) A 300-A, para 55.

7 *Brogan and Ors v United Kingdom* (1988) A 145-B, at, para 53

8 (1994) A 300-A, paras 50–69. See also 37555/97, *O'Hara v United Kingdom* (14 March 2000) (complaint of the failure of the respondent government at any stage during domestic proceedings to provide evidence to support a bare allegation that information had been received by the police which constituted reasonable suspicion that the applicant had been involved in a terrorist murder: declared admissible).

9 Eg *Erdagöz v Turkey* 1997-VI, 2300, paras 49–53 (serious assault and attempted murder).

10 *K-F v Germany* 1997-VII, 2657, paras 61–62 (suspicion that applicant would abscond without paying rent).

11 In consequence, for the purposes of ensuring compatibility with ECHR, Art 5, there is probably no meaningful distinction in Scottish procedure between detention for questioning (under the 'six–hour detention power') and detention following upon arrest (whether or not criminal proceedings are ultimately taken), even although detention for questioning is not part of a process which necessarily involves the detainee being brought before a competent court: the crucial issue would be the existence or otherwise of 'reasonable suspicion' at the outset of detention.

DETENTION TO PREVENT THE COMMISSION OF CRIME

4.58   This purpose is interpreted restrictively. In *Lawless v Ireland*, the state argued that the phrase 'effected for the purpose of bringing him before the competent legal authority' qualified only the heading referring to reasonable suspicion of commission of offence, with the consequence that 'when it is reasonably considered necessary to prevent his committing an offence' should be interpreted as standing alone without the need to ensure judicial supervision. The European Court of Human

Rights disagreed, noting that such an argument would result in the possibility that 'anyone suspected of harbouring an intent to commit an offence could be arrested and detained for an unlimited period on the strength merely of an executive decision'[1]. The sub-paragraph cannot thus authorise 'a policy of general prevention directed against an individual or a category of individuals who ... present a danger on account of their continuing propensity to crime; it does no more than afford [states] a means of preventing a concrete and specific offence'[2]. Similarly, in *Ječius v Lithuania*, domestic law provided for detention with a view to preventing the commission of offences. The applicant had been taken into custody to prevent his involvement in three specific offences of banditism, criminal association and terrorising a person. A month later, he was again charged with murder, a charge which had earlier been dropped. The European Court of Human Rights again observed that detention under the sub-paragraph could only take place within the context of criminal proceedings for alleged past offences, and thus preventive detention of the nature applied to the applicant was incompatible with the Convention[3].

In certain circumstances the sub-paragraph may justify the continuing detention of an individual after the expiry of any court-authorised loss of liberty. In *Eriksen v Norway*, the applicant had developed a tendency to become aggressive after suffering brain damage, and over a period of years had been detained in prison or in mental hospitals. Shortly before the expiry of authorisation granted by a trial court to use 'security measures' to detain the appellant, the police sought and were given approval to keep him in detention for several additional weeks to allow an up-to-date medical report to be obtained. The Court accepted that this period of detention fell within the scope of both sub-paragraphs (a) and (c). The former heading applied since the extension was directly linked to the initial conviction and imposition of 'security measures' on account of the appellant's likely risk of re-offending even although the authority for these had expired. Sub-paragraph (c) also justified detention because of the applicant's previous mental history and record of assaults which had provided substantial reasons for believing he would commit further offences if released[4].

1 *Lawless v Ireland* (1961) A 3, Law, para 14.
2 *Guzzardi v Italy* (1980) A 39, at para 102.
3 (31 July 2000), paras 50–52.
4 1997-III, 839, paras 78–87. Cf *Erkalo v Netherlands* 1998-VI, 2464, paras 50–60 (failure to request an extension to a placement order had resulted in a period of unauthorised detention).

DETENTION TO PREVENT A SUSPECT FROM ABSCONDING

4.59 The final category of permissible detention under the European Convention on Human Rights, Article 5, paragraph (1)(c) is deprivation of liberty to prevent an individual absconding after having committed an offence in order to bring him before a competent judicial authority. The danger of flight must be considered carefully in each case: such factors as the ease of leaving the jurisdiction, the possibility of a heavy sentence and the lack of domestic ties will all be relevant in assessing its likelihood and thus the 'reasonableness' of any state detention[1]. This issue is considered in greater detail in discussion of conditional release pending trial[2].

1 Cf *Wemhoff v Germany* (1978) A 7, Law, paras 13–15.
2 At para 4.79 below.

ECHR, Article 5, paragraph 1(d): Detention of minors for educational supervision and for bringing minors before competent legal authorities

4.60   The European Convention on Human Rights, Article 5, paragraph 1(d) has generated little case law. Detention of minors[1] for 'educational supervision' or to bring them before a 'competent legal authority' are distinct purposes[2]. Deprivation of liberty for educational supervision implies that the nature of the detention supports this objective in some manner. In *Bouamar v Belgium*, the applicant had been detained on numerous occasions in an adult remand prison since no suitable juvenile institution had been available. The state's argument that this was justified for 'educational supervision' was rejected because of the regime of virtual isolation in which the applicant was held, the lack of sufficiently trained staff to provide education, and the absence of any educational programme. While an interim custody measure could be adopted as a preliminary to educational supervision, any such imprisonment must be 'speedily followed by actual application of such a regime in a setting (open or closed) designed and with sufficient resources for the purpose'[3]. The general reference to detention of a minor 'by lawful order ... for the purpose of bringing him before the competent legal authority' without further qualification as to any specific state purpose suggests approval of domestic schemes to divert minors from the ordinary criminal process[4]. In the case of a young person in public care, educational supervision 'must embrace many aspects of the exercise [by the authority] of parental rights for the benefit and protection of the person concerned', and thus the phrase cannot 'be equated rigidly with notions of classroom teaching'[5].

1 The definition of 'minority' is one for the national legal system: 8500/79, *X v Switzerland* (1979) DR 18, 238. For discussion of CPT standards in respect of juveniles deprived of their liberty, see *Ninth General Report* CPT/Inf (99) 12, paras 20–41.
2 *Bouamar v Belgium* (1988) A 129, para 46.
3 (1988) A 129, at para 50.
4 See the comments in *Bouamar v Belgium* (1988) A 129, at para 48. In 8500/79, *X v Switzerland* (1979) DR 18, 238, the detention of a minor for eight months in an 'observation centre' prior to disposal of criminal charges was deemed to have been imposed 'for the purpose of bringing him before the competent authority'. More recently, in *T v United Kingdom* (16 December 1999) and *V v United Kingdom* (16 December 1999), paras 74–78, and 73–77 respectively, the Court clearly endorsed (in discussing the European Convention on Human Rights, Art 3) a welfare-based approach to juvenile justice as being in line with the UN Standard Minimum Rules for the Administration of Juvenile Justice ('The Beijing Rules') and the UN Convention on the Rights of the Child. Cf Council of Europe *Prison Overcrowding and Prison Population Inflation: Recommendation No R (99) 22 and Report* (2000) p 33 (in 1997, the rate per 100,000 of the national population who were juvenile prisoners ranged (in western Europe) between 1.2 (in Finland) to 4.6 (in the United Kingdom); within the UK, the proportion of juveniles in the prison population was 1.9% in Northern Ireland, 3.9% in England and Wales, and 4.4% in Scotland).
5 33670/96, *Koniarska v United Kingdom* (12 October 2000) (complaint of a minor held in secure accommodation who had passed the school leaving age and who was suffering from mental disorder that any education offered to her was merely incidental to the real reason for her detention: inadmissible).

DECISIONS OF DOMESTIC COURTS ON DETENTION FOR EDUCATIONAL SUPERVISION

4.61 In domestic cases, it has been accepted that the placing of a child in secure accommodation (eg by order of a children's hearing) involves a deprivation of liberty, but that it is consistent with detention for the purpose of educational supervision within the meaning of the European Convention on Human Rights, Article 5(1)(d)[1]. In an English case, it was observed that:

> 'the concept of "educational supervision" goes well beyond either normal parental control or academic lessons taught in the classroom, but, to the extent that the arrangements for the welfare of the child interfere with his liberty beyond the interference envisaged in normal parental control, and to avoid any arbitrary exercise of power by a local authority, judicial authorisation is required[2]'.

1 *S v Miller* 2001 SLT 531; *Re K (A Child) (Secure Accommodation Order: Right to Liberty)* [2001] Fam 377. These cases followed *Koniarska v United Kingdom* (12 October 2000).
2 *Re K (A Child) (Secure Accommodation Order: Right to Liberty)* [2001] Fam 377 per Judge LJ at para116: followed in *S v Miller* per Lord President Rodger of Earlsferry at para 46.

ECHR, Article 5, paragraph (1)(e): (i) Detention of persons of unsound mind, vagrants, alcoholics, drug addicts, etc

4.62 'The lawful detention of persons for the prevention of the spreading of infectious diseases, of persons of unsound mind, alcoholics or drug addicts, or vagrants' justifies deprivation of liberty both on public safety grounds as well as to further the well-being of the individual who is detained[1]. Detention for the prevention of the spreading of infectious diseases has not given rise to case law under the European Convention on Human Rights, but there is some jurisprudence on loss of liberty of vagrants and of persons of unsound mind and, more recently, on detention of alcoholics and drug addicts.

1 *Guzzardi v Italy* (1980) A 39, at para 98.

VAGRANTS

4.63 The definition of 'vagrant' is primarily a matter of domestic law, as long as this reflects the generally accepted meaning of the term for the purposes of the European Convention on Human Rights[1]. A state may not seek to apply the label for an improper purpose[2].

1 *De Wilde, Ooms and Versyp v Belgium* (the 'Vagrancy cases') (1971) A 12, para 68.
2 *Guzzardi v Italy* (1980) A 39, para 98 (the fact that the European Convention on Human Rights, Art 5(1)(e) justified detention in part to protect the public could not by extension be made to apply to individuals who are considered still more dangerous).

MENTAL HEALTH DETENTION

4.64 More significantly, the European Convention on Human Rights, Article 5 has proved to be an important source of procedural rights for mental health patients[1]. Recognising that judicial competence in mental welfare is limited and that medical understanding is continually developing, the European Court of Human Rights has deliberately left open the interpretation of 'unsound mind' in terms of sub-paragraph (1)(e), and instead has developed safeguards for those deprived of their liberty under this heading, requirements initially established in *Winterwerp v Netherlands*. To justify detention under this heading, first, the existence of 'unsound mind' must be reliably established on objective medical grounds; second, the individual's actual mental condition must justify detention[2]; and third, continuing detention must be supported and justified by the continuing need for such based on the current mental condition of the patient[3]. In all circumstances, no deprivation of liberty can be considered as justified under this heading if the opinion of a medical expert has not been sought[4]. These requirements also apply to the re-detention of former in-patients who are recalled to hospital[5]. Here, the regime under which an individual is detained will be relevant in assessing the legality of the deprivation of liberty, since there is an expectation that the conditions of treatment reflect the justification for detention[6].

In this way the protection of mental health patients has been advanced significantly in that all the circumstances surrounding the loss of liberty will now call for careful scrutiny. Procedural due diligence on the part of state officials will be essential, although the European Court of Human Rights has accepted that any substantive determination of mental illness justifying detention calls for a certain latitude on the part of medical experts. In *Johnson v United Kingdom*, the applicant had been convicted of assault and confined to a mental hospital. Ultimately, a mental health tribunal had decided that his mental illness had ended but that he still required a period of rehabilitation under medical supervision before it could be certain that no recall to hospital would be necessary, and accordingly it had ordered his discharge but conditional upon his residence in a suitable hostel. Implementation had been deferred until such accommodation could be found, but this was made difficult by the lack of appropriate hostels and problems which arose during a period of trial leave. The applicant remained for most of this time a patient in a secure hospital, although subsequent reviews confirmed that he was not suffering from mental disorder. Eventually, some three-and-a-half years later, he had been given an absolute discharge. The Court clarified that a finding that deprivation of liberty on the ground of mental condition is no longer justified does not necessarily imply a right to immediate and unconditional release since this would unacceptably fetter the exercise of expert medical opinion as to what the best interests of a patient require, particularly since the determination of a medical condition cannot be made with absolute accuracy. The Court also recognised that assessment of patients in this category must take into account the protection of the community[7]. However, in such cases it is 'of paramount importance that appropriate safeguards are in place so as to ensure that any deferral of discharge is consonant with the purposes of Article 5(1) and with the aim of the restriction in sub-paragraph (e)' and above all to ensure that any discharge 'is not unreasonably delayed'. Here, the state's delay resulted in a violation of Article 5[8].

---

1 See further Thorold 'Implications of the ECHR for United Kingdom Mental Health Legislation' [1996] EHRLR 619. For discussion of CPT standards in relation to involuntary placement in psychiatric establishments, see *Eighth General Report* CPT/Inf (98)12, paras 25–28.

2 That is, the assessment must be based on the current state of mental health and not solely on events taking place in the past if a significant period of time has elapsed: *Varbanov v Bulgaria* (5 October 2000), para 47.

3 *Winterwerp v Netherlands* (1979) A 33, para 39. Cf *Luberti v Italy* (1985) A 75, paras 27–29; *Ashingdane v United Kingdom* (1985) A 93, paras 40–42, 48–49. See too 44872/98, *Magalhães Pereira v Portugal* (30 March 2000) (detention on the basis of a medical opinion noting that the applicant required long-term psychiatric opinion for schizophrenia; a court-instructed report obtained some seven months later indicated that the applicant's condition had stabilised, and that he could be released on condition he accepted psychiatric support and continued to take his medicine, but no action taken by the domestic court; further, there was a two-month delay before a court considered whether the applicant's detention should continue after he was re-arrested following a seven-month period of unauthorised liberty: application declared admissible).

4 *Varbanov Bulgaria* (5 October 2000), paras 46–49 (detention ordered by a prosecutor to obtain a medical opinion to assess the need for proceedings with a view to the psychiatric internment of the applicant: the Court observed (at para 47) that in urgent cases or where a person is arrested because of his violent behaviour a medical opinion should be obtained immediately following the start of the detention; in all other instances prior consultation should be necessary and even where there is a refusal to appear for medical examination, a preliminary medical assessment on the basis of the file is required).

5 *X v United Kingdom* (1981) A 46, paras 41–46.

6 *Ashingdane v United Kingdom* (1985) A 93, at para 44: 'in principle, the "detention" of a person as a mental health patient will only be "lawful" for the purposes of [Article 5(1)(e)] if effected in a hospital, clinic or other appropriate institution authorised for that purpose', although this sub-paragraph 'is not in principle concerned with suitable treatment or conditions'. See too *Aerts v Belgium* 1997-V, 1939, paras 45–50, discussed at para 4.39 above.

7 Cf *Luberti v Italy* (1984) A 75, para 29.

8 1997-VII, 2391, paras 58–68.

DECISIONS OF DOMESTIC COURTS ON MENTAL HEALTH DETENTION

4.65 The European Convention on Human Rights, Article 5(1)(e) was considered by the Court of Session in *A v The Scottish Ministers*[1]. The case concerned statutory applications made by three patients detained in the State Hospital, all of whom had been convicted of homicide and were suffering from a mental disorder at the time of their conviction. In their applications they sought their discharge on the basis that they were no longer requiring medical treatment: at the time when two of the applications were made, that was the only basis on which the patients could lawfully be detained. While those applications were pending, the Mental Health (Public Safety and Appeals) (Scotland) Act 1999 was passed and brought into force. It had the effect of requiring the court to refuse such applications where it was necessary, in order to protect the public from serious harm, that the patient continue to be detained in a hospital, whether for medical treatment or not. The applicants then argued that the 1999 Act was incompatible with ECHR, Article 5(1)(e) (and also Article 5(4)). The court derived from the authorities on Article 5(1)(e) the following principles.

The admission and detention of a person of unsound mind must be in conformity with a procedure laid down in domestic law. The domestic law relating to the detention of such persons must conform to three criteria:

(i) a true mental disorder must be established before a competent authority on the basis of objective medical expertise;

(ii) the mental disorder must be of a kind or degree warranting compulsory confinement; and

(iii)   the validity of the patient's continued detention depends upon the
        persistence of such a disorder.

Article 5(1)(e) does not require that the detention of persons of unsound
mind be for the purpose of treatment, but it should be in a hospital, clinic
or other appropriate institution authorised for the purpose. Detention
under Article 5(1)(e) is justified where it is necessary to serve a legitimate
social purpose, which may be the protection of the public. The court held
that the 1999 Act was in conformity with these principles. More generally,
the court observed that the right to liberty enshrined in Article 5 arises in
areas where social policy comes into play, for example when decisions
have to be taken about the circumstances in which persons may have to be
detained for the protection of the rest of the community from harm. The
application of Article 5 thus involves holding a balance between the interests of the community (enshrined in Article 2) and the rights of the individual. Where a democratically elected legislature has applied its mind to
achieving a fair balance, the court considered that it should give due
deference to the assessment which the legislature had made of the policy
issues involved. The court's decision in respect of Article 5(4) is discussed
below[2].

   The continued detention of a patient by reasons of the non-availability
of the after-care facilities necessary for the patient's care and treatment in
the community, despite the exercise of all reasonable endeavours, does not
violate Article 5[3]. Further, since it is contrary to the Convention to detain a
patient compulsorily unless it can be shown that the patient is suffering
from a mental disorder which warrants detention, a statutory test which
allowed the continued detention of the patient where it could not be
shown that his mental condition did *not* warrant detention (ie placing the
onus on the patient to justify his discharge, rather than upon the authorities to justify his detention) was held to contravene Article 5[4].

1   2001 SC 1. This decision has been upheld by the JCPC: 15 October 2001, unreported.
2   At para 4.86 below.
3   *R (K) v Camden and Islington Health Authority* [2001] 3 WLR 553.
4   *R (H) v Mental Health Review Tribunal, North and East London Region* [2001] 3 WLR 512.

ALCOHOLICS AND DRUG ADDICTS

4.66   The European Court of Human Rights in *Litwa v Poland* sought to
clarify the extent of any power of detention of an alcoholic under the sub-
paragraph. The applicant, who had been behaving offensively while
drunk, had been taken to a 'sobering up' centre where he had been
detained for six-and-a-half-hours. For the Court, while the normal
meaning of an 'alcoholic' implied addiction to alcohol, the term was used
in the European Convention on Human Rights, Article 5(1)(e) in a context
which includes reference to other categories of individuals who may be
deprived of their liberty both to protect public safety and for their own
interests. Thus the detention of 'alcoholics' could not be restricted merely
to persons medically so diagnosed but had to include detention of individuals 'whose conduct and behaviour under the influence of alcohol
pose a threat to public order or themselves', and where detention is 'for
the protection of the public or their own interests, such as their health or

personal safety'[1]. By clear analogy, a similar approach should apply in cases of drug abuse[2]. The decision, though, seems limited to any justification for short-term deprivation of liberty; any exercise of a power to order the detention of an individual for longer-term treatment for alcoholism or for drug dependency should certainly be justified by reference to criteria similar to the *Winterwerp* judgment (that is, any existence of dependency and treatment necessitating deprivation of liberty should be reliably established by qualified health professionals).

1 (4 April 2000), paras 60–61.
2 See *Bizzotto v Greece* 1996-V, 1724, paras 31–35, discussed at para 4.53 above.

ECHR, Article 5, paragraph (1)(f): Illegal immigration, deportation and extradition

4.67 The European Convention on Human Rights, Article 5(1)(f) provides for 'the lawful arrest or detention of a person to prevent his effecting an unauthorised entry into the country or of a person against whom action is being taken with a view to deportation or extradition'. Any state action under this heading must be taken in good faith[1]. Detention must be with a view to achieving one of the three listed purposes and not merely to prevent flight[2] or for any covert aim[3]. While the Convention does not provide any right to reside in a particular country or any guarantee against being deported or extradited[4], denial of entry to, or expulsion from, a country may give rise to other human rights guarantees[5].

Strasbourg review will be restricted to 'examining whether there is a legal basis for the detention and whether the decision of the courts on the question of lawfulness could be described as arbitrary in light of the facts of the case'[6]. No deportation order need be in force since deprivation of liberty is authorised where action is being taken 'with a view to deportation'[7], but deportation proceedings must not be unduly prolonged or be of excessive duration. The period of detention pending determination whether to extradite in *Kolompar v Belgium* lasted 32 months, and in *Quinn v France* some 23 months. In the former instance much of the delay was attributable to repeated attempts by the applicant to seek release, and consequently no violation was established[8]; but in the latter case, the Court accepted that there had been successive delays attributable to state authorities which rendered the time taken to reach a decision excessive[9]. This testing of 'due diligence' may on occasion, however, call for detailed scrutiny of the factual situation which may also overlap with Article 3 consideration of whether there are substantial grounds for believing that deportation would carry a real risk of ill-treatment, and such state caution to prevent such an outcome may itself justify prolongation of deportation proceedings. For example, in *Chahal v United Kingdom*, a high-profile supporter of Sikh separatism had been detained for over six years pending determination of various appeals concerning the British Government's decision to return him to India. The Court considered that there was no breach of Article 5 under this heading. It was 'neither in the interests of the individual applicant nor in the general public interest in the administration of justice that such decisions be taken hastily, without due regard to all the relevant issues and evidence'. Determination of issues of 'an extremely serious and weighty nature' called for thorough examination by state authorities, and in the circumstances, there was no corresponding lack of diligence, so that the periods of time complained of either individually or taken together could not be regarded as excessive[10].

1 *Bozano v France* (1986) A 111, paras 53–60. See, too, 51564/99, *Conka and Others v Belgium* (13 March 2001) (arrest and deportation of Roma after they had been summoned to report to a police station to give information relating to their asylum applications: admissible). On Art 5(1)(f) generally see *R (Saadi) v Secretary of State for the Home Department* (19 October 2001, unreported), CA.

2 8081/77, *X v United Kingdom* (1977) DR 12, 207.

3 Cf *Bozano v France* (1986) A 111, paras 53–60.

4 1983/63, *X v Netherlands* (1965) YB 8, 228 at 264; 29493/95, *Aslan v Malta* (3 February 2000) (immigration officers refused the applicant entry on account of visa problems; he was subsequently detained in a cell pending his return to Libya from where he had come; there had been sufficient grounds for refusing him entry and his complaint was thus inadmissible).

5 Eg under the European Convention on Human Rights, Art 3 (protection against torture etc) and Art 8 (respect for family life): see further paras 4.37 above and 6.12 below. The use of force to effect a removal order has been considered by the CPT: see *Seventh General Report* CPT/Inf (97) 10, para 36. See also Lambert *The Position of Aliens in Relation to the European Convention on Human Rights* (2001).

6 9174/80, *Zamir v United Kingdom* (1983) DR 40, 42. See too 6871/75, *Caprino v United Kingdom* (1980) DR 22, 5.

7 6871/75, *Caprino v United Kingdom* (1978) DR 12, 14 at 20.

8 (1992) A 235-C, paras 37–43.

9 (1995) A 311, paras 44–49. See too *Amuur v France* 1996-III, 826, at para 43 (detention 'must not deprive the asylum-seeker of the right to gain effective access to the procedure for determining refugee status'), discussed further, at para 4.49 above. 'Effective access' may on occasion require the provision of free legal assistance: cf 9174/80 *Zamir v United Kingdom* (1983) DR 40, 42 (complexity of the issues and the applicant's limited command of English). For discussion of CPT standards relating to foreign nationals deprived of their liberty, see *Seventh General Report* CPT/Inf (97) 10, paras 24–36.

10 1996-V, 1831, paras 110–117. The Court did determine that any deportation to India would result in a violation of ECHR, Art 3: see para 4.37 above. The Art 5(4) issue is considered at para 4.98 below.

Procedural guarantees following deprivation of liberty

4.68   The remaining provisions of the European Convention on Human Rights, Article 5 provide guarantees to persons deprived of their liberty: to notification of the reasons adduced by the authorities; to take proceedings to test the lawfulness of detention; and to compensation where there has been a violation of the article. Additional guarantees to be brought promptly before a judge and to trial within a reasonable time or to release pending trial exist for those deprived of their liberty under Article 5(1)(c). There is some duplication here with the provisions of Article 6, but Article 5 requires there to be special diligence on the part of authorities in respect of persons who have been deprived of their liberty. Article 5's provisions are thus best considered as constituting separate and independent rights which produce their own effects[1]. These rights are in addition to other safeguards for persons deprived of their liberty[2].

1 *Stögmüller v Austria* (1969) A 9, Law, para 5

2 In particular, protection against ill-treatment under Art 3: see para 4.21 above. Evidence improperly obtained from a detainee through compulsion may also violate Art 6 guarantees: see para 5.70 below. The CPT has also published statements of expectations concerning detainees in 'substantive' sections of its annual reports. For discussion of CPT

standards in respect of persons detained in police custody or in prison, see *Second General Report* CPT/Inf (92) 3, paras 36–55; *Sixth General Report* CPT/Inf (96) 21, paras 14–16; and *Seventh General Report* CPT/Inf (97) 10, paras 12–15; for discussion of health care services for prisoners and involuntary placement in psychiatric institutions, see *Third General Report* CPT/Inf (93) 12, paras 30–77 and *Eighth General Report* CPT/Inf (98) 12, paras 25–58 respectively; and for discussion of foreign national, juvenile, and women detainees, see *Seventh General Report* (CPT/Inf (97) 10, paras 24–36, *Ninth General Report* CPT/Inf (99) 12, paras 20–41, and *Tenth General Report* CPT/Inf (2000) 13, paras 21–28 respectively.

Article 5(2): Prompt advising of reasons for detention

4.69 The purpose of the European Convention on Human Rights, Article 5(2) is to ensure that a detainee is adequately informed of the reasons for his detention so as to permit him to judge the lawfulness of the state action and, if he thinks fit, to take advantage of the right under Article 5(4) to challenge it. This is an 'integral part of the scheme of protection afforded by Article 5'[1]. The reference to 'arrest' in the text extends beyond the realm of the criminal law[2], and the giving of reasons applies to all of the categories provided for under Article 5(1), and not just to persons arrested or detained under Article 5(1)(c)[3]. Content, manner and time of notification are important. The legal basis for the detention together with the essential facts relevant to the lawfulness of the decision must be given in 'simple, non-technical language' that an individual can understand[4]. This does not, however, extend to a need to make the individual aware of the grounds for suspicion of involvement in an offence[5]. These requirements cannot be abridged merely because an individual is considered unable or unsuitable to receive the information; in such a case, the details must be given to a representative such as his lawyer or guardian[6]. Further, the information must be given 'promptly', but 'it need not be related in its entirety by the arresting officer at the very moment of the arrest'. In *Van der Leer v Netherlands*, the applicant had discovered only by accident and some ten days subsequently that she was being detained compulsorily in a hospital, a breach of Article 5(2) which was rendered all the more serious since the applicant originally had entered the hospital as a voluntary patient and thus had been unable to appreciate any factual change in her circumstances[7]. A failure to provide information may alternatively, or in addition, raise an issue under Article 5(4) if the failure to supply information has resulted in an individual being denied a proper opportunity to challenge the legality of his detention[8].

1 *Fox, Campbell and Hartley v United Kingdom* (1990) A 182, at para 40.
2 *Van der Leer v Netherlands* (1990) A 170-A, paras 27–28.
3 *X v United Kingdom* (1981) A 46, para 66.
4 *Fox, Campbell and Hartley v United Kingdom* (1990) A 182, at para 40.
5 8022/77, 8025/77, 8027/77, *McVeigh, O'Neill and Evans v United Kingdom* (1981) DR 25, 15. In the opinion of the Commission, a person arrested upon suspicion of an offence should also be asked whether he admits or denies the allegation: 8098/77, *X v Germany* (1978) DR16, 111 at 114.
6 7215/75, *X v United Kingdom* (1980) B 41, opinion of the Commission, paras 102–108
7 (1990) A 170-A, paras 27–30.
8 *X v United Kingdom* (1981) A 46, para 66. See, too, 51564/99, *Conka and Others v Belgium* (13 March 2001) (arrest of Roma after they had been summoned to report to a police station to give information relating to their asylum applications: admissible under paras (1), (2) and (4)).

4.70   However, some latitude appears evident in cases involving serious and organised criminal activity. In *Fox, Campbell and Hartley v United Kingdom*, the applicants had been given only minimal information as to the legal basis for their detention, but within a few hours had been interrogated at length as to their suspected involvement in proscribed terrorist organisations. The European Court of Human Rights determined that in the circumstances the reasons for the detention had thereby been brought to the notice of the applicants within the constraints of 'promptness'[1]. On the other hand, the Court found a breach of Article 5(2) in *Ireland v United Kingdom* where, following executive instructions given to military police, detainees under anti-terrorism laws were not informed of the grounds for deprivation of liberty but merely advised that they were being held pursuant to the provisions of emergency legislation[2].

1 (1990) A 182, paras 40–42; followed in *Murray v United Kingdom* (1994) A 300-A, paras 71–80 (lack of any more 'probing examination' attributable to the applicant's refusal to refuse any further questions). See too 40451/98, *Kerr v United Kingdom* (7 December 1999) (applicant had been interviewed 39 times by police officers during the week that followed his arrest: it could thus be inferred that he was apprised of the reasons for the arrest); and 37555/97, *O'Hara v United Kingdom* (14 March 2000) (applicant was given only the most minimal of information on the reasons for his arrest but, six hours later, interrogation lasting four hours followed: this part of the application was rejected as manifestly ill-founded).
2 (1978) A 25, para 198.

DOMESTIC COMPLIANCE WITH ARTICLE 5(2)

4.71   In order to comply with the European Convention on Human Rights, Article 5(2), the Crown has since 20 May 1999 (when the relevant parts of the Scotland Act 1998 came into force) adopted a practice of serving on the accused what is known as a 'custody statement' in cases in which it intends to seek a remand in custody. The statement indicates the outlines of the evidence in support of the Crown case in order to inform the accused of the reasons for his arrest. Similarly, in cases in which a petition warrant is sought, the practice has been adopted of including in the petition a brief indication of the information which the Crown had received and upon which arrest and detention were sought. Challenges to these practices have been unsuccessful[1].

1 *Vannet v Hamilton* 1999 SCCR 558; *Brown v Selfridge* 1999 SCCR 809.

Article 5(3): Pre-trial detention – (i) Prompt appearance before a judge

4.72   The aim of the paragraph is to ensure that a person detained is brought before a judge so that the lawfulness of detention can be assessed, and a determination made as to whether the individual should be released or detained in custody pending determination of guilt or innocence[1]. The European Convention on Human Rights, Article 5(3) applies only to detentions which fall within the scope of paragraph (1)(c)[2], that is, for 'the lawful arrest or detention of a person effected for the purpose of bringing him before the competent legal authority on reasonable suspicion of having committed an offence or where it is reasonably considered necessary to prevent his committing an offence or fleeing after having done so'. It thus does not apply where a person has been provisionally released[3] or is already serving a sentence of imprisonment imposed after conviction for a criminal offence[4]. The prompt involvement of a judge is also considered an important safeguard against ill-treatment while in custody[5]. Article 5(3) rights must be granted automatically, and cannot be made dependent upon a specific request by an accused person[6]. The responsibilities of the judge can be summarised as those of reviewing all the circumstances militating for or against detention, deciding whether a continuation of detention can be justified in accordance with legal criteria, recording the detailed reasons for determining that an accused should be remanded in custody awaiting trial, and ordering release if there are insufficient reasons for continuing detention[7].

1 *Brogan and Ors v United Kingdom* (1988) A 145-B, para 58; cf *Sabeur Ben Ali v Malta* (29 June 2000), paras 28–32 at para 29 (failure to provide 'prompt, automatic review of the merits of detention).

2 *De Wilde, Ooms and Versyp v Belgium* (the 'Vagrancy cases') (1971) A 12, para 71.

3 8233/78 *X v United Kingdom* (1979) DR 17, 122.

4 5020/71 (20 March 1972).

5 Cf *Kurt v Turkey* 1998-III 1152, at para 123: ('The requirements of Article 5 (3) and (4) with their emphasis on promptitude and judicial control assume particular importance in this context. Prompt judicial intervention may lead to the detection and prevention of life-threatening measures or serious ill-treatment which violate the fundamental guarantees contained in Articles 2 and 3 of the Convention. . . . What is at stake is both the protection of the physical liberty of individuals as well as their personal security in a context which, in the absence of safeguards, could result in a subversion of the rule of law and place detainees beyond the reach of the most rudimentary forms of legal protection'.)

6 *Aquilina v Malta* 1999-III, 225, para 49.

7 E g *T W v Malta* (29 April 1999), paras 41–44; and *Neumeister v Austria* (1968) A 8, Law, para 5: ('It is essentially on the basis of the reasons given in the decisions on the applications for release pending trial, and of the true facts mentioned by the Applicant in his appeals, that the Court is called upon to decide whether or not there has been a violation [of the guarantee]'.) This principle applies also in situations where domestic law provides for a presumption in favour of relevant factors justifying the continuation of pre-trial detention since the shifting of the burden of proof to a detainee to show that the presumption does not apply 'is tantamount to overturning the rule of Article 5 of the Convention': *Ilijkov v Bulgaria* (26 July 2001), paras 84–85 at para 85.

The meaning of 'promptly'

4.73 'Promptly' suggests more latitude than is accorded by the French text's use of the word '*aussitôt*' which, literally, means 'immediately'. Some applications have given rise to clear breaches of the European Convention on Human Rights, Article 5(3). In *McGoff v Sweden*, an individual was not brought before a judicial officer for 15 days, an interval the European Court of Human Rights had no difficulty in considering unsatisfactory[1]. In *Brogan and Ors v United Kingdom*, there had been failures to involve any judicial official of any kind, let alone 'promptly'. The shortest period of detention had lasted four days and six hours, a period which the Court indicated in any case would have been in excess of that permitted by Article 5[2]. In its reports, the Commission seemed to adopt a yardstick of four days[3], with any period of detention exceeding 96 hours being considered a breach of Article 5(3)[4]. The Court has never adopted such a rigid approach, but in its decisions arrives at a similar result[5], and in *Taş v Turkey*, for example, observed that only in exceptional cases could a period exceeding four days before a detainee is released or brought before a judicial officer be justified[6]. Scottish practice may on occasion violate this requirement. As the Committee for the Prevention of Torture noted in one of its reports, 'at least in theory, a person arrested very early on a Friday morning might not be taken before a court until the following Tuesday morning, were the Monday to be a court holiday'[7].

1 (1984) A 83, para 27. See, too, the three Dutch military criminal procedures cases where applicants were held for periods between seven and fourteen days before being brought before a judge where the Court considered that, 'even taking account of the exigencies of military life', such periods were in excess of what was permissible: *De Jong, Baljet and Van der Brink v Netherlands* (1984) A 77, paras 52–53; *Van der Sluijs, Zuiderveld and Klappe v Netherlands* (1984) A 78, para 49; and *Duinhof and Duijf v Netherlands* (1984) A 79, para 41.
2 *Brogan and Ors v United Kingdom* (1988) A 145-B, paras 61–62. Following upon the Court's decision in *Brogan*, the United Kingdom Government made use of the power contained in the European Convention on Human Rights, Art 15 to derogate from its Convention obligations under para (3) in respect of the detention of persons suspected of involvement in terrorist activities. The derogation was protected by the Human Rights Act 1998, s 1(2) which provides that the relevant articles of the Convention are to be given effect subject to any designated derogation or reservation. The derogation was withdrawn upon the entry into force of the Terrorism Act 2000. See further para 4.46 above.
3 11256/84, *Egue v France* (1988) DR 57, 47 (domestic law which permits detention up to four days in principle in conformity); and cf the earlier decision in 2894/66, *X v Netherlands* (1966) YB 9, 564 at 569.
4 Cf 10990/84, *Riga v Italy* (1987) DR 55, 69. In 4960/71, *X v Belgium* (1972) CD 42, 49 at 55, however, the Commission accepted a delay of five days, but in the special circumstances where the prisoner needed hospitalisation.
5 Cf *Sakik and Ors v Turkey* 1997-VII, 2609, para 45 (in light of *Brogan v United Kingdom* (1988) A 145-B, even if suspicions concerned terrorist activities, not possible to consider detention without judicial intervention lasting 12 and 14 days as appropriate).
6 (14 November 2000), para 86 (30 days' incommunicado detention authorised by the public prosecutor was incompatible with paras (3) and (4), and the lack of available compensation for these breaches violated para (5)). Several other cases have found violations of pre-trial detention by the Turkish authorities: e g *Demir and Ors v Turkey* 1998-VI, 2640, paras 39–58 (23 and 16 days; not strictly required by the European Convention on Human Rights, Art 15 derogation relied upon by the state). An instance of exceptional circumstances is 37388/97, *Rigopoulos v Spain* 1999–II, 435 (arrest of captain of a ship at sea two weeks' sailing from the nearest Spanish territory; delay of 16 days in bringing the suspect before a judge in all the circumstances did not constitute a violation of ECHR, Art 5(3): application inadmissible).
7 CPT/Inf (96) 11, at para 278 (Scottish courts however sat on 26 December 2000 and 2 January 2001 (both of which were Tuesdays) so as to address this problem in part).

'Other judicial officer'

4.74 The provision refers to a 'judge or other officer authorised by law to exercise judicial power', and thus a certain amount of choice in the ordering of arrangements is available to domestic legal systems. The essential requirements are laid down in *Schiesser v Switzerland,* where the applicant had been detained on remand and brought before a local district attorney who had decided that he should be remanded in custody pending trial. The issue arose whether the district attorney was 'an officer authorised by law to exercise judicial power'. The European Court of Human Rights considered that three conditions had to be satisfied:

(i)   independence of the parties (although this did not preclude an 'officer' being subordinate in some degree to other judges or 'officers' as long as they themselves enjoyed similar independence);

(ii) the requirement to follow appropriate judicial procedures in hearing the case; and

(iii) discharge of the tasks of 'reviewing the circumstances militating for or against detention, of deciding, by reference to legal criteria, whether there are reasons to justify detention and of ordering release if there are no such reasons'[1].

In more recent decisions it has been made clear that impartiality must both exist and be seen to exist because of the need to inspire and maintain public confidence in the criminal process[2]. In *Skoogström v Sweden*, for example, the Commission considered the Swedish public prosecutor not to have fulfilled any of the requirements: first, he combined both investigatory and prosecution roles; second, he did not himself hear the individual; and third, there were doubts as to whether his decisions were taken with reference to legal criteria[3]. The matter is of most relevance in continental jurisdictions with inquisitorial systems of justice, or in military justice procedures. In *Hood v United Kingdom*, the applicant had been arrested and brought before his commanding officer and held in detention for some four months before being tried by a court-martial. The Court ruled that the powers and position of the commanding officer (who was responsible for discipline and for determining the necessity of pre-trial detention but who could also play a central role in any subsequent prosecution) were such that he could not be regarded as independent of the parties at the relevant time; further, the Court agreed that misgivings about the commanding officer's impartiality were also objectively justified[4].

1 *Schiesser v Switzerland* (1979) A 34, para 31; see too *Assenov and Ors v Bulgaria* 1998-VIII, 3264, paras 144–150 ('investigator' before whom an accused was brought lacked the power to make legally binding decisions as to detention or release and thus was not sufficiently independent).

2 *Huber v Switzerland* (1990) A 188, para 43; *Brincat v Italy* (1992) A 249-A, paras 17–21.

3 (1984) A 83 (friendly settlement at Court stage: opinion of the Commission, paras 73–83). See too *Niedbala v Poland* (4 July 2000), paras 48–57 (public prosecutors combined investigative and prosecutorial roles along with acting as guardian of the public interest: insufficient guarantees of independence).

4 (18 February 1999), paras 52–61. See too *Stephen Jordan v United Kingdom* (14 March 2000), paras 26–30. British law has now been amended: Armed Forces Act 1996. For earlier military justice cases, see *De Jong, Baljet and Van den Brink, v Netherlands* (1984) A 77, paras 40, 48–51; *van der Sluijs, Zuiderveld and Klappe v Netherlands* (1984) A 78, paras 43–46; and *Duinhof and Duijf v Netherlands* (1984) A 79, paras 34–42.

Article 5(3): Pre-trial detention – (ii) Trial within a reasonable time or release pending trial

4.75 The aim of the second guarantee contained in the European Convention on Human Rights, Article 5(3) is to ensure that the state does not unreasonably prolong any pre-trial detention. The text cannot be read, however, as providing states with the alternative of trial within a reasonable time or of granting provisional release[1]. 'The reasonableness of the time spent by an accused person in detention up to the beginning of his trial must be assessed in relation to the very fact of his detention. Until conviction he must be presumed innocent, and the purpose [of Article

5(3)] is essentially to require his provisional release once his continuing detention ceases to be reasonable[2]'.

1   *Wemhoff v Germany* (1968) A 7, Law, para 4.
2   *Neumeister v Austria* (1968) A 8, Law, at para 4.

Power to order release

4.76   The judge or judicial officer before whom the detainee is brought 'promptly' must be able to order the conditional release of the accused pending trial. Here there was an issue of incompatibility for Scots law which limited the right of releasing a person pending trial on murder to the Lord Advocate or to the High Court since, until the enactment of the Bail, Judicial Appointments, etc (Scotland) Act 2000, the sheriff before whom the detainee was brought had no power to order bail, a situation which was clearly in violation of the European Convention on Human Rights, Article 5's requirements. In *Ireland v United Kingdom*, the European Court of Human Rights remarked that, even had the applicants appeared promptly before the 'commissioners' whose task was to rule on executive detention orders, the state would still not have complied with Article 5(3) since these officials had no power to require release from custody[1]. More particularly, in *Caballero v United Kingdom*, the British Government itself conceded that English law's prohibition of release on bail of any person charged with a designated crime where the individual had previously been imprisoned for any offence of a similar level of seriousness was a violation of Article 5(3)[2].

Subsequently, in *SBC v United Kingdom*, the Court decided to examine the matter itself without relying upon a similar concession again made by the respondent state. It approved the Commission's reasoning in its report in *Caballero* that a crucial feature of the paragraph's safeguards was that of judicial control of executive interference with an individual's right to liberty of person. In order to minimise the risk of arbitrariness in pre-trial detention, the judge 'having heard the accused himself, must examine all the facts arguing for and against the existence of a genuine requirement of public interest justifying, with due regard for the presumption of innocence, a departure from the rule of respect for the accused's liberty', and this implied that a judge must have the power to order the release of an accused[3].

1   (1978) A 25, para 199.
2   (8 February 2000), paras 18–21. See too 30307/96, *BH v United Kingdom* [1998] EHRLR 334. For discussion, see Leach 'Automatic Denial of Bail and the European Convention' [1999] Crim LR 300; and 'Editorial: Bail and Human Rights' [2000] Crim LR 69 for discussion of the English response to incorporation of the European Convention on Human Rights, Art 5(3).
3   (19 June 2001), paras 19–24 at para 22 (violations of ECHR, Art 5(3) and (5) established).

Conditional release on guarantees to appear for trial

4.77   Release of a detainee may be made conditional on guarantees to appear for trial. Such guarantees are not restricted to the deposit of a monetary surety[1]. While the European Convention on Human Rights, Article 5(3) does not imply any right to release on bail as such, it places an obligation upon the state to offer release on whatever terms are required to secure the presence of the accused at any subsequent trial, whenever the sole reason for detaining an individual on remand is the risk of his absconding[2]. In calculating the requisite amount or determining the guarantees to be secured, the state authorities may take into account any relevant personal factors of the individual (for example, his means and his relationship with the person supplying security). The issue is 'the degree of confidence that is possible that the prospect of loss of the security or of action against the guarantors in case of his non-appearance at the trial will act as a sufficient deterrent to dispel any wish on his part to abscond'[3], rather than any financial amount involved in the case. To this end, the individual must co-operate by providing information on his financial means[4], but this does not necessarily absolve the state authorities from considering other relevant information which they themselves possess[5].

1 10670/83, *Schmid v Austria* (1995) DR 44, 195.
2 *Wemhoff v Germany* (1968) A 7, Law, para 15 (choice of conditions to be imposed will normally in financial cases involve the deposit of bail or monetary security).
3 *Neumeister v Austria* (1968) A 8, Law, para 14.
4 8224/78, *Bonnechaux v Switzerland* (1979) DR 18, 100.
5 8339/78, *Schertenleib v Switzerland* (1980) DR 23, 37.

DECISIONS OF DOMESTIC COURTS AND LEGISLATIVE REFORM IN RELATION TO BAIL

4.78   More generally, Scottish law and practice relating to bail have undergone significant change in response to the incorporation of the European Convention on Human Rights, Article 5(3). Certain changes were made by the Bail, Judicial Appointments, etc (Scotland) Act 2000. In particular, the Act placed a duty on the sheriff or judge to consider whether to grant bail at the accused's first appearance in court without the need for an application, so as to satisfy the need for an automatic judicial review of detention; it repealed provisions which precluded the sheriff from considering bail where a person had been charged with or convicted of murder or treason, or where a person had been charged with or convicted of attempted murder, culpable homicide, rape or attempted rape and had a previous conviction for one of these offences or for murder or manslaughter; it provided that where an accused was already in custody for another matter, the court was required to consider bail for the new offence; and it enabled the accused to appeal to the High Court against the decision of a sheriff to refuse bail on first appearance or the refusal of an application made prior to committal, bringing the right of appeal of a person arrested on petition into line with that of a person charged on complaint and with that of the prosecutor. A further change was effected by the decision of the High Court of Justiciary in *Burn, Petitioner*. The petitioner's application for bail had been opposed by the Crown on the ground that it had further inquiries to carry out which would be prejudiced by his release on bail. They did not give any further information about the inquiries. The sheriff refused bail, in accordance with the approach laid down in an earlier decision of the High Court. In the instant case, the High Court held that the previous approach did not meet the requirements of Article 5(3), as it effectively enjoined the sheriff not to consider the merits of the accused's continued detention for himself but to defer to the statement by the Crown. The court held that in future the Crown must provide sufficient general information relating to the particular case to allow the sheriff to consider the merits of their motion that the accused should be committed to prison and detained there for further examination. It is not necessary for the Crown to disclose operational details. On the other hand, where for example the Crown opposed bail on the ground of the risk that the accused would interfere with witnesses, it should be in a position to explain the basis for that fear. Where opposition to bail is based on some such ground and the relevant inquiry is completed before the date for further examination (ie within eight days), the Crown should bring the matter back before the sheriff so that he can, if so advised, order the accused's release from custody[1].

The effect of Article 5 on the English law governing bail was also considered with care in *R (Director of Public Prosecutions) v Havering Magistrates' Court*. The court noted that the breach of a bail condition did not in itself entitle a court to withdraw bail, since it would not constitute a justification for detention under Article 5. The breach of a condition might be some evidence, even powerful evidence, of a relevant risk arising. Article 5 did not require proof of material facts by the production of evidence or subject to cross-examination of witnesses. What was necessary was that the court should come to an honest and rational opinion on the material put before it, taking proper account of the quality of that material and ensuring that the defendant had a full and fair opportunity to comment on and answer that material[2].

1   2000 SCCR 384.
2   [2001] 1 WLR 805.

Release or 'trial within a reasonable time'

4.79   The quality of the evidence used initially to justify detention on 'reasonable suspicion' may in time become weaker and hence insufficient to sustain the loss of liberty[1]. However, the continuation of 'reasonable suspicion' will be insufficient in itself to justify the continuation of pretrial detention. 'The persistence of a reasonable suspicion that the person arrested has committed an offence is a condition *sine qua non* for the lawfulness of the continued detention, but after a certain lapse of time it no longer suffices'[2] since the grounds for the continuing refusal of release pending trial also require to be both relevant and sufficient. In *Ječius v Lithuania*, for example, the only reasons adduced by the state for the persistence of the applicant's detention on remand on suspicion of murder and which had lasted almost 15 months had been the gravity of the offence and the strength of evidence against him. For the European Court of Human Rights, while the reasonableness of the suspicion may have initially justified the detention, it could not in itself constitute a 'relevant and sufficient' ground for the continuation of the custody for this length of time and, accordingly, there had been a violation of the guarantee[3]. Domestic courts must consequently 'examine all the circumstances arguing for or against the existence of a genuine requirement of public interest justifying, with due regard to the principle of the presumption of innocence, a departure from the rule of respect for individual liberty and set them out in their decisions on the applications for release'[4], and not simply apply a presumption that detention is justified solely on account of the gravity of the charges[5]. Relevant reasons justifying continuing detention include the danger that the accused if liberated would suppress evidence or bring pressure to bear on witnesses[6] or collude with accomplices[7] or flee to escape justice[8], or commit additional offences[9], or that his release would provoke public disorder[10] or place the accused in a position of danger from others[11]. On the other hand, his state of health is not a relevant factor under the European Convention on Human Rights, Article 5[12]. Since the sufficiency of such reasons may change with time, they must be able to be challenged periodically in accordance with paragraph (4).

1 Cf *Labita v Italy* (6 April 2000), paras 156–161 (detention initially justified upon uncorroborated hearsay statements made by a former member of the Mafia, but no further evidence to corroborate the allegations had been uncovered during inquiries, and no account had been taken of the fact that the accusations against the applicant had been based on evidence which had become weaker rather than stronger).
2 *Jecius v Lithuania* (31 July 2000), at para 93; cf *Punzelt v Czech Republic* (25 April 2000), paras 71–82 (detention pending extradition on charges of fraud and forgery: no violation on account of the refusal to release on bail).
3 (31 July 2000), para 94 (the Court noted that the suspicion in any case had not been proved substantiated by the trial court which had acquitted the applicant).
4 *Tomasi v France* (1992) A 241-A, at para 84.
5 *Ilijkov v Bulgaria* (26 July 2001), paras 81–87 at para 87 ('by failing to address concrete relevant facts and by relying solely on a statutory presumption based on the gravity of the charges and which shifted to the accused the burden of proving that there was not even a hypothetical danger of absconding, re-offending or collusion, the authorities prolonged the applicant's detention on grounds which cannot be regarded as sufficient': violation). See also *Kreps v Poland* (26 July 2001), paras 42–45 (reliance by the state upon the serious nature of the offences and the need to ensure proper conduct of the trial without adequate consideration of relevant factors recognised by Convention case law: violation).
6 *Wemhoff v Germany* (1968) A 7, Law, paras 13–14; cf *Letellier v France* (1991) A 207, paras 37–39 (any initial and genuine fear of pressure being brought to bear on witnesses would diminish with the passing of time).
7 *Ringeisen v Austria* (1971) A 13, paras 105–106; *I A v France* 1998-VII, 2951, para 109.
8 *Wemhoff v Germany* (1968) A 7, Law, paras 13–14; *Neumeister v Austria* (1968) A 8, Law, paras 9–12; *Letellier v France* (1991) A 207, paras 40–43.
9 *Stögmüller v Austria* (1969) A 9, Law, paras 13–14; *Matznetter v Austria* (1969) A 10, Law, paras 7–9.
10 *Letellier v France* (1991) A 207, paras 47–51.
11 Eg *I A v France* 1998-VII, 2951, para 108.
12 *Kudla v Poland* (26 October 2000), para 93; *Jabłoński v Poland* (21 December 2000), para 82. Cf paras 4.34–4.35 above, for discussion of European Convention on Human Rights, Art 3 considerations.

4.80 'Trial within a reasonable time' under the European Convention on Human Rights, Article 5(3) will thus initially involve assessment of whether pre-trial detention was justified by reasons which were both relevant and sufficient, but the European Court of Human Rights in addition will consider whether the proceedings have been unduly prolonged by avoidable delay[1]. Inactivity on the part of prosecuting officials will suggest a lack of due diligence[2], but the requirement 'must not stand in the way of the efforts of the judges to clarify fully the facts in issue, to give both the defence and the prosecution all facilities for putting forward their evidence and stating their cases and to pronounce judgment only after careful reflection'[3]. The behaviour of the applicant himself may be a factor in the prolonging of pre-trial detention[4]. The question of time held on remand is unlikely often to cause difficulty in Scots law on account of the 110-day rule[5]. In practical terms, the approach taken to determination of the 'reasonableness' of time spent in pre-trial detention in other European

countries[6] continues to be a significant weakness in Strasbourg jurisprudence. It seems to reflect an unwillingness to impose upon states the basic
task of making sufficient resources available to ensure effective and
speedy justice. In several European countries, the high percentage of
remand prisoners (in some cases, over 40 per cent of the total prison population) is not considered unreasonable[7]. Further, pre-trial detention in
excess of four years can in some cases be deemed acceptable[87], and even
those few judgments which condemn particular lengthy detention hardly
encourage optimism that a more demanding approach is being adopted[9].
There is no suggestion of a maximum period of pre-trial detention beyond
which continuing detention is likely to be unacceptable as, for example,
with the 110-day-rule in Scots law. There is an unfortunate contrast
between the concern expressed for the initial safeguard of a 'prompt'
appearance before a judicial officer under the first part of Article 5(3), and
the protracted investigations permitted thereafter. The Court's reasoning
has also been criticised on a number of grounds. First, if 'the justifiable
length of an investigation' was 'automatically co-extensive with the justifiable length of pre-trial detention', then 'it would be possible to conceive
of a case of such extreme complexity as to justify a detention of, say, ten
years or more'[10]. In any case, 'complexity' here is primarily judged by
reference to the efficiency and effectiveness of national law enforcement
resources, while the harm which detention can occasion to the resources
available to an accused for his defence does not appear to have been taken
into account. Second, the importance attached to the consideration that
the period of pre-trial detention will probably be deducted from any
sentence imposed on conviction (or at least taken into account) does not
sit altogether happily with the presumption of innocence. Third, it is still
more difficult to understand why the full exercise of an applicant's rights
under domestic law permitting him to seek to secure release or to refuse to
co-operate with investigating or prosecuting authorities should justify
even lengthier detention[11].

1 *Wemhoff v Germany* (1968) A 7, Law, para 16. For recent examples of Strasbourg scrutiny
   of the relevancy and sufficiency of reasons, see *I A v France* 1998-VII, 2951 (63-month
   detention period deemed violation of the European Convention on Human Rights, Art
   5(3)), and *Jabłoński v Poland* (21 December 2000) (detention on remand in excess of 57
   months considered excessive). The safeguard replicates to some extent the guarantee to a
   hearing 'within a reasonable time' under ECHR, Art 6(1), but special diligence is expected
   where an accused is in detention: *Herczegfalvy v Austria* (1992) A 244, para 71.
2 Eg *Assenov and Ors v Bulgaria* 1998-VIII, 3264, paras 151–158 (12-month period in which
   virtually no action was taken by investigatory authorities); *Punzelt v Czech Republic* (25
   April 2000), paras 71–82 (reasons for detention which lasted over 30 months were relevant and sufficient, but lack of due diligence on the part of the courts).
3 *Wemhoff v Germany* (1968) A 7, Law, at para 17.
4 8339/78, *Schertenleib v Switzerland* (1980) DR 23, 137 at paras 185–187.
5 On the situation where an accused is committed in respect of one offence is then
   committed in respect of another offence, causing the 110-day period to run afresh (*Ross v
   HM Advocate* 1990 SCCR 182), some assistance may be gained *from R (Wardle) v Crown
   Court at Leeds* [2001] 2 WLR 865 which considered Art 5(3) in the context of a broadly
   analogous situation under English law.
6 Continental systems may provide that execution of a sentence cannot take place until
   after disposal of any pending appeal, and label any detention after conviction but
   pending determination of appeal as a continuation of pre-trial detention. Cf *B v Austria*
   (1990) A 175, paras 34–40 (as the trial court had pronounced guilt, given a statement of its
   principal reasons, had imposed a sentence of imprisonment and also ordered continuing

detention pending disposal of the appeal, this detention fell to be considered as deprivation of liberty after conviction).

7 See further Council of Europe *Prison Overcrowding and Prison Population Inflation: Recommendation No R (99) 22 and Report* (2000) pp 31 and 36 (pre-trial detention rates in 1997 per 100,000 of population range from 4 (Iceland) to over 35 (France, Italy, Portugal and Turkey); in central and eastern Europe, the rates range from 10 (FYRO Macedonia) to 174 (Russian Federation). The figures for Scotland and England and Wales were 16 and 17 respectively). For an overview of European (and other) systems, see Dünkel and Vagg (eds) *Untersuchungshaft and Untersuchungshaftvollzug: Waiting for Trial* (2 vols, 1994).

8 *W v Switzerland* (1993) A 254-A, paras 31–43. See too *Contrada v Italy* 1998-V, paras 54–68 (reasons for 31-month detention of senior police officer accused by Mafia informants of serious crimes considered relevant and sufficient throughout this period). See too *Van der Tang v Spain* (1995) A 321, paras 60–75 (while the Court would have welcomed 'more detailed reasoning' for the reasons for pre-trial detention, there was still an 'evident and significant risk' of absconding; and the state was also entitled to conjoin the cases of co-accused, even although the applicant's case itself did not appear particularly complex).

9 Cf *Muller v France* 1997-II, 374, paras 35–48 (four-year detention of individual who had immediately accepted guilt to allow conjoining of case with co-accused 'necessary and sufficient' reason; but some undue delay on part of state authorities in the circumstances); *Vaccaro v Italy* (16 November 2000), at para 44 ('the considerable duration' of the pre-trial detention 'should have been based on particularly convincing reasons'); *IA v France* 1998-VII, 2951, paras 96–112 (63-month-long detention considered 'excessive'); and *Scott v Spain* 1996-VI, 2382, paras 75–84 (pre-trial detention of 4 years and 16 days not justified: while real risk of absconding, the case was not complex and special diligence had not been observed).

10 Dissenting judgment of Judge Cremona in *Matznetter v Austria* (1969) A 10.

11 Eg 8224/78, *Bonnechaux v Switzerland* (1979) DR 18, 100 at 147.

Article 5(4): Judicial determination of the lawfulness of deprivation of liberty

4.81 The inspiration for the European Convention on Human Rights, Article 5(4) allowing a detainee access to a court to challenge the lawfulness of the deprivation of liberty is found in the remedy of *habeas corpus* in Anglo–American jurisprudence. The guarantee involves provision of review of both procedural and substantive requirements of domestic law together with the reasonableness of the suspicion justifying the continuing loss of liberty; however, it does not as such imply a right of appeal against a decision imposing or continuing detention[1], although where domestic law does indeed provide such a right of appeal, the appellate body itself must comply with the requirements of the paragraph[2]. 'Lawfulness', quite simply, has the meaning given to it under Article 5(1), and thus is tested 'in the light not only of the requirements of domestic law, but also of the text of the Convention, the general principles embodied therein and the aims of the restrictions permitted by Article 5(1)'[3]. All forms of deprivation of liberty are covered by the guarantee[4], for the essential purpose is to provide the individual with an effective review of the legality of his original detention and any continuing detention. Periodic review of deprivation of liberty must be available during pre-trial detention[5], and also after conviction and sentence where the sentence contains any element which is indeterminate[6]. This guarantee applies concurrently with paragraph (3) in respect of those detained on suspicion of having committed an offence or to prevent commission or flight under paragraph (1)(c)[7], but if the national authorities release the individual before it is practicable for any hearing to

occur (as, for example, where there has been detention followed by immediate expulsion from a state's territory) the applicant will be deemed not
to have suffered any harm under this heading and will be unable to use
para (4) to challenge the legality of the original deprivation of liberty[8]. The
procedures for challenge must have a judicial character and provide
appropriate safeguards[9]. Once the legal justification for detention ceases,
the detainee must be released without undue delay[10].

1 *Ječius v Lithuania* (31 July 2000), at para 100 ('the provision speaks of "proceedings" and
   not of appeals').
2 *Toth v Austria* (1991) A 224, para 84; *Grauzinis v Lithuania* (10 October 2000), para 32.
3 *Brogan and Ors v United Kingdom* (1988) A 145-B, para 65; *E v Norway* (1990) A 181-A, para
   49.
4 *De Wilde, Ooms and Versyp v Belgium* ('Vagrancy cases') (1971) A 12, para 73.
5 Cf *Assenov and Ors v Bulgaria* 1998-VIII, 3264, paras 162–165 (domestic law only permitted
   remand prisoners one opportunity to challenge lawfulness of detention; lack of any
   further opportunity to have continuing detention (of two years) determined led to violation).
6 Where a fixed sentence of imprisonment is imposed for the purposes of punishment, the
   supervision required by Article 5(4) is incorporated in that court decision: *V v United
   Kingdom* (16 December 1999), para 199; 32072/96, *Mansell v United Kingdom* (2 July 1997)
   F Ct HR. These decisions were applied in relation to the recall of a prisoner released on
   licence in *Varey v The Scottish Ministers* 2001 SC 162.
7 *De Jong, Baljet and Van den Brink v Netherlands* (1984) A 77, para 57.
8 7376/76, *X and Y v Sweden* (1976) DR 7, 123. The European Convention on Human Rights,
   Art 5(4) is in general regarded as the *lex specialis* concerning complaints of unlawful
   deprivation of liberty, and thus where a *detained* applicant also invokes ECHR, Art 13
   (which requires an effective remedy to be provided in domestic law to challenge arguable
   breaches of the Convention), the Court will normally declare the Art 13 issue inadmissible if it has admitted the Article 5(4) complaint for further determination: see eg
   37555/97, *O'Hara v United Kingdom* (14 March 2000).
9 See *R (DPP) v Havering Magistrates' Court* [2001] 1 WLR 805.
10 Cf *Quinn v France* (1995) A 311, paras 39–43 (a court ordered release of the applicant but
   this was delayed to allow the public prosecutor to be notified; the Court accepted that
   while some delay in executing such an instruction is understandable, the particular delay
   (of 11 hours) resulted in a violation of ECHR, Art 5(1)).

The notion of 'incorporated supervision'

4.82   The purpose of the European Convention on Human Rights,
Article 5(4) is to secure judicial overview of the legality of deprivation of
liberty. Where the particular detention has been ordered by a court,
'incorporated supervision' will be deemed to have taken place: that is,
the responsibility for ensuring judicial scrutiny will be accepted as having been discharged by the original tribunal. The most straightforward
example of 'incorporated supervision' will occur where a fixed term of
imprisonment is imposed after 'conviction by a competent court' in
terms of Article 5(1)(a); more complex issues may arise, however, where
prisoners have been transferred between countries in terms of international agreements[1]. For incorporated supervision requirements to be satisfied, it is essential that the procedure adopted is of a judicial character
which provides appropriate guarantees to the individual. In *De Wilde,
Ooms and Versyp v Belgium*, the applicants had been brought before a
magistrate who had placed them at the 'disposal' of the government in
terms of vagrancy laws. The failure to provide a further review body
having the attributes of a 'court' to allow review of the decisions of the
magistrate (who was acting in an administrative capacity rather than as a

judicial officer) resulted in a violation of the paragraph[2]. In *Winterwerp v Netherlands*, neither the original detention of the applicant under mental health legislation ordered by the local mayor nor the subsequent confirmation of the deprivation of liberty by the court afforded the applicant or any representative of his the opportunity to be heard, and there was thus no opportunity of testing the legality of detention[3]. In the related cases of *T v United Kingdom* and *V v United Kingdom*, the setting of the punitive 'tariff' element in an indeterminate sentence had been the responsibility of the Home Secretary rather than a task assigned to an independent tribunal and, accordingly, there had been a violation of fair hearing guarantees under Article 6. Further, on this account, it was not possible to conclude that the supervision required by Article 5(4) had been incorporated in the trial court's sentence[4].

1 See *Drodzd and Janousek v France and Spain* (1992) A 240, paras 104–111; *Iribarne Pérez v France* (1995) A 325-C, paras 26–33.
2 *De Wilde, Ooms and Versyp v Belgium* ('Vagrancy cases') (1971) A 12, paras 76–80.
3 (1979) A 33, paras 54–61.
4 (16 December 1999), paras 105–121; (16 December 1999), paras 106–122. The position of life prisoners is discussed at para 4.87 below.

Periodic review of continuing detention

4.83 More significantly, the European Convention on Human Rights, Article 5(4) may require judicial scrutiny of the lawfulness of continuing pre-trial or post-conviction detention since the circumstances under which the original decision to detain was taken may have changed: for example, an individual may have ceased to qualify as 'dangerous' or 'of unsound mind'[1]. The form of deprivation of liberty involved will largely determine the regularity with which periodic review is required: review of pre-trial detention is called for at monthly intervals, but other forms of loss of liberty such as the committal of persons to a mental hospital may allow lengthier intervals between reviews[2]. Further, where the detention in question has followed upon conviction of a criminal offence, periodic review of continuing detention may still be called for. In the early case of *Van Droogenbroeck v Belgium*, the applicant had been sentenced to imprisonment for two years and in addition had been placed 'at the disposal of the government' for ten years as having a persistent tendency to crime. Since 'persistent tendency' and 'danger to society' were 'essentially relative concepts [which involved] monitoring the development of the offender's personality and behaviour in order to adapt his situation to favourable or unfavourable changes in his circumstances', periodic review was necessary[3]. Likewise, if a sentence of imprisonment contains an element which is indeterminate, Article 5(4) may demand periodic review to ensure that continuing detention continues to be lawful.

1 Cf *Soumare v France* 1998-V, 2201, para 38 (imposition of fine with imprisonment if in default; lawfulness of imprisonment was thus dependent upon applicant's solvency, a factor which could change through time, and thus periodic review of detention was required).
2 In jurisprudence, this matter strictly falls within the question as to the 'speedy' availability of review (see para 4.100 below) but in this work is given separate treatment.
3 (1982) A 50, para 49.

REVIEW OF PRE-TRIAL DETENTION

4.84   Review of pre-trial detention may be required at intervals of one month because of the Convention's insistence that detention on remand is to be strictly limited[1]. The review must permit consideration of both the continuing reasonableness of the suspicion which initially justified the deprivation of liberty as well as the relevancy and sufficiency of the grounds for refusal to release on bail. In *Ječius v Lithuania*, for example, although the appellate courts had noted that the lawfulness of the appli- cant's detention was open to question, they had failed to address his complaints and thus the applicant had been denied the opportunity of contesting the procedural and substantive conditions which had been essential for the continuing lawfulness of the pre-trial detention[2].

1   *Bezicheri v Italy* (1989) A 164, para 21; *Assenov and Ors v Bulgaria* 1998-VIII, 3264, at para 162 (review of pre-trial detention must be available 'at short intervals'); *Jabłoński v Poland* (21 December 2000), paras 91–94 at 94 (while a period of 43 days 'may prima facie appear not to be excessively long', in light of the circumstances this was considered an excessive delay).
2   (31 July 2000), paras 101–102. See too *Grauslys v Lithuania* (10 October 2000), paras 53–55.

MENTAL HEALTH DETENTION

4.85   Mental condition is perhaps the clearest example of a condition susceptible to change through time[1] and which will thus call for periodic review at regular intervals[2]. Issues have arisen in relation to both the avail- ability of review[3] and the nature of the safeguards available[4] in mental health cases[5], but whether the right to take proceedings exists may well depend upon careful categorisation of the deprivation of liberty. In *Silva Rocha v Portugal*, an individual who had been declared to be a danger to the public on account of a mental disorder had been placed in custody for a minimum of three years. While the trial court had concluded that the facts as established constituted aggravated homicide, it had also decided that the applicant could not be held criminally responsible for his actions and thus had ordered his placement in a psychiatric institution. Only at the end of this period was he entitled under domestic law to take proceed- ings to test whether his mental condition required his continuing deten- tion. For the Strasbourg Court, the deprivation of liberty had been lawful both as a conviction within the meaning of the European Convention on Human Rights, Article 5(1)(a) and also as a 'security measure' applied to a 'person of unsound mind' in terms of paragraph (1)(e). The offence and the risk posed to others had justified the applicant's detention for at least three years, and the requirement of 'incorporated supervision' had been met at the time the detention was ordered by the trial court. It followed that only after the expiry of this period would the requirement of 'periodic review' be triggered. Earlier cases were distinguished on account of the specific findings in the present instance by the trial court of the indi- vidual's dangerousness and his likelihood of re-offending[6]. This decision is not without difficulty, as it seems to collapse the all-important distinc- tion accepted in earlier decisions between the elements of retribution and protection of the public in the imposition of custodial sentences.

How often review is required is not clearly established by case law. In *Herzcegfalvy v Austria*, the Court considered that delays between automatic reviews of detention on the ground of mental illness of fifteen months and two years were unreasonable[7]. The emerging principle sees to be that domestic arrangements must be sufficiently flexible to reflect the self-evident fact that there are significant differences in the personal circumstances of each individual detained, and where a patient is seen to be making real progress, review should be available[8].

1 See Mason 'The Legal Aspects and Implications of Risk Assessment' [2000] Med L Rev 69.
2 Cf *Megyeri v Germany* (1992) A 237-A, para 22 ('reasonable intervals' for mental health reviews not defined).
3 In 10213/82, *Gordon v United Kingdom* (1985) DR 47, 36 an individual confined to a mental hospital by a criminal court under the Mental Health (Scotland) Act 1960 challenged his return to a secure hospital after having spent a period in an ordinary mental hospital with leave privileges. Scots law did not make provision for periodic review of the need for continuing detention at the time when the application was made, a deficiency which had been condemned by the Court when it considered similar English legislation as failing to meet the requirements of the European Convention on Human Rights, Art 5(4): cf *X v United Kingdom* (1981) A 46. Accordingly, the Commission applied the Court's decision, but since Scots law was subsequently amended (by virtue of the Mental Health (Amendment) (Scotland) Act 1983) to meet the problem, the Committee of Ministers resolved that no further action was required (Resolution DH(86)9). See also *Croke v Ireland* (21 December 2000) (complaints by mental health detainee as to the absence of an independent review prior to initial detention (or immediately thereafter) and in respect of the absence of a periodic, independent and automatic review of his detention thereafter: friendly settlement achieved in light of the Irish Government's intention to secure an amendment to domestic law); and 44872/98, *Magalhães Pereira v Portugal* (30 March 2000) (repeated attempts by an applicant, a former lawyer, to secure release on the basis of a report suggesting that he could be released on condition he accepted psychiatric support and continued to take his medicine rejected by the domestic courts on the basis that his mental illness prevented him from comprehending the abstract concept of habeas corpus: application declared admissible).
4 *X v United Kingdom* (1981) A 46, paras 55–62; cf *Johnson v United Kingdom* 1997-VII, 2391, paras 50–68 and 72 (issue considered under ECHR, Art 5(1) rather than para (4)).
5 In *Hirst v United Kingdom* (24 July 2001), para 41, the Court was not persuaded that it was possible to distinguish between cases of mental disorder resulting in detention on the ground of mental illness and those resulting in indeterminate imprisonment on the grounds of mental instability posing risks of dangerousness.
6 1996-V, 1913, paras 26–32.
7 (1992) A 244, paras 75–78 (a period of nine months between reviews was not, however, criticised).
8 Cf *Hirst v United Kingdom* (24 July 2001), paras 38 and 42.

DECISIONS OF DOMESTIC COURTS ON REVIEW OF MENTAL HEALTH DETENTION

4.86 The effect of the European Convention on Human Rights, Article 5(4) in the context of mental health detention was considered by the Court of Session in *A v The Scottish Ministers*, the facts of which have already been discussed[1]. The applicants argued in the first place that the introduction of the 'serious harm' test was inconsistent with Article 5(4) because it meant that the review of the lawfulness of the patient's detention was not confined to an examination of the continuing existence of the matters – in particular, a mental disorder requiring treatment – on the basis of which the patient had been originally detained. This argument was held to be unsound. Since the 'serious harm' test applied also to the Scottish Ministers' power to order the patient's discharge, it could constitute a (new) lawful ground for the patient's detention. Article 5(4) therefore required that that new ground should be susceptible of periodic review. The fact that the ground to be reviewed was different from the original ground for detention did not make the review unlawful under Article 5. The applicants further argued that the review required by Article 5(4) must comply with the principle of the rule of law; and it was argued that the retrospective application of the Mental Health (Public Safety and Appeals) (Scotland) Act 1999 to pending proceedings violated that principle. The court considered Strasbourg jurisprudence concerning Article 6, and concluded that the principle of the rule of law and the notion of a fair hearing would generally preclude any interference with a court's conduct of a patient's application for release with the purpose of influencing its determination. Such interference could, however, be justified on compelling grounds of general interest: any interference would have to be proportionate to the public interest which it sought to secure, and the court had to treat any reasons adduced to justify such an interference with the greatest possible degree of circumspection. In the instant case, however, it was hard to imagine a more compelling public interest than the protection of the public from violent or lethal attacks by persons with a prior history of homicide related to an untreatable mental disorder; and the measure of retrospection was a proportionate means of achieving the protection of the public[2].

1 See para 4.65 above.
2 2001 SC 1. This decision has been upheld by the JCPC: 15 October 2001, unreported. Other domestic decisions are cited at paras 4.65, 4.99 and 4.100.

LIFE IMPRISONMENT AND DETENTION WITHOUT LIMIT OF TIME

4.87 Issues under the European Convention on Human Rights, Article 5(4) have also arisen in cases concerning sentences of life imprisonment. In the United Kingdom, such a sentence is mandatory when a person aged 21 or over is convicted of murder, and can also be imposed at the discretion of the court in other cases. The corresponding sentence in the case of a person aged between 18 and 21 is one of detention for life; where a person under 18 is convicted of murder, the mandatory sentence is one of detention without limit of time. The Strasbourg case law to date has accepted that there is a justifiable difference in the treatment of mandatory and discretionary life prisoners. In the case of *Thynne, Wilson and Gunnell v United Kingdom* the Court held that, unlike mandatory life sentences, a discretionary life sentence is imposed not only because the offence is a serious one but because, in addition to the need for punishment, the accused is considered to be a danger to the public. Such sentences were therefore composed of a punitive element and a security element. Once the prisoner had served the 'tariff' or punitive part of the sentence, the justification for further detention was continuing dangerousness: something which was susceptible of change. Once the punitive element of the sentence had expired, Article 5(4) therefore required that the prisoner's continued detention should be reviewed by a court-like body at regular intervals[1]. The earlier case of *Weeks v United Kingdom* had also established that the Parole Board could not be considered to be a 'court-like body' unless it had the power to decide, rather than merely to advise Ministers. In that case a discretionary life prisoner had been released but then recalled to prison by executive order. Since any decision to recall the applicant on any ground inconsistent with the objectives of the sentence could have been a breach of Art 5(1), the Court held that the applicant was entitled to judicial scrutiny of the lawfulness of his recall[2].

What 'regular intervals' meant was not, however, settled in Strasbourg jurisprudence. Some clarification is now available: and the key principle is that domestic arrangements for periodic review must be sufficiently flexible to allow the timing of reviews to be dependent upon the particular circumstances of each individual rather than administrative convenience. In *Oldham v United Kingdom*, the European Court on Human Rights considered that the system of automatic review of discretionary life sentences at periods of two years or less as determined by the Secretary of State violated the requirements of Article 5(4) since this had been insufficiently adaptable to allow the applicant to seek earlier release after completion of rehabilitative work which had been required of him on his recall to prison[3]. Further, in *Hirst v United Kingdom*, the Court held that delays of twenty-one months and two years between reviews in a case in which the applicant had been sentenced to life imprisonment for manslaughter on the ground of diminished responsibility were unreasonable. While the Court did not want to rule on the maximum permissible period between reviews which should apply to such categories of life prisoner, established case law indicated in the case of persons detained on mental health grounds that periods between reviews of fifteen months and two years had not been considered reasonable. In the applicant's case, the mental disorder had arisen not in the context of mental illness but of mental instability posing risks of dangerousness, and the Court could not accept there were grounds for accepting that the latter category was less susceptible to change over time[4].

1 (1990) A 190-A, para 76; cf 21681/93 *W, H and A v United Kingdom* (16 January 1995) (applicants at liberty at time of application and thus not 'victims', therefore unable to challenge issue of revocation of life licence).
2 (1984) A 117, paras 56–58.
3 (26 September 2000), paras 28–37 (at para 32, the Court distinguished the Commission's report in 20488/92, *AT v United Kingdom* (29 November 1995) where a period of almost two years before review of a discretionary life sentence was considered not justified in circumstances where the Parole Board had recommended review within one year).
4 (24 July 2001), paras 36–44, citing *Herzegfalvy v Austria* (1992) A 244, discussed at para 4.85 above (the lack of recommendation for earlier review of the case and considerations of rehabilitation and monitoring had been insufficient to justify the delays between reviews as there had been evidence that the applicant had made progress in behaviour).

4.88 In *Hussain v United Kingdom* and *Singh v United Kingdom*, the European Court of Human Rights held that the principles set out in *Thynne, Wilson and Gunnell v United Kingdom*[1] and *Weeks v United Kingdom*[2] applied also to persons sentenced to an indeterminate period of detention (in Scotland, detention without limit of time) for murders committed by them when they were under the age of 18. The Court considered that an indeterminate term of detention for a convicted young person, which may last as long as that person's life, can be justified only by considerations based on the need to protect the public, considerations which must of necessity take into account any developments in the young offender's personality and attitude as he or she grows older. Failure to respect the maturation process implied that young persons would be treated as having forfeited their liberty for the rest of their lives, a situation which might give rise to questions under the European Convention on Human Rights, Article 3.

Against that background, that the only justifiable ground for continued detention after any punitive 'tariff' had been served was a characteristic which was susceptible to change with the passage of time, the Court held that such persons were entitled under Article 5(4) to have the grounds for their continued detention reviewed by a court at reasonable intervals[3].

In the cases of *T v United Kingdom* and *V v United Kingdom* the Court again drew a distinction between the sentencing of an adult murderer and that of a juvenile. It held that Article 6 applies to the process of setting a punishment period or tariff for a person convicted of murder aged under 18 (and, it would follow, for a discretionary life prisoner also), and that the punishment period should therefore be fixed by a court and not by the executive[4]. The Court further held that the failure to fix any new tariff, following the quashing of the original tariff fixed by the Home Secretary, meant that the applicants' entitlement to access to a tribunal for periodical review of the continuing lawfulness of their detention (as required by Article 5(4), following the *Hussain* and *Singh* judgments) had not been met[5].

1   (1990) A 190-A.
2   (1987) A 114.
3   1996-I, 252, paras 50–62, and 1996-I, 280, paras 58–70. See further McDiarmid 'Children who Murder: What is Her Majesty's Pleasure?' [2000] Crim L R 547.
4   This was already the position in Scots law (unlike English law) by virtue of the Crime and Punishment (Scotland) Act 1997, s 16 which amended the Prisoners and Criminal Proceedings (Scotland) Act 1993, s 2 so as to extend the discretionary life prisoner provisions to murderers under 18 in light of the Court's decisions in *Hussain v United Kingdom* 1996-I, 252 and *Singh v United Kingdom* 1996-I, 280.
5   (16 December 1999) paras 92–100 and paras 93–101 respectively.

4.89   To date, the European Court of Human Rights has refused to apply the same approach to mandatory life sentences, despite some comments by domestic judges that in practice the differences between a mandatory and a discretionary life sentence were narrowing. In *Wynne v United Kingdom* the court held that a mandatory life sentence belonged to a different category from a discretionary life sentence since it is imposed automatically as a punishment for the offence of murder irrespective of considerations about the dangerousness of the offender[1]. It follows that, in mandatory life sentences, the original trial and appeals system satisfy the guarantee of the European Convention on Human Rights, Article 5(4), and there is no additional right to challenge the lawfulness of continued detention. This approach was reiterated by the Commission in *Ryan v United Kingdom*, which concerned a murderer under 21. The Commission accepted that the administrative arrangements for setting a tariff and thereafter considering release fell within the scope of the punishment imposed at the trial[2].

1   (1994) A 294-A, paras 33–38.
2   32875/96 (1 July 1998).

DOMESTIC COMPLIANCE WITH STRASBOURG CASE LAW ON REVIEW OF SENTENCES OF LIFE IMPRISONMENT OR DETENTION WITHOUT LIMIT OF TIME

4.90   As a result of the decisions in *Thynne, Wilson and Gunnell* and *Weeks*, the legislation governing discretionary sentences of life imprisonment (or detention for life) in Scotland was amended by the Prisoners and Criminal

Proceedings (Scotland) Act 1993, s 2. Where a court passes such a sentence, the sentencing judge has a discretion to set a 'designated part' (the period required to be served to satisfy punishment and deterrence) when sentencing the prisoner. In determining the length of the designated part the court considers the seriousness of the offence (and any matters associated with it), previous convictions, and the stage, if any, at which the prisoner pleaded guilty, but not his dangerousness[1]. The court should refrain from setting a designated part only in those rare cases where it is intended that the prisoner should remain in custody for the rest of his life. Once the designated part has expired (and at two-yearly intervals thereafter), the prisoner is entitled to require the Scottish Ministers to refer his case to the Parole Board. In practice, cases are referred automatically and are reviewed more frequently if that is recommended by the Parole Board. If the Parole Board is satisfied that it is no longer necessary for the protection of the public that the prisoner should be confined, it will direct the Scottish Ministers to release him. For these purposes the Board is constituted as a Designated Life Tribunal. The Scottish Ministers are bound to give effect to the Board's direction. The prisoner is released on life licence, and is liable to recall to custody if he fails to comply with the conditions of his licence. Further, as a result of the decisions in *Hussain* and *Singh*, the Crime and Punishment (Scotland) Act 1997, s 16 amended the Prisons and Criminal Proceedings (Scotland) Act 1993, s 2 so as to extend the discretionary life prisoner provisions to murderers under 18.

1 *Clark v HM Advocate* 1997 SCCR 416; *O'Neill v HM Advocate* 1999 SCCR 300.

4.91 Under the arrangements in force until recently[1], the Scottish Ministers had a discretionary power to release mandatory life prisoners following a recommendation of the Parole Board and after consultation with the judiciary. In practice, a non-statutory committee, the Preliminary Review Committee, met in private and considered each case after approximately four years had been served. It was chaired by a civil servant. It recommended to the Scottish Ministers the date for the first review by the Parole Board of the prisoner's suitability for release on life licence. The Scottish Ministers then decided on the timing of the first review in the light of the Committee's recommendation and representations from the prisoner. At the review, the Board focused on the question whether the risk to the public associated with the prisoner's release on life licence was acceptable. The Board made a recommendation to the Scottish Ministers. If the recommendation was in favour of release, the Scottish Ministers were required to consult the judiciary, and invite representations from the prisoner, before deciding whether to accept the recommendation. The release of such prisoners was also affected by the '20-year policy', introduced in 1984, under which prisoners convicted of certain categories of murder could expect to spend not less than 20 years in custody unless there were exceptional circumstances.

Although these procedures relating to adult mandatory life prisoners appeared to be compatible with the European Convention on Human Rights, Articles 5(4) and 6, in terms of existing Strasbourg jurisprudence, the Scottish Ministers considered that there was a risk of a domestic court taking a different view[2]. The Convention Rights (Compliance) (Scotland)

Act 2001 has accordingly brought the arrangements for the sentencing and release of adult mandatory life prisoners into line with those applying to discretionary life prisoners and prisoners sentenced for a murder committed before the age of 18. The 2001 Act also enhances the security of tenure of Parole Board members and ensures that the reappointment and removal of members is not at the discretion of the Scottish Executive, so as to ensure that the Board satisfies the requirements of Article 6.

1 Ie those operating until the relevant provisions of the Convention Rights (Compliance) (Scotland) Act 2001 entered into force on 8 October 2001.
2 The Divisional Court declined to do so, but with expressions of reluctance, in *R (Anderson) v Secretary of State for the Home Department* (22 February 2001, unreported).

EARLY RELEASE OF PRISONERS

4.92   The European Convention on Human Rights cannot, however, be taken to require a domestic legal system to conform to arrangements existing in related jurisdictions to help secure the early release of prisoners. In *Nelson v United Kingdom*, the applicant claimed that differences between Scots and English law in the release of persons sentenced to imprisonment while still minors were discriminatory. Scots law did not provide remission of sentence (as distinct from parole or release on licence) for juvenile offenders, and the applicant alleged that since there was no objective or reasonable justification for such distinctions in the domestic laws of the United Kingdom, this violated Convention guarantees. The Commission considered the application manifestly ill-founded since the Convention did not confer a general right to question the length of any sentence. However, it acknowledged that if any aspect of sentencing policy did appear to affect individuals in a discriminatory way, there could well be an issue under Article 5 taken together with Article 14. Here, distinctions in sentencing policy based upon age reflected the state's need to ensure flexibility in treatment, and differences between the 'penal legislation of two regional jurisdictions' were not related to personal status[1]. Challenges which seek to secure the early release of prisoners under other Convention provisions have also generally been unsuccessful[2].

1 11077/84 (1986) DR 49, 170. Cf Kilkelly *The Child and the European Convention on Human Rights* (1999) p 55, who notes that in 1995 the UN Committee on the Rights of the Child considered this situation was inconsistent with the UN Convention on the Rights of the Child in examining the United Kingdom's report: see UN Doc CRC/C/SR.205, paras 8–11.
2 Cf 11553/85, *Hobgen v United Kingdom* (1986) DR 46, 231 (introduction of more stringent requirements for parole leading to disappointment on part of prisoner not a violation of the European Convention on Human Rights, Art 3).

DOMESTIC REFORM OF PRISON DISCIPLINE

4.93   The deprivation of liberty (through the imposition of additional days, or loss of remission) as a punishment for breaches of prison discipline was suspended in Scotland as from 11 June 2001 on account of concerns that these forms of punishment, imposed by a prison governor, might be at risk of successful challenge under the European Convention on Human Rights[1].

1 The Divisional Court had held otherwise in *R (Greenfield) v Secretary of State for the Home Department* [2001] 1 WLR 1731. See para 5.22, n 6.

Testing the lawfulness of detention

4.94 The effectiveness of domestic procedures in providing review is assessed by considering the proceedings as a whole, since initial short-comings may subsequently be considered to have been remedied by subsequent safeguards[1]. Three general expectations exist: first, the remedy permitting review must be effective and sufficiently certain; second, it must be available through a 'court' enjoying independence and impartiality, able to exact procedural safeguards for the applicant, and also have the power to order the release of the individual; and third, the remedy must be available 'speedily'.

1 *Winterwerp v Netherlands* (1979) A 33, para 62.

AN EFFECTIVE AND SUFFICIENTLY CERTAIN REMEDY

4.95 Effectiveness implies the domestic remedy must be able to secure examination of both discretionary and substantive elements of the decision, not merely whether there has been an abuse of power or defect in the procedure[1]. In *Van Droogenbroeck v Belgium*, for example, one remedy that the state argued met the requirements of the European Convention on Human Rights, Article 5(4) was founded upon old and isolated provisions which had no bearing on the statute under consideration; two remedies were based upon unsettled legal rules which were still evolving; a right to statutory appeal could only address whether detention should be terminated earlier (rather than whether it was lawful); and another remedy could not have resulted in the court ordering the release of the individual[2]. In considering the question whether domestic law provides such a remedy, the European Court of Human Rights will thus take account not only of formal remedies but also the context in which they operate as well as the applicant's personal circumstances[3].

1 *E v Norway* (1990) A 181-A, para 60; cf *Ireland v United Kingdom* (1978) A 25, para 200 (remedies provided at best limited domestic judicial review); *Soumare v France* 1998-V, 2201, para 43 (unresolved issue of French law relied upon by the state).
2 (1982) A 50, paras 49–56.
3 Eg *R M D v Switzerland* 1997-VI, 2003, para 47 (applicant was expecting to be transferred from one canton to another and thus was in a position of great legal uncertainty); *Sakik and Ors v Turkey* 1997-VII, 2609, para 53 (no example of any detainee having successfully invoked particular provisions of domestic law: lack of precedents indicated the uncertainty of these remedies in practice); *Vodenicarov v Slovakia* (21 December 2000), paras 33–45 (possibility of consideration by constitutional court considered an insufficiently certain remedy).

4.96 It is not entirely clear whether Scots law is adequate in this regard. There is one case which suggests an error in Strasbourg's understanding of domestic law concerning the availability of remedies to challenge detention, and domestic law may still be inconsistent with the requirement of the European Convention on Human Rights, Article 5. In *Harkin v United Kingdom* a Northern Ireland citizen who had landed at a Scottish port and subsequently had been detained under prevention of terrorism legislation claimed that British law did not provide an effective remedy to challenge the legality of detention as called for by Article 5(4). The

Commission disposed of this issue by reaffirming an earlier decision that the remedy of habeas corpus was sufficient to meet Convention requirements[1] without being made aware that this English law remedy is not available in Scots law[2].

1 8022/77, 8125/77 and 8027/77, *McVeigh, O'Neill and Evans v United Kingdom* (1981) DR 25, 15.
2 11539/85 (1986) DR 48, 237. Cf *X v United Kingdom* (1981) A 46, paras 58–59 (habeas corpus remedy did not allow a court to examine the medical grounds for detention, and thus was an insufficient remedy for the European Convention on Human Rights, Art 5(4).

PROVISION OF A 'COURT' FOLLOWING JUDICIAL PROCEDURES AND ABLE TO ORDER THE RELEASE OF A DETAINEE

4.97 Review must be available through an independent and impartial[1] 'court' following established procedures and which can order the release of the person detained. Again, what qualifies as a 'court' is interpreted widely, a matter primarily determined by the provision of appropriate judicial procedures[2]. There need not be full 'equality of arms', but an individual must be accorded basic and fundamental procedural guarantees. For example, in *Sanchez-Reisse v Switzerland*, the applicant had been denied the opportunity to make representations in support of his request for release pending a decision whether to extradite him. The European Court of Human Rights considered that in the circumstances he should have been provided with the 'benefit of an adversarial procedure' which could have been discharged by permitting him to submit written comments or by allowing him to appear in person before the court[3].

The procedures required by the European Convention on Human Rights, Article 5(4) will depend upon the particular nature of the detention in issue: that is, 'the Convention requires a procedure of a judicial character with guarantees appropriate to the kind of deprivation of liberty in question'. In other words, the procedures adopted for the purposes of this paragraph need not have provided in all instances the same level of guarantee as would be required by Article 6[4]. This, though, leaves some uncertainty in the jurisprudence, but there are also recent suggestions of a strengthening of procedural requirements, at least in reviews of pre-trial detention. Certainly, in the case of detention falling within the ambit of Article 5 (1)(c) (that is, a person held on detention on suspicion of committing an offence or where detention is reasonably considered necessary to prevent the commission of an offence or the flight of an offender) a hearing will be required[5] in which the principle of equality of arms between the prosecutor and the detained person is respected[6] and where the actual presence of the detainee may be necessary[7]. At the very least, there must be an opportunity to know the case to be met. Indeed, the opportunity to challenge in an effective manner the statements or views put forward by the prosecutor to justify the continuation of pre-trial detention in certain instances will presuppose that the defence be given access to relevant documents. In *Lamy v Belgium*, the judge and the prosecutor had enjoyed access to a detailed investigation file, but the defence had been armed only with such information as could be gleaned from the charges. This was deemed insufficient to permit the applicant to challenge his detention effectively since 'appraisal of the need for a remand in custody and the subsequent assessment of guilt are too closely linked for access to documents to be refused in the former place when the law requires it in the latter case'[8]. As the Court put it in *Garcia Alva v Germany*, the state's legitimate goal in ensuring the efficient investigation of criminal investigations 'cannot be pursued at the expense of substantial restrictions on the rights of the defence'. In consequence, in challenging the continuing lawfulness of pre-trial detention, an accused must be accorded 'a sufficient opportunity to take cognisance of statements and other pieces of evidence underlying them, such as the results of the police and other investigations, irrespective of whether the accused is able to provide any indication as to the relevance for his defence of the pieces of evidence which he seeks to be given access to'[9]. Other categories of detainee may expect similar opportunities. In *Weeks v United Kingdom*, a recalled prisoner did not have the right of full disclosure of documents available to the Parole Board. Such did not 'allow proper participation of the individual adversely affected by the contested decision, this being one of the principal guarantees of a judicial procedure' for the purposes of Article 5[10]. In *Hussain v United Kingdom*, the applicant had only at a late stage been given sight of the reports to be considered by the Parole Board, while in *Singh v United Kingdom*, the prisoner had secured the right to see the reports which had been considered by the Parole Board after seeking judicial review. In neither instance had there been a right to be present at the review of the case. For the Court, 'where a substantial term of imprisonment may be at stake and where characteristics pertaining to [an applicant's] personality and level of maturity are of importance in deciding on his dangerousness', an adversarial hearing with legal representation and the possibility of calling and examining witnesses was appropriate[11].

1 The fact that the judge who determines the question of an accused's detention will also serve as the trial judge examining the merits of the criminal case will not of itself justify fears that he is not impartial since the questions to be considered in each case are different: *Ilijkov v Bulgaria* (26 July 2001), para 97. Cf *D N v Switzerland* (29 March 2001), paras 40–57 (the judge rapporteur who was the sole psychiatric expert among the judges and the only person who had interviewed the applicant had previously expressed on two occasions his opinion the applicant should not be released from mental health detention: objective grounds for believing this judge lacked the necessary impartiality).

2 *De Wilde, Ooms and Versyp v Belgium* (1971) A 12, para 78.

3 (1986) A 107, paras 48–51 at para 51.

4 *Megyeri v Germany* (1992) A 237-A, para 22.

5 *Kampanis v Greece* (1995) A 318-B, paras 47–59; *Wloch v Poland* (19 October 2000), para 126.

6 *Nikolova v Bulgaria* 1999-II, 203, para 58; *Ilijkov v Bulgaria* (26 July 2001), paras 101–105.

7 Eg *Grauzinis v Lithuania* (21 December 2000), at para 34 ('given what was at stake for the applicant, ie his liberty', in addition to factors such as the lapse of time between decisions 'and the re-assessment of the basis for the remand, the applicant's presence was required throughout the pre-trial remand hearings . . . in order to be able to give satisfactory information and instructions to his counsel').

8 (1989) A 151, para 29. See too *Wloch v Poland* (19 October 2000), paras 128–132 (restricted right of access to the court which determined the question of the lawfulness of the detention at a time when the applicant's lawyers had not been given access to the case file: violation of the European Convention on Human Rights, Art 5(4)).

9 (13 February 2001), paras 39–43 at paras 42 and 41.

10 (1987) A 114, para 66 (lack of disclosure of records rendered the procedures of the Parole Board defective).

11 *Hussain v United Kingdom* 1996-I, 252, at paras 58–61; *Singh v United Kingdom* 1996-I, 280, at paras 65–69.

4.98   Although there is no specific right to seek legal assistance in terms of the European Convention on Human Rights, Article 5(4), in certain circumstances legal representation may be required to ensure the effectiveness of any adversarial hearing, for example if the individual is young[1]. The same principle may apply in the case of a person detained on mental health grounds[2]. It also goes without saying that a court in discharging its obligations under Article 5(4) must have available to it the information it requires to be able to come to an assessment of whether the deprivation of liberty has been lawful. This issue has arisen in the context of assertions of national security concerns. In *Chahal v United Kingdom*, the restricted procedural rights then available under British immigration law and the limited effectiveness of judicial review in cases involving issues of national security resulted in an Article 5(4) violation, the European Court of Human Rights noting that legal techniques existed in other countries which could meet national security concerns and at the same time provide 'a substantial measure of procedural justice' to individuals[3].

1   *Bouamar v Belgium* (1988) A 129, para 60.
2   *Winterwerp v Netherlands* (1979) A 33, para 60. Cf 44872/98, *Magalhães Pereira v Portugal* (30 March 2000) (appointment by a judge of a civil servant working in the secure hospital where the applicant was detained to serve as the applicant's representative since the lawyer appointed as his representative was not present: application admissible).
3   1996-V, 435, paras 130–133.

4.99   The 'court' must also have the power to order release. Concerns under the European Convention on Human Rights, Article 5(4) have thus arisen in the context of British mental health law where review tribunals formerly had no authority to order the release of a patient[1]. The powers and procedures of Parole Boards have also in the past been considered wanting since they only had the power to advise Ministers[2]. Despite the introduction of new opportunities for individuals to have sight of the materials being considered at review hearings, the lack of any general power to order a prisoner's release continued to prevent these bodies from satisfying Article 5(4) requirements[3].

1   *X v United Kingdom* (1981) A 46, paras 55–62. Scots law was subsequently changed by the Mental Health (Amendment) (Scotland) Act 1999. Cf 28212/95, *Benjamin and Wilson v United Kingdom* (23 October 1997) (discretionary life sentence prisoners who had been transferred to special hospitals had no right to a review hearing: application declared admissible). See also *R (Von Brandenburg) v East London and the City Mental Health NHS Trust* [2001] 3 WLR 588.
2   In *Weeks v United Kingdom* (13 February 2001), at paras 60–69; and *Thynne, Wilson and Gunnell v United Kingdom* (1990) A 190-A, at para 80.
3   Following these two cases, new interim arrangements seeking to give Parole Boards strengthened powers were again challenged in *Curley v United Kingdom* (28 March 2000), paras 32–34 (detention during HM pleasure for ten years after expiry of tariff; lack of speedy review by body capable of ordering release). Cf *Ječius v Lithuania* (31 July 2000), para 101 (civil proceedings brought by the applicant against the prison administration were irrelevant for the purpose of para (4) since the domestic courts were not able to order the applicant's release; in any event, the civil courts had confined themselves to the question whether formal orders existed authorising the detention rather than its underlying lawfulness). The Convention Rights (Compliance)(Scotland) Act 2001 has amended the law governing parole, see paras 4.90–4.91 above.

4.100 Finally, the review must be 'speedily' available, tested in accordance with the particular circumstances. Both access to a review procedure and the time taken to arrive at a decision are covered[1]. This right is distinguishable from the right an accused person has to be brought 'promptly' before a court under the European Convention on Human Rights, Article 5(3)[2]. Determination of this requirement is dependent on the particular circumstances of each case, and care must be taken in comparing cases or even predicting the likely response of the European Court of Human Rights. Certainly, the examination of the effectiveness of procedural review and the question of speed of review are not wholly separate[3]. In *Sanchez-Reiss v Switzerland*, the applicant's attempts to secure his release pending determination of an extradition decision took 31 and 46 days respectively to be decided, periods labelled 'unwarranted' and 'excessive' by the Court[4]. In *Sakik and Others v Turkey*, requests for release on bail pending trial took a minimum of 12 days to be considered, periods the Court considered incompatible with the guarantee[5]. States are further expected to organise their judicial systems in such a way as to comply with the requirements of the Convention, and thus domestic procedures which involve some complexity may not be relied upon by a state to justify delays in determining requests for release[6]. Nor may a state plead heavy workloads, since the Court considers that Convention obligations require states to organise their legal systems so as to comply with its requirements[7]. Delays calculated in months – rather than in weeks – appear to be in breach of the requirement of speed; but further fine tuning in clarifying whether shorter periods of delay would be acceptable is awaited[8].

1 Access to a review procedure involves discussion of delays between automatic reviews of detention, matters discussed above in respect to the reasonableness of the length of periods between reviews; see paras 4.83–4.89 above.

2 *De Jong, Baljet and Van den Brink v Netherlands* (1984) A 77, paras 57–58

3 Cf *Wloch v Poland* (19 October 2000), paras 131–135 (initial proceedings were 'speedy' but not effective; even assuming subsequent proceedings were effective, they were not 'speedy').

4 *Sanchez-Reiss v Switzerland* (1986) A 107, at paras 59–60.

5 1997-VII, 2609, para 51.

6 *M B v Switzerland* (30 November 2000), paras 27–39, and *G B v Switzerland* (30 November 2000), paras 36–43 (two-tier procedure for determining release from pre-trial detention: delays considered to violate Art 5(4)).

7 Eg *E v Norway* (1990) A 181-A, paras 63–67.

8 Cf *Koendjbiharie v Netherlands* (1990) A 185-B (four-month delay before pre-trial review completed); *E v Norway* (1990) A 181-A, (two-month period which included a five-week delay before a hearing took place); *Erkalo v Netherlands* 1998-VI, 2464, paras 61–64, (complaint that request for release was neither determined speedily nor in accordance with domestic law was disposed of under Art 5(1) rather than para (4), but the Commission had considered that the 16-day period taken did satisfy this requirement). See too *Musial v Poland* 1999-II, 155, at para 44 (delay of 20 months in mental health review 'incompatible with the notion of speediness'unless there are exceptional circumstances); *Vodeničarov v Slovakia* (21 December 2000), paras 33–36 (procedure to review the lawfulness of detention in a mental hospital had been initiated by the applicant but disregarded by the national authorities when they confined him in a mental hospital: violation of Article 5(4)). In *R(C) v Mental Health Review Tribunal London South and South West Region* (3 July 2001, unreported), CA, a practice of routinely listing applications by patients compulsorily detained under the Mental Health Act 1983 for hearing eight weeks after the application date was held to be incompatible with Art 5(4).

Article 5(5): enforceable right to compensation for unlawful deprivation of liberty

4.101   Persons deprived of their liberty in contravention of the European Convention on Human Rights, Article 5 must have a right to compensation. At its most straightforward, Article 5(5) requires the state to provide an enforceable claim for compensation where there has been a violation of any other provision of Article 5[1]. The right thus arises in relation to any deprivation of liberty which was unlawful in domestic law, or which (although lawful in domestic law) is found to have violated Convention guarantees[2]. This paragraph was initially underutilised by applicants. The provision complements the right under Article 41 to 'just satisfaction' for violation of the Convention which is a matter for determination by the European Court of Human Rights; the right to compensation under Article 5(5) must be made available in domestic courts against state authorities responsible for the unlawful arrest or detention, although the guarantee has not been interpreted as requiring any minimum level of payment, or even that any payment should be more than merely nominal[3]. In the past, the United Kingdom's failure to incorporate the Convention into domestic law has resulted in the establishment of violations of this provision[4], although it was accepted that where a civil action of damages against the police for wrongful arrest and detention was available, this would constitute an enforceable right to compensation as required by the guarantee[5]. Where the Convention forms part of domestic law, the Court will consider the constitutional effect of incorporation to ensure that the protection afforded by Article 5(5) is available with sufficient certainty and thus is effective[6].

The obligation is met where an individual is able to seek such a remedy, but any resultant payment of compensation will not deprive an individual of the status of 'victim' for the purposes of considering whether any other guarantee under Article 5 has been breached[7]. The paragraph does not preclude domestic law from requiring compensation to be made available only where the 'victim' can show he has suffered either pecuniary or non-pecuniary damage, and the Court itself has increasingly reflected this principle in its own judgments on Article 41[8]. In *Wassink v Netherlands*, the applicant had been confined to a psychiatric hospital in breach of domestic procedural provisions. The Court considered that national law did provide an adequate right to compensation, but here it would have been exceptionally difficult to establish that any damage had occurred since formal compliance with national law (and thus with the Convention) would have been most likely in any case to have led to his detention[9]. However, a merely illusory right to compensation is insufficient[10]. It also requires the state to refrain from imposing any hurdle which would have the effect of qualifying the clear language of the paragraph, as in *Tsirlis and Kouloumpas v Greece* where a domestic court had decided that the applicants were not entitled to compensation since their unlawful deprivation of liberty had been on account of their own gross negligence[11]. Other challenges are foreseeable. In *Benham v United Kingdom*, the applicant had challenged the immunity of magistrates from civil proceedings in English law which provided that a magistrate could be held liable in damages only if acting in excess of jurisdiction, or for action taken maliciously or without reasonable and probable cause. The issue was avoided in this case since the Court decided that no Article 5 violation had arisen[12].

1 Cf *Benham v United Kingdom* 1996-III, 738, para 50.
2 Cf *N C v Italy* (11 January 2001), paras 44–47 and 61 (applicability of this provision in respect of pre-trial detention under para (1)(c) where the Court's task is to consider whether the evidence which the authorities had knowledge of at the relevant time was reasonably sufficient).
3 Just satisfaction under Art 41 will also address any violation of Art 5(5), but awards tend to be low. Cf *Curley v United Kingdom* (28 March 2000), at para 46 (Parole Board had twice recommended the applicant's release; ten-year delay before review by a body complying with Art 5(4) requirements; the Court accepted the applicant 'must have suffered feelings of frustration, uncertainty and anxiety which cannot be compensated solely by the findings of violations': £1,500 awarded for non-pecuniary damage). In *Steel and Ors v United Kingdom* 1998-VII, 2719, para 122, three protestors each imprisoned for seven hours following peaceful exercise of freedom of expression were each awarded £500.
4 Eg *Brogan and Ors v United Kingdom* (1988) A 145, paras 66–67; followed in a similar case involving British anti-terrorist legislation, *Fox, Campbell and Hartley* (1990) A 182, para 46; and in *Thynne, Wilson and Gunnell v United Kingdom* (1990) A 190, para 82 concerning review of discretionary life sentences; *Hood v United Kingdom* (18 February 1999), para 69, and *Stephen Jordan v United Kingdom* (14 March 2000), para 33 concerning military justice procedures.
5 *Steel and Ors v United Kingdom* 1998-VII, 2719, para 83.
6 *Ciulla v Italy* (1989) A 148, para 44.
7 10868/84, *Woukam Moudefo v France* (1987) DR 51, 62; 11256/84, *Egue v France* (1988) DR 57, 47.
8 Cf *Caballero v United Kingdom* (8 February 2000), at paras 30–31 (just satisfaction in several cases awarded only in respect of 'damage resulting from a deprivation of liberty that the applicant would not have suffered if he or she had had the benefit' of Art 5, and a finding of a violation could thus constitute sufficient just satisfaction in respect of any non-pecuniary damage suffered: in the present case where release on bail was not competent, an award of £1,000 was appropriate since it was accepted the applicant would have had a good chance of release on bail prior to trial).
9 *Wassink v Netherlands* (1990) A 185-A, para 38.
10 *Sakik and Ors v Turkey* 1997-VII, 2609, para 60 (no example of any litigant obtaining compensation by reliance upon domestic law, and thus no effective enjoyment of right ensured with sufficient degree of certainty).
11 1997-III, 909, paras 65–66.
12 1996-III, 738, paras 48–50.

CHAPTER 5

Fair administration of justice

INTRODUCTION

5.01 Procedural propriety and the prohibition of the retroactive imposition of criminal liability lie at the heart of any legal system grounded in the rule of law. The European Convention on Human Rights, Articles 6 and 7 codify those crucial principles of the fair administration of justice which form the bedrock of European legal tradition. Yet while these principles may appear self-evident, they have not always been matched by appropriate domestic provision. The central importance of Article 6[1] is reflected in the volume and scope of applications claiming violation of its guarantees[2]. This provision has been employed by applicants to challenge aspects of criminal, civil and administrative procedures of European legal systems, and the European Court of Human Rights has been at pains to protect the fundamental notion of the effective delivery of fair justice against competing and conflicting contemporary trends: for example, the modern administrative state may seek to promote efficiency in the delivery of public services through relaxed application of due process guarantees; reform of criminal process at domestic level may purport to achieve greater effectiveness through modification of long-held principles considered necessary to protect an accused; or an increasingly litigious society may find that enhanced awareness of civil rights and obligations giving rise to heightened expectations is not met by the allocation of additional financial and judicial resources. Study of this rich and complex resultant case law can be somewhat intimidating, if not less than rewarding, since many of the opinions and judgments tend to reflect the peculiarities of legal systems based upon differing constitutional principles[3]: on the other hand, much of the approach to interpretation has been developed in a number of leading cases which establish key tenets of general application. In contrast, Article 7, which embodies the related principles 'that only the law can define a crime and prescribe a penalty [and] the criminal law must not be extensively construed to an accused's detriment'[4], has produced only limited jurisprudence. In large measure this reflects the codified nature of the criminal law in the majority of European states, but the Court has not found it difficult to accommodate legal systems based on the continuing evolution of the common law by applying the basic criterion of whether criminal liability is reasonably foreseeable[5].

---

1 *De Cubber v Belgium* (1984) A 86, para 30. For further consideration of the provision, see Stavros *The Guarantees for Accused Persons under Article 6 of the European Convention on Human Rights* (1993); and Grotrian *Article 6 of the European Convention on Human Rights: The Right to a Fair Trial* (1994). For a wider perspective on procedural fairness, see Galligan *Due Process and Fair Procedures* (1996).

2 Eissen *The Length of Civil and Criminal Proceedings in the Case-Law of the European Court of Human Rights* (1996) at pp 7 and 8 suggests that in the Court's first 25 years (ie until the end of 1995) 339 of the 554 judgments delivered (ie over 60%) concerned this provision to some extent; and of these judgments, half concerned 'reasonable time'. If anything, the quantity of case load concerning Art 6 has grown: by June 30 2001, the 'new' Court had given 1,284 judgments, of which 768 (or just under 60%) alone concerned length of proceedings cases.

3 Soyer and de Salvia 'Article 6' in Pettiti, Decaux and Imbert *La Convention Européenne des Droits de l'Homme* (1st edn, 1995) at p 241: '[the jurisprudence of the Commission and Court] est touffue, car elle s'élabore à partir d'innombrables espèces, d'autant plus variées qu'elles surgissent dans des systèmes juridiques très divers, voire dissemblables (common law, droit écrit – Etats monistes, Etats dualistes)'. For comparative discussion of fair hearing guarantees and criminal procedures in Europe, see Fennell, Harding, Jörg and Swart *Criminal Justice in Europe: A Comparative Study* (1995); Council of Europe, *The Right to a Fair Trial* (European Commission for Democracy through Law) (2000); and Council of Europe *Criminal Justice and Criminal Procedures* (2001). For discussion of the emergence of a 'European' system of criminal justice, see de Salvia 'Principles Directeurs d'une Procedure Pénale européenne: la Contribution des Organs de la Convention européenne des Droits de l'Homme' in *Collected Courses of the Academy of European Law* vol V-2 (1997) pp 59–134.

4 *S W v United Kingdom* (1995) A 335-B at para 35.

5 *S W v United Kingdom* (1995) A 335-B, paras 36–44, discussed at para 5.139 below.

5.02   Most challenges concerning the administration of justice raised to date by Scottish applications to Strasbourg have concerned the European Convention on Human Rights, Article 6's guarantees of a fair hearing in civil and criminal cases. The particular features of Scots law which have been scrutinised include issues as to the right of access to courts, security measures during trials, criminal appeals, bias on the part of jurors, the non-availability of legal aid in criminal cases, and certain aspects of the children's hearing system. Similarly, since the entry into force of the Scotland Act 1998, the majority of key challenges considered by the courts have founded upon aspects of Article 6[1]. This situation has been replicated since the entry into force of the Human Rights Act 1998 across the entire United Kingdom. The conclusion for each legal system drawn from the case law is that the maintenance of standards of fairness in the administration of justice requires constant vigilance.

1 See written answer of the Lord Advocate of 9 January 2001, WA S1W-4775: between 20 May 1999 and 29 November 2000, 969 devolution issues were raised in Crown Office proceedings of which 824 (or some 85%) concerned Art 6; and 36 of the 37 issues decided against the Crown concerned issues relating to Art 6, of which 30 related to 'trial within a reasonable time'. Of the remaining issues, 2 concerned Art 3; 42 concerned Art 5; 10 concerned Art 7; and 71 concerned Art 8.

General principles of interpretation of Article 6 and relationship with other guarantees

5.03   The text of the European Convention on Human Rights, Article 6 is one of the most detailed of the substantive rights in the Convention. The Strasbourg authorities have sought to give Article 6(1) a purposive interpretation that furthers the principle of fairness in the administration of justice. The European Court of Human Rights has often reiterated that in a democratic society based upon the rule of law, 'the right to a fair administration of justice holds such a prominent place that a restrictive interpretation of Article 6(1) would not correspond to the aim and the purpose of that provision'[1]. Any tendency, however, to regard its sub-divisions as constituting a number of discrete guarantees has been firmly resisted by the Court: the whole provision is composed of elements 'which are distinct but stem from the same basic idea and which, taken together, make up a single right not specifically defined'[2]. Paragraph (1) thus refers to the rights to:

- 'a fair and public hearing';
- 'within a reasonable time';
- 'by an independent and impartial tribunal established by law'; and
- which pronounces its judgment publicly except in defined and narrowly construed circumstances.

Additionally, a person accused of a criminal offence acquires further minimum rights conferred by paragraphs (2) and (3), including the rights:

- to be presumed innocent until proven guilty;
- to be informed of the charge against him;
- to have adequate time and facilities to prepare his defence;
- to defend himself or have legal assistance;
- to examine (and have examined) witnesses; and
- to the free use of an interpreter.

In addition to these textual provisions, the Court will also insist that judicial proceedings are broadly adversarial in character and that the domestic rules of evidence applied meet a certain standard. 'In sum, the whole makes up the right to a fair hearing'[3].

1 Cf *Delcourt v Belgium* (1970) A 11, at para 25.
2 *Golder v United Kingdom* (1975) A 18, at para 28.
3 *Golder v United Kingdom* (1975) A 18 at para 36.

5.04 The right under the European Convention on Human Rights, Article 6 is to 'fairness' rather than to 'justice'. The European Court of Human Rights has consistently refused to allow itself to be looked upon as a court of fourth instance and will not examine the merits of an application to consider, for example, whether a conviction has been wrongly secured[1]. In other words, the ultimate question to be determined by the Court is whether the proceedings as a whole were fair. This in consequence requires consideration of all the particular facts of each case[2], including any decision taken by an appellate court[3] and any failure on the part of state authorities to implement a court decision[4]. Thus while there may appear on the face of the facts to have been some breach of a particular element which forms part of the wider concept of a fair hearing, it will always be necessary to consider the overall impact of this on the proceedings[5]. Similarly, the mere fact that evidence has been led which was obtained in violation of domestic law or even of a Convention guarantee will not of itself render the trial unfair[6]. On the other hand, however, the Court has sought to interpret the guarantees in Article 6 to render them 'practical and effective as opposed to theoretical and illusory'. This may mean that, while an applicant who has been acquitted or where there has been a lack of substantive proceedings in a case cannot generally claim to be a 'victim', in certain circumstances it may still be possible to establish a violation of Article 6 where to hold otherwise would prevent examination of complaints of a violation of fair hearing guarantees[7].

1   Eg 14739/89, *Callaghan and Ors v United Kingdom* (1989) DR 60, 296 (refusal to allow new evidence to be considered by a jury rather than by the Court of Appeal; Art 6(2) was not applicable to reference proceedings at appellate level, and application declared inadmissible).
2   *Krasa v Switzerland* (1993) A 254-B, para 30.
3   *Stanford v United Kingdom* (1994) A 282-A, para 24.
4   *Hornsby v Greece* 1997-II 495, paras 39–45 (failure to implement a final court decision for over five years was considered a violation of Art 6(1)).
5   Cf *Ankerl v Switzerland* 1996-V, 1553, para 38 (difference in treatment in respect of the manner in which evidence was taken from the parties' witnesses, but not one which could be taken to have placed one party at a substantial disadvantage, and thus no breach of Art 6).
6   Eg *Khan v United Kingdom* (12 May 2000) discussed further at para 5.69 below.
7   Eg *Minelli v Switzerland* (1983) A 62, paras 37–38 (expiry of limitation period preventing determination of guilt; but despite the lack of a conviction, the court indicated the probable guilt of the applicant: violation of Art 6(2)); *Funke v France* (1993) A 256-A, paras 39–40 (conviction for failure to supply information, but criminal proceedings in respect of initial inquiries were never initiated); *Sekanina v Austria* (1993) A 266-A, paras 22–31 (acquittal of the applicant but refusal of compensation because of suspicion of guilt contrary to the presumption of innocence); *Allenet de Ribemont v France* (1995) A 308, paras 32–37 (public comments of police officers suggestive of an accused's guilt of charges even though the proceedings on those charges were subsequently discontinued); *Quinn v Ireland* (21 December 2000), paras 43–46 and *Heaney and McGuinness v Ireland* (21 December 2000), paras 43–46 (applicants had been 'charged' for the purposes of Article 6, even though in the first case the applicant had not been charged with a substantive offence; and the two applicants in the second case had not been formally charged when they were required to give information contrary to Art 6(1)).

Relationship between Article 6 and other Convention provisions

5.05   Applicants will frequently challenge both the reasons for a particular decision and the manner in which it was taken, and thus applications will often allege a violation of the European Convention on Human Rights, Article 6 at the same time as seeking to rely upon another substantive provision of the Convention. However, there may be implicit positive obligations upon a state to provide procedural protection under other Convention guarantees. In child care cases falling within the scope of Article 8, for example, the European Court of Human Rights has stressed that while this provision 'contains no explicit procedural requirements, the decision-making process leading to measures of interference must be fair and such as to afford due respect to the interests safeguarded'[1]. Under Articles 2 and 3 there may now be responsibilities for ensuring that an applicant has the right to participate in an independent and public scrutiny of allegations that unlawful lethal force or unnecessary violence has been used by public officials[2]. Article 5 case law now indicates that the determination of whether there has been a 'deprivation of liberty' may involve questioning whether appropriate procedural safeguards have been accorded[3], while periodic review of the lawfulness of continuing detention under Article 5(4) implies access to a 'court' enjoying independence and impartiality and able to order the release of the individual[4]. Further, when assessing the proportionality of an interference with property rights under Protocol 1, Article 1, the Court will consider the degree of protection from arbitrariness that is afforded by the proceedings in a case, and in particular whether the quality of the procedures has ensured that due account has been taken of the interests of an applicant before arriving at a decision affecting property rights[5].

1 *McMichael v United Kingdom* (1995) A 307-B, at para 87; see para 6.23 below. Cf European Convention on the Exercise of Children's Rights (ETS No 160) (1996) not yet ratified by the UK.
2 *McCann and Ors v United Kingdom* (1995) A 324, paras 161–164 (Art 2); *Assenov v Bulgaria* 1998-VIII, 3264, para 102 (Art 3); see paras 4.08 and 4.27 above.
3 *Amuur v France* 1996-III, 827, paras 50–54; see para 4.49 above.
4 Eg *Hussain v United Kingdom* 1996-I, 252, paras 58–61; see paras 4.87–4.99 above.
5 Eg *Hentrich v France* (1994) A 296-A, paras 45–49; see para 8.16 below.

RELATIONSHIP WITH ARTICLE 13

5.06 The primary responsibility for securing European Convention on Human Rights guarantees falls upon member states[1]. The subsidiary nature of the Strasbourg Court is appreciated more clearly when Articles 1, 13 and 35(1) are considered together. Article 1 specifies that contracting states 'shall secure to everyone within their jurisdiction the rights and freedoms defined [in the Convention]; Article 13 provides that 'everyone whose rights and freedoms as set forth in this Convention are violated shall have an effective remedy before a national authority'; and Article 35(1) requires exhaustion of domestic remedies before an application may be brought before the Court[2]. Article 1 does not require formal incorporation of the Convention into domestic law[3]. The key provision from the perspective of an applicant is thus Article 13 which 'guarantees the availability of a remedy at a national level to enforce – and hence to allege non-compliance with – the substance of the Convention rights and freedoms in whatever form they may happen to be secured in the domestic legal order'[4]. In other words, Article 13 must provide the opportunity to challenge domestic law or practice wherever there is an 'arguable' claim that there has been a violation of the Convention, although the provision 'cannot reasonably be interpreted so as to require a remedy in domestic law in respect of any supposed grievance under the Convention that an individual may have, no matter how unmeritorious his claim may be'[5]. However, the constitutional diversity of European legal systems is respected. The Court has accommodated concepts such as sovereignty of parliament and, in consequence, 'Article 13 does not guarantee a remedy allowing a contracting state's laws as such to be challenged before a national authority on the ground of being contrary to the Convention or equivalent domestic norms'[6]. For the purposes of Article 13, for a remedy to be effective in domestic law it must exist with sufficient certainty[7], it must be adequate in the sense of addressing the substance of the issue raised and allowing relief to be granted[8], and it must be available to the individual[9].

1 *Handyside v United Kingdom* (1976) A 24, para 48; *Akdivar and Ors v Turkey* 1996-IV, 1192, para 65.
2 See further, para 2.25 above.
3 *Lithgow and Ors v United Kingdom* (1986) A 102, para 205. In practice, all states except for Ireland have now incorporated the Convention into domestic law, and Ireland is now taking steps to do so (see www.irlgov.ie/justice/Publications/Human%20Rights/B2601.pdf for the Irish Government's proposals which differ in significant ways from the method adopted under the Human Rights Act in the UK).

4 *Boyle and Rice v United Kingdom* (1988) A 131, at para 52. See further Harris, O'Boyle and Warbrick *Law of the European Convention on Human Rights* (1995) pp 443–461.
5 *Boyle and Rice v United Kingdom* (1988) A 131, at para 52. In consequence, an applicant cannot allege breach of Art 13 alone; but the Court may find a violation of Art 13 even where it has determined that there has been no breach of any other guarantee: Cf *Klass and Ors v Germany* (1983) A 28, paras 65–72.
6 *Leander v Sweden* (1987) A 116, at para 77.
7 Cf *Costello-Roberts v United Kingdom* (1993) A 247-C, paras 37–40 (civil action for assault was considered an effective remedy in English law to challenge corporal punishment; while the Commission had been of the opinion such a remedy would not have been effective, 'the effectiveness of a remedy . . . does not depend on the certainty of a favourable outcome. . .').
8 Cf *Silver and Ors v United Kingdom* (1981) A 61, paras 115–119.
9 Eg *Aydin v Turkey* 1997-VI, 1866, paras 104–107.

5.07   An intention to furnish aggrieved parties with domestic remedies for complaints related to the European Convention on Human Rights lies behind the enactment of the Human Rights Act 1998 in the United Kingdom and provides the reason advanced for the exclusion of Article 13 from the list of 'Convention rights' in that legislation[1]. While Article 13 cannot thus be relied upon directly in domestic proceedings, some understanding of this guarantee may nevertheless assist in gaining an appreciation of the importance of Article 6 in the Strasbourg scheme of protection of human rights since the Court appears to be moving gradually towards an expectation that Article 13 requirements will be met through the determination by domestic courts of claims of violation of substantive Convention guarantees. There is an obvious and close relationship between the two provisions: Article 6 guarantees access to a court for the determination of disputes, while Article 13 requires states to ensure that 'everyone whose rights and freedoms as set forth in this Convention [and optional Protocols] are violated shall have an effective remedy before a national authority . . .'. The difficulty is that Article 6 guarantees access to a court for the determination of all 'civil rights and obligations', while Article 13 only applies to the enforcement of Convention guarantees, which may or may not also involve 'civil rights'. Certainly, Article 13 responsibilities may be secured by means other than judicial hearings, and 'although no single remedy may itself satisfy the requirements of Article 13, the aggregate of remedies provided for under domestic law may do so'[2]. Further, the Court may consider another Convention guarantee to be the *lex specialis* (rather than Article 13) in considering whether domestic law provides adequate safeguards[3]; elsewhere in the Convention, it has also shown itself unwilling to address a complaint under Article 13 if it has already examined the issue of the availability of a remedy in domestic law under another substantive provision[4]. In any case, the Court has not always been consistent in its disposal of Article 13 arguments[5]. Disposal of an Article 6 point will often render discussion of any Article 13 argument unnecessary[6], but on the other hand, the Court on occasion has preferred to consider Article 6 questions concerning access to a court for the purposes of vindicating substantive Convention rights under the more general Article 13 obligation of securing an effective remedy in domestic law[7].

1 *Montgomery v HM Advocate* 2000 SCCR 1044, 1093; *Stott v Brown* 2001 SCCR 62 per Lord Hope of Craighead. Cf comments by the Lord Chancellor at 583 HL Official Report (5th series) cols 475–477 (18 November 1997) and 584 HL Official Report (5th series) cols 1265–1267 (19 January 1998) (the Human Rights Act 1998 would give effect to the purpose

of Art 13, and thus incorporation of this provision was unnecessary; but that domestic courts could still have regard to Art 13). One practical effect of non-incorporation of Art 13 in Scots law is that an interdict remains incompetent against the Crown in respect of executive action and which is contrary to Convention rights.

2 *Silver and Ors v United Kingdom* (1983) A 61, at para 113. See further van Dijk and van Hoof *Theory and Practice of the European Convention on Human Rights* (3rd edn, 1998) pp 419 and 696–710.

3 Thus Art 5(4) rather than Art 13 will be the relevant provision to examine whether domestic law permits scrutiny of the lawfulness of detention: see para 4.81 above.

4 Eg *X and Y v Netherlands* (1985) A 91, para 36 (availability of remedy considered in the context of Art 8). See too discussion of the relationship between Art 13 and Arts 2 and 3 discussed at paras 4.09 and 4.28 above.

5 Cf van Dijk and van Hoof *Theory and Practice of the European Convention on Human Rights* (3rd edn, 1998) at p 697: 'every single element of Article 13 still gives rise to difficulties of interpretation'; and Harris, O'Boyle and Warbrick *Law of the European Convention on Human Rights* (1995) at p 443: 'if the general principles which [Article 13] embodies are now tolerably clear, they are not free from criticism'. See also Frowein 'Art 13 as a Growing Pillar of Convention Law' in Mahoney, Matscher, Petzold and Wildhaber (eds) *Protecting Human Rights: The European Perspective* (2000) pp 545–550.

6 *Hentich v France* (1994) A 296-A, at para 65: the requirements of Art 13 'are less strict than, and are here absorbed by, those of Article 6 para 1'. See too, e g, *Mats Jacobsson v Sweden* (1990) A 180-A, para 38; *Pizzetti v Italy* (1993) A 257-C, para 21; *Putz v Austria* 1996-I, 312, para 41.

7 E g *Menteş and Ors v Turkey* 1997-VIII, 2689, paras 86–88 (destruction of homes and property).

Additional Convention guarantees in the criminal process

5.08 As noted, paragraphs (2) and (3) of the European Convention on Human Rights, Article 6 are of relevance in the determination of criminal charges, which Article 7 prohibits the retroactive imposition of the criminal law or of a heavier criminal sanction than the appropriate penalty in force when the criminal act was committed and thus guaranteeing application of the maxims of *nullum crimen sine lege* and *nulla poene sine lege*. Additionally, Protocol 7 makes provision for a right of appeal in criminal matters, for a right to compensation for wrongful conviction, and for a right not to be tried or punished again in criminal proceedings in a state where the individual has already been finally acquitted or convicted in accordance with national law. The United Kingdom is yet to ratify Protocol 7[1], and thus it may be difficult to argue that the principle of *non bis in idem* which prohibits an individual from being tried twice could apply as an aspect of the general right of fairness under Article 6[2]. However, where a state has made provision for a system of criminal appeals in domestic law, the conduct of the appellate courts will also be open to scrutiny under Article 6, irrespective of whether the state in question has ratified this optional Protocol[3].

1 As at 31 August 2001, 31 of the 43 Council of Europe states had ratified Protocol 7. The Government has indicated that it intends to ratify this Protocol at an early stage: *Bringing Rights Home* (Cm 3782) para 4.15.

2 Cf *Maaouia v France* (5 October 2000), para 36 (provisions had to be construed in the light of the entire Convention system, and the terms of Protocol 7, Art 1 which provided additional procedural guarantees applicable to the expulsion of aliens thus implied that Art 6 did not apply in this regard). See, similarly, Reid *A Practitioner's Guide to the European Convention on Human Rights* (1998) p 78.

3 For recent authority, see *Belziuk v Poland* 1998-II, 558, para 37. Cf *Monnell and Morris v United Kingdom* (1987) A 115, para 54 (not contested that leave to appeal proceedings formed part of the determination of a criminal charge).

SCOPE OF ARTICLE 6

5.09   Consideration of the scope of the European Convention on Human Rights, Article 6 is of crucial importance. Paragraph (1) provides that the bundle of rights which together constitute a fair hearing apply in the determination of 'civil rights and obligations' or of 'any criminal charge'. A substantial (but not always coherent or consistent[1]) jurisprudence has emerged as to the interpretation of these concepts. The trend has been to widen the interpretation given to each, and particularly to that of 'civil rights and obligations' which has enjoyed perhaps rather more of an incremental than principled development. Each concept is recognised as having an autonomous meaning which is not dependent upon the characterisation given by the domestic legal system[2].

1   Especially in relation to 'civil rights and obligations'. See, e g, van Dijk 'The Interpretation of 'Civil Rights and Obligations' by the European Court of Human Rights – One More Step to Take', in Matscher and Petzold (eds) *Protecting Human Rights: The European Dimension* (1988) pp 131–143.
2   *König v Germany* (1978) A 27, para 89 ('civil rights'); *Engel and Ors v Netherlands* (1976) A 22, paras 81–82 ('criminal charge').

Civil rights and obligations

5.10   The principal issue is the applicability of the European Convention on Human Rights, Article 6 to proceedings other than those normally disposed of in the ordinary civil courts or to issues which fall outside the ambit of private law as traditionally understood. Invariably, litigation in the civil courts between two private individuals or legal persons will fall within the scope of the guarantee[1], but the accommodation within Article 6 of administrative proceedings and issues involving some element of public law has been achieved not without intellectual difficulty. This threshold question of whether there exists a 'determination' of 'civil rights and obligations' and thus whether Article 6 guarantees apply has resulted in case law which has been described as 'confusing'[2] and as resulting in an 'undesirable situation' for both individuals and state authorities[3]. A more positive view is that the jurisprudence is at least 'progressive'[4].

In determining whether there is an issue which affects 'civil rights and obligations, four conditions must be satisfied:

(i)   there must be a genuine claim or dispute (in French, *contestation*);
(ii)   this dispute must relate to a right or obligation in domestic law;
(iii) this right or obligation must be broadly civil in character; and
(iv)   the outcome of the dispute must be directly decisive for the right or obligation.

1   Including enforcement proceedings and other proceedings ancillary to a court decision with a view to resolving a civil dispute: *Scollo v Italy* (1995) A 315-C, para 44 and *Immobiliare Saffi v Italy* 1999-V, 73, paras 62–63 (although domestic law labelled police assistance in enforcing a court decree as 'administrative', Art 6 rights would be merely illusory if they did not cover implementation of judicial decisions).
2   Gomien, Harris and Zwaak *Law and Practice of the European Convention on Human Rights and the European Social Charter* (1996) at p 177.

3 Van Dijk and van Hoof *Theory and Practice of the European Convention on Human Rights* (3rd edn, 1998) at 404. (At pp 392–394, the authors argue for recourse to the *travaux préparatoires* to help gain clarity as to what the drafters intended, noting that an earlier version of the English text read 'rights and obligations in a suit at law').

4 Reid *A Practitioner's Guide to the European Convention on Human Rights* (1988) at p 58.

The existence of a dispute or 'contestation'

5.11   The French text refers to 'contestations sur ses droits et obligations de charactère civil', while the English version refers merely to the 'determination' of such rights. From *contestation* has come a requirement that there exists a 'dispute' which has at least an arguable basis in domestic law. However, 'conformity with the spirit of the Convention requires that this word should not be construed too technically and that it should be given a substantive rather than a formal meaning'[1]. In *Le Compte, van Leuven and de Meyere v Belgium*, the Court accepted that the applicants' denial of allegations of professional misconduct and their challenge to their suspension by a professional body were sufficient to give rise to the necessary 'dispute'. 'Disputes' can thus relate not only to the actual existence of a civil right, 'but also to its scope or the manner in which it may be exercised'[2]. They can concern questions of either law or fact[3], and may thus involve claims to or the assertion of rights in respect of such matters as entitlement to a pension[4], access by parents to children taken into care[5], compensation for wrongful imprisonment[6], the award of costs in civil litigation[7], and the rights to carry on trading under licence[8], to practise a profession[9], to receive compensation for culpable misconduct or other negligence on the part of state authorities[10], and to exploit land[11]. Indeed, a suggestion found in the Court's decision in *Moreira de Azevedo v Portugal* acknowledges that the issue of 'dispute' is not likely to pose much difficulty. The applicant had intervened in a criminal prosecution against an alleged assailant, as he was entitled to do, but had not expressly sought civil compensation from the wrongdoer. The Court accepted that the intervention itself was enough to constitute a 'dispute' since it gave rise to an implicit claim for compensation and thus a *contestation* could be said to have existed[12].

On the other hand, in *Van Marle v Netherlands*, the applicants had been denied registration as chartered accountants after unsuccessfully sitting a test which sought to assess professional competency. The Court considered this assessment of professional skill as 'akin to a school or university examination' and 'so far removed from the exercise of the normal judicial function that the safeguards in Article 6 cannot be taken as covering resultant disagreements' even although in domestic law the appeal board was considered to be a tribunal. On this basis, it held there was no 'dispute' within the meaning of the requirement[13].

1 *Le Compte, van Leuven and de Meyere v Belgium* (1981) A 43, at para 45.
2 (1981) A 43, para 45.
3 *Benthem v Netherlands* (1985) A 97, at para 32.
4 *Deumeland v Germany* (1986) A 100, para 59; *Salerno v Italy* (1992) A 245-D, paras 15–16. Cf 39712/98, *La Parola and Ors v Italy* (30 November 2000) (request for further financial assistance in respect of a disabled minor who was already in receipt of benefit on a permanent basis: proceedings were not aimed at determining a dispute but rather entitlement to the additional aid requested, and thus Art 6 was inadmissible).

5 *O v United Kingdom* (1987) A 120, paras 58–59.
6 *Baraona v Portugal* (1987) A 122, paras 38 and 41.
7 *Beer v Austria* (6 February2001), paras 11–13.
8 *Pudas v Sweden* (1987) A 125-A, para 34; *Tre Traktörer v Sweden* (1989) A 159, para 40; *Editions Périscope v France* (1992) A 234-B, paras 37–38. Cf *Marjanic Kervöelen v France* (27 March 2001), paras 27–30 (automatic expiry of a licence if no alcohol had been sold for three years: loss of licence was thus not the result of an administrative or judicial act (as in cases such as *Tre Traktörer*), and in consequence, Art 6 was inapplicable).
9 *H v Belgium* (1987) A 127-B, para 43 (an advocate could expect to be readmitted after ten years' suspension: upon satisfaction of the prescribed requirements. Art 6 was applicable since the professional body had to determine whether these conditions had been satisfied); *Kraska v Switzerland* (1993) A 254-B, paras 24–27 (attempt to seek authorisation to practise again as a doctor after licence had been withdrawn).
10 *Neves e Silva v Portugal* (1989) A 153-A, para 37.
11 *Allan Jacobsson v Sweden* (1989) A 163, paras 67–70 (prolongation of building prohibition challenged by applicants; respondent government claimed there was no 'right' to build in existence until a permit had been granted: the Court determined that in the circumstances it could be argued that the applicant had a claim to a 'right' to a permit). See also *Thery v France* (1 February 2000), paras 22–23 (the applicant's asserted right to cultivate his farmland was considered to be a subsidiary right relating to the manner in which a right of property was exercised and thus qualified as a civil right). In *R (Alconbury Developments Ltd) v Secretary of State for the Environment, Transport and the Regions* [2001] 2 WLR 1389 the determination of a called-in planning application was held to involve a 'contestation'.
12 (1994) A 189, at para 66 ('in so far as the French word *'contestation'* would appear to require the existence of a dispute, if indeed it does so at all, the facts of the case show that there was one'). Cf *Hamer v France* 1996-III, 1029, paras 73–79 (no 'dispute' was established in a similar set of circumstances where French law specifically required a civil party seeking to intervene in a criminal process with a view to obtaining compensation to lodge a claim for compensation).
13 (1986) A 101, paras 36–37 at para 36; but cf 39615/98, *Motière v France* (28 March 2000), paras 16–21 (applicant who had worked as a body builder sought a further qualification but had been refused this by the decision of the responsible state official; while the applicant did not have a right to such a qualification she was nevertheless entitled to a lawful examination process in domestic law, a matter amenable to judicial review which the applicant had sought: the Court proceeded upon the basis that there was thus a dispute over a civil right within the meaning of Art 6(1) in considering the reasonableness of the length of proceedings).

Dispute concerning a right with an arguable basis in domestic law

5.12   As with the approach adopted in determining whether a 'dispute' exists, this requirement is considered in a manner which is in keeping with maximising the scope of the guarantee. The claim must further be based upon a right recognised by the national legal system: that is, it must be one which has at least an arguable basis in domestic law[1]. There is no restriction on the issue which may form part of a claim, and so the 'arguable basis' may involve even a challenge to the lawfulness of legal rules[2]. The fact that a domestic court has agreed to hear an action will be sufficient to meet this test. In *Salerno v Italy*, the applicant had sought membership of a pension fund for notaries but the action had been dismissed by the domestic courts. The respondent government asserted that as the substance of his claim had already been determined, a fresh action brought by him some two years later could not be said to have been based upon any arguable claim. The European Court of Human Rights, however, considered that the domestic courts had acknowledged this fresh claim as sufficiently tenable in holding the action admissible and, accordingly, these new proceedings fell within the scope of the European Convention on Human Rights, Article 6[3].

On the other hand, if domestic law restricts the scope of a substantive right or indeed expressly or implicitly excludes a particular right there can be no 'arguable claim', for Article 6 'does not in itself guarantee any particular content for "rights and obligations" in the substantive law of the contracting states'[4]. An applicant must still meet requirements of title and interest to sue, and cannot seek to use Article 6 to establish a 'dispute' where none is recognised by domestic law[5]. In *James v United Kingdom*, tenants of property in England had been given the statutory right to convert their legal interests to those of owners. The applicants (who had held the freehold rights) had thereby been deprived of their property through the exercise of the statutory right by their former tenants, but the applicants had no remedy in domestic law to seek to challenge the transfer of property since satisfaction of the statutory conditions by the tenants had the immediate effect of changing the nature of the legal relationship. The legislation did not confer any right to challenge by appeal or review. The Court held that no Article 6 issue was in existence since there was no *contestation* over any right 'which [could] be said, at least on arguable grounds, to be recognised under domestic law'[6]. Similarly, in *Powell and Rayner v United Kingdom*, statute limited the rights of those affected by aircraft noise to seek remedies for nuisance. Again, the Court ruled that no Article 6 issue consequently arose since there was no relevant civil right in domestic law that could be enforced[7]. Further, an applicant must show that he has taken any necessary prior steps required by domestic law in order to qualify as the holder of a 'right' he seeks to enforce in the domestic courts. In *McMichael v United Kingdom*, the natural father of a child born outwith wedlock sought to assert that determination by a children's hearing of access rights to his child had violated his Article 6 rights. Scots law did not automatically confer parental rights upon an unmarried father, but instead required such a parent to make an application to a court for an order giving him these rights. In this particular case, the applicant had not done so, and consequently, the Court determined that the care proceedings did not involve any dispute over a civil right since he had not obtained legal recognition of his status as a father[8].

In these cases, the question whether domestic law recognises a substantive right is crucial[9]. Purely discretionary authority conferred upon a public authority and which is unfettered by legal rule may not give rise to such a right or obligation. In *Masson and Van Zorn v Netherlands*, provisions of Dutch law specified that a person acquitted of a criminal charge 'shall' have various expenses refunded to him in certain cases, and 'may' be entitled to have other outlays reimbursed where the court accepted that 'reasons in equity' existed for this. The Court held that 'the grant to a public authority of such a measure of discretion indicates that no actual right is recognised in law'[10]. Where substantive or procedural bars exist so as to 'remove from the jurisdiction of the courts a whole range of civil claims or confer immunities from civil liability on large groups or categories of persons', different considerations may apply. The distinction is not always a clear one. In *Fayed v United Kingdom*, the applicants had been prevented from bringing an action of defamation against a government inspector whose report had labelled the applicants as dishonest. English law considered these reports as privileged and thus conferred an immunity from suit in respect of any action of defamation. The Court reiterated that Article 6 could not create by means of judicial interpretation a right which was not recognised in the relevant domestic legal system. It also rejected the applicants' arguments that an official investigatory body in discharging its functions should be open to challenge by means of an action of defamation since such an interpretation 'would in practice unduly hamper the effective regulation in the public interest of complex financial and commercial activities'. However, it did try to distinguish this situation from one in which procedural bars prevented or limited the bringing of legal action to enforce a claim to a right with an established legal basis[11]. In such cases there may well be an Article 6 issue on account of restrictions on the right of access to a court, as discussed below[12].

1 Eg *Zander v Sweden* (1993) A 279-B, at para 22 (the Court 'has first to ascertain whether there was a dispute (*'contestation'*) over a 'right' which can be said, at least on arguable grounds, to be recognised under domestic law').

2 *Procola v Luxembourg* (1995) A 326, para 37 (dispute whether ministerial orders fixing milk quotas made in respect of EC law could be given retrospective effect); *Süßmann v Germany*, 1996-IV, 1158, paras 38–46 (a challenge in the Federal Constitutional Court to amendments to a pension scheme for civil servants fell within the scope of Art 6).

3 (1992) A 245-D, para 16. See too *Siegel v France* (28 November 2000), paras 33–38 (failure to accept that Art 6 applied in respect of division of an estate carried out by notaries at the request and under the control of a court would have excluded supervision over a judicial procedure, and accordingly Art 6 applied).

4 *H v Belgium* (1987) A 127-B at para 40.

5 Cf 45053/98, *Association des Amis de Saint-Raphaël et de Frejus and Ors v France* (29 February 2000) (applicant association which sought to challenge the grant of building permits had not been party to domestic legal proceedings but had merely sought to defend the general interest: neither on this basis nor on other grounds was there any Art 6 dispute).

6 (1986) A 98, at para 81.

7 (1990) A 172, para 36.

8 (1995) A 307-B, para 77. See too 34308/96, *Yildrim v Austria* (19 October 1999) (a married father was unable to have proceedings to contest paternity instituted by the public prosecutor after his own action was time-barred: application declared inadmissible).

9 See, too, 7729/76, *Agee v United Kingdom* (1977) DR 7, 164 (recognition by domestic law of parliamentary privilege attaching to statements made in the course of parliamentary proceedings: hence there was no right in domestic law to raise an action against a minister who made allegedly defamatory statements and in consequence there was no 'civil right' involved for the purposes of Art 6); *Mennitto v Italy* (5 October 2000), paras 24–28 (argument by the state that the applicant's request for payment of an allowance for his disabled child involved not a right but only a legitimate interest which was protected only indirectly and as far as was consistent with the public interest: the Court held that in the circumstances the applicant could claim on arguable grounds a right to receive the full amount of the allowance, and thus it was not necessary to consider whether the autonomous concept of a right for the purposes of Art 6(1) covered only a 'personal right' or also a 'legitimate interest').

10 (1995) A 327-A, paras 48–52 at para 51; see too *Leutscher v Netherlands* 1996-II, 427, para 24. Cf *Georgiadis v Greece*, 1997-III, 949, paras 27–36 (criminal procedure code established a right to compensation except where the detainee was intentionally or through gross negligence responsible for his detention: claims for compensation fell within the scope of Art 6(1)); and *Werner v Austria* 1997-VII, 2496, paras 34–36 (entitlement to compensation where suspicion of commission of an offence has been dispelled).

11 (1994) 294-B, paras 56–63 at para 62.

12 At para 5.30 below.

Rights and obligations which are 'civil' in nature

5.13   If the claim does not concern a right that is broadly civil in character, then no issue in terms of the European Convention on Human Rights,

Article 6 will arise. In determining whether the right is civil in character for the purposes of Article 6, the matter is determined by the substantive nature of the issue rather than by its domestic classification or the capacity in which the state or other agency is operating. In other words, the character of the right is decisive, rather than the form of the proceedings. Private rights are clearly civil rights[1], but civil rights will extend to rights other than private rights since rights derived from public law and private rights which are made dependent upon authorisation by a body recognised as being of a public law nature may be considered as 'civil' rights. This matter was established in a number of early Court judgments. In *Ringeisen v Austria*, the applicant had sought the necessary approval for a contract for the purchase of agricultural heritable property from an administrative commission. This consent had been refused, and the appellant challenged the fairness of proceedings by alleging bias on the part of this body. The Commission considered the Article 6 issue inapplicable as it took the view that 'civil rights and obligations' could only apply to legal relationships between private individuals and not to relationships in which the individual is confronted with those exercising public or state authority. The Commission had noted that, at the time of the drafting of the Convention, European states had widely differing administrative and legal systems for dealing with planning matters, but at the same time that certain issues were normally excluded from judicial review. This narrow interpretation of the meaning of 'civil rights and obligations' was, however, rejected by the Court. It was not the character of the authority but the character of the right which had to determine the scope of this notion. 'Civil rights and obligations' had to be interpreted to include 'all proceedings the result of which is decisive for private rights and obligations', and thus the proceedings of the administrative authority were subject to Article 6 requirements[2]. Similarly, the right to carry on a particular profession is essentially civil, even when this is made subject to authorisation from an administrative agency or other public body. In *König v Germany*, the applicant who was a medical specialist running his own clinic had been prevented first from operating his clinic and then from practising as a doctor. Both decisions had involved the revocation of necessary authorisations by the state government which had subsequently been upheld by administrative tribunals. The Court considered that the right to operate a clinic was essentially of a private character and one which was not affected by the imposition of any state power of supervision in the interests of public health since it was a 'commercial activity carried on with a view to profit'. Nor was this assessment altered by the exercise of supervisory powers by the relevant medical professional body as the medical profession still retained its character of a traditional liberal profession, even despite the nationalisation of health services and the introduction of state regulation. What was conclusive in determining whether a right was a 'civil right' was thus not the government's claim to be acting within a sovereign or privileged capacity but instead the essential character of the right[3].

The subsequent case law indicates that a relatively wide but still not unrestricted scope is given to 'civil rights and obligations'. Several rights are clearly civil in nature and certainly fall within the scope of Article 6, for example, the right to occupy a house[4], or the determination of a parent's

right of access to children[5]. Less obvious issues have also been accommodated within the guarantee such as grants of (or revocations or refusals to
renew) licences[6] or certificates of fitness[7] which are required for the
carrying on of some trade or economic activity, the award of a state
subsidy for the pursuit of an economic activity[8], the right to be registered
as an association[9], and planning determinations which have a direct
impact upon an applicant's rights to use and enjoy his property[10]. The
right to personal reputation, so far as protected by the law of defamation,
will qualify as a civil right[11]. The principle behind these decisions seems to
be that if the right is patrimonial in nature, it is likely to be considered as
falling within the scope of Article 6[12] unless it clearly falls within one of the
recognised exceptions which have not yet been revised by the Court. The
lack of clarity in the jurisprudence in this area leaves domestic courts in
implementing the Human Rights Act 1998 with two options: either to treat
'civil' as largely synonymous with 'private'[13], or to read (from the juxta-
position of 'criminal charge' in the text) 'civil rights' as including most
rights of a public law nature[14]. The consequence of taking the narrower
approach is that such would be inconsistent with the aims of maximising
protection for the individual and of furthering the rule of law; while the
wider interpretation could potentially impose new and far-reaching
restraints upon the exercise of unfettered administrative discretion[15].

1 Cf *Zimmerman and Steiner v Switzerland* (1983) A 66, at para 22 (it was not in dispute that
   the rights in issue 'being personal or property rights – were private, and therefore 'civil'
   within the meaning' of Art 6(1)).
2 (1971) A 13, at para 94.
3 (1978) A 27, paras 92–94. See too *Le Compte, Van Leuven and De Meyere v Belgium* (1981) A
   43, paras 48–49, and *Albert and Le Compte v Belgium* (1983) A 58, para 28 (suspensions and
   revocations of licences to practise medicine by local medical councils had been upheld on
   appeal; the Court in each case applied the *König* decision, holding that the right to practise medicine involved a private relationship between a doctor and his patients normally
   based upon contractual obligations, and thus one which involved a civil right within the
   meaning of Art 6).
4 E g *Gillow v United Kingdom* (1986) A 109, para 68.
5 E g *Olsson v Sweden (No 1)* (1988) A 130, paras 88–90.
6 E g *Benthem v Netherlands* (1985) A 97, para 36 (refusal to grant a licence to operate a liquid
   petroleum gas installation); *Pudas v Sweden* (1989) A 125-A, paras 35–37 (revocation of
   licence to operate a taxi service on a particular route); *Tre Traktörer AB v Sweden* (1989) A
   159, paras 41–43 (revocation of restaurant licence to sell alcohol); *Zander v Sweden* (1993)
   A 279-B, paras 26–27 (challenge to the grant of a permit for the dumping of refuse). For a
   Scottish example, see *Catscratch Ltd v City of Glasgow Licensing Board* (4 June 2001, unreported), Ct of S.
7 *Kingsley v United Kingdom* (7 November 2000), paras 43–45 (revocation of certificate that
   an individual was a 'fit and proper person' to run a gaming establishment).
8 E g *Société Anonyme 'Sotiris et Nikos Koutras ATTEE' v Greece* (16 November 2000),
   discussed at para 5.29 below.
9 *APEH Üldözötteinek Szövetsége, Iványi, Róth and Szerdahelyi v Hungary* (5 October 2000),
   paras 30–36 (Art 6 applicable in a case challenging the fairness of non-contentious court
   registration proceedings: associations could only obtain their legal existence by virtue of
   court registration and thus the position of an unregistered association was very different
   from that of a legal entity, and it was the applicant association's very capacity to become
   a subject of civil rights and obligations under domestic law that was at stake).
10 E g *Sporrong and Lönnroth v Sweden* (1982) A 52, para 79 (imposition of planning restrictions); *Allan Jacobsson v Sweden* (1989) A 163, paras 67–71 (there was an arguable claim
   to a building permit upon satisfaction of the necessary conditions rather than by way
   of grant through unfettered administrative discretion); *Mats Jacobbson v Sweden* (1990)
   A 180-A, paras 29–35 (dispute over lawfulness of amendment to plan which would

have the effect of annulling rights existing under the original plan); *Skärby v Sweden* (1990) A 180-B, paras 27–29 (dispute whether the applicants were covered by an exemption permitting the construction of buildings despite a prohibition order made by a commission); *Bryan v United Kingdom* (1995) A 335-A, para 31 (applicability of Art 6 to planning enforcement challenge: not contested).

11 *Tolstoy Miloslavsky v United Kingdom* (1995) A 316-B, para 58. In 31382/96, *Kurzac v Poland* (25 February 2000) the Court accepted that proceedings to have a deceased brother's conviction for anti-Soviet activities during the 1939–45 war annulled had as its aim the restoration of the reputation of the applicant's family and thus Art 6 was applicable.

12 *Procola v Luxembourg* (1995) A 326, paras 38–40 (payment of disputed additional levies under challenged ministerial orders purporting to implement EC 'milk quota' policy could be considered as a deprivation of possessions and thus involved determination of a 'civil right').

13 Cf *König v Germany* (1978) A 27, at para 95 (the Court did not find it necessary to determine whether 'civil rights and obligations' 'extends beyond those rights which have a private nature').

14 Van Dijk and van Hoof *Theory and Practice of the European Convention on Human Rights* (3rd edn, 1998) at p 406 propose that the most appropriate solution for reducing uncertainty and thereby maximising Art 6 protection is to treat Art 6 as applicable 'to all cases in which a determination by a public authority of the legal position of a private party is at stake, regardless of whether the rights and obligations involved are of a private character'. This was the position advocated in the dissenting opinion in *Ferrazzini v Italy* (12 July 2001), but effectively rejected by the majority of the Grand Chamber which (by 11 votes to 6) confirmed existing case law which excluded tax proceedings from the scope of Art 6.

15 See further Bradley 'Administrative Justice: A Developing Human Right' (1995) 1 EPL 347.

DECISIONS OF THE DOMESTIC COURTS ON 'CIVIL RIGHTS AND OBLIGATIONS'

5.14 The English courts have held that applications for a sex offender order[1], an anti-social behaviour order[2], or the condemnation of goods seized by HM Customs and Excise[3], are 'civil proceedings' rather than criminal proceedings. In one such case Lord Woolf LCJ gave the following reasons for his conclusion:

> 'First, this is clearly a two-stage exercise: the obtaining of the order, and proceedings for breach of the order. Secondly, I rely on the fact that the process is one which is generally used for civil proceedings. Thirdly, I rely on the fact that there is no punishment properly involved here; there is, at most, a restriction on the activities of those subject to the order. Fourthly, I rely on the fact that the objective of making an order, as is clear from the statutory provisions and their historical background, is designed not to punish but to protect; it is not an order made to deprive those subject to the order of any of their normal rights. It is an order, however, which impinges on those rights, but does so for the protection of a section of the public who would otherwise be likely to be subjected to conduct of a socially disruptive nature by those subject to the order. Finally, the administrative nature of the proceedings, involving the requirement that it "appears" to the relevant authority is inconsistent with the proceedings being criminal[4].'

A children's hearing determines civil rights and obligations, even if the ground of referral is the commission of an offence[5]. The absence of any penal sanction, in particular, indicates that proceedings are not to be classified as criminal[6]. Tax assessments do not normally involve civil rights and obligations[7]. An unresolved question is whether, under the Scotland Act 1998 and the Human Rights Act 1998, rights (or some of them) in terms of the European Convention on Human Rights should themselves be regarded as 'civil rights' within the meaning of Article 6(1).

1 *B v Chief Constable of Avon and Somerset Constabulary* [2001] 1 WLR 340.
2 *R (McCann) v Manchester Crown Court* [2001] 1 WLR 358.
3 *Goldsmith v Customs and Excise Commissioners* [2001] 1 WLR 1673.
4 *R (McCann) v Manchester Crown Court* [2001] 1 WLR 358 at para 24.
5 *S v Miller* 2001 SLT 531.
6 *B v Chief Constable of Avon and Somerset Constabulary* [2001] 1 WLR 340 per Lord Bingham LCJ at para 28; *R (McCann) v Manchester Crown Court* [2001] 1 WLR 358 per Lord Woolf LCJ at para 31; *S v Miller* 2001 SLT 531 per LP Rodger of Earlsferry at para 22.
7 *Eagerpath Ltd v Edwards* [2001] STC 26. As to the position of objectors to a planning application, see *R (Vetterlein) v Hampshire County Council* (14 June 2001, unreported), QBD.

PUBLIC LAW ISSUES EXCLUDED FROM 'CIVIL RIGHTS AND OBLIGATIONS'

5.15   There are limits to the scope of 'civil rights and obligations'. Political rights such as the right to stand for election and to sit in the legislature fall outwith the category of civil rights[1], as do other public law rights which do not have the necessary economic base[2] to qualify as a civil right, such as questions concerning freedom of movement[3], immigration and deportation[4]. In *Maaouia v France*, the applicant had sought to have set aside a deportation order made by a criminal court. The European Court of Human Rights considered that this did not involve the determination of a 'civil right' for the purposes of the article, even although the exclusion order would have had a major impact upon the applicant's private and family life and employment prospects. The provisions of the European Convention on Human Rights had to be construed in the light of the entire Convention system, and the terms of Protocol 7, Article 1 which France had ratified provided additional procedural guarantees applicable to the expulsion of aliens thus implying that Article 6 did not apply in this regard[5]. On the other hand, the Court seems to have revised its position on whether the right to liberty can be considered as a civil right within the meaning of Article 6[6]. However, even public law matters with particular financial consequences for an individual may escape Article 6 concern. Determination of tax liability is considered a public law issue and does not qualify as a 'civil right'[7], a position recently reconfirmed by the Grand Chamber in *Ferrazzini v Italy* in determining that the public nature of the relationship between the taxpayer and the tax authority remained predominant over any pecuniary interest in such matters[8]. Administrative penalties which escape application of the designation of 'criminal charge' may, however, still give rise to issues involving determination of a civil right or obligation[9].

1 *Pierre-Bloch v France* 1997-VI, 2206, paras 50–51.
2 Cf *Tinnelly and Sons Ltd and McElduff and Ors v United Kingdom* 1998-IV, 1633, paras 61–62 (dispute arising out of discrimination in the award of public procurement contracts concerned 'civil rights').
3 28979/95 and 30343/96, *Adams and Benn v United Kingdom* (1997) DR 88, 137 (questions arising under EC Treaty, Art 8A (1) concerning freedom of movement and residence within the EU are not covered by ECHR, Art 6(1)).
4 3225/67, *X, Y, Z, V and W v United Kingdom* (1968) CD 25, 117 (admission of aliens); 9285/89, *X Y and Z v United Kingdom* (1982) DR 29, 205 (expulsion of aliens). Note, however, that expulsions may give rise to Art 8 issues concerning private and family life which may require to be taken into account in decision-making: see para 6.12 below.
5 (5 October 2000), paras 35–38. Nor did the matter constitute a 'criminal charge' merely on

account that the order had been made by a criminal court following upon a conviction: para 39.

6 In *Neumeister v Austria* (1968) A 8, at para 23, the Court considered that acceptance of such an interpretation would give 'excessively wide scope . . . to the concept of 'civil rights'. In *Ireland v United Kingdom* (1978) A 25, para 235, the Court left this question open. More recently, in *Aerts v Belgium* 1998-V, 1939, para 59, the Court acknowledged that the right to liberty was a civil right, and thus the determination by domestic courts of the compatibility of the applicant's detention with domestic and Convention law fell within the scope of Art 6.

7 *Schouten and Meldrum v Netherlands* (1994) A 304, at para 50 (an 'obligation which is pecuniary in nature [which] derives from tax legislation or is otherwise part of normal civic duties in a democratic society' will belong 'exclusively to the realm of public law' and will thus not fall within the scope of Art 6(1)). See too 49210/99, *Charlambos v France* (8 February 2000) and 49289/99, *Bassan v France* (8 February 2000) (Art 6 was generally inapplicable to tax proceedings; and it was not enough merely to show that proceedings were of a pecuniary nature to qualify as 'civil rights and obligations': applications inadmisible). Cf *Hentrich v France* (1994) A 296-A, para 56 (taxation authority's decision to exercise a right of pre-emption involving an interference with property rights and based upon reasons which were too summary and general to allow the applicant to mount a reasoned challenge: violation of Art 6). This approach was followed by the Court of Appeal in *Eagerpath Ltd v Edwards* [2001] STC 26.

8 (12 July 2001), paras 24–31. Cf the dissenting opinion which carries an exhaustive survey of existing case law of public law issues which are considered to fall within the scope of Art 6.

9 For discussion of administrative penalties, see para 5.22 below. Cf *Bendenoun v France* (1994) A 284, paras 46–47 (predominance of aspects with a criminal connotation rendered the surcharge a criminal charge; such a system of tax surcharges imposed as penalties was not inconsistent with Art 6, providing a taxpayer could challenge a decision in a court affording Art 6 guarantees). See McFarlane 'Customs and Excise Legislation and the Human Rights Act' 2000 SLT (News) 327, for discussion of powers of customs officers to seize goods and impose fines.

APPLICATION TO CIVIL SERVICE EMPLOYMENT DISPUTES

5.16 A distinction had been drawn over time in the Court's case law between public service employment disputes which concerned recruitment, careers and termination of service of civil and other public servants, and those which were deemed 'purely' or 'essentially' economic such as the payment of salaries or pensions to retired civil servants or other public officials. In the latter case, disputes were treated generally as falling within the scope of the European Convention on Human Rights, Article 6[1]; in the former instance, the jurisprudence was unsatisfactory. This area of case law provided little clear guidance, and was acknowledged by the Grand Chamber of the Court in its recent case of *Pellegrin v France* as containing a 'margin of uncertainty' calling for revision[2]. The applicant who had been a civil servant working overseas as a technical adviser had not had his contract of employment renewed on account of a finding of medical unfitness. He had challenged this finding in the administrative courts, but after some nine years was still awaiting a decision, and accordingly sought to argue in Strasbourg that he had been denied a determination within a reasonable time in terms of Article 6(1). The Court first noted that the current practice in European states was that both established civil servants (who, in France, were subject to public law rules) and officials under contract (regulated by domestic private law) frequently performed similar duties. To resolve the issue of the scope of Article 6 solely on the basis of the domestic applicability of public or private legal provisions would lead to inequality of treatment between European states as well as between individuals within a particular state performing equivalent duties. The Court thus adopted a new criterion of functionality based upon a public servant's duties and responsibilities to determine the applicability of Article 6. The only disputes excluded from the scope of Article 6(1) were to be those complaints raised by public servants whose duties involve 'wield[ing] a portion of the State's sovereign power' where the state has 'a legitimate interest in requiring of these servants a special bond of trust and loyalty'. Clear illustrations of such office-holders, said the Court, were members of the police service and armed forces. Applying this criterion to the particular case, the Court held that Article 6 was not applicable since the applicant's post had involved considerable responsibilities in the area of public finance while exercising public law duties designed to protect the general interests of the state[3].

Disputes which are deemed 'purely' or 'essentially' economic and which in the past might have been considered to fall within the scope of Article 6 will now have to be considered in light of the ruling in *Pellegrin v France*[4]. Applying its test as to whether public sector employees participate directly in the exercise of public law powers and perform duties which are designed to safeguard state interests, the Court has held that appeal court judges who were contending that they were entitled to a higher salary fell within this category and thus Article 6 was not applicable[5]. On the other hand, a dispute concerning pension rights of retired judges who no longer exercise state authority was considered to involve Article 6 issues in *Dimitrios Georgiadis v Greece*[6].

This functionality test should not be applied too restrictively, however, as the Grand Chamber warned subsequently in *Frydlender v France*. The applicant again had been advised that he was not to have his short-term contract working abroad renewed, on this occasion on account of unsatisfactory performance of duties. Applying its reasoning in *Pellegrin*, the Court decided that the employment dispute in this instance did fall within the scope of Article 6. The applicant had worked for a department which was responsible to the Ministry for Economic Affairs (rather than to the Ministry of Foreign Affairs) and his duties had involved the promotion of exports of French products through giving advice and assistance to official and semi-official bodies and to individual exporters or importers. Both the nature of these duties and the relatively low level of responsibilities indicated that he had not been 'carrying out any task which could be said to entail, either directly or indirectly, duties designed to safeguard the general interests of the State'. Were the Court to hold otherwise and accept the contentions of the state that staff in this department were by analogy or extension, and irrespective of their duties or responsibilities, to be considered as exercising public law powers, the object and purpose of Article 6 would be compromised[7]. In time, further clarification of the scope of Article 6 in this area will come with the development of case law. For example, Article 6 has been recently held to apply to disputes relating to contracts of employment of medical staff[8] and to lawyers working as criminologists in state institutions[9].

1 E g *Cazenave de la Roche v France* 1998-III, 1314, paras 42–44 (award of damages to a former civil servant covered a purely economic right). Cf *Huber v France* 1998-I, 105, paras 36–37 (decision to send a civil servant on compulsory leave of absence did not involve an Art 6

issue as this decision concerned her career; the existence of a pecuniary element in the form of a question concerning salary was not relevant). *Maillard v France* 1998-III, 1292, paras 39–41 (pecuniary element merely incidental to primary issue which concerned the applicant's career: Art 6 inapplicable).

2 Accordingly, earlier but still recent decisions in this area cannot now be relied upon: eg *Neigel v France* 1997-II, 399 (reinstatement of shorthand typist: Art 6 inapplicable); *Argento v Italy* 1997-V, 1775 (recruitment and grade assignation did not involve a 'civil right').

3 (8 December 1999), paras 64–71 at para 65. The 'functional criterion' is based upon EU law: cf para 66 (regard was had for guidance to categorisation of activities and posts listed by the European Commission (OJEC No C 72 of 18 March 1988) in view of the derogation from freedom of movement of workers in respect of 'employment in the public service' (EEC Treaty, Article 48(4)), a derogation interpreted restrictively by the European Court of Justice (149/79, *Commission v Belgium* [1980] ECR 3881). The 1988 Communication categorised activities according to whether or not they involved 'direct or indirect participation in the exercise of powers conferred by public law and duties designed to safeguard the general interests of the State'. For an example of an early application of the *Pellegrin* principle, see 31631/96, *Procaccini v Italy* (30 March 2000), paras 13–14 (employment dispute involving a school caretaker; Art 6 applicable as this role did not involve participation in the exercise of powers conferred by public law). Art 6 was not considered applicable in the resolution of a dispute concerning expatriation allowances paid to civil servants working abroad: 42646/98, *Martinez-Caro de la Concha Castañeda and Ors v Spain* (7 March 2000) (inadmissible). See also 45004/98, *Stańczuk v Poland* (14 June 2001) (refusal to reinstate a former secret services agent recruited under the Communist regime: the applicant had not demonstrated that in domestic law he had an arguable claim to have the unfavourable decision reversed; further, the proceedings concerned the dismissal of a public officer working for secret services of the police and which involved the exercise of state powers conferred on the police by public law: inadmissible).

4 (8 December 1999).

5 36401/97, *Kajanen and Tuomaala v Finland* (18 October 2000) (inadmissible). See also 47936/99, *Pitkevitch v Russia* (8 February 2001) (dispute relating to the dismissal of a judge for abuse of her office: inadmissible).

6 (28 March 2000), paras 20–21.

7 (27 June 2000), paras 27–41 at para 39.

8 *Sattonet v France* (2 August 2000), paras 28–30 (contract of director of medical-educational psychology centre).

9 *Castanheira Barros v Portugal* (26 October 2000), paras 26–33.

SOCIAL WELFARE PROVISION

5.17 Application of these principles to social security provision illustrates the incremental manner in which the scope of the European Convention on Human Rights, Article 6 has expanded. In the 1986 case of *Feldbrugge v Netherlands*, the Court for the first time considered that social welfare benefits could fall within the definition of 'civil rights and obligations'. The case concerned a decision to stop the payment of sickness allowances to the applicant after she had been found fit to work. The Court acknowledged that there was no common European approach to the question of whether statutory health insurance schemes were to be treated as a private law right or (as in the Netherlands) as a public law matter; but in any case, the categorisation of such schemes even within a domestic legal system could vary depending upon the basis of the benefit in question. The public law features of social welfare schemes included their statutory and compulsory basis and their administration through state agencies; their private law features involved the economic and personal nature of the claims, their similarity to private schemes of insurance and their link with employment. On balance, the Court was prepared to label the case as dominated by private law concerns, and thus the case was considered to involve determination of a civil right[1]. By 1993, in *Salesi v Italy*, the Court was able to assert that the impact of its decision in *Feldbrugge*, as well as application of a general concern for equality of treatment, warranted 'taking the view that today the general rule is that Article 6(1) does apply in the field of social insurance'. While the particular case concerned welfare assistance as opposed to a scheme of insurance, the differences between these 'cannot be regarded as fundamental at the present stage of the development of social security law'. Here, again, private law features were found to predominate: the applicant had 'suffered an interference with her means of subsistence and was claiming an individual, economic right flowing from specific rules laid down in a statute' which came within the jurisdiction of the ordinary rather than administrative courts in Italy[2]. Subsequent decisions suggest that the factor whether determination of welfare entitlement is made by an administrative tribunal rather than by a non-specialised court is now of little relevance[3]. The conclusion is that with the exception of welfare benefits of a purely discretionary nature, social security entitlements will fall to be determined as involving civil rights[4].

1   (1986) A 99, paras 29–40. Similarly, in *Deumeland v Germany* (1986) A 100, paras 60–74, it was considered that the payment of a supplementary pension to the widow of a man killed in an industrial accident involved a predominance of private law issues and thus Art 6 was applicable.
2   (1993) A 257-E, at para 19.
3   Cf *Schüler-Zgraggen v Switzerland* (1993) A 263, para 46 (the Court applied its reasoning in *Salesi* to deem Art 6(1) applicable in this case which again involved a non-contributory invalidity pension).
4   See also *Tričković v Slovenia* (12 June 2001), paras 36-41 (claim for an advance on the applicant's military pension concerned an Art 6 issue). But cf 39712/98, *La Parola and Ors v Italy* (30 November 2000) (request for further financial assistance in respect of a disabled minor who was already in receipt of benefit on a permanent basis: proceedings were not aimed at determining a dispute but rather entitlement to the additional aid requested, and thus Art 6 was inadmissible). For discussion of recent cases concerning social welfare entitlement involving allegations of discrimination under Art 14, see para 3.47 above. For a domestic example, see *R (Husain) v Asylum Support Adjudicator* (5 October 2001, unreported), QBD.

SOCIAL WELFARE CONTRIBUTIONS

5.18   A similar approach as to whether disputes concerning contributions to social security schemes fall within the European Convention on Human Rights, Article 6 was taken in *Schouten and Meldrum v Netherlands*. The European Court of Human Rights accepted it was not sufficient merely to show that a dispute was pecuniary in nature since payments arising out of normal civic duties such as the determination of tax liability were excluded as belonging exclusively to the field of public law. However, certain additional features of social security contributory schemes including their close relationship with contracts of employment required to be taken into account. In the particular case, the Court considered that the private law features of the scheme were of greater significance than any public law elements and, accordingly, a dispute over contributions fell within the scope of the guarantee[1].

1   (1994) A 304, paras 49–60.

The outcome of the dispute must determine the right or obligation

5.19 The term 'determination' found in the English text requires that the outcome of the dispute must be 'directly decisive' for the civil right or obligation[1]: that is, the proceedings should result in a clear consequence for a civil right, 'mere tenuous connections or remote consequences not being sufficient to bring Article 6(1) into play'[2]. Interlocutory proceedings concerning the taking of interim measures (such as an interim interdict) do not involve the 'determination' of civil rights[3]. In other instances, this requirement will rarely cause difficulty[4]. In *Ringeisen v Austria*, the decisions of the administrative commission were judged to determine the rights between the applicant and the other party to the sale even although the tribunal's decision itself was of a public law character[5]. In *Le Compte, van Leuven and de Meyere v Belgium*, medical practitioners had been suspended pending the determination of whether the doctors had breached professional rules. The Court decided that these proceedings before disciplinary bodies clearly fell within the scope of Article 6 since their outcome directly determined whether the applicants could continue to practise[6]. But any impact on civil rights which is considered too remote will fail the test. Thus the Commission determined in *X v United Kingdom* that the consequences of a deportation order on employment or other private law rights fell outwith the scope of the article[7], and the Court in *Fayed v United Kingdom* held that the proceedings before inspectors appointed to investigate a take-over of a company had not been directly decisive of (or indeed even involved the determination of) the applicants' civil right to reputation[8]. Similarly, if the proceedings cannot have any bearing on an applicant's rights on account of a failure by the applicant to take any necessary steps to be entitled to recognition as a beneficiary of a right, these proceedings cannot be said to be able to lead to a 'determination' necessary to bring Article 6 into play[9].

1 *Ringeisen v Austria* (1971) A 13, at para 94.
2 *Fayed v United Kingdom* (1994) A 294-B, at para 56; *Masson and Van Zon v Netherlands* (1995) A 327-A, at para 44.
3 39754/98, *APIS v Slovakia* (13 January 2000).
4 Cf van Dijk and van Hoof *Theory and Practice of the European Convention on Human Rights* (3rd edn, 1998) at p 397: 'It is sufficient that the outcome of the (claimed) judicial proceedings may be "decisive for", or may "affect", or may "relate to" the determination and/or the exercise of the right, or the determination and/or the fulfilment of the obligation, as the case may be; the effects need not be legal but may also be purely factual.' For a domestic illustration (in the context of housing law), see *R (Johns and McLellan) v Bracknell Forest DC* [2001] 33 HLR 45.
5 (1971) A 13, para 94.
6 (1981) A 43, para 48.
7 7902/77 (1977) DR 9, 224.
8 (1994) A 294-B, paras 66–68. Cf *Fayed v United Kingdom* (1994) A 294-B, paras 60–61 (discussion of the distinction between investigative and dispositive proceedings).
9 Cf *McMichael v United Kingdom* (1995) A 307–B, paras 76–77 (failure of an unmarried father to take steps to secure parental rights in respect of his child); *Hamer v France* 1996-III, 1029, paras 73–79 (failure of the applicant who had intervened in criminal proceedings to make a specific claim for civil damages as required by domestic law).

Criminal charges

5.20   The 'determination' of a 'criminal charge' gives rise to guarantees in terms of the European Convention on Human Rights, Article 6[1]. As with 'civil rights and obligations', the notion of a 'criminal charge' is given an autonomous interpretation[2] and one which is dependent upon a substantive rather than a formal meaning of the term[3] since 'a restrictive interpretation of Article 6(1) would not correspond to the aim and purpose of that provision'[4]. A particular legal dispute may require consideration as to whether Article 6 is applicable on account both that it gives rise to the determination of a criminal charge as well as of a civil right and obligation[5]. There are two principal issues: first, the stage at which in a criminal investigation and process a 'criminal charge' can be said to exist; and second, the circumstances in which a matter considered by domestic law as merely disciplinary or enforced through administrative penalty will fall nevertheless to be considered as a 'criminal charge' for the purpose of the guarantee.

1   The question whether there is a 'determination' is normally subsumed under discussion of the existence of a 'criminal charge', although on occasion the issues may be distinct: eg *JJ v Netherlands* 1998-II, 603, paras 35–40 (appeal to Supreme Court against imposition of fiscal penalty which qualified as a 'criminal charge' declared inadmissible solely on account of the applicant's failure to pay the court registration fee: this gave rise to an Art 6 issue since a successful appeal would have been decisive for the determination of a criminal charge).

2   *Adolf v Austria* (1982) A 49, para 30.

3   *Deweer v Belgium* (1980) A 35, para 44.

4   *Delcourt v Belgium* (1970) A 11, at para 25.

5   Thus if in a particular instance it is considered that a matter is purely disciplinary or otherwise does not involve a 'criminal charge', the matter may still give rise to Art 6 considerations under 'civil rights': eg *Air Canada v United Kingdom* (1995) A 316-A, para 56 (application of Art 6 not disputed); *Aerts v Belgium* 1998-V, 1939, para 59 (lawfulness of detention of person of unsound mind did not give rise to determination of a criminal charge but did involve the right to liberty which was a civil right). Cf 11882/85, *C v United Kingdom* (1987) DR 54, 162 (the applicant had been employed as a janitor at a Scottish school but had been dismissed for petty theft following a hearing before a local authority educational officer and the school's headmaster; a criminal charge of theft had been dismissed in the criminal courts. While Art 6(1) did not apply in every instance of internal disciplinary proceedings in the public service, where a contract of employment (as in the present case) permits access to the civil courts and tribunals for the resolution of disputes, then such recourse may be said to have 'determined' an individual's civil rights).

The concept of a 'charge'

5.21   The first issue is of importance in identifying the stage at which rights in terms of the European Convention on Human Rights, Article 6 come into play under not only paragraph (1) but also paragraphs (2) and (3)[1]. The concept of a 'charge' is not dependent upon domestic law. In *Deweer v Belgium*, the Court considered a criminal charge to be 'the official notification given to an individual by the competent authority of an allegation that he has committed a criminal offence', approving the Commission's test of whether the situation of the suspect has been 'substantially affected[2]. This notification can take whatever form provided for by domestic law[3] and may be constituted by arrest[4], issue of an arrest[5] or a search[6] warrant, by official notification that a prosecution is being instigated[7], by the opening of a preliminary investigation[8], by the bringing

of a private prosecution'[9], or by other official measures carrying the implication of such an allegation and which similarly 'substantially affect the
situation of the suspect', and thus it is possible for Article 6 rights to apply
even although an individual has not been formally charged in domestic
law with an offence[10]. In certain circumstances an individual may also still
claim to be a 'victim' of Article 6's procedural guarantees even although a
subsequent decision not to pursue criminal charges against him is taken[11].

1 Eg *Lutz v Germany* (1987) A 123, para 52.
2 (1980) A 35, at para 46; see too *Eckle v Germany* (1982) A 51, para 73; *Foti and Ors v Germany* (1982) A 56, para 52.
3 Eg *Corigliano v Italy* (1982) A 57, paras 34–35 (the date judicial notification was served on a suspect was the date on which there was a 'charge'); *Belilos v Switzerland* (1988) A 132, para 10 (laying of an information by police officers).
4 Eg *B v Austria* (1990) A 175, para 48.
5 Eg *Boddaert v Belgium* (1992) A 235-D, para 35.
6 Eg *Eckle v Germany* (1982) A 51, paras 73–75.
7 Eg *Mori v Italy* (1991) A 197-C, para 14 (date of formal notification); *Colacioppo v Italy* (1991) 197–D, para 13 (receipt of judicial notice of criminal proceedings).
8 Eg *Ringeisen v Austria* (1971) A 13, para 110.
9 Eg *Minelli v Switzerland* (1983) A 62, para 28 (private prosecution for defamation).
10 *Deweer v Belgium* (1980) A 35, at para 46. Eg *Angelucci v Italy* (1991) A 196-C, para 13 (appointment of defence counsel); *Raimondo v Italy* (1994) A 281-A, para 42 (court order of confiscation of seized goods); *Quinn v Ireland* (21 December 2000), para 42, and *Heaney and McGuinness v Ireland* (21 December 2000), para 42 (applicants were required to answer questions before they had been formally charged with offences; the Court considered that the making of these requirements had thus 'substantially affected' their situation). Cf 39519/98, *Padin Gestoso v Spain* 1999-II, 347 (investigative measures prior to the bringing of a criminal charge did not directly affect the situation of the applicant, and thus Art 6(1) was inapplicable at this stage).
11 *Heaney and McGuinness v Ireland* (21 December 2000), paras 43–46; *Quinn v Ireland* (21 December 2000), paras 43–46 (while in general the lack of subsequent criminal proceedings deprives an individual of status of 'victim' of breach of Art 6 rights, this principle has been refined in certain cases to ensure rights are practical and effective). See further para 5.04 above.

Determining whether a charge is 'criminal'

5.22 The decision to label certain offences as 'disciplinary' or 'administrative' rather than as 'criminal' will not necessarily exclude the application of guarantees in terms of the European Convention on Human
Rights, Article 6. While it is recognised that states are entitled to distinguish between the criminal law and disciplinary codes, this cannot allow
states to escape their responsibilities for ensuring the fair administration
of justice under Article 6 or to avoid the prohibition against retroactive
imposition of sanction under Article 7[1]. In *Engel and Ors v Netherlands*, the
Court considered the proper categorisation of military discipline sanctions imposed upon service personnel by reference to three criteria. First,
the nature of the classification of the offence in domestic law was relevant:
if 'criminal', this will be sufficient to bring the issue within the scope of
Article 6, but if 'disciplinary' this will not be conclusive and will only
provide a starting-point for further evaluation. Second, the nature of the
offence itself required to be assessed: a prohibition directed against a
specific group such as service personnel may in principle rightly be
considered as disciplinary, but it is also appropriate to take into account
comparative practices applying in other European states. Third, the

severity of the penalty which could be imposed upon a determination of guilt was of importance: the more 'appreciably detrimental' the potential sanction, the greater the likelihood that the offence will be considered as criminal, especially if the penalty could involve not inconsiderable loss of liberty[2].

The Court's judgment in this early case which laid down the principles by which 'criminal charge' is to be interpreted – the *Engel* criteria – has subsequently been applied in other instances. For example, in *Öztürk v Germany*, the applicant had collided with a parked car and subsequently had been served with a notice imposing a fine and costs. After an unsuccessful appeal against this notice, he had been ordered to pay additional costs and expenses including the fees of an interpreter. His application challenged the violation of the right to a free interpreter under Article 6(3)(e), but the state responded that the case had not involved a criminal charge. The Court first noted that the ambit of the criminal law normally included 'offences that make their perpetrator liable to penalties intended, inter alia, to be deterrent and usually consisting of fines and of measures depriving the person of his liberty'. Further, the type of road traffic offence in question was classified by the overwhelming majority of European legal systems as criminal as opposed to administrative, and it was a legal rule which was directed 'not towards a given group possessing a special status – in the manner . . . of disciplinary law – but towards all citizens in their capacity as road users' enforced by a sanction that was punitive. Accordingly, the imposition of the administrative penalty (even although it was relatively light) constituted the determination of a criminal charge[3]. In *Weber v Switzerland*, the applicant had been fined by a court for breaching the confidentiality of judicial proceedings in which he was a party. The Court again considered that this had involved a criminal rather than a disciplinary sanction: the legal rule prohibiting disclosure was directed against the population as a whole, and the maximum fine could in certain circumstances have been converted into a term of imprisonment[4]. In *Maaouia v France*, however, the Court refused to label as 'criminal' deportation or exclusion orders made following a conviction, noting that these were considered as essentially administrative by most countries since they involved preventive measures taken within the context of immigration control[5]. Other cases have revolved around the potential severity of the sentence. In *Campbell and Fell v United Kingdom*, prison disciplinary offences covered not only matters of internal discipline but also behaviour which was criminal according to domestic law and punishable by loss of remission of almost three years. The Court took into account the particularly grave character of the offences with which Campbell was charged and the substantial loss of remission (of some 570 days) in determining that Article 6 was applicable to the proceedings of the Board of Visitors[6]. In *Benham v United Kingdom*, the imprisonment of the applicant for the wilful refusal or culpable neglect to pay the community charge (or 'poll tax') was considered to involve a criminal charge despite English law's classification of the court proceedings as civil: the law was of general application, the proceedings, which were brought by a local authority, contained a punitive element, and the maximum penalty (three months' imprisonment) was itself relatively severe[7]. In contrast, in *Phillips v United Kingdom*, the Court ruled that a confiscation order made under the Drug Trafficking Act 1994 following the applicant's conviction did not involve the determination of a 'criminal charge'. While refusal to pay the amount of the compensation order would have resulted in an additional two years' imprisonment, the purpose of the proceedings was neither the acquittal nor the conviction of the applicant[8].

1 *Engel and Ors v Netherlands* (1976) A 22, para 81. For illustrations of the use of administrative sanctions in EU states, see *The System of Administrative and Penal Sanctions in the Member States of the European Communities* (2 vols, 1994).
2 *Engel and Ors v Netherlands* (1976) A 22, paras 80–85 at para 82 (the imposition of two days' strict arrest upon a soldier for breach of military discipline was deemed insufficient to bring the matter within the category of 'criminal'); see too 7341/76, *Eggs v Switzerland* (1979) DR 15, 35 (loss of liberty through imposition of five days' strict arrest for breach of military discipline considered insufficient to establish a 'criminal' offence).
3 (1984) A 73, paras 53–54 at para 53. See too *Lauko v Slovakia* 1998-VI, 2492, paras 56–59 and *Kadubec v Slovakia* 1998-VI, 2518, paras 50–53 (applicability of Art 6 in relation to minor road traffic violations); but cf 43862/98, *Inocêncio Portugal* (11 January 2001) (a pecuniary sanction, even a substantial one, imposed for breach of planning regulations and which would not have resulted in imprisonment in default of payment could not be said to be a punitive measure of general application to all citizens: Art 6 inapplicable).
4 (1990) A 177, paras 33–34. See too *Bendenoun v France* (1994) A 284, para 47 (tax surcharges, potentially applied to all citizens as taxpayers, were intended not as financial compensation but as a punishment and a deterrence to others and thus were 'criminal'); *Schmautzer v Austria* (1995) A 328-A, paras 27–28 (domestic law's labelling as 'administrative *offences*' to be disposed of under 'administrative *criminal* procedure' and the imposition of a fine with the alternative of imprisonment for failure to pay were sufficient to establish the offences as 'criminal'). Cf *Pierre-Bloch v France* 1997-VI, 2206, paras 53–61 (penalty equal to amount of unauthorised expenditure incurred by an election candidate and forfeiture of seat as an MP did not involve a criminal charge: matter was regulated by electoral rather than by criminal law; and the measures differed in crucial respects from criminal penalties).
5 (5 October 2000), para 39.
6 (1984) A 80, paras 69–73. Cf 6224/73, *Kiss v United Kingdom* (1976) DR 7, 55 (80 days' loss of remission insufficient to give rise to a 'criminal charge'); 11691/85, *Pelle v France* (1986) DR 50, 263 (imposition of 12 days' aggravation of detention conditions and risk of loss of 18 days' remission did not give rise to an Art 6 issue). In *R (Greenfield) v Secretary of State for the Home Dept* [2001] 1 WLR 1731, the imposition of 21 days' additional detention for having taken a controlled drug was held not to fall within the scope of Art 6, being a disciplinary matter rather than the determination of a criminal charge. The same view was taken in *R (Carroll) v Secretary of State for the Home Department* (16 February 2001, unreported), QBD. The use of additional days and loss of remission as punishments was however suspended in Scotland as from 11 June 2001, the Scottish Prison Service having been advised that these forms of punishment might be at risk of successful challenge under the Convention. In *Matthewson v The Scottish Ministers* (28 June 2001, unreported), Ct of S, the possibility that the outcome of the disciplinary hearing might affect the prisoner's prospects of being recommended by the Parole Board for release on licence was held not to render Art 6 applicable for the hearing. As to the fixing of the 'tariff' element of a life sentence, see paras 4.87ff above.
7 1996-III, 738, para 56. See too *Demicoli v Malta* (1991) A 210, paras 31–34 (failure to pay a fine could result in a maximum period of 60 days' imprisonment and thus Art 6 applied); *A P, M P and T P v Switzerland* 1997-V, 1477, paras 39–43 and *E L, R L and J O-L v Switzerland*, 1997-V, 1509, para 44 (nature and severity of tax penalties which were not intended as pecuniary compensation but were essentially punitive: Art 6 applicable); *Garyfallou AEBE v Greece* 1997-V, 1821, 32–35 paras 29–35 (fine for violation of trade regulations classified not as an administrative but as a criminal penalty); *Malige v France* 1998-VII, 2922, paras 34–40, (sanction of deducting penalty points from a driving licence which had the possible consequence of disqualification from driving involved the determination of a criminal charge). Cf 45282/99, *Blokker v Netherlands* (7 November 2000) (administrative decision to require the applicant to undergo a training course at his own expense after his conviction for drink-driving under threat of loss of his driving licence should he refuse involved verification of suitability and did not involve a criminal charge).

8 (5 July 2001), paras 28–36; but cf paras 37–47 (the making of the order was still covered by Art 6(1) as this followed on from the initial prosecution, and the guarantee covered the proceedings in their entirety).

DECISIONS OF DOMESTIC COURTS ON THE MEANING OF A 'CRIMINAL CHARGE'

5.23   The approach outlined in, for example, the judgment in *Engel and Ors v Netherlands*[1] has been applied by United Kingdom courts in a number of contexts, such as proceedings involving insane offenders[2], children's hearings[3], sex offender orders[4], anti-social behaviour orders[5], the condemnation of goods seized by HM Customs and Excise[6] and the withdrawal of bail[7]. These decisions have emphasised in particular that the absence of any penal sanction indicates that the proceedings in question are not to be classified as criminal for the purposes of the European Convention on Human Rights, Article 6. Penalty assessments issued by the Inland Revenue and HM Customs and Excise, on the other hand, have been held to constitute criminal charges within the meaning of Art 6[8].

1 (1976) A 22.
2 *R v M* (5 October 2001, unreported), CA.
3 *S v Miller* 2001 SLT 531. See para 5.36 below.
4 *R (McCann) v Manchester Crown Court* [2001] 1 WLR 358. See para 5.14 above.
5 *B v Chief Constable of Avon and Somerset Constabulary* [2001] 1 WLR 340. See para 5.14 above.
6 *Goldsmith v Customs and Excise Commissioners* [2001] 1 WLR 1673.
7 *R (Director of Public Prosecutions) v Havering Magistrates' Court* [2001] 1 WLR 805.
8 *King v Walden* [2001] STC 822; *Customs and Excise Commissioners v Hall* [2001] STC 1188.

CONTEMPT OF COURT

5.24   These criteria can also be applied in respect of determinations by a court of improper behaviour during the course of judicial proceedings, although the outcome of the case law seems to suggest some reluctance to find that the European Convention on Human Rights, Article 6 is applicable, with the possible exception of action taken against a witness for failing to appear before a court[1]. In *Ravnsborg v Sweden*, the applicant had been fined for making improper comments in written pleadings. The Court was not, however, satisfied that this exercise of judicial authority amounted to the determination of a criminal charge. Since there was room for doubt as to whether the imposition of sanctions for disturbing the good order of court proceedings was considered as criminal by Swedish law, the Court turned its attention to assessment of the nature of the offence and of the nature and degree of severity of the penalty. Noting that such a power to sanction disorderly behaviour was a common feature of European legal systems and essentially involved a determination by a judge of his own accord that a breach of good order had occurred, the Court considered that this power was closer to exercise of disciplinary authority than the imposition of a sanction for violation of the criminal law. This conclusion was clearly influenced by practical considerations: courts require to respond to inappropriate behaviour 'even if it is neither necessary nor practicable to bring a criminal charge'. Further, even although the fine could be converted to a term of imprisonment, this could only be done in limited circumstances and in separate proceedings, and in any case the prescribed maximum fine was not high enough to warrant the classification of 'criminal'[2]. Similarly, in *Putz v Austria*, the punishment of the applicant for unfounded accusations or offensive remarks made during a hearing and considered disruptive was not considered to fall within the scope of Article 6. The Court followed its ruling in *Ravnsborg* and considered that the nature of these sanctions was essentially disciplinary; and while the maximum fine was substantially higher in this case, a sentence of imprisonment would only arise if the fine was not paid, was limited to ten days' custody, and was subject to appeal[3].

1 *Serves v France* 1997-VI, 2159, para 42.
2 (1994) A 283-B, paras 33–35, at para 34 (the maximum fine was approximately £100).
3 1996-I, 312, paras 31–37 (the maximum prescribed fine was approximately £500). However, cf *T v Austria* (14 November 2000), paras 61–67 (imposition of fine without a hearing for abuse of process (submitting a fraudulent declaration of means in support of an application for legal aid); the fine imposed was approx £1,500 and was converted into ten days' imprisonment for non-payment: absence of safeguards which had been in place *Ravnsborg v Sweden* (1994) A 283-B taken together with what was at stake for the applicant were sufficiently important to warrant classifying the matter as 'criminal'). Proceedings for breach of an order of the court may well be in a different position from disorderly behaviour in court: cf *Murbarak v Murbarak* [2001] 1 FLR 698, concerned with English committal proceedings.

FORFEITURE PROCEEDINGS CONSEQUENTIAL UPON CRIMINAL ACTS COMMITTED BY A THIRD PARTY

5.25 Proceedings leading to the seizure of property consequential upon acts for which third parties are prosecuted will not involve a 'criminal charge'. In *AGOSI v United Kingdom*, the forfeiture of gold coins owned by the applicant company but smuggled by a third party was considered as a measure 'consequential upon' the criminal behaviour of third parties. Since the company had not been prosecuted, state action of this kind 'cannot of itself lead to the conclusion that, during the proceedings complained of, any "criminal charge", for the purposes of Article 6, could be considered as having been brought against the applicant company'[1]. Similarly, in *Air Canada v United Kingdom*, the seizure of an aircraft in which drugs had been found did not involve a criminal charge against the airline company, even although the company had only been able to recover its property by the payment of a substantial sum of money[2].

1 (1986) A 108, para 65.
2 (1995) A 316-A, paras 52–55.

ACCESS TO AN INDEPENDENT AND IMPARTIAL COURT OR TRIBUNAL

5.26 The European Convention on Human Rights, Article 6(1) guarantees practical and effective access for the determination of civil rights and criminal liability to a court or tribunal established by law which enjoys the attributes of independence and impartiality and which is able to determine all aspects of the dispute and thereafter to give a binding judgment. Article 6 does not extend to guaranteeing a right to trial by jury in states where the legal system makes use of them[1], but where a jury has formed part of the judicial process, it will require to meet expectations of independence and impartiality[2].

1 Cf 14739/89, *Callaghan v United Kingdom* (1989) DR 60, 296 (trial by jury was not an essential aspect of a determination of a criminal charge; and thus the refusal to allow new evidence to be considered by a jury (rather than by an appeal court) did not give rise to an Art 6 issue).
2 See para 5.43 below.

Practical and effective access to a court or tribunal

5.27   Practical and effective access implies the right to have a legal issue brought before a court or tribunal without improper or impractical difficulties. States are left with a free choice as to the means of facilitating access, for example, through the provision of a legal aid scheme[1]. Access to a court also extends to enforcement of court judgments which have become final since otherwise the concept of a fair hearing would cease to have any real meaning[2]. Access is not concerned solely with the conduct of proceedings already initiated. In the early case of *Golder v United Kingdom*, the refusal to allow a prisoner to contact a lawyer without the prior approval of a government minister was held to violate the European Convention on Human Rights, Article 6(1). The applicant had sought to consult a legal adviser with a view to instigating civil proceedings against a prison officer and thus exculpate himself of a charge made against him by the same officer. The Court clarified that the right to initiate legal proceedings had to be read into Article 6(1) as an inherent element having regard to its object and purpose. Were the paragraph to cover only an action already commenced in the courts, a state could 'do away with its courts, or take away their jurisdiction to determine certain classes of civil actions and entrust it to organs dependent upon the Government', a situation which would be 'indissociable from a danger of arbitrary power'[3]. However, the right of access to a court is not absolute. 'There is room, apart from the bounds delimiting the very content of any right, for limitations permitted by implication', and such regulation may 'vary in time and place according to the needs and resources of the community and of individuals'[4]. Any limitation must pursue an aim which is legitimate and have a reasonable relationship of proportionality between the means selected and the purpose of the restriction. Provided further that any limitation does not 'restrict or reduce the access left to the individual in such a way or to such an extent that the very essence of the right is impaired'[5], a certain margin of appreciation covers domestic determination of access to a court.

1 *Airey v Ireland* (1979) A 32, para 26. See further para 5.35 below. For discussion of legal aid in criminal cases, see paras 5.127 and 5.128 below.
2 Eg *Antonakopoulos, Vortsela and Antonakopoulos v Greece* (14 December 1999), paras 24–27; *Dimitrios Georgiadis v Greece* (28 March 2000), paras 22–27. See further para 5.37 below.
3 (1975) A 18, paras 25–40, at para 35.
4 *Golder v United Kingdom* (1975) A 18, at para 38, citing *Belgian Linguistics case* (1968) A 6, Law, para 5. For example, the Government is not bound to grant special leave to remain in the United Kingdom in favour of any litigant in proceedings which cannot satisfactorily be conducted from abroad: *Nwokoye v Secretary of State for the Home Department* (20 June 2001, unreported), Ct of S.
5 *Ashingdane v United Kingdom* (1985) A 93, paras 55–60, at para 57. In extraordinary circumstances or states of emergency, there may be a finding that there is effectively no access to the judicial system: cf *Akdivar and Ors v Turkey* 1996-IV, 1192, para 70 (discussion of exhaustion of domestic remedies).

DECISIONS OF DOMESTIC COURTS ON ACCESS TO A COURT

5.28 A rule of procedure requiring a particular claim to be made by a particular form of process does not entail any contravention of the European Convention on Human Rights, Article 6(1)[1]. The right of access applies to criminal as well as civil proceedings[2]. Other relevant domestic decisions are noted elsewhere[3].

1 *Renyana-Stahl Anstalt v MacGregor* (29 March 2001, unreported), Ct of S.
2 See eg *R v Charles* (31 January 2001, unreported), CA (extension of time limit for lodging application for leave to appeal).
3 See para 5.27, n 4 above (grant of special leave to remain), 5.29, n 2 (vexatious litigants), 5.31 (domestic rules excluding liability or enforcement), 5.36 (legal aid) below.

Restrictions on capacity to pursue civil actions or appeals on points of law

5.29 Such limitations can involve restrictions of capacity to sue, providing always that the tests of legitimate aim and proportionality can be met. In *Ashingdane v United Kingdom*, for example, limitations on access to courts by mental health patients were considered as necessary for preventing the undue harassment of health staff[1]. In *H v United Kingdom* restrictions placed on the applicant as a designated vexatious litigant were accepted by the Commission as not limiting the applicant's right of access completely, and as not disproportionate to the legitimate aim of ensuring the proper administration of justice in Scotland[2]. In *Lithgow v United Kingdom*, a statutory scheme for the collective settlement of disputes concerning compensation for industries taken into state ownership had required shareholders to have recourse solely to the relevant compensation tribunal. This arrangement was deemed neither as impairing the right of access to a court, nor as inappropriate given the state's aim of avoiding multiple claims[3]. In *Tolstoy Miloslavsky v United Kingdom*, an order requiring the applicant to pay security for costs before appellate proceedings could be instituted was upheld as pursuing the legitimate aim of protecting the other party to the action from irrecoverable costs[4]. On the other hand, in *Philis v Greece*, a limitation on legal capacity which had prevented the applicant from recovering payment of fees without direct recourse to his professional organisation was not considered justifiable since the very essence of the right of access to a court had been impaired[5]. A violation was also found in *Canaea Catholic Church v Greece* where the legal personality of the church had been called into question by its failure to comply in time with domestic law governing acquisition of legal personality and by a subsequent court decision that it had no capacity to take legal proceedings. For the Court, this injured the very substance of the right of access to a court[6]. Similarly, in *Société Anonyme 'Sotiris et Nikos Koutras ATTEE' v Greece*, the inadmissibility of the applicant company's application for judicial review on account of an error for which it was not responsible was considered to constitute a violation of its right to access to a court[7].

1 (1985) A 93, para 58 (partial restrictions upon the right to sue the Secretary of State or the relevant health authority were considered neither to impair the essence of access to a court nor to be disproportionate: para 59).
2 11559/85 (1985) DR 45, 182 (restrictions imposed by virtue of the Vexatious Actions (Scotland) Act 1898); followed in *Lord Advocate v Bell* (23 March 2001, unreported), Ct of S

and in *Ebert v Official Receiver* [2001] 3 All ER 942. See also *A-G v Wheen* [2001] IRLR 91; cf
Cachia v Faluyi [2001] 1 WLR 1966.
3 (1986) A 102, paras 195–196.
4 (1995) A 316-B, paras 59–67. In contrast, the Court established a violation in *Garcia Manibardo
    v Spain* (15 February 2000), paras 36–45 (the applicant's appellate action had been ruled
    inadmissible by the domestic courts on account of her failure to deposit a sum of money,
    but this decision had been taken at a stage before her legal aid application had been con-
    sidered: this led to a disproportionate interference with her right of access to a court and
    thus a violation of Art 6(1)); and in *Kreuz v Poland* (19 June 2001), paras 52–67 (fee required
    to initiate an action amounted to the average annual salary in the country: this excessive
    amount constituted a disproportionate restriction on the right of access to a court).
5 (1991) A 209, paras 59–65.
6 1997-VIII, 2843, paras 32–42.
7 (16 November 2000), paras 17–23. See too *Annoni di Gussola and Debordes and Omer v France*
    (14 November 2000), paras 48–59 (failure of applicants to comply with court order to pay
    designated sums resulted in refusal of appeal court to deal with legal merits of the appeal;
    while the obligation to execute the judgment appealed against pursued a legitimate aim,
    the appeal court had failed to consider the precariousness of the applicants' financial situ-
    ation and had failed to give a reasoned judgment: the decision was thus disproportionate
    and a violation of right of access to a court). Cf 46275/99, *Arvanitakis v France* (5 December
    2000) (no 'manifestly excessive consequences' in refusing to admit an appeal on points of
    law for failure to execute the judgment appealed against).

RULES EXCLUDING OR RESTRICTING CIVIL LIABILITY

5.30 In general, limitations on the right to sue through application of
rules concerning prescription and limitation of actions will be considered
as justifiable[1]. Limitations may also involve immunities such as a defence
of absolute or qualified privilege. This matter is not without difficulty. A
state's positive obligations under the European Convention on Human
Rights may require domestic law to ensure that certain civil rights are
recognised[2]. On the other hand, only a civil right with an arguable basis in
domestic law will fall within the scope of Article 6. Immunity from suit
which excludes a course of action by virtue of substantive provisions of
domestic law (for example, in respect of an advocate's conduct of legal proceedings) is thus properly considered as an issue involving the applicability of Article 6 rather than access to a court[3]. If, on the other hand, a
limitation is essentially procedural in character, then the matter is more
properly one examined under Article 6 as a question of restriction of access
to a court. The distinction between a substantive and procedural limitation
may be a fine one, as acknowledged in *Fayed v United Kingdom*. The applicants had sought to challenge in an action of defamation statements made
in a report of inspectors who had been appointed to investigate the take-
over of a company. Such statements were covered by a defence of privilege
in domestic law. The Court accepted that a state was entitled to determine
the extent to which independent investigation into large public companies
should run the inevitable 'risk of some uncompensated damage to reputation'. Attaching privilege to the reports could thus be considered a legitimate and proportionate response for furthering the supervision of public
companies and to help ensure their proper conduct, although 'it may
sometimes be no more than a question of legislative technique whether
[such a] limitation is expressed in terms of the right or its remedy'[4]. This
matter will thus call for some care. If the civil right sought to be asserted
does not have an arguable basis in domestic law, it will not fall within the
scope of Article 6[5]. This was made clear by the court in *Z and Ors v United*

Kingdom[6]. This case concerned the compatibility with the Convention of the decision of the House of Lords in *X (Minors) v Bedfordshire County Council*[7]. The Court made it clear that Article 6 does not in itself guarantee any particular content for civil rights and obligations in national law, although other articles, such as Article 8 and Protocol 1, Article 1, might do so. It was not enough to bring Article 6 into play that the non-existence of a cause of action under domestic law might be described as having the same effect as an immunity, in the sense of not enabling the applicant to sue for a given category of harm. The applicants had been the victims of a breach of Article 3, and ought therefore to have had a remedy under domestic law; but that gave rise to an issue under Article 13, not Article 6[8].

1 Eg *Stubbings and Ors v United Kingdom* 1996-IV, 1487, paras 51–57 (limitation period of six years from attaining majority for bringing an action alleging child abuse did not impair the right of access to a court). Cf *De Geouffre de la Pradelle v France* (1992) A 253-B, paras 34–35 (notification of administrative action only after the expiry of the time limit for challenge: discussed at para 5.33 below). For consideration of retroactive extension of limitation periods in criminal cases, see *Coëme and Ors v Belgium* (22 June 2000), discussed at para 5.140 below. For a domestic example, see *Family Housing Association v Donnellan* (12 July 2001, unreported), Ch D.
2 See further paras 3.07–3.10 above.
3 The Crown's immunity from suit is thus considered as a restriction on liability imposed by substantive law: cf 10475/83, *Dyer v United Kingdom* (1984) DR 39, 246.
4 (1994) A 294-B, paras 65–83 at paras 81 and 67 respectively.
5 See para 5.12 above.
6 (10 May 2001), paras 91–104.
7 [1995] 2 AC 633.
8 See also the related case of *TP and KM v United Kingdom*, decided the same day. These two decisions of the Grand Chamber effectively overturn the judgment in *Osman v United Kingdom* 1998-VIII, 3124, paras 133-154 relating to access to court (restriction on ability to sue a chief constable for the negligent actions of his officers in failing to prevent the death of the first applicant's husband and the serious wounding of the second applicant on account of the rule in *Hill v Chief Constable of West Yorkshire* [1989] AC 53; the rule was considered by the Court not as an absolute bar to any such proceeding but as one allowing a court to assess on the basis of reasoned arguments whether the particular case was one in which the rule should be applied or not: and thus the failure to allow the applicants to argue that the exclusion of liability should not be imposed was deemed a violation of Article 6).

DECISIONS OF DOMESTIC COURTS ON RULES EXCLUDING CIVIL LIABILITY

5.31 The European Convention on Human Rights, Article 6 does not preclude a state from granting immunity to a foreign state as required by international law[1]. It has also been held that the statutory bar to enforcement of consumer credit agreements which do not contain the prescribed terms is incompatible with Article 6(1)[2].

1 *Holland v Lamper-Wolfe* [2000] 1 WLR 1573.
2 *Wilson v First County Ltd (No 2)* [2001] 3 WLR 42.

Interference in article 6 rights by the legislature

5.32 Where a limitation takes the form of legislation which has the effect of influencing the outcome of a judicial determination of a dispute falling within the scope of the European Convention on Human Rights, Article 6 by depriving an applicant of his chance of winning the litigation, the European Court of Human Rights will scrutinise the reasons advanced for this interference with particular care, mindful of the dangers inherent for respect for the rule of law and the notion of a fair trial. 'However, Article 6(1) cannot be interpreted as preventing any interference by the authorities with pending legal proceedings to which they are a party'[1], but any interference with legal rights which takes the form of legislative provisions with retrospective effect must be justified 'on compelling grounds of the general interest'[2], and it will thus always be a question on the facts whether an interference of this kind is justifiable. In *Stran Greek Refineries and Stratis Andreadis v Greece*, the applicants had been granted an enforceable arbitration award in their favour awarding them compensation against the state. The legislature had thereafter enacted a statute with the purpose of annulling the outcome of the judicial proceedings. For the Court, this legislative intervention at a time when the state was a party to litigation in such a manner as to ensure that the ultimate outcome of the proceedings would be favourable to its case amounted to a violation of the guarantee[3]. In contrast, in *National and Provincial Building Society, Leeds Permanent Building Society and Yorkshire Building Society v United Kingdom*, legislation which deprived the applicant societies of their opportunity of being successful in restitution proceedings against the Inland Revenue was considered not to have violated Article 6: the statute had been passed at a time when judicial review proceedings had not even been at the stage of an inter partes hearing; there had been 'even more compelling public-interest motives' than had been the case in the *Stan Greek Refineries* case; recourse to retroactive tax legislation was a feature of several legal systems; and the applicant societies must have been aware that there was a probability that the exemption from taxation upon which they had relied would be subject to parliamentary intervention[4].

1 *National and Provincial Building Society, etc v United Kingdom* 1997-VII, 2325, paras 105–113 at para 112.
2 *Agoudimos and Cefallonian Sky Shipping Co v Greece* (28 June 2001), paras 30–35 at para 30.
3 (1994) A 301-B, paras 44–50. See too *Papageorgiou v Greece* 1997-VI, 2277, paras 37–40; and *Anagnostopoulos and Ors v Greece* (7 November 2000), paras 19–21. Cf *Pressos Compania Naviera and Ors v Belgium* (1995) A 332, paras 28–44 (retroactive exemption from liability for negligence and thus denial of a right of compensation was considered a violation of Protocol 1, Art 1: in the circumstances, there was no need to consider any issue arising under Art 6). See further para 8.05 below).
4 1997-VII, 2325, paras 105–113 at para 112. See too *Truhli v Croatia* (28 June 2001), paras 25–28 (the applicant had been a former officer in the Yugoslav army who had unsuccessfully raised proceedings in the administrative court in respect of the reduction of his army pension; two constitutional complaints had been terminated on the basis that legislation which had come into force in the meantime had confirmed the position with regard to the pensions and had introduced new pensions provisions, and a third constitutional complaint in respect of the decisions taken by the administrative court had been dismissed on the ground that the decisions at issue were based on the relevant laws: no violation of the right of access to a court since the applicant had availed himself of the right of access to the administrative court, and the fact that the constitutional court had decided to terminate other proceedings did not restrict the exercise of this right in such a way or to such an extent that the very essence of the right was impaired).

State responsibilities in ensuring practical and effective access

5.33   The right of access must be one which is practical and effective rather than merely illusory. This implies at the outset that the legal system provides a 'sufficiently coherent and clear' indication of any decision affecting an individual's rights to allow the party concerned the opportunity of legal challenge[1]. In *De Geouffre de la Pradelle v France*, the applicant had certainly enjoyed the theoretical possibility of challenging an administrative decision affecting his property rights, but the Court considered his right of access to a court had been violated. Not only was the law on conservation areas of considerable complexity, but also the applicant had not been notified of the decision until two months after the decree had been published in the *Official Gazette* and then only when the time limit for raising an action had expired[2].

1 *De Geouffre de la Pradelle v France* (1992) A 253-B, at para 35.
2 (1992) A 253-B, paras 28–35.

5.34 Practical and effective access can in certain circumstances also imply access to records held by public authorities to enable a litigant to proceed with his case. In *McGinley and Egan v United Kingdom*, former servicemen who had claimed their health problems were directly linked to their time in the armed forces had been prevented from gaining access to documents they believed would have established that they had been exposed to dangerous doses of radiation. The European Court of Human Rights accepted that the state's failure to produce such documents without good cause could have led to a violation of the right to a fair hearing, but since the applicants had inexplicably failed to use a procedure which had been available to try to obtain the evidence, there could be no finding of denial of effective access to a court or of unfairness[1]. The effect of public interest immunity certificates may thus pose problems in securing effective access to a court. In *Tinnelly and Sons Ltd and Ors and McElduff and Ors v United Kingdom*, a firm of contractors and a number of self-employed joiners had alleged discrimination in the allocation of contracts and employment. In each case, their complaints had been submitted to the Employment Commission which was charged with promoting equality of opportunity in Northern Ireland; but in each instance, the Commission's inquiries had been blocked by the issue of certificates by the Secretary of State to the effect that the decisions taken had involved acts 'done for the purpose of safeguarding national security or of protecting public safety or public order'. While the Court was mindful of the security concerns at stake, it could establish no reasonable relationship of proportionality between the protection of national security relied on and the impact of the certificates on the applicants' right of access to a court. In particular, there had been no independent scrutiny of the reasons advanced for the issue of the certificates, nor any evidence as to why the applicants had been considered a security risk. The Court could not accept that such matters were inappropriate for independent judicial determination, for 'even if national security considerations are present and constitute a highly material aspect of the case', satisfactory arrangements existed in other contexts which both safeguarded national security and also provided individuals with a substantial degree of procedural justice. In short, 'the right guaranteed to an applicant under Article 6(1) of the Convention to submit a dispute to a court or tribunal in order to have a determination of questions of both fact and law cannot be displaced by the *ipse dixit* of the executive'[2].

1 1998-III, 1334, paras 85–90.
2 1998-IV, 1633, paras 72–79 at para 77.

LEGAL AID

5.35 There is no specific mention of a right to civil legal aid in the European Convention on Human Rights, Article 6 (unlike the reference to legal assistance for criminal defendants in paragraph (3)(d)[1]) and the choice of means to ensure practical and effective access to a court is left to states. The provision of legal aid or other state-funded assistance is one such method[2]. In *Airey v Ireland*, the Court considered the failure to provide legal aid to a woman without sufficient financial resources to instruct legal representatives to seek a judicial separation from her husband had rendered her theoretical right to a hearing ineffective. In determining there was a violation of access to a court, the Court indicated that legal aid could only be required in cases where a litigant could not present his own case properly and effectively and where there was a reasonable prospect of success. There could be no duty to supply free legal aid to every litigant seeking to enforce a 'civil right': nonetheless, the provision of free legal representation for civil matters would be necessary either where the complexity of the case made this indispensable or where domestic law makes legal representation compulsory[3]. Further, there are suggestions that the subject matter of the 'dispute' in question may be a relevant factor. In *Munro v United Kingdom*, the Commission accepted the lack of civil legal aid in defamation proceedings in Scotland did not give rise to a violation since the protection of reputation was not as crucial an issue as matters such as regulation of personal or family relationships[4].

1　See paras 5.127–5.128 below.
2　*Andronicou and Constantinou v Cyprus* 1997-VI, 2059, paras 199–201 (offer of *ex gratia* payment from the Attorney General considered adequate).
3　(1979) A 32, paras 24 and 26.
4　10594/83 (1987) DR 52, 158 at 165 (defamation claims are open to abuse and thus restrictions on availability of the action are commonly found in European legal systems; in any case, the substance of the issue had already been tested in a tribunal: no violation of Art 6). See too 37371/97, *Nicholas v Cyprus* (14 March 2000) (no indication that an action had been dismissed on account of the unavailability of legal aid; and the applicant could have represented himself in defamation proceedings: application was thus inadmissible). Cf 46311/99, *McVicar v United Kingdom* (10 May 2001) (the applicant, a journalist, had to defend himself on account of a lack of legal aid against an action of defamation raised by an athlete whom he had accused of using prohibited drugs to enhance his performance: admissible).

DECISIONS OF DOMESTIC COURTS ON LEGAL AID AND LEGISLATIVE REFORM

5.36 In *S v Miller*[1], the Court of Session held that the European Convention on Human Rights, Article 6 in principle required legal representation in proceedings where deprivation of liberty was at stake, and might therefore require the provision of legal aid, where necessary in the interests of justice, in proceedings before a children's hearing. Further, the Convention Rights (Compliance) (Scotland) Act 2001 amends the powers of Scottish Ministers to enable the Scottish Legal Aid Board to make civil legal assistance available for certain proceedings before tribunals and other bodies where Article 6 may require the provision of legal aid to meet the requirements for a fair hearing, while other provisions concern the availability of legal aid in criminal matters[2].

1　2001 SLT 531; see also *S v Miller (No 2)* (7 August 2001, unreported), Ct of S.
2　See paras 5.129 and 5.130 below.

Enforcement of court decisions

5.37 The right of access to a court would be merely illusory if a decision of a domestic court could remain inoperative. 'It would be inconceivable that Article 6 should describe in detail procedural guarantees afforded to litigants – proceedings that are fair, public, and expeditious – without protecting the implementation of judicial decisions', and thus execution of court judgments is regarded as an integral part of a determination[1]. The principle applies to the failure of administrative authorities to take measures necessary to comply with a final and binding court decision[2]. However, some delay in enforcement may be acceptable on account of competing and compelling interests. For example, in *Immobiliare Saffi v Italy*, the European Court of Human Rights accepted that a stay of execution of a judicial decision 'for such period as is strictly necessary' to enable a satisfactory solution to public order problems to be found could be justified 'in exceptional circumstances'. In this case, enforcement of an order against a tenant for possession of his home had frequently been postponed on account of what the state claimed was a threat of serious public disorder justifying first refusal to provide police assistance and then the introduction of a legal power conferring the right on local prefects to intervene in the enforcement of possession orders, a right not made subject to effective judicial review. While accepting that states may intervene in enforcement proceedings by making use of their margin of appreciation in controlling the use of property in exceptional circumstances, 'the consequence of such intervention should not be that execution is prevented, invalidated or unduly delayed or, still less, that the substance of the decision is undermined'. Here, the legislation had the effect of annulling a court decision since the lack of effective judicial review of the decisions of the prefect had deprived the applicant company of its right to rely upon a favourable judicial determination of its dispute with one of its tenants, a situation incompatible with the rule of law[3].

1 *Hornsby v Greece* 1997-II, 495, at para 40 (at para 41: this is of greater importance in respect of administrative proceedings where executive failure to comply with a judicial decision brings into question the concept of legality: 'the administrative authorities form one element of a State subject to the rule of law and their interests accordingly coincide with the need for the proper administration of justice').
2 *Hornsby v Greece* 1997-II, 495, paras 42–45 (failure to comply with a court decision following a decision of the European Court of Justice).
3 1999-V, 73, paras 69–74 at para 69. See too *Antonetto v Italy* (20 July 2000), paras 27–30 (impossibility of enforcing a judgment by the *Conseil d'Etat* to demolish a building built illegally next to the applicant's property: violation of Art 6); and *G L v Italy* (3 August 2000), paras 35–41 (further discussion of the extent of a state's interests in delaying implementation of a judicial decision in exceptional cases). The withdrawal of a tax assessment following a successful appeal, and the issuing of a different assessment, does not offend against this principle: *Bennett v Customs and Excise Commissioners (No 2)* [2001] STC 137.

An independent and impartial tribunal established by law

5.38 The European Convention on Human Rights, Article 6(1) refers to 'an independent and impartial tribunal established by law'. 'Established by law' implies there is a legal basis for the very existence of the tribunal, no matter how specialised its jurisdiction[1]. It may also give rise to questions as to whether a tribunal or court's composition has been in conformity with domestic law, although such issues may in practice be subsumed by consideration of the tribunal's compatibility with Convention requirements[2]. Certainly, defects at first instance may be subsequently cured by a court with full jurisdiction to review the initial decision[3]. Much of the case law concentrates on questions of independence and impartiality. Judicial independence from the parties or the executive or legislature is determined by scrutiny of appointment and terms of office and protection against outside pressure, and impartiality denotes a lack of bias or prejudice. The principles are of general applicability to adjudicatory bodies whether constituted by professional or lay judges or involving jurors[4]. At times, however, the question of impartiality may not be readily disassociated from that of independence, and these two issues may be considered together[5]. Further, the maxim that justice must not only be done but also be seen to be done is of considerable importance[6]: the outward appearance of independence and objective impartiality will be considered necessary to help sustain public confidence in the administration of justice in democratic societies[7].

The importance of appearance was stressed in the judgment in *Kress v France* where a majority of the Grand Chamber found the procedures of the French *Conseil d'Etat* to violate the guarantee. The involvement of an independent officer whose task is to give guidance to the court – an *avocat général* or *procureur général* – is a common feature in many European legal systems (and in the European Court of Justice). The applicant first challenged the lack of 'equality of arms' on the ground that she had not been informed of the submissions of this officer (the 'Government Commissioner') in advance of the hearing. Since these had not been disclosed to either side, the Court considered that it could not be said that the applicant had been placed at a disadvantage; further, although she had not been able to respond orally, she had taken advantage subsequently of the opportunity to comment by means of a written memorandum before the court gave its judgment. Sufficient procedural safeguards had thus been accorded. But this assessment was also of importance in evaluating the impartiality of the court. The Government Commissioner had retired with the court during its deliberations, and although he did not have a vote, the Grand Chamber ruled (by a majority of ten votes to seven) that this had led to a breach of the requirement of the appearance of impartiality. Arguments that the Commissioner was in effect a judge and that his expression of his opinion during the hearing had contributed to the transparency of decision-making were considered inconsistent on account of the absence of the right to vote. Crucially, acceptance that the Commissioner's role had called for appropriate procedural safeguards to protect the adversarial nature of proceedings was also of relevance in assessing the impartiality of the court. The Commissioner's public expression of the merits of the arguments submitted could legitimately be interpreted as siding with one of the parties against the other, and it was thus possible to 'imagine that a party may have a feeling of inequality if, after hearing the Commissioner make submissions unfavourable to his case at the end of the public hearing, he sees him withdraw with the judges of the trial bench to attend the deliberations held in the privacy of chambers' where he would enjoy 'if only to outward appearances, an additional opportunity to bolster his submissions in private, without fear of contradiction'. Such a situation had to be assessed in light of the 'public's increased sensitivity to the fair administration of justice'. Regardless of the Commissioner's acknowledged objectivity, there were insufficient guarantees that the presence of the Commissioner during deliberations would not influence the court's outcomes, and thus there was a violation of Article 6(1)[8].

1 *Lithgow and Ors* (1986) A 102, para 201.
2 Cf *Piersack v Belgium* (1982) A 53, para 33 (domestic question avoided by the Court which established a lack of impartiality under Art 6). Cf *Oberschlick v Austria (No 1)* (1991) A 204, para 50 (judges disqualified by domestic law from sitting in second set of proceedings: national law recognised that their impartiality was open to doubt, and thus there was a violation of Art 6).
3 See paras 5.82–5.85 below.
4 *Holm v Sweden* (1993) A 279-A, para 30.
5 Cf *Ettl and Ors v Austria* (1987) A 117, paras 37–41 and *Stallinger and Kuso v Austria* 1997-II, 660, para 37 (land consolidation decisions taken by land reform boards whose members included civil servants, but whose independence and impartiality were considered not to have been compromised); *Langborger v Sweden* (1989) A 155, paras 34–35 (specialised lay assessors adjudicating upon disputes between landlords and tenants had been nominated by and retained close links with associations having an interest in such issues: legitimate fears in the circumstances that the assessors lacked independence and impartiality); *Incal v Turkey* 1998-IV, 1547, para 71 (there were legitimate grounds for doubting the impartiality and independence of a national security court established to try cases of terrorism); and 28972/95 *Ninn-Hansen v Denmark* (18 May 1999) (lay judges appointed by Parliament to sit on a court of impeachment: no legitimate doubts as to independence or impartiality of judges, and application declared inadmissible).
6 *Campbell and Fell v United Kingdom* (1984) A 80, paras 80–81 (thus weight to be given to prisoners' perceptions that the tribunal which also exercised supervisory responsibilities was not independent; but such perceptions were not in the circumstances sufficient to establish an actual lack of independence).
7 *Piersack v Belgium* (1982) A 53, para 30 (prosecutor who may have dealt with case subsequently sat as a judge in the same matter: impartiality open to doubt); *Sramek v Austria* (1984) A 84, para 42.
8 (7 June 2001), paras 72–88 (at para 86, the Court noted that the Advocate General of the European Court of Justice does not participate in deliberations). The case may have some bearing upon the Court's disposal of a pending challenge to the practice of a clerk retiring with magistrates to help advise them in their deliberations (44564/98, *Mort v United Kingdom*), although the *Kress* decision does seem to be one in which the prior and public expression of opinion was crucial to the disposal of the question of impartiality.

A tribunal established by law

5.39 A 'tribunal' is characterised by its judicial function, that is, a body having the power to give a binding decision[1] after determination of questions of fact and law within its competence[2] and which follows a prescribed procedure[3]. In other words, the term 'is not necessarily to be understood as signifying a court of law of the classic kind, integrated within the standard judicial machinery of the country'[4]. Its composition may include members who are not judges providing always that the appearance of independence is maintained[5]. 'Tribunals' may include regular courts as well as specialised tribunals[6], professional disciplinary bodies[7] and administrative authorities discharging non-judicial as well as judicial functions[8]. On occasion, a tribunal may be charged with additional functions which are non-judicial in nature. In such circumstances, the question will always be whether the requirements of the European Convention on Human Rights as to independence and impartiality have been met in a particular case, for 'neither Article 6 nor any other provision of the Convention requires States to comply with any theoretical constitutional concepts as such'[9]. In *McGonnell v United Kingdom*, the applicant challenged a decision of the Bailiff of Guernsey who combined responsibilities as a judicial officer with powers as a member of the island's executive and legislature. At an earlier stage, the Bailiff had been involved in the consideration of a development plan which had subsequently formed the subject of the judicial proceedings. In holding that the requirements of Article 6(1) had not been met, the European Court of Human Rights noted that direct involvement in the legislative process or in the making of executive rules 'is likely to be sufficient to cast doubt on the judicial impartiality of a person subsequently called on to determine a dispute over whether reasons exist to permit a variation from the wording of the legislation or rules at issue'[10].

1 *Benthem v Netherlands* (1985) A 97, para 40 (administrative litigation division of Council of State only tendered advice; while the advice was normally followed, the division had no power to issue a binding decision).

2 *Coëme and Ors v Belgium* (22 June 2000), paras 105–108 (trial of a government minister and four others in the Court of Cassation which had exclusive jurisdiction to try criminal charges involving ministers, but the court had no established jurisdiction to try the other co-accused who had been indicted to stand trial along with the minister on account of the connection between the charges; while it had been foreseeable that the rules on connection of trials would be applied in the light of academic opinion and domestic case law, the Court ruled that such indications could not have justified the conclusion that the rule on connection was 'established by law' within the meaning of Art 6: violation).

3 *Belilos v Switzerland* (1988) A 132, para 64.

4 *Campbell and Fell v United Kingdom* (1981) A 46, at para 53.

5 *Belilos v Switzerland* (1988) A 132, paras 66–67 (tribunal included legally qualified civil servant from police headquarters sitting in a personal capacity, but who did not enjoy the appearance of impartiality); *Ettl and Ors v Austria* (1987) A 117, paras 38–40 (civil servants were a majority on adjudicatory bodies, but this in itself did not contravene Art 6(1); noted that most legal systems contain examples of professional judges sitting alongside specialists).

6 Eg *Engel and Ors v Netherlands* (1976) A 22, para 89 (military courts); *McMichael v United Kingdom* (1995) A 307-B, para 80 (children's hearings); *British-American Tobacco v United Kingdom* (1995) A 331, para 77 (appeals division of Patent Office).

7 Eg *Le Compte, Van Leuven and De Meyere v Belgium* (1981) A 43, paras 57–58 (appeals council comprised of medical practitioners and judges in equal number and presided over by a judge; method of election of medical members could not support any suggestion of bias).

8 Eg *Belilos v Switzerland* (1988) A 132, paras 65–66 (a police board was both an administrative authority and a judicial body). However, where members of a tribunal successively perform different and conflicting responsibilities, this will probably be sufficient to call the tribunal's impartiality into account: *Procola v Luxembourg* (1995) A 326, paras 44–45 (advisory and judicial functions discharged by members of *Conseil d'Etat*; legitimate doubts as to impartiality of several members who had ruled on the lawfulness of a regulation they had previously scrutinised in their advisory capacity).

9 *McGonnell v United Kingdom* (8 February 2000), at para 51.

10 (8 February 2000), paras 49–58, at para 58 (issues of independence and impartiality treated together). Following *McGonnell*, the Lord Chancellor announced that he would take care not to sit in cases where to do so would violate Art 6: HL Official Report (5th series) cols 655–657 (2 March 2000).

An independent and impartial tribunal

INDEPENDENCE

5.40   The extent of the independence of the decision-making body from the parties to a case and from other organs of government or other external influence is determined by assessing such matters as the 'manner of appointment of its members and the duration of their terms of office, the existence of guarantees against outside pressures and the question whether the body presents an appearance of independence'[1]. Appointment of judges and tribunal members by the Executive is commonplace throughout Europe, and this in itself will not cast doubt on a tribunal's independence[2]. Similarly, appointment by the legislature will not imply a lack of independence[3]. Further, 'the absence of formal recognition [of the irremovability of judges] in law does not in itself imply lack of independence provided that it is recognised in fact and that the other necessary guarantees are present'[4]. Accordingly, the length of the term of appointment will be a relevant factor in determining the extent of the independence of members of a tribunal. In *Ringeisen v Austria*, members of a regional commission had been appointed for a term of office of five years, a term which the European Court of Human Rights decided was satisfactory when considered alongside other guarantees of independence[5]. In *Campbell and Fell v United Kingdom*, a three-year term of office for members of a prison disciplinary board was considered 'admittedly short' but understandable given the unpaid nature of the task and the difficulties in finding volunteers to serve[6]. In *McMichael v United Kingdom*, the applicants argued that the manner of appointment and removal of members of the children's hearing system in Scotland was such that panel members did not enjoy sufficient independence. Members were appointed by the Secretary of State for such period as he specified, and could be removed by him with the consent of the Lord President. In practice, members were appointed initially for two years and usually thereafter for an additional five years and were removed only in exceptional circumstances. The Commission in its report had agreed with the applicants that panel members were not sufficiently independent, but the Court considered it unnecessary to arrive at any decision on this matter on account of a finding of violation of the European Convention on Human Rights, Article 6 on another ground[7].

1 *Campbell and Fell v United Kingdom* (1981) A 46, at para 78 (prison disciplinary board appointed by Home Secretary but not subject to any instructions; considered in all the circumstances to meet test of independence). Cf 44305/98 and 49150/99, *Snooks v United Kingdom* and *Dowse v United Kingdom* (conviction of both applicants for drug-related offences in courts in Jersey which consist of a judge of law (the deputy bailiff) and two judges of fact (the jurats, who are appointed by an electoral college of the legal profession, the judiciary and the executive): communicated).
2 *Belilos v Switzerland* (1988) A 132, at para 66 (appointment by the executive is not in itself sufficient 'to cast doubt on the independence and impartiality of the person concerned, especially as in many Contracting States it is the executive which appoints judges').
3 *Sramek v Austria* (1984) A 84, para 38.
4 *Campbell and Fell v United Kingdom* (1981) A 46, at para 80.
5 (1971) A 13, para 97.
6 (1981) A 46, at para 80.
7 (1995) A 307-B, para 78; see further para 5.58 below.

5.41 The subordination of members of the tribunal to outside influence will certainly raise issues of independence[1]. Particular difficulties have arisen with British military justice. In *Findlay and Ors v United Kingdom*, applicable rules required that the convening officer in disciplinary hearings was closely linked to the prosecuting authorities, was superior in rank to the members of the court martial, and also had the power to dissolve the court martial and to refuse to confirm its decision in certain instances. In these circumstances, the European Court of Human Rights concluded a court martial could not satisfy the requirement of independence[2]. Further, there must be no legitimate doubt or misgiving on the part of a party to proceedings that a member of the tribunal may appear to lack independence. In determining this question, 'the standpoint of the accused is important without being decisive. What is decisive is whether his doubts can be held to be objectively justified'[3]. Internal organisational issues are thus of concern, and an actual lack of independence is not relevant to this further assessment which proceeds upon the appearance of lack of independence. In *Sramek v Austria*, for example, a civil servant on a tribunal was directly subordinate to a colleague who was presenting the government's case[4], and in *Belilos v Switzerland*, the applicant had been convicted of a petty offence by a board which included a civil service lawyer who worked for the police[5].

1 Cf 58442/00, *Lavents v Latvia* (7 June 2001) (withdrawal of judges following statements in the press by the Prime Minister and the Minister for Justice contesting their decision in respect of the applicant who was facing charges in connection with the collapse of the major bank in the country: admissible).
2 1997-I, 263, paras 73–80. See too, eg, *Coyne v United Kingdom* 1997-V, 1842, paras 56–58; *Hood v United Kingdom* 1999-I, 465, paras 73–79; *Wilkinson and Allen v United Kingdom* (6 February 2001), paras 21–26; and *Mills v United Kingdom* (5 June 2001), paras 22–27. The law has now been amended by the Armed Forces Act 1996. However, an application challenging the compatibility of these reforms with the Convention has recently been declared admissible: 38784/97, *Morris v United Kingdom* (3 July 2001).
3 *Incal v Turkey* 1998-IV, 1547, at para 71 (national security courts established to try offences against the state's territorial integrity included military judges; while the independence and impartiality of the civilian judges were not in doubt, there were legitimate fears as to whether the presence of military judges could allow the courts to be unduly influenced by irrelevant considerations). See too *Cyprus v Turkey* (10 May 2001), paras 357–359 (legislative practice of trying civilians by military courts in northern Cyprus: violation of Art 6).
4 (1984) A 84, para 42.
5 (1988) A 132, paras 66–67 at para 67 (legitimate doubts as to the 'independence and organisational impartiality' of the board).

IMPARTIALITY

5.42   Impartiality is also assessed in terms of a subjective test of whether there is any actual bias or prejudice through personal conviction on the part of a member of the tribunal towards the issue or the parties; and further by means of an objective test of whether there exist any ascertainable facts which give rise to any legitimate doubts as to impartiality[1]. Impartiality on the part of the judge is to be presumed unless there is some proof to the contrary[2]. However, it is often possible to be satisfied that there is no actual 'personal conviction' in existence on the part of a member of a tribunal, but that there are still legitimate doubts as to his objective impartiality. Assessment of this issue must take place in the light of the public's increased sensitivity to the importance of fair and transparent administration of justice[3]. The objective test involves consideration of 'whether the judge offered guarantees sufficient to exclude any legitimate doubt in this respect[4]' and not whether the appellant held apprehensions, however understandable[5]. Thus in *Piersack v Belgium*, the trial judge at an earlier stage had been head of the section in the public prosecutor's office which had been responsible for the proceedings against the applicant. While the European Court of Human Rights accepted that there had been no evidence of actual bias, it felt that there were reasonable doubts as to the outward appearances of impartiality[6]. In *Kingsley v United Kingdom*, the Gaming Board had in earlier proceedings expressed the opinion that the applicant was not a fit and proper person to hold a certificate approving him to hold a management position in the industry; after holding a hearing in private, the Board formally found this to be the case. The Court agreed with the applicant that these proceedings were not accompanied by the necessary appearance of impartiality[7]. On the other hand, where a judge has ruled on a preliminary question of whether an accused should be remanded in custody pending trial, this in itself does not normally give rise to any reasonable question of objective impartiality which would be sufficient to render the trial of the individual unfair[8]. In *De Haan v Netherlands*, a judge had presided in a tribunal along with two lay assessors in a case involving an objection against a decision for which he himself was responsible, a matter which the Court considered gave rise to objectively justified fears as to the tribunal's impartiality[9]. However, this situation can be contrasted with one in which an intervening higher court has set a decision aside and remitted it back for fresh determination. Here, there is no general requirement that a superior court is bound to send the case back to a tribunal with a different constitution[10]. Similarly, it will always be a question whether a change in the composition of a court during legal proceedings will give rise to a legitimate doubt as to its impartiality[11]. The requirement of impartiality applies to all bodies which may qualify as 'tribunals' for the purposes of the European Convention on Human Rights, Article 6, and so the question of the lack of objective impartiality may even arise in the determination of an alleged breach of parliamentary privilege[12].

1 *Hauschildt v Denmark* (1989) A 154, para 46. For further discussion, see van Dijk 'Article 6(1) of the Convention and the Concept of "Objective Impartiality"' in Mahoney, Matscher, Petzold and Wildhaber (eds) *Protecting Human Rights: The European Perspective* (2000) pp 1495–1510.
2 *Le Compte, Van Leuven and De Meyere v Belgium* (1981) A 43, para 58. See also 63226/00, *Craxi v Italy* (14 May 2001) (the fact that a judge has ruled on similar cases in the past is not in itself enough to throw doubt on his impartiality); but cf *Debled v Belgium* (1994) A 292-B, paras 36–37 at para 37 (professional disciplinary authority involving the participation of judges dealing with charges identical to those the judges themselves had faced 'can pose problems' under Art 6).
3 *Kress v France* (7 June 2001), para 82, discussed at para 5.38 above.
4 *Fey v Austria* (1993) A 255-A, para 28. See too 25130/94, *Lie and Bernstein v Norway* (16 December 1999) (application challenging the determination of a judge on the question of compensation for the length of criminal proceedings in which he had sat as a trial judge declared inadmissible as there were no legitimate grounds for fearing the judge had any preconceived ideas when dealing with the subsequent claim to compensation); *Tierce and Ors v San Marino* (25 July 2000), paras 77–83 (the same judge had dealt with the judicial investigation and trial at first instance and the preparation of the file for the appeal hearing: in the circumstances, objective fears as to impartiality justified); *Wettstein v Switzerland* (21 December 2000), paras 43–50 (lack of impartiality of two judges in administrative proceedings in circumstances where the judges had acted either directly as lawyers, or through their office partner, against the applicant in separate proceedings); 43505/98, *Salaman v United Kingdom* (15 June 2000) (trial judge and an appeal court judge had not disclosed the fact of their membership of the freemasons in a case where one of the parties was also a freemason: membership of the freemasons was not in itself enough to cast doubt over impartiality, and the applicant had not provided any further evidence to substantiate his fears: inadmissible); 39731/98, *Sigurðsson v Iceland* (14 June 2001)

(impartiality of a judge whose spouse's debts were allegedly reduced by a bank party to the proceedings with which he was dealing; in domestic law, it was in the first place for a judge to determine whether there were reasons which would justify withdrawal from a case, and thus the lack of challenge by the applicant did not involve failure to exhaust domestic remedies: admissible). See also *R(DPP) v Acton Youth Court* [2001] 1 WLR 1828 (judge can conduct trial after making preliminary ruling in favour of Crown).

5 *Nortier v Netherlands* (1993) A 267, para 33.
6 (1982) A 53, paras 30–31; see too *Oberschlick v Austria (No 1)* (1991) A 204, para 50 (breach of rule prohibiting any judge who had dealt with a matter in initial proceedings from hearing the case on appeal; disposal of appeal thus was by a court whose impartiality was specifically recognised as open to doubt); and similarly, *Castillo Algar v Spain* 1998-VIII, 3103, paras 43–51.
7 (7 November 2000), paras 49–50.
8 *Sainte-Marie v France* (1992) A 253-A, paras 32–34; 43715/98, *Garrido Guerrero v Spain* (2 March 2000) (a judge had earlier taken part in confirmation of an indictment purely as a procedural matter and thus there were no legitimate doubts as to his impartiality) and *Ilijkov v Bulgaria* (26 July 2001), para 97. See too *Gautrin and Others v France* 1998-III, 1009, paras 57–60 at para 59 (professional tribunals had a 'worrying connection' in the context of the particular dispute with competitors of an organisation appearing before them). Cf *Hauschildt v Denmark* (1989) A 154, para 52 (judges at pre-trial stage had to be satisfied of a 'particularly confirmed suspicion' of guilt; here, circumstances did establish legitimate doubts as to objective impartiality).
9 1997-IV, 1379, paras 50–55.
10 *Thomann v Switzerland* 1996-III, 806, paras 32–37 (the imposition of any such requirement would slow down the administration of justice).
11 For recent examples, see, e g *Academy Trading Ltd and Ors v Greece* (4 April 2000), paras 43–47 (the retirement of a judge had required a fresh hearing to be held in which two judges who had taken part in earlier deliberations took part again; however (by four votes to three) the Court considered that the applicants had not established any illegality or radical departure from normal court practice sufficient to establish a want of impartiality); *Daktaras v Lithuania* (10 October 2000), paras 30–38 (the President of the Criminal Division of the Supreme Court had combined the role of prosecutor, had appointed the judge *rapporteur*, and was to constitute the court which was to examine the case: insufficient guarantees to exclude any legitimate doubt as to the absence of inappropriate pressure on the Supreme Court led to a violation of Art 6); *Rojas Morales v Italy* (16 November 2000), paras 31–35 (charges of criminal conspiracy and international drug-trafficking: violation of Art 6 because of the lack of appearance of impartiality of the trial court).
12 *Demicoli v Malta* (1991) A 210, paras 39–41 (punishment of editor of periodical by House of Representatives which included the two MPs who had been criticised and subsequently raised the matter of breach of privilege: objective impartiality open to doubt).

ISSUES RELATING TO JURIES

5.43 Where a jury forms part of an adjudicatory tribunal, similar considerations of independence and impartiality apply[1]. The handful of judgments of the European Court of Human on Rights in this area concentrate upon whether there were legitimate doubts as to a jury's objective impartiality rather than the existence of actual bias on the part of a juror or jurors[2], but the outcomes have not always been consistent. Objective impartiality was in question in *Holm v Sweden* where a majority of the jurors hearing a libel case had been active members of a political party which in the past had directly owned and still indirectly controlled the publishing company defending the action. The Court considered that the court's independence and impartiality were open to doubt[3]. A similar conclusion as to the existence of a legitimate doubt as to impartiality was reached in *Remli v Fance* where a juror had been overheard to say 'what's more, I'm a racist' and the trial court had refused to take any formal note of this event or any remedial action since the statement had been made outwith the courtroom. Both cases appear to subsume the question of possible subjective bias into that of objective appearance of impartiality[4].

In contrast, in the Scottish case of *Pullar v United Kingdom*, no violation of the European Convention on Human Rights, Article 6 was established. After a guilty verdict had been returned, it transpired that one of the members of the jury had been an employee of the principal prosecution witness and had personally known another of the witnesses. The Court (by five votes to four) disagreed with the Commission's assessment and held that there had been no violation of the requirement of objective impartiality. The particular juror at the centre of the dispute had been merely a junior employee, had been facing redundancy, and had no personal knowledge of the issues in the case. Of some importance for the majority of the Court were the safeguards offered by the system of jury trial in Scotland including the random method of selection of jurors and the nature of the charge by the presiding judge to the jury which reminded its members that they were to consider in a dispassionate manner the evidence presented[5]. Similarly, in *Gregory v United Kingdom*, the Court did not consider that there was any violation of Article 6. The trial judge had been passed a note reading 'Jury showing racial overtones. 1 member to be excused'. There had been no admission on the part of any juror of the making of racist remarks, and the allegation was vague. The trial judge had dealt with the matter by reminding them of their oath and instructing them to disregard any prejudice, and the Court accepted that this approach was sufficient to deal with any question of perceived bias[6].

However, a recent case suggests a more critical approach is called for in dealing with allegations of juror bias. In *Sander v United Kingdom*, a juror had passed a note to the judge towards the end of a trial expressing concerns that the jury was likely to determine the matter on the basis of racial prejudice. The judge had reminded the jury that they had taken an oath, and invited any juror who felt unable to try the case fairly to advise him. The judge then had received a letter signed by all members of the jury refuting the allegations of racial bias, and a second letter from a juror apologising for any racist statements he may have made which had resulted in the suggestion of prejudice. The jury thereafter had found the applicant guilty but had returned a verdict of not guilty in respect of another co-defendant from an Asian background. The Court did not accept that there had been any breach of the jury's subjective impartiality. While it was clear from the initial note to the trial judge and from the letter of apology written by a juror that at least one juror had made racist jokes, this could not be taken as establishing actual bias. On the other hand, there were legitimate grounds for believing that objective impartiality was in question. English law protected the secrecy of jury deliberations, and thus it had not been possible for the judge to question jurors as to the nature and content of the racist statements. The letter from the jury had to be considered alongside the admission from the individual juror of having made racist statements, the judge's admonition to the jury was considered unlikely to have changed a juror's racist attitudes and, accordingly, the jury's objective impartiality had been open to doubt[7]. Here, the Court placed far less reliance than it had in *Pullar v United Kingdom*[8] or *Gregory v United Kingdom*[9] upon the power of the judge to address questions of prejudice by simple admonition but without explaining why a different approach was called for[10].

1   *Gregory v United Kingdom* 1997-I, 296, para 43. However, there is no specific right to trial by jury under the Convention, nor can one be implied even in states whose legal systems make use of juries: cf 14739/89, *Callaghan v United Kingdom* (1989) DR 60, 296 (trial by jury was not an essential aspect of a determination of a criminal charge; and thus the refusal to allow new evidence to be considered by a jury (rather than by an appeal court) did not give rise to an Art 6 issue).

2   Cf 8403/78, *Jespers v Belgium* (1980) DR 22, 100 (virulent press campaign may adversely affect the fairness of a trial and thus invoke state responsibility, particularly if sparked off by a state authority). Reid *A Practitioner's Guide to the European Convention on Human Rights* (1998) p 99 notes that no finding of unfair trial based on prejudicial pre-trial publicity has yet been established, but that probably 'it would take more than close media interest in a case and it would be likely that the fact[s] that the jurors took oaths, and would be warned to discount news coverage, would be regarded as offsetting prejudice'. See further para 7.40 below. Additional security measures which can be shown to have been necessary in the circumstances will not be considered to have unduly influenced a jury as to the dangerousness of the accused: 11837/85, *Auguste v France* (1990) DR 69,104.

3   *Holm v Sweden* (1993) A 279-A, paras 32–33.

4   1996-II, 559, paras 46–48.

5   1996-III, 783, paras 36–41.

6   1997-I, 296, paras 43–50.

7   (9 May 2000), paras 29–35.

8   1996-III, 783.

9   1997-I, 296.

10 The Court attempted to distinguish *Gregory* on the facts, but did so rather unconvincingly: (9 May 2000), para 34. See the dissenting judgment of Sir Nicholas Bratza (the facts of *Gregory* 'bear a strong similarity to those in the present case'). The English courts have ruled that a misdirection to a jury does not necessarily result in a breach of Art 6: *R v Francom* [2001] 1 Cr App R 237.

DECISIONS OF DOMESTIC COURTS ON INDEPENDENCE AND IMPARTIALITY

5.44   Although Scots law has for centuries contained a variety of principles designed to ensure the independence and impartiality of courts and tribunals, the effect given to the European Convention on Human Rights, Article 6 by the Scotland Act 1998 and the Human Rights Act 1998 has resulted in a large number of challenges based on the Convention and in some significant changes to existing institutions and practices.

INDEPENDENCE

5.45   The first Scottish case to raise this issue was *Starrs v Ruxton*[1], which concerned a temporary sheriff appointed under the Sheriff Courts (Scotland) Act 1971, s 11(2). Such a sheriff was appointed by the Executive for a year at a time, and the appointment was subject to recall by the Executive at any time and for any reason. The appointment could also be effectively recalled by the Executive's not allocating any work to the temporary sheriff. It had become recognised that the normal route to appointment as a permanent sheriff was by way of appointment as a temporary sheriff (which was normally, but not invariably, renewed annually). The court held that the absence of any security of tenure was fatal to the compatibility of the system of temporary sheriffs with the European Convention on Human Rights, Article 6. Following the decision in *Starrs v Ruxton*, the Bail, Judicial Appointments, etc (Scotland) Act 2000 abolished the office of temporary sheriff and replaced it with the office of part-time sheriff (with security of tenure). The 2000 Act also reformed the system of appointment and removal of Justices of the Peace, prevented politically nominated Justices from performing court duties, and prevented local authorities from bringing prosecutions in the District Court (where the legal assessor advising the justices would be an employee of the local authority). These changes were all designed to ensure that the District Court fulfilled the Article 6 requirement of independence and impartiality.

The use of temporary judges of the Court of Session was challenged in *Clancy v Caird*[2], but without success. Appointment as a temporary judge was for a term of three years and carried security of tenure within that period. They were deployed as required by the Lord President. Although the appointment was part-time, the common law rules on declinature of jurisdiction, together with the judicial oath, adequately guaranteed against any conflict of interest. In these circumstances, the temporary judge constituted an independent and impartial tribunal. In addition, the court held that the pursuer had waived his right to an independent and impartial tribunal (*esto* the temporary judge did not constitute such a tribunal) by failing to object at the outset of the case. In that connection, Lord Coulsfield observed:

> 'It is, I think, not irrelevant to bear in mind what sort of litigation this is. It is, in every possible respect, a private dispute between private parties .... It is the sort of dispute which parties might well have agreed to dispose of by arbitration or by summary procedure or by commercial procedure. In these circumstances, in my opinion, the pursuer must be held to have passed from any objection to the disposal of the case by a temporary judge when he failed to raise any objection to the allocation of the temporary judge to hear the case or, at latest, to object at the start of the proof.'

The implications of *Starrs v Ruxton* were explored in *Millar v Dickson*[3], which concerned a number of cases in which persons had been convicted or sentenced in proceedings before temporary sheriffs, no objection having been taken to the proceedings at any earlier stage. It was held by the High Court of Justiciary that the objection came too late, and that the complainers had tacitly waived their right to an independent and impartial tribunal.

That decision was reversed by the Judicial Committee of the Privy Council in a judgment which strongly endorsed the importance of judicial independence. In *Clark v Kelly*[4] the question was raised whether a trial before the District Court amounted to a fair and public hearing by an independent and impartial tribunal. It was argued that the clerk of court was a member of the court and did not have the security of tenure required by Article 6(1), and that the practice whereby the clerk retired with the justices to advise them on points of law was in breach of the accused's right to a public hearing. The court, however, held that the clerk was not a member of the District Court; and, under reference to *Delcourt v Belgium*[5] and *Borgers v Belgium*[6], that private communication between an impartial legal adviser and the justices was not incompatible with Article 6(1). The court emphasised the importance of the justices raising in open court any matter upon which the parties might reasonably wish to comment.

1 1999 SCCR 1052.
2 2000 SC 441. For recent English discussion, see *Locabail (UK) Ltd v Bayfield Properties Ltd* [2000] 2 WLR 870.
3 2001 SCCR 741.
4 2000 SCCR 821. A similar challenge to the role played by the clerk to the magistrates' court

in England and Wales has been communicated to the UK Government: 44564/98, *Mort v United Kingdom*. This decision predates the judgment in *Kress v France* (7 June 2001), discussed at para 5.38 above.
5 (1970) A 11.
6 (1991) A 214.

IMPARTIALITY

5.46   The High Court of Justiciary has been held to be an impartial tribunal when reviewing the compatibility with the European Convention on Human Rights of its own Acts of Adjournal[1]. The impartiality of a judge, forming part of an appeal court, was successfully challenged in *Hoekstra v HM Advocate (No 2)*[2] on the basis of a newspaper article which the judge had written, in which he was strongly critical of the Convention in general and Article 8 in particular. The article was published shortly after the issue of an opinion by the court, over which he had presided, in an appeal based on Article 8. The court (differently composed) upheld the challenge. It stressed that, in reaching that conclusion, it attached particular importance to the tone of the language and the impression which the author deliberately gave that his hostility to the operation of the Convention as part of Scots law was both long-standing and deep-seated; and that the position would have been very different if all that he had done was to publish, say, an article in a legal journal drawing attention, in moderate language, to what he perceived to be the drawbacks of incorporation. Judges were entitled to criticise (or to welcome) developments in the law; but what they could not do with impunity was to publish either criticism or praise of such a nature or in such language as to give rise to a legitimate apprehension that, when called upon in the course of their judicial duties to apply that particular branch of the law, they would not be able to do so impartially.

1 *Dickson v HM Advocate* 2001 SCCR 397.
2 2000 SCCR 367. For another example of a case where a judge might be thought to lack impartiality, see *Re Medicaments and Related Classes of Goods (No 2)* [2001] ICR 564. Changes have been introduced in England and Wales to the procedures for dealing with contempt of court, apparently with Art 6 in mind: *Practice Direction (Magistrates' Courts: Contempt)* [2001] 1 WLR 1254.

JURIES

5.47   A number of cases in the Scottish courts have concerned the impartiality of juries. In *Montgomery v HM Advocate*[1] the issue concerned the prejudicial effect of pre-trial publicity. The Judicial Committee held that the question was not confined to the residual effect of the publicity on the minds of each of the jurors but that account must also be taken of the part which the trial judge would play; and that, on the facts of the case, the directions which the judge might be expected to give to the jury would be sufficient to remove any legitimate doubt that might exist prior to trial about the objective impartiality of the jury. The Judicial Committee also made it clear that the right of the accused to a fair trial by an independent and impartial tribunal was unqualified. The disclosure to a jury that an accused has previously been charged with a criminal offence[2], or has previously been convicted of an offence[3], has been held not to contravene the European Convention on Human Rights, Article 6(1). The fact that a defence witness, who was a convicted prisoner, was handcuffed while giving evidence has also been held not to contravene Article 6(1)[4]. In a case concerned with the contamination of the public water supply of Edinburgh, and its consequent interruption for a period of time, it was held that an Edinburgh jury would constitute an impartial tribunal: only part of the Edinburgh area had been affected; the addresses of jurors were disclosed; three years had passed since the events in question; and the standard procedures and directions would provide sufficient safeguards[5]. On the other hand, where a juror failed to disclose personal knowledge of dishonest conduct on the part of the accused, and that knowledge came to light after the verdict had been reached, in a case in which the credibility of the accused was of critical importance, it was held that objectively justified and legitimate doubts as to the impartiality of the jury could not be excluded[6]. It has been held in England that the Human Rights Act 1998 does not permit the court to inquire into the deliberations of juries[7].

1 2000 SCCR 1044. The same issue was also discussed in *HM Advocate v Fraser* 2000 SCCR 412, and *Aspinall v HM Advocate* (27 March 2000, unreported), HCJ.
2 *Boyd v HM Advocate* 2000 SCCR 962.
3 *Andrew v HM Advocate* 2000 SLT 402.
4 *Trotter v HM Advocate* 2000 SCCR 968.
5 *Crummock (Scotland) Ltd v HM Advocate* 2000 SCCR 453.
6 *McLean v HM Advocate* 2001 SCCR 526.
7 *R v Qureshi* (23 July 2001, unreported), CA.

'TRIBUNALS' OTHER THAN THE ORDINARY COURTS

5.48 Independence and impartiality have also been considered in a number of cases concerned with bodies other than the ordinary courts. The leading cases have concerned planning law, disciplinary tribunals and children's hearings. In relation to planning law, the case of *County Properties Ltd v The Scottish Ministers*[1] concerned decisions by the Scottish Ministers to call in an application for listed building consent following an objection by Historic Scotland (an executive agency of the Scottish Ministers), and to appoint a part-time reporter to hold a public local inquiry and report to the Scottish Ministers. It was admitted that neither the reporter nor the Scottish Ministers was an independent and impartial tribunal. It was however argued that the statutory right of appeal to the court secured compliance with the European Convention on Human Rights, Article 6(1), following *Bryan v United Kingdom*[2]. At first instance, the court distinguished *Bryan* on its facts, having regard to three factors:

1 *Bryan* had concerned a delegated decision, and the facts (as to which the court had only a limited power of review) were found by the inspector following a quasi-judicial process, whereas in *County Properties* the decision would be made by the Scottish Ministers.
2 In *Bryan*, the only objection based on Article 6 concerned the Secretary of State's power to revoke the inspector's appointment, and the consequent lack of independence, whereas in *County Properties* the Scottish Ministers were *iudex in sua causa*, since they were deciding an issue between the petitioners and their own executive agency; and the limitations on the court's power to review their decision on the facts was therefore a matter of greater significance.

3   Since the decision on listed building consent depended largely on aesthetic and planning judgment, the scope for the court to interfere with the Scottish Ministers' decision on appeal was even more restricted than the scope for review of matters of pure fact, with which the *Bryan* case had been concerned.

A similar conclusion was reached in *Lafarge Redland Aggregates Ltd v The Scottish Ministers*[3], again in an unusual factual context. The case concerned a planning application which had been called in for determination by the Secretary of State on the recommendation of Scottish Natural Heritage (SNH). A public inquiry was then held at which SNH were the principal objectors. Persons who gave evidence on behalf of other objectors subsequently joined the board of SNH. Following the inquiry, the Scottish Ministers decided to seek advice concerning the application from SNH. This was held to be incompatible with Article 6(1), since SNH could not be seen as impartial. The judgment would appear to proceed on a similar footing to *County Properties Ltd v The Scottish Ministers*, but the issues arising under Article 6 were not discussed in detail.

The decision in *County Properties Ltd v The Scottish Ministers* was reversed on appeal in view of the decision of the House of Lords in the English case of *R (Alconbury Developments Ltd) v Secretary of State for the Environment, Transport and the Regions*[4]. In this important and welcome decision it was held that a planning application involved the determination of 'civil rights' within the meaning of Article 6, and it was accepted that the Secretary of State was not an independent and impartial tribunal. Nevertheless, decisions taken by him were not incompatible with Article 6 provided they were subject to review by an independent and impartial tribunal which had as full jurisdiction as the nature of the decision required. In so far as the decision involved questions of administrative policy, it was not necessary for the reviewing body to redetermine the merits of the decision. The powers of the court to review, by way of judicial review, the legality of the decision and the procedures followed was sufficient to ensure compliance with Article 6.

1   2000 SLT 965; reversed 2001 SLT 1125.
2   (1996) A335-A, discussed at para 5.85 below.
3   2001 SC 298.
4   [2001] 2 WLR 1389. See also *R (Kathro) v Rhondda Cynon Taff County Borough Council* (6 July 2001, unreported), QBD (planning authority determining own application).

5.49   The independence and impartiality of a disciplinary tribunal came under scrutiny in *Tehrani v United Kingdom Central Council for Nursing, Midwifery and Health Visiting*[1], which concerned disciplinary proceedings against a registered nurse. The body regulating the nursing profession had a committee which considered complaints about nurses and instituted disciplinary proceedings, and another committee which heard and decided those proceedings. The same individuals served from time to time on both committees, but not in respect of the same case. There was a right of appeal to the Court of Session. It was held that the disciplinary proceedings could lead to a determination of civil rights and obligations, within the meaning of Article 6(1), having regard to decisions of the European Court of Human Rights concerning disciplinary proceedings, since they could result in the person's losing the status of a registered nurse and in consequence being prevented, in practice if not in law, from pursuing a career as a nurse in the United Kingdom. It was not however necessary that the disciplinary committee be an independent and impartial tribunal, if the requirements of Article 6(1) were met by the right of appeal to the Court of Session. Construing the statutory right of appeal so as to be compatible with Convention rights (as required by the Human Rights Act 1998, s 3), it was agreed that the right of appeal required to be viewed as unrestricted, and as allowing a complete re-hearing of any case in which the disciplinary committee had decided that the nurse's name should be removed from the register. Considered as a whole, the disciplinary proceedings therefore met the requirements of Article 6(1). A similar approach was adopted by the Privy Council in *Preiss v General Dental Council*[2]. Disciplinary charges brought on behalf of the General Dental Council were determined by its Professional Conduct Committee. That Committee had a preponderance of members of the Council, and was chaired by the president of the Council, who had also acted as preliminary screener. It was held that the Committee was not an independent and impartial tribunal within the meaning of Art 6. Compliance with the Convention was however secured by the right of appeal (on fact as well as law) to the Privy Council itself.

1 2001 SC 581.
2 [2001] 1 WLR 1926. Contrast *R (Nicolaides) v General Medical Council* (27 July 2001, unreported), QBD, where the claimant was only reprimanded and Art 6 was therefore not engaged.

5.50 The independence of the children's hearing was challenged unsuccessfully in *S v Miller*[1]. Noting that the members of the hearing were unpaid lay people appointed and trained with the aim of providing assistance to children, the court held that the fact that they did not enjoy the kind of security of tenure associated with judges of courts of the classic kind did not mean that they were not independent. There was no evidence that they had ever been influenced by the executive or that they lacked independence of judgment. They could not be removed without the consent of an independent judge, and in practice no member had been removed except on account of a refusal to take part in training.

1 2001 SLT 531.

5.51 A permanent president of a court-martial does not lack the independence and impartiality required by the European Convention on Human Rights, Article 6(1)[1]. It has been held that employment tribunals, as constituted in 1999, could not be regarded as an independent and impartial tribunal in cases involving the Secretary of State for Trade and Industry, but that subsequent administrative changes have secured their independence and impartiality[2].

1 *R v Spear* [2001] QB 804. As to courts-martial, see also *R v Williams* (30 July 2001, unreported) Courts-Martial Appeal Ct.
2 *Scanfuture UK Ltd v Secretary of State for Trade and Industry* [2001] IRLR 416. See also *R (Husain) v Asylum Support Adjudicator* (5 October 2001, unreported), QBD.

5.52   Certain reforms have been effected by the Convention Rights (Compliance) (Scotland) Act 2001 in order to ensure compliance with the European Convention on Human Rights, Article 6(1) in the sentencing of life prisoners. The punitive part of a mandatory life sentence is to be fixed by the court, and that release is to be decided on by the Parole Board for Scotland. The constitution of the Parole Board is reformed so as to ensure its independence and impartiality. Reforms to the Lyon Court are also effected to ensure its independence and impartiality.

WHAT CONSTITUTES A FAIR HEARING?

5.53   Of paramount importance in the jurisprudence of the European Convention on Human Rights, Article 6 is the overarching and all-pervading notion of 'fairness'. In applying this assessment, the European Court of Human Rights will consider the proceedings as a whole, so that account will be taken of relevant appellate hearings[1] with allowance being made for the possibility that a defect at first instance may be cured at a subsequent stage[2]. The ultimate question is whether the proceedings as a whole were fair[3]. This allows the Court to consider a range of issues which are not specifically mentioned in the text of Article 6. Three main constituent elements of a fair hearing emerge as being of particular importance: proceedings which are adversarial in character; fair rules of evidence; and the issuing of a fair and reasoned judgment.

1 *Delcourt v Belgium* (1970) A 11, para 25; *Monnell and Morris v United Kingdom* (1987) A 115, para 54; *Ekbatani v Sweden* (1988) A 134, para 24; *Belziuk v Poland*, 1998-II, 558, para 37. Cf 12002/86, *Grant v United Kingdom* (1988) DR 55, 218 (during appeal proceedings, the applicant's counsel had sensed that the High Court of Justiciary was coming round to the opinion that the trial court's sentence of six years' imprisonment was too light and accordingly had attempted to abandon the appeal but was not given permission to do so; the sentence was thereafter increased to ten years' imprisonment. In declaring the application inadmissible as manifestly ill-founded, the Commission considered that the proceedings had to be looked at as a whole, and it was inevitable that an appeal court must form an 'initial inclination or view' from the appeal papers and other materials from the trial court before the opening of the appeal hearing. Furthermore, the court had benefitted from hearing submissions on the sentence. Scots law did permit an individual to abandon his appeal, but in this case the motion to seek authority to do so had been made after the start of the hearing).

2 Eg *De Cubber v Belgium* (1984) A 86, para 33 (the trial judge had been the investigating judge and thus could be supposed to have formed a view as to the applicant's guilt or innocence, but the appeal court had not quashed the conviction on this particular ground: the Court noted that the opportunity for the subsequent curing of defects was the justification for the requirement that an applicant exhaust domestic remedies in terms of Art 35(1)). See further para 5.82 below.

3 Or 'what the proper administration of justice required': *Vaudelle v France* (30 January 2001), paras 57–66 (conviction and imprisonment *in absentia* of the applicant who had been placed under supervisory guardianship on account of deterioration of his mental facilities without the national authorities having taken additional steps to try to examine him and summoning him to appear: violation). Cf *Gillow v United Kingdom* (1986) A 109, paras 70–71 (no unfairness disclosed through the failure to make available a tape recording of a hearing); *Barberà, Messegue and Jabardo v Spain* (1988) A 146, paras 76–89 (brevity

of trial on serious charges and failure to adduce crucial evidence); *Colak v Germany* (1988) A 147, paras 31–32 (assurance given by the president of the court to the defence before the court had deliberated did not constitute unfairness); *Stanford v United Kingdom* (1984) A 282-A, paras 24–31 (applicant's difficulties in hearing the court proceedings did not give rise to a situation of unfairness as the applicant was represented by skilled counsel); *Kraska v Switzerland* (1993) A 254-B, paras 28–33 (allegation that a judge gave his opinion without an adequate knowledge of the case found not to have been established); *Kremzow v Austria* (1993) A 268-B, para 72 (practice of circulating a draft judgment in advance amongst judges which did not bind them did not indicate any unfairness); 63716/00, *Sawoniuk v United Kingdom* (29 May 2001) (conviction of applicant for murder committed during the 1939-45 war: the Convention does not impose any time-limit in respect of war crime prosecutions, and there was no suggestion that the criminal proceedings were unfair: inadmissible).

5.54 The requirements inherent in the concept of a 'fair hearing' in the determination of civil rights and obligations are, though, perhaps less demanding than in the determination of criminal charges on account of the presence of additional detailed guarantees provided by paragraphs (2) and (3) which apply in criminal cases. 'Thus, although these provisions have a certain relevance outside the strict confines of criminal law[1]. . ., the Contracting States have greater latitude when dealing with civil cases concerning civil rights and obligations than they have when dealing with criminal cases'[2]. However, 'fairness' is a standard both broader than and transcendent of the collective minimum rights for criminal defendants contained in the European Convention on Human Rights, Article 6(2) and (3), which in any case merely 'represent specific applications of the general principle of a fair trial'[3]. In consequence, the application of a single and generalised standard of fairness which increasingly now comes across in Court judgments has resulted in some lack of clarity in jurisprudence. Additional considerations determining the assessment of the fairness of a criminal trial are, in short, best considered as specific applications of the general requirement to ensure a fair hearing under the first paragraph, particularly since these subsequent provisions are themselves non-exhaustive and constituent elements of a fair criminal process[4]. In other words, the Court will normally consider the application of paragraphs (2) and (3) in conjunction with the disposal of any paragraph (1) question. Where the difficulty lies is in the Court's somewhat unsatisfactory tendency, particularly in recent cases, to neglect to examine complaints under paragraph (3) if a violation of the general fairness requirement in paragraph (1) has already been established. Arguably, the effect of this approach has been gradually to diminish the clarity and coherence with which the distinction between the specific individual guarantees can be drawn: while it is clear that certain minimum rights are being protected, one cannot be sure exactly of which paragraph a failure to observe those rights will fall foul.

1 *Albert and Le Compte v Belgium* (1983) A 58, para 39.
2 *Dombo Beheer BV v Netherlands* (1993) A 274, at para 32.
3 *Pakelli v Germany* (1983) A 64, at para 42.
4 *Deweer v Belgium* (1980) A 35, para 56.

Proceedings which are adversarial in character

5.55   An adversarial hearing is a vital characteristic in both criminal and civil proceedings. Efforts are made throughout the European Convention on Human Rights to limit the inquisitorial functions of tribunals and courts in favour of an approach which permits challenge, contradiction and counter-evidence[1]. The right to an adversarial hearing ought to translate into 'the opportunity for the parties ... to have knowledge of and comment on all evidence adduced or observations filed ... with a view to influencing the court's decision'[2]. In the majority of instances, this right is most effectively secured by a public hearing in the presence of all parties, with provision for each party to participate and contribute on an equal footing. Where the nature of proceedings does not allow for this optimum, however, the European Court of Human Rights will assess the extent to which a fair balance between the rights of the parties and the requirements of justice has been struck. Infringements of the right to adversarial proceedings may not result exclusively from imbalances that favour one party unfairly over the other; they can also occur when *both* parties are denied knowledge of or opportunity to comment on a piece of evidence before the court. In *Krcmár v Czech Republic*, a violation was established where the constitutional court failed to disclose pivotal documentary evidence to either party in a case concerning nationalisation of a family company under the communist regime. The applicants, who were asserting a civil right to restitution, had thus been denied the chance to comment on documents which had undoubtedly influenced the court's decision[3].

1   See eg paras 6.23 and 8.16 below. This statement is of particular validity in the context of deprivation of liberty of a criminal suspect: see paras 4.97–4.98 above.
2   *Vermeulen v Belgium* 1996-I, 224, at para 33.
3   (3 March 2000), paras 41–46. See too *Kamasinski v Austria* (1989) A 168, paras 87–93.

'Equality of arms'

5.56   Adversarial proceedings are closely related to the notion of 'equality of arms'[1]. 'Equality of arms' requires that 'each party must be afforded a reasonable opportunity to present his case – including his evidence – under conditions which do not place him at a substantial disadvantage vis-à-vis his opponent'[2]. This is only one aspect of the wider concept of a fair civil or criminal trial and thus must be considered in terms of the overall fairness of the proceedings[3] with the result that certain differences in the procedural situation of parties which are not deemed prejudicial may be overlooked[4].

1   Cf *Belziuk v Poland*, 1998-II, 558, paras 37–39 at para 37 ('the principle of equality of arms is only one feature of the wider concept of a fair trial, which also includes the fundamental right that criminal proceedings should be adversarial'; here, the principle of equality of arms and the right to adversarial proceedings both required that the applicant should have been allowed to attend the hearing and to contest the prosecutor's submissions). See further Emmerson 'Prosecution Disclosure in Criminal Cases' (2000) 40 Med Sci Law 125. It is unsatisfactory for the fairness of criminal proceedings to depend on the goodwill and co-operation of the prosecution: the accused has the right to put forward a full and complete defence. See *R v A (No 2)* [2001] 2 WLR 1546, para 41.
2   *Bönisch v Austria* (1985) A 92, paras 29–35 (defence expert witness to be accorded the same facilities as one appointed by the prosecution); *Dombo Beheer BV v Netherlands* (1993) A 274,

at para 33; *Hentrich v France* (1994) A 296-A, at para 56; and *Stran Greek Refineries and Stratis Andreadis v Greece* (1994) A 301-B, at para 46. See too *Reinhardt and Slimane-Kaïd v France* 1998-II, 640, paras 105–107 (communication of the report and draft judgment of the judge *rapporteur* to the *advocat général* but not to the appellant prior to a hearing: violation of Art 6); *Beer v Austria* (6 February 2001), paras 17–21 (non-communication of appeal against an order relating to costs: violation of Art 6). The word 'opportunity' should be emphasised. A party which fails to prepare adequately for a hearing, having had a reasonable opportunity to do so, cannot complain of a breach of Art 6: *Thomson Pettie Tube Products Ltd v Hogg* (4 May 2001, unreported), Ct of S.

3 *Ruiz-Mateos v Spain* (1993) A 262, para 63.
4 *Kremzow v Austria* (1993) A 268-B, para 75 (differences in time limits for submitting pleadings and for responding were not deemed material); *Ankerl v Switzerland*, 1996-V, 1553, para 38 (evidence of one party was not able to be taken on oath, but she was still able to address the court and give evidence; in consequence, there was no breach of Art 6). Cf *Dombo Beheer v Netherlands* (1993) A 274, dissenting judgment of Judge Martens joined by Judge Pettiti: 'in relation to litigation concerning civil rights and obligations, the concept of "equality of arms" can only have a formal meaning: both parties should have an equal opportunity to bring their case before the court and to present their arguments and their evidence'. It cannot imply substantive implications requiring adaptation of substantive rules of procedure and evidence 'in order to guarantee both parties substantively equal chances of success'.

5.57   The Judicial Committee of the Privy Council acknowledged this approach in *Buchanan v McLean*[1]:

'At first sight there is bound to be some measure of inequality of arms as between the prosecutor, who has all the resources of the state at his disposal, and an accused who has to make do with the services that are available by way of criminal legal aid. But in *M v United Kingdom*[2] the Commission recognised that financial restraints may be necessary to ensure the most cost effective use of the funds available for legal aid. It can be assumed that, as the procurator fiscal service is funded by public money, there are pressures on that side also to ensure cost effectiveness. What has to be demonstrated is that the prosecutor in this case will enjoy some particular advantage that is not available to the defence or that would otherwise be unfair.'

1 2001 SCCR 475, at para 40, per Lord Hope of Craighead.
2 App 9728/82 (1983) DR 36, 155.

KNOWLEDGE OF THE CASE TO BE MET

5.58   'Equality of arms' may call for positive steps on the part of judicial or other state authorities to ensure that parties have a proper knowledge of the case to be met. This will normally involve disclosure of evidence to allow the opportunity to respond effectively. In *Kerojärvi v Finland*, the court had not sought to have made available to the unrepresented appellant either relevant files or a legal opinion relating to an insurance claim. For the European Court of Human Rights, the procedure followed by the domestic tribunal had not been such as to allow the applicant's proper participation[1]. In *McMichael v United Kingdom*, the fairness of the Scottish system of children's hearings was found wanting on the lack of equality of arms. An infant had been made subject to compulsory measures of care on the grounds that lack of parental care was 'likely to cause him unnecessary suffering or seriously to impair his health or development'[2]. Both the children's hearing which took the decision and the sheriff court which reviewed the disposal had sight of social reports, but these reports had been withheld from the parents who had only been made aware of the general substance of their contents. The Court considered that there had been a violation of the European Convention on Human Rights, Article 6(1)'s guarantee of a fair hearing through the failure to disclose vital documents to the parents which in consequence had meant that their ability to participate in the hearing and to assess prospects of success in an appeal had been unduly restricted[3].

1 (1995) A 322, paras 40–43. See also *KS v Finland* (31 May 2001), paras 21–24, and *KP v Finland* (31 May 2001), paras 25–28 (failure to disclose opinions on the merits of the applicants' claims for social welfare entitlement: violation of Art 6(1) in each instance); and *FR v Switzerland* (28 June 2001), paras 34-41 (failure to disclose opinion of tribunal before proceedings in Federal Insurance Court).
2 In terms of the Social Work (Scotland) Act 1968, s 32(c). See also *S v Miller* 2001 SLT 531.
3 (1995) A 307-B, paras 80–84. For further discussion of Scots practice, see Hallett and Murray 'Children's Rights and the Scottish Children's Hearing System' (1999) 7 Int Jo Children's Rights 31.

5.59 Within the context of a criminal case, the application of this principle is more rigorous since paragraphs (2) and (3) impose additional safeguards[1]. It requires that 'both prosecution and defence must be given the opportunity to have knowledge of and comment on the observations filed and the evidence adduced by the other party'. However domestic law seeks to secure this end, 'it should ensure that the other party will be aware that observations have been filed and will get a real opportunity to comment thereon'[2]. Where evidence has been withheld on public interest grounds, the European Court of Human Rights will not consider whether non-disclosure was strictly necessary as this is generally a matter for domestic courts but rather will 'ascertain whether the decision-making procedure applied in each case complied, as far as possible, with the requirements of adversarial proceedings and equality of arms and incorporated adequate safeguards to protect the interests of the accused'[3]. In each instance, however, the proceedings as a whole have to be assessed. In *Edwards v United Kingdom*, the police had not disclosed to the defence that one of the victims had failed to identify the applicant from a police photograph album after having made a statement that she thought she would be able to recognise her assailant, nor that fingerprints had been found at the scene of the crime. The Court confirmed that there is a duty upon the prosecutor to make available all material evidence whether or not favourable to an accused, and that the failure to provide this can render the proceedings defective. The referral of the case by the Home Secretary to the Court of Appeal when these failures had come to light had, however, in the present case remedied these defects[4]. In contrast, the Court considered there had been a violation of Article 6 in the case of *Rowe and Davis v United Kingdom*. The applicants and a co-defendant had been convicted of murder, robbery and assault primarily on the evidence of four accessories. During the trial, the defence had sought to allege that three of these witnesses had deliberately lied in order to exculpate themselves, and that two had been influenced by a substantial sum of reward money offered by the police. The prosecutor refused to disclose to the defence whether any of the witnesses had claimed a reward or had been paid, and the trial court had declined to order disclosure after being shown certain documents by the prosecutor. The Court held that entitlement to disclosure of relevant evidence could never be an absolute right since competing interests (such as national security, the need to protect witnesses at risk of reprisals, and safeguarding police investigation methods) had to be weighed against the rights of an accused: indeed 'in some cases it may be necessary to withhold certain evidence from the defence so as to preserve the fundamental rights of another individual or to safeguard an important public interest'. In each case, however, 'only such measures restricting the rights of the defence which are strictly necessary' were permissible. Here, determination of the need to conceal information had been made by the prosecution itself without judicial intervention, and this could not meet Article 6 requirements. Nor had the review by the Court of Appeal of the undisclosed evidence in ex parte hearings with the benefit of submissions from the Crown but in the absence of the defence cured the defect: the appeal court had been left to rely for an understanding of the material's possible relevance on transcripts of the trial hearings and on the account of the issues given by prosecuting counsel. The conclusion was that the trial had been unfair[5]. The principle is thus that the prosecuting and investigating authorities must disclose material in their possession (or to which they could gain access) which may assist the accused in exculpating himself or in mitigating sentence as well as material which may assist in undermining the credibility of prosecution witnesses[6].

1 *Dombo Beheer BV v Netherlands* (1993) A 274, paras 32–33. See Sharpe 'Article 6 and the Disclosure of Evidence in Criminal Trials' [1999] Crim LR 273.
2 *Brandstetter v Austria* (1991) A 211, at para 67; *Lobo Machado v Portugal* 1996-I, 195, para 31; *Belziuk v Poland* 1998-II, 558, para 37.
3 *Rowe and Davis v United Kingdom* (16 February 2000), at para 62.
4 (1992) A 247-B, paras 33–39.
5 (16 February 2000), paras 59–67 at para 61 (the Court considered the matter in terms of para (1)'s guarantees of fair process, finding it unnecessary to consider whether paras (3)(b) and (3)(d) were of relevance). See also the related cases of *Jasper v United Kingdom* (16 February 2000) and *Fitt v United Kingdom* (16 February 2000). *Rowe and Davis* was considered in *R v Smith (Joe)* [2001] 1 WLR 1031 and *Re Doubtfire* [2001] 2 Cr App R 13.
6 8403/78, *Jespers v Belgium* (1981) DR 27, 61, para 58; *Edwards v United Kingdom* (1992) A 247-B, Commission opinion, para 50.

DECISIONS OF THE DOMESTIC COURTS ON 'EQUALITY OF ARMS'

5.60   The right of the defence, in criminal proceedings, to recover material in the possession of the Crown has been considered in the light of the European Convention on Human Rights, Article 6 in recent Scottish cases. *McLeod v HM Advocate*[1], decided prior to the incorporation of the Convention into Scots law but after consideration of Convention jurisprudence, concerned the recovery by the defence of statements given by witnesses to the police. Until then it had been the practice of the Crown to object in the public interest to the disclosure of such statements as a class of document. In the submissions made in that case, however, the Crown departed from that approach, while preserving the possibility that a public interest objection might be taken to the disclosure of such statements in the circumstances of a particular case. In that context, Lord Justice General Rodger said:

'The upshot of this important declaration is that in future it will only be where the Crown raise a public interest objection to recovery on specific grounds, relating to the actual document in question, that the court will need to decide whether the public interest in securing a fair trial requires it to order production of the document despite that objection. It can be expected that, in reaching its view, the court will continue to attach the weight which it has always hitherto attached to an expression of view by the Lord Advocate as to the public interest in maintaining the confidentiality of any document'[2].

1 1998 SCCR 77.
2 1998 SCCR 77 at 90.

5.61   In cases where the public interest issue does not arise, however, 'the Crown have a duty at any time to disclose to the defence information in their possession which would tend to exculpate the accused'[1]. The defence can also recover documents by an application for an order for production, or for commission and diligence:

> 'I consider, however, that an accused person who asks the court to take the significant step of granting a diligence for the recovery of documents, whether from the Crown or from a third party, does require to explain the basis on which he asks the court to order the haver to produce the documents. The court does not grant such orders unless it is satisfied that they will serve a proper purpose and that it is in the interests of justice to grant them. This in turn means that the court must be satisfied that an order for the production of the particular documents would be likely to be of material assistance to the proper preparation of the accused's defence.[2]'

In *Maan, Petitioner*[3] it was held that the Crown's duty of disclosure extends not only to information which bears directly on the guilt or innocence of the accused, but also to information which would tend to undermine the credibility of a Crown witness.

1 1998 SCCR 77 at 98.
2 1998 SCCR 77 at 99.
3 2001 SCCR 172. In this case it was also said: 'The court must consider on the one hand the public interest in securing for the accused a fair trial, and on the other hand the public interest put forward as justifying non-disclosure.... It is ... for the court to decide whether the former interest outweighs the latter.' This, with respect, appears (if understood literally) to be a questionable approach, and to differ from the approach outlined in *McLeod v HM Advocate* 1998 SCCR 77. Although the accused's right to disclosure is not absolute, it is nevertheless necessary to ensure that he receives a fair trial (see *Rowe and Davis v United Kingdom* (16 February 2000), para 61). The right to a fair trial is not something to be balanced against other considerations: *R v Forbes* [2001] 1 AC 473, para 24; *R v A (No 2)* [2001] 2 WLR 1546, para 38.

INTERVENTION BY LAW OFFICERS

5.62   The right to equality of arms extends to the opportunity for the parties to a case 'to have knowledge of and comment on all evidence adduced or observations filed, even by an independent member of the national legal service, with a view to influencing the court's decision'[1]. This principle holds for cases in which it is maintained that, at a criminal appeal hearing, the prosecutor is present in his capacity as guardian of the public interest but where it is clear that his intervention seeks to have a conviction upheld and where his role is thus that of a prosecuting authority[2]. Similarly, it applies where a law officer is present to assist the court in the determination of a civil matter but his task in reality is that of assisting the defending party to an action. For example, in *APEH Uldozotteinek Szovetsege, Ivanyi, Roth and Szerdahelyi v Hungary*, both the public prosecutor's office and the Attorney General had intervened in non-contentious civil proceedings involving an application to register the applicant association, but the domestic court had not advised the association of these facts. For the Court, the intervention by the public prosecutor may well have had a repercussion on the outcome of the case, and while it was not possible to assess the impact if any of the submissions made by the Attorney General, ' the principle of equality of arms does not depend on further, quantifiable unfairness flowing from a procedural inequality' since 'it is a matter for the parties to assess whether a submission deserves a reaction and it is inadmissible for one party to make submissions to a court without the knowledge of the other and on which the latter has no opportunity to comment'[3]. In contrast, in *Kress v France*, the Court found no violation on the facts of the case. The applicant had raised an action of damages in the administrative courts against a hospital authority, and had ultimately appealed on points of law to the *Conseil d'Etat*. She had not been informed of the submissions of the Government Commissioner in advance, and had been unable to respond to these orally at the hearing but had subsequently submitted a memorandum to the court before it gave judgment. The Court noted that the submissions had not been communicated to either side or even to the judges in advance of the hearing, and thus there had been no violation of the principle of equality of arms since the applicant had not been placed at a disadvantage vis-à-vis her opponent. Further, litigants were afforded sufficient safeguards by the court's procedures, for while the applicant had not had the opportunity to reply during the hearing to the submissions, she had made use of the opportunity to respond in writing in a memorandum[4].

1 *Vermeulen v Belgium* 1996-I, 224, at para 33.
2 *Van Orshoven v Belgium* 1997-III, 1039, paras 37–38; see too *Voisine v France* (8 February 2000), paras 25–26 (failure to communicate the submissions of the *advocat général* to the applicant).
3 (5 October 2000), paras 40–44 at para 42.
4 (7 June 2001), paras 72–76 (but there was a violation of the requirement of independence and impartiality through the participation of the Commissioner in the court's deliberations, even although the Commissioner was acknowledged to be objective and did not have a vote: see para 5.38 above).

THE RIGHT OF ATTENDANCE AT A COURT HEARING

5.63 The requirement of an 'equality of arms' is satisfied through allowing both sides to be present or at least be represented at each stage of the proceedings[1]. It goes without saying that an adversarial hearing is most likely to be secured where the parties are accorded a right of attendance at an oral hearing. There is an obvious link with the guarantee of a right to a public hearing, a provision which is designed to protect litigants against the secret administration of justice and maintain public confidence in the judicial system[2]. However, just as the right of a public hearing is not an absolute right, so too the right of attendance at an oral hearing is determined according to the extent to which fairness dictates that attendance would be considered necessary. This is assessed by factors such as the nature of the hearing, its meaning in the context of the proceedings as a whole, and the importance of what is at stake for the parties[3].

1 Cf *Neumeister v Austria* (1968) A 8, Law, para 22.
2 See paras 5.87–5.90 below. The observation, in *R (on the application of Morgan Grenfell & Co Ltd) v Special Commissioners* [2001] 1 All ER 535, 548, that 'the article 6 right to an oral hearing is usually thought to be associated with and to flow from a right to a public hearing' would, however, be unduly limiting if it were understood as meaning that there could not be a right to an oral hearing unless there were also a right to a public hearing.
3 Cf *Allan Jacobsson v Sweden (No 2)* 1998-I, 154, paras 47–49 (applicant's submissions to the Supreme Administrative Court were not of such a nature as to require an oral hearing to allow their proper determination).

5.64   The matter is of particular importance in a criminal process where the right conferred by the European Convention on Human Rights, Article 6, paragraph (3)(c) on an accused to defend himself in person is also in play[1]. It is of the utmost importance that an accused should be able to attend in person at his trial[2]. However, there is no requirement that an individual should be present at all stages of criminal proceedings. A trial in the absence of an accused is not in principle incompatible with Article 6, providing always that an individual can obtain a fresh determination of the merits of the charge as regards both facts and law[3]. In particular, 'the personal attendance of the defendant does not necessarily take on the same significance for an appeal or nullity hearing as it does for a trial hearing'[4]. The right of attendance is essentially considered by the effect absence will have on the fairness of proceedings, and in particular the consequent inability of the court to assess directly the evidence of the defendant. In determining whether Article 6 will require a public hearing and the attendance of the individual, 'regard must be had in assessing this question, inter alia, to the special features of the proceedings involved and the manner in which the defence's interests were presented and protected before the appellate court, particularly in the light of the issues to be decided by it, and their importance for the appellant'[5]. In *Belziuk v Poland*, the applicant who had been sentenced to three years' imprisonment had sought to contest his conviction and to adduce evidence in support of his case but had not been allowed to be present at the hearing, even although he had elected not to be legally represented. The European Court of Human Rights considered that a fair hearing required a direct assessment of the evidence given by the applicant in person thus allowing him the opportunity both to challenge the submissions of the public prosecutor and also to present evidence in support of his appeal. The absence of counsel was not material since under paragraphs (1) and (3)(c) taken together an individual had the right to be present at his appeal and to defend himself in person[6]. Where an appellate court is called upon to examine factual issues and points of law and carry out an overall determination of guilt or innocence, it is thus considered vital that an accused can give evidence in person to allow the court to assess directly the evidence. In *Tierce and Ors v San Marino*, the domestic appeal courts had jurisdiction to decide factual issues as well as points of law without a hearing in public. Where an appeal court considered that further investigations were necessary, an investigative hearing could be held before the judicial officer responsible for investigations on appeal. In this case, the appellate court had been called upon to examine the entire issue of the guilt or innocence of the applicants as well as determine points of law. The court had revised the legal characterisation of the first applicant's conduct as involving fraud rather than misappropriation without directly assessing evidence adduced by the applicant in person, even though the requisite element of intent differed. Similarly, in relation to the second and third applicants the appellate court had established requisite intent, again without taking direct evidence. The Court determined that in these circumstances the appellate court should have permitted the applicants to give direct evidence in person, and thus there had been a violation of Article 6(1) in each case[7].

1 See paras 5.123–5.125 below.
2 *Poitrimol v France* (1993) A 277-A, para 34; cf *Pelladoah v Netherlands* (1994) A 297-B, paras 37–41; *Stefanelli v San Marino* (8 February 2000), paras 19–22 (trial judge sentenced the applicant to four-and-a-half years' imprisonment but without holding a public hearing or even seeing the accused: violation of Art 6(1)).
3 *Poitrimol v France* (1993) A 277-A, para 31; and see also *Medenica v Switzerland* (14 June 2001), paras 53–60 (the applicant had been prevented from attending his trial by a judicial decision preventing him leaving the USA: no violation).
4 *Kremzow v Austria* (1993) A 268-B, paras 58–63 at para 58 (the applicant was legally represented in appellate proceedings considering pleas of nullity and appeals against sentence, and he was able to make submissions through his counsel: no breach of para (1) or of (3)(c)).
5 *Kremzow v Austria* (1993) A 268-B, paras 58–59 at para 59. See also *Helmers v Sweden* (1991) A 212-A, paras 31–32; *Belziuk v Poland* 1998-II, 558, para 37.
6 1998-II, 558, paras 37–38. See too *Botten v Norway* 1996-I, 145, para 52.
7 (25 July 2000), paras 92–102.

THE RIGHT TO PARTICIPATE EFFECTIVELY IN PROCEEDINGS

5.65 Fairness implies the opportunity of effective participation, a notion which itself is bound up with discussion of effective access to a court through the provision of legal aid[1], of knowledge of the case to be met[2], and of the right to interpretation facilities[3]. 'Equality of arms' at the most basic presupposes the right of each side to call its own witnesses, including expert witnesses[4]. In *Dombo Beheer v Netherlands*, the applicant company had sought to establish the basis of an oral agreement between it and a bank. However, it had been denied the opportunity to call its own representative as the domestic courts had identified this individual with the company itself, a situation the European Court of Human Rights accepted as having placed the applicant at a substantial disadvantage in comparison with the bank[5]. In exceptional cases, the European Convention on Human Rights, Article 6 may also call for consideration of the manner in which a hearing is held. In the related cases of *T v United Kingdom* and *V v United Kingdom*, the Court was asked for the first time to consider the position of children as accused persons. The two applicants who had been eleven years old at the time of their trial for the murder of an infant for which they were convicted sought to argue that the formality and ritual of the adult criminal court had prevented their effective participation. The Court considered that the trial must have seemed at times both incomprehensible and intimidating, and it was not sufficient in the circumstances for the purposes of Article 6(1) that the applicants had been represented by skilled and experienced counsel. Indeed, certain of the steps taken to modify the courtroom for the accused (for example, by raising the height of the dock) had resulted in a heightening of their sense of discomfort; and there was also evidence that the accused had been suffering from post-traumatic stress disorder. Their complaints that they had found the trial sufficiently distressing and had not been able to discuss their defence meaningfully with their legal representatives were accepted by the Court which held that the applicants had been denied a fair hearing[6].

1 See para 5.35 above and (in relation to criminal trials) paras 5.127–5.130 below.
2 See paras 5.58–5.59 above.
3 See para 5.137 below (in relation to criminal trials).
4 *Bönisch v Austria* (1985) A 92, paras 32–35.
5 (1993) A 274, paras 34–35.
6 (16 December 1999), paras 83–89 and paras 85–91, respectively.

DOMESTIC COURT DECISIONS ON EFFECTIVE PARTICIPATION

5.66   Article 6 is not necessarily breached where a court refuses to adjourn a hearing in order to enable one party to obtain legal representation, the other parties being legally represented. The Court of Appeal so held in a case concerned with care proceedings, where an adjournment to enable the parents to obtain fresh representation (following the withdrawal of their counsel) would have resulted in delay which would have been incompatible with the rights of the children[1].

1 *Re B and T (Care Proceedings: Legal Representation)* [2001] 1 FLR 485. As to disabled litigants, see *R (King) v Isleworth Crown Court* (15 January 2001, unreported), QBD.

Fair rules of evidence

5.67   Rules of evidence are essentially matters for domestic regulation[1]. The European Court of Human Rights 'is not called upon to rule in general whether it is permissible to exclude the evidence of a person in civil proceedings to which he is a party', far less to examine the 'law of evidence in civil procedure *in abstracto*'; under the European Convention on Human Rights, Article 6, the Court's task is limited to considering whether the proceedings in their entirety were 'fair', but this may involve examination of the method in which evidence was obtained[2] and subsequently admitted in proceedings[3], including the use of evidence from anonymous witnesses or witnesses who are not called to give evidence[4]. In short, evidentiary issues can have some bearing on the fairness of proceedings, although the Court's approach to such questions is often rather pragmatic.

1 Eg 13274/87, *TS and FS v Italy* (1990) DR 66, 164 (Art 6 does not require examination of the compatibility of questioning with domestic law).
2 Eg *Barbera, Messegué and Jabardo v Spain* (1988) A 146, para 68; *Delta v France* (1990) A 191 A, para 35; *Ferrantelli and Santangelo v Italy* 1996-III, 937, para 48; *Magee v United Kingdom* (6 June 2000), discussed at para 5.70 below.
3 *Dombo Beheer BV v Netherlands* (1993) A 274, para 31.
4 See paras 5.132–5.135 below (in relation to criminal trials).

DOMESTIC COURT DECISIONS ON FAIR RULES OF EVIDENCE

5.68   Scottish cases concerning the European Convention on Human Rights have included a number of cases relating to the law of evidence.

Cases concerning hearsay evidence[1] and evidence given anonymously[2] are considered below. Cases concerning irregularly obtained evidence[3] and self-incrimination[4] are considered in the next sections. Generally, the Scottish courts have adopted the same approach as the European Court of Human Rights, namely treating evidence as essentially a matter for regulation by domestic law, subject to the requirement of Article 6 of the Convention that the proceedings in their entirety must be fair. This has implications for the timing of any challenge and for the question whether any incompatibility with the Convention arises from an act of the prosecutor (and is therefore to be dealt with as a devolution issue under the Scotland Act 1998) or from an act of the court (to be dealt with under the Human Rights Act 1998). In *HM Advocate v Robb*[5], for example, the court observed:

> 'It is when and only when the court has determined the admissibility of the evidence, and when, if appropriate, the trial judge has directed the jury on the use of the evidence that any question of the fairness of the trial can be considered.'

1 Para 5.133 (criminal proceedings). Article 6 does not require the exclusion of hearsay evidence in civil proceedings: *R (Chingham) v Marylebone Magistrates Court* (11 January 2001, unreported), QBD.
2 Para 5.136.
3 Para 5.71 below.
4 Paras 5.76 and 5.77 below.
5 1999 SCCR 971 at 977.

The admissibility of irregularly obtained evidence

5.69 The admissibility of evidence improperly obtained is in principle a matter for domestic tribunals. The outcome is that, even where the European Court of Human Rights has established that the state has obtained evidence in violation of domestic law or of a guarantee under the European Convention on Human Rights and has led this evidence in a criminal trial, this will not in itself render the proceedings unfair. In *Schenck v Switzerland*, for example, the applicant had been convicted of incitement to murder his wife partly on the basis of a recording of a conversation made with him but taped without his knowledge or consent. He complained that the use of unlawfully obtained evidence had rendered his trial unfair. The Court did not 'exclude as a matter of principle and in the abstract that unlawfully obtained evidence ... may be admissible', but its task centred upon an assessment of the fairness of the trial. In this case, the rights of the defence had not been disregarded: the applicant had sought unsuccessfully to challenge the authenticity of the recording and also its use in evidence; further, the conviction had not been solely based upon the recordings. In the circumstances, the Court considered that the trial had not been unfair[1]. The principle is more vividly illustrated in *Khan v United Kingdom*. The applicant had been one of a number of visitors to the house of an individual who was being investigated for drugs trafficking and in which the police had installed a listening device. At one point in a conversation which was being recorded, the applicant admitted dealing in drugs. During his trial, the applicant had sought to challenge the admissibility of the evidence obtained through the surveillance, but after the judge had declined to exercise his powers to exclude this, the applicant had pled guilty to an alternative charge and thereafter been sentenced to three years' imprisonment. In contrast with the *Schenck* case, the Court had at the outset of the case established that there had been a breach of the applicant's Article 8 rights[2] and, further, the conviction had been based solely on the evidence from the surveillance; but in line with this earlier judgment, the Court noted that the trial judge had specifically considered the question of admissibility and decided to admit the evidence. In ruling that there had been no violation of the requirement of fairness guaranteed by Article 6(1), the Court attached considerable weight to the fact that had the admission of evidence given rise to substantive unfairness, the national courts would have had discretion to exclude it[3].

1 (1988) A 140, paras 46–47 at para 46. Cf *Lüdi v Switzerland* (1992) A 238, paras 38–40 (in terms of Art 8, telephone intercept deemed necessary in a democratic society, and use of an undercover agent did not involve 'private life').
2 See para 6.25 below. In the *Schenck* case (1988) A 140, para 53, the Court had considered it unnecessary to rule on this matter.
3 (12 May 2000), paras 36–40.

5.70   On the other hand, there is little discussion as to the fairness of evidence obtained under ill-treatment which may give rise to consideration of the guarantees provided by the European Convention on Human Rights, Article 3[1]. However, the clear thrust of Strasbourg jurisprudence is that the rationale behind Convention protection for the right to silence and the right not to incriminate oneself includes protection of an accused against improper compulsion with a view to minimising the risk of a miscarriage of justice[2]. Furthermore, for the purposes of Article 3, ill-treatment by state authorities inflicted for a particular purpose such as to extract a confession or information is treated as an aggravated violation of the guarantee[3]. It would thus be consistent with maximising the scope of protection of an individual to treat the admission of evidence obtained in this way as a violation of a fair trial. Domestic determination that a confession has been given voluntarily is not conclusive. In *Magee v United Kingdom,* the applicant had been held incommunicado in a Northern Ireland holding centre and interviewed for extended periods on five occasions by police officers operating in relays before he confessed his part in the planning of a terrorist attack. His initial request for access to a solicitor had been refused. He complained that he had been kept in virtual solitary confinement in a coercive environment and prevailed upon to incriminate himself, relying in part on the findings of the European Committee for the Prevention of Torture (the CPT) that the detention conditions in the holding centre were unacceptable[4]. While the domestic court had found that the applicant had not been ill-treated and that the confession had been voluntary, the incriminating statements had formed the basis of the prosecution case against him. The Court ultimately concluded that denial of access to a lawyer for over 48 hours and in a situation where the rights of the defence had been irretrievably prejudiced was incompatible with the rights of the accused under paragraphs (1) and (3)(c) of Article 3. For the Court, 'the austerity of the conditions of his detention and his exclusion from outside contact were intended to be psychologically coercive and conducive to breaking down any resolve he may have manifested at the beginning of his detention to remain silent'; thus, in such circumstances, the applicant 'as a matter of procedural fairness, should have been given access to a solicitor at the initial stages of the interrogation as a counterweight to the intimidating atmosphere specifically devised to sap his will and make him confide in his interrogators'[5].

1 Cf *Ferrantelli and Santangelo v Italy* 1996-III, 937, paras 47–50 (allegations that confessions had been obtained through ill-treatment: domestic investigations had established that the allegations were unsubstantiated).
2 Eg *John Murray v United Kingdom* 1996-I, 30, discussed at para 5.79 below. For recent discussion, see *Quinn v Ireland* (21 December 2000), para 40; and *Heaney and McGuinness v Ireland* (21 December 2000), para 40.
3 *Aksoy v Turkey* 1996-VI, 2260, para 64; see further para 4.20 above.
4 Cf *Report to the United Kingdom Government*, CPT/Inf(94) 17, at para 109: 'Even in the absence of overt acts of ill-treatment, there is no doubt that a stay in a holding centre may be – and is perhaps designed to be – a most disagreeable experience. The material conditions of detention are poor ... and important qualifications are, or at least can be, placed upon certain fundamental rights of persons detained by the police (in particular, the possibilities for contact with the outside world are severely limited throughout the whole period of detention and various restrictions can be placed on the right of access to a lawyer). To this must be added the intensive and potentially prolonged character of the interrogation process. The cumulative effect of these factors is to place persons detained at the holding centres under a considerable degree of psychological pressure. The CPT must state, in this connection, that to impose upon a detainee such a degree of pressure as to break his will would amount, in its opinion, to inhuman treatment.'
5 (6 June 2000), paras 38–46 at para 43.

DOMESTIC COURT DECISIONS ON THE ADMISSIBILITY OF IRREGULARLY OBTAINED EVIDENCE

5.71   United Kingdom courts dealing with questions of admissibility of evidence which is said to have been obtained in contravention of rights in terms of the European Convention on Human Rights have applied the *Schenk v Switzerland*[1] and *Khan v United Kingdom*[2] judgments. In *R v P*[3], for example, Lord Hobhouse of Woodborough said:

> 'The critical question is the fairness of the trial. Questions of the admissibility of evidence are not governed by Article 8. The fair use of intercept evidence at a trial is not a breach of Article 6 even if the evidence was unlawfully obtained.... The defendant is not entitled to have the unlawfully obtained evidence excluded simply because it has been so obtained. What he is entitled to is an opportunity to challenge its use and admission in evidence and a judicial assessment of the effect of its admission upon the fairness of the trial.'

1 (1988) A 140.
2 (12 May 2000).
3 [2001] 2 WLR 463. See also *A-G's Reference (No 3 of 1999)* [2001] 2 AC 91, especially per Lord Cooke of Thorndon; *R v Loveridge* (11 April 2001, unreported), CA. Cf *HM Advocate v McLean* 2000 SCCR 987.

Incitement to criminal activity

5.72   In *Teixeira de Castro v Portugal*, the European Court of Human Rights was called upon to consider the use of undercover agents. As part of a drug trafficking operation, two plain-clothes police officers had approached the applicant whose name had been given to them and had asked him to supply heroin. The applicant had procured the drug from a third party who had in turn obtained them from another person, and had been arrested when he had handed over sachets of the drug. Relying on the European Convention on Human Rights, Article 6, he complained that he had not had a fair trial in that he had been incited to commit an offence by plain-clothes police officers who had acted on their own initiative as *agents provocateurs* and without judicial supervision. For the Court, the behaviour of the officers had gone beyond those of undercover agents 'because they instigated the offence and there is nothing to suggest that without their intervention it would have been committed' and so, 'right from the outset, the applicant was definitively deprived of a fair trial'. Although recognising that the rise in organised crime called for appropriate measures, the fair administration of justice could not be 'sacrificed for the sake of expedience' since the public interest could not be used to justify the admission of evidence obtained through police incitement. In other words, the use of undercover agents must be restricted and accompanied by appropriate safeguards[1]. In contrast, in the earlier case of *Lüdi v Switzerland* which the Court distinguished in *Teixeira de Castro*[2], the applicant had been convicted on evidence obtained by an undercover police officer during the course of a preliminary investigation under judicial authority, a matter which did not give rise to any question of unfairness[3].

1 1998-IV, 1451, paras 34–39 at paras 36 and 39.
2 1998-IV, 1451, para 37.
3 (1992) A 238, paras 40–41 and 44–50 (violation established because of refusal to call the undercover agent as a witness).

DOMESTIC COURT DECISIONS ON INCITEMENT TO CRIMINAL ACTIVITY

5.73   The decision in *Teixera de Castro v Portugal*[1] is, on its facts, probably consistent with existing Scots law[2]. Some of the passages in the Court's judgment, if applied literally in Scotland, would however cause acute problems (eg the emphasis on the absence of judicial supervision of the police operation, and on the absence of evidence as to the accused's criminal propensities). Subsequent English cases have emphasised that the judgment has to be interpreted in the light of its specific context. In particular, the Court of Appeal has noted that the decision in *Teixera de Castro* is specifically directed to the actions of police officers and the safeguards properly to be applied to them in the course of covert operations. On that basis, the Court of Appeal distinguished the question of the admissibility of evidence obtained by an investigative journalist acting as an *agent provocateur*. The court also commented that the *Teixera de Castro* judgment contains no analysis of the meaning or scope of the expression 'fair trial' as used in the European Convention on Human Rights, Article 6, and in particular of its apparent extension from the procedural fairness of criminal proceedings consequent upon a charge, to the issue whether the proceedings constitute an abuse of process[3]. The deployment of plain-clothes police officers to make random test purchases in order to detect illicit trading has also been held not to contravene Article 6[4].

1 1998-IV, 1451.
2 *Weir v Jessop (No 2)* 1991 SCCR 636.
3 *R v Shannon* [2001] 1 WLR 51.
4 *Nottingham City Council v Amin* [2000] 1 WLR 1071. See now *R v Loosely* (25 October 2001, unreported), HL.

The right to remain silent and the right not to incriminate oneself

5.74 While the text of the European Convention on Human Rights, Article 6 does not specifically mention either the right to remain silent when being questioned by the police or the privilege against self-incrimination, these are 'generally recognised international standards which lie at the heart of the notion of a fair procedure under Article 6'[1] and which are based upon the assumption that the prosecution proves its case without recourse to methods involving coercion or oppression[2]. In particular, the right not to incriminate oneself is closely linked with the presumption of innocence under paragraph (2)[3] and concerns respect for 'the will of an accused person to remain silent' rather than use of compulsory powers to obtain real evidence, that is 'material ... which ha[s] an existence independent of the will of the suspect, such as inter alia documents acquired pursuant to a warrant, breath, blood and urine samples and bodily tissue for the purposes of DNA testing'[4]. Interferences with the right to remain silent or the right against self-incrimination are likely to take the form of either imposition of penalties for failing to answer questions, or the application of evidentiary rules allowing adverse inferences to be drawn from silence or the direct or indirect use of statements obtained under compulsion. No Article 6 issue arises, however, if the coercion against a person 'charged' with an offence within the meaning of Article 6[5] falls short of a direct attempt to have him incriminate himself[6].

It will always be a question on the facts whether statements have been given voluntarily or under compulsion. In *Kamasinski v Austria*, the appellant complained that questions put to him by the presiding judge had resulted in the shifting of the burden of proof from the prosecution onto the defence through exercise of the power to put questions. However, the European Court of Human Rights considered that the law provided merely an option which an accused could decide to make use of in his own interest and did not impose an obligation to answer any question put, and thus there was no suggestion that the presumption of innocence had been undermined[7]. The matter is also illustrated by the Court's determination in *Staines v United Kingdom* that the application was inadmissible under Article 6(1) and (2). The applicant had been a chartered accountant who had been convicted of illegal share-dealing practices by advising her father to buy shares in a company the subject of a take-over bid. The advice had been given after social contact with another accountant who had been considered to be a 'connected person' in possession of unpublished and price-sensitive information. The applicant had been interviewed several years after the share purchase by Department of Trade and Industry inspectors and had confirmed that no improper information had been disclosed to her. Thereafter, she had been summoned to a formal interview during which she was under a legal duty to answer questions on oath but had adhered to her earlier voluntary statements. In time, she was prosecuted and found guilty. The Court confirmed that the right not to incriminate oneself protected an individual from being convicted on the ground of statements or evidence given by means of oppression or coercion and against the will of the accused. Here, however, the applicant had already given unsolicited and voluntary statements, had been consistent at all times in the account she had given, and far from challenging the prosecution's reliance on the statements given on oath to the inspectors had attempted to found upon them to establish an unwavering line of defence[8].

1 *John Murray v United Kingdom* 1996-I, 30, at para 45. Cf Art 14(3)(g) of the International Covenant on Civil and Political Rights. See further Naismith 'Self-Incrimination: Fairness or Freedom?' [1997] EHRLR 229; Poole 'The Right of Silence, the ECHR and the Trial within a Trial' (1998) SLPQ 310; O'Boyle 'Freedom from Self-Incrimination and the Right to Silence: A Pandora's Box?' in Mahoney, Matscher, Petzold and Wildhaber (eds) *Protecting Human Rights: The European Perspective* (2000) pp 1021–1038.
2 *Saunders v United Kingdom*, 1996-IV, 2044, para 68
3 Cf *Saunders v United Kingdom* 1996-IV, 2044, para 68 (right against self-incrimination is closely linked to the presumption of innocence). Thus the use in evidence of documents delivered up under compulsion, but not containing statements made under compulsion, does not contravene Art 6: *A-G's Reference (No 7 of 2000)* [2001] 1 WLR 1879.
4 *Saunders v United Kingdom* 1996-IV, 2044, at para 69. See too 43486/98 *Tirado Ortiz and Lozano Martin v Spain* (15 June 1999). The right not to incriminate oneself applies also to witnesses who are regarded as co-suspects: cf *Lucà v Italy* (27 February 2001), para 33.
5 See para 5.21 above.
6 *Serves v France* 1997-VI, 2159, paras 46–47 (sanction imposed for refusal to take an oath was designed to ensure that statements were truthful rather than to force a witness to give evidence which was potentially self-incriminating).
7 (1989) A 168, paras 94–95.
8 (16 May 2000).

IMPOSITION OF SANCTIONS FOR FAILURE TO ANSWER QUESTIONS OR TO PROVIDE INCRIMINATING EVIDENCE

5.75 The imposition of a penalty on a person 'charged' with a criminal offence within the meaning of the European Convention on Human Rights, Article 6 for refusal to answer questions or to hand over real evidence which is incriminating may violate the protection against the right to remain silent. In *Funke v France*, customs officers had instigated proceedings against the applicant in an attempt to obtain incriminating documents which they believed existed since the authorities were unable or unwilling to obtain these documents by other means. The proceedings had resulted in a conviction and the imposition of a fine and a penalty for each additional day that the documents were not disclosed. The European Court of Human Rights considered that the guarantee against self-incrimination under paragraph (1) had been breached, and that there was thus no need to consider the issue of the presumption of innocence under paragraph (2)[1]. More recently, in the related cases of *Heaney and McGuinness v Ireland* and *Quinn v Ireland*, the Court again confirmed that the imposition of sanctions for failing to answer questions could violate Article 6. The applicants had been arrested on suspicion of serious criminal charges and required under domestic law to answer questions put to them. Their refusal had led to each being convicted and sentenced to imprisonment for six months. The Court rejected the state's argument that the domestic law in question was a proportionate response to the threat to public order posed by terrorism, considering that such concerns 'cannot justify a provision which extinguishes the very essence of the applicants' rights to silence and against self-incrimination'[2].

Similarly, in *J B v Switzerland*, the Court held that the obligation to submit documents to the tax authorities in the context of tax proceedings violated Article 6. The applicant had admitted that he had made investments without properly declaring the income, but had refused to submit documents requested by the tax authorities which had imposed substantial disciplinary fines. For the Court, although the proceedings were not expressly classified as constituting either supplementary tax proceedings or tax evasion proceedings, they had served both purposes since throughout the proceedings the tax authorities could have imposed a fine for the criminal offence of tax evasion. This offence involved the determination of a 'criminal charge' for the purposes of Article 6, and thus the authorities had been attempting to compel the applicant to submit documents which could have contained information constituting tax evasion[3].

1 (1993) A 256-A, para 44. Contrast *R v Hertfordshire County Council, ex p Green Environmental Industries* [2000] 2 AC 412; *R (Bright) v Central Criminal Court* [2001] 1 WLR 662.
2 *Heaney and McGuinness v Ireland* (21 December 2000), paras 53–59 at para 58, and *Quinn v Ireland* (21 December 2000), paras 53–60, at para 59 (violation of paras (1) and (2) on account of the close relationship with the presumption of innocence).
3 (3 May 2001), paras 63–71.

USE OF STATEMENTS OBTAINED UNDER COMPULSION

5.76 Cases involving powers under UK statutes to require a suspect to provide answers to questions put to him in complex fraud cases have been considered by the European Court of Human Rights. In *Saunders v United Kingdom*, inspectors had been appointed by the Secretary of State for Trade and Industry to investigate the acquisition of a company by another of which the applicant had been chief executive following allegations of unlawful share support. The inspectors could require individuals to answer the questions put to them, and failure to do so could lead to a determination of contempt of court and the imposition of a fine or a prison sentence of up to two years[1]. The Government had argued that only statements made which were self-incriminating could fall within the privilege against self-incrimination, a submission rejected by the Court on the ground that any testimony obtained under compulsion had the potential of being subsequently deployed in criminal proceedings by the prosecution case even to seek to undermine the credibility of an accused, a matter which could be especially harmful where credibility is assessed by a jury. Indeed, in the instant case, extensive use had been made of the transcript by the prosecution, suggesting that the transcripts of answers had been of assistance in establishing the applicant's dishonesty. Without deeming it necessary to determine whether the right not to incriminate oneself is absolute or subject to justification in certain circumstances, the Court in ruling that there had been an infringement of the right not to incriminate oneself also confirmed that the general requirements of fairness contained in the European Convention on Human Rights, Article 6 are applicable in all types of criminal offences 'without distinction from the most simple to the most complex'[2].

1 In terms of the Companies Act 1985, ss 434 and 436.
2 1996-IV, 2044, paras 69–76 at para 74. See too the related case of *I J L, G M R and A K P v United Kingdom* (19 September 2000), paras 82–83. See further Riley '*Saunders* and the Power to Obtain Information in Community and UK Competition Law' (2000) 25 ELRev 575. Other recent cases include *DC, HS and AD v United Kingdom* (14 September 1999) and; *WGS and MLS v United Kingdom* (23 November 1999).

DOMESTIC COURT DECISIONS ON THE USE OF STATEMENTS OBTAINED UNDER COMPULSION

5.77   The implications of the judgment in *Saunders v United Kingdom*[1] were considered by the Scottish courts in *Stott v Brown*[2], which concerned a requirement made of a motorist to give information to the police as to the identity of the driver of her car at a time when the driver was alleged to have committed an offence, non-compliance with the requirement being itself a criminal offence. The accused was suspected of driving her car while under the influence of drink, and was required to give the police information as to who had been driving the car at the material time. She replied that she was. She then gave a positive breath test, and was charged. The High Court of Justiciary held that for evidence to be led of her reply would contravene the protection against self-incrimination provided by the European Convention on Human Rights, Article 6(1). Although it was argued that such a conclusion would render it difficult to prosecute certain motoring offences, the court noted that Article 6(1) applies to the determination of 'any criminal charge', and that in its *Saunders* judgment the Court had said:

> 'It does not accept the Government's argument that the complexity of corpo-rate fraud and the vital public interest in the investigation of such fraud and the punishment of those responsible could justify such a marked departure as that which occurred in the present case from one of the basic principles of a fair procedure. Like the Commission, it considers that the general require-ments of fairness contained in Article 6, including the right not to incrimi-nate oneself, apply to criminal proceedings in respect of all types of criminal offences without distinction from the most simple to the most complex. The public interest cannot be invoked to justify the use of answers compulsorily obtained in a non-judicial investigation, to incriminate the accused during the trial proceedings[3].'

The court noted that it was accepted that to compel the accused to go into the witness box and admit that she had been driving the car at the mate-rial time would infringe Article 6(1). To compel her to make the admission prior to the trial, and allow the admission to be led in evidence, would allow that protection to be circumvented. The Privy Council however took a different view and reversed the decision of the High Court of Justiciary, holding that the rule against self-incrimination was not absolute and that the public interest justified the requirement in question.

The wider implications of *Stott v Brown* were made clear by the House of Lords in the subsequent case of *R v Forbes*:

> 'Reference was made in argument to the right to a fair trial guaranteed by article 6 of the European Convention on Human Rights. That is an absolute right. But, as the Judicial Committee of the Privy Council has very recently held in *Stott v Brown*, the subsidiary rights comprised within that article are not absolute, and it is always necessary to consider all the facts and the whole history of the proceedings in a particular case to judge whether a defendant's right to a fair trial has been infringed or not[4].'

1   1996-IV, 2044.
2   2001 SCCR 62. See Di Rollo 'Section 172 – An Unconventional Approach?' 2001 SLT (News) 13; Duff 'Section 172 – why the Privy Council Got it Right' 2001 SLT (News) 87; Pillay 'Self-incrimination and Article 6: The Decision of the Privy Council in *Procurator Fiscal v Brown*' [2001] EHRLR 78.

3 2001 SCCR 62, at para 74.
4 [2001] 1 AC 473, para 24. See also *A-G's Reference (No 7 of 2000)* [2001] 1 WLR 1879; and *R v Dimsey* [2001] 3 WLR 843.

5.78 The use of statements obtained under compulsory powers may also give rise to an issue of fairness under the European Convention on Human Rights, Article 6 in civil proceedings[1]. This matter was considered by the Court of Appeal in a case concerned with disqualification proceedings, where it was observed[2]:

> 'The issue of fair trial is one that must be considered in the round, having regard to all relevant factors. The relevant factors include (but are not limited to): (i) that disqualification proceedings are not criminal proceedings, and are primarily for the protection of the public, but do nevertheless often involve serious allegations and almost always carry a degree of stigma for anyone who is disqualified; (ii) that there are degrees of coercion involved in different investigative procedures available in corporate insolvency, and these differences may be reflected in different degrees of prejudice involved in the admission, in disqualification proceedings, of statements obtained by such procedures; and (iii) that in this field as in most other fields, it is generally best for issues of fairness or unfairness to be decided by the trial judge, either at a pre-trial review or in the course of the trial.'

1 Cf 39031/97, *DC, HS and AD v United Kingdom* (14 September 1999) and 38172/97, *WGS and MSLS v United Kingdom* (23 November 1999).
2 *Official Receiver v Stern* [2001] 1 All ER 633, 659.

THE DRAWING OF ADVERSE INFERENCES FROM SILENCE

5.79 The right to remain silent and the privilege against self-incrimination may also be compromised by the drawing of adverse inferences from the refusal to answer questions. In *John Murray v United Kingdom*, the question facing the European Court of Human Rights was whether the drawing of inferences from the right to silence was compatible with the European Convention on Human Rights, Article 6. While the right to remain silent was a generally recognised international standard, there was no guidance as to whether it was an absolute right in the sense that its exercise could not be taken into account in the assessment of evidence at trial stage. For the Court, it was 'self-evident that it is incompatible with the immunities under consideration to base a conviction solely or mainly on the accused's silence or on a refusal to answer questions or to give evidence himself'.

However, it was 'equally obvious that these immunities cannot and should not prevent that the accused's silence, in situations which clearly call for an explanation from him, be taken into account in assessing the persuasiveness of the evidence adduced by the prosecution'. In deciding whether Article 6 was infringed by the drawing of adverse inferences from an accused's silence, it was thus necessary to consider 'all the circumstances of the case, having particular regard to the situations where inferences may be drawn, the weight attached to them by the national courts in their assessment of the evidence and the degree of compulsion inherent in the situation'. Here, the applicant was able to remain silent and he remained a non-compellable witness; his refusal to answer did not constitute a criminal offence or contempt of court; and a conviction could not be based solely upon exercise of the right to silence. While denial of access to a solicitor had implications for the rights of the defence, on this point there was no indication that the applicant had not appreciated the significance of the warning that inferences could be drawn from his silence prior to access to his solicitor, and thus there had been no unfairness or infringement of the presumption of innocence[1].

In each case, the facts must be considered with some care. In *Condron and Ors v United Kingdom*, the Court considered that there had been a denial of a fair hearing. During an interview with police, the applicants, who were suspected of drug-trafficking, had refused to answer questions on the advice of their solicitor who considered that they were not fit to do so as they were suffering from drug withdrawal symptoms. This explanation was put to the jury which was given an option of whether to draw an adverse inference from the applicants' failure to explain what had been taking place as a police surveillance team had observed the applicants passing certain items to other individuals. Although the appeal court had criticised the trial judge's direction to the jury, it had nevertheless considered that the convictions were safe. The Court, however, reiterated that particular caution is required before an accused's silence can be invoked against him since basing a conviction wholly or mainly upon an accused person's refusal to answer a question would be incompatible with the Convention. Here, the applicants had advanced an explanation for their refusal to answer questions. The particular charge to the jury, however, had left the jury free to draw an adverse inference were it to have been satisfied that the explanation was plausible rather than instructing it to refuse to draw any such inference in such a situation. Since juries did not give reasons for their decisions, it was impossible to ascertain what weight had been given to the refusal to answer questions, and accordingly there had been a violation of paragraph (1)[2]. A similar violation was found in *Telfner v Austria*. Here, the applicant had been convicted of a driving offence in circumstances where it was open to the accused to have given a contrary version of events without having to inculpate another person as the driver of the vehicle at the relevant time. The victim of the accident had identified the registration number but not the driver of a car registered in the name of the applicant's mother but regularly driven by other members of the family. Police officers had observed the applicant driving the car in the past and thus considered him as the main driver of the car and as the suspect; additionally, suspicion had fallen upon him on account of his absence from home when police had called to make inquiries. In court, the applicant had pled not guilty to the charge of causing injury by negligent driving, stating only that he had not been the driver but declining to give any further evidence. Neither his mother nor his sister had testified, and the victim had again confirmed his inability to identify the driver. For the Court, the case was not one which involved the operation of legal presumptions. It again clarified that it is acceptable in terms of Article 6(2) to draw inferences from silence, but only 'where the courts freely evaluate the evidence before them, provided that the evidence adduced is such that the only common-sense inference to be drawn from the accused's silence is that he had no answer to the case against him'. Here, and in contrast with the *John Murray* case, the trial court had relied upon two uncorroborated elements of evidence which could not be taken to have constituted 'a case against the applicant which would have called for an explanation from his part'. The conclusion was thus that 'in requiring the applicant to provide an explanation although they had not been able to establish a convincing prima facie case against him, the courts shifted the burden of proof from the prosecution to the defence'. In consequence, there has been a violation of the presumption of innocence[3].

1   1996-I, 30, paras 44–58 at para 47. See too, *Averill v United Kingdom* (6 June 2000); *Quinn v Ireland* (21 December 2000), para 40; *Heaney and McGuinness v Ireland* (21 December 2000), para 40; cf 38642/97, *Serves v France* (4 May 2000) (reports drafted for military administrative disciplinary charges and subsequently used in criminal proceedings were not the only evidence used in the trial; nor had the applicant alleged he had been unable to cross-examine the officer who had compiled the reports: and thus the application was inadmissible). *John Murray* has been distinguished in Scottish cases on the basis that the provision that adverse inferences might be drawn from silence has no parallel in Scottish procedure. See *HM Advocate v Robb* 1999 SCCR 971 (accused refused presence of solicitor during police interviews); *HM Advocate v Campbell* 1999 SCCR 980 (identification parade held without presence of accused's solicitor); also *Paton v Ritchie* 2000 SCCR 151.
2   (2 May 2000), paras 63–68. See further Jennings, Ashworth and Emmerson 'Silence and Safety: The Impact of Human Rights Law' [2000] Crim LR 879.
3   (20 March 2001), paras 15–20 at paras 17 and 18. The Court additionally considered that speculation that the applicant had been under the influence of alcohol at the time of the offence, while not directly relevant to establishing guilt, contributed 'to the impression that the courts had a preconceived view of the applicant's guilt' (at para 19). For discussion of the presumption of innocence and the burden of proof, see paras 5.109–5.110 below.

The right to a reasoned judgment

5.80   In general, the European Convention on Human Rights, Article 6 obliges courts to give reasons for their judgment[1]. The giving of reasons is generally implicit in the concept of a fair trial since reasons inform the parties of the basis of the decision and enable them to exercise any right of appeal available to them, and also enable the public to understand the rationale for judicial decisions. The giving of reasons can thus be regarded as being implied in certain of the express requirements of Article 6, such as 'a fair and public hearing', the public pronouncement of judgment, and the provision of adequate facilities for the preparation of the defence in criminal cases. At the same time, states enjoy considerable freedom in the choice of the appropriate means to ensure that their judicial systems comply with the requirements of Article 6[2]. Thus the extent of the duty to give reasons varies according to the nature of the decision.

> 'It is moreover necessary to take into account, inter alia, the diversity of the submissions that a litigant may bring before the courts and the differences existing in the Contracting States with regard to statutory provisions, customary rules, legal opinion and the presentation and drafting of judgments. That is why the question whether a court has failed to fulfil the obligation to state reasons, deriving from Article 6 of the Convention, can only be determined in the light of the circumstances of the case'[3].

The right to a reasoned judgment imposes on domestic courts a duty, in principle, to examine and address the arguments and evidence put forward by the parties to a case[4]. A reasoned judgment does not however have to deal with every matter raised, provided it indicates the grounds on which the decision is based with sufficient clarity[5]. The reasons given must be valid in law[6]. They must be available in time to enable any right of appeal to be exercised[7].

In relation to jury trials, the Commission held inadmissible a complaint about the failure of the Belgian assize court to issue reasons, observing that the requirement that reasons be given must accommodate the particular nature of the procedure in jury trials, where the jury are not required, or are not able, to give reasons for their verdict. The Commission also observed that their decision was not susceptible to appeal on the facts[8].

1 *Hadjianastassiou v Greece* (1992) A 252-A, para 33.
2 *Hadjianastassiou v Greece* (1992) A 252-A, para 33.
3 *Ruiz Torija v Spain* (1994) A 303-A, para 29; *Hiro Balani v Spain* (1994) A 303-B.
4 *Quadrelli v Italy* (11 January 2000), para 34; *Ruiz Torija v Spain* (1994) A 303-A, para 19.
5 *Van der Hurk v Netherlands* (1994) A 288, para 61; *Georgiadis v Greece* 1997-III, 949, para 43; *Helle v Finland* 1997-VIII, 2911, para 55; *Higgins v France* 1998-I, 44, para 42.
6 *De Moor v Belgium* (1994) A 292-A, paras 54–55.
7 *Hadjianastassiou v Greece* (1992) A 252-A, paras 35–37; cf *Zoon v Netherlands* (7 December 2000), paras 36–51. See too 44305/98 and 49150/99, *Snooks v United Kingdom* and *Dowse v United Kingdom* (convictions for drug-related offences in the Jersey courts which consisted of a judge of law (the deputy bailiff) and two judges of fact (the jurats): in the first application, the deputy bailiff gave his summing-up to the jurats in public, while it was done in private in the latter case; in both instances, the deputy bailiff retired with the jurats when the latter were to reach their verdicts, for which no reasons were given: communicated).
8 15957/90, *R v Belgium* (1992) DR 72, 195. In a case concerned with the Contempt of Court Act 1981, s 8, the Commission accepted the necessity, in general, of preventing disclosure of the deliberations of a jury in a criminal trial: 24770/94, *Associated Newspapers Ltd v United Kingdom* (30 November 1994).

DOMESTIC COURT DECISIONS ON THE DUTY TO GIVE REASONS

5.81   The duty to give reasons has been discussed in several cases before United Kingdom courts[1], and in particular there have been several Scottish cases concerned with the implications of this aspect of the European Convention on Human Rights, Article 6 for civil jury trials. In one case, where it is argued that the provisions of the Human Rights Act 1998 preclude the allowance of a jury trial in every action of damages for personal injuries, the issue on the merits has not yet been determined[2]. In another case, an argument that the Human Rights Act 1998 required the court to introduce a new test for the allowance of a new trial on the ground that the damages were excessive – intervening when the court considered the damages to be in excess of what a judge would have awarded, rather than (as under existing law) when the damages were in excess of what any reasonable jury could award – was rejected[3]. In a further case, it was argued that in the particular circumstances of the case, which included a disputed claim for past and future loss of earnings, the inability of the jury to give reasons for any award for loss of earnings would prevent the defenders from exercising a right of appeal. The argument was rejected, the court holding that the approach taken to the determination of a motion for a new trial, when the amount of damages was called into question, did not require detailed reasons to be given by a jury before the right to such a new trial could be exercised[4].

1 See eg *Stefan v General Medical Council* [1999] 1 WLR 1293, 1300–1301; *Flannery v Halifax Estate Agencies Ltd* [2001] 1 WLR 377, 381.

2 *Gunn v Newman* 2001 SC 525 (OH) and 2001 SLT 776, unreported, Ct of S.
3 *McLeod v British Railways Board* 2001 SC 534.
4 *Sandison v Graham Begg Ltd* (30 March 2001, unreported), Ct of S. It should be noted that the form of issue should reflect the issues in dispute. The jury's verdict, answering the questions put to it, when taken with the terms of the presiding judge's charge and the evidence before the jury, should enable any motion for a new trial to be fully considered: cf 15957190, *R v Belgium* (1992) DR 72, 195.

Remedying defects at first instance

5.82 The European Convention on Human Rights, Article 6 does not guarantee a right to an appeal[1], but where a state has made provision for a system of appeals in domestic law, the provision will be applicable in accordance with the principle that the fairness of the proceedings as a whole is what stands to be assessed[2]. This may in turn allow a state to escape liability for a violation of Article 6 where the reviewing court has corrected the defect, for example by providing guarantees of independence and impartiality[3] or a public hearing[4]. If the proceedings concern the determination of a serious criminal charge, however, then the requirements of Article 6 must in general be met at first instance[5]. Further, in terms of Article 35 an applicant is expected to exhaust domestic remedies before bringing an application to the Strasbourg Court, and this will normally involve making use of channels of appeal and review accorded by domestic law[6]. Issues such as effective access to appeal courts through the provision of legal aid[7] and the extent of the right to a public hearing and to participate in the hearing[8] are thus of relevance in appeal proceedings.

1 ECHR, Protocol 7, Art 2 provides for a right of appeal in criminal matters, but the UK has not yet ratified this protocol.
2 E g *Belziuk v Poland* 1998-II, 558, at para 37: 'criminal proceedings form an entity and the protection afforded by Article 6 does not cease with the decision at first instance. A State is required to ensure also before courts of appeal that persons amenable to the law shall enjoy before these courts the fundamental guarantees contained in this Article'.
3 See paras 5.40–5.42 above.
4 See paras 5.87–5.89 below.
5 *Findlay v United Kingdom* 1997-I, 263, para 79. Contrast *Öztürk v Germany* A 73, para 56; *Lutz v Germany* A 123, para 57. Even in criminal proceedings concerning serious charges, however, certain defects at first instance can be remedied by subsequent procedure on appeal: see e g *Edwards v United Kingdom* (1992) A 247-B; followed in *R v Craven* [2001] 2 Cr App R 12.
6 See para 2.25 above.
7 Cf para 5.127–5.128 below (in relation to criminal proceedings).
8 See para 5.89 below.

Curing defects through review of administrative decision-making by a court with 'full jurisdiction'

5.83 The matter may be of particular importance in considering whether a court can subsequently cure a defect which has arisen at first instance. For example, the availability of review or appeal may be crucial in ensuring that the determination of civil rights and obligations has involved access to a court. In terms of the European Convention on Human Rights, Article 6, the court or tribunal hearing the determination in question must be able to deal with all aspects of the dispute, including questions of fact and of law[1]. Stated simply, 'the concept of "full jurisdiction" involves that the reviewing court not only considers the complaint but has the ability to quash the impugned decision and to remit the case for a new decision by an impartial body' if the review court does not itself then take the decision[2]. An issue may also arise as to the qualification for the purposes of Article 6(1) of a professional body which itself does not comply with the requirements of a fair trial. If the body is subject to appeal on all relevant aspects of the case, then this aspect of Article 6 will be deemed to have been satisfied[3]. The outcome will be different where the appeal court is more properly a court exercising judicial review of the legality rather than of the merits. In particular, where review is limited to consideration of whether a public authority has not acted unlawfully, unreasonably or unfairly, this is unlikely to be adequate[4]. In *W v United Kingdom*, while the Court accepted that judicial review of wardship proceedings allowed the domestic courts to consider the issue of access by a parent to his child who had been taken into public care, such proceedings could only examine the lawfulness of the decision rather than its merits. Since no tribunal was able to determine this latter matter, there was deemed to be a violation of Article 6's requirement of access to a court[5]. Similarly, in *Kingsley v United Kingdom*, the Court considered that the scope of judicial review had been insufficient to cure its finding that the Gaming Board had not been an impartial tribunal in determining to revoke the applicant's certificate that he was a 'fit and proper person' to run a casino. It was 'generally inherent in the notion of judicial review that, if a ground of challenge is upheld, the reviewing court has power to quash the impugned decision, and that either the decision will then be taken by the review court, or the case will be remitted for a fresh decision by the same or a different body'. However, neither the High Court nor the Court of Appeal in disposing of the application for review based on allegations of illegality, irrationality (or *Wednesbury* unreasonableness) or procedural impropriety had the power to remit the case for a first decision by the Board or by another independent tribunal, and thus there had been a violation of Article 6[6].

1 *Le Compte, van Leuven and de Meyere v Belgium* (1981) A 43, para 51.
2 *Kingsley v United Kingdom* (7 November 2000) at para 58.
3 Cf *Albert and Le Compte v Belgium* (1983) A 58, para 36 (lack of public hearing not subsequently remedied by public character of Court of Cassation hearing as this court did not take cognisance of the merits of the case).
4 Eg *O v United Kingdom* (1987) A 120, para 63 (review of decision to take a child into public care). Cf *Oerlemans v Netherlands* (1991) A 219, paras 56–57 (civil courts able to carry out a full review of all administrative acts, and thus met the requirements of Art 6(1)); *Fischer v Austria* (1995) A 312, paras 29 and 33 (constitutional court had limited competence in considering whether an administrative decision was in conformity with the Constitution and thus did not have the requisite jurisdiction; but the administrative court so qualified as it could consider all points made by the applicant without declining jurisdiction).
5 (1987) A 121, paras 79–82.
6 (7 November 2000), paras 51–59 (at para 53: the subject matter of the decision appealed against was 'a classic exercise of administrative discretion', and thus the Court did not agree with the applicant that the benefit of a full court hearing on both the facts and the law in initially determining the revocation of his certificate had been required: the panel had been advised by officials who were experts in the gaming industry even if the members taking the decision lacked this expertise, and the procedure had thus been an appropriate one).

DOMESTIC COURT DECISIONS ON THE REMEDYING OF DEFECTS AT FIRST INSTANCE

5.84   Domestic decisions concerning the review of decisions by disciplinary and other tribunals have been discussed above[1].

1 Paragraphs 5.48–5.49.

Review of planning decisions

5.85   There seems, however, to have been some recent relaxation of expectations in at least cases involving planning law where full review of the facts may not be required[1]. Limited judicial control of administrative decision-making is a common feature found in most European legal systems[2]. In the past, it was clear that judicial review would not have been deemed to comply with the guarantee unless it involved a full review of measures concerning those civil rights affected by planning decisions[3].

The compatibility of British arrangements with Article 6 requirements was examined in *Bryan v United Kingdom*. The applicant had sought to challenge a planning inspector's findings of fact (rather than of law) in the High Court. The planning inspector had dismissed the applicant's appeal after an inquiry into an enforcement notice served by the Secretary of State which had required the demolition of two buildings. It was accepted that the inspector who was a civil servant in the department headed by the Secretary of State had not been sufficiently independent to qualify as an independent adjudicator, and in consequence the Court turned to the issue of whether the scope of judicial review was sufficient to provide the necessary control by a judicial body and thus cure the defect of lack of independence. While the appeal had been restricted to matters of law, the Court noted that the inspector's decision could also have been quashed on legal grounds which related to established facts such as perverse or irrational drawing of inferences from facts, or a determination that findings of fact were not supported by the evidence. Further, the procedure before the inspector had provided considerable procedural safeguards, and in any case the applicant had not sought to challenge the primary facts established. For the Court, the conclusion that questions both of fact as well as of law could have been adequately addressed by the domestic courts satisfied the requirements of Article 6(1)[4].

Recently, the Grand Chamber has confirmed this interpretation in the related cases of *Chapman v United Kingdom* and *Jane Smith v United Kingdom*. The applicants were gipsies by birth who had bought land on which they intended to live in order to maintain their traditional gipsy lifestyle and culture. They complained that enforcement measures taken against them for contravening planning regulations violated Convention rights including respect for family life and the protection of property; in addition, they alleged that their right to a fair trial under Article 6 had been violated since the decisions to uphold enforcement proceedings and to refuse planning permission had been made by inspectors employed by the Secretary of State rather than by an independent and impartial tribunal. As in the *Bryan* case, no appeal was possible against the inspector's decision to a court of law because the challenged issues were of fact and not of law. The applicant's argument was essentially that *Bryan* had been decided on its particular facts, and the review by the High Court could neither examine whether the planning inspector had given adequate weight to the needs of the gipsy family in pursuing their lifestyle nor the proportionality of a measure interfering with her rights. The Court, however, again considered that the scope of judicial review of decisions taken after a public procedure before an inspector 'enabled a decision to be challenged on the basis that it was perverse, irrational, had no basis on the evidence or had been made with reference to irrelevant factors or without regard to relevant factors' was sufficient to comply with the European Convention on Human Rights, Article 6[5].

1 See further Jones 'Property Rights, Planning Law and the European Convention' [1996] EHRLR 233; Corner 'Planning, Environment, and the ECHR' [1998] Jo Plan & Env Law 301; and Hart 'The Impact of the ECHR on Planning & Environmental Law' [2000] Jo Plan & Env Law 117.
2 *Bryan v United Kingdom* (1995) A 335-A, para 47.
3 *Sporrong and Lönnroth v Sweden* (1982) A 52, para 86 (admissibility of application for judicial review did not involve a full review of the issues, and thus this remedy did not satisfy Art 6(1)).
4 (1995) A 335-A, paras 39–47.
5 (18 January 2001), paras 122–125 at para 124; (18 January 2001), paras 133–134 at para 133.

DECISIONS OF DOMESTIC COURTS ON THE REVIEW OF PLANNING DECISIONS

5.86   Decisions of domestic courts concerning planning decisions have concerned the 'independent and impartial tribunal' requirement and the 'reasonable time' requirement, and are discussed elsewhere[1].

1 Paragraphs 5.48 above and 5.107 below.

Public hearing and judgment pronounced in open court

5.87   The European Convention on Human Rights, Article 6 (1) provides for a public hearing and further that 'judgment shall be pronounced publicly'. These aspects of a fair trial initially appear the least complex. There is detailed provision for the exclusion of the press and the public from all or part of the trial, to protect either collective interests (that is 'in the interests of morals, public order or national security in a democratic society'); individual concerns (that is 'where the interests of juveniles or the protection of the private life of the parties so require'); or the integrity of the particular proceedings (that is, 'to the extent strictly necessary in the opinion of the court in special circumstances where publicity would prejudice the interests of justice'). However, the requirements of public hearing and public judgment should not be read too literally as they are interpreted in accordance with the purposes of the guarantees and there is thus some flexibility in their application. Here, the Court has identified two principal goals: the protection of litigants against the secret administration of justice; and the maintenance of public confidence in the judicial system. 'By rendering the administration of justice visible, publicity contributes to the achievement of the aim of Article 6(1), namely a fair trial, the guarantee of which is one of the fundamental principles of any democratic society'[1]. A 'public hearing' thus principally applies to proceedings at first instance[2] rather than to the summary disposal of 'screening' decisions[3] or hearings at appeal stage where other considerations such as securing the expeditious disposal of court business come into play[4]. The lack of a public hearing at second or third instance will normally be considered acceptable where the proceedings concern questions of law or leave to appeal[5] where such questions can be considered without oral hearing through written pleadings[6]. Indeed, a public hearing may not be required where an appellate court can additionally reconsider questions of fact[7], but where an appeal court is called upon to make a full assessment of an individual's guilt, fairness will require direct assessment of the individual's own evidence given in person[8]. Further, since the requirement of public pronouncement of judgment is to permit public scrutiny of the administration of justice, this may be achieved through other means as long as the principle of public access to judgments is secured[9], for example, through the deposit of the full text of any appellate decision in the court registry[10].

1 *Axen v Germany* (1983) A 72, at para 25. As regards the special considerations which apply to proceedings involving children, see eg *V v United Kingdom* (16 December 1999).
2 And to other closely related proceedings such as proceedings for compensation for detention following upon an acquittal where such proceedings are recognised by domestic law: eg *Szücs v Austria* 1997-VII, 2468, paras 44–48; *Werner v Austria* 1997-VII, 2496, paras 48–51; cf *Lamanna v Austria* (10 July 2001), paras 29–32 (public pronouncement of appellate court decision on compensation for detention remedied the lack of public hearing at first instance).
3 *Bulut v Austria* 1996-II, 346, paras 40–42.
4 *Ekbatani v Sweden* (1988) A 134, para 31; *K D B v Netherlands* 1998-II, 620, para 39.
5 Cf *Helmers v Sweden* (1991) A 212-A, paras 36–39 (circumstances of appellate proceedings requiring presence of applicant in person to help determine questions of law, also taking into account seriousness of what was at stake (professional reputation and career)); *Elsholz v Germany* (13 July 2000), paras 62–66 (lack of psychological expert evidence and failure by the Regional Court to conduct a further hearing when the applicant's appeal raised questions of fact and law which could not adequately be resolved on the basis of the written submissions alone: violation of Art 6(1)).
6 *Sutter v Switzerland* (1984) A 74, para 30 (military appeal court).
7 *Jan-Åke Andersson v Sweden* (1991) A 212-B, paras 27 and 29 (no questions of fact or of law which could not have been resolved from the case file, and thus no requirement of a public hearing).
8 Cf *Ekbatani v Sweden* (1988) A 134, para 32 (absence of full rehearing in public constituted a violation of Art 6).
9 Cf *Szücs v Austria* 1997-VII, 2468, para 42, and *Werner v Austria* and 1997-VII, 2496, para 45.
10 *Pretto and Ors v Italy* (1983) A 71, at para 27 (principle applies 'at any rate as regards cassation proceedings').

5.88 Limitations on public hearing or pronouncement of judgment must properly satisfy one or more of these permissible grounds such as reasons of public order and security[1] or protection of professional confidence and privacy[2]. A recent judgment helps clarify the Court's approach. In *B v United Kingdom and P v United Kingdom*, the applicants had each instituted proceedings seeking custody of their sons and had asked in each case for a public hearing and public delivery of the judgments. Each of these requests had been refused, and the applicants had further been prohibited from disclosing any documents used in the proceedings. For the Court, the exclusion of the press and public in cases involving custody upon divorce or separation were prime examples where private hearings might be justified to protect the privacy of the child and parties to the proceedings. Further, in such hearings it was crucial that parents and others felt able to express themselves candidly on highly personal issues without fear of public curiosity or comment to allow the court to gain as full and accurate a picture as possible of the merits of the range of options open to it. Nor was the Court prepared to accept that the absence of public delivery of the judgment had violated the European Convention on Human Rights, Article 6, since any individual who had been able to establish an interest in child residence cases could consult or obtain a copy of the full text of orders and judgments made at first instance, while appellate court decisions in cases of special interest were routinely published to allow scrutiny of the disposal of such proceedings[3].

1 *Campbell and Fell v United Kingdom* (1984) A 80, paras 87–88 (prison disciplinary hearings). But cf *Riepan v Austria* (14 November 2000), paras 27–34 (criminal trial involving charges of dangerous menace took place in the prison where the applicant was serving an 18-year prison sentence for murder and burglary: violation of Art 6(1); and not remedied by subsequent proceedings: paras 35–41).

2 This suggests that appropriate scrutiny is required of any reason advanced: cf *Le Compte, Van Leuven and De Meyere v Belgium* (1981) A 43, para 59 (professional disciplinary body was not considering medical treatment of patients, and thus did not involve professional secrecy or protection of private life); *Diennet v France* (1995) A 325-A, paras 33–35 (disciplinary proceedings only concerned a doctor's method of consultation by correspondence and no suggestion that professional confidence would be breached).

3 (24 April 2001), paras 35–49 (para 52: in the circumstances, there was no need to examine the complaints under Art 10).

5.89   The guarantee applies with equal measure to administrative tribunals determining civil rights[1], to disciplinary tribunals considering criminal charges[2], and also, as the Court made clear in *Scarth v United Kingdom*, to arbitration proceedings for the recovery of debt[3]. However, the absence of a public hearing may be remedied on appeal[4]. Generally, a litigant need not show he has suffered actual prejudice since violation of the guarantees will be sufficient to qualify him as a 'victim'[5], but an individual involved in proceedings (including relevant professional disciplinary hearings) may waive his entitlement to a public hearing by 'his own free will and in an unequivocal manner'[6] providing always that the case does not raise an issue of public interest[7]. A waiver may be made by implication, for example, by failing expressly to request an oral hearing where the practice of a court or tribunal is not to hear the parties unless such a request is made[8].

1 *Ringeisen v Austria* (1971) A 13, para 98. See too *Stallinger and Kuso v Austria* 1997-II, 666, paras 50–51 (practice of administrative court not to hear the parties unless a party requested a hearing; here, the applicants had expressly requested an oral hearing which had been refused on the grounds that such was unlikely to clarify the case further: violation of right to a public hearing).

2 That is, within the meaning of Art 6(1): *Engel and Ors v Netherlands* (1976) A 22, para 89. See paras 5.20–5.25 above. In *Findlay v United Kingdom* 1997-I, 263, para 80, the Court decided it was not necessary to consider the lack of public hearings in courts-martial on account of a finding that the tribunal had lacked independence and impartiality.

3 (22 July 1999), paras 28–29 (application for hearing in public refused by the arbiter who conducted the hearing in private).

4 Defects at first instance (in particular, during disciplinary hearings held by professional bodies) may, on the other hand, be remedied where the superior court has full power to review all the issues, including questions of sanction: *Diennet v France* (1995) A 325-A, para 33; *Helle v Finland* 1997-VIII, 2911, paras 45–48. See also *Lamanna v Austria* (10 July 2001), paras 29–32 (public pronouncement of appellate court decision on compensation for detention remedied the lack of public hearing at first instance). Cf *Gautrin and Ors v France*

1998-III, 1009, paras 39–43 (the fact that the applicants would have had a public hearing had they appealed to the *Conseil d' Etat* from the decisions of the regional and national councils of the professional body which was precluded from holding public hearings was irrelevant: here, there had been no issue involving professional secrecy or the protection of private life, and there was a violation of Art 6); *Riepan v Austria* (14 November 2000), paras 35–41 (criminal trial which took place in a prison was not remedied by subsequent proceedings); and *Malhous v Czech Republic* (12 July 2001), paras 55–63 (land tribunal proceedings held in private were not remedied by review courts).

5 *Engel and Ors v Netherlands* (1976) A 22, para 89.

6 *Albert and Le Compte v Belgium* (1983) A 58, at para 35; *H v Belgium* (1987) A 127-B, para 54; *Pauger v Austria* 1997-III, 881, paras 58–62 (the applicant, a professor of public law, was considered to have waived unequivocally his right to a public hearing before the constitutional court); *Rolf Gustafson v Sweden* 1997-IV, 1149, para 47 (failure to request hearing before a board led to the reasonable conclusion the applicant had waived this right). Cf *De Weer v Belgium* (1980) A 35, paras 48–54 (waiver of criminal hearing through payment of administrative fine deemed 'tainted by restraint'); *Werner v Austria* 1997-VII, 2496, para 48 (applicant could not be criticised for failing to request a public hearing where such an application would have had no prospect of success).

7 *Schüler-Zgraggen v Switzerland* (1993) A 263, para 58. Cf *Pauger v Austria* 1997-III, 881, paras 62–63 (principle of equality between widows and widowers as regards pension entitlement had already been decided by the constitutional court, and thus the present case raised no issue of public interest warranting a public hearing).

8 *Zumtobel v Austria* (1993) A 268-A, para 34 ('dispute' raised no questions of public interest); cf *Fischer v Austria* (1995) A 312, para 44 (express request made for oral hearing at first instance court but refused on the ground this would not be likely to help to clarify the merits of the case; breach of 'public hearing' requirement in the circumstances).

DECISIONS OF DOMESTIC COURTS ON THE RIGHT TO A 'PUBLIC HEARING'

5.90 The Scottish courts have had to deal with a small number of cases concerned with the 'public hearing' requirement. In *Hoekstra v HM Advocate (No 1)*[1] it was held that a site visit by a jury to view productions (three tonnes of cannabis resin, and two vessels) which were too large to be produced in court, under the supervision of an officer of the court, and the accused being present (although unable to be present with every juror throughout their tour of the vessel), did not infringe the principle of a public hearing. The evidence, the submissions and the judge's directions to the jury had all been heard in public. The fact that, for practical reasons, the circumstances under which the jury had viewed objects too large to be produced in the courtroom had not involved the public or the accused being present with every juror throughout did not involve an infringement of the principle that there should be public scrutiny of the administration of justice. In *Clark v Kelly*[2] a challenge to justices of the District Court receiving legal advice in private from their clerk failed.

1 2000 SCCR 263. See also para 5.45 above, see also *Degnan v HM Advocate* 2001 SCCR 810 (case adjourned by minute).

2 2000 SCCR 821.

Length of proceedings: judicial determination within a 'reasonable time'

5.91 Justice delayed is justice denied. The reasonableness of the length of civil or criminal proceedings has given rise to substantial case law[1], but little of it concerning the United Kingdom[2]. The proceedings are considered as a whole, including (if relevant) appellate and constitutional proceedings. Two questions arise: first, calculation of the period of time to be taken into account; and second, consideration of whether this period is 'reasonable'. This latter issue requires assessment of the complexity of the factual or legal issues raised, the conduct of the applicant, and the conduct of the domestic authorities as assessed in light of what was at stake for the individual[3].

1 By 30 June 2001, the 'new' Court had given 1,284 judgments of which 768 (or just under 60%) concerned length of proceedings cases. The bulk of these involved Italy, Portugal and France. Cf Eissen *The Length of Civil and Criminal Proceedings in the Case-Law of the European Court of Human Rights* (1996) p 8 (in 165 of the 554 judgments (ie some 30%) delivered by the Court in its first 25 years, the issue of 'reasonable time' was considered). This section draws from this work written by the former Registrar of the Court.
2 Violations of 'reasonable time' have been established in *H v United Kingdom* (1987) A 120, paras 70–86 (2 years and 7 months in seeking access to a child); *Darnell v United Kingdom* (1993) A 272, para 21 (some 9 years before final decision regarding unfair dismissal in employment tribunals); 21437/93, *Dougan v United Kingdom* 1997 SCCR 56 (11 years between accused's failure to appear for trial and execution of non-appearance warrant); *Robins v United Kingdom* 1997-V, 1801, paras 30–35 (more than 4 years for relatively straightforward dispute over costs to be determined); and *Howarth v United Kingdom* (21 September 2000) paras 25–30, discussed at para 5.98 below.
3 *Zimmerman and Steiner v Switzerland* (1983) A 66, para 24.

5.92   The issue of reasonableness in criminal proceedings is also relevant in terms of the European Convention on Human Rights, Article 5(3)'s guarantee of 'trial within a reasonable time or to release pending trial'. In certain cases lengthy pre-trial detention may give rise to violations of both Article 5 and Article 6. There is thus some overlap in the content of each consideration. However, the focus in the first instance is upon the relevancy and sufficiency of reasons justifying continuing detention and any lack of due diligence on the part of the prosecutor, while the latter guarantee requires consideration of such matters as complexity of the case and conduct of the accused as well as that of the prosecutor. The crucial distinction is in the latitude given to the prosecutor. In *I A v France*, for example, pre-trial detention lasting some 63 months was found to violate Article 5(3), but the length of the criminal proceedings themselves which had amounted to some 81 months did not breach Article 6(1)'s guarantee of reasonableness on account of the complex factual issues[1].

1 1998-VII, 2951, paras 99–112, 116–122; see further paras 4.79–4.80 above.

Calculation of the period

START OF THE PERIOD

5.93   In criminal matters, calculation of the period begins with the point at which a person is charged with an offence[1]. As discussed above, the concept of 'charge' is given an autonomous meaning under the European Convention on Human Rights rather than any formal definition found in domestic legal systems[2], and denotes the 'official notification given to an individual by the competent authority of an allegation that he has committed a criminal offence'[3]. Invariably the start of this period will take place before the first court appearance and may be constituted by interview[4], arrest[5], issue of an arrest[6] or a search[7] warrant, by official notification that a prosecution is being investigated[8], by the opening of a preliminary investigation[9], or other official measures carrying the implication of a similar allegation and which similarly 'substantially affect the situation of the suspect'[10]. The reasonableness of the time taken for the 'determination' of any criminal charge thus clearly applies to pre-trial proceedings as much as it does to the period after the first appearance for trial. For example, in *Angelucci v Italy*, the period which fell to be considered began with the appointment of defence counsel, and ended more than eight years later with the pronouncement that there was no case to answer or alternatively (a few days later) when the time limit for an appeal against this decision expired[11].

1 Or in some cases, from the date of the state's acceptance of the right of individual petition if this is later, although assessment of the 'reasonableness' of the time will take account of the state of proceedings at this date: e g *Foti and Ors v Italy* (1982) A 56, para 53.

2 See paras 5.21–5.22 above

3 *Deweer v Belgium* (1980) A 35, paras 42 and 44 (concept has to be understood within the meaning of the Convention; the Court has to look behind formalities and consider the realities of the procedure).

4 *Howarth v United Kingdom* (21 September 2000), para 20 (interview by officers of the Serious Fraud Office in connection with allegations of market rigging, theft and false accounting).

5 E g *B v Austria* (1990) A 175, para 48.

6 E g *Boddaert v Belgium* (1992) A 235-D, para 35.

7 *Eckle v Germany* (1982) A 51, para 75.

8 E g *Mori v Italy* (1991) A 197-C, para 14 (date of formal notification); *Colacioppo v Italy* (1991) 197-D, para 13 (receipt of judicial notice of criminal proceedings).

9 *Ringeisen v Austria* (1971) A 13, para 110. See too *I L J, G M R and A K P v United Kingdom* (19 September 2000), paras 130–132 (the period to be considered for assessing the reasonableness of the length of the proceedings ran from the dates when the first and second applicants were charged and the third applicant was arrested).

10 *Deweer v Belgium* (1980) A 35, at para 46; *Eckle v Germany* (1982) A 51, para 73. See also *Angelucci v Italy* (1991) A 196-C, para 13 (appointment of defence counsel); *Raimondo v Italy* (1994) A 281-A, para 42 (court order of confiscation of seized goods); *Löffler v Austria* (3 October 2000), para 19 (starting-point to be taken as date when criminal proceedings were re-opened (following earlier investigations which had resulted in a conviction) as only after that time was the applicant again someone charged with a criminal offence). Cf *Reinhardt and Slimane-Kaïd v France* 1998-II, 640, para 93 (first applicant had been taken into custody in connection with investigations concerning the second applicant; and in consequence neither this measure nor a search of her home to obtain evidence against the second applicant was an 'official notification' to her that a criminal offence had been alleged).

11 (1991) A 196-C, paras 13 and 15.

5.94 As far as the determination of civil rights and obligations is concerned, calculation of the period of 'reasonable time' normally begins from the time an action is instituted in a court or tribunal[1]. In most cases, this will involve the date of institution of proceedings in a local court[2] or specialised court or tribunal[3] of first instance, unless a higher court has exclusive jurisdiction to hear the matter[4]. In certain circumstances, however, the period may begin at an earlier stage as with the application for interim relief[5], the making of a confiscation order[6], the submission of a preliminary claim for compensation[7], or the lodging of an objection[8] or request to a public authority[9]. The key issue is whether a 'dispute' can be said to exist. In *Lithgow and Ors v United Kingdom*, negotiations between various companies subject to nationalisation and the Department of

Industry had sought to agree the amount of compensation payable to shareholders. At this stage, only one company had instituted proceedings before a statutory arbitration tribunal, although at any point the negotiations seeking to achieve common agreement could have been broken off and the matters referred to the tribunal. The Court considered that the period for calculating the 'reasonable time' requirement only ran from the point when formal reference was made to the tribunal[10].

1 *Erkner and Hofauer v Austria* (1987) A 117, para 64. In certain cases, however, this will be from the date of the state's acceptance of the right of individual petition if later, although in assessing the issue of 'reasonableness', the stage of the proceedings at this date will be taken into account: eg *Pretto and Ors v Italy* (1983) A 71, para 30.

2 Eg *Guincho v Portugal* (1984) A 81, para 29.

3 Eg *Buchholz v Germany* (1981) A 42, para 48 (commencement of action in Labour Court).

4 Eg *Zimmer and Steiner v Switzerland* (1983) A 66, paras 25–32 (administrative appeal against decision of assessment commission determined by federal supreme court).

5 Eg *Cesarini v Italy* (1992) A 245-B, para 16 (request for emergency order).

6 Eg *Raimondo v Italy* (1994) A 281-A, para 42.

7 Eg *Vallée v France* (1994) A 289-A, para 33 (compensation for infected blood transfusions).

8 Eg *König v Germany* (1978) A 27, para 98 (objection to withdrawal of authority to practise as a doctor); *Van Vlimmeren and van Ilveerenbeck v Netherlands* (26 September 2000), paras 34–36 (period for calculation of reasonableness of time taken to determine a claim for compensation for flood damage began when the applicants had informed the relevant commission that they held it responsible).

9 Eg *Olsson v Sweden (No 2)* (1992) A 250, para 101 (submission of request to council for termination of state care of applicant's children).

10 (1986) A 102, para 199. Cf *H v France* (1989) A 162-A, para 49 (question as to whether preliminary legal aid procedure should be included was avoided given the total length (seven-and-a-half years) of the civil proceedings).

END OF THE PERIOD

5.95   The entirety of the duration of the proceedings including any appeal stage is assessed: that is, the period 'extends right up to the decision which disposes of the dispute'[1]. In criminal cases, the aim of this aspect of the European Convention on Human Rights, Article 6 is to ensure persons accused of an offence 'do not have to lie under a charge for too long and that the charge is determined', and consequently it is necessary to consider all stages of a criminal process[2] including any proceedings before an appeal court which can determine the merits of a prosecution[3]. In *Howarth v United Kingdom*, the applicant had been convicted of theft and conspiracy to defraud and had been sentenced to community service. He had lodged a notice of appeal against conviction, and the Attorney General had also made a reference to the English Court of Appeal for a review of the applicant's sentence. Some two years after the conviction and after he had completed the community service order, the applicant's appeal against conviction was dismissed but the Attorney General's reference resulted in the imposition of a sentence of imprisonment of 20 months. The Court determined that the proceedings were only concluded with the determination of the reference, and thus the period to be considered for the purposes of Article 6 was just over four years[4].

1 *Erkner and Hofauer v Austria* (1997) A 117, at para 65.

2 *Wemhoff v Germany* (1968) A 7, at para 18.

3 *Neumeister v Austria* (1968) A 8, para 19.

4 (21 September 2000), para 20.

5.96 In civil matters, the period will terminate when a judgment becomes final, either at first instance level[1] or after the time for lodging an appeal has expired[2], or after an appeal court has refused leave to appeal[3], or final disposal by a supreme court[4] or a constitutional court[5]. Disposal of the question of costs also forms part of the proceedings[6]. To engage the state's responsibility under this aspect of the European Convention on Human Rights, Article 6(1), it is not necessary that such a stage has been reached in domestic proceedings: proceedings which are still pending may give rise to a violation of 'reasonable time'[7]. Proceedings not related to the final determination of the decision (as, for example, an application for the reopening of a case which is more properly regarded as a fresh set of proceedings[8]) are disregarded. The proceedings may also be deemed to have ended at a stage earlier than a final judicial determination on the merits, for example, where the parties secure a friendly settlement[9] or when proceedings are otherwise discontinued[10]. However, it may also continue beyond the date any court decision is secured to include the length of enforcement proceedings when any 'dispute' can only be said to be finally settled at this stage. In *Silva Pontes v Portugal*, for example, a court had upheld the applicant's claim for damages for injuries arising out of a road accident but in accordance with domestic law reserved for the subsequent enforcement proceedings the question of the transport costs incurred to enable hospital treatment after the accident. The Court considered that these subsequent enforcement proceedings were not simply to secure the payment of a civil award but also to determine the amount of damages due, and accordingly this stage in the proceedings also fell to be calculated since the right to damages could only have been finally resolved at this stage[11]. In *Scollo v Italy*, the applicant had sought the assistance of a bailiff in enforcing an eviction notice to eject a tenant from property. The bailiff in turn had in turn on numerous occasions but without success requested police assistance. The Court considered the period to be assessed for the purposes of Article 6 ended on the day that the tenant left of his own accord, the additional delay on the part of the police authorities being included in the calculation[12]. Similarly, in *Dimitrios Georgiadis v Greece*, the failure of the authorities to comply with an enforceable court decision concerning the amount of a supplementary pension due to a retired judge was considered a violation of Article 6, the Court noting that the execution of a judgment was an integral part of a 'hearing' within the meaning of the guarantee without which the concepts of a fair hearing and of the rule of law would cease to have any meaning[13].

1 Eg *Milasi v Italy* (1987) A 119-C, para 14 (date of judgment by court).
2 Eg *Ridi v Italy* (1992) A 229-B, para 14.
3 Eg *H v United Kingdom* (1987) A 120, para 70 (refusal of appeal committee to grant leave to appeal to the House of Lords).
4 Eg *Zimmerman and Steiner v Switzerland* (1983) A 66, para 23.
5 Eg *Deumeland v Germany* (1986) A 100, para 77 (reversing earlier approach in *Buchholz v Germany* (1981) A 42); *Gast and Popp v Germany* (25 February 2000) paras 69–82 (lawfulness of charges of espionage on behalf of the former German Democratic Republic considered by the Constitutional Court).
6 *Robins v United Kingdom* 1997-V, 1801, para 30 (period of 50 months from the determination of the substantive dispute to the dismissal by the Court of Appeal of an appeal against the judgment on costs).
7 Eg *Erknauer and Hofauer v Austria* (1987) A 117, para 65 (period under consideration already exceeded sixteen-and-a-half years: violation). In certain circumstances, the issue

of length of proceedings will be subsumed under consideration of the general right to a court: eg *Immobiliare Saffi v Italy* 1999-V, 73, para 75.
8 *Deumeland v Germany* (1986) A 100, para 77.
9 Eg *Caleffi v Italy* (1991) A 206-B, para 16.
10 Eg *Mori v Italy* (1991) A 197-C, para 14 (court decision that an offence was time-barred).
11 (1994) A 286-A, paras 33–36.
12 (1995) A 315-C, para 44.
13 (28 March 2000), paras 22–27.

Determining the 'reasonableness' of the period

5.97 Each case is considered on its own merits by reference to 'the complexity of the factual or legal issues raised by the case, to the conduct of the applicants and the competent authorities and to what was at stake for the former', but only delay which is the responsibility of the state will be calculated[1]. In other words, consideration of whether the guarantee has been breached will be dependent upon careful consideration of the particular facts, rather than simple calculation of the period of time. However, in certain situations where there is inordinate delay which on the face of it exceeds what appears 'reasonable time', the state will be expected to provide an explanation and adequate justification for this[2]. Inadequate resources (as in low staffing levels) will not be accepted as an excuse: in *Zimmerman and Steiner v Switzerland*, administrative proceedings which had dragged on for three and a half years were considered to have breached the guarantee since no adequate steps had been taken to deal with a backlog that was clearly foreseeable[3]. There is, though, no overall trend which can be drawn from the reported case law: 'there is the risk that the Court will sometimes be regarded as over-indulgent and sometimes as too severe'[4]. The Court is required to reach an overall assessment of whether particular proceedings were concluded within a 'reasonable time', taking into account the issue at stake and any delay attributable to the applicant rather than to the state authorities[5]. Failure to adhere to limits laid down in domestic law does not in itself result in a finding of unreasonable time[6]. Accordingly, the case law can give at best an indication of the type of case which has arisen and the approach adopted by the Court: a period of delay similar to that in the *Zimmerman and Steiner* case can just as readily be considered not to give rise to any violation in the particular circumstances[7].

1 *Zimmerman and Steiner v Switzerland* (1983) A 66, at para 24.
2 Eg *Eckle v Germany* (1982) A 51, para 80 (proceedings lasting 17 years and 10 years); *Corigliano v Italy* (1982) A 57, para 47 (two periods of delay of 13 and 14 months where absence of preliminary investigation measures).
3 (1983) A 66, at para 29 (temporary backlog will not engage state liability provided remedial action reflecting the urgency and importance of the matter for the individual is taken with requisite promptness; however, if the problem of resources becomes prolonged 'and becomes a matter of structural organisation, such methods are no longer sufficient and the State will not be able to postpone further the adoption of effective measures'). After a welter of cases each finding violations of 'reasonable time' requirement, Italy eventually notified the Committee of Ministers that it was appointing an additional 4,700 judges, and the state also carried out reform of civil procedure: cf *Ciricosta and Viola v Italy* (1995) A 337-A, para 31. See too *Pammel v Germany* 1997-IV, 1096, paras 68–73 at para 69 (the 'chronic overload' which had affected the German Constitutional Court for some 20 years could not justify excessively long proceedings; however a 'temporary backlog' of business will not entail a violation of Article 6 if appropriate remedial action is taken). Cf *Süßmann v Germany* 1996-IV, 1158, para 60 (implications of German reunification treaty resulting in

the dismissal of some 300,000 former GDR civil servants had resulted in significant increase in the court's workload).

4 Eissen *The Length of Civil and Criminal Proceedings in the Case-Law of the European Court of Human Rights* (1996) at p 40.

5 Eg *Duclos v France* 1996-VI, 2163 at para 86 ('while the applicant's conduct was not beyond reproach, most of the delays were due to the conduct of the administrative and judicial authorities': a period of eight years and eight months taken to determine payment of a life annuity for applicant who was disabled and unemployed 'cannot be regarded as reasonable'). In a series of cases involving Greece the Court has also examined the effect of withdrawal of labour by striking lawyers: eg *Papageorgiou v Greece* 1997-VI, 2277, paras 44–49 at para 48 (the Court was 'not unaware' of the complications which prolonged strikes can have; such events are not the responsibility of a state, but efforts subsequently made to reduce any resultant delays are to be considered in the assessment of reasonable time).

6 Eg *Wiesinger v Austria* (1990) A 213, para 60; *G v Italy* (1992) A 228-F, para 17 (but cf the position in respect of a person detained under Art 5: see para 4.51 above).

7 Eg *Pretto and Ors v Italy* (1981) A 71, para 37 (three years and six months (on top of two years before recognition of right of individual petition) in civil proceedings considered reasonable).

COMPLEXITY OF THE CASE

5.98 The nature of the proceedings may help determine what constitutes a 'reasonable time'. The case may give rise to complexity in the establishment of the facts (where, for example, there are a significant number of witnesses[1] or amount of evidence[2], or on account of the complexity or nature of any charges[3]) or of the law (including difficulties with statutory interpretation[4] or EU or international law[5]). In *I J L, G M R and A K P v United Kingdom*, the applicants who had been convicted for offences arising out of the take-over of the Distillers Group by Guinness challenged the reasonableness of the length of the proceedings. The Court considered the period to be assessed was around four-and-a-half years, but in view of the complexity of the case and the conduct of the parties, the Court concluded that the criminal charges against the applicants had been determined within a reasonable time[6]. Similarly, in *C P and Ors v France*, criminal proceedings lasting some eight years and involving eighteen accused were considered to have involved considerable complexity on account of the scale of the fraudulent activity. The investigating magistrate had pursued his responsibilities with energy, and in the circumstances, the Court again held that there was no violation of the guarantee[7]. In contrast, in *Howarth v United Kingdom*, while the Court accepted that the combination of the appeals of the applicant and co-defendants and the Attorney General's reference had 'rendered the proceedings more complex than they would otherwise have been', by the time the first instance proceedings had ended the transcripts of the trial had been available and the issues had been aired. Nor had the Attorney General's reference been regarded by the appeal court as having given rise to any particular difficulty. There were thus no convincing reasons for the delay of two years in determining the appeal, and there was a violation of Article 6[8].

Despite early dicta to the effect that the complexity of domestic procedures should not be considered an exculpatory factor[9], the Court is prepared to recognise that uncertainty in jurisdictional matters can help explain some delay as well as to exculpate the applicant from using procedures which ultimately prove inappropriate. In *Allenet de Ribemont v France*, the complexities of French law in allocating jurisdiction between the administrative courts and the ordinary civil courts was accepted as a factor to be taken into account in explaining part of the reasons for the length of proceedings involving the applicant's action for compensation[10]. Similarly, in *Katte Klitsche de la Grange v Italy* where an important issue had arisen in proceedings concerning environmental and planning law and which potentially had considerable repercussions for domestic law, the Court accepted that this factor was of relevance in considering the question of reasonableness[11].

1 E g *König v Germany* (1978) A 27, paras 102–105 (significant number of witnesses with difficulties in tracing several who had changed their names or addresses: but reasonable time still exceeded).

2 E g *Neumeister v Austria* (1968) A 8, para 21 (case record exceeded 10,000 pages plus large number of other documents).

3 E g *Boddaert v Belgium* (1992) A 235-D, para 38 (separate investigations into two serious but interdependent crimes: no violation); *Dobbertin v France* (1993) A 256-D, at para 42 (sensitive nature of offences relating to national security could not 'on their own justify the total length of the proceedings': violation).

4 E g *Pretto and Ors v Italy* (1983) A 71, para 32 (application of recent statute of some complexity: no violation).

5 E g *Beaumartin v France* (1994) A 296-B, paras 32–33 (wording and interpretation of bilateral treaty: violation because of lengthy periods of inactivity); *Pafitis and Ors v Greece* 1998-I, 436, paras 94–95 at 95: (reference to the European Court of Justice took two-and-a-half years to be answered; but to take this period which could appear relatively long into account 'would adversely affect the system instituted by [TEU, Art 234] and work against the aim pursued in substance in that Article'). Delays in the disposal of work by the ECJ are lengthening, with every prospect of the current average of 21 months for the Court to decide on references to increase: see e g 'Report of the French Government to the Inter-Governmental Conference', paper CONFER 4726/00. Amendments to the Court's Rules of Procedure are designed to speed up disposals: OJ L122 24.5.2000 p 43.

6 (19 September 2000), paras 133–138.

7 (1 August 2000), paras 26–35.

8 (21 September 2000), paras 25–30 at para 26 (at para 28: the fact the applicant had completed his non-custodial sentence was 'not strictly relevant to the Court's consideration of the reasonableness of the length of the proceedings').

9 *König v Germany* (1978) A 27, at para 100 ('eminently praiseworthy concern' to enforce individual rights, but should such measures 'result in a procedural maze, it is for the State alone to draw the conclusions and, if need be, to simplify the system').

10 (1995) A 308, para 46.

11 (1994) A 293-B, paras 57–62. See, too, *Süßmann v Germany* 1996-IV, 1158, para 56 and *Gast and Popp v Germany* (25 February 2000), para 75 (constitutional court is entitled to prioritise cases rather than deal with cases in chronological order).

CONDUCT OF THE PARTIES

5.99 Since it is the state which is liable to be held responsible for undue delay in the determination of civil obligations or criminal charges under the European Convention on Human Rights, Article 6(1), only delays attributable to it in some way are relevant in the assessment of whether the 'reasonable time' requirement has been breached[1]. State responsibility can arise where the state itself is a party to a civil action or where the state is involved as the prosecuting authority[2]. In such cases, delays on the part of public officials in the submission of evidence[3], refusal to hand over vital evidence to a litigant[4], or failure either to secure the services of official translators[5] or to separate proceedings to help expedite their conclusion[6] will be considered relevant factors in the assessment. On the other hand, delays which cannot be attributable to the state include an accused's disappearance[7] or refusal to appoint a defence lawyer[8] in criminal cases, and in civil matters the initiating of an action in the wrong forum[9], the lodging of numerous and lengthy submissions[10] or delay in responding to observations or submissions by the other party[11].

1 In exceptional circumstances, the political situation in a state may excuse state responsibility for delay: eg *Acquaviva v France* (1995) A 333-A, para 57 (departure of witnesses from Corsica for personal safety; consequent need to transfer jurisdiction to another court). Cf *Moreira de Azevedo v Portugal* (1990) A 189, para 74 (recognition of implementation of reforms of legal system after ending of dictatorship, but no indication in the case that acceleration of progress in the criminal proceedings had been achieved).
2 *Buchholz v Germany* (1981) A 42, para 49.
3 Eg *H v United Kingdom* (1987) A 120, paras 73–77.
4 Eg *Allenet de Ribemont v France* (1995) A 308, para 64.
5 Eg *Mansur v Turkey* (1995) A 319-B, para 64.
6 Cf *Kemmache v France* (1991) A 218, paras 66–67.
7 Eg *Girolami v Italy* (1991) A 196-E, para 13 (period of 14 months when the accused had absconded disregarded from the assessment).
8 Eg *Corigliano v Italy* (1983) A 57, paras 41–43 (at para 42: 'Article 6 does not require the person concerned actively to co-operate with the judicial authorities').
9 *Allenet de Ribemont v France* (1995) A 308, paras 52 and 53 (delay of 2 years and 7 months for determination of jurisdiction by administrative court disregarded); cf *Paccione v Italy* (1995) A 315-A, para 20 (procedural defect should have resulted in immediate determination by court rather than result in needless investigation).
10 Eg *Stoidis v Greece* (17 May 2001), paras 18 and 20 at para 18 (issue rendered complex by the applicant's invoking of 65 grounds of appeal in 'numerous and voluminous' submissions).
11 Eg *Phocas v France* 1996-II, 519, para 72.

CONDUCT OF THE JUDICIAL AUTHORITIES IN RESPECT OF THE IMPORTANCE OF THE ISSUE AT STAKE

5.100 Additionally, state responsibility can be engaged where courts or tribunals fail to deal expeditiously with a civil case involving private parties[1]. Delays attributable to the private parties to an action can still thus involve violation of the guarantee: even where the conduct of a civil action is in the hands of the parties to the action, this will not 'dispense the courts from ensuring the expeditious trial of the action'[2]. The matter is of considerable relevance where the subject matter in a civil case is of particular importance to a party. In *A and Ors v Denmark*, the applicants had sought damages after contracting AIDS. They were deemed by the Court responsible 'to a significant extent' for the protracting of the civil proceedings through having sought substantial numbers of adjournments and having delayed agreement on the appointment of experts. However, the readiness of the domestic court to grant each adjournment request and its failure to use its power to give directions to speed up the action in a case in which clearly exceptional diligence was required on account of the applicants' reduced life expectancy resulted in a violation of the European Convention on Human Rights, Article 6(1)[3]. In *Bock v Germany*, the Court criticised the prolongation of an action of divorce which had been attributable to the court's 'excessive amount of activity' in focusing upon the petitioner's mental health rather than disposing of any issue of capacity at the earliest moment. The 'abnormal' length of the proceedings which had lasted over nine years was considered unreasonable, 'regard being had to the particular diligence required in cases concerning civil status and capacity'[4]. Particular diligence has also been held to attach to cases involving social welfare claims[5], parental rights in relation to custody and access to children in care[6], compensation cases involving road traffic[7], claims for payment for professional services[8] and even constitutional questions which could have major social and economic implications[9].

In criminal proceedings, 'mitigation of sentence and discontinuation of prosecution granted on account of the excessive length of proceedings do not in principle deprive the individual concerned of his status as a victim' of a violation of Article 6, but such a rule 'is subject to an exception when the national authorities have acknowledged either expressly or in substance, and then afforded redress for, the breach of the Convention'[10], for example 'by reducing the sentence in an express and measurable manner'[11].

1 E g *Styranowski v Poland* 1998-VIII, 3367, para 56 (two periods of inactivity on the part of the judicial authorities amounting to 15 months: in the circumstances, violation of Art 6).
2 *Guincho v Portugal* (1984) A 81, at para 32.
3 1996-I, 85, paras 74–81 at para 74. See also *Van Vlimmeren and van Ilverenbeek v Netherlands* (26 September 2000), paras 33–37 at para 33 (violation of Art 6 in respect of compensation proceedings in relation to a land consolidation project: noted that 'even if proceedings are dealt with as expeditiously as possible once they get under way, a reasonable time may still have been exceeded if an individual was unable for a considerable time to put his claims before a tribunal without sufficiently weighty and pertinent reasons for that delay').
4 (1989) A 150, at paras 47–49.
5 E g *Deumeland v Germany* (1986) A 100, para 90 (11-year delay in determination of widow's supplementary pension: violation); cf *Süßmann v Germany* 1996-IV, 1158, para 61 (reduction in supplementary pension rights determined after some three years and five months did not result in a violation as the matter was not one of urgency).
6 E g *H v United Kingdom* (1987) A 120, para 85 (two years and seven months to determine access to child in care: violation).
7 *Silva Pontes v Portugal* (1994) A 286-A, paras 37–42 (11 years to determine compensation claim arising out of a road traffic accident: special diligence was appropriate).
8 *Doustaly v France* 1998-II, 850, paras 46–48 (fees amounted to more than 30% of an architect's annual turnover).
9 *Ruiz-Mateos v Spain* (1993) A 262, para 52 (compatibility of nationalisation legislation with the constitution).
10 *Eckle v Germany* (1982) A 51, at para 66.
11 *Beck v Norway* (26 June 2001), at para 27.

DOMESTIC COURT DECISIONS ON A HEARING WITHIN A 'REASONABLE TIME'

5.101 Since the European Convention on Human Rights was given domestic legal effect in Scotland[1], cases concerned with the right to have a judicial determination within a 'reasonable time' have formed the largest category of cases to come before the Scottish courts, reflecting experience in Strasbourg. The first case of this kind, *HM Advocate v Little*[2], demonstrated the significance of Article 6(1) when compared with the traditional Scottish approach[3] to the effect of delay. The accused was charged with sexual offences against three children, allegedly committed between 1978 and 1989. He was charged by the police in January 1988 with offences against two of the children. In April 1988 the Crown decided to take no further proceedings. In November 1997 he was charged by the police with offences against the third child, and he appeared on petition in respect of those offences in March 1998. In February 1999 he was indicted in respect of the offences against all three children. He challenged the proceedings in respect of the charges concerning the first two children, both at common law and under Article 6(1). The common law challenge was unsuccessful.

In relation to Article 6(1), it was agreed that the appropriate standing-point was the date when the accused was charged by the police, even though under Scottish procedure that was not a charge by the authority competent to commence or proceed with court proceedings[4]. It was also agreed that each case would depend on its own facts and circumstances, and that, in assessing the reasonableness of the time, factors which were relevant included the complexity of the proceedings, the accused's conduct and the conduct of the authorities. The delay, of 11 years (from being charged by the police to being indicted) was one which called for satisfactory explanation by the Crown. The explanation given was that further information had come to light in 1997 which apparently provided some support for the earlier allegations and warranted a re-assessment of whether it was in the public interest that proceedings be instituted. This was not regarded by the court as a satisfactory explanation, since its acceptance would mean that the Crown could keep open the question of possible proceedings for a period of many years, defeating the purpose of this part of Article 6[5]. The court also rejected the argument that the accused had to show specific actual prejudice, beyond the prejudice inherent in the infringement of the right. Although the court was referred to Strasbourg authorities indicating that a person whose trial was unreasonably delayed could not claim to be the victim of a violation if the breach of Article 6 was acknowledged by the national authorities and redressed (eg by a reduction in sentence)[6], it upheld a plea in bar of trial in respect of the charges in question[7]. There was no fully developed argument as to whether it was necessary to have regard to the public interest in the prosecution of crime, or to the Convention rights of others. As 'historical' child sex abuse cases form a category which is particularly prone to lengthy delay, for a variety of reasons[8], it is perhaps necessary to bear in mind in this context the positive obligation under Article 3 to ensure that the criminal law protects the rights of children[9], as well as the rights of the accused under Article 6.

1 Delay was also raised in the earlier case of *Ucak v HM Advocate* 1998 SCCR 517, which concerned delay in the hearing of an appeal.
2 1999 SCCR 625.
3 See *McFadyen v Annan* 1992 SCCR 186.
4 Consistently with 21437/93, *Dougan v United Kingdom* (11 January 1995) 1997 SCCR 56. It has been said that there may be 'considerable scope for argument' whether a detainee under of the Criminal Procedure (Scotland) Act 1995, s 14 is a person who has been 'charged' for the purposes of Art 6: *HM Advocate v Robb* 1999 SCCR 971, 974. See further para 5.21 above.
5 Ie to avoid that a person charged should remain too long in a state of uncertainty about his fate: *Stögmüller v Austria* (1969) A 9, Law, para 5.
6 Indeed, in *Beck v Norway* (26 June 2001) para 27 the Court held that there had been no violation of Art 6 where the national court had acknowledged the delay in the proceedings and had afforded adequate redress by way of a reduction in sentence.
7 The Court of Appeal (dealing with this issue under s 6 of the Human Rights Act 1998) has held that, where the reasonable time requirement has been breached, a variety of remedies are available, and in particular that a reduction in sentence may be an appropriate remedy. On its approach, the proceedings should be stayed only where the defendant has suffered prejudice interfering with his right to a fair trial which cannot otherwise be remedied: *Attorney-General's Reference (No 2 of 2001)* [2001] 1 WLR 1869. A similar view was taken, in respect of both s 6 of the Human Rights Act 1998 and s 57(2) of the Scotland Act 1998, in *HM Advocate v Rourke* (10 October 2001, unreported), HCJ. This decision is under appeal at the time of writing. See also *Mills and Cochrane v HM Advocate* (1 August 2001, unreported), HCJ (delay after conviction can be remedied by a reduction in sentence).

8 Eg the difficulty of obtaining sufficient evidence for proceedings to be considered to be in the public interest; and the change in public attitudes since the 1960s and 1970s.
9 See para 4.29 above; and para 6.35 below, for discussion of positive duties under Art 8.

5.102   The first case of this kind to be considered by the High Court on appeal was *McNab v HM Advocate*[1], in which a person who had previously pled guilty to a charge of attempted murder, and been sentenced to a long term of imprisonment, was charged with murder following the victim's death. A period of 11 months elapsed before the accused was indicted for murder (the starting-point being taken as the date when the accused was officially informed that she was to be prosecuted for murder). The plea in bar of trial was repelled. As in *HM Advocate v Little*, the court held that the accused did not require to show that prejudice had been or was likely to be suffered in consequence of the delay. How long was more than 'a reasonable time' was a matter which had to be assessed in each instance according to the particular circumstances. There was no universally applicable norm. A number of factors might be relevant and there was not an exhaustive list. The court observed that it was necessary to take into account not only the need to avoid delay in the particular case, but also what was required in order to meet the needs of other cases, and that it was unrealistic to expect all cases to progress towards trial at the same speed. The fact that the accused was serving a long sentence of imprisonment and had pled guilty to the earlier charge also narrowed what was at stake for her. The period which had elapsed was not prima facie unreasonable, and the Crown did not require further to explain or justify it.

Subsequent cases have followed the approach established in those early authorities, and have clarified some additional points. In *McLean v HM Advocate*[2], it was held that investigations and other actings of social work authorities (in another case concerned with offences against a child), prior to any criminal charge, have no bearing on the assessment of time under Article 6(1). In *Robb v HM Advocate*[3] (concerned with the sexual abuse of children), it was conceded that the starting point was the date when the accused was informed of allegations and interviewed under caution. A delay of three years and nine months, without satisfactory explanation, was held to be unreasonable. The court, however, observed:

> 'If at the beginning of the relevant period there is a clear insufficiency of evidence, or if the competent authorities reasonably then consider that to be the position, the passage of time thereafter, with no further proceedings being taken, will often be unsurprising.... And while the provision in Article 6(1) is designed to avoid a person remaining too long in a state of uncertainty about his fate, it does not seem to us to be unreasonable to keep the file open for review, when serious allegations have been made. A lapse of time in unchanging circumstances may not be "attributable" to the State or entail unreasonable delay on the part of the State.'

1   1999 SCCR 930.
2   2000 SCCR 112.
3   2000 SCCR 354. See also *Reilly v HM Advocate* 2000 SCCR 879: starting-point was when official notification of allegation given, not when accused informed by complainer that the matter had been reported to the police, or when police investigations started; similarly *Dyer v Watson* 2000 SLT 751. This approach can be contrasted with that adopted by the Court of Appeal in *Attorney General's Reference (No 2 of 2001)* [2001] 1 WLR 1869:

'Ordinarily ... the commencement of the computation in determining whether a reason-able time has elapsed will start with either a defendant being charged or being served with a summons as a result of information being laid before the magistrates. There will however be situations where a broader approach is required ... [T]here could be a period prior to a person being formally charged under English law if the situation was one where the accused has been substantially affected by the actions of a state so as a matter of substance to be in no different position from a person who has been charged ... [T]here may be some stage prior to an accused being formally charged in accordance with our domestic law where, as a result of the actions of a state linked to an investigation, when [she] he has been materially prejudiced in his position ... In the ordinary way an interrogation or an inter-view of a suspect by itself does not amount to a charging of that suspect for the purpose of the reasonable time requirement in Article 6(1).'

It is submitted that the Court of Appeal's approach is to be preferred.

5.103 In *HM Advocate v McGlinchey*[1], where proceedings had been delayed by six months through the trial judge's failure to provide his report to the High Court of Justiciary expeditiously, the court made obser-vations for the first time about the difference between the time regarded as normal in Scottish procedure and that regarded as normal in some other European legal systems:

'If in applying the Convention a court were simply to concentrate on the standards to be expected in its own domestic system, then this would lead to article 6(1) of the Convention being applied differently in different Contracting States ... More particularly, such an approach could have the apparently perverse result that a breach of the Convention would be estab-lished more readily in a Contracting State where proceedings were generally relatively fast than in a Contracting State where proceedings generally moved more slowly. ... we are applying the international standard which is set by the Convention[2].'

In the particular case, although there was an unexplained period of inactivity, the total length of the proceedings was not exceptional or unreasonable. This approach has been followed in subsequent cases[3]. That a shortage of resources is not necessarily an adequate explana-tion was made clear in *Docherty v HM Advocate*[4]. Equally, however, the fact that greater expedition could be achieved through the deploy-ment of more resources does not in itself demonstrate any unreason-able delay:

'[I]n general, and subject to questions of prioritisation between particular cases, timescales reflect available resources, and any claim that a case or cases are not coming to trial within a reasonable time, on the basis that greater resources would result in better timescales, would need averments (as opposed to simple assertions or assumptions) indicating that the existing timescales produced a period of time between charge and trial which was not reasonable[5].'

The court has also observed:

'Part at least of the *raison d'être* of the venerable system of public prosecution in Scotland is indeed that independent, legally qualified, prosecutors should examine police reports and should identify, discuss and resolve concerns about the case before deciding whether to embark upon serious proceedings ... These procedures take time. But it is time which is, generally at least, well spent in the interests of justice and in the interests of securing a fair trial. Attempts by the courts to second-guess the procurator fiscal and to say that he or she had been unduly cautious, had pursued an unnecessarily detailed line of enquiry or had exaggerated the difficulties of some course of action, could only have a chilling effect on the work of conscientious procurators fiscal. It would be wrong to apply the Convention in such a way as to bring that about[6].'

1 2000 SCCR 593.
2 2000 SCCR 593 at 610, per the Lord Justice-General (Rodger). Lord Coulsfield observed (at 615) that 'the extent to which proceedings have or have not complied with the standards and norms of a particular jurisdiction is relevant, as one, but only one, of the circumstances of the case'. This approach might be contrasted with that followed in *HM Advocate v Hynd* 2000 SCCR 644, where a period of two years and one month in bringing an accused to trial on charges of sexual abuse of three children was held to constitute an unreasonable delay.
3 See the cases cited at para 1.54.
4 2000 SCCR 717. See also *O'Brien v HM Advocate* 2001 SCCR 542.
5 *Gibson v HM Advocate* 2001 SCCR 62; similarly *Mitchell v HM Advocate* 2001 SCCR 110; *HM Advocate v Wright* 2001 SCCR 509.
6 *Valentine v HM Advocate* 2001 SCCR 727.

5.104 In relation to prioritisation, the court has emphasised the importance of prejudice to the accused:

'In deciding upon priorities, a wide discretion is inevitable. Almost every case will have some feature which can be said to point to this being given priority. But all such features must be weighed in what will be quite imprecise but practical processes of 'prioritisation'. That implies no unreasonableness. We would add one specific comment. While prejudice is not an essential element in breach of Article 6(1), it is in our opinion obvious that if the passage of time is likely to be prejudicial to the accused in a given case, that will weigh heavily in favour of giving that case priority over others where such prejudice is not regarded as likely. In this respect absence of prejudice is very relevant to the issue of reasonableness[1].'

1 *Valentine v HM Advocate* (6 July 2001, unreported), HCJ. See also the dissenting opinion of Lord Hamilton in *Dyer v Watson* 2001 SCCR 430.

5.105 Other criminal cases illustrate particular circumstances, for example a delay occasioned by the scientific complexity of the case[1], the preparation of a complex case of fraud[2] or embezzlement[3], other difficulties of investigation[4], or the need for expedition in cases involving child accused[5].

1 *Crummock (Scotland) Ltd v HM Advocate* 2000 SCCR 453.
2 *Docherty v HM Advocate* 2000 SCCR 717.
3 *Reilly v HM Advocate* 2000 SCCR 879.
4 *Gibson v HM Advocate* 2001 SCCR 51.
5 *HM Advocate v P* 2001 SCCR 210; *Kane v HM Advocate* 2001 SCCR 621.

5.106 This line of authority, in holding that the elapse of an unreasonable time automatically entails the consequence that the prosecution must be discontinued, is plainly capable of having unfortunate effects. On this approach, no regard can be paid to the public interest in the trial of accused persons or to the interest of victims of crime. The decisions have proceeded on the basis that s 57(2) of the Scotland Act 1998 prevents the Crown from continuing with a prosecution after a reasonable time has elapsed. This approach is perhaps open to question on a number of bases[1].

1 See *HM Advocate v Rourke* (10 October 2001, unreported), HCJ. This decision is under appeal at the time of writing. See also *Mills and Cochrane v HM Advocate* (1 August 2001, unreported), HCJ, where post-conviction delay was remedied by a reduction in sentence.

5.107 The European Convention on Human Rights, Article 6(1) has less often been invoked in respect of delays in civil proceedings. In *Lafarge Redland Aggregates Ltd v The Scottish Ministers*[1], it was held that a delay in determining a called-in planning application contravened Article 6(1). In *Re Abermeadow Ltd*[2] delay was considered in relation to proceedings for the disqualification of a company director. In *King v Walden*[3] delay was considered in relation to penalty proceedings under revenue law.

1 2001 SC 298.
2 [2000] 2 BCLC 824.
3 [2001] STC 822. Delay in the determination of an appeal against an assessment was considered in *Bennett v Customs and Excise Commissioners (No 2)* [2001] STC 137.

ADDITIONAL GUARANTEES APPLYING TO CRIMINAL PROCEEDINGS: PARAGRAPHS (2) AND (3) OF ARTICLE 6

5.108 Persons facing a 'criminal charge' enjoy additional guarantees under the European Convention on Human Rights, Article 6, paragraphs (2) and (3)[1]. In *Lutz v Germany*, the Court confirmed that the notion of 'criminal charge' in paragraph (1) and the phrases 'charged with a criminal offence' found in paragraphs (2) and (3) indicate that 'the three paragraphs of Article 6 [refer] to identical situations'[2]. The consequences of this were clarified in *Deweer v Belgium* in which the Court noted that these two latter paragraphs 'represent specific applications of the general principle stated in paragraph 1, [since] the presumption of innocence embodied in paragraph 2 and the various rights of which a non-exhaustive list appears in paragraph 3 ("minimum rights", "*notamment*") are constituent elements, amongst others, of the notion of a fair trial in criminal proceedings'[3].

It is important to emphasise that these additional provisions must be read in the context of Article 6 as a whole, that is, they are to be construed in the light of paragraph (1)'s general notion of a fair trial[4]. The ultimate question will always be whether the proceedings as a whole achieved the necessary degree of fairness required by Article 6[5]. Not only is this consistent with the Court's approach under issues arising exclusively under paragraph (1), it also acknowledges that there is in practice considerable overlap between the particular elements of a fair trial guaranteed in these additional paragraphs. Indeed, an applicant may well seek to rely upon two or more specific textual provisions which cannot be examined as if they were discrete guarantees. For example, in *Daud v Portugal*, the applicant had complained that he had been denied a fair trial because of inadequate legal assistance, the shortcomings of his officially assigned lawyers, the refusal of his application for a judicial investigation and of his application to submit evidence, and the poor quality of the interpreting during the proceedings. He sought to rely upon paragraphs (1) and (3)(c) and (e) of Article 6. At the outset of its assessment, the Court indicated it would examine these complaints successively under paragraph 3(c) and (e) but 'without isolating that paragraph from the common core to which it belongs'[6]. While this approach emphasises that Article 6 is comprised of elements 'which are distinct but stem from the same basic idea and which, taken together, make up a single right not specifically defined'[7] and thus the guarantee must be considered as a whole, it does so at some expense of coherency in jurisprudence. Often the Court will spend less effort than it ought to on clarifying the exact parameters of these latter provisions. It also can lead to the situation where the Court establishes that there has been a lack of compliance with a particular aspect of Article 6, but that the proceedings as a whole were still fair and thus there has been no breach of the guarantee[8].

1   For the definition of 'criminal charge' see para 5.21 above. See further Ashworth 'Article 6 and the Fairness of Trials' [1999] Crim L R 261.
2   (1987) A 123, at para 52.
3   (1980) A 35, at para 56.
4   17265/90, *Baragiola v Switzerland* (1993) DR 75, 76.
5   In any case, these principles of fairness are also applicable in the determination of civil rights and obligations: matters such as adequate time and facilities for the preparation of a case, the availability of legal aid, and the right to examine and to cross-examine witnesses all are accommodated in paragraph (1)'s concerns of fairness and effective access to a court: see paras 5.35 and 5.53–5.65 above.
6   1998-II, 739, at para 33.
7   *Golder v United Kingdom* (1975) A 18, at para 28.
8   As, for example, in *Edwards v United Kingdom* (1992) A 247–B, para 33 (the applicant alleged that the failure of the police to disclose relevant evidence to the defence meant that he had been denied the opportunity to examine police witnesses and thus had not been on an equal footing with the prosecution as required by para (3)(d); the Court held that in the circumstances of the case it was unnecessary to examine the relevance of this specific sub-paragraph to the case as the allegations amounted to a complaint that the proceedings had been unfair).

Para 6(2): the presumption of innocence

5.109   The European Convention on Human Rights, Article 6, paragraph (2) provides that 'everyone charged with a criminal offence shall be presumed innocent until proved guilty according to law'. Whether a person is 'charged' with a criminal offence is determined by general considerations as to whether there exists a 'criminal offence' for the purposes of paragraph (1)[1]. In straightforward terms, it requires at least that 'when carrying out their duties, the members of a court should not start with the preconceived idea that the accused has committed the offence charged; the burden of proof is on the prosecution, and any doubt should benefit the accused'[2]. The presumption of innocence relates primarily to the establishment of proof of guilt and not to issues of punishment following upon a determination of guilt[3]. Failure to observe the presumption of innocence may be remedied by a higher court subsequently correcting the defect[4]. More recently, the European Court of Human Rights has also read into this principle a prohibition against imposing criminal liability in respect of acts committed by a deceased person, as 'inheritance of the guilt of the dead is not compatible with the standards of criminal justice in a society governed by the rule of law'[5].

1 *Lutz v Germany* (1987) A 123, para 52; see further para 5.21 above.
2 *Barberà Messegué and Jabardo v Spain* (1988) A 146, at para 77.
3 *Engel v Netherlands* (1976) A 22, para 90; *Phillips v United Kingdom* (5 July 2001) para 35; cf *Bernard v France* 1998-II, 867, paras 37–41 (a psychiatric examination to establish whether the applicant suffered a psychological disorder which could help explain his behaviour and which thus proceeded upon the hypothesis that the applicant had committed the offences did not in the circumstances violate the presumption of innocence).
4 *Adolf v Austria* (1982) A 49, paras 39–40 (a lower court's judgment could have been read as suggesting the applicant was guilty of an offence but one which did not call for punishment; but this judgment had to be read alongside that of the supreme court which clarified that the applicant had been cleared of any guilt).
5 *A P, M P and T P v Switzerland* 1997-V, 1477, paras 44–48 at para 48; and *E L, R L and J O-L v Switzerland* 1997-V, 1509, paras 49–53 (the applicants had been subjected to criminal sanction for tax evasion allegedly committed by the applicants' deceased husbands or fathers).

The burden of proof

5.110 Rules of strict liability which place the burden of proof on the accused through the operation of presumptions of fact or law may give rise to considerations under the European Convention on Human Rights, Article 6(2), but only in exceptional cases will the application of such rules amount to an incompatibility. In principle, domestic law may penalise the occurrence of an objective fact irrespective of criminal negligence or intent. In *Salabiaku v France*, the applicant had been found in possession of drugs by customs officers as he was entering the country. French law provided that the mere fact of possession of goods unlawfully imported resulted in the establishment of criminal liability. In finding there was no violation of the paragraph, the Court confirmed that the sub-paragraph clearly did not preclude the application of such rules of strict liability. It was for states to determine the content of the criminal law and the constituent elements of any defined offence unless this had an impact upon one of the substantive guarantees under the Convention. However, presumptions of fact or law required to be confined within appropriate and reasonable limits, for otherwise 'the national legislature would be free to strip the trial court of any genuine power of assessment and deprive the presumption of innocence of its substance, if the words "according to law" were construed exclusively with reference to domestic law'. In this case, the domestic courts had assessed the question of guilt on the basis of evidence presented rather than merely having relied upon the presumption. Further, the presumption based upon the fact of possession had not been subsequently rebutted by any evidence which would have helped the applicant avoid its application. In consequence, there was no violation of the guarantee[1]. Presumptions which are rebuttable (for example, by allowing an accused to establish error or necessity) and are accompanied by an assessment of all the evidence presented before a court establishes guilt will be deemed to have been applied in a manner consistent with the guarantee[2].

1 (1988) A 141-A, paras 28–30 at para 28.
2 *Pham Hoang v France* (1992) A 243, paras 34–36. See too 26280/95, *Bates v United Kingdom* (16 January 1996), 28846/95, *Foster v United Kingdom* (16 January 1996) 26279/95, and *Brock v United Kingdom* (16 January 1996), cited in Reid *A Practitioner's Guide to the European Convention on Human Rights* (1998) p 119 (no violation of the presumption where owners of certain dogs are required to overcome a rebuttable presumption that the dogs were of a breed or class deemed dangerous)

CONFISCATION ORDERS UNDER DRUG TRAFFICKING LEGISLATION

5.111   The European Convention on Human Rights, Article 6(2) has been considered by the Scottish courts in a series of cases concerned with applications for confiscation of the proceeds of drugs trafficking, culminating in the decision of the Privy Council in *HM Advocate v McIntosh*[1]. Such an application can be made following a conviction of a drug trafficking offence. If such an application is made, the court is required to assess the value of the proceeds of the accused's drug trafficking. In doing so, it can assume that any property acquired by him during the six years prior to his being indicted, or any expenditure by him during that period, was financed by drug trafficking, unless that assumption is shown to be incorrect. The statutory scheme thus enables the court to assume that the accused's involvement in drug trafficking has been far more extensive than the offence of which he has been convicted, unless the accused establishes a legitimate explanation of his financial affairs. In *HM Advocate v McSalley*[2], for example, the accused had been convicted on the basis that he had acted as a custodian of drugs for one day for a payment of £100; but the proceeds of his drug trafficking, calculated on the basis of the foregoing assumptions, were assessed at almost £20,000. In *HM Advocate v McIntosh*, the High Court decided that a person against whom a confiscation order was sought was 'charged with a criminal offence' within the meaning of Article 6(2), and that the statutory assumptions were inconsistent with the presumption of innocence guaranteed by that provision[3]. The Privy Council, on the other hand, held that Article 6(2) had no application (essentially because the accused was not 'charged with a criminal offence' during the confiscation proceedings but was, instead, faced with a sentencing procedure in respect of the offence of which he had previously been convicted), and that the statutory assumptions were in any event compatible with Article 6(2), being a proportionate means of achieving the legitimate aim of punishing and deterring drug trafficking.

1 2001 SCCR 191. For discussion of the presumption of innocence in Scots law, see Summers 'Presumption of Innocence' 2001 JR 37.
2 2000 JC 485.
3 The Court of Appeal reached a similar conclusion on the first point, but not the second, in *R v Benjafield* [2001] 2 All ER 609.

5.112   Subsequently, in *Phillips v United Kingdom* the European Court of Human Rights was able to rule upon the compatibility of confiscation orders made under the Drug Trafficking Act 1994 with the presumption of innocence under the European Convention on Human Rights, Article 6(2). The applicant had been sentenced to imprisonment in connection with the importation of a large quantity of cannabis. At a subsequent confiscation hearing, the judge had concluded that property acquired by the applicant had been met out of payments received in connection with drug trafficking, and had made a confiscation order to the extent of £100,000. The United Kingdom Government sought to argue that Article 6(2) did not apply as the confiscation order was to be considered as a penalty imposed upon the conviction for drug trafficking rather than involving the determination of a 'criminal charge'; the applicant sought to rely upon Lord Prosser's analysis in *HM Advocate v McIntosh*[1] in the High Court. The Court first sought to consider whether the applicant had indeed been 'charged with a criminal offence' in terms of paragraph (1). Applying its standard criteria[2], the Court first noted that domestic law did not classify the proceedings as criminal. When next considering the type and severity of the penalty and the nature of the proceedings, the Court observed that refusal to pay the amount of the compensation order could result in an additional two years' imprisonment. However, the purpose of the proceedings was neither the acquittal nor the conviction of the applicant. While Article 6(2) certainly governed criminal proceedings in their entirety, 'the right to be presumed innocent [under this guarantee] arises only in connection with the particular offence "charged"'. Thus once an accused person has been proved guilty of an offence, the paragraph 'can have no application in relation to allegations made about the accused's character and conduct as part of the sentencing process, unless such accusations are of such a nature and degree as to amount to the bringing of a new "charge" within the autonomous Convention meaning [of the term]'. Article 6(2) was thus inapplicable[3].

1 2001 SCCR 191.
2 See para 5.21 above.
3 (5 July 2001), paras 28–36; and cf paras 37–47 (Art 6(1) was, however, applicable, but there had been no denial of the right of a fair hearing since the statutory assumptions had not been applied in order to determine guilt but to assess the proper amount at which the confiscation order should be assessed; and the assessment had been carried out by a court following judicial procedures and involving prior disclosure of the case to be met, a public hearing etc).

OTHER DOMESTIC COURT DECISIONS CONCERNING THE PRESUMPTION OF INNOCENCE

5.113 Article 6(2) has also been considered by the English courts in a number of criminal cases concerning statutory provisions which place upon the accused the burden of proving a statutory defence. Such cases have concerned the Prevention of Terrorism (Temporary Provisions) Act 1989, s 16A[1], and the Misuse of Drugs Act 1971, s 28[2]. The courts have followed the approach taken by the European Court of Human Rights, examining whether the placing of the burden of proof on the accused has an objective justification and is not disproportionate. In the context of penalty assessments issued by the Inland Revenue, it has been held that statutory provisions as to the effect of earlier commissioners' decisions do not violate Art 6(2)[4].

1 *R v DPP, ex p Kebilene* [2000] 2 AC 326.
2 *R v Lambert* [2001] 2 WLR 211.
3 *King v Walden* [2001] STC 822. See also *Parker v DPP* [2001] 165 JP 213 (irrebuttable presumption under Road Traffic Offenders Act 1988, s 15).

Orders made after a determination of innocence

5.114 The presumption of innocence may be called into question by a judicial order after a prosecution has been discontinued or where an accused has been acquitted where the order 'amounts in substance to a determination of the accused's guilt'[1]. This may occur through, for example, the rejection of a claim for compensation for detention where this decision can be seen 'as a consequence, and to some extent, the concomitant of the decision on [criminal liability]'[2]. In *Minelli v Switzerland*, a private prosecution for defamation based upon the publication of a newspaper article had been declared extinguished on account of limitation. However, the court ordered the accused to bear certain court costs and to pay compensation to private prosecutors in respect of their expenses. The European Court of Human Rights considered that the domestic assize court which had determined that the publication 'would very probably have led to the conviction' of the applicant had thus treated the allegations of the private prosecutors as having been proved even although these comments had been couched in cautious terms. Such an appraisal was, however, one which was 'incompatible with respect for the presumption of innocence'[3]. The presumption of innocence is thus violated where there has been a judicial determination which reflects an opinion of guilt without either a finding of guilt or even the opportunity to present a defence. Inappropriate statements made by English judges in dealing with requests for costs after the acquittals of defendants have resulted in similar findings of violations of paragraph (2) on this ground in several applications[4].

1   *Lutz v Germany* (1987) A 123, at para 60; *Englert v Germany* (1987) A 123, paras 37–40; *Nölkenbockhoff v Germany* (1987) A 123, paras 35–40. In Scots law, is an acquittal on a verdict of 'not proven' a determination of a 'state of suspicion' without an actual finding of guilt (cf *Lutz* at para 62)? The suggestion can be rebutted in three ways: the verdict is historically the antecedent to the development of a 'not guilty' verdict (which was more of a resounding affirmation of innocence); it has no consequences which could be said to 'amount in substance to a determination of guilt' (as with a refusal to allow expenses as in *Lutz*); and it provides an effective means of ensuring that 'any doubt should benefit the accused' (cf *Barberà, Messegué and Jabardo v Spain* (1988) A 146). On the other hand, in the public perception the verdict probably on occasion carries with it a 'state of suspicion'.
2   *Sekanina v Austria* (1993) A 266-A, paras 22–31 at para 22 (domestic law recognised a right to compensation for pre-trial detention following the acquittal of the applicant; the court determining this issue relied heavily upon the trial court's case file and rejected the claim; thereby, it cast doubt on the applicant's innocence and the decision of the trial court and this gave rise to a violation of para (2)). See too *Asan Rushiti v Austria* (21 March 2000), paras 27–32 (there had been no new assessment of guilt; but the court in determining the question of compensation had voiced certain suspicions after an acquittal had been earlier recorded, a matter considered incompatible with the presumption of innocence).
3   (1983) A 62, paras 37 and 38 at para 37.
4   22401/93, *D F v United Kingdom* (24 October 1995); 22613/93, *Moody v United Kingdom* (16 January 1996); and 22614/93, *Lochrie v United Kingdom* (18 January 1996); and cited by Reid *A Practitioner's Guide to the European Convention on Human Rights* (1998) p 119.

Statements made by other public officials

5.115   The obligation to respect the presumption of innocence also applies to other public officials. In *Allenet de Ribemont v France*, two senior police officers during a press conference had referred to the applicant who had just been arrested as one of the instigators of a murder. While acknowledging that the European Convention on Human Rights, Article 6(2) cannot prevent the public being informed of the progress of criminal investigations, the Court confirmed that it does require the relevant authorities to act 'with all the discretion and circumspection necessary if the presumption of innocence is to be respected'. The statement in this case had been a clear declaration that the applicant was guilty. This had both encouraged public belief in the applicant's guilt and also tainted the objective assessment of the relevant facts, and thus resulted in a finding of violation of paragraph (2)[1]. In contrast, the Court held in *Daktaras v Lithuania*, that paragraph (2) had not been breached since not only the actual words used by a public official but also the context in which the statement was made have to be considered. Here, the prosecutor had asserted that the applicant's guilt had been 'proved' in the course of a reasoned decision at a preliminary stage of proceedings in rejecting the applicant's request to discontinue the prosecution, and not, as in the *Allenet de Ribemont* case, in a context independent of the criminal proceedings themselves. While the Court considered the term 'proved' had been unfortunate, the reference had not been to whether the applicant's guilt had been established by the evidence, but to the question whether the case file had disclosed sufficient evidence of the applicant's guilt to justify proceeding to trial[2].

1 (1995) A 308, paras 35–41 at para 38.
2 (10 October 2000), paras 40–45. See too *Adolf v Austria* (1982) A 49, paras 36–41.

The drawing of inferences from the right of silence

5.116 This matter is further discussed above[1].

1 See para 5.79 above.

Domestic court discussion of 'proved guilty according to law'

5.117 It has been held that a material irregularity at a trial, such as a misdirection by the trial judge, may mean that the accused has not been proved guilty 'according to law' within the meaning of the European Convention on Human Rights, Article 6(2). Nevertheless, such an irregularity will not automatically require the conviction to be quashed[1].

1 *R v Williams* (14 March 2001, unreported), CA.

Paragraph (3)(a) notification of the accusation

5.118 The European Convention on Human Rights, Article 6, paragraph (3) provides for five additional guarantees which are specifically stated to be the minimum rights of an accused person, and which are thus best considered as specific aspects of a fair trial in the determination of criminal charges[1]. First, sub-paragraph (a) provides that everyone charged with a criminal offence[2] is to be 'informed promptly, in a language which he understands and in detail, of the nature and cause of the accusation against him'. Article 6(3)(a) is given a straightforward and non-technical meaning. Where a person is taken into custody, this provision to some extent replicates the requirement under Article 5(2) that a person arrested is 'informed promptly, in a language which he understands, of the reasons for his arrest and of any charge against him'[3]. Since Article 6(3)(a) is designed to ensure an accused is 'provided with sufficient information as is necessary to understand fully the extent of the charges against him with a view to preparing an adequate defence', the adequacy of this information is assessed by reference to paragraph (3)(b)'s guarantee of adequate time and facilities for the preparation of the defence and also in terms of paragraph (1)'s more general right to a fair hearing[4]. It normally is satisfied by giving the accused details of the offences, victim, locus and relevant dates[5]. No particular formalities are prescribed, but since the purpose is to enable the accused to prepare his defence, the details provided must be sufficient to achieve this goal[6]. The information required may be given verbally[7]. A mere clerical error which does not affect the substance of the notification of the components of the charge[8] or failure to specify an aggravating circumstance which is implicit in the factual basis of the charge[9] will not result in a breach of the obligation. There may, too, be a certain responsibility on an accused to take advantage of any opportunity to seek further clarification of a charge. In *Campbell and Fell v United Kingdom*, a prisoner who had been charged with the prison disciplinary offence of 'mutiny' claimed that the offence was of such complexity that he had not been able to understand what it involved. The Court rejected this contention, pointing out that the prisoner could have sought clarification but had failed to do this, on one occasion indeed refusing to attend a hearing where this information could have been made available[10]. On the other hand, a violation of violation of this provision was established in *Mattoccia v Italy*. The applicant had been accused of the rape of an eleven-year-old handicapped girl, but no specification of the charge other than it had occurred 'in Rome, in November 1985' had been provided even by the stage of the service of the indictment and at a time when the prosecuting authorities had obtained more precise details of the date and locus of the alleged offence. The state had sought to argue that an earlier request for access to the case file could have provided the applicant with the necessary information, but in the view of the Court, the requirement of sub-paragraph (a) 'rests entirely on the prosecuting authorities and cannot be complied with passively by making information available without bringing this to the attention of the defence'. While it was recognised that cases of rape raise particularly sensitive issues and more so where the victim is young or mentally handicapped, in the present instance the applicant had faced exceptional levels of difficulty in preparing his defence thus resulting in a violation of his rights[11].

1 *F C B v Italy* (1991) A 208-B, para 29.
2 Including a disciplinary offence which falls within the scope of 'criminal charge': *Albert and Le Compte v Belgium* (1983) A 58, para 39. See para 5.22 above. 'Charged' is given an autonomous meaning which refers not to a formal but a material situation; a person is certainly 'charged' once committed for trial: 10889/84, *C v Italy* (1988) DR 56, 40.
3 See paras 4.69 and 4.70 above. The purpose of Art 5(2) is to allow the lawfulness of the deprivation of liberty to be tested.
4 *Mattoccia v Italy* (25 July 2000), at para 60.
5 *Brozicek v Italy* (1989) A 167, para 42.
6 Cf 14723/89, *Erdogan v Turkey* (1992) DR 73, 81 (information in arrest warrant sufficient in the circumstances; non-service of indictment attributable to the applicant).
7 8361/78, *X v Netherlands* (1981) DR 27, 37.
8 *Gea Catalán v Spain* (1995) A 309, paras 28–29.
9 *De Salvador Torres v Spain* 1996-V, 1577, paras 30–32 (embezzlement of public funds aggravated by nature of the accused's position as a public official which he had never sought to dispute).
10 (1984) A 80, para 96.
11 (25 July 2000), paras 58–72 at para 65 (violation of paras (3)(a) and (3)(b) taken together with para (1)).

5.119   The requirement to provide information in a language which the accused understands will be of concern where the authorities cannot establish that an individual has sufficient understanding of the language normally used in official communications[1]. It is up to the state to take any necessary action rather than for the accused to seek assistance. While the sub-paragraph does not specify that relevant information concerning the charge should be in writing or even translated into written form and thus cannot imply a right to have court files translated[2], the indictment is of such central importance in a criminal process that an accused who is not provided with a translated copy of this document is liable to be considered as having been placed at a disadvantage[3].

1 *Brozicek v Italy* (1989) A 167, para 41 (applicant was not of Italian origin and did not reside in Italy, and had difficulty understanding the contents of official communications sent in Italian).
2 6185/73, *X v Austria* (1975) DR 2, 68.
3 Cf *Kamasinski v Austria* (1989) A 168, para 79–80 (the charges were relatively straightforward as regards the facts and the law; the indictment was six pages long; the applicant had been questioned on the charges at length and with the assistance of interpreters: no violation).

DOMESTIC COURT DECISIONS ON NOTIFICATION OF THE ACCUSATION

5.120   The European Convention on Human Rights, Article 6(3)(a) was unsuccessfully invoked in the Scottish case of *McLean v HM Advocate*[1], where the accused was indicted in 1999 on a charge that he had assaulted a child 'between 1 November 1994 and 27 November 1994'. Details were given of the nature and location of the assault, but the Crown was unaware of the precise date. The court held that sufficient information had been given:

> 'The amount of detail which is required may vary with the nature of the allegation. . . . [T]here will be many cases in which the Crown cannot know the precise date on which a crime was committed.'

The difficulties involved where the accused requires the assistance of a translator were considered in *Ucak v HM Advocate*[2].

1 *McLean v HM Advocate* 2000 SCCR 112. See also *McMaster v HM Advocate* 2001 SCCR 517.
2 1998 SCCR 517.

Paragraph (3)(b): adequate time and facilities for the preparation of the defence

5.121   The European Convention on Human Rights, Article 6, sub-paragraphs (a) and (b) are clearly inter-dependent[1]. The right to have adequate time and facilities to prepare the defence presupposes that an accused has been accorded sufficient information as to 'the nature and cause of the accusation against him', and this latter provision may involve the taking of positive measures by a court, for example, by postponing or adjourning the hearing[2], certainly if this is required to allow an accused proper time to instruct his legal representative[3]. The aim is to ensure that an accused 'is afforded a reasonable opportunity to present his defence in conditions that do not place him at a disadvantage vis-à-vis his opponent'[4]. Whether adequate time has been accorded is a matter for assessment at each stage of the proceedings[5] taking into account all the circumstances and features of a case[6]. The requirement certainly involves adequate opportunity for an accused to consult with his legal representative, although this on occasion may be subject to necessary limitation[7] and does not imply the right to unrestricted consultation with counsel[8]. More particularly, it may require positive action on the part of the state in allowing access to the case file (including information which could be of assistance in the preparation of the defence)[9]. Thus in *Jespers v Belgium*, the Commission took the view that the sub-paragraph implied the right of the accused to acquaint himself with the results of any investigations carried out[10]. Further, the sub-paragraph may require the taking of other forms of action by the authorities on behalf of the accused, unless this is unlikely to serve any useful purpose in the preparation of the defence case[11].

1   10857/84, *Bricmont v Belgium* (1986) DR 48, 106; 14723/89, *Erdogan v Turkey* (1992) DR 73, 81; *Mattoccia v Italy* (25 July 2000), discussed at para 5.118 above.

2   *Goddi v Italy* (1984) A 76, para 31.

3   *Campbell and Fell v United Kingdom* (1984) A 80, paras 98–99 (a prisoner was advised of the charges against him five days before the disciplinary board was due to sit; the Court considered that in all the circumstances he had been given adequate time to prepare his defence, noting that in any case he did not request an adjournment).

4   *Bulut v Austria* 1996-II, 346, at para 47.

5   7628/76, *X v Belgium* (1977) DR 9, 169; 7909/74, *X and Y v Austria* (1978) DR 15, 160.

6   Cf *Vacher v France* 1996-VI, 2138, paras 27 30 (appeal dismissed in a shorter than average period which may have taken the applicant by surprise; placing the onus on the applicant to find out when a prescribed period of time ran was incompatible with the diligence states must show in ensuring that Art 6 rights are effective); *Twalib v Greece* 1998-IV, 1415, paras 40–43 (court-appointed lawyer who replaced the applicant's counsel who had not appeared at first instance proceedings had been afforded very little time to prepare the defence in a case of some seriousness: but, on appeal, his lawyer did not attempt to suggest the conviction was unsafe); and *Dallos v Hungary* (1 March 2001), paras 47–53 (initial conviction of aggravated embezzlement was reclassified on appeal as aggravated fraud; while this impaired the applicant's opportunity to defend himself in respect of this latter charge, the appellate court had reviewed all aspects of the case with the power to have acquitted the applicant and the applicant had enjoyed the opportunity to put forward his defence to the reformulated charge: no violation of Art 6(3)(a) and (b)); and 55173/00, *Le Pen v France* (10 May 2001) (conviction of the applicant for assault was reclassified by the appeal court as one of assault of a person vested with public authority: inadmissible).

7   Cf 8339/78, *Schertenleib v Switzerland* (1979) DR 17, 180 (the applicant was detained in solitary confinement but able to consult his lawyer frequently and without impediment: no violation; but observed that the sub-paragraph cannot be interpreted as giving an unrestricted right of access); 11219/84, *Kurup v Denmark* (1985) DR 42, 287 (prohibition on defence counsel from discussing with the applicant statements of witnesses who were interviewed outwith his presence to protect their anonymity).

8   7854/77, *Bonzi v Switzerland* (1978) DR 12, 185 (applicant held in solitary confinement but still able to consult his lawyer: no violation).

9   However, the right is not unrestricted: 7412/76, *Haase v Germany* (1977) DR 11, 78 (allegations of espionage involving disclosure of some 80,000 pages of reports of a technical nature; certain restrictions on access to the case file for national security purposes were considered appropriate); *Kamasinski v Austria* (1989) A 168, paras 87–99 (domestic law restricted access to the case file to an accused's legal representative, a restriction not incompatible with the sub-paragraph). Cf *Foucher v France* 1997-II, 452, paras 31–38 at para 35 (applicant had chosen to represent himself as he was entitled to do; consequently, the reasoning in *Kamasinski* did not apply and the applicant ought to have been allowed access to his case file: violation of Art 6(3)(b) taken with para (1)).

10   8403/78 (1981) DR 27, 61 .

11   *Bricmont v Belgium* (1989) A 158, paras 91–93 (neither an audit of accounts nor the making available of a production would have been of use in the trial; and thus no violation of Art 6(1) and (3)(b) taken together). See also 11396/85, *Ross v United Kingdom* (1986) DR 50, 179 (request by a prisoner preparing his appeal before the High Court of Justiciary for specified legal textbooks, statutes and case reports but which were not readily available: there were practical limits to the steps the prison authorities could reasonably have been

expected to take, and in the circumstances of the case there had been no apparent violation of Art 6: the application was manifestly ill-founded). Cf 11058/84, *F v United Kingdom* (1986) DR 47, 230 (seizure and examination of files and tape recordings an accused had prepared as part of his defence but which ultimately were not relied upon by the prosecutor: no violation).

DOMESTIC COURT DECISIONS ON PREPARATION OF THE DEFENCE

5.122 The High Court of Justiciary has considered whether the Crown infringes the rights of the defence under Article 6(3) (b) and (c) by citing as a witness an expert who has been instructed on behalf of the defence, communications between the expert and the defence and material prepared for the purposes of the defence being treated as confidential under domestic law[1].

1 *Wales v HMA* 2001 SCCR 633.

Paragraph (3)(c): legal representation and assistance

5.123 The European Convention on Human Rights, Article 6(3)(c) provides an accused person with three inter-related rights: 'to defend himself in person'; to defend himself 'through legal assistance of his own choosing'; and 'if he has not sufficient means to pay for legal assistance, to be given it free when the interests of justice so require'[1]. When read alongside sub-paragraph (d) which provides for the right to examine witnesses, it also implies a right for an accused person to be present at his trial[2]. The right of legal representation, however, cannot be made conditional upon an accused's attendance at his trial[3]. These rights must be practical and effective and not merely illusory or theoretical[4]. The majority of cases have concerned the second and third aspects of the provision, since without the services of a legal practitioner, an accused person will not be able to make 'a useful contribution to the examination of the legal issues arising'[5]. However, an accused is certainly able to waive his right to a lawyer[6]. 'Assistance' implies that a legal representative has had the opportunity of adequate time and facilities to prepare the case for the defence, and there is thus a clear link between this sub-paragraph and sub-paragraph (b)[7]. It goes without saying that an accused's right to communicate with his legal representative out of earshot of any other party is a fundamental aspect of a fair trial, and the grounds advanced for any restriction on this right will be scrutinised with particular vigilance[8].

1 Cf *Pakelli v Italy* (1983) A 64, para 31.
2 *Botten v Norway* 1996-I, 123, paras 48–53 (the supreme court overturned an acquittal and imposed a sentence in the absence of the applicant; the court to some extent had required to assess the facts and the applicant's personality and character without the benefit of his presence, matters which could not as a matter of fair trial have been considered properly: violation); *Zana v Turkey* 1997-VII, 2533, paras 68–73 (security court had convicted and sentenced the applicant to 12 months' imprisonment in his absence and without requesting his attendance: taking into account what was at stake for the applicant, the court was unable to give judgment without benefit of assessment of the applicant's evidence given in person: violation).
3 *Krombach v France* (13 February 2001), paras 84–91.
4 *Artico v Italy* (1980) A 37, para 33; cf *Goddi v Italy* (1984) A 76, paras 27–30 (accused was in prison and not brought before the court; his lawyer did not attend the hearing; and a court-

appointed lawyer had not had the opportunity of acquainting himself with the case or taking instructions: thus there had been no 'practical and effective' defence).

5 *Pakelli v Germany* (1983) A 64, at para 38. See too *Van Pelt v France* (23 May 2000), paras 62–70 (refusal to allow the legal representation of an accused who was absent from the trial amounted to a violation of Arts 6(1) and (3)(c): the impossibility for the applicant's lawyers to make submissions on the merits of the case contravened the right of every accused to be effectively represented by a lawyer which was a fundamental feature of the right to a fair trial, and a right an accused did not forfeit merely by not being present at the hearing).

6 *Foucher v France* 1997-II, 452, para 35. Cf *Melin v France* (1993) A 261-A, paras 24–25 (applicant had practised as a lawyer, and in the circumstances, he was under a responsibility to show due diligence in the preparation of his case). See further paras 3.12–3.15 above.

7 *Campbell and Fell v United Kingdom* (1984) A 80, para 99.

8 *S v Switzerland* (1991) A 220, para 48 (the authorities feared that there was a risk of collusion between the applicant's court-appointed lawyer and other defence counsel: but such collaboration with a view to co-ordinating a common defence strategy is not out of the ordinary; and at no time was it suggested the lawyer had breached his professional code of ethics or the law).

5.124   Restrictions on the right of access to legal assistance to particular aspects of the proceedings will not in themselves be deemed incompatible with the guarantee if these can be reconciled with the interests of justice[1]. Access to a legal adviser during detention by the police may become of particular concern where inferences may be drawn from an individual's silence or refusal to answer questions. In *Averill v United* Kingdom, for example, the Court held that the denial of access to a solicitor during the first 24 hours of detention failed to comply with the requirements of the sub-paragraph when taken in conjunction with paragraph (1). The applicant had been held and interrogated under caution on suspicion of involvement in terrorist-related murders in Northern Ireland. Failure to allow access to legal assistance during this period had compromised his rights on account of the 'fundamental dilemma' facing such a detainee in such circumstances: a decision to remain silent could allow inferences to be drawn against him at a trial, but answering questions could also have prejudiced his defence without the risk of such inferences being removed in all instances. As a matter of fairness, the possibility of irretrievable prejudice to the rights of an accused through the existence of this dilemma meant that the applicant should have been guaranteed access to his solicitor before his interrogation began[2].

1 Eg *Engel and Ors v Netherlands* (1976) A 22, para 91 (legal representation restricted to discussion of the legal issues in dispute; and since the applicants were not incapable of furnishing explanations on the simple facts of the case, there was no violation of the sub-paragraph).

2 (6 June 2000), paras 55–61 at para 59. See too *Magee v United Kingdom* (6 June 2000), paras 38–46 (use of statements obtained from a suspect in a coercive environment and without providing him with the benefit of legal assistance: violation of para (1) when taken with (3)(c). A further complaint of discrimination under Art 14 on the grounds that individuals arrested under prevention of terrorism legislation applying elsewhere in the UK were entitled to immediate access to a solicitor was dismissed since differences in treatment fell to be explained in terms of geographical location and not personal characteristics: paras 47–51). See further para 5.70 above.

5.125   The right to an oral hearing before a trial judge is also implicit within the context of the European Convention on Human Rights, Article 6, paragraph (1) and this sub-paragraph may also be of relevance in considering the question whether the attendance of an applicant in person at appeal proceedings is necessary[1]. In other words, inherent in the notion of a fair trial is the accused's right to attend a first instance hearing, and provided this has occurred, there may be justification in certain cases for not holding an appeal hearing in public[2]. In *Cooke v Austria*, for example, the Court considered that the applicant's appeal based upon a plea of nullity did not require his presence before the supreme court, but that the refusal to allow him to attend the hearing of his appeal against sentence had led to a violation of Article 6(1) and (3)(c): the supreme court was called upon to consider whether the sentence should be reduced or increased, and this could not be determined without allowing the court to gain a proper appreciation of the character of the applicant and thus it was essential that he should have been given the chance to attend and to participate[3].

1 See para 5.64 above.
2 *Tierce and Ors v San Marino* (25 July 2000), para 95.
3 (8 February 2000), paras 40–44. See too *Pobornikoff v Austria* (3 October 2000), paras 24–33. Cf *Prinz v Austria* (8 February 2000), paras 34–46 (no violation through the court's refusal to allow a legally-represented appellant to attend a hearing considering a plea of nullity which only involved issues of law and thus did not require his presence where he was legally represented).

DOMESTIC COURT DECISIONS ON LEGAL ASSISTANCE

5.126   The Scottish courts have dealt with a number of cases in which the accused has complained that he was not given, or was refused, access to a solicitor when he was interviewed by the police[1] or during an identification parade[2]. The court has held that the absence of access to a solicitor at the stage of police interview does not necessarily result in a breach of the European Convention on Human Rights, Article 6, given the fact that no adverse inference can be drawn from the suspect's silence at that stage[3] and that he is cautioned. The court has not however excluded the possibility that unfairness might result in particular circumstances. In practice, some Scottish police forces have responded to the incorporation of the Convention by allowing solicitors to be present when suspects are interviewed.

1 *HM Advocate v Robb* 1999 SCCR 971; *Paton v Ritchie* 2000 SCCR 151; *Dickson v HM Advocate* 2001 SCCR 397.
2 *HM Advocate v Campbell* 1999 SCCR 980.
3 See *Paton v Ritchie* 2000 SCCR 151, 156–157. In *Hoekstra v HM Advocate (No 1)* 2000 SCCR 263 the court held that the accused's silence when interviewed by the police could be treated as relevant to the credibility of his evidence in court. The decision was set aside: *Hoekstra v HM Advocate (No 2)* 2000 SCCR 367. Other cases concerning Art 6(3)(c) are discussed at paras 5.122 and 5.129–130.

Provision of free legal assistance

5.127   The right to legal assistance or aid is normally dependent upon two conditions: inability to pay for the services of counsel; and the existence of factors suggesting that the interests of justice require the provision of legal aid[1]. The provision of legal assistance by the state may also be required at appeal stage. Despite the wording of the second aspect of the provision (which refers to the right of an accused to be represented by a legal representative 'of his own choosing'), where free legal aid is made available this is subject to limitation: in appointing counsel, the wishes of the accused should certainly be taken into account, but can be overridden where there are relevant and sufficient reasons for this[2]. The issue of determination of the financial circumstances of an accused person has not given rise to much consideration[3]. On the other hand, significantly more discussion of whether free representation is required in the 'interests of justice' has taken place. Factors of relevance will include the seriousness of the offence and of the likely penalty if convicted[4]; and certainly at appeal stage, the likelihood of success. Application of any pre-determined and unofficial policy may violate the guarantee. In *McDermitt v United Kingdom*, a stipendiary magistrate in Glasgow had rejected an application for legal aid in a criminal case involving a breach of the peace and assault of a police officer on the ground that as a matter of personal policy the magistrate considered that the 'interests of justice' could not be deemed to apply to charges of breach of the peace or of resisting arrest by a police officer. In this case, the matter was disposed of by way of friendly settlement in the form of an ex gratia payment by the government and acceptance that the application for legal aid had not been appropriately dealt with by the magistrate[5]. In *Perks and Ors v United Kingdom*, the lack of legal aid in proceedings in English courts relating to the non-payment of the community charge was considered a violation of Article 6(1) taken with (3)(c). It was clear that the applicants had lacked sufficient financial means to pay for legal representation, and having regard to the complexity of the law and the potential severity of the penalty for non-payment (which had indeed involved imprisonment), the interests of justice had required that the applicants should have benefited from free legal representation[6].

1 *Quaranta v Switzerland* (1991) A 205, para 27.
2 *Croissant v Germany* (1992) A 237-B, para 29; 8295/78, *X v United Kingdom* (1978) DR 15, 242.
3 Eg *Pakelli v Italy* (1983) A 64, at para 34 (it was impossible in practice for the Court to determine whether the accused had insufficient means to pay for his lawyer at the time of his trial: while there were factors indicating he was indigent, these were not sufficient to prove this beyond reasonable doubt; but taking into account his offer to the domestic court to show his lack of financial means and 'in the absence of clear indications to the contrary, they lead the Court to regard the first of the two conditions ... as satisfied').
4 *Quaranta v Italy* (1991) A 205, at para 33 (the imposition of a sentence of more than 18 months' imprisonment was 'not a legal impossibility'; the maximum statutory penalty was three years' imprisonment; and even though the applicant was only sentenced to six months' imprisonment, 'free legal assistance should have been afforded by reason of the mere fact that so much was at stake').
5 11711/85 (1987) DR 52, 244.
6 (12 October 1999), paras 75–76, following *Benham v United Kingdom* 1996-III, 738, paras 57–64 (severity of penalty faced by the applicant and the complexity of the law required that legal aid should have been made available).

5.128   In *Monnell and Morris v United Kingdom*, the applicants complained of the lack of legal aid at appeal stage. In rejecting the complaint, the European Court of Human Rights noted that each applicant had enjoyed free legal representation at trial and after conviction in being advised whether there existed any arguable grounds for appeal. The 'interests of justice' could not be 'taken to require an automatic grant of legal aid whenever a convicted person, with no objective likelihood of success, wishes to appeal after having received a fair trial at first instance in accordance with the European Convention on Human Rights, Article 6'[1]. The

right of access to the criminal appeal court traditionally recognised by
Scots law, however, did result in a tension between this 'open door' policy
and the principle of 'equality of arms' where legal aid had been refused. In
three cases, the Court seemed to consider an appellant's rights in Scotland
as more illusory than real. Where a convicted person's grounds of appeal
were considered as having no likelihood of success, no legal aid was made
available; and in any case, the code of professional ethics of the Faculty of
Advocates prohibited an advocate acting on an appellant's behalf in such
circumstances. However, a convicted but unrepresented appellant was
still entitled to address the court, and thus a situation could arise where
the appeal court became convinced that the case did indeed raise some
legal issue of difficulty. In *Granger v United Kingdom*, the applicant had
given statements to the police in connection with serious charges of wilful
fire-raising and murder in which he had named the persons he believed
responsible. At the trial he denied having made any such statements, and
was subsequently convicted of perjury. He had been granted legal aid to
cover the preparation, trial, and initial appeal stages of his case, but
further legal aid for representation at the appeal hearing was refused by a
legal aid committee which had received counsel's opinion that there were
no reasonable prospects of success[2]. The applicant decided to present his
own appeal and read out a statement presented by his solicitor who had
continued to give him advice but who had been precluded from
appearing since he had no rights of audience. The appeal court then
decided that it could not dispose of the appeal without first obtaining a
transcript of parts of the evidence, and adjourned the hearing. The appeal
subsequently failed. In Strasbourg, the Court considered that there had
been a violation of paragraph (3)(c) taken together with paragraph (1). A
matter of some complexity calling for an adjournment had arisen during
the appeal, and the Court considered that legal aid at least for the
adjourned hearing should have been made available since the applicant
had not been in a position to oppose the arguments advanced by the
Crown or even fully to comprehend the prepared address he had read out.
In short, the appeal court had not had the benefit of 'expert legal argument
from both sides on a complex issue'[3]. A subsequent practice direction
made by the Lord Justice-General advised the appeal court to adjourn and
recommended that the refusal of legal aid be reviewed in such cases[4]. This
allowed the disposal by the Commission of several other pending applications from Scotland[5], and thereafter statute also provided that legal aid
should be granted if an individual had established 'substantial grounds'
for any criminal appeal and it was 'reasonable in the particular circumstances' that it should be awarded[6]. However, these solutions were later
found wanting in the related cases of *Boner v United Kingdom*[7] and *Maxwell
v United Kingdom*[8]. In each, the factual situation which had arisen in
Granger was distinguished in that the legal issues had not been particularly complex, but the crucial matter was the inability of each applicant
who had been denied legal aid at the appeal stage to make an effective
contribution to the proceedings. During Boner's trial, a prospective prosecution witness had entered the courtroom and spoken to a co-accused.
The trial judge exercised his discretion to permit the witness to give
evidence[9], but after his conviction, Boner sought to have this discretion
reviewed on appeal. In the second case, Maxwell's appeal had concerned

his instructions to his representatives and the reliability and sufficiency of evidence. In neither instance had counsel concluded that there was any reasonable prospect of success and thus neither appellant had been legally represented. The Court again found a breach of Article 6(3)(c) in both applications. The Court attached importance to the severity of the penalty imposed by the trial courts (imprisonment for eight years and five years respectively) and 'the limited capacity of an unrepresented appellant to present a legal argument', leading to the finding that the interests of justice again had required the provision of legal aid[10].

1   (1987) A 115, at para 67, applying *Benham v United Kingdom* 1996-III, 738, paras 57–64 (severity of likely penalty and complexity of the legal issues both required that the applicant be accorded legal aid).
2   In terms of the Legal Aid (Scotland) Act 1967, s 1(7).
3   (1990) A 174, paras 42–48 at para 47. (The Commission had been of the opinion that paragraph (3)(c) alone had been violated, and that no separate issue had arisen under para (1).)
4   In such circumstances, legal aid would in practice be awarded: cf *Boner v United Kingdom* (1994) A 300-B, paras 30–1; *Maxwell v United Kingdom* (1994) A 300-C, paras 27–28.
5   Eg 14778/89, *Higgins v United Kingdom* (1992) DR 73, 95.
6   By virtue of the Legal Aid (Scotland) Act 1986, s 25(2).
7   (1994) A 300-B.
8   (1994) A 300-C.
9   In terms of the Criminal Justice (Scotland) Act 1975, s 140.
10 *Boner v United Kingdom* (1994) A 300-B, paras 40–44; *Maxwell v United Kingdom* (1994) A 300-C, paras 37–41. The judgments are probably best appreciated as examples of the application of the principle of equality of arms: see para 5.56 above. The 'open door' policy relied to a large extent (as the Court at least noted) upon the principle that 'counsel cannot properly occupy the time of the court in advancing arguments which he knows to be without foundation'. The judgments do not address this point. The concurring opinion of the British judge, Sir John Freeland, perhaps further confuses the issues by seeming to read the text's reference to the 'interests of justice' as if this reads as the 'appearance of injustice'. Leave to appeal in such instances is now required by virtue of the Criminal Justice (Scotland) Act 1995, s 42. See too *Pham Hoang v France* (1995) A 243, paras 40–41 (the applicant had been acquitted at first instance but convicted on appeal and subsequently had sought to challenge the compatibility of the customs code with the Convention; the refusal of legal aid taken with his lack of legal training resulted in his inability to develop and present complex legal arguments: violation of Art 6); *Biba v Greece* (26 September 2000), paras 26–31 (the applicant had been convicted of murder and sentenced to life imprisonment but had been denied access to the appeal court on account that legal aid was not available and he had been unable to pay for legal representation: violation of Art 6(1) and (3)(c)).

DOMESTIC COURT DECISIONS ON FREE LEGAL ASSISTANCE AND PROPOSED LEGISLATIVE REFORMS

5.129   The Scottish courts have considered issues relating to legal aid and the European Convention on Human Rights, Article 6(3)(c) in a number of cases. In *Shaw, Petitioner*[1], dealing with the withdrawal of a legal aid certificate, the court held that an order withdrawing legal aid should be made only where, by reason of specified conduct of the accused, it would be unreasonable for the solicitor to continue to act on his behalf, and the order would be a proportional response to the accused's conduct when measured against any potential effects on his right to a fair trial. In *Buchanan v McLean*[2] the court considered a scheme under which a fixed sum of £500 was payable as legal aid for all work done in respect of a summary prosecution up to the first 30 minutes of any trial. It was argued that the system placed the solicitor in a situation which was in conflict with the client's interest, as the solicitor would maximise his remuneration by minimising the outlays devoted to the case (for example, by advising the client to plead guilty), and could find himself unable economically to prepare the case fully. It was also argued that there was an inequality of arms and an appearance of disadvantage to an accused. It was accepted that, in the instant case, the solicitor had done and would continue to do all that was necessary for the accused's defence, in accordance with the relevant professional codes.The court accepted that there might be cases in which the client would be affected in such a way that a breach of Article 6(3)(b) or (c) would occur. The court did not, however, accept that such a breach was inevitable in every case, or in the instant case. The court accepted that the fixed payment would not be sufficient to meet outlays and remuneration in the instant case, but that did not deprive the accused of a fair trial given his solicitor's willingness to prepare the case fully despite the lack of remuneration.

1 1998 SCCR 672.
2 2001 SCCR 475. The same issue was raised earlier in *Gayne v Vannet* 2000 SCCR 5, prior to incorporation.

5.130 Following the decision of the High Court of Justiciary in *Buchanan v McLean*[1], cases predictably occurred in which solicitors refused to represent accused persons on the basis that the fixed fees available were inadequate, and in at least one of which a plea in bar was consequently upheld[2]. The Scottish Executive responded to that development, and to the decision in *Buchanan v McLeod*, by proposing amendments to the legal aid system. Under the Convention Rights (Compliance) (Scotland) Act 2001 the Scottish Legal Aid Board is given a discretion to exempt cases from the fixed payment scheme where an accused would be deprived of the right to a fair trial as a result of the solicitor being paid under the scheme. The Board is also empowered to employ solicitors to represent accused persons who would otherwise be unrepresented. In addition, the Act enables measures to be taken to extend the availability of legal aid in proceedings before tribunals[3].

1 2000 SCCR 682.
2 *McLeod v Glendinning* (February 2001, unreported), Sh Ct (see *Buchanan v McLean* 2001 SCCR 475 eg per Lord Hobhouse of Woodborough at para 78).
3 This will enable the Scottish Ministers to address the legal aid issue discussed in *S v Miller* 2001 SLT 531.

The effectiveness of legal representation

5.131 Several cases have considered the effectiveness of the legal representation provided by the state. The appointment of more than one legal representative at different stages of a criminal process is not in itself incompatible with the European Convention on Human Rights, Article 6, but the implications of this should be considered with some care[1]. The fact that a lawyer has been nominated to represent an accused does not in itself ensure effective assistance since the legal representative nominated may be unwilling or unable to act. In these cases, there will be a positive duty upon the state to replace the nominated lawyer 'or cause him to fulfil his responsibilities'[2]. This responsibility may also extend to the taking of appropriate action by the courts[3]. The issue may require detailed examination of the particular circumstances of each case. Minor shortcomings in representation will rarely be judged prejudicial. In *Kamasinski v Austria* the European Court of Human Rights conceded that some of the applicant's complaints had some substance (his defence could perhaps have been conducted in another way, and his lawyer had to some extent acted contrary to what the applicant considered to be in his own best interests), but could not be satisfied that the circumstances of his legal representation during the trial indicated a failure to provide effective legal assistance[4]. In contrast, the situation in *Daud v Portugal* was such as to lead to a violation of the sub-paragraph when read with paragraph (1). The first officially assigned lawyer had not taken any action on the applicant's behalf because of illness, and the applicant was only told of the appointment of his second lawyer three days before the beginning of his trial. This period was considered inadequate to have allowed the lawyer to master the complex file, to visit the applicant in prison, and to prepare his defence. The state had also been aware of 'a manifest shortcoming' on the part of the first lawyer and of the applicant's difficulties in securing a practical and effective defence. It was also clear that the trial court should have been aware that the applicant had not had any proper legal assistance, and thus ought to have adjourned the trial on its own initiative. The Court reiterated that assigning counsel to an individual does not in itself discharge state obligations, although a state cannot be deemed responsible for every shortcoming of a legal aid lawyer on account of the legal profession's independence which implied that 'the conduct of the defence is essentially a matter between the defendant and his counsel'. Only where the lack of 'effective representation is manifest or sufficiently brought to their attention in some other way' would state responsibility be engaged[5].

1 *Croissant v Germany* (1992) A 237-B, para 27.
2 *Artico v Italy* (1980) A 37 paras 33–36 at para 33 (no effective assistance from a nominated lawyer; state inactivity despite attempts by the accused to remedy the situation resulted in a breach of the requirement). This does not mean an individual has unlimited choice in selecting legal representation: 7572/76 etc, *Ensslin v Germany* (1978) DR 14, 64.
3 *Alimena v Italy* (1991) A 195-D, paras 18–20 (disposal of an appeal by the court without the presence of the applicant's lawyer).
4 (1989) A 168, paras 63–71. Cf 37477/97, *Milone v Italy* (23 March 1999) (non-representation of the applicant in appellate proceedings owing to his lawyer being on strike: a state cannot be held responsible for a failure on the part of a lawyer chosen by the applicant, and application declared inadmissible); 45995/99, *Rutkowski v Poland* (19 October 2000) (refusal of a court-appointed lawyer to lodge an appeal after having studied the case file and considered there were no grounds: application declared inadmissible, but observed that the authorities could not remain passive where an issue concerning legal assistance has been brought to their attention); and 53590/99, *Franquesa Freixas v Spain* (21 November 2000) (the lawyer asigned to the applicant (who was himself a lawyer) had not been a specialist in criminal law; but the applicant had not furnished any plausible evidence that the lawyer had been incompetent: inadmissible as manifestly ill-founded).
5 1998 II, 739, paras 37 43 at para 38. See too *Imbrioscia v Switzerland* (1993) A 275, paras 38–44; *Stanford v United Kingdom* (1994) A 282-A, paras 27–32.

Paragraph (3)(d): the right to call and to cross-examine witnesses

5.132 The European Convention on Human Rights, Article 6, sub-paragraph (3)(d) provides that everyone charged with a criminal offence has the rights 'to examine or have examined witnesses against him and to obtain the attendance and examination of witnesses on his behalf under the same conditions as witnesses against him'. The matter is closely related to the requirement that proceedings be adversarial in nature[1]. While the text refers specifically to 'witnesses', general fairness considerations require experts to be treated in a similar fashion[2]. In essence, the rights of an accused must include 'an adequate and proper opportunity to challenge and question a witness against him, either at the time the witness was making his statement or at some later stage of the proceedings'[3]. At the very least, an accused must have a real opportunity to cross-examine key witnesses against him[4]. It does not, however, entail 'the attendance and examination of every witness on the accused's behalf' as 'its essential aim, as is indicated by the words "under the same conditions" is a full "equality of arms" in the matter', and thus domestic courts may properly assess the question of the relevance of any proposed evidence within the confines of ensuring a fair trial[5]. Nor does it preclude special arrangements for the taking of evidence from high-ranking officials as long as there is the opportunity to challenge such evidence in an adversarial manner[6]. Similarly, while evidence in a criminal trial must in principle be produced at a public hearing in the accused's presence to allow it to be challenged through adversarial proceedings, the use of statements obtained at earlier stages of a criminal process (for example, during police inquiries or at judicial examination) is not inconsistent with the provision provided the rights of the defence have been respected[7]. Thus the Court did not find a breach of the provision in *Artner v Austria*. It had not been possible to secure the attendance of the victim at the hearing, but her written statements had been read out before the trial court and had been corroborated by other evidence, and in these circumstances it was not possible to conclude that the rights of the defence had been infringed to such an extent that there had been a violation of a fair trial[8].

1 See para 5.55 above.
2 *Bönisch v Austria* (1985) A 92, para 29 (complaints under para (3)(d) considered under the general requirements of para (1); an expert witness allegedly independent was more akin to an expert witness for the prosecution; there had been no opportunity for the defence to obtain their own expert, and consequently there was a violation of para (1)).
3 *Kostovski v Netherlands* (1989) A 166, at para 41.
4 *A M v Italy* (14 December 1999), paras 24–28 (conviction based exclusively on statements taken in the USA before the trial: violation of Art 6(1) taken along with Art 6(3)(d)). Cf 43373/98, *CG v United Kingdom* (11 April 2001) (allegations that the trial judge had persistently interrupted and hectored the applicant's defence counsel so frequently as to bar the proper cross-examination of a Crown witness: admissible).
5 *Engel and Ors v Netherlands* (1976) A 22, at para 91. Cf *Pisano v Italy* (27 July 2000), paras 21–29 (refusal to call a defence witness following the applicant's conviction for the murder of his wife: no violation established of Art 6(1) or in combination with Art 6(3)(d)); *Perna v Italy* (25 July 2001), paras 26–31 (failure to allow a journalist facing a criminal charge of defamation of the public prosecutor to cross-examine the complainant, but no indication as to what additional information would have been obtained in the particular case, and no violation of Art 6(1) taken with (3)(d). Cf para 26: 'it is not sufficient for an accused to complain that he was not permitted to examine certain witnesses; he must also support his request to call witnesses by explaining the importance of doing so and it must be necessary for the court to take evidence from the witnesses concerned in order to be able to establish the true facts', a principle which also applies to the complainant in a defamation case).
6 *Bricmont v Belgium* (1989) A 158, paras 77–89.
7 *Saïdi v France* (1993) A 261-C, paras 43–44 (pre-trial statements constituted the sole basis of the applicant's conviction, but at no stage was the applicant able to examine the witnesses

who had made the statements; and accordingly there had been a breach of paras (1) and (3)(d)); 35253/97, *Verdam v Netherlands* (31 August 1999) (statements made by rape victims to police officers were used in evidence at the subsequent trial; despite the absence of these witnesses at the trial, one witness had been examined by the accused's lawyer, and the conviction was corroborated by other evidence: application declared inadmissible).
8 (1992) A 242-A, paras 19–24.

DOMESTIC COURT DECISIONS ON THE RIGHT TO CALL AND TO CROSS-EXAMINE WITNESSES

5.133   The Scottish courts have had to consider the European Convention on Human Rights, Article 6(3)(d) in a number of cases. One of these concerned the protection of a vulnerable witness, and is discussed below[1]. The other cases have considered hearsay evidence. In *McKenna v HM Advocate*[2] the accused was charged with murder. The deceased had died when he was with the accused and another man, and must have been killed by one or other of them. The other man had made statements to the police and had then died. In advance of the trial the Crown served a notice under the Criminal Procedure (Scotland) Act 1995, s 259 intimating its intention to lead those statements in evidence. The accused then objected on the basis that the use of the statements would be contrary to Article 6(3)(d). It was accepted that there might be other evidence from a number of sources pointing to the accused's guilt. The court held that it could not be said, out of context of the evidence at the trial, that the admission of the evidence of the statements would necessarily be a breach of the accused's Convention rights. The court also noted that the requirement for corroboration ensured that the statement could never constitute the entire basis for conviction, and distinguished on that basis the decision in *Saidi v France*[3]. The court also noted that in *Trivedi v United Kingdom*[4] the Commission had held inadmissible an application concerning reliance on the hearsay statement of a witness who had become incapacitated and could not appear at the trial. The decision in *McKenna* has been followed in a case concerned with a witness who became mentally ill and incapable of giving evidence, where an objection (at the trial) to the admission of tape-recorded evidence given at an earlier trial was repelled[5], and in another case concerned with a deceased witness[6].

1 Para 5.136 below.
2 2000 SCCR 159.
3 (1993) A 261-C.
4 31700/96 (1997) DR 89, 136.
5 *HM Advocate v Nulty* 2000 SCCR 431.
6 *HM Advocate v Bain* 2001 SCCR 461. This decision is under appeal.

5.134   In England and Wales, the European Convention on Human Rights, Article 6 has been considered in relation to the leading of evidence, in a rape trial, as to the complainant's previous sexual history[1].

1 *R v A (No 2)* [2001] 2 WLR 1546.

Protection of vulnerable witnesses

5.135   The European Court of Human Rights has accepted that special arrangements may be appropriate in certain cases to protect vulnerable witnesses, for example by withholding their identity or by screening them while they are giving evidence in court. However, such measures taken on the ground of expediency cannot be allowed to interfere with the fundamental right to a fair trial[1]. The matter is considered in terms of the fairness of the admissibility of evidence. Over the course of judgments in this area, the Court has elaborated its approach.

In *Kostovski v Netherlands*, convictions had been based upon statements made to the police and to the examining magistrate by witnesses who had wished to remain anonymous in order to protect their identity. The defence had only been given the opportunity to submit written questions to one of the witnesses indirectly through the examining magistrate. For the Court, 'if the defence is unaware of the identity of the person it seeks to question, it may be deprived of the very particulars enabling it to demonstrate that he or she is prejudiced, hostile or unreliable', a situation giving rise to obvious dangers. Further, the absence of the witnesses had precluded the trial courts from observing their demeanour under questioning, and while the courts had observed caution in evaluating their statements, 'this can scarcely be regarded as a proper substitute for direct observation'. While Article 6 did not preclude reliance on information given by anonymous witnesses at the investigation stage, 'the subsequent use of anonymous statements as sufficient evidence to found a conviction, as in the present case, is a different matter' which had involved limitations on defence rights irreconcilable with fair trial guarantees, even taking into account the need to respond to the threat imposed by organised crime[2].

In *Lüdi v Switzerland*, statements had been given by an undercover police officer whose actual identity was not known to the applicant, but whom he had met on five occasions. The state had sought to argue that the need to protect the undercover agent's anonymity was vital in order to continue with the infiltration of drug-dealers, but the Court considered that the legitimate interest in protecting the identity of a police officer engaged in such investigations could have been met in a manner which was also consistent with respect for the interests of the defence. Here, neither the investigating judge nor the trial courts had been willing to hear the officer as a witness or to carry out a confrontation to allow his statements to be contrasted with the applicant's assertions, nor had the defence enjoyed even the opportunity to question the officer to attempt to cast doubt on his credibility, and thus there had been a violation of the guarantee[3].

In *Doorson v Netherlands*, the Court sought to provide a comprehensive statement of its approach. Again, the issue concerned the protection of witnesses in the prosecution of an individual suspected of drug dealing. The Court first reiterated that the use of anonymous witness statements was not in itself incompatible with the Convention since the protection of a witness's rights to life, liberty of the person, and respect for private and family life all were relevant considerations. Accordingly states 'should organise their criminal proceedings in such a way that those interests are not unjustifiably imperilled' by balancing the interests of the defence with those of witnesses required to testify. A decision to protect the anonymity of a witness had to be justified by reasons which were both relevant and also sufficient in each case to ensure that the interests of a witness properly outweighed those of the accused. Further, 'handicaps under which the defence laboured' must be 'sufficiently counterbalanced by the procedures followed by the judicial authorities', for example by allowing counsel to ask whatever questions were deemed appropriate other than those which could result in the identification of the witness. Finally, any evidence obtained from witnesses 'under conditions in which the rights of the defence cannot be secured to the extent normally required by the Convention' must be treated with particular care, and thus a conviction should not be based solely or even to a decisive extent upon evidence from anonymous witnesses. Here, the Court was satisfied that 'counterbalancing' procedures had been in place, and it was sufficiently clear that the trial court had not based its conviction of the applicant solely or to a decisive extent on the evidence of the two anonymous witnesses[4].

On the other hand, in *Van Mechelen and Ors v Netherlands*, the Court held that there had been a violation of Article 6 since the defence had not only been unaware of the identity of the police officers but had also been prevented from observing their demeanour while under direct questioning and thus from testing their reliability. The state had not been able to explain to the Court's satisfaction why such extreme limitations on the rights of an accused had been required, and there was a failure to counterbalance the handicaps under which the defence laboured in presenting its case. Further, the Court considered that the position of a police officer in such situations 'is to some extent different from that of a disinterested witness or a victim' on account of his close link with the prosecution, and consequently the use of an anonymous police witness 'should be resorted to only in exceptional circumstances'[5].

1   *Kostovski v Netherlands* (1989) A 166, para 44. See, too, Committee of Ministers Recommendation R (97) 13 (10 September 1997) 'Intimidation of Witnesses and the Rights of the Defence'; Costigan and Thomas 'Anonymous Witnesses' [2000] NILQ 326.
2   (1989) A 166, paras 38–45 at paras 42–44; see too *Windisch v Austria* (1990) A 186, paras 25–32.
3   (1992) A 238, paras 44–50 (violation of para (3)(d) in conjunction with para (1)). This case was distinguished in *Teixeira de Casto v Portugal* 1998-IV, 1451, para 37 discussed at para 5.72 above (undercover police officers had incited the commission of an offence leading to a violation of Art 6(1): in *Lüdi*, the police officer had been sworn in, the investigating judge had been aware of his mission and a preliminary investigation had been opened).
4   1996-II, 446, paras 67–76 at paras 70, 72 and 76 (circumstances justifying the retention of anonymity of two witnesses considered as appropriate, and their evidence had been treated with the necessary caution and circumspection).
5   1997-III, 691, paras 56–65 at para 56.

DOMESTIC COURT DECISIONS ON THE PROTECTION OF VULNERABLE WITNESSES

5.136   These cases were considered by the High Court of Justiciary in *HM Advocate v Smith*[1], which concerned an application by the Crown prior to a trial to allow undercover police officers to give evidence without revealing their true identities (other than to the trial judge, if required) and while concealed from the public and the press (but not the accused, their lawyers or the jury) by screens. The officers had been involved in a drug trafficking investigation, and it was averred that their safety and their effectiveness in future operations would be jeopardised if these precautions were not taken. The court granted the application.

1   2000 SCCR 910. See also *Re Al Fawwaz* [2001] 4 All ER 149.

Paragraph (3)(e): free assistance of an interpreter

5.137 The European Convention on Human Rights, Article 6(3)(e) provides that an accused has the right to have the 'free assistance of an interpreter if he cannot understand or speak the language used in court'. The provision is given a common-sense and straightforward interpretation. It requires the provision of an interpreter to allow the translation of documents and the interpretation of statements necessary for a fair trial[1], but does not require a written translation of every document in the process since the assistance required is that only necessary to allow the accused 'to have knowledge of the case against him and to defend himself, notably by being able to put before the court his version of events'[2]. This, too, may require the state authorities to ensure the quality of interpretation provided is adequate to achieve this goal: a state does not discharge its obligations merely by appointing and paying for an interpreter[3]. 'Free' is unqualified. In *Luedicke, Belkacem and Koç v Germany*, the Court declined to read into the provision any suggestion that an accused could be made to bear the costs of interpretation if convicted since this would amount to 'limiting in time the benefit of the Article' depriving it of much of its effect 'for it would leave in existence the disadvantages that an accused who does not understand or speak the language used in court suffers as compared with an accused who is familiar with that language', a disadvantage the provision sought to attenuate[4].

1 *Luedicke, Belkacem and Koç v Germany* (1978) A 29, para 48. The difficulties involved where the accused requires the assistance of a translator were considered in *Ucak v HM Advocate* 1998 SCCR 517.
2 *Kamasinski v Austria* (1989) A 168, para 74.
3 *Kamasinski v Austria* (1989) A 168, para 74.
4 (1978) A 29, paras 42–48. See too *Öztürk v Germany* (1984) A 73, paras 57–58.

ARTICLE 7: PROHIBITION AGAINST RETROACTIVE CRIMINAL OFFENCES OR PENALTIES

5.138 The European Convention on Human Rights, Article 7 embodies fundamental aspects of the rule of law and provides additional safeguards against arbitrariness in the criminal process through the prohibition of retroactive imposition of criminal liability or penalty[1]. Paragraph (1) provides first that 'no one shall be held guilty of any criminal offence on account of any act or omission which did not constitute a criminal offence under national or international law at the time when it was committed' and second, that no heavier penalty may be imposed 'than the one that was applicable at the time the criminal offence was committed'. The guarantee only applies to proceedings which lead to a conviction or the imposition of a criminal penalty, and will thus not apply to decisions affecting rules of evidence[2], bankruptcy proceedings[3], extradition[4] or release on parole[5]. The nature and purpose of the provision was succinctly stated by the Court in *Kokkinakis v Greece*: it not only prohibits retrospective application of the criminal law to the disadvantage of an accused, but more generally 'embodies ... the principle that only the law can define a crime and prescribe a penalty (*nullum crimen, nulla poene sine lege*) and the principle that the criminal law must not be extensively construed to an accused's detriment, for instance by analogy'[6]. No derogation from this provision is permissible in time of war or other national emergency in terms of Article 15[7]. Paragraph (2) seeks to protect the prosecution of crimes against humanity including war crimes and genocide recognised as criminal in accordance with the general principles of law 'recognised by civilised nations', a phrase wider than customary international law or legal obligations based upon international treaty[8].

1 For recent discussion, see Jones 'Common Law Crimes and the Human Rights Act 1998' 2000 SLT (News) 95; and Buxton 'The Human Rights Act and the Substantive Criminal Law' [2000] Crim LR 331; and Soyer 'L'Article 7 de la Convention existe-t-il?' in Mahoney, Matscher, Petzold and Wildhaber (eds) *Protecting Human Rights: The European Perspective* (2000) pp 337–1346.
2 6683/74, *X v United Kingdom* (1975) DR 3, 95.
3 8988/80, *X v Belgium* (1981) DR 24, 198.
4 7512/76, *X v Netherlands* (1976) DR 6, 184.
5 11653/85, *Hogben v United Kingdom* (1986) DR 46, 231.
6 (1993) A 260–A, at para 52. An example of an extensive construction of a legal rule by analogy and which violated Art 7 is found in *Baskaya and Okçuoglu v Turkey* (8 July 1999), para 42 (imprisonment of publisher under a provision of domestic law relating only to editors). For a domestic example, see *Smith v Donnelly* 2001 SCCR 800.
7 See paras 3.06 and 4.46 above.
8 But see *Streletz, Kessler and Krenz v Germany* and *K-H v Germany* (22 March 2001), paras 90.105 and 92.105 respectively (international law may be of relevance in assessing whether, at the time of commission, acts were defined with sufficient accessibility and foreseeability). Cf 268/57, *X v Belgium* (1957) 1 YB 239 at 240–241. See too 51891/99, *Naletilic v Croatia* (4 May 2000) (applicant facing charges of crimes against humanity and breaches of the Geneva Conventions before the International Criminal Tribunal for Former Yugoslavia: application under ECHR, Art 7 was inadmissible for, even if it applied, it would have done so under para (2) rather than para (1)). British law makes provision for the trial and punishment of such offences in statutes such as the Genocide Act 1969, the Criminal Justice Act 1988, s 134 (in respect of acts of torture), and the War Crimes Act 1991 (crimes committed in German-occupied territories during the 1939–45 war).

Retroactive application of criminal offences

5.139 Conduct which was not criminal at the time it occurred may not be treated as such by virtue of the retroactive application of the criminal law. The provision further reflects the importance attached by the European Convention on Human Rights to the principle that domestic law must be adequately accessible[1]. Within the context of the criminal code, an individual must be able to know 'from the wording of the relevant provision and, if need be, with the assistance of the courts' interpretation of it, what acts and omissions will make him liable'[2]. Consequently, the retroactive extension of the period of prescription for criminal offences gives rise to Article 7 issues[3]. The prohibition extends to criminal liability imposed both by statute and by development of the common law. However, as illustrated by two related applications in which the removal by the English criminal courts of an immunity which protected an accused in certain circumstances against a criminal charge of rape was considered, absolute legal certainty is by no means required on account of the very nature of a court's responsibilities in interpreting the law: the test is one of reasonable foreseeability as determined by the quality of the law in question and even where this requires an individual to take appropriate legal advice[4].

In *S W v United Kingdom* and in *C R v United Kingdom*, the applicants had sought during their trials to rely upon a common law principle that a husband could not be found guilty of the rape of his wife. According to the applicants, a series of recent court decisions had indeed affirmed this general principle, but in each of their trials the English courts had revised the principle so as to lead to the conviction of the applicants for rape and attempted rape respectively. The Court was not convinced, however, that in either case the requirements of Article 7 had been breached. At the outset of its assessment, the Court accepted that there was an 'inevitable element of judicial interpretation' inherent in any legal rule on account of the need for elucidation of any doubtful issue and for the law's adaptation to new and changing circumstances, and indeed that in European legal systems 'the progressive development of the criminal law through judicial law-making is a well entrenched and necessary part of legal tradition'. Providing always that 'the resultant development is consistent with the essence of the offence and could reasonably be foreseen', the gradual clarification and development of rules of criminal liability through judicial interpretation was thus not inconsistent with Article 7. Here, domestic law on marital rape had developed in such a way as to have resulted in the removal of the immunity as a reasonably foreseeable event; in any case, the abandonment of the principle was entirely consistent with the Convention's concern for the protection of human dignity[5].

This concern to uphold physical integrity was also apparent in the related cases of *Streletz, Kessler and Krenz v Germany* and *K-HW v Germany*. The applicants in the first case had been senior government ministers in East Germany who had been directly responsible for a 'shoot to kill' policy to deal with those seeking to escape to the west, while the applicant in the second case had been a border guard who had shot dead an East German citizen in 1972. Each applicant had subsequently been convicted after reunification of the two German states of intentional homicide under the relevant provisions of East Germany's criminal code. The Court considered that the domestic law applying at the time of the commission of the offences had been defined with sufficient accessibility and foreseeability, and while there had been a broad divide between legal provision and official practice, the first three applicants themselves had largely been responsible for this situation. Further, the Court felt compelled to consider applicable rules of international law dealing with protection of the right to life and of freedom of movement. These principles – particularly the pre-eminence of the right to life – justified a strict interpretation by the Federal courts of the legal provisions in force in the former communist state. Nor could even a private soldier such as the applicant in the second case show total and blind obedience to official orders which were in clear violation of both East German law and international legal norms. Accordingly, no violation of Article 7 was established[6]. This approach which stresses the importance of fundamental values found elsewhere in the Convention, was followed by the English courts, in respect of the scope of the defence of reasonable chastisement, in *R v H (Assault of Child: Reasonable Chastisement)*[7].

1 Cf the requirements of 'lawful', etc under Art 5, and of 'prescribed by law' or 'in accordance with law' under Arts 8–11. See paras 3.34–3.38 and 4.51 above and paras 6.20, 7.23 and 8.12–8.13 below.

2 *Kokkinakis v Greece* (1993) A 260-A, at para 52. See too *G v France* (1995) A 325-B, paras 24–27 (consistent case law on the notions of 'violence' and 'abuse of authority'; further, retrospective legislation operated in favour of the applicant: no violation of Art 7(1)).

3 *Coëme and Ors v Belgium* (22 June 2000), paras 145–151, discussed at para 5.140 below.

4 Cf *Cantoni v France* 1996-V, 1614, paras 29–36 (the manager of a supermarket ought to have appreciated that he ran the risk of prosecution for the unlawful sale of medicinal products; and consequently there was no violation of Article 7). See too 8141/78, *X v Austria* (1978) DR 16, 141 (the degree of precision must be assessed by reference of the particular technical knowledge of the individuals to whom the law is addressed). For a Scottish example (relating to breach of the peace) see *Smith v Donnelly* (31 July 2001, unreported), HCJ.

5 (1995) A 335-B, paras 34–47 at para 36; (1995) A 335-C, paras 32–44 at para 34. For critical discussion, see Osbourne 'Does the End Justify the Means? Retrospectivity, Article 7 and the Martial Rape Exemption' [1996] EHRLR 406. See too 8710/79, *X Ltd and Y v United Kingdom* (1982) DR 28, 77 (domestic courts may clarify but not change the constituent elements of a common law crime to the detriment of an accused).

6 (22 March 2001), paras 49–107 and paras 44–113 respectively (at para 106 in each case the Court noted that the offences could also have given rise to international legal rules on crimes against humanity, but found it unnecessary to consider this point further). See too 46362/99, *Glassner v Germany* (28 June 2001) (application of these principles in respect of the conviction of a former East German public prosecutor in respect of his submissions seeking a sentence which was particularly harsh in respect of a dissident: inadmissible).

7 [2001] 2 FLR 431.

5.140   Retroactive application of provisions extending the time in which a prosecution can be raised may not on the other hand give rise to a violation of the European Convention on Human Rights, Article 7, as illustrated by *Coëme and Ors v Belgium* where two of the applicants had been found guilty of forgery and uttering forgeries, offences classified as crimes (*crimes*) in domestic law but which had been treated in the prosecution as less serious offences (*délits*) on account of extenuating circumstances. Determination of whether the offences had been time-barred had been accordingly considered by the domestic courts having regard to the limitation period for these less serious indictable offences, a period which, however, had been extended on account of the retrospective application of a statute which allowed the extension of this period. For the Court, this did not give rise to a violation of Article 7. Domestic law followed the general principle that procedural rules apply immediately to proceedings that are under way, save where expressly provided to the contrary, and treated laws modifying rules on limitation as legislation on matters of jurisdiction and procedure rather than affecting the criminal nature of the behaviour when it took place[1].

1 (22 June 2000), paras 145–151.

Retroactive imposition of a heavier criminal penalty

5.141   The second aspect of the European Convention on Human Rights, Article 7(1) contains a prohibition on the retroactive imposition of a heavier penalty than the one applying at the time of the act or omission[1]. For the Court, the concept of a 'penalty' has to be given an autonomous Convention meaning to render Article 7 an effective guarantee: that is, it will be necessary to go behind appearances to examine the substance of a measure[2]. An increase in the length of imprisonment which may be imposed for default in the payment of a fine will fall within the scope of the guarantee[3]. However, in *Ibbotson v United* Kingdom, the Commission clarified that a requirement to register under the Sex Offenders Act 1997 in respect of offences committed before the statute came into force was not a 'penalty' for the purposes of Article 7. While the registration followed upon a conviction for a criminal offence, the essential nature of the requirement was preventative rather than punitive[4]. Nor does Article 7 prohibit the imposition of a heavier sentence on appeal[5].

1 *Ecer and Zeyrek v Turkey* (27 February 2001), paras 29–36 (the applicants were sentenced in terms of a statute which had increased the maximum penalty in respect of terrorist offences but in relation to an offence carried out before the legislation came into effect; the Court rejected the state's contention that the offence had been a continuing one and the reference in the indictment to the period before the entry into force of the statute had referred only to the commencement of the offence on account of the lack of a clear finding to this effect by the trial court: violation).
2 *Welch v United Kingdom* (1995) A 307-A, para 27.
3 *Jamil v France* (1995) A 317-B, paras 30–36 (four-month period of imprisonment upon default increased to two years; violation of Art 7(1)).
4 40146/98 (21 October 1998). This approach was followed, in relation to football banning orders, in *Gough v Chief Constable of Derbyshire* [2001] 4 All ER 289.
5 *Howarth v United Kingdom* (21 September 2000), paras 28 and 31, at para 28: (the fact that the applicant had completed his non-custodial sentence was 'not strictly relevant to the Court's consideration of the reasonableness of the length of the proceedings' for the purposes of Art 6; nor did the facts disclose any violation of Art 3).

DECISIONS OF THE DOMESTIC COURTS ON RETROACTIVE IMPOSITION OF A HEAVIER PENALTY

5.142 The imposition of automatic life sentences for a second serious offence under English legislation enacted in 1997 was challenged in *R v Offen*[1] as being incompatible with the European Convention on Human Rights, Article 7 where the first offence pre-dated the 1997 legislation. The court however held that the life sentence was imposed in respect of the second offence alone: the offender was not being sentenced again, or having his sentence increased, for the earlier offence.

1 [2001] 1 WLR 253.

CONFISCATION ORDERS UNDER THE DRUGS TRAFFICKING LEGISLATION

5.143 Particular issues have arisen in relation to the Drug Trafficking Offences Acts in the United Kingdom in regard to confiscation orders applying to the proceeds of crimes which took place before the statute entered into force[1]. In *Welch v United Kingdom*, the applicant had been sentenced to 22 years' imprisonment for drug trafficking in respect of offences occurring before the entry into force of the 1986 legislation, and in addition had a confiscation order under the statute imposed upon him requiring the payment of some £60,000. He asserted that the confiscation order was in the nature of a penalty: an order could only be made following upon a criminal conviction, by confiscating the proceeds (as opposed to the profits) of drug dealing the order went beyond the notions of reparation and prevention, and the orders made took into account the degree of the accused's culpability. The UK Government argued that an order sought to deprive only the profits of drug trafficking and to remove the value of the proceeds from possible future use in the drugs trade. In consequence, it was thus essentially a confiscatory and preventive measure. The Commission had agreed with these submissions from the state, but only by a decision of seven votes to seven with a casting vote being decisive in ruling that there had been no violation of Article 7. For the Court, the starting-point was whether the measure was imposed following a criminal conviction, but other factors were also of relevance in the assessment including 'the nature and purpose of the measure in question; its characterisation under national law; the procedures involved in the making and implementation of the measure; and its severity'. In the present case, the conclusion was that the confiscation order was indeed a 'penalty' within the meaning of Article 7. The imposition of a confiscation order was not only dependent upon the establishment of a criminal conviction, but the legislative background of the 1986 Act also suggested that the statute's purpose as well as being preventive in addition contained punitive elements. In particular, there was ' a strong indication of . . . a regime of punishment' because of the 'sweeping statutory assumptions . . . that all property passing through the offender's hands over a six-year period is the fruit of drug trafficking unless he can prove otherwise'. Further, 'the fact that the confiscation order is directed to the proceeds involved in drug dealing and is not limited to actual enrichment or profit; the discretion of the trial judge, in fixing the amount of the order, to take into consideration the degree of culpability of the accused; and the possibility of imprisonment in default of payment by the offender' all pointed to the conclusion that the retroactive application of the legislation in the particular case violated Article 7[2].

In *Welch*, the Court also sought to stress that the judgment 'did not call into question in any respect the powers of confiscation conferred on the courts as a weapon in the fight against the scourge of drug trafficking'[3]. The Commission had the opportunity to reiterate this in declaring a subsequent application inadmissible. In *Taylor v United Kingdom*, the appellant had been convicted in 1986 of drug trafficking in respect of offences committed between 1974 and 1979, and again in 1994 in respect of offences committed between 1990 and 1993. On the latter occasion, the trial court had also made a confiscation order for more than £15 million under the 1986 Act, relying on the applicant's own admission that he had benefited from drug trafficking during 1974 and 1979, and on the evidence tendered during the proceedings in respect of the second period between 1990 and 1993. The applicant sought to challenge the confiscation order but only insofar as it concerned this earlier period. Following *Welch*, the Commission accepted that the confiscation order constituted a 'penalty' for the purposes of Article 7. However, the Commission was able to distinguish *Welch* since the confiscation order was properly a 'penalty' imposed in respect of the offences committed between 1990 and 1993 rather than between 1974 and 1979. The key issue was that the applicant when committing these later offences had been aware that he was liable to a confiscation order which could have concerned earlier proceeds from crime since the 1986 Act had been in force for some time. What was crucial was the legislation's provisions which linked the power to make a confiscation order to the accused's having 'benefited' from criminal drug trafficking rather than to his conviction, and thus there had been no retroactive application of the law 7[4].

1 See further Bell 'The ECHR and the Proceeds of Crime Legislation' [2000] Crim LR 783. For discussion of dismissals of challenges based upon Art 6(2) by the Privy Council in *HM Advocate v McIntosh* 2001 SCCR 191 (reversing the earlier decision of the High Court of Justiciary) and subsequently by the Court in *Phillips v United Kingdom* (5 July 2001) see para 5.112 above.

2 (1995) A 307-A, paras 26–36 at paras 28 and 33.

3 (1995) A 307-A, at para 36.

4 31209/96, *Taylor v United Kingdom* (10 September 1997) ('according to the Act a person may be considered to have 'benefited' from drug trafficking without having been convicted, while a person who has been convicted is not necessarily considered to have benefited. Following this logic, the Crown Court, in order to make the confiscation order, did not rely on the applicant's previous conviction but on his own admission that he had 'benefited' from drug trafficking between 1974 and 1979'). See too *Elton v United Kingdom* 32344/96 (11 September 1997) (complaints that a confiscation order violated Art 6(2) as well as Art 7 declared inadmissible).

CHAPTER 6

Private and family life; and education

INTRODUCTION

6.01 Family life is at the heart of the protection accorded by the European Convention on Human Rights, Articles 8 and 12 and Protocol 1, Article 2[1]. Article 12 guarantees the right to marry and to found a family; Article 8(1) provides that 'everyone has the right to respect for his private and family life, his home and his correspondence'; and Protocol 1, Article 2 requires that the religious and philosophical convictions of parents are taken into account in the provision of education by the state. These articles reflect commonplace values found in domestic legal systems, and together provide a European framework for the domestic regulation of family life. The scope of each guarantee, however, varies. Article 12's focus is upon the traditional or nuclear family unit. As such, it is of limited application and, within the United Kingdom, has been relied upon primarily by prisoners seeking to enter into a legal relationship of marriage. Protocol 1, Article 2 calls for respect for parents' religious and philosophical convictions in the education of their children. Here, the protection is conferred upon the holders of parental rights irrespective of marital status. In contrast, Article 8 protection extends far beyond the family as a traditionally understood legal entity. Its central concern is protection for the home and the determination of family relationships. These guarantees are buttressed by other Convention concerns such as fair hearings in determination of family law disputes[2] and protection for the physical integrity of family members[3]. The provisions also concern development of personality and choice of lifestyle. Most obviously, Protocol 1, Article 2 provides for access to education while the scope of Article 8 further extends to determination of personal relationships and complements other safeguards for an individual's moral and physical integrity[4]. None of these rights is, however, immune from a state's right to take measures derogating from its obligations in time of emergency in terms of Article 15[5].

Article 8 is at the centre of this protection. The textual link in the guarantee between private life, family life, home and correspondence allows for considerable interplay between these related notions[6] and also a more teleological interpretation of the text than perhaps is evident elsewhere in the Convention. The case law is predominantly dynamic in character, although paradoxically the European Court of Human Rights can on occasion restrict 'lifestyle choices' through the operation of the doctrine of margin of appreciation in situations where there is little European consensus[7]. Article 8 jurisprudence may perhaps appear to lack coherence, but this is more a reflection of the particular issues raised to date by applicants rather than of any fundamental refusal on the part of the Court to recognise additional claims as worthy of discussion. Further advances are possible, above all in the development of positive duties to secure 'respect' for private and family life in contrast to the essentially negative duty upon states to refrain from interference with individual rights.

1 The European Convention on Human Rights, Protocol 7, Art 5 also provides for equality of rights and responsibilities between spouses, but the UK has not yet ratified this protocol.
2 In particular, fair hearing considerations can often arise in discussion of Art 8 concerns as to child care determinations: see further para 6.23 below.
3 Under ECHR, Art 2, near relations of a deceased may enforce obligations upon a state as 'victims', while deportation or extradition may also give rise to Art 3 considerations: see paras 4.03 and 4.37 above. A further link between Arts 3 and 8 is developing to protect physical integrity in situations falling short of violation of Art 3: see para 6.35 below. Article 5 issues may also arise in respect of the exercise of parental decision-making (cf *Nielsen v Denmark* (1988) A 144, discussed at para 4.47, above) or detention for the educational supervision of a child: see para 4.60 above.
4 In particular, ECHR, Arts 3 and 5 are concerned with physical integrity, while Art 9 protects freedom of thought and conscience and Art 11 the right of association. See paras 4.20ff above and paras 7.04–7.13 and 7.52–7.56 below.
5 See further para 3.06 above.
6 Cf *Klass v Germany* (1978) A 28, para 41 (telephone conversations are covered by notions of 'private life' and 'correspondence'); *López Ostra v Spain* (1994) A 303-C, para 51 (pollution could affect enjoyment of home in such a way as to affect private and family life).
7 E g *Sheffield and Horsham v United Kingdom* 1998-V, 2011, paras 51–61 (no requirement on the part of a state to alter register of births to recognise post-operative transsexual identity); *Laskey, Jaggard and Brown v United Kingdom* 1997-I, 1120, paras 42–51 (prohibition on sadomasochistic practices upheld).

ARTICLE 12: THE RIGHTS TO MARRY AND TO FOUND A FAMILY

6.02   The European Convention on Human Rights, Article 12 provides two separate but related rights: to marry; and to found a family. In each case, the right is subject to regulation by domestic legal systems; further, Strasbourg interpretation has lacked the creativity displayed elsewhere in this area. The right to marry is restricted to the traditional form of marriage between men and women as the foundation of a family unit. Accordingly, and despite the possible application of Article 14's prohibition of discrimination in the enjoyment of rights, the guarantee cannot support any claim of persons of the same biological sex (either as homosexuals, or where one party is a transsexual of the same biological sex as the other party) to marry[1]. This right is further restricted to the 'formation of marital relations not their dissolution', and Article 12 does not imply any right to divorce[2].

1 *Rees v United Kingdom* (1986) A 106, para 49; cf *T, Petitioner* 1997 SLT 724 at 734.
2 *Johnston v Ireland* (1986) A 112, at paras 52 and 54 ('in a society adhering to the principle of monogamy, [a restriction on divorce cannot] be regarded as injuring the substance of the right guaranteed by Article 12'). Cf *Airey v Ireland* (1979) A 32, para 24 (lack of legal aid to allow applicant to pursue judicial separation denied her any effective means of access to a court required by the European Convention on Human Rights, Art 6).

6.03   Domestic formalities and issues of legal capacity must be complied with[1], and the European Convention on Human Rights, Article 12 cannot be used to extend domestic rules on capacity to contract marriage[2] or to require that effect should be given to marriages contracted elsewhere and based upon principles of capacity not recognised by domestic law[3]. However, national law may not 'restrict or reduce the right in such a way or to such an extent that the very essence of the right is impaired'[4], and this may call for assessment of the purpose and effect of any legal rule which restricts marriage. Failure to allow convicted prisoners serving lengthy sentences of imprisonment to marry have been deemed to interfere with the essence of the guarantee[5]. Restrictions placed upon individuals seeking to remarry where divorce is recognised can also pose difficulties. In *F v Switzerland* a temporary restriction lasting three years had prohibited the applicant from marrying again following his third divorce. The European Court of Human Rights acknowledged that while a state has a legitimate interest in seeking to protect the stability of the institution of marriage, the temporary prohibition in question was disproportionate. It could not be said to protect the interests of any future spouse, nor did the prohibition encourage measured reflection on the part of the applicant, 'a person of full age in possession of his mental facilities'[6].

1 Cf 22404/93, *Senine Vadbolski and Demonet v France* (1994) DR 79, 79 (failure to comply with domestic formalities to obtain a declaration of facts by repute in lieu of a birth certificate which the applicant could not obtain but required for marriage: inadmissible).

2 11579/85, *Khan v United Kingdom* (1986) DR 48, 253 (Muslim couple of 21 and 14 married in accordance with Islamic law; male convicted for having sexual relations with under-age girl: application manifestly ill-founded); cf 14501/89, *A and A v Netherlands* (1992) DR 72, 118 (no violation of the European Convention on Human Rights, Art 8 in respect of failure to allow child of polygamous marriage to join his father and his second wife). Cf *Pellegrini v Italy* (30 July 2001), paras 40–48 (breach of fairness requirements under ECHR, Art 6 in proceedings before a Vatican ecclesiastical court lacking impartiality and which had annulled the applicant's marriage on the basis of consanguinity).

3 2991–92/66, *Alam and Khan; and Singh v United Kingdom* (1967) CD 24, 116 (friendly settlement). While this case appears to suggest that states are under no obligation to recognise polygamous marriages, the issues were considered under Art 8 rather than Art 12.

4 *Rees v United Kingdom* (1986) A 106 at para 50; 7114/75, *Hamer v United Kingdom* (1979) DR 24, 5, para 62 (domestic law may determine formalities (such as notice and publicity) and contractual issues determined on grounds of public interest (such as capacity, consent, prohibited degrees of consanguinity)); 11089/84, *Lindsay v United Kingdom* (1986) DR 49, 181 (taxation arrangements did not interfere with the right to marry); and 31401/96, *Sanders v France* (1996) DR 87, 160 (rules designed to preclude marriages of convenience not per se contrary to Art 12).

5 7114/75, *Hamer v United Kingdom* (1979) DR 24, 5 (five-year sentence of imprisonment); 8186/78, *Draper v United Kingdom* (1980) DR 24, 72 (life imprisonment). McManus *Prisons, Prisoners and the Law* (1994) p 70 suggests that it has not been practice in Scotland to limit prisoners' rights to marry; and, given that Scots law allows marriages to be conducted anywhere, the ceremony can be held within the prison. The Marriage (Scotland) Act 1977 makes no explicit provision for prisoners, and a prisoner's right to marry is not mentioned in any of the prison statutes or rules. In practice, prisoners held on remand are not permitted to marry someone who is to be a witness at their forthcoming trial (thereby rendering the witness non-compellable).

6 (1987) A 128, at paras 30–40. The Court noted (at para 33) that Switzerland alone retained such a provision requiring delay before marriage and was thus in an 'isolated position', but was not on this account alone willing to find a violation of ECHR, Art 12, especially since the issue of matrimony was 'so closely bound up with the cultural and historic traditions of each society and its deep-rooted ideas about the family'. This sentiment could equally apply to the approach taken in *Johnston v Ireland* (1986) A 112 which involved a prohibition on divorce. In Scots law, it may be questioned whether there is an adequate justification for requiring a five-year period to elapse before a divorce can be granted on the basis of separation of the spouses where a party to a marriage refuses to consent to a divorce.

6.04 The associated right of a married couple to found a family (including by means of adoption[1]) is likewise subject to compliance with applicable rules of domestic law. The issue has been of some concern to married prisoners in the handful of European countries (as in the United Kingdom) where prisoners are not permitted conjugal visits. The Commission has not been sympathetic to applications raising this matter[2]. This case law helps clarify that the right to marry under the European Convention on Human Rights, Article 12 must be considered independently of any right to consummate the marriage, or thereby to found a family. However, the provision cannot support a claim that the legal effects of marriage should also apply to relationships and situations comparable with marriage[3], although discrimination in the enjoyment of Convention rights on the basis of birth or status may give rise to a question under Article 14[4].

1 8896/80, *X v Netherlands* (1981) DR 24, 176 (complaint based on an inability to meet substantive domestic law provisions declared inadmissible); cf 6482/74, *X v Belgium and Netherlands* (1976) DR 7, 75 and 31924/96, *Di Lazarro v Italy* (1997) DR 90, 134 (right to found a family by means of adoption implies the existence of a couple, and thus cannot include adoption by an unmarried person). 36515/97, *Frette v France* (12 June 2001) (rejection on the grounds of his 'life style' of a request for authorisation to adopt a child lodged by an unmarried homosexual man: inadmissible under Arts 12 and 14 since neither provision guarantees a right of adoption; but admissible under Art 8). See also *T, Petitioner* 1997 SLT 724 at 734. In *Briody v St Helen's and Knowsley Area Health Authority* (29 June 2001, unreported), CA, Art 12 was considered in relation to the recoverability of damages to finance the birth of a child by surrogacy.

2 Cf 6564/74, *X v United Kingdom* (1975) DR 2, 105 (complaint by long-term prisoner of a denial of conjugal rights: the situation a prisoner finds himself in 'falls under his own responsibility' and thus the application was declared manifestly ill founded); 7114/75, *Hamer v United Kingdom* (1979) DR 24, 5 (parties must decide if they wish to marry in circumstances where cohabitation is not possible); and 32094/96 and 32568/96, *E L H and P B H v United Kingdom* (1997) DR 91, 61 (refusal to authorise conjugal visits for prisoners amounted to an interference with Art 8 rights, but was considered necessary for the prevention of crime or disorder). Such decisions focus upon the rights of prisoners, rather than the rights of spouses of prisoners. In certain applications involving the United Kingdom, friendly settlements have been secured: e g 17142/90, *G S, R S v United Kingdom* (10 July 1991); and 20004/92, *R J and W J v United Kingdom* (7 May 1993) (the Government accepted that facilities for artificial insemination treatment would be made available). In *R (Mellor) v Secretary of State for the Home Department* [2001] 3 WLR 533, the refusal of artificial insemination facilities to prisoners, other than in exceptional circumstances, was held not to contravene Art 8(2) or Art 12. 'Exceptional circumstances' would be such as would involve a disproportionate interference with a human right. An example of such a situation might be where the conception of a child was only possible for a limited period which fell within the period of imprisonment. In general, however, the inability of a prisoner to procreate is accepted as an aspect of the loss of rights and pleasures imposed as a punishment. Most European countries (in particular, those of central and east Europe) permit conjugal visits, a practice welcomed by the European Committee for the Prevention of Torture as of importance in safeguarding relationships with spouses as long as such visits take place in conditions which respect human dignity: cf *Irish Report*, CPT/Inf (95) 14, para 161.

3 *Marckx v Belgium* (1979) A 31, para 67.

4 See paras 3.40–3.65 above and para 6.44 below.

ARTICLE 8: RESPECT FOR PRIVATE AND FAMILY LIFE; HOME AND CORRESPONDENCE

6.05 The European Convention on Human Rights, Article 8[1] requires respect for private life, family life, home and correspondence. These concepts are closely related and on occasion are indistinguishable[2]. The focus is upon protection of family relationships and the moral and physical integrity of the individual, including development of personality, choice of lifestyle and establishment of relationships[3]. The provision may not only involve the negative duty upon a state to refrain from arbitrary interference with an individual's rights, but also impose a positive duty to adopt specific measures designed to secure respect for these guarantees[4]. Treatment of this article is best considered in three parts: discussion of the scope or application of the guarantee; discussion of what constitutes an 'interference'; and examination of those circumstances where a state interference will be deemed justified. Article 8 interpretation is still underdeveloped if not somewhat lacking in coherence and consistency[5]. Jurisprudence concentrates upon a number of disparate areas such as sexual orientation, child care, state surveillance, prisoners' correspondence and deportation, although there is still potential for further incursion into areas such as privacy and development of issues such as environmental protection[6].

1 For surveys of Art 8 case law, see eg Cohen-Jonathan 'Respect for Private and Family Life' in Macdonald, Matscher and Petzold (eds) *The European System for the Protection of Human Rights* (1993) pp 405–444; Farran 'Recent Commission Decisions and Reports Concerning Article 8' (1996) 21 EL Rev HRC 14–28; Feldman 'The Developing Scope of Article 8' [1997] EHRLR 265; Warbrick 'The Structure of Article 8' [1998] EHRLR 32; Naismith 'Private and Family Life, Home and Correspondence' in da Salvia and Villiger (eds) *The Birth of European Human Rights Law* (1998) pp 141–164; and Cousirrat-Coustère 'Famille et Convention Européene des Droits de l'Homme', in Mahoney, Matscher, Petzold and Wildhaber (eds) *Protecting Human Rights: The European Perspective* (2000) pp 281-307.
2 Eg *Stjerna v Finland* (1994) A 299-B, para 37 (use of name involves identification with a family and thus concerns private and family life); *López Ostra v Spain* (1994) A 303-C, para 51 (environmental pollution may affect ability to enjoy homes in such a manner as to affect private and family life).
3 In consequence, the scope of Art 8 is broad enough to encompass even the choice of family names: *Burghartz v Switzerland* (1994) A 280-B, para 24; *Guillot v France* 1996-V, 1593 paras 23–27.
4 Eg *Marckx v Belgium* (1979) A 31, para 31 (existence of legal safeguards which allow integration 'from the moment of birth' of a child into his family); *Airey v Ireland* (1979) A 32, paras 32–33 (effective access to a court for action of judicial separation); *Stubbings v United Kingdom* 1996-IV, 1487, paras 64–65 (effective deterrence of child sex abuse through protection provided by civil and criminal law). See further para 6.19 below. For domestic examples, see *Venables v News Group Newspapers Ltd* [2001] 2 WLR 1038 and *Re W and B; Re W (Care Plan)* [2001] 2 FLR 582.
5 Cf opinion of Judge Wildhaber in *Stjerna v Finland* (1994) A 299-B, discussed by Warbrick 'The Structure of Article 8' [1998] EHRLR 32.
6 See eg Upton 'The European Convention on Human Rights and Environmental law' [1998] JPL 315; Thornton and Tromans 'Human Rights and Environmental Wrongs. Incorporating the ECHR: Some Thoughts on the Consequences for UK Environmental Law' (1999) 11 J Env L 35; Hart 'The Impact of the ECHR on Planning and Environmental law' [2000] JPL 117.

Scope of Article 8 protection

Respect for family life

DETERMINING THE EXISTENCE OF 'FAMILY LIFE'

6.06   In contrast with the European Convention on Human Rights, Article 12, 'family life' has been interpreted creatively in line with changing social attitudes. In the determination of whether 'family life' exists, it will be necessary to consider all the circumstances of the case, including the intentions of the individuals involved and the stability of their relationships. The key requirement will normally be cohabitation or the existence of other factors indicating that a 'relationship has sufficient constancy to create de facto 'family ties'[1]. Thus 'the question of the existence or non-existence of 'family life' is essentially a question of fact depending upon the existence of close personal ties'[2] and is not determined solely by domestic legal status[3]. Certainly, a lawful and genuine marriage involving cohabitation between two persons of the opposite sex[4] will fall within the scope of the article. However, a relationship outwith marriage may also qualify as a 'family'[5], and the scope of Article 8 may also further extend to situations in which a full family life has not yet been established as long as there is a genuine intention to cohabit and to lead a normal family life[6]. The actual circumstances surrounding any relationship are thus of the essence. Further, since near relatives can play a vital role in families, 'family life' may also extend to ties between relatives such as grandparents and children[7], siblings[8] and, in certain circumstances, between an uncle and a nephew[9].

1   *Kroon and Ors v Netherlands* (1994) A 297-C, at para 30. Relevant factors include whether a couple cohabits, length of relationship, existence of children, etc: see eg *Keegan v Ireland* (1994) A 290, para 36. Cf 14501/89, *A and A v Netherlands* (1992) DR 72, 118 (recognition of 'family life' in polygamous marriage where there had been frequent contact between father and son). *X, Y and Z v United Kingdom* 1997-II, 619, paras 36 and 37 (the Court recognised that there were de facto family ties between a transsexual, his partner of the same biological sex and a child born to the latter by artificial insemination).
2   11468/85, *K v United Kingdom* (1986) DR 50, 199 at 207.
3   See further, Karsten 'Atypical Families and the Human Rights Act: The Rights of Unmarried Fathers, Same Sex Couples and Transsexuals' [1999] EHRLR 195.
4   16106/90, *B v United Kingdom* (1990) DR 64, 278 (homosexual relationships fall within the meaning of private life for the purposes of Art 8). The status of such a partnership under Art 8 would presumably change if domestic law made provision for a legal union between two persons of the same biological sex: cf Reid *A Practitioner's Guide to the European Convention on Human Rights* (1998) p 261: 'in those countries where gay marriages are allowed, it may be that the [Court] would have to accept that "family" relationships could be formed and any inequalities there would be harder to justify'. For a recent development in English law see *Fitzpatrick v Sterling Housing Association* [2000] AC 27 (homosexual partner of deceased tenant held entitled to succeed to the tenancy as either the spouse of the deceased or as a member of his family residing with him at the time of death).
5   *Johnston and Ors v Ireland* (1986) A 112, para 56 (15 years' cohabitation, but each party legally unable to divorce and thus remarry).
6   *Abdulaziz, Cabales and Balkandali v United Kingdom* (1985) A 94, paras 62–63. Cf 15817/89, *Wakefield v United Kingdom* (1990) DR 66, 251 (prisoner requested transfer to prison in Scotland to be near his fiancée; the Commission considered that the relationship between the applicant and his fiancée did not fall within the scope of family life envisaged by Art 8).

7 *Marckx v Belgium* (1979) A 31, para 45 (ties with near relatives covered since 'such relatives may play a considerable part in family life'); *Bronda v Italy* 1998-IV, 1476, para 51. Cf *Hokkanen v Finland* (1994) A 299-A, para 45 (a child was brought up by grandparents while its father was in prison; the Court decided that there were sufficient links to establish a 'family life' since the father retained legal powers over the child and had continuously sought access; but the question of grandparents' interests in 'family life' appears not to have been argued by the Government).
8 *Moustaquim v Belgium* (1991) A 193, para 36.
9 *Boyle v United Kingdom* (1994) A 282-B (friendly settlement) (refusal of a local authority to allow applicant access to his nephew with whom he had formed close bonds before the child was removed from its mother on suspicion of child abuse: the Commission found that the bonds supported 'family life').

PARENTS AND CHILDREN

6.07   Ties between a parent and a child clearly fall within the scope of the European Convention on Human Rights, Article 8 which thus encompasses a broad range of decisions taken by a parent on behalf of a child, including decisions in respect of education[1], health care[2] and discipline, but always having regard to other countervailing rights of the child[3]. More particularly, a decision to take a child into care or to allocate custody to one parent upon divorce or separation will give rise to an Article 8 issue. 'The mutual enjoyment by parent and child of each other's company constitutes a fundamental element of family life'[4], irrespective of the legal nature of the union existing between the biological parents. The existence of family life between a parent and child is again determined by the actual circumstances of each case, but there appears to be a stronger presumption in favour of the existence of such ties. Thus for the purposes of Article 8 a 'family life' between a child and an adult who is not the biological parent[5] of the child may be established where one parent is a step-parent or through legal or social ties involving adoption[6] or fostering[7]. Nor is the tie between a parent and a child dependent upon the continuing cohabitation of its parents. Any child born of a union recognised as constituting a 'family' is '*ipso jure* part of that relationship', and thus

> 'from the moment of the child's birth and by the very fact of it, there exists between him and his parent a bond amounting to "family life", even if the parents are not then living together'[8].

In certain circumstances, the article may indeed require respect for the construction of a personal or family identity through the provision of access to records concerning the upbringing of a child in care[9]. However, 'family life' ties are not indefinite. Subsequent events will break the bond between a child and its parent or other adult in a family relationship through any intervening loss of contact considered substantial enough to break these ties[10]. Most obviously, the loss of dependency upon the parent through maturation of the young person will bring 'family life' to an end[11], although the mere fact that a child is taken into care will not do so[12], nor will a parent's failure to contribute to the costs of a child's upbringing and care[13]. The consequence is that a parent who does not enjoy parental rights in domestic law may still be able to rely upon Article 8 guarantees. In *Keegan v Ireland*, an unmarried father had sought court approval to be recognised as his child's guardian after the child had been placed for adoption shortly after her birth but without his knowledge. The European

Court of Human Rights accepted that the adoption process was an inter-ference with the father's rights under Article 8[14]. Conversely, a parent who is still recognised by domestic law as enjoying parental rights may not be able to satisfy the tests for enjoyment of Article 8 guarantees where the link between the parent and the child has become tenuous[15].

1 See paras 6.53–6.55 below.
2 *Nielsen v Denmark* (1988) A 144, para 61 (the hospitalisation by a mother of a child who was not mentally ill in a psychiatric ward was not a 'deprivation of liberty' for the purposes of Art 5: see para 4.47 above).
3 For example, in terms of Art 3's prohibition of degrading treatment: eg *A v United Kingdom* 1998-VI, 2692, discussed at para 4.29 above. See further, eg van Bueren *International Law on the Rights of the Child* (1995); Verhellen (ed) *Monitoring Children's Rights* (1996); Detrick *A Commentary on the United Nations Convention on the Rights of the Child* (1999); and de Boer-Buquicchio 'The Protection of Children's Rights in Europe and the UN Convention on the Rights of the Child' in Mahoney, Matscher, Petzold and Wildhaber (eds) *Protecting Human Rights: The European Perspective* (2000) pp 345–363. The European Convention on the Exercise of Children's Rights (ETS 160 (1996)) entered into force in July 2000, but has not yet been ratified by the United Kingdom. For discussion of the practical difficulties facing children in enforcing their rights under the ECHR, see Reid 'Article 25 of the Convention: Application by Children' in de Salvia and Villiger (eds) *The Birth of European Human Rights Law* (1998) pp 301–307. It provides a number of procedural measures to allow children to exercise their rights more effectively in partic-ular, in family legal proceedings. Courts (and any person appointed to act on behalf of a child) have responsibilities in facilitating the exercise of rights by children (such as the right to be informed and the right to express their views either themselves or through other persons or bodies).
4 *Olsson v Sweden (No 1)* (1988) A 130 at para 59.
5 Cf 16944/90, *Maassen v Netherlands* (1993) DR 74, 120 (the Commission refused to consider whether the donation of sperm for the purpose of enabling a woman to take advan-tage of artificial insemination to become pregnant gave the donor any Art 8 rights; actual contact between donor and child were insufficient in the particular case to establish family life). See, too, *X, Y and Z v United Kingdom* 1997-II, 619, discussed at para 6.11 below.
6 9993/82, *X v France* (1992) DR 31, 241 (judicial decision withdrawing applicant's parental authority in respect of her adopted son: the relations between adoptive parents and an adopted child are as a rule family relations protected by Art 8).
7 8257/78, *X v Switzerland* (1978) DR 13, 248 (complaint by the applicant that the court's decision to grant custody of her foster child to the parents was an interference with her private and family life, but it was not necessary to consider whether interference amounted to family life, as the separation undoubtedly affected her private life).
8 *Berrehab v Netherlands* (1988) A 138, at para 21.
9 *Gaskin v United Kingdom* (1989) A 160, paras 36–37.
10 Cf *Berrehab v Netherlands* (1988) A 138, para 21 (frequency, regularity and length of contact with daughter after ending of cohabitation with child's mother such as to maintain ties of 'family life'); *Gul v Switzerland* 1996-I, 159, paras 32–43 (refusal by the state to allow a child to join his father who had left his home country when the child was three months old in circumstances suggesting the father had never attempted to develop a family life; further, a 'family life' could have been established in Turkey in any case).
11 Cf 26494/95, *J T v United Kingdom* (30 March 2000) (failure to allow the applicant, who had been detained for some time as a psychiatric patient, to have her mother replaced as her 'nearest relative' by a social worker in view of the difficult relationship she had with her mother: friendly settlement whereby the UK Government indicated that domestic legislation would be amended to provide the detainee with the power to apply to court to have the 'nearest relative' replaced where the patient reasonably objected to a certain person acting in that capacity, and to exclude certain persons from acting as 'nearest rela-tive').
12 *Eriksson v Sweden* (1989) A 156, para 58.
13 *Kroon v Netherlands* (1994) A 297-C, para 30.
14 (1994) A 290, paras 46–55. See also *McMichael v United Kingdom* (1995) A 307-B, paras 86–90, discussed at para 6.23 below.

15 Eg *Söderbäck v Sweden* 1998-VII, 3086, discussed at para 6.38, n 2 below. Additional issues may arise where a parent seeks to resist a requirement to return a child abducted from abroad under the Child Abduction and Custody Act 1985 on account of possible incompatibility with ECHR: see Karsten 'Atypical Families and the Human Rights Act' [1999] EHRLR 195 at 201. Cf 22920/93, *M B v United Kingdom* (1994) DR 77, 108 (a person who is not the guardian or legal representative of a child cannot bring a complaint under Art 8 on behalf of that child).

6.08 The European Convention on Human Rights does not require that a father must enjoy equality of treatment with the mother of a child. While Protocol 7, Article 5 specifically provides that 'spouses shall enjoy equality of rights and responsibilities', by implication, where a state has not ratified this Protocol certain differences in treatment are not incompatible with the Convention[1]. In *Petrovic v Austria*, a father had his claim for parental leave allowance rejected by an employment office since at that time only mothers could qualify. While agreeing with the Commission that payment of social welfare assistance by the state was made with a view to promoting family life, the Court did not accept that the discrimination violated Article 8 when taken with Article 14. Of crucial importance was the lack of any common European standard in determining whether social security provision for parental leave should be paid to fathers. Although most states were moving gradually towards according a high priority to equality of the sexes, there was still no uniformity in this aspect of welfare provision. Accordingly, the state was entitled to a wider margin of appreciation in its assessment of whether there was a need for a difference of treatment between mothers and fathers[2].

1 The United Kingdom has not ratified this Protocol, and it is thus not a 'Convention right' for the purposes of the Human Rights Act 1998.
2 1998-I, 579, paras 22–43 (the Commission had considered by a majority of 25 to 5, that there had been a violation. For the two dissenting judges on the Court, the lack of any standard European norm 'was not conclusive'; and while states were not under a duty in terms of Art 8 to pay any such allowance, if they chose to do so it would not be appropriate to do this in a discriminatory manner).

CHILDREN BORN OUTSIDE MARRIAGE

6.09 The status of illegitimacy for most purposes has ceased throughout Europe to carry legal disabilities, and the European Convention on Human Rights, Article 14 provides that 'birth or other status' may not be used as a ground for discrimination in the provision of rights under the Convention[1]. This provision taken along with Article 8 has resulted in the successful challenge of national laws which discriminate on this ground. In *Marckx v Belgium*, domestic law required an unmarried mother to follow certain legal procedures in order to establish a legal bond with her child; further, the rights of inheritance on intestacy of a recognised illegitimate child were less than those of a child born within marriage. The European Court of Human Rights noted that the text of Article 8 did not distinguish between family units constituted through marriage and those outwith wedlock, and considered that to imply any such interpretation would both be inconsistent with the general principle that Convention guarantees apply to 'everyone', as well as contrary to Article 14's prohibition of any discrimination in the enjoyment of Convention rights on grounds including 'birth'[2].

1 The language of the UN Convention on the Rights of the Child is arguably tighter: Art 2 provides that states must ensure that rights under the treaty are made available to each child 'without discrimination of any kind irrespective of the child's or his parent's or other legal guardian's race, colour, . . . birth or other status'.
2 (1979) A 31, paras 28–65 (various violations of Art 8 taken alone, of Art 8 taken in conjunction with Art 14, of Art 14 taken in conjunction with Art 8, and of Art 14 taken in conjunction with Protocol 1, Art 1). The Court noted (at para 52) that while inheritance rights are normally exercised only upon death when 'family life' undergoes a fundamental change, 'this does not mean that no issue concerning such rights may arise before death: the distribution of the estate may be settled . . . by the making of a will or of a gift on account of a future inheritance [and] therefore represents a feature of family life that cannot be disregarded'.

6.10   The lack of any common European consensus on parental rights has allowed the Commission and the European Court of Human Rights to decline to insist that domestic law treats unmarried fathers and mothers equally[1]. In *McMichael v United Kingdom*, the Court upheld the distinction in Scots law[2] between the automatic conferment of parental rights on a married father and the requirement placed upon an unmarried father to take some form of positive step to acquire these rights (such as through an application to a court) as being a proportionate response in achieving the legitimate aim of distinguishing between fathers who had some justifiable claim and those whose status lacked sufficient merit[3].

1 The weaker standing of an unmarried father is found elsewhere in Europe: eg 9639/82, *B, R and J v Germany* (1984) DR 36, 130 (differences in treatment could be justified; no practical effect on children; the weaker position of the father was mainly a consequence of a choice on the part of the unmarried parents; and the father's disadvantage was proportionate to the aim of the regulation which was to protect the child).
2 Formal equality as regards the exercise of parental rights is specifically rejected by Scots law. Under the Children (Scotland) Act 1995, a father will automatically enjoy parental rights (including, in terms of s 2, the rights to have the child living with him or otherwise to regulate the child's residence; to control, guide and direct the child's upbringing in a manner appropriate to the child's stage of development; to maintain personal relations and direct contact with the child on a regular basis where the child is not living with him; and to act as the child's legal representative) only if married to the mother (at the time of conception or subsequently); if unmarried, to acquire such rights he must draw up an agreement with the mother and have this registered (s 4) or alternatively apply for parental rights through a court order (s 11). In England, it has been held that natural fathers should normally be informed of adoption proceedings even if they do not have statutory 'parental responsibility' (in which event they would be entitled to notice of the proceedings as of right) if the factual relationship between the father and the child constitutes family life within the meaning of Art 8: *Re H* [2001] 1 FLR 646. See also *Re P* (care proceedings: father's application to be joined as party) [2001] 1 FLR 781; *Re M* (adoption: rights of natural father) [2001] 1 FLR 745.
3 (1995) A 307-B, para 98.

WIDENING THE SCOPE OF ARTICLE 8 PROTECTION THROUGH AN EMERGING AND DEVELOPING EUROPEAN CONSENSUS

6.11   Where there is considerable variation amongst states in domestic approaches to issues in the area of family law, the practical effect (as illustrated by cases such as *Petrovic v Austria*) is likely to be that the European Court of Human Rights will prove unwilling to enlarge the scope of the guarantee[1]. Just as Article 12 has not been recognised as supporting any right of homosexuals, or transsexuals of the same biological sex as the other party, to marry, so Article 8 is also more cautious than some domestic legal systems which take a more liberal attitude in the regulation of family and private life. For example, Article 8 cannot at present be used to imply a positive duty upon states to grant parental rights to post-operative transsexuals. In *X, Y and Z v United Kingdom*, the state had refused to register a transsexual as the father of a child born to his partner by artificial insemination of the donor. The Court accepted that there were de facto family ties linking the three applicants and thus domestic law had to ensure the integration of the child into the family from as early a stage in the child's life as was practicable. However, the lack of any common European standard on the issue of parental rights for transsexuals meant that states had a wide margin of appreciation in regulating this area in which general state interests (including protection of the integrity of domestic family law) outweighed any individual interest[2].

1 But cf *Guillot v France* 1996-V, 1593, paras 21–22 (willingness to consider whether refusal to register applicants' daughter by a name used by her but not officially recognised by the French state involved an interference).

2 1997-II, 619, paras 38–52 (at para 50 the Court observed that the first applicant was 'not prevented in any way from acting as [the child's] father in the social sense'). See, too, *T, Petitioner* 1997 SLT 724 at 736B (sexual orientation was only one factor to be taken into account in an adoption case).

IMMIGRATION, DEPORTATION AND EXTRADITION

6.12 The European Convention on Human Rights, Article 8 cannot in itself be used to found a right to live as a family unit in any particular country since international law recognises a state's right to control immigration into its territory. However, consideration of whether the article imposes a duty on the immigration authorities to admit any relative of settled immigrants will be dependent upon the particular facts of each case[1]. It will be more readily accepted that there exists a 'family life' giving rise to an Article 8 issue in cases involving extradition and deportation when an individual can be said to have dominant and long-established family roots and relationships in the country from which he faces expulsion. Here, the determination of the existence of 'family life' will involve consideration of a wider range of circumstances, such as whether his near relatives also reside in the state, his language, education and upbringing, length of residence, and extent of existing links with the country to which a state intends expelling the individual[2].

1 Cf *Cruz Varas and Ors v Sweden* (1991) A 201, para 88 (no evidence to show that the applicants could not establish a family life in their home country); *Gül v Switzerland* 1996-I, 159, paras 38–43 (no duty upon state to admit applicant's son since there were no obstacles to developing a family life in the country where the son was living and had been brought up); *Ahmut v Netherlands* 1996-VI, 2017, paras 67–73 (a father had arranged for his son to be schooled abroad, often visited his son abroad, and had dual nationality; the Court determined that a fair balance had been struck between the applicants' interests and the public interest in controlling immigration).

2 Eg *Moustaquim v Belgium* (1991) A 193; *Beldjoudi v France* (1992) A 234-A, paras 67–76 (marriage and subsequent establishment of matrimonial home in France for 20 years had established 'family life', despite lengthy periods of enforced separation of spouses through imprisonment); *Nasri v France* (1995) A 320-B, paras 43–46 (deportation of deaf and dumb applicant of limited education whose parents and nine siblings lived in France had been ordered after his conviction for gang rape; the Court established that in all the

circumstances the deportation would violate Art 8); *Dalia v France* 1998-I, 76, para 45 (the permanent exclusion of a woman who had joined her mother and seven siblings in France and who subsequently gave birth to a child in the country gave rise to an Art 8 issue; but the order imposed after a conviction for drug-trafficking was considered justified); *Baghli v France* (30 November 1999), paras 45–49 (expulsion of an Algerian national convicted of drug-trafficking who had arrived in France at the age of two, who had lived most of his life there, and whose close family were resident there, but who had not taken French nationality and who had retained some links with the country of birth: no violation of Art 8 in view of the serious breach of public order his behaviour had occasioned); and *Boultif v Switzerland* (2 August 2001), paras 39–56 (expulsion of the applicant who had entered the country with a tourist visa, married a Swiss national, and been sentenced to a two-year prison sentence for robbery and other offences: since it was practically impossible for him to live with his family outside Switzerland and he presented only a comparatively limited danger to public order, the interference with respect for family life was not proportionate and thus constituted a violation of Art 8). Scottish examples include *Abdadou v Secretary of State for the Home Dept* 1998 SC 504, and *Akhtar v Secretary of State for the Home Dept* 2001 SLT 1239. For recent domestic discussion at appellate level, see *R v Secretary of State for the Home Department ex p Isiko* [2001] 1 FLR 930; *R (Samaroo) v Secretary of State for the Home Department* (17 July 2001, unreported), CA.

DOMESTIC COURT DECISIONS ON THE SCOPE OF 'FAMILY LIFE'

6.13   The refusal of citizenship is not in itself a failure to respect or interference with family life[1]. It has been held that the non-availability of damages for the birth of a healthy child (following *McFarlane v Tayside Health Board*[2]) is not incompatible with Art 8[3].

1   *R (Montana) v Secretary of State for the Home Dept* [2001] 1 WLR 552.
2   2000 SC (HL) 1.
3   *Greenfield v Irwin* [2001] 1 WLR 1279.

Respect for home

6.14   'Home' is closely related to both 'family life' and 'private life'[1]. The facts must support the establishment of a 'home', and this is determined by factors such as nature and length of residence, and intention[2]. However, the mere intention to establish a home in the future is insufficient[3]. Respect for 'home' may give rise to questions including physical intrusion into a home[4] to carry out a search[5], planning and control decisions[6], environmental nuisances which have a substantial impact upon enjoyment of the property[7], and possibly also non-physical intrusion through telephone tapping[8]. However, the concept does not include questions relating to rights or obligations arising from a lease[9] or compulsory purchase[10] or other matters which more properly fall within the scope of the European Convention on Human Rights, Protocol 1, Article 1 which protects property rights[11]. The guarantee is essentially a civil and not an economic right, and thus cannot be interpreted as requiring states to provide a 'home' for every family[12]. Otherwise, 'home' is usually given an interpretation consistent with maximising the scope of the Article. In *Gillow v United Kingdom,* the applicants had lived on Guernsey for some four years during which period they had bought a house. During an absence from the island for almost 19 years, they had retained ownership of the house and maintained an intention to return to Guernsey. The European Court of Human Rights considered that in these circumstances there were sufficient continuing links with the house to allow it to be considered their 'home'[13].

Even if the home has been established unlawfully in terms of domestic law, there may still be a 'home' deserving state respect in terms of Article 8. In *Buckley v United Kingdom*, the applicant had purchased land and had then occupied a caravan on this property with her children but in contravention of planning controls. The facts of the case, including length of residence, absence of any intention to move elsewhere and integration of her eldest children into the local school, allowed the Court to categorise the issue of failure to provide retrospective planning consents as one concerning the right to respect for 'home'[14].

Further, 'home' may extend beyond the domestic sphere. *Niemietz v Germany* involved a court-authorised search of a lawyer's office. In deciding that in certain circumstances business premises could fall within the scope of 'home', the Court remarked that any precise distinction between office and home would often be difficult to draw 'since activities which are related to a profession or business may well be conducted from a person's private residence and activities which are not so related may well be carried on in an office or commercial premises'[15].

1 Cf *López Ostra v Spain* (1994) A 303-C, at para 51 (severe environmental pollution may prevent enjoyment of homes in such a way as to affect private and family life).

2 Cf *Mentes and Ors v Turkey* 1997-VIII, 2689, para 73 (occupation of a house for significant periods annually was sufficient to establish an Art 8 interest).

3 *Loizidou v Turkey* 1996-VI, 2216, para 66.

4 12474/86, *Kanthak v Germany* (1988) DR 58, 94 (the question whether the applicant's camping car could be considered a 'home' was left unresolved).

5 Eg *Murray v United Kingdom* (1994) A 300-A, paras 84–86 (entry and search by military personnel); *Chappell v United Kingdom* (1989) A 152-A, para 51 (Anton Piller orders).

6 Eg *Buckley v United Kingdom* 1996-IV, 1271, para 54; *Mentes v Turkey* 1997-VIII, 2689, para 73 (destruction of homes by security forces constituted a 'particularly grave interference').

7 Eg *Powell and Rayner v United Kingdom* (1990) A 172, para 40 (airport noise).

8 *Klass v Germany* (1978) A 28, para 41 (point raised but not decided).

9 *Langborger v Sweden* (1989) A 155, paras 38–39 (power to negotiate rent conferred on tenants' association).

10 10825/84, *Howard v United Kingdom* (1987) DR 52, 198 (compulsory purchase order for the applicant's house was justified by Art 8(2) as being necessary for the protection of the rights of others who would benefit from the development).

11 See paras 8.03–8.10 below.

12 *Velosa Barreto v Portugal* (1995) A 334, para 24 (a landlord had sought recovery of possession of a rented house; the Court accepted that legislation sought to protect tenants and had a tendency to promote the economic well-being of the country and thus had a legitimate aim; the landlord had failed to show that he had any need of the property and the state was under no obligation to give a landlord the right to recover possession of a rented house on request and in any circumstances).

13 (1986) A 109, para 46.

14 1996-IV, 1271, para 54. Cf 26662/95, *Varey v United Kingdom* (21 December 2000) (friendly settlement in relation to complaint that planning enforcement measures taken in respect of the applicants' occupation of land which they had bought in order to maintain their traditional gipsy lifestyle and culture violated Art 8). See now *Porter v South Buckinghamshire DC* (12 October 2001, unreported), CA. An eviction order has been held to fall within the scope of Art 8: *Poplar Housing and Regeneration Community Association Ltd v Donoghue* [2001] 3 WLR 183.

15 *Niemietz v Germany* (1992) A 251-B, paras 30–31. This decision mirrors the approach adopted by the UN Human Rights Committee in the interpretation given to the International Covenant on Civil and Political Rights, Art 17: see General Comment 16(32), ORGenAss, 40th Session, Supplement No 40 (A/40/40) (1985): 'the term "home" . . . is to be understood to indicate the place where a person resides or carries out his usual

occupation'. The *Niemietz* judgment was briefly considered in *R (on the application of Morgan Grenfell & Co Ltd) v Special Commissioner* [2001] 1 All ER 535. In *R (Pamplin) v Law Society* (30 March 2001, unreported), QBD, Art 8 was held to have no application to a transcript of a police interview concerning the applicant's activities as a solicitor's clerk.

Private life

6.15 'Private life' includes 'the physical and moral integrity of the person, including his or her sexual life'[1], and the quality of private life as affected by the amenities of his home[2]. The concept can accommodate a range of issues, including educational provision[3], infliction of corporal[4] and other forms of punishment or treatment falling short of violations of the European Convention on Human Rights, Article 3[5], telephone tapping and electronic surveillance[6], data collection[7], use of family names[8], arbitrary denial of citizenship[9], legal determination of personal status[10] access to information on personal identity[11], forcible medical examination[12], involuntary medical treatment[13], excessive delay in providing medical treatment[14], recognition of transsexualism[15], and the criminalisation of homosexual conduct[16]. Nor was the Court in *Niemietz v Germany* willing to restrict 'private life' to 'an '"inner circle" in which the individual may live his own personal life as he chooses and to exclude therefrom entirely the outside world not encompassed within that circle'. In this case, the Court accepted that the concept of private life 'must also comprise to a certain degree the right to establish and develop relationships with other human beings'. Thus Article 8 could not be assumed 'to exclude activities of a professional or business nature since it is, after all, in the course of their working lives that the majority of people have a significant, if not the greatest, opportunity of developing relationships with the outside world'[17]. This decision illustrates the dynamic interpretation given to 'private life' under Article 8 and one which is wider than 'privacy' as traditionally understood in Anglo–American jurisprudence which is concerned more with the restricted notion of protection against unwanted publicity[18]. Indeed, development of a notion of privacy in Strasbourg jurisprudence is relatively underdeveloped: for example, there is little guidance on such matters as whether publication by the press of an individual's photograph can give rise to an Article 8 issue[19]. This situation can be explained more by the scarcity of applications raising such issues than by any refusal to recognise these claims as worthy of Article 8 discussion. The development of protection against over intrusive surveillance or against unjustified dissemination of information concerning private life through media publication by use of Article 8 principles may be appropriate by courts and other public bodies under the Human Rights Act 1998[20].

1 *X and Y v Netherlands* (1985) A 91, para 22.
2 *Powell and Rayner v United Kingdom* (1990) A 172, para 40. Cf *Botta v Italy* 1998-I, 412, paras 27–35 (the failure of the state to take measures to ensure that private bathing establishments allow access to disabled persons falls outwith the scope of Art 8 since there is no conceivable direct link with the applicant's private life). For an English example concerned with the flooding of a house, see *Marcic v Thames Water Utilities Ltd* [2001] 3 All ER 698; *Marcic v Thames Water Utilities Ltd (No 2)* [2001] 4 All ER 326.
3 *Belgian Linguistics* case (1968) A 6, Law, para 7.
4 *Costello-Roberts v United Kingdom* (1993) A 247-C, para 36.
5 Cf *Raninen v Finland* 1997-VIII, 2804, paras 63–64 (the applicant had been handcuffed when he was taken from prison to a military hospital: while the Court did not exclude the

possibility that Art 8 could be regarded as affording protection in relation to conditions during detention which do not meet the level of severity required by Art 3, in this case, however, there was not sufficient evidence to warrant a finding that there had been a breach of Art 8).

6 Eg *Klass v Germany* (1978) A 28, para 41; *Khan v United Kingdom* (12 May 2000), para 25.

7 Eg *Lingens v Austria* (1986) A 103, paras 37–47.

8 *Stjerna v Finland* (1994) A 299-B.

9 31414/96, *Karassev v Finland* 1999-II, 403 (while the Convention did not guarantee the right to the citizenship of a particular state, in certain cases arbitrary denial of citizenship could give rise to an Art 8 issue).

10 18643/91, *Benes v Austria* (1992) DR 72, 271 (annulment of marriage was an interference in the circumstances with respect for private life).

11 *Gaskin v United Kingdom* (1989) A 160, paras 36–37 (personal file containing history and development of child who had been in foster care).

12 *Matter v Slovakia* (5 July 1999), para 64.

13 *Peters v Netherlands* (1994) DR 77, 75; cf *Re A (Children) (Conjoined Twins: Surgical Separation)* [2001] Fam 147; *NHS Trust A v M* [2001] Fam 348. See also *R (Pretty) v DPP* (18 October 2001, unreported) (assisted suicide).

14 32647/96, *Passannante v Italy* (1998) DR 94, 91 (where a state has assumed responsibilities for health care, an excessive delay which is likely to have an impact on a patient's health may give rise to an Art 8 issue; but, on the facts of the case, there was no evidence of any such impact: inadmissible).

15 Eg *Rees v United Kingdom* (1986) A 106, paras 34–35; *B v France* (1992) A 232-C, paras 48–62.

16 Eg *Dudgeon v United Kingdom* (1983) A 45.

17 *Niemietz v Germany* (1992) A 251-B, at para 29. Cf 23953/94, *Reiss v Austria* (1995) DR 82, 51 (public showing of obscene videos in a bar: the extent to which business premises are covered by Art 8 protection depends on the nature of the premises and the activities carried out, and here the conviction of the applicant did not involve an interference with Art 8 rights). See also *Ward v Scotrail Railways Ltd* 1999 SC 255 (sexual harassment at work).

18 Eg 7654/76, *Van Oosterwijck v Belgium* (1980) B 36, paras 51–52 (report of the Commission).

19 Cf *Friedl v Austria* (1995) 305-B, Commission report, paras 49–52 (police photographing of demonstrators was not an Art 8 violation); 28122/95, *Hutcheon v United Kingdom* (27 November 1996) (75 ft-high security tower build beside applicant's home did not constitute an Art 8 violation since the applicant had not shown she was under surveillance and, in any case, visual surveillance was within normal police duties); 28851–28852/95, *Spencer v United Kingdom* (1998) DR 92, 56 (publication of photograph of celebrity taken with telephoto lens while she was walking in the grounds of private clinic: failure to exhaust domestic remedies). In *R v Loveridge* (11 April 2001, unreported), CA, the filming of persons by the police at a court, without their knowledge, for the purpose of comparing those pictures with CCTV footage taken at a robbery, was held to be an infringement of Art 8(1). For a valuable discussion, see Naismith 'Photographs, Privacy and Freedom of Expression' [1996] EHRLR 150.

20 See para 6.34 below.

Correspondence

6.16 The scope of respect for 'correspondence' is obviously related closely to 'private life' and 'family life'[1]. The actual content of the communication is irrelevant, and business or non-private 'correspondence' also falls within the guarantee[2]. Thus where the challenge is to an interference with expression contained in correspondence, the *lex specialis* governing the application is the European Convention on Human Rights, Article 8, rather than Article 10[3]. The term clearly covers communication by means of letter, telegram[4] and telephone conversations[5], and most certainly use of e-mail. It may also involve the seizure of magazines[6]. The scope of 'respect for correspondence' is in practice unlikely to cause difficulty.

1 Cf *Funke v France* (1993) A 256-A, para 48 (house search and seizures conceded by state to have involved private life; found by Commission additionally to have involved respect for home; and also respect for correspondence by the Court).

2 *A v France* (1993) A 277-B, paras 36–37 (police tapping of conversations relating to serious crimes); *Halford v United Kingdom* 1997-III, 1004, paras 43–52 (interception of conversations of senior police officer relating both to police work and to merely private matters); *Kopp v Switzerland* 1998-II, 524, para 50 (interception of telephone calls made to and from a law firm). In *R (on the application of Morgan Grenfell & Co Ltd) v Special Commissioner* [2001] 1 All ER 535 the Divisional Court appear to have accepted that the instructions to and advice received from counsel in relation to a tax-related scheme devised by a merchant bank, held in the possession of the merchant bank, fell within Art 8. There was no detailed analysis.

3 Eg *Campbell v United Kingdom* (1992) A 233, discussed further at para 6.47 below.

4 21482/93, *Christie v United Kingdom* (1994) DR 78, 119 (applicant's telexes were routinely intercepted; this was held to be an interference with the guarantees of Art 8); *Messina v Italy* (1993) A 257-H, para 30.

5 Telephone conversations may also be covered by the notion of 'private life': *Klass and Ors v Germany* (1978) A 28, para 41. Additionally, telephone calls between family members will also be covered by the notion of 'family life': *Margareta and Roger Andersson v Sweden* (1992) A 226-A, para 72.

6 7308/75, *X v United Kingdom*, DR 16, 32 (seizure of pornographic magazine).

Determining whether there has been an 'interference'

6.17   The duty imposed by the European Convention on Human Rights, Article 8, paragraph (1) upon states to ensure 'respect' for private and family life, home and correspondence can involve both negative and positive duties: that is, obligations not only to refrain from taking state action which interferes with the guarantee, but also in certain circumstances the duty to take positive action to ensure domestic law encourages or ensures effective 'respect' in the conduct of private and family life relationships and activities. Normally, the question whether a state by its action has failed to refrain from interfering[1] with an individual's rights is a straightforward one. In respect of private life, there will be an interference when state action has a direct impact upon an individual's rights as, for example, with the storage and release of information concerning an individual's private life[2]. Similarly, there will be an interference with the right to respect for 'home' through state action such as house searches by state officials[3], or by authorising activity which has a direct impact on enjoyment of the amenities of a home[4]. Delays in determining issues involving parental rights may result in an interference with respect for 'family life'[5]. Impeding the initiation of correspondence (as for example by requiring that a prisoner obtain official permission before contacting a solicitor[6]), delaying a communication (for example, through opening and reading mail[7]), or intercepting a conversation (for example, by telephone tapping[8]) clearly give rise to Article 8 issues, as will the release to a third party of information gathered for a legitimate purpose[9]. Interception by itself will constitute an 'interference', and the question of whether there has been any subsequent use of recordings is not a relevant consideration in this assessment[10].

1 The Court makes use of the notion of 'interference' found in the opening words of para 2 in order to discuss whether any para 1 issue has arisen.

2 *Leander v Sweden* (1987) A 116, para 48.

3 Eg *Funke v France* (1993) A 256-A, para 48; *Murray v United Kingdom* (1994) A 300-A, paras 84–86.
4 *Powell and Rayner v United Kingdom* (1990) A 172, para 40 (noise of aircraft when using Heathrow Airport); *López Ostra v Spain* (1994) A 303-C, para 51 (severe pollution from waste treatment plant close to applicant's home).
5 *H v United Kingdom* (1987) A 120 paras 89–90 (delays in determining whether a child born to father with history of drug abuse and violent behaviour and mother recently discharged from mental hospital should be freed for adoption).
6 *Golder v United Kingdom* (1975) A 18, para 43.
7 *Silver and Ors v United Kingdom* (1983) A 61, paras 83–84; *Campbell v United Kingdom* (1992) A 233, para 32.
8 *Malone v United Kingdom* (1984) A 82, para 64. However, the use of electronic 'bugging devices' in private homes is more likely to fall within respect for private life and home life: cf 12175/86, *Hewitt and Harman v United Kingdom* (1989) DR 67, 88 (applicants subject to telephone and mail intercepts by government surveillance agents; it was not contested that this constituted an interference with the applicants' Art 8 rights); 20271/92 *Redgrave v United Kingdom* (1 September 1993) (the applicant, who was a well-known actress and a member of the Marxist party, discovered an electronic listening device in her house).
9 *Malone v United Kingdom* (1984) A 82 para 84 (release of information to the police on calls made on a telephone line, collated to ensure a telephone subscriber is correctly billed).
10 *Kopp v Switzerland* 1998-II, 524 , paras 51–53 (recorded conversations not disclosed to the prosecutor and subsequently destroyed).

6.18 Some jurisprudence indicates that an individual can indeed be a 'victim' of an interference even where there has been no actual or obvious application of state action. The mere existence of certain legal provisions (for example, those which render certain forms of homosexual conduct criminal[1]) may also be sufficient without the necessity of establishing application of the legal powers: the 'chilling effect' upon an individual's behaviour may in itself constitute an interference with respect for private life. A similar approach may in certain circumstances be taken in regard to covert surveillance which by its very nature is hidden or not obvious. For example, the very existence of legislation authorising telephone tapping which thus creates the 'menace of surveillance' may in certain circumstances amount to an 'interference'[2] where the applicant is a member of a class reasonably likely to be subjected to surveillance measures[3].

1 Eg *Dudgeon v United Kingdom* (1981) A 45, para 41, discussed at para 6.41 below.
2 Eg *Klass and Ors v Germany* (1978) A 28, at para 41, discussed at para 6.24 below.
3 Cf *Malone v United Kingdom* (1984) A 82, para 64; and 12015/86, *Hilton v United Kingdom* (1988) DR 57, 108 (collection of data on the applicant's private life for a security check for an appointment to a post in the broadcasting services; the Commission determined that someone who shows a reasonable likelihood that the authorities have collected and retained data on his or her private life may claim to be a victim of Art 8).

Positive duties

6.19 In addition to this essentially negative requirement to refrain from action impinging upon Article 8 rights, a state may be under a positive obligation to ensure that domestic law adequately reflects the guarantee's requirements. Convention rights must be effective. A failure to provide adequate legal safeguards to ensure implementation of human rights guarantees or an inability or unwillingness to enforce any such safeguard may result in an 'interference', although the choice of means by a state in determining how best to meet these obligations is likely to be covered by a margin of appreciation[1]. Generally applicable rules of private law which fail to ensure 'respect' for Article 8 rights may thus violate Convention guarantees, as in the case of legal rules which permit discriminatory treatment of illegitimate children[2] or make it impossible for a mother to deny the husband's paternity of her child[3] or fail to provide a natural father with an opportunity to be consulted before his child is placed for adoption[4] or allow the surveillance of individuals by other private parties without adequate legal safeguards[5]. Further, the state may be under an obligation to ensure that such rights can be effectively enforced through the provision of legal representation. In *Airey v Ireland*, the appellant had been unable to institute proceedings to enable her to obtain a judicial separation since legal aid was not available for such actions. The European Court of Human Rights ruled that the state was under an obligation to ensure that parties to a marriage were accorded the right to relieve themselves of the legal duty to cohabit when appropriate, and that this right must be 'effectively accessible' through ensuring proper access to a court by the provision of legal aid[6]. Similar concerns will apply to a state's responsibility to enforce the decisions of a court which seek to protect Article 8 rights[7].

However, whether a positive obligation can be assumed to exist under Article 8 is not without difficulty. 'Regard must be had to a fair balance that has to be struck between the general interest of the community and the interests of the individual, the search for which balance is inherent in the whole of the Convention[8]. This assessment is also affected by the extent to which European states have adopted a common approach to a particular issue or whether there remains considerable variation in domestic legal systems[9], an issue which is also relevant in any assessment of whether an interference is 'necessary in a democratic society'. The Court will also be concerned not to lose sight of the essential core of each concept. 'Private life' concerns an individual's physical and psychological integrity and the development of personality through relations with others, and so may involve positive obligations on the part of state authorities[10]. However, claims which concern 'interpersonal relations of such broad and indeterminate scope that there can be no conceivable direct link' between the measures sought by the applicant and his private life, fall outwith the scope of Article 8[11]. In any case, however, the Court has subsequently recognised that 'the boundaries between the State's positive and negative obligations ... do not lend themselves to precise definition' and, indeed, it has accepted that the principles that underlie an assessment of whether there has been a violation of the guarantee are similar[12]. In consequence, the labelling of state obligations as positive or negative may have little practical importance, and the starting-point for any assessment of an Article 8 question will often be the purpose of the guarantee in seeking to provide protection against arbitrary state decision-making or interference.

---

1 *X and Y v Netherlands* (1985) A 91, para 24. For recent discussion, see Ovey 'The Margin of Appreciation and Article 8' (1998) 19 HRLJ 10; Arai 'The Margin of Appreciation Doctrine in the Jurisprudence of Article 8 of the European Convention on Human Rights' (1998) 16 NQHR 41–61.
2 *Marckx v Belgium* (1979) A 31, para 31.
3 *Kroon and Ors v Netherlands* (1994) A 297-C, para 36 (domestic law prevented recognition

of a child by its natural father without a denial of paternity by the applicant's former husband who was untraceable; positive obligation to allow a family to establish legal family ties as soon as possible).

4 *Keegan v Ireland* (1994) A 290, at para 51 ('secret placement of [a] child for adoption without the applicant's knowledge or consent' in circumstances where it was accepted 'family life' existed).

5 Cf 41953/98, *Verliere v Switzerland* (28 June 2001) discussed at para 6.24 below.

6 *Airey v Ireland* (1979) A 32, para 32; cf *Johnston v Ireland* (1986) A 112, paras 51–58 (the Convention is to be read as a whole; and thus there was no positive duty to ensure the availability of divorce when the article was read alongside Art 12).

7 *Hokkanen v Finland* (1994) A 299-A, paras 60–62 (non-enforcement of access and custody rights against the grandparents of child).

8 *Rees v United Kingdom* (1986) A 106, at para 37.

9 Eg *Sheffield and Horsham v United Kingdom* 1998-V, 2011, paras 55–58 (no consensus amongst European states on question of registering change of sex): discussed further at para 6.45 below.

10 Eg *Stubbings v United Kingdom* 1996-IV, 1487, paras 64–65 (effective deterrence of child sex abuse through protection provided by civil and criminal law): discussed at para 6.35 below.

11 *Botto v Italy* 1998-I, 412, at para 35 (physically disabled applicant sought to gain access to beach facilities while on holiday at a place distant from his normal home).

12 *Keegan v Ireland* (1994) A 290, at para 49.

Assessing whether an 'interference' is justified

6.20 In terms of the European Convention on Human Rights, Article 8, paragraph (2), any interference with respect for private or family life or home or correspondence must be 'in accordance with the law', have a legitimate aim, and be 'necessary in a democratic society'. These three requirements are replicated in other provisions of the Convention[1]. The first calls for scrutiny of both the extent to which state activity is covered by domestic legal rules, and also the quality of these rules themselves. The interference must have some legal basis in domestic law[2]. Further, the law must be adequately accessible and possess sufficient clarity. Absolute certainty and clarity are not essential, however, since 'many laws are inevitably couched in terms which, to a greater or lesser extent, are vague and whose interpretation and application are questions of practice'[3], and, as long as there is reasonable foreseeability of the consequences of any action, the requirement will be satisfied[4]. Finally, the law itself must conform to the notion of the rule of law in that there must be some safeguard against arbitrariness in its application[5]. Strasbourg supervision of compliance with domestic legislation is limited: the initial responsibility for securing the interpretation of such law rests with the national courts[6]. In relation to the United Kingdom, this aspect of paragraph (2) has been of particular importance in cases involving interception of communications where domestic law has failed to provide sufficient regulation of state activities[7]. Use of covert surveillance techniques continues to pose questions as to the adequacy of legal guarantees against arbitrary interference with Article 8 rights[8].

1 In particular, in Arts 9–11. See further paras 3.33–3.39 and 3.66–3.78 above.

2 Eg *Eriksson v Sweden* (1989) A 156, para 65 (restrictions on access to children did not have the requisite basis in domestic law).

3 Eg *Olsson v Sweden (No 1)* (1988) A 130, at para 62 (circumstances in which a child may

require to be taken into care 'are so variable that it would scarcely be possible to formulate a law to cover every eventuality').

4 In *Silver and Ors v United Kingdom* (1983) A 61, paras 85–90, the Court considered that Prison Rules which admittedly did not have the force of law could still be taken into account for the purpose of considering whether the test of foreseeability was satisfied.

5 *Malone v United Kingdom* (1984) A 82, paras 67–68.

6 *Chappell v United Kingdom* (1989) A 152-A, paras 52–57.

7 *Malone v United Kingdom* (1984) A 82, paras 69–80 (no legal regulation for issue of warrants authorising interceptions); *Halford v United Kingdom* 1997-III, 1004, para 51 (no legal regulation of interception of domestic calls on internal communications systems operated by public authorities).

8 Cf *Khan v United Kingdom* (12 May 2000), paras 26–28 (failure to provide statutory framework for use by police of electronic 'bugging' device). The Regulation of Investigatory Powers (Scotland) Act 2000, s 65(2) will exempt the police and the security and intelligence agencies from challenge in a court of law and will instead require complaints to be dealt with by a tribunal: see further para 6.29 below. In *Khan v United Kingdom* (12 May 2000), paras 45–47, the Court did not consider that the system of investigation of complaints by the police had the requisite safeguard of independence required by Art 13. In *R v Loveridge* (11 April 2001, unreported), CA, the filming of persons by the police without their knowledge, at a court, was held to be unlawful and therefore contrary to Art 8(2).

6.21   In contrast, the second requirement, that an interference must meet the test of 'legitimate aim', will seldom pose a problem. Invariably any interference can be brought under one of the listed aims of the European Convention on Human Rights, Article 8, paragraph (2): that is, national security, public safety, national economic well-being, prevention of disorder or crime, protection of health, protection of morals, or protection of the rights of others.

6.22   The real complexity lies in the determination of the third requirement: whether any interference is 'necessary in a democratic society'. The phrase suggests some 'pressing social need'[1]; requires the reasons for any interference to be both 'relevant' and 'sufficient'; and involves a test of proportionality in assessing whether the relationship between the action taken and the aim of the intervention is acceptable[2]. The recognition of a margin of appreciation confers a certain amount of discretion on state authorities[3], but the European Court of Human Rights will still expect domestic decision-makers to show that they have addressed this test. Some consideration of contemporary European standards, too, may be relevant to this assessment, since it will be easier to condemn any interference as not being 'necessary in a democratic society' where domestic law or practice is out of line with standards generally applied elsewhere in Europe[4]. Where there has been a particularly grave interference with Article 8 rights, however, the Court's approach to the assessment of necessity is likely to be peremptory. In *Menteş and Ors v Turkey*, for example, where the Court accepted that Turkish security forces had destroyed the applicants' homes and expelled them from their village, the Court simply noted that these measures were 'devoid of justification' in establishing a violation of the provision[5].

1 *Dudgeon v United Kingdom* (1983) A 45, at paras 51 and 53.

2 Eg *Olsson (No 2) v Sweden* (1992) A 250, paras 87–91; *Re S (Sexual Abuse Allegations: Local Authority Response)* [2001] 2 FLR 776.

3 For recent discussion, see Ovey 'The Margin of Appreciation and Article 8' (1998) 19 HRLJ 10; Arai 'The Margin of Appreciation Doctrine in the Jurisprudence of Article 8 of the ECHR' (1998) 16 NQHR 41.

4 Eg *Dudgeon v United Kingdom* (1981) A 45, para 60 (the majority of other European states had decriminalised homosexual behaviour).
5 1997-VIII, 2689, paras 70–73 at para 73.

Procedural safeguards in decision-making

6.23 Within the context of Article 8, the necessity of any interference may also require a determination of whether the decision-making process giving rise to the interference has been fair and has afforded due respect to the rights protected by this guarantee, even although the article itself makes no specific reference to procedural propriety[1]. The approach taken by Strasbourg is that due process requirements help protect against arbitrary decision-making by public authorities in such issues as surveillance or interception of communications[2] and search of premises[3]. This matter is of particular importance in child care cases where there is acceptance of limited international judicial competence in reviewing domestic decisions but a corresponding high level of insistence that proceedings are open and fair. For example, in *W v United Kingdom*, the European Court of Human Rights considered that such decision-making was both sensitive and difficult, and it was thus prepared to accord the local authority a measure of discretion. However, acceptance of a margin of appreciation on the part of decision-makers did not allow the state to exclude the natural parents from deliberations. Since a decision to place a child in care is likely to restrict significantly or even terminate the link with its natural parents, the decision-making process must be such as to ensure that the views of the parents can be ascertained and duly considered[4]. In *McMichael v United Kingdom*, the Court reiterated that failure to accord the parents of a child subject to care proceedings taken through the Scottish system of children's hearings the requisite procedural safeguards could also give rise to an Article 8 issue. While access to a court for the determination of civil rights and obligations was required by Article 6, ensuring 'respect' for family life also implied the provision of fair decision-making procedures during purely administrative proceedings under Article 8[5]. Indeed, there may be a positive obligation on the state to make information held by it available to parents even in the absence of any request. In *TP and KM v United Kingdom*, the failure to determine promptly the question of whether to disclose to a mother the contents of an interview with a young child which led to the child being taken into care was considered a violation of Article 8. During the interview, the child had alleged she had been sexually assaulted and had identified the perpetrator as someone no longer living with her mother, but a doctor and social worker had proceeded upon the basis that the alleged abuser was the mother's boyfriend then living in the home, and had instigated action which resulted in the child being taken into care. When the mother had sought access to the video, this had been opposed. Her solicitors eventually obtained a transcript of the interview in which it was clear that her daughter had exonerated her mother's current boyfriend. Although it accepted that the initial care measure had been justified, the Court concluded that the subsequent procedures had failed to protect the Article 8 interests of both the mother and her daughter. Resolution of the issue whether to disclose the video of the interview and its transcript should have been determined promptly to allow the mother 'an effective opportunity' to challenge the allegations that her daughter could not return safely to her care. While a parent could not enjoy an absolute right to access to all information held by a local authority in these circumstances, 'the potential importance of the contents of such interviews renders it necessary for careful consideration to be given to whether they should be disclosed to the parents'. However, since a local authority could not be regarded as able to determine such a question in an objective way, the authority's failure to submit the issue to the court for determination had deprived her of 'an adequate involvement in the decision-making process concerning the care of her daughter and thereby of the requisite protection of their interests'[6].

1 *W v United Kingdom* (1987) A 121, para 63; *McMichael v United Kingdom* (1995) 307-B, para 87.
2 See para 6.27 below.
3 See para 6.30 below.
4 (1987) A 121, paras 62–70.
5 (1995) 307-B, paras 87–93 (an unmarried father did not enjoy automatic parental rights in Scots law and thus had no standing in proceedings under Art 6. The Court also emphasised the different nature of interests protected by Arts 6 and 8, and in this case the repercussions on 'a fundamental element of the family life' of the applicant was such as to warrant an examination of Art 8. In respect of the mother, these two articles provided parallel safeguards, and in light of the state's concession that children's hearing and sheriff court proceedings were unfair in the context of Art 6, the Court also found Art 8 violations).
6 (10 May 2001), paras 78 –83 at paras 81 and 83 (at para 82: 'the positive obligation on the Contracting State to protect the interests of the family requires that this material be made available to the parent concerned, even in the absence of any request by the parent').

Particular substantive issues arising under Article 8

Surveillance and interception of communications

6.24 Surveillance and interception of communications by police and the security services are accepted as tactics necessitated by the threat posed by organised crime[1]. Use of either will clearly fall within the scope of the European Convention on Human Rights, Article 8 and will invariably involve an 'interference'. Indeed, an applicant need merely establish that he is a member of a class reasonably likely to have his communications intercepted to qualify as a 'victim' for the purposes of Article 8[2]. State interference can involve data-gathering[3], interception of communications[4], or use of electronic listening devices[5]. Monitoring of e-mails would most certainly be covered[6]. It is immaterial that the information gathered or the purpose of the surveillance does not relate to 'private life' but rather to the public interest, for example, in order to investigate crime[7] or to ensure the proper discharge of public office[8]. Nor is it material that the interception takes place on a telephone line belonging to another person[9]. Further, the existence of an interference is assessed irrespective of whether any subsequent use is ever made of the surveillance[10]. However, the state action must probably go beyond mere observation and involve active monitoring of individuals or data-gathering[11]. In *Friedl v Austria*, police officers had photographed and videoed a demonstration, but claimed that no steps had been taken thereafter to try to trace the identity of any of the participants. The European Court of Human Rights accepted that there were no reasons of public policy preventing the case being struck from its list after a friendly settlement was achieved[12]. In *Murray v United Kingdom*, army personnel had entered the applicant's house in order to effect arrests. During the subsequent search, photographs were taken. The Court seems to have accepted as implicit that the retention of the photographs involved an interference with Article 8[13].

There may be, too, a positive obligation on states to ensure effective respect for private life through application of domestic law in regard to surveillance carried out by private individuals or bodies. For example in *Verliere v Switzerland*, the applicant complained of surveillance measures carried out by private detectives. Following a road accident, the applicant had lodged a claim for compensation alleging that she was suffering the after-effects of injuries, but her insurers had doubts about the genuineness of her claim, and had instructed private detectives to investigate. Swiss law, though, recognised both civil and criminal remedies to protect privacy, and the applicant had sought to make use of these processes. The domestic courts had sought to analyse carefully the competing interests of the applicant and of the insurance company, and had decided that the latter's obligation to verify the justification for the claim outweighed those of the applicant. In considering that the domestic courts had thus discharged the positive obligation inherent in ensuring effective respect for private life, the Court declared the application inadmissible[14].

1 *Klass and Ors v Germany* (1978) A 28, paras 46–48. See further, Uglow 'Covert Surveillance and the ECHR' [1999] Crim LR 287.

2 Cf *Halford v United Kingdom* 1997-III, 1004 paras 47–48 and 56–60 (the Court found it established that there was a reasonable likelihood that calls from her office telephone had been intercepted, but not that there had been any interception of calls made from her home telephone); *Klass and Ors v Germany* (1978) A 28, para 41; 12015/86, *Hilton v United Kingdom* (1988) DR 57, 108 (no reasonable likelihood that security services had retained personal information).

3 Eg *Leander v Sweden* (1987) A 116, para 48 (secret police file containing details of applicant's private life); 12015/86, *Hilton v United Kingdom* (1988) DR 57, 108 (collection of data for security check); 23413/94, *Christie v United Kingdom* (1994) DR 78, 119 (interception of telexes); *Amann v Switzerland* (16 February 2000), paras 65–67 (storage of cards concerning details of applicant's private life). Cf 25099/94, *Martin v Switzerland* (1995) DR 81,136 (archiving of police register for 50 years may not involve an interference).

4 Eg *Malone v United Kingdom* (1984) A 82, para 64 (telephone tapping). See also *R v P* [2001] 2 WLR 463.

5 *Khan v United Kingdom* (12 May 2000), para 25 (evidence obtained by tape-recording of conversations).

6 The Regulation of Investigatory Powers (Scotland) Act 2000 now regulates telephone and e-mail surveillance: see para 6.29 below.

7 *A v France* (1993) A 277-B, para 36–37 (monitoring of murder suspect]).

8 Eg *Halford v United Kingdom* 1997-III, 1004, paras 44–52 (interception of calls made by a senior police officer on internal communications system).

9 *Lambert v France* 1998-V, 2230, para 21.

10 *Kopp v Switzerland* 1998-II, 524.

11 The purpose of any surveillance may also help determine the question of whether there has been any interference with Art 8 rights: *Malone v United Kingdom* (1984) A 82, para 84 (Art 8 issue where information gathered for a legitimate purpose is disclosed to a third party for another reason).

12 (1995) A 305-A (Austria notified the Court that it was introducing independent administrative tribunals to deal with complaints of police photography).

13 (1994) A 300-A, para 88. Cf 32200–32201/96, *Herbecq and Association 'Ligue des Droits de l'Homme' v Belgium* (1998) DR 92, 92 (surveillance without recording of public places involved surveillance of public conduct, and did not give rise to an Art 8 issue).

14 41953/98 (28 June 2001).

6.25   The aim of any surveillance will invariably fall within one or more of the recognised interests such as national security, public safety, or prevention of crime or disorder. Thus, the initial focus of the case law is likely to be in determining whether the interference is 'in accordance with the law'. Most obviously, an unauthorised interception, which takes place without legal basis, will constitute a violation of the European Convention on Human Rights, Article 8[1]. However, the law must also provide sufficient legal regulation to protect against arbitrary interference: that is, the law must also meet the tests of accessibility and foreseeability[2], and legal rules which leave the authorities with too much latitude will fail this test[3]. In *Malone v United Kingdom*, the European Court of Human Rights found that the scope and manner of exercise of powers to intercept communications were not prescribed with sufficient certainty, and reiterated that 'in accordance with law' not only referred to the existence of domestic law but also to its quality, which had to be compatible with the notion of the rule of law. Domestic law must thus determine with sufficient clarity both the scope and manner of exercise of any discretionary authority conferred[4]. The legal situation in Britain has, on a number of occasions, failed to meet these standards. In *Halford v United Kingdom*, the Court found that domestic law failed to regulate the monitoring or interception of calls made on an internal telecommunications system[5]. More recently, in *Khan v United Kingdom*, the use of electronic covert listening devices by English police forces, regulated only by Home Office guidelines which were neither binding nor publicly accessible, were found not to fulfil the demands of Article 8[6].

1 *A v France* (1993) A 277-B, paras 38–39 (unauthorised interception); *Foxley v United Kingdom* (20 June 2000), para 35 (interception of mail after expiry of order).
2 *Lambert v France* 1998-V, 2230, paras 23–28.
3 *Petra v Romania* 1998-VII, 2844, para 37; cf *Rotaru v Romania* (4 May 2000), paras 55–63 (complaint that the Romanian intelligence service held a file containing information on the applicant's private life and that it was impossible to refute the untrue information that he had been a member of an extremist political organisation: domestic law did not define the kind of information that could be recorded, the categories of people against whom or the circumstances in which surveillance measures could be taken, the procedure to be followed, or limits on the age of information held or the length of time for which it could be kept; and, accordingly, domestic law did not indicate with reasonable clarity the scope and manner of exercise of the relevant discretion).
4 (1984) A 82, at paras 67–68. This decision resulted in the enactment of the Interception of Communications Act 1985. See too *Valenzuela Contreras v Spain* 1998-V, 1909, paras 49–61. See further Jantaramassagarn 'UK Wiretapping Law: Public versus Private Systems, Warrants and Admission of Intercepted Materials' (1999) 4 Comm Law 95.
5 1997-III, 1004. See McDermott and Miller 'Monitoring Calls – A Potential Human Rights Problem at Work' (1999) 4 Comms L 186.
6 (12 May 2000), paras 26–28 (the Court noted that the Police Act 1997 now provides a statutory framework for such practices). See too 27237/95, *Govell v United Kingdom* (14 January 1998) (drilling of hole into living room wall and installation of surveillance devices; the Commission noted the lack of any statutory framework to regulate the use of covert listening devices, and that Home Office Guidelines were neither legally binding nor publicly accessible: violation of Art 8, and of Art 13 since the system of investigation of complaints by the Police Complaints Authority did not 'meet the requisite standards of independence needed to constitute sufficient protection against the abuse of authority' (at para 69)); 48539/99, *Allan v United Kingdom* (use of covert surveillance against a detainee in order to obtain evidence: communicated).

6.26   In *R v Loveridge*[1], the filming of persons by the police at a court, without the persons' knowledge, was held to be unlawful under domestic law and therefore in contravention also of the European Convention on Human Rights, Article 8.

1   (11 April 2001, unreported), CA.

SAFEGUARDS AGAINST ABUSE

6.27   Determination of whether surveillance or interception of communications is 'necessary in a democratic society' tends to focus upon the assessment of the existence and effectiveness of safeguards prohibiting misuse. Certainly, it would be most difficult for a state to justify why the interception of communications with a legal adviser was necessary. In *Foxley v United Kingdom*, a postal packet re-direction order made under the English Insolvency Act 1986 in favour of the trustee in bankruptcy had led to the opening, reading and copying of correspondence from the applicant's legal advisers. The European Court of Human Rights could not be persuaded that there was any pressing social need for this, bearing in mind the principles of confidentiality and professional privilege attaching to relations between a lawyer and his client[1]. Otherwise, consideration of the reasons for any interception or monitoring are normally subsumed by an assessment of whether the legal framework provides adequate safeguards against arbitrary application or misuse. The basis for this approach is twofold: first, a wide margin of appreciation covers application of surveillance which aims to protect national security or to prevent or investigate criminal activity; and second, the article cannot require state disclosure that the surveillance has been ordered or carried out since this would defeat the very purpose of the measure[2]. Thus the Court will be more concerned to ensure that domestic safeguards have taken into account circumstances such as

> 'the nature, scope and duration of the possible measures, the grounds required for ordering such measures, the authorities competent to permit, carry out and supervise such measures, and the kind of remedy provided by the national law'[3].

Supervisory control of the exercise of executive action is in principle most appropriately discharged by judicial officers[4], although other arrangements which provide independent and 'effective and continuous control' of surveillance are acceptable[5]. Sufficient safeguards against arbitrariness were assumed to exist in *Leander v Sweden*[6] which concerned the collection of personal data. However, in the related cases of *Kruslin v France* and *Huvig v France* safeguards against arbitrariness in telephone tapping were considered wanting[7].

1   (20 June 2001), paras 43–46, citing *Campbell v United Kingdom* (1992) A 233, discussed at para 6.47 below. The principle also applies to correspondence with the Strasbourg Court: *Petra v Romania* 1998-VII, 2844, paras 35–36. Cf 28808/95, *Valle v Finland* (7 December 2000) (complaints of applicant subject to compulsory psychiatric care that restrictions on visits and telephone calls were unlawful, and (in terms of Art 13) that there was no effective remedy in domestic law to challenge restrictions on telephone calls from his lawyer: friendly settlement achieved).

2 *Klass and Ors v Germany* (1978) A 28, at para 58 (failure to inform a person subjected to surveillance cannot be incompatible with Art 8 since 'it is this very fact which ensures the efficacy of the "interference" ').
3 *Klass v Germany* (1978) A 28, at para 50.
4 Eg 10439–10441/83, *Mersch v Luxembourg* (1985) DR 43, 34.
5 *Klass v Germany* (1978) A 28, at para 56 (Parliamentary Board and a commission both of which were independent of those carrying out the surveillance and able to give objective rulings on measures ordered by the relevant government minister); 21482/53, *Christie v United Kingdom* (1994) DR 78, 119 (British arrangements (an independent tribunal subject to scrutiny by a commissioner holding high judicial office) contained in the Interception of Communications Act 1985 were considered acceptable).
6 (1987) A 116, paras 54–56 (scope of discretion to make entries in police register was limited by law (entries required to satisfy the test of necessity for attainment of specific objectives) and detailed provision of conditions had to be satisfied before information could be communicated).
7 (1990) A 176-A, paras 34–36 and (1990) A 176-B, paras 33–34 (categories of persons liable to interception not defined; no limits on duration of intercepts; no specification of procedure for reports; procedure for transmitting reports intact unspecified). See, too, *Kopp v Switzerland* 1998-II, 524 (interception of calls made to a lawyer without adequate safeguards for client confidentiality; and failure to determine with sufficient certainty the scope, etc of interceptions).

6.28   Further challenges to British law and practice are possible. Scrutiny of whether CCTV is 'in accordance with law'[1] and is accompanied by adequate safeguards will take place in the pending case of *Peck v United Kingdom* which involves the disclosure and subsequent television broadcast of video footage taken by a local authority of an incident involving the applicant's attempted suicide[2]. Data-gathering by police forces involving retention of DNA samples[3] and matching personal data held by different government agencies[4] may give rise to questions involving compatibility with the European Convention on Human Rights, Article 8.

1 The statutory basis for CCTV installation is minimal: the Criminal Justice and Public Order Act 1994, s 163 merely provides that local authorities may establish CCTV systems in consultation with chief constables. Planning control requirements were largely removed by the Town and Country Planning (General Permitted Development) (Scotland) Amendment Order 1996, SI 1996/1266.
2 44647/98 (15 May 2001) (application declared admissible). In *R v Brentwood Council, ex p Peck* (1998) EMLR 697 the domestic courts determined that a local authority had the power to distribute the video footage. See further Wadham 'Remedies for Unlawful CCTV Surveillance' (2000) 150 NLJ 1173 and 1236. Subsequent complaints to the Broadcasting Standards Commission and to the Independent Television Commission were upheld, but a third complaint to the Press Complaints Commission was rejected because of the events having taken place in a public street open to public view. Under Art 8, however, there must be a genuine doubt as to whether the test of proportionality is met. This issue in part may now have been cured by the Data Protection Act 1998 which requires registration of CCTV systems and compliance with the principles of data protection; before this Act came into force, prohibition of misuse of CCTV relied primarily upon a voluntary and largely ignored code of practice (BS 7958).
3 Cf *Under the Microscope: Thematic Inspection Report on Scientific and Technical Support*, report of HM Inspector of Constabulary for England and Wales (2000), para 2.23 (English police forces are holding DNA samples taken from suspects found not guilty or where the prosecution is discontinued without legal authority; it is estimated that in the lifetime of the National DNA database, as many as 50,000 samples may be being held when they should have been removed). In Scotland, retention of samples taken from people who are subsequently found not guilty is prohibited by the Criminal Procedure (Scotland) Act 1995, s 18.
4 Cf *Report of the Data Protection Commissioner* (HC Paper 575 (2000)) at para 2.23 (proposals for increased data-matching as part of the national fraud initiative 'may well contravene the Human Rights Act . . . because of lack of safeguards for individuals').

DOMESTIC LEGISLATIVE REFORM

6.29 In order to secure compliance with the European Convention on Human Rights, Article 8, the use of covert investigation techniques in Scotland was put on a statutory footing by the Regulation of Investigatory Powers (Scotland) Act 2000. That Act applies to the Scottish police and the National Criminal Intelligence Service. The use by Scottish police of some other techniques (interference with property and wireless telegraphy) was already covered by the Police Act 1997. UK public authorities that operate in Scotland, such as HM Customs and Excise and the Security Service, are regulated by the Regulation of Investigatory Powers Act 2000. The Intelligence Services Act 1994 and the Police Act 1997 also apply to UK public authorities operating in Scotland. The focus of the Regulation of Investigatory Powers (Scotland) Act 2000 is on 'directed surveillance', 'intrusive surveillance' and the conduct and use of covert human intelligence sources. 'Directed surveillance' is surveillance which is covert and which is undertaken in relation to a specific investigation in order to obtain information about, or identify, a particular person or to determine who is involved in a matter under investigation. 'Intrusive surveillance' is surveillance which is covert and carried out in relation to anything taking place on residential premises or in any private vehicle. This type of surveillance may take place by means either of a person or device located inside a residential premises or a private vehicle, or by means of a device placed outside which provides a product of equivalent quality and detail to the product which would be obtained from a device located inside. The use of 'covert human intelligence sources' covers the use of informants, agents and undercover officers. Less intrusive forms of surveillance where there is a general awareness on the part of the public that surveillance is taking place, such as CCTV for crime prevention, public order or traffic management purposes, are excluded from the authorisation process.

Search of premises

6.30 Similar issues arise in respect of search of premises[1] as with surveillance or interception of communications. It is also accepted that searches undertaken in order to obtain evidence may be necessary in the fight against crime; and the European Court of Human Rights will consider the relevancy and sufficiency of any reasons adduced to justify a search primarily by ensuring that the relevant domestic legislation and practice provide adequate and effective safeguards against abuse[2]. Warrants authorising searches which are drawn in broad terms are unlikely to satisfy the European Convention on Human Rights, Article 8[3]. In *Funke v France,* customs officers had searched the appellant's house and had removed certain documents. The appellant argued that the search was not properly prescribed by domestic law, but the Court declined to address this question as it was able to dispose of the matter on the basis of lack of effective procedural safeguards against abuse of search powers. Here, customs officers had exclusive competence in assessing crucial matters such as the length and scale of any customs inquiry. When this was considered along with the lack of any requirement of a judicial warrant for a search, the Court was of the opinion that domestic law was 'too lax and full of loopholes' for the interference to have been strictly proportionate to the legitimate aim of protecting the economic well-being of the country[4]. In contrast, in *Camenzind v Switzerland* the Court accepted that relevant Swiss law did provide effective safeguards. The case involved a search in order to seize an unauthorised cordless telephone that the applicant had admitted having used. Relevant safeguards included the authorisation of searches by warrant which could only be issued by a limited number of designated and senior officers on carefully prescribed grounds, and the requirement that searches were carried out by specially trained officials with the presence of a public officer at the premises to ensure that the search was properly conducted[5].

1   Including business premises in certain circumstances: *Niemietz v Germany* (1992) A 251-B, paras 29–33, discussed at para 6.15 above. Cf 12474/86, *Kanthak v Germany* (1988) DR 58, 94 (question whether the applicant's camping car could be considered a 'home' was left unresolved).
2   *Camenzind v Switzerland* 1997-VIII, 2880, para 45. As to the granting of search warrants under the Misuse of Drugs Act 1971, s 23, see *Birse v HM Advocate* 2000 SCCR 505.
3   Eg *Niemietz v Germany* (1992) A 251-B, para 37; cf *Chappell v United Kingdom* (1989) A 152-A, paras 59–61 (English 'Anton Piller' order sufficiently limited in scope). Cf 62002/00, *Tamosius v United Kingdom* (premises of a lawyer searched under warrant by the Inland Revenue on two occasions on suspicion of tax fraud without the presence of any independent observer; the lawfulness of the warrants had been upheld as not being dependent upon specificity but only upon reasonable suspicion: communicated). Procedure under the Administration of Justice (Scotland) Act 1972, s 1 was reformed with effect from 2 October 2000 so as to ensure compliance with Art 8. See RCS 1994, Ch 64, as substituted by the Act of Sederunt (Rules of the Court of Session Amendment No 4) (Applications under s 1 of the Administration of Justice (Scotland) Act 1972) 2000, SSI 2000/319; and Charteris 'Sun Sets on Dawn Raids' 2000 SLT (News) 271.
4   (1993) A 256-A, paras 51–59 at para 57. See too *Crémieux v France* (1995) A 256-B, paras 38–40; and *Miailhe v France* (1993) A 256-C, paras 36–39. As to tax investigations, see also *R (Banque Internationale à Luxembourg) v Inland Revenue Commissioners* [2000] STC 708.
5   1997-VIII, 2880, paras 41–47.

6.31   The method of carrying out a search must also be proportionate[1]. In *McLeod v United Kingdom*, police officers had secured entry to a house to assist the applicant's former husband and his solicitor to remove certain items of property following a court order requiring the applicant to hand over the property. The former husband honestly but mistakenly believed that agreement to collect the items had been reached, but the police officers failed to check the terms of the court order when advising the applicant's mother (the applicant herself not being present initially) that their action was based upon a judicial instruction. The domestic courts had accepted that the police officers had behaved properly, since they had believed that there was a real and imminent risk of a breach of the peace. While accepting that the power of the police to enter private premises without a warrant to deal with or prevent a breach of the peace was defined with sufficient precision and was clearly for the legitimate aim of preventing disorder or crime, the European Court of Human Rights found that that the means employed by the police officers were disproportionate to the legitimate aim pursued. Scrutiny of the court order would have shown that the property was to be handed over rather than collected and that the applicant still had some days left in which to do so; further, the appellant's absence when the police arrived should have suggested there was then minimal risk of disorder[2].

1 E g *Murray and Ors v United Kingdom* (1994) A 300-A, paras 90–94 (entry into and search of a family home by army personnel in order to arrest the first applicant who was suspected of involvement in terrorist activities was accompanied by the confinement of other members of her family in another room for a short period; the manner of the search was judged proportionate in view of the threat posed to democratic society by organised terrorism).
2 1998-VII, 2724, paras 38–58.

Disclosure of personal data

6.32   The disclosure of personal data without the express consent of the individual concerned may give rise to Article 8 considerations[1]. Medical records in particular may contain highly sensitive information about an individual, and ensuring respect for the confidentiality of these records is considered to be crucial in order to maintain public confidence in the health services[2]. This aspect of Article 8 essentially protects the patient or client, although justification for the confidentiality of records may well also involve the protection of professional advisers and other third parties[3]. Where personal records have been disclosed, the questions which will arise will relate to the relevance and sufficiency of the reasons, and the extent to which the disclosure was 'subjected to important limitations and accompanied by effective and adequate safeguards against abuse'[4]. These issues will be of particular importance in instances where disclosure of personal information has been made in accordance with regulations or upon the order of a court during the course of legal proceedings. In *M S v Sweden,* a state clinic had disclosed the applicant's health records, including information that she had undergone an abortion, to the social insurance office which was dealing with her claim for compensation for an alleged injury sustained while at work. The European Court of Human Rights accepted that Article 8 applied as it could not be inferred that the applicant, in initiating the claim for compensation, had waived her right to confidentiality. The assessment of whether the disclosure of the records was necessary had been left to the state authorities without allowing the applicant the opportunity to be consulted or informed beforehand. It was accepted that this interference was in accordance with domestic law and had the legitimate aim of determining whether public funds should compensate her for the alleged injury and thus was in the interests of the 'economic well-being of the country'. However, the applicant challenged the disclosure of the abortion and the absence of her participation in the determination that disclosure of this information was 'necessary in a democratic society'. The Court accepted that the state had a genuine need to transmit medical records from one public authority to another to allow it to verify whether the applicant met the tests required for compensation, and that this information had indeed been relevant to the determination of the claim. Further, and crucially, the information disclosed was itself subject to protection ensuring it remained confidential. Not only clinical staff but also the social insurance officers who received the data were under duties enforceable by sanction to treat the information as confidential. Accordingly there had been no breach of Article 8[5].

1 For discussion of English law, see Barber 'Privacy and the Police: Private Right, Public Right, or Human Right?' [1998] PL 19. EU law now provides safeguards in this area: Directive (EC) 95/46, implemented in the UK by virtue of the Data Protection Act 1998. See Auldhouse 'Data Protection, Privacy and the Media' (1999) 4 Comms L 8–15.

2 *M S v Sweden* 1997–IV, 1437, paras 35 and 41. See too Committee of Ministers Recommendation No R (97) 5 on the protection of medical data (13 February1997). For discussion of English criminal procedure, see 'Access to Medical Records: PACE and Excluded Material' [1996] Med L Rev 319; Corker 'Involuntary Disclosure of Private Medical Records' (1998) 38 Med Sci Law 138. The *M S* judgment was distinguished in *De Keyser Ltd v Wilson* [2001] IRLR 324, which concerned references to a litigant's private life in the opposing party's letter of instruction to their medical expert.

3 Cf *Gaskin v United Kingdom* (1989) A 160, para 49.

4 *Z v Finland* 1997-I, 323, at para 103 (disclosure of applicant's infection with HIV from confidential medical records, in proceedings where applicant's husband was prosecuted for attempting manslaughter of another by deliberately subjecting her to risk of HIV infection; and limited period of confidentiality of ten years also held to be in breach of Art 8).

5 1997-IV, 1437, paras 31–44. The Scottish procedures governing the recovery of medical (and other) records for use in legal proceedings are capable of meeting the issues identified in these cases. The court will order their recovery only if they are relevant to the issues in the proceedings; and a commissioner appointed by the court will ensure that only documents falling within the scope of the court's order are recovered (unless, by agreement between the parties, the optional procedure is adopted). In addition, the party recovering the documents is under an obligation not to use them for any purpose other than the conduct of the proceedings in respect of which they have been recovered: *Iomega Corporation v Myrica (UK) Ltd (No 2)* 1999 SLT 796. A difficulty under Art 8 might however arise where the documents concerned a person who was neither a party nor the haver. In such a situation, 'respect' for that person's private life would probably require that he be given intimation of the application for the recovery of the documents.

6.33   Conversely, an Article 8 issue may arise in respect of a refusal to grant an individual access to his personal records held by public authorities. In *Gaskin v United Kingdom*, the applicant had been taken into care as a six-month old child following his mother's death and had been cared for by a succession of foster parents. After attaining majority, he had attempted to gain access to his case papers which contained various reports written by his doctors, teachers, social workers, and probation officers. This access was denied, however, on the basis that the effective conduct of a child care system justified the treating of such reports as confidential except where the express consent of the contributor to disclosure had been given. The European Court of Human Rights accepted that 'confidentiality of public records is of importance for receiving objective and reliable information' and that this could also be necessary to protect third parties who contributed information. However, the state was also under an obligation to ensure that the applicant's right to receive 'the information necessary to know and to understand their childhood' was properly considered when the consent of a contributor to disclosure was not available through, for example, the involvement of an independent authority which could make an assessment of the competing interests between state and individual[1].

1 (1989) A 160, at paras 42–49. Cf *Leander v Sweden* (1987) A 116, which the Court distinguished in *Gaskin*. See too 39393/98, *M G v United Kingdom* (3 July 2001) (denial of access to personal records: admissible).

Privacy and press freedom

6.34   Incorporation into domestic law of the European Convention on Human Rights guarantee of 'respect for private life' may give rise to questions as to the adequacy of protection against media intrusion[1]. The Human Rights Act 1998 will not necessitate the formulation of a new law of privacy, but it is likely have a significant effect upon the Press Complaints Commission and associated bodies such as the Broadcasting Standards Commission[2]. It is not inconceivable that the domestic courts, too, may wish to extend protection by reflecting Article 8 considerations in their decisions[3]. Intrusions of privacy purportedly justified as being in the public interest but which disclose merely immoral or offensive behaviour or which may inhibit the development of relationships (including in certain cases professional relationships) may require to be subjected to more rigorous tests of public interest and proportionality.

The lack of any specific right of privacy in Scots law will not in itself give rise to an Article 8 issue as it has been accepted that English law (where similarly there is no such right) protects privacy through other means such as the civil law of defamation[4]. In any case, the scope of Article 8 is not as broad as proponents of a new domestic law of privacy would perhaps wish. The Commission has accepted that respect for private life includes 'the right to privacy, the right to live as far as one wishes, protected from publicity'[5]. However, this is subject to the qualification that the facts disclose a situation in which there is an expectation of privacy. There will be no such expectation where an individual by his own actions brings 'his private life into contact with public life'[6]. Nor is there any Article 8 issue where objection is taken to a photograph which has been taken in such a way as to depict what could have been seen by any member of the public[7], presumably as long as this involves a record of observation rather than more active surveillance or data collection[8]. In any case, the question of privacy and press intrusion cannot be considered in isolation from the consideration of freedom of expression under Article 10[9] which includes the freedom 'to receive and impart information and ideas without interference by public authority. Under Article 10, there is a presumption in favour of freedom of speech as a means to the enhancement of democracy and development of the person: 'pluralism, tolerance and broadmindedness' are crucial to the maintenance of democratic society[10]. Differing levels of protection of speech are thus justified, depending upon the issue at stake. Political expression and debate on matters of public concern call for the highest safeguards, and this can imply reduced protection for the personal privacy of those in the political arena who have voluntarily placed themselves in a public position of accountability[11]. Balancing respect for private life with freedom of expression is thus likely to involve consideration of how best to maintain the Press's role in contributing to the democratic accountability of political figures with the need to reflect fundamental Convention values such as tolerance and broadmindedness.

1 These questions were discussed, but not answered, in *Douglas v Hello! Ltd* [2001] 2 WLR 992. See also *Clibbery v Allan* [2001] 2 FLR 819 (family proceedings in chambers); and *R (British Broadcasting Corporation) v Broadcasting Standards Commission* [2000] 3 WLR 1327 (surreptitious filming inside shops).

2 Human Rights Act 1998, s 6(3) (definition of 'public authorities'): see paras 1.72–1.76 above. Cf Singh 'Privacy and the Media after the Human Rights Act' [1998] EHRLR 712; Whittle 'The Human Rights Act: a View from the Broadcasting Standards Commission' (1999) 4 Comm Law 3; Pinker 'Human Rights and Self-Regulation of the Press' (1999) 4 Comm Law 51.

3 See further, Thomson 'Privacy and Prior Restraint after the Human Rights Act' (2000) 5 Com Law 54; Murdoch 'Incorporation and Interpretation of Guarantees for Respect for Private Life: A Threat to Press Freedom?' in Miller (ed) *Human Rights: A Modern Agenda* (2000) pp 51–66. For an international and comparative study, see Michael *Privacy and Human Rights* (1994).

4 27436/95 and 28406/95, *Stewart-Brady v United Kingdom* (1997) DR 90, 45 (a state need not provide legal aid for actions of defamation for harm to reputation). Cf 28851–28852/95, *Spencer v United Kingdom* (1998) DR 92, 56 (complaint concerning newspaper article containing details of personal and family problems; action for breach of confidence now sufficiently certain in domestic law, and the applicants could have been expected to utilise this: inadmissible for failure to exhaust domestic remedies). For discussion of whether Scots common law could provide adequate protection for privacy, see Rodger 'Human Rights: Surveillance and Intrusion' in Mahoney and Mahoney *Human Rights in the Twenty-First Century: A Global Challenge* (1993) pp 817–827.

5 Cf 6825/74, *X v Iceland* (1976) DR 5, 86.

6 Cf 6959/75, *Brüggeman and Scheuten v Germany* (1977) DR 10, 100 at 115.

7 Naismith 'Photographs, Privacy and Freedom of Expression' [1996] EHRLR 150 at p 153; however, at p 156 the author cites the Commission decision in 20683/92, *N v Portugal* (20 February 1995) in which the conviction of a magazine publisher for defamation and invasion of privacy involving the publication of photographs of a businessman involved in sexual activities with a number of women was accepted as proportionate for protection of the rights of individuals for the purposes of Art 10. See further para 6.15 above.

8 Cf *Friedl v Austria* (1995) A 305-A, discussed at para 6.24 above.

9 Cf the Human Rights Act 1998, s.12 which provides that courts are to have particular regard to the importance of freedom of expression in deciding whether to grant any relief which could affect this right; further, where the material in issue is 'journalistic, literary or artistic', courts are also to have regard to the extent to which the material has (or is about to) become available in the public domain, whether it would be in the public interest for the material to be published, and any relevant privacy code (such as the Press Complaints Commission's code of 26 November 1997). See Rasaiah 'Current Legislation, Privacy and the Media in the UK' (1998) 3 Comm Law 183; and Samuels 'The Rights of Privacy and Freedom of Expression: The Drafting Challenge' (1999) 20 Stat LR 66.

10 *Handyside v United Kingdom* (1976) A 24, at para 49.

11 Eg *Lingens v Austria* (1986) A 103, at paras 42–44 (publication of articles criticising the Austrian Chancellor's fitness for office had resulted in a successful private defamation action; the Court considered that this was a form of censure likely to inhibit political discussion and debate and thus 'liable to hamper the press in performing its task as purveyor of information and public watchdog'. Further, 'the limits of acceptable criticism are . . . wider as regards a politician as such than as regards a private individual' since a politician 'inevitably and knowingly lays himself open to close scrutiny of his every word and deed'. Accordingly, while protection of reputation is a recognised ground for state interference and will extend to protection of the reputation of politicians, 'in such cases the requirements of such protection have to be weighed in relation to the interests of open discussion of political issues'). In *Fayed v United Kingdom* (1994) A 294-B, at para 75, the Court extended this to businessmen actively involved in the affairs of major public companies who also 'inevitably and knowingly lay themselves open to close scrutiny of all their acts' not only by the media but also by inspectors and other institutions representing the public interest. It would be difficult to extend this principle further to include media celebrities: the private life of a film star is unlikely to involve questions of democratic accountability. See further paras 7.27–7.29 below.

Protection against violations of physical and moral integrity

6.35   The European Convention on Human Rights, Article 8 provides additional protection of physical and moral integrity. In this respect, it complements protection available under Article 3 in that circumstances which do not meet the threshold test for inhuman and degrading treatment or punishment may nevertheless fall within the scope of respect for private life. Indeed, the guarantee may impose positive obligations upon a state to adopt measures or to take action to further 'respect' for Article 8 concerns[1]. In *Costello-Roberts v United Kingdom*, for example, the majority of the European Court of Human Rights did not consider that the corporal punishment inflicted on a young school pupil in a private school could be said to have attained the minimum level of severity required to constitute inhuman or degrading treatment under Article 3, but did accept that Article 8 in certain situations could afford some additional protection for the physical integrity of an individual. However, on the facts of the application (and taking into account that the schooling of a child 'necessarily involves some degree of interference with his or her private life'), no violation of Article 8 was established[2]. The positive obligation to ensure protection for physical or moral integrity may also take the form of providing effective deterrence and punishment through criminal prosecution. In *X and Y v Netherlands*, a mentally handicapped 16-year-old girl had been sexually assaulted while resident in a home. The girl's father had complained to the police on her behalf, but the public prosecutor had decided not to institute proceedings since domestic law required such complaints to be made by the alleged victim. The Court ruled that the lack of proceedings in the criminal courts failed to provide the appellant with sufficient protection since the opportunity available to the victim to raise a civil action would have been insufficient on its own to vindicate Article 8 requirements in light of the 'fundamental values and essential aspects of private life' involved in the particular case[3]. Whether adequate protection in this manner has been provided is a question to be determined on the particular facts of the case[4]. In *Stubbings v United Kingdom*, victims of child sex abuse had found themselves prevented by a limitation statute from raising civil actions against the perpetrators. In finding that Article 8 had not been violated, the Court noted the provision did not require the provision of unlimited civil remedies, certainly where the criminal law also provided protection where there was sufficient evidence for a prosecution[5]. Paradoxically, discharge of Article 8 responsibilities involving the protection of vulnerable individuals may itself give rise to other considerations under this guarantee. While the registration of sex offenders will generally be considered to be justifiable, this will probably require to be accompanied by adequate safeguards to ensure that any legitimate disclosure of this information to third parties is not abused[6].

1 Cf *Whiteside v United Kingdom* (1994) DR 76, 80 (refusal of the court to grant injunction against the husband in a case of alleged domestic violence: inadmissible on account of failure to exhaust domestic remedies, but the Commission noted there could exist a positive duty to protect against persistent and distressing harassment).
2 (1993) A 247-C, at para 36 (cf paras 27–28: a state remains responsible for a breach of Convention guarantees committed in the course of the provision of education in a private school, since the assumption of responsibilities in the field of regulation of education is sufficient to establish liability in certain circumstances in respect of private educational institutions).
3 (1985) A 91, at paras 23–27 (the Court decided it was not necessary to consider the application of Art 3; nor whether Art 14 was relevant). Cf 39272/98, *M C v Bulgaria* (alleged failure of the public prosecutor to investigate effectively a complaint of rape, and legal requirement of proof of actual physical resistance in domestic law: communicated). See further Andrews 'The Right to take Proceedings for Sexual Assaults' (1985) 10 EL Rev 295. For domestic discussion, see *Ward v Scotrail Railways Ltd* 1999 SC 255 (sexual harassment).
4 Cf *Osman v United Kingdom* 1998-VIII, 3124, paras 128–130 (not established that the police knew or ought to have known at the time that an individual represented a real and immediate risk; nor was there any evidence implicating the individual in attacks on the family home).

5 1996-IV, 1487, paras 58–67.
6 The Sex Offenders Act 1997 covers not only those convicted of an offence (or found not guilty by reason of insanity), but also those cautioned for any offence covered by Sch 1. The provision applies to crimes committed before the entry into force of the statute, and thus gave rise to Art 7 consideration, but the Commission considered registration not to have any penal effect: 40146/98 *Ibbotson v UK* (21 October 1998) (conviction in 1996 of applicant and imprisonment, discussed by Ovey at [1999] Crim LR 153). Cf Cobley 'Keeping Track of Sex Offenders – Part 1 of the Sex Offenders Act 1997' (1997) 60 MLR 69. There is now a question whether the inclusion on the register of a conviction for homosexual activity with a consenting male under 18 is still appropriate in light of *Sutherland v United Kingdom*, discussed at para 6.44 below. Cf Soothill and Francis 'Sexual Reconviction and the Sex Offenders Act 1997' (1997) 147 NLJ 1285 and 1324; Barber 'Privacy and the Police: Private Right, Public Right, or Human Right?' [1998] PL 19; Power 'Gay Men and Part 1 of the Sex Offenders Act 1997' (1998) 1 Web JCLI; Power 'The Crime and Disorder Act 1998: Sex Offenders, Privacy and the Police' [1999] Crim LR 3.

Child custody and access; and state assumption of care

6.36   The European Convention on Human Rights, Article 8 provides safeguards against arbitrary interference by the state in the development and maintenance of family relationships[1], including decisions concerning the regulation of custody or access of children upon divorce or separation or the removal of children from their parents[2]. Invariably, cases focus upon whether decisions taken have been 'necessary in a democratic society'; but inevitably, given the nature of Strasbourg supervision, Article 8 jurisprudence in this area provides limited protection. There is no specific right under the Convention to custody or access, and a high level of margin is accorded to domestic decision-makers in determining such issues or whether a child should be placed in care. Rather, review will focus upon whether the reasons for an interference with family life have been relevant and sufficient, and whether the decision-making process has been fair.

1 As noted, 'family life' is given a broad interpretation, and can include relationships between grandparents and grandchildren and de facto family arrangements: see paras 6.06–6.07 above.
2 24875/94, *Logan v United Kingdom* (1996) DR 86, 74 (regulations relate to maintenance payments of absent parents and so the legislation does not by its nature affect family life); and 20357/92, *Whiteside v United Kingdom* (1994) DR 76, 80 (refusal of the court to grant injunction against the husband in a case of alleged domestic violence: inadmissible on account of failure to exhaust domestic remedies, but the Commission noted that there could exist a positive duty to protect against persistent and distressing harassment).

6.37   The European Court of Human Rights has accepted that it is not appropriate for it to substitute its judgment for that of the national author-ities who have the advantage of having direct contact with the relevant parties in determining the crucial issue of what is in the best interests of the child[1]. Further, views as to when it is appropriate to place a child in care vary considerably in Europe and depend upon such factors 'as tradi-tions relating to the role of the family and to State intervention in family affairs and the availability of resources for public measures'[2]. These issues are also complicated by the emerging case law under the European Convention on Human Rights, Articles 3 and 8 which stress a state's posi-tive obligations to take action to protect the physical and moral well-being of children[3]. The result is that in most cases, a wide margin of appreciation is accorded to domestic decision-makers in determining custody questions or whether a child should be taken into care, and the absence of any general European approach to child care and restricted judicial competence in reviewing decisions of care professionals may militate against any more rigorous Strasbourg supervision.

Some examination of case law illustrates the Court's approach. In the leading case of *Olsson v Sweden (No 1)*, a married couple had challenged the decision by the local authority to place their three children in separate foster homes at considerable distances away from the parents, the procedure involved, and the refusal to terminate the care arrangements. The deliberations had been taken after several case conferences, with the parents having been present at one of these sessions; later, further decisions had been taken restricting the parents' access rights. The Court confirmed that Strasbourg review was not confined to merely determining whether the decision-makers had exercised their discretion 'reasonably, carefully and in good faith', but extended to consideration of whether the reasons adduced were both relevant and sufficient. A minority of the Court (following a majority of the Commission) considered that the state had not shown that the reasons adduced could support the interference. The majority of the Court, however, was prepared to accept that the domestic court had given reasons which were both relevant (such as the parents' inability to provide a satisfactory home environment, the children's social and educational retardation, and the lack of success of other preventive measures) and in all the circumstances also sufficient after taking into account the substantial investigations that had taken place into the family background. Similarly, there had been relevant and sufficient reasons for holding that the care arrangements should not have been terminated. However, the manner in which the care decision had been implemented did give rise to a violation of Article 8 since it had involved the placement of the three children in separate homes and at some distance from the parents. While there was nothing to suggest that the public authority had acted other than in good faith, the measures taken were not consistent with its ultimate goal of reintegrating the children into the family unit[4]. This case does suggest that some scrutiny of any stated reasons for a care decision is appropriate, at least to ensure that the measures selected can be shown to be in line with the purported aim of state intervention. Other cases suggest an even less demanding review of domestic determinations. The failure to enforce custody orders was considered rather unconvincingly in *Hokkanen v Finland* where a child's grandparents had proven reluctant to hand over a child who had been in their care for several years to its father. The Court declined to consider whether Article 8 could require forcible measures to be used, merely noting that in certain circumstances preparatory measures may be required to secure the co-operation of all parties to such a dispute. In any case, it noted that ' the interests as well as the rights and freedoms of all concerned must be taken into account, and more particularly the best interests of the child and his or her rights under Article 8'. Ultimately, the crucial element in this instance was that the authorities had 'taken all necessary steps to facilitate reunion as can reasonably be demanded in the special circumstances of each case'[5].

1 Cf 47457/99 and 47458/99, *Tiemann v France and Germany* (27 April 2000) (decision of courts in Germany to order the return of the children of the applicant to their mother who was living in France; and refusal of the French courts to order the return of the children to Germany: applications declared inadmissible). Respect for family life may, however, give greater weight to parental decision-making than those rights of a child for respect for private life or under other guarantees: cf *Nielsen v Denmark* (1988) A 144, discussed at para 4.47 above (placement by a mother of her 12-year old son, who was not mentally ill, in psychiatric hospital).

2 *Johansen v Norway* 1996-III, 979, at para 54.

3 See para 6.35 above. See too 46544/99, *Kutzner v Germany* (10 July 2001) (removal of child from its parents who were considered intellectually incapable of looking after it: admissible).

4 (1988) A 130, paras 66–83. See too *Margareta and Roger Andersson v Sweden* (1992) A 226, at para 96 (prohibition of contact by correspondence and telephone by parents with children taken into care were relevant, 'but do not sufficiently show that it was necessary to deprive the applicants of almost every means of maintaining contact with each other for a period of approximately one and a half years. Indeed, it is questionable whether the measures were compatible with the aim of reuniting the applicants'). For a domestic example, see *Re B (adoption order)* [2001] 2 FLR 26.

5 (1994) A 299-A, at para 58 (violation established in respect of one period of time taking into account the limited steps to reunite the father with his child). See too *Bronda v Italy*, 1998-IV, 1476, paras 52–63 (failure to return a child to its original family contrary to an appeal court decision considered not to violate Art 8; reasons for allowing a child to remain with foster parents were both relevant and sufficient, the court attaching special weight to the overriding interest of the child); *Nuutinen v Finland* (27 June 2000), paras 129–138 (in the continuous re-assessment of the child's best interests the national authorities could have reasonably formulated a recommendation that the access rights should be revoked until the child had reached a more mature age; and having regard to the margin of appreciation afforded to the state, and the authorities had taken all necessary steps with a view to enforcing the access rights as could reasonably be demanded in the very difficult conflict at hand: no violation of Art 8); *Scozzari and Giunta v Italy* (13 July 2000), paras 148–151, 169–183, 201–216 and 221–227 (complaints of infringements of Art 8 in that the applicant's parental rights had been suspended, her children had been taken into care, the authorities had delayed before finally allowing her to see the children, too few contact visits had been organised and the authorities had placed the children in a home: certain violations of Art 8 established, but not in respect of the second applicant's complaint concerning the discounting of the possibility of her being given the care of her grandsons and delay in organising contact with them).

6.38   There are several qualifications, however. First, the European Court of Human Rights will wish to examine carefully any domestic decision which has been influenced by a factor based upon discriminatory treatment and which thus may violate the European Convention on Human Rights, Article 14 when taken together with Article 8[1]. Second, the removal of a child from a parent should in principle be seen as a temporary measure, and the ultimate aim must be to establish the reunion between parent and child. Thus the Court will apply a stricter scrutiny of the justifications advanced for restrictions on parental rights of access[2]. Third, the Court is concerned to ensure that fair decision-making procedures which give due recognition to Article 8 guarantees have been in place to help ensure that there has been due 'respect' shown for family life considerations[3]. These complement any applicable Article 6 interests[4]. In other words, procedures in child care or custody cases must allow parents adequate involvement in the decision-making process and also be carried out with sufficient expedition so as to avoid undue delay since this may lead to de facto determination of child care questions through the establishment of new ties with any foster parents or other carers[5].

Fourth, as the Court made clear in *Ignaccolo-Zenide v Romania*, Article 8 must be construed in the light of the Hague Convention of 1980 on Civil Aspects of International Child Abduction. The case concerned the failure of the domestic authorities to enforce a court order granted by the Romanian courts in favour of the applicant to allow her to be reunited with her two children who had been taken by their father from the USA to Romania. The Court reiterated that the article imposed positive obligations inherent in an effective 'respect' for family life which included the right for parents to have measures taken by the state with a view to reuniting them with their children. However, this obligation could not be absolute, on account both of the need for preparation before the reunion with a child who has been living for any length of time with the other parent and also of the limited scope for the use of coercion. The key question was whether the national authorities had taken all reasonable steps in the particular circumstances of the case to facilitate the enforcement of the court order, bearing in mind the need to take into account the paramount interests of the child and his own rights under Article 8. Here, initial steps to enforce the order had been taken promptly but then had been followed by minimal efforts; no proper preparation had been made for the children's return (for example, by arranging meetings of child psychiatrists and psychologists); and the authorities had not implemented the measures set out in the Hague Convention, Article 7 to secure the children's return to the applicant. In these circumstances, a violation of the European Convention on Human Rights, Article 8 was established[6].

Fifth, unduly harsh or oppressive interferences will be subject to particular scrutiny. There are certainly limits to what will be recognised as acceptable. In *K and T v Finland*, for example, a Chamber of the Court accepted that there had been a violation of the provision. The application had been brought by a mother and her cohabiting partner, the father of the younger of the mother's three children. The mother had been diagnosed on several occasions as suffering from schizophrenia, and various care measures (both emergency and 'normal') had been taken which restricted the access of the parents to the children. Most of the administrative proceedings had not involved oral hearings. The chamber determined that the reasons given and the methods used were arbitrary: the applicants had not even been given the opportunity of beginning a family life with a new-born daughter who had been placed in care immediately, and a care order concerning a son had been taken on the basis of purported risks none of which had been relevant since he was already in a safe home environment. There was also a violation of Article 8 in respect of the state's failure to consider with any seriousness the question of termination of the care orders despite some suggested improvement in the position of the mother[7]. The judgment was accepted for referral to the Grand Chamber which in consequence reheard the case. However, it approached the matter by considering the emergency care order separately from the normal care order since the two orders were of different natures and had involved different decision-making processes. Unanimously, the Grand Chamber held that the taking of the 'normal' care orders in each case had been in accordance with Article 8 since the applicants had been properly involved in the proceedings and it had been reasonable to conclude that care measures were in the best interests of the children. The Grand Chamber also found that there had been a violation of the state's responsibilities to take proper steps to try to reunite the family. However, by a majority, the Court ruled that the state had not shown that there had been 'extraordinarily compelling reasons' for the taking of the new-born baby into care at the time of its birth. Such a measure was 'extremely harsh', and the 'shock and disarray felt by even a perfectly healthy mother are easy to imagine'. Less draconian measures to deal with the situation had existed, but the state could not show that these had been considered[8].

1 Eg *Salgueiro da Silva Mouta v Portugal* (21 December 1999), discussed at para 6.44 below; *Hoffman v Austria* (1993) A 255-C, paras 32–36 (decision on child custody heavily influenced by consideration that mother was a Jehovah's Witness: the Court considered that this discrimination had no objective or reasonable justification).

2 *Johansen v Norway* 1996-III, 979, paras 64–84 (order made to take applicant's daughter into public care; complaint concerned the deprivation of her parental rights, the termination of her access to her daughter, the excessive length of the proceedings and their lack of fairness; only violation concerned lack of access and termination of parental rights which had not been supported by relevant and sufficient reasons); cf *Söderbäck v Sweden* 1998-VII, 3086, paras 22–35 (an adoption order had the effect of cutting all legal ties between the applicant and his daughter who had enjoyed only infrequent and limited contact; there were de facto family ties between the mother, the adoptive father and the daughter which had been in existence for over five years; and thus, given the adoption order's formalisation of these ties, it could not be said that any adverse effects on the applicant's relationships with the child had been disproportionate); *E P v Italy* (16 November 1999), paras 62–70 (absolute and irreversible ending of relationship between mother and daughter on the basis of the mother's pathological behaviour towards her child was based upon factual inaccuracies and without sufficiently rigorous analysis of the situation by the authorities: violation of Art 8).

3 See para 6.23 above. The European Convention on the Exercise of Children's Rights (ETS No 160) (1996) (not yet ratified by the United Kingdom) seeks to provide procedural measures to allow children to exercise their rights more effectively, in particular, in family legal proceedings.

4 Cf *McMichael v United Kingdom* (1995) A 307-B, para 87 and 91. See too *Elsholz v Germany* (13 July 2000), paras 48–53 (a domestic court had concluded that a child's development would be endangered if he had to take up contacts with the applicant (his father) contrary to his mother's will, but had arrived at this conclusion without having ordered an independent psychological report and in the absence of sufficient involvement of the applicant in the decision-making process: violation of Art 8). Article 6, however, only applies where there is a civil right or obligation recognised by domestic law or where parental interests are sufficiently vital so as to require domestic law to allow access to a court: 11468/85, *K v United Kingdom* (1986) DR 50 199; (1988) DR 56, 138 (child removed from natural father and placed with foster parents by the local authority: friendly settlement); *Paulsen-Medalen and Svensson v Sweden* 1998-I, 131, para 42 (delay of some 30 months in determining appeal by mother against taking children into care: violation of Art 6(1)).

5 *H v United Kingdom* (1987) A 120, at paras 89–90. For similar cases involving the taking of children into care, see *O v United Kingdom* (1987) A 120; *W, B and R v United Kingdom* (1987) A 121; *Keegan v Ireland* (1994) A 290. Cf *Bronda v Italy* 1998-IV, 1476, paras 61–63 (substantial judicial delays etc could 'appear incomprehensible and unacceptable' in a sensitive case in which 'the passage of time may have irreversible effects on the child's mental equilibrium, since she is forced to live in a state of uncertainty'; but the Court was ultimately satisfied that the decisions taken were based on both relevant and sufficient reasons).

6 (25 January 2000), paras 101–113.

7 (27 April 2000), paras 143–146, 155–164.

8 (12 July 2001) paras 164–170, 173–174, 177–179, 192–194 (on the other hand, a majority of the Court did accept that the emergency care order in respect of an older child had been justified: this would not have had as great an impact; the child was already physically separated from his family; and the applicants' lack of participation in the process was understandable so as not to add to the stress facing the applicants at the time of the birth of another child).

6.39 The Children (Scotland) Act 1995, s 11(7)(a) (which governs the circumstances in which an order (including a contact order) may be made in relation to parental responsibilities and rights) has been held to be in conformity with the European Convention on Human Rights, Article 8[1]. The implications of Article 8 for child care procedures have been considered with care by the English courts[2].

1 *White v White* 2001 SLT 485. A similar conclusion was reached, in respect of English legislation, in *Payne v Payne* [2001] 2 WLR 1826 which concerned the removal of a child from the jurisdiction, allegedly in breach of the non-custodial parent's rights under Art 8. The paramountcy of the interests of the child, under Art 8(2), was affirmed in *Re L (A Child) (Contact: Domestic violence)* [2001] Fam 260.
2 *Re W and B; Re W (Care Plan)* [2001] 2 FLR 582. In relation to the case of mentally handicapped adults, see *Re F (Adult: Court's jurisdiction)* [2001] Fam 38.

Sexuality

6.40 Sexuality concerns a most intimate aspect of private life, and any state interference such as the imposition of a sanction in respect of homosexual behaviour will call for the most searching scrutiny of the reasons advanced for this[1]. Further, the justification for any 'pressing social need' for discriminatory treatment based upon sexual orientation is likely to pose particular difficulties for a state under the European Convention on Human Rights, Article 14. Here most clearly is an illustration of the Convention as a 'living instrument'. Advances in European social attitudes are of considerable relevance, and some of the earliest case law must certainly now be disregarded[2]. In this area, too, are applications of the hallmarks of pluralism, tolerance and broadmindedness as the keystones of European democratic society[3]. On the other hand, the jurisprudence remains cautious when the claims assert respect for family life[4]. In *X and Y v United Kingdom*, for example, the Commission refused to accept that the deportation of one member of a homosexual couple gave rise to an Article 8 issue unless it could have been shown that the couple could not have lived elsewhere, and that the requisite link with the state which sought to deport the individual in question could have been said to be a material element in the relationship[5].

1 See further van Dijk 'The Treatment of Homosexuality under the ECHR' in Waaldijk and Clapham (eds) *Homosexuality: A European Community Issue* (1993) pp 179–206; Wintemute *Sexual Orientation and Human Rights* (1995); and Heinze *Sexual Orientation: A Human Right* (1995).
2 Eg 7215/75, *X v the United Kingdom* (1978) DR 19, 66 (age of homosexual consent fixed at 21 justified as being necessary for the protection of the rights of others); 17279/90, *W Z v Austria* (13 May 1992) (prohibition of males over the age of 19 from engaging in homosexual acts with a person of the same sex who was under that age compatible with the Convention): reports cited and now doubted in *Sutherland v United Kingdom* (27 March 2001), report of the Commission, paras 59–60.
3 *Lustig-Prean and Beckett v United Kingdom* (27 September 1999), para 80.
4 See paras 6.06 and 6.11 above but cf 36515/97, *Frette v France* (12 June 2001) (rejection on the grounds of his 'life style' of a request for authorisation to adopt a child lodged by an unmarried homosexual man: admissible under Art 8). For discussion of British law, see Wintemute 'Current Topic: Lesbian and Gay Britons, the Two Europes, and the Bill of Rights Debate' [1997] EHRLR 466; Bailey-Harris 'Lesbian and Gay Family Values and the Law' [1999] Fam Law 560.

5 9369/81 (1983) DR 32, 220. A complaint concerning the threatened expulsion from the
   UK of an individual cohabiting in a long-term homosexual relationship and who is
   suffering from AIDS has been communicated: 47061/99, *Cardoso and Johansen v United
   Kingdom*.

HOMOSEXUALITY

6.41   Many of the leading cases have challenged British law. In *Dudgeon v
United Kingdom*, the European Court of Human Rights examined
Northern Ireland legislation which treated homosexual behaviour
between consenting adult males as a criminal offence. While the applicant
had not actually faced prosecution, the Court accepted that the existence
of this law was enough to constitute an interference with his Article 8
rights on account of the continuous and direct effect it had on his private
life. Further, the state could not show sufficient indication of a pressing
social need for such legislation either on account of risk of harm to any
vulnerable section of the community or the protection of public morals.
The fact that members of the public could be 'shocked, offended or
disturbed' could not by itself justify the prosecution of private homosexual acts[1]. More recently, in *A D T v United Kingdom*, the Court extended
this approach to criminal laws which penalised homosexual activities in
private involving more than two individuals. The applicant had been
convicted of gross indecency after video tapes showing the applicant and
four others engaging in consensual homosexual acts not involving any
physical harm had been seized by the police. The Court considered that
the circumstances did not justify any state interference on the grounds of
protection of health or morals. Taking into account the restricted number
of participants, as well as the fact that the videos were for personal
consumption and would not enter the public domain, the activities were
considered genuinely 'private'. In short, there were insufficient reasons
both for the existence of the English legislation criminalising homosexual
acts between men in private, and the present prosecution and conviction[2].
In light of this decision, the Convention Rights (Compliance) (Scotland)
Act 2001 repealed the relevant section of the equivalent Scottish statute[3].

1 (1981) A 45, paras 41 and 60 at para 60. It is not entirely clear the extent to which an applicant must show that he falls within a class of person who is liable to prosecution under
   such legislation to qualify as a 'victim': cf *Sutherland v United Kingdom* (27 March 2001),
   report of the Commission, paras 34–37; and 10389/83, *Johnson v United Kingdom* (1986) DR
   47, 72 (violation of respect for private life requires that domestic law continuously and
   directly affects his private life). See, too, *Norris v Ireland* (1988) A 142, para 46; *Modinos v
   Cyprus* (1993) A 259, para 25.
2 (31 July 2000), paras 37–39; see Davenport 'None of the Law's Business' (2000) 150 NLJ
   1233.
3 Ie the Criminal Law (Consolidation) (Scotland) Act 1995, s 13(2)(a).

6.42   However, the notion of 'private life' in the area of sexual practices
'cannot be stretched indefinitely', as illustrated by *Laskey, Jaggard and
Brown v United Kingdom*. The applicants sought to challenge their convictions for assault in respect of consensual sado-masochistic acts involving
over 40 other homosexual men over a ten-year period. The Court
observed that the European Convention on Human Rights, Article 8 did
not extend to every form of sexual activity carried out behind closed
doors, and questioned whether the organisation and scope of the activities

could be said to have taken them outwith the character of 'private life'. Without deciding this point, it distinguished other cases which had concerned only private sexual behaviour from the present application which involved 'significant injury or degree of wounding which could not be characterised as trifling or transient'. Taking into account the serious nature of the harm inflicted, the Court considered that both relevant and sufficient reasons had been established for the prosecution and conviction of the applicants, and that these measures were proportionate to the aim of protecting health[1]. That the applicants and other participants were all homosexual males was thus of incidental relevance; and this case is best considered as an illustration of the principle that the scope of Article 8 in the area of private life is not unlimited[2].

1 1997-I, 29, paras 36–51 at 45. The Court specifically stated (at para 51) that it did not consider it necessary to consider the issue in respect of protection of morals, but this finding, however, 'should not be understood as calling into question the prerogative of the State on moral grounds to seek to deter acts of the kind in question'.
2 Cf *Laskey, Jaggard and Brown v United Kingdom* 1997-I, 29, concurring opinion of Judge Pettiti: 'The concept of private life cannot be stretched indefinitely' and 'the fact that the behaviour concerned takes place on private premises does not suffice to ensure complete immunity and impunity. ... The protection of private life means the protection of a person's intimacy and dignity, not the protection of his baseness or the promotion of criminal immoralism'.

DECISIONS OF THE DOMESTIC COURTS ON SEXUALITY

6.43 A sex offender order (prohibiting the defendant from seeking contact with children, associating with children, residing in a house where children were present, or working with children) has been held to be in accordance with the European Convention on Human Rights, Article 8(2) where, on the evidence, it was necessary, and went no further than was necessary, to protect the public from serious harm[1].

1 *B v Chief Constable of the Avon and Somerset Constabulary* [2001] 1 WLR 340. See also para 6.44.

DISCRIMINATION

6.44 Other cases have considered the impact of discriminatory policies against homosexuals which can give rise to questions under the European Convention on Human Rights, Article 8 alone, or this guarantee taken along with Article 14's general prohibition of discrimination[1]. Differences in treatment based upon sexual orientation are subject to particular scrutiny[2]. For example, in *Salgueiro da Silva Mouta v Portugal*, the refusal to grant custody of the daughter of a marriage to the father, who was by then living in a homosexual relationship, on the ground that such an environment could not be a healthy one in which to raise a child, was considered a violation of Article 8 taken together with Article 14[3].

Differences in the ages of consent as between heterosexuals and homosexuals were similarly considered a violation of Article 8 taken along with Article 14 by the Commission in *Sutherland v United Kingdom*. British law prohibited homosexual acts between males over the age of 16 but under the age of 18 years, while the minimum age for heterosexual activity was 16. The Commission could find no objective and reasonable justification for the distinction, even after attaching some weight to recent deliberations by the British Parliament which had considered the reasoning that certain young men between the ages of 16 and 18 did not yet have a settled sexual orientation and thus required protection. However, Parliament had also discussed current medical findings which now suggest that sexual orientation is already fixed in both sexes by the age of 16, and thus the Commission could not accept arguments that the law required to protect young men over this age. In considering Parliament's conclusion that society was entitled to indicate disapproval of homosexual conduct by displaying its preference for children to 'follow a heterosexual way of life', the Commission applied the Court's dictum in *Dudgeon v United Kingdom*[4] that preference for a heterosexual lifestyle could not constitute an objective or reasonable justification[5]. Following this report, amending legislation was introduced which equalised the age of consent for homosexual acts, and thus the Court subsequently struck out the case[6].

In *Lustig-Prean and Beckett v United Kingdom*, the Ministry of Defence's absolute policy of excluding homosexuals from the armed forces was challenged by applicants who complained that the investigations into their homosexuality and their subsequent discharge from the Royal Navy had violated Article 8. The English Court of Appeal had confirmed this policy to be lawful in terms of both domestic and applicable European Union law. In Strasbourg, the Court accepted that the purpose of the investigations and the policy of dismissal was to ensure the operational effectiveness of the armed forces, matters covered by the aims of 'interests of national security' and 'prevention of disorder'. Accordingly the principal question was whether the policy was 'necessary in a democratic society'. Here, the investigations were of an exceptionally intrusive character and had continued well after the applicants had confirmed their sexual orientation, and the Court could find no convincing or weighty reasons for this. The state had further attempted to justify the policy of instant discharge irrespective of an individual's conduct or service record on the grounds that the presence of open or suspected homosexuals in the armed forces would have had a substantial and negative effect on morale, citing an internal survey in support. The Court, however, was not persuaded of the reliability or validity of the report whose conclusions were based solely upon predisposed bias against a minority of service personnel of homosexual orientation. This could not amount to sufficient justification, given the lack of any concrete evidence to substantiate any alleged damage to morale or operational effectiveness[7].

1   For Art 14, see paras 3.40–3.65 above.
2   See further Conway 'Are Human Rights Homosexual Rights?' (2000) 150 NLJ 506; and Kirby 'Developments in Gay Rights' (2000) 150 NLJ 550.
3   (21 December 1999), paras 21–36. It is doubtful whether the dicta in *T, Petitioner* 1997 SLT 724 at 734 concerning Arts 8 and 14 reflect the current interpretation of the Convention. See *Pearce v Governing Body of Mayfield School* [2001] IRLR 669 per Hale LJ for a discussion of Arts 8 and 14 and sexual orientation.
4   (1981) A 45.
5   (27 March 2001), report of the Commission, of 1 July 1997, paras 55–66.
6   (27 March 2001), paras 16–21. Domestic law was amended by virtue of the Sexual Offences (Amendment) Act 2000.
7   (27 September 1999), paras 80–105. The Court declined to consider the Art 14 issue (at para 108), noting that this matter 'amounts in effect to the same complaint, albeit seen from a different angle'.

TRANSSEXUALS

6.45 The European Court of Human Rights has hitherto proved itself reluctant to recognise any positive duty upon the United Kingdom to recognise an individual's change of sexual identity[1]. Repeated challenges by post-operative transsexuals to governmental refusal to alter or otherwise amend information recorded on an individual's birth certificate so as to help protect private life concerns have failed, unless the particular facts of the case have allowed the Court to accept that these concerns have reached a particular degree of seriousness. The grounds for refusing these applications are inevitably that any detriment suffered by an applicant has not been sufficient to outweigh the recognition of a wide margin of appreciation on the part of states on account of the 'complex scientific, legal, moral and social issues' involved on which there is, as yet, no common European consensus[2]. State interests in upholding the integrity of the system of registration of births for purposes associated with succession rights or according access to this data by third parties with a legitimate interest in receiving such information[3] are thus given preference over individual concerns of privacy. In the most recent challenge to British law, *Sheffield and Horsham v United Kingdom*, the two applicants had been registered at birth as males, but each had undergone gender re-assignment treatment. Both applicants complained of practical difficulties encountered as a result of the state's insistence on the use of purely biological criteria to determine sex and its refusal to recognise officially their change of sexual identity. The Commission had accepted the applicants were subject to a 'real and continuous risk of intrusive and distressing enquiries and to an obligation to make embarrassing disclosures', and further that there was now a clear trend in European states towards legal recognition of gender re-assignation. A majority of the Court, however, felt that the continuation of any 'sufficiently broad consensus' on the legal reaction to a change of sex together with a lack of 'noteworthy scientific developments' made it inappropriate to depart from its earlier case law, and in any case the appellants had not shown that their difficulties were anything more than embarrassment and distress and thus these were not of sufficient seriousness to override the state's margin of appreciation[4].

Only in one case, *B v France*, has the Court accepted that the inconveniences faced by an individual were sufficiently serious to result in a violation of Article 8. The applicant had been recorded as male at birth, had undergone medical treatment, and subsequently regarded herself as female. She had been unable to obtain an amendment to the civil status register allowing her to have her change of forename recorded, with the consequence that all official documents and even bank accounts continued to be in the name recorded at birth. The Court accepted that this involved the frequent, if not daily, necessity of disclosing details of her private life, and thus distinguished these facts from those which had arisen in earlier cases involving the United Kingdom. Here, individual rights did outweigh state interests[5]. This area of jurisprudence is probably best considered as one in which revision is likely. The relative weight of the majority decision in *Sheffield and Horsham* (eleven votes to nine) suggests that there is a real likelihood that consideration of recent medical understanding and changing social attitudes will prompt review of this case law in the near future[6].

The English courts have held that a male-to-female transsexual is to be treated as a biological male and therefore not a woman for the purposes of marriage. The Court acknowledged that the situation was unsatisfactory and that there was a need to reconsider the legal position of transsexuals, but concluded that that was a matter for the legislature rather than the courts[7].

1 See, further, Andrews and Sherlock 'Transexuals' Rights and the European Convention' (1992) 17 EL Rev 561; Karsten 'Atypical Families and the Human Rights Act: The Rights of Unmarried Fathers, Same Sex Couples and Transsexuals' [1999] EHRLR 195; and Council of Europe *Transsexualism in Europe* (2000). For the autobiography of an applicant in one of the leading cases, see Cossey *My Story* (1991).
2 See *Rees v United Kingdom* (1986) A 106, para 37; *Cossey v United Kingdom* (1990) A 184, paras 32–42; *Stubbings v United Kingdom* 1996-IV, 1487, paras 63–67; *X, Y and Z v United Kingdom* 1997-II, 619, paras 41–52 at para 52.
3 *Rees v United Kingdom* (1986) A 106, paras 42–43.
4 1998-V, 2011, at paras 49–61.
5 (1992) A 232-C, paras 48–62; differences in English and French law and practice were specifically discussed (at paras 49–51), thus justifying the distinguishing (but not the over-ruling) of earlier decisions involving the United Kingdom.
6 See, especially, the joint partly dissenting opinions of Judges Bernhardt and others noting that information provided by Liberty suggested that only four states (including the UK) still refused to change birth certificate entries in respect of post-operative transsexuals, while at least 23 of the 37 European states surveyed did so.
7 *Bellinger v Bellinger* (17 July 2001, unreported), CA.

Environmental protection

6.46 Certain environmental concerns have now been accommodated within the European Convention on Human Rights, Article 8's require-ment of effective respect for private and family life and home[1]. Such issues may also arise under related guarantees[2]. Real threats to the enjoyment of home and family life posed by identifiable individuals in the form of harassment, victimisation or vandalism may also give rise to a positive obligation on the part of state authorities to take effective action to protect physical integrity[3]. Otherwise, the complaints must amount to allegations of serious environmental pollution which has a direct and harmful impact upon the applicant or his family: the Convention does not provide any general right against industrial or commercial development[4]. In *López Ostra v Spain*, the Court accepted that the failure to take steps to address the significant levels of pollution generated by a treatment plant situated only a few metres from the applicant's home was a violation of Article 8 which required the state to take steps to ensure the effective protection of the applicant's right to respect for her private and family life. The plant's operation had had a marked effect on the health of the applicant, and indeed the pollution had required the evacuation of local residents from their homes for a lengthy period[5]. Further, there may now be a positive duty upon the state to make available any necessary or essential informa-tion to allow those affected by a clear and obvious environmental hazard to assess the risk of continuing to live in a particular locality. In *Guerra and Ors v Italy*, a fertiliser plant with a history of accidents which had resulted in the hospitalisation of many residents had eventually been subject to inspection and inquiry. However, local townspeople, who would have been most vulnerable in the event of a further accident at the factory, were not provided with information until after a significant delay. The Court considered that there had been a failure on the part of the authorities to secure the applicants' rights under Article 8[6]. These two cases must be read carefully. Both involved extraordinary and proven threats to health. Other challenges to less hazardous environmental nuisances have not resulted in violations. Thus in *Powell and Rayner v United Kingdom*, the Court considered that the state's decision to deal with the nuisance of aircraft noise by means of regulation rather than through the device of civil action for nuisance fell clearly within its margin of appreciation[7].

1 Including nomadic lifestyles: cf 9278/81 and 9415/81, *G and E v Norway* (1983) DR 35, 30 (flooding of area traditionally used by Sana reindeer herders gave rise to Art 8 issue, but justified by para (2)).
2 Potentially fatal risks can give rise to Art 2 issues (cf *LCB v United Kingdom* 1998-III, 1390, discussed at para 4.12 above); environmental concerns may have an impact upon property considerations under Protocol 1, Art 1 (eg *Fredlin v Sweden* (1990) A 192); and fair hearing requirements may exist in determination of environmental and planning questions under Art 6 (eg *Bryan v United Kingdom* (1995) A 335-A, discussed at para 5.85 above).
3 Cf *Osman v United Kingdom* 1998-VIII, 3124, paras 128–130 (the facts did not support any finding that the police had failed to take appropriate steps in all the circumstances).
4 Cf 7407/76, *X and Y v Germany* (1976) DR 5, 161 (no right to nature preservation contained in the Convention, and application by environmental group seeking to prevent use of marshland manifestly ill-founded). See further Boyle and Anderson (eds) *Human Rights Approaches to Environmental Protection* (1998); Javis and Sherlock 'The ECHR and the Environment' (1999) 24 EL Rev HR 15; Thornton and Tromans 'Human Rights and Environmental Wrongs' (1999) 11 J Env L 35.
5 (1994) A 303-C, paras 50–58. See further Sands 'Human Rights, Environment and the *López Ostra* Case' [1996] EHRLR 597. Cf 20357/92, *Whiteside v United Kingdom* (1994) DR 76, 80 (positive obligations on a state may extend to providing protection against persistent harassment); and 53157/99 et al *Lediayeva and Ors v Russia* (failure of authorities to rehouse residents of an area recognised as dangerously polluted: communicated).
6 1998-I, 210, paras 57–60. See too *McGinley and Egan v United Kingdom* 1998-III, 1334, paras 98–103 discussed at para 4.12 above.
7 (1990) A 172, paras 41–44. See too 7889/77, *Arondelle v United Kingdom* (1982) DR 26, 5 (friendly settlement) and 9310/81, *Baggs v United Kingdom* (1987) DR 52, 59 (friendly settlement). See also *R (Vetterlein) v Hampshire County Council* (14 June 2001, unreported), QBD.

Prisoners' rights

6.47   The European Convention on Human Rights, Article 8 has been interpreted as requiring prison authorities to assist prisoners to maintain effective contact with their close relatives and friends[1], but always having regard to the 'ordinary and reasonable requirements of imprisonment and to the resultant degree of discretion' which must be accorded to the national authorities in regulating contact in order to maintain security and good order[2]. The notion of implied limitations on prisoners' rights through loss of liberty which influenced early Commission decisions and reports has long been rejected, and restrictions on prisoners' rights must be shown to meet the test of being 'necessary in a democratic society'[3]. The guarantee has proved to be of most use in challenging censorship of prisoners' mail where Court decisions have led to the progressive reduction of the ability of state authorities to interfere with prisoners' correspondence to the extent strictly necessary to meet state interests[4]. In *Campbell v United Kingdom*, correspondence with a solicitor which related to various civil and criminal matters and with the European Commission on Human

Rights had been interfered with by the Scottish prison authorities on the ground that the only way to establish whether correspondence contained prohibited material was to read it. The Court considered that while the state could justify the 'interferences' as falling within the legitimate state aim of preventing disorder or crime, the necessity of the particular interferences had not been established. 'The fact that the opportunity to write and to receive letters is sometimes the prisoner's only link to the outside world' should not be overlooked; further, consultation with a lawyer required to take place under circumstances 'which favour full and uninhibited discussion'. Only when state authorities had reasonable cause to believe that a letter from a legal representative 'contains an illicit enclosure which the normal means of detection have failed to disclose' should a letter be opened – but not read – and with the provision of 'suitable guarantees' such as opening the letter in the presence of the prisoner[5]. A similar principle of proportionality applies in regard to other forms of prisoners' correspondence: while 'some measure of control is not of itself incompatible with the Convention, . . . the resulting interference must not exceed what is required by the legitimate aim pursued'[6].

1 For discussion of prisoners' contacts with journalists under Art 10, see Richardson 'Prisoners' Rights to Free Speech – the Consequences of Implementation of the ECHR into the UK Legal System' (1998) 3 Comms L 123.
2 *Boyle and Rice v United Kingdom* (1988) A 131, at para 74.
3 *Golder v United Kingdom* (1975) A 18, at para 44.
4 In particular, in *Golder v United Kingdom* (1975) A 18; *Silver and Ors v United Kingdom* (1983) A 61; *Campbell and Fell v United Kingdom* (1984) A 80; *Boyle and Rice v United Kingdom* (1988) A 131; *Schönenberger and Durmaz v Switzerland* (1988) A 137. The Scottish case of *McCallum v United Kingdom* (1990) A 183, paras 10–31, involved a challenge to the stopping of letters written to the applicant's solicitor, his Member of Parliament, a journalist, an academic, and a public prosecutor. The state conceded – as in *Boyle and Rice* – that these interferences constituted breaches of Art 8. See too 10621/83, *McComb v United Kingdom* (1986) DR 50, 81 (friendly settlement involving the introduction of new prison standing orders narrowing the power of the authorities to censor correspondence with a legal adviser: but these standing orders were subsequently found wanting in the later case of *Campbell v United Kingdom* (1992) A 233).
5 (1992) A 233, paras 44–53 at para 48.
6 *Pfeifer and Plankl v Austria* (1992) A 227, paras 46–48 at 46 (deletion of jokes about prison staff which were considered insulting). See too 8231/78, *T v United Kingdom* (1982) DR 28, 5 (blanket prohibition on communication of artistic or scientific material not justified); *Calogero Diana v Italy* 1996-V, 1765; *Domenichini v Italy* 1996-V, 2195, paras 32–33 (too much latitude left to the authorities in deciding the scope and manner of the exercise of their discretion in censoring mail). For examples of recent findings of violation of respect for prisoners' correspondence, see *Demirtepe v France* (21 December 1999); *Messina v Italy (No 2)* (28 September 2000); *Rinzivillo v Italy* (21 December 2000); and *Peers v Greece* (19 April 2001), paras 81–84 at 84 (risk of drugs being contained in a letter from the Secretariat of the European Commission on Human Rights was 'so negligible that it must be discounted': violation). For discussion of interference with the correspondence of mental health patients, see *Herczegfalvy v Austria* (1992) A 244, paras 88–91 (forwarding of letters to a patient's guardian to decide whether the letters should be sent on had no legal basis: violation). See also *R (Daly) v Secretary of State for the Home Dept* [2001] 2 WLR 1622.

6.48   The European Convention on Human Rights, Article 8 has been of reduced utility where a prisoner has sought increased visiting rights[1] or location in a prison closer to his home[2]. In *Boyle and Rice v United Kingdom*, for example, one of the complaints concerned restrictions on special leave entitlement. The European Court of Human Rights considered that an annual visit entitlement which totalled twelve visits of one hour each did not violated the guarantee, nor that the particular circumstances in which one of the applicants had been refused compassionate leave supported any such claim[3]. The Court has also proved reluctant to become involved in matters of internal prison administration, preferring instead to recognise a high degree of discretion to deal with such matters on the part of prison authorities. Similarly, the maintenance of internal security may be readily accepted as justification for intrusions into private life, such as the imposition of solitary confinement[4], strip searches or drug testing[5].

1 Eg 9054/80, *X v United Kingdom* (1982) DR 30, 113 (restrictions on visits with persons campaigning about prison medical treatment did not violate Art 8).
2 Eg 14462/88, *Ballantyne v United Kingdom* (12 April 1991) (decision to place applicant in Peterhead prison several hundred miles distant from his family rather than in a local prison; Art 8 did not confer a general right on prisoners to choose the place of their detention, and in any case the applicant's move to a prison offering a more secure regime was as a consequence of his behaviour; separation from family is an inevitable consequence of imprisonment: inadmissible); 23241/94, *Hacisüleymanoğlu v Italy* (1994) DR 79, 121 (the European Convention on Transfer of Sentenced Prisoners does not require a state to transfer a prisoner; and the distance between a prisoner and his family is an inevitable consequence of detention); 15817/89, *Wakefield v United Kingdom* (1990) DR 66, 251 (engagement did not constitute 'family life' but did involve 'private life'; and the conditions imposed on the visits by a prisoner temporarily transferred to a Scottish prison with his fianceé were considered justified); and 70258/01, *Selmani v Switzerland* (28 June 2001) (deportation of a prisoner's wife and children did not give rise to an Art 8 issue: while separation and distance from families are inevitable consequences of detention, where exceptionally the detention of a prisoner at a distance from his family which renders any visit highly difficult if not impossible may constitute an interference with family life, the lack of means to travel could not be taken into account for practical reasons. Here, in any case, the prisoner was serving a short sentence and communication through writing and telephone was possible).
3 (1988) A 131, paras 74–82.
4 8317/78, *McFeely v United Kingdom* 20 DR 44, para 82.
5 21780/93, *TV v Finland* DR 76, 140 (disclosure of prisoner's HIV status to prison staff was an interference with respect for his private life; but justified as necessary, and no evidence of any wider disclosure); 21132/93 *Peters v Netherlands* (1996) DR 77, 75 and 20872/92, *A B v Switzerland* (1995) DR 80, 66 (compulsory medical intervention, in this case urine tests undergone by prisoners, constitutes an interference with respect for private life; but is justified as necessary for the prevention of crime and disorder). Cf *Matter v Slovakia* (5 July 1999), paras 64–72 (forcible examination of mental health detainee justified on the grounds of his own interests). Strip searching was held to be compatible with Art 8 in *R (Carroll) v Secretary of State for the Home Dept* (16 February 2001, unreported), QBD.

DECISIONS OF DOMESTIC COURTS ON PRISONERS' RIGHTS

6.49   The refusal of artificial insemination facilities to prisoners has been held to be justifiable under the European Convention on Human Rights, Article 8(2)[1]. A prison service policy that children should cease to reside with their mothers in prison when they become 18 months old has been held to be compatible with Art 8(2) only if it is operated in a flexible manner which involves a consideration of individual circumstances[2].

1 *R (Mellor) v Secretary of State for the Home Dept* [2001] 3 WLR 533. As to Art 12, see para 604.
2 *R (P) v Secretary of State for the Home Dept* [2001] 1 WLR 2002.

STANDARD-SETTING BY THE EUROPEAN COMMITTEE FOR THE PREVENTION OF TORTURE

6.50   The Committee for the Prevention of Torture and Inhuman or Degrading Treatment or Punishment (the CPT)[1] has had some limited impact upon prison policy in Council of Europe member states. Its starting-point is that the maintenance of contact between a prisoner and his family and close friends is not only a fundamental human right but is also of crucial importance in helping ensure that the prisoner's eventual re-integration into his family and community will be effective. Thus limitations on visits, written correspondence or telephone conversations should be based solely upon security concerns of an appreciable nature or resource considerations, and the aim should be the promotion of contact. The Committee's recommendations to states stress that there should be some flexibility as regards the application of rules on visits and telephone contacts where a prisoner is located some distance from his family and where in consequence it is difficult for regular visits to take place. Such prisoners, for example, should be permitted to accumulate visiting time entitlement, and enjoy enhanced telephone contact. Letters sent by inmates should not be immediately recognisable as having been sent from a prison, visiting accommodation should also be appropriate to facilitate communication and, where families live some distance from a prison, some flexibility in visiting arrangements should be possible[2]. The CPT has also been prepared to consider specific problems facing non-nationals, and has encouraged states to utilise the European Convention on the Transfer of Sentenced Persons to permit the remainder of sentences to be served in home institutions.

1 See para 2.34 above.
2 *Second General Report*, CPT/Inf (92) 3, paras 51–52; see further Murdoch 'The Work of the Council of Europe's Torture Committee' (1994) 5 EJIL 220.

PROTOCOL 1, ARTICLE 2: EDUCATION RIGHTS

6.51   In providing for a right to education, the Euopean Convention on Human Rights, Protocol 1, Article 2 recognises the duty upon a state to respect parents' religious and philosophical convictions in exercising its powers and responsibilities in this area[1]. 'It is in the discharge of a natural duty towards their children – parents being primarily responsible for the "education and teaching" of their children – that parents may require the State to respect their religious and philosophical convictions', and thus this right 'corresponds to a responsibility closely linked to the enjoyment and the exercise of the right to education'[2]. There is an obvious link between the provision of education and respect for private and family life under Article 8, and also with guarantees of freedom of thought, conscience and religion under Article 9 and of freedom of expression under Article 10[3]. The general prohibition of discrimination in the enjoyment of Convention rights in terms of Article 14 can also give rise to considerations of equal treatment in the provision of education[4]. The overall thrust of the jurisprudence, though, suggests that Strasbourg takes a cautious approach to interpretation[5]. This probably reflects the Court's awareness of limited judicial competence in an aspect of Convention protection which transgresses upon social and cultural human rights rather than being firmly located within the sphere of civil and political rights.

1 See further Lonby 'Rights in Education under the ECHR' (1983) 46 MLR 345; Wildhaber 'Right to Education and Parental Rights' in Macdonald, Matscher and Petzold (eds) *The European System for the Protection of Human Rights* (1993) pp 531–551; and Evans *Religious Liberty and International Law in Europe* (1997) pp 342–362.

2 *Kjeldsen, Busk Madsen and Pedersen v Denmark* (1976) A 23, at para 52.

3 *Kjeldsen, Busk Madsen and Pedersen v Denmark* (1976) A 23, at para 52 (provision to be read alongside Arts 8–10 and thus curriculum matters are in principle for the state); *Belgian Linguistics* case (1968) A 6, at para 7: (state educational measures which affect Art 8 rights in an unjustifiable manner, e g 'by separating parents from their children in an arbitrary way' are open to challenge).

4 Cf *Kjeldsen, Busk Madsen and Pedersen v Denmark* (1976) A 23, para 56 (provision of sex education is not similar to religious instruction and was consistent with Art 14's requirements).

5 See Bradley 'Scope for Review: The Convention Rights to Education and the Human Rights Act 1998' [1999] EHRLR 395.

The right to education

6.52   The European Convention on Human Rights, Protocol 1, Article 2 first provides that 'no person shall be denied the right to education'. This sentence dominates the article: any interpretation given to the right of parents to have philosophical convictions taken into account must not conflict with the primary right to education enjoyed by the child[1]. It involves access to educational facilities existing at a given time[2]. It also extends to official recognition of completed studies in order to be able to derive profit from the education received[3], although any such recognition of studies completed abroad may be subject to an examination in terms of domestic regulation[4]. State regulation of education is permitted as long as this does not injure the very substance of the guarantee[5]. Suspension of a pupil from a school imposed as a disciplinary measure will not give rise to a violation of the article, providing that the pupil has access to another educational facility[6]. There is some jurisprudence which suggests that the right to education is concerned primarily with elementary studies and not with advanced or higher education[7], and thus limiting entry to higher studies to those candidates who have attained a sufficient level of achievement to undertake such studies successfully does not constitute a violation[8]. Further, providing there is no 'denial of the substance of the right at issue' and that the right to access to educational facilities is a real rather than an illusory one[9], Protocol 2, Article 1 cannot substantiate a claim to be educated in a particular language[10] or in a particular country[11] or to be educated in a private school[12], or a claim of a private school to receive state funding[13] or to be exempted from ordinary planning controls[14], although the guarantee does protect the right to establish and to run private schools subject to state regulation to ensure the quality of education[15]. Nor does a requirement that students should belong to an association interfere with the right to education[16].

1 *Campbell and Cosans v United Kingdom* (1982) A 48, para 36; 44888/98 *Martins Casimiro and Cerveira Ferreira v Luxembourg* (27 April 1999) (a refusal to grant a general exemption from attending school on Saturdays on religious grounds to the sons of the applicants, Seventh Day Adventists, could be regarded as an interference with the manifestation of belief, but no general dispensation could be recognised which would adversely affect a child's right to education which prevailed over the parents' rights to have their religious convictions taken into account: the application was deemed inadmissible).

2 *Belgian Linguistics* case (1968) A 6, Law, para 4. Cf *Coster v United Kingdom* (18 January 2001), para 137; *Lee v United Kingdom* (18 January 2001), para 125; and *Jane Smith v United Kingdom* (18 January 2001), para 129 (complaints that enforcement of planning controls

had effectively deprived the applicants' children and grandchildren of the right to education: no violation on account of the applicants having failed to substantiate their allegations). In respect of a child deprived of his liberty for educational supervision, the nature of the detention conditions must support this purpose to justify application of Art 5(1)(d): *Bouamar v Belgium* (1988) A 129, discussed at para 4.60 above.

3 *Belgian Linguistics* case (1968) A 6, Law, para 4. See further Convention on the Recognition of Qualifications concerning Higher Education in the European Region (ETS 165 (1997)).

4 7864/77, *X v Belgium* (1978) DR 16, 82; 11655/85, *Glazewska v Sweden* (1985) DR 45, 300 (no requirement to recognise professional status acquired abroad).

5 *Campbell and Cosans v United Kingdom* (1982) A 48, paras 40– 41 (suspension of pupil for an academic year pending acceptance by parents that he should be punished in a manner contrary to their convictions was not reasonable and in any case fell outwith the state's power of regulation: violation of the child's right to education in terms of the first sentence, and of respect for parents' convictions in terms of the second sentence). The assumption of state responsibilities in the field of regulation of education is sufficient to establish liability in certain circumstances in respect of private educational institutions: cf *Costello-Roberts v United Kingdom* (1993) A 247-C, paras 27–28.

6 14524/89, *Yanasik v Turkey* (1993) DR 74, 14.

7 5962/72, *X v United Kingdom* (1975) DR 2, 50; 7671/76, *15 Foreign Students v United Kingdom* (1977) DR 9, 185; 14524/89, *Yanasik v Turkey* (1993) DR 74, 14; and 24515/94, *Sulak v Turkey* (1996) DR 84, 98. But cf van Dijk and van Hoof *Theory and practice of the European Convention on Human Rights* (3rd edn, 1998) at p 644: the Commission's position that Art 2 is concerned primarily with elementary education 'is corroborated neither by the text of Article 2 nor by the Court's case-law'.

8 11655/85, *Glazewska v Sweden* (1985) DR 45, 300. Cf 8844/80, *X v United Kingdom* (1980) DR 23, 228 (failure to allow a student with a poor first year performance and attendance to continue with studies). See too 60856/00, *Eren v Turkey* (the applicant passed examinations which would have allowed him access to university studies at his third attempt, but the results were annulled on the ground that the marks seemed too high in comparison with those which he had obtained in previous years: communicated).

9 *Cyprus v Turkey* (10 May 2001), paras 277–280 at paras 277 and 278 (children of Greek Cypriot parents living in an enclave in Turkish-occupied northern Cyprus wishing to continue their education in the Greek language beyond primary school had been required to transfer to secondary schools in the southern part of the island; while confirming that Protocol 1, Art 2 'does not specify the language in which education must be conducted in order that the right to education be respected', the Court ruled that there had been a violation of the right to education in this case. The key point was that no appropriate secondary school facilities were available: while secondary schooling was available either in Turkish- or in English-language schools and thus there had been no denial of education in the strict sense, these options were unrealistic. The authorities had assumed responsibility for Greek-language primary schooling, and thus 'the failure . . . to make continuing provision for it at the secondary-school level must be considered in effect to be a denial of the substance of the right at issue': violation of Protocol 1, Art 2).

10 *Belgian Linguistics* case (1968) A 6, Law, para 6.

11 *R (Holab) v Secretary of State for the Home Dept* [2001] 1 WLR 1359.

12 14688/89, *Simpson v United Kingdom* (1989) DR 64, 188 (no requirement that a disabled child should be educated in a private school with the state paying the fees where a place was available in a state school with special facilities for handicapped pupils).

13 6853/74, *40 Mothers v Sweden* (1977) DR 9, 27; 23419/94, *Verein Gemeinsam Lernen v Austria* (1995) DR 82, 41

14 20490/92, *Iskon and Ors v United Kingdom* (1994) DR 76, 90.

15 11533/85, *Jordebo Foundation of Christian Schools and Jordebo v Sweden* (1987) DR 51, 125.

16 6094/73, *Association X v Sweden* (1977) DR 9, 5 (a students' association was not considered a trade union for the purposes of Art 11).

Provision of education in conformity with parents' religious and philosophical convictions

6.53 The second sentence of the European Convention on Human Rights, Protocol 1, Article 2 provides that 'in the exercise of any functions which it assumes in relation to education and to teaching, the State shall respect the right of parents to ensure such education and teaching in conformity with their own religious and philosophical convictions'. The right to respect for religious and philosophical convictions belongs to the parents of a child and not to the child itself[1] or to any school or religious association[2]. The fact that a child has been taken into care does not extinguish parental rights in this area[3], although a mother whose child has been adopted by another person no longer enjoys rights in this regard[4]. As noted, parental interests are considered to be secondary to the child's basic right to education[5]. 'Education' suggests 'the whole process whereby, in any society, adults endeavour to transmit their beliefs, culture and other values to the young', while 'teaching or instruction refers in particular to the transmission of knowledge and to intellectual development'[6]. 'Respect' suggests more than mere acknowledgment or even that a parent's views have been taken into account, and instead 'implies some positive obligation on the part of the State'[7]. The matter may arise in regard to the content and implementation of curriculum, but will not extend to the provision of a specific form of teaching through, for example, the placement of a child in a particular school[8]. 'Philosophical convictions' suggests views 'as are worthy of respect in a "democratic society" ... and are not incompatible with human dignity' and which also 'attain a certain level of cogency, seriousness, cohesion and importance'. These include settled beliefs which refer to 'a weighty and substantial aspect of human life and behaviour'. However, linguistic preferences are not 'philosophical convictions' since this would distort the ordinary meaning of the term[9].

1 *Erikkson v Sweden* (1989) A 156, para 93.
2 Cf 11533/85, *Jordebo Foundation of Christian Schools and Jordebo v Sweden* (1987) DR 51, 125 (the parents of pupils in a private school which was refused permission to provide the higher stage of compulsory education qualified as 'victims', but not the school itself).
3 *Olsson v Sweden (No 1)* (1988) A 103, para 95 (but 'no serious indication' that atheist parents were concerned that children were being given a religious upbringing); 10554/83, *Aminoff v Sweden* (1985) DR 43, 120 (decision to remove a child from its adoptive mother; subsequent complaint by the mother that the child's education is contrary to her wishes declared admissible); 10723/83, *Widén v Sweden* (1986) DR 48, 93 (decision to remove two children from their mother; in consequence, mother unable to place them in a private religious school: friendly settlement).
4 7626/76, *X v United Kingdom* (1977) DR 11, 160.
5 See para 6.52 above. Cf 10233/83, *Family H v United Kingdom* (1984) DR 37, 105 (a state may require parents who have chosen to educate their children at home to co-operate in the assessment of their children's educational standards).
6 *Campbell and Cosans v United Kingdom* (1982) A 48, at para 33.
7 *Campbell and Cosans v United Kingdom* (1982) A 48, at para 37; *Valsamis v Greece* 1996-VI, 2312, at para 27.
8 14135/88, *P D and L D v United Kingdom* (1989) DR 62, 292 and 13887/88, *Graeme v United Kingdom* (1990) DR 64, 158 (placement of disabled children in special schools against the wishes of the parents; no violation); and 25212/94, *Klerks v Netherlands* (1995) DR 82, 129 (respect for parents' convictions does not require the admission of a severely handicapped child to an ordinary school). See too 10228/82 and 10229/82, *W & D M v United Kingdom* and *M & H I v United Kingdom* (1984) DR 37, 96 (state education provision included both single-sex grammar schools and mixed-sex comprehensive schools; parents sought to assert that the failure to place their children in the former type of school on account of a shortage of places violated their philosophical convictions: application declared inadmissible).
9 *Belgian Linguistics* case (1968) A 6, Law, para 6; cf *Cyprus v Turkey* (10 May 2001), at para 278: (the authorities were aware that Greek Cypriot parents living in an enclave in northern

Cyprus wished their children's education 'to be completed through the medium of the Greek language', and while this education was available in the southern part of the island, it could not be maintained that this possibility 'suffice[d] to fulfil the obligation laid down in Article 2 of Protocol No 1, having regard to the impact of that option on family life').

6.54   The United Kingdom's obligations under this provision are subject to a reservation made at the time of ratification and protected by the Human Rights Act 1998 to the effect that this particular obligation applies only in so far as 'it is compatible with the provision of efficient instruction and training, and the avoidance of unreasonable public expenditure'[1]. In any case, a state is not required to provide a financial subsidy to a particular form of education to meet its obligations: rather, the duty is to 'respect' such convictions in the provision of any existing form of education[2]. In *X and Y v United Kingdom* the applicants complained that the state did not provide funding to a Rudolf Steiner school which provided their children with education in accordance with their commitment to the 'anthroposophical movement'. The complaint was rejected as manifestly ill-founded even without having to consider Britain's reservation since the Commission considered that this article could not be interpreted as obliging the state to establish or support any educational establishment serving any particular set of religious beliefs or convictions. In any case, the Commission was of the opinion that the state had indeed shown 'respect' by granting the school charitable status and by extending an assisted places scheme to it[3].

1   The reservation appears in the Human Rights Act 1998, Sch 3, as given effect to by s 1(2). The reservation was referred to in 14135/88, *P D and L D v United Kingdom* (1989) DR 62, 292.
2   10476/83, *W & K L v Sweden* (1985) DR 45, 143.
3   9461/81 (1982) DR 31, 210.

6.55   In each instance, the European Court of Human Rights must first determine whether parents are entitled to rely upon the provision to secure respect for their philosophical and religious convictions, and then consider whether the state has indeed respected these convictions[1]. The outcome of such an assessment is not always obvious. For example, in *Valsamis v Greece* and in *Efstratiou v Greece*, pupils who were Jehovah's Witnesses had been punished for failing to attend parades commemorating the country's national day. The parents of the pupils had sought exemptions from the requirement to take part in the parades on account of their belief that such events were incompatible with their firmly held pacifism. The Court accepted that Jehovah's Witnesses enjoyed the status of a 'known religion' and thus parents were entitled to rely upon the right to respect for these convictions. While the Court expressed surprise 'that pupils can be required on pain of suspension from school – even if only for a day – to parade outside the school precincts on a holiday', it considered that the nature of these parades (even taking into account the involvement of military personnel) contained nothing which could offend the applicants' pacifist convictions[2].

Perhaps more evidently, curriculum setting and planning are matters which fall within the competence of the domestic authorities, and in which judicial expertise is limited[3]. In *Kjeldsen, Busk Madsen and Pedersen v Denmark*, parents objected to the provision of sex education to their children. In a crucial part of the judgment which encapsulates the manner in which conflicting interests of the state, of pupils and of their parents are expected to be resolved, the Court drew a distinction between the imparting of knowledge even of a directly or indirectly religious or philosophical nature, and teaching which sought to inculcate a particular value or philosophy which did not respect the views of a parent. The provision does not 'permit parents to object to the integration of such teaching or education in the school curriculum, for otherwise all institutionalised teaching would run the risk of proving impracticable' since most school subjects involved 'some philosophical complexion or implications'. However, a school has to ensure that the education provided by way of teaching or instruction conveyed information and knowledge 'in an objective, critical and pluralistic manner'. The key guarantee is against the state pursuing an 'aim of indoctrination that might be considered as not respecting parents' religious and philosophical convictions', this being 'the limit that must not be exceeded'[4].

On the other hand, 'the imposition of disciplinary penalties is an integral part of the process whereby a school seeks to achieve the object for which it was established, including the development and moulding of the character and mental powers of its pupils'[5], and thus an issue such as the use of corporal punishment may not simply be dismissed as a matter merely of internal administration. In *Campbell and Cosans v United Kingdom*, parents of pupils in Scottish schools objected to the practice of administering the belt or tawse. The Court accepted that the applicants' views met the test of philosophical conviction in that they related to a 'weighty and substantial aspect of human life and behaviour, namely the integrity of the person', and thus the state's failure to respect these convictions violated the guarantee[6].

1 *Valsamis v Greece* 1996-VI, 2312, para 26.
2 1996-VI, 2312, paras 26–33 at para 31; 1996-VI, 2347, paras 27–34 at para 32 (public celebration of democracy and human rights not vitiated by presence of military; similarly, no violation of Art 9).
3 *Kjeldsen, Busk Madsen and Pedersen v Denmark* (1976) A 23, para 53.
4 (1976) A 23, at para 53. See also 17187/90, *Bernard v Luxembourg* (1993) DR 75, 57 (requirement to attend moral and social education in the absence of any allegation of indoctrination did not give rise to an interference with Art 9 rights); and Parliamentary Assembly Recommendation 1412 (1999) reiterating the importance of the history and philosophy of religion in school curricula with a view to protecting young persons from the illegal activities of sects.
5 *Valsamis v Greece*, 1996-VI, 2312, at para 29.
6 (1982) A 48, paras 33–37 at para 36. Corporal punishment was ultimately prohibited in state schools, and in relation to pupils in state assisted places at independent schools, by the Education (Scotland) Act 1980, s 48A as amended by the Education Act 1993, s 294.

Discrimination

6.56 The European Convention on Human Rights, Article 14 when taken together with Protocol 1, Article 2 prohibits discriminatory treatment which does not pursue a legitimate aim or is proportionate[1]. These articles cannot, however, be read as implying any right for a child to be educated in a particular language, or for parents to insist that education is provided using their language of choice[2]. At the most, it prohibits the imposition of any discriminatory treatment which has 'as its basis or reason a personal characteristic ("status") by which persons or groups are distinguishable from each other'[3], and which falls within the scope of the right to education[4]. Operation of the Scottish system of publicly funded denominational education, though, may well give rise to issues. One question may be whether refusal to accord Muslim parents the facilities of public-sector denominational schooling in communities in which there is a real demand for this meets Convention expectations where similar demands from parents of other faiths have been accommodated[5].

1 See paras 3.40–3.65 above.
2 *Belgian Linguistics* case (1968) A 6, Law, para 11.
3 *Kjeldsen, Busk Madsen and Pedersen v Denmark* (1976) A 23, at para 56.
4 Thus differences of treatment in the funding arrangements of students attending Scottish universities based upon residence status would presumably escape censure since there is some doubt as to whether higher education falls within the ambit of the article, and the guarantee cannot imply the requirement to provide any particular financial support. In any case, there could presumably be an arguable case that any difference in treatment pursued a legitimate aim and was not disproportionate.
5 Cf Murdoch 'Religion, Education and the Law' (1989) 34 JLSS 258 at 261. See too Arthur 'British Human Rights Legislation and Religiously Affiliated Schools and Colleges' (1998) 10 Ed Law 225.

CHAPTER 7

Civil and political liberties: thought, expression, assembly and association; and free elections

INTRODUCTION

7.01 The European Convention on Human Rights, Articles 9, 10 and 11 guarantee freedom of thought, conscience and religion, expression, assembly and association. The guarantees are closely linked, in terms of both substantive content[1] and textual formulation[2]. These civil liberties are crucial for the protection of collective political freedom and the development of individual identity as shaped through personal attitudes and beliefs. Protocol 1, Article 3 further guarantees the holding of free elections at reasonable intervals by secret ballot. Policy issues shape much of the jurisprudence, for the European Court of Human Rights has been at pains to highlight the particular importance of these rights in maintaining democratic discussion[3], accountability[4], pluralism and tolerance[5]. None of these guarantees is absolute, for a state may interfere with each right, providing always that this is done in accordance with domestic law and is 'necessary in a democratic society' for the achievement of prescribed interests[6]. A state may also take measures derogating from its obligations in time of emergency, in terms of Article 15[7]. Further, Article 16 provides that 'nothing in Articles 10, 11 and 14 shall be regarded as preventing the High Contracting Parties from imposing restrictions on the political activity of aliens'[8].

1 Cf *Young, James and Webster v United Kingdom* (1981) A 44 at para 57: 'the protection of personal opinion afforded by Articles 9 and 10 in the shape of freedom of thought, conscience and religion and of freedom of expression is also one of the purposes of freedom of association as guaranteed by Article 11'.

2 That is, paragraph (1) of each article makes provision for the general right, while paragraph (2) recognises certain state interests which may justify interference with individual freedoms.

3 E g *Barfod v Denmark* (1989) A 149, at para 29 (importance of 'not discouraging members of the public, for fear of criminal or other sanctions, from voicing their opinions on issues of public concern').

4 E g *Lingens v Austria* (1986) A 103, at paras 41 and 42 ('it is 'incumbent [upon the press] to impart information and ideas on political issues, [and] freedom of the press affords the public one of the best means of discovering and forming an opinion of the ideas and attitudes of political leaders').

5 Cf *Handyside v United Kingdom* (1976) A 24, at para 49 (expression was crucial for promotion of 'pluralism, toleration and broadmindedness').

6 For discussion of the general limitations in the European Convention on Human Rights, Arts 8–11, see paras 3.33–3.78 above.

7 See further para 3.06 above.

8 Cf *Piermont v France* (1995) A 314, paras 62–64 (possession of EU citizenship by the German applicant who was also a Member of the European Parliament did not allow ECHR, Art 16 to be raised against her by the respondent state in respect of violation of her Art 10 rights when expelled from a French overseas territory represented in the European Parliament).

7.02   Since the European Convention on Human Rights is to be read as a whole[1], the substantive content of each guarantee may be influenced by competing considerations[2]. In any case, factual circumstances may give rise to simultaneous challenges under two or more of these guarantees, although the European Court of Human Rights will invariably dispose of an application under only one article when it considers that the merits of the application can be addressed adequately in this way[3]. In practical terms, the bulk of the jurisprudence lies in Article 10, with Articles 9 and 11 generating much less in the way of case law. Protocol 1, Article 3 is probably more of symbolic than practical use since the variety of different voting systems and constitutional arrangements amongst European states justifies a wide margin of appreciation[4]. The duties upon a state go beyond the responsibilities of refraining from interfering with the rights of individuals. Each guarantee can require positive action on the part of the state to ensure that the right is an effective right[5].

1 *Belgian Linguistics case* (1968) A 6, at para 1.
2 Eg *Kjeldsen, Busk Madsen and Pedersen v Denmark* (1976) A 23, paras 52 and 53 (parental interests in education under the European Convention on Human Rights, Protocol 1, Art 2 to be interpreted in a way consistent with Arts 8, 9 and 10); *Otto-Preminger-Institut v Austria* (1994) A 295-A, para 56 (permissible restrictions on expression under ECHR, Art 10 read alongside promotion of religious tolerance under Art 9); *News Verlags v Austria* (11 January 2000), para 56 (restrictions on prejudicial pre-trial publicity under ECHR, Art 10(2) consistent with accused's rights under Art 6(1) and (2)).
3 Eg *Young James and Webster v United Kingdom* (1981) A 44, para 66 (disposal under ECHR, Art 11 rather than in terms of Arts 9 or 10); *Kokkinakis v Greece* (1993) A 260-A, para 54 (dissemination of religious beliefs considered under ECHR, Art 9 rather than Art 10); *Steel and Ors v United Kingdom* 1998-VII, 2719, para 113 (various protests both peaceful and non-peaceful considered under ECHR, Art 10 rather than Art 11).
4 Cf *Mathieu-Mohin and Clerfayt v Belgium* (1987) A 113, para 54. For discussion of 'margin of appreciation', see paras 3.85–3.90 above.
5 The notion of positive obligations first appears under ECHR, Art 11 and is then developed in Arts 9 and 10: cf *Plattform 'Ärzte für das Leben' Austria* (1988) A 139, discussed at para 7.49 below; *Otto-Preminger-Institut v Austria* (1994) A 295-A, discussed at para 7.07 below; and *Özgür Gündem v Turkey* (16 March 2000), discussed at para 7.15 below. ECHR, Protocol 1, Art 3 is exclusively secured through positive state action: *Mathieu-Mohin and Clerfayt v Belgium* (1987) A 113, discussed at para 7.57 below.

7.03   The Human Rights Act 1998 makes specific provision for freedom of expression (s 12) and for the freedom of thought, conscience and religion of religious organisations (s 13). These provisions are the results of amendments made during parliamentary stages, and require to be taken into account in any relevant domestic proceeding. They may have little practical impact; but if a court is unduly influenced by either provision in its interpretation of the European Convention on Human Rights, it is not inconceivable that this could be corrected by application to the Strasbourg Court[1].

1 See paras 1.90–1.92 above; and paras 7.10 and 7.25–7.26 below. The issue of how a court would consider a case involving the balancing of expression with respect for religious belief where the Human Rights Act 1998, ss 12 and 13 are themselves in issue seems not to

have been considered, but would in any case most likely be resolved by reference to existing Strasbourg case law: cf *Otto-Preminger Institut v Austria* (1994) A 295-A, discussed at para 7.07 below.

FREEDOM OF THOUGHT, CONSCIENCE AND RELIGION

The scope of 'freedom of thought, conscience and religion'

7.04   The European Convention on Human Rights, Article 9[1] is at the heart of individual identity and protection of that 'true religious pluralism'[2] which is a hallmark of a democratic society: it is fundamental for religious belief[3] 'but it is also a precious asset for atheists, agnostics, sceptics and the unconcerned'[4]. No distinction is drawn between religious and other beliefs: beliefs which relate to a 'weighty and substantial aspect of human life and behaviour' are worthy of protection[5]. The provision covers individual thought, conscience and religion[6], and collective manifestation[7] of that opinion or belief with others. Consequently, the concerns it raises are closely allied to other Convention guarantees and in particular to protection of expression, peaceful assembly, and respect for religious and philosophical convictions of parents in the provision of state education for their children under Articles 10 and 11 and Protocol 1, Article 2 respectively. Freedom of religion issues may even arise in respect of loss of liberty under Article 5[8]. The guarantee is also buttressed by Article 14's prohibition of discrimination on the grounds inter alia of religious and political opinion[9]. However, the guarantee is not absolute. Paragraph (2) provides that any state interference with thought, conscience or religion may relate only to a manifestation of belief or practice, and thus while the holding (or changing) of convictions appears to be an absolute right[10], certain grounds for limiting other aspects of Article 9 on account of countervailing interests are recognised. Further, the case law is not always satisfactory[11].

The guarantees provided by Article 9 relate in essence to the right to hold philosophical or religious convictions, to change these beliefs, and to manifest these individually or in common with others[12]. Thus issues giving rise to consideration under this article include impositions of religious oaths[13] or requirements to attend religious ceremonies[14] and restrictions on proselytism[15] or on places of worship[16] or on the disposal of the remains of the deceased[17]. The scope of the provision does not extend to such issues as the non-availability of divorce[18], allegations of discriminatory treatment in the application of tax regulations[19], or deprivation of a religious organisation's material resources[20]. Nor can the guarantee imply any right of a taxpayer to demand that the state allocates his payments to particular purposes[21], or the use of any particular language in exercising freedom of thought[22].

1 See further, Shaw 'Freedom of Thought, Conscience and Religion' in Macdonald, Matscher and Petzold (eds) *The European System for the Protection of Human Rights* (1993) pp 445–463; Evans *Religious Liberty and International Law in Europe* (1997) pp 262–341; Cullen 'The Emerging Scope of Freedom of Conscience' (1997) 22 EL Rev HR 32; Edge 'The European Court of Human Rights and Religious Rights' (1998) 47 ICLQ 680; Edge

'Religious Rights and Choice under the ECHR' [2000] 3 Web JCLI; Moon and Allen 'Substantive Rights and Equal Treatment in Respect of Religion and Belief' [2000] EHRLR 580; Naismith 'Religion and the European Convention on Human Rights' (2001) HR & UK P, Issue 1, 8; and Costa 'La Convention Européenne des Droits de l'Homme et les Sectes' in Mahoney, Matscher, Petzold and Wildhaber (eds) *Protecting Human Rights: The European Perspective* (2000) pp 273–280. For an international perspective, see van der Vyver and Witte (eds) *Religious Human Rights in Global Perspective* (2 vols, 1996); and for comparative discussion of ECHR and US Supreme Court approaches to claims based on religious or philosophical belief, see Stavros 'Freedom of Religion and Claims for Exemption from Generally Applicable, Neutral Laws: Lessons from Across the Pond? [1997] EHRLR 607. For an overview of related international instruments, see Durham 'Freedom of Religion or Belief: Laws Affecting the Structuring of Religious Communities', OSCE Briefing Paper ODHIR 1999/4; and Tahzib *Freedom of Religion and Belief* (1996).

2   *Manoussakis and Ors v Greece* 1996-IV, 1346, at para 44.

3   Cf *Kokkinakis v Greece* (1993) A 260-A, at para 31: 'bearing witness in words and deeds is bound up with the existence of religious convictions'. There is an onus on an applicant to establish that a particular 'religion' exists, although the Strasbourg organs may attempt to avoid any such determination: 7291/75, *X v United Kingdom* (1977) DR 11, 55 (prisoner claimed to be a member of the 'Wicca' faith; Commission observed that the applicant had not established any factual basis for the existence of this religion); cf 12587/86, *Chappell v United Kingdom* (1987) DR 53, 241 (question whether Druidism could be classified as a 'religion' avoided).

4   *Kokkinakis v Greece* (1993) A 260-A, at para 31. See too *Re Crawley Green Road Cemetery, Luton* [2001] Fam 308.

5   *Campbell and Cosans v United Kingdom* (1982) A 48, at para 36 (in relation to philosophical convictions under the European Convention on Human Rights, Protocol 1, Art 2); and 16311/90–6313/90, *Hazar, Hazar and Acik v Turkey* (1991) DR 72, 200 (offence of belonging to the Communist Party: admissible under ECHR, Art 9). Cf Harris, O'Boyle and Warbrick *Law of the European Convention on Human Rights* (1995) at 357: 'the line between a philosophy and a political programme may yet be hard to draw'. See too *Refah Partisi (The Welfare Party), Erbakan, Kazan and Tekdal v Turkey* (31 July 2001), para 80, discussed at para 7.54 below (prohibition on a political party which sought to introduce Islamic law contrary to the state's secular constitution upheld, in part since the values of such a legal system were contrary to those of the Convention).

6   23380/94, *C J, J J and E J v Poland* (1996) DR 84, 46 (ECHR, Art 9 primarily protects personal beliefs and faiths, that is, the area often referred to as the *forum internum*, and acts intimately related to these beliefs).

7   A church or other religious organisation can claim to be a 'victim' of a violation of a Convention guarantee under ECHR, Art 25 in relation to freedom of religion: 7805/77, *X and Church of Scientology v Sweden* (1979) DR 16, 68 (Church in lodging an application under ECHR, Art 9 does so in a representative capacity on behalf of its members); but a church or legal person cannot claim to be victim of freedom of conscience: 11921/86, *Verein Kontakt-Information-Therapie and Hagen v Austria* (1988) DR 57, 81. Other associations or corporate bodies may lack the standing of 'victim': cf 11308/84, *Vereniging Rechtswinkels Utrecht v Netherlands* (1986) DR 46, 200 (prisoners' rights association, while motivated by idealism, could not qualify as 'victim' either in its own capacity or as a representative body). In *Canea Catholic Church v Greece* 1997-VIII, 2843, the Court found a violation of ECHR, Art 6(1) taken alone and with Art 14 (legal capacity of Greek Catholic Church to take legal proceedings was restricted, and thus the very substance of 'right to a court' was impaired; further, no formalities or restrictions were imposed on the Orthodox Church or the Jewish community, and there was no objective or reasonable justification for such a difference of treatment). Cf 34614/96, *Scientology Kirche Deutschland v Germany* (1997) DR 89, 163 (only the members of an association and not the association itself could claim to be a 'victim' of ECHR, Art 8's guarantee of respect for private life).

8   *Tsirlis and Kouloumpas v Greece* 1997-III, 909, paras 56–63 (refusal of authorities to exempt ministers of certain religions from military service contrary to domestic law: issue considered under ECHR, Art 5); *Riera Blume and Ors v Spain* (14 October 1999), paras 25–35 (holding of sect members on the order of a judge to allow their 'de-programming': not in accordance with domestic law, and thus violation of ECHR, Art 5), discussed at para 4.47 above.

9 Eg *Thlimmenos v Greece* (6 April 2000), discussed at para 7.13 below. See further paras 3.40–3.65 above.
10 While ECHR, Art 15 allows for derogation in time of public emergency etc, it is difficult to see how a state could in practice 'take measures' to interfere with the holding of convictions.
11 For a critical perspective of Court judgments in this area, see Evans *Religious Liberty and International Law in Europe* (1997) pp 281–341.
12 *Kokkinakis v Greece* (1993) A 260-A, para 31.
13 *Buscarini and Ors v San Marino* 1999-I, 605, para 34.
14 Cf *Valsamis v Greece* 1996-VI, 2312, paras 21–37 (no interference with ECHR, Art 9 rights).
15 *Kokkinakis v Greece* (1993) A 260-A, paras 31–33, discussed at para 7.12 below.
16 *Manoussakis and Ors v Greece* 1996-IV, 1346, paras 36–53, discussed at para 7.11 below.
17 *Re Durrington Cemetery* [2001] Fam 33 (interment in accordance with Jewish law); *Re Crawley Green Road Cemetery, Luton* [2001] Fam 308 (interment of humanist in unconsecrated ground).
18 *Johnston and Ors v Ireland* (1986) A 112, paras 62–63 (issues considered under ECHR, Arts 8, 12 and 14).
19 *Darby v Sweden* (1990) A 187, paras 28–35 (application disposed of under ECHR, Protocol 1, Art 1 taken with Art 14; the Court considered that the establishment of a particular church in a state did not give rise to any Art 9 issue if membership is voluntary (para 35)).
20 *Holy Monasteries v Greece* (1994) A 301-A, paras 86–87 (matters considered under ECHR, Protocol 1, Art 1 since the complaint did not concern 'objects intended for the celebration of divine worship').
21 10358/83, *C v United Kingdom* (1983) DR 37, 142 (a Quaker opposed the use of any tax paid by him for military purposes; the Commission noted Art 9 could not always guarantee the right to behave in the public sphere (eg refusing to pay tax) in a manner dictated by belief); and 53072/99, *Alujer Fernandez and Caballero Garcia v Spain* (14 June 2001) (the impossibility for members of a church to earmark part of their income tax for the support of their church as was possible for members of the Roman Catholic Church did not give rise to a violation of Art 9 taken with Art 14: the state had a certain margin of appreciation in such a matter on which there was no common European practice).
22 2333/64, *Inhabitants of Leeuw-St Pierre v Belgium* (1968) YB 11, 228.

Manifestations of religion or belief

7.05   It may be necessary to determine whether an issue falling within the scope of the guarantee involves a 'manifestation' of religion or belief through 'worship, teaching, practice [or] observation', for the European Convention on Human Rights, Article 9, paragraph (2) provides that a state may legitimately interfere only with such a 'manifestation'. A 'practice' may be the broadest of these four forms of 'manifestation' but, as the Commission clarified in *Arrowsmith v United Kingdom*, this 'does not cover each act which is motivated or influenced by a religion or a belief'. The applicant had been convicted for distributing leaflets to soldiers which were critical of government policy in Ulster. The Commission accepted that any public declaration which proclaimed the idea of pacifism and urged acceptance of a commitment to the belief in non-violence would fall to be considered as a 'normal and recognised manifestation of pacifist belief'. However, the leaflets in question did not so qualify as they focused not upon the promotion of non-violent means for dealing with political issues but with British policy in Northern Ireland. Accordingly, the distribution of leaflets which failed to express the authors' own pacifist values could not be a 'manifestation' of a belief for the purposes of Article 9 even although the distribution of the leaflets had been motivated by a belief in pacifism. The issue was, however, admissible under Article 10[1]. Similarly excluded from 'manifestations' of belief are the physical chastisement of children on religious grounds[2] and the placing of advertisements of a commercial nature concerning religious objects[3]. On the other hand, matters such as proselytism[4], general participation in the life of a religious community[5], following a diet dictated by religion[6] or slaughtering animals in accordance with religious prescriptions[7] will qualify.

1 7050/75, *Arrowsmith v United Kingdom* DR 19, 5, at paras 71–72. See too 22838/93, *Van der Dungen v Netherlands* (1995) DR 80, 147 (distribution of anti-abortion material outside a clinic did not involve expression of the applicant's religious beliefs); and 41615/98, *Zaoui v Switzerland* (18 January 2001) (publication of political propaganda on behalf of an Islamic group resulting in the confiscation of means of communication: activities did not concern the expression of a religious belief, and thus inadmissible under the European Convention on Human Rights, Art 9). See also *R (Pretty) v DPP* (18 October 2001, unreported), QBD (assisted suicide).
2 Eg 8811/79, *Seven Individuals v Sweden* (1982) DR 29, 104 (prohibition of parental chastisement of children even where practice is based upon religious beliefs not a breach of ECHR, Art 9).
3 7805/77, *X and the Church of Scientology v Sweden* (1979) DR 16, 68, para 4 (distinction drawn between 'informational' advertisements which may fall within ECHR, Art 9, and those which seek to sell goods for profit which do not).
4 *Kokkinakis v Greece* (1993) A 260-A, discussed at para 7.12 below. See too 50963/99, *Al-Nashif and Others v Bulgaria* (25 January 2001) (deportation on account of having taught Islamic religion without proper authorisation: admissible).
5 *Hasan and Chaush v Bulgaria* (26 October 2000), paras 60–65 (ECHR, Art 9 to be interpreted in light of Art 11).
6 Cf 13669/88, *DS and ES v United Kingdom* (1990) DR 65, 245 (restriction on ability of Orthodox Jews to obtain 'kosher' meat; failure to exhaust domestic remedies and thus inadmissible).
7 *Jewish Liturgical Association Cha'are Shalom Ve Tsedek v France* (27 June 2000), para 74, discussed at para 7.08 below.

Positive obligations

7.06   The duty upon the state to refrain from interfering with thought, conscience or religious belief may extend in certain circumstances to the taking of positive steps to provide respect for these rights. This may include responsibility for reconciling competing religious claims in a manner which promotes pluralism and tolerance[1]. The state will be expected to recognise the religious needs of those deprived of their liberty by ensuring the provision of religious observances[2] and respecting the religious practices of detainees unless these are considered inconsistent with the maintenance of good order[3]. There may also be a duty to recognise exemptions from general civic or legal obligations[4]. However, because of the European Convention on Human Rights, Article 4, which makes specific provision for 'service of a military character', Article 9 cannot probably in itself imply any right of recognition of conscientious objection to compulsory military service[5] although any discriminatory treatment may give rise to Convention issues[6].

1 *Kokkinakis v Greece* (1993) A 260-A, para 33.
2 Cf *Guzzardi v Italy* (1980) A 39, para 110 (applicant had not specifically requested provision of services, and consequently no issue in terms of the European Convention on Human Rights, Art 9 arose). For discussion of diet, see, eg 5947/72, *X v United Kingdom* (1976) DR 5, 8 (diet which respected religious faith had been available to a prisoner: inadmissible).
3 Cf 6886/75, *X v United Kingdom* (1976) DR 5, 100 (prisoner sought access to martial arts book as part of his religious beliefs: refusal justified under ECHR, Art 9(2) by the security threat posed).
4 Cf *Jewish Liturgical Association Cha'are Shalom Ve Tsedek v France* (27 June 2000), para 76 (exception permitting ritual slaughter of animals was an example of discharge of a positive

obligation under ECHR, Art 9). In contrast, see 44888/98, *Martins Casimiro and Cerveira Ferreira v Luxembourg* (27 April 1999) (a refusal to grant a general exemption from attending school on Saturdays on religious grounds to the sons of the applicants, Seventh Day Adventists, could be regarded as an interference with the manifestation of belief, but no general dispensation could be recognised which would adversely affect a child's right to education which prevailed over the parents' rights to have their religious convictions taken into account: application deemed inadmissible); and the related cases of *Valsamis v Greece* and *Efstratiou v Greece* 1996-VI, 2312, paras 37–38, 1996-VI, 2347, paras 38–39, discussed at para 7.08 below. See further Stavros 'Freedom of Religion and Claims for Exemption from Generally Applicable, Neutral Laws: Lessons from Across the Pond?' [1997] EHRLR 607.

5 7705/76, *X v Germany* (1977) DR 9, 196 (no right to be exempted from compulsory civilian service where the state recognises this as an alternative to military service). However, by 2000, only three Council of Europe states (Albania, FYRO Macedonia, and Turkey) with military service did not recognise alternative civilian service: see Council of Europe 'Report of the Committee on Legal Affairs and Human Rights on the Exercise of the Right of Conscientious Objection to Military Service', doc 8809, 13 July 2000. It is not clear whether the Court in future would read into ECHR, Art 9 a right to recognition of alternative civilian service in a clear case where an individual otherwise would be compelled to act contrary to fundamental religious beliefs. The issue was raised but avoided in 32438/96, *Stefanov v Bulgaria* (3 May 2001) (prison sentence imposed on Jehovah's Witness for his refusal to undertake military service; the Constitution provided that substitute civilian service should be regulated by statute, but no such law had been enacted: friendly settlement providing that all convictions of certain citizens for failing to undertake military service would be quashed where citizens had been willing to undertake civilian service). See further Rodotà 'Conscientious Objection to Military Service' in *Freedom of Conscience: Proceedings of the Leiden Seminar* (1993) pp 95–106; Gunn 'Adjudicating Rights of Conscience under the European Convention on Human Rights', in van der Vyver and Witte (eds) *Religious Human Rights in a Global Perspective* (1996) pp 305–330; and para 4.42 above.

6 See *Thlimmenos v Greece* (6 April 2000), discussed at para 7.13 below; cf 10600/83, *Johansen v Norway* (1985) DR 44, 155 (limited exemptions of certain ministers of religion from military service: no breach of the European Convention on Human Rights, Art 9 taken together with Art 14); 10410/83, *N v Sweden* (1984) DR 40, 203 (question whether exemptions from military service were operated in a discriminatory manner: no violation).

7.07   Any tension in society occasioned by religious differences should be addressed by the state not through elimination of pluralism but by encouraging mutual tolerance and understanding[1]. This may involve positive protection for religious sensibilities of adherents of particular faiths by preventing or punishing the display of insulting or offensive material which could discourage adherents from practising or professing their faith through ridicule. However, any attempt to achieve an appropriate balance between the freedom to express controversial ideas which may appear offensive, and protection for thought, conscience and religion is not likely to be a straightforward one, and may involve restrictions on rights in terms of the European Convention on Human Rights, Article 10 which appear unduly responsive to religious sensitivities. In *Otto-Preminger-Institut v Austria*, the authorities had seized and ordered the forfeiture of a film which ridiculed the beliefs of Roman Catholics. In interpreting Article 10's guarantee of freedom of expression, the European Court of Human Rights accepted that those who manifest their religious convictions 'must tolerate and accept the denial by others of their religious beliefs and even the propagation by others of doctrines hostile to their faith'.

However, the Court also considered that national authorities could deem it necessary to take action to protect believers against 'provocative portrayals of objects of religious veneration' where such constitute 'malicious violation of the spirit of tolerance, which must also be a feature of democratic society'[2]. Similarly, in *Wingrove v United Kingdom*, the Court rejected a complaint brought under Article 10 concerning the refusal of the British Board of Film Classification to license a video considered blasphemous, an interference which was deemed justified as for the protection of the rights of Christians[3]. In both these cases, the Court stressed that objection was taken to the manner in which the opinions had been expressed rather than to the content of the opinions themselves[4].

1 *Serif v Greece* (14 December 1999), para 53. Cf 53430/99, *Féderation Chrétienne des Temoins de Jehovah v France* (inclusion of Jehovah's Witnesses in a list of sects considered dangerous by a parliamentary commission and which allegedly triggered a policy of repression: communicated).
2 (1994) A 295-A, at para 47. Cf 33490/96 and 34055/96, *Dubowska and Skup v Poland* (1997) DR 89, 156 (criminal investigations were instituted into the display of a picture causing offence to religious sensitivities, but the conclusion that no offence had been committed did not involve a failure to protect the applicants' rights under ECHR, Art 9).
3 1996-V, 1937, paras 57–65. Cf an earlier approach of the Commission in 17439/90, *Choudhury v United Kingdom* (5 March 1991) (failure to extend protection of the law of blasphemy in England to other religions including the Muslim faith did not directly interfere with the applicant's freedom to manifest his belief: inadmissible).
4 *Otto-Preminger-Institut v Austria* (1994) A 295-A, para 56; *Wingrove v United Kingdom* 1996-V, 1937, para 60. See too 8710/79, *X Ltd and Y v United Kingdom* (1982) DR 28, 77 (protection accorded by English law of blasphemy justified as 'necessary in a democratic society': no violation of ECHR, Art 10).

Interferences

7.08 The facts must support a finding that there has been an 'interference' with rights in terms of the European Convention on Human Rights, Article 9. This issue is not as clear as determining whether there has been an interference with freedom of expression under Article 10[1]. A believer's right to freedom of religion includes the expectation that his religious community will be able to function free from arbitrary state intervention, so a failure by the state to remain neutral in exercising powers of registration of a religious community will involve an interference with freedom to manifest belief[2]. There can, however, be some difficulty in treating any perceived incompatibility between contractual or other duties and personal belief or principle as an interference[3], unless there are special features in the case which are accepted as of particular weight[4].

Even where a complaint has been obviously motivated by deep and sincere conviction, there may not be a finding that an interference has taken place. In the related cases of *Valsamis v Greece* and *Efstratiou v Greece*, pupils who were Jehovah's Witnesses had been punished for failing to attend parades commemorating the country's national day because of their belief that such events were incompatible with their firmly held pacifism. The Court considered that the nature of these parades (even taking into account the involvement of military personnel) contained nothing which could offend the applicants' pacifist convictions[5]. The decision seems unconvincing: the dissenting judges could discern no ground for holding that participation in a public event designed to show solidarity with symbolism which was anathema to personal religious belief could be 'necessary in a democratic society'[6]. In *Jewish Liturgical Association Cha'are Shalom Ve Tsedek v France*, a religious body sought to challenge a refusal by the authorities to grant the necessary permission to allow it to perform the slaughter of animals for consumption in accordance with its ultra-orthodox beliefs. Another Jewish organisation had received approval for the slaughter of animals according to its own rites which differed only marginally from those of the applicant association. Further, meat prepared in a manner consistent with the applicant association's beliefs was also available from other suppliers in a neighbouring country. On these grounds, the Court determined that there had been no interference since it had not been made impossible for the association's adherents to obtain meat slaughtered in a manner considered appropriate[7]. This decision is also unsatisfactory. It suggests that there are limits to the state's responsibilities to respect cultural pluralism without explaining the grounds for this or where these limits lie.

1 See para 7.20 below. Cf *Cyprus v Turkey* (10 May 2001), paras 245–246 at para 245: (restrictions placed on the freedom of movement of Greek Cypriots in northern Turkey 'considerably curtailed their ability to observe their religious beliefs, in particular their access to places of worship outside their villages and their participation in other aspects of religious life': violation of the European Convention Human Rights, Art 9).

2 *Hasan and Chaush v Bulgaria* (26 October 2000), para 82 (favouring of one faction in a leadership dispute between rivals for the post of Chief Mufti of Muslims living in the country); and 45701/99, *Mitropolia Basarabiei Si Exarhatul Plairuilor and Ors v Moldova* (7 June 2001) (refusal to grant official recognition to a church declared admissible).

3 See *Kalaç v Turkey* 1997-IV, 1199, paras 28–31 at para 28 (voluntary acceptance of restrictions on rights by the applicant when joining the armed forces which may adopt disciplinary regulations to prohibit conduct 'inimical to an established order reflecting the requirements of military service'); 8160/78, *X v United Kingdom* (1981) DR 22, 27 (refusal of rearrangement of teacher's timetable to allow him to attend the mosque not a violation as he had previously accepted an offer of employment without making any such request; but the Commission considered that in certain circumstances dismissal could raise an issue under ECHR, Art 9); 29107/95, *Stedman v United Kingdom* (1997) DR 89, 104 (employee who was a Christian dismissed because of refusal to work on Sundays: the Commission considered that dismissal was because of refusal to work certain hours rather than her religious beliefs); Cf 16278/90, *Karaduman v Turkey* (1993) DR 74, 93 (dress regulations of a secular university prohibiting the wearing of a headscarf did not constitute an interference with ECHR, Art 9 rights); and 42393/98, *Dahlab v Switzerland* (15 February 2001) (ban imposed on a Muslim teacher from wearing an Islamic veil at work: inadmissible). Cf 41556/98, *Tekin v Turkey* (nurse prohibited from wearing an Islamic shawl in higher education training institution: communicated). The issue may also arise under ECHR, Art 10: e g 12242/86, *Rommelfanger v Germany* (1989) DR 62, 151 (dismissal of a doctor employed in a Roman Catholic hospital for expressing views on abortion not in conformity with the Church's teaching: inadmissible).

4 Cf *Buscarini and Ors v San Marino* 1999-I, 605, paras 34–41 at para 39 ('interference' where applicants who were elected to parliament were required to take a religious oath on the Bible as a condition of sitting; making the 'exercise of a mandate intended to represent different views of society within Parliament subject to a prior declaration of commitment to a particular set of beliefs' was contradictory and thus a violation of ECHR, Art 9); but cf 39511/98, *McGuiness v United Kingdom* 1999-V, 481 (elected representatives required to take an oath of allegiance to the monarch; application declared inadmissible under ECHR, Art 10 since the oath could be viewed simply as an affirmation of loyalty to the UK's constitutional principles). See too 24875/94, *Logan v United Kingdom* (1996) DR 86, 74 (applicant asserted that the duty to pay maintenance payments had the effect of restricting his ability to visit Buddhist places of worship; the Commission considered that the complaint did not disclose any effective restriction on freedom to practise his religion); and 31876/96 et al, *Tepeli and Others v Turkey* (hearing of 12 June 2001) (compulsory retiral of 41 members of the armed forces, allegedly upon the basis of religious and political beliefs).

5 1996-VI, 2312, paras 37–38; 1996-VI, 2347, paras 38–39 (public celebration of democracy and human rights not vitiated by presence of military; similarly, no violation of ECHR, Protocol 1, Art 2).

6 Cf too the dissenting opinion of the Commission President, Trechsel, who considered that the issue was more appropriate for deliberation under ECHR, Art 11.
7 (27 June 2000), paras 73–85. The Court also noted that, even if there had been an interference, this would have pursued the aim of protection of public health and order and would not have been considered disproportionate. The decision of the majority of the Court (12 to 5) differs sharply from the majority of the Commission (14 to 3) which had been of the opinion that there had been a violation of ECHR, Art 9 taken along with Art 14. The Court on this point considered that the difference of treatment was limited in scope and also met the test of proportionality, and no ECHR, Art 14 question arose (at paras 86–88).

Assessing whether a limitation on 'manifestation' of religion or belief meets the requirements of paragraph (2)

7.09   The European Court of Human Rights, Article 9, paragraph (2) provides that any state interference with thought, conscience or religion may only relate to manifestation of belief. As with related guarantees under the Convention, the state must establish that any interference with the guarantee is 'prescribed by law', has a legitimate aim, and is 'necessary in a democratic society'. The lawfulness of any interference will rarely cause a problem in this area[1]; similarly the application of a recognised state interest (restricted under the paragraph to the protection of public safety, public order, health and morals and the rights and freedoms of others[2]) will seldom prove to be controversial.

1 But cf *Tsirlis and Kouloumpas v Greece* 1997-III, 909, paras 56–63 (detention following unlawful refusal to excuse certain ministers of religion from military service; issue determined under the European Convention on Human Rights, Art 5); *Hasan and Chaush v Bulgaria* (25 October 2000), paras 84–89 (domestic law did not provide substantive criteria for the registration of religious denominations and leadership: violation of ECHR, Art 9).
2 Unlike Arts 8, 10 and 11, national security is not recognised as such an aim in this guarantee.

Human Rights Act 1998, s 13

7.10   Some attempt is made by the Human Rights Act 1998 to give particular weight to freedom of thought, conscience and religion in any domestic determination of an issue under the European Convention on Human Rights, Article 9. The 1998 Act, s 13(1) provides that 'if a court's determination of any question arising under this Act might affect the exercise by a religious organisation (itself or its members collectively) of the Convention right to freedom of thought, conscience and religion, it must have particular regard to the importance of that right'[1]. The intention is to protect the common faith or views of members of a church or other religious body 'against attack, whether by outsiders or by individual dissidents'[2]. However, the extent to which churches (including established churches) are bound by Convention requirements is not entirely clear in existing jurisprudence[3].

1 'Court' includes a tribunal: Human Rights Act 1998, s 13(2).
2 312 HC Official Report (6th series) col 1021, 20 May 1998 (Home Secretary). See further Thorp 'The Human Rights Bill: Churches and Religious Organisations', House of

Commons Research paper 98/26 (1998); Cumper 'The Protection of Religious Rights under Section 13 of the Human Rights Act 1998' [2000] PL 254.

3 See further Naismith 'Religion and the European Convention on Human Rights' (2001) HR & UK P, 8 at 19, discussing 21283/93, *Tyler v United Kingdom* (1994) DR 77, 81 (dismissal of a clergyman after determination by an ecclesiastical court of the Church of England that he had been guilty of adultery: no finding of violation of ECHR, Art 6 requirement of independence in the circumstances). Cf 24019/94, *Finska Fösamlingen I Stockholm and Hautaniemi v Sweden* (1996) DR 85, 94 (Lutheran Church and its parishes were non-governmental organisations, and thus decisions of the Church Assembly concerning freedom of religion did not engage state responsibility under Art 9); but see too *Pellegrini v Italy* (20 July 2001), paras 40–48 (breach of fairness requirements under Art 6 in proceedings before a Vatican ecclesiastical court lacking impartiality).

'Necessary in a democratic society'

7.11   The crucial question is likely to be whether an interference was 'necessary in a democratic society'. As with the European Convention on Human Rights, Articles 8, 10 and 11, the interference complained of must correspond to a pressing social need, be proportionate to the legitimate aim pursued, and be justified by relevant and sufficient reasons[1]. The proportionality of a limitation on manifestation of belief is considered carefully, for while there is recognition of some margin of appreciation on the part of national decision-makers, the quality of reasons adduced for an interference must support the requisite test which requires 'very strict scrutiny'[2]. Certainly, the 'pressing social need' of any state limitation on manifestation of religious belief may involve promoting public safety considerations[3]. Particular and more difficult issues, however, have arisen in relation to unorthodox religious sects or minority faiths where justification is based upon protection of public order or protection against exploitation of individuals[4]. The promotion of pluralism and tolerance is normally at the heart of the Court's approach. In *Serif v Greece*, the applicant had been elected as a mufti, a Muslim religious leader, and had begun to exercise the functions of that office but without receiving the necessary state authority. The public prosecutor had sought to protect the authority of another mufti who had been officially recognised, considering that this would help relieve the tensions developing between Muslim factions, and apparently also as between Greece and Turkey. In consequence, the applicant was convicted of having usurped the functions of a minister of a 'known religion', an interference which the Court accepted as pursuing the legitimate aim of protecting public order. However, the Court was not persuaded that there was any pressing social need for the conviction. There had been no instance of local disturbance, and any inter-state diplomatic difficulty was no more than a remote possibility. In any case, the function of the state was to promote pluralism rather than to seek to eliminate it[5]. In *Manoussakis and Ors v Greece*, domestic law required religious organisations to obtain formal approval for the use of premises for worship. Jehovah's Witnesses had sought unsuccessfully to obtain permission, and thereafter had been convicted of operating an unauthorised place of worship. The Court accepted that national authorities had the right to take measures designed to determine whether activities undertaken by a religious association were potentially harmful to others, but this could not allow the state to determine the legitimacy of either the

beliefs or the means of expressing such beliefs. Here, the 'apparently innocent requirement of an authorisation to operate a place of worship had
been transformed from a mere formality into a lethal weapon against the
right to freedom of religion'[6].

1 See further paras 3.66–3.78 above.
2 *Manoussakis and Ors v Greece* 1996-IV, 1346, at para 40.
3 7992/77 *X v United Kingdom* (1978) DR 14, 234 (objection by Sikhs to wearing crash helmets
   when driving motorcycles; legal requirement considered justified).
4 But see Parliamentary Assembly Recommendation 1412 (1999) on the illegal activities of
   sects and calling for domestic action against 'illegal practices carried out in the name of
   groups of a religious, esoteric or spiritual nature', and to provide and exchange information on such sects.
5 (14 December 1999), paras 49–54.
6 1996-IV, 1346, paras 44–53 at para 41 (tendency on the part of the Greek state and Orthodox
   Church to restrict the activities of other faiths; severity of sanction not proportionate to legitimate aims of protection of public order and rights of others). See too 28626/95, *Christian
   Association of Jehovah's Witnesses v Bulgaria* (1997) DR 90, 77 (suspension of the association's
   registration followed by arrests, dispersal of meetings held in public and private locations
   and confiscation of religious materials declared admissible under the European Convention
   on Human Rights, Arts 6, 9–11 and 14; (9 March 1998) friendly settlement ultimately
   achieved); 26308/95, *Institute of French Priests and Ors v Turkey* (14 December 2000) (decision by the Turkish courts to register a plot of land belonging to the Institute in the name
   of state bodies on the ground that the Institute was no longer eligible for treatment as a religious body as it had let part of its property for various sporting activities: friendly settlement secured after a life tenancy in favour of the priests representing the Institute was
   conferred). Cf *Canea Catholic Church v Greece* 1997-VIII, 2843 (discriminatory treatment in
   the recognition of legal personality of a church dealt with under ECHR, Arts 6 and 14).

7.12   Manifestation of belief through 'teaching' includes the right to pros-
elytise by attempting to persuade others to convert to another religion. In
Kokkinakis v Greece, a Jehovah's Witness had been sentenced to imprisonment for proselytism which was specifically prohibited by the Greek
Constitution and by statute. The European Court of Human Rights
accepted that the right to try to convince others to convert to another faith
was included within the scope of the guarantee, 'failing which ...
"freedom to change [one's] religion or belief", enshrined in Article 9,
would be likely to remain a dead letter'[1]. While accepting that the prohibition was prescribed by law and had the legitimate aim of protecting the
rights of others, the Court, however, could not accept that the interference
could be justified as necessary in a democratic society. A distinction had to
be drawn between 'bearing Christian witness' or evangelicalism and
'improper proselytism' involving undue influence or even force, especially upon weak and vulnerable members of society. The former was
accepted by Christians as part of the Church's mission; the latter was
incompatible with respect for beliefs and opinion. The failure of the
domestic courts to specify the reasons for the conviction meant that the
state could not show that there was a pressing social need for the conviction, and thus the sentence was not proportionate to the aim of the protection of others[2].

1 *Kokkinakis v Greece* (1993) A-260A at para 31.
2 *Kokkinakis v Greece* (1993) A-260A, paras 31–50. The Court in its judgment (para 48) made
   use of a report of the World Council of Churches. See too *Larissis v Greece* 1998-I, 362, paras
   40–61 (conviction of senior officers for proselytism of three airmen under their command
   held not to be a breach of ECHR, Art 9; but there was a violation in respect of conviction
   for proselytism of civilians). Cf Naismith 'Religion and the European Convention on

Human Rights' (2001) HR & UK P Issue 1, 8 at 13 who warns against too ready use of the concept of abuse since there would 'be a real danger of the right to communicate one's beliefs under Article 9 being restricted in a manner inconsistent with the liberal interpretation ... given to the more general right of freedom of expression guaranteed by Article 10 of the Convention').

Religious discrimination

7.13   Religious beliefs may also involve consideration of discriminatory treatment in employment and give rise to questions under the European Convention on Human Rights, Article 9 or this provision taken along with Article 14[1]. *Thlimmenos v Greece* concerned a person who had been refused admission as a chartered accountant because of a criminal conviction. The conviction in question arose from his refusal to wear military uniform, during a period of general mobilisation, on account of his religious beliefs as a Jehovah's Witness. The Court noted that access to a profession was not as such covered by the Convention, but treated the complaint as one of discrimination on the basis of the exercise of freedom of religion. Although states could legitimately exclude certain classes of offenders from various professions, the particular conviction in question could not suggest dishonesty or moral turpitude. The treatment of the applicant therefore did not have a legitimate aim, and was in the nature of a disproportionate sanction (additional to the substantial period of imprisonment he had already served). There was accordingly a violation of Article 14 taken in conjunction with Article 9[2].

1   Eg *Hoffman v Austria* (1993) A 255-C, discussed at para 3.58 above.
2   (6 April 2000), paras 39–49 (consideration of issue under the European Convention on Human Rights, Art 9 alone not necessary in view of the finding of violation). Cf 40130/98, *Riondel v Switzerland* (14 October 1999) (withdrawal of licence permitting applicant to run a private security agency on account of his connections with a sect whose beliefs were considered potentially destabilising for public order declared inadmissible).

FREEDOM OF EXPRESSION

The scope of 'freedom of expression'

7.14   The European Convention on Human Rights, Article 10 seeks to protect freedom of expression[1]. The text specifically provides that the freedom 'to hold opinions and to receive and impart information and ideas without interference by public authority' is included. The article has generated a substantial amount of case law, and it is now possible to state with some certainty the principles which have emerged. There is no one judicial approach; rather, the European Court of Human Rights will be influenced in particular by the particular type of speech issue at stake[2]. The justification for free speech is drawn both from its importance in a pluralist society and also as a means of self-fulfilment[3]: the presumption is that expression acts as a tool for the enhancement of democracy as well as for individual personal development. One central aim is the furtherance of 'pluralism, tolerance and broadmindedness without which there is no "democratic society"', and thus ideas or information which 'offend, shock or disturb the State or any sector of the population' are as much covered as those 'favourably received or regarded as inoffensive or as a matter of indifference'[4]. As well as political speech, Article 10 covers artistic expression 'which affords the opportunity to take part in the public exchange of cultural, political and social information and ideas of all kinds'[5], and commercial information and advertisements[6]. The Court has also drawn a distinction between facts (whose existence can be proved or disproved) and value judgments (which are not susceptible to proof and thus are worthy of enhanced protection[7], providing always that the factual basis for such judgments are 'substantially correct' and made in good faith[8]). The scope of Article 10 covers a broad range of means of expression[9] and also protects freedom to receive information[10]. It may thus extend to access to means of communication[11] including the reception and transmission of broadcasts[12].

1 See further Lester 'Freedom of Expression' in Macdonald, Matscher and Petzold (eds) *The European System for the Protection of Human Rights* (1993) pp 465–491. For a comprehensive survey of Strasbourg case law, see Council of Europe *Case-Law Concerning Article 10 of the European Convention on Human Rights* (2001). For a discussion of the European Convention on Human Rights, Art 10 and its application in the UK (and in Austria), see Oetheimer *L'Harmonisation de la Liberté d'Expresion en Europe* (2001).

2 Cf Mahoney 'Universality versus Subsidiarity in the Strasbourg Case Law on Free Speech' [1997] EHRLR 364; Lester of Herne Hill 'Universality versus Subsidiarity: A Reply' [1998] EHRLR 73.

3 The classic justification for freedom of expression is found in J S Mill *On Liberty* (1848) para 2. See, further, Barendt *Freedom of Speech* pp 28–36; Nieuwenhuis 'Freedom of Speech: USA v Germany and Europe' (2000) 18 NQHR 195. It is not clear whether ECHR, Art 10 extends to expression through choice of clothes, although protection may exist in employment law. Cf 11674/85, *Stevens v United Kingdom* (1986) DR 46, 245 at para 2 (expression 'may include the right for a person to express his ideas through the way he dresses'). Cf 16278/90, *Karaduman v Turkey* (1993) DR 74, 93 (dress regulations of a secular university prohibiting the wearing of a headscarf did not constitute an interference with ECHR, Art 9 rights); and 42393/98, *Dahlab v Switzerland* (15 February 2001) (ban imposed on a Muslim teacher from wearing an Islamic veil at work: inadmissible under ECHR, Art 9). For a full discussion, see Kuhn 'Student Dress Codes in the Public Schools' (1996) 25 Jo Law and Educ 83; Clayton and Pitt 'Dress Codes and Freedom of Expression' [1997] EHRLR 54; Parry and Parry 'Implications of the Human Rights Act 1988 for Schools' (2000) 12 Ed Law 279 at 281.

4 *Handyside v United Kingdom* (1976) A 24, at para 49. It follows under ECHR, Protocol 1, Art 2 that the state may determine school curricular issues and impart factual information concerning religious or philosophical matters, provided always it does so in an 'objective, critical and pluralistic manner': *Kjeldsen, Busk Madsen and Pedersen v Denmark* (1976) A 23 at para 53.

5 *Müller and Ors v Switzerland* (1988) A 133, at para 27.

6 *Markt intern Verlag GmbH and Klaus Beerman v Germany* (1989) A 165, para 35 (statements published in a specialised bulletin critical of a mail-order firm); *Groppera Radio AG and Ors v Switzerland* (1990) A 173, para 55 (light music and commercials retransmitted by cable originating in another country); cf *Casado Coca v Spain* (1994) A 285-A, paras 54–55 (ban on professional advertising by lawyers).

7 Thus in *Lingens v Austria* (1986) A 103, at para 46, the Court was critical of domestic law which placed the onus of proving the truthfulness of the offending comments upon the accused, but since the expression complained of essentially concerned value judgments, the Court noted that the requirement to prove the truthfulness of the allegations 'is impossible of fulfilment and it infringes freedom of opinion itself, which is a fundamental part of the right secured by Article 10'. See too *Thorgeir Thorgeirson v Iceland* (1992) A 239, at para 65 (domestic law requiring the accused to prove the truthfulness of his allegations of police brutality, an 'unreasonable, if not impossible task'); *Feldek v Slovakia* (12 July

2001), paras 85–90 (value judgment concerning a minister's background in a fascist organisation). The distinction between facts and value judgments is also drawn in domestic legal systems in the UK. For a suggestion that the approach adopted by the English courts is open to challenge, see Young 'Fact, Opinion and the Human Rights Act 1998: Does English Law need to Modify its Definition of Statements of Opinion?' (2000) OJLS 89.

8 *Schwabe v Austria* (1992) A 242-B, at para 34 (defamation conviction for comment made about politician; the Court found a breach of ECHR, Art 10, as the applicant could not have been considered to have exceeded the limits of freedom of expression). See also *Jerusalem v Austria* (27 February 2001), at paras 42–43 ('the requirement to prove the truth of a value judgment is impossible to fulfil and infringes freedom of opinion ... [but] even where a statement amounts to a value judgment, the proportionality of an interference may depend on whether there exists a sufficient factual basis for the impugned statement, since even a value judgment without any factual basis to support it may be excessive'); and *Perna v Italy* (25 July 2001), paras 40–45 at paras 42 and 44 (defamation proceedings in relation (a) to a statement concerning a public prosecutor ('when he entered the State Legal Service he swore a threefold oath of obedience – to God, to the Law and to [the Communist Party]'), a 'symbolic image [which was] admittedly hard-hitting' but one with an uncontested factual basis which thus could not be considered excessive and thus protected by Art 10; and (b) allegations concerning the prosecutor which were not covered by Art 10 protection unless they had a factual basis, 'especially considering the seriousness of such accusations, since they were allegations of fact susceptible of proof', but since the newspaper article failed to supply supporting evidence or corroboration of the allegations context, the assertions had 'overstepped the limits of acceptable criticism' and thus fell outside Art 10 protection).

9 However, where the challenge is to an interference with expression through interference with correspondence, the *lex specialis* governing the application is ECHR, Art 8 rather than Art 10: see para 6.16 above.

10 For discussion of the right to freedom of information, see Cohen-Jonathan 'Transparence, Démocratie et Effectivité des Droits fondamentaux dans la Convention Européenne des Droits de l'Homme' in Mahoney, Matscher, Petzold and Wildhaber (eds) *Protecting Human Rights: The European Perspective* (2000) pp 245–263. Cf *Cyprus v Turkey* (10 May 2001), at para 252 (vetting of school books ostensibly sought to identify material which could harm inter-communal relations, but the reality was that a significant number of books were subjected to unilateral censorship which 'far exceeded the limits of confidence-building methods and amounted to a denial of the right to freedom of information').

11 Eg 8317/78, *McFeely v United Kingdom* (1980) DR 20, 44 (restrictions imposed on prisoners as to means of communication (no access to television, radio etc) justified for prevention of disorder); and 41615/98, *Zaoui v Switzerland* (18 January 2001) (confiscation of fax machine and preventing access to the Internet constituted interferences, but were justified on security and public order grounds). The European Convention on Human Rights, Art 10 does not guarantee a right to access to broadcasting facilities: 25060/94, *Haider v Austria* (1995) DR 83, 66 (complaint by applicant that the reporting of news events concerning him did not meet the requirements of plurality, information and objectivity as required by Art 10: application declared inadmissible). Nor can it imply protection against deportation for a journalist who is not a national of the state involved: 7729/76, *Agee v United Kingdom* (1977) DR 7, 164.

12 *Autronic AG v Switzerland* (1990) 178, at para 47: 'Article 10 applies not only to the content of information but also to the means of transmission or reception since any restriction imposed on the means necessarily interferes with the right to receive and impart information' (refusal by state to permit reception of satellite transmissions from another state: violation of ECHR, Art 10). Cf 10462/83, *B v Germany* (1984) DR 37, 155 (ECHR, Art 10 does not guarantee a right to install an antenna for an amateur radio station); and 17713/91, *Schindewolf v Germany* (2 September 1991) (removal of unauthorised aerial on planning grounds: inadmissible). See also *BBC Petitioners* 2000 SCCR 533 at 561 and 577 (refusal of permission to televise a trial).

Positive obligations

7.15 The primary duty imposed upon a state is the negative one of refraining from interfering with freedom of expression[1]. In certain cases, a state will also have positive obligations to take steps to safeguard the rights of individuals by providing protection against unlawful acts by others designed to restrict or inhibit free speech[2]. This may apply even where the relations between an employer and an employee are governed by rules of private law. In *Fuentes Bobo v Spain*, a television producer had been dismissed after making comments which had been considered critical of the management of the state broadcasting company. The European Court of Human Rights rejected the state's contentions that it could not be held responsible for the applicant's dismissal since the television station was a private law undertaking, and clarified that in certain cases there could be a positive obligation on the state to ensure that freedom of expression was properly respected in such circumstances. Here, the severity of the penalty imposed could not be supported by any pressing social need and consequently there was a violation of the guarantee[3]. The European Convention on Human Rights, Article 10, on the other hand, does not go as far as to establish any general duty to allow access to personal information held by state authorities, but merely prevents any governmental restriction on receiving information that others wish or may be willing to impart[4]. In certain circumstances, however, the Convention imposes positive responsibilities upon the state to make available information held by it, for example in respect of protection of life under Article 2[5] or where this concerns respect for private or family life under Article 8[6].

1 Other initiatives of the Council of Europe have, however, sought to stress positive responsibilities of the state in ensuring equality of access to the media for minority groups and in encouraging journalistic independence and pluralism: see further, Resolution MCM (94) 20 (4th European Ministerial Conference on Mass Media Policy); and Recommendation No R(96)10 (Guaranteeing Independence of Public Service Broadcasting).

2 *Özgür Gündem v Turkey* (16 March 2000), paras 41–46 (deliberate and concerted attacks upon journalists, distributors etc associated with the newspaper; no action taken by the state despite requests by the newspaper: the Court reiterated key importance of free expression and held the state had failed to comply with its positive duty to protect the newspaper). Cf the related cases of *Yasa v Turkey* 1998-VI, 2411, paras 118–120 (attacks on newsagents considered under ECHR, Arts 2 and 13); *Tekin v Turkey* 1998-IV, 1504 (detention and ill-treatment of journalists etc: not established that loss of liberty was because of the applicant's occupation, and consequently no violation of ECHR, Art 10).

3 (29 February 2000), paras 44–50.

4 *Leander v Sweden* (1987) A 116, para 74 (prohibition on national security grounds on gaining access to personal information on applicant held by state authorities: no violation of ECHR, Art 10); *Open Door and Dublin Well Woman v Ireland* (1992) A 246-A, para 55; (access to information on abortion facilities); *Guerra and Ors v Italy* 1998-I, 210, paras 52–54 at para 53 (question whether there was a positive duty upon a state to publish a report on a serious environmental hazard: the Commission considered such was an essential method of protecting health and well-being, but the Court reiterated its position that ECHR, Art 10 could not require any positive duty 'to collect and disseminate information of its own motion'). Cf 38406/97, *Albayrak v Turkey* (16 November 2000) (sanctions imposed upon a judge for having read a newspaper and having watched television both of which were pro-Kurdish: admissible).

5 Eg *McGinley and Egan v United Kingdom* 1998-III, 1334, paras 85–90; see para 4.12 above.

6 Eg *Gaskin v United Kingdom* (1989) A 160, paras 42–49; *T P and K M v United Kingdom* (10 May 2001), paras 78–83. See paras 6.33 and 6.23 respectively above.

The media and freedom of expression

7.16 Protection of the media is considered a vital feature of a democracy[1]. Journalists act as a conduit for information and thereby have a vital role in contributing to public discussion and debate and in acting in a 'watchdog' role through investigative journalism. This justifies a high level of protection for the media[2], but it carries with it certain responsibilities for journalists. The media may have a responsibility to verify in advance factual statements that are potentially defamatory where this does not involve 'an unreasonable, if not impossible task'[3], although 'the press should normally be entitled, when contributing to public debate on matters of legitimate concern, to rely on the contents of official reports without having to undertake independent research'[4]. Further, competing considerations such as the responsibility to respect private life under the European Convention on Human Rights, Article 8 may justify restrictions on expression on the ground of protection of individual privacy[5]. However, particular weight is accorded to media attempts to promote discussion and debate on matters of legitimate public concern. In *Lingens v Austria*, the applicant had been punished for publishing articles in a newspaper criticising the head of state's fitness for office. The Court considered that such sanctions operated as a form of censure which would be likely to inhibit future political discussion and debate and thus were 'liable to hamper the press in performing its task as purveyor of information and public watchdog' since 'freedom of the press ... affords the public one of the best means of discovering and forming an opinion of the ideas and attitudes of political leaders'[6]. This sentiment shapes much of the application of Article 10. In *Castells v Spain*, a Member of Parliament had been convicted for criticising in the press the government's apparent failure to investigate terrorist activities (the responsibility for which he had attributed to the government) without having been allowed to try to prove the allegations by way of defence in court. The importance of a free press was again emphasised in aiding democratic communication between the electorate and those chosen as its representatives: 'it gives politicians the opportunity to reflect and comment on the preoccupations of public opinion; it thus enables everyone to participate in the free political debate which is at the very core of the concept of a democratic society'[7]. In such circumstances, 'the dominant position which the Government occupies makes it necessary for it to display restraint in resorting to criminal proceedings, particularly where other means are available for replying to the unjustified attacks and criticisms of its adversaries or the media'[8]. Similar concerns apply to the perceived role of the media in scrutinising the administration of justice[9].

1 Eg *Goodwin v United Kingdom* 1996-II, 483 at para 39 ('protection of journalistic sources is one of the basic conditions for press freedom'); *Thoma v Luxembourg* (29 March 2001), para 64 (there had to be 'particularly cogent reasons' for punishing a journalist for assisting in the dissemination of statements made by another person since this would seriously hamper the contribution of the press to discussion of matters of public interest). Cf 52207/99, *Banković and Ors v Belgium and 16 other States* (NATO bombing of Radio-Television Serbia during the Kosovo campaign: communicated). The *Goodwin* judgment was considered by the Court of Appeal in *Ashworth Hospital Authority v MGN Ltd* [2001] 1 WLR 515 (disclosure of source of 'leak' of patient records from hospital). Other recent English cases include *Kelly v BBC* [2001] 2 WLR 253 (broadcasting of interview with child

who was a ward of court) and *R (Wagstaff) v Secretary of State for Health* [2001] 1 WLR 292 (holding of inquiry in private).

2 For the purposes of ECHR, Art 10, 'victims' of interference with the guarantee can include newspaper companies, journalists and editors but not trade union associations: 11553/85 and 11658/85, *Hodgson and Ors v United Kingdom* (1987) DR 51, 136 (National Union of Journalists could not be a 'victim' for the purposes of the application); 15404/89, *Purcell and Ors v Ireland* (1991) DR 70, 262 (even although unions considered themselves guardians of collective interests of their members, their rights were not affected by the challenged measures, and thus they were not 'victims'). In 25798/94, *BBC v United Kingdom* (1996) DR 84, 129 and again in 34324/96, *BBC Scotland, McDonald, Rodgers and Donald v United Kingdom* (23 October 1997), the Commission left open the question of whether a state public service broadcaster could qualify as a 'victim'. See further, Tierney 'Press Freedom and Public Interest: The Developing Jurisprudence of the European Court of Human Rights' [1998] EHRLR 419; Lester of Herne Hill and Schiffrin 'The European Convention on Human Rights and Media Law', in Barendt (ed) *IV Yearbook of Copyright and Media Law* 353; and Costigan 'Human Rights and the Police Seizure of Journalists' Material' (2000) 5 Comms L 197; and Ress 'Media Law in the Context of the European Union and the European Convention on Human Rights' in Mahoney, Matscher, Petzold and Wildhaber (eds) *Protecting Human Rights: The European Perspective* (2000) pp 1173–1196. Other Council of Europe initiatives in this area stress the importance of a free press and of co-operation in broadcasting: see eg European Convention on Transfrontier Television (ETS 132, 1989) and amending Protocol (ETS 171, 1998); and more generally, 'Recommendations and Resolutions adopted by the Parliamentary Assembly of the Council of Europe in the Media Field', doc DH-MM (97) 3; 'Recommendations and Declarations adopted by the Committee of Ministers in the Media Field, doc DH-MM (98) 2; and Council of Europe *Media and Democracy* (1998).

3 Cf *Thorgeir Thorgeirson v Iceland* (1992) A 239, at para 65 (newspaper articles reported numerous allegations of police brutality made by others and sought an independent inquiry; conviction of journalist was in part based upon his failure to justify the allegations which had not been established as without foundation).

4 *Bladet Tromsø and Stensaas v Norway* 1999-III, 289, at para 68.

5 This matter is discussed under ECHR, Art 8: see para 6.34 above.

6 *Lingens v Austria* (1986) A 103, at para 42.

7 *Castells v Spain* (1992) A 236, at para 43. See, too, *Oberschlick v Austria (No 1)* (1991) A 204, paras 57–63 (conviction of applicant for criminal libel).

8 (1992) A 236, at para 6, noting that the government may react nevertheless 'appropriately and without excess' to unfounded defamatory accusations.

9 Eg *Prager and Oberschlick v Austria* (1995) A 313, para 34; see further para 7.42 below.

Protection for journalistic sources

7.17   This underlying policy also implies recognition of the importance of protection for journalists' sources which is acknowledged as a fundamental prerequisite for a free press. In *Goodwin v United Kingdom*, on the application of a private company, a court made a disclosure order against a journalist which required him to disclose the identity of the source who had supplied him with unsolicited information on the company's financial activities. The journalist had refused to comply with the order and had been fined. It was accepted that this interference pursued a legitimate aim, but the applicant alleged that any compulsion to disclose sources had to be limited to the most exceptional circumstances where there were vital public or individual interests at stake to satisfy the test of pressing social need. In light of the injunction prohibiting any publication of the information, the Court considered whether the disclosure order could have served any additional purposes. While there were undoubtedly relevant reasons for the order (such as identifying any disloyal employee), it was not possible to say that the reasons were sufficient, and a violation of the European Convention on Human Rights, Article 10 was established[1].

However, where a criminal trial is involved and the liberty of an individual may be at stake, the pressing social need for disclosure of sources may be more readily justified[2].

1 1996-II, 483, paras 36–46.
2 25798/94, *BBC v United Kingdom* (1996) DR 84, 129 (requirement to disclose material which had been filmed during riots, for the purposes of evidence in a criminal trial, did not violate ECHR, Art 10).

DECISIONS OF THE DOMESTIC COURTS ON PROTECTION OF JOURNALISTS' SOURCES

7.18 These judgments of the European Court of Human Rights were considered by the Court of Appeal in *Ashworth Hospital Authority v MGN Ltd*. The case concerned the disclosure of the source of a 'leak' to the press of medical records held by Ashworth Hospital relating to one of the 'Moors murderers'. The court held that an order for disclosure was justified. Lord Phillips of Worth Maltraves MR observed:

> 'It seems to me that the approach of the European Court to the question of whether disclosure of a source is 'necessary' involves a single exercise in which the court considers not merely whether, on the facts of the particular case, disclosure of the source is necessary to achieve the legitimate aim but, more significantly, whether the achievement of the legitimate aim on the facts of the instant case is so important that it overrides the public interest in protecting journalistic sources in order to ensure free communication of information to and through the press[1].'

In relation to the latter point, the disclosure of confidential medical records to the press was an attack on an area of confidentiality which should be safeguarded in any democratic society, the protection of patient information being of vital concern[2]. Laws LJ added:

> 'It is in my judgment of the first importance to recognise that the potential vice – the 'chilling effect' – of court orders requiring the disclosure of press sources is in no way lessened, and certainly not abrogated, simply because the case is one in which the information actually published is of no legitimate, objective public interest. Nor is it to the least degree lessened or abrogated by the fact (where it is so) that the source is a disloyal and greedy individual, prepared for money to betray his employer's confidences. The public interest in the non-disclosure of press sources is constant, whatever the merits of the particular publication, and the particular source[3].'

1 [2001] 1 WLR 515 at para 90. See also *John v Express Newspapers* [2000] 1 WLR 1931.
2 [2001] 1 WLR 515 at para 99.
3 [2001] 1 WLR 515 at para 101.

Licensing of broadcasting and cinemas

7.19 The European Convention on Human Rights, Article 10(1) additionally provides that states are not to be prevented 'from requiring the licensing of broadcasting, television or cinema enterprises'. This permits states to regulate the technical aspects of broadcasting rather than the actual content of broadcasts themselves[1]. For example, in *Vgt Verein Gegen Tierfabriken v Switzerland*, a television advertisement prepared by an animal protection society denouncing the industrial rearing of pigs and encouraging people to eat less meat was rejected by a broadcasting authority because of domestic law which prohibited the broadcasting of advertisements of a political nature. While the European Court of Human Rights accepted that the prohibition pursued a legitimate aim in preventing financially strong groups from obtaining an advantage in politics, it found that the limitation of the prohibition solely to radio and television broadcasts was not particularly pressing, and that the primary aim of the advertisement had been to participate in an ongoing general debate on animal protection. Accordingly, it had not been shown that the interference with free speech had been relevant and sufficient[2]. Further, both the object or purpose and the scope of any exercise of the power to license must be in accordance with the overall context of the guarantee of freedom of expression, and in particular with the requirement that any licensing determination meets the exacting tests of paragraph (2)[3]. In *Informationsverein Lentia and Ors v Austria*, the Court accepted that a state broadcasting monopoly which protected public service broadcasting and which satisfied quality and balance concerns through the operation of state supervision could meet the requirements of paragraph (1). However, since a licensing determination could also involve other factors such as 'the nature and objectives of a proposed station, its potential audience at national, regional or local level, the rights and needs of a specific audience and the obligations deriving from international legal instruments', further consideration of the acceptability of any refusal to allow commercial broadcasting was required in terms of the general principles applying under paragraph (2). The Court in the particular case was not persuaded that there was any pressing social need for the continuation of any such restriction, nor that this was proportionate to the state aim of preventing the establishment of a private broadcasting monopoly[4].

1 Licence restrictions on contents need to satisfy standard ECHR, Art 10 concerns: cf 15404/89, *Purcell and Ors v Ireland* (1991) DR 70, 262 (prohibition on broadcasting of interviews with members of a political party: inadmissible); 18714/91, *Brind and Ors v United Kingdom* (1994) DR 77, 42 (prohibition on broadcasting spoken comments by supporters of organisations linked with Sinn Fein: inadmissible) See further Krüger and Buquicchio-de Boer 'The Case-Law of the European Commission of Human Rights Concerning the Application of Article 10 ECHR' in Cassese and Clapham (eds) *Transfrontier Television in Europe: The Human Rights Dimension* (1990) pp 98–112.
2 (28 June 2001), paras 35–79.
3 *Groppera Radio AG and Ors v Switzerland* (1990) A 173, para 61. Cf 8266/78, *X v United Kingdom* (1978) DR 16, 190 (prosecution for advertising broadcasts of a pirate radio station: inadmissible); 8962/80, *X and Y v Belgium* (1982) DR 28, 112 (prosecution for unlawful use of CB radio; inadmissible).
4 (1993) A 276, paras 32–43 at para 32. See too *Telesystem Tirol Kabeltelevision v Austria* 1997-III, 970 (refusal to allow company to broadcast cable television programmes on account of state monopoly: friendly settlement and case struck off the list); *Radio ABC v Austria* 1997-VI, 2180, paras 30–38; and *Tele 1 Privatfernsehgesellschaft v Austria* (21 September 2000), para 35 (refusal to grant radio operating licence violation of ECHR, Art 10 following *Informationsverein Lentia* case and after consideration of subsequent domestic legislative proceedings).

Establishing whether there has been an 'interference'

7.20   The guarantee protects both the content of the message sought to be communicated and the manner and form in which it is made. Neither the type of information in question nor the category of individual seeking to exercise freedom of expression is relevant in the assessment of whether there has been any state interference[1]. In the language of the European Convention on Human Rights, Article 10, paragraph (2), 'interferences' can involve 'formalities, conditions, restrictions or penalties'. In practical terms, these can take the form of seizure and confiscation of a publication[2] or film[3]; grant of an injunction (temporary or permanent) restraining publication of a newspaper article[4] or the right to make comment in the press[5]; refusal to grant a video a certificate permitting distribution[6] or to allow re-transmission of television signals[7]; the vetting of school books before distribution[8]; the imposition of disciplinary[9] or criminal sanctions following publication[10] or for refusal to reveal information sources[11]; the making of a civil award of damages against an author[12]; dismissal from (rather than refusal of access to) public employment because of political sympathies[13] or refusal to re-appoint to a post on account of expression of opinions[14]; and expulsion from a territory for participation in a protest[15].

1 Cf *Hadjianastassiou v Greece* (1992) A 252, para 39 (freedom of expression applies to servicemen; and information relating to military issues is also protected).

2 Eg *Handyside v United Kingdom* (1976) A 24 (seizure of English translation of *Little Red Schoolbook*).

3 *Otto-Preminger-Institut v Austria* (1994) A 295-A.

4 Eg *Sunday Times v United Kingdom (No 1)* (1979) A 30; and *Sunday Times v United Kingdom (No 2)* (1991) A 217 (restraints against publication of articles on testing of thalidomide and of extracts from unauthorised memoirs of secret service agent).

5 *Barthold v Germany* (1985) A 90 (prohibition on veterinary surgeon who operated an emergency hours service from making critical comment in local press about lack of such facilities on account of professional code of ethics and unfair competition statute).

6 *Wingrove v United Kingdom* 1996-V, 1937 (refusal to grant a certificate by British Board of Film Classification on the grounds that the work was blasphemous).

7 Eg *Groppera Radio AG v Switzerland* (1990) A 173; *Autronic AG v Switzerland* (1990) A 178. As to the televising of a trial, or the use of encrypted television signals, see *BBC, Petitioners* 2000 SCCR 533.

8 *Cyprus v Turkey* (10 May 2001), para 252.

9 Where the disciplinary body can reasonably be held to be a 'public authority' through its recognition by domestic law and responsibilities towards protection of the public: eg as in *Le Compte, Van Leuven and De Meyere v Belgium* (1981) A 43, para 64 (sanctions imposed by medical professional bodies); and *Casado Coca v Spain* (1994) A 285-A, para 38 (action taken by Bar Council).

10 Eg *Castells v Spain* (1992) A 236; *Jersild v Denmark* (1994) A 298 (television journalist convicted for assisting in dissemination of racist statements).

11 *Goodwin v United Kingdom* 1996-II, 483 (disclosure order made against journalist to reveal sources for information).

12 Eg *Tolstoy Miloslavsky v United Kingdom* (1995) A 316-B (award of £1.5 million, three times the amount of the previous highest award, and made by a jury without 'adequate or effective safeguards ... against a disproportionately large award' (at para 51)). See too 55120/00, *Independent News and Media plc and Independent Newspapers (Ireland) Ltd v Ireland* (damages in favour of a leading politician assessed by a jury at IEP 300,000, the highest amount ever awarded in the state: communicated).

13 *Vogt v Germany* (1995) A 323 (dismissal of civil servant for communist sympathies); cf *Glasenapp v Germany* (1986) A 104 and *Kosiek v Germany* (1986) A 105 (failure to grant tenure to probationary civil servants because of membership of extremist political party not considered interference with ECHR, Art 10).

14 *Wille v Liechtenstein* (28 October 1999), paras 36–51 (refusal by the sovereign to re-appoint the applicant who was president of the administrative court after he had given an academic lecture which sought to explore whether the sovereign was subject to the jurisdiction of the constitutional court). It is not, however, clear whether failure merely to promote an individual inter alia on the basis of his opinions would similarly constitute an interference.

15 Eg *Piermont v France* (1995) A 314.

DECISIONS OF DOMESTIC COURTS ON 'INTERFERENCES'

7.21   In an English case, the holding of an inquiry (into the deaths of Dr Harold Shipman's patients) in private was held to be an interference both with the freedom of relatives to receive information from witnesses and with the freedom of the media to report the proceedings[1]. In the later English case of *Ashdown v Telegraph Group Ltd*, it was accepted that the law of copyright was capable of restricting the right to freedom of expression, so as to engage Article 10 of the European Convention on Human Rights, in circumstances in which it was important that ideas and information (which are not in themselves protected by copyright) should be conveyed using the form of words devised by a particular author[2].

1 *R (Wagstaff) v Secretary of State for Health* [2001] 1 WLR 292.
2 (18 July 2001, unreported), CA.

Assessing whether an interference meets the requirements of paragraph (2)

7.22   A determination that there has been an 'interference' by a public authority of a right which falls within the scope of the European Convention on Human Rights, Article 10 will trigger consideration of whether such an interference is nevertheless justified under paragraph (2). This determination calls in turn for scrutiny of three separate issues: first, whether the interference falls within one of the prescribed state interests; second, whether it is 'prescribed by law'; and third, whether the interference in any case was 'necessary in a democratic society'.

7.23   The first issue will rarely, if ever, pose difficulty since normally it will be possible for the state to rely upon one of the listed legitimate aims for an interference. These state aims comprise competing state or public interests (protection of national security, territorial integrity, public safety, prevention of disorder[1] or crime, protection of health or morals[2], and maintenance of the authority and impartiality of the judiciary), and private or individual interests (protection of the reputation or rights of others[3], and prevention of disclosure of information received in confidence). Nor is 'prescribed by law' likely to pose much difficulty in cases under the European Convention on Human Rights, Article 10[4], although in the recent case of *Hashman and Harrup v United Kingdom*, English law on binding over to keep the peace was found wanting on this head. Hunt saboteurs had been found by a court not to have committed a breach of the peace but nevertheless had been bound over to keep the public peace by being required to pay a surety. The nature of breach of the peace and of behaviour considered *contra bones mores* in English law had been considered in an earlier case concerning Article 5[5], but in that instance there had been an actual finding of breach of the peace and the binding-over order had been imposed as a sanction. In the present case, the European Court of Human Rights considered that the order was entirely prospective in effect, and that in consequence it was not possible to consider that the applicants knew what behaviour was being prohibited. Accordingly, there was a violation of Article 10 as the interference had not been 'prescribed by law'[6].

1 Including prevention of disorder 'within the confines of a special social group': *Engel and Ors v Netherlands* (1976) A 22, para 98 and *Vereinigung Demokratischer Soldaten Österreichs and Gubi v Austria* (1994) A 302, para 32 (maintenance of military discipline); to protect the right of peaceful assembly and procession: *Chorherr v Austria* (1993) A 266-B (conviction for breach of the peace during a military ceremony); and maintenance of international telecommunications order: *Groppera Radio AG and Ors v Switzerland* (1990) A 173, paras 69–70 (international co-operation on usage of limited radio frequencies).
2 Including protection of the morals of the young: *Handyside v United Kingdom* (1976) A 24, para 52.
3 Including commercial reputation: *Markt Intern Verlag GmbH and Klaus Beermann* (1989) A 165, para 31.
4 Cf *Tammer v Estonia* (6 February 2001), para 38 (although the relevant provision of the criminal code was worded in rather general terms, it still satisfied the test of 'prescribed by law'). 'Prescribed by law' is discussed further at paras 3.33–3.39 above.
5 *Steel v United Kingdom* 1998-VII, 2719, paras 70–75 and 94 (orders to be bound over to keep the peace and be of good behaviour met the test of 'lawfulness' since the elements of breach of the peace were adequately defined by English law). See para 4.51 above.
6 (25 November 1999), paras 35–41.

7.24   It is the 'necessary in a democratic society' test which is likely to be at the heart of any issue in terms of the European Convention on Human Rights, Article 10. The balancing of interests in speech with competing public or private interests provides much of the substantive case law associated with the article. The test to be applied under paragraph (2) is, in principle, a demanding one. The exceptions 'must be narrowly interpreted and the necessity for any restrictions must be convincingly established'[1]. The interference complained of must correspond to a pressing social need', be proportionate to the legitimate aim pursued, and be justified by relevant and sufficient reasons[2]. 'Pressing social need' suggests a compelling reason rather than one which is merely ' "admissible", "ordinary", "useful", "reasonable" or "desirable" '; but the test is not as high as 'indispensable'[3]. Further, the interference must be proportionate to the legitimate aim pursued, and this requires consideration of the relationship between the means selected and the stated aim. Finally, the reasons advanced by the state for the interference must be considered first in terms of their relevancy and then their sufficiency in the particular case. Prior restraints affecting the media, in particular, call for the closest scrutiny: news is a 'perishable commodity' and even the shortest of delays in authorising publication may significantly diminish its interest[4]. The European Court of Human Rights will require to satisfy itself that domestic decision-makers 'applied standards which were in conformity with the principles embodied in Article 10 and, moreover, that they based their decisions on an acceptable assessment of the relevant facts'[5].

The outcome is that the level of protection ultimately accorded depends upon the particular circumstances, including 'the nature of the restriction in question, the degree of interference, the nature of the type of opinions or information involved, the societal or political context of the case, the persons involved, the type of medium involved, the public involved'[6]. Decisions, too, will reflect the underlying aims and values of the European Convention on Human Rights: political expression which contributes to democratic discussion will attract the highest safeguards, while there will be a wide margin of appreciation recognised on the part of state authorities in cases involving less worthy expression such as obscenity or blasphemy. The variety of factors, underlying values, and practical concerns render the jurisprudence a rich if at times complex one[7].

1 *Vogt v Germany* (1995) A 323, at para 52
2 *Sunday Times (No 1) v United Kingdom* (1979) A 30, para 62.
3 *Handyside v United Kingdom* (1976) A 24, at para 48.
4 *Sunday Times v United Kingdom (No 2)* (1991) A 217, at para 51.
5 *Vogt v Germany* (1995) A 323, at para 52. In relation to domestic law, see eg *Kelly v BBC* [2001] 2 WLR 253, 264, and the authorities cited there.
6 Voorhoof 'Guaranteeing the Freedom and Independence of the Media', in Council of Europe, *Media and Democracy* (1998) pp 35–59 at p 53.
7 Further, it may be possible to identify two or more legitimate state aims for a particular interference with speech: eg *Observer and Guardian Newspapers v United Kingdom* (1991) A 216, para 56 (injunctions prohibiting publication justified both as necessary for the maintenance of the authority of the judiciary (in the sense of protection of litigants' rights) and also national security); *Castells v Spain* (1992) A 236, para 39 (penalty imposed for criticism of government fell both under prevention of disorder and protection of reputation of others).

Human Rights Act 1998, s 12

7.25   The Human Rights Act 1998, s 12 seeks to ensure that courts pay particular regard to freedom of expression in general. Where it is claimed or appears that any material is journalistic, literary or artistic, the court must have regard to any relevant privacy code and to the extent to which material has or is about to become available to the public or it is in the public interest for material to be published[1]. It is difficult to see what additional purpose will be served by this provision. It merely encapsulates the general approach to interpretation of the European Convention on Human Rights, Article 10; but if the courts were to construe the provision as adversely affecting the application of countervailing Convention guarantees (for example, Article 8's requirement of respect for private life) a litigant who was unsuccessful in the domestic courts could bring proceedings in Strasbourg[2].

1 Human Rights Act 1998, s 12(4). In determining whether relief should be granted, where the person against whom application for relief is sought is not present or represented, the court cannot grant relief unless satisfied the applicant has taken all practicable steps to notify the respondent except in circumstances where there are compelling reasons for not notifying the respondent: s 12(2). No relief is to be granted so as to restrain publication before trial unless the court is satisfied the applicant is likely to establish that publication should not be allowed: s 12(3). See Samuels 'The Rights of Privacy and Freedom of Expression: The Drafting Challenge' (1999) 20 Stat LR 66.
2 Cf comments made by the Home Secretary at 315 HC Official Report (6th series) col 543, 2 July 1998: 'So far as we are able in a manner consistent with the Convention and its jurisprudence, we are saying to the courts that whenever there is a clash between article 8 rights and article 10 rights, they must pay particular attention to the article 10 rights.' See Fiddick 'The Human Rights Bill: Privacy and the Press', House of Commons Research paper 98/25 (1998); Singh 'Privacy and the Media after the Human Rights Act' [1998] EHRLR 712.

INTERPRETATION OF THE HUMAN RIGHTS ACT 1998, S 12 BY DOMESTIC COURTS

7.26   The Human Rights Act 1998, s 12 was considered in *Ashdown v Telegraph Group Ltd*[1], where it was said that section 12 did no more than underline the need to have regard to contexts in which the Strasbourg jurisprudence had given particular weight to freedom of expression, while at the same time drawing attention to considerations which might nevertheless justify restricting that right.

Section 12 was considered in greater detail in *Douglas v Hello! Ltd*. In relation to s 12(3), it was said:

'The subsection does not seek to give a priority to one Convention right over another. It is simply dealing with the interlocutory stage of proceedings and with how the court is to approach matters at that stage in advance of any ultimate balance being struck between rights which may be in potential conflict. In requires the court to look at the merits of the case and not merely to apply the *American Cynamid* test[2]. Thus the court has to look ahead to the ultimate stage and be satisfied that the scales are likely to come down in the applicant's favour. That does not conflict with the Convention, since it is merely requiring the court to apply its mind to how one right is to be balanced, on the merits against another right, without building in additional weight on one side. In a situation ... where the non-article 10 right is of fundamental importance to the individual, such as the article 2 right to life, the merits will include not merely the evidence about how great is the risk of that right being breached, but also a consideration of the gravity of the consequences for an applicant if the risk materialises[3].'

In relation to HRA 1998, s 12(4), the court noted that privacy is dealt with in the Code of Practice ratified by the Press Complaints Commission in November 1997, clause 3:

'[I]n any case where the court is concerned with issues of freedom of expression in a journalistic, literary or artistic context, it is bound to pay particular regard to any breach of the rules set out in clause 3 of the code, especially where none of the public interest claims set out in the preamble to the code is asserted. A newspaper which flouts clause 3 of the code is likely in those circumstances to have its claim to an entitlement to freedom of expression trumped by article 10(2) considerations of privacy[4].'

It was also observed that HRA 1998, s 12(4) 'puts beyond question the direct applicability of at least one article of the Convention as between one private party to litigation and another – in the jargon, its horizontal effect[5].'

The requirement in HRA 1998, s 12(3) that the applicant 'is likely to establish' that publication should not be allowed was considered again in *Imutran Ltd v Uncaged Campaigns Ltd*, where it was said that:

'Theoretically and as a matter of language likelihood is slightly higher in the scale of probability than a real prospect of success. But the difference between the two is so small that I cannot believe that there will be many (if any) cases which would have succeeded under the *American Cynamid* test but will now fail because of the terms of s 12(3) of the 1998 Act[6].'

1 (18 July 2001, unreported), CA, para 12. See also *Imutran Ltd v Uncaged Campaigns Ltd* [2001] 2 All ER 385, para 20.
2 Ie the test of (1) whether there is a serious issue to be tried and (2) the balance of convenience.
3 [2001] 2 WLR 992, at para 150, per Keene LJ. See also paras 134–137, per Sedley LJ; and *Venables v News Group Newspapers Ltd* [2001] 2 WLR 1038.
4 [2001] 2 WLR 992, para 94, per Brooke LJ. As to judicial review of decisions of the Press Complaints Commission concerning clause 3, see *R (Ford) v Press Complaints Commission* (31 July 2001, unreported), QBD.

5 [2001] 2 WLR 992 para 133, per Sedley LJ. Section 12(4) was also applied in *A-G v Times Newspapers Ltd* [2001] 1 WLR 885. The horizontal effect of Art 10 was implicit in *Thomas v News Group Newspapers Ltd* (18 July 2001, unreported), CA.
6 [2001] 2 All ER 385 at para 17 per Sir Andrew Morritt V-C.

Determining whether an interference is 'necessary in a democratic society': particular issues

Public debate and personal reputation

7.27   The highest level of protection under the European Convention on Human Rights, Article 10 attaches to expression which contributes to the maintenance and furtherance of public debate and the enhancement of democratic accountability. The necessity 'in a democratic society' for an interference with discussion on matters of general public concern[1] will call for sensitive assessment. Only the most compelling reasons will outweigh free speech, even when such expression is considered harmful to the protection of individual reputation. In short, 'there is little scope under [Article 10(2)] for restrictions on political speech or on debate on questions of public interest'[2]. In such cases, the status of the applicant as well as that of the party whose reputation is under threat will be of relevance. In *Lingens v Austria* the applicant, who was a journalist, had been punished for publishing articles criticising the Chancellor of Austria as 'immoral' or 'undignified' for his protection of former Nazis. The European Court of Human Rights considered that these criticisms could have been said to have been well founded, and had been made in good faith. The particular role of the press in helping the public come to an assessment of their leaders was acknowledged as of critical importance; further 'the limits of acceptable criticism are ... wider as regards a politician as such than as regards a private individual' since a politician 'inevitably and knowingly lays himself open to close scrutiny of his every word and deed'. Accordingly, while protection of the reputation of individuals is a recognised ground for state interference under ECHR, Article 10, paragraph (2) and extends to protection of the reputation of politicians, 'in such cases the requirements of such protection have to be weighed in relation to the interests of open discussion of issues'[3]. In *Fayed v United Kingdom*, the Court applied this approach to businessmen actively involved in the affairs of major public companies who also 'inevitably and knowingly lay themselves open to close scrutiny of all their acts' not only by the media but also by inspectors and other institutions representing the public interest[4], and subsequently in *Jerusalem v Austria*, to private individuals and associations when they enter the arena of public debate[5]. Language may be provocative and still attract protection. Action taken in relation to offensive speech directed against public figures such as politicians and high-profile businessmen will not in itself and as a matter of course be easier to justify than more moderately worded criticism. Certainly, a politician 'who expresses himself [in such a manner as to shock] exposes himself to a strong reaction on the part of journalists and the public' and thus should expect strong comment in return[6]. In other words 'a degree of exaggeration should be tolerated in a heated and continuing public debate of affairs of general concern, where on both sides professional reputations are at stake'[7]. The importance attached to promotion of open debate thus implies that statements attacked on the basis that they are defamatory may require to be considered in their wider context[8] and with considerable care[9] to ensure that Convention expectations are met. Strasbourg jurisprudence may point to possible difficulties with certain substantive rules of defamation in Scots and English law[10].

1 The Court has refused to draw any distinction between the narrower idea of 'political discussion' and 'discussion of other matters of public concern', preferring a wide approach to determination of what helps constitute a healthy 'democratic society': *Thorgeir Thorgeirson v Iceland* (1992) A 239, at para 64.

2 *Feldek v Slovakia* (12 July 2001), at para 74.

3 (1986) A 103, at para 42. See too *Lopes Gomes da Silva v Portugal* (28 September 2000), paras 31–37 (prosecution for criminal libel concerning a candidate for election considered disproportionate: violation of ECHR, Art 10). Cf *Demicoli v Malta* (1991) A 210, paras 39–41 (satirical newspaper attack upon MPs punished under parliamentary privilege rules: matter considered under Art 6 with violation established because of procedural impropriety).

4 (1994) A 294-B, at para 75 (discussing enforcement of the right to a good reputation under ECHR, Art 6).

5 (27 February 2001), paras 38–39.

6 *Oberschlick v Austria (No 1)* (1991) A 204, at para 61 (private prosecution for defamation against applicant who alleged that racist comments made by politician were similar to those made by the Nazis); *Oberschlick v Austria (No 2)* 1997-IV, 1275, paras 29–35 (conviction of journalist for insulting the leader of the right-wing Austrian Freedom Party by calling him 'an idiot' in an article after he had made a speech glorifying the Austrians who had fought in the 1939–45 war: the politician had clearly intended being provocative, the article had provided an objective assessment of the speech, and the insult was not a gratuitous personal attack); *Feldek v Slovakia* (12 July 2001), paras 77–90 (use of harsh language concerning a minister's background but made in good faith and with the aim of protecting the development of democracy in a newly-established state emerging from totalitarian rule: violation). Cf *Constantinescu v Romania* (27 June 2000), paras 66–78 (trade union leader could have voiced criticism of previous leadership without having used the offensive description of 'receivers of stolen property').

7 *Nilsen and Johnsen v Norway* (25 November 1999), at para 52.

8 Cf *Bladet Tromsø and Stensaas v Norway* 1999-III, 281, paras 61–73 (relevant reasons for award of damages against a journalist for defamation of seal-hunters (protection of the reputation of the hunters), but the reasons were not sufficient to outweigh public interest in public debate on issue of concern: impugned statements were part of a series of articles which involved a wide range of opinions and which sought to encourage proper public debate); *Bergens Tidende and Ors v Norway* (2 May 2000), paras 51–60 (defamation award of approximately £375,000 in favour of a cosmetic surgeon held a violation of ECHR, Art 10; correct accounts of treatment were accurately recorded in a balanced article and thus the reasons for interference were not sufficient); and *Marônek v Slovakia* (19 April 2001), paras 54–60 (award of damages for defamation equivalent to 25 times the average monthly salary against the applicant who had written an open letter in a newspaper complaining about his failure to gain possession of a state-owned flat allocated to him and the behaviour of the occupants of the property: the letter urged others with a similar problem to take joint action since he considered that resolution of the issue was a matter of public concern and also crucial for strengthening the rule of law in a new democracy; the statements did not appear excessive, most of the events on which he had relied had already been made public, and the reasons invoked by the domestic courts did not justify the relatively high damages awarded and thus there was no reasonable relationship of proportionality between the measures applied by the domestic courts and the legitimate aim pursued).

9 Cf *Nilsen and Johnsen v Norway* (25 November 1999), paras 43–53 (five statements made by the applicants who were police officers about findings of police violence by an academic researcher were considered defamatory: the Court considered that three of the statements could not be said to have exceeded the limits of permissible criticism for the purposes of ECHR, Art 10; the findings of defamation had not been supported by sufficient reasons nor were they proportionate to the aim of protecting the academic's reputation).

10 For a recent example of balancing expression with protection of a political figure in English law, see *Reynolds v Times Newspapers and Ors* [2001] 2 AC 127. See also *Loutchansky v Times Newspapers Ltd* [2001] 3 WLR 404; *Branson v Bower* (24 May 2001, unreported), CA; *Berezovsky v Forbes* (31 July 2001, unreported), CA. For current discussion of Scots legal principles, see Norrie *Defamation and Related Actions* (1995) pp 125–149; and for defamation awards, see Thomson *Delictual Liability* (2nd edn, 1999) pp 258–259. For discussion of political speech and defamation (and the effect of the Defamation Act 1996, s 13 which provides MPs with additional protection against press criticism) see Williams 'Only Flattery is Safe: Political Speech and the Defamation Act 1996' (1997) 60 MLR 388; Bonnington 'UK Defamation Practice and the Defamation Act 1996' (1997) 2 SLPQ 202; Sharland and Loveland 'The Defamation Act 1996 and Political Libels' [1997] PL 113; Loveland 'Political Libels and Qualified Privilege: A British Solution to a British Problem' [1997] PL 428; Loveland 'Reforming Libel Law: The Public Law Dimension' (1997) 46 ICLQ 561; Lester of Herne Hill 'Private Lives and Public Figures: Freedom of Political Speech in a Democracy' (1999) 4 Comms L 43.

7.28 This approach also covers discussion or expression of opinion in relation to contentious historical events. In *Tolstoy Miloslavsky v United Kingdom*, the question arose whether the amount of damages awarded for defamation – £1.5 million – was disproportionate to the legitimate aim of protecting the reputation or rights of a person in respect of actions performed by him in his capacity as a public officer at the end of the 1939–45 war. While the European Court of Human Rights considered that the failure to prescribe any maximum amount of compensation a jury could make did not in itself render the interference one which was not 'prescribed by law', the Court nevertheless considered that the size of the particular award together with the lack of adequate and effective safeguards against a disproportionately large award resulted in a violation of the European Convention on Human Rights, Article 10[1].

1 (1995) A 316-B, paras 46–51.

7.29 On the other hand, the European Court of Human Rights has been reluctant to extend this approach to expression unduly critical of civil servants or other public officials who cannot be taken to have 'knowingly la[in] themselves open to close scrutiny' unlike politicians. Thus it is open for a state to punish 'offensive and abusive verbal attacks' against civil servants or public officials since these individuals 'must enjoy public confidence in conditions free of undue perturbation if they are to be successful in performing their tasks'[1]. Robust (if not insulting) expression directed against public officials such as police officers or judges[2] who cannot readily engage in political debate or public response thus will more readily justify state interference to protect their reputation and rights, particularly in the absence of substantiated or corroborated evidence[3] or good faith, since the media should be able to discharge their function of contributing to political debate and accountability without exceeding generally acceptable standards[4]. Again, however, the context in which statements considered defamatory of public officials are made requires to be considered with sensitivity. In *Thoma v Luxembourg*, a journalist had been ordered to pay nominal damages and costs to some 60 Forestry Commission officials who had raised an action of defamation in respect of remarks made during a radio programme. The journalist had quoted from a newspaper article written by another journalist suggesting that Forestry Commission officials were corruptible, but when doing so had clearly indicated that he was quoting the strongly worded comments of another individual. The domestic court had considered that by failing to distance himself formally from the quote he had thus endorsed the views put forward and had also led listeners to believe that the allegations were true. For the Court, there had to be 'particularly cogent reasons' for punishing a journalist for helping disseminate statements made by others since otherwise this would seriously hamper the contribution of the press to discussion of matters of public interest. The topic discussed in the programme concerned a matter of general interest which had been widely debated in the local media. While it was reasonable to accept that the journalist had adopted to some extent the content of the quotation in issue, the determination that he had not acted without malice, essentially on account of his failure to distance himself systematically from the views of the other journalist, could not constitute 'particularly cogent reasons' capable of justifying the interference with free speech. Such a general requirement upon journalists was not reconcilable with the media's role of providing information on current events, opinions and ideas, and thus there had been a violation of the European Convention on Human Rights, Article 10[5].

1 *Janowski v Poland* 1999-I, 187, paras 31–35 at para 33 (punishment for intervening out of civic concern in a street incident in which municipal guards were called 'dumb' and 'oafish': the majority of the Court considered that even accepting law enforcement officers were trained how to respond to abusive language, the insults had taken place in a public place in front of others and while the officers were carrying out their duties and thus sufficient grounds existed for the conviction).

2 E g *Schopfer v Switzerland* 1998-III, 1042, paras 28–34 (disciplinary penalties imposed by the Bar on a lawyer following criticism of judges at a press conference held not a violation of ECHR, Art 10). For further discussion of attacks upon the judiciary, see para 7.42 below. See also *Thorgeir Thorgeirson v Iceland* (1992) A 239, paras 63–69 (strongly worded allegations of police brutality: onus on accused to establish veracity of allegations considered unreasonable and a violation of ECHR, Art 10).

3 *Perna v Italy* (25 July 2001), paras 44-45 at para 44 (serious and factual allegations concerning a public prosecutor but unsupported by evidence or corroboration which had 'overstepped the limits of acceptable criticism in that they had no factual basis').

4 Cf Art 10(2) which specifically acknowledges that the exercise of free speech carries with it certain duties and responsibilities. In *Lingens v Austria* (1986) A 103, para 46, the Court accepted that there had been no absence of good faith on the part of the applicant. Cf *Castells v Spain* (1992) A 236, paras 47–48 (the applicant had been unable to plead truth or good faith by means of defence in the domestic criminal court).

5 (29 March 2001), paras 50–66 at para 64 ('raisons particulièrement sérieuses') (the Court accepted that even though the journalist had not identified any individual by name, the comparatively small size of Luxembourg and the limited number of Commission staff meant that the officials concerned had been easily identifiable to listeners.)

Expression and participation in the democratic process

7.30 Special protection is accorded to expression associated with the exercise of democracy or discussion of constitutional issues[1]. Free speech is of particular importance for Members of Parliament, political parties and their activists since 'they represent their electorate, draw attention to their preoccupations and defend their interests', and in consequence, an interference with the rights under the European Convention on Human Rights, Article 10 of a politician calls for 'the closest scrutiny'[2]. In *Castells v Spain*, the European Court of Human Rights went as far as to suggest that the boundaries of acceptable criticism had to be wider as regards a member of the executive (rather than a parliamentarian or other politician) since the maintenance of democracy required close scrutiny. An elected senator had been convicted of the offence of insulting the government through the publication of an article critical of the situation in the Basque region; here, the fact that the applicant was an elected Member of Parliament was of considerable relevance in determining that there had been a breach of Article 10[3]. Even virulent language which may be considered seditious may be protected. In *Incal v Turkey*, the applicant was a member of the executive committee of a political party who had been punished for distributing leaflets considered separatist propaganda seeking to incite insurrection. The penalties imposed involved imprisonment for six-and-a-half months, debarment from entering the civil service, and restrictions upon further political activities. While mindful of the problems posed by terrorism, the Court considered the 'radical' nature of the penalties disproportionate bearing in mind that the authorities under domestic law could have required changes to be made in the leaflet before publication. Restraint on the part of prosecutors was called for in such cases[4].

However, there may be a fine line between political expression which is considered worthy of protection and that which seeks to undermine democracy and thus is deemed incompatible with the Convention because of ECHR, Article 17 which prohibits the abuse of Convention rights[5]. Such considerations may have had some part to play in the disposal of applications challenging restrictions on broadcasts with members of political parties considered to have links with terrorist organisations[6].

Indeed, restrictions on expression may on occasion and perhaps paradoxically be justified in order to protect democratic institutions from longer-term harm, as illustrated by *Ahmed v United Kingdom*, where restrictions on the political activities of senior local government officers were upheld[7]. Further, speech which is considered particularly insulting may escape protection. In *Wabl v Austria*, a Member of Parliament asserted that an article critical of him constituted 'Nazi journalism'. The Austrian courts had granted the newspaper concerned an injunction prohibiting the applicant from repeating the statement. The Court considered that this interference was supported by reasons which were both relevant and sufficient as there was a particular stigma in Austria attaching to activities inspired by National Socialism, and the remark was not only polemical but offensive. The restraint was also proportionate since it concerned only repetition of this term and the applicant had still been free to voice his opinion about the newspaper in other ways[8].

1 Cf *Thorgeir Thorgeirson v Iceland* (1992) A 239, at para 64 (there is 'no warrant' in ECHR, Art 10 jurisprudence for distinguishing 'between political discussion and discussion of other matters of concern'). See too *Wille v Liechtenstein* (28 October 1999), paras 67–70 (refusal by the sovereign to re-appoint the applicant who was president of the administrative court after he had given an academic lecture which sought to explore whether the sovereign was subject to the jurisdiction of the constitutional court: while a judge had to show particular restraint in the expression of views, the opinions he had stated were tenable and had been expressed in an appropriate way and accordingly the interference was not 'necessary in a democratic society'). For further discussion, see Mowbray 'The Role of the European Court of Human Rights in the Promotion of Democracy' [1999] PL 703; and Fenwick and Phillipson 'Public Protest, The Human Rights Act and Judicial Responses to Political Expression' [2000] PL 627.

2 *Incal v Turkey* 1998-IV, 1547, at para 46.
3 *Castells v Spain* (1992) A 236, paras 42 and 46. Cf *Piermont v France* (1995) A 314 at para 76: 'a person opposed to official ideas and positions must be able to find a place in the political arena' (expulsion of a German MEP from a French overseas territory after participation in a demonstration).
4 1998-IV, 1547, paras 46–58. See too further cases decided by the Grand Chamber on 8 July 1999 involving the punishment of 'separatist' expression claimed by the state as incitement to violence or insurrection: *Ceylan v Turkey; Arslan v Turkey; Gerger v Turkey; Polat v Turkey; Karataş v Turkey; Erdoğdu and İnce v Turkey* 1999-IV, 185; *Başkaya and Okcuoğlu v Turkey* 1999-IV, 261; *Okcuoğlu v Turkey; Sürek and Özdemir v Turkey; Sürek v Turkey (No 2);* and *Sürek v Turkey (No 4)* (all held to be violations of ECHR, Art 10). Cf the cases decided the same day of *Sürek v Turkey (No 1)* 1999-IV, 353; and *Sürek v Turkey (No 3)* (no violation of Art 10 established).
5 ECHR, Art 10 may not be applied in a manner inconsistent with the intention of Art 17 in permitting speech to be used in such a way as to be 'aimed at the destruction of any of the rights and freedoms' listed in the Convention: cf *Lehideux and Isorni v France* 1998-VII, 2864, paras 50–58 (supporters of the Pétain regime who took out an advertisement in a newspaper were convicted of defending war crimes and collaboration; the Court considered that the statements did not fall within clearly established historical facts such as the holocaust, denial or rejection of which would have removed the statements from Art 10 protection in light of Art 17, and affirmed that speech striking at the Convention's underlying values would not attract protection: here, though, the criminal convictions were considered disproportionate and thus a violation of Art 10, and accordingly, it was unnecessary to consider Art 17).
6 15404/89, *Purcell and Ors v Ireland* (1991) DR 70, 262 (prohibition on broadcasting of interviews with members of a political party: inadmissible); 18714/91, *Brind and Ors v United Kingdom* (1994) DR 77, 42 (prohibition on broadcasting spoken comments by supporters of organisations linked with Sinn Fein: inadmissible). See too 39511/98, *McGuiness v United Kingdom* 1999-V, 481 (elected representatives required to take an oath of allegiance to the monarch; application declared inadmissible under Art 10 since the oath could be viewed simply as an affirmation of loyalty to the UK's constitutional principles). This decision can be contrasted with *Buscarini and Ors v San Marino* 1999-I, 251, paras 34–41 at para 39 (interferences with ECHR, Art 9 rights where applicants who were elected to parliament were required to take a religious oath on the Bible as a condition of sitting, making the 'exercise of a mandate intended to represent different views of society within Parliament subject to a prior declaration of commitment to a particular set of beliefs' which could not be considered appropriate).
7 1998-VI, 2356, discussed at para 7.37 below.
8 (21 March 2000), paras 38–45. See also *Constantinescu v Romania* (27 June 2000), paras 66–78 (prosecution of trade union leader for published comments labelling previous leadership as 'receivers of stolen property': conviction justified as for the protection of the rights of others). Cf *Jerusalem v Austria* (27 February 2001), paras 32–47 (injunction against a member of a municipal council from repeating allegations that a sect had fascist tendencies and was totalitarian; the applicant in court had sought unsuccessfully to offer evidence in support of her assertions that the value judgments were fair comment: violation).

7.31 Issues under the European Convention on Human Rights, Article 10 may also arise in regards to the regulation of electoral campaigns. Free speech and free elections 'together form the bedrock of any democratic system' and ECHR, Article 10 and Protocol 1, Article 3 'are interrelated and operate to reinforce each other', although the two provisions may come into conflict with each other at election time when it may be appropriate to place certain restrictions on free speech[1]. In *Bowman v United Kingdom*, the applicant challenged the prohibition found in the Representation of the People Act 1983 against the incurring of unauthorised expenditure of more than £5 with a view to promoting the return of a particular candidate in a parliamentary election. As the director of an anti-abortion pressure group, she had arranged for the distribution of leaflets in individual constituencies outlining the views of each of the candidates on this subject. The European Court of Human Rights considered that the restriction on expression did pursue the legitimate aim of protecting the rights of electoral candidates, but found the means selected disproportionate in the light of the lack of restraints at national or regional campaign level[2]. However, the determination of access to broadcast facilities is covered by a margin of appreciation on the part of state authorities, and it has proved difficult for applicants to use the Convention to challenge domestic arrangements[3].

1 *Bowman v United Kingdom* 1998-I, 175, paras 41–43 at para 42.
2 1998-I, 175, at paras 45–47. See further Davis 'Bowman *v* United Kingdom – a Case for the Human Rights Act? [1998] PL 592; Reville 'Freedom of Expression in Party Election Broadcasts' [1998] CIL 100; and Ghaleigh 'Election Spending and Freedom of Expression' (1999) 58 CLJ 431.
3 E g 4750/71, *M v United Kingdom* (1972) CD 40, 29 (refusal of BBC to give broadcasting time to a political party declared inadmissible); 24744/94, *Huggett v United Kingdom* (1995) DR 82, 98 (rules determining allocation of broadcasting time were not arbitrary: inadmissible).

DECISIONS OF DOMESTIC COURTS ON EXPRESSION RELATING TO POLITICAL EVENTS

7.32   In an English case concerned with the unauthorised publication of an extract from a leading politician's private diary, following which proceedings were brought by the politician for breach of copyright, it was said that in most circumstances the principle of freedom of expression would be sufficiently protected if there was a right to publish information and ideas set out in another's literary work, without copying the very words which that person had employed to convey the information or express the idea. In such circumstances it would normally be necessary in a democratic society that the author of the work should have his property in his own creation protected. There would, however, be occasions when it was in the public interest not merely that information should be published, but that the public should be told the very words used by a person, notwithstanding that the author enjoyed copyright in them. In circumstances where the right of freedom of expression came into conflict with the protection afforded by the Copyright, Designs and Patents Act 1988, the court was bound in so far as possible, to apply the Act in a manner that accommodated the right of freedom of expression[1]. Usually this might be done by declining to grant an injunction, ie allowing the newspaper to copy the exact words, but indemnifying the author for any loss or accounting to him for any profit. In the rare case where it was in the public interest that the words should be copied without any sanction, this could be permitted under the statutory 'public interest' exception[2].

1 *Ashdown v Telegraph Group Ltd* (18 July 2001, unreported), CA.
2 Notably under the Berne Convention 1971 and various EC Directives.

Maintenance of public order and safety

7.33   The maintenance of public order and public safety may justify restrictions on expression, provided always that the test of necessity can be met[1]. In *Steel and Ors v United Kingdom*, the first two applicants had been involved in hunt sabotage and disruption of road construction work respectively and had been detained pending appearance before a court for 44 and 17 hours in each case; the final three applicants had taken part in a peaceful protest against the sale of military equipment by distributing leaflets in a conference centre which had led to their detention for seven hours. The European Court of Human Rights considered each case on its own merits. In respect of the first two protestors, the Court accepted that there had been a continuing risk of disorder inherent in each of the protest activities and thus their arrest and detention by police officers could not be said to have been disproportionate. However, the measures taken against the remaining three applicants were considered disproportionate because of the entirely peaceful nature of their protest[2].

1   For discussion of restrictions upon prisoners on these grounds, see *R v Secretary of State for the Home Department, ex p Simms* [2000] 2 AC 115.
2   1998-VII, 2719, paras 102–111. Contrast *Hutchinson v Newbury Magistrates Court* (9 October 2000, unreported), QBD. Cf *Chorherr v Austria* (1993) A 266-B, paras 31–33 (arrest of counter-demonstrator at military parade justified to protect the public peace: non-violation of ECHR, Art 10); cf *Piermont v France* (1995) A 314, paras 76–86 (expulsion of MEP from French overseas territory following her participation in a demonstration not justified). See also *R (Farrakhan) v Secretary of State* for the Home Dept (1 October 2001, unreported), QBD.

7.34   Greater latitude may be shown by the Court in considering interferences justified by a state on the grounds of current national security concerns. In *Zana v Turkey*, a former mayor had been prosecuted for statements published in a newspaper indicating his support for an illegal terrorist liberation movement. Since the statements had been made at a time of serious disturbances in south-east Turkey, it was accepted that the prosecution had sought to maintain national security and public safety. In determining the necessity for the interference, the statement could not be considered in isolation but had to be assessed against the background of terrorist attacks carried out on civilians. The interview, which was carried in a major national newspaper, thus had to be regarded as likely to exacerbate an already explosive situation, and in consequence the penalty imposed could reasonably have been regarded as supported by a pressing social need. Further, the reasons adduced by the Turkish state were relevant and sufficient, and the actual penalty imposed was also deemed proportionate to the legitimate aims pursued[1].

1   1997-VII 2533, paras 55–62 (factual situation distinguished in *Incal v Turkey* 1998-IV, 1547, discussed at para 7.30 above). See too 35402/97, *Hogefeld v Germany* (20 January 2000) (the applicant was allowed only one interview with a journalist during her trial on terrorist offences and on condition she did not refer to her organisation or her trial; these restrictions were considered a reasonable response to the pressing social need to ensure she did not encourage sympathisers to carry on with the campaign of terrorism, and the application was considered inadmissible). For a domestic example where the safety of private individuals outweighed freedom of expression, see *Venables v News Group Newspapers Ltd* [2001] 2 WLR 1038.

Racially offensive, etc speech

7.35   Where expression attacks those values of 'pluralism, tolerance and broadmindedness' which underlie the European Convention on Human Rights, Article 10, assessment of whether Article 17 comes into play is necessary. This provision prohibits the abuse of any Convention right which could undermine other guarantees, an issue which will arise in the consideration of 'hate speech'[1]. However, a sensitive assessment of intent and outcome will always be necessary. In *Jersild v Denmark*, a television journalist had been fined for having aided and abetted the dissemination of racially offensive statements. The television programme had featured interviews with young people who had expressed racist views on immigrant groups as part of a programme seeking to expose the existence of racism in Danish society. The European Court of Human Rights accepted that the medium of communication was of relevance in determining the extent of a journalist's duties or responsibilities, and that audiovisual media such as television 'have often a much more immediate and powerful effect than the print media'. However, in all the circumstances, the Court accepted that the broadcast had neither the purpose nor the unintended outcome of dissemination of racist views, and thus the conviction was not justified by ECHR, Article 10, paragraph (2)[2]. Journalism which seeks to expose rather than to promote extremism and intolerance will thus fall within the scope of ECHR, Article 10 protection.

The English courts have refused to strike out an action brought against a newspaper for statutory harassment, the newspaper's argument being that if the statute were interpreted consistently with Article 10 no action would be in the circumstances complained of. The Court of Appeal held that the plaintiff had pleaded an arguable case that the *Sun* had harassed her by publishing racist criticism of her which was foreseeably likely to stimulate a racist reaction on the part of their readers and cause her distress[3].

1 12194/86, *Kühnen v Germany* (1988) DR 56, 205 (prosecution for publishing material promoting fascism: conviction 'necessary in a democratic society'); 36773/97, *Nachtmann v Austria* (9 September 1998) (punishment for denial of holocaust; the Court reiterated that ECHR, Art 10 could not be invoked in a sense incompatible with Art 17); 32307/96, *Schimanek v Austria* (1 February 2000) (applicant involved in activities inspired by National Socialism, a totalitarian doctrine 'incompatible with democracy and human rights' whose adherents 'undoubtedly pursue aims of the kind referred to in Article 17', and the conviction was thus justified by Art 10(2) as read together with Art 17). See further Bindman 'Outlawing Holocaust Denial' (1997) NLJ 466 and 468; Jones *Human Rights: Group Defamation, Freedom of Expression and the Law of Nations* (1998); Cooper and William 'Hate Speech, Holocaust Denial and International Human Rights Law' (1999) EHRLR 593; and Nieuwenhuis 'Freedom of Speech: USA *v* Germany and Europe' (2000) 18 NQHR 195.
2 (1994) A 298, paras 25–36. The Court also took account of the state's obligations under the UN Convention on the Elimination of All Forms of Racial Discrimination in assessing whether the conviction was justified (at paras 30–31).
3 *Thomas v News Group Newspapers Ltd* (18 July 2001, unreported), CA.

Public sector employment and military service

7.36   Guarantees of freedom of expression under the European Convention on Human Rights, Article 10 apply to civil servants and other public sector employees[1], police officers[2] and service personnel[3]. However, restrictions on access to the civil service or public office upon grounds of qualification or fitness for office based on belief or expression fall outwith the scope of Convention guarantees[4]. The purported state aim in restricting expression on the part of public sector officials is likely to be national security or the protection of democratic institutions[5], and while a wide margin of appreciation is recognised on the part of domestic authorities in deciding whether such an interference is justified as 'necessary in a democratic society', this is still subject to the supervisory jurisdiction of the European Court of

Human Rights since any contrary approach would leave substantial numbers of citizens without ECHR, Article 10 guarantees and significant areas of activity immune from commentary and press scrutiny.

National security is certainly recognised as conferring a particularly wide margin of appreciation on domestic decision-makers[6], and the Court will be reluctant to interfere with the punishment of disclosures of classified information by members of the armed services[7]. Military order may also justify restrictions on expression where a real threat to military discipline exists. In *Engel and Ors v Netherlands*, conscript soldiers had been punished for distribution of pamphlets to other soldiers. The Court indicated that it would take into account such factors as the general nature of military life and the corresponding responsibilities of armed force personnel, and in the circumstances of the case concluded that there had been 'well-founded reasons for considering that [the applicants] had attempted to undermine military discipline'[8]. On the other hand, there will be a more critical assessment of any state justification for restriction of opinions of military personnel where these concern general service conditions and do not pose an immediate threat to good order. In *Vereinigung Demokratischer Soldaten Österreichs and Gubi v Austria*, the Court rejected allegations that the applicants' periodical represented a threat to military effectiveness. While the tenor of the complaints voiced was often polemical, the publication could not be said to have 'overstepped the bounds of what is permissible in the context of a mere discussion of ideas, which must be tolerated in the army of a democratic State'[9]. Further, circulation of military or security information which is considered no longer sensitive or which has entered the public domain will be difficult to restrict since justification of censorship or imposition of post-publication sanction is unlikely to be considered necessary to achieve the aim of protecting state security[10].

1 Cf 11389/85, *Morrissens v Belgium* (1988) DR 56, 127 (suspension of teacher after attacking superiors on television; considered justified as necessary for the protection of reputation and rights of others).
2 Cf *Rekvényi v Hungary* (20 May 1999), paras 46–50.
3 Eg *Hadjianastassiou v Greece* (1992) A 252, para 39 (freedom of expression applies to servicemen; and information relating to military issues also protected).
4 *Glasenapp v Germany* (1986) A 104, paras 50–53; *Kosiek v Germany* (1986) A 105, paras 36–39 (conditions of appointment of civil servants involved an obligation to uphold democratic constitutional values, conditions deemed not to have been satisfied in respect of the applicants who were members of extremist political parties); *Leander v Sweden* (1987) A 116, paras 71–73 (access sought to confidential files concerning the applicant which had been used by military authorities to determine that he was not qualified for a particular post; the Court considered that the essence of the challenge was to the assessment of relevant information by the authorities to ensure the applicant was qualified for the post, and accordingly there had been no violation of his freedom to express opinions).
5 Eg *Vogt v Germany* (1995) A 323, at para 51 ('the civil service is the guarantor of the Constitution and democracy'); *Ahmed and Ors v United Kingdom* 1998-VI, 2356, para 52 (protection of the rights of council members and electorate through effective local political democracy).
6 *Zana v Turkey* 1997-VII, 2533, discussed at para 7.34 above.
7 *Hadjianastassiou v Greece* (1992) A 252, paras 45–47 (disclosure of information on weaponry technology punished by military court). See also *R v Shayler* (28 September 2001, unreported), CA (unauthorised disclosure of information by former member of security services: no public interest defence).
8 (1976) A 22 at para 101: the Court noted that the applicants had not been denied their freedom of expression, merely that they had been punished for their 'abusive exercise' of this right.

9 (1994) A 302, at para 38. See too *Grigoiades v Greece* 1997-VII, 2575, paras 46–47 (letter containing intemperate remarks, but made in the context of a general criticism of the army as an institution and not disseminated to a wider audience: this was considered to have had only an insignificant impact on military discipline, and thus prosecution and the conviction were not necessary in a democratic society).

10 Eg *Vereiniging Weekblad Bluf! v Netherlands* (1995) A 306-A, discussed at para 7.46 below.

7.37 More generally, restrictions on expression by public-sector employees purportedly to meet long-term state interests will require to satisfy the test of 'pressing social need'. Reasons for any interference must also be relevant and sufficient, and the relationship between means and ends must be proportionate. In *Vogt v Germany*, a teacher had been dismissed from her post because of political activities deemed incompatible with a duty of political loyalty to the constitutional order of the state. While accepting the historical background to the imposition of the obligation, the European Court of Human Rights considered that the post did not carry any particular security risk, nor was there any evidence that the applicant had sought to indoctrinate her pupils or even had made any anti-constitutional statements outside school. Accordingly, the conclusion was that the real ground for dismissal had been her active membership of the Communist Party, including her candidature in public elections, and while the reasons advanced by the state were relevant, they were not 'sufficient to establish convincingly that it was necessary in a democratic society to dismiss her'[1]. Assessment may be more difficult when the state argues that the protection of democracy compels restrictions on free expression. In *Ahmed and Ors v United Kingdom*, a majority of the Court accepted such a justification in respect of the imposition of a requirement of political neutrality, which included limitations on expression, on some 12,000 senior local authority officials. The Court did not accept the applicants' argument that there had to be a clear threat to the stability of the state before the protection of effective democracy could be invoked as a justification for limitations on rights under the European Convention on Human Rights, Article 10, but preferred to recognise that a state could take steps to safeguard democratic institutions when it considered this was justified. While the Commission had been of the opinion that the state had shown no pressing need for the restrictions, the majority of the Court accepted that the conclusions of a committee set up to consider how best to maintain the political neutrality of officials with a view to protecting local democracy were sufficient to establish a need for regulation. Further, the means selected were sufficiently proportionate since they had made use of a focused and function-based approach which sought to avoid partisan commentary[2].

1 (1995) A 323, paras 57–61 at para 60.

2 1998-VI, 2356, paras 57–65 (challenges to regulations made in terms of the Housing and Local Government Act 1989).

Protection of privacy

7.38 The European Convention on Human Rights, Article 8 requires respect for private and family life, and while incorporation of the Convention into British law need not lead to the development of a new law of privacy, more searching examination of any intrusion into privacy will be necessary. Media discussion which may inhibit the development of personal relationships will call for more rigorous tests of social need and proportionality[1].

1 See para 6.34 above. For an (unusual) example, see *Venables v News Group Newspapers Ltd* [2001] 2 WLR 1038.

Contempt of court

7.39 The European Convention on Human Rights, Article 10, paragraph (2) specifically identifies maintenance of the 'authority and impartiality of the judiciary' as a legitimate aim which may justify interference with expression. Insertion of this particular interest in Article 10 appears to have been at the insistence of the United Kingdom which was concerned to ensure that British contempt of court law was protected[1]. The balance to be achieved is between on the one hand protection of public discussion of matters of legitimate interest in a democracy, and on the other prevention of interference in a particular court proceeding or of undermining faith in the judicial process more generally. There are thus two principal concerns: protection of the integrity of any particular court proceeding; and protection of the reputation of the legal system in the longer term. Different considerations apply to each. It may be easier to determine whether any interference corresponds to a 'pressing social need' and is proportionate to the aim of protecting the rights of litigants or of an accused in a particular trial, than it is in cases where the general 'authority' of the court system is called into question.

1 *Sunday Times v United Kingdom* (1979) A 30; at para 60, the Court noted that, even assuming that the drafters of the Convention had added maintaining the 'authority and impartiality of the judiciary' specifically to provide for the continuation of British contempt of court law, this would not have resulted in the transposition of contempt law as it stood at the time of ratification since the phrase had to be read as an autonomous concept in which the 'necessity' of any interference would have to be assessed on a case-by-case basis. The Contempt of Court Act 1981 was enacted in response to a finding of a violation of ECHR, Art 10 in this case (as acknowledged in *Cox and Griffiths, Petitioners* 1998 SCCR 561 at 568; and in *HM Advocate v Scottish Media Newspapers and Ors*, 1999 SCCR 599).

PREJUDICING THE OUTCOME OF COURT PROCEEDINGS

7.40 The European Convention on Human Rights calls for a balance between the press's rights and responsibilities under Article 10 and the interests of litigants or accused under Article 6[1]. Restrictions on prejudicial pre-trial publicity will be consistent with an accused's rights to a fair hearing under Article 6(1) and to the presumption of innocence under Article 6(2)[2]. There is, however, both recognition of the watchdog role of the media in the administration of justice in helping ensure a fair trial[3] as well as acceptance that a judicial proceeding may attract legitimate public and press discussion, particularly where a public figure is involved and in which case the limits of acceptable comment will be wider[4]. In *Worm v Austria*, the applicant had been punished for publishing an article calculated to interfere with the trial of a former Finance Minister and Vice-Chancellor of Austria. The Court accepted that the reasons for the conviction were relevant: the conviction did not impinge upon the applicant's right to provide information in an objective manner about the trial of a political figure. The article instead had concerned an unfavourable assessment of evidence presented at the trial including a clear statement of opinion on the accused's guilt. The reasons adduced to justify interference were also sufficient: the domestic courts had taken into account the impugned article in its entirety, and it was not possible to conclude that the article was incapable of warranting the domestic court's conclusion as to its potential for influencing the outcome of the trial. Nor was the sanction imposed disproportionate, given the amount of the fine imposed and the fact that the publishing firm was made jointly and severally liable for payment along with the applicant[5]. Similarly, the Commission in *BBC Scotland, McDonald, Rodgers and Donald v United Kingdom* accepted that use of the *nobile officium* by the High Court of Justiciary to prevent the screening of a documentary concerning allegations of brutality against prisoners was justified to protect the rights of three prison officers who were shortly to stand trial on charges of assaulting prisoners, even although the programme would not have featured any of the accused[6]. In contrast, in *News Verlags v Austria*, the Court did not consider that a prohibition order made on the application of an accused person preventing the publishing of any report containing his photograph was justified. The court order had been directed against the applicant company alone, and other publishers had remained free of any restraint. While the Court acknowledged that the prohibition of prejudicial pre-trial publicity was a relevant reason for prohibiting any such publication, the reasons could not be considered sufficient in the particular case, nor was there any reasonable relationship of proportionality with the legitimate aim of protecting the rights of the accused person[7].

1 Cf 11553/85 and 11685/85, *Hodgson and Ors v United Kingdom* (1987) DR 51, 136 (restrictions on televised reporting of court proceedings; inadmissible). See further Bonnington 'The Media Reporting of Court Proceedings' (1998) 3 SLPQ 329; for discussion of English law, see Cram 'Minors' Privacy, Free Speech and the Courts' [1997] PL 410; and Cram 'Automatic Reporting Restrictions in Criminal Proceedings and Article 10, ECHR' [1998] EHRLR 742.

2 *News Verlags v Austria* (11 January 2000), para 56.

3 *Axen v Germany* (1983) A 72 para 25.

4 *Worm v Austria* 1997-V, 1534, para 50. See too *Du Roy and Malaurie v France* (3 October 2000), paras 28–37 (absolute and general ban on publication of reports on pending criminal proceedings involving political figures but not instigated by the public prosecutor: the measure was disproportionate and thus a violation of ECHR, Art 10).

5 1997-V, 1534 paras 52–59 at para 52.

6 34324/96 (23 October 1997) (the Contempt of Court Act 1981 did not apply as the broadcast had not been made; but the High Court applied the Act's test and held that that there was more than a minimal risk of prejudice to the fairness of the trial. Transmission was delayed until after the trial by means of an order made under the court's discretionary and inherent power, even although the last recorded use of the *nobile officium* in this way had been a century or so ago. The Commission considered the reasoning adduced by the High Court (in *Muir v BBC* 1996 SCCR 584) and concluded that the interference was both 'prescribed by law' and 'necessary in a democratic society'. The Commission again raised but avoided answering the question whether the BBC as a public broadcaster properly qualified as a 'victim').

7 (11 January 2000), paras 55–60. At para 58, the Court indicated that any prohibition of a suspect's photograph would itself require to be justified on a case-by-case basis. See too *Weber v Switzerland* (1990) A 177, paras 47–52 (press conference organised by the applicant did not prejudice the fairness of judicial proceedings against him since most of the information had already been disclosed and the proceedings were almost complete).

DECISIONS OF DOMESTIC COURTS ON PRE-TRIAL PUBLICITY

7.41   Scottish cases on contempt of court since 1998 have shown a change in attitude in the part of the court, with a much greater emphasis being placed on the freedom of press and the adoption of a robust attitude to juries. The court has made it clear that it will be only in exceptional circumstances that prejudicial pre-trial publicity will prevent an accused from receiving a fair trial from a jury, as required by the European Convention on Human Rights, Article 6; and, equally, it will only be in unusual circumstances that publicity will 'create a substantial risk that the course of justice will be seriously impeded or prejudiced', as required by the Contempt of Court Act 1981, s 2(2). Both the change in attitude (as a result of the enactment of the 1981 Act, and thus as a result of ECHR, Article 10, which the 1981 Act was intended to implement), and the link between the test under the 1981 Act, s 2 and the question whether a jury would be likely to be significantly influenced by the publication in question, were made clear in *Cox and Griffiths, Petitioners*[1] and subsequent cases[2].

1 1998 SCCR 561, especially at 568–569 per the Lord Justice-General, Lord Rodger of Earlsferry.
2 Eg *HM Advocate v Scottish Media Newspapers Ltd* 1999 SCCR 599; *Galbraith v HM Advocate* 2000 SCCR 935; *BBC, Petitioners* (2 May 2001, unreported), HCJ. See also *R v Sherwood, ex p Telegraph Group* (3 May 2001, unreported), CA; *Re X (Disclosure of Information)* [2001] 2 FLR 440 (disclosure to press of affidavit evidence in matrimonial proceedings: no contempt); *Clibbery v Allan* [2001] 2 FLR 819 (disclosure of evidence conveyed in chambers: no injunction).

PROTECTING THE INTEGRITY OF THE JUDICIARY

7.42 The European Court of Human Rights takes a more searching approach in cases involving interferences with expression purportedly justified by the need to protect the integrity of the courts[1]. In the *Sunday Times (No 1) v United Kingdom* case, the Court noted that the 'authority and impartiality of the judiciary' particularly covered 'the notion that the courts are, and are accepted by the public at large as being, the proper forum for the ascertainment of legal rights and obligations and the settlement of disputes relative thereto; further that the public at large have respect for and confidence in the courts' capacity to fulfil that function'[2]. While judges also enjoy rights in terms of the European Convention on Human Rights, Article 10, it is recognised that they must of necessity show restraint in expressing their opinions[3]. Each interference through the application of contempt of court laws will call for exacting scrutiny. In *De Haes and Gijsels v Belgium*, two journalists who had criticised named judges and the Advocate General for cowardice and for political bias in their disposal of a case involving sexual abuse of children had been convicted of criminal defamation. The Court reiterated that in a state based upon the rule of law, the judiciary required protection against destructive and unfounded criticism, especially since judges themselves were precluded from answering back. In the circumstances, however, the Court decided that there was a violation of ECHR, Article 10 since the 'severely critical' opinions expressed in a 'polemical and even aggressive tone' could be justified as 'proportionate to the stir and indignation caused by the matters alleged'. The guarantee protected both substance and form of expression: 'journalistic freedom also covers possible recourse to a degree of exaggeration, or even provocation'[4]. However, bad faith or insulting language will remove any Article 10 protection[5]. In *Prager and Oberschlick v Austria* , the Court decided that harsh criticisms of a judge's personal integrity fell outwith ECHR, Article 10 protection since these had not been made in good faith and had violated principles of professional ethics, even although the Court recognised that the role of the media in both reporting and commenting on the administration of justice was of fundamental importance in a democratic society[6]. A similar conclusion was reached in *Barfod v Denmark* where the applicant had been fined for publishing an article suggesting that two lay judges had been motivated by bias in determining his tax case in favour of the government which was also the 'employer' of the judges. The Court rejected the applicant's assertions that the criticism should be seen as part of wider political debate as to judicial impartiality, accepting the state's arguments that the article had been a direct attack unsupported by evidence upon two judges which had been likely to lower their esteem in public opinion[7].

1 See Addo 'Are Judges Beyond Criticism under Article 10 of the European Convention on Human Rights?' (1998) 47 ICLQ 425. The maintenance of the authority of the judiciary may also justify interference with the freedom of expression of judges: 47936/99, *Pitkevich v Russia* (8 February 2001) (district court judge who was a member of an evangelical sect had been dismissed for allegedly having proselytised during judicial hearings: inadmissible).
2 (1979) A 30 at para 55. See also 14132/88 *Channel 4 Television v United Kingdom* (1989) DR 61, 285; and *Harris v Harris* [2001] 2 FLR 895.
3 *Wille v Liechtenstein* (28 October 1999), para 64 (at para 67: the lecture given by a judge concerned constitutional issues which by their very nature were political, but this in itself was not a reason for sanctioning the judge whose comments in any case were shared by many).
4 1997-I, 233, paras 37–49 at paras 46 and 48.
5 Applications considered inadmissible on this point include 30339/96, *Bossi v Germany* (15 April 1997) (written appeal pleadings included references to the trial judge's lack of moral fibre and incompetence); 26602/95, *WR v Austria* (30 June 1997) (judicial opinion labelled 'ridiculous' by a lawyer); 26601/95, *Leiningen-Westerburg v Germany* (1997) DR 88, 85 (judge referred to fellow members of the judiciary variously as 'whores' or 'turds', and suggested that they were open to bribery).
6 (1995) A 313, paras 34–38. See too *Schöpfer v Switzerland* 1998-III, 1042, paras 28–34 (disciplinary penalties imposed by the bar on a lawyer following criticism of judges at a press conference held not to be a violation of ECHR, Art 10: it was legitimate to expect lawyers to help maintain public confidence in administration of justice).
7 (1989) A 149, paras 34–35.

Commercial speech

7.43 Expression concerning information essentially of a commercial nature also falls within the ambit of protection of the European Convention on Human Rights, Article 10[1], and both individuals and companies can claim to be 'victims' of interferences with freedom of expression[2]. In *Barthold v Germany*, a veterinary surgeon had been prohibited by competition law and professional conduct rules from making comments about the lack of after-hours care for animals. The applicant himself operated a clinic, and colleagues alleged that he had been using his concerns about the inadequate emergency service to gain unfair publicity. However, the European Court of Human Rights held that any publicity was secondary to the principal content of the article and the nature of the issue being put to the public at large, and as such, the restrictions on his speech were disproportionate and there had been a violation of ECHR, Article 10[3]. However, the Court has proved to be more restrictive in its application of Article 10 in instances where the public interest in open debate is less obvious, and has accepted that a number of factors may justify restrictions on speech which properly can be considered as purely commercial[4]. Here, a certain margin of appreciation is 'essential in commercial matters, and in particular, in an area as complex and fluctuating as that of unfair competition' where issues of business confidentiality, protection of consumers, and fairness to enterprises can all be of relevance[5]. Nevertheless, the sufficiency of such reasons[6], as well as the proportionality of the measures to the aim sought to be achieved[7], will still require to be established.

1 *Markt Intern Verlag GmbH and Klaus Beerman v Germany* (1989) A 165, para 26. See further Skouris (ed) *Advertising and Constitutional Rights in Europe* (1994). See also *R (Matthias Rath Bv) v Advertising Standards Authority Ltd* [2001] HRLR 22; *R (Smithkline Beecham plc) v Advertising Standards Authority Ltd* (17 January 2001, unreported), QBD.

2 *Autronic AG v Switzerland* (1990) A 178, para 47; *Hertel v Switzerland* 1998-VI, 2300, paras 31, 46–51 (unfair competition laws prevented expression of opinion that microwave-cooked food was dangerous to health; violation of ECHR, Art 10 established).

3 (1985) A 90, paras 55–58. At para 42, the Court rejected any attempt to distinguish clearly between factual data and 'elements which go more to manner of presentation than to substance' and which may thus have an advertising or 'publicity-like effect'. See too *Colman v United Kingdom* (1993) A 258-D (General Medical Council (GMC) restrictions on advertising by medical practices: the case was struck off the list following the achievement of a friendly settlement involving revision of the GMC's rules on advertising restrictions); *Casado Coca v Spain* (1994) A 285-A, paras 50–56 (disciplinary action against lawyer who had advertised his professional services not considered a violation).

4 Cf *Open Door Counselling and Dublin Well Women v Ireland* (1992) A 246 (restraints upon counselling agencies from providing pregnant women with information on available abortion facilities abroad were considered: the Court noted that the corporate applicants were engaged in the counselling of pregnant women in the course of which counsellors neither advocated nor encouraged abortion but confined themselves to an explanation of the available options and thus these restraints were disproportionate).

5 *Markt Intern Verlag GmbH and Klaus Beermann v Germany* (1989) A 165, paras 33–37 (prohibition on publisher and editor of specialist commercial bulletin from repeating information).

6 Thus in *Groppera Radio AG and Ors v Switzerland* (1990) A 173, the Court (at para 73) listed and approved the factors advanced by the state in justifying restrictions on the company's rights to retransmit broadcasts from Italy. However, in *Autronic AG v Switzerland* (1990) A 178, paras 61–63, the Court was not persuaded that the state's refusal to allow retransmission without consent of the broadcaster of uncoded broadcast signals from a satellite was justified, primarily on account of an international convention specifically permitting such.

7 Eg *Jacubowski v Germany* (1994) A 291-A, paras 26–30 (prohibition on journalist from circulating material critical of former employer considered proportionate: applicant retained right to defend himself elsewhere).

Maintenance of public morality

7.44 Artistic expression clearly falls within the ambit of the European Convention on Human Rights, Article 10[1], but where state authorities claim that interference is necessary for the protection of morals, the European Court of Human Rights recognises that there is a wide margin of appreciation on the part of the state, and appears to defer readily to national decision-making. The justification for this rests primarily upon the lack of objectivity in interpreting the term 'morals'. As the Court held in the early case of *Handyside v United Kingdom*, there is no uniform European approach to the protection of public morality since views on morality vary 'from time to time and from place to place, especially in our era which is characterised by a rapid and far-reaching evolution of opinion on the subject'. More particularly, the Strasbourg authorities have recognised that their competence in such questions is limited. 'By reason of their direct and continuous contact with the vital forces of their countries', national authorities are better placed to determine whether a matter is necessary to achieve a particular state aim. Strasbourg supervision is thus limited, at most, to consideration of whether the state has advanced reasons for any interference which are relevant and sufficient[2], and of whether any penalty is disproportionate[3]. 'Relevant' reasons may include evidence of public opinion on a particular matter of morality[4]; while an assessment of the 'sufficiency' of such reasons to justify an interference is likely to be limited to a cursory examination of whether the state can show that a domestic decision-maker had a reasonable basis for considering that the interference was necessary for the protection of morals. Thus in the *Handyside* case, the Court noted that the offending publication, *The Little Red Schoolbook*, could have been interpreted by young people 'as an encouragement to indulge in precocious activities harmful for them or even to commit certain criminal offences', and thus domestic courts 'were entitled, in the exercise of their discretion, to think that [the work] would have pernicious effects on the morals of many children and adolescents who would read it'[5]. In *Müller and Ors v Switzerland*, the Court accepted (after having inspected the works of art in question) that it was not unreasonable for the domestic courts to have considered paintings displayed in a public exhibition as 'liable grossly to offend the sense of sexual propriety of persons of ordinary sensitivity'. The imposition of a criminal penalty for publishing obscenity and the confiscation of the paintings thus did not involve a breach of the guarantee[6]. The deference shown to decision-making by national authorities in such instances can at times seem difficult to reconcile with the Court's stated intention of promoting 'pluralism, toleration and broadmindedness', particularly where the moral values appear to be deeply held by a significant sector of society[7]. The practical consequence for artistic expression is that it is accorded little in the way of protection under ECHR, Article 10[8].

1 Cf *Müller v Switzerland* (1988) A 133, para 43.
2 (1976) A 24, paras 48–50 at para 48.
3 E g 31211/96, *Hoare v United Kingdom* (2 July 1997) (30 months' imprisonment for distribution of obscene video cassettes to a restricted circle of customers outwith the video certification scheme, and where no artistic merit was claimed for the works, considered proportionate to the legitimate aim pursued).
4 Cf *Open Door and Dublin Well Woman v Ireland* (1992) A 246-A, para 63 (domestic anti-abortion laws based upon 'profound moral values' as indicated by referendum result); *Otto-Preminger-Institut v Austria* (1994) A 295-A, para 56 (Roman Catholic religion was the faith of the 'overwhelming majority' of population in particular locality). Such factors may, though, not be relevant in other Convention guarantees where local public opinion conflicts with prevailing values in the member states: e g *Tyrer v United Kingdom* (1978) A 26, para 31 (birching supported by local population); *Dudgeon v United Kingdom* (1981) A 45, paras 57–61 (majority of Northern Irish were against legalisation of homosexuality).
5 (1976) A 24, at para 52.
6 (1988) A 133, paras 36–43 at para 36. The question of accessibility to the offending material may be relevant in such circumstances. In *Handyside v United Kingdom* (1976) A 24, the publication had been specifically targeted at young people, while in *Müller v Switzerland* (1988) A 133, the paintings had been displayed in an art gallery which was open to members of the public without payment. On the other hand, in *Otto-Preminger-Institut v Austria*, below, the film in question was to be screened to paying adults at a late hour of the day. Cf *Scherer v Switzerland* (1994) A 287 (screening of pornographic video in private club; nature of the establishment was not apparent to passers-by, but customers knew about it through advertisements placed in specialist magazines etc; domestic court distinguished

factual circumstances from *Müller* in that no unwilling adult or young person had been confronted with the film, but nevertheless still considered punishment was appropriate: the Commission was of the opinion there had been a violation of ECHR, Art 10, but the Court struck the case off its list after the applicant's death).

7 For a defence of this approach, see Mahoney 'Universality versus Subsidiarity in the Strasbourg Case Law on Free Speech' [1997] EHRLR 364; for a response, see Lester of Herne Hill 'Universality versus Subsidiarity: A Reply' [1998] EHRLR 73.
8 Cf Geus 'Quelle Libérte d'Expression pour l'Artiste?' in de Salvia and Villiger (eds) *The Birth of European Human Rights Law* (1998) pp 81–91.

7.45 Artistic expression which challenges religious belief in a manner considered offensive may also justify state interference. In *Otto-Preminger-Institut v Austria*, a seizure order had been made against a film on the ground that it ridiculed particular beliefs of the Roman Catholic Church. While accepting that those who manifest their religious convictions 'must tolerate and accept the denial by others of their religious beliefs and even the propagation by others of doctrines hostile to their faith', the European Court of Human Rights considered that national authorities could consider it necessary to take action to protect believers against 'provocative portrayals of objects of religious veneration' where such constitute 'malicious violation of the spirit of tolerance, which must also be a feature of democratic society'[1]. A similar approach was adopted in *Wingrove v United Kingdom*, where the refusal of the British Board of Film Classification to grant a distribution certificate for a video was challenged. The Court accepted that the English law on blasphemy contained adequate safeguards to protect against arbitrary decision-making, and that the decision by the Board in the particular case had not been unreasonable[2].

1 (1994) A 295-A, at para 47.
2 1996-V, 1937, paras 57–65 (the Court itself viewed the film). For discussion, see Ghandi and James 'The English Law of Blasphemy and the ECHR' [1998] EHRLR 430.

Determining 'necessity' where there has been prior publication

7.46 Where information has already entered the public domain through prior publication, it may be difficult to establish either that the reasons for interference are sufficient or that the measures taken are proportionate. In *Weber v Switzerland*, a journalist had been convicted for disclosing information relating to a pending judicial procedure at a press conference in violation of domestic law which sought to protect the confidentiality of judicial investigations. Much of this information had already been disclosed at an earlier press conference, and in the circumstances the European Court of Human Rights determined that the necessity of protecting the confidentiality of the information no longer existed[1]. Similarly, in *Observer and Guardian Newspapers v United Kingdom* which concerned attempts to prevent the publication of extracts from the 'Spycatcher' memoirs by a former member of the UK security service, the Court accepted there had been relevant grounds for an interference both to protect national security and to prevent prejudice to the Government's position as a litigant. However, the Court drew a distinction between the period from the initial granting of temporary injunctions against newspapers until the time when much of the information became available through publication abroad, and the period after such publication which had involved worldwide dissemination of the book's content. In the first period, the Court accepted that the grounds for restraining publication were also sufficient; but in the second period (and after publication of the book in the USA) this was no longer the case[2]. In *Vereniging Weekblad 'Bluf! v Netherlands*, a magazine containing the results of a confidential survey had been seized and withdrawn from sale, but only after substantial numbers of the publication had already been sold. On this ground, the Court held that the seizure was disproportionate[3].

1 (1990) A 177, paras 51 and 52. See, too, 10038/82, *Harman v United Kingdom* (1984) DR 38, 53 and (1986) DR 46, 57 (finding of contempt of court made against solicitor for allowing journalist to have sight of documents which had been read out in open court: friendly settlement ultimately achieved with change of domestic law to preclude the publication of any document disclosed in court proceedings from being considered a contempt of court).
2 (1991) A 216, paras 62–68. See, similarly, *Sunday Times v United Kingdom (No 2)* (1991) A 217, paras 50–55. For discussion, see Lord Oliver 'Spycatcher Case: Confidence, Copyright and Contempt' in Shetreet (ed), *Free Speech and National Security* (1991).
3 (1995) A 306-A, paras 40–46 (at para 45, the Court acknowledged that while the withdrawal of the magazine was no longer justified, 'it would have been quite possible, however, to prosecute the offenders').

ASSEMBLY AND ASSOCIATION

Scope of Article 11

7.47   The European Convention on Human Rights, Article 11 protects the rights of peaceful assembly and of association with others. These two interrelated rights are fundamental aspects of political life. They also have a close relationship with other Convention concerns such as the manifestation of religious and philosophical convictions and freedom of expression, concerns which must be taken into account in the application of Article 11[1]. In particular, 'the protection of opinions and the freedom to express them is one of the objectives of the freedoms of assembly and association'[2]. The article also has certain implications for aspects of employment law, such as the right to join trade unions which is specifically recognised in paragraph (1), although this provision may be of more limited utility than some commentators would wish[3].

1 Cf *Young, James and Webster v United Kingdom* (1981) A 44, para 57, discussed at para 7.53 below; *Socialist Party of Turkey and Ors v Turkey* 1998-III, 1233, para 41 (ECHR, Art 11 to be considered in the light of Art 10). Cf *Steel and Ors v United Kingdom* 1998-VII, 2719, para 113 (peaceful protest considered under Art 10 rather than Art 11); *Hashman and Harrup v United Kingdom* (25 November 1999), para 24 (complaint under Art 11 not pursued before the Court, and merits considered under Art 10).
2 *United Communist Party of Turkey and Ors v Turkey* 1998-I, 1 at para 42.
3 See Hendry 'The Human Rights Act, Article 11, and the Right to Strike' [1998] EHRLR 582; Christie 'Bringing Rights to the Workplace?' 2000 JR 73; Palmer 'Human Rights: Implications for Labour Law' (2000) 59 CLJ 168. The European Social Charter seeks to protect employment rights which are of the nature of economic and social rights: see para 2.39 above.

7.48   The format of the European Convention on Human Rights, Article 11 follows that of Articles 8, 9 and 10: that is, paragraph (1) first recognises the freedoms of peaceful assembly and association, and paragraph (2) thereafter permits interferences on the grounds of listed state interests where prescribed by law and 'necessary in a democratic society'[1]. The legitimate interests recognised include national security, public safety, the prevention of disorder or crime, and the individual aims of protection of health or morals or the rights and freedoms of others. It will invariably be possible to bring an interference under one of these heads, and satisfying the test of 'prescribed by law' has not often proved to be a matter of difficulty[2]. In this area, the critical question again has concerned scrutiny of the necessity of an interference which must correspond to a pressing social need, be proportionate to the legitimate aim pursued, and be justified by relevant and sufficient reasons. ECHR, Article 11, paragraph (2) makes specific provision for state restrictions on the exercise of these rights by 'members of the armed forces, of the police or the administration of the state', an issue considered below in respect of the withdrawal of recognition of trade union membership[3].

1 See further paras 3.33–3.39 and 3.66–3.78 above.
2 Cf *NF v Italy* (2 August 2001), paras 26-34 (the applicant, a judge, was a former freemason who was reprimanded after his resignation from his lodge during the course of disciplinary proceedings for having undermined the prestige of the judiciary in terms of a directive read in conjunction with an earlier decree; however, the terms of the directive had not been sufficiently clear to allow even a judge trained in the law to realise that a magistrate joining an official masonic lodge could face disciplinary action: the sanction was thus not 'forseeable' and thus not 'prescribed by law', and the interference involved a violation of Art 11).
3 See para 7.56 below.

Positive obligations

7.49   The guarantee can require positive action on the part of the state. 'Genuine, effective freedom of peaceful assembly' cannot be secured simply by a duty upon the state itself not to interfere, but must entail positive state assistance to those seeking to meet and to protest through protection against those opposed to the expression of the particular opinion, since 'in a democracy the right to counter-demonstrate cannot extend to inhibiting the exercise of the right to demonstrate'[1]. In *Plattform 'Ärzte für das Leben' v Austria*, the European Court of Human Rights considered an application from an association of doctors campaigning against abortion legislation who had their protest disrupted by groups opposed to their views and complained that the police had given them insufficient protection. The Court held that the European Convention on Human Rights, Article 11 imposed a duty upon public authorities to take such reasonable measures as were appropriate in order to allow a lawful demonstration to take place peacefully, although the state had a wide discretion in its choice of methods and there could not be an absolute guarantee of protection for participants against those opposed to the expression of such views[2].

1 *Plattform 'Ärzte für das Leben' v Austria* (1988) A 139, at para 32.
2 (1988) A 139, paras 32 and 34 (no violation established in the circumstances).

Peaceful assembly

7.50 An 'assembly'[1] can take the form of either a meeting or a procession, and can take place either on private property or in a public space[2]. The European Convention on Human Rights, Article 11 applies irrespective of whether the assembly is unlawful in terms of domestic law, although the qualification of 'peaceful' does suggest that any meeting seeking to provoke violence falls outwith the scope of the guarantee[3]. It is a right enjoyed not only by the participants in but also by the organisers of a demonstration, including any association or corporate body[4]. There will be an 'interference' with this right where an assembly or procession is prohibited[5] or where there is a sanction imposed for the exercise of the right[6], but the mere fact that an assembly or procession requires prior approval does not itself constitute an interference[7].

1 See further Fitzpatrick and Taylor 'Trespassers *Might* Be Prosecuted: The European Convention and Restrictions on the Right to Assemble' [1998] EHRLR 292; Fenwick 'The Right to Protest, the Human Rights Act and the Margin of Appreciation' (1999) 62 MLR 491.
2 8191/78, *Rassemblement Jurassien v Switzerland* (1979) DR 17, 93; 8440/78, *Christians Against Racism and Fascism v United Kingdom* (1980) DR 21, 138. Cf 33689/96, *Anderson and Ors v United Kingdom* (1997) DR 91, 79 (exclusion of applicants from a shopping centre because of misconduct did not give rise to an Art 11 issue in the absence of any history of their having used the centre for any assembly or association: the guarantee is not intended to protect assembly for purely social purposes).
3 13079/87, *G v Germany* (1989) DR 60, 256 (obstruction of a road by way of protest does not constitute a violent demonstration); and 8440/78, *Christians Against Racism and Fascism v United Kingdom* (1980) DR 21, 138 (peaceful nature of assembly cannot be lost by violent nature of any counter-demonstration).
4 8440/78, *Christians Against Racism and Fascism v United Kingdom* (1980) DR 21, 138.
5 8440/78, *Christians Against Racism and Fascism v United Kingdom* (1980) DR 21, 138.
6 13079/87, *G v Germany* (1989) DR 60, 256.
7 8191/78, *Rassemblement Jurassien v Switzerland* (1979) DR 17, 93. See too 25522/94, *Rai and Ors v United Kingdom* (1995) DR 81, 146 (prohibition on meetings in Trafalgar Square not an 'interference': the policy was not designed to discriminate between different organisations but instead to prevent disorder, and the applicants could meet elsewhere).

Assessing whether any interference meets the requirements of para (2)

7.51 Under the European Convention on Human Rights, Article 11, paragraph (2), any interference must be prescribed by law, seek to achieve one of the prescribed legitimate interests, and meet the 'necessary in a democratic society' test. Again, this latter test is likely to be the key issue. In *Christians Against Racism and Fascism v United Kingdom*, the Commission considered a blanket prohibition order which had been imposed on all forms of procession. The question of proportionality was tackled by considering whether the security and public order reasons justified the prohibition, and whether the same ends could have been achieved by less onerous alternatives. In the circumstances, the order was considered to be reasonable[1]. This case suggests recognition of a fairly wide margin of appreciation on the part of state authorities, but now has to be read alongside judgments of the European Court of Human Rights which seem to demand greater care in scrutinising interferences with political protest. In *Ezelin v France*, an office-bearer of an association of lawyers had taken part in a duly authorised protest during which offensive comments had been directed by other participants at the police and made about the judiciary. He had been disciplined for having neither disassociated himself from the disorder nor having expressed disapproval. For the Court, although the sanctions imposed were minimal, they were considered disproportionate since the applicant had not committed any blameworthy act, and even lawyers should not be discouraged 'for fear of disciplinary sanctions, from making clear their beliefs'[2].

1 8440/78 (1980) DR 21, 138.
2 (1991) A 202, paras 37–41, 51–53 at para 52.

Freedom of association

7.52 Freedom of association[1] involves a general right or liberty of individuals 'to join without interference by the state in association in order to attain various ends'[2], and thus an 'association' is a more formal or organised concept than an 'assembly'[3]. The scope of the freedom does not, however, extend to any right merely to socialise or to be in the company of others[4] let alone to insist upon the right to join an association against the association's wishes[5]. More crucially, it does not apply to institutions with a public law nature which pursue public interests. In *Le Compte, Van Leuven and De Meyere v Belgium*, for example, a statutory body charged with the professional regulation of medical practitioners through administrative, disciplinary and rule-making means was considered not to be an 'association' covered by the European Convention on Human Rights, Article 11[6].

1 'Association' is given an autonomous meaning; and the domestic legal system's classification has only relative value and constitutes no more than a starting-point: *Chassagnou and Ors v France* 1999-III, 21, paras 99–102. See further, Tomuschat 'Freedom of Association' in Macdonald, Matscher and Petzold (eds) *The European System for the Protection of Human Rights* (1993) pp 493–513; Lewis-Anthony 'Case Law of Article 11, ECHR' in Council of Europe, *Freedom of Association: Proceedings of Reykjavik Seminar* (1994) pp 31–48; Cullen Freedom of Association as a Political Right' (1999) 24 EL Rev HR 30; and Fenwick and Phillipson 'Public Protest, the Human Rights Act and Judicial Responses to Political Expression' [2000] PL 627.
2 6094/73, *Association X v Sweden* (1978) DR 9, 5.
3 Gomien, Harris and Zwaak *Law and Practice of the European Convention on Human Rights and the European Social Charter* (1996) p 304.
4 Cf 8317/78, *McFeely v United Kingdom* (1980) DR 20, 44 (prisoner held in solitary confinement could not rely upon ECHR, Art 11 to claim to 'association').
5 10550/83, *Cheall v United Kingdom* (1985) DR 42, 178 (the right to join a trade union could not be interpreted as conferring a general right to join the union of one's choice irrespective of the rules of the union). This judgment was applied in *Royal Society for the Protection of Animals v Attorney General* [2001] 3 All ER 530.
6 (1981) A 43, paras 64–65 (establishment of the professional body did not prevent doctors from joining other associations, and thus the obligation to be subject to the body in no way limited ECHR, Art 11 rights). Cf *Sigurdur A Sigurjónsson v Iceland* (1993) A 264, paras 31–37 (taxicab drivers' association considered predominantly a private law organisation: compulsion to join the association against the applicant's wishes gave rise to an ECHR, Art 11 issue).

Interferences

7.53 The European Convention on Human Rights, Article 11 has both a positive and a negative aspect: protection for associations and their members; and protection against compulsion to join an association. The positive aspect was considered briefly in *Vogt v Germany*, where a teacher had been dismissed from her post because of her failure to disassociate herself from a political party, membership of which was considered incompatible with her office as a civil servant. This was considered to be an interference with ECHR, Article 11, paragraph (1)[1]. An association can also claim to be the victim of a violation of Article 11 in its own right. In *Grande Oriente d'Italia de Palazzo Giustiniani v Italy*, an association of a number of Italian masonic lodges challenged the adoption of a law requiring candidates for public office to declare that they were not freemasons. The Court accepted that the association was protected by Article 11, and since the measure could well have resulted in a loss of membership and prestige, there had been an 'interference'[2]. The negative aspect was at issue in *Young, James and Webster v United Kingdom*, where three employees of British Rail had been dismissed after the introduction of an obligation to join a trade union. The European Court of Human Rights accepted that even assuming that the negative aspect of ECHR, Article 11 does not carry as much weight as the positive right to associate, the threat of dismissal and consequent loss of livelihood were serious interferences which went to the very heart of the essence of the guarantee, particularly since the compulsion also gave rise to considerations under Articles 9 and 10[3]. Article 11 thus protects individuals against any abuse of a trade union's dominant position in the workplace[4].

There may also be an interference with the right of association through failure to recognise legal personality or refusal to grant registration[5]. This may call into question a state's commitment to the promotion of pluralist views and democratic debate. In *Sidiropoulos and Ors v Greece*, some 50 individuals living in northern Greece had sought to establish a cultural association called 'Home of Macedonian Civilisation' which the domestic courts had refused to register for several reasons including the prevention of disorder and protection of the state's cultural identity. This refusal was deemed to give rise to an issue in terms of ECHR, Article 11[6]. However, the article cannot be taken as requiring an association to be given title and interest to sue in a legal action where otherwise it would not be recognised as having standing[7].

1 (1995) A 323, para 64 (matter ultimately disposed of under ECHR, Art 10: see para 7.37 above). See too 11002/84, *Van der Heijden v Netherlands* (1985) DR 41, 264 (termination of employment on account of membership of a political party was considered justified for the protection of the rights of others since the party concerned had views contrary to the welfare of immigrants which the employer sought to promote).
2 (2 August 2001), paras 15–16. This decision seems to suggest that a low threshold test is required to establish 'victim' status for an association under Art 11. The Court held (paras 24-26 and 30-32) that the measure was deemed disproportionate and thus not 'necessary in a democratic society'; and further, that it did not properly fall within the category of lawful restriction on the exercise of rights by members of the administration of the state'. Cf 43505/98, *Salaman v United Kingdom* (15 June 2000) (trial judge and an appeal court judge had not disclosed the fact of their membership of the freemasons in a case where one of the parties was also a freemason: membership of the freemasons was not in itself enough to cast doubt over impartiality as required by ECHR, Art 6, and the applicant had not provided any further evidence to substantiate his fears: inadmissible).
3 (1981) A 44, paras 55 and 57 (but (at para 55) compulsion to join a trade union 'may not always be contrary to the Convention'). See too *Sibson v United Kingdom* (1993) A 258-A (applicant had no objection to trade union membership on the grounds of any conviction,

no closed shop agreement was in place, and dismissal was not inevitable; no violation established); and *Sigurdur A Sigurjónsson v Iceland* (1993) A 264, noted at para 7.52 fn 6 above. Cf 52562/99, *Sørensen v Denmark* (a student who was offered a summer job was advised that membership of a trade union affiliated to the national union would be obligatory if he secured a post; when offered a post, he was advised the terms of his employment would be regulated by an agreement between the company and a particular union specified by the company; his refusal to join this union led to his dismissal: communicated).

4   15533/89, *Englund and Ors v Sweden* (1994) DR 77, 10.

5   28626/95, *Christian Association of Jehovah's Witnesses v Bulgaria* (1997) DR 90, 77 (suspension of the association's registration declared admissible; (9 March 1998) friendly settlement achieved). However, refusal of registration because of the association's name being considered misleading will not result in a violation: *Apeh Üldözötteinek Szövetsege, Ivanyi, Róth and Szerdaheli v Hungary* (5 October 2000), paras 30–44 (association refused registration in the name of 'Alliance of [National Tax Authority's] Persecutees' as this was considered defamatory and to prevent any impression that the association was linked to the tax authority: case considered under ECHR, Art 6).

6   1998-IV, 1594, para 31 (interference was a disproportionate response to the legitimate aim of protecting national security and prevention of disorder). But compare decisions of the Commission which appear to take a less liberal approach: 8652/79, *X v Austria* (1981) DR 26, 89 (the dissolution by the state of two organisations intended to provide support for the 'Moon' sect (or 'Moonies') was not a violation of ECHR, Art 11); 9905/82, *A Association and H v Austria* (1984) DR 36, 187 (prohibition of meeting supporting reunification with Germany necessary for national security given the state's international obligations to respect neutrality); 23892/94, *A C R E P v Portugal* (1995) DR 83, 57 (association seeking to promote Portuguese monarchy and constitutional order of 1838 dissolved by judicial decision: inadmissible in view of the state's margin of appreciation in determining whether this was necessary to prevent disorder).

7   9234/81, *X Association v Germany* (1981) DR 26, 270.

Assessing whether any interference meets the requirements of para (2)

7.54   Under the European Convention on Human Rights, Article 11, paragraph (2), any interference must be prescribed by law, seek to achieve one of the listed legitimate state interests, and meet the 'necessary in a democratic society' test. In applying the test of 'necessary in a democratic society', association is accorded particular protection in the maintenance of pluralist opinion and democracy, and thus the exceptions recognised by paragraph (2) have to be construed strictly. This principle will apply to situations where domestic law compels an individual to join an association which is contrary to his own convictions. In such circumstances, the European Court of Human Rights will consider whether a fair balance has been struck between individual and collective interests[1]. In *Young, James and Webster v United Kingdom*, the Court noted various surveys and official reports which indicated that trade unions could still have fulfilled their purpose in furthering their members' interests without compelling non-union employees to join, thus helping establish that the dismissal of the three employees had been a disproportionate measure[2]. Where action is taken against a political party, particular scrutiny is required. In *United Communist Party of Turkey and Ors v Turkey*, the applicant association had been dissolved by the country's constitutional court on the grounds that the party had called itself 'communist' contrary to domestic law, and further that the party was seeking to promote the division of the state by encouraging Kurdish separatism. On the first point the Court considered that choice of name could never in itself justify dissolution without other relevant and sufficient reasons; on the second, there could not be any justification for such a step simply because the party sought to stimulate public debate in the political arena. A principal characteristic of democracy is 'the possibility it offers of resolving a country's problems through dialogue, without recourse to violence, even where they are irksome'. Nor was it appropriate for the state to seek to rely upon ECHR, Article 17 since the party could not be said to have had any responsibility for promoting terrorism or seeking the destruction of the rights of others[3]. In contrast, in *Refah Partisi (The Welfare Party), Erbakan, Kazan and Tekdal v Turkey*, a bare majority of the Court held that the dissolution of the Welfare Party by the constitutional court had not resulted in a violation of ECHR, Article 11. Steps had been taken against the party because of its objectives which sought the establishment of the 'Sharia', a system of Islamic law, and a theocratic government in violation of the state's strictly secular constitution. For the Court, the enjoyment of freedom of association on the part of a political party campaigning for legislative changes or alteration of legal and constitutional structures state was dependent upon two conditions: first, the means used to seek to secure these ends had to be entirely lawful and democratic; and second, the proposed changes had themselves to be compatible with fundamental democratic principles. It thus followed that political parties which sought change through violent means or whose political aims were incompatible with democracy or sought to suppress democratic rights and freedoms could not rely upon the Convention. In determining this issue, it was necessary to have regard not only to the party's own programme but also to the pronouncement of its leaders: here, the leaders of the Welfare Party had not only declared an intention to introduce certain features of Islamic law which embodied values contrary to those found in the Convention, but also had left open the issue as to the appropriateness of non-democratic methods to obtain and retain political power[4].

1   Cf *Chassagnou and Ors v France* 1999-III, 21, paras 109–117 (the obligatory membership of hunting association against the convictions of the applicant which also involved the transfer of rights over members' land to allow the hunting association to attain its objects went well beyond achieving a fair balance between conflicting interests and could not be considered as proportionate to the aim pursued. The Court (paras 118–121) also established a violation of ECHR, Art 11 taken in conjunction with Art 14).
2   (1981) A 44, paras 63–65.
3   1998-I, 1, paras 51–61 at para 57. See too *Socialist Party and Ors v Turkey* 1998-III, 1233, paras 41–54 at 47 (the fact that a separatist programme 'is considered incompatible with the current principles and structures of the Turkish State does not make it incompatible with the rules of democracy'). Cf 6741/74, X v Italy (1976) DR 5, 83 (repression of groups seeking to restore the fascist party may be considered necessary in a democratic society); and *Freedom and Democracy Party (ÖZDEP) v Turkey* (8 December 1999), paras 37–48 (the Court could find nothing in the party's programme which could be taken to constitute a call to violence or rejection of constitutional principles, and the dissolution of the party was thus deemed a violation of ECHR, Art 11).
4   (31 July 2001), paras 42–52, 63–83. Cf the dissenting judgment which stresses the importance of pluralism and the lack of any pressing danger to the Turkish state posed by the party.

Trade unions

7.55   The European Convention on Human Rights, Article 11, paragraph (1) makes specific reference to the 'right to form and to join trade unions'[1]. The concluding words 'for the protection of his interests' imply that trade unions not only must be permitted[2] but also in some manner be allowed to express the interests of their members[3]. This can be achieved through the use of collective agreements[4] or recognition of the right to strike[5]. Further, there may be an obligation to make some special provision for trade union representatives[6], but in each instance the choice of means is covered by recognition of a margin of appreciation on the part of the state. In any case, the right of association may also involve recognition of a right of *non-association* which provides protection against compulsion to join any association, as in the case of *Young, James and Webster v United Kingdom* discussed above[7].

1 Cf 6094/73, *Association X v Sweden* (1977) DR 9, 5 (students' union not a 'trade union'). See further, Hepple 'Freedom to Form and Join or not to Join Trade Unions' in Council of Europe *Freedom of Association: Proceedings of Reykjavik Seminar* (1984) pp 161–174.

2 Including having the right to draw up their own rules: 10550/83, *Cheall v United Kingdom* (1985) DR 42, 178.

3 7361/76, *Trade Union X v Belgium* (1978) DR 14, 40. Cf 7990/77, *X v United Kingdom* (1981) DR 24, 57 (no duty upon prison authorities to assist a prisoner on a pre-release employment scheme to have his trade union rights respected); and 53574/99, *UNISON v United Kingdom* (court injunction prohibiting strike action after failing to obtain assurances that employees' rights would be maintained with the transfer of business activities to a private company: communicated).

4 *National Union of Belgian Police v Belgium* (1975) A 19, paras 38 and 39; *Swedish Engine Drivers' Union v Sweden* (1976) A 20, paras 39 and 40.

5 *Schmidt and Dahlström v Sweden* (1976) A 21, para 36 (noting the right to strike contained in the European Social Charter); but cf 28910/95, *National Association of Teachers in Further and Higher Education v United Kingdom* (1998) DR 93, 63 (the right to strike is not expressly provided for in the European Convention on Human Rights, and may be regulated by domestic law; and a requirement that a trade union disclose the names of its members entitled to vote on whether to take industrial action was not in the circumstances a disproportionate interference with ECHR, Art 11 rights).

6 Cf 57742/00, *Sanchez Navajas* (21 June 2001) (deduction of salary for time spent by a trade union representative on study of new legislation concerning trade union elections on the basis that the study was to further the representative's interests rather than those of members of the union: while it was possible to deduce from ECHR, Art 11 when read with Art 28 of the (revised) European Social Charter a limited right of trade union representatives to such facilities to allow the effective discharge of their union responsibilities, in this case it could not be shown that the study had been strictly necessary, and non-payment of salary did not affect the substance of the right guaranteed by EHCR, Art 15: inadmissible).

7 See para 7.53 above,.

7.56 The European Convention on Human Rights, Article 11, paragraph (2) further provides that lawful restrictions may be placed on the exercise of these rights by 'members of the armed forces, of the police or the administration of the state'. The categories, particularly the latter, should be interpreted narrowly[1]. For example, in *Grande Oriente d'Italia de Palazzo Giustiniani v Italy*, the Court could not accept that the adoption of a law requiring candidates for public office to declare that they were not freemasons involved the imposition of lawful restrictions on members of the administration of the state since the categories subject to the requirement went beyond the narrow meaning of the term[2]. However, this provision will imply a wide margin of appreciation for states if national security considerations exist. In *Council of Civil Service Unions v United Kingdom*, where the right of employees at the government's communications monitoring centre to join a trade union had been removed, the Commission considered that there was no violation of ECHR, Article 11.

'Administration of the state' was to be read in the context of references to the armed forces and police, and the Commission was satisfied that the employees in question could be considered to fall within the category covered by the second sentence of paragraph (2). 'Restrictions' could also include a complete prohibition; and even if the qualification 'lawful' included not only the requirement of having some basis in domestic law but also protection against arbitrariness, both of these conditions had been met. In any case, states had to be given 'a wide discretion when securing the protection of their national security'[3]. Similarly, in *Rekvényi v Hungary*, a general constitutional ban on political activities by police officers and members of the security services which also involved a prohibition on membership of any political party was accepted as having the intended aim of depoliticising these services and thereby helping consolidate pluralist democracy. The Court took particular account of the recent history of the state which had only recently emerged from a totalitarian system of government in which the direct commitment of police officers to the ruling party's values had been expected[4].

1 Cf *Vogt v Germany* (1995) A 323, paras 66–68 at para 67: ('administration of the state' to be interpreted narrowly; issue of whether teacher who was civil servant included avoided in the particular case).
2 (2 August 2001), paras 30–32.
3 11603/85 (1987) DR 50, 228, at 241. Cf 12719/87, *Frederiksen v Denmark* (1988) DR 56, 237 (payment of reasonable compensation for dismissal on account of trade union membership deprives the individual of status of 'victim').
4 (20 May 1999), paras 58–62 (application concerned both ECHR, Arts 10 and 11 (cf paras 46–50) police officers could still articulate political opinions under Art 10 and thus the measure was not disproportionate).

THE RIGHT TO FREE ELECTIONS

Scope of Protocol 1, Article 3

7.57   The Preamble to the European Convention on Human Rights acknowledges that the maintenance of justice and peace is dependent not only upon a shared understanding and observance of human rights, but also upon 'effective political democracy'. This end is in large part secured by such rights as freedom of expression, protest, and thought which further political dialogue, while the jurisprudence of the European Court of Human Rights emphasises the values of pluralism and tolerance as the essential hallmarks of democratic society. ECHR, Protocol 1, Article 3 initially was considered more as of symbolic importance in confirming the importance of institutional arrangements than as a provision which conferred individual rights[1], but it is now clear that this guarantee does secure the rights to vote and to stand as a candidate in elections to the legislature[2]. Accordingly, the article requires the discharge of positive obligations by states. In *Mathieu-Mohin and Clerfayt v Belgium*, the Court confirmed as inappropriate any suggestion that the article should be given a restrictive interpretation and rejected the argument that individual rights could not be derived from the provision. The 'inter-state colouring of the wording ... does not reflect any difference of substance from the other substantive clauses in the Convention and Protocols' and could be explained by the 'desire to give greater solemnity to the commitment undertaken and ... the fact that the primary obligation in the field concerned is not one of abstention or non-interference, as with the majority of the civil and political rights, but one of adoption by the state of positive measures to "hold" democratic elections'[3]. In interpreting 'effective political democracy', there is probably no implicit suggestion of the notion of the right to self-determination which is found in international law[4], although the Court in *Incal v Turkey* did accept that ECHR, Article 10 also protected expression which called for the dissolution of an existing state[5]. However, the rights protected by this article are not absolute: the rights exist only in relation to elections for the 'legislature'; and the provision comfortably accommodates the wide variety of arrangements for electoral and parliamentary systems found throughout Europe[6].

1 Cf 3321–3/67 and 3344/67, *Greek case* (1969) YB 12, at 179 (provision 'presupposes the existence of a representative legislature, elected at reasonable intervals').
2 6745/74 and 6746/74, *W, X, Y and Z v Belgium* (1975) DR 2, 110; 9267/81, *Moureaux and Ors v Belgium* (1983) DR 33, 97. See further de Meyer 'Electoral Rights' in Macdonald, Matscher and Petzold (eds) *The European System for the Protection of Human Rights* (1993) pp 553–569; Marks 'The European Convention on Human Rights and its "Democratic Society"' (1997) 66 BYIL 209; Herndl 'The Case-Law of the Commission as Regards the Right to Free Elections' in da Salvia and Villiger (eds) *The Birth of European Human Rights Law* (1998) pp 91–99; and Cremona 'The Right to Free Elections in the European Convention on Human Rights' in Mahoney, Matscher, Petzold and Wildhaber (eds) *Protecting Human Rights: The European Perspective* (2000) pp 309–323.
3 (1987) A 113, paras 48–54 at para 50.
4 Franck 'The Emerging Right to Democratic Governance' (1992) 86 AJIL 46.
5 1998-IV, 1547, discussed at para 7.30 above. Similarly, the Court has found violations of ECHR, Art 11 in respect of the dissolution of political parties which advocate the dissolution of a state using non-violent means: e g *United Communist Party of Turkey and Others v Turkey* 1998-I, 1, discussed at para 7.54 above.
6 See further Davis 'Constitutional Reform in the United Kingdom and the Right to Free and Fair Elections' [1999] EHRLR 411; Doherty and Reid 'Voting Rights for the European Parliament: Whose Responsibility?' [1999] EHRLR 420.

The right to vote; and ensuring the 'free expression of the opinion of the people'

7.58 The European Convention on Human Rights, Protocol 1, Article 3 requires states to ensure that appointment to the legislature is by 'free' elections at 'reasonable intervals' through a 'secret ballot' and 'under conditions which will ensure the free expression of the opinion of the people'[1]. This aim is also supplemented by protection for political speech under ECHR, Article 10[2]. States may impose conditions on the right to vote[3] such as those relating to residency[4] or exercise of the franchise on national territory[5] or disqualification for conviction of offences deemed incompatible with civic duties[6], provided that the very essence of the right is not impaired. The article does not preclude imposition of a duty upon citizens to vote[7]. However, the provision cannot be used to secure a particular voting system, such as one based upon proportional representation, to seek to ensure that each vote is of equal value[8]. In

Mathieu-Mohin and Clerfayt v Belgium, the Court acknowledged that assessment of arrangements for exercise of the franchise had to involve consideration of the political evolution of the state concerned: 'features that would be unacceptable in the context of one system may accordingly be justified in the context of another, at least so long as the chosen system provides for conditions which will ensure the 'free expression of the opinion of the people in the choice of the legislature'[9]. The avoidance of inappropriate judicial involvement in political questions is thus achieved by recognising a wide margin of appreciation on the part of states in determining voting arrangements. The case concerned Belgium's rather fragile stability and a requirement placed upon a French-speaking linguistic minority to vote for candidates willing to use Flemish. The Court found no violation of the article on the grounds that French-speaking voters had the same rights as Flemish-speaking voters, and any linguistic requirement was not such a disproportionate limitation so as to thwart the 'free expression of the opinion of the people'[10]. Similarly, the use of different electoral systems in the United Kingdom (in particular, in Northern Ireland) with a view to protecting the interests of a minority does not interfere with the free expression of democratic opinion[11]. Nor is a state precluded from providing financial support to parties on the ground that this would hinder the aim of the provision[12].

1   Cf 60983/00, *Zhermal v Russia* (allegation of irregularity in electoral process in the return of a candidate with a relative (as opposed to an absolute) majority: communicated).
2   See paras 7.27–7.31 above.
3   6745/74 and 6746/74, *W, X, Y, Z v Belgium* (1975) DR 2, 110.
4   7566/76, *X v United Kingdom* (1976) DR 9, 121 (the residence requirement in UK's electoral law was not unreasonable or arbitrary, and was thus compatible with ECHR, Protocol 1, Art 3); 8612/79, *Alliance des Belges de la CEE v Belgium* (1979) DR 15, 259 (Belgian legislation governing participation of Belgian nationals in elections was not inconsistent with ECHR, Protocol 1, Art 3).
5   7730/76, *X v United Kingdom* (1979) DR 15, 137 (non-residents less likely to have understanding of electoral issues and contact with candidates); 8987/80, *X and Association Y v Italy* (1981) DR 24, 192.
6   8701/79, *X v Belgium* (1979) DR 18, 250 (deprivation of right to vote for collaborating with German occupying forces during the 1939–45 war and thus for uncitizenlike conduct does not violate free expression of the opinion of the electorate in the choice of the legislature); 9914/82, *H v Netherlands* (1983) DR 33, 242 (restriction on right of persons convicted for refusing to serve in the military on the grounds of conscience where the individual refused to comply with formalities allowing acquisition of objector status) but cf *Thlimmenos v Greece* (6 April 2000), discussed at para 7.13 above. The disqualification of serving prisoners from voting was held not to contravene ECHR, Protocol 1, Art 3 (alone, or taken together with Art 14 of the Convention), in *R (Pearson) v Secretary of State for the Home Dept* (4 April 2001, unreported), QBD.
7   1718/62, *X v Austria* (1965) YB 8, 168 at 172–173 ('the term "free elections" does not mean elections in which voting is not compulsory but elections in which the exercise of electoral choice is free').
8   8941/80, *X v Iceland* (1981) DR 27, 145 (a system which results in return of successful candidate in one constituency with fewer votes than in other constituencies does not infringe 'free expression of the opinion of the people'); 8765/79, *The Liberal Party v United Kingdom* (1980) DR 21, 211 (both the simple majority system and proportional representation are compatible with ECHR, Protocol 1, Art 3); and 56618/00, *Federación Nacionalista Canaria v Spain* (7 June 2001) (challenge to rule requiring a party to secure a minimum percentage of votes cast in order to obtain a seat in Parliament: inadmissible).
9   (1987) A 113, at para 54. Cf 8873/80, *X v United Kingdom* (1982) DR 28, 99 (ratification of ECHR, Protocol 1 by the UK could not have been intended to interfere with the settled relationship between Westminster and Jersey so as to allow Channel Island residents the right to vote in British parliamentary elections).

10 (1987) A 113, para 57. See too *Matthews v United Kingdom* 1999-I, 251, at para 64 ('The Court makes it clear at the outset that the choice of electoral system by which the free expression of the opinion of the people in the choice of the legislature is ensured – whether it be based on proportional representation , the "first-past-the-post" system or some other arrangement – is a matter in which the State enjoys a wide margin of appreciation').
11 8364/78, *Lindsay v United Kingdom* (1979) DR 15, 247.
12 6850/74, *X, Y and Z v Germany* (1976) DR 5, 90.

The rights to stand as a candidate and to sit as a representative

7.59 As with the right to vote, the right to stand as a candidate is not absolute, and a state may prescribe formalities such as the registration as a political party[1], the requirement of securing a minimum level of support from registered electors[2] or the enrolment in a particular language[3]. In this regard, concerns under the European Convention on Human Rights, Article 11 may also be relevant[4]. The provision also guarantees the right of a candidate duly elected to sit in the legislature, again subject to restrictions considered reasonable[5]. In *Gitonas and Ors v Greece*, the election of five MPs had been annulled on account of their disqualification as holders of public office. The Court confirmed that the right to sit in a legislature was not absolute, but was subject to such implied limitations as a state considered necessary taking into account the historical and political development of the country with a view to ensuring the proper functioning of democratic institutions. The disqualification of civil servants and other categories of holders of public office from standing as candidates and from sitting in the legislature was a feature found in many other European states and helped ensure that candidates enjoyed 'equal means of influence'; it also 'protect[ed] the electorate from pressure from such officials who, because of their position, are called upon to take many – and sometimes important – decisions and enjoy substantial prestige in the eyes of the ordinary citizen'. Accordingly, there was no violation of ECHR, Protocol 1, Article 3[6].

1 6850/74, *X, Y and Z v Germany* (1976) DR 5, 90.
2 7008/75, *X v Austria* (1976) DR 6, 120; and 25035/94, *Magnago and Südtiroler Volkspartei v Italy* (1996) DR 85, 112 (requirement that a political party must secure a minimum of the national vote as a condition for allocation of seats pursues the legitimate aim of promoting a legislature which contains sufficiently representative opinion and is not discriminatory).
3 *Mathieu-Mohin and Clerfayt v Belgium* (1987) A 113, para 57.
4 See para 7.54 above. See too *Refah Partisi (The Welfare Party), Erbakan, Kazan and Tekdal v Turkey* (31 July 2001), paras 85-86 (the dissolution of the Welfare Party and the imposition of disqualification from sitting in Parliament or holding other political offices on the party's leaders was justified in terms of Art 11, and thus did not give rise to a violation in terms of Protocol 1, Article 3).
5 10316/83, *M v United Kingdom* (1984) DR 37, 129 (disqualification on the basis of membership of another legislature). See too *Buscarini and Ors v San Marino* 1999-I, 605, paras 34–41 at para 39 ('interference' with ECHR, Art 9 rights where applicants who were elected to parliament were required to take a religious oath on the Bible as a condition of sitting; making the 'exercise of a mandate intended to represent different views of society within Parliament subject to a prior declaration of commitment to a particular set of beliefs' was contradictory and thus a violation of Art 9); but cf 39511/98, *McGuiness v United Kingdom* 1999-V, 481 (elected representatives required to take an oath of allegiance to the monarch; application declared inadmissible under Article 10 since oath could be viewed simply as an affirmation of loyalty to the UK's constitutional principles); and 36909/97, *Gaulieder v*

Slovakia (18 May 2000) (member of parliament elected in respect of a party list had his office terminated upon his resignation from the parliamentary group: friendly settlement).
6 1997-IV, 1217, paras 39–44 at para 40.

'Legislature'

7.60   The rights secured by the European Convention on Human Rights, Protocol 1, Article 3 apply in relation to the 'legislature', a term which is interpreted in the light of political institutions established by the constitution of each state[1]. The key question appears to be the level of law-making power entrusted to the institution: a 'legislature' must have the powers both to initiate legislation as well as to adopt it. Municipal councils cannot be considered as legislative bodies[2] but regional legislatures within a federal constitutional structure will qualify[3]. In *Booth-Clibborn v United Kingdom*, the Commission had to consider whether English metropolitan county councils constituted 'legislatures' for the purposes of the Convention. Although they were able to create byelaws, this power was delegated by the national parliament which had complete control over the extent and nature of the councils' powers, and thus councils were not legislatures within the meaning of the Convention[4].

1 6745/74 and 6746/74, *X, Y and Z v Belgium* (1975) DR 2, 110; 9267/81, *Moureaux and Ors v Belgium* (1983) DR 33, 97.
2 5155/71, *X v United Kingdom* (1976) DR 6, 13.
3 7008/75, *X v Austria* (1976) DR 6, 120; 27311/95, *Jan Timke v Germany* (1995) DR 82, 158; and 23450/94, *Polacco and Garofala v Italy* (1997) DR 90, 5.
4 11391/85 (1985) DR 43, 236. The Scottish Parliament should certainly qualify as a 'legislature' for the purposes of the article: even although it remains constitutionally subordinate to Westminster, its legislative powers (unlike the Welsh Assembly) involve much more than the exercise of delegated regulatory power, and are arguably more akin to those of a state legislature in a federal system of government.

7.61   These principles have been applied to questions concerning elections to the European Parliament. In early decisions, the Commission considered that the drafters of the European Convention on Human Rights had only intended to cover elections to national legislatures, and also doubted whether in any case the European Parliament had the requisite powers and functions to qualify as a 'legislature': it was primarily an advisory body with only limited legislative authority[1]. However, the entry into force of the Single European Act of 1986 enhanced the Parliament's status, as acknowledged by the Commission in *Fournier v France*[2]. The leading case is now *Matthews v United Kingdom* in which the Court was asked to consider whether Britain's failure to extend the right to vote in elections to the European Parliament to residents of Gibraltar raised any issue under this provision. The application also raised the wider question of whether states which were bound by the European Convention on Human Rights had positive responsibilities under this treaty in determining the manner in which they discharged their duties under EU law. Community law itself limited the franchise for European parliamentary elections, but the United Kingdom could have chosen to extend relevant EC legislation to become part of domestic law in Gibraltar. For the Court, since Community legislation can affect the population of Gibraltar 'in the same way as legislation which enters the domestic legal order . . . there is no difference between European and domestic legislation', and thus the European Parliament fell to be considered as a 'legislature' on account of the supremacy of Community law over national law. No reason had been made out which could justify exclusion of the European Parliament from the scope of the guarantee simply 'on the ground that it is a supranational, rather than a purely domestic, representative organ'. Examination of the European Parliament's powers after the Maastricht Treaty of 1992 indicated that it was now 'sufficiently involved' both in legislative processes leading to the passage of certain EU legislation and also in the general democratic supervision of the activities of the European Community to such an extent that it could be taken to constitute part of the 'legislature' of Gibraltar. Further, there was 'no reason why the United Kingdom should not be required to 'secure' the rights [under Article 1] . . . in respect of European legislation, in the same way as those rights are required to be 'secured' in respect of purely domestic legislation'. The provision 'enshrines a characteristic of an effective political democracy', but there was no indication that steps had been taken to ensure the representation of the population of Gibraltar in the European Parliament. While the choice of electoral system is covered by a wide margin of appreciation, the 'very essence of the applicant's right to vote' had been completely denied leading to the conclusion that there has been a violation of ECHR, Protocol 1, Article 3[3].

1 8364/78, *Lindsay and Ors v United Kingdom* (1979) DR 15, 247; and 8612/79, *Alliance des Belges de la CEE v Belgium* (1979) DR 15, 259 (question not resolved in either application); 11123/84, *Tête v France* (1987) DR 54, 52 (European Parliament could not yet be considered a 'legislature').
2 11406/85, (1988) DR 55, 130.
3 1999-I, 251, paras 34–65 at paras 44 and 65.

CHAPTER 8

Property rights

INTRODUCTION: PROTOCOL 1, ARTICLE 1

8.01 The right to property can involve a general guarantee either of eligibility to hold property[1] or of protection against improper state expropriation[2]. It is in this second sense that the European Convention on Human Rights protects property rights. While the text of Protocol 1, Article 1 provides for the right of peaceful enjoyment of property, at the same time it recognises that the public interest may justify deprivation or control over the use of possessions upon satisfaction of prescribed conditions[3]. The article comprises three distinct but connected rules[4]: first, a rule of general applicability that 'every natural or legal person is entitled to the peaceful enjoyment of property'; second, a rule that 'no one shall be deprived of his possessions except in the public interest and subject to the conditions provided for by law and by the general principles of international law'; and, third, explicit recognition that states may seek to control the use of property by providing that a state continues to enjoy the right without impairment 'to enforce such laws as it deems necessary to control the use of property in accordance with the general interest or to secure the payment of taxes or other contributions or penalties'. Any interference must meet the test of legal certainty, be justified by the general or public interest, and have a reasonable degree of proportionality between the means selected and the ends sought to be achieved to ensure that a fair balance between individual and collective interests has been struck. However, property rights have a strong claim to be considered more akin to economic rather than civil rights, and Strasbourg supervision in this area is covered by recognition of a wide margin of appreciation on the part of state authorities[5]. In consequence, the case law has concentrated upon ensuring that any state interference is lawful and meets the test of proportionality in achieving a fair balance between individual and collective interests, but even this latter issue may in practice involve no more than ascertaining whether a reasonable scheme for compensation has been established. Under Article 15, a state may take measures derogating from its obligations in time of emergency[6].

1 Cf Universal Declaration of Human Rights, Art 17(1): 'Everyone has the right to own property alone as well as in association with others.'
2 See further Waldron *The Right to Private Property* (1988) pp 16–27.
3 *Sporrong and Lönnroth v Sweden* (1982) A 52, para 61. See further, Sermet *The European Convention on Human Rights and Property Rights* (rev edn, 1998); McBride 'The Right to Property' (1996) 21 EL Rev HRC 40; Jones 'Property Rights, Planning Law and the European Convention' [1996] EHRLR 233; Winisdoerffer 'Margin of Appreciation and Article 1 of Protocol No 1' (1998) 19 HRLJ 18; Corner 'Planning, Environment, and the ECHR' [1998] JPL 301; Kitson 'The ECHR and Local Plans' [1998] JPL 321; Hart 'The Impact

of the ECHR on Planning & Environmental Law' [2000] JPL 117; O'Neill 'The Protection of Fundamental Rights in Scotland as a General Principle of Community Law' [2000] EHRLR 18; and Pellonpää 'Reflections on the Notion of "Deprivation of Possessions" in Article 1 of the First Protocol to the European Convention on Human Rights' in Mahoney, Matscher, Petzold and Wildhaber (eds) *Protecting Human Rights: The European Perspective* (2000) pp 1087–1105. For a comprehensive study of the subject, see Mittelburger *Der Eigentumsschutz nach Art 1 des Ersten Zusatsprotokolls zur EMKR im Lichte der Rechtsprechung der Strassburger Organe* (2000).

4 *Sporrong and Lönnroth v Sweden* (1982) A 52, para 61; *James and Ors v United Kingdom* (1986) A 98, para 37; *Erknauer and Hofauer v Austria* (1987) A 117, para 73; *Poiss v Austria* (1987) A 117, para 63; *Air Canada v United Kingdom* (1995) A 316-A, paras 29–30.

5 Inclusion of a right to property proved to be controversial at the time of drafting of the European Convention on Human Rights, and ultimately it was not included in the main Convention. At this time, several west European states (including the United Kingdom) were taking steps to nationalise significant aspects of economic activities. See further Robertson 'The European Convention on Human Rights: Recent Developments' (1951) 28 BYIL 359.

6 For further discussion of Art 15, see paras 3.06 and 4.46 above.

8.02   The European Convention on Human Rights, Protocol 1, Article 1 is also often invoked in conjunction with Article 6 which guarantees a fair hearing in the determination of civil rights, since interference with property rights invariably also raises issues under this heading[1]. However, a tendency on the part of the European Court of Human Rights to avoid discussion of property issues on the ground that that the merits of the application can be disposed of under Article 6 alone can, on occasion, threaten to blur the boundaries of the guarantee[2].

1 E g *Sporrong and Lönnroth v Sweden* (1982) A 52, para 79; *G L v Italy* (3 August 2000), paras 20–26 and 31–41 (failure to implement court decision concerning recovery of possession of a flat: violation of the European Convention on Human Rights, Art 6(1) and Protocol 1, Art 1). Cf *Brigandì v Italy* (1991) A 194-B, paras 31–32 (question whether the length of proceedings had resulted in a deprivation of property avoided in light of the finding under ECHR, Art 6); *British-American Tobacco v United Kingdom* (1995) A 331, para 91 (issue whether a patent application was a 'possession' was avoided as the question of availability of judicial remedy was considered under ECHR, Art 6(1)).

2 Cf *Lobo Machado v Portugal* 1996-I, 195 (dissenting opinion of the President of the Commission (report of 19 May 1994): the conclusion that no distinct question arises in relation to ECHR, Protocol 1, Art 1 may lead to the misunderstanding that a possible violation of the guarantee for property rights was covered by a finding of violation of Art 6, and thus a specific finding that there was no violation of this provision was appropriate).

THE SCOPE OF PROTOCOL 1, ARTICLE 1

8.03   The European Convention on Human Rights, Protocol 1, Article 1 itself refers to 'possessions' rather than to 'property', but in substance the two terms are synonymous[1]. In any case, 'possessions' is given an autonomous meaning and will include a wide and varied range of economic interests and assets including ownership of a house[2], goodwill of a business[3], non-registered title[4] or disputed title[5] to heritable property, entitlement to rent[6], a security right *in rem*[7], an award made under arbitration[8], a patent[9], a concession to work land owned by others[10], and a claim to compensation[11] or to social welfare entitlements[12]. Thus domestic classification of property rights will not be conclusive as the term has an autonomous meaning for the purposes of the Convention[13]. However, the article will cover only existing rights and assets and not future claims to property[14] except where there is at least a legitimate expectation of obtaining effective enjoyment of a property right[15] since the 'possession' must be sufficiently established in its existence[16]. Further, an application which in effect involves a claim to pursue a hobby or interest will fall outwith the scope of the provision[17]. Nor does the imposition of a duty to provide professional services without remuneration involve interference with the peaceful enjoyment of property[18], even although in discharging the responsibility outlays are incurred or the opportunity cost involved may result in a loss of revenue. Further, the provision cannot be interpreted as providing any guarantee of a particular quality of environment surrounding a property[19]. Finally, the facts complained of must involve an exercise of governmental authority rather than exclusively concern relationships of a private nature[20].

1 *Marckx v Belgium* (1979) A 31, para 63.
2 *Akdivar and Ors v Turkey* 1996-IV, 1192, para 88 and *Selçuk and Asker v Turkey* 1998-II, 891, para 86 (deliberate burning of homes by security forces; violation of both the European Convention on Human Rights, Art 8 and Protocol 1, Art 1); *The Former King of Greece and Ors v Greece* (23 November 2000), paras 60–66 (estates owned by the applicants as private persons rather than as members of the royal family considered 'possessions'); cf 19217/91, *Durini v Italy* (1994) DR 76, 76 (the right to live in a home which is not owned is not a 'possession').
3 *Van Marle v Netherlands* (1986) A 101, para 41 (goodwill of business conducted by chartered accountants).
4 *Holy Monasteries v Greece* (1994) A 301-A, paras 58–66.
5 *Iatridis v Greece* 1999-II, 75, paras 54–55 (the applicant inherited three-quarters of a tract of land and subsequently purchased the remaining quarter: but the state refused to recognise him as the owner and he was ordered to vacate the premises he had built without compensation: while it was not for the European Court of Human Rights to take the place of the national courts and determine whether the land in question belonged to the state or not, it noted that as the applicant had operated a cinema on the land for 11 years under a formally valid lease, and as he had built up a regular clientele, this constituted an asset for the purposes of ECHR, Protocol 1, Art 1).
6 *Mellacher and Ors v Austria* (1989) A 169, paras 40–41.
7 *Gasus Dosier- und Födertechnik v Netherlands* (1995) A 306-B, para 53. A creditor's right to recover the loan or to enforce a security was treated as falling within ECHR, Protocol 1, Art 1 in *Wilson v First County Trust Ltd* [2001] QB 407 and *Wilson v First County Trust Ltd (No 2)* [2001] 3 WLR 42; contrast *Family Housing Association v Donnellan* (12 July 2001, unreported), Ch D.
8 *Stran Greek Refineries v Greece* (1994) A 301–B, paras 59–62.
9 12633/87, *Smith Kline and French Laboratories v Netherlands* (1990) DR 66, 70.
10 *Matos e Silva and Ors v Portugal* 1996-IV, 1092, para 75 (unchallenged rights over land had existed for over a century, and the applicants derived revenue from the land: sufficient to establish a 'possession').
11 *Pressos Compania Naviera and Ors v Belgium* (1995) A 332, para 31.
12 *Gaygusuz v Austria* 1996-IV, 1129, para 41 (emergency assistance). Cf 36120/97, *Crossland v United Kingdom* (9 November 1999); and 38890/97 *Leary v UK* and 36578/97, *Cornwell v UK* (25 April 2000) (discrimination in the payment of social welfare benefits upon death: friendly settlements).
13 *Gasus Dosier- und Födertechnik v Netherlands* (1995) A 306-B, para 53 (immaterial whether a right to a concrete mixer was considered a right of ownership or as a security right *in rem*). Cf *British-American Tobacco v United Kingdom* (1995) A 331, para 91 (issue of whether a patent application was a 'possession' was avoided).
14 *Marckx v Belgium* (1979) A 31, at para 50 (the guarantee does not apply to the acquisition

of possessions 'whether on intestacy or through voluntary dispositions'); *Inze v Austria* (1987) A 126, paras 37–38.

15   19819/92, *Størksen v Norway* (1994) DR 78, 88 (revocation of a fishing licence upon a firm's insolvency and refusal to grant a new licence to the applicant who had been a shareholder did not involve an interference with 'possessions': future loss of earnings does not constitute a 'possession' unless income has been earned or an enforceable claim to income exists); and 33071/96 *Malhous v Czech Republic* (13 December 2000) (proceedings for restitution of land seized by the communist state: the hope of recognition of the survival of a property right some 50 years after expropriation could not be a 'possession'; and no legitimate expectation that the post-communist legislation would result in the return of the property: inadmissible under ECHR, Protocol 1, Art 1).

16   *Stran Greek Refineries and Stratis Andreadis v Greece* (1994) A 301-B, paras 58–62 (question was whether an arbitration award was 'sufficiently established to be enforceable' rather than 'merely to furnish the applicants with the hope that they would secure recognition of the claim put forward': here, the final and binding nature of the award constituted a 'possession'). Cf *National and Provincial Building Society v United Kingdom* 1997-VII, 2325, paras 62–70 (the Court proceeded on the assumption that claims for restitution were 'possessions').

17   See e g 37664–37665/97 and others, *R C and A W A and Ors v United Kingdom* (1998) DR 94, 119 (prohibition of possession of small-calibre pistols prevented the applicants from continuing with their hobby which they claimed was a 'possession': application inadmissible as manifestly ill-founded).

18   *Van der Mussele v Belgium* (1983) A 70, paras 47–49.

19   9310/81, *Rayner v United Kingdom* (1986) DR 47, 5; 13728/88, *S v France* (1990) DR 65, 250 (construction of a nuclear power plant close to a residence: application inadmissible).

20   *Gustafsson v Sweden* 1996-II, 637, para 60 (stoppage in deliveries between the applicant and his suppliers or deliverers did not involve a question under ECHR, Protocol 1, Art 1); cf 12947/87, *Association of General Practitioners v Denmark* (1989) DR 62, 226 (contractual rights to fee adjustments constituted a 'possession').

8.04   An applicant may be a natural or legal person, but in each case must satisfy the requirement of being a 'victim'. Shareholders seeking to challenge state action taken against companies can do so

> 'only in exceptional circumstances, in particular where it is clearly established that it is impossible for the company to apply to the Convention institutions through the organs set up under its articles of incorporation or – in the event of liquidation – through its liquidation'[1].

1   *Agrotexim and Ors v Greece* (1995) A 330-A, para 66.

DETERMINING WHETHER THERE HAS BEEN AN INTERFERENCE: THE THREE 'RULES'

The first rule: peaceful enjoyment of property

8.05   The three rules established by the European Convention on Human Rights, Protocol 1, Article 1 are closely connected. 'The first rule, set out in the first paragraph, is of a general nature and enunciates the principle of the peaceful enjoyment of property'. However, 'before enquiring whether the first general rule has been complied with, [the Court] must determine whether the last two are applicable' since these latter rules involve particular categories of interference with property rights[1]. This first rule, while subsidiary, is still of importance, for even if there has been no deprivation or control over property, the facts may still amount to an interference with the peaceful enjoyment of property[2]. For example, in *Stran Greek Refineries and Statis v Greece*, an arbitration award which was final and binding in favour of the applicants had been subsequently annulled by legislation, thus rendering it impossible for the applicants to secure enforcement of the award made. While the legislative measure was neither an expropriation of property nor a measure to control the use of property, the European Court of Human Rights accepted that it nevertheless constituted an interference with the applicants' right of property, and thus in turn called for an assessment of whether a fair balance had been struck between community interests and individual rights[3]. Similarly, where the applicability of the second or third rule is in doubt, the issue may be considered under this first rule concerning the peaceful enjoyment of possessions[4].

1 *James and Ors v United Kingdom* (1986) A 98, at paras 37 and 71.
2 Eg *Sporrong and Lönnroth v Sweden* (1982) A 52, para 65; *Poiss v Austria* (1987) A 117, paras 62–64; *Katte Klitsche de la Grange v Italy* (1994) A 293-B, para 40.
3 (1994) A 301-B, paras 61–69.
4 *Beyeler v Italy* (5 January 2000), paras 100–106 (the painting 'Portrait of a Young Peasant' by Vincent Van Gogh had been purchased by the applicant and had remained in his possession for several years before the state had exercised a right of pre-emption; under domestic law the sale had been held to be null and void: the Commission was of the opinion that the applicant had never become the owner of the painting and thus could not assert a right under the European Convention on Human Rights, Protocol 1, Art 1, but the Court accepted that the applicant had a proprietary interest recognised under domestic law which constituted a 'possession' for the purposes of the article, and further that the factual complexity of the case was such that it could not be classified in a precise category but instead fell to be considered in light of the general rule requiring peaceful enjoyment of possessions).

8.06 The European Convention on Human Rights, Protocol 1, Article 1 protects against interference with the *enjoyment* of possessions, and thus a broad range of state activity which interferes with any of the normal consequences arising out of ownership or possession will be recognised as giving rise to an issue under the guarantee, including the seizure and destruction of books considered obscene[1], limitations placed on the right to dispose of possessions after death[2], de facto appropriation of property caused by 'planning blight'[3] or protracted building prohibitions[4], nationalisation of private property[5], forfeiture of smuggled goods[6], adoption of development plans[7], and revocation of a licence to sell alcohol in a restaurant[8] or of a land exploitation permit[9] or planning consents[10]. Further, a hindrance can amount to a violation of the peaceful enjoyment of possessions just as much as a legal impediment. In *Loizidou v Turkey*, the applicant, a Cypriot national, had claimed to be the owner of several plots of land in northern Cyprus to which she had been denied access by the Turkish occupying forces. The European Court of Human Rights held that the continuous denial of access to her property must be regarded as an interference with her rights under Protocol 1, Article 1, and, while this interference could not be regarded as either a deprivation of property or a control of use within the meaning of the first and second paragraphs of the provision, it clearly fell within the ambit of an interference with the peaceful enjoyment of possessions[11]. On the other hand, the interference must be sufficiently definite. The provisional transfer of property which is not designed to restrict or control its use will not constitute an interference with property rights[12], nor will the provisional confiscation of property[13]. The English courts have held that tax avoidance legislation which lifts the corporate veil is not an interference with the peaceful enjoyment of possessions[14].

1 *Handyside v United Kingdom* (1976) A 24, para 61.
2 *Marckx v Belgium* (1979) A 31, para 63.
3 *Sporrong and Lönnroth v Sweden* (1982) A 52, paras 60–61; *Papamichalopoulos and Ors v Greece* (1993) A 260-B, para 41.
4 *Allan Jacobsson* (1989) A 163, para 52.
5 *Lithgow and Ors v United Kingdom* (1986) A 102, para 105.
6 *AGOSI v United Kingdom* (1986) A 108, para 49. In *HM Advocate v McSalley* 2000 JC 485, it was noted that a confiscation order under the Proceeds of Crime (Scotland) Act 1995, s 1 was an order for the payment of a sum of money rather than an order appropriating or transferring ownership of any property. It was held that such an order would in any event be compatible with the European Convention on Human Rights, Protocol 1, Art 1 of if a fair balance had been struck between the demands of the general interest of the community and the requirements of the protection of the individual's fundamental rights. In assessing that question of proportionality, it was necessary to keep in mind the underlying purpose of such orders, namely the combating of drug trafficking and the protection of the public from the evils and dangers of illegal drugs. In *HM Advocate v McIntosh* 2001 SCCR 191, it was observed that there was no discernible breach of ECHR, Protocol 1, Art 1. These issues have been clarified by the judgment of the European Court of Human Rights in *Phillips v United Kingdom* (5 July 2001), paras 50–54 where it was held that a confiscation order fell within the scope of Protocol 1, Art 1(2) but was compatible with the article.
7 *Phocas v France* 1996-II, 519, paras 49–52.
8 *Tre Traktörer v Sweden* (1989) A 159, para 53; cf *Catscratch Ltd v City of Glasgow Licensing Board (No 1)* 2001 SCLR 817.
9 *Fredin v Sweden* (1990) A 192, para 40.
10 *Pine Valley Developments and Ors v Ireland* (1991) A 222, para 51.
11 1996-VI, 2216, paras 60–64 (the Court took a much wider view than the Commission which had considered the application as essentially involving freedom of movement). See further White 'Tackling Political Disputes Through Individual Applications' [1998] EHRLR 61.
12 *Erkner and Hofauer v Austria* (1987) A 117, paras 73–79; *Poiss v Austria* (1987) A 117, paras 62–69; *Prötsch v Austria* 1996-V, 1812, para 42.
13 *Raimondo v Italy* (1994) A 281-A, para 36.
14 *R (Professional Contractors Group Ltd) v Inland Revenue Commissioners* [2001] STC 618.

The second rule: deprivation of property

8.07   Deprivation of property is the most radical form of interference with property rights[1]. The second sentence of the European Court of Human Rights, Protocol 1, Article 1 provides that deprivation of possessions may occur only where it is 'in the public interest and subject to the conditions provided for by law and by the general principles of international law'. 'Deprivation' includes expropriation and other loss of rights which flow from the legal consequences of property[2]. This will include, for example, property taken under compulsory powers[3]. It may also include the retroactive removal of liability for acts of negligence and which has the effect of depriving individuals of legal claims for compensation[4]. The deprivation must be definitive and involve an irrevocable expropriation or transfer of property rights[5]. Mere provisional seizure of goods[6] or of heritable property[7] is insufficient to give rise to a 'deprivation'. A legal obligation to make financial contributions of a modest amount does not involve a 'deprivation' of property[8], nor does the removal of a licence or imposition of planning controls which leads to a detrimental impact on a business[9].

1 *James and Ors v United Kingdom* (1986) A 98, para 71.

2 Eg *James and Ors v United Kingdom* (1986) A 98, para 38 (conversion of leasehold properties into freehold properties in favour of former tenants); *Lithgow and Ors v United Kingdom* (1986) A 102, paras 105–107 (nationalisation of private property); *AGOSI v United Kingdom* (1986) A 108, para 51 (forfeiture of coins); *Håkansson and Sturesson v Sweden* (1990) A 171-A, paras 42–43 (compulsory sale of heritable property); *Hentrich v France* (1994) A 296-A, para 35 (exercise of the right of pre-emption); *Holy Monasteries v Greece* (1994) A 301-A, paras 61–66 (statutory transfer of land to the state; even although no administrative eviction order had been yet made against the applicants, this was no guarantee that none would be issued in light of the attitude of the authorities to the matter: and a deprivation of possessions had occurred).

3 *Zubani v Italy* 1996-IV, 1067, paras 45–49; *Katikaridis and Ors v Greece* 1996-V, 1673 paras 45–51, and *Tsomtsos and Ors v Greece* 1996-V, 1699, paras 40–42 (Greek law created an irrebuttable presumption that the owners of the properties on major roads benefited when the roads were widened, and required the owners to contribute to the costs of expropriation; and while it was legitimate to take into account the benefit derived from the works by the adjoining owners, the system of compensation was too inflexible and did not take into account the diversity of situations in which an owner might have received little or no benefit or been caused varying degrees of loss: thus the system was 'manifestly without reasonable foundation').

4 *Pressos Compania Naviera and Ors v Belgium* (1995) A 332, para 34 (statutory exemption of providers of pilot services from delictual liability).

5 *Raimondo v Italy* (1994) A 281-A, para 29 (confiscation of property did not have the effect in domestic law of transferring property rights until an irrevocable decision had been taken, and no such decision had been taken on account of the applicant's legal challenge).

6 *Handyside v United Kingdom* (1976) A 24, para 62.

7 *Erknauer and Hofauer v Austria* (1987) A 117, para 74; *Poiss v Austria* (1987) A 117, para 64; *Wiesinger v Austria* (1991) A 213, para 72.

8 *Langborger v Sweden* (1989) A 155, paras 40–41; contrast *Aston Cantlow and Wilmcote with Billesley Parochial Church Council v Wallbank* [2001] 3 All ER 393.

9 *Tre Traktörer v Sweden* (1989) A 159, para 55 (licence for the sale of alcohol); *Fredin v Sweden* (1991) A 192, paras 43–47 (revocation of licence to exploit a gravel pit); *Pine Valley Developments Ltd and Ors v Ireland* (1991) A 222, para 56 (imposition of planning controls).

8.08   The key issue is whether there has been a real deprivation of property. Since the European Convention on Human Rights seeks to guarantee rights that are practical and effective, this may include a de facto expropriation as well as a formal expropriation[1]. In each instance, the particular facts of the case will call for close examination as to whether expropriation has indeed occurred. In *Sporrong and Lönnroth v Sweden*, for example, the European Court of Human Rights considered that the permits granted to the municipal authorities to allow them to expropriate the applicants' property had imposed limitations on their right of property which had become precarious and thus affected the value of the premises in question. However, and crucially, the right of property had not disappeared, and the grant of the permits could not be said to have amounted in substance to a de facto deprivation of property since the applicants had continued to utilise their property and could even have disposed of it through sale. In consequence, there had been no 'deprivation of possessions' within the meaning of the second sentence[2]. In contrast, in *Papamichaelopoulos and Ors v Greece*, the Court considered that there had been a clear 'deprivation' of property through the occupation of land belonging to the applicants by the military authorities who had established a naval base and holiday resort on the land. Although ownership of the land had not passed to the state, the loss of all ability on the part of the applicants to dispose of it had resulted in a de facto expropriation of the property[3].

1 *Sporrong and Lönnroth v Sweden* (1982) A 52, para 63; *Raimondo v Italy* (1994) A 281-A, para 29.

2 *Sporrong and Lönnroth v Sweden* (1982) A 52, at para 63. See too *Allan Jacobsson v Sweden* (1989) A 163, para 54 (protracted building prohibitions); and *Mellacher and Ors v Austria* (1989) A 169, paras 43–44 (imposition of system of fixed rents was not a de facto appropriation); *Brumarescu v Romania* (28 October 1999), paras 74–80 at 77 (nationalisation of property which was then resold to the tenants who had been the original owners: the Court accepted this was a case of de facto expropriation).
3 (1993) A 260-B, paras 41–46.

DECISIONS OF DOMESTIC COURTS ON DEPRIVATION OF PROPERTY

8.09   It has been held that a limitation period preventing the bringing of an action for the recovery of possession of land in the face of 12 years' adverse possession does not deprive the person of his possessions, or alternatively is in any event justified in the public interest[1]. In another English case, the effect of flooding on the value of a house was held to constitute a partial expropriation[2]. The discharge of a land obligation has been treated as deprivation of property[3].

1 *J A Pye (Oxford) Ltd v Graham* [2001] 2 WLR 1293; *Family Housing Association v Donnellan* (12 July 2001, unreported), Ch D.
2 *Marcic v Thames Water Utilities Ltd* [2001] 3 All ER 698.
3 *Strathclyde Joint Police Board v Elderslie Estates Ltd* (17 August 2001, unreported), Lands Tr.

The third rule: control over the use of property

8.10   The third sentence which forms the second paragraph of the European Convention on Human Rights, Protocol 1, Article 1 provides that the first and second rules do not 'in any way impair the right of a state to enforce such laws as it deems necessary to control the use of property in accordance with the general interest or to secure the payment of taxes or other contributions or penalties'[1]. Control of the use of property may involve the seizure of goods by state authorities[2], the prohibition on the importation of goods[3], imposition of rent control[4] or of planning controls[5], a requirement that hunting rights are transferred to an association[6], and even revocation of a licence which has an economic impact on the conduct of a business[7]. However, initial steps taken by public authorities which do not have the purpose or consequence of limiting or controlling the use of property will not fall within the scope of the second paragraph[8].

1 Taxation policy is covered by a wide margin of appreciation, but is still subject to the requirement that interferences with property rights are not manifestly without reasonable foundation: cf *National and Provincial Building Society v United Kingdom* 1997-VII, 2325, paras 56–70 (the Court proceeded on the assumption that claims for restitution were possessions). Litigation costs are 'contributions': 15434/89, *Antoniades v United Kingdom* (1990) DR 64, 232 .
2 E g *Handyside v United Kingdom* (1976) A 24, para 62; *Air Canada v United Kingdom* (1995) A 316-A, paras 33–34.
3 *AGOSI v United Kingdom* (1986) A 108, para 51 (forfeiture of smuggled coins formed a constituent element of the procedures for control of use of gold coins, and thus was better considered as involving control of use rather than deprivation of property).
4 *Mellacher and Ors v Austria* (1989) A 169, paras 43–45; *Spadea and Scalabrino v Italy* (1995) 315–B, paras 26–28, and *Scollo v Italy* (1995) A 315-C, paras 27–28 (emergency measures regulating residential property leases); *Velosa Barreto v Portugal* (1995) A 334, para 35; see also 15434/89, *Antoniades v United Kingdom* (1990) DR 64, 232 (determination that an agreement is a protected tenancy rather than an occupation under licence does not constitute a deprivation of possessions).
5 *Pine Valley Developments and Ors v Ireland* (1991) A 222, para 56.

6 *Chassagnou and Ors v France* 1999-III, 21, para 74.
7 *Tre Traktörer v Sweden* (1989) A 159, para 55 (revocation of licence to sell alcohol in a restaurant); *Fredin v Sweden* (1991) A 192, paras 43–47 (revocation of permit to exploit a gravel pit); *Vendittelli v Italy* (1994) A 293-A, para 38 (sequestration of flat); *Spadea and Scalabrino v Italy* (1995) A 315-B, paras 26–28, and *Scollo v Italy* (1995) A 315-C, paras 27–28 (emergency housing controls).
8 *Sporrong and Lönroth v Sweden* (1982) A 52, paras 64–65; *Erkner and Hofauer v Austria* (1987) A 117, para 74; *Poiss v Austria* (1987) A 117, para 64.

ASSESSING WHETHER AN INTERFERENCE IS JUSTIFIED

8.11 Under the European Convention on Human Rights, Protocol 1, Article 1 any interference with property rights must satisfy three tests:

(i)   the state interference must meet the test of legal certainty;
(ii)   it must be justified by the general or public interest; and
(iii) there must be a reasonable degree of proportionality between the means selected and the ends sought to be achieved to ensure that a fair balance between individual and collective interests has been maintained.

These tests apply to any interference with property rights falling within the Article's scope. In *Handyside v United Kingdom*, the European Court of Human Rights had initially drawn a distinction between the concept of 'necessity' as it appears elsewhere in the Convention (as, for example, in the context of Article 10(2)) and in the second paragraph of Protocol 1, Article 1, and had suggested that in terms of this latter provision states were recognised as having exclusive authority for judging the necessity of any state action; and the Court had thus restricted its responsibilities under the guarantee to 'supervising the lawfulness and the purpose of the restriction in question'[1]. In subsequent cases, however, the Court reconsidered its approach and clarified that the second paragraph of the article must be interpreted in accordance with the principles applying in any assessment carried out under the first paragraph since the text 'must be construed in the light of the principles laid down in the article's first sentence'[2]. Further, even although there are no explicit procedural requirements laid down in the second paragraph of Article 1 – that is, in respect of the third rule – in assessing whether a fair balance has been struck between individual and collective interests, the Court will evaluate the procedures used and whether these have given the applicant a reasonable opportunity of putting his case as well as allowing due consideration of other factors of relevance[3].

1 (1976) A 24, at para 62.
2 *Gasus Dosier- und Fördertechnik v Netherlands* (1995) A 306-B, at para 62.
3 *AGOSI v United Kingdom* (1986) A 108, paras 54–55 at para 55 (in confiscation cases, there is a trend in European domestic practice that the behaviour of the owner of goods is taken into account in considering whether smuggled goods should be returned; any such assessment should involve consideration of the degree of fault or care displayed by the owner).

Examining the lawfulness of state action

8.12 Deprivation of property may take place only 'subject to the conditions provided for by law and by the general principles of international law'. However, as discussed, scrutiny of the lawfulness of state action will apply to all forms of interference with property rights, and not just to those falling within the second rule. Unless there is an interference with the property rights of non-nationals, the focus is likely to be on domestic rather than international law, for, in relation to the taking by a state of property belonging to its own nationals, general principles of international law will not be applicable[1].

Certainly, an interference which is not authorised by domestic law will result in a violation of the article[2]. For example, in *Vasilescu v Romania*, the applicant's house had been searched by the police without a warrant in connection with a police investigation into the unlawful possession of valuables by her husband. The police had seized a substantial number of gold coins which were deposited into a bank and retained even after all charges had been dropped. In Strasbourg, the state conceded that the reasons for removal of the coins had been unlawful. In these circumstances, the Court held that the continuing retention of the items in question had amounted to a de facto confiscation not authorised by law and thus incompatible with the applicant's rights to the peaceful enjoyment of her possessions[3].

1 *James and Ors v United Kingdom* (1986) A 98, paras 64–66; *Lithgow and Ors v United Kingdom* (1986) A 102, para 112. See further Lambert *The Position of Aliens in Relation to the European Convention on Human Rights* (2001) pp 24–26. Cf *Loizidou v Turkey* 1996-VI, 2216, paras 39–47 (international law did not recognise the 'Turkish Republic of Northern Cyprus' as a state; the Turkish state which was occupying northern Cyprus was thus responsible for the interference with property rights); and *Cyprus v Turkey* (10 May 2001), para 61.
2 *Iatridis v Greece* 1999-II, 75, paras 54–62 (while the applicant's eviction had had a basis in domestic law, the eviction order had been subsequently quashed as the conditions for issuing it had not been fulfilled; since no appeal lay against that decision, from then on occupation of the property by the state was unlawful: violation of the European Convention on Human Rights, Protocol 1, Art 1).
3 1998-III, 1064, paras 48–53.

8.13   However, as with the interpretation given to 'law' or 'lawful' elsewhere in the European Convention on Human Rights, this requirement relates not only to the conformity of a measure with the provisions of domestic law[1] but also as to whether the quality of domestic law is compatible with the rule of law[2]. In particular, under this provision, the legal justification for an interference with property rights must be sufficiently clear and precise to allow individuals to be aware of the possibility of such an interference, and further the law must not be applied unfairly. In *Hentich v France*, for example, the European Court of Human Rights considered that a power of pre-emption which was available to the tax authorities to substitute themselves for any purchaser of property had operated 'arbitrarily and selectively and was scarcely foreseeable', and further that 'as applied to the applicant, did not sufficiently satisfy the requirements of precision and foreseeability implied by the concept of law within the meaning of the Convention'[3]. In *Belvedere v Italy*, the applicant company owned a hotel and adjacent land which gave patrons of the hotel direct access to the sea. The local authority had approved a road building scheme over this land, and subsequently had taken possession and started work. The Court accepted arguments that domestic law on constructive expropriation had evolved in such a way as to lead to the rule being applied inconsistently, and that this could result in unforeseeable or arbitrary outcomes and thus deprive litigants of effective protection of their rights. The scheme was considered in consequence not to have met the test of lawfulness[4]. In contrast, in *Spacek v Czech Republic*, the Court accepted that the implementation of income tax legislation had sufficient legal basis in domestic law and met the requirements of accessibility and foreseeability. While the rules and regulations were not published in any official gazette in the form of a decree or ruling and so could not amount to binding legislation, the Court noted that 'the term "law" is to be understood in its substantive sense and not in its formal one'; and, further, that the Convention did not lay down any 'specific requirements as to the degree of publicity to be given to a particular legal provision'. Here, the applicant company had been aware of the ways in which the Ministry of Finance published its accounting principles, and thus at the least should have consulted specialists about any transitional problems. Accordingly, no violation of the guarantee was established[5].

1 Cf *Pine Valley Developments and Ors v Ireland* (1991) A 222, para 57 (not disputed that an interference was in conformity with planning law); *Raimondo v Italy* (1994) A 281-A, para 36 (significant delay in regularising the legal status of some of the applicant's possessions, and thus the interference was not provided for by law).
2 *James and Ors v United Kingdom* (1986) A 98, para 67.
3 (1994) A 296-A, at para 42.
4 (30 May 2000), paras 56–58. See too *Carbonara and Ventura v Italy* (30 May 2000), paras 61–72.
5 (9 November 1999), paras 54–61 at para 57.

Determining the general or public interest for an interference

8.14 The text of the European Convention on Human Rights, Protocol 1, Article 1 specifies that deprivation of property must be in the 'public interest', while controls over the use of property are to be 'in accordance with the general interest' or otherwise to secure the payment of taxes or other contributions or penalties. The two phrases – 'public interest' and 'general interest' – are best considered as expressing the same idea[1]. Certainly, the failure by public authorities to respect a judicial determination concerning property (as, for example, by continuing to occupy premises despite a judicial order recognising rights of private ownership[2]) is unlikely to satisfy the test of 'public interest'. A wide margin of appreciation is appropriate in applying these tests, since what an applicant is likely to be challenging in effect is the social or economic policy behind a decision affecting his property rights. The elimination of social injustice is properly a responsibility of the legislature; and in any case policy-making of this nature is not amenable to international judicial scrutiny. In consequence, what is in the 'general' interest is given the widest interpretation and, in practice, the test is restricted to assessment of whether state action can be deemed to be 'manifestly unreasonable'[3]. Thus:

> 'the taking of property effected in pursuance of legitimate economic, social, economic or other policies may be "in the public interest", even if the community at large has no direct use or enjoyment of the property taken'[4].

Policy decisions such as the need for import controls[5] or rent restrictions[6] or for measures to deal with tax evasion[7] or the collection of taxes[8] or drug smuggling[9], or to prevent illegal sales or uncontrolled development of land[10] or the seizure of property which appears to be the proceeds of organised crime[11], are thus invariably respected. This approach also applies to implementation of planning and other infrastructure decisions in the areas of housing[12], licensing[13], town planning[14], road improvements[15], environmental protection[16] and rationalisation of the use of agricultural land[17], and even forfeiture of bail for failure to appear before the courts[18].

1 *James and Ors v United Kingdom* (1986) A 98, para 43.
2 *Zwierzyński v Poland* (19 June 2001), paras 68–74 (no conceivable 'public interest' in such circumstances; and public authorities had a particular moral responsibility to lead by example in observing legal decisions).
3 *James and Ors v United Kingdom* (1986) A 98, at para 49.
4 *James and Ors v United Kingdom* (1986) A 98, at para 45.
5 *AGOSI v United Kingdom* (1986) A 108, para 52.
6 *Mellacher and Ors v Austria* (1989) A 169, paras 45–47.
7 *Hentrich v France* (1994) A 296-A, para 39; *Gasus Dosier und Fördertechnik v Netherlands* (1995) A 306-B, para 61.
8 *National and Provincial Building Society v United Kingdom* 1997-VII, 2325, para 79.
9 *Air Canada v United Kingdom* (1995) A 316-A, paras 41–42.
10 *Holy Monasteries v Greece* (1994) A 301-A, para 69.
11 *Raimondo v Italy* (1994) A 281-A, paras 27–30.
12 *James and Ors v United Kingdom* (1986) A 98, at para 47 (housing is a 'prime social need' which cannot simply be left to the operation of market forces); *Spadea and Scalabrino v Italy* (1995) A 315-B, paras 30–32; *Scolla v Italy* (1995) A 315-C, paras 29–30.
13 *Tre Traktörer v Sweden* (1989) A 159, para 57.
14 *Allan Jacobbson v Sweden* (1989) A 163, para 57; *Phocas v France* 1996-II, 519, paras 54–55.
15 *Phocas v France* 1996-II, 519, para 55; *Katikaridis and Ors v Greece* 1996-V, 1673, para 45; *Tsomtsos and Ors v Greece* 1996-V, 1699, para 36.
16 *Fredin v Sweden* (1991) A 192, para 48; *Pine Valley Developments and Ors v Ireland* (1991) A 222, para 57; *Matos e Silva and Ors v Portugal* 1996-IV, 1092, paras 87–88.
17 *Håkansson and Sturesson v Sweden* (1990) A 171-A, para 44; *Prötsch v Austria* 1996-V, 1812, para 44.
18 10577/83, *G v Germany* (1985) DR 42, 195.

Proportionality

8.15   An interference with property under the European Convention on Human Rights, Protocol 1, Article 1 also requires to satisfy the test of proportionality: that is, there must also be 'a reasonable relationship of proportionality between the means employed and the aim sought to be realised'[1]. This allows the European Court of Human Rights to assess 'whether a fair balance was struck between the demands of the general interest of the community and the requirements of the protection of the individual's fundamental rights'[2]. The test also applies to the reference in the second paragraph to the 'securing the payment of taxes' which explicitly recognises the power of states to enact such fiscal legislation as they consider desirable, but always provided that such measures 'do not amount to arbitrary confiscation'[3]. As noted, determination of what is in the public interest is covered by a wide margin of appreciation, and while an interference which is of benefit only to certain individuals or to a minority sector of the public may still qualify as in the general interest, the requirement of proportionality will protect an applicant from having to bear what may be considered 'an individual and excessive burden'[4]. Again, though, the Court will be reluctant to establish that the implementation of measures considered appropriate to deal with pressing social problems such as housing shortages are disproportionate[5]. In practice, it is likely to restrict its considerations to whether there are adequate safeguards to protect the individual and whether a right of compensation exists, unless the cumulative effect of a range of circumstances suggests that a fair balance has not been struck.

Two recent Italian cases illustrate the Court's approach. Both concern the adoption of general development plans which had an impact upon the applicant companies' property rights but which in each instance had not subsequently been implemented, thus leading to an interference with the right of peaceful enjoyment of property. In *Cooperativa La Laurentina v Italy*, the applicant company had been aware that exploitation of its land was conditional upon adoption by the authorities of a detailed development plan but, for some 35 years, the council had taken no action. However, it would also have been possible for the company to have sought to enter into a development agreement, an opportunity which the company had not pursued. Further, at the stage the land could only be used for building houses, the rights of the company had largely been preserved since it could still have sold the land, the value of the property had considerably increased, and the company had been able to continue receiving rent. In these circumstances the Court held that the 'fair balance' between public and private interests had not been upset[6]. In contrast, in *Elia Srl v Italy*, the Court found that there had been a violation of the guarantee. A general development plan adopted in 1974 had set aside the applicant company's land for the creation of a public park and, to this end, the council imposed an absolute ban on building which continued until the adoption of a detailed development plan more than 20 years later when the land was finally expropriated. For the Court, the combination of the situation of complete uncertainty the company found itself in as regards the future of its property (despite repeated requests for information and the raising of legal action), the considerable diminution in its prospects of being able to sell its land, and the lack of compensation in domestic law all suggested that the 'fair balance' on this occasion had not been met[7].

1 *James and Ors v United Kingdom* (1986) A 98, at para 50; for domestic discussion, see *Malekshad v Howard de Walden Estates Ltd* [2001] 3 WLR 824. See also the related cases of *Chapman v United Kingdom, Coster v United Kingdom, Lee v United Kingdom*, and *Jane Smith v United Kingdom* (18 January 2001), paras 120, 133, 121, and 125 respectively (planning enforcement notices served against the applicants: measures were necessary to protect the environment, and not disproportionate in striking a fair balance: no violation of the European Convention on Human Rights, Protocol 1, Art 1 in light of the Court's disposal of these issues under Art 8).

2 *Sporrong and Lönnroth v Sweden* (1982) A 52, at para 69.

3 *Gasus Dosier- und Fördertechnik v Netherlands* (1995) A 306-B, paras 59–74 at para 59 (citing relevant *travaux préparatoires*).

4 *James and Ors v United Kingdom* (1986) A 98, at para 50. Cf 20471/92, *Kustannus Oy Vapaa Ajattelija AB and Ors v Finland* (1996) DR 85, 29 (a rule providing that tax incorrectly collected would not be reimbursed if below a certain amount did not impose an excessive burden).

5 E g *Spadea and Scalabrino v Italy* (1995) A 315-B, paras 36–41; *Scollo v Italy* (1995) A 315-C, paras 35–40; Cf *Immobiliara Saffi v Italy* 1999-V, 73.

6 (2 August 2001), paras 58–64, and 93–115.
7 (2 August 2001), paras 76–84.

Safeguards against arbitrary decision-making

8.16   In assessing the proportionality of an interference with property rights, the European Court of Human Rights will consider the degree of protection from arbitrariness that is afforded by the proceedings in a case[1]. This may involve an assessment of the information made available by the public authorities to relevant parties[2], and thus there is some relationship with the requirement that the law be sufficiently clear to allow individuals to be aware that there may be an interference with their rights. It may also call for scrutiny of the quality of decision-making processes to ensure that due account could have been taken of the interests of an applicant. For example, in *AGOSI v United Kingdom*, the Court examined whether British law, which provided for the confiscation of gold coins smuggled into the country, allowed reasonable account to be taken of relevant considerations such as the degree of fault of the legal owners of the coins[3]. In *Hentrich v France*, the Court considered that a power of pre-emption which was available to the tax authorities to substitute themselves for any purchaser of property belonging to an individual suspected of tax evasion had not been accompanied by sufficient protection against arbitrariness. As a 'selective victim' of this power of pre-emption, the applicant 'bore an individual and excessive burden' which could only have been regarded as legitimate were she not to have been denied the possibility of challenging the measure[4]. An applicant will be expected to make use of the available procedures provided by domestic law to this end[5], but fair hearing defects (such as delay in the decision-making process which results in considerable and prolonged uncertainty) may themselves lead to a finding that there has been a disproportionate burden placed on the applicant[6]. This assessment, however, also calls for consideration of the applicant's own behaviour. For example, in *Phocas v France*, the applicant had owned and run commercial premises at the spot where one road crossed another. In 1960, a scheme for improving the crossroads had been adopted and, on this basis, the applicant had transferred his greengrocery business to other premises. He asserted that he could not have reasonably let his property to another trader since in the event of expropriation he would have been liable for the payment of compensation. He had also been prevented from converting the building to other uses, but had refused to sell the building to the authorities because of the derisory price that he considered they were offering. For the Commission, the applicant's right of property had been rendered so unstable and uncertain over a lengthy period of time that the conclusion was that no fair balance had been struck between the public interest and the private interest. In contrast, a majority of the Court concluded that there had been no violation. Domestic law had afforded the applicant a remedy, but he had not followed the appropriate procedures available to him, and so eventually had found this remedy time-barred. Since the applicant was responsible for this situation, the conclusion was that there was no violation of the guarantee[7].

1 *Hentrich v France* (1994) A 296-A, at para 45.
2 *Fredin v Sweden* (1991) A 192, paras 54–55 (applicants were reasonably aware that a permit

to exploit a gravel pit would possibly be withdrawn in the future and thus had no legitimate expectations that they would be able to carry on operations for anything other than a short period of time); *Pine Valley Developments and Ors v Ireland* (1991) A 222, para 59 (applicants were engaged on a commercial venture which carried a certain amount of risk, and were aware of a relevant zoning plan and the opposition of the local authority to their proposed development: thus the annulment of the permission could not be regarded as disproportionate).

3 (1986) A 108, paras 54–55 (no violation established).

4 (1994) A 296-A, paras 45–49 at para 49.

5 Eg *Air Canada v United Kingdom* (1995) A 316-A, paras 44–48 (the scope of judicial review could have provided the applicants with sufficient safeguards to challenge the confiscation of an aircraft in which drugs had been found; further, the requirement to pay £50,000 to secure the release of the aircraft was not considered a disproportionate measure in view of the aim of preventing the importation of drugs).

6 *Matos e Silva and Ors v Portugal* 1996-IV, 1092, paras 92–93 (no progress in proceedings for some 13 years); cf *Prötsch v Austria* 1996-V, 1812, paras 46–48 (provisional transfer of property lasted some six years, but this was not regarded as unreasonably long in all the circumstances since the applicants had enjoyed an opportunity to challenge the lawfulness of the allotment and the domestic court had concluded that the applicants had suffered no damage and in fact had benefited from the transfer); *Beyeler v Italy* (5 January 2000), paras 114–122 (delay in determining whether to exercise a power of pre-emption in respect of a painting had resulted in the authorities deriving an unjust enrichment from the uncertainty that existed during the period and to which they had largely contributed: this was incompatible with the requirement of a fair balance); *Immobiliare Saffi v Italy* 1999-V, 73, paras 47–59 (failure to enforce eviction of a tenant accepted in the circumstances as having the legitimate aim of preventing social tension and public disorder, but system of staggering enforcement orders over a six-year period had resulted in a state of uncertainty for the applicant company which was disproportionate); and similarly *AO v Italy* (30 May 2000) and *GL v Italy* (3 August 2000).

7 1996-II, 519, paras 56–60. For domestic examples, see *Westerhall Farms v The Scottish Ministers* (25 April 2001, unreported), Ct of S and *Shepherd v The Scottish Ministers* (1 May 2001, unreported), Ct of S (slaughter of animals to prevent spread of foot and mouth disease); *Wilson v First County Trust Ltd (No 2)* [2001] 3 WLR 42 (statutory bar on enforcement of consumer credit agreement which failed correctly to state amount of credit).

Compensation for expropriation

8.17 An interference with property rights should in principle be redressed by a right of compensation[1]. This applies not only to formal or de facto expropriation of property[2], but also to other interferences with the peaceful enjoyment of possessions[3]. The scheme of compensation payable will be material to the assessment of whether a fair balance has been struck between community and individual interests, and failure to pay compensation of an amount reasonably related to the value of the property taken or otherwise subject to interference will normally constitute a disproportionate interference with property rights[4]. In *Holy Monasteries v Greece*, the Greek legislature had expropriated land belonging to the applicants without making provision for compensation. The Commission had accepted that there had been exceptional circumstances justifying the lack of compensation, including the manner in which the property had been acquired and used and the dependency of the applicants on the Greek Orthodox Church which in turn had been dependent upon the state. For the Court, however, the expropriation had imposed too excessive a burden on the applicants, and thus a fair balance between their interests and those of the community had not been achieved[5]. In *Pressos Compania Naviera and Ors v Belgium*, the retrospective extinguishing by statute of claims available to victims of pilot accidents for high awards of damages for negligence following a judicial decision, without payment by way of compensation of an amount reasonably related to the value of the claims, was similarly considered a disproportionate interference with property rights[6].

1   For discussion of recent cases, see further Anderson 'Compensation for Interference with Property' [1999] EHRLR 543; and McBride 'Compensation, Restitution and Human Rights in Post-Communist Europe' (2000) 13 Interights Bull 3.
2   *James and Ors v United Kingdom* (1986) A 98, paras 54–56 at para 54 (the taking of property without compensation can only be justified in exceptional circumstances since otherwise the right would be 'largely illusory and ineffective'); *The Former King of Greece and Ors v Greece* (23 November 2000), paras 84–99 (deprivation of property by statute without compensation considered a violation of the articles); cf *Katte Klitsche de la Grange v Italy* (1994) A 293-B, paras 47–48 (no compensation payable under domestic law since the applicant's property had not been subject to expropriation: no breach of the European Convention on Human Rights, Protocol 1, Art 1).
3   Eg *Sporrong and Lönnroth v Sweden* (1982) A 52, para 73 (individual and excessive burden could only have been rendered legitimate were the applicants to have had the opportunity of seeking a reduction of applicable time limits or the payment of compensation); *Erkner and Hofauer v Austria* (1987) A 117, paras 76–79 (applicants still awaited clarification of the final fate of their property after 16 years and the resultant compensation: this amounted to a disproportionate burden, and thus a violation of the guarantee). This line of authority was discussed in *Booker Aquaculture Ltd v Secretary of State for Scotland* 2001 SC 9.
4   Eg *Platakou v Greece* (11 January 2001), paras 55–57.
5   (1994) A 301-A, paras 71–75.
6   (1995) A 332, paras 38–44.

8.18   In determining the amount of compensation payable, it is legitimate for the state to take into account any material benefits derived by others such as adjacent proprietors of land which has been expropriated[1]. However, as the European Court of Human Rights made clear in *Lithgow and Ors v United Kingdom* and later in *Holy Monasteries v Greece*, there is no guarantee of a right to full compensation since there may be legitimate public interest objectives in play which 'may call for less than reimbursement of the full market value'[2]. In the *Lithgow* case, state nationalisation of shipbuilding and aircraft concerns on the Clyde and elsewhere in Britain had been challenged by eight individuals and companies, principally upon the issue of calculation of the compensation which fell to be paid. The Court held that a right to compensation was implied by the European Covention on Human Rights, Protocol 1, Article 1, but did not accept that any scheme adopted must meet the full market cost of any property affected since state interests in achieving social justice or economic reform had also to be taken into account[3].

1   Cf *Katikaridis and Ors v Greece* 1996-V, 1673, paras 45–51 and *Tsomtsos and Ors v Greece* 1996-V, 1699, paras 40–42 (Greek law created an irrebuttable presumption that the owners of the properties on major roads benefited when roads are widened and required the owners to contribute to the costs of expropriation; while it was legitimate to take into account the benefit derived from the works by the adjoining owners, the system of compensation was too inflexible and did not take into account the diversity of situations in which an owner may have received little or no benefit or caused varying degrees of loss: thus the system was 'manifestly without reasonable foundation').
2   (1986) A 102, at para 121; *Holy Monasteries v Greece* (1994) A 301-A, at para 71.
3   *Lithgow and Ors v United Kingdom* (1986) A 102, paras 120–22. See too *Phocas v France* 1996-II, 519, paras 59–60 (applicant had accepted expropriation compensation, and thus domestic law afforded a remedy sufficient to meet the article's requirements).

8.19 More recent cases, however, suggest that the European Court of Human Rights will be more critical of compensation terms which appear unreasonable because of undue delay in the payment of compensation[1]. In particular, the Court has shown itself prepared to take into account the impact of inflation on claims for damages and compensation in a series of Turkish cases. For example, in *Akkus v Turkey*, the Turkish water board had expropriated agricultural land belonging to the applicant in order to construct a hydroelectric dam, but had initially paid in compensation only one quarter of the value of the land (a figure increased on appeal) and with payment of statutory default interest set at a rate of 30 per cent per annum. The applicant sought to argue that the calculation of interest should have been based upon the prevailing rate of inflation (some 70 per cent per annum) rather than upon the rate of statutory interest. The Court reiterated that the adequacy of compensation would be diminished if it were not to be paid within a reasonable time, since delay would reduce its real value. In the instant case, it had taken the state authorities 17 months after the court judgment to pay the additional compensation together with interest at a rate less than half of the annual rate of inflation. The difference between the value of the applicant's compensation as finally determined and the value when paid had thus caused the applicant to sustain a further loss in addition to that caused by the expropriation, and by deferring payment for such a period the authorities had rendered the compensation inadequate[2]. In *Aka v Turkey*, the applicant's complaint concerned the insufficiency of the statutory interest intended to compensate for the high monetary depreciation during the period since the commencement of the proceedings for compensation, rather than the delay in paying additional compensation which had been the issue in the *Akkus* case. The Court again acknowledged that the national authorities have a margin of appreciation in determining compensation, and even 'that it may be important for them to limit the amount of interest payable on debts due by the state', but it was still incumbent upon the Court to 'verify whether the "fair balance" between the demands of the general interest and the requirements of the protection of the individual's fundamental rights has been preserved'. Once more, the conclusion was that the difference between the real value of the amounts due to the applicant when the land was expropriated and when they were actually paid had caused the applicant to sustain an additional and separate loss which, when taken together with the loss of his land, could be said to have upset the fair balance that should have been maintained[3].

1 *Zubani v Italy* 1996-IV, 1067, paras 45–49 (the law providing for compensation did not enter into force until some eight years after the land was taken, and thus a fair balance between protecting the right of property and the demands of the general interest had not been struck); *Guillemin v France* 1997-I, 149, paras 53–56 (compensation for loss sustained can only constitute adequate reparation where it also takes into account the damage arising from the length of the deprivation, and further must be paid within a reasonable time; here, proceedings were still continuing after five years and compensation had not begun to be paid: violation of the guarantee); *Almeida Garrett, Mascarenhas Falcão and Ors v Portugal* (11 January 2000), paras 49–55 (period of 24 years without final compensation having been paid: violation of the European Convention on Human Rights, Art 6).

2 1997-IV, 1300, paras 27–30.

Implementation of policies which affect other Convention rights

8.20   The margin of appreciation recognised as belonging to the state authorities in relation to implementation of policies which have a direct bearing on other Convention concerns falling within the civil and political (rather than the economic or social) sphere may be less generous. In *Chassagnou and Ors v France*, the applicants were farmers in a region where the owners of smallholdings below a certain size were required to transfer hunting rights over their properties to an approved hunters' association. Following upon the transfer of these rights, the owners became members of the association and were entitled to hunt anywhere on lands over which the association had hunting rights, but only in exceptional cases would compensation be available where landowners could show that they had suffered loss of profits. As members of an anti-hunting movement, the applicants complained that the compulsory transfer of the hunting rights over their land interfered with their right to peaceful enjoyment of their possessions. For the European Court of Human Rights, there had to be a 'reasonable relationship' of proportionality between the means employed and the aim pursued. In assessing whether this had been achieved, the Court acknowledged that the state had a

> 'wide margin of appreciation with regard to choosing the means of enforcement and to ascertaining whether the consequences of enforcement are justified in the general interest for the purpose of achieving the object of the law in question'.

However, while the legislation was in the general interest in avoiding unregulated hunting and attempting to encourage the rational management of game stocks,

> 'compelling small landowners to transfer hunting rights over their land so that others can make use of them in a way which is totally incompatible with their beliefs imposes a disproportionate burden'

which could not be justified under the Article[1].

1   1999-III, 21, para 74 at paras 75 and 85. The decision is in contrast with the Commission's opinion in 11763/85, *Banér v Sweden* (1989) DR 60, 128 (extension of public rights of fishing in Swedish waters, but no evidence of economic loss). Cf Harpum 'Hunting Rights and Human Rights' (1999) 58 CLJ 481 (discussion of whether legislation conferring a general right of open access to the countryside in the face of opposition from landowners would require to be accompanied by compensation).

APPENDIX 1

Human Rights Act 1998

1998 CHAPTER 42

An Act to give further effect to rights and freedoms guaranteed under the European Convention on Human Rights; to make provision with respect to holders of certain judicial offices who become judges of the European Court of Human Rights; and for connected purposes.

[9th November 1998]

BE IT ENACTED by the Queen's most Excellent Majesty, by and with the advice and consent of the Lords Spiritual and Temporal, and Commons, in this present Parliament assembled, and by the authority of the same, as follows:—

Introduction

1 The Convention Rights

(1) In this Act 'the Convention rights' means the rights and fundamental freedoms set out in—
(a) Articles 2 to 12 and 14 of the Convention,
(b) Articles 1 to 3 of the First Protocol, and
(c) Articles 1 and 2 of the Sixth Protocol,
as read with Articles 16 to 18 of the Convention.

(2) Those Articles are to have effect for the purposes of this Act subject to any designated derogation or reservation (as to which see sections 14 and 15).

(3) The Articles are set out in Schedule 1.

(4) The Secretary of State may by order make such amendments to this Act as he considers appropriate to reflect the effect, in relation to the United Kingdom, of a protocol.

(5) In subsection (4) 'protocol' means a protocol to the Convention—
(a) which the United Kingdom has ratified; or
(b) which the United Kingdom has signed with a view to ratification.

(6) No amendment may be made by an order under subsection (4) so as to come into force before the protocol concerned is in force in relation to the United Kingdom.

NOTES

Initial Commencement
  To be appointed
  To be appointed: see s 22(3).

Appointment
> Appointment: 2 October 2000: see SI 2000/1851, art 2.

2 Interpretation of Convention rights

(1) A court or tribunal determining a question which has arisen in connection with a Convention right must take into account any—

(a) judgment, decision, declaration or advisory opinion of the European Court of Human Rights,

(b) opinion of the Commission given in a report adopted under Article 31 of the Convention,

(c) decision of the Commission in connection with Article 26 or 27(2) of the Convention, or

(d) decision of the Committee of Ministers taken under Article 46 of the Convention,

whenever made or given, so far as, in the opinion of the court or tribunal, it is relevant to the proceedings in which that question has arisen.

(2) Evidence of any judgment, decision, declaration or opinion of which account may have to be taken under this section is to be given in proceedings before any court or tribunal in such manner as may be provided by rules.

(3) In this section 'rules' means rules of court or, in the case of proceedings before a tribunal, rules made for the purposes of this section—

(a) by the Lord Chancellor or the Secretary of State, in relation to any proceedings outside Scotland;

(b) by the Secretary of State, in relation to proceedings in Scotland; or

(c) by a Northern Ireland department, in relation to proceedings before a tribunal in Northern Ireland—

    (i) which deals with transferred matters; and

    (ii) for which no rules made under paragraph (a) are in force.

NOTES

Initial Commencement
> *To be appointed*
> To be appointed: see s 22(3).

Appointment
> Appointment: 2 October 2000: see SI 2000/1851, art 2.

Subordinate Legislation
> Act of Adjournal (Criminal Procedure Rules Amendment No 2) (Human Rights Act 1998) 2000, SSI 2000/315.
> Act of Sederunt (Rules of the Court of Session Amendment No 6) (Human Rights Act 1998) 2000, SSI 2000/316.

Legislation

3 Interpretation of legislation

(1) So far as it is possible to do so, primary legislation and subordinate legislation must be read and given effect in a way which is compatible with the Convention rights.

(2) This section—

(a) applies to primary legislation and subordinate legislation whenever enacted;

(b) does not affect the validity, continuing operation or enforcement of any incompatible primary legislation; and

(c) does not affect the validity, continuing operation or enforcement of any incompatible subordinate legislation if (disregarding any possibility of revocation) primary legislation prevents removal of the incompatibility.

NOTES

Initial Commencement
To be appointed
To be appointed: see s 22(3).

Appointment
Appointment: 2 October 2000: see SI 2000/1851, art 2.

4 Declaration of incompatibility

(1) Subsection (2) applies in any proceedings in which a court determines whether a provision of primary legislation is compatible with a Convention right.

(2) If the court is satisfied that the provision is incompatible with a Convention right, it may make a declaration of that incompatibility.

(3) Subsection (4) applies in any proceedings in which a court determines whether a provision of subordinate legislation, made in the exercise of a power conferred by primary legislation, is compatible with a Convention right.

(4) If the court is satisfied—
(a) that the provision is incompatible with a Convention right, and
(b) that (disregarding any possibility of revocation) the primary legislation concerned prevents removal of the incompatibility,
it may make a declaration of that incompatibility.

(5) In this section 'court' means—
(a) the House of Lords;
(b) the Judicial Committee of the Privy Council;
(c) the Courts-Martial Appeal Court;
(d) in Scotland, the High Court of Justiciary sitting otherwise than as a trial court or the Court of Session;
(e) in England and Wales or Northern Ireland, the High Court or the Court of Appeal.

(6) A declaration under this section ('a declaration of incompatibility')—
(a) does not affect the validity, continuing operation or enforcement of the provision in respect of which it is given; and
(b) is not binding on the parties to the proceedings in which it is made.

NOTES

Initial Commencement
To be appointed
To be appointed: see s 22(3).

Appointment
Appointment: 2 October 2000: see SI 2000/1851, art 2.

5 Right of Crown to intervene

(1) Where a court is considering whether to make a declaration of incompatibility, the Crown is entitled to notice in accordance with rules of court.

(2) In any case to which subsection (1) applies—

(a) a Minister of the Crown (or a person nominated by him),

(b) a member of the Scottish Executive,

(c) a Northern Ireland Minister,

(d) a Northern Ireland department,

is entitled, on giving notice in accordance with rules of court, to be joined as a party to the proceedings.

(3) Notice under subsection (2) may be given at any time during the proceedings.

(4) A person who has been made a party to criminal proceedings (other than in Scotland) as the result of a notice under subsection (2) may, with leave, appeal to the House of Lords against any declaration of incompatibility made in the proceedings.

(5) In subsection (4)—

'criminal proceedings' includes all proceedings before the Courts-Martial Appeal Court; and

'leave' means leave granted by the court making the declaration of incompatibility or by the House of Lords.

NOTES

Initial Commencement
> *To be appointed*
> To be appointed: see s 22(3).

Appointment
> Appointment: 2 October 2000: see SI 2000/1851, art 2.

Subordinate Legislation
> *UK*
> Criminal Appeal (Amendment) Rules 2000, SI 2000/2036.
> *Scotland*
> Act of Adjournal (Criminal Procedure Rules Amendment No 2) (Human Rights Act 1998) 2000, SSI 2000/315.
> Act of Sederunt (Rules of the Court of Session Amendment No 6) (Human Rights Act 1998) 2000, SSI 2000/316.

Public authorities

6 Acts of public authorities

(1) It is unlawful for a public authority to act in a way which is incompatible with a Convention right.

(2) Subsection (1) does not apply to an act if—

(a) as the result of one or more provisions of primary legislation, the authority could not have acted differently; or

(b) in the case of one or more provisions of, or made under, primary legislation which cannot be read or given effect in a way which is compatible with the Convention rights, the authority was acting so as to give effect to or enforce those provisions.

(3) In this section 'public authority' includes—

(a) a court or tribunal, and

(b) any person certain of whose functions are functions of a public nature,

but does not include either House of Parliament or a person exercising functions in connection with proceedings in Parliament.

(4) In subsection (3) 'Parliament' does not include the House of Lords in its judicial capacity.

(5) In relation to a particular act, a person is not a public authority by virtue only of subsection (3)(b) if the nature of the act is private.

(6) 'An act' includes a failure to act but does not include a failure to—
(a) introduce in, or lay before, Parliament a proposal for legislation; or
(b) make any primary legislation or remedial order.

NOTES

Initial Commencement
  To be appointed
  To be appointed: see s 22(3).

Appointment
  Appointment: 2 October 2000: see SI 2000/1851, art 2.

---

7 Proceedings

(1) A person who claims that a public authority has acted (or proposes to act) in a way which is made unlawful by section 6(1) may—
(a) bring proceedings against the authority under this Act in the appropriate court or tribunal, or
(b) rely on the Convention right or rights concerned in any legal proceedings,
but only if he is (or would be) a victim of the unlawful act.

(2) In subsection (1)(a) 'appropriate court or tribunal' means such court or tribunal as may be determined in accordance with rules; and proceedings against an authority include a counterclaim or similar proceeding.

(3) If the proceedings are brought on an application for judicial review, the applicant is to be taken to have a sufficient interest in relation to the unlawful act only if he is, or would be, a victim of that act.

(4) If the proceedings are made by way of a petition for judicial review in Scotland, the applicant shall be taken to have title and interest to sue in relation to the unlawful act only if he is, or would be, a victim of that act.

(5) Proceedings under subsection (1)(a) must be brought before the end of—
(a) the period of one year beginning with the date on which the act complained of took place; or
(b) such longer period as the court or tribunal considers equitable having regard to all the circumstances,
but that is subject to any rule imposing a stricter time limit in relation to the procedure in question.

(6) In subsection (1)(b) 'legal proceedings' includes—
(a) proceedings brought by or at the instigation of a public authority; and
(b) an appeal against the decision of a court or tribunal.

(7) For the purposes of this section, a person is a victim of an unlawful act only if he would be a victim for the purposes of Article 34 of the Convention if proceedings were brought in the European Court of Human Rights in respect of that act.

(8) Nothing in this Act creates a criminal offence.

(9) In this section 'rules' means—

(a) in relation to proceedings before a court or tribunal outside Scotland, rules made by the Lord Chancellor or the Secretary of State for the purposes of this section or rules of court,

(b) in relation to proceedings before a court or tribunal in Scotland, rules made by the Secretary of State for those purposes,

(c) in relation to proceedings before a tribunal in Northern Ireland—

    (i)   which deals with transferred matters; and

    (ii) for which no rules made under paragraph (a) are in force,

    rules made by a Northern Ireland department for those purposes,

and includes provision made by order under section 1 of the Courts and Legal Services Act 1990.

(10) In making rules, regard must be had to section 9.

(11) The Minister who has power to make rules in relation to a particular tribunal may, to the extent he considers it necessary to ensure that the tribunal can provide an appropriate remedy in relation to an act (or proposed act) of a public authority which is (or would be) unlawful as a result of section 6(1), by order add to—

(a) the relief or remedies which the tribunal may grant; or

(b) the grounds on which it may grant any of them.

(12) An order made under subsection (11) may contain such incidental, supplemental, consequential or transitional provision as the Minister making it considers appropriate.

(13) 'The Minister' includes the Northern Ireland department concerned.

NOTES

Initial Commencement
> *To be appointed*
> To be appointed: see s 22(3).

Appointment
> Appointment: 2 October 2000: see SI 2000/1851, art 2.

Subordinate Legislation
> *UK*
> Proscribed Organisations Appeal Commission (Human Rights Act Proceedings) Rules 2001, SI 2001/127 (made under sub-s 7(9)(a), (b)).
> *Scotland*
> Human Rights Act 1998 (Jurisdiction) (Scotland) Rules 2000, SSI 2000/301.

---

8 Judicial remedies

(1) In relation to any act (or proposed act) of a public authority which the court finds is (or would be) unlawful, it may grant such relief or remedy, or make such order, within its powers as it considers just and appropriate.

(2) But damages may be awarded only by a court which has power to award damages, or to order the payment of compensation, in civil proceedings.

(3) No award of damages is to be made unless, taking account of all the circumstances of the case, including—

(a) any other relief or remedy granted, or order made, in relation to the act in question (by that or any other court), and

(b) the consequences of any decision (of that or any other court) in respect of that act, the court is satisfied that the award is necessary to afford just satisfaction to the person in whose favour it is made.

(4) In determining—
(a) whether to award damages, or
(b) the amount of an award,
the court must take into account the principles applied by the European Court of Human Rights in relation to the award of compensation under Article 41 of the Convention.

(5) A public authority against which damages are awarded is to be treated—
(a) in Scotland, for the purposes of section 3 of the Law Reform (Miscellaneous Provisions) (Scotland) Act 1940 as if the award were made in an action of damages in which the authority has been found liable in respect of loss or damage to the person to whom the award is made;
(b) for the purposes of the Civil Liability (Contribution) Act 1978 as liable in respect of damage suffered by the person to whom the award is made.

(6) In this section—
'court' includes a tribunal;
'damages' means damages for an unlawful act of a public authority; and
'unlawful' means unlawful under section 6(1).

NOTES

Initial Commencement
> *To be appointed*
> To be appointed: see s 22(3).

Appointment
> Appointment: 2 October 2000: see SI 2000/1851, art 2.

---

9 Judicial acts

(1) Proceedings under section 7(1)(a) in respect of a judicial act may be brought only—
(a) by exercising a right of appeal;
(b) on an application (in Scotland a petition) for judicial review; or
(c) in such other forum as may be prescribed by rules.

(2) That does not affect any rule of law which prevents a court from being the subject of judicial review.

(3) In proceedings under this Act in respect of a judicial act done in good faith, damages may not be awarded otherwise than to compensate a person to the extent required by Article 5(5) of the Convention.

(4) An award of damages permitted by subsection (3) is to be made against the Crown; but no award may be made unless the appropriate person, if not a party to the proceedings, is joined.

(5) In this section—
'appropriate person' means the Minister responsible for the court concerned, or a person or government department nominated by him;
'court' includes a tribunal;
'judge' includes a member of a tribunal, a justice of the peace and a clerk or other officer entitled to exercise the jurisdiction of a court;

'judicial act' means a judicial act of a court and includes an act done on the instructions, or on behalf, of a judge; and
'rules' has the same meaning as in section 7(9).

NOTES

Initial Commencement
  To be appointed
  To be appointed: see s 22(3).

Appointment
  Appointment: 2 October 2000: see SI 2000/1851, art 2.

Subordinate Legislation
  Human Rights Act 1998 (Jurisdiction) (Scotland) Rules 2000, SSI 2000/301.

Remedial action

10 Power to take remedial action

(1) This section applies if—

(a) a provision of legislation has been declared under section 4 to be incompatible with a Convention right and, if an appeal lies—

    (i) all persons who may appeal have stated in writing that they do not intend to do so;

    (ii) the time for bringing an appeal has expired and no appeal has been brought within that time; or

    (iii) an appeal brought within that time has been determined or abandoned; or

(b) it appears to a Minister of the Crown or Her Majesty in Council that, having regard to a finding of the European Court of Human Rights made after the coming into force of this section in proceedings against the United Kingdom, a provision of legislation is incompatible with an obligation of the United Kingdom arising from the Convention.

(2) If a Minister of the Crown considers that there are compelling reasons for proceeding under this section, he may by order make such amendments to the legislation as he considers necessary to remove the incompatibility.

(3) If, in the case of subordinate legislation, a Minister of the Crown considers—

(a) that it is necessary to amend the primary legislation under which the subordinate legislation in question was made, in order to enable the incompatibility to be removed, and

(b) that there are compelling reasons for proceeding under this section,
he may by order make such amendments to the primary legislation as he considers necessary.

(4) This section also applies where the provision in question is in subordinate legislation and has been quashed, or declared invalid, by reason of incompatibility with a Convention right and the Minister proposes to proceed under paragraph 2(b) of Schedule 2.

(5) If the legislation is an Order in Council, the power conferred by subsection (2) or (3) is exercisable by Her Majesty in Council.

(6) In this section 'legislation' does not include a Measure of the Church Assembly or of the General Synod of the Church of England.

(7) Schedule 2 makes further provision about remedial orders.

NOTES

Initial Commencement
> *To be appointed*
> To be appointed: see s 22(3).

Appointment
> Appointment: 2 October 2000: see SI 2000/1851, art 2.

Other rights and proceedings

11 Safeguard for existing human rights

A person's reliance on a Convention right does not restrict—
(a) any other right or freedom conferred on him by or under any law having effect in any part of the United Kingdom; or
(b) his right to make any claim or bring any proceedings which he could make or bring apart from sections 7 to 9.

NOTES

Initial Commencement
> *To be appointed*
> To be appointed: see s 22(3).

Appointment
> Appointment: 2 October 2000: see SI 2000/1851, art 2.

---

12 Freedom of expression

(1) This section applies if a court is considering whether to grant any relief which, if granted, might affect the exercise of the Convention right to freedom of expression.

(2) If the person against whom the application for relief is made ('the respondent') is neither present nor represented, no such relief is to be granted unless the court is satisfied—
(a) that the applicant has taken all practicable steps to notify the respondent; or
(b) that there are compelling reasons why the respondent should not be notified.

(3) No such relief is to be granted so as to restrain publication before trial unless the court is satisfied that the applicant is likely to establish that publication should not be allowed.

(4) The court must have particular regard to the importance of the Convention right to freedom of expression and, where the proceedings relate to material which the respondent claims, or which appears to the court, to be journalistic, literary or artistic material (or to conduct connected with such material), to—
(a) the extent to which—
    (i) the material has, or is about to, become available to the public; or
    (ii) it is, or would be, in the public interest for the material to be published;
(b) any relevant privacy code.

(5) In this section—
'court' includes a tribunal; and
'relief' includes any remedy or order (other than in criminal proceedings).

NOTES

Initial Commencement
  To be appointed
  To be appointed: see s 22(3).

Appointment
  Appointment: 2 October 2000: see SI 2000/1851, art 2.

13 Freedom of thought, conscience and religion

(1) If a court's determination of any question arising under this Act might affect the exercise by a religious organisation (itself or its members collectively) of the Convention right to freedom of thought, conscience and religion, it must have particular regard to the importance of that right.

(2) In this section 'court' includes a tribunal.

NOTES

Initial Commencement
  To be appointed
  To be appointed: see s 22(3).

Appointment
  Appointment: 2 October 2000: see SI 2000/1851, art 2.

Derogations and reservations

14 Derogations

(1) In this Act 'designated derogation' means—

. . .

any derogation by the United Kingdom from an Article of the Convention, or of any protocol to the Convention, which is designated for the purposes of this Act in an order made by the Secretary of State.

(2) . . .

(3) If a designated derogation is amended or replaced it ceases to be a designated derogation.

(4) But subsection (3) does not prevent the Secretary of State from exercising his power under subsection (1)... to make a fresh designation order in respect of the Article concerned.

(5) The Secretary of State must by order make such amendments to Schedule 3 as he considers appropriate to reflect—
(a) any designation order; or
(b) the effect of subsection (3).

(6) A designation order may be made in anticipation of the making by the United Kingdom of a proposed derogation.

NOTES

Initial Commencement
  To be appointed
  To be appointed: see s 22(3).

Appointment
> Appointment: 2 October 2000: see SI 2000/1851, art 2.

Amendment
> Sub-s (1): words omitted repealed by SI 2001/1216, art 2(a).
> Date in force: 1 April 2001: see SI 2001/1216, art 1.
> Sub-s (2): repealed by SI 2001/1216, art 2(b).
> Date in force: 1 April 2001: see SI 2001/1216, art 1.
> Sub-s (4): reference omitted repealed by SI 2001/1216, art 2(c).
> Date in force: 1 April 2001: see SI 2001/1216, art 1.

15 Reservations

(1) In this Act 'designated reservation' means—
(a) the United Kingdom's reservation to Article 2 of the First Protocol to the Convention; and
(b) any other reservation by the United Kingdom to an Article of the Convention, or of any protocol to the Convention, which is designated for the purposes of this Act in an order made by the Secretary of State.

(2) The text of the reservation referred to in subsection (1)(a) is set out in Part II of Schedule 3.

(3) If a designated reservation is withdrawn wholly or in part it ceases to be a designated reservation.

(4) But subsection (3) does not prevent the Secretary of State from exercising his power under subsection (1)(b) to make a fresh designation order in respect of the Article concerned.

(5) The Secretary of State must by order make such amendments to this Act as he considers appropriate to reflect—
(a) any designation order; or
(b) the effect of subsection (3).

NOTES

Initial Commencement
> *To be appointed*
> To be appointed: see s 22(3).

Appointment
> Appointment: 2 October 2000: see SI 2000/1851, art 2.

16 Period for which designated derogations have effect

(1) If it has not already been withdrawn by the United Kingdom, a designated derogation ceases to have effect for the purposes of this Act—
. . .
> at the end of the period of five years beginning with the date on which the order designating it was made.

(2) At any time before the period—
(a) fixed by subsection (1). . ., or
(b) extended by an order under this subsection,
comes to an end, the Secretary of State may by order extend it by a further period of five years.

(3) An order under section 14(1). . . ceases to have effect at the end of the period for consideration, unless a resolution has been passed by each House approving the order.

(4) Subsection (3) does not affect—
(a) anything done in reliance on the order; or
(b) the power to make a fresh order under section 14(1). . . .

(5) In subsection (3) 'period for consideration' means the period of forty days beginning with the day on which the order was made.

(6) In calculating the period for consideration, no account is to be taken of any time during which—
(a) Parliament is dissolved or prorogued; or
(b) both Houses are adjourned for more than four days.

(7) If a designated derogation is withdrawn by the United Kingdom, the Secretary of State must by order make such amendments to this Act as he considers are required to reflect that withdrawal.

NOTES

Initial Commencement
   To be appointed
   To be appointed: see s 22(3).

Appointment
   Appointment: 2 October 2000: see SI 2000/1851, art 2.

Amendment
   Sub-s (1): words omitted repealed by SI 2001/1216, art 3(a).
      Date in force: 1 April 2001: see SI 2001/1216, art 1.
   Sub-s (2): in para (b) words omitted repealed by SI 2001/1216, art 3(b).
      Date in force: 1 April 2001: see SI 2001/1216, art 1.
   Sub-s (3): reference omitted repealed by SI 2001/1216, art 3(c).
      Date in force: 1 April 2001: see SI 2001/1216, art 1.
   Sub-s (4): in para (b) reference omitted repealed by SI 2001/1216, art 3(d).
      Date in force: 1 April 2001: see SI 2001/1216, art 1.

Subordinate Legislation
   Human Rights Act (Amendment) Order 2001, 2001/1216 (made under sub-s (7)).

---

17 Periodic review of designated reservations

(1) The appropriate Minister must review the designated reservation referred to in section 15(1)(a)—
(a) before the end of the period of five years beginning with the date on which section 1(2) came into force; and
(b) if that designation is still in force, before the end of the period of five years beginning with the date on which the last report relating to it was laid under subsection (3).

(2) The appropriate Minister must review each of the other designated reservations (if any)—
(a) before the end of the period of five years beginning with the date on which the order designating the reservation first came into force; and
(b) if the designation is still in force, before the end of the period of five years beginning with the date on which the last report relating to it was laid under subsection (3).

(3) The Minister conducting a review under this section must prepare a report on the result of the review and lay a copy of it before each House of Parliament.

NOTES

Initial Commencement
   To be appointed
   To be appointed: see s 22(3).

Appointment
   Appointment: 2 October 2000: see SI 2000/1851, art 2.

Judges of the European Court of Human Rights

18 Appointment to European Court of Human Rights

(1) In this section 'judicial office' means the office of—
(a) Lord Justice of Appeal, Justice of the High Court or Circuit judge, in England and Wales;
(b) judge of the Court of Session or sheriff, in Scotland;
(c) Lord Justice of Appeal, judge of the High Court or county court judge, in Northern Ireland.

(2) The holder of a judicial office may become a judge of the European Court of Human Rights ('the Court') without being required to relinquish his office.

(3) But he is not required to perform the duties of his judicial office while he is a judge of the Court.

(4) In respect of any period during which he is a judge of the Court—
(a) a Lord Justice of Appeal or Justice of the High Court is not to count as a judge of the relevant court for the purposes of section 2(1) or 4(1) of the Supreme Court Act 1981 (maximum number of judges) nor as a judge of the Supreme Court for the purposes of section 12(1) to (6) of that Act (salaries etc);
(b) a judge of the Court of Session is not to count as a judge of that court for the purposes of section 1(1) of the Court of Session Act 1988 (maximum number of judges) or of section 9(1)(c) of the Administration of Justice Act 1973 ('the 1973 Act') (salaries etc);
(c) a Lord Justice of Appeal or judge of the High Court in Northern Ireland is not to count as a judge of the relevant court for the purposes of section 2(1) or 3(1) of the Judicature (Northern Ireland) Act 1978 (maximum number of judges) nor as a judge of the Supreme Court of Northern Ireland for the purposes of section 9(1)(d) of the 1973 Act (salaries etc);
(d) a Circuit judge is not to count as such for the purposes of section 18 of the Courts Act 1971 (salaries etc);
(e) a sheriff is not to count as such for the purposes of section 14 of the Sheriff Courts (Scotland) Act 1907 (salaries etc);
(f) a county court judge of Northern Ireland is not to count as such for the purposes of section 106 of the County Courts Act (Northern Ireland) 1959 (salaries etc).

(5) If a sheriff principal is appointed a judge of the Court, section 11(1) of the Sheriff Courts (Scotland) Act 1971 (temporary appointment of sheriff principal) applies, while he holds that appointment, as if his office is vacant.

(6) Schedule 4 makes provision about judicial pensions in relation to the holder of a judicial office who serves as a judge of the Court.

(7) The Lord Chancellor or the Secretary of State may by order make such transitional provision (including, in particular, provision for a temporary increase in the maximum number of judges) as he considers appropriate in relation to any holder of a judicial office who has completed his service as a judge of the Court.

NOTES

Initial Commencement
   Royal Assent
   Royal Assent: 9 November 1998: see s 22(2).

Parliamentary procedure

19 Statements of compatibility

(1) A Minister of the Crown in charge of a Bill in either House of Parliament must, before Second Reading of the Bill—
(a) make a statement to the effect that in his view the provisions of the Bill are compatible with the Convention rights ('a statement of compatibility'); or
(b) make a statement to the effect that although he is unable to make a statement of compatibility the government nevertheless wishes the House to proceed with the Bill.

(2) The statement must be in writing and be published in such manner as the Minister making it considers appropriate.

NOTES

Initial Commencement
   To be appointed
   To be appointed: see s 22(3).

Appointment
   Appointment: 24 November 1998: see SI 1998/2882, art 2.

Supplemental

20 Orders etc under this Act

(1) Any power of a Minister of the Crown to make an order under this Act is exercisable by statutory instrument.

(2) The power of the Lord Chancellor or the Secretary of State to make rules (other than rules of court) under section 2(3) or 7(9) is exercisable by statutory instrument.

(3) Any statutory instrument made under section 14, 15 or 16(7) must be laid before Parliament.

(4) No order may be made by the Lord Chancellor or the Secretary of State under section 1(4), 7(11) or 16(2) unless a draft of the order has been laid before, and approved by, each House of Parliament.

(5) Any statutory instrument made under section 18(7) or Schedule 4, or to which subsection (2) applies, shall be subject to annulment in pursuance of a resolution of either House of Parliament.

(6) The power of a Northern Ireland department to make—
(a) rules under section 2(3)(c) or 7(9)(c), or
(b) an order under section 7(11),
is exercisable by statutory rule for the purposes of the Statutory Rules (Northern Ireland) Order 1979.

(7) Any rules made under section 2(3)(c) or 7(9)(c) shall be subject to negative resolution; and section 41(6) of the Interpretation Act (Northern Ireland) 1954 (meaning of 'subject to negative resolution') shall apply as if the power to make the rules were conferred by an Act of the Northern Ireland Assembly.

(8) No order may be made by a Northern Ireland department under section 7(11) unless a draft of the order has been laid before, and approved by, the Northern Ireland Assembly.

NOTES

Initial Commencement
    Royal Assent
    Royal Assent: 9 November 1998: see s 22(2).

21 Interpretation, etc

(1) In this Act—
'amend' includes repeal and apply (with or without modifications);
'the appropriate Minister' means the Minister of the Crown having charge of the appropriate authorised government department (within the meaning of the Crown Proceedings Act 1947);
'the Commission' means the European Commission of Human Rights;
'the Convention' means the Convention for the Protection of Human Rights and Fundamental Freedoms, agreed by the Council of Europe at Rome on 4th November 1950 as it has effect for the time being in relation to the United Kingdom;
'declaration of incompatibility' means a declaration under section 4;
'Minister of the Crown' has the same meaning as in the Ministers of the Crown Act 1975;
'Northern Ireland Minister' includes the First Minister and the deputy First Minister in Northern Ireland;
'primary legislation' means any—
    (a) public general Act;
    (b) local and personal Act;
    (c) private Act;
    (d) Measure of the Church Assembly;
    (e) Measure of the General Synod of the Church of England;
    (f) Order in Council—
        (i) made in exercise of Her Majesty's Royal Prerogative;
        (ii) made under section 38(1)(a) of the Northern Ireland Constitution Act 1973 or the corresponding provision of the Northern Ireland Act 1998; or
        (iii) amending an Act of a kind mentioned in paragraph (a), (b) or (c);
and includes an order or other instrument made under primary legislation (otherwise than by the National Assembly for Wales, a member of the Scottish Executive, a Northern Ireland Minister or a Northern Ireland department) to the extent to which it operates to bring one or more provisions of that legislation into force or amends any primary legislation;
'the First Protocol' means the protocol to the Convention agreed at Paris on 20th March 1952;

'the Sixth Protocol' means the protocol to the Convention agreed at Strasbourg on 28th April 1983;

'the Eleventh Protocol' means the protocol to the Convention (restructuring the control machinery established by the Convention) agreed at Strasbourg on 11th May 1994;

'remedial order' means an order under section 10;

'subordinate legislation' means any—

(a) Order in Council other than one—

    (i) made in exercise of Her Majesty's Royal Prerogative;

    (ii) made under section 38(1)(a) of the Northern Ireland Constitution Act 1973 or the corresponding provision of the Northern Ireland Act 1998; or

    (iii) amending an Act of a kind mentioned in the definition of primary legislation;

(b) Act of the Scottish Parliament;

(c) Act of the Parliament of Northern Ireland;

(d) Measure of the Assembly established under section 1 of the Northern Ireland Assembly Act 1973;

(e) Act of the Northern Ireland Assembly;

(f) order, rules, regulations, scheme, warrant, byelaw or other instrument made under primary legislation (except to the extent to which it operates to bring one or more provisions of that legislation into force or amends any primary legislation);

(g) order, rules, regulations, scheme, warrant, byelaw or other instrument made under legislation mentioned in paragraph (b), (c), (d) or (e) or made under an Order in Council applying only to Northern Ireland;

(h) order, rules, regulations, scheme, warrant, byelaw or other instrument made by a member of the Scottish Executive, a Northern Ireland Minister or a Northern Ireland department in exercise of prerogative or other executive functions of Her Majesty which are exercisable by such a person on behalf of Her Majesty;

'transferred matters' has the same meaning as in the Northern Ireland Act 1998; and

'tribunal' means any tribunal in which legal proceedings may be brought.

(2) The references in paragraphs (b) and (c) of section 2(1) to Articles are to Articles of the Convention as they had effect immediately before the coming into force of the Eleventh Protocol.

(3) The reference in paragraph (d) of section 2(1) to Article 46 includes a reference to Articles 32 and 54 of the Convention as they had effect immediately before the coming into force of the Eleventh Protocol.

(4) The references in section 2(1) to a report or decision of the Commission or a decision of the Committee of Ministers include references to a report or decision made as provided by paragraphs 3, 4 and 6 of Article 5 of the Eleventh Protocol (transitional provisions).

(5) Any liability under the Army Act 1955, the Air Force Act 1955 or the Naval Discipline Act 1957 to suffer death for an offence is replaced by a liability to imprisonment for life or any less punishment authorised by those Acts; and those Acts shall accordingly have effect with the necessary modifications.

NOTES

Initial Commencement

    Royal Assent

    Sub-s (5): Royal Assent: 9 November 1998: see s 22(2).

To be appointed
Sub-ss (1)–(4): To be appointed: see s 22(3).

Appointment
Sub-ss (1)–(4): Appointment: 2 October 2000: see SI 2000/1851, art 2.

22 Short title, commencement, application and extent

(1) This Act may be cited as the Human Rights Act 1998.

(2) Sections 18, 20 and 21(5) and this section come into force on the passing of this Act.

(3) The other provisions of this Act come into force on such day as the Secretary of State may by order appoint; and different days may be appointed for different purposes.

(4) Paragraph (b) of subsection (1) of section 7 applies to proceedings brought by or at the instigation of a public authority whenever the act in question took place; but otherwise that subsection does not apply to an act taking place before the coming into force of that section.

(5) This Act binds the Crown.

(6) This Act extends to Northern Ireland.

(7) Section 21(5), so far as it relates to any provision contained in the Army Act 1955, the Air Force Act 1955 or the Naval Discipline Act 1957, extends to any place to which that provision extends.

NOTES

Initial Commencement
Royal Assent
Royal Assent: 9 November 1998: see s 22(2).

Subordinate Legislation
Human Rights Act 1998 (Commencement) Order 1998, SI 1998/2882 (made under sub-s (3)).
Human Rights Act 1998 (Commencement No 2) Order 2000, SI 2000/1851 (made under sub-s (3)).

SCHEDULE 1
The Articles[1]

Part II
The First Protocol[2]

Part III
The Sixth Protocol[3]

SCHEDULE 2
Remedial Orders

Section 10

Orders

1 (1) A remedial order may—
(a) contain such incidental, supplemental, consequential or transitional provision as the person making it considers appropriate;
(b) be made so as to have effect from a date earlier than that on which it is made;
(c) make provision for the delegation of specific functions;
(d) make different provision for different cases.

(2) The power conferred by sub-paragraph (1)(a) includes—
(a) power to amend primary legislation (including primary legislation other than that which contains the incompatible provision); and
(b) power to amend or revoke subordinate legislation (including subordinate legislation other than that which contains the incompatible provision).

(3) A remedial order may be made so as to have the same extent as the legislation which it affects.

(4) No person is to be guilty of an offence solely as a result of the retrospective effect of a remedial order.

Procedure

2 No remedial order may be made unless—
(a) a draft of the order has been approved by a resolution of each House of Parliament made after the end of the period of 60 days beginning with the day on which the draft was laid; or
(b) it is declared in the order that it appears to the person making it that, because of the urgency of the matter, it is necessary to make the order without a draft being so approved.

Orders laid in draft

3 (1) No draft may be laid under paragraph 2(a) unless—
(a) the person proposing to make the order has laid before Parliament a document which contains a draft of the proposed order and the required information; and

---

1 Not reproduced here. For the text of ECHR, Arts 2–12, 14–18, see appendix 3.
2 Not reproduced here. For the text of Protocol 1, Arts 1–3, see appendix 3.
3 Not reproduced here. For the text of Protocol 6, Arts 1–2, see appendix 3.

(b) the period of 60 days, beginning with the day on which the document required by this sub-paragraph was laid, has ended.

(2) If representations have been made during that period, the draft laid under paragraph 2(a) must be accompanied by a statement containing—
(a) a summary of the representations; and
(b) if, as a result of the representations, the proposed order has been changed, details of the changes.

Urgent cases

4 (1) If a remedial order ('the original order') is made without being approved in draft, the person making it must lay it before Parliament, accompanied by the required information, after it is made.

(2) If representations have been made during the period of 60 days beginning with the day on which the original order was made, the person making it must (after the end of that period) lay before Parliament a statement containing—
(a) a summary of the representations; and
(b) if, as a result of the representations, he considers it appropriate to make changes to the original order, details of the changes.

(3) If sub-paragraph (2)(b) applies, the person making the statement must—
(a) make a further remedial order replacing the original order; and
(b) lay the replacement order before Parliament.

(4) If, at the end of the period of 120 days beginning with the day on which the original order was made, a resolution has not been passed by each House approving the original or replacement order, the order ceases to have effect (but without that affecting anything previously done under either order or the power to make a fresh remedial order).

Definitions

5 In this Schedule—
'representations' means representations about a remedial order (or proposed remedial order) made to the person making (or proposing to make) it and includes any relevant Parliamentary report or resolution; and
'required information' means—
(a) an explanation of the incompatibility which the order (or proposed order) seeks to remove, including particulars of the relevant declaration, finding or order; and
(b) a statement of the reasons for proceeding under section 10 and for making an order in those terms.

Calculating periods

6 In calculating any period for the purposes of this Schedule, no account is to be taken of any time during which—
(a) Parliament is dissolved or prorogued; or
(b) both Houses are adjourned for more than four days.

[**7** (1) This paragraph applies in relation to—
(a) any remedial order made, and any draft of such an order proposed to be made,—

(i)   by the Scottish Ministers; or

(ii) within devolved competence (within the meaning of the Scotland Act 1998) by Her Majesty in Council; and

(b) any document or statement to be laid in connection with such an order (or proposed order).

(2) This Schedule has effect in relation to any such order (or proposed order), document or statement subject to the following modifications.

(3) Any reference to Parliament, each House of Parliament or both Houses of Parliament shall be construed as a reference to the Scottish Parliament.

(4) Paragraph 6 does not apply and instead, in calculating any period for the purposes of this Schedule, no account is to be taken of any time during which the Scottish Parliament is dissolved or is in recess for more than four days.]

NOTES

Initial Commencement
To be appointed
To be appointed: see s 22(3).

Appointment
Appointment: 2 October 2000: see SI 2000/1851, art 2.

Amendment
Para 7: inserted by SI 2000/2040, art 2(1), Schedule, Pt I, para 21.
Date in force: 27 July 2000: see SI 2000/2040, art 1(1).

SCHEDULE 3
Derogation and Reservation

Sections 14 and 15

Part I

. . .

NOTES

Amendment
Repealed by SI 2001/1216, art 4.
Date in force: 1 April 2001: see SI 2001/1216, art 1.

. . .

NOTES

Amendment
Repealed by SI 2001/1216, art 4.
Date in force: 1 April 2001: see SI 2001/1216, art 1.

Part II
Reservation

At the time of signing the present (First) Protocol, I declare that, in view of certain provisions of the Education Acts in the United Kingdom, the principle affirmed in the second sentence of Article 2 is accepted by the United Kingdom only so far as it is compatible with the provision of efficient instruction and training, and the avoidance of unreasonable public expenditure.

Dated 20 March 1952. Made by the United Kingdom Permanent Representative to the Council of Europe.

NOTES

Initial Commencement
   To be appointed
   To be appointed: see s 22(3).

Appointment
   Appointment: 2 October 2000: see SI 2000/1851, art 2.

SCHEDULE 4
JUDICIAL PENSIONS

Section 18(6)

Duty to make orders about pensions

1 (1) The appropriate Minister must by order make provision with respect to pensions payable to or in respect of any holder of a judicial office who serves as an ECHR judge.

(2) A pensions order must include such provision as the Minister making it considers is necessary to secure that—
(a) an ECHR judge who was, immediately before his appointment as an ECHR judge, a member of a judicial pension scheme is entitled to remain as a member of that scheme;
(b) the terms on which he remains a member of the scheme are those which would have been applicable had he not been appointed as an ECHR judge; and
(c) entitlement to benefits payable in accordance with the scheme continues to be determined as if, while serving as an ECHR judge, his salary was that which would (but for section 18(4)) have been payable to him in respect of his continuing service as the holder of his judicial office.

Contributions

2 A pensions order may, in particular, make provision—
(a) for any contributions which are payable by a person who remains a member of a scheme as a result of the order, and which would otherwise be payable by deduction from his salary, to be made otherwise than by deduction from his salary as an ECHR judge; and
(b) for such contributions to be collected in such manner as may be determined by the administrators of the scheme.

Amendments of other enactments

3 A pensions order may amend any provision of, or made under, a pensions Act in such manner and to such extent as the Minister making the order considers necessary or expedient to ensure the proper administration of any scheme to which it relates.

Definitions

4 In this Schedule—
'appropriate Minister' means—
   (a) in relation to any judicial office whose jurisdiction is exercisable exclusively in relation to Scotland, the Secretary of State; and
   (b) otherwise, the Lord Chancellor;

'ECHR judge' means the holder of a judicial office who is serving as a judge of the Court;

'judicial pension scheme' means a scheme established by and in accordance with a pensions Act;

'pensions Act' means—

    (a) the County Courts Act (Northern Ireland) 1959;

    (b) the Sheriffs' Pensions (Scotland) Act 1961;

    (c) the Judicial Pensions Act 1981; or

    (d) the Judicial Pensions and Retirement Act 1993; and

'pensions order' means an order made under paragraph 1.

NOTES

Initial Commencement

    Royal Assent

    Royal Assent: 9 November 1998: see s 22(2).

Scotland Act 1998

1998 CHAPTER 46

An Act to provide for the establishment of a Scottish Parliament and Administration and other changes in the government of Scotland; to provide for changes in the constitution and functions of certain public authorities; to provide for the variation of the basic rate of income tax in relation to income of Scottish taxpayers in accordance with a resolution of the Scottish Parliament; to amend the law about parliamentary constituencies in Scotland; and for connected purposes.

[19th November 1998]

BE IT ENACTED by the Queen's most Excellent Majesty, by and with the advice and consent of the Lords Spiritual and Temporal, and Commons, in this present Parliament assembled, and by the authority of the same, as follows:—

1–27, 37–43, 59–97, 104–106, 108–125, 128, Schs 1–5, 7–9 *(outside the scope of this work).*

PART I
THE SCOTTISH PARLIAMENT

Legislation

28 Acts of the Scottish Parliament

(1) Subject to section 29, the Parliament may make laws, to be known as Acts of the Scottish Parliament.

(2) Proposed Acts of the Scottish Parliament shall be known as Bills; and a Bill shall become an Act of the Scottish Parliament when it has been passed by the Parliament and has received Royal Assent.

(3) A Bill receives Royal Assent at the beginning of the day on which Letters Patent under the Scottish Seal signed with Her Majesty's own hand signifying Her Assent are recorded in the Register of the Great Seal.

(4) The date of Royal Assent shall be written on the Act of the Scottish Parliament by the Clerk, and shall form part of the Act.

(5) The validity of an Act of the Scottish Parliament is not affected by any invalidity in the proceedings of the Parliament leading to its enactment.

(6) Every Act of the Scottish Parliament shall be judicially noticed.

(7) This section does not affect the power of the Parliament of the United Kingdom to make laws for Scotland.

NOTES

Initial Commencement
   To be appointed
   To be appointed: see s 130.

Appointment
   Appointment: 1 July 1999: see SI 1998/3178, art 2(1).

29 Legislative competence

(1) An Act of the Scottish Parliament is not law so far as any provision of the Act is outside the legislative competence of the Parliament.

(2) A provision is outside that competence so far as any of the following paragraphs apply—
(a) it would form part of the law of a country or territory other than Scotland, or confer or remove functions exercisable otherwise than in or as regards Scotland,
(b) it relates to reserved matters,
(c) it is in breach of the restrictions in Schedule 4,
(d) it is incompatible with any of the Convention rights or with Community law,
(e) it would remove the Lord Advocate from his position as head of the systems of criminal prosecution and investigation of deaths in Scotland.

(3) For the purposes of this section, the question whether a provision of an Act of the Scottish Parliament relates to a reserved matter is to be determined, subject to subsection (4), by reference to the purpose of the provision, having regard (among other things) to its effect in all the circumstances.

(4) A provision which—
(a) would otherwise not relate to reserved matters, but
(b) makes modifications of Scots private law, or Scots criminal law, as it applies to reserved matters,
is to be treated as relating to reserved matters unless the purpose of the provision is to make the law in question apply consistently to reserved matters and otherwise.

NOTES

Initial Commencement
   To be appointed
   To be appointed: see s 130.

Appointment
   Appointment: 1 July 1999: see SI 1998/3178, art 2(1).

30 Legislative competence: supplementary

(1) Schedule 5 (which defines reserved matters) shall have effect.

(2) Her Majesty may by Order in Council make any modifications of Schedule 4 or 5 which She considers necessary or expedient.

(3) Her Majesty may by Order in Council specify functions which are to be treated, for such purposes of this Act as may be specified, as being, or as not being, functions which are exercisable in or as regards Scotland.

(4) An Order in Council under this section may also make such modifications of—

(a) any enactment or prerogative instrument (including any enactment comprised in or made under this Act), or

(b) any other instrument or document,

as Her Majesty considers necessary or expedient in connection with other provision made by the Order.

NOTES

Initial Commencement
To be appointed
To be appointed: see s 130.

Appointment
Appointment: 6 May 1999: see SI 1998/3178, art 2(2), Sch 3.

Subordinate Legislation
Scotland Act 1998 (Modifications of Schedules 4 and 5) Order 1999, SI 1999/1749 (made under sub-ss (2), (4)).
Scotland Act 1998 (Transfer of Functions to the Scottish Ministers etc) Order 2000, SI 2000/1563 (made under sub-s (3)).
Scotland Act 1998 (Modifications of Schedule 4) Order 2000, SI 2000/1831 (made under sub-s (2)).
Scotland Act 1998 (Modifications of Schedule 5) Order 2000, SI 2000/3252 (made under sub-s (2)).
Scotland Act 1998 (Transfer of Functions to the Scottish Ministers etc) (No 2) Order 2000, SI 2000/3253 (made under sub-s (3)).
Scotland Act 1998 (Modification of Schedule 5) Order 2001, SI 2001/1456 (made under sub-s (2)).

---

31 Scrutiny of Bills before introduction

(1) A member of the Scottish Executive in charge of a Bill shall, on or before introduction of the Bill in the Parliament, state that in his view the provisions of the Bill would be within the legislative competence of the Parliament.

(2) The Presiding Officer shall, on or before the introduction of a Bill in the Parliament, decide whether or not in his view the provisions of the Bill would be within the legislative competence of the Parliament and state his decision.

(3) The form of any statement, and the manner in which it is to be made, shall be determined under standing orders, and standing orders may provide for any statement to be published.

NOTES

Initial Commencement
To be appointed
To be appointed: see s 130.

Appointment
Appointment: 1 July 1999: see SI 1998/3178, art 2(1).

---

32 Submission of Bills for Royal Assent

(1) It is for the Presiding Officer to submit Bills for Royal Assent.

(2) The Presiding Officer shall not submit a Bill for Royal Assent at any time when—

(a) the Advocate General, the Lord Advocate or the Attorney General is entitled to make a reference in relation to the Bill under section 33,

(b) any such reference has been made but has not been decided or otherwise disposed of by the Judicial Committee, or

(c) an order may be made in relation to the Bill under section 35.

(3) The Presiding Officer shall not submit a Bill in its unamended form for Royal Assent if—

(a) the Judicial Committee have decided that the Bill or any provision of it would not be within the legislative competence of the Parliament, or

(b) a reference made in relation to the Bill under section 33 has been withdrawn following a request for withdrawal of the reference under section 34(2)(b).

(4) In this Act—

'Advocate General' means the Advocate General for Scotland,

'Judicial Committee' means the Judicial Committee of the Privy Council.

NOTES

Initial Commencement
> *To be appointed*
> To be appointed: see s 130.

Appointment
> Appointment: 1 July 1999: see SI 1998/3178, art 2(1).

33 Scrutiny of Bills by the Judicial Committee

(1) The Advocate General, the Lord Advocate or the Attorney General may refer the question of whether a Bill or any provision of a Bill would be within the legislative competence of the Parliament to the Judicial Committee for decision.

(2) Subject to subsection (3), he may make a reference in relation to a Bill at any time during—

(a) the period of four weeks beginning with the passing of the Bill, and

(b) any period of four weeks beginning with any subsequent approval of the Bill in accordance with standing orders made by virtue of section 36(5).

(3) He shall not make a reference in relation to a Bill if he has notified the Presiding Officer that he does not intend to make a reference in relation to the Bill, unless the Bill has been approved as mentioned in subsection (2)(b) since the notification.

NOTES

Initial Commencement
> *To be appointed*
> To be appointed: see s 130.

Appointment
> Appointment: 1 July 1999: see SI 1998/3178, art 2(1).

34 ECJ references

(1) This section applies where—

(a) a reference has been made in relation to a Bill under section 33,

(b) a reference for a preliminary ruling has been made by the Judicial Committee in connection with that reference, and

(c) neither of those references has been decided or otherwise disposed of.

(2) If the Parliament resolves that it wishes to reconsider the Bill—

(a) the Presiding Officer shall notify the Advocate General, the Lord Advocate and the Attorney General of that fact, and

(b) the person who made the reference in relation to the Bill under section 33 shall request the withdrawal of the reference.

(3) In this section 'a reference for a preliminary ruling' means a reference of a question to the European Court under Article 177 of the Treaty establishing the European Community, Article 41 of the Treaty establishing the European Coal and Steel Community or Article 150 of the Treaty establishing the European Atomic Energy Community.

NOTES

Initial Commencement
> *To be appointed*
> To be appointed: see s 130.

Appointment
> Appointment: 1 July 1999: see SI 1998/3178, art 2(1).

35 Power to intervene in certain cases

(1) If a Bill contains provisions—

(a) which the Secretary of State has reasonable grounds to believe would be incompatible with any international obligations or the interests of defence or national security, or

(b) which make modifications of the law as it applies to reserved matters and which the Secretary of State has reasonable grounds to believe would have an adverse effect on the operation of the law as it applies to reserved matters,

he may make an order prohibiting the Presiding Officer from submitting the Bill for Royal Assent.

(2) The order must identify the Bill and the provisions in question and state the reasons for making the order.

(3) The order may be made at any time during—

(a) the period of four weeks beginning with the passing of the Bill,

(b) any period of four weeks beginning with any subsequent approval of the Bill in accordance with standing orders made by virtue of section 36(5),

(c) if a reference is made in relation to the Bill under section 33, the period of four weeks beginning with the reference being decided or otherwise disposed of by the Judicial Committee.

(4) The Secretary of State shall not make an order in relation to a Bill if he has notified the Presiding Officer that he does not intend to do so, unless the Bill has been approved as mentioned in subsection (3)(b) since the notification.

(5) An order in force under this section at a time when such approval is given shall cease to have effect.

NOTES

Initial Commencement
> *To be appointed*
> To be appointed: see s 130.

Appointment
> Appointment: 1 July 1999: see SI 1998/3178, art 2(1).

36 Stages of Bills

(1) Standing orders shall include provision—
(a) for general debate on a Bill with an opportunity for members to vote on its general principles,
(b) for the consideration of, and an opportunity for members to vote on, the details of a Bill, and
(c) for a final stage at which a Bill can be passed or rejected.

(2) Subsection (1) does not prevent standing orders making provision to enable the Parliament to expedite proceedings in relation to a particular Bill.

(3) Standing orders may make provision different from that required by subsection (1) for the procedure applicable to Bills of any of the following kinds—
(a) Bills which restate the law,
(b) Bills which repeal spent enactments,
(c) private Bills.

(4) Standing orders shall provide for an opportunity for the reconsideration of a Bill after its passing if (and only if)—
(a) the Judicial Committee decide that the Bill or any provision of it would not be within the legislative competence of the Parliament,
(b) a reference made in relation to the Bill under section 33 is withdrawn following a request for withdrawal of the reference under section 34(2)(b), or
(c) an order is made in relation to the Bill under section 35.

(5) Standing orders shall, in particular, ensure that any Bill amended on reconsideration is subject to a final stage at which it can be approved or rejected.

(6) References in subsection (4), sections 28(2) and 38(1)(a) and paragraph 7 of Schedule 3 to the passing of a Bill shall, in the case of a Bill which has been amended on reconsideration, be read as references to the approval of the Bill.

NOTES

Initial Commencement
To be appointed
To be appointed: see s 130.

Appointment
Appointment: 1 July 1999: see SI 1998/3178, art 2(1).

PART II
THE SCOTTISH ADMINISTRATION

Ministers and their staff

44 The Scottish Executive

(1) There shall be a Scottish Executive, whose members shall be—
(a) the First Minister,
(b) such Ministers as the First Minister may appoint under section 47, and
(c) the Lord Advocate and the Solicitor General for Scotland.

(2) The members of the Scottish Executive are referred to collectively as the Scottish Ministers.

(3) A person who holds a Ministerial office may not be appointed a member of the Scottish Executive; and if a member of the Scottish Executive is appointed to a Ministerial office he shall cease to hold office as a member of the Scottish Executive.

(4) In subsection (3), references to a member of the Scottish Executive include a junior Scottish Minister and 'Ministerial office' has the same meaning as in section 2 of the House of Commons Disqualification Act 1975.

NOTES

Initial Commencement
  To be appointed
  To be appointed: see s 130.

Appointment
  Sub-ss (1)(a), (b), (2)–(4): Appointment: 6 May 1999: see SI 1998/3178, art 2(2), Sch 3.
  Sub-s (1)(c): Appointment: 20 May 1999: see SI 1998/3178, art 2(2), Sch 4.

---

45 The First Minister

(1) The First Minister shall be appointed by Her Majesty from among the members of the Parliament and shall hold office at Her Majesty's pleasure.

(2) The First Minister may at any time tender his resignation to Her Majesty and shall do so if the Parliament resolves that the Scottish Executive no longer enjoys the confidence of the Parliament.

(3) The First Minister shall cease to hold office if a person is appointed in his place.

(4) If the office of First Minister is vacant or he is for any reason unable to act, the functions exercisable by him shall be exercisable by a person designated by the Presiding Officer.

(5) A person shall be so designated only if—
(a) he is a member of the Parliament, or
(b) if the Parliament has been dissolved, he is a person who ceased to be a member by virtue of the dissolution.

(6) Functions exercisable by a person by virtue of subsection (5)(a) shall continue to be exercisable by him even if the Parliament is dissolved.

(7) The First Minister shall be the Keeper of the Scottish Seal.

NOTES

Initial Commencement
  To be appointed
  To be appointed: see s 130.

Appointment
  Appointment: 6 May 1999: see SI 1998/3178, art 2(2), Sch 3.

---

46 Choice of the First Minister

(1) If one of the following events occurs, the Parliament shall within the period allowed nominate one of its members for appointment as First Minister.

(2) The events are—

(a) the holding of a poll at a general election,

(b) the First Minister tendering his resignation to Her Majesty,

(c) the office of First Minister becoming vacant (otherwise than in consequence of his so tendering his resignation),

(d) the First Minister ceasing to be a member of the Parliament otherwise than by virtue of a dissolution.

(3) The period allowed is the period of 28 days which begins with the day on which the event in question occurs; but—

(a) if another of those events occurs within the period allowed, that period shall be extended (subject to paragraph (b)) so that it ends with the period of 28 days beginning with the day on which that other event occurred, and

(b) the period shall end if the Parliament passes a resolution under section 3(1)(a) or when Her Majesty appoints a person as First Minister.

(4) The Presiding Officer shall recommend to Her Majesty the appointment of any member of the Parliament who is nominated by the Parliament under this section.

NOTES

Initial Commencement
To be appointed
To be appointed: see s 130.

Appointment
Appointment: 6 May 1999: see SI 1998/3178, art 2(2), Sch 3.

47 Ministers

(1) The First Minister may, with the approval of Her Majesty, appoint Ministers from among the members of the Parliament.

(2) The First Minister shall not seek Her Majesty's approval for any appointment under this section without the agreement of the Parliament.

(3) A Minister appointed under this section—

(a) shall hold office at Her Majesty's pleasure,

(b) may be removed from office by the First Minister,

(c) may at any time resign and shall do so if the Parliament resolves that the Scottish Executive no longer enjoys the confidence of the Parliament,

(d) if he resigns, shall cease to hold office immediately, and

(e) shall cease to hold office if he ceases to be a member of the Parliament otherwise than by virtue of a dissolution.

NOTES

Initial Commencement
To be appointed
To be appointed: see s 130.

Appointment
Appointment: 6 May 1999: see SI 1998/3178, art 2(2), Sch 3.

48 The Scottish Law Officers

(1) It is for the First Minister to recommend to Her Majesty the appointment or removal of a person as Lord Advocate or Solicitor General for Scotland; but he shall not do so without the agreement of the Parliament.

(2) The Lord Advocate and the Solicitor General for Scotland may at any time resign and shall do so if the Parliament resolves that the Scottish Executive no longer enjoys the confidence of the Parliament.

(3) Where the Lord Advocate resigns in consequence of such a resolution, he shall be deemed to continue in office until the warrant of appointment of the person succeeding to the office of Lord Advocate is granted, but only for the purpose of exercising his retained functions.

(4) Subsection (3) is without prejudice to section 287 of the Criminal Procedure (Scotland) Act 1995 (demission of office by Lord Advocate).

(5) Any decision of the Lord Advocate in his capacity as head of the systems of criminal prosecution and investigation of deaths in Scotland shall continue to be taken by him independently of any other person.

(6) In Schedule 2 to the House of Commons Disqualification Act 1975 (Ministerial offices) and Part III of Schedule 1 to the Ministerial and other Salaries Act 1975 (salaries of the Law Officers), the entries for the Lord Advocate and the Solicitor General for Scotland are omitted.

NOTES

Initial Commencement
To be appointed
To be appointed: see s 130.

Appointment
Sub-s (1): Appointment (for the purpose of enabling the First Minister to recommend the appointment of the Lord Advocate and Solicitor General for Scotland to take effect from a date not earlier than 20 May 1999): 6 May 1999: see SI 1998/3178, art 2(2), Sch 3.
Sub-s (1): Appointment (for remaining purposes): 20 May 1999: see SI 1998/3178, art 2(2), Sch 4.
Sub-ss (2)–(6): Appointment: 20 May 1999: see SI 1998/3178, art 2(2), Sch 4.

---

49 Junior Scottish Ministers

(1) The First Minister may, with the approval of Her Majesty, appoint persons from among the members of the Parliament to assist the Scottish Ministers in the exercise of their functions.

(2) They shall be known as junior Scottish Ministers.

(3) The First Minister shall not seek Her Majesty's approval for any appointment under this section without the agreement of the Parliament.

(4) A junior Scottish Minister—
(a) shall hold office at Her Majesty's pleasure,
(b) may be removed from office by the First Minister,
(c) may at any time resign and shall do so if the Parliament resolves that the Scottish Executive no longer enjoys the confidence of the Parliament,
(d) if he resigns, shall cease to hold office immediately, and
(e) shall cease to hold office if he ceases to be a member of the Parliament otherwise than by virtue of a dissolution.

50 Validity of acts of Scottish Ministers etc

The validity of any act of a member of the Scottish Executive or junior Scottish Minister is not affected by any defect in his nomination by the Parliament or (as the case may be) in the Parliament's agreement to his appointment.

51 The Civil Service

(1) The Scottish Ministers may appoint persons to be members of the staff of the Scottish Administration.

(2) Service as—
(a) the holder of any office in the Scottish Administration which is not a ministerial office, or
(b) a member of the staff of the Scottish Administration,
shall be service in the Home Civil Service.

(3) Subsection (1) and the other enactments conferring power to appoint such persons shall have effect subject to any provision made in relation to the Home Civil Service by or under any Order in Council.

(4) Any Civil Service management function shall be exercisable by the Minister for the Civil Service in relation to the persons mentioned in subsection (2) as it is exercisable in relation to other members of the Home Civil Service; and, accordingly, section 1 of the Civil Service (Management Functions) Act 1992 (delegation of functions by Ministers) shall apply to any such function as extended by this section.

(5) Any salary or allowances payable to or in respect of the persons mentioned in subsection (2) (including contributions to any pension scheme) shall be payable out of the Scottish Consolidated Fund.

(6) Section 1(2) and (3) of the Superannuation Act 1972 (delegation of functions relating to civil service superannuation schemes etc) shall have effect as if references to a Minister of the Crown (other than the Minister for the Civil Service) included the Scottish Ministers.

(7) The Scottish Ministers shall make payments to the Minister for the Civil Service, at such times as he may determine, of such amounts as he may determine in respect of—

(a) the provision of pensions, allowances or gratuities by virtue of section 1 of the Superannuation Act 1972 to or in respect of persons who are or have been in such service as is mentioned in subsection (2), and

(b) any expenses to be incurred in administering those pensions, allowances or gratuities.

(8) Amounts required for payments under subsection (7) shall be charged on the Scottish Consolidated Fund.

(9) In this section—

'Civil Service management function' means any function to which section 1 of the Civil Service (Management Functions) Act 1992 applies and which is vested in the Minister for the Civil Service,

'the Home Civil Service' means Her Majesty's Home Civil Service.

NOTES

Initial Commencement
> *To be appointed*
> To be appointed: see s 130.

Appointment
> Sub-ss (1)–(3), (5), (6), (8), (9): Appointment: 6 May 1999: see SI 1998/3178, art 2(2), Sch 3.
> Sub-ss (4), (7): Appointment (for the purpose of enabling any delegation of civil service management functions or any determination of payments to be made to come into force not earlier than 6 May 1999): 25 January 1999: see SI 1998/3178, art 2(2), Sch 1.
> Sub-ss (4), (7): Appointment (for remaining purposes): 6 May 1999: see SI 1998/3178, art 2(2), Sch 3.

Ministerial functions

52 Exercise of functions

(1) Statutory functions may be conferred on the Scottish Ministers by that name.

(2) Statutory functions of the Scottish Ministers, the First Minister or the Lord Advocate shall be exercisable on behalf of Her Majesty.

(3) Statutory functions of the Scottish Ministers shall be exercisable by any member of the Scottish Executive.

(4) Any act or omission of, or in relation to, any member of the Scottish Executive shall be treated as an act or omission of, or in relation to, each of them; and any property acquired, or liability incurred, by any member of the Scottish Executive shall be treated accordingly.

(5) Subsection (4) does not apply in relation to the exercise of—
(a) functions conferred on the First Minister alone, or
(b) retained functions of the Lord Advocate.

(6) In this Act, 'retained functions' in relation to the Lord Advocate means—
(a) any functions exercisable by him immediately before he ceases to be a Minister of the Crown, and
(b) other statutory functions conferred on him alone after he ceases to be a Minister of the Crown.

(7) In this section, 'statutory functions' means functions conferred by virtue of any enactment.

NOTES

Initial Commencement
To be appointed
To be appointed: see s 130.

Appointment
Appointment (except in so far as relating to the Lord Advocate): 6 May 1999: see SI 1998/3178, art 2(2), Sch 3.
Appointment (for remaining purposes): 20 May 1999: see SI 1998/3178, art 2(2), Sch 4.

---

53 General transfer of functions

(1) The functions mentioned in subsection (2) shall, so far as they are exercisable within devolved competence, be exercisable by the Scottish Ministers instead of by a Minister of the Crown.

(2) Those functions are—
(a) those of Her Majesty's prerogative and other executive functions which are exercisable on behalf of Her Majesty by a Minister of the Crown,
(b) other functions conferred on a Minister of the Crown by a prerogative instrument, and
(c) functions conferred on a Minister of the Crown by any pre-commencement enactment,
but do not include any retained functions of the Lord Advocate.

(3) In this Act, 'pre-commencement enactment' means—
(a) an Act passed before or in the same session as this Act and any other enactment made before the passing of this Act,
(b) an enactment made, before the commencement of this section, under such an Act or such other enactment,
(c) subordinate legislation under section 106, to the extent that the legislation states that it is to be treated as a pre-commencement enactment.

(4) This section and section 54 are modified by Part III of Schedule 4.

NOTES

Initial Commencement
To be appointed
To be appointed: see s 130.

Appointment
Appointment: 1 July 1999: see SI 1998/3178, art 2(1).

---

54 Devolved competence

(1) References in this Act to the exercise of a function being within or outside devolved competence are to be read in accordance with this section.

(2) It is outside devolved competence—
(a) to make any provision by subordinate legislation which would be outside the legislative competence of the Parliament if it were included in an Act of the Scottish Parliament, or
(b) to confirm or approve any subordinate legislation containing such provision.

(3) In the case of any function other than a function of making, confirming or approving subordinate legislation, it is outside devolved competence to exercise the function (or exercise it in any way) so far as a provision of an Act of the Scottish Parliament conferring the function (or, as the case may be, conferring it so as to be exercisable in that way) would be outside the legislative competence of the Parliament.

NOTES

Initial Commencement
   To be appointed
   To be appointed: see s 130.

Appointment
   Appointment: 1 July 1999: see SI 1998/3178, art 2(1).

55 Functions exercisable with agreement

(1) A statutory provision, or any provision not contained in an enactment, which provides for a Minister of the Crown to exercise a function with the agreement of, or after consultation with, any other Minister of the Crown shall cease to have effect in relation to the exercise of the function by a member of the Scottish Executive by virtue of section 53.

(2) In subsection (1) 'statutory provision' means any provision in a pre-commencement enactment other than paragraph 5 or 15 of Schedule 32 to the Local Government, Planning and Land Act 1980 (designation of enterprise zones).

NOTES

Initial Commencement
   To be appointed
   To be appointed: see s 130.

Appointment
   Appointment: 1 July 1999: see SI 1998/3178, art 2(1).

56 Shared powers

(1) Despite the transfer by virtue of section 53 of any function under—
(a) section 17(1) of the Ministry of Transport Act 1919 (power to make advances for certain purposes),
(b) any Order in Council under section 1 of the United Nations Act 1946 (measures to give effect to Security Council decisions),
(c) section 9 of the Industrial Organisation and Development Act 1947 (levies for scientific research, promotion of exports, etc),
(d) section 5 of the Science and Technology Act 1965 (funding of scientific research),
(e) section 1 of the Mineral Exploration and Investment Grants Act 1972 (contributions in respect of mineral exploration),
(f) sections 10 to 12 of the Industry Act 1972 (credits and grants for construction of ships and offshore installations),
(g) sections 2, 11(3) and 12(4) of the Employment and Training Act 1973 (power to make arrangements for employment and training etc and to make certain payments),
(h) sections 7 to 9 and 11 to 13 of the Industrial Development Act 1982 (financial and other assistance for industry), and

(i) sections 39 and 40 of the Road Traffic Act 1988 (road safety information and training),
the function shall be exercisable by a Minister of the Crown as well as by the Scottish Ministers.

(2) Despite the transfer of any other function by virtue of section 53, the function shall, if subordinate legislation so provides, be exercisable (or be exercisable so far as the legislation provides) by a Minister of the Crown as well as by the Scottish Ministers.

(3) Subordinate legislation under subsection (2) may not be made so as to come into force at any time after the function in question has become exercisable by the Scottish Ministers.

(4) Any power referred to in section 53(2)(a) to establish, maintain or abolish a body, office or office-holder having functions which include both—
(a) functions which are exercisable in or as regards Scotland and do not relate to reserved matters, and
(b) other functions,
shall, despite that section, be exercisable jointly by the Minister of the Crown and the Scottish Ministers.

(5) In subsection (4), 'office-holder' includes employee or other post-holder.

NOTES

Initial Commencement
   To be appointed
   To be appointed: see s 130.

Appointment
   Sub-ss (1), (3)–(5): Appointment: 1 July 1999: see SI 1998/3178, art 2(1).
   Sub-s (2): Appointment (for the purpose of enabling subordinate legislation to be made to come into force not earlier than 1 July 1999): 25 January 1999: see SI 1998/3178, art 2(2), Sch 1.
   Sub-s (2): Appointment (for remaining purposes): 1 July 1999: see SI 1998/3178, art 2(1).

Subordinate Legislation
   Scotland Act 1998 (Concurrent Functions) Order 1999, SI 1999/1592 (made under sub-s (2)).

---

57 Community law and Convention rights

(1) Despite the transfer to the Scottish Ministers by virtue of section 53 of functions in relation to observing and implementing obligations under Community law, any function of a Minister of the Crown in relation to any matter shall continue to be exercisable by him as regards Scotland for the purposes specified in section 2(2) of the European Communities Act 1972.

(2) A member of the Scottish Executive has no power to make any subordinate legislation, or to do any other act, so far as the legislation or act is incompatible with any of the Convention rights or with Community law.

(3) Subsection (2) does not apply to an act of the Lord Advocate—
(a) in prosecuting any offence, or
(b) in his capacity as head of the systems of criminal prosecution and investigation of deaths in Scotland,

which, because of subsection (2) of section 6 of the Human Rights Act 1998, is not unlawful under subsection (1) of that section.

NOTES

Initial Commencement
To be appointed
To be appointed: see s 130.

Appointment
Sub-s (1): Appointment: 1 July 1999: see SI 1998/3178, art 2(1).
Sub-s (2): Appointment: 6 May 1999: see SI 1998/3178, art 2(2), Sch 3.
Sub-s (3): Appointment: 20 May 1999: see SI 1998/3178, art 2(2), Sch 4.

Subordinate Legislation
Paying Agency (National Assembly for Wales) Regulations 1999, SI 1999/2223 (made under sub-s (1)).
Hill Livestock (Compensatory Allowances) (Enforcement) Regulations 1999, SI 1999/3315 (made under sub-s (1)).
Hill Livestock (Compensatory Allowances) Regulations 1999, SI 1999/3316 (made under sub-s (1)).
Harbour Works (Environmental Impact Assessment) Regulations 1999, SI 1999/3445.

---

58 Power to prevent or require action

(1) If the Secretary of State has reasonable grounds to believe that any action proposed to be taken by a member of the Scottish Executive would be incompatible with any international obligations, he may by order direct that the proposed action shall not be taken.

(2) If the Secretary of State has reasonable grounds to believe that any action capable of being taken by a member of the Scottish Executive is required for the purpose of giving effect to any such obligations, he may by order direct that the action shall be taken.

(3) In subsections (1) and (2), 'action' includes making, confirming or approving subordinate legislation and, in subsection (2), includes introducing a Bill in the Parliament.

(4) If any subordinate legislation made or which could be revoked by a member of the Scottish Executive contains provisions—
(a) which the Secretary of State has reasonable grounds to believe to be incompatible with any international obligations or the interests of defence or national security, or
(b) which make modifications of the law as it applies to reserved matters and which the Secretary of State has reasonable grounds to believe to have an adverse effect on the operation of the law as it applies to reserved matters,
the Secretary of State may by order revoke the legislation.

(5) An order under this section must state the reasons for making the order.

NOTES

Initial Commencement
To be appointed
To be appointed: see s 130.

Appointment
Appointment: 6 May 1999: see SI 1998/3178, art 2(2), Sch 3.

PART IV
THE TAX-VARYING POWER

Juridical

98 Devolution issues

Schedule 6 (which makes provision in relation to devolution issues) shall have effect.

NOTES

Initial Commencement
To be appointed
To be appointed: see s 130.

Appointment
Appointment: 6 May 1999: see SI 1998/3178, art 2(2), Sch 3.

---

100 Human rights

(1) This Act does not enable a person—
(a) to bring any proceedings in a court or tribunal on the ground that an act is incompatible with the Convention rights, or
(b) to rely on any of the Convention rights in any such proceedings,
unless he would be a victim for the purposes of Article 34 of the Convention (within the meaning of the Human Rights Act 1998) if proceedings in respect of the act were brought in the European Court of Human Rights.

(2) Subsection (1) does not apply to the Lord Advocate, the Advocate General, the Attorney General or the Attorney General for Northern Ireland.

(3) This Act does not enable a court or tribunal to award any damages in respect of an act which is incompatible with any of the Convention rights which it could not award if section 8(3) and (4) of the Human Rights Act 1998 applied.

(4) In this section 'act' means—
(a) making any legislation,
(b) any other act or failure to act, if it is the act or failure of a member of the Scottish Executive.

NOTES

Initial Commencement
To be appointed
To be appointed: see s 130.

Appointment
Appointment: 6 May 1999: see SI 1998/3178, art 2(2), Sch 3.

---

101 Interpretation of Acts of the Scottish Parliament etc

(1) This section applies to—
(a) any provision of an Act of the Scottish Parliament, or of a Bill for such an Act, and
(b) any provision of subordinate legislation made, confirmed or approved, or purporting to be made, confirmed or approved, by a member of the Scottish Executive,
which could be read in such a way as to be outside competence.

(2) Such a provision is to be read as narrowly as is required for it to be within competence, if such a reading is possible, and is to have effect accordingly.

(3) In this section 'competence'—
(a) in relation to an Act of the Scottish Parliament, or a Bill for such an Act, means the legislative competence of the Parliament, and
(b) in relation to subordinate legislation, means the powers conferred by virtue of this Act.

NOTES

Initial Commencement
> *To be appointed*
> To be appointed: see s 130.

Appointment
> Appointment: 1 July 1999: see SI 1998/3178, art 2(1).

102 Powers of courts or tribunals to vary retrospective decisions

(1) This section applies where any court or tribunal decides that—
(a) an Act of the Scottish Parliament or any provision of such an Act is not within the legislative competence of the Parliament, or
(b) a member of the Scottish Executive does not have the power to make, confirm or approve a provision of subordinate legislation that he has purported to make, confirm or approve.

(2) The court or tribunal may make an order—
(a) removing or limiting any retrospective effect of the decision, or
(b) suspending the effect of the decision for any period and on any conditions to allow the defect to be corrected.

(3) In deciding whether to make an order under this section, the court or tribunal shall (among other things) have regard to the extent to which persons who are not parties to the proceedings would otherwise be adversely affected.

(4) Where a court or tribunal is considering whether to make an order under this section, it shall order intimation of that fact to be given to—
(a) the Lord Advocate, and
(b) the appropriate law officer, where the decision mentioned in subsection (1) relates to a devolution issue (within the meaning of Schedule 6),
unless the person to whom the intimation would be given is a party to the proceedings.

(5) A person to whom intimation is given under subsection (4) may take part as a party in the proceedings so far as they relate to the making of the order.

(6) Paragraphs 36 and 37 of Schedule 6 apply with necessary modifications for the purposes of subsections (4) and (5) as they apply for the purposes of that Schedule.

(7) In this section—
'intimation' includes notice,
'the appropriate law officer' means—
(a) in relation to proceedings in Scotland, the Advocate General,
(b) in relation to proceedings in England and Wales, the Attorney General,
(c) in relation to proceedings in Northern Ireland, the Attorney General for Northern Ireland.

NOTES
Initial Commencement
   To be appointed
   To be appointed: see s 130.

Appointment
   Appointment: 1 July 1999: see SI 1998/3178, art 2(1).

103 The Judicial Committee

(1) Any decision of the Judicial Committee in proceedings under this Act shall be stated in open court and shall be binding in all legal proceedings (other than proceedings before the Committee).

(2) No member of the Judicial Committee shall sit and act as a member of the Committee in proceedings under this Act unless he holds or has held—
(a) the office of a Lord of Appeal in Ordinary, or
(b) high judicial office as defined in section 25 of the Appellate Jurisdiction Act 1876 (ignoring for this purpose section 5 of the Appellate Jurisdiction Act 1887).

(3) Her Majesty may by Order in Council—
(a) confer on the Judicial Committee in relation to proceedings under this Act such powers as Her Majesty considers necessary or expedient,
(b) apply the Judicial Committee Act 1833 in relation to proceedings under this Act with exceptions or modifications,
(c) make rules for regulating the procedure in relation to proceedings under this Act before the Judicial Committee.

(4) In this section 'proceedings under this Act' means proceedings on a question referred to the Judicial Committee under section 33 or proceedings under Schedule 6.

NOTES
Initial Commencement
   To be appointed
   To be appointed: see s 130.

Appointment
   Sub-ss (1), (2), (4): Appointment: 6 May 1999: see SI 1998/3178, art 2(2), Sch 3.
   Sub-s (3): Appointment (for the purpose of enabling subordinate legislation to be made to come into force not earlier than 6 May 1999): 25 January 1999: see SI 1998/3178, art 2(2), Sch 1.
   Sub-s (3): Appointment (for remaining purposes): 6 May 1999: see SI 1998/3178, art 2(2), Sch 3.

Subordinate Legislation
   Judicial Committee (Devolution Issues) Rules Order 1999, SI 1999/665 (made under sub-s (3)(c)).
   Judicial Committee (Powers in Devolution Cases) Order 1999, SI 1999/1320 (made under sub-s (3)(a)).

Supplementary powers

107 Legislative power to remedy ultra vires acts

Subordinate legislation may make such provision as the person making the legislation considers necessary or expedient in consequence of—

(a) an Act of the Scottish Parliament or any provision of an Act of the Scottish Parliament which is not, or may not be, within the legislative competence of the Parliament, or
(b) any purported exercise by a member of the Scottish Executive of his functions which is not, or may not be, an exercise or a proper exercise of those functions.

NOTES

Initial Commencement
To be appointed
To be appointed: see s 130.

Appointment
Appointment: 1 July 1999: see SI 1998/3178, art 2(1).

Subordinate Legislation
Scotland Act 1998 (Regulation of Care (Scotland) Act 2001) Order 2001, SI 2001/2478.

PART VI
SUPPLEMENTARY

Final provisions

126 Interpretation

(1) In this Act—
'body' includes unincorporated association,
'constituencies' and 'regions', in relation to the Parliament, mean the constituencies and regions provided for by Schedule 1,
'constituency member' means a member of the Parliament for a constituency,
'the Convention rights' has the same meaning as in the Human Rights Act 1998,
'document' means anything in which information is recorded in any form (and references to producing a document are to be read accordingly),
'enactment' includes an Act of the Scottish Parliament, Northern Ireland legislation (within the meaning of the Northern Ireland Act 1998) and an enactment comprised in subordinate legislation, and includes an enactment comprised in, or in subordinate legislation under, an Act of Parliament, whenever passed or made,
'financial year' means a year ending with 31st March,
'functions' includes powers and duties, and 'confer', in relation to functions, includes impose,
'government department' means any department of the Government of the United Kingdom,
'the Human Rights Convention' means—
    (a) the Convention for the Protection of Human Rights and Fundamental Freedoms, agreed by the Council of Europe at Rome on 4th November 1950, and
    (b) the Protocols to the Convention,
    as they have effect for the time being in relation to the United Kingdom,
'Minister of the Crown' includes the Treasury,
'modify' includes amend or repeal,
'occupational pension scheme', 'personal pension scheme' and 'public service pension scheme' have the meanings given by section 1 of the Pension Schemes Act 1993, . . .
'the Parliament' means the Scottish Parliament,
'parliamentary', in relation to constituencies, elections and electors, is to be taken to refer to the Parliament of the United Kingdom,

'prerogative instrument' means an Order in Council, warrant, charter or other instrument made under the prerogative,

'the principal appointed day' means the day appointed by an order under section 130 which is designated by the order as the principal appointed day,

'proceedings', in relation to the Parliament, includes proceedings of any committee or sub-committee,

'property' includes rights and interests of any description,

'regional member' means a member of the Parliament for a region,

'Scotland' includes so much of the internal waters and territorial sea of the United Kingdom as are adjacent to Scotland,

'Scottish public authority' means any public body (except the Parliamentary corporation), public office or holder of such an office whose functions (in each case) are exercisable only in or as regards Scotland,

'the Scottish zone' means the sea within British fishery limits (that is, the limits set by or under section 1 of the Fishery Limits Act 1976) which is adjacent to Scotland,

'standing orders' means standing orders of the Parliament,

'subordinate legislation' has the same meaning as in the Interpretation Act 1978 and also includes an instrument made under an Act of the Scottish Parliament,

'tribunal' means any tribunal in which legal proceedings may be brought.

(2) Her Majesty may by Order in Council determine, or make provision for determining, for the purposes of this Act any boundary between waters which are to be treated as internal waters or territorial sea of the United Kingdom, or sea within British fishery limits, adjacent to Scotland and those which are not.

(3) For the purposes of this Act—

(a) the question whether any function of a body, government department, office or office-holder relates to reserved matters is to be determined by reference to the purpose for which the function is exercisable, having regard (among other things) to the likely effects in all the circumstances of any exercise of the function, but

(b) bodies to which paragraph 3 of Part III of Schedule 5 applies are to be treated as if all their functions were functions which relate to reserved matters.

(4) References in this Act to Scots private law are to the following areas of the civil law of Scotland—

(a) the general principles of private law (including private international law),

(b) the law of persons (including natural persons, legal persons and unincorporated bodies),

(c) the law of obligations (including obligations arising from contract, unilateral promise, delict, unjustified enrichment and negotiorum gestio),

(d) the law of property (including heritable and moveable property, trusts and succession), and

(e) the law of actions (including jurisdiction, remedies, evidence, procedure, diligence, recognition and enforcement of court orders, limitation of actions and arbitration),

and include references to judicial review of administrative action.

(5) References in this Act to Scots criminal law include criminal offences, jurisdiction, evidence, procedure and penalties and the treatment of offenders.

(6) References in this Act and in any other enactment to the Scottish Administration are to the office-holders in the Scottish Administration and the members of the staff of the Scottish Administration.

(7) For the purposes of this Act—
(a) references to office-holders in the Scottish Administration are to—
  (i) members of the Scottish Executive and junior Scottish Ministers, and
  (ii) the holders of offices in the Scottish Administration which are not ministerial offices, and
(b) references to members of the staff of the Scottish Administration are to the staff of the persons referred to in paragraph (a).

(8) For the purposes of this Act, the offices in the Scottish Administration which are not ministerial offices are—
(a) the Registrar General of Births, Deaths and Marriages for Scotland, the Keeper of the Registers of Scotland and the Keeper of the Records of Scotland, and
(b) any other office of a description specified in an Order in Council made by Her Majesty under this subsection.

(9) In this Act—
(a) all those rights, powers, liabilities, obligations and restrictions from time to time created or arising by or under the Community Treaties, and
(b) all those remedies and procedures from time to time provided for by or under the Community Treaties,
are referred to as 'Community law'.

(10) In this Act, 'international obligations' means any international obligations of the United Kingdom other than obligations to observe and implement Community law or the Convention rights.

(11) In this Act, 'by virtue of' includes 'by' and 'under'.

NOTES

Initial Commencement
   Royal Assent
   Royal Assent: 19 November 1998: (no specific commencement provision).

Amendment
   Sub-s (1): in definition 'occupational pension scheme', 'personal pension scheme', 'public service pension scheme' words omitted repealed by the Welfare Reform and Pensions Act 1999, s 88, Sch 13, Pt I.
      Date in force: 25 April 2000: see SI 2000/1047, art 2(2)(b), Schedule, Pt II.

Subordinate Legislation
   Scotland Act 1998 (Commencement) Order 1998, SI 1998/3178 (made under sub-s (1)).
   Scottish Adjacent Waters Boundaries Order 1999, SI 1999/1126 (made under sub-s (2)).
   Scottish Administration (Offices) Order 1999, SI 1999/1127 (made under sub-s (8)(b)).

127 Index of defined expressions

In this Act, the expressions listed in the left-hand column have the meaning given by, or are to be interpreted in accordance with, the provisions listed in the right-hand column.

Expression	*Provision of this Act*
Act of the Scottish Parliament	Section 28(1)
Advocate General	Section 32(4)
Auditor General for Scotland	Section 69
Body	Section 126(1)
By virtue of	Section 126(11)

Expression	*Provision of this Act*
Clerk, and Assistant Clerk	Section 20 and paragraph 3 of Schedule 2
Community law	Section 126(9)
Constituencies and constituency member	Section 126(1)
The Convention rights	Section 126(1)
Cross-border public authority	Section 88(5)
Devolved competence (in relation to the exercise of functions)	Section 54
Document	Section 126(1)
Enactmen	Sections 113(6) and 126(1)
Financial year	Section 126(1)
Functions	Section 126(1)
Government department	Section 126(1)
The Human Rights Convention	Section 126(1)
International obligations	Section 126(10)
Judicial Committee	Section 32(4)
Legislative competence	Section 29
Member of the Scottish Executive	Section 44(1)
Members of the staff of the Scottish Administration	Section 126(7)
Minister of the Crown	Section 126(1)
Modify	Section 126(1)
Occupational pension scheme, personal pension scheme and public service pension scheme	Section 126(1)
Office-holders in the Scottish Administration	Section 126(7)
Offices in the Scottish Administration which are not ministerial offices	Section 126(8)
Open power	Section 112(3)
The Parliament	Section 126(1)
'parliamentary' (in relation to constituencies, elections and electors)	Section 126(1) Section 21(1)
The Parliamentary corporation	
Pre-commencement enactment	Section 53(3)
Prerogative instrument	Section 126(1)
Presiding Officer	Section 19
Principal appointed day	Section 126(1)
Proceedings	Section 126(1)
Property	Section 126(1)
Regional list (in relation to a party)	Section 5(4)
Regional returning officer	Section 12(6)
Regional vote	Section 6(2)
Regions and regional member	Section 126(1)
Registered political party	Section 5(9)
Reserved matters	Schedule 5
Retained functions (in relation to the Lord Advocate)	Section 52(6)
Scotland	Section 126(1) and (2)
Scots criminal law	Section 126(5)
Scots private law	Section 126(4)
Scottish Administration	Section 126(6)
Scottish Ministers	Section 44(2)
Scottish public authority	Section 126(1)

Expression	*Provision of this Act*
Scottish public authority with mixed functions or no reserved functions	Paragraphs 1 and 2 of Part III of Schedule 5
Scottish Seal	Section 2(6)
The Scottish zone	Section 126(1)
Staff of the Parliament	Paragraph 3 of Schedule 2
Standing orders	Section 126(1)
Subordinate legislation	Section 126(1)
Tribunal	Section 126(1)

NOTES

Initial Commencement
Royal Assent
Royal Assent: 19 November 1998: (no specific commencement provision).

129 Transitional provisions etc

(1) Subordinate legislation may make such provision as the person making the legislation considers necessary or expedient for transitory or transitional purposes in connection with the coming into force of any provision of this Act.

(2) If any of the following provisions come into force before the Human Rights Act 1998 has come into force (or come fully into force), the provision shall have effect until the time when that Act is fully in force as it will have effect after that time: sections 29(2)(d), 57(2) and (3), 100 and 126(1) and Schedule 6.

NOTES

Initial Commencement
Royal Assent
Royal Assent: 19 November 1998: (no specific commencement provision).

Subordinate Legislation
UK
Scotland Act 1998 (Transitional and Transitory Provisions) (Subordinate Legislation under the Act) Order 1998, SI 1998/3216 (made under sub-s (1)).
Scotland Act 1998 (Transitory and Transitional Provisions) (Finance) Order 1999, SI 1999/441 (made under sub-s (1)).
Scotland Act 1998 (Consequential Modifications) (No 1) Order 1999, SI 1999/1042 (made under sub-s (1)).
Scotland Act 1998 (Transitory and Transitional Provisions) (Grants to Members and Officeholders) Order 1999, SI 1999/1081 (made under sub-s (1)).
Scotland Act 1998 (Transitory and Transitional Provisions) (Scottish Parliamentary Pension Scheme) Order 1999, SI 1999/1082 (made under sub-s (1)).
Scotland Act 1998 (Transitory and Transitional Provisions) (Standing Orders and Parliamentary Publications) Order 1999, SI 1999/1095 (made under sub-s (1)).
Scotland Act 1998 (Transitory and Transitional Provisions) (Statutory Instruments) Order 1999, SI 1999/1096 (made under sub-s (1)).
Scotland Act 1998 (Transitory and Transitional Provisions) (Salaries and Allowances) Order 1999, SI 1999/1097 (made under sub-s (1)).
Scotland Act 1998 (Transitory and Transitional Provisions) (Salaries and Allowances) Order 1999, SI 1999/1097 (made under sub-s (1)).
Scotland Act 1998 (Transitory and Transitional Provisions) (Administration of the Parliament) Order 1999, SI 1098 (made under sub-s (1)).
Scotland Act 1998 (General Transitory, Transitional and Savings Provisions) Amendment Order 1999, SI 1999/1334 (made under sub-s (1)).
Scotland Act 1998 (Transitory and Transitional Provisions) (Members Interests) Order 1999, SI 1999/1350 (made under sub-s (1)).

Scotland Act 1998 (Transitory and Transitional Provisions) (Complaints of Maladministration) Order 1999, SI 1999/1351 (made under sub-s (1)).
Scotland Act 1998 (Transitory and Transitional Provisions) (Laying of Reports) Order 1999, SI 1999/1594 (made under sub-s (1)).
Scotland Act 1998 (Transitory and Transitional Provisions) (Complaints of Maladministration) Amendment Order 1999, SI 1999/1595 (made under sub-s (1)).
Scotland Act 1998 (Transitory and Transitional Provisions) (Grants to Members and Officeholders and Scottish Parliamentary Pension Scheme) Amendment Order 1999, SI 1999/1891 (made under sub-s (1)).
Scotland Act 1998 (Transitory and Transitional Provisions) (Finance) Amendment Order 1999, SI 1999/3273 (made under sub-s (1)).
Scotland
Scotland Act 1998 (Transitory and Transitional Provisions) (Appropriations) Amendment Order 1999, SSI 1999/175 (made under sub-s (1)).
Scotland Act 1998 (Transitory and Transitional Provisions) (Appropriations) Amendment (Scotland) Order 2000, SSI 2000/69 (made under sub-s (1)).

SCHEDULE 6
Devolution Issues

Section 98

Part I
Preliminary

1 In this Schedule 'devolution issue' means—
(a) a question whether an Act of the Scottish Parliament or any provision of an Act of the Scottish Parliament is within the legislative competence of the Parliament,
(b) a question whether any function (being a function which any person has purported, or is proposing, to exercise) is a function of the Scottish Ministers, the First Minister or the Lord Advocate,
(c) a question whether the purported or proposed exercise of a function by a member of the Scottish Executive is, or would be, within devolved competence,
(d) a question whether a purported or proposed exercise of a function by a member of the Scottish Executive is, or would be, incompatible with any of the Convention rights or with Community law,
(e) a question whether a failure to act by a member of the Scottish Executive is incompatible with any of the Convention rights or with Community law,
(f) any other question about whether a function is exercisable within devolved competence or in or as regards Scotland and any other question arising by virtue of this Act about reserved matters.

2 A devolution issue shall not be taken to arise in any proceedings merely because of any contention of a party to the proceedings which appears to the court or tribunal before which the proceedings take place to be frivolous or vexatious.

NOTES

Initial Commencement
To be appointed
To be appointed: see s 130.

Appointment
Appointment: 6 May 1999: see SI 1998/3178, art 2(2), Sch 3.

Part II

Proceedings in Scotland

Application of Part II

3 This Part of this Schedule applies in relation to devolution issues in proceedings in Scotland.

Institution of proceedings

4 (1) Proceedings for the determination of a devolution issue may be instituted by the Advocate General or the Lord Advocate.

(2) The Lord Advocate may defend any such proceedings instituted by the Advocate General.

(3) This paragraph is without prejudice to any power to institute or defend proceedings exercisable apart from this paragraph by any person.

Intimation of devolution issue

5 Intimation of any devolution issue which arises in any proceedings before a court or tribunal shall be given to the Advocate General and the Lord Advocate (unless the person to whom the intimation would be given is a party to the proceedings).

6 A person to whom intimation is given in pursuance of paragraph 5 may take part as a party in the proceedings, so far as they relate to a devolution issue.

Reference of devolution issue to higher court

7 A court, other than the House of Lords or any court consisting of three or more judges of the Court of Session, may refer any devolution issue which arises in proceedings (other than criminal proceedings) before it to the Inner House of the Court of Session.

8 A tribunal from which there is no appeal shall refer any devolution issue which arises in proceedings before it to the Inner House of the Court of Session; and any other tribunal may make such a reference.

9 A court, other than any court consisting of two or more judges of the High Court of Justiciary, may refer any devolution issue which arises in criminal proceedings before it to the High Court of Justiciary.

References from superior courts to Judicial Committee

10 Any court consisting of three or more judges of the Court of Session may refer any devolution issue which arises in proceedings before it (otherwise than on a reference under paragraph 7 or 8) to the Judicial Committee.

11 Any court consisting of two or more judges of the High Court of Justiciary may refer any devolution issue which arises in proceedings before it (otherwise than on a reference under paragraph 9) to the Judicial Committee.

Appeals from superior courts to Judicial Committee

12 An appeal against a determination of a devolution issue by the Inner House of the Court of Session on a reference under paragraph 7 or 8 shall lie to the Judicial Committee.

13 An appeal against a determination of a devolution issue by—

(a) a court of two or more judges of the High Court of Justiciary (whether in the ordinary course of proceedings or on a reference under paragraph 9), or

(b) a court of three or more judges of the Court of Session from which there is no appeal to the House of Lords,

shall lie to the Judicial Committee, but only with leave of the court concerned or, failing such leave, with special leave of the Judicial Committee.

NOTES

Initial Commencement
   To be appointed
   To be appointed: see s 130.

Appointment
   Appointment: 6 May 1999: see SI 1998/3178, art 2(2), Sch 3.

PART III

PROCEEDINGS IN ENGLAND AND WALES

Application of Part III

14 This Part of this Schedule applies in relation to devolution issues in proceedings in England and Wales.

Institution of proceedings

15 (1) Proceedings for the determination of a devolution issue may be instituted by the Attorney General.

(2) The Lord Advocate may defend any such proceedings.

(3) This paragraph is without prejudice to any power to institute or defend proceedings exercisable apart from this paragraph by any person.

Notice of devolution issue

16 A court or tribunal shall order notice of any devolution issue which arises in any proceedings before it to be given to the Attorney General and the Lord Advocate (unless the person to whom the notice would be given is a party to the proceedings).

17 A person to whom notice is given in pursuance of paragraph 16 may take part as a party in the proceedings, so far as they relate to a devolution issue.

Reference of devolution issue to High Court or Court of Appeal

18 A magistrates' court may refer any devolution issue which arises in proceedings (other than criminal proceedings) before it to the High Court.

19 (1) A court may refer any devolution issue which arises in proceedings (other than criminal proceedings) before it to the Court of Appeal.

(2) Sub-paragraph (1) does not apply to—

(a) a magistrates' court, the Court of Appeal or the House of Lords, or

(b) the High Court if the devolution issue arises in proceedings on a reference under paragraph 18.

20 A tribunal from which there is no appeal shall refer any devolution issue which arises in proceedings before it to the Court of Appeal; and any other tribunal may make such a reference.

21 A court, other than the House of Lords or the Court of Appeal, may refer any devolution issue which arises in criminal proceedings before it to—
(a) the High Court (if the proceedings are summary proceedings), or
(b) the Court of Appeal (if the proceedings are proceedings on indictment).

References from Court of Appeal to Judicial Committee

22 The Court of Appeal may refer any devolution issue which arises in proceedings before it (otherwise than on a reference under paragraph 19, 20 or 21) to the Judicial Committee.

Appeals from superior courts to Judicial Committee

23 An appeal against a determination of a devolution issue by the High Court or the Court of Appeal on a reference under paragraph 18, 19, 20 or 21 shall lie to the Judicial Committee, but only with leave of the High Court or (as the case may be) the Court of Appeal or, failing such leave, with special leave of the Judicial Committee.

NOTES

Initial Commencement
To be appointed
To be appointed: see s 130.

Appointment
Appointment: 6 May 1999: see SI 1998/3178, art 2(2), Sch 3.

Part IV
Proceedings in Northern Ireland

Application of Part IV

24 This Part of this Schedule applies in relation to devolution issues in proceedings in Northern Ireland.

Institution of proceedings

25 (1) Proceedings for the determination of a devolution issue may be instituted by the Attorney General for Northern Ireland.

(2) The Lord Advocate may defend any such proceedings.

(3) This paragraph is without prejudice to any power to institute or defend proceedings exercisable apart from this paragraph by any person.

Notice of devolution issue

26 A court or tribunal shall order notice of any devolution issue which arises in any proceedings before it to be given to the Attorney General for Northern Ireland and the Lord Advocate (unless the person to whom the notice would be given is a party to the proceedings).

27 A person to whom notice is given in pursuance of paragraph 26 may take part as a party in the proceedings, so far as they relate to a devolution issue.

Reference of devolution issue to Court of Appeal

28 A court, other than the House of Lords or the Court of Appeal in Northern Ireland, may refer any devolution issue which arises in any proceedings before it to the Court of Appeal in Northern Ireland.

29 A tribunal from which there is no appeal shall refer any devolution issue which arises in any proceedings before it to the Court of Appeal in Northern Ireland; and any other tribunal may make such a reference.

References from Court of Appeal to Judicial Committee

30 The Court of Appeal in Northern Ireland may refer any devolution issue which arises in proceedings before it (otherwise than on a reference under paragraph 28 or 29) to the Judicial Committee.

Appeals from Court of Appeal to Judicial Committee

31 An appeal against a determination of a devolution issue by the Court of Appeal in Northern Ireland on a reference under paragraph 28 or 29 shall lie to the Judicial Committee, but only with leave of the Court of Appeal in Northern Ireland or, failing such leave, with special leave of the Judicial Committee.

NOTES

Initial Commencement
To be appointed
To be appointed: see s 130.

Appointment
Appointment: 6 May 1999: see SI 1998/3178, art 2(2), Sch 3.

Part V
General

Proceedings in the House of Lords

32 Any devolution issue which arises in judicial proceedings in the House of Lords shall be referred to the Judicial Committee unless the House considers it more appropriate, having regard to all the circumstances, that it should determine the issue.

Direct references to Judicial Committee

33 The Lord Advocate, the Advocate General, the Attorney General or the Attorney General for Northern Ireland may require any court or tribunal to refer to the Judicial Committee any devolution issue which has arisen in proceedings before it to which he is a party.

34 The Lord Advocate, the Attorney General, the Advocate General or the Attorney General for Northern Ireland may refer to the Judicial Committee any devolution issue which is not the subject of proceedings.

35 (1) This paragraph applies where a reference is made under paragraph 34 in relation to a devolution issue which relates to the proposed exercise of a function by a member of the Scottish Executive.

(2) The person making the reference shall notify a member of the Scottish Executive of that fact.

(3) No member of the Scottish Executive shall exercise the function in the manner proposed during the period beginning with the receipt of the notification under sub-paragraph (2) and ending with the reference being decided or otherwise disposed of.

(4) Proceedings relating to any possible failure by a member of the Scottish Executive to comply with sub-paragraph (3) may be instituted by the Advocate General.

(5) Sub-paragraph (4) is without prejudice to any power to institute proceedings exercisable apart from that sub-paragraph by any person.

Expenses

36 (1) A court or tribunal before which any proceedings take place may take account of any additional expense of the kind mentioned in sub-paragraph (3) in deciding any question as to costs or expenses.

(2) In deciding any such question, the court or tribunal may award the whole or part of the additional expense as costs or (as the case may be) expenses to the party who incurred it (whatever the decision on the devolution issue).

(3) The additional expense is any additional expense which the court or tribunal considers that any party to the proceedings has incurred as a result of the participation of any person in pursuance of paragraph 6, 17 or 27.

Procedure of courts and tribunals

37 Any power to make provision for regulating the procedure before any court or tribunal shall include power to make provision for the purposes of this Schedule including, in particular, provision—
(a) for prescribing the stage in the proceedings at which a devolution issue is to be raised or referred,
(b) for the sisting or staying of proceedings for the purpose of any proceedings under this Schedule, and
(c) for determining the manner in which and the time within which any intimation or notice is to be given.

Interpretation

38 Any duty or power conferred by this Schedule to refer a devolution issue to a court shall be construed as a duty or (as the case may be) power to refer the issue to the court for decision.

NOTES

Initial Commencement
To be appointed
To be appointed: see s 130.

Appointment
Appointment: 6 May 1999: see SI 1998/3178, art 2(2), Sch 3.

Subordinate Legislation
UK
Act of Sederunt (Devolution Issues Rules) 1999, SI 1999/1345 (made under para 37).
Act of Adjournal (Devolution Issues Rules) 1999, SI 1999/1346 (made under para 37).

Act of Sederunt (Proceedings for Determination of Devolution Issues Rules) 1999, SI 1999/1347 (made under para 37).

Employment Tribunals (Constitution and Rules of Procedure) (Scotland) Regulations 2001, SI 2001/1170 (made under para 37).

Employment Tribunals (Constitution and Rules of Procedure) (Scotland) (Amendment) Regulations 2001, SI 2001/1460 (made under para 37).

Scotland

Act of Adjournal (Criminal Procedure Rules Amendment) (Miscellaneous) 2000, SSI 2000/65 (made under para 37).

Act of Sederunt (Rules of the Court of Session Amendment) (Miscellaneous) 2000, SSI 2000/66 (made under para 37).

Convention for the Protection of Human Rights and Fundamental Freedoms

Rome, 4.X1.1950

THE GOVERNMENTS SIGNATORY HERETO, being members of the Council of Europe;

Considering the Universal Declaration of Human Rights proclaimed by the General Assembly of the United Nations on 10th December 1948;

Considering that this Declaration aims at securing the universal and effective recognition and observance of the Rights therein declared;

Considering that the aim of the Council of Europe is the achievement of greater unity between its members and that one of the methods by which that aim is to be pursued is the maintenance and further realisation of human rights and fundamental freedoms;

Reaffirming their profound belief in those fundamental freedoms which are the foundation of justice and peace in the world and are best maintained on the one hand by an effective political democracy and on the other by a common understanding and observance of the human rights upon which they depend;

Being resolved, as the governments of European countries which are like-minded and have a common heritage of political traditions, ideals, freedom and the rule of law, to take the first steps for the collective enforcement of certain of the rights stated in the Universal Declaration,

Have agreed as follows:

NOTES

1. Headings added according to the provisions of Protocol No. 11 (ETS No. 155).

Article 1[1]
Obligation to respect human rights

The High Contracting Parties shall secure to everyone within their jurisdiction the rights and freedoms defined in Section 1 of this Convention.

SECTION 1[1] — RIGHTS AND FREEDOMS

Article 2[1]
Right to life

1 Everyone's right to life shall be protected by law. No one shall be deprived of his life intentionally save in the execution of a sentence of a court following his conviction of a crime for which this penalty is provided by law.

2 Deprivation of life shall not be regarded as inflicted in contravention of this article when it results from the use of force which is no more than absolutely necessary:

a   in defence of any person from unlawful violence;
b   in order to effect a lawful arrest or to prevent the escape of a person lawfully detained;
c   in action lawfully taken for the purpose of quelling a riot or insurrection.

Article 3[1]
Prohibition of torture

No one shall be subjected to torture or to inhuman or degrading treatment or punishment.

Article 4[1]
Prohibition of slavery and forced labour

1 No one shall be held in slavery or servitude.

2 No one shall be required to perform forced or compulsory labour.

3 For the purpose of this article the term 'forced or compulsory labour' shall not include:

a   any work required to be done in the ordinary course of detention imposed according to the provisions of Article 5 of this Convention or during conditional release from such detention;
b   any service of a military character or, in case of conscientious objectors in countries where they are recognised, service exacted instead of compulsory military service;
c   any service exacted in case of an emergency or calamity threatening the life or well-being of the community;
d   any work or service which forms part of normal civic obligations.

Article 5[1]
Right to liberty and security

1 Everyone has the right to liberty and security of person. No one shall be deprived of his liberty save in the following cases and in accordance with a procedure prescribed by law:

a   the lawful detention of a person after conviction by a competent court;
b   the lawful arrest or detention of a person for noncompliance with the lawful order of a court or in order to secure the fulfilment of any obligation prescribed by law;
c   the lawful arrest or detention of a person effected for the purpose of bringing him before the competent legal authority on reasonable suspicion of having committed an offence or when it is reasonably considered necessary to prevent his committing an offence or fleeing after having done so;
d   the detention of a minor by lawful order for the purpose of educational supervision or his lawful detention for the purpose of bringing him before the competent legal authority;
e   the lawful detention of persons for the prevention of the spreading of infectious diseases, of persons of unsound mind, alcoholics or drug addicts or vagrants;
f   the lawful arrest or detention of a person to prevent his effecting an unauthorised entry into the country or of a person against whom action is being taken with a view to deportation or extradition.

2 Everyone who is arrested shall be informed promptly, in a language which he understands, of the reasons for his arrest and of any charge against him.

3 Everyone arrested or detained in accordance with the provisions of paragraph 1.c of this article shall be brought promptly before a judge or other officer authorised by law to exercise judicial power and shall be entitled to trial within a reasonable time or to release pending trial. Release may be conditioned by guarantees to appear for trial.

4 Everyone who is deprived of his liberty by arrest or detention shall be entitled to take proceedings by which the lawfulness of his detention shall be decided speedily by a court and his release ordered if the detention is not lawful.

5 Everyone who has been the victim of arrest or detention in contravention of the provisions of this article shall have an enforceable right to compensation.

Article 6[1]
Right to a fair trial

1 In the determination of his civil rights and obligations or of any criminal charge against him, everyone is entitled to a fair and public hearing within a reasonable time by an independent and impartial tribunal established by law. Judgment shall be pronounced publicly but the press and public may be excluded from all or part of the trial in the interests of morals, public order or national security in a democratic society, where the interests of juveniles or the protection of the private life of the parties so require, or to the extent strictly necessary in the opinion of the court in special circumstances where publicity would prejudice the interests of justice.

2 Everyone charged with a criminal offence shall be presumed innocent until proved guilty according to law.

3 Everyone charged with a criminal offence has the following minimum rights:

   a   to be informed promptly, in a language which he understands and in detail, of the nature and cause of the accusation against him;

   b   to have adequate time and facilities for the preparation of his defence;

   c   to defend himself in person or through legal assistance of his own choosing or, if he has not sufficient means to pay for legal assistance, to be given it free when the interests of justice so require;

   d   to examine or have examined witnesses against him and to obtain the attendance and examination of witnesses on his behalf under the same conditions as witnesses against him;

   e   to have the free assistance of an interpreter if he cannot understand or speak the language used in court.

Article 7[1]
No punishment without law

1 No one shall be held guilty of any criminal offence on account of any act or omission which did not constitute a criminal offence under national or international law at the time when it was committed. Nor shall a heavier penalty be imposed than the one that was applicable at the time the criminal offence was committed.

2 This article shall not prejudice the trial and punishment of any person for any act or omission which, at the time when it was committed, was criminal according to the general principles of law recognised by civilised nations.

Article 8[1]
Right to respect for private and family life

1 Everyone has the right to respect for his private and family life, his home and his correspondence.

2 There shall be no interference by a public authority with the exercise of this right except such as is in accordance with the law and is necessary in a democratic society in the interests of national security, public safety or the economic well-being of the country, for the prevention of disorder or crime, for the protection of health or morals, or for the protection of the rights and freedoms of others.

Article 9[1]
Freedom of thought, conscience and religion

Everyone has the right to freedom of thought, conscience and religion; this right includes freedom to change his religion or belief and freedom, either alone or in community with others and in public or private, to manifest his religion or belief, in worship, teaching, practice and observance.

2 Freedom to manifest one's religion or beliefs shall be subject only to such limitations as are prescribed by law and are necessary in a democratic society in the interests of public safety, for the protection of public order, health or morals, or for the protection of the rights and freedoms of others.

Article 10[1]
Freedom of expression

1 Everyone has the right to freedom of expression. This right shall include freedom to hold opinions and to receive and impart information and ideas without interference by public authority and regardless of frontiers. This article shall not prevent States from requiring the licensing of broadcasting, television or cinema enterprises.

2 The exercise of these freedoms, since it carries with it duties and responsibilities, may be subject to such formalities, conditions, restrictions or penalties as are prescribed by law and are necessary in a democratic society, in the interests of national security, territorial integrity or public safety, for the prevention of disorder or crime, for the protection of health or morals, for the protection of the reputation or rights of others, for preventing the disclosure of information received in confidence, or for maintaining the authority and impartiality of the judiciary.

Article 11[1]
Freedom of assembly and association

1 Everyone has the right to freedom of peaceful assembly and to freedom of association with others, including the right to form and to join trade unions for the protection of his interests.

2 No restrictions shall be placed on the exercise of these rights other than such as are prescribed by law and are necessary in a democratic society in the interests of national security or public safety, for the prevention of disorder or crime, for the protection of health or morals or for the protection of the rights and freedoms of others. This article shall not prevent the imposition of lawful restrictions on the exercise of these rights by members of the armed forces, of the police or of the administration of the State.

Article 12[1]
Right to marry

Men and women of marriageable age have the right to marry and to found a family, according to the national laws governing the exercise of this right.

Article 13[1]
Right to an effective remedy

Everyone whose rights and freedoms as set forth in this Convention are violated shall have an effective remedy before a national authority notwithstanding that the violation has been committed by persons acting in an official capacity.

Article 14[1]
Prohibition of discrimination

The enjoyment of the rights and freedoms set forth in this Convention shall be secured without discrimination on any ground such as sex, race, colour, language, religion, political or other opinion, national or social origin, association with a national minority, property, birth or other status.

Article 15[1]
Derogation in time of emergency

1 In time of war or other public emergency threatening the life of the nation any High Contracting Party may take measures derogating from its obligations under this Convention to the extent strictly required by the exigencies of the situation, provided that such measures are not inconsistent with its other obligations under international law.

2 No derogation from Article 2, except in respect of deaths resulting from lawful acts of war, or from Articles 3, 4 (paragraph 1) and 7 shall be made under this provision.

3 Any High Contracting Party availing itself of this right of derogation shall keep the Secretary General of the Council of Europe fully informed of the measures which it has taken and the reasons therefor. It shall also inform the Secretary General of the Council of Europe when such measures have ceased to operate and the provisions of the Convention are again being fully executed.

Article 16[1]
Restrictions on political activity of aliens

Nothing in Articles 10, 11 and 14 shall be regarded as preventing the High Contracting Parties from imposing restrictions on the political activity of aliens.

Article 17[1]
Prohibition of abuse of rights

Nothing in this Convention may be interpreted as implying for any State, group or person any right to engage in any activity or perform any act aimed at the destruction of any of the rights and freedoms set forth herein or at their limitation to a greater extent than is provided for in the Convention.

Article 18[1]
Limitation on use of restrictions on rights

The restrictions permitted under this Convention to the said rights and freedoms shall not be applied for any purpose other than those for which they have been prescribed.

SECTION II[1] — EUROPEAN COURT
OF HUMAN RIGHTS

Article 19
Establishment of the Court

To ensure the observance of the engagements undertaken by the High Contracting Parties in the Convention and the Protocols thereto, there shall be set up a European Court of Human Rights, hereinafter referred to as 'the Court'. It shall function on a permanent basis.

Article 20
Number of judges

The Court shall consist of a number of judges equal to that of the High Contracting Parties.

Article 21
Criteria for office

1 The judges shall be of high moral character and must either possess the qualifications required for appointment to high judicial office or be jurisconsults of recognised competence.

2 The judges shall sit on the Court in their individual capacity.

3 During their term of office the judges shall not engage in any activity which is incompatible with their independence, impartiality or with the demands of a full-time office; all questions arising from the application of this paragraph shall be decided by the Court.

Article 22
Election of judges

1 The judges shall be elected by the Parliamentary Assembly with respect to each High Contracting Party by a majority of votes cast from a list of three candidates nominated by the High Contracting Party.

2 The same procedure shall be followed to complete the Court in the event of the accession of new High Contracting Parties and in filling casual vacancies.

Article 23
Terms of office

1 The judges shall be elected for a period of six years. They may be re-elected. However, the terms of office of one-half of the judges elected at the first election shall expire at the end of three years.

2 The judges whose terms of office are to expire at the end of the initial period of three years shall be chosen by lot by the Secretary General of the Council of Europe immediately after their election.

3 In order to ensure that, as far as possible, the terms of office of one-half of the judges are renewed every three years, the Parliamentary Assembly may decide, before proceeding to any subsequent election, that the term or terms of office of one or more judges to be elected shall be for a period other than six years but not more than nine and not less than three years.

4 In cases where more than one term of office is involved and where the Parliamentary Assembly applies the preceding paragraph, the allocation of the terms of office shall be effected by a drawing of lots by the Secretary General of the Council of Europe immediately after the election.

5 A judge elected to replace a judge whose term of office has not expired shall hold office for the remainder of his predecessor's term.

6 The terms of office of judges shall expire when they reach the age of 70.

7 The judges shall hold office until replaced. They shall, however, continue to deal with such cases as they already have under consideration.

Article 24
Dismissal

No judge may be dismissed from his office unless the other judges decide unanimously that he has ceased to fulfil the required conditions.

Article 25
Registry and legal secretaries

The Court shall have a registry, the functions and organisation of which shall be laid down in the rules of the Court. The Court shall be assisted by legal secretaries.

Article 26
Plenary Court

The plenary Court shall

a   elect its President and one or two Vice-Presidents for a period of three years; they may be re-elected;
b   set up Chambers, constituted for a fixed period of time;
c   elect the Presidents of the Chambers of the Court; they may be re-elected;
d   adopt the rules of the Court, and
e   elect the Registrar and one or more Deputy Registrars.

Article 27
Committees, Chambers and Grand Chamber

1 To consider cases brought before it, the Court shall sit in committees of three judges, in Chambers of seven judges and in a Grand Chamber of seventeen judges. The Court's Chambers shall set up committees for a fixed period of time.

2 There shall sit as an *ex officio* member of the Chamber and the Grand Chamber the judge elected in respect of the State Party concerned or, if there is none or if he is unable to sit, a person of its choice who shall sit in the capacity of judge.

3 The Grand Chamber shall also include the President of the Court, the Vice-Presidents, the Presidents of the Chambers and other judges chosen in accordance with the rules of the Court. When a case is referred to the Grand Chamber under Article 43, no judge from the Chamber which rendered the judgment shall sit in the Grand Chamber, with the exception of the President of the Chamber and the judge who sat in respect of the State Party concerned.

Article 28
Declarations of inadmissibility by committees

A committee may, by a unanimous vote, declare inadmissible or strike out of' its list of cases an application submitted under Article 34 where such a decision can be taken without further examination. The decision shall be final.

Article 29
Decisions by Chambers on admissibility and merits

1 If no decision is taken under Article 28, a Chamber shall decide on the admissibility and merits of individual applications submitted under Article 34.

2 A Chamber shall decide on the admissibility and merits of inter-State applications submitted under Article 33.

3 The decision on admissibility shall be taken separately unless the Court, in exceptional cases, decides otherwise.

Article 30
Relinquishment of jurisdiction to the Grand Chamber

Where a case pending before a Chamber raises a serious question affecting the interpretation of the Convention or the protocols thereto, or where the resolution of a question before the Chamber might have a result inconsistent with a judgment previously delivered by the Court, the Chamber may, at any time before it has rendered its judgment, relinquish jurisdiction in favour of the Grand Chamber, unless one of the parties to the case objects.

Article 31
Powers of the Grand Chamber

The Grand Chamber shall

a   determine applications submitted either under Article 33 or Article 34 when a Chamber has relinquished jurisdiction under Article 30 or when the case has been referred to it under Article 43; and

b   consider requests for advisory opinions submitted under Article 47.

Article 32
Jurisdiction of the Court

1 The jurisdiction of the Court shall extend to all matters concerning the interpretation and application of the Convention and the protocols thereto which are referred to it as provided in Articles 33, 34 and 47.

2 In the event of dispute as to whether the Court has jurisdiction, the Court shall decide.

Article 33
Inter-State cases

Any High Contracting Party may refer to the Court any alleged breach of the provisions of the Convention and the protocols thereto by another High Contracting Party.

Article 34
Individual applications

The Court may receive applications from any person, non-governmental organisation or group of individuals claiming to be the victim of a violation by one of the High Contracting Parties of the rights set forth in the Convention or the protocols thereto. The High Contracting Parties undertake not to hinder in any way the effective exercise of this right.

Article 35

Admissibility criteria

1 The Court may only deal with the matter after all domestic remedies have been exhausted, according to the generally recognised rules of international law, and within a period of six months from the date on which the final decision was taken.

2 The Court shall not deal with any application submitted under Article 34 that

a   is anonymous; or
b   is substantially the same as a matter that has already been examined by the Court or has already been submitted to another procedure of international investigation or settlement and contains no relevant new information.

3 The Court shall declare inadmissible any individual application submitted under Article 34 which it considers incompatible with the provisions of the Convention or the protocols thereto, manifestly ill-founded, or an abuse of the right of application.

4 The Court shall reject any application which it considers inadmissible under this Article. It may do so at any stage of the proceedings.

Article 36
Third party intervention

1 In all cases before a Chamber of the Grand Chamber, a High Contracting Party one of whose nationals is an applicant shall have the right to submit written comments and to take part in hearings.

2 The President of the Court may, in the interest of the proper administration of justice, invite any High Contracting Party which is not a party to the proceedings or any person concerned who is not the applicant to submit written comments or take part in hearings.

Article 37
Striking out applications

1 The Court may at any stage of the proceedings decide to strike an application out of its list of cases where the circumstances lead to the conclusion that

a   the applicant does not intend to pursue his application; or
b   the matter has been resolved; or
c   for any other reason established by the Court, it is no longer justified to continue the examination of the application.

However, the Court shall continue the examination of the application if respect for human rights as defined in the Convention and the protocols thereto so requires.

2 The Court may decide to restore an application to its list of cases if it considers that the circumstances justify such a course.

Article 38
Examination of the case and friendly settlement proceedings

1 If the Court declares the application admissible, it shall

a   pursue the examination of the case, together with the representatives of the parties, and if need be, undertake an investigation, for the effective conduct of which the States concerned shall furnish all necessary facilities;

b   place itself at the disposal of the parties concerned with a view to securing a friendly settlement of the matter on the basis of respect for human rights as defined in the Convention and the protocols thereto.

2 Proceedings conducted under paragraph 1.b shall be confidential.

Article 39
Finding of a friendly settlement

If a friendly settlement is effected, the Court shall strike the case out of its list by means of a decision which shall be confined to a brief statement of the facts and of the solution reached.

Article 40
Public hearings and access to documents

1 Hearings shall be in public unless the Court in exceptional circumstances decides otherwise.

2 Documents deposited with the Registrar shall be accessible to the public unless the President of the Court decides otherwise.

Article 41
Just satisfaction

If the Court finds that there has been a violation of the Convention or the protocols thereto, and if the internal law of the High Contracting Party concerned allows only partial reparation to be made, the Court shall, if necessary, afford just satisfaction to the injured party.

Article 42
Judgments of Chambers

Judgments of Chambers shall become final in accordance with the provisions of Article 44, paragraph 2.

Article 43
Referral to the Grand Chamber

1 Within a period of three months from the date of the judgment of the Chamber, any party to the case may, in exceptional cases, request that the case be referred to the Grand Chamber.

2 A panel of five judges of the Grand Chamber shall accept the request if the case raises a serious question affecting the interpretation or application of the Convention or the protocols thereto, or a serious issue of general importance.

3 If the panel accepts the request, the Grand Chamber shall decide the case by means of a judgment.

Article 44
Final judgments

1 The judgment of the Grand Chamber shall be final.

2 The judgment of a Chamber shall become final

    a   when the parties declare that they will not request that the case be referred to the Grand Chamber; or

    b   three months after the date of the judgment, if reference of the case to the Grand Chamber has not been requested; or

    c   when the panel of the Grand Chamber rejects the request to refer under Article 43.

3 The final judgment shall be published.

Article 45
Reasons for judgments and decisions

1 Reasons shall be given for judgments as well as for decisions declaring applications admissible or inadmissible.

2 If a judgment does not represent, in whole or in part, the unanimous opinion of the judges, any judge shall be entitled to deliver a separate opinion.

Article 46
Binding force and execution of judgments

1 The High Contracting Parties undertake to abide by the final judgment of the Court in any case to which they are parties.

2 The final judgment of the Court shall be transmitted to the Committee of Ministers, which shall supervise its execution.

Article 47
Advisory opinions

1 The Court may, at the request of the Committee of Ministers, give advisory opinions on legal questions concerning the interpretation of the Convention and the protocols thereto.

2 Such opinions shall not deal with any question relating to the content or scope of the rights or freedoms defined in Section 1 of the Convention and the protocols thereto, or with any other question which the Court or the Committee of Ministers might have to consider in consequence of any such proceedings as could be instituted in accordance with the Convention.

3 Decisions of the Committee of Ministers to request an advisory opinion of the Court shall require a majority vote of the representatives entitled to sit on the Committee.

Article 48
Advisory jurisdiction of the Court

The Court shall decide whether a request for an advisory opinion submitted by the Committee of Ministers is within its competence as defined in Article 47.

Article 49
Reasons for advisory opinions

1 Reasons shall be given for advisory opinions of the Court.

2 If the advisory opinion does not represent, in whole or in part, the unanimous opinion of the judges, any judge shall be entitled to deliver a separate opinion.

3 Advisory opinions of the Court shall be communicated to the Committee of Ministers.

Article 50
Expenditure on the Court

The expenditure on the Court shall be borne by the Council of Europe.

Article 51
Privileges and immunities of judges

The judges shall be entitled, during the exercise of their functions, to the privileges and immunities provided for in Article 40 of the Statute of the Council of Europe and in the agreements made thereunder.

SECTION III[1,2] — MISCELLANEOUS PROVISIONS

NOTES
1. Headings in this section added according to the provisions of Protocol No. 11 (ETS No. 155).
2. The articles of this section are renumbered according to the provisions of Protocol No. 11. (ETS No. 155).

Article 52[1]
Inquiries by the Secretary General

On receipt of a request from the Secretary General of the Council of Europe any High Contracting Party shall furnish an explanation of the manner in which its internal law ensures the effective implementation of any of the provisions of the Convention.

Article 53[1]
Safeguard for existing human rights

Nothing in this Convention shall be construed as limiting or derogating from any of the human rights and fundamental freedoms which may be ensured under the laws of any High Contracting Party or under any other agreement to which it is a Party.

Article 54[1]
Powers of the Committee of Ministers

Nothing in this Convention shall prejudice the powers conferred on the Committee of Ministers by the Statute of the Council of Europe.

Article 55[1]
Exclusion of other means of dispute settlement

The High Contracting Parties agree that, except by special agreement, they will not avail themselves of treaties, conventions or declarations. in force between them for the purpose of submitting, by way of petition, a dispute arising out of the interpretation or application of this Convention to a means of settlement other than those provided for in this Convention.

Article 56[1]
Territorial application

1[2] Any State may at the time of its ratification or at any time thereafter declare by notification addressed to the Secretary General of the Council of Europe that the present Convention shall, subject to paragraph 4 of this Article, extend to all or any of the territories for whose international relations it is responsible.

2 The Convention shall extend to the territory or territories named in the notification as from the thirtieth day after the receipt of this notification by the Secretary General of the Council of Europe.

3 The provisions of this Convention shall be applied in such territories with due regard, however, to local requirements.

4[2] Any State which has made a declaration in accordance with paragraph 1 of this article may at any time thereafter declare on behalf of one or more of the territories to which the declaration relates that it accepts the competence of the Court to receive applications from individuals, non-governmental organisations or groups of individuals as provided by Article 34 of the Convention.

NOTES
1. Heading added according to the provisions of Protocol No. 11 (ETS No. 155).
2. Text amended according to the provisions of Protocol No. 11 (ETS No. 155).

Article 57[1]
Reservations

1 Any State may, when signing this Convention or when depositing its instrument of ratification, make a reservation in respect of any particular provision of the Convention to the extent that any law then in force in its territory is not in conformity with the provision. Reservations of a general character shall not be permitted under this article.

2 Any reservation made under this article shall contain a brief statement of the law concerned.

Article 58[1]
Denunciation

1 A High Contracting Party may denounce the present Convention only after the expiry of five years from the date on which it became a party to it and after six months' notice contained in a notification addressed to the Secretary General of the Council of Europe, who shall inform the other High Contracting Parties.

2 Such a denunciation shall not have the effect of releasing the High Contracting Party concerned from its obligations under this Convention in respect of any act which, being capable of constituting a violation of such obligations, may have been performed by it before the date at which the denunciation became effective.

3 Any High Contracting Party which shall cease to be a member of the Council of Europe shall cease to be a Party to this Convention under the same conditions.

4[2] The Convention may be denounced in accordance with the provisions of the preceding paragraphs in respect of any territory to which it has been declared to extend under the terms of Article 56.

NOTES
> 1. Heading added according to the provisions of Protocol No. 11 (ETS No. 155).
> 2. Text amended according to the provisions of Protocol No. 11 (ETS No. 155).

Article 59[1]
Signature and ratification

1 This Convention shall be open to the signature of the members of the Council of Europe. It shall be ratified. Ratifications shall be deposited with the Secretary General of the Council of Europe.

2 The present Convention shall come into force after the deposit of ten instruments of ratification.

3 As regards any signatory ratifying subsequently, the Convention shall come into force at the date of the deposit of its instrument of ratification.

4 The Secretary General of the Council of Europe shall notify all the members of the Council of Europe of the entry into force of the Convention, the names of the High Contracting Parties who have ratified it, and the deposit of all instruments of ratification which may be effected subsequently.

Done at Rome this 4th day of November 1950, in English and French, both texts being equally authentic, in a single copy which shall remain deposited in the archives of the Council of Europe. The Secretary General shall transmit certified copies to each of the signatories.

Protocol [No. 1] to the Convention for the Protection of Human Rights and Fundamental Freedoms[1]

Paris, 20.III.1952

THE GOVERNMENTS SIGNATORY HERETO, being members of the Council of Europe,

Being resolved to take steps to ensure the collective enforcement of certain rights and freedoms other than those already included in Section 1 of the Convention for the Protection of Human Rights and Fundamental Freedoms signed at Rome on 4 November 1950 (hereinafter referred to as 'the Convention'),

Have agreed as follows:

NOTES

    1. Headings of articles added and text amended according to the provisions of Protocol No. 11 (ETS No. 155) as from its entry into force.

Article 1
Protection of property

Every natural or legal person is entitled to the peaceful enjoyment of his possessions. No one shall be deprived of his possessions except in the public interest and subject to the conditions provided for by law and by the general principles of international law.

The preceding provisions shall not, however, in any way impair the right of a State to enforce such laws as it deems necessary to control the use of property in accordance with the general interest or to secure the payment of taxes or other contributions or penalties.

Article 2
Right to education

No person shall be denied the right to education. In the exercise of any functions which it assumes in relation to education and to teaching, the State shall respect the right of parents to ensure such education and teaching in conformity with their own religious and philosophical convictions.

Article 3
Right to free elections

The High Contracting Parties undertake to hold free elections at reasonable intervals by secret ballot, under conditions which will ensure the free expression of the opinion of the people in the choice of the legislature.

Article 4[1]
Territorial application

Any High Contracting Party may at the time of signature or ratification or at any time thereafter communicate to the Secretary General of the Council of Europe a declaration stating the extent to which it undertakes that the provisions of the present Protocol shall apply to such of the territories for the international relations of which it is responsible as are named therein.

Any High Contracting Party which has communicated a declaration in virtue of the preceding paragraph may from time to time communicate a further declaration modifying the terms of any former declaration or terminating the application of the provisions of this Protocol in respect of any territory.

A declaration made in accordance with this article shall be deemed to have been made in accordance with paragraph 1 of Article 56 of the Convention.

NOTES

1. Text amended according to the provisions of Protocol No. 11 (ETS No. 155).

Article 5
Relationship to the Convention

As between the High Contracting Parties the provisions of Articles 1, 2, 3 and 4 of this Protocol shall be regarded as additional articles to the Convention and all the provisions of the Convention shall apply accordingly.

Article 6
Signature and ratification

This Protocol shall be open for signature by the members of the Council of Europe, who are the signatories of the Convention; it shall be ratified at the same time as or after the ratification of the Convention. It shall enter into force after the deposit of ten instruments of ratification. As regards any signatory ratifying subsequently, the Protocol shall enter into force at the date of the deposit of its instrument of ratification.

The instruments of ratification shall be deposited with the Secretary General of the Council of Europe, who will notify all members of the names of those who have ratified.

Done at Paris on the 20th day of March 1952, in English and French, both texts being equally authentic, in a single copy which shall remain deposited in the archives of the Council of Europe. The Secretary General shall transmit certified copies to each of the signatory governments.

Protocol No. 4 to the Convention for the Protection of Human Rights and Fundamental Freedoms securing certain rights and freedoms other than those already included in the Convention and in the First Protocol thereto[1]*

Strasbourg, 16.IX.1963

The governments signatory hereto, being members of the Council of Europe,

Being resolved to take steps to ensure the collective enforcement of certain rights and freedoms other than those already included in Section 1 of the Convention for the Protection of Human Rights and Fundamental Freedoms signed at Rome on 4th November 1950 (hereinafter referred to as the 'Convention') and in Articles 1 to 3 of the First Protocol to the Convention, signed at Paris on 20th March 1952,

Have agreed as follows:

NOTES
    1. Headings of articles added and text amended according to the provisions of Protocol No. 11 (ETS No. 155) as from its entry into force.

Article 1
Prohibition of imprisonment for debt

No one shall be deprived of his liberty merely on the ground of inability to fulfil a contractual obligation.

Article 2
Freedom of movement

1 Everyone lawfully within the territory of a State shall, within that territory, have the right to liberty of movement and freedom to choose his residence.

2 Everyone shall be free to leave any country, including his own.

3 No restrictions shall be placed on the exercise of these rights other than such as are in accordance with law and are necessary in a democratic society in the interests of national security or public safety, for the maintenance of ordre public, for the prevention of crime, for the protection of health or morals, or for the protection of the rights and freedoms of others.

4 The rights set forth in paragraph 1 may also be subject, in particular areas, to restrictions imposed in accordance with law and justified by the public interest in a democratic society.

* Protocol not ratified by the United Kingdom.

Article 3
Prohibition of expulsion of nationals

1 No one shall be expelled, by means either of an individual or of a collective measure, from the territory of the State of which he is a national.

2 No one shall be deprived of the right to enter the territory of the state of which he is a national.

Article 4
Prohibition of collective expulsion of aliens

Collective expulsion of aliens is prohibited.

Article 5
Territorial application

1 Any High Contracting Party may, at the time of signature or ratification of this Protocol, or at any time thereafter, communicate to the Secretary General of the Council of Europe a declaration stating the extent to which it undertakes that the provisions of this Protocol shall apply to such of the territories for the international relations of which it is responsible as are named therein.

2 Any High Contracting Party which has communicated a declaration in virtue of the preceding paragraph may, from time to time, communicate a further declaration modifying the terms of any former declaration or terminating the application of the provisions of this Protocol in respect of any territory.

3[1] A declaration made in accordance with this article shall be deemed to have been made in accordance with paragraph 1 of Article 56 of the Convention.

4 The territory of any State to which this Protocol applies by virtue of ratification or acceptance by that State, and each territory to which this Protocol is applied by virtue of a declaration by that State under this article, shall be treated as separate territories for the purpose of the references in Articles 2 and 3 to the territory of a State.

5[2] Any State which has made a declaration in accordance with paragraph 1 or 2 of this Article may at any time thereafter declare on behalf of one or more of the territories to which the declaration relates that it accepts the competence of the Court to receive applications from individuals, non-governmental organisations or groups of individuals as provided in Article 34 of the Convention in respect of all or any of Articles 1 to 4 of this Protocol.

NOTES
> 1. Text amended according to the provisions of Protocol No. 11 (ETS No. 155).
> 2. Text added according to the provisions of Protocol No. 11 (ETS No. 155).

Article 6[1]
Relationship to the Convention

As between the High Contracting Parties the provisions of Articles 1 to 5 of this Protocol shall be regarded as additional Articles to the Convention, and all the provisions of the Convention shall apply accordingly.

NOTES
> 1. Text amended according to the provisions of Protocol No. 11 (ETS No. 155).

Article 7
Signature and ratification

1 This Protocol shall be open for signature by the members of the Council of Europe who are the signatories of the Convention; it shall be ratified at the same time as or after the ratification of the Convention. It shall enter into force after the deposit of five instruments of ratification. As regards any signatory ratifying subsequently, the Protocol shall enter into force at the date of the deposit of its instrument of ratification.

2 The instruments of ratification shall be deposited with the Secretary General of the Council of Europe, who will notify all members of the names of those who have ratified.

In witness whereof the undersigned, being duly authorised thereto, have signed this Protocol.

Done at Strasbourg, this 16th day of September 1963, in English and in French, both texts being equally authoritative, in a single copy which shall remain deposited in the archives of the Council of Europe. The Secretary General shall transmit certified copies to each of the signatory states.

Protocol No. 6 to the Convention for the Protection of Human Rights and Fundamental Freedoms concerning the Abolition of the Death Penalty[1]

Strasbourg, 28.IV.1983

The member States of the Council of Europe, signatory to this Protocol to the Convention for the Protection of Human Rights and Fundamental Freedoms, signed at Rome on 4 November 1950 (hereinafter referred to as 'the Convention'),

Considering that the evolution that has occurred in several member States of the Council of Europe expresses a general tendency in favour of abolition of the death penalty;

Have agreed as follows:

NOTES
1. Headings of articles added and text amended according to the provisions of Protocol No. 11 (ETS No. 155) as from its entry into force.

Article 1
Abolition of the death penalty

The death penalty shall be abolished. No-one shall be condemned to such penalty or executed.

Article 2
Death penalty in time of war

A State may make provision in its law for the death penalty in respect of acts committed in time of war or of imminent threat of war; such penalty shall be applied only in the instances laid down in the law and in accordance with its provisions. The State shall communicate to the Secretary General of the Council of Europe the relevant provisions of that law.

Article 3
Prohibition of derogations

No derogation from the provisions of this Protocol shall be made under Article 15 of the Convention.

Article 4[1]
Prohibition of reservations

No reservation may be made under Article 57 of the Convention in respect of the provisions of this Protocol.

NOTES
1. Text amended according to the provisions of Protocol No. 11 (ETS No. 155).

Article 5
Territorial application

1 Any State may at the time of signature or when depositing its instrument of ratification, acceptance or approval, specify the territory or territories to which this Protocol shall apply.

2 Any State may at any later date, by a declaration addressed to the Secretary General of the Council of Europe, extend the application of this Protocol to any other territory specified in the declaration. In respect of such territory the Protocol shall enter into force on the first day of the month following the date of receipt of such declaration by the Secretary General.

3 Any declaration made under the two preceding paragraphs may, in respect of any territory specified in such declaration, be withdrawn by a notification addressed to the Secretary General. The withdrawal shall become effective on the first day of the month following the date of receipt of such notification by the Secretary General.

Article 6
Relationship to the Convention

As between the States Parties the provisions of Articles 1 and 5 of this Protocol shall be regarded as additional articles to the Convention and all the provisions of the Convention shall apply accordingly.

Article 7
Signature and ratification

The Protocol shall be open for signature by the member States of the Council of Europe, signatories to the Convention. It shall be subject to ratification, acceptance or approval. A member State of the Council of Europe may not ratify, accept or approve this Protocol unless it has, simultaneously or previously, ratified the Convention. Instruments of ratification, acceptance or approval shall be deposited with the Secretary General of the Council of Europe.

Article 8
Entry into force

1 This Protocol shall enter into force on the first day of the month following the date on which five member States of the Council of Europe have expressed their consent to be bound by the Protocol in accordance with the provisions of Article 7.

2   In respect of any member State which subsequently expresses its consent to be bound by it, the Protocol shall enter into force on the first day of the month following the date of the deposit of the instrument of ratification, acceptance or approval.

Article 9
Depositary functions

The Secretary General of the Council of Europe shall notify the member States of the Council of:

a   any signature;
b   the deposit of any instrument of ratification, acceptance or approval;
c   any date of entry into force of this Protocol in accordance with Articles 5 and 8;
d   any other act, notification or communication relating to this Protocol.

In witness whereof the undersigned, being duly authorised thereto, have signed this Protocol.

Done at Strasbourg, this 28th day of April 1983, in English and in French, both texts being equally authentic, in a single copy which shall be deposited in the archives of the Council of Europe. The Secretary General of the Council of Europe shall transmit certified copies to each member State of the Council of Europe.

Protocol No. 7 to the Convention for the Protection of Human Rights and Fundamental Freedoms[1*]

Strasbourg, 22.XI.1984

The member States of the Council of Europe signatory hereto,

Being resolved to take further steps to ensure the collective enforcement of certain rights and freedoms by means of the Convention for the Protection of Human Rights and Fundamental Freedoms signed at Rome on 4 November 1950 (hereinafter referred to as 'the Convention'),

Have agreed as follows:

NOTES

    1. Headings of articles added and text amended according to the provisions of Protocol No. 11 (ETS No. 155) as from its entry into force.

Article 1
Procedural safeguards relating to expulsion of aliens

1 An alien lawfully resident in the territory of a State shall not be expelled therefrom except in pursuance of a decision reached in accordance with law and shall be allowed:

  a   to submit reasons against his expulsion,
  b   to have his case reviewed, and
  c   to be represented for these purposes before the competent authority or a person or persons designated by that authority.

2 An alien may be expelled before the exercise of his rights under paragraph 1.a, b and c of this Article, when such expulsion is necessary in the interests of public order or is grounded on reasons of national security.

Article 2
Right of appeal in criminal matters

1 Everyone convicted of a criminal offence by a tribunal shall have the right to have his conviction or sentence reviewed by a higher tribunal. The exercise of this right, including the grounds on which it may be exercised, shall be governed by law.

2 This right may be subject to exceptions in regard to offences of a minor character, as prescribed by law, or in cases in which the person concerned was tried in the first instance by the highest tribunal or was convicted following an appeal against acquittal.

Article 3
Compensation for wrongful conviction

When a person has by a final decision been convicted of a criminal offence and when subsequently his conviction has been reversed, or he has been pardoned, on the ground that a new or newly discovered fact shows conclusively that there has

---

* Protocol not ratified by the United Kingdom.

been a miscarriage of justice, the person who has suffered punishment as a result of such conviction shall be compensated according to the law or the practice of the state concerned, unless it is proved that the nondisclosure of the unknown fact in time is wholly or partly attributable to him.

Article 4
Right not to be tried or punished twice

1 No one shall be liable to be tried or punished again in criminal proceedings under the jurisdiction of the same state for an offence for which he has already been finally acquitted or convicted in accordance with the law and penal procedure of that state.

2 The provisions of the preceding paragraph shall not prevent the reopening of the case in accordance with the law and penal procedure of the State concerned, if there is evidence of new or newly discovered facts, or if there has been a fundamental defect in the previous proceedings, which could affect the outcome of the case.

3 No derogation from this Article shall be made under Article 15 of the Convention.

Article 5
Equality between spouses

Spouses shall enjoy equality of rights and responsibilities of a private law character between them, and in their relations with their children, as to marriage, during marriage and in the event of its dissolution. This Article shall not prevent States from taking such measures as are necessary in the interests of the children.

Article 6
Territorial applications

1 Any State may at the time of signature or when depositing its instrument of ratification, acceptance or approval, specify the territory or territories to which this Protocol shall apply and state the extent to which it undertakes that the provisions of this Protocol shall apply to this or these territories.

2 Any state may at any later date, by a declaration addressed to the Secretary-General of the Council of Europe, extend the application of this Protocol to any other territory specified in the declaration. In respect of such territory the protocol shall enter into force on the first day of the month following the expiration of a period of two months after the date of receipt by the Secretary-General of such declaration.

3 Any declaration made under the two preceding paragraphs may, in respect of any territory specified in such declaration, be withdrawn or modified by a notification addressed to the Secretary-General. The withdrawal or modification shall become effective on the first day of the month following the expiration of a period of two months after the date of receipt of such notification by the Secretary-General.

4[1] A declaration made in accordance with this Article shall be deemed to have been made in accordance with paragraph 1 of Article 56 of the Convention.

5 The territory of any State to which this Protocol applies by virtue of ratification, acceptance or approval by that State, and each territory to which this Protocol is applied by virtue of a declaration by that State under this Article, may be treated

as separate territories for the purpose of the reference in Article 1 to the territory of a State.

6² Any State which has made a declaration in accordance with paragraph 1 or 2 of this Article may at any time thereafter declare on behalf of one or more of the territories to which the declaration relates that it accepts the competence of the Court to receive applications from individuals, non-governmental organisations or groups of individuals as provided in Article 34 of the Convention in respect of Articles 1 to 5 of this Protocol.

NOTES

1. Text amended according to the provisions of Protocol No. 11 (ETS No. 155).
2. Text added according to the provisions of Protocol No. 11 (ETS No. 155).

Article 7¹
Relationship to the Convention

As between the States Parties, the provisions of Article 1 to 6 of this Protocol shall be regarded as additional Articles to the Convention, and all the provisions of the Convention shall apply accordingly.

NOTES

1. Text amended according to the provisions of Protocol No. 11 (ETS No. 155).

Article 8
Signature and ratification

This Protocol shall be open for signature by member States of the Council of Europe which have signed the Convention. It is subject to ratification, acceptance or approval. A member State of the Council of Europe may not ratify, accept or approve this Protocol without previously or simultaneously ratifying the Convention. Instruments of ratification, acceptance or approval shall be deposited with the Secretary General of the Council of Europe.

Article 9
Entry into force

1 This Protocol shall enter into force on the first day of the month following the expiration of a period of two months after the date on which seven member States of the Council of Europe have expressed their consent to be bound by the Protocol in accordance with the provisions of Article 8.

2 In respect of any member State which subsequently expresses its consent to be bound by it, the Protocol shall enter into force on the first day of the month following the expiration of a period of two months after the date of the deposit of the instrument of ratification, acceptance or approval.

Article 10
Depositary functions

The Secretary General of the Council of Europe shall notify all the member States of the Council of Europe of:

a   any signature;
b   the deposit of any instrument of ratification, acceptance or approval;
c   any date of entry into force of this Protocol in accordance with Articles 6 and 9;
d   any other act, notification or declaration relating to this Protocol.

In witness whereof the undersigned, being duly authorised thereto, have signed this Protocol.

Done at Strasbourg this 22nd day of November 1984, in English and French, both texts being equally authentic, in a single copy which shall be deposited in the archives of the Council of Europe. The Secretary General of the Council of Europe shall transmit certified copies to each member State of the Council of Europe.

Index